THE UNFINISHED NATION

A Concise History of the American People

THE UNFINISHED NATION

A Concise History of the American People

Fourth Edition

ALAN BRINKLEY

Columbia University

Boston Burr Ridge, IL Dubuque, IA Madison, WI New York
San Francisco St. Louis Bangkok Bogotá Caracas Kuala Lumpur
Lisbon London Madrid Mexico City Milan Montreal New Delhi
Santiago Seoul Singapore Sydney Taipei Toronto

The McGraw-Hill Companies

Higher Education

THE UNFINISHED NATION: A CONCISE HISTORY OF THE AMERICAN PEOPLE
Published by McGraw-Hill, a business unit of The McGraw-Hill Companies, Inc., 1221 Avenue of the Americas, New York, NY, 10020.

This book is printed on acid-free paper.

pbk 1 2 3 4 5 6 7 8 9 0 DOC/DOC 0 9 8 7 6 5 4 3
hc 2 3 4 5 6 7 8 9 0 DOC/DOC 0 9 8 7 6 5 4 3

ISBN 0-07-256554-3 (softcover)
ISBN 0-07-256561-6 (hardcover)

Publisher: *Lyn Uhl*
Senior sponsoring editor: *Steve Drummond*
Developmental editor: *Kristen Mellitt*
Editorial assistant: *Kimberly McGrath*
Marketing manager: *Katherine Bates*
Senior media producer: *Sean Crowley*
Lead project manager: *Susan Trentacosti*
Production supervisor: *Carol A. Bielski*
Freelance design coordinator: *Gino Cieslik*
Supplement associate: *Kathleen Boylan*
Supplement developmental editor: *Kate Scheinman*
Associate photo research coordinator: *Natalia Peschiera*
Associate art editor: *Cristin Yancey*
Photo researcher: *PhotoSearch, Inc.*
Cover and interior design: *Maureen McCutcheon*
Typeface: *10.5/12 Janson*
Compositor: *Shepherd Inc.*
Printer: *R.R. Donnelley and Sons, Inc.*

Library of Congress Cataloging-in-Publication Data

Brinkley, Alan.
The unfinished nation : a concise history of the American people / Alan Brinkley.—4th ed.
p. cm.
Includes bibliographical references and index.
Contents: v. 1. To 1877 — v. 2. From 1865.
ISBN 0-07-256554-3 (softcover : alk. paper) — ISBN 0-07-256562-4 (v. 1 : softcover : alk. paper) — ISBN 0-07-256563-2 (v. 2 : softcover : alk. paper)
1. United States—History. I. Title
E178.1B827 2004
973—dc21 2003046457

www.mhhe.com

About the Author

ALAN BRINKLEY is the Allan Nevins Professor of History at Columbia University. He is the author of *Voices of Protest: Huey Long, Father Coughlin, and the Great Depression*, which won the 1983 National Book Award; *American History: A Survey; The End of Reform: New Deal Liberalism in Recession and War*; and *Liberalism and Its Discontents.* He was educated at Princeton and Harvard, and he has taught at Harvard (where he was awarded the Joseph R. Levenson Memorial Teaching Award), Princeton, the City University of New York Graduate School, and Oxford University, where he was the Harmsworth Professor of American History. He is a member of the American Academy of Arts and Sciences, a member of the board of the New York Council for the Humanities, and chairman of the board of the Century Foundation.

Brief Contents

Contents

Chapter Three

Society and Culture in Provincial America *58*

Chapter Four

The Empire in Transition *90*

Chapter Five

The American Revolution *116*

Chapter Six

The Constitution and the New Republic *146*

Chapter Seven

The Jeffersonian Era *166*

Chapter Eight

Varieties of American Nationalism *200*

Chapter Nine

Jacksonian America 222

Chapter Ten

America's Economic Revolution *248*

Chapter Fifteen

Reconstruction and the New South *396*

Chapter Sixteen

The Conquest of the Far West *428*

Chapter Nineteen

From Stalemate to Crisis *514*

Chapter Twenty

The Imperial Republic *534*

Chapter Twenty-One

The Rise of Progressivism *556*

I WANT YOU
FOR U.S. ARMY
NEAREST RECRUITING STATION

Work Pays America!
PROSPERITY

Chapter Twenty-Eight

America in a World at War *720*

Chapter Twenty-Nine

The Cold War *750*

Chapter Thirty

The Affluent Society *778*

Chapter Thirty-One

The Ordeal of Liberalism *812*

Chapter Thirty-Three

From "The Age of Limits" to the Age of Reagan *878*

Chapter Thirty-Four

The Age of Globalization *908*

List of Illustrations

LIST OF ILLUSTRATIONS

List of Maps and Charts

LIST OF MAPS AND CHARTS

LIST OF MAPS AND CHARTS

Preface

The story of the American past, which is the subject of this book, has undergone many transformations in recent decades. The past itself has not changed, of course, but the way Americans understand it has changed dramatically. And in the wake of those changes have come both new forms of presentation and bitter controversies.

In one sense, American history is thriving as almost never before as a part of American popular culture. Historical museums and exhibitions have multiplied and have attracted large audiences. Popular writing on history—both nonfiction and novels—has grown in popularity. History is a continuing presence on television, in films, and increasingly on the Internet. The popular appetite for American history seems to be almost boundless. At the same time, however, historical scholarship has become the source of increasing debate—among historians themselves, among the various publics historians try to reach, and among politicians, some of whom attack the historical profession for what they claim is an excessively critical view of the past.

Both the growing popularity of history and the growing controversies surrounding it reflect the character of our time. Ours is an era of rapid and bewildering change, which encourages people—particularly in the aftermath of the attacks of September 11, 2001—to look to the past for guidance and reassurance, and for reminders of what many believe were simpler, stabler times. But the turbulence of our age has also encouraged historians to ask new questions of the past—and thus to reinterpret it—in an effort to understand the tensions and contests that preoccupy us today. As the population of the United States has become more diverse and as groups that once stood outside the view of scholarship have thrust themselves into its center, historians have labored to reveal the immense complexity of their country's past. As America's economy and culture and power become more deeply involved in the life of the rest of the world, historians struggle to see the ways in which global forces have shaped the nation's development. Historical narratives once recounted little beyond the experiences of great men and the unfolding of great public events. Today, they attempt to tell a more complicated story—one that includes private as well as public lives, ordinary people as well as celebrated ones, differences as well as unity, international phenomena as well as national ones. This newer history seems fragmented at times, because it attempts to embrace so many more areas of human experience than the older narratives. It is often disturbing, because it reveals failures and injustices as well as triumphs. But it is also richer, fuller, and better suited to helping us understand our own diverse and contentious world.

I have tried in this book to consider both the diversity and the unity that have characterized the American experience. The United States is, and has always been, a nation of many cultures. To understand its history, we must understand the experiences of the many groups who have shaped American society—the many worlds that have developed within it based on region, religion, class, ideology, race, gender, and ethnicity.

But the United States is not simply a collection of different cultures. It is also a great nation. And as important as understanding its diversity is understanding the forces that have drawn it together and allowed it to survive and flourish despite division. The United States has constructed a remarkably stable and enduring political system, which touches the lives of all Americans. It has developed an immense and highly productive national economy that affects the working and consuming lives of virtually everyone and reaches all across the globe. It has created a mass popular culture that colors the experiences and assumptions of almost all Americans, and of the people of much of the rest of the world as well. One can admire these unifying forces for their contributions to America's considerable success as a nation, or condemn them for creating—or failing to address—injustices. But no one proposing to understand the history of the United States can afford to ignore them.

In this fourth edition of *The Unfinished Nation*, I have tried to tell the complicated and fascinating story of America for students of history and for general readers. Those familiar with earlier editions will find a thorough editing and updating of all chapters, reflecting recent scholarship. Beyond that, there are three areas of special emphasis in this revision:

1. Greater attention to the global context of United States history, including a new feature called "America in the World."
2. Expanded coverage of science and technology.
3. Extensive new material on environmental history.

In addition, new chapter introductions and marginal notes throughout the text should make it more accessible to readers. And the most visible change is the introduction of full color maps, images, and other graphics to the book—and an expanded map and illustration program to take advantage of this change.

I trust that this edition will introduce readers to enough different aspects of American history to make them aware of its extraordinary richness and complexity. But I hope, too, that it will provide readers some sense of the shared experiences of Americans and of the forces that have sustained the United States as a nation.

My thanks to Kevin Murphy for his assistance on this edition. I am, as always, grateful to the many people at McGraw-Hill who have helped with the editing and production of this book: Lyn Uhl, Steve Drummond, Jim Strandberg, Susan Trentacosti, Gino Cieslik, Kim McGrath, Carol Bielski, Holly Rudelitsch, Natalia Peschiera, and Cristin Yancey. I am also grateful to the teachers and scholars who reviewed the manuscript and offered suggestions for revision: S. Charles Bolton, *University of Arkansas*,

Little Rock; Steven Boyd, *University of Texas, San Antonio;* Mike Haridopolos, *Brevard Community College;* Mark D. Van Ells, *Queensborough Community College;* B. R. Burg, *Arizona State University;* Yolanda Chávaz Leyva, *University of Texas, El Paso;* Gregory Wilson, *University of Akron;* Beverly Garrison, *Oral Roberts University;* Kenneth W. Townsend, *Coastal Carolina University;* Joanne Kropp, *University of Texas, El Paso;* Anita Ashendel, *Texas A & M University;* Donald Rakestraw, *Georgia Southern University;* Josh Rothman, *University of Alabama;* David Freligh, *Phillips Community College;* Victor Triary, *Middlesex Community College;* Alex Wellek, *Quinnipiac University;* Margaret Orelup, *Keene State College;* Dr. Robert Tracy McKenzie, *University of Washington;* Jeffrey A. Kaufmann, *Muscatine Community College;* Jack Hammersmith, *West Virginia University;* Wendy Gunderson, *Collin County Community College;* Elizabeth Osborn, *Indiana University;* Alexander Knott, *University of Northern Colorado;* William Virden, *University of Northern Colorado;* and David Cullin, *Collin County Community College.*

I am grateful, finally, to those readers of the book who have offered me unsolicited comments, criticisms, and corrections. I hope they will continue to do so. Suggestions can be sent to me at the Department of History, Columbia University, New York, NY 10027, or by e-mail at ab65@columbia.edu.

Alan Brinkley

THE UNFINISHED NATION

A Concise History of the American People

Frobisher and the Eskimos In 1577, the English explorer Martin Frobisher embarked on an elusive search that enchanted a generation of Europeans—the search for the "Northwest Passage," a waterway through North America to the Pacific. He sailed into the Arctic regions of eastern Canada, deep into Baffin Bay, before finding his route blocked by impassable ice. Along the way, he encountered groups of Baffinland Eskimos, who—as this John White drawing (repainted by his contemporary Hans Sloan) shows—attacked his party. Even outnumbered, the Frobisher party had the advantage of firearms and escaped serious harm. *(British Museum, London/The Bridgeman Art Library, NY)*

TIME LINE

16,000-14,000 B.C.	1492	1497	1502	1518-1530	1519-1522
Asians migrate to North America	Columbus discovers America	Cabot explores North America	African slaves arrive in Spanish America	Smallpox ravages Indians	Magellan circumnavigates globe

CHAPTER ONE

THE MEETING OF CULTURES

America before Columbus
Europe Looks Westward
The Arrival of the English

The discovery of America did not begin with Christopher Columbus. It started many thousands of years earlier when human beings first crossed an ancient land bridge from eastern Siberia across the Bering Strait into what is now Alaska. These early migrants, thought to be mostly of Mongolian stock, were truly the first Americans. Humans never developed in the Americas; the people had to find it. The early arrivals from Siberia began the first of two great migrations that would make the western hemisphere eventually the site of some of the largest and most important civilizations in the world.

Over the course of many centuries, migrants from Russia and probably also from other areas of Asia and from the Pacific Islands spread out through the lands of North and South America and created great civilizations. But beginning in the fifteenth century A.D., Europeans began to encounter the Americas as well—and began to launch their own great migrations into what they called the New World. This early period of contact between American and European civilization was sometimes friendly and sometimes mutually beneficial. But mostly, it was catastrophic for the American natives (or "Indians," as Europeans called them), both because they were not able to match European technologies in battle and because they were highly vulnerable to European diseases. Plagues from Europe decimated the native population in many parts of the Americas and made the European conquest of the continents much easier. By the late sixteenth century, Europeans had established a claim to all the lands of the Americas and actual control over much of it.

1558	1565	1587	1603	1607	1608	1609
Elizabeth I becomes English queen	St. Augustine, Florida, founded	"Lost Colony" established on Roanoke Island	James I becomes English king	Jamestown founded	French establish Quebec	Spanish found Santa Fe

AMERICA BEFORE COLUMBUS

No one is certain when the first migrations into the Americas began; recent estimates suggest that they started between 14,000 and 16,000 years ago. They were probably a result of the development of stone-tipped spears and other hunting implements that made it possible for humans to pursue large animals from Asia into North America. Year after year, a few at a time, these nomadic peoples entered the new continent and moved deeper into its heart. Perhaps as early as 8,000 B.C., the migrations reached the southern tip of South America. By the end of the fifteenth century A.D., when the first important contact with Europeans occurred, America was the home of many millions of men and women. Scholars estimate that well over 50 million people—and perhaps as many as 75 million—lived in the Americas by 1500 and that perhaps 10 million lived in the territory that now constitutes the United States.

The Civilizations of the South

Incan and Aztec Empires

Elaborate societies emerged in South and Central America and in Mexico. In Peru, the Incas created a powerful empire of perhaps 6 million people. They developed a complex political system and a large network of paved roads that welded together the populations of many tribes under a single government. In Central America and on the Yucatan Peninsula of Mexico, the Mayas built a sophisticated culture with a written language, a numerical system similar to the Arabic, an accurate calendar, and an advanced agricultural system. They were succeeded by the Aztecs, a once-nomadic warrior tribe from the north. In the late thirteenth century, the Aztecs established a precarious rule over much of central and southern Mexico and built elaborate administrative, educational, and medical systems. They also developed a harsh religion that required human sacrifice. Their Spanish conquerors discovered the skulls of 100,000 victims in one location when they arrived in 1519.

The economies of these societies were based primarily on agriculture, but there were also substantial cities. Tenochtitlán, the Aztec capital built on the site of present-day Mexico City, had a population of over 100,000 in 1500. The Mayas (at Mayapan and elsewhere) and the Incas (in such cities as Cuzco and Machu Picchu) produced elaborate settlements with striking religious and ceremonial structures. These civilizations accomplished all this without some of the important technologies that Asian and European civilizations possessed. As late as the sixteenth century, no American society had yet developed wheeled vehicles.

INDIANS OF NEW FRANCE The drawing is by the cartographer Charles Bécard de Granville, who was employed by the French government to make maps of its territories in North America. Granville also produced drawings of the flora and fauna of the region and of the natives he encountered. This depiction of Indian hunters traveling by river dates from approximately 1701. (Codex Canadiensis, *by Louis Nicolas, from the Collection of Gilcrease Museum, Tulsa)*

The Civilizations of the North

Hunting and Gathering

The peoples north of Mexico developed less elaborate but still substantial civilizations. Inhabitants of the northern regions of the continent subsisted on some combination of hunting, gathering, and fishing. They included the Eskimos of the Arctic Circle, who fished and hunted seals; the big-game hunters of the northern forests, who led nomadic lives based on pursuit of moose and caribou; the tribes of the Pacific Northwest, whose principal occupation was salmon fishing and who created substantial permanent settlements along the coast; and a group of tribes spread through relatively arid regions of the Far West, who developed successful communities based on fishing, hunting small game, and gathering edible plants.

Other societies in North America were agricultural. Among the most developed were those in the Southwest. The people of that arid region built large irrigation systems, and they constructed towns of stone and adobe structures. In the Great Plains region, too, most tribes were engaged in sedentary farming (corn and other grains) and lived in large permanent settlements.

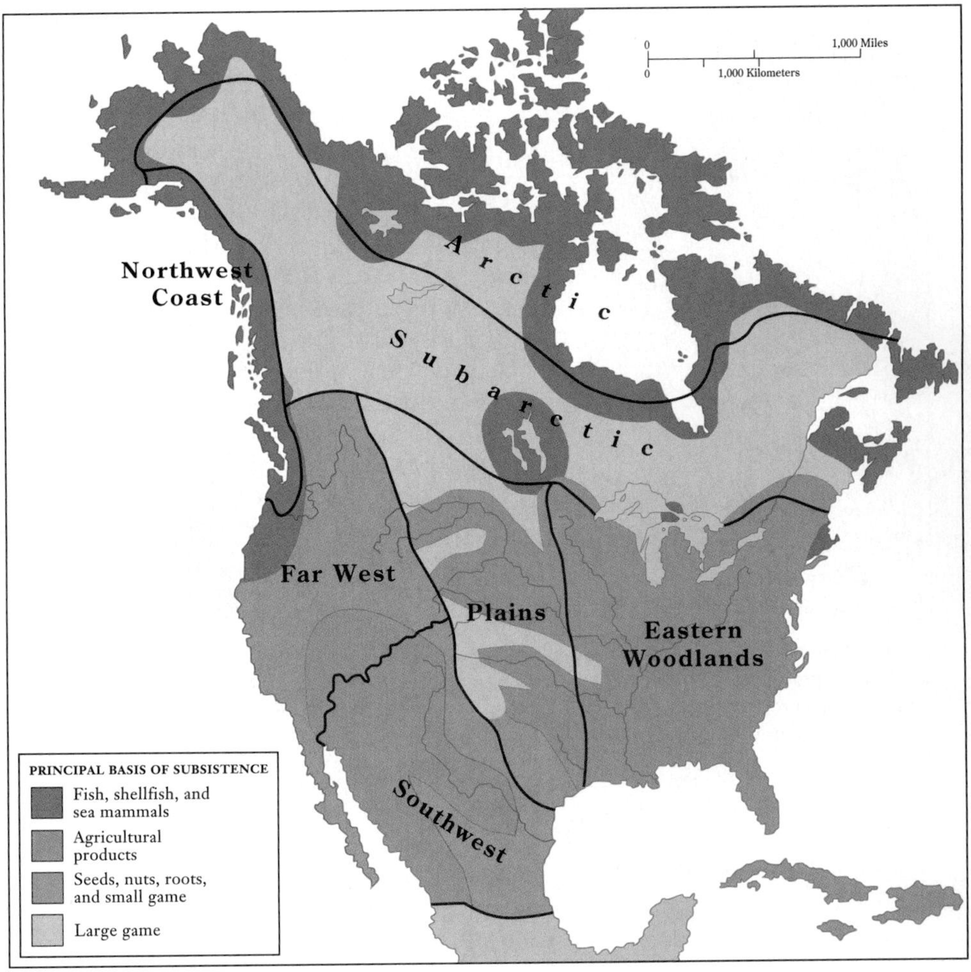

HOW THE EARLY NORTH AMERICANS LIVED This map shows the various ways in which the native tribes of North America supported themselves before the arrival of European civilization. Like most precommercial peoples, the native Americans survived largely on the resources available in their immediate surroundings. Note, for example, the reliance on the products of the sea of the tribes along the northern coastlines of the continent, and the way in which tribes in relatively inhospitable climates in the North—where agriculture was difficult—relied on hunting large game. Most native Americans were farmers. ◆ *What different kinds of farming would have emerged in the very different climates of the agricultural regions shown on this map?*

For an interactive version of this map go to www.mhhe.com/unfinishednation4ch1maps

The eastern third of what is now the United States—much of it covered with forests and inhabited by the Woodland Indians—had the greatest food resources of any area of the continent. Most of the many tribes of the region engaged in farming, hunting, gathering, and fishing simultaneously. In the South there were permanent settlements and large trading networks based on the corn and other grains grown in the rich lands of the

Mississippi River valley. Cahokia, a trading center located near present-day St. Louis, had a population of 40,000 at its peak in A.D. 1200.

Cahokia

The agricultural societies of the Northeast were more mobile. Farming techniques there were designed to exploit the land quickly rather than to develop permanent settlements. Many of the tribes living east of the Mississippi River were linked together loosely by common linguistic roots. The largest of these language groups consisted of the Algonquin tribes, which lived along the Atlantic seaboard from Canada to Virginia; the Iroquois Confederacy, which was centered in what is now upstate New York; and the Muskogean tribes, which consisted of the tribes in the southernmost region of the eastern seaboard. Alliances among the various Indian societies (even among those with common languages) were fragile.

Religion was usually closely linked with the natural world on which the tribes depended. Native Americans worshipped many gods, whom they associated variously with crops, game, forests, rivers, and other elements of nature.

All tribes assigned women the jobs of caring for children, preparing meals, and gathering certain foods. But the allocation of other tasks varied from one society to another. Some tribal groups reserved farming tasks almost entirely for men. Among other groups, women tended the fields, while men engaged in hunting, warfare, or clearing land. Because women and children were often left alone for extended periods while men were away hunting or fighting, women in some tribes tended to control the social and economic organization of the settlements.

Gender Relations

EUROPE LOOKS WESTWARD

Europeans were almost entirely unaware of the existence of the Americas before the fifteenth century. A few early wanderers—Leif Eriksson, an eleventh-century Norse seaman, and others—had glimpsed parts of the New World on their voyages. But even if their discoveries had become common knowledge (and they did not), there would have been little incentive for others to follow. Europe in the Middle Ages (roughly A.D. 500–1500) was too divided and decentralized to inspire many great ventures. By the end of the fifteenth century, however, conditions in Europe had changed, and the incentive for overseas exploration had grown.

Commerce and Nationalism

Two changes in particular encouraged Europeans to look toward new lands. One was a result of the significant growth in Europe's population in the fifteenth century. The

European Population Growth

Black Death, a catastrophic epidemic of the bubonic plague that began in Constantinople in 1347, had killed (according to some estimates) more than a third of the people of the continent. But a century and a half later, the population had rebounded. With that growth came a reawakening of commerce. A new merchant class was emerging to meet the rising demand for goods from abroad. As trade increased, and as advances in navigation made long-distance sea travel more feasible, interest in expanding trade even further grew quickly.

The second change was the emergence of new governments that were more united and powerful than the feeble political entities of the feudal past. In the western areas of Europe in particular, strong new monarchs were eager to enhance the commercial development of their nations.

Ever since the early fourteenth century, when Marco Polo and other adventurers had returned from Asia bearing exotic spices, cloths, and dyes, and even more exotic tales, Europeans who craved commercial glory had dreamed above all of trade with the East. For two centuries, that trade had been limited by the difficulties of the long overland journey to the Asian courts. But in the fourteenth century, as the maritime talents of several western European societies increased, talk of finding a faster, safer sea route to East Asia began.

Portuguese Exploration

The Portuguese were the preeminent maritime power in the fifteenth century largely because of Prince Henry the Navigator, who devoted much of his life to the promotion of exploration. In 1486, after Henry's death, the Portuguese explorer Bartholomeu Dias rounded the southern tip of Africa (the Cape of Good Hope); and in 1497–1498, Vasco da Gama proceeded all the way around the cape to India. But the Portuguese were not the first to encounter the New World.

Christopher Columbus

Christopher Columbus was born and reared in Genoa, Italy, and spent his early seafaring years in the service of the Portuguese. By the time he was a young man, he had developed great ambitions. He believed he could reach East Asia by sailing west, across the Atlantic, rather than east, around Africa. Columbus thought the world was far smaller than it actually is. He also believed that the Asian continent extended farther eastward than it actually does. Most important, he did not realize that anything lay to the west between Europe and the lands of Asia.

Columbus failed to enlist the leaders of Portugal behind his plan, so he turned instead to Spain. The marriage of Spain's two most powerful regional rulers, Ferdinand of Aragon and Isabella of Castile, had produced the strongest and most ambitious monarchy in Europe. Columbus appealed to Queen Isabella for support for his proposed westward voyage, and in 1492, she agreed. Commanding ninety men and three ships—the *Niña*, the *Pinta*, and the

Columbus's First Voyage

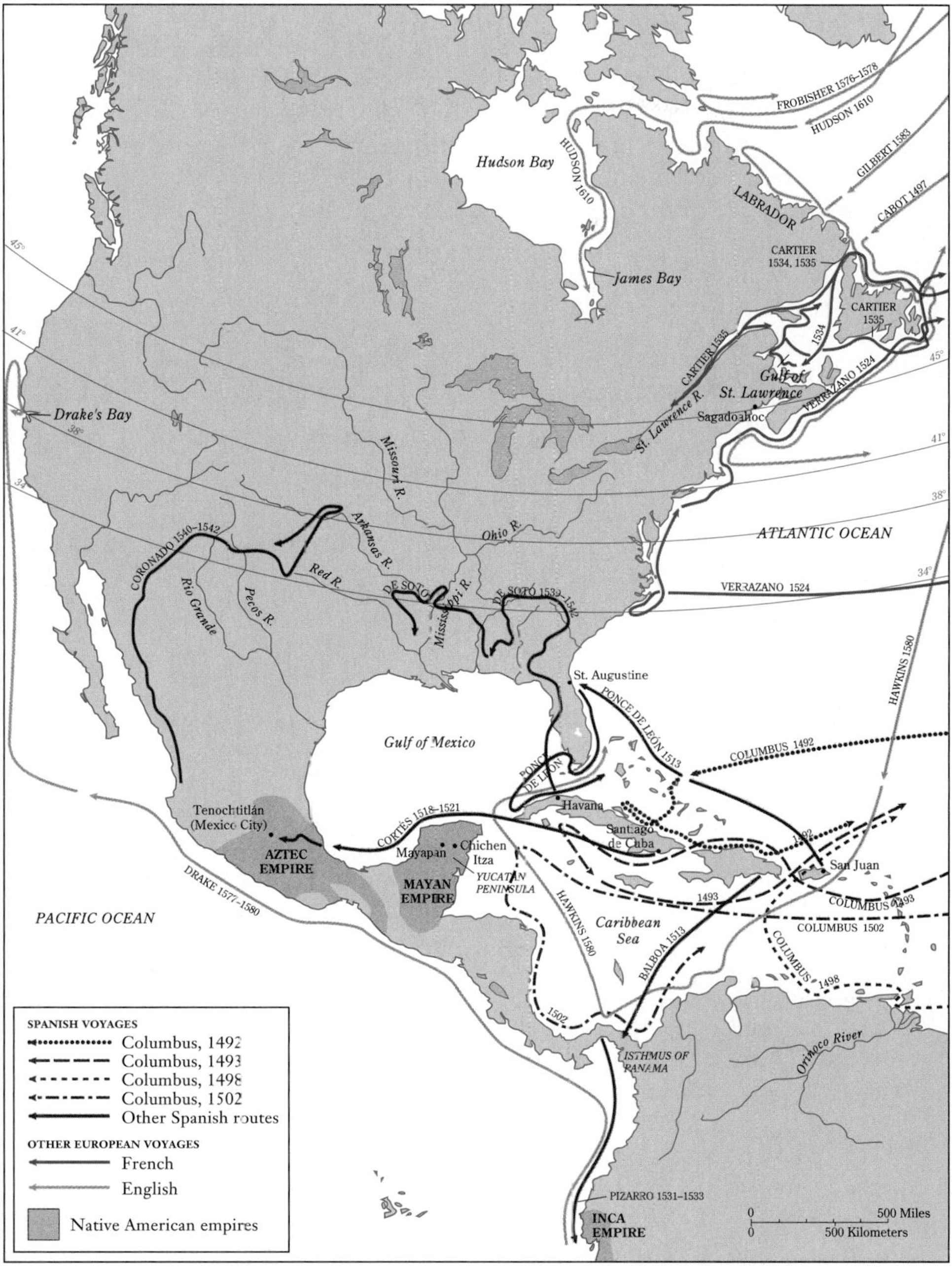

EUROPEAN EXPLORATION AND CONQUEST, 1492–1583 This map shows the many voyages of exploration to and conquest of North America launched by Europeans in the late fifteenth and sixteenth centuries. Note how Columbus and the Spanish explorers who followed him tended to move quickly into the lands of Mexico, the Caribbean, and Central and South America, while the English and French explored the northern territories of North America. ◆ *What factors might have led these various nations to explore and colonize these different areas of the New World?*

For an interactive version of this map go to www.mhhe.com/unfinishednation4ch1maps

Santa María—Columbus left Spain in August 1492 and sailed west into the Atlantic. Ten weeks later, he sighted land and assumed he had reached an island off Asia. In fact, he had landed in the Bahamas. When he pushed on and encountered Cuba, he assumed he had reached China. He returned to Spain, bringing with him several captured natives as evidence of his achievement. (He called the natives "Indians" because he believed they were from the East Indies in the Pacific.)

But Columbus did not, of course, bring back news of the great khan's court in China or any samples of the fabled wealth of the Indies. And so a year later, he tried again, this time with a much larger expedition. As before, he headed into the Caribbean, discovering several other islands and leaving a small and short-lived colony on Hispaniola. On a third voyage, in 1498, he finally reached the mainland and cruised along the northern coast of South America. He then realized, for the first time, that he had encountered not a part of Asia but a separate continent.

Columbus's celebrated accomplishments made him a popular hero for a time, but he ended his life in obscurity. Ultimately, he was even unable to give his name to the land he had revealed to the Europeans. That distinction went instead to a Florentine merchant, Amerigo Vespucci, who wrote a series of vivid descriptions of the lands he visited on an expedition to the New World and helped popularize the idea that the Americas were new continents.

Partly as a result of Columbus's initiative, Spain began to devote greater resources and energy to maritime exploration. In 1513 the Spaniard Vasco de Balboa crossed the Isthmus of Panama and became the first known European to gaze westward upon the great ocean that separated America from China. Seeking access to that ocean, Ferdinand Magellan, a Portuguese in Spanish employ, found the strait that now bears his name at the southern end of South America, struggled through the stormy narrows and into the ocean (so calm by contrast that he christened it the *Pacific*), and then proceeded to the Philippines. There Magellan died in a conflict with the natives, but his expedition went on to complete the first known circumnavigation of the globe (1519–1522). By 1550, Spaniards had explored the coasts of North America as far north as Oregon in the west and Labrador in the east.

Circumnavigation of the Globe

The Spanish Empire

In time, Spanish explorers in the New World stopped thinking of America simply as an obstacle to their search for a route to the East and began instead to consider it a possible source of wealth in itself. The Spanish claimed for themselves the whole of the New World, except for a piece of it (today's Brazil) that was reserved by a papal decree for the Portuguese.

The early Spanish colonists settled on the islands of the Caribbean. But then, in 1518, Hernando Cortés, who had been an unsuccessful Spanish government official in Cuba for fourteen years, decided to lead a small military expedition (about 600 men) against the Aztecs in Mexico and their powerful emperor, Montezuma, after hearing stories of great treasures there. His first assault on Tenochtitlán, the Aztec capital, failed. But Cortés and his army had unwittingly exposed the natives to smallpox. An epidemic of that deadly disease, to which the natives, unlike the Europeans, had developed no immunity, decimated the Aztec population and made it possible for the Spanish to triumph in their second attempt at conquest. Through his ruthless suppression of the surviving natives, Cortés established himself as one of the most brutal of the Spanish "conquistadores" (conquerors). Twenty years later, Francisco Pizarro conquered the Incas in Peru and opened the way for other advances into South America.

"Conquistadores"

The conquistadores had cleared the way for the first Spanish settlers in America. They were interested only in exploiting the American stores of gold and silver, and they were fabulously successful. For 300 years, beginning in the sixteenth century, the mines of Spanish America yielded more than ten times as much gold and silver as the rest of the world's mines together. After the first wave of conquest, however, most Spanish settlers in America traveled to the New World for other reasons. Many went in hopes of profiting from agriculture, and they helped establish elements of European civilization permanently in America. Other Spaniards—priests, friars, and missionaries—went to America to spread the Christian religion; through their efforts, the influence of the Catholic Church ultimately extended throughout South and Central America and Mexico.

THE MEXICANS STRIKE BACK In this vivid scene from the Duran Codex, Mexican artists illustrate a rare moment in which Mexican warriors gained the upper hand over the Spanish invaders. Driven back by native fighters, the Spanish have taken refuge in a room in the royal palace in Tenochtitlán while brightly attired Mexican warriors besiege them. Although the Mexicans gained a temporary advantage in this battle, the drawing illustrates one of the reasons for their inability to withstand the Spanish in the longer term. The Spanish soldiers are armed with rifles and crossbows, while the Indians carry only spears and shields. *(Oronoz Archivo)*

By the end of the sixteenth century, the Spanish Empire included the Caribbean islands, Mexico, and southern North America. It also spread into South America and included what is now Chile, Argentina, and Peru. In 1580, when the Spanish and Portuguese monarchies temporarily united, Brazil came under Spanish jurisdiction as well.

Northern Outposts

St. Augustine and Santa Fe

In 1565, the Spanish established the fort of St. Augustine in Florida, their first permanent settlement north of Mexico. But it was little more than a small military outpost. A more substantial colonizing venture began in the Southwest in 1598, when Don Juan de Onate traveled north from Mexico with a party of 500, claimed for Spain some of the lands of the Pueblo Indians in what is now New Mexico, and began to establish a colony. Onate granted *encomiendas* (the right to exact tribute and labor from the natives on large tracts of land) to favored Spaniards. In 1609, Spanish colonists founded Santa Fe. By 1680, there were over 2,000 Spanish colonists living among about 30,000 Pueblos. The economic heart of the colony was cattle and sheep, raised on the *ranchos* that stretched out around the small towns Spanish settlers established.

In 1680, the colony was nearly destroyed when the Pueblos rose in revolt. Despite widespread conversions to Catholicism, most natives (including the converts) continued to practice their own religious rituals. In 1680, Spanish priests and the colonial government were trying to suppress these rituals. In response, Pope, an Indian religious leader, led an uprising that killed hundreds of European settlers, captured Santa Fe, and drove the Spanish from the region. Twelve years later the Spanish returned, resumed seizing Pueblo lands, and crushed a last revolt in 1696.

After the revolts, many Spanish colonists seemed to understand that they could not hope to prosper in New Mexico in constant conflict with a native population that greatly outnumbered them. Although the Spanish intensified their efforts to assimilate the Indians, they also now permitted the Pueblos to own land. They stopped commandeering Indian labor, and they tacitly tolerated the survival of tribal religious rituals. There was significant intermarriage between Europeans and Indians. By 1750, the Spanish population had grown modestly to about 4,000. The Pueblo population had declined (through disease, war, and migration) to about 13,000—less than half what it had been in 1680. New Mexico had by then become a reasonably stable but still weak and isolated outpost of the Spanish Empire.

Assimilation and Accommodation

Biological and Cultural Exchanges

European and native cultures never entirely merged in the Spanish Empire. Nevertheless, the arrival of whites launched a process of interaction between different peoples that left no one unchanged.

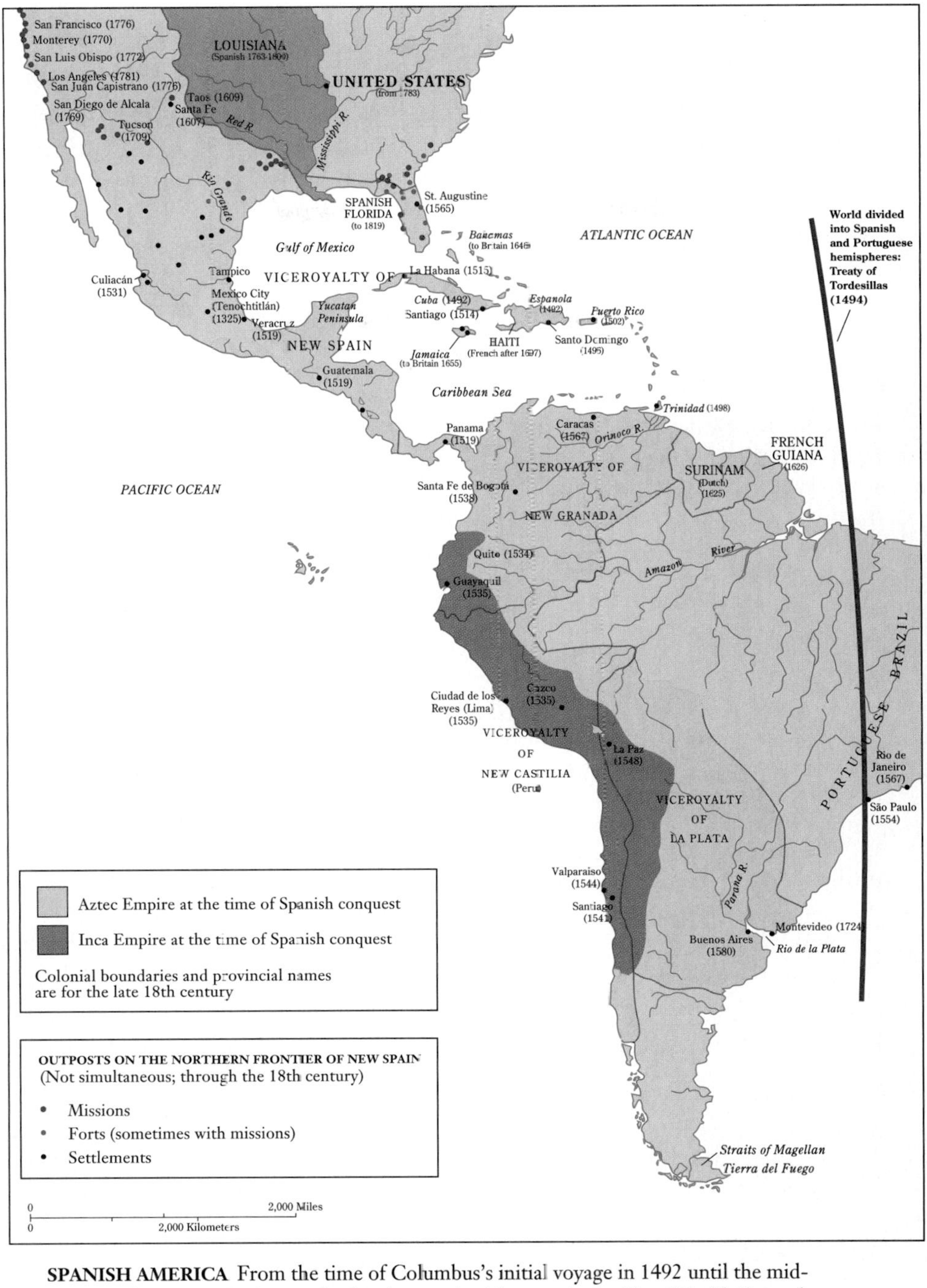

SPANISH AMERICA From the time of Columbus's initial voyage in 1492 until the mid-nineteenth century, Spain was the dominant colonial power in the New World. From the southern regions of South America to the northern regions of the Pacific northwest, Spain controlled one of the world's vastest empires. Note how much of the Spanish empire was simply grafted upon the earlier empires of native peoples—the Incas in what is today Chile and Peru, and the Aztecs across much of the rest of South America, Mexico, and the Southwest of what is now the United States. ◆ *What characteristics of Spanish colonization would account for their preference for already settled regions?*

For an interactive version of this map go to www.mhhe.com/unfinishednation4ch1maps

Debating the Past

THE AMERICAN POPULATION BEFORE COLUMBUS

No one knows how many people lived in the Americas in the centuries before Columbus. But scholars, and others, have spent more than a century debating the question. Interest in this question survives because the debate over the pre-Columbian population is closely connected to the much larger debate over the consequences of European settlement of the Western Hemisphere.

Throughout the nineteenth century, Native Americans spoke often of the great days before Columbus when there were many more people in their tribes. The painter and ethnographer George Catlin, who spent much time among the tribes in the 1830s, listened to these oral legends and estimated that there had been 16 million Indians in North America before the Europeans came. Other white Americans dismissed such claims as preposterous, insisting that Indian civilization was far too primitive ever to have sustained a population even as large as a million.

In 1928, James Mooney, an ethnologist at the Smithsonian Institution, drawing from early accounts of soldiers and missionaries in the sixteenth century, came up with the implausibly precise figure of 1.15 million natives who lived north of Mexico in the early sixteenth century. That was a larger figure than nineteenth-century writers had suggested, but still much smaller than the Indians themselves claimed. A few years later, the anthropologist Alfred Kroeber used some of Mooney's methods to come up with an estimate considerably larger than Mooney's, but much lower than Catlin's. He concluded in 1934 that there were 8.4 million people in the Americas in 1492, half in North America and half in the Caribbean and South America.

These low early estimates reflected an assumption that the arrival of the Europeans did not much reduce the native population. But in the 1960s and 1970s, scholars discovered that the early tribes had been catastrophically decimated by European plagues not long after the arrival of Columbus—that the numbers Europeans observed even in the late 1500s were already dramatically smaller than the numbers in 1492. Historians such as William McNeill in 1976 and Alfred Crosby a decade later produced powerful accounts of the near extinction of some tribes and the dramatic depopulation of others in a pestilential holocaust with few parallels in history.

The belief that the native population was much larger in 1492 than it was a few decades later has helped spur much larger estimates of how many people were in America before Columbus. Henry Dobyns, an anthropologist, claimed in 1966 that there were between 10 and 12 million people north of Mexico in 1492, and between 90 and 112 million in all of the Americas. No subsequent scholar has made so high a claim, but most subsequent estimates have been much closer to Dobyns's than to Kroeber's. The geographer William M. Denevan, for example, argued in 1976 that the American population in 1492 was around 55 million and that the population north of Mexico was under 4 million. These are among the lowest of modern estimates, but still dramatically higher than the nineteenth-century numbers.

The vehemence with which scholars, and at times the larger public, have debated these figures does not stem solely from the difficulty inherent in the effort to determine population size. It is also because the debate over the population is part of the debate over whether the arrival of Columbus—and the millions of Europeans who followed him—was a great advance in the history of civilization or an unparalleled catastrophe that virtually exterminated a large and flourishing native population. How to balance the many achievements of European civilization in the New World after 1492 against the terrible destruction of native peoples that accompanied it is, in the end, less a historical question, perhaps, than a moral one.

(text continued from page 12)

Beneficial and Catastrophic Exchanges

That Europeans were exploring the Americas at all was a result of their early contacts with the natives, from whom they had learned of the rich deposits of gold and silver. From then on, the history of the Americas became one of increasing levels of exchanges—some beneficial, some catastrophic—among different peoples and cultures. The first and perhaps most profound result of this exchange was the importation of European diseases to the New World. It would be difficult to exaggerate the consequences of the exposure of Native Americans to such illnesses as influenza, measles, typhus, and above all smallpox. Millions died. In some areas, native populations were virtually wiped out within a few decades of their first contact with whites. On Hispaniola, where Columbus had landed in the 1490s, the native population quickly declined from approximately 1 million to about 500. In the Mayan areas of Mexico, as much as 95 percent of the population perished within a few years of the natives' first contact with the Spanish. Many (although not all) of the tribes north of Mexico, whose contact with European settlers came later and was often less intimate, were spared the worst of the epidemics. But for other areas of the New World, this was a catastrophe at least as grave as, and in some places far worse than, the Black Death that had killed over a third of the population of Europe two centuries before. Europeans, watching this biological catastrophe, saw it as evidence of God's will that they should dominate the New World—and its native population.

The decimation of native populations in the southern regions of the Americas was not, however, purely a result of exposure to infection. It was also a result of the conquistadores' deliberate policy of subjugation and extermination. Their brutality was in part a reflection of the ruthlessness with which Europeans waged war in all parts of the world. It was also a result of their conviction that the natives were "savages"—uncivilized peoples who could be treated as somehow not fully human. By the 1540s, the combined effects of European diseases and European military brutality had all but destroyed the empires of Mexico and South America.

Deliberate Subjugation and Extermination

Not all aspects of the exchange were so disastrous to the Indians. The Europeans introduced to America important new crops (among them sugar and bananas), domestic livestock (cattle, pigs, and sheep), and, perhaps most significant, the horse, which gradually became central to the lives of many natives and transformed their societies.

The exchange was at least as important (and more beneficial) to the Europeans. In both North and South America, the arriving white peoples learned from the natives new agricultural techniques appropriate to the demands of the new land. They discovered new crops—above all maize (corn), which Columbus took back to Europe from his first trip to America. Such foods as squash, pumpkins, beans, sweet potatoes, tomatoes, peppers, and potatoes all found their way into European diets.

New World Crops

In South America, Central America, and Mexico, a society in which Europeans and natives lived in intimate, if unequal, contact with one another emerged. Many natives gradually came to speak Spanish or Portuguese, but they created a range of dialects fusing the European languages with elements of their own. European men outnumbered European women by at least ten to one. As a result, male Spanish immigrants had substantial sexual contact with native women. Intermarriage—often forcible—became frequent. Before long, the population of the colonies came to be dominated (numerically, at least) by people of mixed race, or mestizos.

Virtually all the enterprises of the Spanish and Portuguese colonists depended on an Indian workforce. In some places, Indians were sold into slavery. More often, colonists used a coercive (or "indentured") wage system, under which Indians worked in the mines and on the plantations under duress for fixed periods. That was not, in the end, enough to meet the labor needs of the colonists. As early as 1502, therefore, European settlers began importing slaves from Africa.

Coercive Wage System

Africa and America

Over half of all the immigrants to the New World between 1500 and 1800 were Africans, virtually all of them sent to America against their will. Most came from a large region below the Sahara Desert, known as Guinea.

Europeans and white Americans came to portray African society as primitive and uncivilized. But most Africans were, in fact, civilized peoples with well-developed economies and political systems. The residents of upper Guinea had substantial commercial contact with the Mediterranean world—trading ivory, gold, and slaves for finished goods—and, largely as a result, became early converts to Islam. After the collapse of the ancient kingdom of Ghana around A.D. 1100, they created the even larger empire of Mali, whose trading center at Timbuktu became fabled as a center of education and a meeting place of the peoples of many lands.

Trade States of West Africa

Farther south, Africans were more isolated from Europe and the Mediterranean and were more politically fragmented. The central social unit was the village, which usually consisted of members of an extended family group. Some groups of villages united in small kingdoms. But no large empires emerged in the south. Nevertheless, these southern societies developed extensive trade, both among themselves and, to a lesser degree, with the outside world.

African civilizations developed economies that reflected the climates and resources of their lands. In upper Guinea, fishing and rice cultivation, supplemented by the extensive trade with Mediterranean lands, were the foundation of the economy. Farther south, Africans grew wheat and other food crops, raised livestock, and fished. There were some more nomadic tribes in the interior, who subsisted largely on hunting and gathering. But most Africans were sedentary, farming people.

Matrilineal Societies

As in many Indian societies in America, African families tended to be matrilineal: They traced their heredity through and inherited property from their mothers. Women played a major role, often the dominant role, in trade. In many areas, they were the principal farmers (while the men hunted, fished, and raised livestock), and everywhere, they managed child care and food preparation. Most tribes also divided political power by gender, with men choosing leaders to manage male affairs and women choosing parallel leaders to handle female matters.

In those areas of west Africa where indigenous religions had survived the spread of Islam, people worshiped many gods, whom they associated with various aspects of the natural world and whose spirits they believed lived in trees, rocks, forests, and streams. Most Africans also developed forms of ancestor worship and took great care in tracing family lineage; the most revered priests were generally the oldest people.

African Slavery

Small elites of priests and nobles stood at the top of many African societies. Most people belonged to a large middle group of farmers, traders, crafts workers, and others. At the bottom of society were slaves—men and women who were put into bondage after being captured in wars, because of criminal behavior, or as a result of unpaid debts. African people were generally in bondage for a fixed term, and in the meantime retained certain legal protections (including the right to marry). Children did not inherit their parents' condition of bondage.

Sugar and the Slave Trade

The African slave trade long preceded European settlement in the New World. As early as the eighth century, west Africans began selling small numbers of slaves to traders from the Mediterranean and later to the Portuguese. In the sixteenth century, however, the market for slaves increased dramatically as a result of the growing European demand for sugar cane. The small areas of sugar cultivation in the Mediterranean could not meet the demand, and production soon spread to new areas: to the island of Madeira off the African coast, which

THE ATLANTIC CONTEXT OF EARLY AMERICAN HISTORY

Most Americans understand that our nation has recently become intimately bound up with the rest of the world—that we live in a time sometimes called the "age of globalization." Until recently, however, most historians have examined the nation's past in relative isolation. Among the first areas of American history to re-examine the past in an international perspective is the earliest period of European settlement of the Americas. Many scholars of early American history now examine what happened in the "New World" in the context of what has become known as the "Atlantic World."

The idea of an "Atlantic World" rests in part on the obvious connections between western Europe and the Spanish, British, French, and Dutch colonies in North and South America. All the early European civilizations of the Americas were part of a great imperial project launched by the major powers of Europe. The massive European immigration to the Americas beginning in the sixteenth century, the defeat and devastation of native populations, the creation of European agricultural and urban settlements, and the imposition of imperial regulations on trade, commerce, landowning, and political life—all of these forces reveal the influence of Old World imperialism on the history of the New World.

But the creation of empires is only one part of the creation of the Atlantic World. At least equally important—and closely related—is the expansion of commerce from Europe to the Americas. Although some Europeans traveled to the New World in search of religious freedom, or to escape oppression, or to search for adventure, the great majority of European immigrants were in search of economic opportunity. Not surprisingly, therefore, the European settlements in the Americas were almost from the start intimately connected to Europe through the growth of commerce between them—commerce that grew more extensive and more complex with every passing year. The commercial relationship between America and Europe was responsible not just for the growth of trade, but also for the increases in migration over time—as the demand for labor in the New World drew more and more settlers from the Old World. Commerce was also the principal reason for the rise of slavery in the Americas, and for the growth of the slave trade between European America and Africa. The Atlantic World, in other words, included not just Europe and the Americas, but Africa as well.

Religion was another force binding together the Atlantic World. The vast majority of people of European descent were Christians, and most of them maintained important religious ties to Europe. Catholics, of course, were part of a hierarchical church based in Rome and maintained close ties with the Vatican. But the Protestant faiths that predominated in North America were intimately linked to their European counterparts as well. New religious ideas and movements spread back and forth across the Atlantic with astonishing speed. Great revivals that began in Europe moved quickly to America. The "Great Awakening" of the mid-eighteenth century, for example, began in Britain and traveled to America in large part through the efforts of the English evangelist George Whitefield. American evangelists later carried religious ideas from the New World back to the Old.

The early history of European America was also closely bound up with the intellectual life of Europe. The Enlightenment—the cluster of ideas that emerged in Europe in the seventeenth and eighteenth centuries emphasizing the power of human reason—moved quickly to the Americas, producing considerable intellectual ferment throughout the New World, but particularly in the British colonies in North America and the Caribbean. The ideas of the British philosopher John Locke, for example, helped shape the founding of Georgia. The English Constitution, and the idea of the "rights of Englishmen," shaped the way North Americans shaped their own concepts of politics. Many of the ideas that lay behind the American Revolution were products of British and continental philosophy that had traveled across the Atlantic. The reinterpretation of those ideas by Americans to help justify their drive to independence—by, among others, Thomas Paine—moved back to Europe and helped, among other things, to inspire the French Revolution. Scientific and technological knowledge—another product of the Enlightenment—traveled constantly across the Atlantic and back. Americans borrowed industrial technology from Britain. Europe acquired much of its early knowledge of electricity from experiments done in America. But the Enlightenment was only one part of the continuing intellectual connections within the Atlantic World, connections that spread artistic, scholarly, and political ideas widely through the lands bordering the ocean.

Instead of thinking of the early history of what became the United States simply as the story of the growth of thirteen small colonies along the Atlantic seaboard of North America, the idea of the "Atlantic World" encourages us to think of early American history as a vast pattern of exchanges and interactions—trade, migration, religious and intellectual exchange, and many other relationships—among all the societies bordering the Atlantic: western Europe, western Africa, the Caribbean, and North and South America.

(text continued from page 17)

became a Portuguese colony, and not long thereafter (still in the sixteenth century) to the Caribbean islands and Brazil. Sugar was a labor-intensive crop, and the demand for African workers in these new areas of cultivation was high. At first the slave traders were overwhelmingly Portuguese. By the seventeenth century, the Dutch had won control of most of the market. In the eighteenth century, the English dominated it. (Despite some recent claims, Jews were never significantly involved in the slave trade.) By 1700, slavery had spread well beyond its original locations in the Caribbean and South America and into the English colonies to the north.

THE ARRIVAL OF THE ENGLISH

England's first documented contact with the New World came only five years after Spain's. In 1497, John Cabot (like Columbus, a native of Genoa) sailed to the northeastern coast of North America on an expedition sponsored by King Henry VII, in an unsuccessful search for a northwest passage through the New World to the Orient. But nearly a century passed before the English made any serious efforts to establish colonies in America.

Incentives for Colonization

Interest in colonization grew in part as a response to social and economic problems in sixteenth-century England. The English people suffered from frequent and costly European wars, and they suffered from almost constant religious strife within their own land. Many suffered, too, from harsh economic changes in their countryside. Because the worldwide demand for wool was growing rapidly, landowners were converting their land from fields for crops to pastures for sheep. The result was a reduction in the amount of land available for growing food. England's food supply declined at the same time that the English population was growing—from 3 million in 1485 to 4 million in 1603. To some of the English, the New World began to seem attractive because it offered something that was growing scarce in England: land.

Scarce Land

At the same time, new merchant capitalists were prospering by selling the products of England's growing wool-cloth industry abroad. At first, most exporters did business almost entirely as individuals. In time, however, merchants formed companies, whose charters from the king gave them monopolies for trading in particular regions. Investors in these companies often made fantastic profits, and they were eager to expand their trade.

Central to this trading drive was the emergence of a new concept of economic life known as mercantilism. Mercantilism rested on the belief that one person or nation could grow rich only at the expense of another, and that a nation's economic health depended, therefore, on selling as much as possible to foreign lands and buying as little as possible from them. The principles of mercantilism spread throughout Europe in the sixteenth and seventeenth centuries. One result was the increased attractiveness of acquiring colonies, which could become the source of raw materials and a market for the colonizing power's goods.

Mercantilism

In England, the mercantilistic program thrived at first on the basis of the flourishing wool trade with the European continent, and particularly with the great cloth market in Antwerp. In the 1550s, however, that glutted market began to collapse, and English merchants had to look elsewhere for overseas trade. Some English believed colonies would solve their problems. They would create markets, alleviate poverty, and siphon off the surplus population. Perhaps most important, colonial commerce would allow England to acquire products for which the nation had previously been dependent on foreigners—products such as lumber, naval stores, and silver and gold.

Religious Motives of Colonization

There were also religious motives for colonization—a result of the Protestant Reformation. It had began in Germany in 1517, when Martin Luther challenged some of the basic practices and beliefs of the Roman Catholic Church. Luther quickly won a wide following among ordinary men and women in northern Europe. When the pope excommunicated him in 1520, Luther began leading his followers out of the Catholic Church entirely.

The Swiss theologian John Calvin went even further than Luther had in rejecting the Catholic belief that human behavior could affect an individual's prospects for salvation. Calvin introduced the doctrine of predestination. God "elected" some people to be saved and condemned others to damnation; each person's destiny was determined before birth, and no one could change that predetermined fate. But those who accepted Calvin's teachings came to believe that the way they led their lives might reveal to them their chances of salvation. A wicked or useless existence would be a sign of damnation; saintliness, diligence, and success could be signs of grace. Calvinism created anxieties among its followers, but it also produced a strong incentive to lead virtuous, productive lives. The new creed spread rapidly throughout northern Europe and produced (among other groups) the Huguenots in France and the Puritans in England.

The English Reformation

The English Reformation was at first more a result of a political dispute between the king and the pope than of these doctrinal revolts. In 1529 King Henry VIII, angered by the refusal of the pope to grant him a divorce from his Spanish wife, broke England's ties with the Catholic Church and established himself as the head of the Christian faith in his country. After Henry's death, his Catholic daughter, Queen Mary, restored England's allegiance to Rome and persecuted those who resisted. But when Mary died in 1558, her half-sister, Elizabeth I, became England's sovereign and once again severed the nation's connection with the Catholic Church, this time for good.

To many English people, however, the new Church of England was not reformed enough. Some had been affected by the teachings of the European Reformation, and they clamored for reforms that would "purify" the church. As a result, they became known as Puritans.

Puritan Separatists

The most radical Puritans, known as Separatists, were determined to worship in their own independent congregations, despite English laws that required all subjects to attend regular Anglican services. But most Puritans did not wish to leave the Church of England. They wanted, rather, to simplify Anglican forms of worship and reform the leadership of the church. Like the Separatists, they grew increasingly frustrated by the refusal of political and ecclesiastical authorities to respond to their demands.

Puritan discontent grew rapidly after the death of Elizabeth, the last of the Tudors, and the accession of James I, the first of the Stuarts, in 1603. Convinced that kings ruled by divine right, James quickly antagonized the Puritans by resorting to illegal and arbitrary taxation, by favoring English Catholics in the granting of charters and other favors, and by supporting "high-church" forms of ceremony. By the early seventeenth century, some religious nonconformists were beginning to look for places of refuge outside the kingdom.

England's first experience with colonization came not in the New World but in neighboring Ireland. The English had long laid claim to the island, but only in the late sixteenth century did serious efforts at colonization

Lessons of Irish Colonization

begin. The long, brutal process by which the English attempted to subdue the Irish led to an important assumption about colonization that the English would take with them to America: the belief that settlements in foreign lands must retain a rigid separation from the native populations. Unlike the Spanish in America, the English in Ireland tried to build a separate society of their own, peopled with emigrants from England itself. They would take that concept with them to the New World.

The French and the Dutch in America

English settlers in North America were to encounter not only natives but also other Europeans who were, like them, driven by mercantilist ideas. There were scattered North American outposts of the Spanish Empire and, more important, there were French and Dutch settlers who were also vying for a stake in the New World.

France founded its first permanent settlement in America at Quebec in 1608, less than a year after the English started their first at Jamestown. The colony's population grew very slowly, but the French exercised an influence in the New World disproportionate to their numbers, because of their relationships with Native Americans. Unlike the early English settlers, the French forged close ties with natives deep inside the continent. French Jesuit missionaries established some of the first contacts between the two peoples. More important were the *coureurs de bois*—adventurous fur traders and trappers—who also penetrated far into the wilderness and developed an extensive trade that became one of the underpinnings of the French colonial economy. The French traders formed partnerships with the Indians. They often lived among the natives and married Indian women. The fur trade helped open the way for French agricultural estates (or *seigneuries*) along the St. Lawrence River and for the development of trade and military centers at Quebec and Montreal.

Disproportionate French Influence

New Amsterdam

The Dutch, too, were establishing a presence in North America. Holland in the early seventeenth century was one of the leading trading nations of the world. In 1609 an English explorer in the employ of the Dutch, Henry Hudson, sailed up the river that was to be named for him in what is now New York State. His explorations led to a Dutch claim on that territory. In 1624, not long after the first two permanent English colonies took root in Jamestown and Plymouth, the Dutch created a wedge between them when the Dutch West India Company established a series of permanent trading posts on the Hudson, Delaware, and Connecticut Rivers that soon became the colony of New Netherland. Its principal town, New Amsterdam, was on Manhattan Island.

The First English Settlements

The first permanent English settlement in the New World was established at Jamestown, in Virginia, in 1607. But for nearly thirty years before that, English merchants and adventurers had been engaged in a series of failed efforts to create colonies in America.

Through much of the sixteenth century, the English had harbored mixed feelings about the New World. They were intrigued by its possibilities, but they were also leery of Spain, which remained the dominant force in America. In 1588, however, King Philip II of Spain sent one of the largest military fleets in the history of warfare—the Spanish Armada—across the English Channel to attack England itself. The smaller English fleet, taking advantage of its greater maneuverability, defeated the armada and, in a single stroke, ended Spain's domination of the Atlantic. This great shift in naval power caused interest in colonizing the New World to grow quickly.

The Spanish Armada

The pioneers of English colonization were Sir Humphrey Gilbert and his half-brother Sir Walter Raleigh—both veterans of earlier colonial efforts in Ireland. In 1578 Gilbert obtained from Queen Elizabeth a six-year patent granting him the exclusive right "to inhabit and possess any remote and heathen lands not already in the possession of any Christian prince." Five years later, after several setbacks, he led an expedition to Newfoundland looking for a good place to build a profitable colony. But a storm sank his ship, and he was lost at sea. The next year, Sir Walter Raleigh secured his own six-year grant from the queen and sent a small group of men on an expedition to explore the North American coast. When they returned, Raleigh named the region they had explored Virginia, in honor of Elizabeth, who was known as the "Virgin Queen."

Gilbert and Raleigh

In 1585 Raleigh recruited his cousin, Sir Richard Grenville, to lead a group of men to the island of Roanoke, off the coast of what is now North Carolina, to establish a colony. Grenville deposited the settlers on the island, destroyed an Indian village as retaliation for a minor theft, and returned to England. The following spring, with supplies and reinforcements from England long overdue, Sir Francis Drake unexpectedly arrived in Roanoke. The dispirited colonists boarded his ships and left.

Raleigh tried again in 1587, sending an expedition to Roanoke carrying ninety-one men, seventeen women, and nine children. The settlers attempted to take up where the first group of colonists had left off. (Shortly after arriving, one of the women gave birth to a daughter, Virginia Dare, the first American-born child of English parents.) John White, the commander of the expedition, returned to England after several weeks, in search of supplies and additional settlers. Because of a war with Spain, he was unable to return to Roanoke for three years. When he did, in 1590, he found the island utterly deserted, with no clue to the fate of the settlers other than the cryptic inscription "Croatoan" carved on a post.

Failed Colony of Roanoke

ROANOKE A drawing by one of the English colonists in the ill-fated Roanoke expedition of 1585 became the basis for this engraving by Theodore DeBry, published in England in 1590. A small European ship carrying settlers approaches the island of Roanoke, at left. The wreckage of several larger vessels farther out to sea and the presence of Indian settlements on the mainland and on Roanoke itself suggest some of the perils the settlers encountered. *(New York Public Library)*

The Roanoke disaster marked the end of Sir Walter Raleigh's involvement in English colonization of the New World. No later colonizer would receive grants of land in America as vast or undefined as those Raleigh and Gilbert had acquired. Yet the colonizing impulse remained very much alive. In the early years of the seventeenth century, a group of London merchants to whom Raleigh had assigned his charter rights decided to renew the attempt at colonization in Virginia. A rival group of merchants, from the area around Plymouth, was also interested in American ventures and was sponsoring voyages of exploration farther north. In 1606 James I issued a new charter, which divided North America between the two groups. The London group got the exclusive right to colonize in the south, and the Plymouth merchants received the same right in the north. Through the efforts of these and other companies, the first enduring English colonies would be established in America.

CONCLUSION

The lands that Europeans eventually named the Americas were the home of many millions of people before the arrival of Columbus. Having migrated from Asia thousands of years earlier, the pre-Columbian Americans spread throughout the Western Hemisphere and eventually created great civilizations. Among the most notable of them were the Incas in Peru, and the Mayas and Aztecs in Mexico. In the regions north of what was later named the Rio Grande, the human population was smaller and the civilizations less advanced than they were further south. Even so, North American natives created a cluster of civilizations that thrived and expanded.

In the century after European contact, these native populations suffered a series of catastrophes that all but destroyed the civilizations they had built: brutal invasions by Spanish and Portuguese conquistadores and a series of plagues inadvertently imported by Europeans. By the middle of the sixteenth century, the Spanish and Portuguese—no longer faced with effective resistance from the native populations—had established colonial control over all of South America and much of North America.

In the parts of North America that would eventually become the United States, the European presence was for a time much less powerful. The Spanish established an important northern outpost in what is now New Mexico, a society in which Europeans and Indians lived together intimately, if unequally. On the whole, however, the North American Indians remained largely undisturbed by Europeans until English, French, and Dutch migrations began in the early seventeenth century.

FOR FURTHER REFERENCE

Alvin M. Josephy, ed., *America in 1492: The World of the Indian Peoples Before the Arrival of Columbus* (1993) and Brian M. Fagan, *The Great Journey: The Peopling of Ancient America* (1987) provide introductions to pre-Columbian history. William M. Denevan, ed., *The Native Population of the Americas in 1492* (1976) and Russell Thornton, *American Indian Holocaust and Survival: A Population History since 1492* (1987) are important contributions to the debate over the size and character of the American population before Columbus. Alfred Crosby, *The Columbian Exchange: Biological and Cultural Consequences of 1492* (1972) explores the results of European-Indian contact both in the Americas and Europe. D. W. Meinig, *The Shaping of America, Vol I: Atlantic America, 1492–1800* (1986) is an account of the early contacts between Europeans and the New World. Gary Nash, *Red, White and Black: The Peoples of Early America* (1982) provides a brief, multiracial survey of colonial America. Philip Curtin, *The Atlantic Slave Trade: A Census* (1969) has become the indispensable starting point for understanding African forced migration to the Americas. An outstanding collection of essays that summarizes modern scholarship on colonial America is Jack P. Green and J. R. Pole, eds., *Colonial British America: Essays in the New History of the Early Modern Era* (1984). *Columbus and the Age of Discovery* (1991) is a seven-part documentary film series on Christopher Columbus, his era, and his legacy.

For quizzes, Internet resources, references to additional books and films, and more, consult this book's Online Learning Center at www.mhhe.com/unfinishednation4.

THE INCONVENIENCIES THAT HAVE HAPPENED TO SOME PERSONS WHICH HAVE TRANSPORTED THEMSELVES

from *England* to *Virginia*, vvithout prouiſions neceſſary to ſuſtaine themſelues, hath *greatly hindred the Progreſſe of that noble Plantation: For preuention of the like diſorders* heereafter, that no man ſuffer, either through ignorance or miſinformation; it is thought requiſite to publiſh this ſhort declaration: wherein is contained a particular of ſuch neceſ*ſaries, as either priuate families or ſingle perſons ſhall haue cauſe to furniſh themſelues with, for their better ſupport at their firſt landing in* Virginia, *whereby alſo greater numbers may receiue in part, directions how to prouide themſelues.*

Apparrell.

Apparrell for one man, and ſo after the rate for more.

	li.	s.	d.
One Monmouth Cap	00	01	10
Three falling bands	—	01	03
Three ſhirts	—	07	06
One waſte-coate	—	02	02
One ſuite of Canuaſe	—	07	06
One ſuite of Frize	—	10	00
One ſuite of Cloth	—	15	00
Three paire of Iriſh ſtockins	—	04	—
Foure paire of ſhooes	—	08	08
One paire of garters	—	00	10
One doozen of points	—	00	03
One paire of Canuaſe ſheets	—	08	00
Seuen ells of Canuaſe, to make a bed and boulſter, to be filled in *Virginia* 8.s. One Rug for a bed 8.s. which with the bed ſeruing for two men, halfe is	—	08	00
Fiue ells coorſe Canuaſe, to make a bed at Sea for two men, to be filled with ſtraw, iiij.s. One coorſe Rug at Sea for two men, will coſt vj.s. is for one	—	05	00
	04	00	00

Victuall.

For a whole yeere for one man, and ſo for more after the rate.

	li.	s.	d.
Eight buſhels of Meale	02	00	00
Two buſhels of peaſe at 3.s.	—	06	00
Two buſhels of Oatemeale 4.s. 6.d.	—	09	00
One gallon of *Aquauitæ*	—	02	06
One gallon of Oyle	—	03	06
Two gallons of Vineger 1.s.	—	02	00
	03	03	00

Armes.

For one man, but if halfe of your men haue armour it is ſufficient ſo that all haue Peeces and ſwords.

	li.	s.	d.
One Armour compleat, light	—	17	00
One long Peece, fiue foot or fiue and a halfe, neere Musket bore	01	02	—
One ſword	—	05	—
One belt	—	01	—
One bandaleere	—	01	06
Twenty pound of powder	—	18	00
Sixty pound of ſhot or lead, Piſtoll and Gooſe ſhot	—	05	00
	03	09	06

Tooles.

For a family of 6. perſons and ſo after the rate for more.

	li.	s.	d.
Fiue broad howes at 2.s. a piece	—	10	—
Fiue narrow howes at 16.d. a piece	—	06	08
Two broad Axes at 3.s. 8.d. a piece	—	07	04
Fiue felling Axes at 18.d. a piece	—	07	06
Two ſteele hand ſawes at 16.d. a piece	—	02	08
Two two-hand-ſawes at 5.s. a piece	—	10	—
One whip-ſaw, ſet and filed with box, file, and wreſt	—	10	—
Two hammers 12.d. a piece	—	02	00
Three ſhouels 18.d. a piece	—	04	06
Two ſpades at 18.d. a piece	—	03	—
Two augers 6.d. a piece	—	01	00
Sixe chiſſels 6.d. a piece	—	03	00
Two percers ſtocked 4.d. a piece	—	00	08
Three gimlets 2.d. a piece	—	00	06
Two hatchets 21.d. a piece	—	03	06
Two froues to cleaue pale 18.d.	—	03	00
Two hand bills 20. a piece	—	03	04
One grindleſtone 4.s.	—	04	00
Nailes of all ſorts to the value of	02	00	—
Two Pickaxes	—	03	—
	06	02	08

Houſhold Implements.

For a family of 6. perſons, and ſo for more or leſſe after the rate.

	li.	s.	d.
One Iron Pot	00	07	—
One kettle	—	06	—
One large frying-pan	—	02	06
One gridiron	—	01	06
Two skillets	—	05	—
One ſpit	—	02	—
Platters, diſhes, ſpoones of wood	—	04	—
	01	08	00

	li.	s.	d.
For Suger, Spice, and fruit, and at Sea for 6. men	00	12	06
So the full charge of Apparrell, Victuall, Armes, Tooles, and houſhold ſtuffe, and after this rate for each perſon, will amount vnto about the ſumme of	12	10	—
The paſſage of each man is	06	00	—
The fraight of theſe prouiſions for a man, will bee about halfe a Tun, which is	01	10	—
So the whole charge will amount to about	20	00	00

Nets, hookes, lines, and a tent muſt be added, if the number of people be greater, as alſo ſome kine.

And this is the vſuall proportion that the Virginia Company *doe beſtow vpon their Tenants which they ſend.*

Whoſoeuer tranſports himſelfe or any other at his owne charge vnto *Virginia*, ſhall for each perſon ſo tranſported before Midſummer 1625. haue to him and his heires for euer fifty Acres of Land vpon a firſt, and fifty Acres vpon a ſecond diuiſion.

Imprinted at London by FELIX KYNGSTON. 1622.

ADVICE TO MIGRANTS This 1622 handbill by the Virginia Company of London provides a detailed list of items that people contemplating a voyage to America should plan to take with them. The list reflects the company's awareness of how few finished goods were yet available in America (and also their realization that they themselves could profit from selling such goods to their passengers). *(Rare Books Division, New York Public Library, Astor, Lenox and Tilden Foundations)*

TIME LINE

1607	1619	1620	1622	1624	1630	1634	1636	1637
Jamestown founded	First African workers in Virginia	Pilgrims found Plymouth Colony	Powhatan Indians attack Virginia	Dutch settle Manhattan	Puritans establish Massachusetts Bay Colony	Maryland founded	Roger Williams founds Rhode Island	Anne Hutchinson expelled from Massachusetts Bay Colony
	Virginia House of Burgesses meets							Pequot War

CHAPTER TWO

TRANSPLANTATIONS AND BORDERLANDS

The Early Chesapeake
The Growth of New England
The Restoration Colonies
Borderlands and Middle Grounds
The Development of Empire

The Roanoke fiasco dampened colonization enthusiasm in England for a time. But the lures of the New World were too strong to be suppressed for very long. By the early seventeenth century, the effort to establish permanent English colonies in the New World had resumed.

The new efforts were much like the earlier, failed ones: private ventures, with little planning or direction from the English government; small, fragile enterprises led by people unprepared for the hardships they were to face. Unlike the Roanoke experiment, they survived, but not before experiencing a series of disastrous setbacks.

Several things shaped the character of these English settlements. First, the colonies were business enterprises, and one of their principal concerns was to produce a profit for their corporate sponsors. Second, because the colonies were tied only indirectly to the crown, they began from the start to develop their own political and social institutions. Third, the English tried to isolate themselves from the Indians and created communities that would be entirely their own: "transplantations" of societies from the Old World to the New. And fourth, almost nothing worked out as they had planned—largely because the English could not effectively isolate themselves from the world around them—a world populated by Native Americans, by colonists, explorers, and traders from Spain, France, the Netherlands, and other parts of Europe, and by forced immigrants from Africa.

1663	1664	1675	1676	1681	1686	1689	1732
Carolina chartered	English capture New Netherlands	King Philip's War	Bacon's Rebellion	Pennsylvania chartered	Dominion of New England	Glorious Revolution in America	Georgia chartered

THE EARLY CHESAPEAKE

Once James I had issued his 1606 charters, the London Company moved quickly and decisively to launch a colonizing expedition headed for Virginia—a party of 144 men aboard three ships, the *Godspeed*, the *Discovery*, and the *Susan Constant*, which set sail for America early in 1607.

The Founding of Jamestown

Only 104 men survived the journey. They reached the American coast in the spring of 1607, sailed into Chesapeake Bay and up a river they named the James, and established their colony on a peninsula. They called it Jamestown.

They chose an inland setting that they believed would offer them security from the natives. But they chose poorly. The site was low and swampy. It was surrounded by thick woods and it bordered the territories of powerful local Indians. The result could hardly have been more disastrous. For seventeen years, one wave of settlers after another attempted to make Jamestown a habitable and profitable colony. Every effort failed. All that could be said of Jamestown at the end of this first period of its existence was that it had survived.

Jamestown's Early Ordeal

The initial colonists ran into serious difficulties from the moment they landed. They had no prior exposure to the infections of the new land and were highly vulnerable to local diseases, particularly malaria. The promoters in London diverted the colonists' energies into futile searches for gold and only slightly more successful efforts to pile up lumber, tar, pitch, and iron for export. These energies would have been better spent on growing food. The promoters also sent virtually no women to Jamestown. Hence, settlers could not establish real households and had no permanent stake in the community.

By January 1608, when ships appeared with additional men and supplies, all but 38 of the first 104 colonists were dead. Jamestown survived largely as a result of the efforts of Captain John Smith, who at age twenty-seven was already a famous world traveler. Leadership in the colony had been bitterly divided until the fall of 1608, when Smith took control. He imposed work and order on the community. He also organized raids on neighboring Indian villages to steal food and kidnap natives. During the colony's second winter, fewer than a dozen died. By the summer of 1609, the colony was showing promise of survival. But Jamestown's ordeal was not over yet.

John Smith

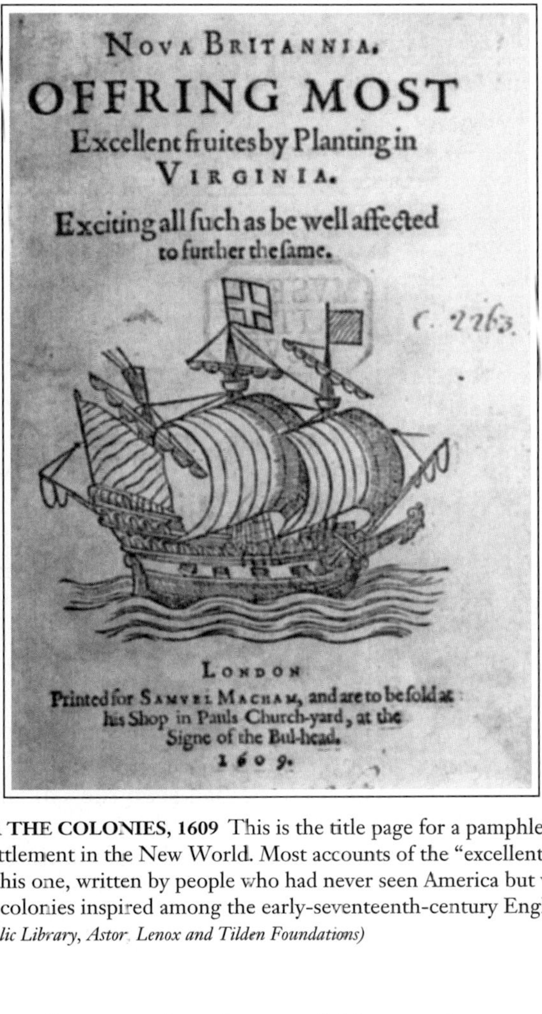

RECRUITING FOR THE COLONIES, 1609 This is the title page for a pamphlet that describes the attractions of settlement in the New World. Most accounts of the "excellent fruites" of life in Virginia were, like this one, written by people who had never seen America but who shared the excitement that the colonies inspired among the early-seventeenth-century English. *(Rare Books Division, New York Public Library, Astor, Lenox and Tilden Foundations)*

Reorganization and Expansion

As Jamestown struggled to survive, the London Company (now renamed the Virginia Company) was already dreaming of bigger things. In 1609, it obtained a new charter from the king, which increased its power and enlarged its territory; and it sent Lord De La Warr to be the colony's first governor. It offered stock in the company to planters who were willing to migrate at their own expense. And it provided free passage to Virginia for poorer people who would agree to serve the company for seven years. In the spring of 1609, the Virginia Company dispatched a fleet of nine vessels with about 600 people aboard (including some women and children) to Virginia.

Disaster followed. One of the Virginia-bound ships was lost at sea in a hurricane. Another ran aground on one of the Bermuda islands and was unable to free itself for months. Many of those who reached Jamestown succumbed to fevers before winter came. The winter of 1609–1610 became known as the "starving time." The local Indians killed off the livestock in the woods and kept the colonists barricaded within their palisade. The Europeans lived on what they could find: "dogs, cats, rats, snakes, toadstools, horsehides," and even the "corpses of dead men," as one survivor recalled. When the migrants who had run aground in Bermuda finally arrived in Jamestown the following May, they found only about 60 emaciated people still alive. The new arrivals took the survivors onto their ship and sailed for home. But as the refugees proceeded down the James, they met an English ship coming up the river—part of a fleet bringing supplies and the colony's first governor, Lord De La Warr. The departing settlers agreed to return to Jamestown. New relief expeditions with hundreds of colonists soon began to arrive, and the effort to turn a profit in Jamestown resumed.

The "Starving Time"

Under the leadership of its first governors, Virginia survived and even expanded. New settlements began lining the river above and below Jamestown. That was partly because of the order and discipline the governors at times managed to impose and because of increased military assaults on the local Indian tribes to protect the new settlements. But it was also because the colonists had at last discovered a marketable crop: tobacco.

Europeans had become aware of tobacco soon after Columbus's first return from the West Indies, where he had seen the Cuban natives smoking small cigars *(tabacos)*, which they inserted in the nostril. By the early seventeenth century, tobacco from the Spanish colonies was already in wide use in Europe. Then in 1612, the Jamestown planter John Rolfe began trying to cultivate the crop in Virginia. Tobacco planting soon spread up and down the James.

The Tobacco Economy

Tobacco growers needed large areas of farmland, and because tobacco exhausted the soil very quickly, the demand for land increased rapidly. As a result, English farmers began establishing plantations deeper and deeper in the interior, isolating themselves from Jamestown and penetrating farther into the territory of the native tribes.

The tobacco economy also created a heavy demand for labor. To entice new workers to the colony, the Virginia Company established what it called the "headright" system. Headrights were fifty-acre grants of land. Those who already lived in the colony received two headrights (100 acres) apiece. Each new settler received a single headright for himself or herself. This system encouraged family groups to migrate together, since the more family members who traveled to America, the more land the family would receive. In addition, anyone who paid for the passage of immigrants to Virginia would receive an extra headright for each arrival. As a result, some colonists were able to assemble large plantations.

The "Headright System"

The company also transported ironworkers and other skilled craftsmen to Virginia to diversify the economy. In 1619, it sent 100 Englishwomen to the colony to become the wives of male colonists. It promised the male colonists the full rights of Englishmen (as provided in the original charter of 1606), an end to strict and arbitrary rule, and even a share in self-government. On July 30, 1619, delegates from the various communities met as the House of Burgesses, the first elected legislature within what was to become the United States.

A month later, Virginia established another important precedent. As John Rolfe recorded, "about the latter end of August" a Dutch ship brought in "20 and odd Negroes." There is some reason to believe that the colonists thought of these first Africans as servants to be held for a term of years and then freed. For a time, moreover, the use of black labor remained limited. Although Africans trickled steadily into the colony, planters continued to prefer European indentured servants until at least the 1670s. But the small group of blacks who arrived in 1619 marked the first step toward the enslavement of Africans within what was to be the American republic.

Birth of American Slavery

The European settlers in Virginia built their society not only on the coerced labor of imported Africans but also on the effective suppression of the local Indians. For two years in the 1610s, Sir Thomas Dale, De La Warr's successor as governor, led unrelenting assaults against the Powhatan Indians, led by (and named for) their formidable chief, Powhatan. In the process, Dale kidnapped Powhatan's young daughter Pocahontas. Several years earlier, Pocahontas had played a role in mediating differences between her people and the Europeans. But now, Powhatan refused to ransom her. Living among the English, Pocahontas gradually adapted to many of their ways. She converted to Christianity and in 1614 married John Rolfe and visited England with him. There she stirred interest among many English in projects to "civilize" the Indians. She died shortly before her planned return to Virginia.

Pocahontas

By the time of Pocahontas's marriage, Powhatan had ceased his attacks on the English in the face of overwhelming odds. But after his death several years later, his brother, Opechancanough, began secretly to plan the elimination of the English intruders. On a March morning in 1622, tribesmen called on the white settlements as if to offer goods for sale; then they suddenly attacked. Not until 347 whites of both sexes and all ages (including John Rolfe) lay dead were the Indian warriors finally forced to retreat. And not until over twenty years later were the Powhatans finally defeated.

By then, however, the Virginia Company in London was defunct. In 1624, James I revoked the company's charter, and the colony came under the control of the crown where it would remain until 1776. The colony, if not the company, had survived—but at a terrible cost. In Virginia's first seventeen years, more than 8,500 white settlers had arrived in the colony, and nearly eighty percent of them had died.

Demise of the Virginia Company

Exchanges of Agricultural Technology

The hostility the early English settlers expressed toward their Indian neighbors was in part a result of their conviction that their own civilization was greatly superior to that of the natives. The English, after all, had great ocean-going vessels, muskets and other advanced implements of weaponry, and many other tools that the Indians had not developed. Indeed, when John Smith and other early Jamestown residents grew frustrated at their inability to find gold, they often blamed the backwardness of the natives. The Spanish in South America, Smith once wrote, had grown rich because the natives there had built advanced civilizations and mined much gold and silver. If Mexico and Peru had been as "ill peopled, as little planted, laboured and manured as Virginia," he added, the Spanish would have found no more wealth than the English did.

Yet the survival of Jamestown was, in the end, largely a result of agricultural technologies developed by Indians and borrowed by the English. Native agriculture was far better adapted to the soil and climate of Virginia than the agricultural traditions the English settlers brought with them. The Indians of Virginia were settled farmers whose villages were surrounded by neatly ordered fields in which grew a variety of crops—beans, pumpkins, vegetables, and above all maize (known to us as corn). Some of the Indian farmlands stretched over hundreds of acres and supported substantial populations.

Indian Agricultural Techniques

The English settlers did not adopt all the Indian agricultural techniques. But the English learned a great deal from the Indians about how to grow food in the New World. In particular, they quickly recognized the value of corn, which proved to be easier to cultivate and which produced much larger yields than any of the European grains the English had known at home. The English also learned the advantages of growing beans alongside corn to enrich the soil. An early settler in New England wrote that the Indians had taught the settlers "to cull out the finest seede, to observe the fittest season, to keepe distance for holes, and fit measure for hills, to worme it, and weede it; to prune it, and dresse it as occasion shall require."

Like the natives, the English quickly learned to combine the foods they grew with food for which they hunted and fished, and here, too, Indian techniques proved of great value. Particularly valuable was the canoe, which was much better at navigating the rivers and streams of Virginia (and later New England) than were any English vessels. Canoes could be made by hollowing out a single log (dugouts) or sewing birchbark around a simple frame and sealing it with resin (birchbark canoes, some of which could hold as many as eighty people). John Smith was a particular admirer of the Indian canoes. The "primitive" civilizations of the natives in fact provided the early settlers with some of their most vital agricultural techniques and technologies.

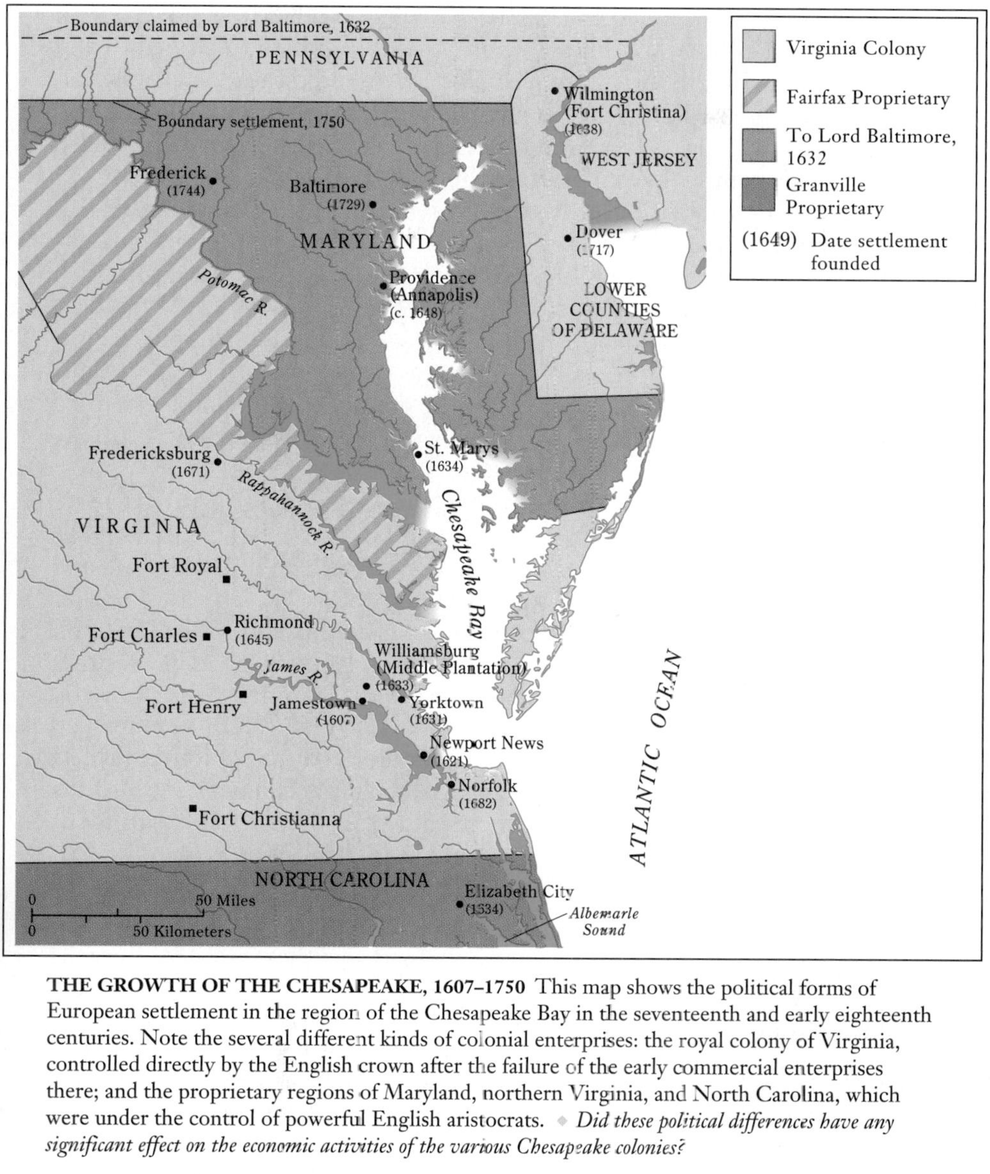

THE GROWTH OF THE CHESAPEAKE, 1607–1750 This map shows the political forms of European settlement in the region of the Chesapeake Bay in the seventeenth and early eighteenth centuries. Note the several different kinds of colonial enterprises: the royal colony of Virginia, controlled directly by the English crown after the failure of the early commercial enterprises there; and the proprietary regions of Maryland, northern Virginia, and North Carolina, which were under the control of powerful English aristocrats. ◆ *Did these political differences have any significant effect on the economic activities of the various Chesapeake colonies?*

Maryland and the Calverts

George Calvert

The Maryland colony ultimately came to look much like Virginia, but its origins were very different from those of its southern neighbor. George Calvert, the first Lord Baltimore, envisioned establishing a colony in America both as a great speculative venture in real estate and as a refuge for English Catholics like himself. Calvert died while still negotiating with the king for a charter to establish a colony in the Chesapeake region. But in 1632 his son Cecilius, the second Lord Baltimore, finally received the charter.

Lord Baltimore named his brother, Leonard Calvert, as governor of the colony. In March 1634, two ships—the *Ark* and the *Dove*—bearing Calvert along with 200 or 300 other colonists, entered the Potomac River, turned into one of its eastern tributaries, and established the village of St. Mary's on a high, dry bluff. Neighboring Indians befriended the settlers and provided them with temporary shelter and with stocks of corn.

The Calverts needed to attract thousands of settlers to Maryland if their expensive colonial venture was to pay. As a result, they had to encourage the immigration of Protestants as well as their fellow English Catholics. The Calverts soon realized that Catholics would always be a minority in the colony, and so they adopted a policy of religious toleration, embodied in the 1649 "Act Concerning Religion." Nevertheless, politics in Maryland remained plagued for years by tensions, and at times violence, between the Catholic minority and the Protestant majority.

"Act Concerning Religion"

At the insistence of the first settlers, the Calverts agreed in 1635 to the calling of a representative assembly—the House of Delegates. But the proprietor retained absolute authority to distribute land as he wished; and since Lord Baltimore granted large estates to his relatives and to other English aristocrats, a distinct upper class soon established itself. By 1640, a severe labor shortage forced a modification of the land-grant procedure; and Maryland, like Virginia, adopted a headright system—a grant of 100 acres to each male settler, another 100 for his wife and each servant, and 50 for each of his children. But the great landlords of the colony's earliest years remained powerful. Like Virginia, Maryland became a center of tobacco cultivation; planters worked their land with the aid, first, of indentured servants imported from England and then, beginning late in the seventeenth century, of slaves imported from Africa.

Bacon's Rebellion

Sir William Berkeley

For more than thirty years, one man—Sir William Berkeley, the royal governor of Virginia—dominated the politics of the colony. He took office in 1642 at the age of thirty-six and with but one brief interruption remained in control of the government until the 1670s. In his first years as governor, he helped open up the interior of Virginia by sending explorers across the Blue Ridge Mountains and crushing a 1644 Indian uprising. The defeated Indians agreed to a treaty ceding to England most of the territory east of the mountains and establishing a boundary west of which white settlement would be prohibited. But the rapid growth of the Virginia population made this agreement difficult to sustain. Between 1640 and 1660, Virginia's population rose from 8,000 to over 40,000. By 1652, English settlers had established three counties in the territory set aside by the treaty for the Indians.

In the meantime, Berkeley was expanding his own powers. By 1670, the vote for delegates to the House of Burgesses, once open to all white men, was restricted to landowners. Elections were rare, and the same burgesses, representing the established planters of the eastern (or tidewater) region of the colony, remained in office year after year. The more recent settlers on the frontier were underrepresented.

Resentment of the power of the governor and the tidewater aristocrats grew steadily in the newly settled lands of the west (often known as the "backcountry"). In 1676, this resentment helped create a major conflict, led by Nathaniel Bacon. Bacon had a good farm in the west and a seat on the governor's council. But like other members of the new backcountry gentry, he chafed at the governor's attempts to hold the line of settlement steady so as to avoid antagonizing the Indians. Bacon's rift with Berkeley was also a result of resentment that Berkeley refused to allow him a piece of the Indian fur trade, which the governor himself controlled.

"Backcountry" Resentment

In 1675, a major conflict erupted in the west between whites and natives. As the fighting escalated, Bacon and other concerned landholders demanded that the governor send the militia. When Berkeley refused, Bacon responded by offering to organize a volunteer army of backcountry men who would do their own fighting. Berkeley rejected the offer. Bacon ignored him and launched a series of vicious but unsuccessful pursuits of the Indian challengers. When Berkeley heard of the unauthorized military effort, he proclaimed Bacon and his men to be rebels. Bacon now turned his army against the governor and, in what became known as Bacon's Rebellion, twice led his troops east to Jamestown. The first time he won a temporary pardon from the governor; the second time, after the governor repudiated the agreement, Bacon burned much of the city and drove the governor into exile. But then Bacon died suddenly of dysentery; and Berkeley soon regained control. In 1677, the Indians reluctantly signed a new treaty that opened new lands to white settlement.

Bacon's Rebellion was evidence of the continuing struggle to define the Indian and white spheres of influence in Virginia. It also revealed the bitterness of the competition among rival elites, and it demonstrated the potential for instability in the colony's large population of free, landless men. One result was that landed elites in both eastern and western Virginia began to recognize a common interest in quelling social unrest from below. That was among the reasons that they turned increasingly to the African slave trade to fulfill their need for labor. African slaves, unlike white indentured servants, did not need to be released after a fixed term and hence did not threaten to become an unstable, landless class.

Consequences of Bacon's Rebellion

THE GROWTH OF NEW ENGLAND

The northern regions of British North America were slow to attract settlers, in part because the Plymouth Company was never able to mount a successful colonizing expedition after receiving its charter in 1606. It did, however, sponsor explorations of the region. Captain John Smith, after his departure from Jamestown, made an exploratory journey for the Plymouth merchants, wrote an enthusiastic pamphlet about the lands he had seen, and called them New England.

Plymouth Plantation

A discontented congregation of Puritan Separatists in England, not the Plymouth Company, established the first enduring European settlement in New England. In 1608, a congregation of Separatists from the hamlet of Scrooby began emigrating quietly (and illegally), a few at a time, to Leyden, Holland, where they could enjoy freedom of worship. But as foreigners in Holland, they had to work at unskilled and poorly paid jobs. They also watched with alarm as their children began to adapt to Dutch society and drift away from their church. Finally, some of the Separatists decided to move again, across the Atlantic, where they hoped to create a stable, protected community where they could spread "the gospel of the Kingdom of Christ in those remote parts of the world."

The Scrooby Separatists

In 1620, leaders of the Scrooby group obtained permission from the Virginia Company to settle in Virginia. The "Pilgrims," as they saw themselves, sailed from Plymouth, England, in September 1620 on the *Mayflower*; thirty-five "saints" (Puritan Separatists) and sixty-seven "strangers" (people who were not part of the congregation) were aboard. In November, after a long and difficult voyage, they sighted land—the shore of what is now known as Cape Cod. That had not been their destination, but it was too late in the year to sail farther south. So the Pilgrims chose a site for their settlement in the area just north of the cape, a place John Smith had labeled "Plymouth" on a map he had drawn during an earlier exploration of New England. Because Plymouth lay outside the London Company's territory, the settlers were not bound by the company's rules. While still aboard ship, the "saints" in the group drew up an agreement, the Mayflower Compact, to establish a government for themselves. Then, on December 21, 1620, they stepped ashore at Plymouth Rock.

Plymouth Founded

The Pilgrims' first winter was a difficult one. Half the colonists perished from malnutrition, disease, and exposure. But the colony survived, in large part because of crucial assistance from local Indians. Trade and other exchanges with the Indians were critical to the settlers and attractive to the natives. The tribes

Pilgrim-Indian Interaction

provided the colonists with furs. They also showed the settlers how to cultivate corn and how to hunt wild animals for meat. After the first autumn harvest, the settlers invited the natives to join them in a festival, the original Thanksgiving. But the relationship between the settlers and the local Indians was not a happy one for long. Thirteen years after the Pilgrims arrived, a devastating smallpox epidemic—a result of natives' exposure to Europeans carrying the disease—wiped out much of the Indian population around Plymouth.

The Pilgrims could not create rich farms on the sandy and marshy soil around Plymouth, but they developed a profitable trade in fish and furs. New colonists arrived from England, and in a decade the population reached 300. The people of Plymouth Plantation chose as their governor the remarkable William Bradford, who governed successfully for many years. The Pilgrims were always poor. As late as the 1640s, they had only one plow among them. But they were, on the whole, content to be left alone to live their lives in what they considered godly ways.

The Massachusetts Bay Experiment

Events in England encouraged other Puritans to migrate to the New World. King James I had pursued repressive policies toward Puritans for years. When he died in 1625, his son and successor, Charles I, was even more hostile to Puritans and imprisoned many of them for their beliefs. The king dissolved Parliament in 1629 (it was not to be recalled until 1640), ensuring that there would be no one in a position to oppose him.

In the midst of this turmoil, a group of Puritan merchants began organizing a new colonial venture in America. They obtained a grant of land in New England for most of the area now comprising Massachusetts and New Hampshire, and they acquired a charter from the king allowing them to create the Massachusetts Bay Company and to establish a colony in the New World. Some members of the Massachusetts Bay Company wanted to create a refuge in New England for Puritans. They bought out the interests of company members who preferred to stay in England, and the new owners elected a governor, John Winthrop. They then sailed for New England in 1630. With 17 ships and 1,000 people, it was the largest single migration of its kind in the seventeenth century. Winthrop carried with him the charter of the Massachusetts Bay Company, which meant that the colonists would be responsible to no company officials in England.

Massachusetts Bay Company

The Massachusetts migration quickly produced several settlements. The port of Boston became the capital, but in the course of the next decade colonists established several other towns in eastern Massachusetts: Charlestown, Newtown (later renamed Cambridge), Roxbury, Dorchester, Watertown, Ipswich, Concord, Sudbury, and others.

The Massachusetts Puritans were not grim or joyless, as many critics would later come to believe, but they were serious and pious. They strove to lead useful, conscientious lives of thrift and hard work, and they honored material success as evidence of God's favor. Winthrop and the other founders of Massachusetts believed they were founding a holy commonwealth, a model—a "city upon a hill"—for the corrupt world to see and emulate. Colonial Massachusetts was a "theocracy," a society in which the church was almost indistinguishable from the state. Residents had no more freedom of worship than the Puritans themselves had had in England.

Winthrop's "City on a Hill"

Like other new settlements, the Massachusetts Bay colony had early difficulties. During the first winter (1629–1630), nearly 200 people died and many others decided to leave. But the colony soon grew and prospered. The nearby Pilgrims and neighboring Indians helped with food and advice. Incoming settlers brought needed tools and other goods. The dominance of families in the colony helped ensure a feeling of commitment to the community and a sense of order among the settlers, and it also ensured that the population would reproduce itself.

The Expansion of New England

It did not take long for English settlement to begin moving outward from Massachusetts Bay. Some people migrated in search of soil more productive than that the stony land around Boston provided. Others left because of the oppressiveness of the church-dominated government of Massachusetts.

Fundamental Orders of Connecticut

The Connecticut River valley, about 100 miles west of Boston, began attracting English families as early as the 1630s because of the valley's fertile lands and its isolation from Massachusetts Bay. In 1635, Thomas Hooker, a minister of Newtown (Cambridge), defied the Massachusetts government, led his congregation west, and established the town of Hartford. Four years later, the people of Hartford and of two other newly founded towns nearby adopted a constitution known as the Fundamental Orders of Connecticut, which created an independent colony with a government similar to that of Massachusetts Bay but gave a larger proportion of the men the right to vote and hold office. (Women were barred from voting virtually everywhere.)

Another Connecticut colony grew up around New Haven on the Connecticut coast. Unlike Hartford, it reflected unhappiness with what its founders considered the increasing religious laxity in Boston. The Fundamental Articles of New Haven (1639) established a Bible-based government even stricter than that of Massachusetts Bay. New Haven remained independent until 1662, when a royal charter officially gave the Hartford colony jurisdiction over the New Haven settlements.

Roger Williams's Dissent

European settlement in what is now Rhode Island was a result of the religious and political dissent of Roger Williams, a controversial young minister who lived for a time in Salem, Massachusetts. Williams was a confirmed Separatist who

CHAPTER THREE

SOCIETY AND CULTURE IN PROVINCIAL AMERICA

The Colonial Population
The Colonial Economies
Patterns of Society
Awakenings and Enlightenments

The British colonies were, most people in both England and America believed, outposts of the British world. And it is true that as the colonies grew and became more prosperous, they also became more English. Some of the early settlers had come to America to escape what they considered English tyranny. But by the early eighteenth century, many, perhaps most, colonists considered themselves Englishmen just as much as the men and women in England itself did.

At the same time, however, life in the colonies was diverging in many ways from that in England simply by the nature of the New World. The physical environment was very different—vaster and less tamed. The population was more diverse as well. The area that would become the United States was a magnet for immigrants from many lands other than England: Scotland, Ireland, the European continent, eastern Russia, the Spanish and French empires already established in America. And English North America became as well the destination for thousands of forcibly transplanted Africans. Equally important, Europeans and Africans were interacting constantly with a native population that for many years outnumbered them.

To the degree that the colonists emulated English society, they were becoming more and more like one another. To the degree that they were shaped by the character of their own regions, they were becoming more and more different. Indeed, the pattern of society in some areas of North America resembled that of other areas scarcely at all.

1720	1734	1739	1740s
Cotton Mather starts smallpox inoculations	Great Awakening begins	George Whitefield arrives in America	Indigo production begins
	Zenger Trial	Great Awakening intensifies	
		Stono Slave rebellion	

THE COLONIAL POPULATION

Immigration and Natural Increase

After uncertain beginnings, the non-Indian population of English North America grew rapidly and substantially, through continued immigration and through natural increase. By the late seventeenth century European and African immigrants outnumbered the natives along the Atlantic coast.

A few of the early settlers were members of the English upper classes, but the dominant element was English laborers. Some came independently, such as the religious dissenters in early New England. But in the Chesapeake, at least three-fourths of the immigrants in the seventeenth century arrived as indentured servants.

Indentured Servitude

The system of temporary servitude developed out of practices in England. Young men and women bound themselves to masters for fixed terms of servitude (usually four to five years) in exchange for passage to America, food, and shelter. Male indentures were supposed to receive clothing, tools, and occasionally land upon completion of their service. In reality, however, many left service with nothing. Most women indentures—who constituted roughly one-fourth of the total in the Chesapeake—worked as domestic servants and were expected to marry when their terms of servitude expired.

Social Problems of Indentured Servitude

By the late seventeenth century, the indentured servant population had become one of the largest elements of the colonial population and was creating serious social problems. Some former indentures managed to establish themselves successfully as farmers, tradespeople, or artisans, and some of the women married propertied men. Others (mostly males) found themselves without land, without employment, without families, and without prospects; and there grew up in some areas, particularly the Chesapeake, a large floating population of young single men who served as a source of social unrest.

Growing Reliance on Slavery

Beginning in the 1670s, a decrease in the birth rate in England and an improvement in economic conditions there reduced the pressures on laboring men and women to emigrate, and the flow of indentured servants declined. Those who did travel to America as indentures now generally avoided the southern colonies, where prospects for advancement were slim. In the Chesapeake, therefore, landowners began to rely much more heavily on African slavery as their principal source of labor.

Birth and Death

Although immigration remained for a time the greatest source of population growth, the most important long-range factor in the increase of the colonial population was its ability to reproduce itself. Marked improvement in the reproduction rate began in New England and the mid-Atlantic colonies in the second half of the seventeenth century, and after the 1650s natural increase became the most important source of population growth in those areas. The New England population more than quadrupled through reproduction alone in the second half of the seventeenth century. This rise was a result not only of families having large numbers of children. It was also because life expectancy in New England was unusually high.

High Death Rate in the South

Conditions improved much more slowly in the South. The high death rates in the Chesapeake region did not begin to decline to the levels of those elsewhere until the mid-eighteenth century. Throughout the seventeenth century, the average life expectancy for European men in the region was just over forty years, and for women slightly less. One in four white children died in infancy, and half died before the age of twenty. Children who survived infancy often lost one or both of their parents before reaching maturity. Widows, widowers, and orphans thus formed a substantial proportion of the white Chesapeake population. Only after settlers developed immunity to local diseases (particularly malaria) did life expectancy increase significantly. Population growth was substantial in the region, but it was largely a result of immigration.

Toward a Balanced Sex Ratio

The natural increases in the population in the seventeenth century were in large part a result of steady improvement in the balance between men and women in the colonies. In the early years of settlement, more than three-quarters of the white population of the Chesapeake consisted of men. And even in New England, which from the beginning had attracted more families (and thus more women) than the southern colonies, 60 percent of the inhabitants were male in 1650. Gradually, however, more women began to arrive in the colonies; and increasing birth rates contributed to shifting the sex ratio (the balance between men and women) as well. Throughout the colonial period, the population almost doubled every twenty-five years. By 1775, the non-Indian population of the colonies was over 2 million.

Medicine in the Colonies

The very high death rates of women who bore children illustrate the primitive nature of medical knowledge and practice in the colonies. Physicians had little or no understanding of infection and sterilization. As a result, many people died from infections contracted during childbirth or surgery. Because communities were unaware of bacteria, many were plagued with infectious diseases transmitted by garbage or unclean water.

One result of the limited extent of medical knowledge was that it was relatively easy for people to enter the field, even without any professional training. The biggest beneficiaries of this were women, who established themselves in considerable numbers as midwives. Midwives assisted women in childbirth, but they also dispensed other medical advice. They were popular because they were usually friends and neighbors of the people they treated, unlike physicians, who were few and therefore not often well known to their patients. Male doctors felt threatened by the midwives and struggled continually to drive them from the field, although they did not make substantial progress in doing so until the nineteenth century.

Midwifery

Midwives and doctors alike practiced medicine on the basis of the prevailing assumptions of their time, most of them derived from the theory of "humoralism" popularized by the great second-century Roman physician Galen. Galen argued that the human body was governed by four "humors" that were lodged in four bodily fluids: yellow bile (or "choler"), black bile ("melancholy"), blood, and phlegm. In a healthy body, the four humors existed in balance. Illness represented an imbalance and suggested the need for removing from the body the excesses of whatever fluid was causing the imbalance. That was the rationale that lay behind the principal medical techniques of the seventeenth century: purging, expulsion, and bleeding. Bleeding was practiced mostly by male physicians. Midwives favored "pukes" and laxatives. The great majority of early Americans, however, had little contact with physicians, or even midwives, and sought instead to deal with illness on their own. The assumption that treating illness was the exclusive province of trained professionals, so much a part of the twentieth century and beyond, lay far in the distance in the colonial era.

"Humoralism"

That seventeenth-century medicine rested so much on ideas produced 1,400 years before is evidence of how little support there was for the scientific method in England and America at the time. Bleeding, for example, had been in use for hundreds of years, during which time there had been no evidence at all that it helped people recover from illness; indeed, if anyone had chosen to look for it, there was considerable evidence that bleeding could do great harm. But what would seem in later eras to be the simple process of testing scientific assumptions was not yet a common part of Western thought. That was one reason that the birth of the Enlightenment in the late seventeenth century—with its faith in human reason and its belief in the capacity of individuals and societies to create better lives—was important not just to politics but to science.

Women and Families in the Colonies

Early Marriages

Because there were many more men than women in seventeenth-century America, few women remained unmarried for long. The average European woman in America married for the first time at twenty or twenty-one years of age. Because of the large numbers of indentured servants who were forbidden to marry until their terms of service expired, premarital sexual relationships were frequent. Children born out of wedlock to indentured women were often taken from their mothers at a young age and themselves bound out as indentured servants.

Women in the Chesapeake could anticipate a life consumed with childbearing. The average wife experienced pregnancies every two years. Those who lived long enough bore an average of eight children apiece (up to five of whom typically died in infancy or early childhood). Since childbirth was one of the most frequent causes of female death, many women did not survive to see their children grow to maturity. Those who did, however, were often widowed, since they were usually much younger than their husbands.

Stable New England Families

In New England, where many more immigrants arrived with family members and where death rates declined far more quickly, family structure was much more stable than in the Chesapeake. The sex ratio was more balanced than in the Chesapeake, so most men could expect to marry. As in the Chesapeake, women married young, began producing children early, and continued to do so well into their thirties. In contrast to the situation in the South, however, northern children were more likely to survive, and their families were more likely to remain intact. Fewer New England women became widows, and those who did generally lost their husbands later in life.

The longer lives in New England meant that parents continued to control their children longer than did parents in the South. Few sons and daughters could choose a spouse entirely independently of their parents' wishes. Men tended to rely on their fathers for land to cultivate. Women needed dowries from their parents if they were to attract desirable husbands. Stricter parental supervision of children meant, too, that fewer women became pregnant before marriage than was the case in the South.

Patriarchal Puritanism

Puritanism placed a high value on the family, and the position of wife and mother was highly valued in Puritan culture. At the same time, however, Puritanism served to reinforce the idea of nearly absolute male authority. A wife was expected to devote herself almost entirely to serving the needs of her husband and the family economy.

AFRICANS BOUND FOR AMERICA Shown here are the below-deck slave quarters of a Spanish vessel en route to the West Indies. A British warship captured the slaver, and a young English naval officer (Lt. Francis Meynell) made this watercolor sketch on the spot. The Africans seen in this picture appear somewhat more comfortable than prisoners on some other slave ships, who were often chained and packed together so tightly that they had no room to stand or even sit. *(National Maritime Museum, London)*

The Beginnings of Slavery in English America

The demand for African servants to supplement the scarce southern labor force existed almost from the first moments of settlement. For a time, however, black workers were hard to find. Not until the mid-seventeenth century, when a substantial commerce in slaves grew up between the Caribbean islands and the southern colonies, did black workers become generally available in North America.

The demand for slaves in North America helped expand the transatlantic slave trade. And as slave trading grew more extensive and more sophisticated, it also grew more horrible. Before it ended in the nineteenth century, it was responsible for the forced immigration of as many as 11 million Africans to North and South America and the Caribbean. In the flourishing slave marts on the African coast, native chieftains brought captured members of rival tribes to the ports. The terrified victims were then packed

The "Middle Passage"

into the dark, filthy holds of ships for the horrors of the "middle passage"—the long journey to the Americas, during which the prisoners were usually kept chained in the bowels of the slave ships and supplied with only minimal food and water. Many slave traders tried to cram as many Africans as possible into their ships to ensure that enough would survive to yield a profit at journey's end. Those who died en route, and many did, were simply thrown overboard. Upon arrival in the New World, slaves were auctioned off to white landowners and transported, frightened and bewildered, to their new homes.

North America was a less important direct destination for African slaves than were such other parts of the New World as the Caribbean islands and Brazil; fewer than 5 percent of the Africans imported to the Americas arrived first in the English colonies. Through most of the seventeenth century, those blacks who were transported to what became the United States came not directly from Africa but from the West Indies. Not until the 1670s did traders start importing blacks directly from Africa to North America. Even then the flow remained small for a time, mainly because a single group, the Royal African Company of England, monopolized the trade and kept prices high and supplies low.

Surging Slave Population

A turning point in the history of the black population in North America was 1697, the year rival traders broke the Royal African Company's monopoly. With the trade now open to competition, prices fell and the number of Africans greatly increased. In 1700, about 25,000 African slaves lived in English North America. Because blacks were so heavily concentrated in a few southern colonies, they were already beginning to outnumber whites in some areas. There were perhaps twice as many black men as black women in most areas, but in some places the African-American population grew by natural increase nevertheless. In the Chesapeake more new slaves were being born than were being imported from Africa. In South Carolina, by contrast, the arduous conditions of rice cultivation ensured that the black population would barely be able to sustain itself through natural increase until much later. By 1760, the number of Africans in the colonies had increased to approximately a quarter of a million, the vast majority of whom lived in the South. By then blacks had almost wholly replaced white indentured servants as the basis of the southern work force.

Ambiguous Legal Status

For a time, the legal and social status of the African laborers remained somewhat fluid. In some areas white and black laborers worked together at first on terms of relative equality. Some blacks were treated much like white hired servants, and some were freed after a fixed term of servitude. By the late seventeenth century, however, a rigid distinction was emerging between blacks and whites. Gradually, the assumption spread that blacks would remain in service permanently and that black children would inherit their parents' bondage. White beliefs about the inferiority of the black race reinforced the growing rigidity of the system, but so did the economic advantages of the system to white slaveowners.

Race-based "Slave Codes"

The system of permanent servitude—American slavery—became legal in the early eighteenth century when colonial assemblies began to pass "slave codes" granting white masters almost absolute authority over their slaves. Only one factor determined whether a person was subject to the slave codes: color. In the colonial societies of Spanish America, people of mixed race were granted a different (and higher) status than pure Africans. English America recognized no such distinctions.

Debating the Past

THE ORIGINS OF SLAVERY

The debate among historians over how and why white Americans created a system of slave labor in the seventeenth century—and how and why they determined that African Americans and no others should populate that system—has been an unusually lively one. At its center is a debate over whether slavery was a result of white racism, or whether racism was a result of slavery.

In 1950, Oscar and Mary Handlin published an influential article comparing slavery to other systems of "unfreedom" in the colonies. What separated slavery from other conditions of servitude, they argued, was that it was restricted to people of African descent, that it was permanent, and that it passed from one generation to the next. The unique characteristics of slavery, the Handlins argued, were part of an effort by colonial legislatures to increase the available labor force. White laborers needed an incentive to come to America; black laborers, forcibly imported from Africa, did not. The distinction between the conditions of white workers and the conditions of black workers was, therefore, based on legal and economic motives, not on racism.

Winthrop Jordan was one of a number historians who later challenged the Handlins' thesis and argued that white racism, more than economic interests, produced African slavery. In *White Over Black* (1968) and other works, Jordan argued that Europeans had long viewed people of color as inferior beings. Those attitudes migrated with white Europeans to the New World, and white racism shaped the treatment of Africans in America from the beginning. Even without the economic incentives the Handlins described, in other words, whites would have been likely to oppress blacks in the New World.

Peter Wood's *Black Majority* (1974), a study of seventeenth-century South Carolina, was one of a number of works that moved the debate back toward social and economic conditions. Wood demonstrated that blacks and whites often worked together on relatively equal terms in the early years of settlement. But as rice cultivation expanded, it became more difficult to find white laborers willing to do the arduous work. The increase in the forcible importation of African slaves was a response to this growing demand for labor. It was also a response to fears among whites that without slavery it would be difficult to control a labor force brought to America against its will. Edmund Morgan's *American Slavery, American Freedom* (1975) argued similarly that the southern labor system was at first relatively flexible and later grew more rigid. In colonial Virginia, he claimed, white settlers did not at first intend to create a system of permanent bondage. But as the tobacco economy grew and created a high demand for cheap labor, white landowners began to feel uneasy about their dependence on a large group of dependent white workers. Such workers were difficult to recruit and control. Slavery, therefore, was less a result of racism than of the desire for whites to find a reliable and stable labor force.

Robin Blackburn's *The Making of New World Slavery* (1996) argues particularly strenuously that, while race was a factor in making the enslavement of Africans easier for whites to justify to themselves, the real reasons for the emergence of slavery were hardheaded economic decisions by ambitious entrepreneurs who realized very early that a slave-labor system in the labor-intensive agricultural world of the American South and the Caribbean was more profitable than a free-labor system. Slavery served the interests of a powerful combination of groups: planters, merchants, industrialists, and consumers. The most important reason for the creation and continuation of the system, therefore, was not racism, but the pursuit of profit. Slavery was not, Blackburn concludes, an antiquated remnant of an older world. It was a recognizably modern labor system that served the needs of an emerging market economy.

(text continued from page 65)

Changing Sources of European Immigration

The most distinctive and enduring feature of the American population was that it brought together peoples of many different races, ethnic groups, and nationalities. North America was home to a substantial population of natives, to a growing number of English immigrants, to forcibly imported Africans, and to substantial non-English groups from Europe.

Religious Refugees

The earliest of these continental European immigrants were about 300,000 French Calvinists, or Huguenots, who left Roman Catholic France for the English colonies of North America after the Edict of Nantes, which had guaranteed them substantial liberties, was revoked in 1685. Many German Protestants emigrated to America to escape similarly arbitrary religious policies and the frequent wars between their principalities and France. The Rhineland of southwestern Germany, known as the Palatinate, was exposed to frequent invasion; more than 12,000 Palatinate Germans fled to England early in the eighteenth century, and approximately 3,000 of them found their way to America. Most settled in Pennsylvania, where they ultimately became known to English settlers as the "Pennsylvania Dutch" (a corruption of the German term for their nationality, *Deutsch*). Other, later German immigrants headed to Pennsylvania as well, among them the Moravians and Mennonites.

Scotch-Irish

The most numerous of the newcomers were the so-called Scotch-Irish—Scotch Presbyterians who had settled in northern Ireland (in the province of Ulster) in the early seventeenth century. Most of the Scotch-Irish in America pushed out to the edges of European settlement and occupied land without much regard for who actually claimed to own it.

There were also immigrants from Scotland itself and from southern Ireland. Scottish Highlanders, some of them Roman Catholics, mainly immigrated into North Carolina. Scottish Presbyterian Lowlanders, fleeing high rents and unemployment, left for America in large numbers shortly before the American Revolution. The Irish migrated steadily over a long period. Many of them abandoned their Roman Catholic religion and much of their ethnic identity after they arrived in America.

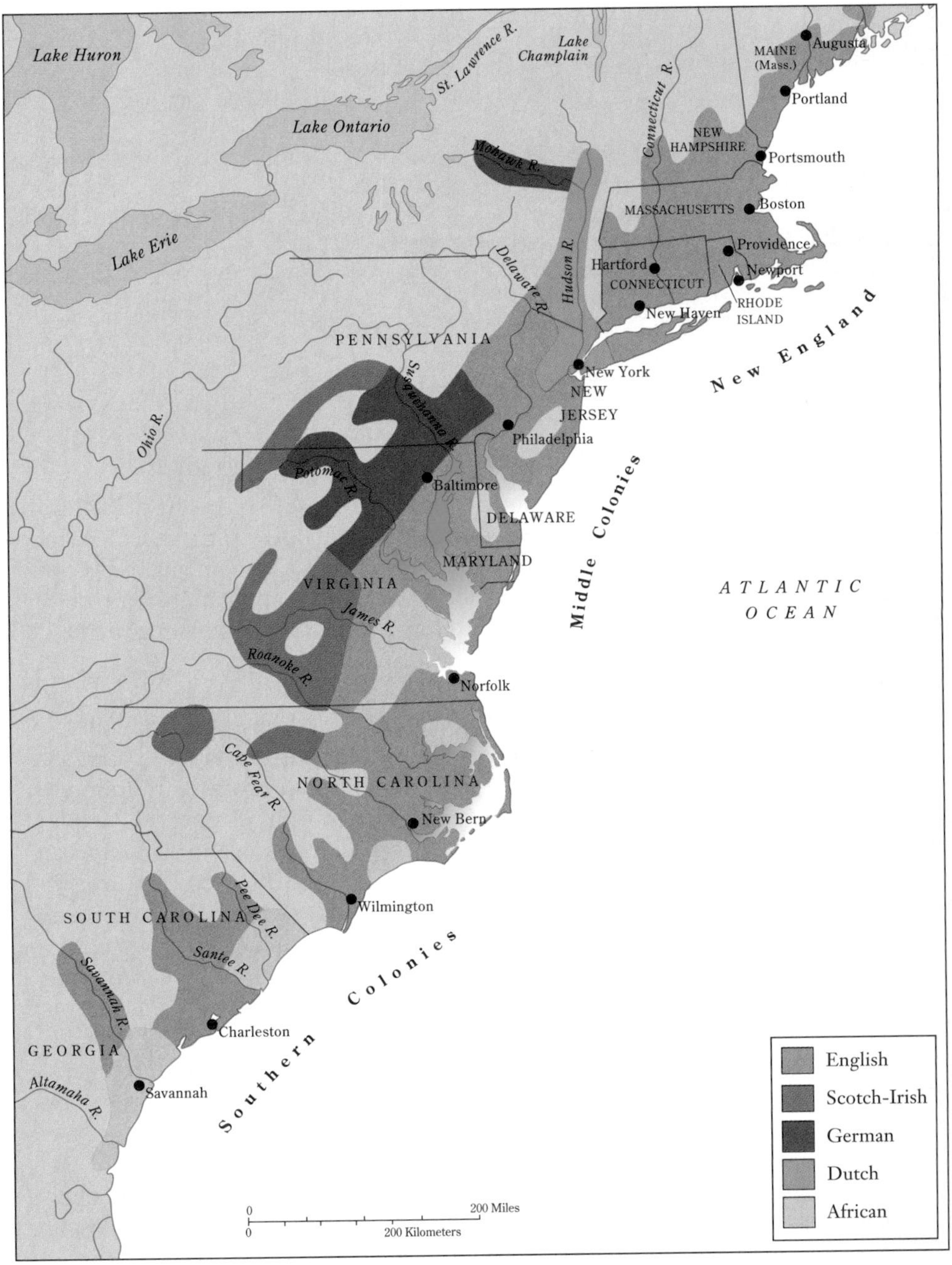

IMMIGRANT GROUPS IN COLONIAL AMERICA, 1760 Even though the entire Atlantic seaboard of what is now the United States had become a series of British colonies by 1760, the population consisted of people from many nations. As this map reveals, English settlers dominated most of the regions of North America. But note the large areas of German settlement in the western Chesapeake and Pennsylvania; the swath of Dutch settlement in New York and New Jersey; the Scotch-Irish regions in the western regions of the South; and the large areas in which Africans were becoming the majority of the population, even if subjugated by the white minority. ◆ *What aspects of the history of these colonies help explain their ethnic composition?*

For an interactive version of this map go to www.mhhe.com/unfinishednation4ch3maps

THE COLONIAL ECONOMIES

Farming dominated almost all areas of European and African settlement in North America throughout the seventeenth and eighteenth centuries. Even so, the economies of the different regions varied markedly.

The Southern Economy

A strong European demand for tobacco enabled some planters in the Chesapeake (Maryland and Virginia) to become enormously wealthy and at times allowed the region as a whole to prosper. But throughout the seventeenth and eighteenth centuries, production of tobacco frequently exceeded demand, and as a result the price of the crop sometimes suffered severe declines. The result was a boom-and-bust cycle in the Chesapeake economy, with the first major bust occurring in 1640.

Boom-and-bust Tobacco Economy

South Carolina and Georgia relied on rice production, since the low-lying coastline with its many tidal rivers made it possible to create rice

SELLING TOBACCO This late-seventeenth-century label was used in the sale of American tobacco in England. The drawing depicts Virginia as a land of bright sunshine, energetic slaves, and prosperous, pipe-smoking planters. *(American Heritage Publishing Co./A Division of Forbes, Inc.)*

paddies that could be flooded and drained. Rice cultivation was so difficult and unhealthy that white laborers generally refused to perform it. Hence planters in South Carolina and Georgia were much more dependent on slaves than were their northern counterparts. African workers were adept at rice cultivation, in part because some of them had come from rice-producing regions of west Africa and in part because they were generally more accustomed to the hot, humid climate than were Europeans and had a greater natural immunity to malaria.

The South's Cash-Crop Economy

Because of their dependence on large-scale cash crops, the southern colonies developed less of a commercial or industrial economy than the colonies of the North. The trading in tobacco and rice was handled largely by merchants based in London and, later, in the northern colonies.

Northern Economic and Technological Life

In the North, as in the South, agriculture continued to dominate, but it was agriculture of a more diverse kind. In northern New England, colder weather and hard, rocky soil made it difficult for colonists to develop the kind of large-scale commercial farming system that southerners were creating. Conditions for agriculture were better in southern New England and the middle colonies, where the soil was fertile and the weather more temperate. New York, Pennsylvania, and the Connecticut River valley were the chief suppliers of wheat to much of New England and to parts of the South. Even there, however, a substantial commercial economy emerged alongside the agricultural one.

Almost every colonist engaged in a certain amount of industry at home. Occasionally these home industries provided families with surplus goods they could trade or sell. Beyond these domestic efforts, craftsmen and artisans established themselves in colonial towns as cobblers, blacksmiths, riflemakers, cabinetmakers, silversmiths, and printers. In some areas, entrepreneurs harnessed water power to run small mills for grinding grain, processing cloth, or milling lumber. And in several places, large-scale shipbuilding operations began to flourish.

Colonial Artisans and Entrepreneurs

The first effort to establish a significant metals industry in the colonies was an ironworks established in Saugus, Massachusetts, in the 1640s. The Saugus works used water power to drive a bellows, which controlled the heat in a charcoal furnace. The carbon from the burning charcoal helped remove the oxygen from the ore and thus reduced its melting temperature. As the ore melted, it trickled down into molds or was taken in the form of simple "sow bars" to a nearby forge to be shaped into iron objects such as pots and anvils. There was also a mill suitable for turning the "sow bars" into narrow rods that blacksmiths could cut into nails. The Saugus works was a technological success but a financial failure. It began operations in 1646; in 1668, its financial problems forced it to close its doors.

Metal works, however, gradually became an important part of the colonial economy. The largest industrial enterprise anywhere in English North America was the ironworks of the German ironmaster Peter Hasenclever in northern New Jersey. Founded in 1764 with British capital, it employed several hundred laborers. There were other, smaller ironmaking enterprises in every northern colony, and there were ironworks as well in several of the southern colonies. Even so, these and other growing industries did not become the basis for the kind of explosive industrial growth that Great Britain experienced in the late eighteenth century—in part because English parliamentary regulations such as the Iron Act of 1750 restricted metal processing in the colonies. Similar prohibitions limited the manufacture of woolens, hats, and other goods. But the biggest obstacles to industrialization in America were an inadequate labor supply, a small domestic market, and inadequate transportation facilities and energy supplies.

Peter Hasenclever's Ironworks

More important than manufacturing were industries that exploited the natural resources of the continent. By the mid-seventeenth century, the flourishing fur trade of earlier years was in decline. Taking its place were lumbering, mining, and fishing. These industries provided commodities that could be exported to England in exchange for manufactured goods. And they helped produce the most distinctive feature of the northern economy: a thriving commercial class.

The Extent and Limits of Technology

Despite the technological progress that was occurring in some parts of America in the seventeenth and eighteenth centuries, much of colonial society was conspicuously lacking in even very basic technological capacities. Up to half the farmers in the colonies were so primitively equipped that they did not even own a plow. Substantial numbers of households owned no pots or kettles for cooking. And only about half the households in the colonies owned guns or rifles. The relatively low levels of ownership of these and other elementary tools was not because such things were difficult to make, but because most Americans remained too poor or too isolated to be able to afford them. Many households had few if any candles, because they were unable to afford candle molds or tallow (wax), or because they had no access to commercially produced candles. In the early eighteenth century, very few farmers owned wagons. Most made do with two-wheeled carts, which were not very efficient for transporting crops to market. The most commonly owned tool on American farms was the axe.

Persistent Colonial Poverty

Even so, few colonists were self-sufficient in the late seventeenth and early eighteenth centuries. A popular image of early American households is of people who grew their own food, made their own clothes, and bought little from anyone else. In fact, relatively few colonial families owned spinning

Myth of Colonial Self-Sufficiency

wheels or looms, which suggests that most people purchased whatever yarn and cloth they needed. Most farmers who grew grain took it to centralized facilities for processing.

In general, unsurprisingly, people who lived in isolated or poor areas owned fewer tools and had less access to advanced technologies than did those in more populous or affluent areas. But throughout the colonies, the ability of people to acquire manufactured implements lagged far behind the economy's capacity to produce them.

The Rise of Colonial Commerce

Obstacles to Trade

Perhaps the most remarkable feature of colonial commerce was that it was able to survive at all. American merchants faced such bewildering obstacles, and lacked so many of the basic institutions of trade, that they managed to stay afloat only with great difficulty. The colonies had almost no gold or silver, and their paper currency was not acceptable as payment for goods from abroad. For many years, colonial merchants had to rely on barter or on money substitutes such as beaver skins.

A second obstacle was lack of information about supply and demand. Traders had no way of knowing what they would find in foreign ports; vessels sometimes stayed at sea for years, journeying from one port to another, trading one commodity for another, attempting to find some way to turn a profit. There was also an enormous number of small, fiercely competitive companies, which made the problem of rationalizing the system even more acute.

Nevertheless, commerce in the colonies survived and grew. There was elaborate trade among the colonies themselves and with the West Indies. The mainland colonies offered their Caribbean trading partners rum, agricultural products, meat, and fish. The islands offered sugar, molasses, and at times slaves in return. There was also trade with England, continental Europe, and the west coast of Africa. This commerce has often been described, somewhat inaccurately, as the "triangular trade," suggesting a neat process by which merchants carried rum and other goods from New England to Africa, exchanged their merchandise for slaves, whom they then transported to the West Indies (hence the term "middle passage" for the dreaded journey—it was the second of the three legs of the voyage), and then exchanged the slaves for sugar and molasses, which they shipped back to New England to be distilled into rum. In reality, the so-called triangular trade in rum, slaves, and sugar was a complicated maze of highly diverse trade routes. Out of this risky trade emerged a group of adventurous entrepreneurs who by the mid-eighteenth century were beginning to constitute a distinct merchant class. The British Navigation Acts protected them from foreign competition in the colonies. They had ready access to the market in England for such colonial products as furs, timber, and American-built ships. But they also

An Emerging Merchant Class

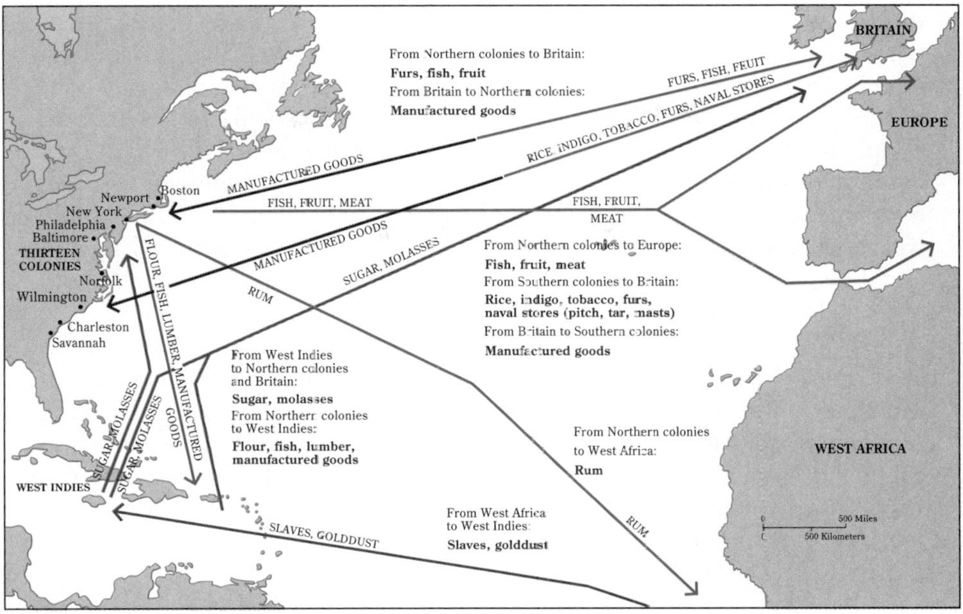

THE "TRIANGULAR TRADE" This map illustrates the complex pattern of trade that fueled the colonial American economy in the seventeenth and eighteenth centuries. A simple explanation of this trade is that the American colonies exported raw materials (agricultural products, furs, and others) to Britain and Europe and imported manufactured goods in return. But while that explanation is accurate, it is not complete, largely because the Atlantic trade was not a simple exchange between America and Europe, but a complex network of exchanges involving the Caribbean, Africa, and the Mediterranean. Note the important exchanges between the North American mainland and the Caribbean islands; the important trade between the American colonies and Africa; and the wide range of European and Mediterranean markets in which Americans were active. Not shown on this map, but also very important to colonial commerce, was a large coastal trade among the various regions of British North America. ◆ *Why did the major ports of trade emerge almost entirely in the northern colonies?*

For an interactive version of this map go to www.mhhe.com/unfinishednation4ch3maps

developed markets illegally outside the British Empire—in the French, Spanish, and Dutch West Indies—where they could often get higher prices for their goods than in the British colonies.

The Rise of Consumerism

Among relatively affluent residents of the colonies, the growing prosperity and commercialism of British America created both new appetites and new opportunities to satisfy them. The result was a growing preoccupation with the consumption of material goods.

Class Differences and Consumerism

One thing that spurred the growth of the eighteenth-century consumerism was the increasing division of American societies by class. As the difference between the upper and lower classes became more glaring, people of means became more intent on demonstrating their own membership in the upper ranks of society. The ability to purchase and display consumer goods was an important way of doing so, particularly for affluent people in cities and towns, who did not have large estates with which they could demonstrate their success. But the growth of consumerism was also a product of the early stages of the industrial revolution. Although there was relatively little industry in America in the eighteenth century, England and Europe were making rapid advances and producing more and more affordable goods for affluent Americans to buy.

To facilitate the new consumer appetites, merchants and traders began advertising their goods in journals and newspapers. Agents of urban merchants—the ancestors of the traveling salesman—fanned out through the countryside, attempting to interest wealthy landowners and planters in the luxury goods now available to them. George and Martha Washington, for example, spent considerable time and money ordering elegant furnishings for their home at Mount Vernon, goods that were shipped to them mostly from England and Europe.

One feature of a consumer society is that things that once were considered luxuries quickly come to be seen as necessities once they are readily available. In the colonies, items that became commonplace after having once been expensive luxuries included tea, household linens, glassware, manufactured cutlery, crockery, furniture, and many other things. Another result of consumerism is the association of material goods—of the quality of a person's home and possessions and clothing, for example—with virtue and "refinement." The ideal of the cultivated "gentleman" and the gracious "lady" became increasingly powerful throughout the colonies in the eighteenth century. In part that meant striving to become educated and "refined"—"gentlemanly" or "ladylike" in speech and behavior. Americans read books on manners and fashion. They bought magazines about London society. And they strove to develop themselves as witty and educated conversationalists. They also commissioned portraits of themselves and their families, devoted large portions of their homes to entertainment, built shelves and cases in which they could display fashionable possessions, constructed formal gardens, and lavished attention on their wardrobes and hairstyles.

PATTERNS OF SOCIETY

Although there were sharp social distinctions in the colonies, the well-defined and deeply entrenched class system of England failed to reproduce itself in America. Aristocracies emerged to be sure; but they tended to rely less on landownership than on control of a substantial work force, and they were generally less secure and less powerful than their English counterparts.

More than in England, white people in America faced opportunities for social mobility—both up and down. There were also new forms of community in America, and they varied greatly from one region to another.

Social Mobility

Masters and Slaves on the Plantation

The plantation system of the American South produced one form of community. The first plantations emerged in the tobacco-growing areas of Virginia and Maryland. Some of the early planters became established aristocrats with vast estates. On the whole, however, seventeenth-century colonial plantations were rough and relatively small. In the early days in Virginia, they were little more than crude clearings where landowners and indentured servants worked side by side in conditions so harsh that death was an everyday occurrence. Most landowners lived in rough cabins or houses, with their servants or slaves nearby. The economy of the plantation was a precarious one. Planters could not control their markets, so even the largest of them were constantly at risk. When prices fell, planters faced the prospect of ruin. The plantation economy created many new wealthy landowners, but it also destroyed many.

Precarious Plantation Economy

The enslaved African Americans, of course, lived very differently. On the smaller farms with only a handful of slaves, it was not always possible for a rigid separation to develop between whites and blacks. But by the early eighteenth century, over three-fourths of all blacks lived on plantations of at least ten slaves, and nearly half lived in communities of fifty slaves or more. In those settings, they were able to develop a society and culture of their own. Although whites seldom encouraged formal marriages among slaves, blacks themselves developed a strong and elaborate family structure. There was also a distinctive slave religion, which blended Christianity with African folklore and which became a central element in the emergence of an independent black culture.

Slave Culture

Nevertheless, black society was subject to constant intrusions from and interaction with white society. Black house servants, for example, were isolated from their own community. Black women were subject to usually unwanted sexual advances from owners and overseers and hence to bearing mulatto children, who were rarely recognized by their white fathers. On some plantations, black workers were treated with kindness and sometimes responded to their owners with genuine devotion. On others, they encountered physical brutality and occasionally even sadism, against which they were virtually powerless.

Slaves often resisted their masters, in large ways and small. The most serious example in the colonial period was the Stono Rebellion in South Carolina in 1739, during which about 100 blacks rose up, seized weapons, killed several whites, and

Stono Rebellion

attempted to escape south to Florida. The uprising was quickly crushed, and most participants were executed. A more frequent form of resistance was simply running away, but that provided no real solution either. For most, there was nowhere to go. Resistance more often took the form of subtle, and often undetected, defiance or evasion of their masters' wishes.

Most slaves, male and female, worked as field hands. But on the larger plantations that aspired to genuine self-sufficiency, some slaves learned trades and crafts: blacksmithing, carpentry, shoemaking, spinning, weaving, sewing, midwifery, and others. These skilled crafts workers were at times hired out to other planters. Some set up their own establishments in towns or cities and shared their profits with their owners. A few were able to buy their freedom.

The Puritan Community

Close-knit Puritan Communities

The characteristic social unit in New England was not the isolated farm but the town. In the early years of colonization, each new settlement drew up a "covenant" binding all residents tightly together both religiously and socially. Colonists laid out a village, with houses and a meetinghouse arranged around a central pasture, or "common." Thus families generally lived with their neighbors close by. They divided up the outlying fields and woodlands among the residents; the size and location of a family's field depended on the family's numbers, wealth, and social station.

Participatory Democracy

Once a town was established, residents held a yearly "town meeting" to decide important questions and to choose a group of "selectmen," who ran the town's affairs. Participation in the meeting was generally restricted to adult males who were members of the church. Only those who could give evidence of being among the elect assured of salvation (the "visible saints") were admitted to full church membership, although other residents of the town were required to attend church services.

New Englanders did not adopt the English system of primogeniture—the passing of all property to the firstborn son. Instead, a father divided up his land among all his sons. His control of this inheritance gave him great power over the family. Often a son would reach his late twenties before his father would allow him to move into his own household and work his own land. Even then, sons would usually continue to live in close proximity to their fathers.

The early Puritan community was a tightly knit organism. Yet as the years passed and the communities grew, strains and tensions began to affect this communal structure. This was partly because of the increasing commercialization of New England society, which introduced new forces into the communities of the region. It was also partly because of population growth. As towns grew larger, residents tended to cultivate lands farther and farther from the community center and, by necessity, to live at

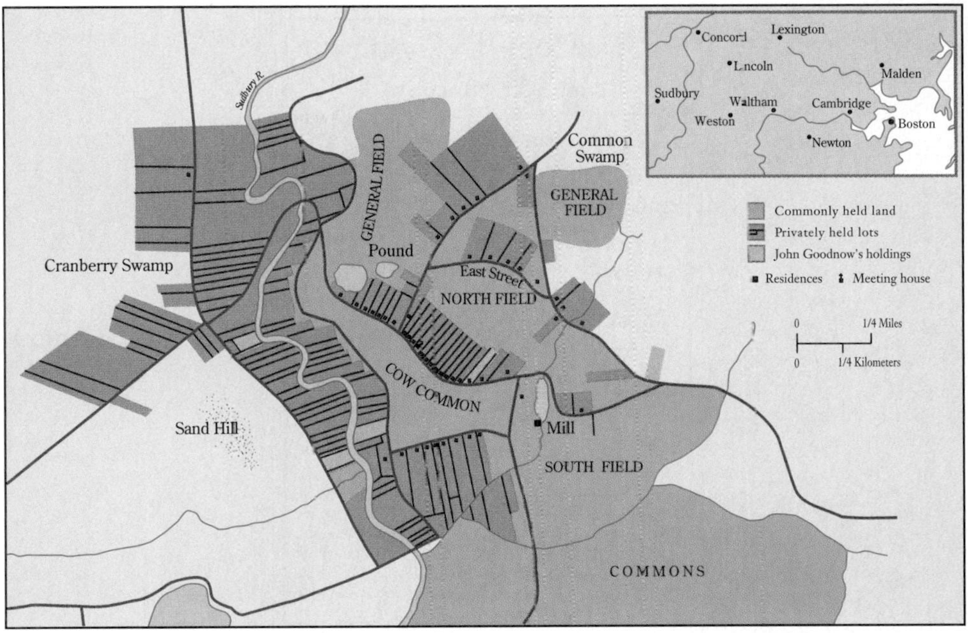

THE NEW ENGLAND TOWN: SUDBURY, MASSACHUSETTS, 17TH CENTURY Just as the plantation was a characteristic social form in the southern colonies, the town was the most common social unit in New England. This map shows the organization of Sudbury, Massachusetts, a town just west of Boston, in its early years in the seventeenth century. Note the location of the houses, which are grouped mostly together around a shared pasture (or "commons") and near the church. Note, too, the outlying fields, which were divided up among residents of the town, even though they were often not connected to the land on which they lived. The map illustrates the holdings of a single resident of Sudbury, John Goodnow, whose house was on the Common, but whose lands were scattered over a number of areas of Sudbury. ◆ *What aspects of New England life might help explain the clustering of residences at the center of the town?* *(From Sumner Chilton Powell,* Puritan Village: The Formation of a New England Town. *Copyright © 1963 by Wesleyan University. Reprinted by permission from Wesleyan University Press)*

Communal Strains and Tensions

increasing distances from the church. The control of land by fathers also created strains. In the first generations, fathers generally controlled enough land to satisfy the needs of all their sons. After several generations, however, there was often too little to go around, particularly in communities surrounded by other towns, with no room to expand outward. The result was that in many communities, groups of younger residents broke off and moved elsewhere to form towns of their own.

The tensions building in Puritan communities could produce bizarre and disastrous events. One example was the widespread hysteria in the 1680s and 1690s over accusations of witchcraft (the human exercise of satanic powers) in New England. The most famous outbreak was in Salem, Massachusetts, where adolescent girls leveled charges of witchcraft against several West Indian servants steeped in voodoo lore. Hysteria spread

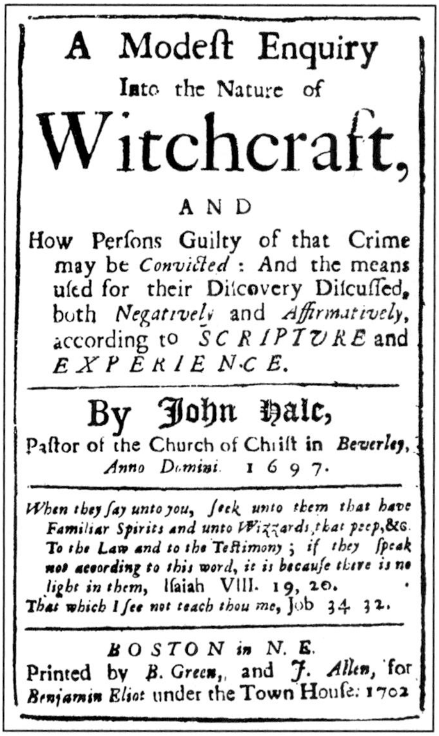

A Modeſt Enquiry
Into the Nature of
Witchcraft,
AND
How Perſons Guilty of that Crime may be *Convicted* : And the means uſed for their Diſcovery Diſcuſſed, both *Negatively* and *Affirmatively*, according to *SCRIPTURE* and *EXPERIENCE*.

By John Hale,
Paſtor of the Church of Chriſt in *Beverley*, *Anno Domini.* 1697.

When they ſay unto you, ſeek unto them that have Familiar Spirits and unto Wizzards, that peep, &c. *To the Law and to the Teſtimony* ; *if they ſpeak not according to this word, it is becauſe there is no light in them,* Iſaiah VIII. 19, 20.
That which I ſee not teach thou me, Job 34. 32.

BOSTON in N. E.
Printed by *B. Green*, and *J. Allen*, for *Benjamin Eliot* under the Town Houſe: 1702

A STUDY OF WITCHCRAFT This pamphlet, originally written in 1697 near the height of the witchcraft phenomenon in New England, was one of many contemporary studies to take the idea of witchcraft seriously. Belief in witches was widespread in early New England society, and many of the charges that seem preposterous to twentieth-century eyes appeared entirely plausible even to educated people of the time. *(Courtesy Peabody Essex Museum, Salem, MA)*

throughout the town, and hundreds of people (most of them women) were accused of witchcraft. Nineteen residents of Salem were put to death before the trials finally ended in 1692; the girls who had been the original accusers later recanted and admitted that their story had been fabricated.

Salem Witch Trials

The Salem experience was not unique. Accusations of witchcraft spread through many New England towns in the early 1690s and centered mostly on women. Research into the background of accused witches reveals that most were middle-aged women, often widowed, with few or no children. Many accused witches were of low social position, were often involved in domestic conflicts, had frequently been accused of other crimes, and were considered abrasive by their neighbors. Others were women who, through inheritance or hard work, had come into possession of substantial property of their own and thus challenged the gender norms of the community.

The witchcraft controversies were also a reflection of the highly religious character of New England societies. New Englanders believed in the power of Satan. Belief in witchcraft was not a marginal superstition rejected by the mainstream. It was a common feature of Puritan religious conviction.

Cities

Colonial Cities

In the 1770s the two largest colonial ports—Philadelphia and New York—had populations of 28,000 and 25,000, respectively, which made them larger than most English urban centers of their time. Boston (16,000), Charles Town (later Charleston), South Carolina (12,000), and Newport, Rhode Island (11,000), were also substantial communities by the standards of the day.

Colonial cities served as trading centers for the farmers of their regions and as marts for international commerce. Their leaders were generally merchants who had acquired substantial wealth. More than in any other area of colonial life (except, of course, in the relationship between masters and slaves), social distinctions were real and visible in urban areas.

Centers of Industry and Education

Cities were the centers of much of what industry there was in the colonies. They were the locations of the most advanced schools and sophisticated cultural activities and of shops where imported goods could be bought. In addition, they were communities with urban social problems: crime, vice, pollution, traffic. Unlike smaller towns, cities needed to set up constables' offices and fire departments and develop systems for supporting the urban poor, whose numbers became especially large in times of economic crisis.

Finally, cities were places where new ideas could circulate and be discussed. There were newspapers, books, and other publications from abroad, and hence new intellectual influences. The taverns and coffeehouses of cities provided forums in which people could gather and debate the issues of the day. That is one reason why the Revolutionary crisis, when it began to build in the 1760s and 1770s, began first in the cities.

AWAKENINGS AND ENLIGHTENMENTS

Intellectual life in colonial America revolved around the conflict between the traditional emphasis on a personal God deeply involved in individual lives, and the new spirit of the Enlightenment, which stressed the importance of science and human reason. The old views placed a high value on a stern moral code in which intellect was less important than faith. The Enlightenment suggested that people had substantial control over their own lives and societies.

The Pattern of Religions

Religious toleration flourished in America to a degree unmatched in any European nation. Settlers in America brought with them so many different religious practices that it proved impossible to impose a single religious code on any large area.

The Church of England was established as the official faith in Virginia, Maryland, New York, the Carolinas, and Georgia. Except in Virginia and Maryland, however, the laws establishing the Church of England as the official colonial religion were largely ignored. Even in New England, where the Puritans had originally believed that they were all part of a single faith, there was a growing tendency in the eighteenth century for different congregations to affiliate with different denominations. In parts of New York and New Jersey, Dutch settlers had established their own Calvinist denomination, Dutch Reformed. American Baptists developed a great variety of sects. All Baptists shared the belief that rebaptism, usually by total immersion, was necessary when believers reached maturity. But while some Baptists remained Calvinists (believers in predestination) others came to believe in salvation by free will.

Multiplying Denominations

Persistent Anti-Catholicism

Protestants extended toleration to one another more readily than they did to Roman Catholics. New Englanders, in particular, viewed their Catholic neighbors in New France (Canada) not only as commercial and military rivals but also as dangerous agents of Rome. In most of the English colonies, however, Roman Catholics were too few to cause serious conflict. They were most numerous in Maryland, and even there they numbered no more than 3,000. Perhaps for that reason they suffered their worst persecution in that colony. After the overthrow of the original proprietors in 1691, Catholics in Maryland not only lost their political rights but also were forbidden to hold religious services except in private houses.

Anti-Semitism

Jews in provincial America totaled no more than about 2,000 at any time. The largest community lived in New York City. Smaller groups settled in Newport and Charleston, and there were scattered Jewish families in all the colonies. Nowhere could they vote or hold office. Only in Rhode Island could they practice their religion openly.

Declining Piety

By the beginning of the eighteenth century, some Americans were growing troubled by the apparent decline in religious piety in their society. The movement of the population westward and the wide scattering of settlements had caused many communities to lose touch with organized religion. The rise of commercial prosperity created a more secular outlook in urban areas. The progress of science and free thought caused at least some colonists to doubt traditional religious beliefs.

Concerns about weakening piety surfaced as early as the 1660s in New England, where the Puritan oligarchy warned of a decline in the power of the church. Ministers preached sermons of despair (known as "jeremiads"), deploring the signs of waning piety. By the standards of other societies or other eras, the Puritan faith remained remarkably strong. But to New Englanders the "declension" of religious piety seemed a serious problem.

The Great Awakening

By the early eighteenth century, similar concerns were emerging in other regions and among members of other faiths. Everywhere, colonists were coming to believe, religious piety was in decline. The result was the first great American revival: the Great Awakening.

The Great Awakening began in earnest in the 1730s and reached its climax in the 1740s. The revival had particular appeal to women (who constituted the majority of converts) and to younger sons of the third or fourth generation of settlers—those who stood to inherit the least land and who faced the most uncertain futures. The rhetoric of the revival emphasized the potential for every person to break away from the constraints of the past and start anew in his or her relationship with God. Such beliefs may have reflected in part the desires of many people to break away from their families or communities and start a new life.

Appeal of the Great Awakening

Powerful evangelists from England helped spread the revival. John and Charles Wesley, the founders of Methodism, visited Georgia and other colonies in the 1730s. George Whitefield, a powerful open-air preacher, made several evangelizing tours through the colonies and drew tremendous crowds. But the outstanding preacher of the Great Awakening was the New England Congregationalist Jonathan Edwards. From his pulpit in Northampton, Massachusetts, Edwards attacked the new doctrines of easy salvation for all. He preached anew the traditional Puritan ideas of the absolute sovereignty of God, predestination, and salvation by God's grace alone. His vivid descriptions of hell could terrify his listeners.

The Great Awakening led to the division of existing congregations (between "New Light" revivalists and "Old Light" traditionalists) and to the founding of new ones. It also affected areas of society outside the churches. Some of the revivalists denounced book learning as a hindrance to salvation. But other evangelists saw education as a means of furthering religion, and they founded or led schools for the training of New Light ministers.

"New Lights" and "Old Lights"

The Enlightenment

The Great Awakening caused one great cultural upheaval in the colonies. The Enlightenment caused another, very different one. The Enlightenment was the product of some of the great scientific and intellectual discoveries in Europe in the seventeenth century—discoveries that revealed the "natural laws" that regulated the workings of nature. The new scientific knowledge encouraged many thinkers to begin celebrating the power of human reason and to argue that rational thought, not just religious faith, could create progress and advance knowledge in the world.

"Natural Law"

In celebrating reason, the Enlightenment encouraged men and women to look to themselves and their own intellect—not just to God—for guidance as to how to live their lives and shape their societies. It helped produce a growing interest in education and a heightened concern with politics and government.

In the early seventeenth century, Enlightenment ideas in America were largely borrowed from Europe—from such great thinkers as Francis Bacon and John Locke of England, Baruch Spinoza of Amsterdam, and René Descartes of France. Later, however, such Americans as Benjamin Franklin, Thomas Paine, Thomas Jefferson, and James Madison made their own important contributions to Enlightenment thought.

Literacy and Technology

White male Americans achieved a high degree of literacy in the eighteenth century. By the time of the Revolution, well over half of all white men could read and write. The literacy rate for women lagged behind the rate for men until the nineteenth century. While opportunities for education beyond the primary level were scarce for men, they were almost nonexistent for women.

The large number of colonists who could read created a market for the first widely circulated publications in America other than the Bible: almanacs. By 1700, there were dozens, perhaps hundreds, of almanacs circulating throughout the colonies and even in the sparsely settled lands to the west. Most families had at least one. Almanacs provided medical advice, navigational and agricultural information, practical wisdom, humor, and predictions about the future—most famously, predictions about weather patterns for the coming year, which many farmers used as the basis of decisions about crops even though the predictions were notoriously unreliable. The most famous almanac in eighteenth-century America was *Poor Richard's Almanac*, published by Benjamin Franklin in Philadelphia.

Poor Richard's Almanac

The wide availability of reading material in colonial America by the eighteenth century was a result of the spread of printing technology. The first printing press began operating in the colonies in 1639, and by 1695 there were more towns in America with printers than there were in England. At first, many of these presses did not get very much use. Over time, however, the rising literacy of the society created a demand for books, pamphlets, and almanacs that the presses rushed to fill.

Publick Occurrences

The first newspaper in the colonies, *Publick Occurrences*, was published in Boston in 1690 using a relatively advanced printing facility. It was the first step toward what would eventually become a large newspaper industry. One reason the Stamp Act of 1765, which imposed a tax on printed materials, created such a furor was because printing technology had by then become central to colonial life.

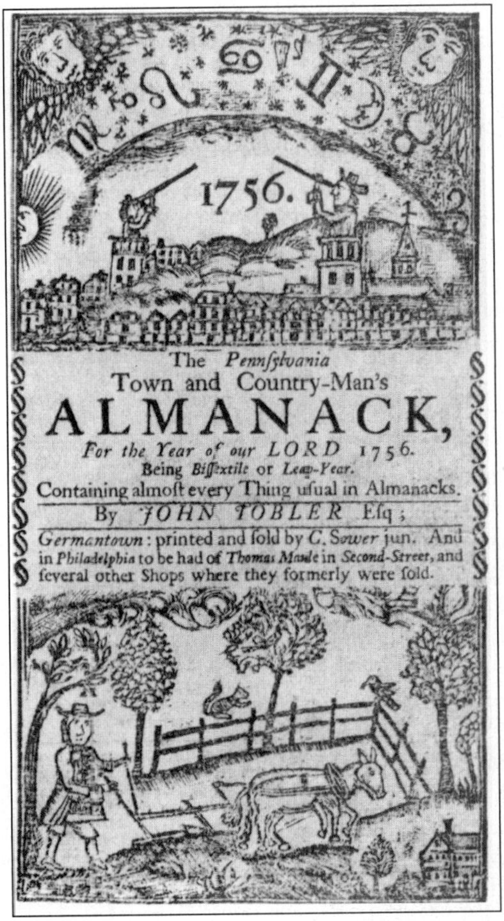

TOWN AND COUNTRY-MAN'S ALMANACK As the population of colonial cities and towns grew, almanacs—originally targeted mainly at farmers—began to appeal to townspeople as well. *(Sinclair Hamilton Collection, Visual Materials Division, Department of Rare Books and Special Collections, Princeton University Library)*

Education

Even before Enlightenment ideas penetrated America, colonists placed a high value on formal education. Some families tried to teach their children to read and write at home, although the heavy burden of work in most agricultural households limited the time available for schooling. In Massachusetts, a 1647 law required that every town support a school; and a modest network of public schools emerged as a result. The Quakers and other sects operated church schools, and in some communities widows or unmarried women conducted "dame schools" by holding private classes in their homes. In cities, master craftsmen set up evening schools for their apprentices.

Growth of Public Education

African Americans had virtually no access to education. Occasionally a master or mistress would teach slave children to read and write; but as the slave system became more firmly entrenched, strong social (and ultimately legal) sanctions developed to discourage such efforts. Indians, too, remained largely outside the white educational system—to a large degree by choice. Some white missionaries and philanthropists established schools for Native Americans and helped create a small population of Indians literate in spoken and written English.

Colonial Higher Education

Harvard, the first American college, was established in 1636 by Puritan theologians who wanted to create a training center for ministers. (The college was named for a Charlestown minister, John Harvard, who had left it his library and half his estate.) In 1693, William and Mary College (named for the English king and queen) was established in Williamsburg, Virginia, by Anglicans. And in 1701, conservative Congregationalists, dissatisfied with the growing religious liberalism of Harvard, founded Yale (named for one of its first benefactors, Elihu Yale) in New Haven, Connecticut. Out of the Great Awakening emerged the College of New Jersey, founded in 1746 and known later as Princeton (after the town in which it was located); one of its first presidents was Jonathan Edwards. Despite the religious basis of these colleges, most of them offered curricula that included not only theology but logic, ethics, physics, geometry, astronomy, rhetoric, Latin, Hebrew, and Greek. King's College, founded in New York in 1754 and later renamed Columbia, was specifically devoted to the spread of secular knowledge. The Academy and College of Philadelphia, founded in 1755 and later renamed the University of Pennsylvania, was also a completely secular institution, established by a group of laymen under the inspiration of Benjamin Franklin.

After 1700, most colonial leaders received their entire educations in America (rather than attending university in England, as had once been the case). But higher education remained available only to a few relatively affluent white men.

The Spread of Science

Growing Interest in Science

The clearest indication of the spreading influence of the Enlightenment in America was an increasing interest in scientific knowledge. Most of the early colleges established chairs in the natural sciences and introduced some of the advanced scientific theories of Europe, including Copernican astronomy and Newtonian physics, to their students. But the most vigorous promotion of science in these years occurred through the private efforts of amateurs and the activities of scientific societies. Leading merchants, planters, and even theologians became corresponding members of the Royal Society of London, the leading English scientific organization. Benjamin Franklin won international fame through his experiments with electricity. Particularly no-

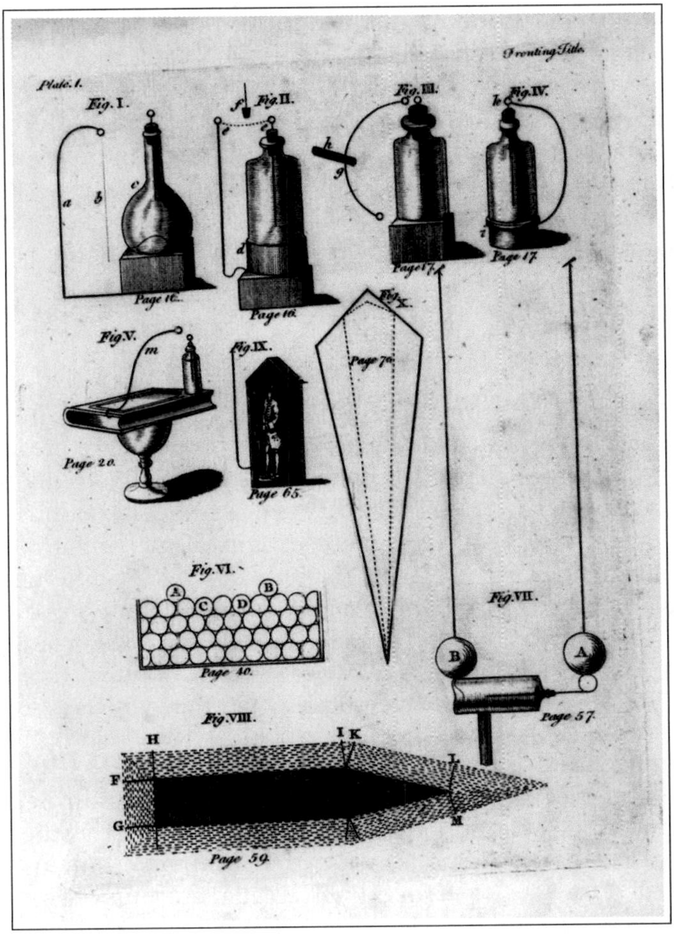

BENJAMIN FRANKLIN ON ELECTRICITY The discovery of electricity was one of the great scientific events of the eighteenth century, even though large-scale practical use of electrical energy emerged much later. Benjamin Franklin was one of the first Americans, and certainly the most famous American, to experiment with electricity. This is the frontispiece for a book, originally published in 1750 in Philadelphia, that describes his "experiments and observations." The pages shown here are from the London edition, which appeared in 1774. *(© Hulton Getty/Getty Images)*

table was his 1747 theory and his 1752 demonstration, using a kite, that lightning and electricity were the same. (Previously, most scientists had believed that there were several distinct types of electricity.) His research on the way in which electricity could be "grounded" led to the development of the lightning rod, which greatly reduced fires and other damage to buildings during thunderstorms.

Smallpox Inoculation

The high value that influential Americans were beginning to place on scientific knowledge was clearly demonstrated by the most daring and controversial scientific experiment of the eighteenth century: inoculation against smallpox. The

Puritan theologian Cotton Mather had learned of experiments in England by which people had been deliberately infected with mild cases of smallpox in order to immunize them against the deadly disease. Despite strong opposition, he urged inoculation on his fellow Bostonians during an epidemic in the 1720s. The results confirmed the effectiveness of the technique. Other theologians took up the cause, along with many physicians. By the mid-eighteenth century, inoculation had become a common medical procedure in America.

Concepts of Law and Politics

In law and politics, as in other parts of their lives, Americans in the seventeenth and eighteenth centuries believed that they were re-creating in the New World the practices and institutions of the Old. But as in other areas, they in fact created something very different. Although the American legal system adopted most of the essential elements of the English system, including such ancient rights as trial by jury, significant differences developed in court procedures, punishments, and the definition of crimes. In England, for example, a printed attack on a public official, whether true or false, was considered libelous. At the 1734–1735 trial of the New York publisher John Peter Zenger, the courts ruled that criticisms of the government were not libelous if factually true—a verdict that removed some colonial restrictions on the freedom of the press.

Powerful Colonial Legislatures

More significant for the future of the relationship between the colonies and England were differences emerging between the American and British political systems. Because the royal government was so far away, Americans created a group of institutions of their own that gave them a large measure of self-government. In most colonies, local communities grew accustomed to running their own affairs with minimal interference from higher authorities. The colonial assemblies came to exercise many of the powers that Parliament exercised in England. Provincial governors (appointed by the king after the 1690s) had broad powers on paper, but their actual influence was limited.

The result of all this was that the provincial governments became accustomed to acting more or less independently of Parliament, and a set of assumptions and expectations about the rights of the colonists took hold in America that was not shared by policymakers in England. These differences caused few problems before the 1760s, because the British did little to exert the authority they believed they possessed. But when, beginning in 1763, the English government began attempting to tighten its control over the American colonies, a great imperial crisis resulted.

CONCLUSION

The English colonies in America grew steadily between the 1650s and the 1750s: in population, in the size of their economies, and in the sophistication—and diversity—of their cultures. Although most white Americans in the 1750s still believed that they were fully a part of the British Empire, they were in fact living in a world that had become very different from that of England.

Many distinct societies developed in the colonies, but the greatest distinction was between the colonies of the North and those of the South. In the North, society was dominated by relatively small family farms and by towns and cities of growing size. A thriving commercial class was developing, and with it an increasingly elaborate urban culture. In the South, there were many family farms as well. But there were also large plantations cultivating tobacco, rice, indigo, and cotton for export. By the late seventeenth century, these plantations were relying heavily on African workers who had been brought to the colonies forcibly as slaves. There were few significant towns and cities in the South, and little commerce other than the marketing of crops.

Diverging North and South

The colonies did, however, also have much in common. Most white Americans accepted common assumptions about racial inequality. That enabled them to tolerate the enslavement of African men and women and to justify a campaign of displacement and often violence against Native Americans. Most white Americans (and, in different ways, most nonwhite Americans as well) were deeply religious. The Great Awakening, therefore, had a powerful impact throughout the colonies. And most white colonists shared a belief in certain basic principles of law and politics, which they considered embedded in the English constitution. Their interpretation of that constitution, however, was becoming increasingly different from that of the parliament in England and was laying the groundwork for future conflict.

FOR FURTHER REFERENCE

Edward Countryman, *Americans: A Collision of Histories* (1996) includes a vivid picture of the many cultures that encountered one another in early America. Bernard Bailyn, *Voyagers to the West: A Passage in the Peopling of America on the Eve of the Revolution* (1986) reveals the complexity and scope of European emigration to North America. Bailyn's *The Origin of America Politics* (1968) remains an excellent introduction to colonial politics.

David Hackett Fischer, *Albion's Seed* (1989) suggests four major folkways for English migrants to America. Jack P. Greene, *Pursuits of Happiness: The Social Development of Early Modern British Colonies and the Formation of American Culture* (1986) is a broad portrait of life in early American communities. Laurel Thatcher Ulrich, *Good Wives: Image and Reality in the Lives of Women in Northern New England, 1650–1750* (1982) offers a typology of women's roles in colonial New England. John Demos, *The Unredeemed Captive: A Family Story of Early America* (1994) is a vivid, unconventional account of the experiences of a New England girl captured by Indians. Robin Blackburn, *The Making of New World Slavery: From the Baroque to the Modern, 1492–1800* (1997) includes an important examination of the character of the institution in colonial America. Philip D. Morgan, *Slave Counterpoint: Black Culture in the Eighteenth-Century Chesapeake and Lowcountry* (1998) is a major study of the early history of slavery. Kathleen M. Brown, *Good Wives, Nasty Wenches, and Anxious Patriarchs: Gender, Race and Power in Colonial Virginia* (1996) places gender at the center of the development of slavery in the Chesapeake. Rhys Isaac, *The Transformation of Virginia, 1740–1790* (1982) uses the methods of cultural anthropology in an influential study of the world of the colonial Virginia gentry. Darren Staloff, *The Making of an American Thinking Class: Intellectuals and Intelligentsia in Puritan Massachusetts* (1998) is an intellectual history of early New England.

For quizzes, Internet resources, references to additional books and films, and more, consult this book's Online Learning Center site at www.mhhe.com/unfinishednation4

THE BOSTON MASSACRE (1770), BY PAUL REVERE This is one of many sensationalized engravings, by Revere and others, of the conflict between British troops and Boston laborers that became important propaganda documents for the Patriot cause in the 1770s. Among the victims of the massacre listed by Revere was Crispus Attucks, probably the first black man to die in the struggle for American independence. *(Burstein Collection/Corbis)*

TIME LINE

1754	1756	1760	1763	1764	1765	1766
Beginning of French and Indian War	Seven Years' War begins	George III becomes king	Peace of Paris Proclamation of 1763	Sugar Act	Stamp Act	Stamp Act repealed Declaratory Act

CHAPTER FOUR

THE EMPIRE IN TRANSITION

Loosening Ties
The Struggle for the Continent
The New Imperialism
Stirrings of Revolt
Cooperation and War

As late as the 1750s, few Americans objected to their membership in the British Empire. The imperial system provided many benefits to the Americans, and for the most part the English government left the colonies alone. By the mid-1770s, however, the relationship between the American colonies and their British rulers had become so strained that the empire was on the verge of unraveling. And in the spring of 1775, the first shots were fired in a war that would ultimately win America its independence. How had it happened? And why so quickly?

LOOSENING TIES

In one sense, it had not happened quickly at all. Ever since the first days of English settlement in North America, the ideas and institutions of the colonies had been diverging from those in Britain. In another sense, however, the Revolutionary crisis emerged in response to relatively sudden

1767	1770	1771	1772	1773	1774	1775
Townshend Duties	Boston Massacre Most Townshend Duties repealed	Regulator movement in North Carolina	Committees of correspondence in Boston Gaspée incident	Tea Act, Boston Tea Party	Intolerable Acts First Continental Congress in Philadelphia	Battles of Lexington and Concord American Revolution begins

changes in the administration of the empire. In 1763 the English government began to enforce a series of policies toward its colonies that brought the differences between the two societies into sharp focus.

A Decentralized Empire

In the fifty years after the Glorious Revolution, the English Parliament established a growing supremacy over the king. Under Kings George I (1714–1727) and George II (1727–1760), the prime minister and his cabinet became the nation's real executives. Because they depended politically on the great merchants and landholders of England, they were less inclined than the seventeenth-century monarchs had been to try to tighten control over the empire, which many merchants feared would disrupt the profitable commerce with the colonies. As a result, administration of the colonies remained loose, decentralized, and inefficient.

Decentralized Colonial Administration

The character of the royal officials in America contributed further to the looseness of the imperial system. Few governors were able men. Many, perhaps most, had used bribery to obtain their offices and continued to accept bribes once they assumed their offices. Some appointees remained in England and hired substitutes to take their places in America.

Assertive Colonial Assemblies

The colonial assemblies, taking advantage of the weak imperial administration, had asserted their own authority to levy taxes, make appropriations, approve appointments, and pass laws for their respective colonies. The assemblies came to look upon themselves as little parliaments, each practically as sovereign within its colony as Parliament itself was in England.

The Colonies Divided

Even so, the colonists continued to think of themselves as loyal English subjects. Many felt stronger ties to England than they did to the other American colonies. Although the colonies had slowly learned to cooperate with one another on such practical matters as intercolonial trade, road construction, and the creation of a colonial postal service, they remained reluctant to cooperate in larger ways, even when, in 1754, they faced a common threat from their old rivals, the French, and France's Indian allies. Delegates from Pennsylvania, Maryland, New York, and New England met in Albany in that year to negotiate a treaty with the Iroquois and tentatively approved a proposal by Benjamin Franklin to set up a "general government" to manage relations with the Indians. War with the French and Indians was already beginning when the Albany Plan was presented to the colonial assemblies. None approved it.

Albany Plan

THE STRUGGLE FOR THE CONTINENT

Seven Years' War

The war that raged in North America through the late 1750s and early 1760s was part of a larger struggle between England and France. The British victory in that struggle, known in Europe as the Seven Years' War, confirmed England's commercial supremacy and cemented its control of the settled regions of North America. In America, however, the conflict, which colonists called the French and Indian War, was also the final stage in a long struggle among the three principal powers in northeastern North America: the English, the French, and the Iroquois.

New France and the Iroquois Nation

By the end of the seventeenth century, the French Empire in America had come to possess a vast territory: the whole length of the Mississippi River and its delta (which they named Louisiana, after their king), and the continental interior as far west as the Rocky Mountains and as far south as the Rio Grande. France claimed, in effect, the entire interior of the continent.

France's Colonial Empire

To secure their hold on these enormous claims, they founded a string of widely separated communities, fortresses, missions, and trading posts. Would-be feudal lords established large estates *(seigneuries)* along the banks of the St. Lawrence River. On a high bluff above the river stood the fortified city of Quebec. Montreal to the south and Sault Sainte Marie and Detroit to the west marked the northern boundaries of French settlement. On the lower Mississippi emerged plantations much like those in the southern colonies of English America, worked by black slaves and owned by "Creoles" (white immigrants of French descent). New Orleans, founded in 1718 to service the French plantation economy, was soon as big as some of the larger cities of the Atlantic seaboard; Biloxi and Mobile to the east completed the string of French settlement.

Both the French and the English were aware that the battle for control of North America would be determined in part by which group could best win the allegiance of native tribes. The English—with their more advanced commercial economy—could usually offer the Indians better and more plentiful goods. But the French offered tolerance. Unlike the English, the French settlers in the interior generally adjusted their own behavior to Indian patterns. French fur traders frequently married Indian women and adopted tribal ways; Jesuit missionaries interacted comfortably with the natives and converted them to Catholicism by the thousands without challenging most of their social customs. By the mid-eighteenth century, therefore, the French had better and closer relations with most of the Indians of the interior than did the English.

The Powerful Iroquois Confederacy

The most powerful native group, however, had remained aloof from both the British and the French. The Iroquois Confederacy—five Indian nations (Mohawk, Seneca, Cayuga, Onondaga, and Oneida) that had formed a defensive alliance in the fifteenth century—had been the most powerful native presence in the Ohio Valley and a large surrounding region since the 1640s. The Iroquois maintained their autonomy by avoiding too close a relationship with either the French or the English. They traded successfully with both groups and astutely played them against each other. As a result, they maintained precarious power in the Great Lakes region.

Anglo-French Conflicts

As long as England and France remained at peace and as long as the precarious balance in the North American interior survived, English and French colonists coexisted without serious difficulty. But after the Glorious Revolution in England, a series of Anglo-French wars erupted in Europe and continued intermittently for nearly eighty years, creating important repercussions in America.

King William's War (1689–1697) produced only a few, indecisive clashes between the English and the French in northern New England. Queen Anne's War, which began in 1701 and continued for nearly twelve years, generated more substantial conflicts. The Treaty of Utrecht, which brought the conflict to a close in 1713, transferred substantial territory from the French to the English in North America, including Acadia (Nova Scotia) and Newfoundland. Two decades later, disputes over British trading rights in the Spanish colonies produced a conflict between England and Spain that soon grew into a much larger European war. The English colonists in America were drawn into the struggle, which they called King George's War; and between 1744 and 1748 they engaged in a series of conflicts with the French. New Englanders captured the French bastion at Louisbourg on Cape Breton Island, but the peace treaty that finally ended the conflict forced them to abandon it.

King George's War

In the aftermath of King George's War, relations among the English, French, and Iroquois in North America quickly deteriorated. The Iroquois (in what appears to have been a major blunder) granted trading concessions in the interior to English merchants for the first time. The French, fearful (probably correctly) that the English were using the concessions as a first step toward expansion into French lands, began in 1749 to construct new fortresses in the Ohio Valley. The English began building up their military forces and building fortresses of their own. The balance of power that the Iroquois had carefully and successfully maintained for so long rapidly disintegrated.

For the next five years, tensions between the English and the French increased. In the summer of 1754 the governor of Virginia sent a militia force (under the command of an inexperienced young colonel, George Washington) into the Ohio Valley to challenge French expansion. Washington built a crude stockade (Fort Necessity) not far from Fort Duquesne, the larger outpost the French were building on the site of what is now Pittsburgh. After the Virginians staged an unsuccessful attack on a French detachment, the French countered with an assault on Fort Necessity, trapping Washington and his soldiers inside. After a third of them died in the fighting, Washington surrendered. The clash marked the beginning of the French and Indian War.

Fort Necessity

The Great War for the Empire

The French and Indian War lasted nearly nine years, and it moved through three distinct phases. During the first of these phases, from the Fort Necessity debacle in 1754 until the expansion of the war to Europe in 1756, it was primarily a local, North American conflict. Virtually all the tribes except the Iroquois were now allied with the French; they launched a series of raids on western English settlements. The English colonists fought largely alone to defend themselves against those raids. The Iroquois feared antagonizing the French and remained largely passive in the conflict. By late 1755, many English settlers along the frontier had withdrawn to the east of the Allegheny Mountains to escape the hostilities.

The second phase of the struggle began in 1756, when the Seven Years' War began. The fighting now spread to the West Indies, India, and Europe itself. But the principal struggle remained the one in North America, where so far England had suffered nothing but frustration and defeat. Beginning in 1757, William Pitt, the English secretary of state (and future prime minister), brought the war for the first time fully under British control. Pitt himself planned military strategy, appointed commanders, and issued orders to the colonists. British commanders began forcibly enlisting colonists (a practice known as "impressment"). Officers also seized supplies from local farmers and tradesmen and compelled colonists to offer shelter to British troops—all generally without compensation. The Americans resented these new impositions and firmly resisted them. By early 1758, the friction between the British authorities and the colonists was threatening to bring the war effort to a halt.

William Pitt Takes Command

Beginning in 1758, therefore, Pitt initiated the third and final phase of the war by relaxing many of the policies that Americans had found obnoxious. He agreed to reimburse the colonists for all supplies requisitioned by the army. He returned control over recruitment to the colonial assemblies. And he dispatched large numbers of additional British troops to America. Finally, the tide of battle began to turn in England's favor. The French had always been outnumbered by the British colonists. After 1756, moreover, they suffered from a series of poor harvests. As a result, they were unable to sustain their early military successes. By mid-1758, British regulars and

RECUITING FOR THE FRENCH AND INDIAN WAR The extravagant promises in this recruiting poster, distributed to colonists during the French and Indian War, suggest how difficult it sometimes was to persuade Americans to fight in the British army. *(Bettmann/Corbis)*

colonial militias were seizing one French stronghold after another. Two brilliant English generals, Jeffrey Amherst and James Wolfe, captured the fortress at Louisbourg in July 1758; a few months later Fort Duquesne fell without a fight. The next year, at the end of a siege of Quebec, the army of General Wolfe struggled up a hidden ravine under cover of darkness, surprised the larger forces of the Marquis de Montcalm, and defeated them in a battle in which both commanders were killed. The dramatic fall of Quebec on September 13, 1759, marked the beginning of the end of the American phase of the war. A year later, in September 1760, the French army formally surrendered to Amherst in Montreal. Peace finally came in 1763, with the Peace of Paris, by which the French ceded to Great Britain some of their West Indian islands, most of their colonies in India and Canada, and all other French territory in North America east of the Mississippi. They ceded New Orleans and their claims west of the Mississippi to Spain, thus surrendering all title to the mainland of North America.

Peace of Paris

The French and Indian War greatly expanded England's territorial claims in the New World. At the same time, the cost of the war greatly enlarged Britain's debt and substantially increased British resentment of the Americans. English leaders were contemptuous of the colonists for what they considered American military ineptitude during the war; they were angry that the colonists had made so few financial contributions to a struggle waged, they believed, largely for American benefit; they were particularly bitter that some colonial merchants had been selling food and other goods to the French in the West Indies throughout the conflict. All these factors combined to persuade many English leaders that a major reorganization of the empire giving London increased authority over the colonies would be necessary in the aftermath of the war.

British Resentment

The war had an equally profound but very different effect on the American colonists. It was an experience that forced them, for the first time, to act in concert against a common foe. And the friction of 1756–1757 over British requisition and impressment policies and the 1758 return of authority to the colonial assemblies seemed to many Americans to confirm the illegitimacy of English interference in local affairs.

For the Indians of the Ohio Valley, the British victory was disastrous. Those tribes that had allied themselves with the French had earned the enmity of the victorious English. The Iroquois Confederacy, which had allied itself with Britain, fared only slightly better. English officials saw the passivity of the Iroquois during the war as evidence of duplicity. In the aftermath of the peace settlement, the Iroquois alliance with the British quickly unraveled. The tribes would continue to contest the English for control of the Ohio Valley for another fifty years; but increasingly divided and increasingly outnumbered, they would seldom again be in a position to deal with their European rivals on terms of military or political equality.

Disastrous Consequences for Native Americans

THE NEW IMPERIALISM

With the treaty of 1763, England found itself truly at peace for the first time in more than fifty years. As a result, the British government could now turn its attention to the organization of its empire. Saddled with enormous debts from the many years of fighting, England was desperately in need of new revenues from its empire. Responsible for vast new lands in the New World, the imperial government believed it must increase its administrative capacities in America. The result was a dramatic and, for England, disastrous redefinition of the colonial relationship.

Burdens of Empire

The experience of the French and Indian War should have suggested that increasing imperial control over the colonies would not be easy. Not only

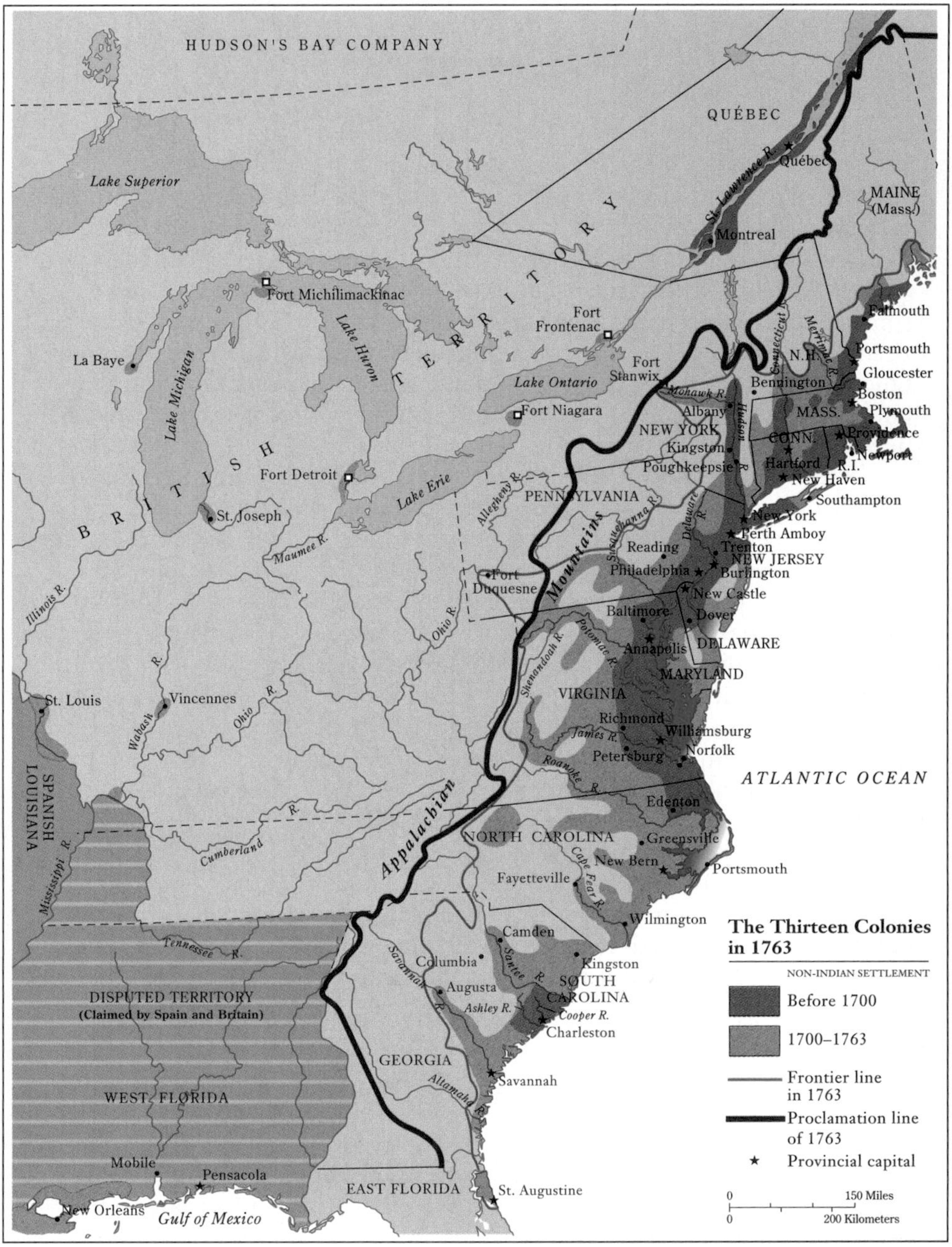

THE THIRTEEN COLONIES IN 1763 This map is a close-up of the thirteen colonies at the end of the Seven Years' War. It shows the line of settlement established by the Proclamation of 1763 (the red line), as well as the extent of actual settlement in that year (the thin green line). Note that in the middle colonies (North Carolina, Virginia, Maryland, and southern Pennsylvania), settlement had already reached the red line—and in one small area of western Pennsylvania moved beyond it—by the time of the Proclamation of 1763. Note also the string of forts established beyond the Proclamation line. ◆ *How do the forts help to explain the efforts of the British to restrict settlement? And how does the extent of actual settlement help explain why it was so difficult for the British to enforce their restrictions?*

For an interactive version of this map go to www.mhhe.com/unfinishednation4ch4maps

had the colonists proved so resistant to British control that Pitt had been forced to relax his policies in 1758, but the colonial assemblies had continued after that to chart a course different from, and often in conflict with, the desires of the government in London. Defiance of imperial trade regulations and other British demands continued. But the most immediate problem for London was its staggering war debt. Landlords and merchants in England were objecting strenuously to any further tax increases, and the colonial assemblies had repeatedly demonstrated their unwillingness to pay for the war effort. Many officials in England believed that only by taxing the Americans directly from London could the empire effectively meet its financial needs.

Britain's Staggering War Debt

At this crucial moment in Anglo-American relations, the government of England was thrown into turmoil by the accession to the throne of George III, who assumed power in 1760. He brought two particularly unfortunate qualities to the office. First, he was determined to reassert the authority of the monarchy. He removed from power the relatively stable coalition of Whigs that had governed the empire for much of the century and replaced it with a new and very unstable coalition of his own. The new ministries that emerged as a result of this change each lasted in office an average of only about two years.

George the Third

The king also had serious intellectual and psychological limitations. He suffered, apparently, from a rare mental disease that produced intermittent bouts of insanity. (Indeed, in the last years of his long reign he was, according to most accounts, unable to perform any official functions.) Yet even when George III was lucid and rational, which was most of the time in the 1760s and 1770s, he was painfully immature and insecure. The king's personality, therefore, contributed both to the instability and to the rigidity of the British government during these critical years.

More directly responsible for the problems that soon emerged with the colonies, however, was George Grenville, whom the king made prime minister in 1763. Grenville shared the prevailing opinion within Britain that the colonists should be compelled to obey the laws and to pay a part of the cost of defending and administering the empire.

George Grenville

The British and the Tribes

With the defeat of the French, frontiersmen from the English colonies had begun immediately to move over the mountains and into tribal lands in the upper Ohio Valley. An alliance of Indian tribes, under the Ottawa chieftain Pontiac, struck back. Fearing that an escalation of the fighting might threaten western trade, the British government—in the Proclamation of 1763—forbade settlers to advance beyond the mountains that divided the Atlantic coast from the interior.

Many Indian groups supported the Proclamation as the best bargain available to them. The Cherokee, in particular, worked actively to hasten the drawing of the boundary, hoping finally to put an end to white movements into their lands. Relations between the western tribes and the British improved for a time, partly as a result of the work of the Indian superintendents the British appointed, who were sympathetic to tribal needs.

In the end, however, the Proclamation of 1763 was ineffective. White settlers continued to swarm across the boundary and continued to claim lands farther and farther into the Ohio Valley. The British authorities failed repeatedly to enforce limits to the expansion. In 1768, new agreements with the western tribes pushed the boundary further west in another effort to create a permanent western boundary for European settlement. But these treaties also failed to stop the white advance. Within a few years, the 1768 agreements were replaced with new ones, which pushed the line of settlement still farther west.

Failure of the Proclamation of 1763

Battles over Trade and Taxes

The Grenville ministry tried to increase its authority in the colonies in other ways as well. Regular British troops were stationed permanently in America, and under the Mutiny Act of 1765 the colonists were required to help provision and maintain the army. Ships of the British navy patrolled American waters to search for smugglers. The customs service was reorganized and enlarged. Royal officials were required to take up their colonial posts in person instead of sending substitutes. Colonial manufacturing was restricted, so that it would not compete with rapidly expanding industries in Great Britain.

Sugar, Stamp, and Currency Acts

The Sugar Act of 1764 raised the duty on sugar while lowering the duty on molasses. It also established new vice-admiralty courts in America to try accused smugglers—thus cutting them off from sympathetic local juries. The Currency Act of 1764 required that the colonial assemblies stop issuing paper money. Most momentously, the Stamp Act of 1765 imposed a tax on every printed document in the colonies: newspapers, almanacs, pamphlets, deeds, wills, licenses. British officials were soon collecting more than ten times as much annual revenue in America as they had been before 1763.

It was difficult for the colonists to resist these unpopular new laws. For one thing, Americans continued to harbor as many grievances against one another as they did against the authorities in London. In 1763, for example, a band of Pennsylvania frontiersmen known as the Paxton Boys descended on Philadelphia to demand tax relief and financial support for their defense against Indians.

Paxton Boys

Bloodshed was averted only by concessions from the colonial assembly. In 1771, a small-scale civil war broke out in North Carolina when the Regulators, farmers of the Carolina upcountry, organized and armed themselves to resist the high taxes that local sheriffs (appointed by the colonial governor) collected. An army of militiamen, most of them from the eastern counties, crushed the revolt.

But the Grenville program helped the colonists overcome their internal conflicts and recognize that the policies from London were a threat to all Americans. Northern merchants would suffer from restraints on their commerce, from the closing of the West to land speculation and fur trading, and from the restriction of opportunities for manufacturing. Southern planters, in debt to English merchants, would be unable to ease their debts by speculating in western land. Small farmers would suffer from the abolition of paper money, which had been the source of most of their loans. Workers in towns faced the prospect of narrowing opportunities, particularly because of the restraints on manufacturing and currency. Everyone stood to suffer from increased taxes.

Persistent Colonial Grievances

Most Americans soon found ways to live with the new British laws without terrible economic hardship. But their political grievances remained. Americans were accustomed to wide latitude in self-government. They believed that colonial assemblies had the sole right to control appropriations for the costs of government within the colonies. By attempting to raise extensive revenues directly from the public, the British government was challenging the basis of colonial political power.

STIRRINGS OF REVOLT

By the mid-1760s, a hardening of positions had begun in both England and America. The result was a progression of events that, more rapidly than imagined, destroyed the British Empire in America.

The Stamp Act Crisis

Effects of the Stamp Act

Grenville could not have devised a better method for antagonizing and unifying the colonies than the Stamp Act of 1765. Unlike the Sugar Act of a year earlier, which affected only a few New England merchants, the tax on printed documents fell on everyone. More alarming than the relatively light taxes, however, was the precedent they seemed to create. In the past, taxes and duties on colonial trade had always been designed to regulate commerce. The Stamp Act, however, was clearly an attempt by England to raise revenue in the colonies without the consent of the colonial assemblies.

"Virginia Resolves"

Few colonists believed that they could do anything more than grumble until the Virginia House of Burgesses aroused Americans to action. Patrick Henry made a dramatic speech to the House in May 1765, concluding with a vague prediction that if present policies were not revised, George III, like earlier tyrants, might lose his head. There were shocked cries of "Treason!" But Henry introduced a set of resolutions (only some of which the assembly passed) declaring that Americans possessed the same rights as the English, especially the right to be taxed only by their own representatives; that Virginians should pay no taxes except those voted by the Virginia assembly; and that anyone advocating the right of Parliament to tax Virginians should be deemed an enemy of the colony. Henry's resolutions were printed and circulated as the "Virginia Resolves."

In Massachusetts at about the same time, James Otis persuaded his fellow members of the colonial assembly to call an intercolonial congress to take action against the new tax. And in October 1765, the Stamp Act Congress, as it was called, met in New York with delegates from nine colonies. In a petition to the British government, the congress denied that the colonies could rightfully be taxed except through their own provincial assemblies.

In the summer of 1765, meanwhile, mobs were rising up in several colonial cities against the Stamp Act. The largest of them was in Boston, where men belonging to the newly organized Sons of Liberty terrorized stamp agents and burned stamps. The mob also attacked such supposedly pro-British aristocrats as the lieutenant governor, Thomas Hutchinson (who had privately opposed passage of the Stamp Act but who felt obliged to support it once it became law). Hutchinson's elegant house was pillaged and virtually destroyed.

Stamp Act Repealed

The crisis finally subsided largely because England backed down. The authorities in London were less affected by the political protests than by economic pressure. Many New Englanders had stopped buying English goods to protest the Sugar Act of 1764, and the Stamp Act caused the boycott to spread. Under pressure from English merchants concerned about the loss of much of their colonial market, Parliament—under a new prime minister, the Marquis of Rockingham—repealed the unpopular law on March 18, 1766. To satisfy his strong and vociferous opponents, Rockingham also pushed through the Declaratory Act, which confirmed parliamentary authority over the colonies "in all cases whatsoever." In their rejoicing over the Stamp Act repeal, most Americans paid little attention to this ominous declaration of Parliament's power.

The Townshend Program

When the Rockingham government's policy of appeasement met substantial opposition in England, the king dismissed the Rockingham ministry and replaced it with a new government led by the aging but still powerful William Pitt, who was now Lord Chatham. Chatham had in the past been sympathetic toward American interests. Once in office, however, he was at times so incapacitated by mental illness that the actual leadership of his administration fell to the chancellor of the exchequer, Charles Townshend.

Townshend had to deal with colonial grievances left over from the Grenville ministry. With the Stamp Act repealed, the greatest American grievance involved the Mutiny (or Quartering) Act of 1765, which required the colonists to provide shelter and supplies for British troops. The colonists objected not so much to quartering or supplying the troops but to being required by London to do so. The Massachusetts and New York assemblies went so far as to refuse to vote the mandated supplies to the troops.

Mutiny Act

Townshend responded in 1767 by disbanding the New York Assembly until the colonists agreed to obey the Mutiny Act. By singling out New York, he believed, he would avoid antagonizing all the colonies at once. He also imposed new taxes (known as the Townshend Duties) on various goods imported to the colonies from England—lead, paint, paper, and tea. Townshend assumed that since these were taxes purely on "external" transactions (imports from overseas), as opposed to the internal transactions the Stamp Act had taxed, the colonists would not object. But all the colonies resented the suspension of the New York Assembly, believing it to be a threat to every colonial government. And all the colonies rejected Townshend's careful distinction between external and internal taxation.

Townshend Duties

Townshend also established a board of customs commissioners in America. The new commissioners virtually ended smuggling in Boston, where they established their headquarters, although smugglers continued to carry on a busy trade in other colonial seaports. The Boston merchants—angry that the new commission was diverting the lucrative smuggling trade elsewhere—helped organize a boycott of British goods that were subject to the Townshend Duties. Merchants in Philadelphia and New York joined them in a nonimportation agreement in 1768, and later some southern merchants and planters also agreed to cooperate. Throughout the colonies, American homespun and other domestic products became suddenly fashionable.

Nonimportation Agreement

Late in 1767, Charles Townshend died. In March 1770, the new prime minister, Lord North, hoping to end the American boycott, repealed all the Townshend Duties except the tea tax.

The Boston Massacre

Before news of the repeal reached America, an event in Massachusetts electrified colonial opinion. The harassment of the new customs commissioners in Boston had grown so intense that the British government had placed four regiments of regular

Rebellious Boston

"THE TORY'S DAY OF JUDGMENT" A mob of American Patriots hoists a Loyalist neighbor up a flagpole in this woodcut, which is obviously sympathetic to the victim. The crowd is shown as fat, rowdy, and drunken. Public humiliations of Tories were not infrequent during the war. More common, however, was seizure of their property. *(The Library of Congress)*

troops in the city. Many of the poorly paid British soldiers looked for jobs in their off-duty hours and thus competed with local workers. Clashes between the two groups were frequent.

On the night of March 5, 1770, a mob of dockworkers, "liberty boys," and others began pelting the sentries at the customs house with rocks and snowballs. Hastily, Captain Thomas Preston of the British regiment lined up several of his men in front of the building to protect it. There was some scuffling; one of the soldiers was knocked down; and in the midst of it all, apparently, several British soldiers fired into the crowd, killing five people.

This murky incident, almost certainly the result of panic and confusion, was quickly transformed by local resistance leaders into the "Boston Massacre." The event became the subject of such lurid (and inaccurate) accounts as the widely circulated pamphlet *Innocent Blood Crying to God from the Streets of Boston.* A famous engraving by Paul Revere portrayed the massacre as a calculated assault on a peaceful crowd. The British soldiers, tried before a jury of Bostonians, were found guilty only of manslaughter and given token punishment. But colonial pamphlets and newspapers convinced many Americans that the soldiers were guilty of official murder.

The leading figure in fomenting public outrage over the Boston Massacre was Samuel Adams. England, he argued, had become a morass of sin and corruption; only in America did public virtue survive. In 1772, he proposed the creation of a "committee of correspondence" in Boston to publicize the grievances against England. Other colonies followed Massachusetts's lead, and a loose intercolonial network of political organizations was soon established that kept the spirit of dissent alive through the 1770s.

"Committee of Correspondence"

The Philosophy of Revolt

Although a superficial calm settled on the colonies after the Boston Massacre, the crises of the 1760s had helped arouse enduring ideological challenges to England and had produced powerful instruments for publicizing colonial grievances. Gradually a political outlook gained a following in America that would ultimately serve to justify revolt.

The ideas that would support the Revolution emerged from many sources. Some were drawn from religious (particularly Puritan) sources or from the political experiences of the colonies. Others came from abroad. Most important, perhaps, were the "radical" ideas of those in Great Britain who stood in opposition to their government. Some were Scots, who considered the English state tyrannical. Others were embittered "country Whigs," who felt excluded from power and considered the existing system corrupt and oppressive. Drawing from some of the great philosophical minds of earlier generations—most notably John Locke—these English dissidents framed a powerful argument against their government.

Sources of Revolutionary Ideology

Central to this emerging ideology was a new concept of what government should be. Because humans were inherently corrupt and selfish, government was necessary to protect individuals from the evil in one another. But because any government was run by corruptible people, the people needed safeguards against its possible abuses of power. Most people in both England and America considered the English constitution the best system ever devised to meet these necessities. By distributing power among the three elements of society—the monarchy, the aristocracy, and the common people—the English political system ensured that no individual or group could exercise authority unchecked by another. Yet by the mid-seventeenth century, dissidents in both England and America had become convinced that the constitution was in danger. A single center of power—the king and his ministers—was becoming so powerful that it could not be effectively checked.

Such arguments found little sympathy in most of England. The English constitution was not a written document or a fixed set of unchangeable rules. It was a general sense of the "way things are done," and most people in England were willing to accept changes in it. Americans, by contrast, drew from their experience with colonial charters, in which the shape and powers of government were permanently inscribed on paper. They resisted the idea of a flexible, changing set of basic principles.

One basic principle, Americans believed, was the right of people to be taxed only with their own consent—a belief that gradually took shape in the widely repeated slogan, "No taxation without representation." Whatever the nature of a tax, it could not be levied without the consent of the colonists themselves.

"No Taxation without Representation"

This clamor about "representation" made little sense to the English. According to English constitutional theory, members of Parliament did not represent individuals or particular geographical areas. Instead, each member represented the interests of the whole nation and indeed the whole empire. The many boroughs of England that had no representative in Parliament, the whole of Ireland, and the colonies thousands of miles away—all were thus represented in the Parliament at London, even though they elected no representatives of their own. This was the theory of "virtual" representation. But Americans, drawing from their experiences with their town meetings and their colonial assemblies, believed in "actual" representation. Every community was entitled to its own representative, elected by the people of that community. Since the colonists had none of their own representatives in Parliament, it followed that they were not represented there. Americans believed that the colonial assemblies played the same role within the colonies that Parliament did within England. The empire, the Americans argued, was a sort of federation of commonwealths, each with its own legislative body, all tied together by loyalty to the king.

"Virtual" and "Actual" Representation

Such ideas illustrated a fundamental difference of opinion between England and America over the question of where ultimate power lay. By arguing that Parliament had the right to legislate for the empire as a whole, but that only the provincial assemblies could legislate for the individual colonies, Americans were in effect arguing for a division of sovereignty. Parliament would be sovereign in some matters, the assemblies in others. To the British,

Sovereignty Debated

such an argument was absurd. In any system of government there must be a single, ultimate authority. And since the empire was, in their view, a single, undivided unit, there could be only one authority within it: the English government of king and Parliament.

Sites of Resistance

The apparent calm in America in the first years of the 1770s hid a growing sense of frustration and resentment about the continued enforcement of the Navigation Acts. Popular anger was visible in occasional acts of rebellion. At one point, colonists seized a British revenue ship on the lower Delaware River. In 1772, angry residents of Rhode Island boarded the British schooner *Gaspée*, set it afire, and sank it.

Colonists kept the growing spirit of resistance alive in many ways, but most of all through writing and talking. Dissenting leaflets, pamphlets, and books circulated widely through the colonies. In towns and cities, men gathered in churches, schools, town squares, and above all in taverns to discuss politics. Indeed, the tavern culture of the colonies was crucial to the growth of Revolutionary sentiment. Taverns were appealing, of course, because they provided alcoholic drinks in a culture where the craving for alcohol was very high. But taverns were also among the few public spaces were people could meet and talk openly. The tavern was a mostly male institution, just as politics was considered a mostly male concern. The combination of male companionship and political conversation emerged naturally out of the tavern culture.

Political Importance of Colonial Taverns

As the Revolutionary crisis deepened, taverns and pubs became the central meeting places for discussions of ideas about resistance. Taverns were also places were resistance pamphlets and leaflets could be distributed, and the settings for meetings for the planning of protests and demonstrations. Massachusetts had the most elaborately developed tavern culture, which was perhaps one reason why the spirit of resistance grew more quickly there than anywhere else.

The Tea Excitement

The Tea Act

The Revolutionary fervor of the 1760s revived, finally, as a result of a new act of Parliament—one that involved the business of selling tea. In 1773, Britain's East India Company was sitting on large stocks of tea that it could not sell in England. It was on the verge of bankruptcy. In an effort to save it, the government passed the Tea Act of 1773, which gave the company the right to export its merchandise directly to the colonies without paying any of the regular taxes that were imposed on the colonial merchants, who had traditionally served as the middlemen in such transactions. With these privileges, the company could undersell American merchants and monopolize the colonial tea trade.

The act angered influential colonial merchants, who feared being replaced by a powerful monopoly. More important, however, the Tea Act revived American passions about the issue of taxation without representation. The law provided no new tax on tea. But the original Townshend duty on the commodity survived; and the East India Company was now exempt from paying it. Lord North had assumed that most colonists would welcome the new law because it would reduce the price of tea to consumers by removing the middlemen. But resistance leaders in America argued that the law, in effect, represented an unconstitutional tax on American merchants. The colonists responded by boycotting tea.

Unlike earlier protests, most of which had involved relatively small numbers of people, the tea boycott mobilized large segments of the population. It also helped link the colonies together in a common experience of mass popular protest. Particularly important to the movement were the activities of colonial women, who led the boycott. The Daughters of Liberty—a women's patriotic organization that was committed to agitating against British policies—proclaimed, "rather than Freedom, we'll part with our Tea."

Daughters of Liberty

In the last weeks of 1773, with strong popular support, leaders in various colonies made plans to prevent the East India Company from landing its cargoes in colonial ports. In Philadelphia and New York, determined colonists kept the tea from leaving the company's ships, and in Charleston, they stored it away in a public warehouse. In Boston, local patriots staged a spectacular drama. On the evening of December 16, 1773, three companies of fifty men each, masquerading as Mohawk Indians, went aboard three ships, broke open the tea chests, and heaved them into the harbor. As the electrifying news of the Boston "tea party" spread, colonists in other seaports staged similar acts of resistance.

The Boston "Tea Party"

Parliament retaliated in four acts of 1774: closing the port of Boston, drastically reducing the powers of self-government in Massachusetts, permitting royal officers in America to be tried in other colonies or in England when accused of crimes, and providing for the quartering of troops by the colonists. These Coercive Acts—or, as they were more widely known in America, "Intolerable Acts"—were followed by the Quebec Act, which extended the boundaries of Quebec to include the French communities between the Ohio and Mississippi Rivers. It also granted political rights to Roman Catholics and recognized the legality of the Roman Catholic Church within the enlarged province. Many colonists feared that a plot was afoot in London to subject Americans to the authority of the pope.

Consequences of the Coercive Acts

The Coercive Acts, far from isolating Massachusetts, made it a martyr in the eyes of residents of other colonies and sparked new resistance up and down the coast. Colonial legislatures passed a series of resolves supporting Massachusetts. Women's groups mobilized to extend the boycotts of British goods and to create substitutes for the tea, textiles, and other commodities they were shunning. In Edenton, North Carolina, fifty-one women signed an agreement in October 1774 declaring their "sincere adherence" to the anti-British resolutions of their provincial assembly and proclaiming their duty to do "every thing as far as lies in our power" to support the "publick good."

COOPERATION AND WAR

Beginning in 1765, colonial leaders developed a variety of organizations for converting popular discontent into action—organizations that in time formed the basis for an independent government.

New Sources of Authority

The passage of authority from the royal government to the colonists themselves began on the local level. In colony after colony, local institutions responded to the resistance movement by simply seizing authority. At times, entirely new institutions emerged.

The most effective of these new groups were the committees of correspondence. Virginia established the first intercolonial committees of correspondence, which helped make possible continuous cooperation among the colonies. After the royal governor dissolved the assembly in 1774, a rump session met in the Raleigh Tavern at Williamsburg, declared that the Intolerable Acts menaced the liberties of every colony, and issued a call for a Continental Congress.

The First Continental Congress

Delegates from all the colonies except Georgia were present when, in September 1774, the First Continental Congress convened in Philadelphia. They made five major decisions. First, they rejected a plan for a colonial union under British authority. Second, they endorsed a relatively moderate statement of grievances, which addressed the king as "Most Gracious Sovereign," but which also included a demand for the repeal of all oppressive legislation passed since 1763. Third, they approved a series of resolutions recommending that military preparations be made for defense against possible attack by the British troops in Boston. Fourth, they agreed to a series of boycotts that they hoped would stop all trade with Great Britain, and they formed a "Continental Association" to see that these agreements were enforced. Finally, the delegates agreed to meet again the following spring.

During the winter, the Parliament in London debated proposals for conciliating the colonists, and early in 1775 Lord North finally won approval for a series of measures known as the Conciliatory Propositions. Parliament proposed that the colonies would tax themselves at Parliament's demand. With this offer, Lord North hoped to separate the American moderates, whom he believed represented the views of the majority, from the extremist minority. But his offer was too little and too late. It did not reach America until after the first shots of war had been fired.

THE ALTERNATIVES OF WILLIAM BURG In the aftermath of the Boston Tea Party, and in response to the Coercive Acts Great Britain enacted to punish the colonists, the First Continental Congress called on Americans to boycott British goods until the Acts were repealed. In this drawing, a prosperous Virginia merchant is seen signing a pledge to honor the nonimportation agreement—unsurprisingly given the alternative, visible in the background of the picture: tar and feathers hanging from a post labeled "A Cure for the Refractory." *(Colonial Williamsburg Foundation)*

Lexington and Concord

"Minutemen"

For months, the farmers and townspeople of Massachusetts had been gathering arms and ammunition and training as "minutemen," preparing to fight on a minute's notice. The Continental Congress had approved preparations for a defensive war, and the citizen-soldiers waited only for an aggressive move by the British regulars in Boston.

General Thomas Gage

In Boston, General Thomas Gage, commanding the British garrison, considered his army too small to do anything without reinforcements. He resisted the advice of

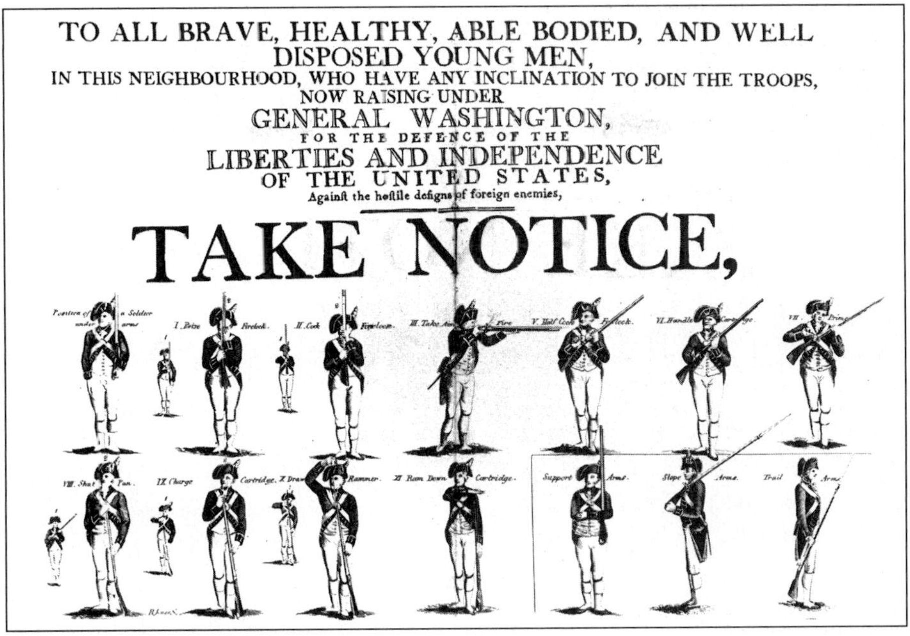

RECRUITING PATRIOTS This Revolutionary War recruiting poster tries to attract recruits by appealing to their patriotism (asking them to defend "the liberties and independence of the United States"), their vanity (by showing the "handsome clothing" and impressive bearing of soldiers), and their greed (by offering them "a bounty of twelve dollars" and "sixty dollars a year"). *(The Library of Congress)*

less cautious officers, who assured him that the Americans would back down quickly before any show of British force. When General Gage received orders to arrest the rebel leaders Sam Adams and John Hancock, known to be in the vicinity of Lexington, he still hesitated. But when he heard that the minutemen had stored a large supply of gunpowder in Concord (eighteen miles from Boston), he decided to act. On the night of April 18, 1775, he sent a detachment of about 1,000 men out toward Lexington. He hoped to surprise the colonials and seize the illegal supplies without bloodshed.

But patriots in Boston were watching the British movements closely, and during the night two horsemen, William Dawes and Paul Revere, rode out to warn the villages and farms. When the redcoats arrived in Lexington the next day, several dozen minutemen awaited them on the town common. Shots were fired and minutemen fell; eight were killed and ten wounded. Advancing to Concord, the British discovered that the Americans had hastily removed most of the powder supply. All along the road back to Boston, the British were harassed by the gunfire of farmers hiding behind trees, rocks, and stone walls. By the end of the day, the British had lost almost three times as many men as the Americans.

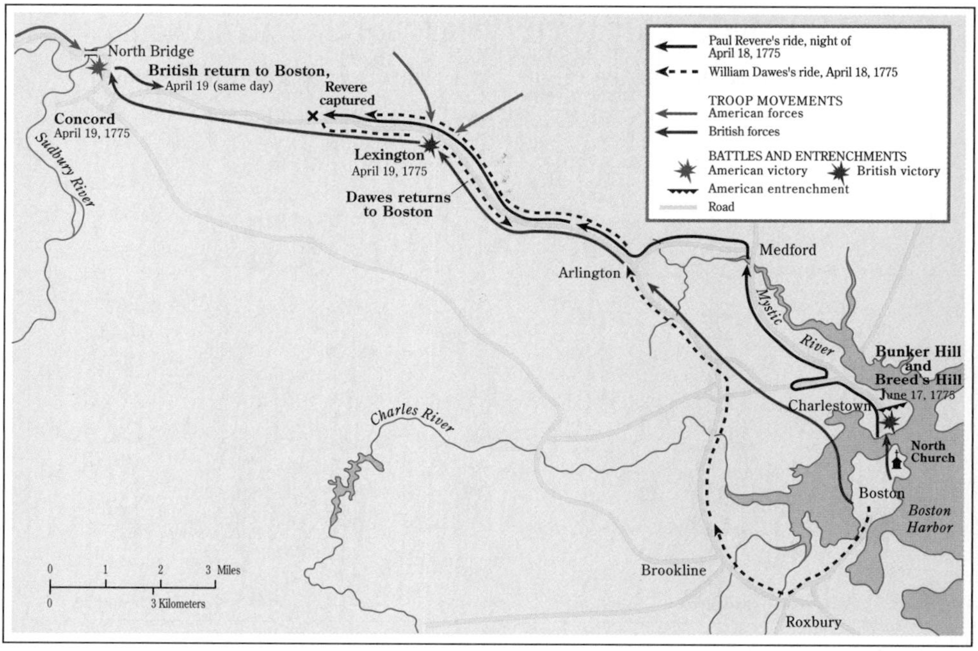

THE BATTLES OF LEXINGTON AND CONCORD, 1775 This map shows the fabled series of events that led to the first battle of the American Revolution. On the night of April 18, 1775, Paul Revere and William Dawes rode out from Boston to warn the outlying towns of the approach of British troops. Revere was captured just west of Lexington, but Dawes escaped and returned to Boston. The next morning, British forces moved out of Boston toward Lexington, where they met armed American minutemen on the Lexington common and exchanged fire. The British dispersed the Americans in Lexington. But they next moved on to Concord, where they encountered more armed minutemen, clashed again, and were driven back toward Boston. All along their line of march, they were harassed by riflemen. ◆ *What impact did the battles of Lexington and Concord (and the later battle of Bunker Hill, also shown on this map) have on colonial sentiment toward the British?*

The first shots—the "shots heard 'round the world," as Americans later called them—had been fired. But who had fired them first? According to one of the minutemen at Lexington, the British commander, Major Thomas Pitcairn, had shouted to the colonists on his arrival, "Disperse, ye rebels!" When they ignored him, he ordered his troops to fire. British officers and soldiers claimed that the minutemen had fired first. Whatever the truth, the rebels succeeded in circulating their account well ahead of the British version, adorning it with tales of British atrocities. The effect was to rally thousands of colonists to the rebel cause.

The War for Independence Begins

It was not immediately clear that the skirmishes at Lexington and Concord were the first battles of a war. But whether people recognized it at the time or not, the War for Independence had begun.

CONCLUSION

When the French and Indian War ended in 1763, it might have seemed reasonable to expect that relations between the English colonists in America and Great Britain itself would have been cemented more firmly than ever. But in fact the end of the French and Indian War altered the imperial relationship forever, in ways that ultimately drove Americans to rebel against English rule and begin a war for independence. To the British, the lesson of the war was that the colonies in America needed firmer control from London. The empire was now much bigger, and it needed better administration. The war had produced great debts, and the Americans—among the principal beneficiaries of the war—should help pay them. And so for more than a decade after the end of the fighting, the British tried one strategy after another to tighten control over and extract money from the colonies.

To the colonists, this effort to tighten imperial rule appeared both a betrayal of the sacrifices they had made in the war and a challenge to their long-developing assumptions about the rights of English people to rule themselves. Gradually, white Americans came to see in the British policies evidence of a conspiracy to establish tyranny in the New World. And so throughout the 1760s and 1770s, the colonists developed ever more overt and effective forms of resistance. By the time the first shots were fired in the American Revolution in 1775, Britain and America had come to view each other as two very different societies. Their differences, which came to seem irreconcilable, propelled them into a war that would change the course of both countries' history.

FOR FURTHER REFERENCE

Fred Anderson, *The Crucible of War: The Seven Years' War and the Fate of Empire in British North America, 1754–1766* (2000) is an excellent account of the critical years in which the British Empire transformed itself through its colonial wars in America. David Armitage, *The Ideological Origins of the British Empire* (2000) examines the ideas of those who promoted and sought to justify Britain's imperial ambitions. Francis Jennings, *The Ambiguous Iroquois Empire* (1984) examines the critical role of the Iroquois in the conflicts over empire in North America. Karen Ordahl Kupperman, *Indians and English: Facing Off in Early America* (2000) is an important study of the complex relationships between settlers and natives. Richard Bushman, *King and People in Colonial Massachusetts* (1987) traces the fracture between Massachusetts colonists and the imperial government. Gary Nash, *The Urban Crucible: The Northern Seaports and the Origins of the American Revolution* (1979) argues that increasing class stratification in northern cities contributed to the coming of the American Revolution. Robert R. Palmer, *The*

Age of Democratic Revolution: Vol. 1, The Challenge (1959) and J. G. A. Pocock, *The Machiavellian Moment* (1975) both place the American Revolution in the context of a transatlantic political culture. Jon Butler, *Becoming America: The Revolution Before 1776* (2000) examines social, religious, and intellectual changes in the American self-image. Bernard Bailyn, *The Ideological Origins of the American Revolution* (1967) was one of the first works by an American historian to emphasize the importance of English republican political thought for the revolutionary ideology of the American colonists.

For quizzes, Internet resources, references to additional books and films, and more, consult this book's Online Learning Center site at www.mhhe.com/unfinishednation4.

THE BRITISH SURRENDER This comtemporary drawing depicts the formal surrender of British troops at Yorktown on October 19, 1781. Columns of American troops and a large French fleet flank the surrender ceremony, suggesting part of the reason for the British defeat. General Cornwallis, the commander of British forces in Virginia, did not himself attend the surrender. He sent a deputy in his place. *(Hulton/Archive/Getty Images)*

TIME LINE

1775	1776	1777	1778	1781
Second Continental Congress	Paine's *Common Sense*	Articles of Confederation adopted	French-America alliance	Articles of Confederation ratified
Washington commands American forces	Declaration of Independence	British defeat at Saratoga		Cornwallis surrenders at Yorktown
	Battle of Trenton			

CHAPTER FIVE

THE AMERICAN REVOLUTION

The States United
The War for Independence
War and Society
The Creation of State Governments
The Search for a National Government

Two struggles occurred simultaneously during the seven years of war that began in April 1775. One was the military conflict with Great Britain. The second was a political conflict within America.

The military conflict was, by the standards of later wars, a relatively modest one. By the standards of its own day, however, it was an unusually savage conflict, pitting not only army against army but the civilian population against a powerful external force. The shift of the war from a traditional, conventional struggle to a new kind of conflict—a revolutionary war for liberation—is what made it possible for the United States to defeat the more powerful British.

At the same time, Americans were wrestling with the great political questions that the conflict necessarily produced: first, whether to demand independence from Britain; then, how to structure the new nation they had proclaimed.

	1783	1784	1786	1787	
	Treaty of Paris	Postwar depression begins	Shays's Rebellion	Northwest Ordinance	

CHAPTER FIVE

THE STATES UNITED

Although some Americans had long been expecting a military conflict with Britain, the actual beginning of hostilities in 1775 found the colonies generally unprepared for war against the world's greatest armed power.

Defining American War Aims

Three weeks after the battles of Lexington and Concord, when the Second Continental Congress met in Philadelphia, delegates from every colony (except Georgia, which had not yet sent a representative) agreed to support the war. But they disagreed about its purpose. At one extreme was a group led by the Adams cousins (John and Samuel), Richard Henry Lee of Virginia, and others, who already favored independence; at the other extreme was a group led by such moderates as John Dickinson of Pennsylvania, who hoped for a quick reconciliation with Great Britain.

Divergent American War Aims

Most Americans believed at first that they were fighting not for independence but for a redress of grievances within the British Empire. During the first year of fighting, however, many of them began to change their minds. The costs of the war were so high that the original war aims began to seem too modest to justify them. Many colonists were enraged when the British began trying to recruit Indians, African slaves, and German mercenaries (the hated "Hessians") against them. When the British government blockaded the colonial ports and rejected all efforts at conciliation, many colonists concluded that independence was the only remaining option.

An impassioned pamphlet crystallized these feelings in January 1776: Thomas Paine's *Common Sense.* Paine, who had emigrated from England to America less than two years before, wanted to turn the anger of Americans away from particular parliamentary measures and toward what he considered the root of the problem—the English constitution itself. It was simple common sense, he wrote, for Americans to break completely with a political system that could inflict such brutality on its own people. *Common Sense* sold more than 100,000 copies in only a few months. It helped create a rapid growth of support for the idea of independence in the early months of 1776.

Common Sense

The Declaration of Independence

In the meantime, the Continental Congress in Philadelphia was moving toward a complete break with England. At the beginning of the summer, it appointed a committee to draft a formal declaration of independence; and on July 2, 1776, it adopted a

Independence Declared

resolution: "That these United Colonies are, and, of right, ought to be, free and independent states; that they are absolved from all allegiance to the British crown, and that all political connexion between them and the state of Great Britain is, and ought to be, totally dissolved." Two days later, on July 4, Congress approved the Declaration of Independence itself, which provided formal justifications for the actions the delegates had taken two days earlier.

Articles of Confederation

The Declaration launched a period of energetic political innovation, as one colony after another reconstituted itself as a "state." By 1781, most states had produced written constitutions for themselves. At the national level, however, the process was more uncertain. In November 1777, finally, Congress adopted a plan for union, the Articles of Confederation. The document confirmed the existing weak, decentralized system.

Thomas Jefferson

Thomas Jefferson, a thirty-three-year-old Virginian, wrote most of the Declaration, with help from Benjamin Franklin and John Adams. The Declaration expressed concepts that had been circulating throughout the colonies over the previous few months in the form of at least ninety other, local "declarations of independence"—declarations drafted up and down the coast by town meetings, artisan and militia organizations, county officials, grand juries, Sons of Liberty, and colonial assemblies. Jefferson borrowed heavily from these texts.

The final document was in two parts. In the first, the Declaration restated the familiar contract theory of John Locke: the theory that governments were formed to protect what Jefferson called "life, liberty and the pursuit of happiness." In the second part, it listed the alleged crimes of the king, who, with the backing of Parliament, had violated his contract with the colonists and thus had forfeited all claim to their loyalty.

Mobilizing for War

Financing the war was difficult, because Congress lacked the authority and the states generally lacked the inclination to impose taxes on the public. Congress had no authority to levy taxes on its own, and when it requisitioned money from the state governments, none contributed more than a small part of its expected share. Congress had little success borrowing from the public, since few Americans could afford to buy bonds. In the end, there was no alternative but to issue paper money. Printing presses turned out enormous amounts of "Continental currency," and the states printed currencies of their own. The result, predictably, was soaring inflation, and Congress soon found that the Continental currency was virtually worthless. Ultimately, it financed the war mostly by borrowing from other nations.

After a first surge of patriotism in 1775, volunteer soldiers were scarce. States had to pay bounties or use a draft to recruit the needed men.

Debating the Past

THE AMERICAN REVOLUTION

The longstanding debate over the origins of the American Revolution has intended to reflect two broad schools of interpretation. One sees the Revolution largely as a political and intellectual event, the other as a social and economic phenomenon.

The Revolutionary generation itself portrayed the conflict as a struggle over ideals, and this interpretation prevailed through most of the nineteenth century. But in the early twentieth century, historians influenced by the reform currents of the progressive era began to identify social and economic forces that they believed had contributed to the rebellion. Carl Becker, for example, wrote in a 1909 study of New York that two questions had shaped the Revolution: "The first was the question of home rule; the second was the question . . . of who should rule at home." The colonists were not only fighting the British; they were also engaged in a kind of civil war, a contest between radicals and conservatives.

Other "progressive" historians elaborated on Becker's thesis. J. Franklin Jameson, writing in 1926, argued, "Many economic desires, many social aspirations, were set free by the political struggle, many aspects of society profoundly altered by the forces thus let loose." Arthur M. Schlesinger maintained in a 1917 book that colonial merchants, motivated by their own interest in escaping the restrictive policies of British mercantilism, aroused American resistance in the 1760s and 1770s.

Beginning in the 1950s, a new generation of scholars began to reemphasize the role of ideology and de-emphasize the role of economic interests. Robert E. Brown (in 1955) and Edmund S. Morgan (in 1956) both argued that most eighteenth-century Americans shared common political principles and that the social and economic conflicts the progressives had identified were not severe. The rhetoric of the Revolution, they suggested, was not propaganda but a real reflection of the ideas of the colonists. Bernard Bailyn, in *The Ideological Origins of the American Revolution* (1967), demonstrated the complex roots of the ideas behind the Revolution and argued that this carefully constructed political stance was not a disguise for economic interests but a genuine ideology, rooted in deeply held convictions about rights and power. The Revolution, he exclaimed, "was above all an ideological, constitutional, political struggle and not primarily a controversy between social groups undertaken to force changes in the organization of the society or the economy."

By the late 1960s, a new generation of historians—many influenced by the New Left—were reviving economic interpretations of the Revolution by exploring the social and economic tensions that they claimed shaped the Revolutionary struggle. Historians cited the actions of mobs in colonial cities, the economic pressures on colonial merchants, the growing climate of economic distress in colonial cities, and other changes in the character of American culture and society as critical prerequisites for the growth of the Revolutionary movement. Gary Nash, attempting to reconcile the emphasis on economic interests with the role of ideology, argued that the two things were not incompatible. "Everyone has economic interests," he claimed, "and everyone . . . has an ideology." Exploring the relationship between the two, he argues, is critical to historians' ability to understand either. Also, as Linda Kerber and others have argued, the newer social interpretations have raised increasing interest in the experience of workers, slaves, women, Native Americans, and other groups previously considered marginal to public life as part of the explanation of the Revolutionary struggle.

Finally, Gordon Wood, in *The Radicalism of the American Revolution* (1992) revived an idea once popular and recently unfashionable: that the Revolution was a genuinely radical event that led to the breakdown of such longstanding characteristics of society as deference, patriarchy, and traditional gender relations. Class conflict may not have caused the Revolution, he argues, but the Revolution had a profound, even radical, effect on society nevertheless.

(text continued from page 119)

REVOLUTIONARY SOLDIERS Jean Baptist de Verger, a French officer serving in America during the Revolution, kept an illustrated journal of his experiences. Here he portrays four American soldiers carrying different kinds of arms: a black infantryman with a light rifle, a musketman, a rifleman, and an artilleryman. *(Anne S.K. Brown Military Collection, Brown University Library)*

At first, the militiamen remained under the control of their respective states. But Congress recognized the need for a centralized military command, and it created a Continental army with a single commander in chief: George Washington. Washington had considerable military experience and was an early advocate of independence; he was admired, respected, and trusted by nearly all Patriots. He took command of the new army in June 1775. With the aid of foreign military experts such as the Marquis de Lafayette from

Washington Takes Charge

France and the Baron von Steuben from Prussia, he built a force that prevailed against the mightiest power in the world. Even more important, perhaps, Washington's steadiness, courage, and dedication to his cause provided the army—and the people—with a symbol of stability around which they could rally.

THE WAR FOR INDEPENDENCE

The British seemed to have overwhelming advantages as the War for Independence began: the greatest navy and the best-equipped army in the world, the resources of an empire, a coherent structure of command. Yet the United States had advantages, too. Americans were fighting on their own ground. They were more committed to the conflict than were the British. And, beginning in 1777, they received substantial aid from abroad.

But the American victory was also a result of a series of blunders and miscalculations by the British in the early stages of the fighting, when England could (and probably should) have won. And it was, finally, a result of the transformation of the war—through three distinct phases—into a new kind of conflict that the British military, for all its strength, was unable to win.

The First Phase: New England

For the first year of the conflict—from the spring of 1775 to the spring of 1776—many English authorities thought that British forces were not fighting a real war, but simply quelling pockets of rebellion in the contentious area around Boston. After the redcoats withdrew from Lexington and Concord in April, American forces besieged them in Boston. In the Battle of Bunker Hill (actually fought on Breed's Hill) on June 17, 1775, the Patriots suffered severe casualties and withdrew. But they inflicted even greater losses on the enemy. The siege continued. Early in 1776, finally, the British decided that Boston was a poor place from which to fight. It was in the center of the most anti-British part of America and tactically difficult to defend because it was easily isolated and surrounded. And so, on March 17, 1776, the redcoats evacuated Boston for Halifax, Nova Scotia, with hundreds of Loyalist refugees.

Bunker Hill

In the meantime, a band of southern Patriots, at Moore's Creek Bridge in North Carolina, crushed an uprising of Loyalists (Americans still loyal to England and its king) on February 27, 1776. And to the north, the Americans began an invasion of Canada. Generals Benedict Arnold and Richard Montgomery unsuccessfully threatened Quebec in late 1775 and early 1776 in a battle in which Montgomery was killed and Arnold wounded.

Invasion of Canada

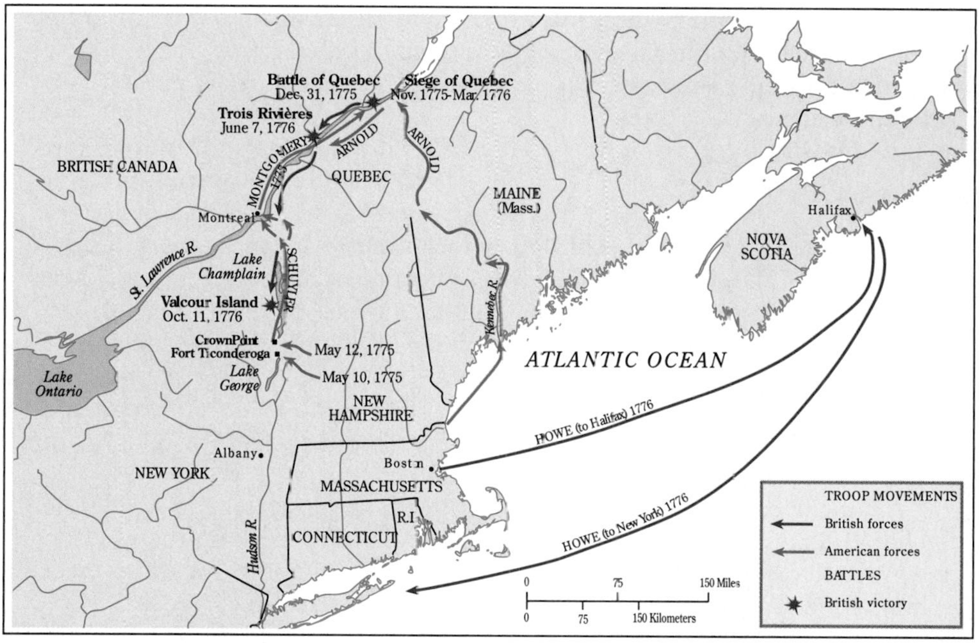

THE REVOLUTION IN THE NORTH, 1775–1776 After initial battles in and around Boston, the British forces left Massachusetts and (after a brief stay in Halifax, Canada) moved south to New York. ◆ *Why would the British have considered New York a better base than Boston?* In the meantime, American forces moved north in an effort to capture British strongholds in Montreal and Quebec, with little success.

For an interactive version of this map go to www. mhhe.com/unfinishednation4ch5maps

By the spring of 1776, it had become clear to the British that the conflict was not just a local phenomenon. The American campaigns in Canada, the agitation in the South, and the growing evidence of colonial unity all suggested that England must prepare to fight a much larger conflict.

The Second Phase: The Mid-Atlantic Region

During the next phase of the war, which lasted from 1776 until early 1778, the British were in a good position to win. Indeed, had it not been for a series of mistakes and misfortunes, they probably would have crushed the rebellion.

The British regrouped quickly after their retreat from Boston. During the summer of 1776, hundreds of British ships and 32,000 British soldiers arrived in New York, under the command of General William Howe. He offered Congress a choice between surrender with royal pardon and a battle against apparently overwhelming odds. To oppose Howe's great force, Washington could muster only about 19,000 soldiers; he had no navy at all. Even so, the Americans

General William Howe

rejected Howe's offer. The British then pushed the Patriot forces off Long Island, forced them to abandon Manhattan, and then drove them in slow retreat over the plains of New Jersey, across the Delaware River, and into Pennsylvania.

The British settled down for the winter in northern and central New Jersey, with an outpost of Hessians at Trenton, on the Delaware River. But Washington did not sit still. On Christmas night 1776, he daringly re-crossed the icy Delaware River, surprised and scattered the Hessians, and occupied Trenton. Then he advanced to Princeton and drove a force of redcoats from their base in the college there. But Washington was unable to hold either Princeton or Trenton and finally took refuge for the rest of the winter in the hills around Morristown. The campaign of 1776 came to an end with the Americans having triumphed in two minor battles and with their main army still intact.

Trenton and Princeton

For the campaigns of 1777 the British devised a strategy to divide the United States in two. Howe would move from New York up the Hudson to Albany, while another force would come down from Canada to meet him. John Burgoyne, commander of the northern force, began a two-pronged attack to the south along both the Mohawk and the upper Hudson approaches to Albany. But having set the plan in motion, Howe abandoned his part of it. Instead of moving north to meet Burgoyne, he went south and captured Philadelphia, hoping that his seizure of the rebel capital would bring the war to a speedy conclusion. Philadelphia fell with little resistance—and the Continental Congress moved into exile in York, Pennsylvania. After launching an unsuccessful Patriot attack against the British on October 4 at Germantown (just outside Philadelphia), Washington went into winter quarters at Valley Forge.

Howe's move to Philadelphia left Burgoyne to carry out the campaign in the north alone. He sent Colonel Barry St. Leger up the St. Lawrence River toward Lake Ontario. Burgoyne himself advanced directly down the upper Hudson Valley and easily seized Fort Ticonderoga. But Burgoyne soon experienced two staggering defeats. In one of them—at Oriskany, New York, on August 6—Patriots held off a force of Indians and Tories commanded by St. Leger. That allowed Benedict Arnold to close off the Mohawk Valley to St. Leger's advance. In the other battle—at Bennington, Vermont, on August 16—New England militiamen mauled a detachment that Burgoyne had sent to seek supplies. Short of materials, with all help cut off, Burgoyne fought several costly engagements and then withdrew to Saratoga, where General Horatio Gates surrounded him. On October 17, 1777, Burgoyne surrendered.

Patriot Victory at Saratoga

The campaign in upstate New York was not just a British defeat. It was a setback for the ambitious efforts of several Iroquois leaders. Although the Iroquois Confederacy had declared its neutrality in the Revolutionary War in 1776, some of its members allied themselves with the

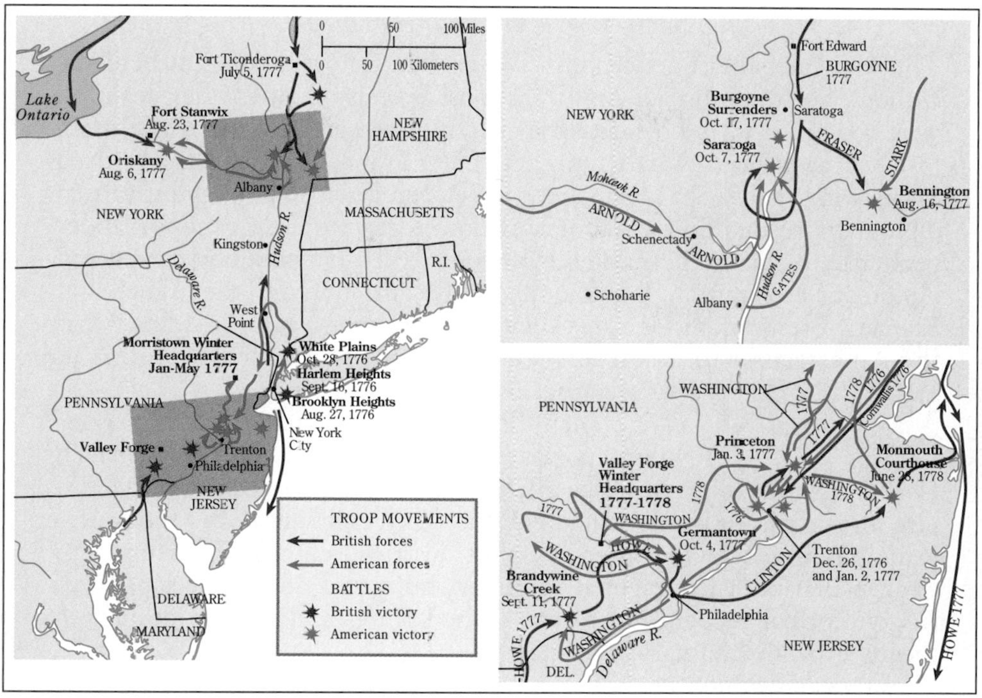

THE REVOLUTION IN THE MIDDLE COLONIES, 1776–1778 These maps illustrate the major campaigns of the Revolution in the middle colonies—New York, New Jersey, and Pennsylvania—between 1776 and 1778. The large map on the left shows the two prongs of the British strategy: first, a movement of British forces south from Canada into the Hudson Valley; and second, a movement of other British forces, under General William Howe, out from New York. The strategy was designed to trap the American army in between the two British movements. ◆ *What movements of Howe helped thwart the plan?* The two smaller maps on the right show a more detailed picture of some of the major battles. The upper one reveals the surprising American victory at Saratoga. The lower one shows a series of inconclusive battles between New York and Philadelphia in 1777 and 1778.

For an interactive version of this map go to www.mhhe.com/unfinishednation4ch5maps

British, among them a Mohawk brother and sister, Joseph and Mary Brant. This ill-fated alliance further divided the already weakened Iroquois Confederacy, because only three of the Iroquois nations (the Mohawk, the Seneca, and the Cayuga) followed the Brants in support of the British. A year after the defeat at Oriskany, Iroquois forces joined British troops in a series of raids on white settlements in upstate New York. Patriot forces under the command of General John Sullivan harshly retaliated, wreaking such destruction on Indian settlements that large groups of Iroquois fled north into Canada to seek refuge. Many never returned.

Securing Aid from Abroad

The leaders of the American effort knew that victory would not be likely without aid from abroad. And their most promising allies, they realized, were the French, who believed they had much to gain from seeing Britain lose a crucial part of its empire. At first, France provided the United States with badly needed supplies but remained reluctant to grant formal diplomatic recognition to the new nation. After the Declaration of Independence, Benjamin Franklin himself went to France to lobby for aid and diplomatic recognition. Franklin quickly became a hero to the French, but France's foreign minister, the Count de Vergennes, wanted evidence that the Americans had a real chance of winning. The British defeat at Saratoga, he believed, offered that evidence.

French Diplomatic Recognition

When the news from Saratoga arrived in London and Paris in early December 1777, a shaken Lord North made a new peace offer: complete home rule within the empire for Americans if they would quit the war. Vergennes feared the Americans might accept the offer and thus destroy France's opportunity to weaken Britain. Encouraged by Franklin, he agreed on February 6, 1778, to give formal recognition to the United States and to provide it with greatly expanded military assistance.

France's decision made the war an international conflict, which over the years pitted France, Spain, and the Netherlands against Great Britain. That helped reduce the resources available for the English effort in America. France was America's most important ally. It furnished the new nation with most of its money and munitions, and it provided a navy and an expeditionary force that were vital to the final, successful phase of the Revolutionary conflict.

The Final Phase: The South

Britain's Southern Strategy

The American victory at Saratoga and the intervention of the French transformed the war. Instead of mounting a full-scale military struggle against the American army, the British now tried to enlist the support of those elements of the American population who were still loyal to the crown. And since Loyalist sentiment was thought to be strongest in the South, and since the English also hoped slaves would rally to their cause, the main focus of the British effort shifted there.

The new strategy was a dismal failure. British forces spent three years (from 1778 to 1781) moving through the South. But they had badly overestimated the extent of Loyalist sentiment. And they had underestimated the logistical problems they would face. Patriot forces could move at will throughout the region, blending in with the civilian population and leaving the British unable to distinguish friend from foe. The British, by contrast, suffered all the disadvantages of an army in hostile territory.

"Revolutionary" Conflict in the South

It was this phase of the conflict that made the war "revolutionary"—not only because it introduced a new kind of warfare, but because it had the effect of mobilizing and politicizing large groups of the population. With the war expanding into previously isolated communities, with many civilians forced to involve themselves whether they liked it or not, the political climate of the United States grew more heated than ever. And support for independence, far from being crushed, greatly increased.

In the North, the fighting settled into a stalemate. Sir Henry Clinton replaced the unsuccessful William Howe in May 1778 and moved what had been Howe's army from Philadelphia back to New York. There the British troops stayed for more than a year. In the meantime, George Rogers Clark led a Patriot expedition over the Appalachian Mountains and captured settlements in the Illinois country from the British and their Indian allies. On the whole, however, there was relatively little military activity in the North after 1778. There was, however, considerable intrigue. In the fall of 1780, American forces were shocked by the exposure of treason on the part of General Benedict Arnold. Convinced that the American cause was hopeless, Arnold conspired with British agents to betray the Patriot stronghold at West Point on the Hudson River. When the scheme was exposed and foiled, Arnold fled to the safety of the British camp, where he spent the rest of the war.

The British did have some significant military successes during this period. On December 29, 1778, they captured Savannah, Georgia. On May 12, 1780, they took the port of Charleston, South Carolina, and advanced into the interior. But although the British were able to win conventional battles, they were constantly harassed by Patriot guerrillas led by such resourceful fighters as Thomas Sumter, Andrew Pickens, and Francis Marion, the "Swamp Fox." Penetrating to Camden, South Carolina, Lord Cornwallis (whom Clinton named British commander in the South) met and crushed a Patriot force under Horatio Gates on August 16, 1780. Congress recalled Gates, and Washington replaced him with Nathanael Greene, one of the ablest of all the American generals of the time.

Even before Greene arrived in the South, the tide of battle had begun to turn against Cornwallis. At King's Mountain (near the North Carolina–South Carolina border) on October 7, 1780, a band of Patriot riflemen from the backwoods killed, wounded, or captured every man in a force of 1,100 New York and South Carolina Tories, upon whom Cornwallis had depended as auxiliaries. Once Greene arrived, he confused and exasperated Cornwallis by dividing the American forces into fast-moving contingents while avoiding open, conventional battles. One of the contingents inflicted what Cornwallis admitted was "a very unexpected and severe blow" at Cowpens on January 17, 1781. Finally, after receiving reinforcements, Greene combined all his forces and maneuvered to meet the British at Guilford Court House, North Carolina. After a hard-fought battle there on March 15, 1781,

Guilford Court House

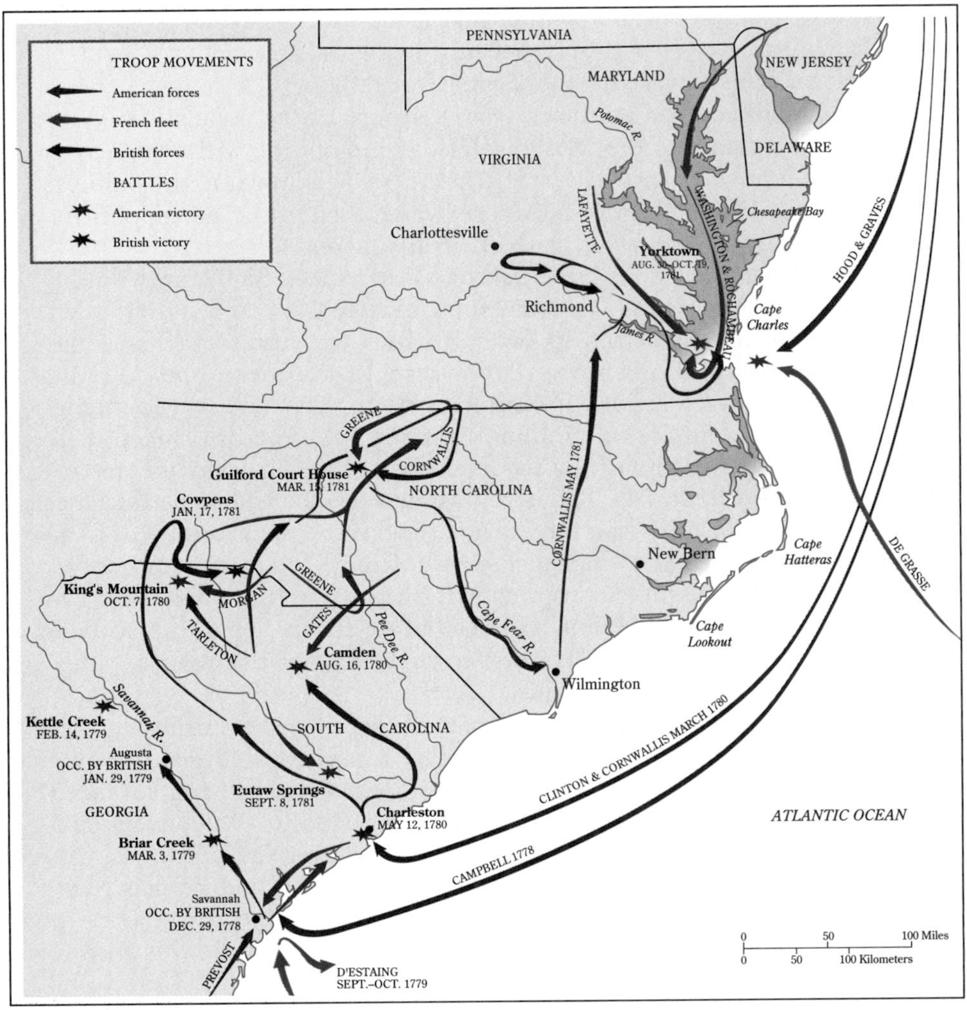

THE REVOLUTION IN THE SOUTH, 1778–1781 The final phase of the American Revolution occurred largely in the South, which the British thought would be a more receptive region for their troops. ◆ *Why did they believe that?* This map reveals the many, scattered military efforts of the British and the Americans in those years, none of them conclusive. It also shows the final chapter of the Revolution around the Chesapeake Bay and the James River. ◆ *What errors led the British to their surrender at Yorktown?*

For an interactive version of this map go to www.mhhe.com/unfinishednation4ch5maps

Greene was driven from the field; but Cornwallis had lost so many men that he decided to abandon the Carolina campaign. Instead, he moved north, hoping to carry on raids in the interior of Virginia. But Clinton, fearful that the southern army might be destroyed, ordered him to take up a defensive position at Yorktown.

Yorktown

At that point, American and French forces descended on Yorktown. Washington and the Count de Rochambeau marched a French-American army from New York to join the Marquis de Lafayette in Virginia, while Admiral de Grasse took a French fleet with additional troops up Chesapeake Bay to the York River. These joint operations caught Cornwallis between land and sea. After a few shows of resistance, he surrendered on October 17, 1781. Two days later, he surrendered his whole army of more than 7,000.

Winning the Peace

Cornwallis's defeat provoked outcries in England against continuing the war. Lord North resigned as prime minister; Lord Shelburne emerged from the political wreckage to succeed him; and British emissaries appeared in France to talk informally with the American diplomats there, of whom the three principals were Benjamin Franklin, John Adams, and John Jay.

Franklin's Skillful Diplomacy

The Americans were under instructions to cooperate with France in their negotiations with England. But Vergennes, the French foreign minister, insisted that France could not agree to any settlement of the war with England until its ally Spain had achieved its principal war aim: winning back Gibraltar from the British. There was no real prospect of that happening soon, and the Americans began to fear that the alliance with France might keep them at war indefinitely. As a result, the Americans began proceeding on their own, without informing Vergennes, and soon drew up a preliminary treaty with Great Britain, which was signed on November 30, 1782. Benjamin Franklin, in the meantime, skillfully pacified Vergennes and avoided an immediate rift in the French-American alliance.

The final treaty was signed September 3, 1783. The agreement was, on the whole, remarkably favorable to the United States. It provided a clear-cut recognition of independence and a large, though ambiguous, cession of territory to the new nation—from the southern boundary of Canada to the northern boundary of Florida and from the Atlantic to the Mississippi. The American people had good reason to celebrate as the last of the British occupation forces embarked from New York.

WAR AND SOCIETY

Historians have long debated whether the American Revolution was a social as well as a political revolution. But whatever the intention of those who launched and fought the war, the conflict had important effects on the nature of American society.

America in the World

THE AGE OF REVOLUTIONS

The American Revolution was a result of specific tensions and conflicts between imperial Britain and its colonies along the Atlantic coast of North America. But it was also both a part, and a cause, of what historians have come to call an "age of revolutions," which spread through much of the world in the last decades of the eighteenth century and the first decades of the nineteenth.

The modern idea of revolution—the overturning of old systems and regimes and the creation of new ones—was a product to a large degree of the ideas of the Enlightenment. Among those ideas was the notion of popular sovereignty, articulated by, among others, the English philosopher John Locke. It introduced the idea that political authority did not derive from the divine right of kings or the inherited authority of aristocracies but from the consent of the governed. A related Enlightenment idea was the concept of individual freedom, which challenged the traditional belief that governments had the right to prescribe the way people act, speak, and even think. Champions of individual freedom in the eighteenth century—among them the French philosopher Voltaire—advocated religious toleration (an end to discrimination against those who did not embrace a nation's dominant or official religion) and freedom of thought and expression. The Enlightenment also helped spread the idea of political and legal equality for all people—the end of special privileges for aristocrats and elites, the right of all citizens to participate in the formation of policies and laws. Jean Jacques Rousseau, a Swiss-French theorist, helped define these new ideas of equality. Together, these Enlightenment ideas formed the basis for challenges to existing social orders in many parts of the western world, and eventually beyond it.

The American Revolution was the first and in many ways most influential of the Enlightenment-derived uprisings against established orders. It served as an inspiration to people in other lands who were trying to find a way to oppose unpopular regimes. In 1789, a little over a decade after the beginning of the American Revolution, revolution began in France—at first through a revolt by the national legislature against the king, and then through a series of increasingly radical challenges to established authority. The monarchy was abolished (and the king and queen publicly executed in 1793), the authority of the Catholic church was challenged and greatly weakened, and at the peak of revolutionary chaos during the Jacobin period (1793–1794), over 40,000 suspected enemies of the revolution were executed and hundreds of thousands of others imprisoned. The radical phase of the revolution came to an end in 1799, when Napoleon Bonaparte, a young general, seized power and began to build a new French empire. But France's *ancien regime* of king and aristocracy never wholly revived.

Together, the French and American revolutions helped inspire uprisings in many other parts of the Atlantic world. In 1791, a major slave uprising began in Haiti and soon attracted over 100,000 rebels. The slave army defeated both the white settlers of the island and the French colonial armies sent to quell their rebellion. Under the leadership of Toussaint L'ouverture, they began to agitate for independence and on January 1, 1804, a few months after Toussaint's death, Haiti established its independence.

The ideas of these revolutions spread next into Spanish and Portuguese colonies in the Americas, particularly among the so-called *creoles*, people of European ancestry born in America. In the late eighteenth century, they began to resist the continuing authority of colonial officials sent from Spain and Portugal and to demand a greater say in governing their own lands. When Napoleon's French armies invaded Spain and Portugal in 1807, they weakened the ability of the European regimes to sustain authority over their American colonies. In the years that followed, revolutions swept through much of Latin America and established independent nations throughout the New World. Mexico became an independent nation in 1821, and provinces of Central America that had once been part of Mexico (Guatemala, El Salvador, Honduras, Nicaragua, and Costa Rica) established their independence three years later. Simon Bolivar, modeling his efforts on those of George Washington, led a great revolutionary movement that won independence for Brazil in 1822 and also helped lead revolutionary campaigns in Venezuela, Ecuador, and Peru—all of which won their independence in the 1820s. At about the same time, Greek patriots—drawing from the examples of other revolutionary nations—launched a movement to win their independence from the Ottoman empire, which finally succeeded in 1830.

The age of revolutions left many new, independent nations in its wake. It did not, however, succeed in establishing the ideals of popular sovereignty, individual freedom, and political equality in all the nations it affected. Slavery survived in the United States and in many areas of Latin America. New forms of aristocracy and even monarchy emerged in France, Mexico, Brazil, and elsewhere. Women—many of whom had hoped the revolutionary age would win new rights for them—made few legal or political gains in this era. But the ideals that the revolutionary era introduced to the western world continued to shape the histories of nations throughout the nineteenth century and beyond.

(text continued from page 129)

Loyalists and Minorities

Estimates differ as to how many Americans remained loyal to England during the Revolution, but it is clear that there were many—at least a fifth (and some estimate as much as a third) of the white population. Some were officeholders in the imperial government. Others were merchants whose trade was closely tied to the imperial system. Still others were people who lived in relative isolation and had simply retained their traditional loyalties. And there were those who, expecting the British to win the war, were simply currying favor with the anticipated victors.

The Loyalists' Plight

Many of these Loyalists were hounded by Patriots in their communities and harassed by legislative and judicial actions. Up to 100,000 fled the country. Those who could afford to moved to England. Others moved to Canada, establishing the first English-speaking community in the province of Quebec. Some returned to America after the war and gradually managed to reenter the life of the nation.

The war weakened other groups as well. The Anglican Church, many of whose members were Loyalists, lost its status as the official religion of Virginia and Maryland. By the time the fighting ended, many Anglican parishes could no longer even afford clergymen. Also weakened were the Quakers, whose pacifism won them widespread unpopularity when they refused to support the war.

Other Protestant denominations, however, grew stronger. Presbyterian, Congregational, and Baptist churches successfully tied themselves to the Patriot cause. And most American Catholics also supported the Patriots and won increased popularity as a result. Shortly after the peace treaty was signed, the Vatican provided the United States with its own hierarchy and, in 1789, its first bishop.

The War and Slavery

For the largest of America's minorities—the African-American population—the war had limited, but nevertheless profound, significance. For some, it meant freedom, because the British enabled many escaped slaves to leave the country as a way of disrupting the American war effort. In South Carolina, for example, nearly a third of all slaves defected during the war.

Exposure to Liberty

For other African Americans, the Revolution meant an increased exposure to the concept, although seldom to the reality, of liberty. Most black Americans could not read, but few could avoid exposure to the new and exciting ideas circulating through the towns and cities, and even at times on the plantations, where they lived. In several communities, slaves exposed to revolutionary ideas engaged in open resistance to white control. In Charleston, South Carolina, for example, Thomas Jeremiah, a free black, was executed after white authorities learned of elaborate plans for a slave uprising.

Slaveowners opposed British efforts to emancipate their slaves, but they also feared that the revolution itself would foment slave rebellions. Although the ideals of the Revolution produced occasional challenges to slavery by white southerners (including laws in Virginia and Maryland permitting slaveowners to free—"manumit"—their slaves if they wished), white support for slavery survived. Southern churches, some of which flirted briefly with voicing objections to the system, quickly rejected the antislavery ideas of the North and worked instead to reinforce ideas about white superiority.

In much of the North, by contrast, the combination of revolutionary sentiment and evangelical Christian fervor helped spread antislavery sentiments widely through society. The first target was the slave trade, which was prohibited by several states (Pennsylvania, Rhode Island, and Connecticut among them). The next target was state laws forbidding owners from freeing their slaves. Quakers and other antislavery activists succeeded in pressuring legislatures to allow legal manumission in all the northern states before the end of the Revolution, and even in Kentucky and Tennessee. The final step was emancipation of slaves. Pennsylvania was the first state to declare slavery illegal within its borders—again in part because of the influence of the fiercely antislavery Quakers—in 1780. One by one, all the northern states except New York and New Jersey abolished slavery before the end of the Revolution. New York followed in 1799 and New Jersey in 1804.

Tension between Liberty and Slavery

The Revolution exposed the continuing tension between the nation's commitment to liberty and its commitment to slavery. To people in our time, and even to some people in revolutionary times, it seems obvious that liberty and slavery are incompatible with one another. But to many white Americans in the eighteenth century, especially in the South, that did not seem obvious. Many white southerners believed, in fact, that enslaving Africans—whom they considered inferior and unfit for citizenship—was the best way to ensure liberty for white people. They feared that without slaves, it would be necessary to recruit a servile white work force in the South, and that the resulting inequalities would jeopardize the survival of liberty. One of the ironies of the American Revolution was that white Americans were fighting both to secure freedom for themselves and to preserve slavery for others.

Native Americans and the Revolution

Indians viewed the American Revolution with considerable uncertainty. Most tribes ultimately chose to stay out of the war. But many Indians feared that the Revolution would replace a ruling group in which they had developed at least some measure of trust (the British, who had tried to limit the expansion of white settlement into tribal land) with one they considered generally hostile to them (the Patriots, who had spearheaded the expansion). Thus some Indians chose to join the English cause. Still others took advantage of the conflict to launch attacks of their own.

In the western Carolinas and Virginia, Cherokee led by Chief Dragging Canoe launched a series of attacks on outlying white settlements in the summer of 1776. Patriot militias responded in great force, ravaging Cherokee lands and forcing the chief and many of his followers to flee west across the Tennessee River. Those Cherokee who remained behind agreed to a new treaty by which they gave up still more land. Some Iroquois, despite the setbacks at Oriskany, continued to wage war against Americans in the West and caused widespread destruction in agricultural areas of New York and Pennsylvania. The retaliating American armies inflicted heavy losses on the Indians, but the attacks continued.

Native Americans Weakened

In the end, the Revolution generally weakened the position of Native Americans in several ways. The Patriot victory increased white demand for western lands. Many whites resented the assistance such nations as the Mohawk had given the British and insisted on treating them as conquered people. Others drew from the Revolution a paternalistic view of the tribes. Thomas Jefferson, for example, came to view the Indians as "noble savages," uncivilized in their present state but redeemable if they were willing to adapt to the norms of white society.

Women's Rights and Women's Roles

New Roles for Women

The long Revolutionary War had a profound effect on American women. The departure of so many men to fight in the Patriot armies left women in charge of farms and businesses. Often, women handled these tasks with great success. But in other cases, inexperience, inflation, the unavailability of male labor, or the threat of enemy troops led to failure. Some women whose husbands or fathers were called away to war did not have even a farm or shop to fall back on. Cities and towns had significant populations of impoverished women, who on occasion led protests against price increases or rioted and looted for food. On several other occasions, women launched attacks on occupying British troops, whom they were required to house and feed at considerable expense.

Not all women stayed behind when the men went off to war. Many joined their male relatives in the camps of the Patriot armies. These female "camp followers" increased army morale and provided a ready source of volunteers to do cooking, laundry, nursing, and other necessary tasks. In the rough environment of the camps, traditional gender distinctions proved difficult to maintain. Considerable numbers of women became involved, at least intermittently, in combat. A few women even disguised themselves as men so as to be able to fight.

The emphasis on liberty and the "rights of man" led some women to begin to question their own position in society. "By the way," Abigail Adams wrote to her husband John Adams in 1776, "in the new code of laws which I suppose it will be necessary for you to make, I desire you would remember the ladies and be more generous and favorable to them than your ancestors." Adams was calling simply for new protections against abusive and tyrannical men. A few women, however, went further. Judith Sargent Murray, one of the leading essayists of the late eighteenth century, wrote in 1779 that women's minds were as good as those of men and that girls as well as boys therefore deserved access to education.

Patriarchy Strengthened

But little changed as a result. Under English common law, an unmarried woman had some legal rights, but a married woman had virtually no rights at all. Everything she owned and everything she earned belonged to her husband. Because she had no property rights, she could not engage in any legal transactions on her own. She could not vote. She had no legal authority over her children. Nor could she initiate a divorce; that, too, was a right reserved almost exclusively to men. After the Revolution, it did become easier for women to obtain divorces in a few states. Otherwise, there were few advances and some setbacks—including the loss of the right of widows to regain their dowries from their husbands' estates. The Revolution, in other words, did not really challenge, but actually confirmed and strengthened, the patriarchal legal system.

But the Revolution did encourage people of both sexes to reevaluate the contribution of women to the family and society. As the new republic searched for a cultural identity for itself, it attributed a higher value to the role of women as mothers. The new nation was, many Americans liked to believe, producing a new kind of citizen, steeped in the principles of liberty. Mothers had a particularly important task, therefore, in instructing their children in the virtues that the republican citizenry now was expected to possess.

The War Economy

The Revolution also produced important changes in the structure of the American economy. After more than a century of dependence on the British imperial system, American commerce suddenly found itself on its own. English ships no longer protected American vessels, but tried to drive them from the seas. British imperial ports were closed to American trade. But this disruption in traditional economic patterns served in the long run to strengthen the American economy. Enterprising merchants in New England and elsewhere began to develop new commerce in the Caribbean and South America. By the mid-1780s, American merchants were also developing an important trade with Asia.

New Patterns of Trade

When English imports to America were cut off, there were desperate efforts throughout the states to stimulate domestic manufacturing of certain necessities. No great industrial expansion resulted, but there was a modest increase in production and an even greater increase in expectations. There was also a substantial increase in trade among the American states.

THE CREATION OF STATE GOVERNMENTS

At the same time that Americans were struggling to win their independence on the battlefield, they were also struggling to create new institutions of government to replace the British system they had repudiated.

The Assumptions of Republicanism

If Americans agreed on nothing else when they began to build new governments for themselves, they agreed that those governments would be republican. To them, that meant a political system in which all power came from the people, rather than from some supreme authority (such as a king). The success of such a government depended on the nature of its citizenry. If the population consisted of sturdy, independent property owners imbued with civic virtue, then the republic could survive. If it consisted of a few powerful aristocrats and a great mass of dependent workers, then it would be in danger. From the beginning, therefore, the ideal of the small freeholder (the independent landowner) was basic to American political ideology.

Another crucial part of that ideology was the concept of equality. The Declaration of Independence had given voice to that idea in its most ringing phrase: "All men are created equal." The innate talents and energies of individuals, not their positions at birth, would determine their roles in society. Some people would inevitably be wealthier and more powerful than others. But all people would have to earn their success. There would be no equality of condition, but there would be equality of opportunity.

Rhetoric of Equality

In reality, of course, the United States was never a nation in which all citizens were independent property holders. From the beginning, there was a sizable dependent labor force, white and black. American women remained both politically and economically subordinate. Native Americans were systematically exploited and displaced. Nor was there ever full equality of opportunity. American society was more open and more fluid than that of most European nations, but the condition of a person's birth was almost always a crucial determinant of success.

Reality of Inequality

Nevertheless, in embracing the assumptions of republicanism, Americans were adopting a powerful, even revolutionary, ideology, and their experiment in statecraft became a model for many other countries.

The First State Constitutions

Two states—Connecticut and Rhode Island—already had governments that were republican in all but name. They simply deleted references to England and the king from their charters and adopted them as constitutions. The other eleven states, however, produced new documents.

The first and perhaps most basic decision was that the constitutions were to be written down, because Americans believed the vagueness of England's unwritten constitution had produced corruption. The second decision was that the power of the executive, which Americans believed had grown too great in England, must be limited. Pennsylvania eliminated the executive altogether. Most other states inserted provisions limiting the power of governors over appointments, reducing or eliminating their right to veto bills, and preventing them from dismissing the legislature. Most important, every state forbade the governor or any other executive officer from holding a seat in the legislature, thus ensuring that, unlike in England, the two branches of government would remain wholly separate.

Curbing Executive Power

But most new constitutions did not embrace direct popular rule. In Georgia and Pennsylvania, the legislature consisted of one popularly elected house. But in every other state, there was an upper and a lower chamber, and in most cases, the upper chamber was designed to represent the "higher orders" of society. There were property requirements for voters—some modest, some substantial—in all states.

Revising State Governments

By the late 1770s, Americans were growing concerned about the apparent instability of their new state governments. Many believed the problem was one of too much democracy. As a result, most of the states began to revise their constitutions to limit popular power. Massachusetts was the first to act on the new concerns. By waiting until 1780 to ratify its first constitution, Massachusetts allowed these changing ideas to shape its government.

Two changes in particular differentiated the Massachusetts and later constitutions from the earlier ones. The first was a change in the process of constitution writing itself. Most of the first documents had been written by state legislatures and thus could easily be amended (or violated) by them. Massachusetts created the constitutional convention: a special assembly of the people that would meet only for the purpose of writing the constitution.

Massachusetts's Constitution

The second change was a significant strengthening of the executive. The 1780 Massachusetts constitution made the governor one of the strongest in any state. He was to be elected directly by the people; he was to have a fixed salary (in other words, he would not be dependent on the good will of the legislature each year for his wages); he would have significant appointment powers and a veto over legislation. Other states followed. Those with weak or nonexistent upper houses strengthened or created them. Most increased the powers of the governor. Pennsylvania, which had no executive at all at first, now produced a strong one. By the late 1780s, almost every state had either revised its constitution or drawn up an entirely new one in an effort to produce stability in government.

Toleration and Slavery

Most Americans continued to believe that religion should play some role in government, but they did not wish to give special privileges to any particular denomination. The privileges that churches had once enjoyed were now largely stripped away. In 1786, Virginia enacted the Statute of Religious Liberty, written by Thomas Jefferson, which called for the complete separation of church and state.

Statute of Religious Liberty

More difficult to resolve was the question of slavery. In areas where slavery was already weak—in New England, where there had never been many slaves, and in Pennsylvania, where the Quakers opposed slavery—it was abolished. Even in the South, there were some pressures to amend or even eliminate the institution; every state but South Carolina and Georgia prohibited further importation of slaves from abroad, and South Carolina banned the slave trade during the war. Virginia passed a law encouraging manumission (the freeing of slaves).

Reasons for Slavery's Persistence

Nevertheless, slavery survived in all the southern and border states. There were several reasons: racist assumptions among whites about the inferiority of blacks; the enormous economic investments many white southerners had in their slaves; and the inability of even such men as Washington and Jefferson, who had moral misgivings about slavery, to envision any alternative to it. If slavery were abolished, what would happen to the black people in America? Few whites believed blacks could be integrated into American society as equals.

THE SEARCH FOR A NATIONAL GOVERNMENT

Americans were much quicker to agree on state institutions than they were on the structure of their national government. At first, most believed that the central government should remain relatively weak and that each state would be virtually a sovereign nation. It was in response to such ideas that the Articles of Confederation emerged.

The Confederation

The Articles of Confederation, which the Continental Congress had adopted in 1777, provided for a national government much like the one already in place. Congress remained the central—indeed the only—institution of national authority. Its powers expanded to give it authority to conduct wars and foreign relations and to appropriate, borrow, and issue money. But it did not have power to regulate trade, draft troops, or levy taxes directly on the people. For troops and taxes it had to make formal requests to the state legislatures, which could—and often did—refuse them. There was no separate executive; the "president of the United States" was merely the presiding officer at the sessions of Congress. Each state had a single vote in Congress, and at least nine of the states had to approve any important measure. All thirteen state legislatures had to approve any amendment of the Articles.

Limited Power of the National Government

During the process of ratifying the Articles of Confederation (which required approval by all thirteen states), broad disagreements over the plan became evident. The small states had insisted on equal state representation, but the larger states wanted representation to be based on population. The smaller states prevailed on that issue. More important, the states claiming western lands wished to keep them, but the rest of the states demanded that all such territory be turned over to the national government. New York and Virginia had to give up their western claims before the Articles were finally approved. They went into effect in 1781.

The Confederation, which existed from 1781 until 1789, was not a complete failure, but it was far from a success. It lacked adequate powers to deal with interstate issues or to enforce its will on the states.

Diplomatic Failures

Postwar Problems with Britain

In the peace treaty of 1783, the British had promised to evacuate American territory; but British forces continued to occupy a string of frontier posts along the Great Lakes within the United States. Nor did the British honor their agreement to make restitution to slaveowners whose slaves the British army had confiscated. There were also disputes over the northeastern boundary of the new nation and over the border between the United States and Florida. Most American trade remained within the British Empire, and Americans wanted full access to British markets; England, however, placed sharp restrictions on that access.

In 1784, Congress sent John Adams as minister to London to resolve these differences, but Adams made no headway with the English, who were never sure whether he represented a single nation or thirteen different ones. Throughout the 1780s, the British government refused even to send a diplomatic minister to the American capital.

Regional Differences over Diplomatic Policy

Confederation diplomats agreed to a treaty with Spain in 1786. The Spanish accepted the American interpretation of the Florida boundary. In return the Americans recognized the Spanish possessions in North America and accepted limits on the right of United States vessels to navigate the Mississippi for twenty years. Southern states, incensed at the idea of giving up their access to the Mississippi, blocked ratification.

The Confederation and the Northwest

The Confederation's most important accomplishment was its resolution of some of the controversies involving the western lands. The Confederation had to find a way to include these areas in the political structure of the new nation. The landed states began to yield their claims to the national government in 1781, and by 1784 the Confederation controlled enough land to permit Congress to begin making policy for the national domain.

Ordinances of 1784 and 1785

The Ordinance of 1784, based on a proposal by Thomas Jefferson, divided the western territory into ten self-governing districts, each of which could petition Congress for statehood when its population equaled the number of free inhabitants of the smallest existing state. Then, in the Ordinance of 1785, Congress created a system for surveying and selling the western lands. The territory

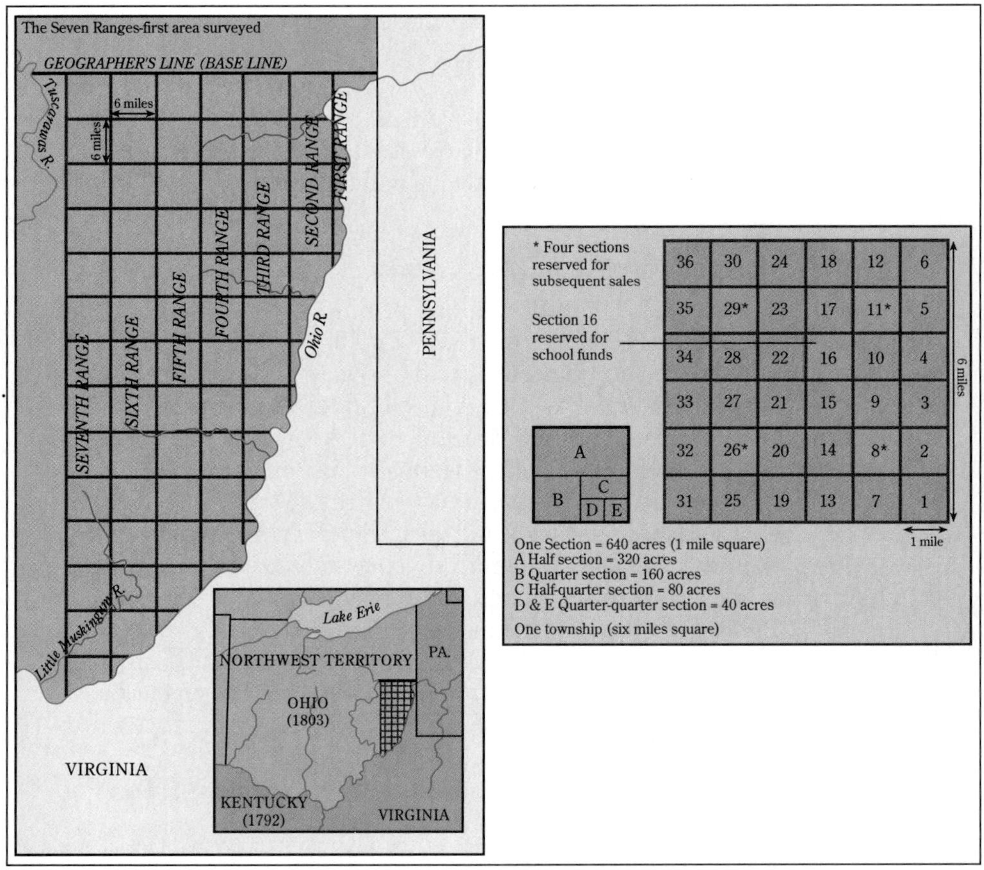

LAND SURVEY: ORDINANCE OF 1785 In the Ordinance of 1785, the Congress established a new system for surveying and selling western lands. These maps illustrate the way in which the lands were divided in an area of Ohio. Note the highly geometrical grid pattern that the Ordinance imposed on these lands. Each of the squares in the larger map on the left was subdivided into 36 sections, as illustrated in the map on the right. ◆ *Why was this grid pattern so appealing to the planners of the western lands?*

north of the Ohio River was to be surveyed and marked off into neat rectangular townships, each divided into thirty-six identical sections. In every township four sections were to be set aside for the United States; the revenue from the sale of one of the other sections was to support creation of a public school.

The precise rectangular pattern imposed on the Northwest Territory—the grid—became a model for all subsequent land policies of the federal government and for many other planning decisions in states and localities. The grid also became characteristic of the layout of many American cities. It had many advantages. It eliminated the uncertainty about property borders that earlier, more informal land systems had produced. It sped the development of the western lands by making land ownership simple and understandable. But it also encouraged a dispersed form of settlement—with each farm family separated from its neighbors—that made the formation of community more difficult. Whatever its consequences, however, the 1785 Ordinance made a dramatic and indelible mark on the American landscape.

The original ordinances proved highly favorable to land speculators and less so to ordinary settlers, many of whom could not afford the price of the land. Congress compounded the problem by selling much of the best land to the Ohio and Scioto Companies before making it available to anyone else. Criticism of these policies led to the passage in 1787 of another law governing western settlement—legislation that became known as the "Northwest Ordinance." The 1787 Ordinance abandoned the ten districts established in 1784 and created a single Northwest Territory out of the lands north of the Ohio; the territory could be divided subsequently into between three and five territories. It also specified a population of 60,000 as a minimum for statehood, guaranteed freedom of religion and the right to trial by jury to residents of the Northwest, and prohibited slavery throughout the territory.

The Northwest Ordinance

The western lands south of the Ohio River received less attention from Congress. The region that became Kentucky and Tennessee developed rapidly in the late 1770s as slaveowning territories, and in the 1780s began setting up governments and asking for statehood. The Confederation Congress was never able to resolve the conflicting claims in that region successfully.

Indians and the Western Lands

On paper at least, the western land policies of the Confederation created a system that brought order and stability to the process of white settlement in the Northwest. But in reality, order and stability came slowly and at great cost, because much of the land was claimed by the Indians. Congress tried to resolve that problem in 1784, 1785, and 1786 by persuading Iroquois, Choctaw, Chickasaw, and Cherokee leaders to sign treaties ceding lands to the United States. But those agreements proved ineffective. In 1786, the leadership of the Iroquois Confederacy repudiated the treaty it had signed two years earlier. Other tribes had never really accepted the treaties affecting them and continued to resist white movement into their lands.

Violence between whites and Indians on the Northwest frontier reached a crescendo in the early 1790s. In 1790 and again in 1791, the Miami, led by the famed warrior Little Turtle, defeated United States forces in two major battles; in the second of those battles, on November 4, 1791, 630 white Americans died in fighting at the Wabash River. Efforts to negotiate a settlement failed because of the Miami's insistence that no treaty was possible unless it forbade white settlement west of the Ohio River. Negotiations did not resume until after General Anthony Wayne led 4,000 soldiers into the Ohio Valley in 1794 and defeated the Indians in the Battle of Fallen Timbers.

Battle of Fallen Timbers

A year later, the Miami signed the Treaty of Greenville, ceding substantial new lands to the United States in exchange for a formal acknowledgment of their claim to the territory they had managed to retain. This was the first time the new federal government recognized the sovereignty of Indian nations; in doing so, it was affirming that Indian lands could be ceded only by the tribes themselves. That hard-won assurance, however, proved a frail protection against the pressure of white expansion.

Debts, Taxes, and Daniel Shays

The postwar depression, which lasted from 1784 to 1787, increased the perennial American problem of an inadequate money supply, a problem that weighed particularly heavily on debtors. The Confederation itself had an enormous outstanding debt that it had accumulated during the Revolutionary War, and few means with which to pay it. It had sold war bonds that were now due to be repaid; it owed money to its soldiers; it had substantial debts abroad. But it had no power to tax. It could only make requisitions of the states, and it received only about one-sixth of the money it requisitioned. The fragile new nation was faced with the grim prospect of defaulting on its obligations.

Fiscal Crisis

This alarming possibility brought to the fore a group of leaders who would play a crucial role in the shaping of the republic for several decades. Robert Morris, the head of the Confederation's treasury; Alexander Hamilton, his young protégé; James Madison of Virginia; and others called for a "continental impost"—a 5 percent duty on imported goods to be levied by Congress and used to fund the debt. Many Americans, however, feared that the impost plan would concentrate too much financial power in the hands of Morris and his allies in Philadelphia. Congress failed to approve the impost in 1781 and again in 1783.

"Continental Import" Rejected

The states had war debts, too, and they generally relied on increased taxation to pay them. But poor farmers, already burdened by debt, considered such policies unfair. They demanded that the state governments issue paper currency to increase the money supply and make it easier for them to meet their obligations. Resentment was especially high among farmers in New England, who felt that the states were squeezing them to enrich already wealthy bondholders in Boston and other towns.

Throughout the late 1780s, therefore, mobs of distressed farmers rioted periodically in various parts of New England. Dissidents in the Connecticut Valley and the Berkshire Hills of Massachusetts rallied behind Daniel Shays, a former captain in the Continental army. Shays issued a set of demands that included paper money, tax relief, a moratorium on debts, and the abolition of imprisonment for debt. During the summer of 1786, the Shaysites concentrated on preventing the collection of debts, private or public, and used force to keep courts from sitting and sheriffs from selling confiscated property. In Boston, members of the legislature denounced Shays and his men as rebels and traitors. When winter came, the rebels ad-

DANIEL SHAYS AND JOB SHATTUCK Shays and Shattuck were the principal leaders of the 1786 uprising of poor Massachusetts farmers demanding relief from their indebtedness. Shattuck led an insurrection in the east, which collapsed when he was captured on November 30. Shays organized the rebellion in the west, which continued until it was finally dispersed by state militia in late February 1787. The following year, state authorities pardoned Shays; even before that, the legislature responded to the rebellion by providing some relief to the impoverished farmers. This drawing is part of a hostile account of the rebellion published in 1787 in a Boston almanac. *(The National Portrait Gallery, Smithsonian Institution/Art Resource, NY)*

vanced on Springfield, hoping to seize weapons from the arsenal there. An army of state militiamen set out from Boston to confront them. In January 1787, this army met Shays's band and dispersed his ragged troops.

Consequences of Shays's Rebellion

As a military enterprise, Shays's Rebellion was a failure, although it produced some concessions to the aggrieved farmers. Shays and his lieutenants, at first sentenced to death, were later pardoned, and Massachusetts offered the protesters some tax relief and a postponement of debt payments. The rebellion had more important consequences for the future of the United States, for it added urgency to the movement to produce a new, national constitution.

CONCLUSION

Between a small, inconclusive battle on a village green in New England in 1775 and a momentous surrender at Yorktown in 1781, the American people fought a great and terrible war against the mightiest military nation in the world. Few would have predicted in 1775 that the makeshift armies of the colonies could withstand the armies and navies of the British empire. But a combination of luck, brilliance, determination, costly errors by the British, and timely aid from abroad allowed the patriots, as they began to call themselves, to make full use of the advantages of fighting on their home soil and to frustrate British designs.

The war was not just a historic military event. It was also a great political one, for it propelled the colonies to unite, to organize, and to declare their independence. Having done so, they fought with even greater determination, defending now not just a set of principles, but an actual, fledgling nation. By the end of the war, they had created new governments at both the state and national level and had begun experimenting with new political forms.

The war was also important for its effects on American society—for the way it shook the existing social order; for the way it caused women to question their place in society; and for the way it spread notions of liberty and freedom throughout a society that in the past had mostly been rigidly hierarchical. Even African-American slaves absorbed some of the ideas of the Revolution, although it would be many years before they would be in any position to make very much use of them.

Victory in the American Revolution solved many of the problems of the new nation, but it also produced others. What should the United States do about its relations with the Indians and with its neighbors to the north and south? What should it do about the distribution of western lands? What should it do about slavery? How should it balance its commitment to liberty with its need for order? These questions bedeviled the new national government in its first years of existence.

FOR FURTHER REFERENCE

Robert Middlekauf, *The Glorious Cause: The American Revolution, 1763–1789* (1985), a volume in the Oxford History of the United States, is a thorough, general history of the Revolution. Edward Countryman, *The American Revolution* (1985) is a useful, briefer overview. Gordon Wood, *The Radicalism of the American Revolution* (1992) emphasizes the profound political change that the Revolution entailed. Charles Royster, *A Revolutionary People at War: The Continental Army and American Character* (1979) suggests the importance of military service for American men. Mary Beth Norton, *Liberty's Daughters: The Revolutionary Experience of American Women, 1750–1800* (1980) demonstrates that the Revolution had a significant impact on the lives of American women as well. Eric Foner, *Tom Paine and Revolutionary America* (1976) connects the leading pamphleteer of the Revolution with urban radicalism in Philadelphia. Pauline Maier, *American Scripture* (1997) is a penetrating study of the making of the Declaration of Independence, and of its impact on subsequent generations of Americans. Colin Calloway, *The American Revolution in Indian Country* (1995) is a new and important study on an often neglected aspect of the war. Sylvia R. Frey, *Water from the Rock: Black Resistance in a Revolutionary Age* (1991) argues that the American Revolution was a major turning point in the history of slavery in the American South. Alfred E.

Young, *The Shoemaker and the Tea Party: Memory and the American Revolution* (1999) examines the role of memory in the making of the revolution. *Liberty* (1997) is a compelling six-hour PBS documentary film history of the American Revolution, from its early origins in the 1760s.

For quizzes, Internet resources, references to additional books and films, and more, consult this book's Online Learning Center site at www.mhhe.com/unfinishednation4.

THE AMERICAN STAR Frederick Kemmelmeyer painted this tribute to George Washington sometime in the 1790s. It was one of many efforts by artists and others to create an iconography for the new republic. *(The Metropolitan Museum of Art, Gift of Edgar William and Bernice Chrysler Barbisch, 1962. (62.256.7) Photograph © 2002 The Metropolitan Museum of Art)*

TIME LINE

1786	1787	1787-1788	1789	1791	1792
Annapolis Conference	Constitutional Convention; Constitution adopted	States ratify Constitution	Washington becomes first president	First Bank of U.S. chartered	Washington reelected
			Bill of Rights		
			French Revolution		
			Judiciary Act		

CHAPTER SIX

THE CONSTITUTION AND THE NEW REPUBLIC

Framing a New Government
Adoption and Adaptation
Federalists and Republicans
Establishing National Sovereignty
The Downfall of the Federalists

By the late 1780s, many Americans had grown dissatisfied with the Confederation. It was, they believed, ridden with factions, unable to deal effectively with economic problems, and frighteningly powerless in the face of Shays's Rebellion. A decade earlier, Americans had deliberately avoided creating a strong national government. Now they reconsidered. In 1787, the nation produced a new constitution and a much more powerful government with three independent branches. Yet the adoption of the Constitution did not complete the creation of the republic. For, while most Americans came to agree that the Constitution was a nearly perfect document, they often disagreed on what that document meant.

FRAMING A NEW GOVERNMENT

The Confederation Congress had become so unpopular and ineffectual by the mid-1780s that it began to lead an almost waiflike existence. In 1783, its members timidly withdrew from Philadelphia to escape army veterans demanding their back pay. They took refuge for a while in Princeton, New Jersey, then moved on to Annapolis, and in 1785 settled in New York. Delegates

1793	1794	1795	1796	1797	1798-1799	1800
Genet Affair	Whiskey Rebellion	Pinckney's Treaty	John Adams elected president	XYZ Affair	Quasi war with France	Jefferson elected president
	Jay's Treaty			Alien and Sedition Acts	Virginia and Kentucky Resolutions	

were often scarce. Only with great difficulty could Congress produce a quorum to ratify the treaty with Great Britain ending the Revolutionary War.

Advocates of Reform

In the 1780s, some of the wealthiest and most powerful groups in the population began to clamor for a stronger national government. By 1786, such demands had grown so intense that even defenders of the existing system reluctantly agreed that the government needed strengthening at its weakest point—its lack of power to tax.

Alexander Hamilton

The most resourceful advocate of a stronger national government was Alexander Hamilton, the illegitimate son of a Scottish merchant in the West Indies, who had become a successful New York lawyer. Hamilton now called for a national convention to overhaul the Articles of Confederation. He found an important ally in James Madison of Virginia, who persuaded the Virginia legislature to convene an interstate conference on commercial questions. Only five states sent delegates to the meeting, which took place at Annapolis, Maryland, in 1786; but the conference approved a proposal drafted by Hamilton for a convention of special delegates from all the states to meet in Philadelphia the next year.

At first there seemed little reason to believe the Philadelphia convention would attract any more delegates than had the Annapolis meeting. Then, early in 1787, the news of Shays's Rebellion spread throughout the nation, alarming many previously apathetic leaders. Most important of all, the rebellion aroused George Washington, who promptly made plans to travel to Philadelphia for the Constitutional Convention. His support gave the meeting wide credibility.

A Divided Convention

The "Founding Fathers"

Fifty-five men, representing all the states except Rhode Island, attended one or more sessions of the convention that sat in the Philadelphia State House from May to September 1787. These "Founding Fathers," as they became known much later, were relatively young men; the average age was forty-four. They were well educated by the standards of their time. Most were wealthy property owners, and many feared what one of them called the "turbulence and follies" of democracy. Yet all retained the Revolutionary suspicion of concentrated power.

The convention unanimously chose Washington to preside over its sessions and then closed its business to the public and the press. It then ruled that each state delegation would have a single vote and that major decisions would require not unanimity, as they did in Congress, but a simple majority. Almost all the delegates agreed that the United States needed a stronger central government. But there agreement ended.

GEORGE WASHINGTON AT MOUNT VERNON Washington was in his first term as president in 1790 when an anonymous folk artist painted this view of his home at Mount Vernon, Virginia. Washington appears in uniform, along with members of his family, on the lawn. After he retired from office in 1797, Washington returned happily to his plantation and spent the two years before his death in 1799 "amusing myself in agricultural and rural pursuits." He also played host to an endless stream of visitors from throughout the country and Europe. *(Gift of Edgar William and Bernice Chrysler Garbisch, © 1998 Board of Trustees, National Gallery of Art, Washington)*

Madison's Virginia Plan

Virginia, the largest state in population, sent a well-prepared delegation to Philadelphia led by James Madison (thirty-six years old), who had devised in some detail a plan for a new "national" government. The Virginia Plan shaped the agenda of the convention from the moment Edmund Randolph of Virginia opened the debate by proposing that "a national government ought to be established, consisting of a supreme Legislative, Executive, and Judiciary." Even that brief description outlined a government very different from the Confederation. But the delegates were so committed to fundamental reform that they approved the resolution after only brief debate.

There was less agreement about the details of Madison's Virginia Plan. It called for a national legislature of two houses. In the lower house, states would be represented in proportion to their population. Members of the upper house were to be elected by the lower house under no rigid system of representation; thus some of the smaller states might at times have no members at all in the upper house.

The New Jersey Plan

The proposal aroused immediate opposition among delegates from the smaller states. William Paterson of New Jersey offered an alternative (the New Jersey Plan) that would have retained the essence of the existing system with its one-house legislature in which all states had equal representation, but which would have given Congress expanded powers to tax and to regulate commerce.

The convention rejected Paterson's proposal, but supporters of the Virginia Plan now realized they would have to make concessions to the small states. They agreed to permit members of the upper house to be elected by the state legislatures.

Many questions remained unresolved. Among the most important was the question of slavery. There was no serious discussion of abolishing slavery during the convention. But other issues were debated heatedly. Would slaves be counted as part of the population in determining representation in Congress? Or would they be considered property, not entitled to representation? Delegates from the states with large slave populations wanted to have it both ways. They argued that slaves should be considered persons in determining representation but as property if the new government levied taxes on the states on the basis of population. Representatives from states where slavery had disappeared or was expected soon to disappear argued that slaves should be included in calculating taxation but not representation.

Compromise

The delegates argued for weeks. By the end of June, as both temperature and tempers rose to uncomfortable heights, the convention seemed in danger of collapsing. But the delegates refused to give up. Finally, on July 2, the convention created a "grand committee," chaired by Franklin and with one delegate from each state, which produced a proposal that became the basis of the "Great Compromise." It called for a two-house legislature. In the lower house, the states would be represented on the basis of population; each slave would be counted as three-fifths of a free person in determining the basis for both representation and direct taxation. In the upper house, the states would be represented equally with two members apiece. On July 16, 1787, the convention voted to accept the compromise.

The "Great Compromise"

In the next few weeks, the convention agreed to another important compromise. To placate southern delegates, who feared the new government would interfere with slavery, the convention agreed to bar the new government from stopping the slave trade for twenty years.

Unresolved Issues

Some significant issues remained unaddressed. Most important was the absence of a list of individual rights, which would restrain the powers of the national government. Madison opposed the idea, arguing that specifying rights that were reserved to the people would, in effect, limit those rights. Others, however, feared that without such protections the national government might abuse its new authority.

The Constitution of 1787

Many people contributed to the creation of the American Constitution, but the most important person in the process was James Madison. Madison had devised the Virginia Plan, and he did most of the drafting of the

Constitution itself. Madison's most important achievement, however, was in helping resolve two important philosophical questions: the question of sovereignty and the question of limiting power.

Popular Sovereignty

How could a national government exercise sovereignty concurrently with state governments? Where did ultimate sovereignty lie? The answer, Madison and his contemporaries decided, was that all power, at all levels of government, flowed ultimately from the people. Thus neither the federal government nor the state governments were truly sovereign. All of them derived their authority from below. The resolution of the problem of sovereignty made possible one of the distinctive features of the Constitution—its division of powers between the national and state governments. The Constitution and the government it created were to be the "supreme law" of the land. At the same time, however, the Constitution left important powers in the hands of the states.

In addition to solving the question of sovereignty, the Constitution produced a distinctive solution to the problem of concentrated authority. Drawing from the ideas of the French philosopher Baron de Montesquieu, most Americans had long believed that the best way to avoid tyranny was to keep government close to the people. A large nation would breed corruption and despotism because the rulers would be so distant from most of the people that there would be no way to control them.

Madison, however, helped break the grip of these assumptions by arguing that a large republic would be less, not more, likely to produce tyranny because no single group would ever be able to dominate it. The idea of many centers of power "checking each other" and preventing any single, despotic authority from emerging also helped shape the internal structure of the federal government. The Constitution's most distinctive feature was its "separation of powers" within the government, its creation of "checks and balances" among the legislative, executive, and judicial branches. The forces within the government would constantly compete with one another. Congress would have two chambers, each checking the other, since both would have to agree before any law could be passed. The president would have the power to veto acts of Congress. The federal courts would be protected from both the executive and the legislature, because judges would serve for life.

"Checks and Balances"

The "federal" structure of the government was designed to protect the United States from the kind of despotism that Americans believed had emerged in England. But it was also designed to protect the nation from another kind of despotism: the tyranny of the people. Shays's Rebellion, most of the founders believed, had been only one example of what could happen if a nation did not defend itself against the unchecked exercise of popular will. Thus in the new government, only the members of the House of Representatives would be elected directly by the people. On September 17, 1787, thirty-nine delegates signed the Constitution.

ADOPTION AND ADAPTATION

The delegates at Philadelphia had greatly exceeded their instructions from Congress and the states. Instead of making simple revisions in the Articles of Confederation, they had produced a plan for a completely different form of government. They feared that the Constitution would not be ratified under the rules of the Articles of Confederation, which required unanimous approval by the state legislatures. So the convention changed the rules, proposing that the new government come into being when nine of the thirteen states ratified the Constitution and recommending that state conventions, not state legislatures, be called to ratify it.

Federalists and Antifederalists

The Congress in New York accepted the convention's work and submitted it to the states for approval. All the state legislatures except Rhode Island elected delegates to ratifying conventions, most of which began meeting in early 1788. Even before the ratifying conventions adjourned, however, a great national debate on the new Constitution had begun.

The Federalist Papers

Supporters of the Constitution had a number of advantages. They were better organized. They had the support of the two most eminent men in America, Franklin and Washington. And they seized an appealing label for themselves: "Federalists"—a term that opponents of centralization had once used to describe themselves—thus implying that they were less committed to a "nationalist" government than in fact they were. The Federalists also had the support of the ablest political philosophers of their time: Alexander Hamilton, James Madison, and John Jay. Those three men, under the joint pseudonym "Publius," wrote a series of essays—widely published in newspapers throughout the nation—explaining the meaning and virtues of the Constitution. The essays were later issued as a book, and they are known today as *The Federalist Papers.*

The "Antifederalists"

The Federalists called their critics "Antifederalists," which suggested that their rivals had nothing to offer except opposition. But the Antifederalists, too, were represented by distinguished leaders of the Revolution, among them Patrick Henry and Samuel Adams. And they had serious and intelligent arguments of their own. They saw themselves as the defenders of the true principles of the Revolution. The Constitution, they believed, would betray those principles. It would increase taxes, weaken the states, wield dictatorial powers, favor the "well-born" over the common people, and abolish individual liberty. But their biggest complaint was that the Constitution lacked a bill of rights. Only by enumerating the natural rights of the people, they argued, could there be any certainty that those rights would be protected.

CELEBRATING THE CONSTITUTION Perhaps because opposition to the Constitution had been so intense, its champions staged elaborate celebrations at the time of ratification in an effort to enhance its legitimacy. In 1788, supporters of the Constitution organized an elaborate parade down Wall Street, which included the ship on wheels (representing the "ship of state") pictured here. Alexander Hamilton, whose name is emblazoned on the ship's banners, was New York's leading advocate of the Constitution. *(North Wind Picture Archives)*

Despite the efforts of the Antifederalists, ratification proceeded quickly during the winter of 1787–1788. The Delaware convention was the first to act. It ratified the Constitution unanimously, as did New Jersey and Georgia. New Hampshire ratified the document in June 1788—the ninth state to do so. It was now theoretically possible for the Constitution to go into effect. A new government could not hope to succeed, however, without Virginia and New York, whose conventions remained closely divided. But by the end of June, first Virginia and then New York had consented to the Constitution by narrow margins—on the assumption that a bill of rights would be added in the form of amendments to the Constitution. North Carolina's convention adjourned without taking action, waiting to see what happened to the amendments. Rhode Island did not even consider ratification.

Completing the Structure

The first elections under the Constitution were held in the early months of 1789. There was never any doubt about who would be the first president. George Washington had presided at the Constitutional Convention, and many who had favored ratification did so only because they expected him to preside over the new government as well. Washington received the votes of all the presidential electors. John Adams, a leading Federalist, became vice president. After a journey from his estate at Mount Vernon, Virginia, marked by elaborate celebrations along the way, Washington was inaugurated in New York on April 30, 1789.

The first Congress served in many ways as a continuation of the Constitutional Convention. Its most important task was drafting a bill of rights. By early 1789, even Madison had come to agree that some sort of bill of rights would be essential to legitimize the new government in the eyes of its opponents. On September 25, 1789, Congress approved twelve amendments, ten of which were ratified by the states by the end of 1791. These first ten amendments to the Constitution comprise what we know as the Bill of Rights. Nine of them placed limitations on Congress by forbidding it to infringe on certain fundamental rights: freedom of religion, speech, and the press; immunity from arbitrary arrest; trial by jury; and others. The Tenth Amendment reserved to the states or the people all powers except those specifically withheld from them or delegated to the federal government.

The Bill of Rights

On the subject of federal courts, the Constitution said only: "The judicial power of the United States shall be vested in one Supreme Court, and in such inferior courts as the Congress may from time to time ordain and establish." It was left to Congress to determine the number of Supreme Court judges to be appointed and the kinds of lower courts to be organized. In the Judiciary Act of 1789, Congress provided for a Supreme Court of six members and a system of lower district courts and courts of appeal. It also gave the Supreme Court the power to make the final decision in cases involving the constitutionality of state laws.

The Constitution referred indirectly to executive departments but did not specify which ones or how many there should be. The first Congress created three such departments—state, treasury, and war—and also established the offices of the attorney general and postmaster general. To the office of secretary of the treasury Washington appointed Alexander Hamilton of New York. For secretary of war he chose a Massachusetts Federalist, General Henry Knox. As attorney general he named Edmund Randolph of Virginia. As secretary of state he chose another Virginian, Thomas Jefferson.

Establishing the Executive Departments

FEDERALISTS AND REPUBLICANS

The framers of the Constitution had dealt with many controversies by papering them over with a series of vague compromises; as a result, the disagreements survived to plague the new government.

At the heart of the controversies of the 1790s was the same basic difference in philosophy that had been at the heart of the debate over the Constitution. On one side stood a powerful group who believed that America required a strong, national government. They envisioned that the country's mission was to become a genuine nation-state, with centralized authority and a complex commercial economy. On the other side stood another group whose members envisioned a more modest national government. The United States should not, this group believed, aspire to be a highly commercial or urban nation. It should remain predominantly rural and agrarian. The centralizers became known as the Federalists and gravitated to the leadership of Alexander Hamilton. Their opponents acquired the name Republicans and gathered under the leadership of Thomas Jefferson and James Madison.

Competing National Visions

Hamilton and the Federalists

For twelve years, the Federalists retained firm control of the new government. That was in part because George Washington had always envisioned a strong national government and as president did little to stop those attempting to create one. But the president, Washington believed, should stand above political controversies, and so he avoided personal involvement in the deliberations of Congress. As a result, the dominant figure in his administration became Alexander Hamilton. Of all the national leaders of his time, Hamilton was one of the most aristocratic in political philosophy; he believed that a stable and effective government required an elite ruling class. Thus the new government needed the support of the wealthy and powerful; and to get that, it needed to give elites a stake in its success. Hamilton proposed, therefore, that the existing public debt be "funded": that the various certificates of indebtedness that the old Congress had issued during and after the Revolution—many of them now in the possession of wealthy speculators—be called in and exchanged for interest-bearing bonds. He also recommended that the states' Revolutionary debts be "assumed" (taken over by the federal government) to cause state bondholders also to look to the central government for eventual payment. Hamilton wanted to create a permanent national debt, with new bonds being issued as old ones were paid off. The result, he believed, would be that the wealthy classes, who were the most likely to lend money to the government, would always have a reason to want the government to survive.

Hamilton's "Funded" Debt Proposal

Hamilton also wanted to create a national bank. It would provide loans and currency to businesses, give the government a safe place for the deposit of federal funds, facilitate the collection of taxes and the disbursement of the government's expenditures, and provide a stable center to the nation's small and feeble banking system. The bank would be chartered by the federal government, but much of its capital would come from private investors.

The funding and assumption of debts would require new sources of revenue. Hamilton recommended two kinds of taxes to complement the receipts anticipated from the sales of public land. One was an excise tax on alcoholic beverages, a tax that would be most burdensome to the whiskey distillers of the backcountry, small farmers who converted part of their corn and rye crops into whiskey. The other was a tariff on imports, which Hamilton saw not only as a way to raise money but as a way to protect domestic industries from foreign competition. In his famous "Report on Manufactures" of 1791, he outlined a plan for stimulating the growth of industry and spoke glowingly of the advantages to society of a healthy manufacturing sector.

"Report on Manufactures"

The Federalists, in short, offered more than a vision of a stable new government. They offered a vision of the sort of nation America should become—a nation with a wealthy, enlightened ruling class, a vigorous, independent commercial economy, and a thriving manufacturing sector.

Enacting the Federalist Program

Few members of Congress objected to Hamilton's plan for funding the national debt, but many did oppose his proposal to exchange new bonds for old certificates of indebtedness on a dollar-for-dollar basis. Many of the original holders had been forced to sell during the hard times of the 1780s to speculators, who had bought them at a fraction of their face value. James Madison, now a representative from Virginia, argued for a plan by which the new bonds would be divided between the original purchasers and the speculators. But Hamilton's allies insisted that the honor of the government required a literal fulfillment of its earlier promises to pay whoever held the bonds. Congress finally passed the funding bill Hamilton wanted.

Objections to the Funding Bill

Hamilton's proposal that the federal government assume the state debts encountered greater difficulty. Its opponents argued that if the federal government took over the state debts, the states with few debts would have to pay taxes to service the states with large ones. Massachusetts, for example, owed much more money than did Virginia. Only by striking a bargain with the Virginians were Hamilton and his supporters able to win passage of the assumption bill.

Compromise on the National Capital

The deal involved the location of the national capital. The Virginians wanted to create a new capital near them in the South. Hamilton and Jefferson met and agreed to exchange northern support for placing the capital in the South for Virginia's votes for the assumption bill. The bargain called for the construction of a new capital city on the banks of the Potomac River, which divided Maryland and Virginia, on land to be selected by George Washington.

Hamilton's bank bill produced the most heated debates. Madison, Jefferson, Randolph, and others argued that because the Constitution made no provision for a national bank, Congress had no authority to create one. But Congress agreed to Hamilton's bill despite these objections, and Washington signed it. The Bank of the United States began operations in 1791.

Hamilton also had his way with the excise tax, although protests from farmers later forced revisions to reduce the burden on the smaller distillers. He failed to win passage of a tariff as highly protective as he had hoped for, but the tariff law of 1792 did raise the rates somewhat.

Division over Hamilton Program

Once enacted, Hamilton's program won the support of manufacturers, creditors, and other influential segments of the population. But others found the Hamilton program less appealing. Small farmers complained that they were being taxed excessively. They and others began to argue that the Federalist program served the interests not of the people but of small, wealthy elites. Out of this feeling an organized political opposition arose.

The Republican Opposition

The Constitution made no reference to political parties. Most of the framers believed that organized parties were dangerous and to be avoided. Disagreement was inevitable on particular issues, but they believed that such disagreements need not and should not lead to the formation of permanent factions.

Establishment of the Federalist Party

Yet not many years had passed after the ratification of the Constitution before Madison and others became convinced that Hamilton and his followers had become a dangerous, self-interested faction. The Federalists had used the powers of their offices to reward their supporters and win additional allies. They were doing many of the same things, their opponents believed, that the corrupt British governments of the early eighteenth century had done.

Because the Federalists appeared to their critics to be creating such a menacing and tyrannical structure of power, there was no alternative but to organize a vigorous opposition. The result was the emergence of an alternative political organization, whose members called themselves "Republicans." (These first Republicans are not institutionally related to the modern Republican Party, which was born in the 1850s.) By the late 1790s, the Republicans were going to even greater lengths than the Federalists to create vehicles of partisan influence. In every state they had formed committees, societies, and caucuses; Republican groups were banding together to influence state and local elections. Neither side was willing to admit that it was acting as a party, nor would either concede the right of the other to exist. This institutionalized factionalism is known to historians as the "first party system."

Formation of the Republican Party

From the beginning, the preeminent figures among the Republicans were Thomas Jefferson and James Madison. Jefferson became the most prominent spokesman for the cause. He promoted a vision of an agrarian republic, in which most citizens would farm their own land. Jefferson did not scorn commercial or industrial activity. But he believed that the nation should be wary of too much urbanization and industrialization.

Regional and Economic Differences

Although both parties had supporters in all parts of the country and among all classes, there were regional and economic differences. The Federalists were most numerous in the commercial centers of the Northeast and in such southern seaports as Charleston; the Republicans were most numerous in the rural areas of the South and the West. The difference in their philosophies was visible in, among other things, their reactions to the progress of the French Revolution. As that revolution grew increasingly radical in the 1790s, the Federalists expressed horror. But the Republicans applauded the democratic, antiaristocratic spirit they believed the French Revolution displayed.

When the time came for the nation's second presidential election, in 1792, both Jefferson and Hamilton urged Washington to run for a second term. The president reluctantly agreed. But while Washington had the respect of both factions, he was, in reality, more in sympathy with the Federalists than with the Republicans.

ESTABLISHING NATIONAL SOVEREIGNTY

The Federalists consolidated their position by acting effectively in two areas in which the old Confederation had not always been successful: the western territories and diplomacy.

Securing the West

Despite the Northwest Ordinance, the old Congress had largely failed to tie the outlying western areas of the country firmly to the national government. Farmers in western Massachusetts had rebelled; settlers in Vermont, Kentucky, and Tennessee had flirted with seceding from the Union. At first, the new government under the Constitution faced similar problems.

In 1794, farmers in western Pennsylvania raised a major challenge to federal authority when they refused to pay the new whiskey excise tax and began terrorizing tax collectors in the region. But the federal government did not leave settlement of the so-called Whiskey Rebellion to the authorities of Pennsylvania. At Hamilton's urging, Washington called out the militias of three states and assembled an army of nearly 15,000—and he personally accompanied the troops into Pennsylvania. At the approach of the militiamen, the rebellion quickly collapsed.

Whiskey Rebellion

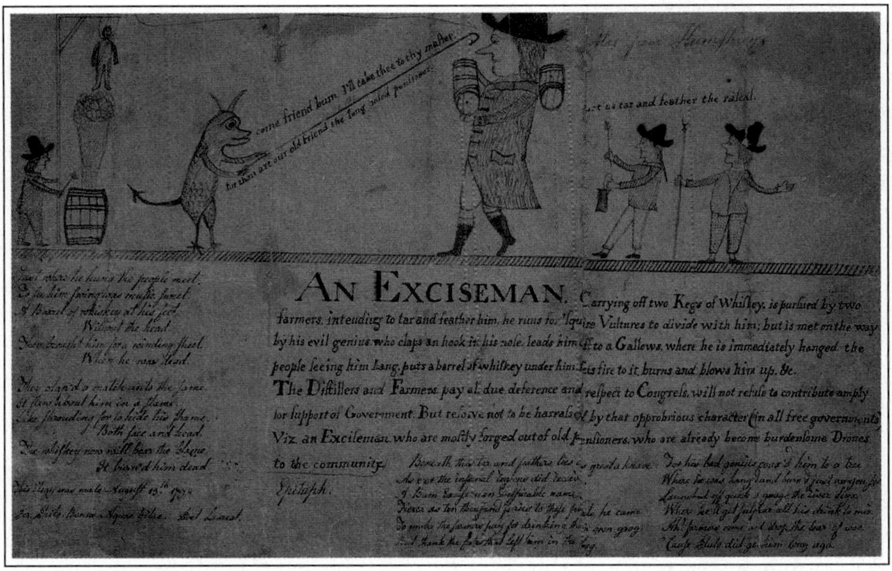

A COMMENT ON THE WHISKEY REBELLION Although Thomas Jefferson and other Republicans claimed to welcome occasional popular uprisings, the Federalists were horrified by such insurgencies as Shays's Rebellion in Massachusetts and, later, the Whiskey Rebellion in Pennsylvania. The Federalist cartoon portrays the rebels as demons who pursue and eventually hang an unfortunate "exciseman" (tax collector), who has confiscated two kegs of rum. *(Courtesy of the Atwater Kent Museum of Philadelphia)*

The federal government won the allegiance of the whiskey rebels through intimidation. It won the loyalties of other western people by accepting new states as members of the Union. The last two of the original thirteen colonies joined the Union once the Bill of Rights had been appended to the Constitution—North Carolina in 1789 and Rhode Island in 1790. Vermont became the fourteenth state in 1791 after New York and New Hampshire agreed to give up their claims to it. Next came Kentucky, in 1792, when Virginia gave up its claim to that region. After North Carolina ceded its western lands to the Union, Tennessee became a state in 1796.

The new government faced a greater challenge in more distant areas of the Northwest and the Southwest. The ordinances of 1784–1787, establishing the terms of white settlement in the West, had produced a series of border conflicts with Indian tribes. The new government inherited these clashes, which continued with few interruptions for nearly a decade.

The Indians' Ambiguous Status

These clashes revealed another issue the Constitution had done little to resolve: the place of the Indian nations within the new federal structure. The Constitution gave Congress power to "regulate Commerce . . . with the Indian tribes." And it bound the new government to respect treaties negotiated by the Confederation, most of which had been with the tribes. But none of this did very much to clarify the precise legal standing of Indians or Indian nations within the United States. The tribes received no direct representation in the new government. Above all, the Constitution did not address the major issue of land. Indian nations lived within the boundaries of the United States, yet they claimed (and the white government at times agreed) that they had some measure of sovereignty over their own land. But neither the Constitution nor common law offered any clear guide to the rights of a "nation within a nation" or to the precise nature of tribal sovereignty.

Maintaining Neutrality

A crisis in Anglo-American relations emerged in 1793 when the new French government established after the revolution of 1789 went to war with Great Britain. Both the president and Congress took steps to establish American neutrality in the conflict, but that neutrality was severely tested.

Early in 1794, the Royal Navy began seizing hundreds of American ships engaged in trade in the French West Indies. Hamilton was deeply concerned. War would mean an end to imports from England, and most of the revenue for maintaining his financial system came from duties on those imports. Hamilton and the Federalists did not trust the State Department, now in the hands of the ardently pro-French Edmund Randolph, to find a solution to the crisis. So they persuaded Washington to name a special commissioner to go to England and negotiate a solution: the chief justice of the Supreme Court, John Jay. Jay was instructed to secure compensation for the recent British assaults on American shipping, to demand withdrawal of British forces from their posts on the frontier of the United States, and to negotiate a commercial treaty with Britain.

Jay's Treaty

The long and complex treaty Jay negotiated in 1794 failed to achieve these goals. But it settled the conflict with Britain, avoiding a likely war. It provided for undisputed American sovereignty over the entire Northwest and produced a reasonably satisfactory commercial relationship with a nation whose trade was important to the United States. Nevertheless, when the terms became known in America, criticism was intense. Opponents of the treaty went to great lengths to defeat it in the Senate, but in the end the Senate ratified what was by then known as Jay's Treaty.

Pinckney's Treaty

Jay's Treaty paved the way for a settlement of important American disputes with Spain. Under Pinckney's Treaty (negotiated by Thomas Pinckney and signed in 1795), Spain recognized the right of Americans to navigate the Mississippi to its mouth and to deposit goods at New Orleans for reloading on oceangoing ships; agreed to fix the northern boundary of Florida along the 31st parallel; and commanded its authorities to prevent the Indians in Florida from launching raids north across the border.

THE DOWNFALL OF THE FEDERALISTS

Since almost everyone in the 1790s agreed that there was no place in a stable republic for organized parties, the emergence of the Republicans as a powerful and apparently permanent opposition seemed to the Federalists a grave threat to national stability. And so when major international perils confronted the government in the 1790s, the temptation to move forcefully against this "illegitimate" opposition was strong.

The Election of 1796

George Washington refused to run for a third term as president in 1796. Jefferson was the obvious presidential candidate of the Republicans that year, but the Federalists faced a more difficult choice. Hamilton had created too many enemies to be a credible candidate. Vice President John Adams, who was directly associated with none of the controversial Federalist achievements, received the party's nomination for president at a caucus of the Federalists in Congress.

The Federalists were still clearly the dominant party. But without Washington to mediate, they fell victim to fierce factional rivalries. Adams defeated Jefferson by only three electoral votes and assumed the presidency as head of a divided party facing a powerful opposition. Jefferson became vice president as a result of finishing second. (Not until the adoption of the Twelfth Amendment in 1804 did electors vote separately for president and vice president.)

John Adams Elected

The Quasi War with France

American relations with Great Britain and Spain improved as a result of Jay's and Pinckney's Treaties. But the nation's relations with revolutionary France quickly deteriorated. French vessels captured American ships on the high seas. The French government refused to receive Charles Cotesworth Pinckney when he arrived in Paris as the new American minister. In an effort to stabilize relations, Adams appointed a bipartisan commission to negotiate with France. When the Americans arrived in Paris in 1797, three agents of the French foreign minister, Prince Talleyrand, demanded a loan for France and a bribe for French officials before any negotiations could begin. Pinckney, a member of the commission, responded, "No! No! Not a sixpence!"

When Adams heard of the incident, he sent a message to Congress urging preparations for war. Before giving the commissioners' report to Congress, he deleted the names of the three French agents and designated them only as Messrs. X, Y, and Z. When the report was published, the "XYZ Affair," as it quickly became

The "XYZ Affair"

known, provoked widespread popular outrage at France's actions and strong popular support for the Federalists' response. For nearly two years, 1798 and 1799, the United States found itself engaged in an undeclared war with France.

Adams persuaded Congress to cut off all trade with France, to abrogate the treaties of 1778, and to authorize American vessels to capture French armed ships on the high seas. In 1798, Congress created the Department of the Navy. The navy soon won a number of duels and captured a total of eighty-five French ships. The United States also began cooperating closely with the British. In response, the French began trying to conciliate the United States. Adams sent another commission to Paris in 1800, and the new French government (headed now by "First Consul" Napoleon Bonaparte) agreed to a treaty with the United States that canceled the old agreements of 1778 and established new commercial arrangements. As a result, the "quasi war" came to a reasonably peaceful end.

The "Quasi War"

Repression and Protest

The conflict with France helped the Federalists increase their majorities in Congress in 1798. They now began to consider ways to silence the Republican opposition. The result was some of the most controversial legislation in American history: the Alien and Sedition Acts.

The Alien and Sedition Acts

The Alien Act placed new obstacles in the way of foreigners who wished to become American citizens, and it strengthened the president's hand in dealing with aliens. The Sedition Act allowed the government to prosecute those who engaged in "sedition" against the government. In theory, only libelous or treasonous activities were subject to prosecution; but since such activities had no clear definition, the law, in effect, gave the government authority to stifle virtually any opposition. The Republicans interpreted the new laws as part of a Federalist campaign to destroy them.

President Adams signed the new laws but was cautious in implementing them. He did not deport any aliens, and he prevented the government from launching a broad crusade against the Republicans. But the Alien Act discouraged immigration and encouraged some foreigners already in the country to leave. And the administration used the Sedition Act to arrest and convict ten men, most of them Republican newspaper editors whose only crime had been criticism of the Federalists in government.

Republican leaders began to look for ways to reverse the Alien and Sedition Acts. Some looked to the state legislatures for help. They developed a theory to justify action by the states against the federal government in two sets of resolutions of 1798–1799, one written (anonymously) by Jefferson and adopted by the Kentucky legislature and the other drafted by Madison and approved by the Virginia legislature. The Virginia and Kentucky Resolutions, as

Virginia and Kentucky Resolutions

CONGRESSIONAL BRAWLERS, 1798 This savage cartoon was inspired by the celebrated fight on the floor of the House of Representatives between Matthew Lyon, a Republican representative from Vermont, and Roger Griswold, a Federalist from Connecticut. Griswold (at right) attacks Lyon with his cane, and Lyon retaliates with fire tongs. Other members of Congress are portrayed enjoying the battle. *(New York Public Library)*

they were known, used the ideas of John Locke and the Tenth Amendment to the Constitution to argue that the federal government had been formed by a "compact" or contract among the states and possessed only certain delegated powers. Whenever a party to the contract, a state, decided that the central government had exceeded those powers, it had the right to "nullify" the appropriate laws.

The Republicans did not win wide support for the nullification idea; they did, however, succeed in elevating their dispute with the Federalists to the level of a national crisis. By the late 1790s, the entire nation was deeply and bitterly politicized. State legislatures at times resembled battlegrounds. Even the United States Congress was plagued with violent disagreements. In one celebrated incident in the chamber of the House of Representatives, Matthew Lyon, a Republican from Vermont, responded to an insult from Roger Griswold, a Federalist from Connecticut, by spitting in Griswold's eye. Griswold attacked Lyon with his cane, Lyon fought back with a pair of fire tongs, and soon the two men were wrestling on the floor.

The "Revolution" of 1800

Election of 1800

These bitter controversies shaped the presidential election of 1800. The presidential candidates were the same as four years earlier: Adams for the Federalists, Jefferson for the

Republicans. But the campaign of 1800 was very different from the one preceding it. Adams and Jefferson themselves displayed reasonable dignity, but their supporters showed no such restraint. The Federalists accused Jefferson of being a dangerous radical and his followers of being wild men who, if they should come to power, would bring on a reign of terror comparable to that of the French Revolution. The Republicans portrayed Adams as a tyrant conspiring to become king, and they accused the Federalists of plotting to impose slavery on the people. The election was close, and the crucial contest was in New York. There, Aaron Burr mobilized an organization of Revolutionary War veterans, the Tammany Society, to serve as a Republican political machine. Through Tammany's efforts, the party carried the city by a large majority, and with it the state. Jefferson was, apparently, elected.

But an unexpected complication soon jeopardized the Republican victory. The Constitution called for each elector to "vote by ballot for two persons." The expectation was that an elector would cast one vote for his party's presidential candidate and the other for his party's vice presidential candidate. To avoid a tie, the Republicans had intended that one elector would refrain from voting for the party's vice-presidential candidate, Aaron Burr. But when the votes were counted, Jefferson and Burr each had 73. No candidate had a majority, and the House of Representatives had to choose between the two top candidates, Jefferson and Burr. Each state delegation would cast a single vote.

The new Congress, elected in 1800 with a Republican majority, was not to convene until after the inauguration of the president, so it was the Federalist Congress that had to decide the question. After a long deadlock, several leading Federalists concluded that Burr was too unreliable to trust with the presidency. On the thirty-sixth ballot, Jefferson was elected.

After the election of 1800, the only branch of the federal government left in Federalist hands was the judiciary. The Adams administration spent its last months in office taking steps to make the party's hold on the courts secure. With the Judiciary Act of 1801, the Federalists reduced the number of Supreme Court justiceships by one but greatly increased the number of federal judgeships as a whole. Adams quickly appointed Federalists to the newly created positions. He also appointed a leading Federalist, John Marshall, to be chief justice of the Supreme Court, a position Marshall held for 34 years. Indeed, there were charges that he stayed up until midnight on his last day in office to finish signing the new judges' commissions. These officeholders became known as the "midnight appointments."

The Judiciary Act of 1801

Even so, the Republicans viewed their victory as almost complete. The nation had, they believed, been saved from tyranny. The exuberance with which the victors viewed the future—and the importance they ascribed to the defeat of the Federalists—was evident in the phrase Jefferson himself later used to describe his election. He called it the "Revolution of 1800."

CONCLUSION

The writing of the Constitution of 1787 was the single most important political event in the history of the United States. In creating a "federal" system of dispersed authority—authority divided among national and state governments, authority divided among an executive, a legislature, and a judiciary—the young nation sought to balance its need for an effective central government against its fear of concentrated and despotic power. The ability of the delegates to the Constitutional Convention to compromise gave evidence of the deep yearning among them for a stable political system. The same willingness to compromise allowed the greatest challenge to the ideals of the new democracy—slavery—to survive intact.

The writing and ratifying of the Constitution settled some questions about the shape of the new nation. The first twelve years under the government created by the Constitution solved others. And yet by the year 1800, a basic disagreement about the future of the nation remained unresolved and was creating bitter divisions and conflicts within the political world. The election of Thomas Jefferson to the presidency that year opened a new chapter in the nation's public history. It also brought to a close, at least temporarily, savage political conflicts that had seemed to threaten the nation's future.

FOR FURTHER REFERENCE

Charles Beard, *An Economic Interpretation of the Constitution of the United States* (1913) is one of the seminal works of modern American historical inquiry, although its interpretation is no longer widely accepted. Gordon Wood, *The Creation of the American Republic* (1969) is the leading analysis of the intellectual path from the Declaration of Independence to the American Constitution. Jack Rakove, *Original Meanings: Politics and Ideas in the Making of the Constitution* (1996) connects the politics of the 1780s with the political ideas embedded in the Constitution. Stanley Elkins and Eric McKitrick, *The Age of Federalism* (1993) provides a detailed overview of political and economic development in the 1790s. Joyce Appleby, *Capitalism and a New Social Order: The Republican Vision of the 1790s* (1984) highlights liberal and capitalist impulses unleashed after the ratification of the Constitution. Joseph Ellis is the author of several highly regarded books on the founders: *After the Revolution: Profiles of Early American Culture* (1979), which examines some of the framers of the new nation; *American Sphinx: The Character of Thomas Jefferson* (1997); *Founding Brothers: The Revolutionary Generation* (2000); and *Passionate Sage: The Character and Legacy of John Adams* (1993). David McCullough, *John Adams* (2001) is a vivid, sympathetic, and outstandingly popular biography.

For quizzes, Internet resources, references to additional books and films, and more, consult this book's Online Learning Center site at www.mhhe.com/unfinishednation4.

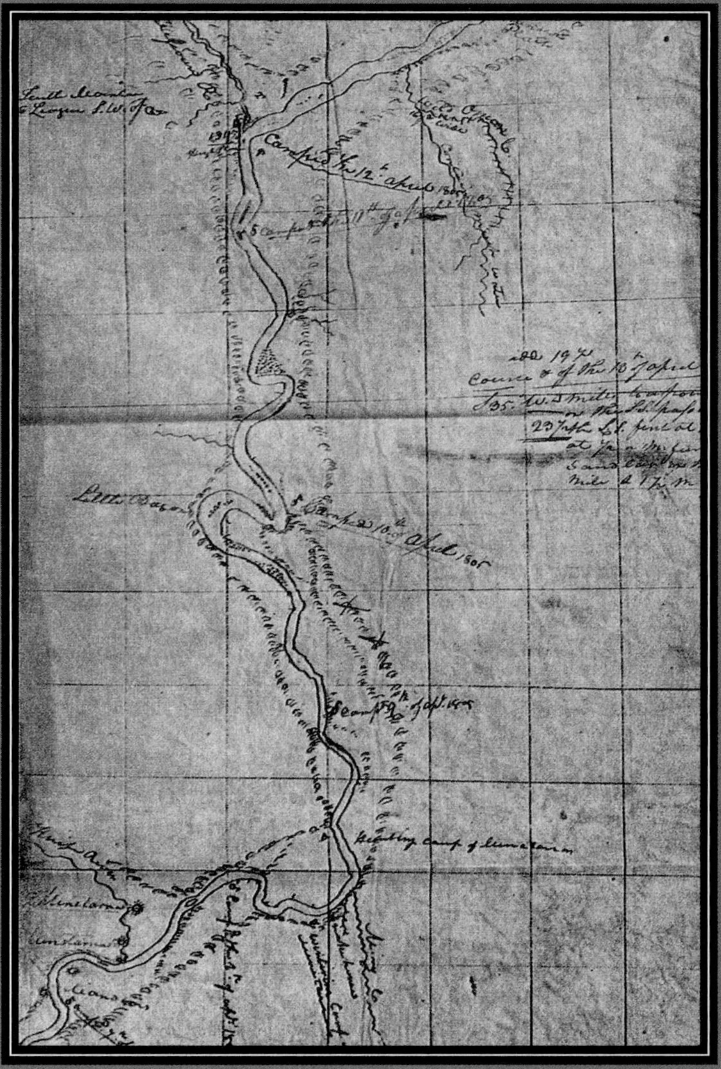

THE JOURNAL OF LEWIS AND CLARK This page is from the journal the explorers Meriwether Lewis and William Clark kept on their famous journey through the territory the United States had acquired in the Louisiana Purchase—and beyond. Shown here is one of the rough maps they drew to describe the lands they had seen. *(© British Museum)*

TIME LINE

	1793	1800	1801	1803	1804-1806	1804	1807	
	Eli Whitney invents cotton gin	U.S. capital moves to Washington	Second Great Awakening begins	Louisiana Purchase	Lewis and Clark expedition	Jefferson reelected	Embargo	
			Marshall chief justice of Supreme Court	*Marbury* v. *Madison*				

CHAPTER SEVEN

THE JEFFERSONIAN ERA

The Rise of Cultural Nationalism
Stirrings of Industrialism
Jefferson the President
Doubling the National Domain
Expansion and War
The War of 1812

Thomas Jefferson and his followers assumed control of the national government in 1801 as the champions of a distinctive vision of America. They favored a society of sturdy, independent farmers, happily free from the workshops, the industrial towns, and the city mobs of Europe. They celebrated localism and republican simplicity. Above all, they proposed a federal government of sharply limited power.

Almost nothing worked out as they had planned, for during their years in power the young republic was developing in ways that made much of their vision obsolete. The American economy became steadily more diversified and complex, making the ideal of a simple, agrarian society impossible to maintain. American cultural life was dominated by a vigorous and ambitious nationalism. And Jefferson himself contributed to the changes by exercising strong national authority at times, and by arranging the greatest single increase in the size of the United States in its history.

1808	1809	1810	1811	1812	1814	1815
Madison elected president	Non-Intercourse Act	Macon's Bill No. 2	Battle of Tippecanoe	U.S. declares war on Great Britain	Hartford Convention	Battle of New Orleans
	Tecumseh Confederacy formed			Madison reelected	Treaty of Ghent	

THE RISE OF CULTURAL NATIONALISM

In many respects, American cultural life in the early nineteenth century reflected the Republican vision of the nation's future. Opportunities for education increased, the nation's literary and artistic life began to free itself from European influences, and American religion began to adjust to the spread of Enlightenment rationalism. In other respects, however, the new culture was posing a serious challenge to Republican ideals.

Educational and Literary Nationalism

Importance of a Virtuous Citizenry

Central to the Republican vision of America was the concept of a virtuous and enlightened citizenry. Republicans believed, therefore, in the creation of a nationwide system of public schools in which all male citizens would receive free education. Such hopes were not fulfilled. Schooling remained primarily the responsibility of private institutions, most of which were open only to those who could afford to pay for them. In the South and in the mid-Atlantic states, most schools were run by religious groups. In New England, private academies were often more secular, many of them modeled on those founded by the Phillips family at Andover, Massachusetts, in 1778, and at Exeter, New Hampshire, three years later. Many were frankly aristocratic in outlook. There were a few educational institutions open to the poor, but not nearly enough to accommodate everyone, and the education they offered was usually clearly inferior to that provided for more prosperous students.

Private secondary schools such as those in New England generally accepted only male students; even many public schools excluded females from the classroom. Yet the late eighteenth and early nineteenth centuries did see some important advances in education for women. As Americans began to place a higher value on the importance of the "republican mother" who would help train the new generation, they began to ask how mothers could raise their children to be enlightened if the mothers themselves were uneducated. Such concerns helped speed the creation of female academies throughout the nation (usually for the daughters of affluent families). In 1789, Massachusetts required that its public schools serve females as well as males. Other states, although not all, soon followed.

Judith Sargent Murray

Some women aspired to more. In 1784, Judith Sargent Murray published an essay defending the right of women to education. Men and women were equal in intellect and equal in potential, Murray argued. Women, therefore, should have precisely the same educational opportunities as men. What was more, they should have opportunities to earn their own livings and to establish roles

THE PENNSYLVANIA HOSPITAL As the ideas of the Enlightenment spread through American culture in the eighteenth and nineteenth centuries, encouraging the belief that every individual was a divine being and could be redeemed from even the most miserable condition, hospitals and asylums—such as this institution in Pennsylvania—began to emerge to provide settings for the redemption of the poor, the ill, and the deviant. *(The Library Company of Philadelphia)*

for themselves in society apart from their husbands and families. Murray's ideas attracted relatively little support.

Because Jefferson and his followers liked to think of Native Americans as "noble savages" (uncivilized but not necessarily uncivilizable) they hoped that schooling the Indians in white culture would "uplift" the tribes. Missionaries and mission schools proliferated among the tribes. There were no comparable efforts to educate enslaved African Americans.

Higher Education

Higher education similarly diverged from Republican ideals. The number of colleges and universities in America grew substantially, from nine at the time of the Revolution to twenty-two in 1800. None of the new schools, however, was truly public. Even universities established by state legislatures relied on private contributions and tuition fees to survive. Scarcely more than one white man in a thousand (and virtually no women, blacks, or Indians) had access to any college education, and those few who did attend universities were, almost without exception, members of prosperous, propertied families.

Medicine and Science

Medicine and science were not always closely connected to one another in the early nineteenth century, but many physicians were working hard to strengthen the link. The University of Pennsylvania created the first American medical school early in the nineteenth century. Most doctors, however, studied medicine by working with an established practitioner. Some American physicians believed in applying new scientific methods to medicine, but they had to struggle against age-old prejudices and superstitions. Efforts to teach anatomy, for example, encountered strong public hostility because of the dissection of cadavers that the study required. Municipal authorities had virtually no understanding of medical science and almost no idea of what to do in the face of the severe epidemics that so often swept their populations; only slowly did they respond to warnings that lack of adequate sanitation programs was to blame for much disease.

Individual patients often had more to fear from their doctors than from their illnesses. Even the leading advocates of scientific medicine often embraced useless and dangerous treatments. George Washington's death in 1799 was probably less a result of the minor throat infection that had afflicted him than of his physicians' efforts to cure him by bleeding and purging.

Decline of Midwifery

The medical profession also used its newfound commitment to the "scientific" method to justify expanding its control over kinds of care that had traditionally been outside its domain. Most childbirths, for example, had been attended by female midwives. In the early nineteenth century, physicians began to handle deliveries themselves. Among the results of that change was a narrowing of opportunities for women and a restriction of access to childbirth care for poor mothers (who could have afforded midwives, but who could not pay the higher physicians' fees).

Cultural Aspirations of the New Nation

Establishing a National Culture

Many Americans dreamed of an American literary and artistic life that would rival the greatest achievements of Europe. The 1772 "Poem on the Rising Glory of America" predicted that America was destined to become the "seat of empire" and the "final stage" of civilization. The Connecticut schoolmaster and lawyer Noah Webster (author of widely used American spellers and dictionaries) echoed such sentiments, arguing that the American schoolboy should be educated as a nationalist. "As soon as he opens his lips," Webster wrote, "he should rehearse the history of his own country; he should lisp the praise of liberty, and of those illustrious heroes and statesmen who have wrought a revolution in her favor."

A growing number of native authors began working to create a strong American literature. Among the most ambitious was the Philadelphia writer Charles Brockden Brown. But his fascination with horror and deviance kept him from developing a popular audience. More successful was Washington Irving of New York, whose popular folk tales, recounting the adventures of such American rustics as Ichabod Crane and Rip Van Winkle, made him the widely acknowledged leader of American literary life in the early eighteenth century.

Religion and Revivalism

The American Revolution had weakened traditional forms of religious practice. It had elevated ideas of individual liberty and reason that challenged many ecclesiastical traditions. By the 1790s, only a small proportion of white Americans were members of formal churches, and ministers were complaining about the "decay of vital piety."

Religious traditionalists were particularly alarmed about the emergence of new, "rational" religious doctrines—theologies that reflected modern, scientific attitudes. "Deism," which had originated among Enlightenment philosophers in France, attracted such educated Americans as Jefferson and Franklin and by 1800 was reaching a moderately broad popular audience. Deists accepted the existence of God, but they considered Him a remote being who, after having created the universe, had withdrawn from direct involvement with the human race and its sins. Religious skepticism also produced the philosophies of "universalism" and "unitarianism." Disciples of these new ideas rejected the traditional Calvinist belief in predestination and the idea of the Trinity. Jesus was only a great religious teacher, they claimed, not the son of God. But religious skepticism appeared more powerful than it actually was, in part because those who clung to more traditional faiths were for a time confused and disorganized. Beginning in 1801, however, traditional religion staged a dramatic comeback in the form of a wave of revivalism known as the Second Great Awakening.

"Deism"

The origins of the Awakening lay in the efforts of conservative theologians to fight the spread of religious rationalism and in the efforts of church establishments to revitalize their organizations. Presbyterians expanded their efforts on the western fringes of white settlement. The Methodists sent itinerant preachers throughout the nation to win recruits for the new church, which soon became the fastest-growing denomination in America. Almost as successful were the Baptists, who found an especially fervent following in the South.

By 1800, the revivalist energies of all these denominations were combining to create the greatest surge of evangelical fervor since the first Great Awakening sixty years before. In only a few years, the revivalists mobilized a large proportion of the American people, and membership in those churches embracing revivalism was mushrooming. At Cane Ridge, Kentucky, in the summer

Cane Ridge

THE CAMP MEETING Camp meetings became a popular feature of evangelical religion in America beginning around 1800. By the 1820s, there were about 1,000 such meetings a year, most of them in the South and the West. This lithograph, which dates from the 1830s, illustrates the central role of women in the religious revivals of the time. *(Lithograph by Kennedy and Lucas, after A. Rider, © The New-York Historical Society)*

of 1801, a group of evangelical ministers presided over the nation's first "camp meeting"—an extraordinary revival that lasted several days and impressed all who saw it with its size (some estimated that 25,000 people attended) and its fervor. Such events became common in subsequent years.

Message of the Second Great Awakening

The basic message of the Second Great Awakening was that individuals must readmit God and Christ into their daily lives; must embrace a fervent, active piety; and must reject the skeptical rationalism that threatened traditional beliefs. Yet the wave of revivalism did not restore the religion of the past. Few denominations any longer accepted the idea of predestination, and the belief that a person could affect his or her own chances for salvation added intensity to the individual's search for salvation. The Awakening, in short, combined a more active piety with a belief in a God whose grace could be attained through faith and good works.

New Roles for Women

One of the striking features of the Awakening was the preponderance of women within it. Female converts far outnumbered males. That may have been in part because of the movement of industrial work out of the home and into the factory. That process, which was making rapid strides in the early nineteenth century, robbed women of one of their most important social roles. Religious enthusiasm provided, among other things, access to a new range of activities associated with the churches—charitable societies ministering to orphans and the poor, missionary organizations, and others—in which women came to play important roles.

In some areas of the country, revival meetings were open to people of all races. From these revivals emerged a group of black preachers who became important figures within the slave community. Some of them translated the apparently egalitarian religious message of the Awakening—that salvation was available to all—into a similarly egalitarian message for blacks in the present world. Out of black revival meetings in Virginia, for example, arose an elaborate plan in 1800 (devised by Gabriel Prosser, the brother of a black preacher) for a slave rebellion and an attack on Richmond. The plan was discovered and foiled in advance by whites, but revivalism continued in subsequent years to create occasional racial unrest in the South.

The spirit of revivalism was particularly strong among Native Americans. Presbyterian and Baptist missionaries were active among the southern tribes and sparked a wave of conversions. But the most important revivalism came from the efforts of Handsome Lake, a Seneca whose seemingly miraculous "rebirth" after years of alcoholism helped give him a special stature within his tribe. Handsome Lake called for a revival of traditional Indian ways. That meant repudiating the individualism of white society and restoring the communal quality of the Indian world. Handsome Lake's message spread through the scattered Iroquois communities that had survived the military and political setbacks of previous decades and inspired many Indians to give up whiskey, gambling, and other destructive customs derived from white society. But Handsome Lake also encouraged Christian missionaries to become active within the tribes, and he urged Iroquois men to abandon their roles as hunters and become sedentary farmers instead. Iroquois women, who had traditionally done the farming, were to move into more domestic roles.

Handsome Lake

STIRRINGS OF INDUSTRIALISM

While Americans were engaged in a revolution to win their independence, an even more important revolution was in progress in England: the emergence of modern industrialism. Power-driven machines were permitting manufacturing to become more rapid and extensive—with profound social and economic consequences. Not since the agrarian revolution thousands of years earlier, when humans had turned from hunting to farming for sustenance, had there been an economic change of a magnitude comparable to the industrial revolution.

The Industrial Revolution

PAWTUCKET BRIDGE AND FALLS One reason for the growth of the textile industry in New England in the early nineteenth century was that there were many sources of water power in the region to run the machinery in the factories. That was certainly the case with Slater's Mill, one of the first American textile factories, which was located in Pawtucket, Rhode Island, alongside a powerful waterfall. This view was painted by an anonymous artist in the 1810s. *(Courtesy The Rhode Island Historical Society)*

Technology in America

Nothing even remotely comparable to the English industrial revolution occurred in America in the first two decades of the nineteenth century. Yet even while Jeffersonians warned of the dangers of rapid economic change, they were witnessing a series of technological advances that would ultimately help ensure that the United States too would be transformed. Some of these technological advances were imported from England. Despite efforts by the British government to prevent the export of textile machinery or the emigration of skilled mechanics, a number of immigrants with advanced knowledge of English technology arrived in the United States eager to introduce the new machines to America. Samuel Slater, for example, used the knowledge he had acquired before leaving England to build a spinning mill in Pawtucket, Rhode Island, for the Quaker merchant Moses Brown in 1790.

The Cotton Gin and the Spread of Slavery

America in the early nineteenth century also produced notable inventors of its own. In 1793, Eli Whitney invented a machine that performed the arduous task of removing the seeds from short-staple cotton quickly and efficiently. It was dubbed the cotton gin ("gin" was a derivative of "engine"). With the device a single operator could clean as much cotton in a few hours as a group of workers had once needed a whole day to do. The results were profound. Soon cotton growing spread throughout the South. (Previously it had been restricted largely to the coast and the Sea Islands, the only places where long-staple cotton—easily cleaned without the cotton gin—could be grown.) Within a decade, the total cotton crop increased eightfold. African-American slavery, which with the decline of tobacco production had seemed for a time to be a dwindling institution, expanded and firmly fixed itself upon the South. The large supply of domestically produced fiber also served as a strong incentive to entrepreneurs in New England and elsewhere to develop a native textile industry.

Whitney was an important figure in the history of American technology for another reason as well—as a major figure in introducing the concept of interchangeable parts to the United States. As machines such as the cotton gin began to be widely used, it became increasingly important that owners of such machines have access to spare parts—and that the parts be made so that they would fit the machines properly. Whitney not only designed the cotton gin, therefore, but designed machine tools that could manufacture its component parts to exact specifications. The U.S. government later commissioned Whitney to manufacture 1,000 muskets for the army. Each part of the gun had to be interchangeable with the equivalent part in every other gun.

Importance of Interchangeable Parts

Interchangeability was of great importance in the United States because of the great distances many people had to travel to reach towns or cities and the relatively limited transportation systems available to them. Interchangeable parts meant that a farmer could repair a machine himself rather than transport it over great distances to a machine shop or armory. But the interchangeability that Whitney championed was not easy to achieve. In theory, many parts were designed to be interchangeable. In reality, the actual manufacturing of such parts was for many years not nearly as precise as it was supposed to be. Farmers and others often had to do considerable fitting before the parts would work in their equipment. Not until later in the nineteenth century would machine tools be developed to the point that parts could be made truly interchangeable.

Transportation Innovations

One of the prerequisites for industrialization is a transportation system that allows the efficient movement of raw materials to factories and of finished goods to markets. The United States had no such system in the early years of the republic, and thus it had no domestic market extensive enough to justify large-scale production. But projects were under way that would ultimately remove the transportation obstacle.

Robert Fulton's Steamboat

One such project was the development of the steamboat. England had pioneered steam power, and even steam navigation, in the eighteenth century, and there had been experiments in America in the 1780s and 1790s in various forms of steam-powered transportation. A major advance emerged out of the efforts of the inventor Robert Fulton and the promoter Robert R. Livingston,

America in the World

THE GLOBAL INDUSTRIAL REVOLUTION

While Americans were engaged in a revolution to win their independence, they were also taking the first steps toward an at least equally important revolution—one that was already in progress in England and Europe. It was the emergence of modern industrialism. Historians differ over precisely when the industrial revolution began, but it is clear that by the end of the eighteenth century it was well under way in many parts of the world. A hundred years later, the global process of industrialization had transformed the societies of Britain, most of continental Europe, Japan, and the United States. Its social and economic consequences were complex and profound and continue today to shape the nature of global society.

For Americans, the industrial revolution was largely a product of rapid changes in Great Britain, the nation with which they had the closest relations. Britain was the first nation to develop significant industrial capacity. The factory system took root in England in the late eighteenth century, revolutionizing the manufacture of cotton thread and cloth. One invention followed another in quick succession. Improvements in weaving drove improvements in spinning, and these changes created a demand for new devices for carding (combing and straightening the fibers for the spinner). Water, wind, and animal power continued to be important in the textile industry; but more important was the emergence of steam power—which began to proliferate after the appearance of James Watt's advanced steam engine (patented in 1769). Cumbersome and inefficient by modern standards, Watt's engine was nevertheless a major improvement over the earlier "atmospheric" engine of Thomas Newcomen. England's textile industry quickly became the most profitable in the world, and it helped encourage comparable advances in other fields of manufacturing as well. Despite the efforts of the British government to prevent the export of English industrial technology, knowledge of the new machines reached other nations quickly, usually through the emigration of people who had learned the technology in British factories.

America benefited the most from English technology, because it received more immigrants from Great Britain than from any other country. But English technology spread quickly to the nations of continental Europe as well. Belgium was the first, developing a significant coal, iron, and armaments industry in the early nineteenth century. France—profiting from the immigration of approximately fifteen thousand British workers with advanced technological skills—had created a substantial industrial capacity in textiles and metals by the end of the 1820s, which in turn contributed to a great boom in railroad construction later in the century. German industrialization progressed rapidly after 1840, beginning with coal and iron production and then, in the 1850s, moving into large-scale railroad construction. By the late nineteenth century, Germany had created some of the world's largest industrial corporations. In Japan, the sudden intrusion of American and European traders helped cause the so-called Meiji reforms of the 1880s and 1890s, which launched a period of rapid industrialization there as well.

Industrialization changed not just the world's economies, but also its societies. First in England, and then in Europe, America, and Japan, social systems underwent wrenching changes. Hundreds of thousands of men and women moved from rural areas into cities to work in factories, where they experienced both the benefits and the costs of industrialization. The standard of living of the new working class, when objectively quantified, was usually significantly higher than that of the rural poor. Most of those who moved from farm to factory, in other words, experienced some improvement in nutrition and other material circumstances, and even in their health. But the psychological costs of being suddenly uprooted from one way of life and thrust into another, fundamentally different, one could outweigh the economic gains. There was little in most workers' prior experience to prepare them for the nature of industrial labor. It was disciplined, routinized work with a fixed and rigid schedule, a sharp contrast to the varying, seasonal work pattern of the rural economy. Nor were many factory workers prepared for life in the new industrial towns and expanding cities. Industrial workers experienced, too, a fundamental change in their relationship with their employers. Unlike rural landlords and local aristocrats, factory owners and managers—the new class of industrial capitalists, many of them accumulating unprecedented wealth—were usually remote and inaccessible figures. They dealt with their workers impersonally, and the result was a growing schism between the two classes—each lacking access to or understanding of the other. Working men and women throughout the globe began thinking of themselves as a distinct class, with common goals and interests. And their efforts simultaneously to adjust to their new way of life and to resist its most damaging aspects sometimes created great social turbulence. Battles between workers and employers became a characteristic feature of industrial life throughout the world.

Life in industrial nations changed at every level. Populations in industrial nations grew rapidly, and people began to live longer. At the same time, industrial cities began to produce great increases in pollution, crime, and—until modern sanitation systems emerged—infectious disease. Around the industrial world, middle classes expanded and came, in varying degrees, to dominate the economy (although not always the culture or the politics) of their nations.

Not since the agrarian revolution thousands of years earlier, when many humans had turned from hunting to farming for sustenance, had there been an economic change of a magnitude comparable to the industrial revolution. Centuries of traditions, of social patterns, of cultural and religious assumptions were challenged and, often, shattered. The tentative stirrings of industrial activity in the United States in the early nineteenth century, therefore, were part of a vast movement that over the course of the next century was to transform much of the globe.

(text continued from page 175)

who made significant advances in steam-powered navigation that made possible the launching of a steamboat large enough to carry passengers. Their *Clermont*, equipped with paddle wheels and an English-built engine, sailed up the Hudson in the summer of 1807.

The "Turnpike Era"

Meanwhile, what was to become known as the "turnpike era" had begun. In 1794, a corporation constructed a toll road running the sixty miles from Philadelphia to Lancaster, Pennsylvania, with a hard-packed surface of crushed stone, which provided a good year-round surface with effective drainage (but was very

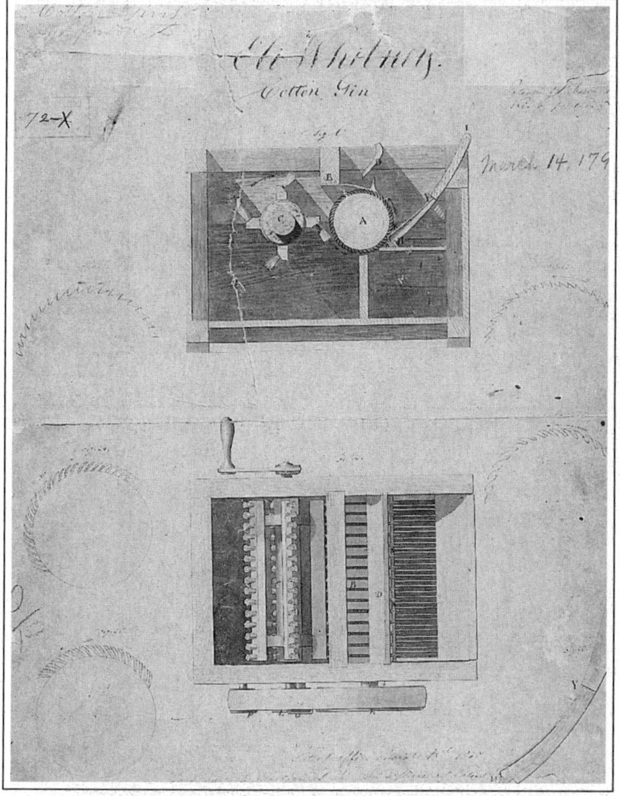

THE COTTON GIN Eli Whitney's cotton gin revolutionized the cotton economy of the South by making the processing of short-staple cotton simple and economical. These 1794 drawings are part of Whitney's application for a federal patent on his device. *(The National Archives and Records Administration)*

expensive to use). The Pennsylvania venture proved so successful that similar turnpikes (so named from the kind of tollgate frequently used) were laid out from other cities to neighboring towns.

The process of building the turnpikes was a difficult one. Companies had to survey their routes with many things in mind, particularly elevation. Horse-drawn vehicles had great difficulty traveling along roads with more than a five-degree incline, which required many roads to take very circuitous routes to avoid climbing straight up steep hills. Building roads over mountains was an almost insurmountable task, and no company was successful in doing so until governments began to participate in the financing of the projects.

Country and City

Despite all the changes, America remained an overwhelmingly rural and agrarian nation. Only 3 percent of the population lived in towns of more than 8,000 in 1800. Even the nation's largest cities could not begin to compare with such European capitals as London and Paris (although Philadelphia, with 70,000 residents, New York, with 60,000, and others were becoming centers of commerce, learning, and urban culture comparable to many of the secondary cities of Europe).

City Life

People who lived in cities and towns lived differently from the vast majority of Americans who continued to work as farmers. Among other things, urban life produced affluence, and affluent people sought increasing elegance and refinement in their homes, their grounds, and their dress. They also looked for diversions—music, theater, dancing, and, for many people, horse racing. It was natural that horse racing would appeal to Americans in this era, when horses were virtually the only means of transportation other than walking for most people. Informal horse racing had begun as early as the 1620s, and the first formal race course opened near New York City in 1665. By the early nineteenth century, horse racing was a popular activity in most areas of the country. The crowds that gathered at horse races were an early sign of the vast appetite for popular, public entertainments that would be an enduring part of American culture.

It was still possible for some to believe that this small, half-formed nation might not become a complex modern society. But the forces already at work would soon lastingly transform the United States. And Thomas Jefferson, for all his commitment to the agrarian ideal, found himself, as president, obliged to confront and accommodate them.

JEFFERSON THE PRESIDENT

Privately, Thomas Jefferson may well have considered his victory over John Adams in 1800 to be what he later termed it: a revolution "as real . . . as that of 1776." Publicly, however, he was restrained and conciliatory, attempting to minimize the differences between the two parties and calm the passions that the bitter campaign had aroused. There was no complete repudiation of Federalist policies, no true "revolution." Indeed, at times Jefferson seemed to outdo the Federalists at their own work.

The Federal City and the "People's President"

The relative unimportance of the federal government during the Jeffersonian era was symbolized by the character of the newly founded national capital, the city of Washington. There were many who envisioned that the raw, uncompleted town would soon emerge as a great and majestic city.

L'Enfant's Vision

The French architect Pierre L'Enfant had designed the capital on a grand scale. Many Americans believed Washington would become the Paris of the United States.

THOMAS JEFFERSON This 1805 portrait by the noted American painter Rembrandt Peale shows Jefferson at the beginning of his second term as president. It also conveys (through the simplicity of dress and the slightly unkempt hair) the image of democratic simplicity that Jefferson liked to project as the champion of the "common man." *(© The New-York Historical Society)*

Reality of Washington, D.C.

In reality, throughout most of the nineteenth century Washington remained little more than a straggling, provincial village. Although the population increased steadily from the 3,200 counted in the 1800 census, it never rivaled that of New York, Philadelphia, or the other major cities of the nation. The city remained a raw, inhospitable community. Members of Congress viewed Washington not as a home but as a place to visit briefly during sessions of the legislature. Most lived in a cluster of simple boardinghouses in the vicinity of the Capitol. It was not unusual for a member of Congress to resign his seat in the midst of a session to return home if he had an opportunity to accept the more prestigious post of member of his state legislature.

Jefferson was a wealthy planter by background, but as president he conveyed to the public an image of plain, almost crude disdain for pretension. He walked like an ordinary citizen to and from his inauguration at the Capitol. In the presidential mansion, which had not yet acquired the name "White House," he disregarded the courtly etiquette of his predecessors. He did not always bother to dress up, prompting the British ambassador to complain of being received by the president in clothes that were "indicative of utter slovenliness and indifference to appearances."

Yet Jefferson managed nevertheless to impress most of those who knew him. He was one of the nation's most intelligent and creative men, with a wider range of interests and accomplishments than any major public figure in American history with the possible exception of Benjamin Franklin. In addition to politics and diplomacy, he was an active architect, educator, inventor, scientific farmer, and philosopher-scientist.

Jefferson the Politician

Jefferson was, above all, a shrewd and practical politician. He worked hard to exert influence as the leader of his party, giving direction to Republicans in Congress by quiet and sometimes even devious means. Although the Republicans had objected strenuously to the efforts of their Federalist predecessors to build a network of influence through patronage, Jefferson used his powers of appointment as an effective political weapon. Like Washington before him, he believed that federal offices should be filled with men loyal to the principles and policies of the administration. By the end of his second term practically all federal jobs were held by loyal Republicans. Jefferson was a popular president during his first term and had little difficulty winning reelection against the Federalist Charles C. Pinckney in 1804. Jefferson won by the overwhelming electoral majority of 162 to 14, and Republican membership of both houses of Congress increased.

Dollars and Ships

Under Washington and Adams, the Republicans believed, the government had been needlessly extravagant. Yearly federal expenditures had nearly tripled between 1793 and 1800. The public debt had also risen, and an extensive system of internal taxation had been erected.

Limiting the Federal Government

The Jefferson administration moved deliberately to reverse these trends. In 1802, the president persuaded Congress to abolish all internal taxes, leaving customs duties and the sale of western lands as the only sources of revenue for the government. Meanwhile, Secretary of the Treasury Albert Gallatin drastically reduced government spending. Although Jefferson was unable entirely to retire the national debt as he had hoped, he did cut it almost in half (from $83 million to $45 million).

Jefferson also scaled down the armed forces. He reduced the already tiny army of 4,000 men to 2,500. He pared down the navy from twenty-five ships in commission to seven. Anything but the smallest of standing armies, he argued, might menace civil liberties and civilian control of government. Yet Jefferson was not a pacifist. At the same time that he was reducing the size of the army and navy, he helped establish the United States Military Academy at West Point, founded in 1802. And when trouble started brewing overseas, he began again to build up the fleet. Such trouble appeared first in the Mediterranean, off the coast of northern Africa.

For years the Barbary states of North Africa—Morocco, Algiers, Tunis, and Tripoli—had been demanding protection money, paid to avoid piracy, from all nations whose ships sailed the Mediterranean. During the 1780s and 1790s the United States, too, had agreed to treaties providing for annual tribute to the Barbary states, but Jefferson showed reluctance to continue this policy of appeasement.

Challenging the Barbary Pirates

In 1801, the pasha of Tripoli forced Jefferson's hand. Unhappy with American responses to his demands, he ordered the flagpole of the American consulate chopped down—a symbolic declaration of war. Jefferson responded cautiously and built up American naval forces in the area over the next several years. Finally, in 1805, he agreed to terms by which the United States ended the payment of tribute to Tripoli but paid a substantial (and humiliating) ransom for the release of American prisoners.

Conflict with the Courts

Having won control of the executive and legislative branches of government, the Republicans looked with suspicion on the judiciary, which remained largely in the hands of Federalist judges. Soon after Jefferson's first inauguration, his followers in Congress launched an attack on this last preserve of the opposition. Their first step was the repeal of the Judiciary Act of 1801, thus eliminating the judgeships to which Adams had made his "midnight appointments."

The debate over the courts led to one of the most important judicial decisions in the history of the nation. Federalists had long maintained that the Supreme Court had the authority to nullify acts of Congress, and the Court itself had actually exercised the power of judicial review in 1796 when it upheld the validity of a law passed by Congress. But the Court's authority in this area would not be secure, it was clear, until it actually declared a congressional act unconstitutional. In 1803, in the case of *Marbury* v. *Madison,* it did so. William Marbury, one of Adams's "midnight appointments," had been named a justice of the peace in the District of Columbia. But his commission, although signed and sealed, had not been delivered to him before Adams left office. When Jefferson took office, his secretary of state, James Madison, refused to hand over the commission. Marbury asked the Supreme Court to direct Madison to perform his official duty. But the Court ruled that while Marbury had a right to his commission, the Court had no authority to order Madison to deliver it. On the surface, therefore, the decision was a victory for the administration. But of much greater importance than the relatively insignificant matter of Marbury's commission was the Court's reasoning in the decision.

Marbury v. Madison

The original Judiciary Act of 1789 had given the Court the power to compel executive officials to act in such matters as the delivery of commissions, and it was on that basis that Marbury had filed his suit. But the Court ruled that Congress had exceeded its authority, that the Constitution defined the powers of the judiciary, and that the legislature had no right to expand them. The relevant section of the 1789 act was, therefore, void. In seeming to deny its own authority, the Court was in fact radically enlarging it. The justices had repudiated a relatively minor power (the power to force the delivery of a commission) by asserting a vastly greater one (the power to nullify an act of Congress).

John Marshall

The chief justice of the United States at the time of the ruling (and until 1835) was John Marshall. A leading Federalist and prominent Virginia lawyer, he had served John Adams as secretary of state. In 1801, just before leaving office, Adams had appointed him chief justice, and almost immediately Marshall established himself as the dominant figure of the Court, shaping virtually all its most important rulings—including, of course, *Marbury* v. *Madison.* Through a succession of Republican presidents, he battled to give the federal government unity and strength. And in so doing, he established the judiciary as a coequal branch of government with the executive and the legislature.

DOUBLING THE NATIONAL DOMAIN

In the same year Jefferson was elected president of the United States, Napoleon Bonaparte made himself ruler of France with the title of first consul. In the year Jefferson was reelected, Napoleon named himself emperor. The two men had little in common, yet for a time they were of great assistance to each other in international politics.

Jefferson and Napoleon

Napoleon's North American Dream

Having failed in a grandiose plan to seize India from the British Empire, Napoleon began to dream of restoring French power in the New World. The territory east of the Mississippi, which France had ceded to Great Britain in 1763, was now part of the United States, but Napoleon hoped to regain the lands west of the Mississippi, which belonged to Spain. In 1800, under the secret Treaty of San Ildefonso, France regained title to Louisiana, which included almost the whole of the Mississippi Valley to the west of the river. The Louisiana Territory would, Napoleon hoped, become the heart of a great French empire in America.

Jefferson was unaware at first of Napoleon's imperial ambitions in America, and for a time he pursued a foreign policy that reflected his well-known admiration for France. But he began to reassess American relations with the French when he heard rumors of the secret transfer of Louisiana. Particularly troubling to Jefferson was French control of New Orleans, the outlet through which the produce of the fast-growing western regions of the United States was shipped to the markets of the world.

Importance of New Orleans

Jefferson was even more alarmed when, in the fall of 1802, he learned that the Spanish intendant at New Orleans (who still governed the city, since the French had not yet taken formal possession of the region) had announced a disturbing new regulation. American ships sailing the Mississippi River had for many years been accustomed to depositing their cargoes in New Orleans for transfer to oceangoing vessels. The intendant now forbade the practice, even though Spain had guaranteed Americans that right in the Pinckney Treaty of 1795.

Westerners demanded that the federal government do something to reopen the river, and the president faced a dilemma. If he yielded to the frontier clamor and tried to change the policy by force, he would run the risk of a major war with France. If he ignored the westerners' demands, he might lose political support. But Jefferson saw another solution. He instructed Robert Livingston, the American ambassador in Paris, to negotiate for the purchase of New Orleans. Livingston, on his own authority, proposed that the French sell the United States the rest of Louisiana as well.

In the meantime, Jefferson persuaded Congress to appropriate funds for an expansion of the army and the construction of a river fleet, and he hinted that American forces might soon descend on New Orleans and that the United States might form an alliance with Great Britain if the problems with France were not resolved. Perhaps in response, Napoleon suddenly decided to offer the United States the entire Louisiana Territory.

Napoleon's Offer

Napoleon had good reasons for the decision. His plans for an empire in America had already gone seriously awry, partly because a yellow fever epidemic had wiped out much of the French army in the New World and partly because the expeditionary force he wished to send to reinforce the troops had been icebound in a Dutch harbor through the winter of 1802–1803. By the time the harbor thawed in the spring of 1803, Napoleon was preparing for a renewed war in Europe. He would not, he realized, have the resources to secure an empire in America.

The Louisiana Purchase

Faced with Napoleon's sudden proposal, Livingston and James Monroe, whom Jefferson had sent to Paris to assist in the negotiations, had to decide whether they should accept it even if they had no authorization to do so. But fearful that Napoleon might withdraw the offer, they decided to proceed. After some haggling over the price, Livingston and Monroe signed an agreement with Napoleon on April 30, 1803.

By the terms of the treaty, the United States was to pay a total of 80 million francs ($15 million) to the French government. The United States was also to grant certain exclusive commercial privileges to France in the port of New Orleans and was to incorporate the residents of Louisiana into the Union with the same rights and privileges as other citizens. The boundaries of the purchase were not clearly defined.

In Washington, the president was both pleased and embarrassed when he received the treaty. He was pleased with the terms of the bargain; but he was uncertain about his authority to accept it, since the Constitution said nothing about the acquisition of new territory. But Jefferson's advisers persuaded him that his treaty-making power under the Constitution would justify the purchase of Louisiana, and Congress promptly approved the treaty. Finally, late in 1803, General James Wilkinson, commissioner of the United States, took formal control of the territory on behalf of the United States. Before long, the Louisiana Territory was organized on the general pattern of the Northwest Territory, with the assumption that it would be divided eventually into states. The first of these was admitted to the Union as the state of Louisiana in 1812.

Jefferson's Ideological Dilemma

Exploring the West

Meanwhile, a series of explorations was revealing the geography of the far-flung new territory to white Americans. In 1803, Jefferson helped plan an expedition that was to cross the continent to the Pacific Ocean, gather geographical facts, and investigate prospects for trade with the Indians. He named as its leader the thirty-two-year-old Meriwether Lewis, a veteran of Indian wars who was skilled in the ways of the wilderness. Lewis chose as a colleague the twenty-eight-year-old William Clark, an experienced frontiersman and Indian fighter. In the spring of 1804, Lewis and Clark, with a company of four dozen men, started up the Missouri River from St. Louis. With the Shoshone woman Sacajawea as their interpreter, they eventually crossed the Rocky Mountains, descended along the Snake and Columbia Rivers, and in the late autumn of 1805 camped on the Pacific coast. In September 1806, they were back in St. Louis with elaborate records of the geography and the Indian civilizations they had observed along the way.

Lewis and Clark

While Lewis and Clark were on their journey, Jefferson dispatched other explorers to other parts of the Louisiana Territory. Lieutenant Zebulon Montgomery Pike, twenty-six years old, led an expedition in the fall of 1805 from St. Louis into the upper Mississippi Valley. In the summer of 1806, he set out again, proceeding up the valley of the Arkansas River and into what later became Colorado. His account of his western travels helped create an enduring (and inaccurate) impression among most Americans that the land between the Missouri and the Rockies was a desert that farmers could never cultivate.

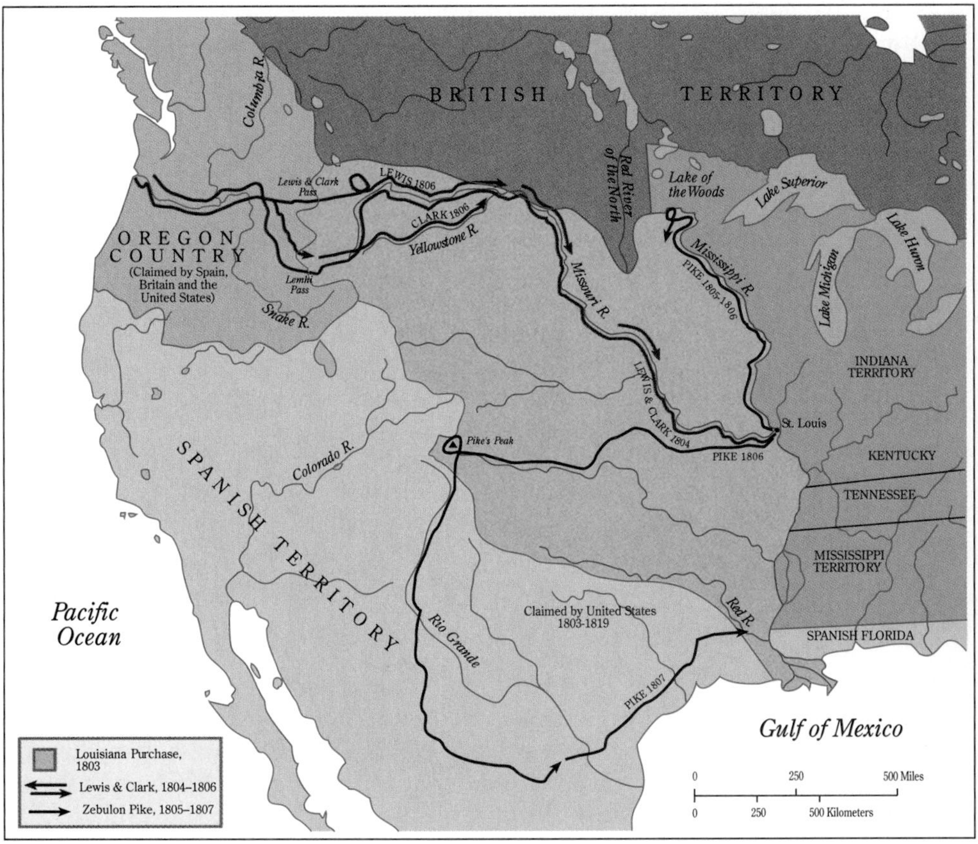

EXPLORING THE LOUISIANA PURCHASE, 1804–1807 When Jefferson purchased the Louisiana territory from France in 1803, he doubled the size of the nation. But few Americans knew what they had bought. The Lewis and Clark Expedition set out in 1804 to investigate the new territories, and this map shows their route, along with that of another inveterate explorer Zebulon Pike. Note the vast distances the two parties covered (including, in both cases, a great deal of land outside the Louisiana Purchase). Note, too, how much of this enormous territory lay outside the orbit of even these ambitious explorations. ◆ *How did the American public react to the addition of these new territories?*

For an interactive version of this map go to www.mhhe.com/unfinishednation4ch7maps

The Burr Conspiracy

Jefferson's triumphant reelection in 1804 suggested that most of the nation approved the new territorial acquisition. But some New England Federalists raged against it. They realized that the more new states joined the Union, the less power the Federalists and their region would retain. In Massachusetts, a group of the most extreme Federalists, known as the Essex Junto, concluded that the only recourse for New England was to se-

Essex Junto

cede from the Union and form a separate "northern confederacy." If a northern confederacy was to have any hope for lasting success as a separate nation, the Federalists believed, it would have to include New York and New Jersey as well as New England. But the leading Federalist in New York, Alexander Hamilton, refused to support the secessionist scheme.

Hamilton and Burr

Federalists in New York then turned to Hamilton's greatest political rival, Vice President Aaron Burr. Burr accepted a Federalist proposal that he become their candidate for governor of New York in 1804, and there were rumors that he had also agreed to support the Federalist plans for secession. Hamilton accused Burr of plotting treason and made numerous private remarks, widely reported in the press, about Burr's "despicable" character. When Burr lost the election, he blamed his defeat on Hamilton's malevolence and challenged him to a duel. Hamilton feared that refusing Burr's challenge would brand him a coward. And so, on a July morning in 1804, the two men met at Weehawken, New Jersey. Hamilton was mortally wounded; he died the next day.

Burr now had to flee New York to avoid an indictment for murder. He found new outlets for his ambitions in the West. Even before the duel, he had begun corresponding with General James Wilkinson, now governor of the Louisiana Territory. Burr and Wilkinson, it seems clear, hoped to lead an expedition that would capture Mexico from the Spanish. But there were also rumors that they wanted to separate the Southwest from the Union and create a western empire that Burr would rule. There is little evidence that these rumors were true.

Whether true or not, many of Burr's opponents chose to believe the rumors—including, ultimately, Jefferson himself. When Burr led a group of armed followers down the Ohio River by boat in 1806, disturbing reports flowed into Washington (the most alarming from Wilkinson, who had suddenly turned against Burr) that an attack on New Orleans was imminent. Jefferson ordered the arrest of Burr and his men as traitors. Burr was brought to Richmond for trial. But Chief Justice Marshall limited the evidence the government could present and defined the charge in such a way that the jury had little choice but to acquit Burr.

The Burr conspiracy was in part the story of a single man's soaring ambitions and flamboyant personality. But it was also a symbol of the larger perils still facing the new nation. With a central government that remained deliberately weak, with ambitious political leaders willing, if necessary, to circumvent normal channels in their search for power, the legitimacy of the federal government—and indeed the existence of the United States as a stable and united nation—remained to be fully established.

EXPANSION AND WAR

Conflicts in Europe and North America

Two very different conflicts were taking shape in the last years of Jefferson's presidency. One was the continuing tension in Europe, which in 1803 escalated once again into a full-scale conflict (the Napoleonic Wars). As fighting between the British and the French increased, each side took steps to prevent the United States from trading with the other. The other conflict occurred in North America itself, a result of the ceaseless westward expansion of white settlement, which was colliding with a native population committed to protecting its lands from intruders. In both the North and the South, the threatened tribes mobilized to resist white encroachments. They began as well to forge connections with British forces in Canada and Spanish forces in Florida. The Indian conflict on land, therefore, became intertwined with the European conflict on the seas, and ultimately helped cause the War of 1812.

Conflict on the Seas

In 1805, at the Battle of Trafalgar, a British fleet virtually destroyed what was left of the French navy. Because France could no longer challenge the British at sea, Napoleon now chose to pressure England in other ways. The result was what he called the Continental System, designed to close the European continent to British trade. Napoleon issued a series of decrees barring British ships and neutral ships touching at British ports from landing their cargoes at any European port controlled by France or its allies. The British government replied to Napoleon's decrees by establishing a blockade of the European coast. The blockade required that any goods being shipped to Napoleon's Europe be carried either in British vessels or in neutral vessels stopping at British ports—precisely what Napoleon's policies forbade.

Embargo and Blockade

America's Predicament

In the early nineteenth century, the United States had developed one of the most important merchant marines in the world, one that soon controlled a large proportion of the trade between Europe and the West Indies. But the events in Europe now challenged that control, because American ships were caught between Napoleon's decrees and Britain's blockade. If they sailed directly for the European continent, they risked being captured by the British navy. If they sailed by way of a British port, they ran the risk of seizure by the French. Both of the warring powers were violating America's rights as a neutral nation. But most Americans considered the British, with their greater sea power, the worse offender—especially since British vessels frequently stopped American ships on the high seas and seized sailors off the decks, making them victims of "impressment."

Impressment

Many British sailors called their navy—with its floggings, its low pay, and its terrible shipboard conditions—a "floating hell." Few volunteered. Most had had to be "impressed" (forced) into the service. At every opportunity they deserted. By 1807, many of these deserters had emigrated to the United States and joined the American merchant marine or the American navy. To check this loss of manpower, the British claimed the right to stop and search American merchantmen and reimpress deserters. They did not claim the right to take native-born Americans, but they did insist on the right to seize naturalized Americans born on British soil. In practice, the British navy often made no careful distinctions, impressing British deserters and native-born Americans alike into their service.

In the summer of 1807, the British went to more provocative extremes. Sailing from Norfolk, with several alleged deserters from the British navy among the crew, the American naval frigate *Chesapeake* was hailed by the British ship *Leopard.* When the American commander, James Barron, refused to allow the British to search the *Chesapeake*, the *Leopard* opened fire. Barron had no choice but to surrender, and a boarding party from the *Leopard* dragged four men off the American frigate.

Chesapeake-Leopard Incident

When news of the *Chesapeake-Leopard* incident reached the United States, there was a great popular clamor for revenge. But Jefferson and Madison tried to maintain the peace. Jefferson expelled all British warships from American waters to lessen the likelihood of future incidents. Then he sent instructions to his minister in England, James Monroe, to demand from the British government an end to impressment. The British government disavowed the actions of the *Leopard's* commanding officer and recalled him; it offered compensation for those killed and wounded in the incident; and it promised to return three of the captured sailors (one of the original four had been hanged). But the British cabinet refused to renounce impressment and instead reasserted its right to recover deserting seamen.

"Peaceable Coercion"

In an effort to prevent future incidents that might bring the nation again to the brink of war, Jefferson persuaded Congress to pass a drastic measure late in 1807. It was known as the Embargo, and it prohibited American ships from leaving the United States for any foreign port anywhere in the world. The law was widely evaded, but it was effective enough to create a serious depression throughout most of the nation. Hardest hit were the merchants and shipowners of the Northeast, most of them Federalists.

Jefferson's Embargo

The presidential election of 1808 came in the midst of this Embargo-induced depression. James Madison was elected president, but the Federalist candidate, Charles Pinckney again, ran much more strongly than he had in 1804. The Embargo was clearly a growing political liability, and Jefferson decided to back down. A few days before leaving office, he approved a bill ending his experiment with what he called "peaceable coercion."

Madison's Non-Intercourse Act

To replace the Embargo, Congress passed the Non-Intercourse Act just before Madison took office. It reopened trade with all nations but Great Britain and France. A year later, in 1810, the Non-Intercourse Act expired and was replaced by Macon's Bill No. 2, which reopened free commercial relations with Britain and France but authorized the president to prohibit commerce with either belligerent if it should continue violating neutral shipping after the other had stopped. Napoleon, in an effort to induce the United States to reimpose the Embargo against Britain, announced that France would no longer interfere with American shipping. Madison announced that an embargo against Great Britain alone would automatically go into effect early in 1811 unless Britain renounced its restrictions on American shipping.

In time, this new, limited embargo persuaded England to repeal its blockade of Europe. But the repeal came too late to prevent war. In any case, naval policies were only part of the reason for tensions between Britain and the United States.

The "Indian Problem" and the British

Given the ruthlessness with which white settlers in North America had dislodged Indian tribes to make room for expanding settlement, it was hardly surprising that ever since the Revolution most Indians had continued to look to England for protection. The British in Canada, for their part, had relied on the Indians as partners in the lucrative fur trade. There had been relative peace in the Northwest for over a decade after Jay's Treaty and Anthony Wayne's victory over the tribes at Fallen Timbers in 1794. But the 1807 war crisis following the *Chesapeake-Leopard* incident revived the conflict between Indians and white settlers. Two important (and very different) men emerged to lead it: William Henry Harrison and Tecumseh.

Conflict between Settlers and Indians

The Virginia-born Harrison, already a veteran Indian fighter at age twenty-six, went to Washington as the congressional delegate from the Northwest Territory in 1799. An advocate of development in the western lands, he was largely responsible for the passage in 1800 of the so-called Harrison Land Law, which enabled white settlers to acquire farms from the public domain on much easier terms than before.

William Henry Harrison

In 1801, Jefferson appointed Harrison governor of Indiana Territory to administer the president's proposed solution to the "Indian problem." Jefferson offered the Indians a choice: they could convert themselves into settled farmers and become a part of white society, or they could migrate west of the Mississippi. In either case, they would have to give up their claims to their tribal lands in the Northwest.

Jefferson's Assimilation Proposal

Jefferson considered the assimilation policy a benign alternative to the continuing conflict between Indians and white settlers. But to the tribes, the new policy seemed far from benign, especially given the bludgeonlike efficiency with which Harrison set out to implement it. He used threats, bribes, trickery, and whatever other tactics he felt would help him. By 1807, the United States had extracted treaty rights to eastern Michigan, southern Indiana, and most of Illinois from reluctant tribal leaders.

Meanwhile, in the Southwest, white Americans were taking millions of acres from other tribes in Georgia, Tennessee, and Mississippi. The Indians wanted desperately to resist, but the separate tribes were helpless by themselves against the power of the United States. They might have accepted their fate passively but for the emergence of two new factors.

One factor was the policy of British authorities in Canada. After the *Chesapeake* incident, they began to expect an American invasion of Canada and took desperate measures for their own defense. Among those measures were efforts to renew friendship with the Indians.

Tecumseh and the Prophet

The second, and more important, factor intensifying the border conflict was the rise of two remarkable native leaders. One was Tenskwatawa, a charismatic religious leader and orator known as "the Prophet." He had experienced a mystical awakening in the process of recovering from alcoholism. Having freed himself from what he considered the evil effects of white culture, he began to speak to his people of the superior virtues of Indian civilization and the sinfulness and corruption of the white world. In the process, he inspired a religious revival that spread through numerous tribes and helped unite them. The Prophet's headquarters at the meeting of Tippecanoe Creek and the Wabash River (known as Prophetstown) became a sacred place for people of many tribes. Out of their common religious experiences, they began to consider joint military efforts as well.

The Prophet's brother Tecumseh—"the Shooting Star," chief of the Shawnees—emerged as the leader of these efforts. Tecumseh understood, as few other Indian leaders had, that only through united action could the tribes hope to resist the steady advance of white civilization. Beginning in 1809, he set out to unite all the tribes of the Mississippi Valley into what became known as the Tecumseh Confederacy. Together, he promised, they would halt white expansion, recover the whole Northwest, and make the Ohio River the boundary between the United States and Indian country. He maintained that Harrison and others, by negotiating treaties with individual tribes, had obtained no real title to land. The land belonged to all the tribes; none of them could rightfully cede any of it without the consent of the others. In 1811, Tecumseh left Prophetstown and traveled down the Mississippi to visit the tribes of the South and persuade them to join the alliance.

The Tecumseh Confederacy

During Tecumseh's absence, Governor Harrison saw a chance to destroy the growing influence of the two Indian leaders. With 1,000 soldiers he camped near Prophetstown, and on November 7, 1811, he provoked an armed conflict. Although the white forces suffered losses as heavy as those of the natives, Harrison drove off the Indians and burned the town.

Battle of Tippecanoe

The Battle of Tippecanoe (named for the creek near which it was fought) disillusioned many of the Prophet's followers, and Tecumseh returned to find the confederacy in disarray. But there were still warriors eager for combat, and by spring of 1812 they were active along the frontier, raiding white settlements and terrifying settlers.

The bloodshed along the western borders was largely a result of the Indians' own initiative, but Britain's agents in Canada had encouraged and helped to supply the uprising. To Harrison and most white residents of the regions, there seemed only one way to make the West safe for Americans: to drive the British out of Canada and annex that province to the United States.

Florida and War Fever

While white "frontiersmen" in the North demanded the conquest of Canada, those in the South looked to the acquisition of Spanish Florida. The territory was a continuing threat to whites in the southern United States. Slaves escaped across the Florida border; Indians in Florida launched frequent raids north. But white southerners also coveted Florida because through it ran rivers that could provide residents of the Southwest with access to valuable ports on the Gulf of Mexico.

Coveted Florida

In 1810, American settlers in West Florida (the area presently part of Mississippi and Louisiana) seized the Spanish fort at Baton Rouge and asked the federal government to annex the territory to the United States. President Madison happily agreed and then began planning to get the rest of Florida, too. The desire for Florida became yet another motivation for war with Britain. Spain was Britain's ally, and a war with England might provide an excuse for taking Spanish as well as British territory.

By 1812, therefore, war fever was raging on both the northern and southern borders of the United States. The demands of the residents of these areas found substantial support in Washington among a group of determined young congressmen who soon earned the name "War Hawks."

"War Hawks"

In the congressional elections of 1810, voters elected a large number of representatives of both parties eager for war with Britain. The most influential of them came from the new states in the West or from the backcountry of the old states in the South. Two of their leaders, both recently elected to the House of Representatives, were Henry Clay of Kentucky and John C. Calhoun of South Carolina, men of great intellect, magnetism, and ambition. Both were supporters of war with Great Britain.

Clay and Calhoun Call for War

Clay was elected Speaker of the House in 1811, and he appointed Calhoun to the crucial Committee on Foreign Affairs. Both men began agitating for the conquest of Canada. Madison still preferred peace but was losing control of Congress. On June 18, 1812, he approved a declaration of war against Britain.

THE WAR OF 1812

The British were not eager for an open conflict with the United States. Even after the Americans declared war, Britain largely ignored them for a time. But in the fall of 1812, Napoleon launched a catastrophic campaign against Russia that left his army in disarray. By late 1813, with the French empire on its way to final defeat, Britain was able to turn its military attention to America.

Battles with the Tribes

In the summer of 1812, American forces invaded Canada through Detroit. They soon had to retreat back to Detroit and in August surrendered the fort there. Other invasion efforts also failed. In the meantime, Fort Dearborn (later Chicago) fell before an Indian attack.

Things went only slightly better for the United States on the seas. At first, American frigates won some spectacular victories over British warships. But by 1813, the British navy was counterattacking effectively, driving the American frigates to cover and imposing a blockade on the United States.

Put-in Bay

The United States did, however, achieve significant early military successes on the Great Lakes. First, the Americans took command of Lake Ontario; this permitted them to raid and burn York (now Toronto), the capital of Canada. American forces then seized control of Lake Erie, mainly through the work of the young Oliver Hazard Perry, who engaged and dispersed a British fleet at Put-in Bay on September 10, 1813. This made possible, at last, a more successful invasion of Canada by way of Detroit. William Henry Harrison pushed up the river Thames into upper Canada and on October 5, 1813, won a victory notable for the death of Tecumseh, who was serving as a brigadier general in the British army. The Battle of the Thames resulted in no lasting occupation of Canada, but it weakened and disheartened the Indians of the Northwest.

In the meantime, another white military leader was striking an even harder blow at the Indians of the Southwest. The Creeks, supplied by the

Spaniards in Florida, had been attacking white settlers near the Florida border. Andrew Jackson, a wealthy Tennessee planter and a general in the state militia, set off in pursuit of the Creeks. On March 27, 1814, in the Battle of Horseshoe Bend, Jackson's men took terrible revenge on the Indians, slaughtering women and children along with warriors. The tribe agreed to cede most of its lands to the United States and retreated westward. The battle also won Jackson a commission as major general in the United States Army, and in that capacity he led his men farther south into Florida. On November 7, 1814, he seized the Spanish fort at Pensacola.

Battles with the British

But the victories over the tribes were not enough to win the war. After the surrender of Napoleon in 1814, England prepared to invade the United States. A British armada sailed up the Patuxent River from Chesapeake Bay and landed an army that marched to nearby Bladensburg, on the outskirts of Washington, where it dispersed a poorly trained force of American militiamen. On August 24, 1814, the British troops entered Washington and put the government to flight. Then they set fire to several public buildings, including the White House, in retaliation for the earlier American burning of the Canadian capital at York.

The British Invasion

Leaving Washington in partial ruins, the invading army proceeded up the bay toward Baltimore. But Baltimore, guarded by Fort McHenry, was prepared. To block the approaching fleet, the American garrison had sunk several ships in the Patapsco River (the entry to Baltimore's harbor), thus forcing the British to bombard the fort from a distance. Through the night of September 13, Francis Scott Key (a Washington lawyer on board one of the British ships) watched the bombardment. The next morning, "by the dawn's early light," he could see the flag on the fort still flying; he recorded his pride in the moment by writing a poem—"The Star-Spangled Banner." The British withdrew from Baltimore, and Key's words were soon set to the tune of an old English drinking song. (In 1931 "The Star-Spangled Banner" became the official national anthem.)

Meanwhile, American forces repelled another British invasion in northern New York; at the Battle of Plattsburgh, on September 11, 1814, they turned back a much more numerous British naval and land force. In the South, a formidable array of battle-hardened British veterans landed below New Orleans and prepared to advance north up the Mississippi. Awaiting the British was Andrew Jackson with a motley collection of Tennesseans, Kentuckians, Creoles, blacks, pirates, and regular army troops drawn up behind earthen breastworks. On January 8, 1815, the redcoats advanced on the American fortifications, but the exposed British forces were no match for Jackson's well-protected men. After the Americans had repulsed several waves of attackers, the British finally retreated, leaving behind 700 dead, 1,400 wounded,

Battle of New Orleans

THE BURNING OF WASHINGTON This dramatic engraving somewhat exaggerates the extent of the blazes in Washington when the British occupied the city in August 1814. But the invaders did set fire to the Capitol, the White House, and other public buildings in retaliation for the American burning of the Canadian capital at York. *(Bettmann/Corbis)*

and 500 prisoners. Jackson's losses: 8 killed, 13 wounded. Only later did news reach North America that the United States and Britain had signed a peace treaty several weeks before the Battle of New Orleans.

The Revolt of New England

With a few notable exceptions, the military efforts of the United States between 1812 and 1815 consisted of a series of failures. As a result, the American government faced increasing opposition as the contest dragged on. In New England, opposition both to the war and to the Republican government that was waging it was so extreme that some Federalists celebrated British victories. In Congress, in the meantime, the Republicans had continual trouble with the Federalist opposition, led by a young congressman from New Hampshire, Daniel Webster.

Federalist Opposition to War

By now the Federalists were very much in the minority in the country as a whole, but they were still the majority party in New England. Some of them began to dream of creating a separate nation in that region. Talk of secession reached a climax in the winter of 1814–1815.

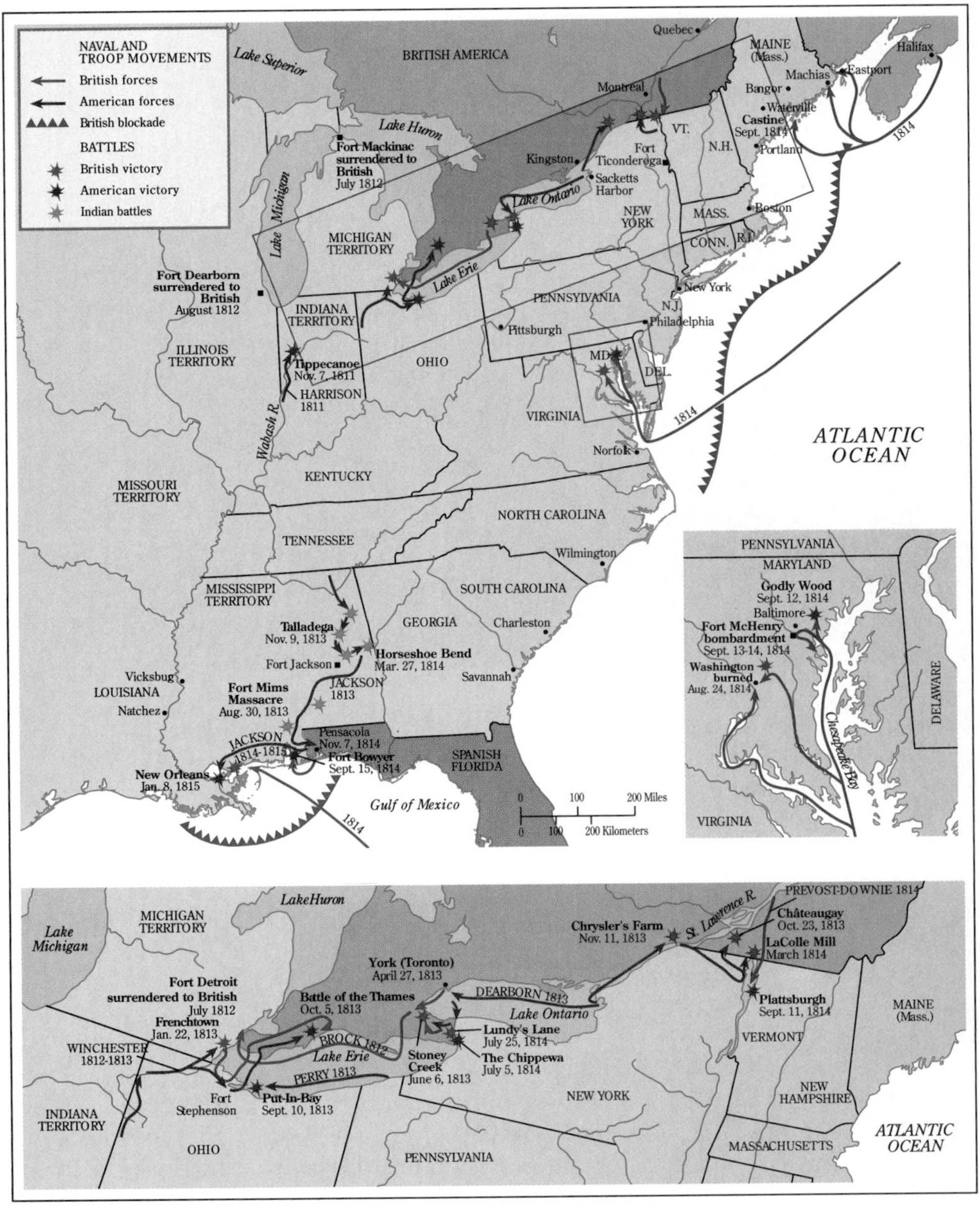

THE WAR OF 1812 These three maps illustrate the military maneuvers of the British and the Americans during the War of 1812. The large map at top shows all the theaters of the war, from New Orleans to southern Canada. The large detail at bottom shows the extended land and water battle along the Canadian border and in the Great Lakes. The small detail in the bottom right corner of the upper map shows the fighting around Washington and Baltimore. Note how in all these theaters, there are about the same number of British and American victories. ◆ *What brought this inconclusive war finally to an end?*

For an interactive version of this map go to www.mhhe.com/unfinishednation4ch7maps

The Hartford Convention

On December 15, 1814, delegates from the New England states met in Hartford, Connecticut, to discuss their grievances against the Madison administration. The would-be seceders at the Hartford Convention were outnumbered by a comparatively moderate majority. But while the convention's report only hinted at secession, it reasserted the right of nullification and proposed seven amendments to the Constitution—amendments designed to protect New England from the growing influence of the South and the West.

Because the war was going so badly, the New Englanders assumed that the Republicans would have to agree to their demands. Soon after the convention adjourned, however, the news of Jackson's victory at New Orleans reached the cities of the Northeast. A day or two later, reports of a peace treaty arrived from abroad. In the changed atmosphere these apparent triumphs produced, the Hartford Convention and the Federalist party came to seem futile, irrelevant, even treasonable.

The Peace Settlement

Treaty of Ghent

Serious negotiations between the United States and Britain began in August 1814, when American and British diplomats met in Ghent, Belgium. John Quincy Adams, Henry Clay, and Albert Gallatin led the American delegation. Although both sides began with extravagant demands, the final treaty did very little except end the fighting itself. The Americans gave up their demand for a British renunciation of impressment and for the cession of Canada to the United States. The British abandoned their call for creation of an Indian buffer state in the Northwest and made other, minor territorial concessions. The treaty was signed on Christmas Eve 1814.

Both sides had reason to accept this skimpy agreement. The British, exhausted and in debt from their prolonged conflict with Napoleon, were eager to settle the lesser dispute in North America. The Americans realized that with the defeat of Napoleon in Europe, the British would no longer have much incentive to interfere with American commerce.

Other settlements followed the Treaty of Ghent. A commercial treaty in 1815 gave Americans the right to trade freely with England and much of the British Empire. The Rush-Bagot agreement of 1817 provided for mutual disarmament on the Great Lakes; eventually (although not until 1872) the Canadian-American boundary became the longest "unguarded frontier" in the world.

Disastrous Consequences for the Indians

For the other parties to the War of 1812—the Indian tribes east of the Mississippi—the conflict proved another disastrous blow to the capacity of Indians to resist white expansion. Tecumseh was dead. The British were gone from the Northwest. The intertribal alliance that Tecumseh and the Prophet had forged was in disarray. The end of the war served to spur white movement westward, into land the Indians were less than ever able to defend.

CONCLUSION

Thomas Jefferson called his election to the presidency the "Revolution of 1800," and his supporters believed that his victory would bring a dramatic change in the character of the nation—a retreat from Hamilton's dreams of a powerful, developing nation and a return to an ideal of a simple agrarian republic.

But American society was changing rapidly, making it virtually impossible for the Jeffersonian dream to prevail. The nation's population was expanding and diversifying. Its cities were growing, and its commercial life was becoming ever more important. In 1803, Jefferson himself made one of the most important contributions to the growth of the United States: the Louisiana Purchase, which dramatically expanded the physical boundaries of the nation—and which began extending white settlement deeper into the continent. In the process, it greatly widened the battles between Europeans and Native Americans.

The growing national pride and commercial ambitions of the United States gradually created another serious conflict with Great Britain: the War of 1812, a war that was settled finally in 1814 on terms at least mildly favorable to the United States. By then, the bitter party rivalries that had characterized the first years of the republic had to some degree subsided, and the nation was poised to enter what became known, quite inaccurately, as the "Era of Good Feelings."

FOR FURTHER REFERENCE

Joseph J. Ellis, *American Sphinx: The Character of Thomas Jefferson* (1997) is a perceptive study of the man. Henry Adams, *History of the United States During the Administration of Jefferson and Adams*, 9 vols. (1889–1891) is one of the great literary achievements of early American historiography. Frank Bergon, ed., *The Journals of Lewis and Clark* (1989) is a concise abridgement of these fascinating accounts of their explorations. James Ronda, *Lewis and Clark Among the Indians* (1984) examines the exploration from a Native American perspective. Thomas C. Cochran, *Frontiers of Change: Early Industrialization in America* (1981) summarizes economic development in the early republic. Jeanne Boydston, *Home and Work: Housework, Wages, and the Ideology of Labor in the Early Republic* (1990) argues that the cultural status of women declined as the market revolution began to transform the American economy. Peter S. Onuf, *The Language of American Nationhood* (2000) examines nationalist rhetoric and ideas in the Jeffersonian era. Joyce Appleby, *Inheriting the Revolution: The First Generation of Americans* (2000) examines the adjustment of the revolutionary generation to the burdens of nationhood. Drew McCoy, *The Elusive Republic: Political Economy in Jeffersonian America* (1980) traces the Jeffersonian struggle to keep the United States free from European-style corruption and decay. Paul Finkleman, *Slavery and the Founders: Race and Liberty in the Age of Jefferson* (1996) considers the problem of slavery in the early Republic. Donald Hickey, *The War of 1812: A Forgotten Conflict* (1989) is an account of the war. Anthony F. C. Wallace, *Jefferson and the Indians: The Tragic Fate of the First Americans* (1999) is a critical study of the impact of Jefferson's policies on the tribes. J. C. A. Stagg, *Mr. Madison's War: Politics, Diplomacy, and Warfare in the Early American Republic, 1783–1830* (1983) argues that James Madison led the United States to war against Great Britain in order to preserve vital American commercial interests, but that he underestimated New England opposition to the war.

For quizzes, Internet resources, references to additional books and films, and more, consult this book's Online Learning Center site at www.mhhe.com/unfinishednation4.

***FOURTH OF JULY PICNIC AT WEYMOUTH LANDING* (C. 1845), BY SUSAN MERRETT** Celebrations of Independence Day, like this one in eastern Massachusetts, became major festive events throughout the United States in the early nineteenth century, a sign of rising American nationalism. *(Susan Torrey Merritt, American, 1826–1879,* Anti-Slavery Picnic at Weymouth Landing, Massachusetts, *c. 1845, watercolor, gouache, and collage on paper, 74.9 × 100 cm, Gift of Elizabeth R. Vaughan, 1950.1846 image © The Art Institute of Chicago)*

TIME LINE

	1815	1816	1818	1819	
	U.S. takes western lands from Indians	Second Bank of U.S. Monroe elected president	Seminole War ends	Panic and depression *Dartmouth College* v. *Woodward; McCulloch* v. *Maryland*	

CHAPTER EIGHT

VARIETIES OF AMERICAN NATIONALISM

Stabilizing Economic Growth
Expanding Westward
The "Era of Good Feelings"
Sectionalism and Nationalism
The Revival of Opposition

Like a "fire bell in the night," as Thomas Jefferson put it, the issue of slavery arose after the War of 1812 to threaten the unity of the nation. The debate began when the territory of Missouri applied for admission to the Union, raising the question of whether it would be a free or a slaveholding state. But the larger issue was whether the vast new western regions of the United States would ultimately move into the orbit of the North or the South.

The Missouri crisis was significant because it was a sign of the sectional crises to come. But at the time, it was also significant because it stood in such sharp contrast to the rising American nationalism of the years following the war. Whatever forces might be working to pull the nation apart, stronger ones were acting for the moment to draw it together.

STABILIZING ECONOMIC GROWTH

The end of the War of 1812 allowed the United States to resume its economic growth and territorial expansion. A vigorous postwar boom led to a disastrous bust in 1819. Brief though it was, the collapse was evidence that the United States continued to lack some of the basic institutions necessary to sustain long-term growth.

1820	1823	1824	1828
Missouri Compromise	Monroe Doctrine	John Quincy Adams elected	Tariff of abominations
Monroe reelected			Jackson elected president

The Government and Economic Growth

Postwar Economic Problems

The War of 1812 produced chaos in shipping and banking, and it exposed dramatically the inadequacy of the existing transportation and financial systems. The aftermath of the war, therefore, saw the emergence of a series of political issues connected with national economic development.

The wartime experience underlined the need for another national bank. After the expiration of the first Bank's charter, a large number of state banks had issued vast quantities of bank notes, creating a confusing variety of currency of widely differing value. It was difficult to tell what any bank note was really worth, and counterfeiting was easy. In response to these problems, Congress chartered a second Bank of the United States in 1816, much like its predecessor of 1791 but with more capital. The national bank could not forbid state banks from issuing notes, but its size and power enabled it to compel the state banks to issue only sound notes or risk being forced out of business.

Second Bank of the United States

Congress also acted to promote manufacturing, which the war (by cutting off imports) had already greatly stimulated. The American textile industry had experienced a particularly dramatic growth. Between 1807 and 1815, the total number of cotton spindles in the country increased more than fifteenfold, from 8,000 to 130,000. Until 1814, the textile factories—most of them in New England—produced only yarn and thread; families operating hand looms at home did the actual weaving of cloth. Then the Boston merchant Francis Cabot Lowell, after examining textile machinery in England, developed a power loom better than its English counterpart. In 1813, in Waltham, Massachusetts, Lowell founded the first mill in America to carry on the processes of spinning and weaving under a single roof.

But the end of the war suddenly dimmed the prospects for American industry. British ships swarmed into American ports and unloaded cargoes of manufactured goods, many priced below cost. In 1816, protectionists in Congress passed a tariff law that effectively limited competition from abroad on a wide range of items, including cotton cloth, despite objections from agricultural interests, who stood to pay higher prices for manufactured goods.

The Protective Tariff

Transportation

Inadequate Transportation System

The nation's most pressing economic need was for improvements in its transportation system. An old debate resumed: Should the federal government help to finance roads and other "internal improvements"? The idea of using government funds to finance road building was not a new one. When Ohio entered the Union in 1803, the federal government agreed that part of the proceeds from the sale of public lands there should finance

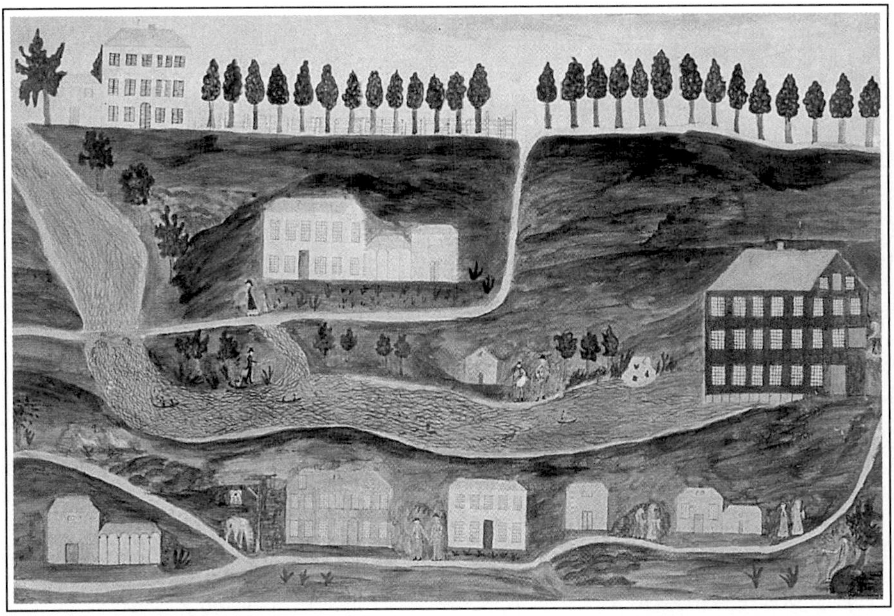

AN EARLY MILL IN NEW ENGLAND This early folk painting of about 1814 shows the small town of East Chelmford, Massachusetts—still primarily agrarian, with its rural houses, open fields, and grazing livestock, but with a small textile mill already operating along the stream, at right. A little more than a decade later, the town had been transformed into a major manufacturing center and renamed for the family that owned the mills: Lowell. (Part of the Town of Chelmsford by Miss Warren. *Abby Aldrich Rockefeller Folk Art Center, Williamsburg, Virginia)*

road construction. And in 1807, Congress enacted a law proposed by the Jefferson administration that permitted using revenues from Ohio land sales to finance a National Road from the Potomac River to the Ohio. By 1818, the highway ran as far as Wheeling, Virginia, on the Ohio River; and the Lancaster Pike, financed in part by the state of Pennsylvania, extended westward to Pittsburgh.

At the same time, steam-powered shipping was expanding rapidly. By 1816, river steamers were beginning to journey up and down the Mississippi to the Ohio River, and up the Ohio as far as Pittsburgh. Steamboats were soon carrying more cargo on the Mississippi than all the earlier forms of river transport—flatboats, barges, and others—combined. They stimulated the agricultural economy of the West and the South by providing access to markets at greatly reduced cost, and they enabled eastern manufacturers to send their finished goods west much more readily.

Nevertheless, serious gaps in the nation's transportation network remained, as experience during the War of 1812 had shown. Once the British blockade had cut off Atlantic shipping, the coastal roads had become choked by the unaccustomed volume of north-south traffic. Congress passed a bill introduced by Representative John C. Calhoun that allowed the

Federally Funded Improvements Debated

THE *CLERMONT'S* ENGINE Robert Fulton's *Clermont* became the first steamboat to travel from New York to Albany (in 32 hours) in 1809. Its great paddle was driven by a powerful piston, which was driven in turn by power generated by a steam boiler. This is Fulton's own drawing of the engine system. *(© The New-York Historical Society)*

use of government funds to finance internal improvements, but Madison, on his last day in office, vetoed it. He supported the purpose of the bill, he explained, but he believed that Congress lacked authority to fund the improvements without a constitutional amendment. For a time, state governments and private enterprise were left on their own to build the transportation network necessary for the growing American economy.

EXPANDING WESTWARD

One reason for the growing interest in internal improvements was the dramatic surge in westward expansion in the years following the War of 1812. By the time of the census of 1820, white settlers had pushed well beyond the Mississippi River, and the population of the western regions was increasing more rapidly than that of the nation as a whole.

The Great Migration

The westward movement of the white American population was one of the most important developments of the century. There were several major reasons for this expansion.

Reasons for Westward Expansion

One reason was population growth, which drove many white Americans out of the East. Between 1800 and 1820, the population nearly doubled—from 5.3 million to 9.6 million. Most Americans were still farmers, and the agricultural lands of the East were by now largely occupied or exhausted. In the South, the spread of the plantation system limited opportunities for new settlers. Another reason was that the West itself was becoming increasingly attractive to white settlers. Land there was much more plentiful than it was in the East. And in the aftermath of the War of 1812, the federal government continued its policy of pushing the Indian tribes farther and farther west. Migrants from throughout the East flocked in increasing numbers to what was then known as the Old Northwest (now part of the Midwest), most of them via the Ohio and Monongahela Rivers. Once on the Ohio, most floated downstream on flatboats, then left the river (often at Cincinnati) and traveled overland with wagons, handcarts, packhorses, cattle, and hogs.

White Settlers in the Old Northwest

Having arrived at their destination, most settlers built lean-tos or cabins and then hewed clearings out of the forest and planted crops of corn to supplement the wild game they caught and the domestic animals they had brought with them. It was a rough and lonely existence. Men, women, and children worked side by side in the fields—and at times had virtually no contact for weeks or months with anyone outside their own families.

Life in the western territories was not, however, entirely solitary or individualistic. Migrants often journeyed westward in groups and built new communities with schools, churches, and stores. The labor shortage in the interior led neighbors to develop systems of mutual aid. They gathered periodically to raise a barn, clear land, or harvest crops.

A Mobile Society

Another common feature of life in the Northwest was mobility. Individuals and families were constantly on the move, settling for a few years in one place and then selling their land (often at a significant profit) and resettling somewhere else. When new areas for settlement opened farther to the west, it was often the people already on the western edges of white settlement—rather than those who remained in the East—who flocked to them first.

The Plantation System in the Old Southwest

In the Old Southwest (now generally known as the Deep South), the new agricultural economy emerged along different lines. The market for cotton continued to grow, and the Southwest contained a broad zone where cotton could thrive. That zone included what was to become known as the Black Belt of central Alabama and Mississippi, a vast prairie with a dark, productive soil.

Cotton and the Expansion of Slavery

The first arrivals in the uncultivated regions of the Old Southwest were usually small farmers who made rough clearings in the forest. But wealthier planters soon followed. They bought up the cleared or partially cleared land, and the original settlers moved farther west and started over again. Success in the wilderness was by no means assured, even for the wealthiest settlers. Many settlers managed to do little more than subsist in their new environment, and others experienced utter ruin. But some planters soon expanded small clearings into vast cotton fields. They replaced the cabins of the early pioneers with more sumptuous log dwellings and ultimately with imposing mansions. They also built up large slave work forces.

New States in the West

The rapid growth of the Old Northwest and Southwest resulted in the admission of four new states to the Union: Indiana in 1816, Mississippi in 1817, Illinois in 1818, and Alabama in 1819.

Trade and Trapping in the Far West

Not many Anglo-Americans yet knew much about or were much interested in the far western areas of the continent. But a significant trade nevertheless began to develop between these western regions and the United States early in the nineteenth century, and it grew steadily for decades.

Mexico, which continued to control Texas, California, and much of the rest of the far Southwest, won its independence from Spain in 1821. Almost immediately, it opened its northern territories to trade with the United States. American traders poured into the region. Merchants from the United States quickly displaced Indian and Mexican traders. In New Mexico, for example, the Missouri trader William Becknell began in 1821 to offer American manufactured goods for sale, priced considerably below the inferior Mexican goods that had dominated the market in the past. Mexico effectively lost its markets in its own colony as a steady traffic of commercial wagon trains began moving back and forth along the Santa Fe Trail between Missouri and New Mexico.

Astor's American Fur Company

Fur traders created a wholly new kind of commerce. After the War of 1812, John Jacob Astor's American Fur Company and others extended their operations from the Great Lakes area westward to the Rockies. At first, fur traders did most of their business by purchasing pelts from the Indi-

THE RENDEZVOUS The annual rendezvous of fur trappers and traders was a major event in the lives of the lonely men who made their livelihoods gathering furs. It was also a gathering of representatives of the many cultures that mingled in the Far West, among them Anglo-Americans, French Canadians, Indians, and Hispanics. *(Denver Public Library)*

ans. But increasingly, white trappers entered the region and joined the Iroquois and other Indians in pursuit of beaver and other furs.

The trappers, or "mountain men," who began trading in the Far West were small in number. But they developed important relationships with the existing residents of the West—Indian and Mexican—and altered the character of society there. White trappers were mostly young, single men. Perhaps unsurprisingly, many of them entered into sexual relationships with Indian and Mexican women. They also recruited the women as helpers in the difficult work of preparing furs and skins for trading. Perhaps two-thirds of the white trappers married Indian or Hispanic women.

Rocky Mountain Fur Company

In 1822, Andrew and William Ashley founded the Rocky Mountain Fur Company and recruited white trappers to move permanently into the Rockies. The Ashleys dispatched supplies annually to their trappers in exchange for furs and skins. The arrival of the supply train became the occasion for a gathering of scores of mountain men, some of whom lived much of the year in considerable isolation.

But however isolated their daily lives, these mountain men were closely bound up with the expanding market economy. Some were employees of the Rocky Mountain Fur Company, earning a salary in return for providing a steady supply of furs. Others trapped on their own and simply sold their furs for cash, but they too depended on merchants from the East for their livelihoods. Whatever the character of the transactions, the bulk of the profits from the trade flowed to the merchants, not the trappers.

Eastern Images of the West

Americans in the East were only dimly aware of the world of the trappers, and the trappers themselves did little to enlighten others. More important in increasing eastern awareness of the West were explorers, many of them dispatched by the United States government. In 1819 and 1820, with instructions from the War Department to find the source of the Red River, Stephen H. Long led nineteen soldiers on a journey up the Platte and South Platte Rivers through what is now Nebraska and eastern Colorado (where he discovered the peak that would be named for him), and then returned eastward along the Arkansas River through what is now Kansas. He failed to find the headwaters of the Red River. But he wrote an influential report on his trip, which echoed the dismissive conclusions of Zebulon Pike fifteen years before. The region "between the Missouri River and the Rocky Mountains," Long wrote, "is almost wholly unfit for cultivation, and of course uninhabitable by a people depending upon agriculture for their subsistence." On the published map of his expedition, he labeled the Great Plains the "Great American Desert."

Exploring the West

THE "ERA OF GOOD FEELINGS"

The expansion of the economy, the growth of white settlement and trade in the West, the creation of new states—all reflected the rising spirit of nationalism that was permeating the United States in the years following the War of 1812. That spirit found reflection for a time as well in the character of national politics.

The End of the First Party System

Ever since 1800, the presidency seemed to have been the special possession of Virginians. After two terms in office Jefferson chose his secretary of state, James Madison of Virginia, to succeed him, and after two more terms, Madison secured the presidential nomination for his secretary of state, James Monroe, also of Virginia. Many in the North were expressing impatience with the so-called Virginia Dynasty, but the Republicans had no difficulty electing their candidate in 1816. Monroe received 183 ballots in the electoral college; his Federalist opponent, Rufus King of New York, received only 34.

The Virginia Dynasty

Monroe was sixty-one years old when he became president. He entered office under what seemed to be remarkably favorable circumstances. With the decline of the Federalists, his party faced no serious opposition. With the conclusion of the War of 1812, the nation faced no important international threats. Some American politicians had dreamed since the first days of the republic of a time in which partisan divisions and factional

THE INAUGURATION OF JAMES MONROE, 1816 The ruins of part of the United States Capitol, burned by the British two years earlier late in the War of 1812, provided a bleak backdrop for James Monroe's first inauguration in 1816. *(Bettmann/Corbis)*

disputes might come to an end. In the prosperous postwar years, Monroe attempted to use his office to realize that dream.

He made that clear, above all, in the selection of his cabinet. For secretary of state, he chose the New Englander and former Federalist John Quincy Adams. Jefferson, Madison, and Monroe had all served as secretary of state before becoming president; Adams, therefore, immediately became the heir apparent, suggesting that the "Virginia Dynasty" would soon come to an end. Speaker of the House Henry Clay declined an offer to be secretary of war, so Monroe named John C. Calhoun instead.

Monroe's Good-will Tour

Soon after his inauguration, Monroe made a good-will tour through the country. In New England, so recently the scene of rabid Federalist discontent, he was greeted everywhere with enthusiastic demonstrations. The *Columbian Centinel*, a Federalist newspaper in Boston, observed that an "era of good feelings" had arrived. And on the surface, at least, the years of Monroe's presidency did appear to be an "era of good feelings." In 1820, Monroe was reelected without opposition. For all practical purposes, the Federalist Party had now ceased to exist.

John Quincy Adams and Florida

Like his father, the second president of the United States, John Quincy Adams had spent much of his life in diplomatic service. And even before becoming secretary of state, he had become one of the great diplomats in American history. He was also a committed nationalist, and he considered his most important task to be the promotion of American expansion.

SEMINOLE DANCE This 1838 drawing by a U.S. military officer portrays a dance by Seminole Indians near Fort Butler in Florida. It was made in the midst of the prolonged Second Seminole War, which ended in 1842 with the removal of most of the tribe from Florida to reservations west of the Mississippi. *(The Huntington Library, San Marino, California)*

His first challenge was Florida. The United States had already annexed West Florida, but that claim was in dispute. Most Americans, moreover, still believed the nation should gain possession of the entire peninsula. In 1817, Adams began negotiations with the Spanish minister, Luis de Onís, in hopes of resolving the dispute and gaining the entire territory for the United States.

In the meantime, however, events were taking their own course in Florida itself. Andrew Jackson, now in command of American troops along the Florida frontier, had orders from Secretary of War Calhoun to "adopt the necessary measures" to stop continuing raids on American territory by Seminole Indians south of the border. Jackson used those orders as an excuse to invade Florida and seize the Spanish forts at St. Marks and Pensacola. The operation became known as the Seminole War.

The Seminole War

Instead of condemning Jackson's raid, Adams urged the government to assume responsibility for it. The United States, he told the Spanish, had the right under international law to defend itself against threats from across its borders. Since Spain was unwilling or unable to curb those threats, America had simply done what was necessary. Jackson's raid demonstrated to the Spanish that the United States could easily take Florida by force. Adams implied that the nation might consider doing so.

Onís realized, therefore, that he had little choice but to come to terms with the Americans. Under the provisions of the Adams-Onís Treaty of 1819, Spain ceded all of Florida to the United States and gave up its claim to territory north of the 42nd parallel in the Pacific Northwest. In return, the American government gave up its claims to Texas.

Adams-Onís Treaty

The Panic of 1819

But the Monroe administration had little time to revel in its diplomatic successes, for the nation was falling victim to a serious economic crisis: the Panic of 1819. It followed a period of high foreign demand for American farm goods and thus of exceptionally high prices for American farmers. The rising prices for farm goods had stimulated a land boom in the western United States. Fueled by speculative investments, land prices soared.

The availability of easy credit to settlers and speculators—from the government (under the land acts of 1800 and 1804), from state banks and wildcat banks, even for a time from the rechartered Bank of the United States—fueled the land boom. Beginning in 1819, however, new management at the national bank began tightening credit, calling in loans, and foreclosing mortgages. This precipitated a series of failures by state banks, and the result was a financial panic. Six years of depression followed.

Tight Credit

Some Americans saw the Panic of 1819 and the widespread distress that followed as a warning that rapid economic growth and territorial expansion would destabilize the nation. But by 1820 most Americans were irrevocably committed to the idea of growth and expansion.

SECTIONALISM AND NATIONALISM

For a brief but alarming moment in 1819–1820, the increasing differences between the North and the South threatened the unity of the United States—until the Missouri Compromise averted a sectional crisis for a time. The forces of nationalism continued to assert themselves, and the federal government began to assume the role of promoter of economic growth.

The Missouri Compromise

When Missouri applied for admission to the Union as a state in 1819, slavery was already well established there. Even so, Representative James Tallmadge, Jr. of New York proposed an amendment to the Missouri statehood bill that would prohibit the further introduction of slaves into Missouri and provide for

Tallmadge Amendment

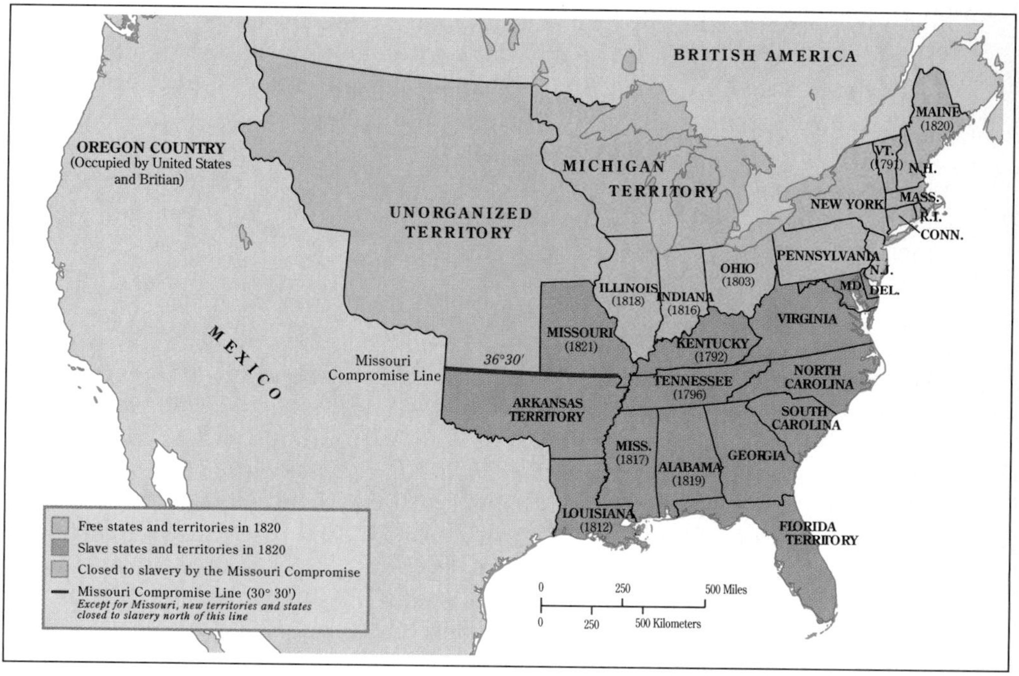

THE MISSOURI COMPROMISE, 1820 This map illustrates the way in which the Missouri Compromise proposed to settle the controversy over slavery in the new western territories of the United States. The compromise rested on the virtually simultaneous admission of Missouri and Maine to the Union, one a free state and the other a slave one. Note the red line extending beyond the southern border of Missouri, which in theory established a permanent boundary between areas in which slavery could be established and areas where it could not be. ◆ *What precipitated the Missouri Compromise?*

For an interactive version of this map go to www.mhhe.com/unfinishednation4ch8maps

the gradual emancipation of those already there. The Tallmadge Amendment provoked a controversy that was to rage for the next two years.

Since the beginning of the republic, new states had come into the Union more or less in pairs, one from the North, another from the South. In 1819, there were eleven free states and eleven slave states; the admission of Missouri would upset that balance. Hence the controversy over slavery and freedom in Missouri.

Crisis Averted

Complicating the Missouri question was the application of Maine (previously the northern part of Massachusetts) for admission as a new (and free) state. Speaker of the House Henry Clay informed northern members that if they blocked Missouri from entering the Union as a slave state, southerners would block the admission of Maine. But Maine ultimately offered a way out of the impasse, as the Senate agreed to combine the Maine and Missouri proposals into a single bill. Maine would be admitted as a free state, Missouri as a slave state. Then Senator Jesse B. Thomas of Illinois proposed an amendment prohibiting slavery in the rest of the Louisiana Purchase territory north of the southern boundary of Missouri (the 36°30′ parallel). The Senate adopted the Thomas Amendment, and Speaker Clay, with great difficulty, guided the amended Maine-Missouri bill through the House.

Nationalists in both North and South hailed this settlement—which became known as the Missouri Compromise—as a happy resolution of a danger to the Union. But the debate over it had revealed a strong undercurrent of sectionalism.

Marshall and the Court

John Marshall served as chief justice of the United States from 1801 to 1835. More than anyone but the framers themselves, he molded the development of the Constitution: strengthening the judicial branch at the expense of the executive and legislative branches, increasing the power of the federal government at the expense of the states, and advancing the interests of the propertied and commercial classes.

Committed to promoting commerce, the Marshall Court staunchly defended the inviolability of contracts. In *Fletcher* v. *Peck* (1810), which arose out of a series of notorious land frauds in Georgia, the Court had to decide whether the Georgia legislature of 1796 could repeal the act of the previous legislature granting lands under shady circumstances to the Yazoo Land Companies. In a unanimous decision, Marshall held that a land grant was a valid contract and could not be repealed even if corruption was involved.

Dartmouth College v. Woodward

Dartmouth College v. *Woodward* (1819) further expanded the meaning of the contract clause of the Constitution. Having gained control of the New Hampshire state government, Republicans tried to revise Dartmouth College's charter to convert the private college into a state university. Daniel Webster argued the college's case. The Dartmouth charter, he insisted, was a contract, protected by the same doctrine that the Court had already upheld in *Fletcher* v. *Peck.* The Court ruled for Dartmouth, proclaiming that corporation charters such as the one the colonial legislature had granted the college were contracts and thus inviolable. The decision placed important restrictions on the ability of state governments to control corporations.

In overturning the act of the legislature and the decisions of the New Hampshire courts, the justices also implicitly claimed for themselves the right to override the decisions of state courts. But advocates of states' rights, especially in the South, continued to challenge its right to do so. In *Cohens* v. *Virginia* (1821), Marshall explicitly affirmed the constitutionality of federal review of state court decisions. The states had given up part of their sovereignty in ratifying the Constitution, he explained, and their courts must submit to federal jurisdiction.

JOHN MARSHALL The imposing figure in this early photograph is John Marshall, the most important chief justice of the Supreme Court in American history. A former secretary of state, Marshall served as chief justice from 1801 until his death in 1835 at the age of 80. Such was the power of his intellect and personality that he dominated his fellow justices throughout that period, regardless of their previous party affiliations or legal ideologies. Marshall established the independence of the Court, gave it a reputation for nonpartisan integrity, and established its powers, which were only vaguely described by the Constitution. *(The National Archives and Records Administration)*

"Implied Powers" Confirmed Meanwhile, in *McCulloch* v. *Maryland* (1819), Marshall confirmed the "implied powers" of Congress by upholding the constitutionality of the Bank of the United States. The Bank had become so unpopular in the South and the West that several of the states tried to drive branches out of business. This case presented two constitutional questions to the Supreme Court: Could Congress charter a bank? And if so, could individual states ban it or tax it? Daniel Webster, one of the Bank's attorneys, argued that establishing such an institution came within the "necessary and proper" clause of the Constitution and that the power

to tax involved a "power to destroy." If the states could tax the Bank at all, they could tax it to death. Marshall adopted Webster's words in deciding for the Bank.

In the case of *Gibbons* v. *Ogden* (1824), the Court strengthened Congress's power to regulate interstate commerce. The state of New York had granted the steamboat company of Robert Fulton and Robert Livingston the exclusive right to carry passengers on the Hudson River to New York City. Fulton and Livingston then gave Aaron Ogden the business of carrying passengers across the river between New York and New Jersey. But Thomas Gibbons, with a license granted under an act of Congress, began competing with Ogden for the ferry traffic. Ogden brought suit against him and won in the New York courts. Gibbons appealed to the Supreme Court. The most important question facing the justices was whether Congress's power to give Gibbons a license to operate his ferry superseded the state of New York's power to grant Ogden a monopoly. Marshall claimed that the power of Congress to regulate interstate commerce (which, he said, included navigation) was "complete in itself" and might be "exercised to its utmost extent." Ogden's state-granted monopoly, therefore, was void.

Federal Primacy Established

The decisions of the Marshall Court established the primacy of the federal government over the states in regulating the economy and opened the way for an increased federal role in promoting economic growth. They protected corporations and other private economic institutions from local government interference. They were, in short, highly nationalistic decisions.

The Court and the Tribes

The nationalist inclinations of the Marshall Court were visible as well in a series of decisions concerning the legal status of Indian tribes within the United States. But these decisions did not simply affirm the supremacy of the United States; they also carved out a distinctive position for Native Americans within the constitutional structure.

The first of the crucial Indian decisions was in the case of *Johnson* v. *McIntosh* (1823). Leaders of the Illinois and Pinakeshaw tribes had sold parcels of their land to a group of white settlers (including Johnson) but had later signed a treaty with the federal government ceding territory that included those same parcels to the United States. The government proceeded to grant homestead rights to new white settlers (among them McIntosh) on the land claimed by Johnson. The Court was asked to decide which claim had precedence. Marshall's ruling, not surprisingly, favored the United States. But in explaining it, he offered a preliminary definition of the place of Indians within the nation. The tribes had a basic right to their tribal lands, he said, that preceded all other American law. Individual American citizens could not buy or take land from the tribes; only the federal government—the supreme authority—could do that.

Worcester v. Georgia

Even more important was the Court's 1832 decision in *Worcester* v. *Georgia*, in which the Court invalidated a Georgia law that attempted to regulate access by U.S. citizens to Cherokee country. Only the federal government could do that, Marshall claimed. The tribes, he explained, were sovereign entities in much the same way Georgia was a sovereign entity—"distinct political communities, having territorial boundaries within which their authority is exclusive." In defending the power of the federal government, he was also affirming, indeed expanding, the rights of the tribes to remain free from the authority of state governments.

The Marshall decisions, therefore, did what the Constitution itself had not done: they defined a place for Indian tribes within the American political system. The tribes had basic property rights. They were sovereign entities not subject to the authority of state governments. But the federal government, like a "guardian" governing its "ward," had ultimate authority over tribal affairs.

Tribal Rights Affirmed

The Latin American Revolution and the Monroe Doctrine

Just as the Supreme Court was asserting American nationalism in the shaping of the country's economic life, so the Monroe administration was asserting nationalism in foreign policy. As always, American diplomacy was principally concerned with Europe. But in the 1820s, dealing with Europe forced the United States to develop a policy toward Latin America.

Americans looking southward in the years following the War of 1812 beheld a gigantic spectacle: the Spanish Empire in its death throes and a whole continent in revolt. Already the United States had developed a profitable trade with Latin America. Many believed the success of the anti-Spanish revolutions would further strengthen America's position in the region.

In 1815, the United States proclaimed neutrality in the wars between Spain and its rebellious colonies. But the United States sold ships and supplies to the revolutionaries, a clear indication that it was not genuinely neutral but was trying to help the insurgents. Finally, in 1822, President Monroe established diplomatic relations with five new nations—La Plata (later Argentina), Chile, Peru, Colombia, and Mexico—making the United States the first country to recognize them.

In 1823, Monroe went further and announced a policy that would ultimately be known (beginning some thirty years later) as the "Monroe Doctrine," even though it was primarily the work of John Quincy Adams. "The American continents," Monroe declared, ". . . are henceforth not to be considered as subjects for future colonization by any European powers." The United States would consider any foreign challenge to the sovereignty of existing American nations an unfriendly act. At the same time, he proclaimed,

The "Monroe Doctrine"

"Our policy in regard to Europe . . . is not to interfere in the internal concerns of any of its powers."

The Monroe Doctrine emerged directly out of America's relations with Europe in the 1820s. Many Americans feared that Spain's European allies (notably France) would assist Spain in an effort to retake its lost empire. Even more troubling was the fear that Great Britain had designs on Cuba. Monroe and Adams wanted to keep Cuba in Spanish hands until it fell to the Americans.

The Monroe Doctrine had few immediate effects, but it was important as an expression of the growing spirit of nationalism in the United States in the 1820s. And it established the idea of the United States as the dominant power in the Western Hemisphere.

THE REVIVAL OF OPPOSITION

Renewed Partisan Divisions

After 1816, the Federalist Party offered no presidential candidate and soon ceased to exist as a national political force. The Republican Party was the only organized force in national politics. By the late 1820s, however, partisan divisions were emerging once again. In some respects, the division mirrored the schism that had produced the first party system in the 1790s. The Republicans had in many ways come to resemble the early Federalist regimes in their promotion of economic growth and centralization. And the opposition objected to the federal government's expanding role in the economy. There was, however, a crucial difference. At the beginning of the century, the opponents of centralization had also often been opponents of economic growth. Now, in the 1820s, the controversy involved not *whether* but *how* the nation should continue to expand.

The "Corrupt Bargain"

"King Caucus" Overthrown

Until 1820, presidential candidates were nominated by caucuses of the two parties in Congress. But in 1824, "King Caucus" was overthrown. The Republican caucus nominated William H. Crawford of Georgia, the favorite of the extreme states' rights faction of the party. But other candidates received nominations from state legislatures and won endorsements from irregular mass meetings throughout the country.

One of them was Secretary of State John Quincy Adams. But he was a man of cold and forbidding manners, with little popular appeal. Another contender was Henry Clay, the Speaker of the House. He had a devoted personal following and a definite and coherent program: the "American System," which proposed creating a great home market for factory and farm producers by raising the protective tariff, strengthening the national bank, and financing internal improvements. Andrew Jackson, the fourth major candidate, had no significant political record—even though he was a new member of the United States Senate. But he was a military hero and had the help of shrewd political allies from his home state of Tennessee.

Jackson received more popular and electoral votes than any other candidate, but not a majority. The Twelfth Amendment to the Constitution (passed in the aftermath of the contested 1800 election) required the House of Representatives to choose among the three candidates with the largest numbers of electoral votes. Crawford was seriously ill. Clay was out of the running, but he was in a strong position to influence the result. Jackson was Clay's most dangerous political rival in the West, so Clay supported Adams, in part because Adams was an ardent nationalist and a likely supporter of the American System. With Clay's endorsement, Adams won election in the House.

Disputed Election

The Second President Adams

The Jacksonians believed their large popular and electoral pluralities entitled their candidate to the presidency, and they were enraged when he lost. But they grew angrier still when Adams named Clay his secretary of state. The State Department was the well-established route to the presidency, and Adams thus appeared to be naming Clay as his own successor. The outrage the Jacksonians expressed at what they called a "corrupt bargain" haunted Adams throughout his presidency.

Adams proposed an ambitiously nationalist program reminiscent of Clay's American System, but Jacksonians in Congress blocked most of it. Adams also experienced diplomatic frustrations. He appointed delegates to an international conference that the Venezuelan liberator, Simón Bolívar, had called in Panama in 1826. But Haiti was one of the participating nations, and southerners in Congress opposed the idea of white Americans mingling with the black delegates. Congress delayed approving the Panama mission so long that the American delegation did not arrive until after the conference was over.

Diplomatic Frustrations

Even more damaging to the administration was its support for a new tariff on imported goods in 1828. This measure originated with the demands of Massachusetts and Rhode Island woolen manufacturers. But to win support from middle and western states, the administration had to accept duties on other items. In the process, it antagonized the original New England supporters of the bill; the benefits of protecting their manufactured goods from foreign competition now had to be weighed against the prospects of having to pay more for raw materials. Adams signed the bill, earning the animosity of southerners, who cursed it as the "tariff of abominations."

The "Tariff of Abominations"

Jackson Triumphant

By the time of the 1828 presidential election, a new two-party system had begun to emerge. On one side stood the supporters of John Quincy Adams, who called themselves the National Republicans and who supported the economic nationalism of the preceding years. Opposing them were the followers of Andrew Jackson, who took the name Democratic Republicans. Adams attracted the support of most of the remaining Federalists; Jackson appealed to a broad coalition that opposed the "economic aristocracy."

But issues seemed to count for little in the end, as the campaign degenerated into a war of personal invective. The Jacksonians charged that Adams as president had been guilty of gross waste and extravagance. Adams's supporters hurled even worse accusations at Jackson. They called him a murderer and distributed a "coffin handbill," which listed, within coffin-shaped outlines, the names of militiamen whom Jackson was said to have shot in cold blood during the War of 1812. (The men had been deserters who were legally executed after sentence by a court-martial.) And they called his wife a bigamist. Jackson had married his beloved Rachel at a time when the pair incorrectly believed her first husband had divorced her. (When Jackson's wife first read of the accusations against her shortly after the election, she collapsed, and a few weeks later, died.)

Jackson Victorious

Jackson's victory was decisive, but sectional. Adams swept virtually all of New England and showed significant strength in the mid-Atlantic region. Nevertheless, the Jacksonians considered their victory as complete and as important as Jefferson's in 1800. Once again, the forces of privilege had been driven from Washington. Once again, a champion of democracy would occupy the White House. America had entered, some Jacksonians claimed, a new era of democracy, the "era of the common man."

CONCLUSION

In the aftermath of the War of 1812, a vigorous nationalism came increasingly to characterize the political and popular culture of the United States. In all regions of the country, white men and women celebrated the achievements of the early leaders of the republic, the genius of the Constitution, and the success of the nation in withstanding serious challenges both from without and within. Party divisions faded.

But the broad nationalism of the so-called era of good feelings disguised some deep divisions. Indeed, the character of American nationalism differed substantially from one region, and one group, to another.

Battles continued between those who favored a strong central government committed to advancing the economic development of the nation and those who wanted a decentralization of power to open opportunity to more people. Battles continued as well over the role of slavery in American life—and in particular over the place of slavery in the new western territories. The Missouri Compromise of 1820 postponed the day of reckoning on that issue—but only for a time.

FOR FURTHER REFERENCE

Frederick Jackson Turner, *The Frontier in American History* (1920) is the classic statement of American exceptionalism; Turner argued that the western frontier endowed the United States with a distinctive, individualist, and democratic national character. John Mack Faragher, *Women and Men on the Overland Trail* (1979) was an early and influential book in the "new western history" that challenged Turner; his *Sugar Creek* (1987) portrays the society of the Old Northwest in the early nineteenth century. Robert V. Remini, *Andrew Jackson and the Course of American Empire: 1767–1821* (1977) emphasizes Andrew Jackson's importance in American territorial expansion in the South prior to 1821 and in the development of American nationalism. Morton J. Horwitz, *The Transformation of American Law, 1780–1865* (1977), an important work in American legal history, connects changes in the law to changes in the American economy. R. Kent Newmyer, *John Marshall and the Heroic Age of the Supreme Court* (2002) is a more sympathetic study of the early Court. Ernest R. May, *The Making of the Monroe Doctrine* (1975) presents the history of a leading principle of American foreign policy.

For quizzes, Internet resources, references to additional books and films, and more, consult this book's Online Learning Center site at www.mhhe.com/unfinishednation4.

DETAIL FROM *THE VERDICT OF THE PEOPLE* (1855), BY GEORGE CALEB BINGHAM This scene of an election-day gathering is peopled almost entirely by white men. Women and blacks were barred from voting, but among white males political rights expanded substantially in the 1830s and 1840s. *(© The Saint Louis Art Museum. Gift of Bank of America)*

TIME LINE

1830	1830–1838	1831	1832	1832–1833	1833
Webster and Hayne debate	Indians expelled from Southeast	Anti-Mason Party holds first convention	Jackson vetoes recharter of Bank of U.S.	Nullification crisis	Jackson removes deposits from Bank of U.S.
			Jackson reelected		Commercial panic

CHAPTER NINE

JACKSONIAN AMERICA

The Rise of Mass Politics
"Our Federal Union"
The Removal of the Indians
Jackson and the Bank War
The Emergence of the Second Party System
Politics After Jackson

Many Americans were growing apprehensive about the future of their republic as the nation expanded. Some feared that the rapid growth of the United States would produce social chaos; they insisted that the country's first priority must be to establish order and a clear system of authority. Others argued that the greatest danger facing the nation was the growth of inequality and privilege: they believed that society's goal should be to eliminate the favored status of powerful elites and make opportunity more widely available. Advocates of this latter vision seized control of the federal government in 1829 with the inauguration of Andrew Jackson.

THE RISE OF MASS POLITICS

Jackson Inaugurated

On March 4, 1829, thousands of Americans from all regions of the country crowded before the United States Capitol to watch the inauguration of Andrew Jackson. After the ceremonies, the crowd poured into a public reception at the White House, where, in their eagerness to shake the new president's hand, they filled the state rooms to overflowing, trampled one another, soiled the

1835	1835-1842	1836	1837-1844	1840	1841
Taney named chief justice of Supreme Court	Seminole War	Specie Circular	Panic and depression	William Henry Harrison elected president	Harrison dies; Tyler becomes president
		Van Buren elected president		Independent Treasury Act	

carpets, and damaged the upholstery. "It was a proud day for the people," wrote Amos Kendall, one of Jackson's closest political associates. Supreme Court justice Joseph Story, a friend and colleague of John Marshall, remarked with disgust: "The reign of King 'Mob' seems triumphant."

In fact, the "age of Jackson" was much less a triumph of the common people than Kendall hoped and Story feared. But it did mark a transformation of American politics. Once restricted to a relatively small elite of property owners, politics now became open to virtually all the nation's white male citizens. In a political sense at least, the era had some claim to the title the Jacksonians gave it: the "era of the common man."

The Expanding Electorate

The Franchise Expanded

Until the 1820s, relatively few Americans had been permitted to vote; most states restricted the franchise to white male property owners or taxpayers or both. But even before Jackson's election, the franchise began to expand. Change came first in Ohio and other new states of the West, which, on joining the Union, adopted constitutions that guaranteed all adult white males—not just property owners or taxpayers—the right to vote and permitted all voters the right to hold public office. Older states, concerned about the loss of their population to the West, began to drop or reduce their own property ownership or taxpaying requirements.

The wave of state reforms was generally peaceful, but in Rhode Island democratization efforts created considerable instability. The Rhode Island constitution barred more than half the adult males in the state from voting in the 1830s. In 1840, the lawyer and activist Thomas L. Dorr and a group of his followers formed a "People's party," held a convention, drafted a new constitution, and submitted it to a popular vote. It was overwhelmingly approved, and the Dorrites began to set up a new government, with Dorr as governor. The existing legislature, however, rejected the legitimacy of Dorr's constitution. And so, in 1842, two governments were claiming to be the real power in Rhode Island. The old state government proclaimed that Dorr and his followers were rebels and began to imprison them. The Dorrites, meanwhile, made an ineffectual effort to capture the state arsenal.

The Dorr Rebellion

The Dorr Rebellion, as it was known, quickly failed, but the episode helped spur the old guard to draft a new constitution that greatly expanded the suffrage.

The democratization process was far from complete. In much of the South, of course, no slaves could vote. In addition, southern election laws continued to favor the planters and politicians of the older counties. Free blacks could not vote anywhere in the South and hardly anywhere in the North. In no state could women vote. Nowhere was the ballot secret, and often it was cast as a spoken vote, which meant that voters could be easily bribed or intimidated. Despite the persisting limitations, however, the number of voters increased much more rapidly than did the population as a whole.

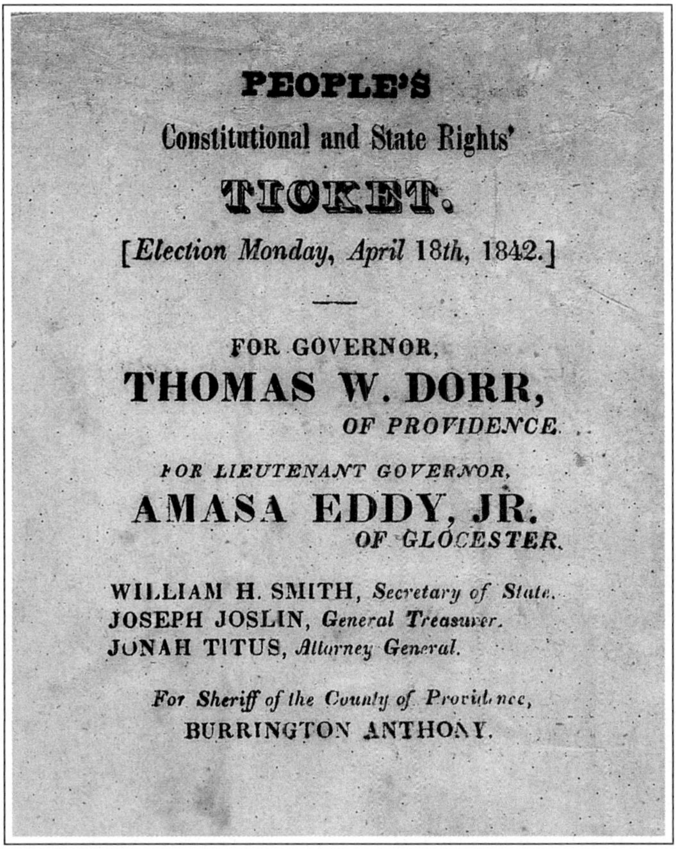

PEOPLE'S
Constitutional and State Rights'
TICKET.
[*Election Monday, April 18th, 1842.*]

FOR GOVERNOR,
THOMAS W. DORR,
OF PROVIDENCE.

FOR LIEUTENANT GOVERNOR,
AMASA EDDY, JR.
OF GLOCESTER.

WILLIAM H. SMITH, *Secretary of State.*
JOSEPH JOSLIN, *General Treasurer.*
JONAH TITUS, *Attorney General.*

For Sheriff of the County of Providence,
BURRINGTON ANTHONY.

THE DORR REBELLION The democratic sentiments that swept much of the nation in the 1830s and 1840s produced, among many other things, the Dorr Rebellion (as its opponents termed it) in Rhode Island. Thomas Dorr was one of many Rhode Islanders who denounced the state's constitution, which limited voting rights to a small group of property owners known as "freeholders." The dissidents crafted a new constitution and submitted it to a vote; a majority of the state's citizens approved it. But the legislature refused to acknowledge its legitimacy, and the result was two separate elections in 1842 for the same state offices. Dorr ran for governor under the new constitution, and was elected by a majority of the people. This "ticket" was what his supporters placed in ballot boxes as they cast their votes. Another candidate, Samuel King, ran under the old constitution, and was elected by the freeholders. Both men were inaugurated, and not until President Tyler threatened federal intervention on behalf of King did the Dorr movement crumble. A year later, however, the state ratified a new constitution extending the franchise. (*Courtesy The Rhode Island Historical Society, RHi X5 304*)

Politics Reformed

One of the most striking political trends of the early nineteenth century was the change in the method of choosing presidential electors. In 1800, the legislatures had chosen the presidential electors in ten states, and the people in only six. By 1828, electors were chosen by popular vote in every state but South Carolina. In the presidential election of 1824, fewer than 27 percent of adult white males had voted. In the election of 1828, the figure was 58 percent; and in 1840, 80 percent.

The Legitimization of Party

Although factional competition was part of American politics almost from the beginning of the republic, acceptance of the idea of party was not. But in the 1820s and 1830s, most Americans gradually came to consider permanent, institutionalized parties to be a desirable part of the political process.

The elevation of the idea of party occurred first at the state level, most prominently in New York. There, Martin Van Buren led a dissident political faction (known as the "Bucktails" or the "Albany Regency"). In the years after the War of 1812 this group began to challenge the established political elite led by the aristocratic governor, De Witt Clinton. They argued that only an institutionalized party, based in the populace, could ensure genuine democracy. The alternative was the sort of closed elite that Clinton had created. For a party to survive, moreover, it must have a permanent opposition. Competing parties would force politicians to remain continually sensitive to the will of the people; they would check and balance each other in much the same way that the different branches of government checked and balanced one another.

By the late 1820s, this new idea of party had spread beyond New York. The election of Jackson in 1828, the result of a popular movement that stood apart from the usual political elites, seemed further to legitimize it.

The Two-Party System

In the 1830s, finally, a fully formed two-party system began to operate at the national level. The anti-Jackson forces began to call themselves the Whigs. Jackson's followers called themselves Democrats, thus giving a permanent name to what is now the nation's oldest political party.

President of the Common Man

Andrew Jackson embraced a distinct and simple theory of democracy. Government, he said, should offer "equal protection and equal benefits" to all its white male citizens and favor no one region or class over another. In practice, that meant launching an assault on what Jackson considered the citadels of the eastern aristocracy and making an effort to extend opportunities to the rising classes of the West and the South.

Jackson's first target was the entrenched officeholders in the federal government. Jackson bitterly denounced what he considered a class of permanent officeholders. Offices, he said, belonged to the people, not to a self-serving bureaucracy. Equally important, a large turnover in the bureaucracy would allow him to reward his own supporters with offices. One of Jackson's allies, William L. Marcy of New York, once explained, "To the

The "Spoils System"

victors belong the spoils"; and patronage, the process of giving out jobs as political rewards, became known as the "spoils system." Although Jackson removed no more

ANDREW JACKSON EN ROUTE TO WASHINGTON, 1829 Only a few weeks after Andrew Jackson's wife died (a result, he believed, of vicious attacks on her by his political enemies), the president-elect began a slow, triumphal procession from Tennessee to Washington, greeted by throngs of admirers in every town through which he passed. *(The Library of Congress)*

than one-fifth of the existing federal officeholders, his embrace of the spoils system helped cement its place in party politics.

Jackson's supporters also worked to transform the process by which presidential candidates were selected. In 1832, the president's followers staged a national convention to renominate him. Through the convention, its founders believed, power in the party would arise directly from the people in a great democratic conclave rather than from such elite political institutions as the congressional caucus.

"OUR FEDERAL UNION"

Jackson's commitment to extending power beyond entrenched elites led him to want to reduce the functions of the federal government. A concentration of power in Washington would, he believed, restrict opportunity to people with political connections. But Jackson was also strongly committed to the preservation of the Union. Thus at the same time that he was promoting an economic program to reduce the power of the national government, he was asserting the supremacy of the Union in the face of a

Debating the Past

JACKSONIAN DEMOCRACY

To many Americans in the 1820s and 1830s, Andrew Jackson was a champion of democracy, a symbol of the spirit of antielitism and egalitarianism that was sweeping American life. Historians, however, have disagreed sharply not only in their assessments of Jackson himself but in their portrayal of American society in his era.

The "progressive" historians of the early twentieth century tended to see Jacksonian politics as a forebear of their own battles against economic privilege and political corruption. Frederick Jackson Turner encouraged scholars to see Jacksonianism as a protest by the people of the frontier against the conservative aristocracy of the East, which they believed restricted their own freedom and opportunity. Jackson represented those who wanted to make government responsive to the will of the people rather than to the power of special interests. The culmination of this progressive interpretation of Jacksonianism was the publication in 1945 of Arthur M. Schlesinger, Jr.'s *The Age of Jackson.* Schlesinger was less interested in the regional basis of Jacksonianism than the disciples of Turner had been. Jacksonian Democracy, he argued, was the effort "to control the power of the capitalist groups, mainly Eastern, for the benefit of non-capitalist groups, farmers and laboring men, East, West, and South." He portrayed Jacksonianism as an early version of modern reform efforts to "restrain the power of the business community."

Richard Hofstadter, in an influential 1948 essay, sharply disagreed. Jackson, he argued, was the spokesman of rising entrepreneurs—aspiring businessmen who saw the road to opportunity blocked by the monopolistic power of Eastern aristocrats. The Jacksonians opposed special privileges only to the extent that those privileges blocked their own road to success. They were less sympathetic to the aspirations of those below them. Bray Hammond, writing in 1957, argued similarly that the Jacksonian cause was "one of enterpriser against capitalist." Other historians saw Jacksonianism less as a democratic reform movement than as a nostalgic effort to restore a lost past. Marvin Meyers's *The Jacksonian Persuasion* (1957) argued that Jackson and his followers looked with misgivings on the new industrial society emerging around them and yearned instead for a restoration of the agrarian, republican virtues of an earlier time.

In the 1960s, historians began taking less interest in Jackson and his supporters and more in the social and cultural bases of American politics in the time of Jackson. Lee Benson's *The Concept of Jacksonian Democracy* (1961) used quantitative techniques to demonstrate the role of religion and ethnicity in shaping party divisions. Edward Pessen's *Jacksonian America* (1969) portrayed America in the Jacksonian era as an increasingly stratified society. This inclination to look more closely at society than at formal "Jacksonianism" has continued into the 1980s and 1990s. Sean Wilentz, in *Chants Democratic* (1984), examined the rise of a powerful class identification among workers in New York, who were attracted less to Jackson than to an artisanal notion of democracy.

Gradually, this attention to the nature of society has led to reassessments of Jackson himself and the nature of his regime. In *Fathers and Children* (1975), Michael Rogin portrays Jackson as a leader determined to secure the supremacy of white men in the United States. Alexander Saxton, in *The Rise and Fall of the White Republic* (1990) makes the related argument that "Jacksonian Democracy" was explicitly a white man's democracy that rested on the subjugation of slaves, women, and Native Americans. But the portrayal of Jackson as a champion of the common man has not vanished from scholarship entirely. The most renowned postwar biographer of Jackson, Robert V. Remini, argues that, despite the flaws in his democratic vision, he was a genuine "man of the people."

(text continued from page 227)

potent challenge. For no sooner had he entered office than his own vice president—John C. Calhoun—began to champion a controversial constitutional theory: nullification.

Calhoun and Nullification

Calhoun had once been an outspoken protectionist and had strongly supported the tariff of 1816. But by the late 1820s, many South Carolinians had come to believe that the "tariff of abominations" was responsible for the stagnation of their state's economy—even though the stagnation was largely a result of the exhaustion of South Carolina's farmland, which could no longer compete effectively with the newly opened and fertile lands of the Southwest. Some exasperated Carolinians were ready to consider a drastic remedy—secession.

Calhoun's future political hopes rested on how he met this challenge in his home state. He did so by developing the theory of nullification. Drawing from the ideas of Madison and Jefferson and citing the Tenth Amendment to the Constitution, Calhoun argued that since the federal government was a creation of the states, the states—not the courts or Congress—were the final arbiters of the constitutionality of federal laws. If a state concluded that Congress had passed an unconstitutional law, then it could hold a special convention and declare the federal law null and void within the state. The nullification doctrine—and the idea of using it to nullify the 1828 tariff—quickly attracted broad support in South Carolina. But it did nothing to help Calhoun's standing within the new administration, in part because he had a powerful rival in Martin Van Buren.

Calhoun's Theory of Nullification

The Rise of Van Buren

Van Buren had won election to the governorship of New York in 1828 and then resigned in 1829 when Jackson appointed him secretary of state. He soon established himself as a member both of the official cabinet and of the president's unofficial circle

Martin Van Buren

of political allies, known as the "Kitchen Cabinet." Van Buren's influence with the president was unmatched and grew stronger still as a result of a quarrel over etiquette that drove a wedge between the president and Calhoun.

Peggy O'Neale was the attractive daughter of a Washington tavern keeper with whom both Andrew Jackson and his friend John H. Eaton had taken lodgings while serving as senators from Tennessee. O'Neale was married, but rumors circulated in Washington in the mid-1820s that she and Senator Eaton were having an affair. O'Neale's husband died in 1828, and she and Eaton were soon married. A few weeks later, Jackson named Eaton secretary of war and thus made the new Mrs. Eaton a cabinet wife. The rest of the administration wives, led by Mrs. Calhoun, refused to receive her. Jackson was furious and demanded that the members of the cabinet accept her into their social world. Calhoun, under pressure from his wife, refused. Van Buren, a widower, befriended the Eatons and thus ingratiated himself with Jackson. By 1831, Jackson had chosen Van Buren to succeed him in the White House, apparently ending Calhoun's dreams of the presidency.

The Webster-Hayne Debate

In January 1830, in the midst of a routine debate over federal policy toward western lands, a senator from Connecticut suggested that all land sales and surveys be temporarily discontinued. Robert Y. Hayne, a young senator from South Carolina, responded, charging that slowing down the growth of the West was a way for the East to retain its political and economic power. He hoped his stance would attract support from westerners in Congress for South Carolina's drive to lower the tariff. Both the South and the West, he argued, were victims of the tyranny of the Northeast. He hinted that the two regions might combine to defend themselves against that tyranny.

States' Rights versus National Power

Daniel Webster, now a senator from Massachusetts, attacked Hayne, and through him Calhoun, for what he considered their challenge to the integrity of the Union—in effect, challenging Hayne to a debate not on public lands and the tariff but on the issue of states' rights versus national power. Hayne responded with a defense of the theory of nullification. Webster then spent two full afternoons delivering what became known as his "Second Reply to Hayne." He concluded with the ringing appeal: "Liberty and Union, now and for ever, one and inseparable!"

Both sides now waited to hear what President Jackson thought of the argument. The answer became clear at the annual Democratic Party banquet in honor of Thomas Jefferson. After dinner, guests delivered a series of toasts. The president arrived with a written text in which he had underscored certain words: "Our Federal Union—It must be preserved." While he spoke, he looked directly at Calhoun. The diminutive Van Buren, who stood on his chair to see better, thought he saw Calhoun's hand shake and a trickle of wine run down his glass as he responded to the president's toast with his own: "The Union, next to our liberty most dear."

The Nullification Crisis

In 1832, finally, the controversy over nullification produced a crisis when South Carolinians responded angrily to a congressional tariff bill that offered them no relief from the 1828 "tariff of abominations." Almost immediately, the legislature summoned a state convention, which voted to nullify the tariffs of 1828 and 1832 and to forbid the collection of duties within the state. At the same time, South Carolina elected Hayne to serve as governor and Calhoun to replace Hayne as senator.

Force Bill Proposed

Jackson insisted that nullification was treason. He strengthened the federal forts in South Carolina and ordered a warship to Charleston. When Congress convened early in 1833, Jackson proposed a force bill authorizing the president to use the military to see that acts of Congress were obeyed. Violence seemed a real possibility.

Clay's Compromise

Calhoun faced a predicament as he took his place in the Senate. Not a single state had come to South Carolina's support. But the timely intervention of Henry Clay, newly elected to the Senate, averted a crisis. Clay devised a compromise by which the tariff would be lowered gradually so that, by 1842, it would reach approximately the same level as in 1816. The compromise and the force bill were passed on the same day, March 1, 1833. Jackson signed them both. In South Carolina, the convention reassembled and repealed its nullification of the tariffs. But unwilling to allow Congress to have the last word, the convention nullified the force act—a purely symbolic act, since the tariff had already been repealed. Calhoun and his followers claimed a victory for nullification, which had, they insisted, forced the revision of the tariff. But the episode taught Calhoun and his allies that no state could defy the federal government alone.

THE REMOVAL OF THE INDIANS

Andrew Jackson's attitude toward the Indian tribes that remained in the eastern United States was simple and clear: He wanted them to move west. Jackson harbored a deep hostility toward the Indians drawn from his earlier experiences leading military campaigns against the tribes. In this he was little different from most white Americans.

White Attitudes toward the Tribes

In the eighteenth century, many whites had shared Thomas Jefferson's view of the Indians as "noble savages," with an inherent dignity that made civilization possible among them. By the first decades of the nineteenth century, however, this attitude was fading, particularly among the whites in the West. They were coming to view Native Americans simply as "savages." That was one reason for the growing white commitment to removing the Indians from all the lands east of the Mississippi. But white westerners also favored removal to put an end to violence and conflict in the western areas of white settlement. Most of all, however, they wanted valuable land that the tribes still possessed.

Events in the Northwest added urgency to the issue of removal. In Illinois, an alliance of Sauk (or Sac) and Fox Indians under Black Hawk fought white settlers in 1831–1832 in an effort to overturn what Black Hawk considered an illegal treaty ceding tribal lands in that state to the United States. The Black Hawk War was notable for the viciousness of the white military efforts. White forces attacked the Indians even when they attempted to surrender, pursued them as they retreated, and slaughtered many of them. But its real impact was to reinforce the determination of whites to remove all the tribes to the West.

The Black Hawk War

The "Five Civilized Tribes"

Even more troubling to the government in the 1830s were the remaining Indian tribes of the South. In western Georgia, Alabama, Mississippi, and Florida lived what were known as the "Five Civilized Tribes"—the Cherokee, Creek, Seminole, Chickasaw, and Choctaw. In 1830, both the federal government and several southern states were accelerating efforts to remove the tribes to the West. Most were too weak to resist, but some fought back.

The Cherokees tried to stop the state of Georgia from taking their lands through an appeal in the Supreme Court, and the Court's rulings in *Cherokee Nation* v. *Georgia* and *Worcester* v. *Georgia* supported the tribe's contention that the state had no authority to negotiate with tribal representatives. But Jackson repudiated the decisions, reportedly responding to news of the rulings with the contemptuous statement: "John Marshall has made his decision. Now let him enforce it." Then, in 1835, the United States government extracted a treaty from a minority faction of the Cherokees that ceded to Georgia the tribe's land in that state in return for $5 million and a reservation west of the Mississippi. The great majority of the 17,000 Cherokees did not recognize the treaty as legitimate. But Jackson sent an army of 7,000 under General Winfield Scott to round them up and drive them westward.

Cherokee Legal Resistance

BLACK HAWK AND WHIRLING THUNDER After his defeat by white settlers in Illinois in 1832, the famed Sauk warrior Black Hawk and his son, Whirling Thunder, were captured and sent on a tour by Andrew Jackson, displayed to the public as trophies of war. They showed such dignity through the ordeal that much of the white public quickly began to sympathize with them. This portrait, by John Wesley Jarvis, was painted on the tour's final stop, in New York City. Black Hawk wears the European-style suit, while Whirling Thunder wears native costume to emphasize his commitment to his tribal roots. Soon thereafter, Black Hawk returned to his tribe, wrote a celebrated autobiography, and died in 1838. *(Bettmann/Corbis)*

Trails of Tears

Removal

About 1,000 Cherokee fled to North Carolina, where eventually the federal government provided them with a small reservation in the Smoky Mountains that survives today. But most of the rest made a long, forced trek to "Indian Territory," what later became Oklahoma, beginning in the winter of 1838. Thousands, perhaps a quarter or more of the émigrés, perished before reaching their unwanted destination. In the harsh new reservations, the survivors remembered the terrible journey as "The Trail Where They Cried," the Trail of Tears.

Between 1830 and 1838, virtually all the Five Civilized Tribes were forced to travel to Indian Territory. The Choctaws of Mississippi and western Alabama were the first to make the trek, beginning in 1830. The army moved out the Creeks of eastern Alabama and western Georgia in 1836. The Chickasaws in northern Mississippi began the long march westward a year later, and the Cherokees, finally, a year after that.

Osceola Defiant

Only the Seminoles in Florida were able to resist the pressures, and even their success was limited. Like other tribes, the Seminoles had agreed under pressure to a settlement by which they ceded their lands to the United States and agreed to move to Indian Territory within three years. Most did move west, but a substantial minority, under the leadership of the chieftain Osceola, balked and staged an uprising beginning in 1835 to defend their lands. (Joining the

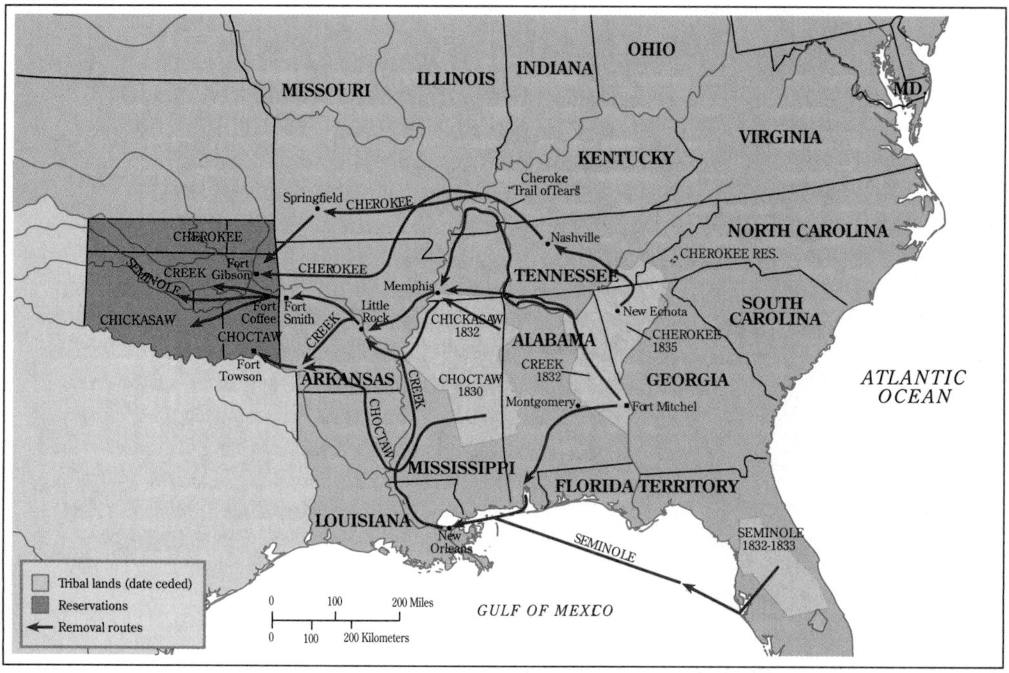

THE EXPULSION OF THE TRIBES, 1830–1835 Andrew Jackson was famous well before he became president for his military exploits against the tribes. Once in the White House, he ensured that few Indians would remain in the southern states of the nation, now that white settlement was increasing there. The result was a series of dramatic "removals" of Indian tribes out of their traditional lands and into new territories west of the Mississippi—mostly in Oklahoma. Note the very long distance many of these tribes had to travel. ◆ *Why was the route of the Cherokees, shown in the upper portion of the map, known as the "Trail of Tears"?*

For an interactive version of this map go to www.mhhe.com/unfinishednation4ch9maps

Indians in their struggle was a group of runaway black slaves, who had been living with the tribe.) Jackson sent troops to Florida, but the Seminoles and their black allies were masters of guerrilla warfare in the jungle-like Everglades. Finally, in 1842, the government abandoned the war. By then, many of the Seminoles had been either killed or forced westward.

The Meaning of Removal

By the end of the 1830s, virtually all the important Indian societies east of the Mississippi had been removed to the West. The tribes had ceded over 100 million acres of eastern land to the federal government; they had received in return about $68 million and 32 million acres in the far less hospitable lands west of the Mississippi. There they lived, divided by tribe into a series of separate reservations, in a territory surrounded by a string of United States forts, in a region whose climate and topography bore little relation to anything they had known before.

What were the alternatives to the removal of the eastern Indians? There was probably never any realistic possibility that the government could stop white expansion westward. But there were, in theory at least, alternatives to the brutal removal policy. The West was filled with examples of white settlers and native tribes living side by side. In the pueblos of New Mexico, in the fur trading posts of the Pacific Northwest, in parts of Texas and California, settlers from Mexico, Canada, and the United States had created societies in which Indians and whites were in intimate contact with each other. Sometimes these close contacts between whites and Indians were beneficial to both sides; often they were cruel and exploitive. But the early multiracial societies of the West did not separate whites and Indians. They demonstrated ways in which the two cultures could interact, each shaping the other.

Alternatives to Removal

By the mid-nineteenth century, however, white Americans had adopted a different model. Much as the early British settlers along the Atlantic coast had established "plantations," from which natives were, in theory, to be excluded, so the western whites of later years believed that Indians could not be partners in the creation of new societies in the West. They were obstacles to be removed and, as far as possible, isolated.

JACKSON AND THE BANK WAR

Jackson was quite willing to use federal power against the Indian tribes. Where white Americans were concerned, however, he was more reluctant. An early example of that was his 1830 veto of a congressional measure providing a subsidy to the proposed Maysville Road in Kentucky. The bill was unconstitutional, Jackson argued, because the road in question lay entirely within Kentucky and was not, therefore, a part of "interstate commerce." But the bill was also unwise because it committed the government to what Jackson considered extravagant expenditures. A similar resistance to federal power lay behind Jackson's war against the Bank of the United States.

Biddle's Institution

The Bank of the United States had a monopoly on the deposits of the federal government, which owned one-fifth of the Bank's stock; it also provided credit to growing enterprises; issued bank notes that served as a dependable medium of exchange throughout the country; and exercised a restraining effect on the less well-managed state banks. Nicholas Biddle, who ran the Bank from 1823 on, had done much to put the institution on a sound and prosperous basis. Nevertheless, many Americans—among them Andrew Jackson—were determined to destroy it.

Nicholas Biddle

"Soft-money" versus "Hard-money"

Opposition to the Bank came from two very different groups: the "soft-money" faction and the "hard-money" faction. Advocates of soft money consisted largely of state bankers and their allies. They objected to the Bank of the United States because it restrained the state banks from issuing notes freely. The hard-money supporters believed that coin was the only safe currency, and they condemned all banks that issued bank notes, including the Bank of the United States. The soft-money advocates were believers in rapid economic growth and speculation; the hard-money forces embraced older ideas of "public virtue" and looked with suspicion on expansion and speculation. Jackson himself supported the hard-money position. He made it clear that he would not favor renewing the charter of the Bank of the United States, which was due to expire in 1836.

Recharter Bill Vetoed

Biddle was a Philadelphia aristocrat, unaccustomed to politics. But in his efforts to save the Bank, he began granting banking favors to influential men. In particular, he relied on Daniel Webster, whom he named the Bank's legal counsel and director of the Boston branch. Webster helped Biddle enlist the support of Henry Clay as well. Clay, Webster, and other advisers persuaded Biddle to apply to Congress for a recharter bill in 1832, four years ahead of the expiration date. Congress passed the recharter bill; Jackson vetoed it; and the Bank's supporters in Congress failed to override the veto. The Bank question then emerged as the paramount issue of the 1832 election, just as Clay had hoped.

In 1832, Clay ran for president as the unanimous choice of the National Republicans. But the "Bank War" failed to provide Clay with the winning issue for which he had hoped. Jackson, with Van Buren as his running mate, won an overwhelming victory with 55 percent of the popular vote and 219 electoral votes.

The "Monster" Destroyed

Jackson was now more determined than ever to destroy the "monster." He could not legally abolish the Bank before the expiration of its charter. But he weakened it by removing the government's deposits from it. His secretary of the treasury believed that such an action would destabilize the financial system and refused to give the order. Jackson fired him and appointed a replacement. When the new secretary similarly procrastinated, Jackson fired him, too, and named a third: Roger B. Taney, the attorney general, a close friend and loyal ally of the president.

Government Deposits Removed

Taney soon began taking the government's deposits out of the Bank of the United States and putting them in a number of state banks. In response, Biddle called in loans and raised interest rates, explaining that without the government deposits the Bank's resources were stretched too thin. His actions precipitated a short recession.

As financial conditions worsened in the winter of 1833–1834, supporters of the Bank sent petitions to Washington urging a rechartering of the Bank. But the Jacksonians blamed the recession on Biddle and refused. The banker finally carried his contraction of credit too far and had to reverse himself to appease the business community. His hopes of winning a recharter of the Bank died in the process. Jackson had won a considerable political victory. But when the Bank of the United States died in 1836, the country was left with a fragmented and chronically unstable banking system that would plague the economy for many years.

Jackson's Political Victory

The Taney Court

In the aftermath of the Bank War, Jackson moved against the most powerful remaining institution of economic nationalism: the Supreme Court. In 1835, when John Marshall died, the president appointed as the new chief justice his trusted ally Roger B. Taney. Taney did not bring a sharp break in constitutional interpretation, but he did help modify Marshall's vigorous nationalism.

Perhaps the clearest indication of the new judicial climate was the celebrated case of *Charles River Bridge* v. *Warren Bridge* of 1837. The case involved a dispute between two Massachusetts companies over the right to build a bridge across the Charles River between Boston and Cambridge. One company had a longstanding charter from the state to operate a toll bridge, a charter that the firm claimed guaranteed it a monopoly of the bridge traffic. Another company had applied to the legislature for authorization to construct a second, competing bridge that would—since it would be toll-free—greatly reduce the value of the first company's charter. The first company contended that in granting the second charter, the legislature was engaging in a breach of contract; and it noted that the Marshall Court, in the *Dartmouth College* case and other decisions, had ruled that states had no right to abrogate contracts. But now Taney supported the right of Massachusetts to award the second charter. The object of government, Taney maintained, was to promote the general happiness, an object that took precedence over the rights of property. A state, therefore, had the right to amend or abrogate a contract if such action was necessary to advance the well-being of the community. The decision reflected one of the cornerstones of the Jacksonian idea: that the key to democracy was an expansion of economic opportunity, which would not occur if older corporations could maintain monopolies.

Charles River Bridge v. Warren Bridge

THE EMERGENCE OF THE SECOND PARTY SYSTEM

Jackson's tactics in crushing first the nullification movement and then the Bank of the United States helped galvanize a growing opposition coalition. It began as a gathering of national political leaders opposed to Jackson's use of power. Denouncing the president as "King Andrew I," they began to refer to themselves as Whigs, after the party in England that traditionally worked to limit the power of the king. With the emergence of the Whigs, the nation once again had two competing political parties. What scholars now call the "second party system" had begun its relatively brief life.

The Two Parties

The philosophy of the Democratic Party in the 1830s bore the stamp of Andrew Jackson. The federal government, the Democrats believed, should be limited in power, except to the degree that it worked to eliminate social and economic arrangements that entrenched privilege and stifled opportunity. The rights of states should be protected except to the extent that state governments interfered with social and economic mobility. Jacksonian Democrats celebrated "honest workers," "simple farmers," and "forthright businessmen" and contrasted them to the corrupt, monopolistic, aristocratic forces of established wealth. Democrats were more likely than Whigs to support territorial expansion, which would, they believed, widen opportunities for aspiring Americans. Among the most radical members of the party—the so-called Locofocos, mainly workingmen and small businessmen and professionals in the Northeast—sentiment was strong for a vigorous, perhaps even violent, assault on monopoly and privilege.

Democrats' Emphasis on Opportunity

The political philosophy that became known as Whiggery favored expanding the power of the federal government and encouraging industrial and commercial development. Whigs were cautious about westward expansion, fearful that rapid territorial growth would produce instability. Their vision of America was of a nation rising to greatness as a commercial and manufacturing power. And although Whigs insisted that their vision would result in increasing opportunities for all Americans, they tended to attribute particular value to the entrepreneurs and institutions that most effectively promoted economic growth.

Whig Calls for Industrial Development

The Whigs were strongest among the more substantial merchants and manufacturers of the Northeast, the wealthier planters of the South, and the ambitious farmers and rising commercial class of the West. The Democrats drew more support from smaller merchants and the workingmen of the Northeast; from Southern planters suspicious of industrial growth; and from westerners who favored a predominantly agrarian economy. Whigs tended to be wealthier than Democrats, tended to have more aristocratic backgrounds, and tended to be more commercially ambitious. But Whigs and Democrats alike were more interested in winning elections than in maintaining philosophical purity. And both parties made adjustments from region to region in order to attract the largest possible number of voters.

In New York, for example, the Whigs developed a popular following through a movement known as Anti-Masonry. The Anti-Mason Party had emerged in the 1820s in response to widespread resentment against the secret and exclusive, hence supposedly undemocratic, Society of Freemasons. Such resentment increased in 1826 when a former Mason, William Morgan, mysteriously disappeared from his home in Batavia, New York, shortly before he was scheduled to publish a book that would allegedly expose the secrets of Freemasonry. The assumption was widespread that Morgan had been abducted and murdered by the vengeful Masons. Whigs seized on the Anti-Mason frenzy to launch spirited attacks on Jackson and Van Buren (both Freemasons), implying that the Democrats were connected with the antidemocratic conspiracy.

Religious and Ethnic Divisions

Religious and ethnic divisions also played an important role in determining the constituencies of the two parties. Irish and German Catholics tended to support the Democrats, who appeared to share their own vague aversion to commercial development and who seemed to respect their cultural values. Evangelical Protestants gravitated toward the Whigs because they associated the party with constant development and improvement. They envisioned a society progressing steadily toward unity and order, and they looked on the new immigrant communities as groups that needed to be disciplined and taught "American" ways.

The Whig Party was more successful at defining its positions and attracting a constituency than it was in uniting behind a national leader. No one person was ever able to command the loyalties of the party in the way Jackson commanded the loyalties of the Democrats. Instead, Whigs tended to divide their allegiance among three major figures: Henry Clay, Daniel Webster, and John C. Calhoun.

The American System

Clay won support from many of those who favored internal improvements and economic development, what he called the American System; such improvements were especially important to people living in the western states. But Clay's image as a devious political operator and his identification with the West was a liability. He ran for president three times and never won. Daniel Webster won broad support among the Whigs with his passionate speeches in defense of the Constitution and the Union; but his close connection with the Bank of the United States and the protective tariff, his reliance on rich men for financial support, and his excessive fondness for brandy prevented him from developing enough of a national constituency to win him the office he so desperately wanted. John C. Calhoun never considered himself a true Whig, and his identification with the nullification controversy in effect disqualified him from national leadership in any case. Yet he sided with Clay and Webster on the issue of the national bank, and he shared with them a strong animosity toward Andrew Jackson.

Van Buren Elected

The Whigs competed relatively evenly with the Democrats in congressional, state, and local races, but they managed to win only two presidential elections in the more than twenty years of their history. Their problems became particularly clear in 1836. The Democrats were united behind Andrew Jackson's personal choice for president, Martin Van Buren. The Whigs could not even agree on a single candidate. Instead, they ran several candidates: in different regions, hoping they might separately draw enough votes from Van Buren to prevent his getting a majority and throw the election to the House of Representatives, where the Whigs might be better able to elect one of their candidates. In the end, however, Van Buren won easily, with 170 electoral votes to 124 for all his opponents.

POLITICS AFTER JACKSON

Andrew Jackson retired from public life in 1837, the most beloved political figure of his age. Martin Van Buren was less fortunate. He could not match Jackson's personal magnetism, and his administration suffered from economic difficulties that hurt both him and his party.

The Panic of 1837

Van Buren's success in the 1836 election was a result in part of a nationwide economic boom. Canal and railroad builders were at a peak of activity. Prices were rising, and credit was plentiful. The land business, in particular, was booming. Between 1835 and 1837, the government sold nearly 40 million acres of public land, nearly three-fourths of it to speculators. These land sales, along with revenues the government received from the tariff of 1833, created a series of substantial federal budget surpluses and made possible a steady reduction of the national debt. From 1835 to 1837, the government for the first and only time in its history was out of debt, with a substantial surplus in the Treasury.

Boom

Congress and the administration now faced the question of what to do with the Treasury surplus. Support soon grew for returning the federal surplus to the states. An 1836 "distribution" act required the federal government to pay its surplus funds to the states each year in four quarterly installments as interest-free, unsecured loans. No one expected the "loans" to be repaid. The states spent the money quickly, mainly to promote the construction of highways, railroads, and canals. The distribution of the surplus thus gave further stimulus to the economic boom. At the same time, the withdrawal of federal funds strained the state banks in which they had been deposited by the government; the banks had to call in their own loans to make the transfer of funds to the state governments.

Congress did nothing to check the speculative fever. But Jackson feared that the government was selling land for state bank notes of questionable value. In 1836 he issued an executive order, the "specie circular." It provided that in payment for public lands, the government would accept only gold or silver coins or currency backed by gold or silver. The specie circular produced a financial panic that began in the first months of Van Buren's presidency. Banks and businesses failed; unemployment grew; there were bread riots in some of the larger cities; and prices fell, especially the price of land. Many railroad and canal projects failed; several of the debt-burdened state governments ceased to pay interest on their bonds, and a few repudiated their debts, at least temporarily. It was the worst depression in American history to that point, and it lasted for five years. It was a political catastrophe for Van Buren and the Democrats.

Bust

The Van Buren Program

The Van Buren administration did little to fight the depression. Some of the steps it took—borrowing money to pay government debts and accepting only specie for payment of taxes—may have made things worse. Other efforts failed in Congress: a "preemption" bill that would have given settlers the right to buy government land near them before it was opened for public sale, and another bill that would have lowered the price of land. Van Buren did succeed in establishing a ten-hour workday on all federal projects by issuing a presidential order, but he had few legislative achievements.

The most important and controversial measure in the president's program was a proposal for a new financial system. Under Van Buren's plan, known as the "independent treasury" or "subtreasury" system, government funds would be placed in an independent treasury in Washington and in subtreasuries in other cities. No private banks would have the government's money or name to use as a basis for speculation. Van Buren called a special session of Congress in 1837 to consider the proposal, which failed in the House. In 1840, the administration finally succeeded in driving the measure through both houses of Congress.

"Independent Treasury" System

The Log Cabin Campaign

As the campaign of 1840 approached, the Whigs realized that they would have to settle on one candidate for president. In December 1839, they

THE SUN.

NUMBER 123.] NEW YORK, FRIDAY, JANUARY 24, 1834. [PRICE ONE CENT.

PUBLISHED DAILY,
BY BENJ. H. DAY & GEO. W. WISNER.
Office 222, William street.

☞ Subscriptions to this paper will be received, if paid in advance, at the rate of 3 dollars per annum. Advertising 30 dollars per annum for one square—single insertion 50 cents.
N. B. Bills for advertising will be sent monthly.

BOSTON AND PROVIDENCE.
TREMONT MAIL STAGES.
Leaves Boston every morning at 5, and Providence at 6 o'clock.
Also, Steam Boat Mail leaves Providence every day, on the arrival of the boats, and arrives in Boston from one to three hours in advance of the principal part of the Stages of the Citizens line.
For Seats or Extra Coaches, in Boston, apply at City Tavern, Brattle-street and Washington Coffee House, 158 Washington street. In Providence, at Tremont Stage Office, corner of Market square and South Main street, and to the Agent on board of the Boats on their arrival. All Baggage and Freight is at the risk of the owner thereof.—Passengers wishing to travel by this line will please not to pay their stage fare on board the Boats.
a17 C. B. WILDER, Agent.

FOR SAWPITTS, NORWALK, AND BRIDGEPORT.
WINTER ARRANGEMENTS.
From the old established pier, east side of the Catharine Market, N. Y.
The splendid low pressure Steam Packet WESTCHESTER, Capt. JOHN BROOKS, will leave the steam pier, foot of Catharine street, East River, every Tuesday, Thursday, and Saturday mornings, at seven o'clock, for the above place, leaving Bridgeport every Monday, Wednesday, and Friday, touching at the above landings each way. d2 tf

LAKE ONTARIO STEAM BOAT NOTICE.
The splendid low pressure steam boat Great Britain, Capt. Whitney, 500 tons, two engines, one hundred and eighty horse power, will, during the present season, leave Prescott every Wednesday morning for Niagara, calling at Brockville, Kingston, Coburg, Port Hope, and York.
Will leave Niagara every Saturday afternoon for Prescott, calling at Oswego, (State of N. Y.) Kingston, and Brockville. s18

EMIGRANT PASSAGE OFFICE, *for steerage passengers from Great Britain and Ireland.*—Persons settled in the United States, who wish to send for their friends from Great Britain or Ireland, can secure their passage at this office, No. 273 Pearl street, on the most moderate terms, in first rate ships, sailing from Liverpool every week, in any of which they can embark at the time most convenient to themselves. The ships are of a very superior class, fitted up with every convenience for the voyage, commanded by skilful and careful men, and the frequency and punctuality of their departure will prevent the heavy expenses often attendant on delay at Liverpool. The greatest care is used to promote the comfort of the passengers, and if they should not come out, the passage money is always returned to the persons from whom it was received. The cheapness of travelling in the steamboats, which are constantly running to Liverpool from the various ports of Ireland, Scotland, and Wales, renders this a very expeditious and economical mode of emigration; and the

MEMOIRS OF TOM JONES.

Fielding, having finished the manuscript of "Tom Jones," and being at the same time hard pressed for money, he went with it to one of your second-rate booksellers, with a view of selling it for what it would fetch at the moment. He left it with this trader in the children of other men's brains, and called upon him the succeeding morning, full of anxiety, both to know at how high a rate his labors were appreciated, as well as how far he migh calculate upon its producing him wherewithal to discharge a debt of some twenty pounds, which he had promised to pay the next day. He had reason to imagine, from the judgment of some literary friends, to whom he had shewn his MS., that it should, at least, produce twice that sum. But alas! when the bookseller, with a significant shrug, showed a hesitation as to publishing the work at all, even the moderate expectations with which our Cervantes had buoyed up his hopes seemed at once to close upon him at this unexpected and distressing information.

"And will you give me no hopes?" said he, in a tone of despair. "Very faint ones, indeed, sir," replied the bookseller, "for I have scarcely any that the book will move." "Well, sir," answered Fielding, "money I must have for it, and little as that may be, pray give me some idea of what you can afford to give for it?" "Why, sir," returned our bookseller, again shrugging up his shoulders, "I have read some part of your 'Jones,' and, in justice to myself, must even think again before I name a price for it;—the book will not move, it is not to the public, nor do I think any inducement can make me offer you more than £25 for it." "And that you will give for it," said Fielding, anxiously and quickly.—"Really, I must think again, and will endeavor to make up my mind by tomorrow." "Well, sir, replied Fielding, "I will look in again tomorrow morning. The book is yours for the £25, but them must positively be laid out for me when I call. I am pressed for the money, and, if you decline, must go elsewhere with my manuscript." "I will see what I can do," returned the bookseller, and so the two parted.

Our author, returning homewards from this unpromising visit, met his friend Thompson, the poet, and told him how the negotiation for the manuscript, he had formerly shown him, stood. The poet, sensible of the extraordinary merit of his friend's production, reproached Fielding with his headstrong bargain, conjured him, if he could do it honorably, to conceal it, and promised him, in that event, to find him a purchaser, whose purse would do more credit to his judgment. Fielding, therefore, posted away to his appointment the next morning with as much apprehension lest the bookseller should stick to his bargain, as he had felt the day before lest he should altogether decline it.—To his great joy, the ignorant trafficker in literature, either from inability to advance the money, or a want of common discrimination, returned the MS. very safely into Fielding's hands. Our author set off, with a gay heart, exclaimed Fielding; "two hundred pounds!" "Indeed, Mr. Fielding," replied Millar, "indeed, I am sensible of your talents; but my mind is made up." "Two hundred pounds!" continued Fielding, in a tone of perfect astonishment, "two hundred pounds did you say?" "Upon my word, sir, I mean no disparagement to the writer or his great merit, but my mind is made up, and I cannot give one farthing more." "Allow me to ask you," continued Fielding, with undiminished surprise,—"Allow me, Mr. Millar, to ask you—whether—you—are—se—*rious?*"—"Never more so," replied Millar, "in all my life, and I hope you will candidly acquit me of every intention to injure your feelings, or depreciate your abilities, when I repeat that I positively cannot afford you more than two hundred pounds for your novel." "Then, my good sir," said Fielding, recovering himself from this unexpected stroke of fortune, "give me your hand, the book is yours. And waiter," continued he, "bring us a couple of bottles of your best port."

Before Millar died, he had cleared eighteen thousand pounds by "Tom Jones," out of which he had the generosity to make Fielding presents at different times to various sums till they amounted to £2000. And he closed his life by bequeathing a handsome legacy to each of Mr. Fielding's sons.

A Slave Sale.—The next party was exceedingly interesting. The principal person was a stout, well built man; or, as the auctioneer called him, "a fellow who was a capital driver." His wife stood by his side—a fine, well proportioned, and really handsome woman, though as black as jet. Her left arm encircled a child about six months old, who rested, in oriental fashion, on the hip bone. To preserve the balance, her body was inclined to the right, where two little urchins clung to her knee; one of whom, evidently much frightened, clasped its mother's hand, and never relinquished it during the sale which followed. The husband looked grave, and somewhat sad; but there was a manliness in the expression of his countenance, which appeared strange in a person placed in so degraded a situation. What struck me most, however, was an occasional touch of anxiety about his eye, as it glanced from bidder to bidder, when new offers were made. It appeared to imply a perfect acquaintance with the characters of the different parties competing for him; and his happiness or misery for life, he might think, turned upon a word! The whole of this pretty group were neatly dressed, and altogether so decorous in their manner, that I felt my interest in them rising at every instant. The two little boys, who appeared to be twins, kept their eyes fixed steadily on their mother's face. At first they were quite terrified, but eventually they became as tranquil as their parents. The struggle amongst the buyers continued for nearly a quarter of an hour, till at length they were knocked down for 290 dollars apiece, or 1,450 dollars for the whole family.—[Extract of a letter from Charleston, S. C.

THE NEW YORK *SUN* This 1834 front page of the *Sun*, which had begun publication a year earlier, contains advertisements, light stories, a description of a slave auction in Charleston, South Carolina, and homespun advice: "Life is short. The poor pittance of several years is not worth being a villain for." *(© The New-York Historical Society)*

William Henry Harrison

held their first nominating convention. Passing over Henry Clay, they chose William Henry Harrison, a renowned soldier and a popular national figure. The Democrats again nominated Van Buren.

The 1840 campaign was the first in which the new and popular "penny press" carried news of the candidates to large audiences. Newspapers of the "penny press" were deliberately livelier and even more sensationalistic than the newspapers of the past, which had been almost entirely directed at the upper classes. The New York *Sun*, the first of the new breed, began publishing in 1833 and was from the beginning self-consciously egalitarian. It soon had the largest circulation in New York. Other, similar papers soon began appearing in other cities—reinforcing the increasingly democratic character of political culture and encouraging the inclination of both parties to try to appeal to ordinary voters as they planned their campaigns.

The campaign of 1840 also illustrated how fully the spirit of party competition had established itself in America. The Whigs—who had emerged as a party largely because of their opposition to Andrew Jackson's common-man democracy—presented themselves in 1840 as the party of the common people. So, of course, did the Democrats. Both parties used the same tech-

WHIG HEADQUARTERS The Whig Party managed in 1840 to disguise its relatively elitist roots by portraying its presidential candidate, the patrician General William Henry Harrison, as a product of a log cabin who enjoyed drinking hard cider from a jug. Pictures of log cabins abounded in Whig campaign posters, as seen in this drawing of a Harrison rally in Philadelphia. *(Bettmann/Corbis)*

Mass Voter Appeal

niques of mass voter appeal; what mattered was not the philosophical purity of the party but its ability to win votes. The Whig campaign was particularly effective in portraying William Henry Harrison, a wealthy member of the frontier elite with a considerable estate, as a simple man of the people who loved log cabins and hard cider. The Democrats, already weakened by the depression, had no effective defense against such tactics. Harrison won the election with 234 electoral votes to 60 for Van Buren and with a popular majority of 53 percent.

The Frustration of the Whigs

But the Whigs found the four years after their resounding victory frustrating and divisive. In large part, that was because their appealing new president died of pneumonia one month after taking office. Vice President John Tyler of Virginia succeeded him.

Tyler was a former Democrat who had left the party in reaction to what he considered Jackson's excessively egalitarian program. But his approach to public policy still showed signs of his Democratic past. The president did agree to bills abolishing Van Buren's independent-treasury system and raising tariff rates. But he refused to support Clay's attempt to recharter the Bank of the United States. And he vetoed several internal improvement bills sponsored by Clay and other congressional Whigs. Finally, a conference of congressional Whigs read Tyler out of the party. Every cabinet member but Webster, who was serving as secretary of state, resigned; five former Democrats took their places. When Webster, too, left the cabinet, Tyler appointed Calhoun, who had rejoined the Democratic Party, to replace him.

A New Political Alignment

A new political alignment was taking shape. Tyler and a small band of conservative southern Whigs were preparing to rejoin the Democrats. Into the common man's party of Jackson and Van Buren was arriving a faction with decidedly aristocratic political ideas, men who thought that government had an obligation to protect and even expand the institution of slavery and who believed in states' rights with almost fanatical devotion.

Whig Diplomacy

In the midst of these domestic controversies, anti-British factions in Canada launched an unsuccessful rebellion against the colonial government there in 1837. When the insurrection failed, some of the rebels took refuge near the United States border and chartered an American steamship, the *Caroline*, to ship them supplies across the Niagara River from New York. British authorities in Canada seized the *Caroline* and burned it, killing one American in the process. Resentment in the United States grew rapidly. At the same time, tensions flared over the boundary between Canada and Maine, which had been in dispute since the treaty of 1783. In 1838, rival groups of Americans and Canadians, mostly lumberjacks, began moving into the Aroostook River region in the disputed area, precipitating a violent brawl between them that became known as the "Aroostook War."

Tensions with Britain

Several years later, in 1841, an American ship, the *Creole*, sailed from Virginia for New Orleans with more than 100 slaves aboard. En route the slaves mutinied, seized possession of the ship, and took it to the Bahamas. British officials there declared the slaves free, and the English government refused to overrule them. Many Americans, especially southerners, were furious.

At this critical juncture a new government eager to reduce tensions with the United States came to power in Great Britain. It sent Lord Ashburton, an admirer of America, to negotiate an agreement on the Maine boundary and other matters. The result was the Webster-Ashburton Treaty of 1842, under which

Webster-Ashburton Treaty

the United States received slightly more than half the disputed area and agreed to a revised northern boundary as far west as the Rocky Mountains. Ashburton also eased the memory of the *Caroline* and *Creole* affairs by expressing regret and promising no future "officious interference" with American ships. Anglo-American relations improved significantly.

During the Tyler administration, the United States established its first diplomatic relations with China. In the Treaty of Wang Hya, concluded in 1844, American diplomats secured the same trading privileges as the English. In the next ten years, American trade with China steadily increased.

Treaty of Wang Hya

In their diplomatic efforts, at least, the Whigs were able to secure some important successes. But by the end of the Tyler administration, the party could look back on few other victories. In the election of 1844, the Whigs lost the White House.

CONCLUSION

The election of Andrew Jackson to the presidency in 1828 represented the emergence of a new political world. Throughout the American nation, the laws governing political participation were loosening and the number of people permitted to vote (which eventually included most white males, but almost no one else) was increasing. Along with this expansion of the electorate was emerging a new spirit of party politics.

Jackson set out as president to entrench his party, the Democrats, in power. He was also a fierce defender of the West and a sharp critic of what he considered the stranglehold of the aristocratic East on the nation's economic life. He sought to limit the role of the federal government in economic affairs and worked to destroy the Bank of the United States, which he considered a corrupt vehicle of aristocratic influence. And he confronted the greatest challenge to American unity yet to have emerged in the young nation—the nullification crisis of 1832–1833—with a strong assertion of the power and importance of the Union. These positions won him broad popularity and ensured his reelection in 1832 and the election of his designated successor, Martin Van Buren, in 1836.

But a new coalition of anti-Jacksonians, who called themselves the Whigs, launched a powerful new party that used much of the same anti-elitist rhetoric the Democrats had used to win support for their own much more nationalist program. Their emergence culminated in the campaign of 1840 with the election of the first Whig president.

FOR FURTHER REFERENCE

Arthur M. Schlesinger, J., *The Age of Jackson* (1945) represents Jacksonian politics as an eastern, urban democratic movement of working men and upper-class intellectuals. Bray Hammond, *Banks and Politics in America from the Revolution to the Civil War* (1957) challenges Schlesinger by arguing that the Bank War was essentially a struggle between different groups of capitalist elites. Howard Bodenhorn, *A History of Banking in Antebellum America: Financial Markets and Economic Development in the Era of Nation-Building* (2000) is a more recent examination of the American banking system in the early republic. Harry L. Watson, *Liberty and Power: The Politics of Jacksonian America* (1990) provides an important newer synthesis of Jacksonian politics. Donald B. Cole, *Martin Van Buren and the American Political System* (1984) examines the emergence of modern notions of party through the career of Van Buren. Richard Hofstadter, *The Idea of a Party System: The Rise of Legitimate Opposition in the United States, 1740–1840* (1969) traces the growing acceptance of the idea of partisan competition. Daniel Walker Howe, *The Political Culture of the American Whigs* (1979) analyzes the careers of several leading Whig politicians including the Whig triumvirate of Calhoun, Clay, and Webster. William V. Freehling, *Prelude to Civil War: The Nullification Controversy in South Carolina* (1966) argues that South Carolina planters' anxiety over the fate of slavery was at the heart of the nullification crisis. Francis P. Prucha, *American Indian Policy in the Formative Years* (1962) is an overview of early Indian policy by the leading scholar of the subject. Michael Rogin, *Fathers and Children: Andrew Jackson and the Destruction of American Indians* (1975) offers a more radical and idiosyncratic perspective on Jackson's career as an Indian fighter using the methods of psychoanalysis. Sean Wilentz, *Chants Democratic: New York City and the Rise of the American Working Class, 1788–1850* (1984) is an important study of working-class ideology during the Jacksonian period.

For quizzes, Internet resources, references to additional books and films, and more, consult this book's Online Learning Center site at www.mhhe.com/unfinishednation4.

THE LOWELL MILLS Fifteen years earlier, Lowell, Massachusetts, had been a small farming village known as East Chelmsford. By the 1840s, when Fitzhugh Lane painted *The Middlesex Company Woolen Mills,* the town had become one of the most famous manufacturing centers in America and a magnet for visitors from around the world. Lane's painting shows female workers, who dominated the labor force in Lowell, entering the factory. (Middlesex Company Woolen Mill, Lowell, MA, *c. 1848. Artist unknown. American Textile History Museum, Lowell, Massachusetts)*

TIME LINE

1817-1825	1830	1830s	1834	1837
Erie Canal constructed	Baltimore and Ohio Railroad begins operation	Immigration from southern Ireland begins	Lowell mills women strike McCormick patents mechanical reaper	Native American Association fights immigration

CHAPTER TEN

AMERICA'S ECONOMIC REVOLUTION

The Changing American Population
Transportation and Communications Revolutions
Commerce and Industry
Men and Women at Work
Patterns of Society
The Agricultural North

When the United States entered the War of 1812, it was still an essentially agrarian nation. There were, to be sure, some substantial cities in America. There was also modest but growing manufacturing, mainly in the Northeast. But the overwhelming majority of Americans were farmers and tradespeople.

By the time the Civil War began in 1861, the United States had transformed itself. Most Americans were still rural people. But even most farmers were now part of a national, and even international, market economy. Equally important, the United States was beginning to challenge the industrial nations of Europe for supremacy in manufacturing. The nation had experienced the beginning of its industrial revolution.

THE CHANGING AMERICAN POPULATION

The American industrial revolution was a result of many factors: advances in transportation and communications, the growth of manufacturing technology, and the development of new systems of business organization, and perhaps above all, population growth.

1844	1845	1846	1847	1852
Morse sends first telegraph message	Native American Party formed	Rotary press invented	John Deere manufactures steel plows	American Party (Know Nothings) formed

Three trends characterized the American population between 1820 and 1840. The population was increasing rapidly. Much of it was moving westward. And much of it was becoming concentrated in towns and cities, where the new residents provided a work force for industry.

Rapid Population Growth

The American population had stood at only 4 million in 1790. By 1820, it had reached 10 million; and by 1840, 17 million. One reason for the growth was improvements in public health; the number and ferocity of epidemics slowly declined, as did the mortality rate as a whole. But the population increase was also a result of a high birth rate. In 1840, white women bore an average of 6.14 children each.

The African-American population increased more slowly than the white population. After 1808, when the importation of slaves became illegal, the proportion of blacks to whites in the nation as a whole steadily declined. The slower increase of the black population was a result of its comparatively high death rate. Slave mothers had large families, but life was shorter for both slaves and free blacks than for whites—a result of the enforced poverty in which virtually all African Americans lived.

Burgeoning Immigration

Immigration, choked off by wars in Europe and economic crises in America, contributed little to the American population in the first three decades of the nineteenth century. Of the total 1830 population of nearly 13 million, the foreign-born numbered fewer than 500,000. Soon, however, immigration began to grow once again. Reduced transportation costs and increasing economic opportunities in America helped stimulate the immigration boom, as did deteriorating economic conditions in some areas of Europe. The migrations introduced new groups to the United States. In particular, the number of immigrants arriving from the southern (Catholic) counties of Ireland began to grow.

Much of this new European immigration flowed into the rapidly growing cities of the Northeast. But urban growth was a result of substantial internal migration as well. As the agricultural regions of New England and other areas grew less profitable, more and more people picked up stakes and moved—some to promising agricultural regions in the West, but many to eastern cities.

Immigration and Urban Growth, 1840–1860

Rapid Urbanization

The growth of cities accelerated dramatically between 1840 and 1860. The population of New York, for example, rose from 312,000 to 805,000 making it the nation's largest and most commercially important city. Philadelphia's population grew over the same twenty-year period from 220,000 to 565,000; Boston's, from 93,000 to 177,000. By 1860, 26 percent of the population of the free states was living in towns (places of 2,500 people or more) or cities, up from 14 percent in 1840. In the South, by contrast, the increase of urban residents was only from 6 percent in 1840 to 10 percent in 1860.

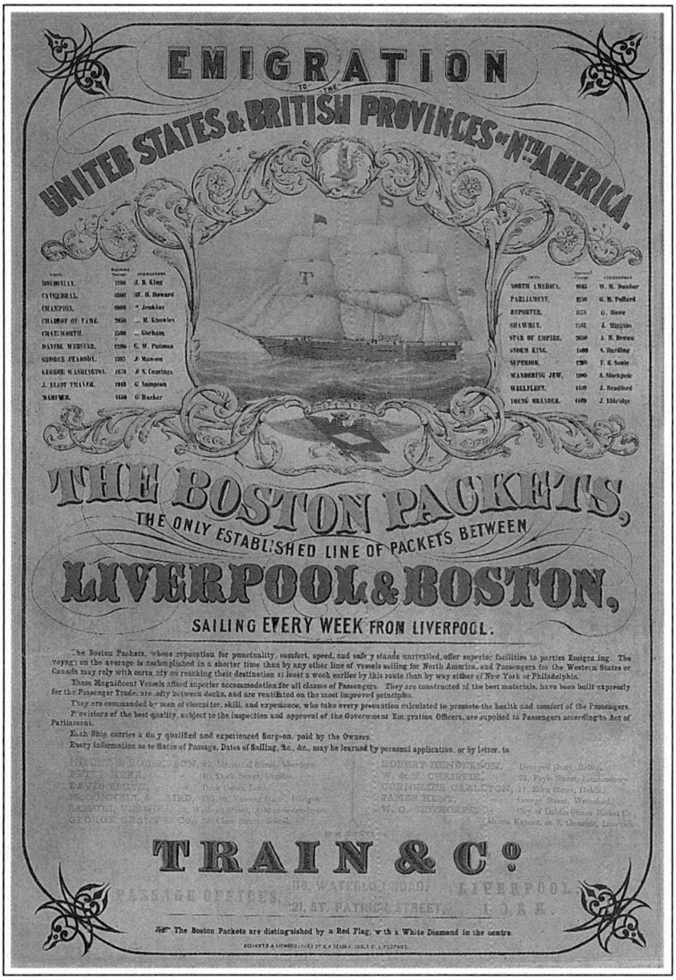

AN APPEAL TO EMIGRANTS This widely distributed advertising card was one of many appeals to potential English and Irish travelers to America in the 1830s and 1840s. Like many such companies, it tried to attract both affluent passengers (by boasting of "superior accommodations") and working-class people of modest means. *(Courtesy of The Bostonian Society/Old State House)*

The booming agricultural economy of the western regions of the nation produced significant urban growth as well. Between 1820 and 1840, communities that had once been small villages or trading posts became major cities: St. Louis, Pittsburgh, Cincinnati, Louisville. All of them became centers of the growing carrying trade that connected the farmers of the Midwest with New Orleans and, through it, the cities of the Northeast. After 1830, however, an increasing proportion of this trade moved from the Mississippi River to the Great Lakes and created major new urban centers that gradually superseded the river ports. Among them were Buffalo, Detroit, Milwaukee, Cleveland, and Chicago.

The enlarged urban population was to a large degree a result of the flow of two major groups of people into cities: the native farmers of the Northeast, who were being forced off the land by competition from the West; and immigrants from Europe. Between 1840 and 1850, more than 1.5 million Europeans moved to America. In the 1850s, the number rose to 2.5 million. Almost half the residents of New York City in the 1850s were recent immigrants. In St. Louis, Chicago, and Milwaukee, the foreign-born outnumbered those of native birth. Few immigrants settled in the South.

Irish and German Immigrants

The newcomers came from many different countries, but the overwhelming majority came from Ireland and Germany. By 1860, there were more than 1.5 million Irish-born and approximately 1 million German-born people in the United States. Most of the Irish stayed in the eastern cities where they landed and became part of the unskilled labor force. The largest single group of Irish immigrants were young, single women, who worked in factories or in domestic service. Germans, who—unlike the Irish—usually arrived with at least some money and often came in family groups, generally moved on to the Northwest, where they became farmers or went into business in the western towns.

The Rise of Nativism

Many politicians eagerly courted the support of the new arrivals. Others, however, viewed the growing foreign population with alarm. Some argued that the immigrants were racially inferior or that they corrupted politics by selling their votes. Others complained that they were stealing jobs from the native work force. Protestants worried that the growing Irish population would increase the power of the Catholic Church in America. Older-stock Americans feared that immigrants would become a radical force in politics. Out of these fears and prejudices emerged a number of secret societies to combat the "alien menace."

Native American Party

The first was the Native American Association, founded in 1837, which in 1845 became the Native American Party. In 1850, it joined with other nativist groups to form the Supreme Order of the Star-Spangled Banner, whose demands included banning Catholics or aliens from holding public office, enacting more restrictive naturalization laws, and establishing literacy tests for voting. The order adopted a strict code of secrecy, which included a secret password: "I know nothing." Ultimately, members of the movement came to be known as the "Know-Nothings."

The Know-Nothings

After the 1852 elections, the Know-Nothings created a new political organization that they called the American Party. It scored an immediate and astonishing success in the elections of 1854. The Know-Nothings did well in Pennsylvania and New York and actually won control of the state government in Massachusetts. Outside the Northeast, however, their progress was more modest. After

1854, the strength of the Know-Nothings declined and the party soon disappeared.

TRANSPORTATION AND COMMUNICATIONS REVOLUTIONS

Just as the industrial revolution required an expanding population, it also required an efficient system of transportation and communications. The first half of the nineteenth century saw dramatic changes in both.

The Canal Age

From 1790 until the 1820s, the so-called turnpike era, the United States had relied largely on roads for internal transportation. But roads alone were not adequate for the nation's expanding needs. And so, in the 1820s and 1830s, Americans began to turn to other means of transportation as well.

The larger rivers became increasingly important as steamboats replaced the slow barges that had previously dominated water traffic. The new riverboats carried the corn and wheat of northwestern farmers and the cotton and tobacco of southwestern planters to New Orleans. From New Orleans, oceangoing ships took the cargoes on to eastern ports or abroad.

Advantages of Canals

But this roundabout river-sea route satisfied neither western farmers nor eastern merchants, who wanted a way to ship goods directly to the urban markets and ports of the Atlantic coast. New highways across the mountains provided a partial solution to the problem. But the costs of hauling goods overland, although lower than before, were still too high for anything except the most compact and valuable merchandise. And so interest grew in building canals.

The job of financing canals fell largely to the states. New York was the first to act. It had the natural advantage of a good land route between the Hudson River and Lake Erie through the only break in the Appalachian chain. But the engineering tasks were still imposing. The distance was more than 350 miles, and the route was interrupted by high ridges and thick woods. After a long public debate, canal advocates prevailed. Digging began on July 4, 1817.

Impact of the Erie Canal

The building of the Erie Canal was the greatest construction project Americans had ever undertaken. The canal itself was basically a simple ditch forty feet wide and four feet deep, with towpaths along the banks for the horses or mules that were to draw the canal boats. But its construction involved hundreds of difficult cuts and fills to enable the canal to pass through hills and over valleys, stone aqueducts to carry it across streams, and eighty-eight locks, of heavy masonry with great wooden gates, to permit ascents and descents. The

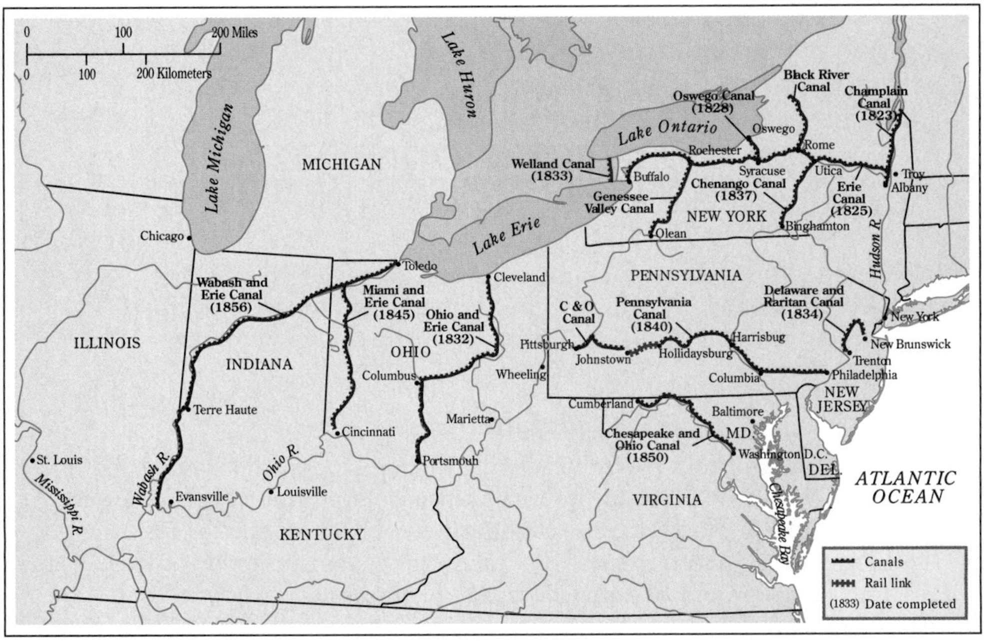

CANALS IN THE NORTHEAST, 1823–1860 The great success of the Erie Canal, which opened in 1825, inspired decades of energetic canal building in many areas of the United States, as this map illustrates. But none of the new canals had anything like the impact of the original Erie Canal, and thus none of New York's competitors—among them Baltimore, Philadelphia, and Boston—were able to displace it as the nation's leading commercial center. ◆ *What form of transportation ultimately displaced the canals?*

For an interactive version of this map go to www.mhhe.com/unfinishednation4ch10maps.

Erie Canal opened in October 1825, amid elaborate ceremonies and celebrations, and traffic was soon so heavy that within about seven years tolls had repaid the entire cost of construction. By providing a route to the Great Lakes, the canal gave New York access to Chicago and the growing markets of the West. The Erie Canal also contributed to the decline of agriculture in New England. Now that it was so much cheaper for western farmers to ship their crops east, people farming marginal land in the Northeast found themselves unable to compete.

The system of water transportation extended farther when the states of Ohio and Indiana, inspired by the success of the Erie Canal, provided water connections between Lake Erie and the Ohio River. These canals made it possible to ship goods by inland waterways all the way from New York to New Orleans.

Increased Settlement in the Northwest

One of the immediate results of these new transportation routes was increased white settlement in the Northwest, because it was now easier for migrants to make the westward journey and to ship their goods back to

RACING ON THE RAILROAD Peter Cooper designed and built the first steam-powered locomotives in America in 1830 for the Baltimore and Ohio railroad. On August 28 of that year, he raced his locomotive (the "Tom Thumb") against a horse-drawn railroad car. This sketch depicts the moment when Cooper's engine overtook the horse-car. *(Museum of the City of New York)*

eastern markets. Much of the western produce continued to go downriver to New Orleans, but an increasing proportion went east to New York. And manufactured goods from throughout the East now moved in growing volume through New York and then to the West via the new water routes.

Rival cities along the Atlantic seaboard took alarm at the prospect of New York's acquiring access to (and control over) so vast a market, largely at their expense. But they had limited success in catching up. Boston, its way to the Hudson River blocked by the Berkshire Mountains, did not even try to connect itself to the West by canal. Philadelphia, Baltimore, Richmond, and Charleston all aspired to build water routes to the Ohio Valley, but never completed them. Some cities, however, saw opportunities in a different and newer means of transportation. Even before the canal age had reached its height, the era of the railroad was beginning.

The Early Railroads

Organizational and Technological Significance

Railroads played a relatively small role in the nation's transportation system in the 1820s and 1830s, but railroad pioneers laid the groundwork in those years for the great surge of railroad building in midcentury. Eventually, railroads became the primary transportation system for the United States. They also eventually became critical sites of development for innovations in technology and corporate organization.

Railroads emerged from a combination of technological and entrepreneurial innovations: the invention of tracks, the creation of steam-powered locomotives, and the development of trains as public carriers of passengers and freight. By 1804, both English and American inventors had experimented with steam engines for propelling land vehicles. In 1820, John Stevens ran a locomotive and cars around a circular track on his New Jersey estate. And in 1825, the Stockton and Darlington Railroad in England became the first line to carry general traffic.

The Baltimore and Ohio

American entrepreneurs quickly grew interested in the English experiment. The first company to begin actual operations was the Baltimore and Ohio, which opened a thirteen-mile stretch of track in 1830. In New York, the Mohawk and Hudson began running trains along the sixteen miles between Schenectady and Albany in 1831. By 1836, more than a thousand miles of track had been laid in eleven states.

The Triumph of the Rails

After 1840, railroads gradually supplanted canals and all other forms of transport. In 1840, the total railroad trackage of the country was under 3,000 miles. By 1860, it was over 27,000 miles. The Northeast developed the most comprehensive and efficient system, with twice as much trackage per square mile as the Northwest and four times as much as the South. Railroads even crossed the Mississippi at several points by great iron bridges. Chicago eventually became the rail center of the West.

The emergence of the great train lines diverted traffic from the main water routes—the Erie Canal and the Mississippi River. By lessening the dependence of the West on the Mississippi, the railroads also helped weaken further the connection between the Northwest and the South.

Importance of Government Funding

Railroad construction required massive amounts of capital. Some of it came from private sources, but much of it came from government funding. State and local governments invested in railroads, but even greater assistance came from the federal government in the form of public land grants. By 1860, Congress had allotted over 30 million acres to eleven states to assist railroad construction.

It would be difficult to exaggerate the impact of the rails on the American economy, on American society, even on American culture. It was, according to one writer, "the resistless chariot of civilization with scythed axles mowing down ignorance and prejudice as it whirls along . . . [driving] the shadows of the past . . . into the dim woods." Where railroads went, towns, ranches, and farms grew up rapidly along their routes. Areas once cut off from markets during winter and other spells of bad weather found that the railroad could transport goods to and from them at any time of year.

Economic Effects of the Railroad

Most of all, the railroads cut the time of shipment and travel. In the 1830s, traveling from New York to Chicago by lake and canal took roughly three weeks. By railroad in the 1850s, the same trip took less than two days.

The railroads were much more than a fast and economically attractive form of transportation. They were also a breeding ground for technological advances; a key to the nation's economic growth; and the birthplace of the modern corporate form of organization. They also became a symbol of the nation's technological prowess. To many people, railroads were the most visible sign of the country's progress and greatness.

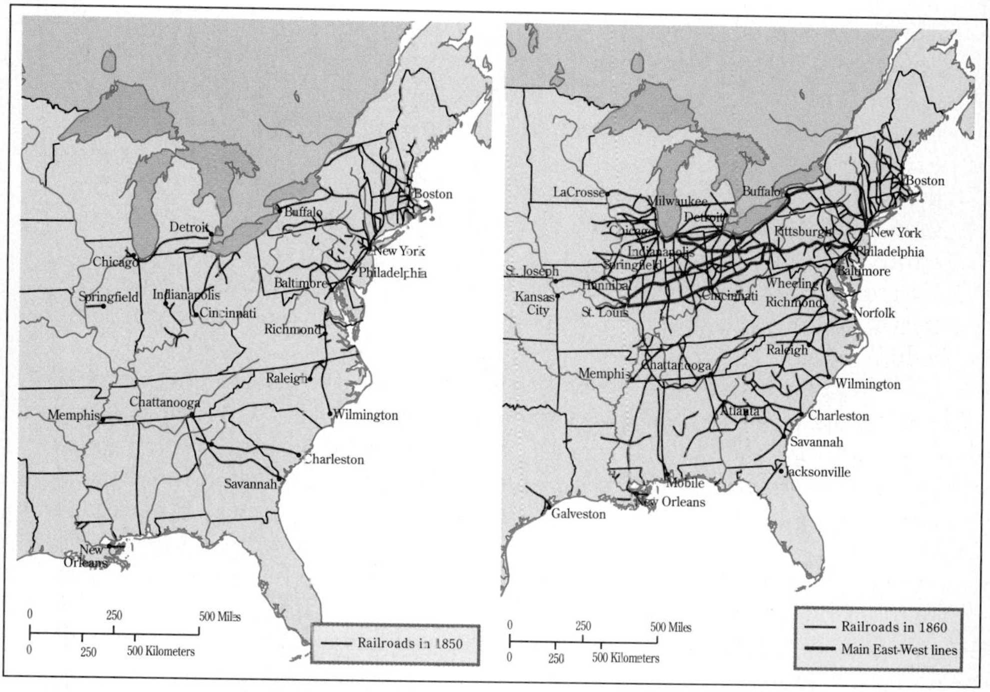

RAILROAD GROWTH, 1850–1860 These two maps illustrate the dramatic growth in the extent of American railroads in the 1850s. Note the particularly extensive increase in mileage in the upper Midwest (known at the time as the Northwest). Note too the relatively smaller increase in railroad mileage in the South. Railroads forged a close economic relationship between the upper Midwest and the Northeast, and weakened the Midwest's relationship to the South. ◆ *How did this contribute to the South's growing sense of insecurity within the Union?*

For an interactive version of this map go to www.mhhe.com/unfinishednation4ch10maps

The Telegraph

What the railroad was to transportation the telegraph was to communication—a dramatic advance over traditional methods and a symbol of national progress and technological expertise.

Before the invention of the telegraph, communication over great distances on land could be achieved only by direct, physical contact. That meant that virtually all long-distance communication relied on the mail, which traveled first on horseback and coach, and later by railroad. There were obvious disadvantages to this system, not the least of which was the difficulty in coordinating the railroad schedules. By the 1830s, experiments with many methods of improving long-distance communication had been conducted, among them using the sun and reflective devices to send light signals as far as 187 miles.

Samuel Morse

In 1832, Samuel F. B. Morse—a professor of art with an interest in science—began experimenting with a different system. Fascinated with the possibilities of electricity,

Morse set out to find a way to send signals along an electrical cable. Technology did not yet permit the use of electrical wiring to send reproductions of the human voice or any complex information. But Morse realized that electricity itself could serve as a communication device—that pulses of electricity could themselves become a kind of language. He experimented at first with a numerical code, in which each number would represent a word on a list available to recipients. Gradually, however, he became convinced of the need to find a more universal telegraphic "language," and he developed what became the Morse Code, in which alternating long and short bursts of electrical current would represent individual letters.

By 1835, Morse had developed his idea for telegraphic communication to the point that he was ready to promote it. Eight years later, Congress appropriated $30,000 for the construction of an experimental telegraph line between Baltimore and Washington; in May 1844, it was complete, and Morse succeeded in transmitting the news of James K. Polk's nomination for the presidency over the wires from Baltimore to Washington. By 1860, more than 50,000 miles of wire connected most parts of the country; a year later, the Pacific Telegraph, with 3,595 miles of wire, opened between New York and San Francisco. By then, nearly all the independent lines had joined in one organization, the Western Union Telegraph Company. The telegraph spread rapidly across Europe as well, and in 1866, the first transatlantic cable was laid across the Atlantic.

Western Union Telegraph Company

One of the first beneficiaries of the telegraph was the growing system of rails. Telegraph wires often ran alongside railroad tracks, and telegraph offices were often located in railroad stations. The telegraph allowed railroad operators to communicate directly with stations in cities, small towns, and even rural hamlets—to alert them to schedule changes, warn them about delays and breakdowns, and convey other information about the movement of the trains. Among other things, this new form of communication helped prevent accidents by alerting stations to problems that in the past engineers had to discover for themselves.

New Forms of Journalism

Another beneficiary of the telegraph was American journalism, which used the wires to get news from around the country—and eventually, the world—that had once taken days, weeks, and even months to reach them, in the space of a few hours. Where once the exchange of national and international news relied on the cumbersome exchange of newspapers by mail, now it was possible for papers to share their reporting. In 1846, newspaper publishers from around the nation formed the Associated Press to promote cooperative news gathering by wire.

Other technological advances spurred the development of the American press. In 1846, Richard Hoe invented the steam cylinder rotary press, making it possible to print newspapers much more rapidly and cheaply than had been possible in the past. Among other things, the rotary press spurred the dramatic growth of mass-circulation newspapers. The New York *Sun*, the most widely circulated paper in the nation, had 8,000 readers in 1834. By 1860, its successful rival the *New York Herald*—benefiting from the speed and economies of production the rotary press made possible, had a circulation of 77,000.

New York Herald

COMMERCE AND INDUSTRY

By the middle years of the nineteenth century, the United States had developed the beginnings of a modern capitalist economy and an advanced industrial capacity. But the economy had developed along highly unequal lines—benefiting some classes and some regions far more than others.

The Expansion of Business, 1820–1840

American business grew rapidly in the 1820s and 1830s in part because of important innovations in business management. Individuals or limited partnerships continued to operate most businesses, and the dominating figures were still the great merchant capitalists, who generally had sole ownership of their enterprises. In some larger businesses, however, the individual merchant capitalist was giving way to the corporation. Corporations had the advantage of combining the resources of a large number of shareholders, and they began to develop particularly rapidly in the 1830s, when some legal obstacles to their formation were removed. Previously, a corporation could obtain a charter only by a special act of a state legislature; by the 1830s, states were beginning to pass general incorporation laws, under which a group could secure a charter merely by paying a fee. The laws also permitted a system of limited liability, in which individual stockholders risked losing only the value of their own investment if a corporation should fail; they were not liable (as they had been in the past) for the corporation's larger losses. These changes made possible much larger manufacturing and business enterprises.

Advantages of Corporations

The Emergence of the Factory

The most profound economic development in mid-nineteenth-century America was the rise of the factory. Before the War of 1812, most manufacturing took place within households or in small workshops. Early in the nineteenth century, however, New England textile manufacturers began using new machines driven by water power that allowed them to bring their operations together under a single roof. This "factory system," as it came to be known, soon penetrated the shoe industry and other industries as well.

Dramatic Industrial Growth

Between 1840 and 1860, American industry experienced particularly dramatic growth. For the first time, the value of manufactured goods was roughly equal to that of agricultural products. More than half of the approximately 140,000 manufacturing establishments in the country in 1860 were located in the Northeast, and they included most of the larger enterprises. The Northeast thus produced more than two-thirds of the manufactured goods and employed nearly three-quarters of the men and women working in manufacturing.

Advances in Technology

Even the most highly developed industries were still relatively immature. American cotton manufacturers, for example, produced goods of coarse grade; fine items continued to come from England. But by the 1840s, significant advances were occurring.

Machine Tools

Among the most important was in the manufacturing of machine tools—the tools used to make machinery parts. The government supported much of the research and development of machine tools, often in connection with supplying the military. For example, a government armory in Springfield, Massachusetts, developed two important tools—the turret lathe (used for cutting screws and other metal parts) and the universal milling machine (which replaced the hand chiseling of complicated parts and dies)—early in the nineteenth century. The precision grinding machine (which became critical to, among other things, the construction of sewing machines) was designed in the 1850s to help the United States Army produce standardized rifle parts. The federal armories such as those at Springfield and Harpers Ferry, Virginia, where these and other tools were developed, became the breeding ground for many technological discoveries. By the 1840s, the machine tools used in the factories of the Northeast were already better than those in most European factories.

One important result of the creation of better machine tools was that the principle of interchangeable parts now found its way into many industries. Eventually, interchangeability would revolutionize watch and clock making, the manufacturing of locomotives, the creation of steam engines, and the making of many farm tools. It would also help make possible bicycles, sewing machines, typewriters, cash registers, and eventually the automobile.

New Sources of Energy

Industrialization was also profiting from the introduction of new sources of energy. Coal was replacing wood and water power. The production of coal, most of it mined around Pittsburgh in western Pennsylvania, leaped from 50,000 tons in 1820 to 14 million tons in 1860. The new power source made it possible to locate mills away from running streams and thus permitted industry to expand still more widely.

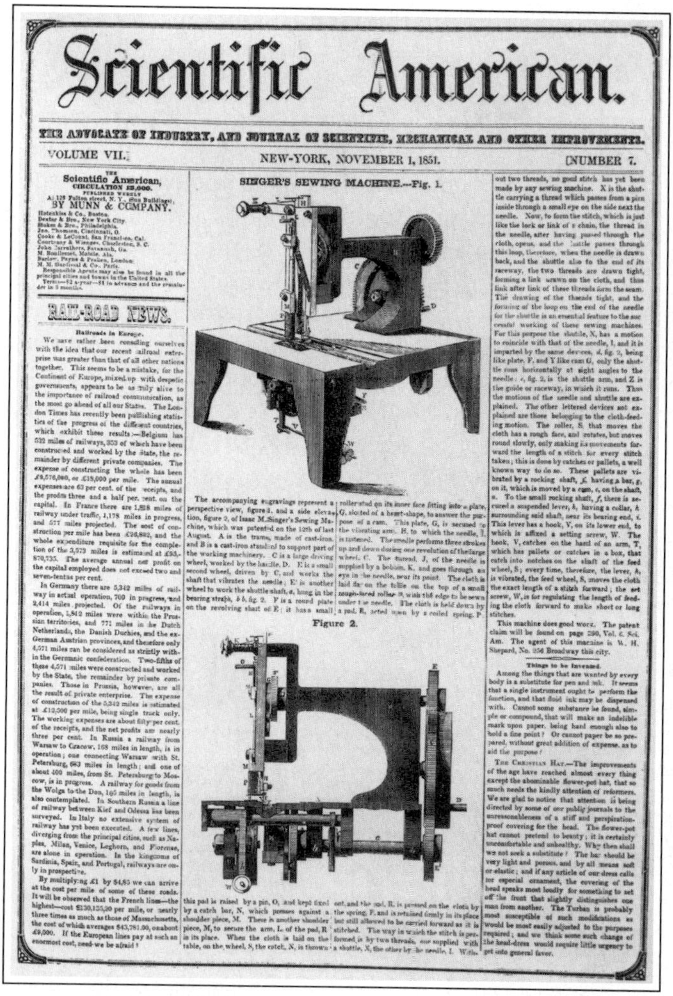

Scientific American.

THE ADVOCATE OF INDUSTRY, AND JOURNAL OF SCIENTIFIC, MECHANICAL AND OTHER IMPROVEMENTS.

VOLUME VII. | NEW-YORK, NOVEMBER 1, 1851. | NUMBER 7.

THE
Scientific American,
CIRCULATION 12,000.
PUBLISHED WEEKLY
At 128 Fulton street, N. Y., (Sun Buildings),
BY MUNN & COMPANY.
Hotchkiss & Co., Boston.
Dexter & Bro., New York City.
Stokes & Bro., Philadelphia.
Jno. Thomson, Cincinnati, O.
Cooke & LeCount, San Francisco, Cal.
Courtenay & Wienges, Charleston, S. C.
John Carruthers, Savannah, Ga.
M. Boullemet, Mobile, Ala.
Barlow, Payne & Parken, London.
M. M. Gardissal & Co., Paris.
Responsible Agents may also be found in all the principal cities and towns in the United States.
Terms—$2 a-year—$1 in advance and the remainder in 6 months.

RAIL-ROAD NEWS.

Railroads in Europe.

We have rather been consoling ourselves with the idea that our recent railroad enterprise was greater than that of all other nations together. This seems to be a mistake, for the Continent of Europe, mixed up with despotic governments, appears to be as fully alive to the importance of railroad communication, as the most go ahead of all our States. The London Times has recently been publishing statistics of the progress of the different countries, which exhibit these results:—Belgium has 532 miles of railways, 353 of which have been constructed and worked by the State, the remainder by different private companies. The expense of constructing the whole has been £9,576,080, or £18,000 per mile. The annual expenses are 63 per cent. of the receipts, and the profits three and a half per cent. on the capital. In France there are 1,828 miles of railway under traffic, 1,178 miles in progress, and 577 miles projected. The cost of construction per mile has been £26,882, and the whole expenditure requisite for the completion of the 3,573 miles is estimated at £95,870,735. The average annual net profit on the capital employed does not exceed two and seven-tenths per cent.

In Germany there are 5,342 miles of railway in actual operation, 700 in progress, and 2,414 miles projected. Of the railways in operation, 1,842 miles were within the Prussian territories, and 771 miles in the Dutch Netherlands, the Danish Duchies, and the ex-German Austrian provinces, and therefore only 4,571 miles can be considered as strictly within the Germanic confederation. Two-fifths of these 4,571 miles were constructed and worked by the State, the remainder by private companies. Those in Prussia, however, are all the result of private enterprise. The expense of construction of the 5,342 miles is estimated at £12,500 per mile, being single track only. The working expenses are about fifty per cent. of the receipts, and the net profits are nearly three per cent. In Russia a railway from Warsaw to Cracow, 168 miles in length, is in operation; one connecting Warsaw with St. Petersburg, 683 miles in length; and one of about 400 miles, from St. Petersburg to Moscow, is in progress. A railway for goods from the Wolga to the Don, 105 miles in length, is also contemplated. In Southern Russia a line of railway between Kief and Odessa has been surveyed. In Italy no extensive system of railway has yet been executed. A few lines, diverging from the principal cities, such as Naples, Milan, Venice, Leghorn, and Florence, are alone in operation. In the kingdoms of Sardinia, Spain, and Portugal, railways are only in prospective.

By multiplying £1 by $4,85 we can arrive at the cost per mile of some of these roads. It will be observed that the French lines—the highest—cost $130,135,20 per mile, or nearly three times as much as those of Massachusetts, the cost of which averages $43,781.00, or about £9,000. If the European lines pay at such an enormous cost, need we be afraid?

SINGER'S SEWING MACHINE.—Fig. 1.

The accompanying engravings represent a perspective view, figure 1, and a side elevation, figure 2, of Isaac M. Singer's Sewing Machine, which was patented on the 12th of last August. A is the frame, made of cast-iron, and B is a cast-iron standard to support part of the working machinery. C is a large driving wheel, worked by the handle, D. E is a small second wheel, driven by C, and works the shaft that vibrates the needle; E' is another wheel to work the shuttle shaft, a, hung in the bearing straps, b b, fig. 2. F is a round plate on the revolving shaft of E; it has a small roller stud on its inner face fitting into a plate, G, slotted of a heart-shape, to answer the purpose of a cam. This plate, G, is secured to the vibrating arm, H, to which the needle, I, is fastened. The needle performs three strokes up and down during one revolution of the large wheel, C. The thread, J, of the needle is supplied by a bobbin, K, and goes through an eye in the needle, near its point. The cloth is laid flat on the table on the top of a small rough-faced roller, S, with the edge to be sewn under the needle. The cloth is held down by a pad, R, acted upon by a coiled spring, P.

Figure 2.

this pad is raised by a pin, O, and kept fixed by a catch bar, N, which presses against a shoulder piece, M. There is another shoulder piece, M, to secure the arm, L, of the pad, R in its place. When the cloth is laid on the table, on the wheel, S, the catch, N, is thrown out, and the pad, R, is pressed on the cloth by the spring, P, and is retained firmly in its place but still allowed to be carried forward as it is stitched. The way in which the stitch is performed is by two threads, one supplied with a shuttle, X, the other by the needle, I. Without two threads, no good stitch has yet been made by any sewing machine. X is the shuttle carrying a thread which passes from a pirn inside through a small eye on the side next the needle. Now, to form the stitch, which is just like the lock or link of a chain, the thread in the needle, after having passed through the cloth, opens, and the shuttle passes through this loop, therefore, when the needle is drawn back, and the shuttle also to the end of its raceway, the two threads are drawn tight, forming a link drawn on the cloth, and thus link after link of these threads form the seam. The drawing of the threads tight, and the forming of the loop on the end of the needle for the shuttle is an essential feature to the successful working of these sewing machines. For this purpose the shuttle, X, has a motion to coincide with that of the needle, I, and it is imparted by the same devices, d, fig. 2, being like plate, F, and Y like cam G, only the shuttle runs horizontally at right angles to the needle; e, fig. 2, is the shuttle arm, and Z is the guide or raceway, in which it runs. Thus the motions of the needle and shuttle are explained. The other lettered devices not explained are those belonging to the cloth-feeding motion. The roller, S, that moves the cloth has a rough face, and rotates, but moves round slowly, only making its movements forward the length of a stitch for every stitch taken; this is done by catches or pallets, a well known way to do so. These pallets are vibrated by a rocking shaft, f, having a bar, g, on it, which is moved by a cam, c, on the shaft, a. To the small rocking shaft, f, there is secured a suspended lever, h, having a collar, k, surrounding said shaft, near its bearing end, i. This lever has a hook, V, on its lower end, to which is affixed a setting screw, W. The hook, V, catches on the hand of an arm, T, which has pallets or catches in a box, that catch into notches on the shaft of the feed wheel, S; every time, therefore, the lever, h, is vibrated, the feed wheel, S, moves the cloth the exact length of a stitch forward; the set screw, W, is for regulating the length of feeding the cloth forward to make short or long stitches.

This machine does good work. The patent claim will be found on page 390, Vol. 6, Sci. Am. The agent of this machine is W. H. Shepard, No. 256 Broadway this city.

Things to be Invented.

Among the things that are wanted by every body is a substitute for pen and ink. It seems that a single instrument ought to perform the function, and that fluid ink may be dispensed with. Cannot some substance be found, simple or compound, that will make an indelible mark upon paper, being hard enough also to hold a fine point? Or cannot paper be so prepared, without great addition of expense, as to aid the purpose?

THE CHRISTIAN HAT.—The improvements of the age have reached almost every thing except the abominable flower-pot hat, that so much needs the kindly attention of reformers. We are glad to notice that attention is being directed by some of our public journals to the unreasonableness of a stiff and perspiration-proof covering for the head. The flower-pot hat cannot pretend to beauty; it is certainly uncomfortable and unhealthy. Why then shall we not seek a substitute? The hat should be very light and porous, and by all means soft or elastic; and if any article of our dress calls for especial ornament, the covering of the head speaks most loudly for something to set off the front that slightly distinguishes one man from another. The Turban is probably most susceptible of such modifications as would be most easily adjusted to the purposes required; and we think some such change of the head-dress would require little urgency to get into general favor.

THE EARLY SEWING MACHINE *Scientific American*, which reported American scientific and technological achievements, was a popular journal in the mid-nineteenth century. Here it gives front-page attention to the design and construction of Isaac Singer's sewing machine, alongside articles trumpeting news of the progress of the railroads and urging the invention of a ballpoint pen. *(Scientific American, 1851)*

The great technological advances in American industry owed much to American inventors. In 1830, the number of inventions patented was 544; in 1860, it stood at 4,778. Several industries provide particularly vivid examples of how a technological innovation could produce a major economic change. In 1839, Charles Goodyear, a New England hardware merchant, discovered a method of vulcanizing rubber (treating it to give it greater strength and elasticity); by 1860, his process had found over 500 uses and had helped create a major American rubber industry. In 1846, Elias Howe of Massachusetts constructed a sewing machine; Isaac Singer made improvements on it, and the Howe-Singer machine was soon being used in the manufacture of ready-to-wear clothing.

Innovations in Corporate Organization

The merchant capitalists remained figures of importance in the 1840s. In such cities as New York, Philadelphia, and Boston, influential mercantile groups operated shipping lines to southern ports or dispatched fleets of trading vessels to the ports of Europe and Asia. But merchant capitalism was declining by the middle of the century. This was partly because British competitors were stealing much of America's export trade, but mostly because there were greater opportunities for profit in manufacturing than in trade. That was one reason why industries developed first in the Northeast: an affluent merchant class already existed there and had the money and the will to finance them. The emerging industrial capitalists soon became the new ruling class, the aristocrats of the Northeast, with far-reaching economic and political influence.

Rise of the Industrial Ruling Class

MEN AND WOMEN AT WORK

In the 1820s and 1830s, factory labor came primarily from the native-born population. After 1840, the growing immigrant population became the most important new source of workers.

Recruiting a Native Work Force

Recruiting a labor force was not an easy task in the early years of the factory system. Ninety percent of the American people in the 1820s still lived and worked on farms. Many of the relatively small number of urban residents were skilled artisans who owned and managed their own shops. The available unskilled workers were not numerous enough to form a reservoir from which the new industries could draw. But dramatic improvements in agricultural production, particularly in the Midwest, meant that each region no longer had to feed itself; it could import the food it needed. As a result, some of the relatively unprofitable farming areas of the East began to decline, and rural people began leaving the land to work in the factories.

Two systems of recruitment emerged to bring this new labor supply to the expanding textile mills. One, common in the mid-Atlantic states, brought whole families from the farm to work together in the mill. The second system, common in Massachusetts, enlisted young women, mostly farmers' daughters in their late teens and early twenties. It was known as the Lowell or Waltham

Lowell System

WOMEN AT WORK This early photograph of female millworkers standing before their machines suggests something of the primitive quality of early factories—dimly lit, cramped, with conditions that offered little protection against accidents. All the women in this picture are wearing hair tightly pulled back, to prevent it from being caught in one of the machines. *(Courtesy George Eastman House)*

system, after the towns in which it first emerged. Many of these women worked for several years in the factories, saved their wages, and then returned home to marry and raise children. Others married men they met in the factories or in town. Most eventually stopped working in the mills and took up domestic roles instead.

Labor conditions in these early years of the factory system, hard as they often were, remained significantly better than they would later become. The Lowell workers, for example, lived in clean boardinghouses and dormitories, which the factory owners maintained for them. They were well fed and carefully supervised. Wages for the Lowell workers were relatively generous by the standards of the time. The women even published a monthly magazine, the *Lowell Offering*.

Yet even these relatively well-treated workers found the transition from farm life to factory work difficult. Forced to live among strangers in a regimented environment, many women had difficulty adjusting to the nature of factory work. However uncomfortable women may have found factory work, they had few other options. Work in the mills was in many cases virtually the only alternative to returning to farms that could no longer support them.

The paternalistic factory system of Lowell did not, in any case, survive for long. In the competitive textile market as it developed in the 1830s and 1840s, manufacturers found it difficult to maintain the high living standards and reasonably attractive working conditions with which they had begun. Wages declined; the hours of work lengthened; the conditions of the boardinghouses deteriorated. In 1834, mill workers in Lowell organized a union—the Factory Girls Association—which staged a strike to protest a 25 percent wage cut. Two years later, the association struck again—against a rent increase in the boardinghouses. Both strikes failed, and a recession in 1837 virtually destroyed the organization. Eight years later the Lowell women, led by the militant Sarah Bagley, created the Female Labor Reform Association and began agitating for a ten-hour day and for improvements in conditions in the mills. The new association also turned to state government and asked for legislative investigation of conditions in the mills. By then, however, the character of the factory work force was changing again. Many mill girls were gradually moving into other occupations: teaching, domestic service, or marriage. And textile manufacturers were turning to a less demanding labor supply: immigrants.

Factory Girls Association

The Immigrant Work Force

The increasing supply of immigrant workers after 1840 was a boon to manufacturers and other entrepreneurs. These new workers, because of their growing numbers and their unfamiliarity with their new country, had even less leverage than the women they at times displaced, and thus they often encountered far worse working conditions. Poorly paid construction gangs, made up increasingly of Irish immigrants, performed the heavy, unskilled work on turnpikes, canals, and railroads. Many of them lived in flimsy shanties, in grim conditions that endangered the health of their families (and reinforced native prejudices toward the "shanty Irish"). Irish workers began to predominate in the New England textile mills as well in the 1840s. Employers began paying piece rates rather than a daily wage and used other devices to speed up production and exploit the labor force more efficiently. The factories themselves were becoming large, noisy, unsanitary, and often dangerous places to work; the average workday was extending to twelve, often fourteen hours; and wages were declining. Women and children, whatever their skills, earned less than most men.

Cheap Immigrant Labor

The Factory System and the Artisan Tradition

Factories were also displacing the trades of skilled artisans. The artisan tradition was as much a part of the older, republican vision of America as the tradition of sturdy yeoman farmers. Independent craftsmen clung to a vision of economic life that was in some ways very different from the one the new capitalist class was promoting. It was a vision based not just on

A TOLEWARE MAKER, C. 1850 By the middle of the nineteenth century, skilled artisans—such as this maker of handcrafted kitchenware—were rapidly being replaced by semiskilled workers producing similar goods in factories. The craftsman pictured here conveys some of the important elements of the vanishing artisanal world: formal dress in the workplace, to suggest his status as a highly skilled craftsman; pride in his workmanship; and a middle-class sensibility that, in the end, made it difficult for artisans to fight the forces driving them toward obsolescence. *(Collection of Zelda P. Mackay, San Francisco, CA)*

the idea of individual, acquisitive success but also on a sense of a "moral community." Skilled artisans valued their independence; they also valued the stability and relative equality within their economic world.

Some artisans made successful transitions into small-scale industry. But others found themselves unable to compete with the new factory-made goods. In the face of this competition from industrial capitalists, skilled workers in cities such as Philadelphia, Baltimore, Boston, and New York formed societies for mutual aid. During the 1820s and 1830s, these craft societies began to combine on a citywide basis and set up central organizations known as trade unions. In 1834, delegates from six cities founded the National Trades' Union, and in 1836, printers and cordwainers (makers of high-quality shoes and boots) set up their own national craft unions.

Deskilling

Hostile laws and hostile courts handicapped the unions. The Panic of 1837 and the depression that followed weakened the movement further. But the failure of these first organizations did not end the efforts by workers to gain control over their productive lives.

Fighting for Control

Workers made continuous efforts to improve their lots. They tried, with little success, to persuade state legislatures to pass laws setting a maximum workday and regulating child labor. The greatest legal victory of industrial workers came in Massachusetts in 1842, when the state supreme court, in *Commonwealth* v. *Hunt*, declared that unions were lawful organizations and that the strike was a lawful weapon. Other state courts gradually accepted the principles of the Massachusetts decision, but employers continued to resist.

Commonwealth v. Hunt

Virtually all the early craft unions excluded women. As a result, women began establishing their own protective unions by the 1850s. Like the male craft unions, the female protective unions had little power in dealing with employers. They did, however, serve an important role as mutual aid societies for women workers.

Many factors combined to inhibit the growth of effective labor resistance. Among the most important was the flood of immigrant laborers into the country. The newcomers were usually willing to work for lower wages than native workers; and because they were so numerous, manufacturers had little difficulty replacing disgruntled or striking workers with eager immigrants. Ethnic divisions and tensions often led workers to channel their resentments into internal bickering rather than into their shared grievances against employers. Another obstacle was the sheer strength of the industrial capitalists, who had not only economic but political and social power.

PATTERNS OF SOCIETY

The industrial revolution was making the United States dramatically wealthier by the year. It was also making society more unequal, and it was transforming social relationships at almost every level.

The Rich and the Poor

The commercial and industrial growth of the United States greatly elevated the average income of the American people. But this increasing wealth was being distributed highly unequally. Substantial groups of the population shared hardly at all in the economic growth: slaves, Indians, landless

Highly Unequal Distribution of Wealth

CENTRAL PARK To affluent New Yorkers, the construction of the city's great Central Park was important because it provided them with an elegant setting for their daily carriage rides—an activity ostensibly designed to expose the riders to fresh air but that was really an occasion for them to display their finery to their neighbors. (WCTU Parade, Great Riot, & Fashionable "Turn-outs" in Central Park. *The Museum of the City of New York)*

farmers, and many of the unskilled workers on the fringes of the manufacturing system. But even among the rest of the population, disparities of income were increasingly marked. Merchants and industrialists were accumulating enormous fortunes; and because there was now a significant number of rich people living in cities, a distinctive culture of wealth began to emerge.

In large cities, people of great wealth gathered together in neighborhoods of astonishing opulence. They founded clubs and developed elaborate social rituals. They looked increasingly for ways to display their wealth—in the great mansions they built, the showy carriages in which they rode, the lavish household goods they accumulated, the elegant social establishments they patronized. New York developed a particularly elaborate high society. The construction of the city's great Central Park, which began in the 1850s, was in part a result of pressure from the members of high society, who wanted an elegant setting for their daily carriage rides.

The Urban Poor

There was also a significant population of genuinely destitute people emerging in the growing urban centers of the nation. These were people who were not merely poor, in the sense of having to struggle to sustain themselves. They were almost entirely without resources, often homeless, dependent on charity or crime or both for survival. Substantial numbers of people actually starved to death or died of exposure. Some of these "paupers," as contemporaries called them, were recent immigrants. Some were widows and orphans, stripped of the family structures that allowed most working-class Americans to survive. Some were people suffering from alcoholism or mental illness, unable to work. Others were victims of native prejudice—barred from all but the most menial employment because of race or ethnicity. The Irish were particular victims of such prejudice.

Harsh Life for Free Blacks

Among the worst victims were free blacks. Most major urban areas had significant black populations. Some of these African Americans were descendants of families that had lived in the North for generations. Others were former slaves who had escaped or been released by their masters. In material terms, at least, life was not always much better for them in the North than it had been in slavery. Most had access to very menial jobs at best. In most parts of the North, blacks could not vote, could not attend public schools, indeed could not use any of the public services available to white residents. Even so, most blacks preferred life in the North, however arduous, to life in the South.

Social Mobility

Despite the contrasts between conspicuous wealth and conspicuous poverty in antebellum America, there was relatively little overt class conflict. For one thing, life, in material terms at least, was better for most factory workers than it had been on the farms or in the European societies from which they had migrated. There was also a significant amount of mobility within the working class, which helped limit discontent. A few workers managed to move from poverty to riches by dint of work, ingenuity, and luck—a very small number, but enough to support the dreams of those who watched them. And a much larger number of workers managed to move at least one notch up the ladder—for example, becoming in the course of a lifetime a skilled, rather than an unskilled, laborer.

Geographical Mobility

More important than social mobility was geographical mobility. Some workers saved money, bought land, and moved west to farm it. But few urban workers, and even fewer poor ones, could afford to make such a move. Much more common was the movement of laborers from one industrial town to another. These migratory workers were often the victims of layoffs, looking for better opportunities elsewhere. Their search may seldom have led to a marked improvement in their circumstances, but the rootlessness of this large segment of the work force—one of the most distressed segments—made effective organization and protest more difficult.

Middle-Class Life

For all the visibility of the very rich and the very poor in antebellum society, the fastest-growing group in America was the middle class. Economic development opened many more opportunities for people to own or work in businesses, to own shops, to engage in trade, to enter professions, and to administer organizations. In earlier times, when ownership of land had been the only real basis of wealth, society had been divided between people with little or no land (people Europeans generally called peasants) and a landed gentry (which in Europe usually became an inherited aristocracy). Once commerce and industry became a source of wealth, these rigid distinctions broke down; many people could become prosperous without owning land, but by providing valuable services.

Rapidly Expanding Middle Class

Middle-class life in the years before the Civil War rapidly established itself as the most influential cultural form of urban America. Middle-class families lived in solid and often substantial homes. Their houses lined city streets, larger in size and more elaborate in design than the cramped, functional rowhouses in working-class neighborhoods—but also far less lavish than the great houses of the very rich. Like the wealthy, middle-class people tended to own their homes. Workers and artisans were increasingly becoming renters.

Middle-class women usually remained in the home and cared for the household, although increasingly they were also able to hire servants—usually young, unmarried immigrant women. One of the aspirations of middle-class women in an age when doing the family's laundry could take an entire day was to escape from some of the drudgery of housework.

New Household Inventions

New household inventions altered, and greatly improved, the character of life in middle-class homes. Perhaps the most important was the invention of the cast-iron stove, which began to replace fireplaces as the principal vehicle for cooking in the 1840s. These wood- or coal-burning devices were hot, clumsy, and dirty by the standards of the twentieth century; but compared to the inconvenience and danger of cooking on an open hearth, they seemed a great luxury. Stoves gave cooks more control over the preparation of food and allowed them to cook several things at once.

Middle-class diets were changing rapidly, and not just because of the wider range of cooking the stove made possible. The expansion and diversification of American agriculture and the ability of farmers to ship goods to urban markets by rail from distant regions greatly increased the variety of food available in cities. Fruits and vegetables were difficult to ship over long distances in an age with little refrigeration, but families had access to a greater variety of meats, grains, and dairy products than they had had in the past. A few households acquired iceboxes, which allowed them to keep fresh meat and dairy products for as long as several days without spoilage. Most families, however, did not yet have any kind of refrigeration. For them, preserving food meant curing meat with salt and preserving fruits in sugar. Diets were generally much heavier and starchier than they are today, and middle-class people tended to be considerably stouter than would be considered healthy or fashionable now.

Middle-class homes came to differentiate themselves from those of workers and artisans in other ways as well. They were more elaborately decorated and furnished. Houses that had once had bare walls and floors now had carpeting, wallpaper, and curtains. The spare, simple styles of eighteenth-century homes gave way to the much more elaborate, even baroque household styles of the Victorian era—styles increasingly characterized by crowded, even cluttered rooms, dark colors, lush fabrics, and heavy furniture and draperies. Middle-class homes also became larger. It became less common for children to share beds and for all members of families to sleep in the same room. Parlors and dining rooms separate from the kitchen—once a luxury reserved largely for the wealthy—became the norm now for the middle class as well. Some urban middle-class homes had indoor plumbing and indoor toilets by the 1850s—a significant advance over the outdoor wells and privies that had been virtually universal only a few years earlier.

The Changing Family

Declining Patriarchy

The new industrializing society produced profound changes in the nature and function of the family. At the heart of the transformation was the movement of families from farms to urban areas. The family patterns of the countryside, where powerful fathers controlled their children's futures by controlling the distribution of land to them, could not survive the move to a city or town. Sons and daughters in urban households were much more likely to leave the family in search of work than they had been in the rural world.

Emergence of Public and Private Spheres

Another important change was the shift of income-earning work out of the home and into the shop, mill, or factory. In the early decades of the nineteenth century, the family itself had been the principal unit of economic activity. Now most income earners left home each day to work elsewhere. A sharp distinction began to emerge between the public world of the workplace and the private world of the family. The world of the family was now dominated not by production but by housekeeping, child rearing, and other primarily domestic concerns.

Accompanying the changing economic function of the family was a decline in the birth rate. In 1800, the average American woman could be expected to give birth to approximately seven children. By 1860, the average woman bore five children. The birth rate fell most quickly in urban areas and among middle-class women.

The "Cult of Domesticity"

The growing separation between the workplace and the home helped cause increasingly sharp distinctions between the social roles of men and women. Those distinctions affected not only factory workers and farmers but members of the growing middle class as well.

Traditional inequalities remained. Women had many fewer legal and political rights than did men, and within the family they remained under the virtually absolute authority of their husbands. Women were seldom encouraged in pursuing education above the primary level. Not until 1837 did any college or university accept women students: Oberlin in Ohio, which educated both women and men; and Mt. Holyoke in Massachusetts, founded by Mary Lyon as an academy for women.

Establishment of Women's Colleges

However unequal the positions of men and women in the preindustrial era, those positions had generally been defined within the context of a household in which all members played important economic roles. In the middle-class family of the new industrial society, by contrast, the husband was assumed to be the principal, usually the only, income producer. The wife was now expected to remain in the home and to engage in largely domestic activities. The image of women changed from one of contributors to the family economy to one of guardians of the "domestic virtues." Middle-class women learned to place a higher value on keeping a clean, comfortable, and well-appointed home; on entertaining; on dressing elegantly and stylishly.

Within their own separate sphere, middle-class women began to develop a distinctive female culture. A "lady's" literature began to emerge. There were romantic novels, which focused on the private sphere that middle-class women now inhabited. There were women's magazines, which focused on fashions, shopping, homemaking, and other purely domestic concerns.

Women's Separate Sphere

This "cult of domesticity," as some scholars have called it, gave many women greater material comfort than they had enjoyed in the past and placed a higher value on their "female virtues." At the same time, it left women increasingly detached from the public world, with few outlets for their interests and energies. Except for teaching and nursing, work by women outside the household gradually came to be seen as a lower-class preserve.

Advantages and Drawbacks

Working-class women continued to work in factories and mills, but under conditions far worse than those that the original, more "respectable" women workers of Lowell and Waltham had experienced. Domestic service became another frequent source of female employment. Now that production had moved outside the household, women who needed to earn money had to move outside their own homes to do so.

Leisure Activities

Leisure time was scarce for all but the wealthiest Americans. Most people worked long hours. Vacations—paid or unpaid—were rare. For most people, Sunday was the only respite from work; and Sundays were generally reserved for religion and rest. For many working-class and middle-class people, therefore, holidays took on

Importance of Holidays

a special importance. That was one reason for the strikingly elaborate celebrations of the Fourth of July in the nineteenth century. The celebrations were not just expressions of patriotism. They were a way of enjoying one of the few nonreligious holidays from work available to most Americans.

In rural America, the erratic pattern of farmwork gave many people some relief from the relentless working schedules of city residents. For urban people, however, leisure was something to be seized in what few free moments they had. Men gravitated to taverns for drinking, talking, and game-playing after work. Women gathered in one another's homes for conversation and card games. For educated people, reading became one of the principal leisure activities. Newspapers and magazines proliferated rapidly, and books became staples of affluent homes. Women were particularly avid readers, and women writers created a new genre of fiction specifically for females—the "sentimental novel," which often offered idealized visions of women's lives and romances.

Vibrant Culture of Public Leisure

There was also a vigorous culture of public leisure. In larger cities, theaters were becoming increasingly popular; and while some of them catered to particular social groups, others attracted audiences that crossed class lines. Wealthy people, middle-class people, workers and their families—all could sometimes be found together watching a performance. Much of the popular theater of the time consisted of melodrama based on popular novels or American myths. But much of it reflected the great love of Shakespeare that extended through all levels of the theater-going population.

By the 1830s, Shakespeare was the most popular playwright in America. American performances of his work tended to be lively, irreverent, and highly inaccurate. Plays were abbreviated and sandwiched into programs containing other popular works. So familiar were many Shakespearean plots that parodies of them were staples of regional theater, through productions of such comedies as *Hamlet and Egglet* or *Julius Sneezer*. American audiences were noisy and rambunctious, and at times crowded onto the stage to participate in battle or crowd scenes. Their loyalties to their favorite actors were so strong that in 1849 there was a major riot at New York's Astor Place Opera House when supporters of a popular American Shakespearean actor, Edwin Forrest, gathered to protest a visit from an eminent English Shakespearean, Charles Macready.

Minstrel shows—in which white actors wearing blackface mimicked (and ridiculed) African-American culture—became increasingly popular. Public sporting events—boxing, horse racing, cockfighting (already becoming controversial), and others—often attracted considerable audiences. Baseball—not yet organized into professional leagues—was beginning to attract large crowds when played in city parks or fields on the edges of towns. A particularly exciting event in many communities was the arrival of the circus.

Popular tastes in public spectacle tended toward the bizarre and the fantastic. Relatively few people traveled; and in the absence of film, radio, television, or even much photography, they hungered for visions of unusual phenomena that contrasted with their normal experiences. People going to the theater or the circus or the museum wanted to see things that amazed and even frightened them. Perhaps the most celebrated provider of such experiences was the famous and unscrupulous showman P. T. Barnum, who opened the American Museum in New York in 1842—not a showcase for art or nature, but a great freak show populated by midgets (the most famous named Tom Thumb), Siamese twins, magicians, and ventriloquists. Barnum was a genius in publicizing his ventures with garish posters and elaborate newspaper announcements. Later, in the 1870s, he launched the famous circus for which he is still best remembered.

P. T. Barnum

One of the ways Barnum tried to draw visitors to his museum was by engaging lecturers. He did so because he understood that the lecture was one of the most popular forms of entertainment in nineteenth-century America. Men and women flocked in enormous numbers to lyceums, churches, schools, and auditoriums to hear lecturers explain the latest advances in science, describe their visits to exotic places, provide vivid historical narratives, or rail against the evils of alcohol or slavery. Messages of social uplift and reform attracted rapt audiences, particularly among women.

THE AGRICULTURAL NORTH

Even in the rapidly urbanizing and industrializing Northeast, and more so in what nineteenth-century Americans called the Northwest (what Americans today call the Midwest), most people remained tied to the agricultural world. But agriculture, like industry and commerce, was becoming increasingly a part of the new capitalist economy.

Growth of Commercial Farming

Northeastern Agriculture

The story of agriculture in the Northeast after 1840 is one of decline and transformation. The reason for the decline was simple: the farmers of the section could no longer compete with the new and richer soil of the Northwest. In 1840, the leading wheat-growing states were New York, Pennsylvania, Ohio, and Virginia; in 1860 they were Illinois, Indiana, Wisconsin, Ohio, and Michigan. In raising corn, Illinois, Ohio, and Missouri supplanted New York, Pennsylvania, and Virginia. In 1840 the most important cattle-raising areas in the country were New York, Pennsylvania, and New England; but by the 1850s the leading cattle states were Illinois, Indiana, Ohio, and Iowa in the West and Texas in the South.

Some eastern farmers responded to these changes by moving west themselves and establishing new farms. Still others moved to mill towns and became laborers. Some farmers, however, remained on the land and turned to the task of supplying food to the growing cities of the East; they raised vegetables (truck farming) or fruit and sold their produce in nearby towns. Supplying milk, butter, and cheese to local urban markets also attracted many farmers in central New York, southeastern Pennsylvania, and various parts of New England.

The Old Northwest

Industrial Growth in the Northwest

Life was different in the states of the Northwest. There was some industry in this region, and in the two decades before the Civil War the section experienced steady industrial growth. There were flourishing industrial and commercial areas in and around Cleveland (on Lake Erie) and Cincinnati, the center of meatpacking in the Ohio Valley. Farther west, Chicago was emerging as the national center of the agricultural machinery and meatpacking industries. Most of the major industrial activities of the West either served agriculture (as in the case of farm machinery) or relied on agricultural products (as in flour milling, meatpacking, whiskey distilling, and the making of leather goods).

Some areas of the Northwest were not yet dominated by whites. Indians remained the most numerous inhabitants of large portions of the upper third of the Great Lakes states until after the Civil War. In those areas, hunting and fishing, along with some sedentary agriculture, remained the principal economic activities.

Rapid Expansion of Farming

For the settlers who populated the lands farther south, the Northwest was primarily an agricultural region. Its rich and plentiful lands made farming a lucrative and expanding activity there. Thus the typical citizen of the Northwest was not the industrial worker or poor, marginal farmer but the owner of a reasonably prosperous family farm.

Industrialization, in both the United States and Europe, provided the greatest boost to agriculture. With the growth of factories and cities in the Northeast, the domestic market for farm goods increased dramatically. The growing national and worldwide demand for farm products resulted in steadily rising farm prices. For most farmers, the 1840s and early 1850s were years of increasing prosperity.

The expansion of agricultural markets had profound effects on sectional alignments in the United States. The Northwest sold most of its products to the Northeast and became an important market for the products of eastern industry. A strong economic relationship was emerging between the two sections that was profitable to both—and that was increasing the isolation of the South within the Union.

Growing Ties between Northeast and Northwest

By 1850, the growing western white population was moving into the prairie regions on both sides of the Mississippi. These farmers cleared for-

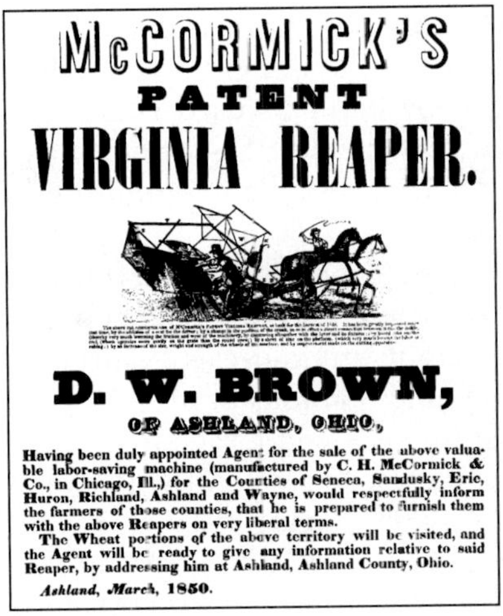

MCCORMICK'S REAPER This 1850 advertisement for the automatic reaper created by Cyrus McCormick was aimed at farmers in Ohio and Illinois. But the reaper's greatest impact was to be in the vast grain-growing regions farther west, which were already attracting large numbers of white settlers and would attract many more in the decades to come. *(International Harvester)*

est lands or made use of fields the Indians had cleared many years earlier. And they began to develop a timber industry to make use of the forests that remained. Wheat was the staple crop of the region, but other crops—corn, potatoes, and oats—and livestock were also important.

New Agricultural Techniques

The Northwest also increased production by adopting new agricultural techniques. Farmers began to cultivate new varieties of seed, notably Mediterranean wheat, which was hardier than the native type; and they imported better breeds of animals, such as hogs and sheep from England and Spain. Most important were improved tools and farm machines. The cast-iron plow remained popular because its parts could be replaced when broken. An even better tool appeared in 1847, when John Deere established at Moline, Illinois, a factory to manufacture steel plows, which were more durable than those made of iron.

McCormick Reaper

Two new machines heralded a coming revolution in grain production. The most important was the automatic reaper, the invention of Cyrus H. McCormick of Virginia. The reaper took the place of sickle, cradle, and hand labor. Pulled by a team of horses, it had a row of horizontal knives on one side for cutting wheat; the wheels drove a paddle that bent the stalks over the knives, which then fell onto a moving belt that carried it into the back of the vehicle. The reaper enabled a crew of six or seven men to harvest in a day as much wheat as fifteen men could harvest using the older methods. McCormick, who had patented his device in 1834, established a factory at Chicago in 1847. By 1860, more than 100,000 reapers were in use on western farms. Almost as important to the grain grower was the thresher—a machine that separated the grain from the wheat stalks. Threshers appeared in large numbers after 1840. Before that, farmers generally flailed grain by hand or used farm animals to tread it. The Jerome I. Case factory in Racine, Wisconsin, manufactured most of the threshers. (Modern "harvesters" later combined the functions of the reaper and the thresher.)

The Northwest was the most self-consciously democratic section of the country. But its democracy was of a relatively conservative type—capitalistic, property-conscious, middle-class. Abraham Lincoln, an Illinois Whig, voiced the economic opinions of many of the people of his section. "I take it that it is best for all to leave each man free to acquire property as fast as he can," said Lincoln. "Some will get wealthy. I don't believe in a law to prevent a man from getting rich; it would do more harm than good. . . . When one starts poor, as most do in the race of life, free society is such that he knows he can better his condition; he knows that there is no fixed condition of labor for his whole life."

Rural Life

Life for farming people varied greatly from one region to another. In the more densely populated areas east of the Appalachians and in the easternmost areas of the Northwest, farmers were usually part of relatively vibrant communities and made extensive use of the institutions of those communities—the churches, schools, stores, and taverns. As white settlement moved further west, farmers became more isolated and had to struggle to find any occasions for contact with people outside their own families.

Although the extent of social interaction differed from one area to another, the forms of interaction were usually very similar. Religion drew farm communities together perhaps more than any other force. Town or village churches were popular meeting places, both for services and for social events—most of them dominated by women. Even in areas with no organized churches, farm families—and, again, women in particular—gathered in one another's homes for prayer meetings, Bible readings, and other religious activities. Weddings, baptisms, and funerals also brought communities together.

Rural Social Interaction

But religion was only one of many reasons for interaction. Farm people joined together frequently to share tasks such as barn raising. On those occasions, families would gather and create a festive atmosphere of celebration. Women prepared large suppers while the men worked on the barn and the children played. Large numbers of families gathered together at harvest time to help bring in crops, husk corn, or thresh wheat. Women came together to share domestic tasks, holding "bees" in which groups of women joined together to make quilts, baked goods, preserves, and other products.

Despite the many social gatherings farm families managed to create, they had much less contact with popular culture and public social life than people who lived in towns and cities. Rural people treasured their links to the outside world—letters from relatives and friends in distant places, newspapers and magazines from cities they had never seen, catalogs advertising merchandise that their local stores never had. Yet many also valued the relative autonomy that a farm life gave them. One reason many rural Americans looked back nostalgically on country life once they moved to the city was that they sensed that in the urban world they did not have as much control over the patterns of their daily lives as they had once known.

CONCLUSION

Between the 1820s and the 1850s, the American economy experienced the beginnings of an industrial revolution—a change that transformed almost every area of life in fundamental ways.

Sources of the Industrial Revolution

The American industrial revolution was a result of many things: population growth, advances in transportation and communication, new technologies that spurred the development of factories capable of mass producing goods, the recruiting of a large industrial labor force, and the creation of corporate bodies capable of managing large enterprises. The new economy expanded the ranks of the wealthy and helped create a large new middle class. It also created high levels of inequality.

Culture in the industrializing areas of the North changed, too, and there were important changes in the structure and behavior of the family, in the role of women, and in the way people used their leisure time and encountered popular culture. The changes helped widen the gap in experience and understanding between the generation of the Revolution and the generation of the mid-nineteenth century. They also helped widen the gap between North and South.

FOR FURTHER REFERENCE

John Bodnar, *The Transplanted: A History of Immigrants in America* (1985) is a useful survey. Matthew Frye Jacobson, *Whiteness of a Different Color: European Immigrants and the Alchemy of Race* (1999) is a wide-ranging cultural history of immigration. Charles G. Sellers, *The Market Revolution: Jacksonian America, 1815–1846* (1991) demonstrates the overwhelming impact of the market revolution on American social and political development. George R. Taylor, *The Transportation Revolution* (1951) is a classic account of economic development in the antebellum period. Christopher Clark, *The*

Roots of Rural Capitalism: Western Massachusetts, 1780–1860 (1990) is an examination of the impact of emerging capitalism on a rural area. Paul Johnson, *A Shopkeeper's Millennium: Society and Revivals in Rochester, New York, 1815–1837* (1978) explores the changing character of class relations in upstate New York in an age of rapid economic development. Alice Kessler-Harris, *Out to Work: A History of Wage-Earning Women in the United States* (1982) is a broad history of women in the wage labor force. Thomas Dublin, *Transforming Women's Work: New England Lives in the Industrial Revolution* (1994) looks in particular at the mill towns of the northeast. Mary Ryan, *Cradle of the Middle Class: The Family in Oneida County, New York, 1790–1865* (1981) demonstrates the relationship between the market revolution and the changing character of middle-class family structure. Christine Stansell, *City of Women: Sex and Class in New York, 1789–1860* (1983) explores the female world of antebellum New York City. Paul W. Gates, *The Farmer's Age: Agriculture, 1815–1860* (1966) is an important overview. Alan Taylor, *William Cooper's Town: Power and Persuasion on the Frontier in the Early American Republic* (1995) examines the early years of Cooperstown, New York, and the impact on it of the rise of the market and of democratic politics. Witold Rybczynski, *A Clearing in the Distance: Frederick Law Olmsted and America in the Nineteenth Century* (1999) is a perceptive and engaging study of the man who, along with Calvert Vaux, designed New York City's Central Park and other important American landscapes.

For quizzes, Internet resources, references to additional books and films, and more, consult this book's Online Learning Center site at www.mhhe.com/unfinishednation4.

THE NEW ORLEANS COTTON EXCHANGE Edgar Degas, the great French impressionist, painted this scene of cotton traders examining samples in the New Orleans cotton exchange in 1873. By this time the cotton trade was producing less impressive profits than those that had made it the driving force of the booming southern economy of the 1850s. Degas's mother came from a Creole family of cotton brokers in New Orleans, and two of the artist's brothers (depicted here reading a newspaper and leaning against a window) joined the business in America. *(Giraudon/Art Resource, NY)*

TIME LINE

1800	1808	1820s	1822	1831
Gabriel Prosser's unsuccessful slave revolt	Slave importation banned	Depression in tobacco prices begins	Denmark Vesey's conspiracy	Nat Turner slave rebellion
		High cotton production in Southwest		

CHAPTER ELEVEN

COTTON, SLAVERY, AND THE OLD SOUTH

The Cotton Economy
Southern White Society
Slavery: The "Peculiar Institution"
The Culture of Slavery

The South, like the North, experienced dramatic growth in the middle years of the nineteen century. Southerners fanned out into the Southwest. The southern agricultural economy grew increasingly productive and increasingly prosperous. Trade in such staples as sugar, rice, tobacco, and above all cotton made the South a major force in international commerce. It also tied the South securely to the emerging capitalist world of the United States and its European trading partners.

Yet despite all these changes, the South experienced a much less fundamental transformation in these years than did the North. It had begun the nineteenth century a primarily agricultural region; it remained overwhelmingly agrarian in 1860. It had begun the century with few important cities and little industry; and so it remained sixty years later. In 1800, a plantation system dependent on slave labor had dominated the southern economy; by 1860, that system had only strengthened its grip on the region. As one historian has written, "The South grew, but it did not develop."

	1833	1837	1846	1849	
	John Randolph frees 400 slaves	Cotton prices plummet	*De Bow's Review* founded	Cotton production boom	

THE COTTON ECONOMY

The most important economic development in the mid-nineteenth-century South was the shift of economic power from the "upper South," the original southern states along the Atlantic coast, to the "lower South," the expanding agricultural regions in the new states of the Southwest. That shift reflected above all the growing dominance of cotton in the southern economy.

The Rise of King Cotton

Declining Tobacco Economy

Much of the upper South continued to rely on the cultivation of tobacco. But the market for that crop was notoriously unstable, and tobacco rapidly exhausted the land on which it grew. By the 1830s, therefore, many farmers in the old tobacco-growing regions of Virginia, Maryland, and North Carolina were shifting to other crops, while the center of tobacco cultivation was moving westward, into the Piedmont area.

The southern regions of the coastal South—South Carolina, Georgia, and parts of Florida—continued to rely on the cultivation of rice, a more stable and lucrative crop. But rice demanded substantial irrigation and needed an exceptionally long growing season (nine months), so cultivation of that staple remained restricted to a relatively small area. Sugar growers along the Gulf Coast, similarly, enjoyed a reasonably profitable market for their crop. But sugar cultivation required intensive (and debilitating) labor and a long growing time; only relatively wealthy planters could afford to engage in it. In addition, producers faced major competition from the great sugar plantations of the Caribbean. Sugar cultivation, therefore, did not spread much beyond a small area in southern Louisiana and eastern Texas. Long-staple (Sea Island) cotton was another lucrative crop, but like rice and sugar, it could grow only in a limited area—the coastal regions of the Southeast.

SLAVERY AND COTTON IN THE SOUTH, 1820 AND 1860 The two maps on the opposite page show the remarkable spread of cotton cultivation in the South in the decades before the Civil War. Both maps show the areas of cotton cultivation (the light-orange colored areas) as well as areas with large slave populations (the darker rust dotted or solid areas). Note how in the top map, which represents 1820, cotton production is concentrated largely in the East, with a few areas scattered among Alabama, Mississippi, Louisiana, and Tennessee. Slavery is concentrated along the Georgia and South Carolina coast, areas in which long-staple cotton was grown, with only a few other areas of highly dense slave populations. By 1860, the South had changed dramatically. Cotton production had spread throughout the lower South, from Texas to northern Florida, and slavery had moved with it. Slavery was also much denser in the tobacco-growing regions of Virginia and North Carolina, which had also grown. ◆ *How did this economic shift affect the white South's commitment to slavery?*

For an interactive version of this map go to www.mhhe.com/unfinishednation4ch11maps

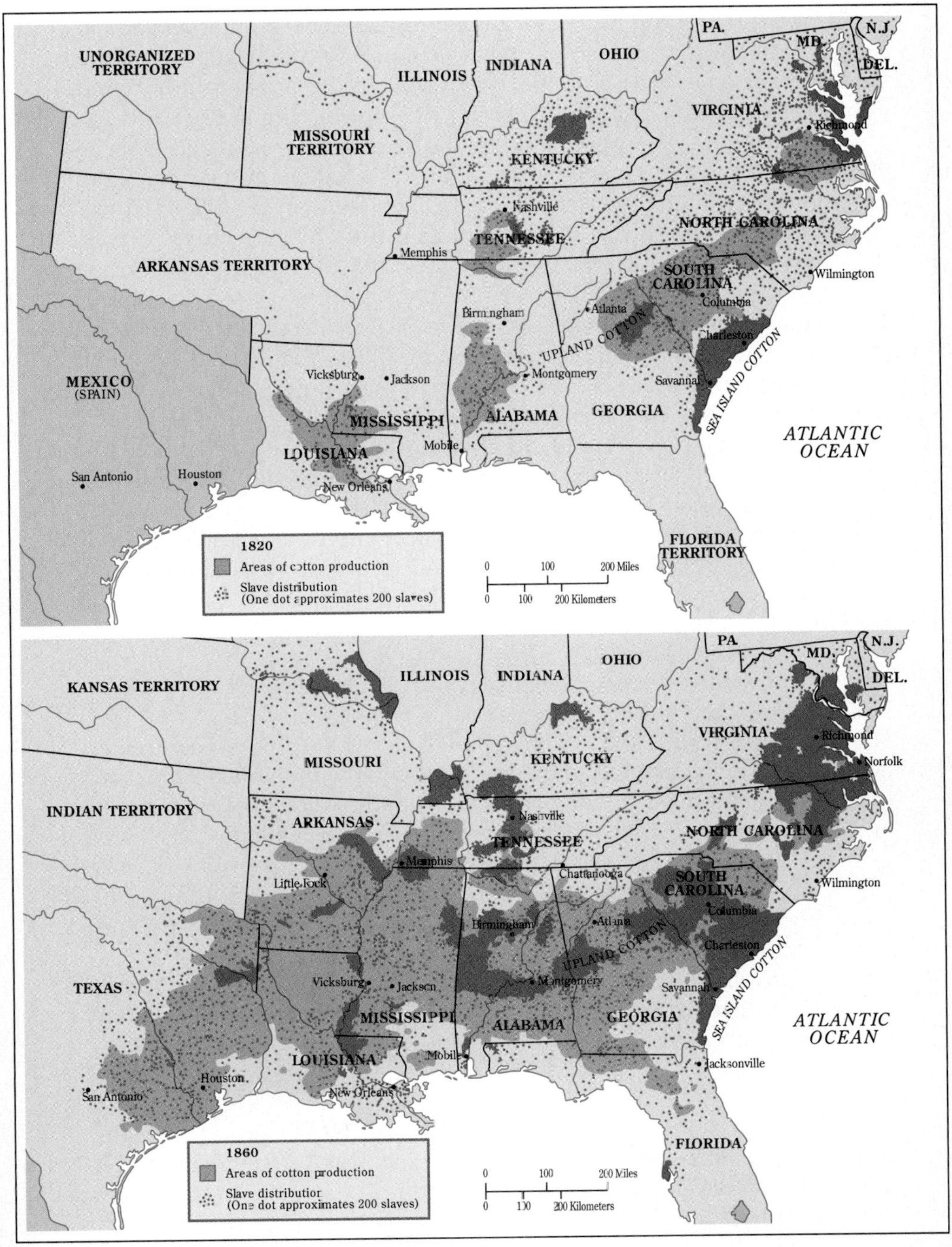
UNORGANIZED TERRITORY
ILLINOIS
INDIANA
OHIO
PA.
N.J.
MD.
DEL.
MISSOURI TERRITORY
VIRGINIA
Richmond
KENTUCKY
Nashville
TENNESSEE
NORTH CAROLINA
Memphis
ARKANSAS TERRITORY
SOUTH CAROLINA
Wilmington
Columbia
Birmingham
Atlanta
UPLAND COTTON
Charleston
Montgomery
MEXICO (SPAIN)
Vicksburg
Jackson
Savannah
SEA ISLAND COTTON
MISSISSIPPI
ALABAMA
GEORGIA
ATLANTIC OCEAN
LOUISIANA
Mobile
San Antonio
Houston
New Orleans
1820
Areas of cotton production
Slave distribution
(One dot approximates 200 slaves)
0 100 200 Miles
0 100 200 Kilometers
FLORIDA TERRITORY
PA.
N.J.
MD.
DEL.
OHIO
ILLINOIS
INDIANA
KANSAS TERRITORY
VIRGINIA
Richmond
Norfolk
MISSOURI
KENTUCKY
INDIAN TERRITORY
Nashville
ARKANSAS
TENNESSEE
NORTH CAROLINA
Memphis
Chattanooga
SOUTH CAROLINA
Wilmington
Little Rock
Columbia
Birmingham
Atlanta
UPLAND COTTON
Charleston
SEA ISLAND COTTON
TEXAS
Vicksburg
Jackson
Montgomery
Savannah
ATLANTIC OCEAN
MISSISSIPPI
ALABAMA
GEORGIA
LOUISIANA
Mobile
Jacksonville
Houston
San Antonio
New Orleans
FLORIDA
1860
Areas of cotton production
Slave distribution
(One dot approximates 200 slaves)
0 100 200 Miles
0 100 200 Kilometers

The decline of the tobacco economy in the upper South, and the inherent limits of the sugar, rice, and long-staple cotton economies farther south, might have forced the region to shift its attention to other, nonagricultural pursuits had it not been for the growing importance of a new product that soon overshadowed all else: short-staple cotton. This was a hardier and coarser strain of cotton that could grow successfully in a variety of climates and in a variety of soils. It was harder to process than the long-staple variety because its seeds were difficult to remove from the fiber. But the invention of the cotton gin had largely solved that problem.

Short-Staple Cotton

Demand for cotton increased rapidly in the nineteenth century with the growth of the textile industry in Britain in the 1820s and 1830s and in New England in the 1840s and 1850s. In response to that demand, beginning in the 1820s, cotton production spread rapidly. From the western areas of South Carolina and Georgia, production moved into Alabama and Mississippi and then into northern Louisiana, Texas, and Arkansas. By the 1850s, cotton had become the linchpin of the southern economy. There were periodic booms and busts, but the cotton economy continued to grow. By the time of the Civil War, cotton constituted nearly two-thirds of the total export trade of the United States. It was little wonder that southern politicians now proclaimed: "Cotton is king!"

Increasing Cotton Cultivation

Cotton production boomed in the newly settled areas of what came to be known as the "lower South" (or, in a later era, the "Deep South"). Some began to call it the "Cotton Kingdom." The prospect of tremendous profits drew settlers to the lower South by the thousands. Some were wealthy planters from the older states, but most were small slaveholders or slaveless farmers who hoped to move into the planter class.

A similar shift, if an involuntary one, occurred in the slave population. Between 1840 and 1860, according to some estimates, 410,000 slaves moved from the upper South to the cotton states—either accompanying masters who were themselves migrating to the Southwest or (more often) sold to planters already there. The sale of slaves to the Southwest became an important economic activity in the upper South.

Rapid Expansion of Slavery

Southern Trade and Industry

In the face of this booming agricultural expansion, other forms of economic activity developed slowly in the South. There was growing activity in flour milling and in textile and iron manufacturing, particularly in the upper South, but industry remained an insignificant force in comparison with the agricultural economy. The total value of southern textile manufactures in 1860 was $4.5 million—a threefold increase over the value of

HAULING THE WHOLE WEEK'S PICKING This watercolor by William Henry Brown, painted in approximately 1842, portrays a slave family loading cotton onto a wagon, presumably after a hard day of picking. Even young children participate in the chores. Brown was an artist known for his silhouettes, a form popular in the nineteenth century. (One of his later subjects was Abraham Lincoln.) This picture is part of a five-foot cutout he made as a gift to a family he was visiting. *(William Henry Brown,* Hauling the Whole Weeks Picking, *1842. The Historic New Orleans Collection, 1975.93.1 & 1975.93.2)*

those goods twenty years before, but only about 2 percent of the value of the cotton exported that year.

Obstacles to Economic Development

The limited nonfarm commercial sector that did develop in the South was largely intended to serve the needs of the plantation economy. Particularly important were the brokers, or "factors," who marketed the planters' crops. The South had only a very rudimentary financial system, and the factors often also served the planters as bankers, providing them with credit. Other obstacles to economic development included the South's inadequate transportation system. Canals were almost nonexistent; most roads were crude and unsuitable for heavy transport; and railroads, although they expanded substantially in the 1840s and 1850s, failed to tie the region together effectively. The principal means of transportation was water. Planters generally shipped their crops to market along rivers or by sea; most manufacturing was in or near port towns.

De Bow's Commercial Review

The South was, therefore, becoming more and more dependent on the manufacturers, merchants, and professionals of the North. Some southerners began to advocate economic independence for the region, among them James D. B. De Bow of New Orleans, whose magazine, *De Bow's Commercial Review*, called for southern commercial and agricultural expansion and economic independence from the North. Yet even *De Bow's Commercial Review* was filled with advertisements from northern manufacturing firms; and its circulation was far smaller in the South than such northern magazines as *Harper's Weekly*.

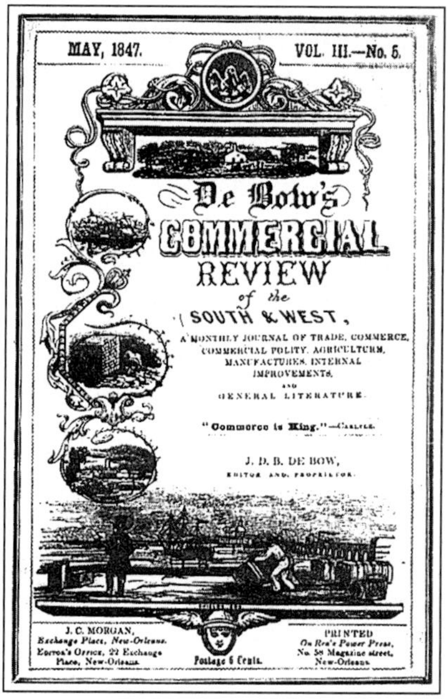
MAY, 1847. VOL. III.—No. 5.

De Bow's COMMERCIAL REVIEW of the SOUTH & WEST,

A MONTHLY JOURNAL OF TRADE, COMMERCE, COMMERCIAL POLITY, AGRICULTURE, MANUFACTURES, INTERNAL IMPROVEMENTS, AND GENERAL LITERATURE.

"Commerce is King."—Carlyle.

J. D. B. DE BOW, EDITOR AND PROPRIETOR.

J. C. MORGAN, Exchange Place, New-Orleans. Editor's Office, 22 Exchange Place, New-Orleans.

Postage 6 Cents.

PRINTED On Rea's Power Press, No. 58 Magazine street, New-Orleans.

DE BOW'S COMMERCIAL REVIEW J. D. B. De Bow, owner and editor of the South's leading magazine, presented his *Review* as a commercial publication—designed for those committed to commerce. But it also contained essays and articles promoting the South's way of life and what many white southerners considered the region's distinctive (and superior) culture. *(Courtesy of Archives and History, Jackson, MI.)*

Sources of Southern Difference

An important question about antebellum southern history is why the region did so little to develop a larger industrial and commercial economy of its own. Why did it remain so different from the North?

Sources of Uneven Development

Part of the reason was the great profitability of the region's agricultural system. In the Northeast, many people had turned to manufacturing as the agricultural economy of the region declined. In the South, the agricultural economy was booming, and ambitious people eager to profit from the emerging capitalist economy had little incentive to look elsewhere. Another reason was that wealthy southerners had so much capital invested in their land and their slaves that they had little left for other investments. Some historians have suggested that the southern climate—with its long, hot, steamy summers—was less suitable for industrial development than the climate of the North.

Distinct Southern Values

But the southern failure to create a flourishing commercial or industrial economy was also in part the result of a set of values distinctive to the South. Many white southerners liked to think of themselves as representatives of a special way of life. Southerners were, they argued, more concerned with a refined and gracious way of life than with rapid growth and development. But appealing as this image was to southern whites, it conformed to the reality of southern society in very limited ways.

SOUTHERN WHITE SOCIETY

Only a small minority of southern whites owned slaves. In 1860, when the white population was just above 8 million, the number of slaveholders was only 383,637. Even with all members of slaveowning families included in the figures, those living in slaveowning households still amounted to perhaps no more than one-quarter of the white population. And only a small proportion of this relatively small number of slaveowners owned slaves in substantial numbers.

The Planter Class

Planter Aristocracy's Dominance

How, then, did the South come to be seen as a society dominated by wealthy landowning planters? In large part, it was because the planter aristocracy exercised power and influence far in excess of their numbers.

White southerners liked to compare their planter class to the old upper classes of England and Europe. In fact, most of the southern upper class was not at all similar to the landed aristocracies of the Old World. In some areas of the upper South, the great aristocrats were indeed people whose families had occupied positions of wealth and power for generations. In most of the South, however, there was no longstanding landed aristocracy. As late as the 1850s, many of the great landowners in the lower South were still first-generation settlers, who had only relatively recently started to live in the comfort and luxury for which they became famous. Large areas of the South had been settled and cultivated for less than two decades at the time of the Civil War.

Nor was the world of the planter nearly as leisured and genteel as the aristocratic myth would suggest. Growing staple crops was a business. Planters were, in many respects, just as much competitive capitalists as the industrialists of the North. Even many affluent planters lived rather modestly, their wealth so heavily invested in land and slaves that there was little left for personal comfort. And white planters, including some substantial ones, tended to move frequently as new and presumably more productive areas opened up to cultivation.

The Aristocratic Ideal

Wealthy southern whites sustained their image of themselves as aristocrats in many ways. They adopted an elaborate code of "chivalry," which obligated white men to defend their "honor," often through dueling. They avoided such "coarse" occupations as trade and commerce; those who did not become planters often gravitated toward the military. The aristocratic ideal also found reflection in the definition of a special role for southern white women.

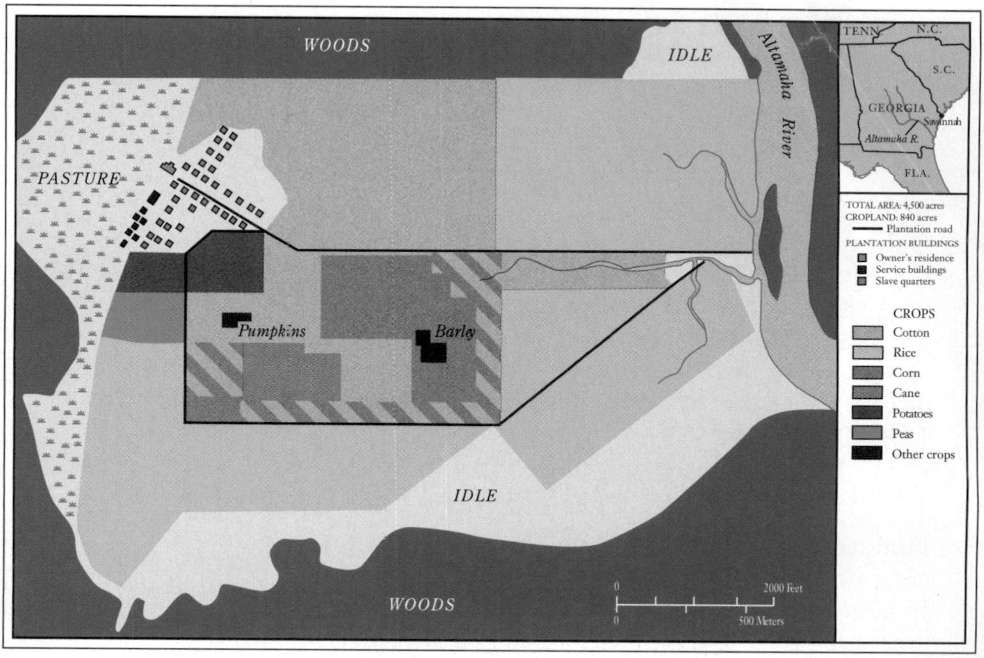

A GEORGIA PLANTATION This map of the Hopeton Plantation in South Carolina shows both how much plantations were connected to the national and world markets, and how much they tried to be self-sufficient. Note the large areas of land devoted to the growing of cotton, rice, and sugar cane, all of them crops for the market. ◆ *Why would a plantation in this part of the South be so much more diversified in the market crops it raised than the cotton plantations in the Mississippi Delta?* Note also the many crops grown for the local market or for consumption by residents of the plantation—potatoes, vegetables, corn, and others. The top left of the map shows the distribution of living quarters, with slaves' quarters grouped together very near the owner's residence. ◆ *Why would planters want their slaves living nearby? Why might slaves be unhappy about being so close to their owners?*

The "Southern Lady"

In some respects, affluent white women in the South occupied roles very similar to those of middle-class white women in the North. Their lives generally centered in the home, where (according to the South's social ideal) they served as companions to and hostesses for their husbands and as nurturing mothers for their children. "Genteel" southern white women seldom engaged in public activities or found income-producing employment.

But the life of the "southern lady" was also in many ways very different from that of her northern counterpart. For one thing, the cult of honor in the region meant that southern white men gave particular importance to the defense of women. In practice, this generally meant that white men were even more dominant and white women even more subordinate in southern culture than they were in the North. Social theorist George Fitzhugh wrote in the 1850s: "Women, like children, have but one right, and that is the right to protection. The right to protection involves the obligation to obey."

Female Subordinance Reinforced

More important in determining the role of southern white women, however, was that the vast majority of them lived on farms, with little access to the "public world" and thus few opportunities to look beyond their roles as wives and mothers. For many white women, living on farms of modest size meant a fuller engagement in the economic life of the family than was becoming typical for middle-class women in the North. These women engaged in spinning, weaving, and other production; they participated in agricultural tasks; they helped supervise the slave work force. On the larger plantations, however, even these limited roles were often considered unsuitable for white women, and the "plantation mistress" became, in some cases, more an ornament for her husband than an active part of the economy or the society. Southern white women also had less access to education than their northern counterparts. The few female "academies" in the South trained women primarily to be suitable wives.

Special Burdens

Southern white women had other special burdens as well. The southern white birth rate remained nearly 20 percent higher than that of the nation as a whole, and infant mortality in the region remained higher than elsewhere. The slave labor system also had a mixed impact on white women. It helped spare many of them from certain kinds of arduous labor, but it also damaged their relationships with their husbands. Male slaveowners had frequent sexual relationships with the female slaves on their plantations; the children of those unions served as a constant reminder to white women of their husbands' infidelities. Black women (and men) were obviously the most important victims of such practices, but white women suffered, too.

The Plain Folk

The typical white southerner was a yeoman farmer. Some of these "plain folk," as they became known, owned a few slaves, with whom they worked and lived more closely than did the larger planters. Some plain folk, most of whom owned their own land, devoted themselves largely to subsistence farming; others grew cotton or other crops for the market, but usually could not produce enough to allow them to expand their operations or even get out of debt.

One reason was the southern educational system. For the sons of wealthy planters, the region provided ample opportunities to gain an education. In 1860 there were 260 southern colleges and universities, public and private, with 25,000 students enrolled in them. But as in the rest of the United States, universities were only within the reach of the upper class. The elementary and secondary schools of the South were not only fewer than but also inferior to those of the Northeast. The South had more than 500,000 illiterate whites, over half the nation's total.

Inadequate Educational Opportunities

The subordination of the plain folk to the planter class raises an important question: Why did lower-class whites not oppose the aristocratic social system from which they benefited so little?

Some nonslaveowning whites did oppose the planter elite, but for the most part in limited ways and in isolated areas. These were mainly the "hill people," who lived in the Appalachian ranges east of the Mississippi, in the Ozarks to the west of the river, and in other "hill country" or "backcountry" areas. Of all southern whites, they were the most isolated from the mainstream of the region's life. They practiced a simple form of subsistence agriculture and owned practically no slaves. They were, in most respects, unconnected to the new commercial economy that dominated the great cotton-planting region of the South.

"Hill People"

Such whites frequently expressed animosity toward the planter aristocracy. The mountain region was the only part of the South to resist the movement toward secession when it finally developed. Even during the Civil War itself, many refused to support the Confederacy.

Far greater in number, however, were the nonslaveowning whites who lived in the midst of the plantation system. Many, perhaps most of them, accepted that system because they were tied to it in important ways. Small farmers depended on the local plantation aristocracy for many things: access to cotton gins, markets for their modest crops and their livestock, credit or other financial assistance in time of need. In many areas, moreover, the poorest resident of a county might easily be a cousin of the richest aristocrat. In the 1850s, the boom in the cotton economy allowed many small farmers to improve their economic fortunes. Some bought more land, became slaveowners, and moved into at least the fringes of plantation society. Others simply felt more secure in their positions as independent yeomen and hence more likely to embrace the fierce regional loyalty that was spreading throughout the white South in these years.

Dependence on the Plantation

There were other white southerners, however, who shared almost not at all in the plantation economy and yet continued to accept its premises. These were known variously as "crackers," "sand hillers," or "poor white trash." Occupying the infertile lands of the pine barrens, the red hills, and the swamps, they lived in genuine squalor. Many owned no land and supported themselves by foraging or hunting. Others worked at times as common laborers for their neighbors. Their degradation resulted partly from dietary deficiencies and disease. They resorted at times to eating clay (hence the tendency of more affluent whites to refer to them disparagingly as "clay eaters"), and they suffered from pellagra, hookworm, and malaria. Planters and small farmers alike held them in contempt.

Even among these southerners—the true outcasts of white society in the region—there was no real opposition to the plantation system or slavery. In part, undoubtedly, this was because these men and women were so benumbed by poverty that they had little strength to protest. But it resulted also from perhaps the single greatest unifying factor among the southern white population: their perception of race. However poor and miserable white southerners might be, they could still look down on the black population of the region and feel a bond with their fellow whites born of a determination to maintain their racial supremacy.

Absence of Class Conflict

SLAVERY: THE "PECULIAR INSTITUTION"

White southerners often referred to slavery as the "peculiar institution." By that they meant not that the institution was odd but that it was distinctive, special. American slavery was indeed distinctive. The South in the mid-nineteenth century was the only area in the Western world—except for Brazil, Cuba, and Puerto Rico—where slavery still existed. Slavery, more than any other single factor, isolated the South from the rest of American society.

Within the South itself, the institution of slavery had paradoxical results. On the one hand, it isolated blacks from whites. As a result, African Americans under slavery began to develop a society and culture of their own. On the other hand, slavery created a unique bond between blacks and whites—masters and slaves—in the South. The two groups may have maintained separate spheres, but each sphere was deeply influenced by the other.

Varieties of Slavery

The slave codes of the southern states forbade slaves to hold property, to leave their masters' premises without permission, to be out after dark, to congregate with other slaves except at church, to carry firearms, or to strike a white person even in self-defense. The codes prohibited whites from teaching slaves to read or write and denied slaves the right to testify in court against white people. The laws contained no provisions to legalize slave marriages or divorces. If an owner killed a slave while punishing him, the act was generally not considered a crime. Slaves, however, faced the death penalty for killing or even resisting a white person and for inciting revolt. The codes also contained extraordinarily rigid provisions for defining a person's race. Anyone with a trace (or often even a rumor) of African ancestry was defined as black.

Slave Codes

Enforcement of the laws, however, was spotty and uneven. Some slaves did acquire property, did learn to read and write, and did assemble with other slaves. White owners themselves handled most transgressions by their slaves and inflicted widely varying punishments. In other words, despite the rigid provisions of law, there was in reality considerable variety within the slave system. Some slaves lived in almost prisonlike conditions,

Debating the Past

THE CHARACTER OF SLAVERY

No issue in American history has produced a more spirited debate than the nature of plantation slavery. The debate began even before the Civil War, when abolitionists strove to expose slavery to the world as a brutal, dehumanizing institution, while Southern defenders of slavery tried to depict it as a benevolent, paternalistic system. But by the late nineteenth century, with white Americans eager for sectional conciliation, most Northern and Southern chroniclers of slavery began to accept a romanticized and unthreatening picture of the Old South and its peculiar institution.

The first major scholarly examination of slavery was Ulrich B. Phillips's *American Negro Slavery* (1918), which portrayed slavery as an essentially benign institution in which kindly masters looked after submissive and generally contented African Americans. Phillips's apologia for slavery remained the authoritative work on the subject for nearly thirty years.

In the 1940s, challenges to Phillips began to emerge. In 1941, for example, Melville J. Herskovits challenged Phillips's contention that black Americans retained little of their African cultural inheritance. In 1943, Herbert Aptheker published a chronicle of slave revolts as a way of challenging Phillips's claim that blacks were submissive and content.

A somewhat different challenge to Phillips emerged in the 1950s from historians who emphasized the brutality of the institution. Kenneth Stampp's *The Peculiar Institution* (1956) and Stanley Elkins's *Slavery* (1959) described a labor system that did serious physical and psychological damage to its victims. They portrayed slavery as something like a prison, in which men and women had virtually no space to develop their own social and cultural lives. Elkins compared the system to Nazi concentration camps and likened the childlike "Sambo" personality of slavery to the tragic distortions of character produced by the Holocaust.

In the early 1970s, an explosion of new scholarship on slavery shifted the emphasis away from the damage the system inflicted on African Americans and toward the striking success of the slaves themselves in building a culture of their own. John Blassingame in 1973 argued that "the most remarkable aspect of the whole process of enslavement is the extent to which the American-born slaves were able to retain their ancestors' culture." Herbert Gutman, in *The Black Family in Slavery and Freedom* (1976), challenged the prevailing belief that slavery had weakened and even destroyed the African-American family. On the contrary, he argued, the black family survived slavery with impressive strength, although with some significant differences from the prevailing form of the white family. Eugene Genovese's *Roll, Jordan, Roll* (1974) revealed how African Americans manipulated the paternalist assumptions that lay at the heart of slavery to build a large cultural space of their own where they could develop their own family life, social traditions, and religious patterns. That same year, Robert Fogel and Stanley Engerman published their controversial *Time on the Cross*, a highly quantitative study that supported some of the claims of Gutman and Genovese about black achievement but that went much further in portraying slavery as a successful and reasonably humane (if ultimately immoral) system. Slave workers, they argued, were better treated and lived in greater comfort than most Northern industrial workers of the same era. Their conclusions produced a storm of criticism.

Some of the most important recent scholarship on slavery extends the notion of slave autonomy to discussions of African-American women. Elizabeth Fox-Genovese's *Within the Plantation Household* (1988) examined the lives of both white and black women on the plantation. She portrayed slave women as defined by their dual roles as members of the plantation work force and anchors of the black family. Slave women, she argued, professed loyalty to their mistresses when forced to serve them as domestics; but their real loyalty remained to their own communities and families.

(text continued from page 291)

rigidly and harshly controlled by their masters. Many (probably most) others enjoyed considerable flexibility and autonomy.

The nature of the relationship between masters and slaves depended in part on the size of the plantation. White farmers with few slaves generally supervised their workers directly and often worked closely alongside them. The paternal relationship between such masters and their slaves could be warm and benevolent. It could also be tyrannical and cruel. In general, African Americans themselves preferred to live on larger plantations, where they had a chance for a social world of their own.

Paternal Relationship

Although the majority of slaveowners were small farmers, the majority of slaves lived on plantations of medium or large size, with substantial slave work forces. Thus the relationship between master and slave was much less intimate for the typical slave than for the typical slaveowner. Substantial planters often hired overseers and even assistant overseers to represent them. "Head drivers," trusted and responsible slaves often assisted by several subdrivers, acted under the overseer as foremen.

Life under Slavery

Slaves generally received an adequate yet simple diet, consisting mainly of cornmeal, salt pork, molasses, and on special occasions fresh meat or poultry. Many slaves cultivated gardens for their own use. Their masters provided them with cheap clothing and shoes. They lived in rough cabins, called slave quarters. The plantation mistress or a doctor retained by the owner provided some medical care, but slave women themselves—as "healers" and midwives, or simply as mothers—were the more important source.

Slaves worked hard, beginning with light tasks as children. Their workdays were longest at harvest time. Slave women worked particularly hard. They generally labored in the fields with the men, and they also handled cooking, cleaning, and child rearing. Many slave families were divided. Husbands and fathers often lived

Work Conditions

RETURNING FROM THE COTTON FIELD In this photograph, South Carolina field workers return after a day of picking cotton, some of their harvest carried in bundles on their heads. A black slave driver leads the way. *(©The New-York Historical Society)*

on neighboring plantations; at times, one spouse (usually the male) would be sold to a plantation owner far away. As a result, black women often found themselves acting in effect as single parents.

High Mortality Rates

Slaves were, as a group, much less healthy than southern whites. After 1808, when the importation of slaves became illegal, the proportion of blacks to whites in the nation as a whole steadily declined. The slower increase of the black population was a result of its comparatively high death rate. Slave mothers had large families, but the enforced poverty in which virtually all African Americans lived ensured that fewer of their children would survive to adulthood than the children of white parents. Even those who did survive typically died at a younger age than the average white person.

Household servants had a somewhat easier life—physically at least—than did field hands. On a small plantation, the same slaves might do both field work and housework. But on a large estate, there would generally be a separate domestic staff: nursemaids, housemaids, cooks, butlers, coachmen. These people lived close to the master and his family, eating the leftovers from the family table. Between the blacks and whites of such households affectionate, almost familial relationships might develop. More often, however, house servants resented their isolation from their fellow slaves and the lack of privacy that came with living in such close proximity to the master's family. Among other things, that proximity meant that their transgressions were more visible than those of field hands. When emancipation came after the Civil War, it was often the house servants who were the first to leave the plantations of their former owners.

Sexual Abuse

Female household servants were especially vulnerable to sexual abuse by their masters and white overseers. In addition to being subjected to unwanted sexual attention from white men, female slaves often received vindictive treatment from white women. Plantation mistresses naturally resented the sexual liaisons between their husbands and female slaves. Punishing their husbands was not usually possible, so they often punished the slaves instead—with arbitrary beatings, increased workloads, and various forms of psychological torment.

Slavery in the Cities

The conditions of slavery in the cities differed significantly from those in the countryside. On the relatively isolated plantations, slaves had little contact with free blacks and lower-class whites, and masters maintained a fairly direct and effective control. In the city, however, a master often could not supervise his slaves closely and at the same time use them profitably. Even if they slept at night in carefully watched backyard barracks, they moved about during the day alone, performing errands of various kinds.

There was a considerable market in the South for common laborers, particularly since, unlike in the North, there were few European immigrants to perform menial chores. As a result, masters often hired out slaves for such tasks. Slaves on contract worked in mining and lumbering (often far from cities), but others worked on the docks and on construction sites, drove wagons, and performed other unskilled jobs in cities and towns. Slave women and children worked in the region's few textile mills. Particularly skilled workers such as blacksmiths or carpenters were also often hired out. After regular working hours, many of them fended for themselves; thus urban slaves gained numerous opportunities to mingle with free blacks and with whites. In the cities, the line between slavery and freedom was less distinct than on the plantation.

Relative Autonomy of Urban Slaves

Free Blacks

There were about 250,000 free blacks in the slaveholding states by the start of the Civil War, more than half of them in Virginia and Maryland. In some cases, they were slaves who had somehow earned money with which they managed to buy their own and their families' freedom. It was most often urban blacks, with their greater freedom of movement and activity, who could take that route. One example was Elizabeth Keckley, a slave woman who bought freedom for herself and her son with proceeds from sewing. She later became a seamstress, personal servant, and companion to Mary Todd Lincoln in the White House. But few masters had any incentive, or inclination, to give up their slaves, so this route was open to relatively few people.

New Restrictions on Manumission

Some slaves were set free by a master who had moral qualms about slavery, or by a master's will after his death—for example, the more than 400 slaves belonging to John Randolph of Roanoke, freed in 1833. From the 1830s on, however, state laws governing slavery became more rigid, in part in response to the fears Nat Turner's revolt (see p. 297) created among white southerners. The new laws made it more and more difficult, and in some cases practically impossible, for owners to set free (or "manumit") their slaves.

A few free blacks attained wealth and prominence. Some owned slaves themselves, usually relatives whom they had bought in order to ensure their ultimate emancipation. In a few cities—New Orleans, Natchez, and Charleston—free black communities managed to flourish relatively unmolested by whites and with some economic stability. Most southern free blacks, however, lived in abject poverty. Yet, great as were the hardships of freedom, blacks usually preferred them to slavery.

Slave Resistance

Slaveowners, and many other white Americans after emancipation, liked to argue that the slaves were generally content, "happy with their lot." That may have been true in some cases. But it is clear that the vast majority of southern blacks yearned for freedom. Evidence for that can be found, if nowhere else, in the reaction of slaves when emancipation finally came. Virtually all reacted to freedom with great joy; relatively few chose to remain in the service of the whites who had owned them before the Civil War.

Adaptation and Resistance

Rather than contented acceptance, the dominant response of blacks to slavery was a complex one: a combination of adaptation and resistance. At the extremes, slavery could produce two very different reactions, each of which served as the basis for a powerful stereotype in white society. One extreme was what became known as the "Sambo"—the shuffling, grinning, head-scratching, deferential slave who acted out the role that he recognized the white world expected of him. More often than not, the "Sambo" pattern of behavior was a charade, a facade assumed in the presence of whites. The other extreme was the slave rebel—the African American who could not bring himself or herself to either acceptance or accommodation but remained forever rebellious.

Slave Revolts

Actual slave revolts were extremely rare, but the knowledge that they were possible struck terror into the hearts of white southerners everywhere. In 1800, Gabriel Prosser gathered 1,000 rebellious slaves outside Richmond; but two Africans gave the

HARRIET TUBMAN WITH ESCAPED SLAVES Harriet Tubman (c. 1820–1913) was born into slavery in Maryland. In 1849, when her master died, she escaped to Philadelphia to avoid being sold out of state. Over the next ten years, she assisted first members of her own family and then up to 300 other slaves to escape from Maryland to freedom. During the Civil War, she served alternately as a nurse and as a spy for Union forces in South Carolina. She is shown here, on the left, with some of the slaves she had helped to free. *(Smith College Museum of Art)*

plot away, and the Virginia militia stymied the uprising before it could begin. Prosser and thirty-five others were executed. In 1822, the Charleston free black Denmark Vesey and his followers—rumored to total 9,000—made preparations for revolt; but again word leaked out, and suppression and retribution followed. On a summer night in 1831, Nat Turner, a slave preacher, led a band of African Americans armed with guns and axes from house to house in Southampton County, Virginia. They killed sixty white men, women, and children before being overpowered by state and federal troops. More than a hundred blacks were executed in the aftermath.

For the most part, however, resistance to slavery took other, less violent forms. Some blacks attempted to resist by running away. A small number managed to escape to the North or to Canada, especially after sympathetic whites and free blacks began organizing secret escape routes, known as the "underground railroad," to assist them in flight. But the odds against a successful escape were very high. The hazards of distance and the slaves' ignorance of geography were serious obstacles. So were the white "slave patrols," which stopped wandering blacks on sight throughout the South demanding to see travel permits. Despite all the obstacles to success, however, blacks continued to run away from their masters in large numbers.

Day-to-day Slave Resistance

But perhaps the most important method of resistance was simply a pattern of everyday behavior by which blacks defied their masters. That whites so often considered blacks to be lazy and shiftless suggests one means of resistance: refusal to work hard. Some slaves stole from their masters or from neighboring whites. Some performed isolated acts of sabotage: losing or breaking tools or performing tasks improperly. In extreme cases, blacks might make themselves useless by cutting off their fingers or even committing suicide. A few turned on their masters and killed them. The extremes, however, were rare. For the most part, blacks resisted by building subtle methods of rebellion into their normal patterns of behavior.

THE CULTURE OF SLAVERY

Resistance was only part of the slave response to slavery. Another was an elaborate process of adaptation. One of the ways blacks adapted was by developing their own, separate culture, one that enabled them to sustain a sense of racial pride and unity.

Slave Religion

A separate slave religion was not supposed to exist. Almost all African Americans were Christians by the early nineteenth century. Some had converted voluntarily and some in response to persuasion or coercion from their masters and Protestant missionaries who evangelized among them. Masters expected their slaves to worship under the supervision of white ministers. Indeed, autonomous black churches were banned by law, and many slaves became members of the same denominations as their owners.

Black Christianity

Nevertheless, blacks throughout the South developed their own version of Christianity, at times incorporating into it such practices as voodoo or other polytheistic religious traditions of Africa. Or they simply bent religion to the special circumstances of bondage.

African-American religion was more emotional than its white counterpart and reflected the influence of African customs and practices. Slave prayer meetings routinely involved fervent chanting, spontaneous exclamations from the congregation, and ecstatic conversion experiences. Black religion was also more joyful and affirming than that of many white denominations. And above all, African-American religion emphasized the dream of freedom and deliverance. In their prayers and songs and sermons, black Christians talked and sang of the day when the Lord would "call us home," "deliver us to freedom," "take us to the Promised Land."

And while their white masters generally chose to interpret such language merely as the expression of hopes for life after death, many blacks themselves used the images of Christian salvation to express their own dream of freedom in the present world.

In cities and towns in the South, some African Americans had their own churches, where free blacks occasionally worshiped alongside slaves. In the countryside, however, slaves usually attended the same churches as their masters. Seating in such churches was usually segregated. Blacks sat in the rear or in balconies. They held their own services later, often in secret, usually at night.

Language and Music

In many areas, slaves retained a language of their own. Having arrived in America speaking many different African languages, the first generations of slaves had as much difficulty communicating with one another as they did with white people. To overcome these barriers, they learned a simple, common language (known to linguists as "pidgin"). It retained some African words, but it drew primarily, if selectively, from English. And while slave language grew more sophisticated as blacks spent more time in America, some features of this early pidgin survived in black speech for many generations.

"Pidgin"

Music was especially important in slave society. Again, the African heritage was an important influence. African music relied heavily on rhythm, and so did black music in America. Africans thought of music as an accompaniment to dance, and so did blacks in America. The banjo became important to slave music. But most important were voices and song.

Field workers often used songs to pass the time; since they sang them in the presence of the whites, they usually attached relatively innocuous words to them. But African Americans also created more politically challenging music in the relative privacy of their own religious services. It was there that the tradition of the spiritual emerged. Through the spiritual, Africans in America not only expressed their religious faith, but also lamented their bondage and expressed continuing hope for freedom.

Importance of Slave Spirituals

Slave songs were rarely written down and often seemed entirely spontaneous; but much slave music was really derived from African and Caribbean traditions passed on through generations. Performers also improvised variations on other songs they had heard. Slaves often created instruments for themselves out of whatever materials were at hand. When the setting permitted it, African Americans danced to their music—dances very different from and much more spontaneous than the formal steps that nineteenth-century whites generally learned. They also used music to accompany another of their important cultural traditions: storytelling.

THE OLD PLANTATION This painting, by an unidentified folk artist of the early nineteenth century, suggests the importance of music in the lives of plantation slaves in America. Banjos, such as the one the black musician at right is playing, were originally African instruments. (The Old Plantantion, *c. 1790–1800. Abby Aldrich Rockefeller Folk Art Museum. Colonial Williamsburg Foundation, Williamsburg, VA)*

The Slave Family

The slave family was the other crucial institution of black culture in the South. Like religion, it suffered from legal restrictions. Nevertheless, what we now call the "nuclear family" consistently emerged as the dominant kinship model among African Americans.

Black women generally began bearing children at younger ages than most whites, often as early as age fourteen or fifteen (sometimes as a result of unwanted sexual relations with their masters). Slave communities did not condemn premarital pregnancy in the way white society did, and black couples would often begin living together before marrying. It was customary, however, for couples to marry—in a ceremony involving formal vows—soon after conceiving a child. Many marriages occurred between slaves living on neighboring plantations. Husbands and wives sometimes visited each other with the permission of their masters, but often such visits had to be in secret, at night. Family ties were generally no less strong than those of whites.

Slave Marriages

When marriages did not survive, it was often because of circumstances over which blacks had no control. Up to a third of all black families were broken apart by the slave trade. That produced some of the other distinctive characteristics of the black family. Extended kinship networks were strong and important, and often helped compensate for the breakup of nuclear families. A slave forced suddenly to move to a new area, far from his or her family, might create fictional kinship ties and become "adopted" by a family in the new community. Even so, the impulse to maintain contact with a spouse and children remained strong long after the breakup of a family. One of the most frequent causes of flight from the plantation was a slave's desire to find a husband, wife, or child who had been sent elsewhere.

Paternalism

However much blacks resented their lack of freedom, they often found it difficult to maintain an entirely hostile attitude toward their owners. They depended on whites for the material means of existence—food, clothing, and shelter—and they relied on them as well for security and protection. There was, in short, a paternal relationship between slave and master—sometimes harsh, sometimes kindly, but always important. That paternalism, in fact, became a vital instrument of white control. By creating a sense of mutual dependence, whites helped reduce resistance to an institution that, in essence, served only the interests of the ruling race.

CONCLUSION

While the North was creating a complex and rapidly developing commercial-industrial economy, the South was expanding its agrarian economy without making many fundamental changes in its character. Great migrations took many southern whites, and even more African-American slaves, into new agricultural areas in the Deep South, where they created a booming "cotton kingdom." The cotton economy created many great fortunes, and some modest ones. It also entrenched the planter class as the dominant force within southern society—both as owners of vast numbers of slaves and as patrons, creditors, landlords, and marketers for the large number of poor whites who lived on the edge of the planter world.

The differences between the North and the South were a result of differences in natural resources, social structure, climate, and culture. Above all, they were the result of the existence within the South of an unfree labor system that prevented the kind of social fluidity that an industrializing society usually requires.

FOR FURTHER REFERENCE

Peter Kolchin, *American Slavery, 1619–1877* (1993) is an excellent recent synthesis of the history of slavery in the United States from the settlement of Virginia through Reconstruction. James Oakes, *Slavery and Freedom* (1990) provides an overview of southern politics and society in the antebellum period. Eugene Genovese's classic study *Roll, Jordan, Roll: The World the Slaves Made* (1974) argues that masters and slaves forged a system of mutual obligations within a fundamentally coercive social system. Genovese's *The Political Economy of Slavery* (1965) argues that slavery blocked southern economic development. James Oakes, *The Ruling Race: A History of American Slaveholders* (1982) argues that slaveowners were hardheaded businessmen and capitalists. Frederick Douglass's *Narrative of the Life of Frederick Douglass,* first published in 1845, is a classic autobiography. Elizabeth Fox-Genovese, *Within the Plantation Household* (1988) argues against the idea that black and white women shared a community of interests on southern plantations. Charles Joyner, *Down by the Riverside: A South Carolina Slave Community* (1984) is a fine study of slavery in a single community. Charles C. Bolton, *Poor Whites of the Antebellum South: Tenants and Laborers in Central North and Northeast Mississippi* (1994) is a good study of a neglected group in the southern population. Bertram Wyatt-Brown, *Southern Honor: Ethics and Behavior in the Old South* (1982) argues that concepts of honor lay at the core of southern white identity in the antebellum period. Steven Hahn, *The Roots of Southern Populism: Yeomen Farmers and the Transformation of the Georgia Upcountry, 1850–1890* (1983) argues that white farmers in upcountry regions of the antebellum South maintained economically self-sufficient communities on the periphery of the market.

For quizzes, Internet resources, references to additional books and films, and more, consult this book's Online Learning Center at www.mhhe.com/unfinishednation4.

***GIRL'S EVENING SCHOOL* (C. 1840), ANONYMOUS** Schooling for women, which expanded significantly in the mid-nineteenth century, included training in domestic arts (as indicated by the sewing table at right), as well as in reading, writing, and other basic skills. *(Unidentified artist, American, c. 1840.* Girls' Evening School. *Graphite pencil and watercolor, 34.3 x 46.0 cm. © 2003 Museum of Fine Arts, Boston. Gift of Maxim Karolik, 53.2431)*

TIME LINE

1821	1826	1830	1831	1833	1837	1840	1841
New York constructs first penitentiary	Cooper's *The Last of the Mohicans*	Joseph Smith publishes the Book of Mormon	The *Liberator* begins publication	American Antislavery Society founded	Horace Mann secretary of Massachusetts Board of Education	Liberty Party formed	Brook Farm founded

CHAPTER TWELVE

ANTEBELLUM CULTURE AND REFORM

The Romantic Impulse
Remaking Society
The Crusade against Slavery

The United States in the mid-nineteenth century was growing rapidly in geographical extent, in population, and in the size and complexity of its economy. Most Americans were excited by the new possibilities that economic growth was providing. But they were also painfully aware of the dislocations that it was creating.

One result of these conflicting attitudes was the emergence of movements to "reform" the nation. Some rested on an optimistic faith in human nature, a belief that within every individual resided a spirit that was basically good and that society should attempt to unleash. A second impulse was a desire for order and control. With their traditional values and institutions being challenged and eroded, many Americans yearned above all for a restoration of stability and discipline. Often, this impulse embodied a conservative nostalgia for better, simpler times. But it also inspired efforts to create new institutions of social control, suited to the realities of the new age.

By the end of the 1840s, however, one issue—slavery—had come to overshadow all others. And one group of reformers—the abolitionists—had become the most influential of all.

1845	1848	1850	1851	1852	1854	1855
Frederick Douglass's autobiography	Women's rights convention at Seneca Falls, N.Y.	Hawthorne's *The Scarlet Letter*	Melville's *Moby Dick*	Beecher Stowe's *Uncle Tom's Cabin*	Thoreau's *Walden*	Whitman's *Leaves of Grass*
	Oneida Community founded					

THE ROMANTIC IMPULSE

"In the four quarters of the globe," wrote the English wit Sydney Smith in 1820, "who reads an American book? or goes to an American play? or looks at an American picture or statue?" The answer, he assumed, was obvious: no one.

American intellectuals were painfully aware of the low regard in which Europeans held their culture, and they tried to create an artistic life that would express their own nation's special virtues. At the same time, many of the nation's cultural leaders were striving for another kind of liberation, which was—ironically—largely an import from Europe: the spirit of romanticism. In literature, in philosophy, in art, even in politics and economics, American intellectuals were committing themselves to the liberation of the human spirit.

The Spirit of Romanticism

Nationalism and Romanticism in American Painting

When Sydney Smith asked in 1820 who looked at an American painting, he was expressing the almost universal belief among European artists that they—and they alone—stood at the center of the world of art. But in the United States, a great many people were, in fact, looking at American paintings—and they were doing so not because the paintings introduced them to the great traditions of Europe, but because they believed Americans were creating important new artistic traditions of their own.

American painters sought to capture the undiluted power of nature by portraying some of the nation's most spectacular and undeveloped areas. The first great school of American painters emerged in New York. Frederic Church, Thomas Cole, Thomas Doughty, and Asher Durand—who were, along with others, known as the Hudson River School—painted the spectacular vistas of the rugged and still largely untamed Hudson Valley. Like Ralph Waldo Emerson and Henry David Thoreau, whom many of the painters read and admired (see pp. 309–310), they considered nature—far more than civilization—the best source of wisdom and fulfillment. In portraying the Hudson Valley, they seemed to announce that in America, unlike in Europe, "wild nature" still existed; and that America, therefore, was a nation of greater promise than the played-out lands of the Old World.

Hudson River School

In later years, some of the Hudson River painters traveled further west. Their enormous canvases of great natural wonders—the Yosemite Valley, Yellowstone, the Rocky Mountains—touched a passionate chord among the public. Some of the most famous of their paintings—particularly the works of Albert Bierstadt and Thomas Moran—traveled around the country attracting enormous crowds.

KINDRED SPIRITS Thomas Cole was one of the early leaders of the Hudson River School of artists in New York, and he is shown here, in a painting by Asher Durand, standing in the wilderness of the Hudson Valley with the great New York poet and editor William Cullen Bryant, a hero of mid-nineteenth-century intellectual life. Durand, who succeeded Cole as a leader of the Hudson Valley School, painted this scene not long after Cole's death. It was inspired by a moving eulogy Bryant had given at Cole's funeral, and Durand concluded that the two men were "kindred spirits" in their reverence for nature. Durand himself once wrote that "art must be a vision of God through nature." (Thomas Cole and William Cullen Bryant *by Asher Durand, New York Public Library, Special Collections)*

An American Literature

The effort to create a distinctively American literature made considerable progress in the 1820s through the work of the first great American novelist: James Fenimore Cooper. What most distinguished his work was its evocation of the American West. Cooper had a lifelong fascination with the human relationship to nature and with the challenges (and dangers) of America's expansion westward. His most important novels—among them *The Last of the Mohicans* (1826) and *The Deerslayer* (1841)—explored the experience of rugged white frontiersmen with Indians, pioneers, violence, and the law. Cooper evoked the ideal of the independent individual with a natural inner goodness—an ideal that many Americans feared was in jeopardy.

Another later group of American writers displayed more clearly the appeal of romanticism to the nation's artists and intellectuals. In 1855, Walt Whitman published his first book of poems, *Leaves of Grass.* His poems celebrated democracy, the liberation of the individual spirit, and the pleasures of the flesh. Whitman helped liberate verse from traditional, restrictive conventions; he also expressed a yearning for emotional and physical release and personal fulfillment—a yearning perhaps rooted in part in his own experience as a homosexual living in a society profoundly intolerant of unconventional sexuality.

Walt Whitman

Less exuberant was Herman Melville, perhaps the greatest American writer of his era. The most important of his novels was *Moby Dick*, published in 1851—the story of Ahab, the powerful, driven captain of a whaling vessel, who was obsessed with his search for Moby Dick, the great white whale that had once maimed him. It was a story of courage and of the strength of human will. But it was also a tragedy of pride and revenge, and an uncomfortable metaphor for the harsh, individualistic, achievement-driven culture of nineteenth-century America.

Literature in the Antebellum South

Edgar Allan Poe

Similarly bleak were the works of the southern writer Edgar Allan Poe, who produced stories and poems that were primarily sad and macabre. His first book, *Tamerlane and Other Poems* (1827), received little recognition. But later works, including his most famous poem, "The Raven" (1845), established him as a major, if controversial, literary figure. Poe evoked images of individuals rising above the narrow confines of intellect and exploring the deeper world of the spirit and the emotions. Yet that world, he seemed to say, contained much pain and horror. Other American writers were contemptuous of Poe's work and his message, but he was ultimately to have a profound effect on European poets.

Poe, however, was something of an exception in the world of southern literature. The South experienced a literary flowering of its own in the mid-nineteenth century, and it produced writers and artists who were, like their northern counterparts, concerned with defining the nature of American society and of the American nation. But white southerners tended to produce very different images of what that society was and should be.

Southern novelists of the 1830s (among them Beverly Tucker, William Alexander Caruthers, and John Pendleton Kennedy) produced historical romances or romantic eulogies of the plantation system of the upper South. The most distinguished of the region's men of letters was William Gilmore Simms. For a time, his work expressed a broad nationalism that transcended his regional background; but by the 1840s he too had become a strong defender of southern institutions—especially slavery—against the encroachments of the North. There was, he believed, a unique quality to southern life that it was the duty of intellectuals to defend.

William Gilmore Simms

One group of southern writers, however, produced works that were more broadly American. These were writers from the fringes of plantation society, who depicted the world of the backwoods rural areas. Augustus B. Longstreet, Joseph G. Baldwin, Johnson J. Hooper, and others focused on ordinary people and poor whites. Instead of romanticizing their subjects, they were deliberately and sometimes painfully realistic. And they seasoned their sketches with a robust, vulgar humor that was new to American literature. These southern realists established a tradition of American regional humor that was ultimately to find its most powerful voice in Mark Twain.

The Transcendentalists

One of the outstanding expressions of the romantic impulse in America came from a group of New England writers and philosophers known as the transcendentalists. Borrowing heavily from German and English writers and philosophers, the transcendentalists embraced a theory of the individual that rested on a distinction between what they called "reason" and "understanding." Reason, as they defined it, had little to do with rationality. It was, rather, the individual's innate capacity to grasp beauty and truth by giving full expression to the instincts and emotions. Understanding, by contrast, was the use of intellect in the narrow, artificial ways imposed by society; it involved the repression of instinct and the victory of externally imposed learning. Every person's goal, therefore, should be liberation from "understanding" and, instead, the cultivation of "reason." Each individual should strive to "transcend" the limits of the intellect and allow the emotions, the "soul," to create an "original relation to the Universe."

Transcendentalist philosophy emerged first in America among a small group of intellectuals centered in Concord, Massachusetts, and led by Ralph Waldo Emerson. A Unitarian minister in his youth, Emerson left the clergy in 1832 to devote himself to writing, teaching, and lecturing. In "Nature" (1836), Emerson wrote that in the quest for self-fulfillment, individuals should work for a communion with the natural world: "in the woods, we return to reason and faith. . . . Standing on the bare ground,—my head bathed by the blithe air, and uplifted into infinite space,—all mean egotism vanishes. . . . I am part and particle of God." In other essays, he was even more explicit in advocating a commitment of the individual to the full exploration of inner capacities.

Ralph Waldo Emerson

Almost as influential as Emerson was Henry David Thoreau. Thoreau went even further in repudiating the repressive forces of society, which produced, he said, "lives of quiet desperation." Each individual should work for self-realization by resisting pressures to conform to society's expectations and responding instead to his or her own instincts. Thoreau's own effort to free himself—immortalized in *Walden* (1854)—led him to build a small cabin in the Concord woods on the edge of Walden Pond, where he lived alone for

Thoreau's Walden

two years as simply as he could, attempting to liberate himself from what he considered society's excessive interest in material comforts. Thoreau's rejection of what he considered the artificial constraints of society extended to his relationship with government. In his 1849 essay "Resistance to Civil Government," he argued that a government that required an individual to violate his or her own morality had no legitimate authority. The proper response was "civil disobedience," or "passive resistance"—a public refusal to obey unjust laws.

The Defense of Nature

As the tributes of Emerson and Thoreau to the power of nature suggest, a small but influential group of Americans in the mid- and late nineteenth century feared the impact of the new capitalist enthusiasms on the integrity of the natural world. "The mountains and cataracts, which were to have made poets and painters," wrote the essayist Oliver Wendell Holmes, "have been mined for anthracite and dammed for water power."

New Understanding of Nature

To the transcendentalists, as well as to others, nature was not just a setting for economic activity, as many farmers, miners, and others believed. It was the source of deep, personal human inspiration—the vehicle through which individuals could best realize the truth within their own souls. Genuine spirituality, they argued, did not come from formal religion, but through communion with the natural world. "In wildness is the preservation of the world," Thoreau once wrote. Humans separated from nature, he believed, would lose a substantial part of their humanity.

In making such claims, the transcendentalists were among the first Americans to anticipate the environmental movement of the twentieth century. They had no scientific basis for their defense of the wilderness, little sense of the twentieth-century notion of the interconnectedness of species. But they did believe in, and articulate, an essential unity between humanity and nature—a spiritual unity, they believed, without which civilization would be impoverished. They looked at nature, they said, "with new eyes," and with those eyes they saw that "behind nature, throughout nature, spirit is present."

Visions of Utopia

Although transcendentalism was at its heart an individualistic philosophy, it helped spawn one of the most famous of all nineteenth-century experiments in communal living: Brook Farm. The dream of the Boston transcendentalist George Ripley, Brook Farm was established in 1841 as an experimental community in West Roxbury, Massachusetts. There, according to Ripley, individuals would gather to create a new society that would permit every member to have full opportunity for self-realization. All residents would share equally in

Failure of Brook Farm

PLAN FOR THE COLONY AT NEW HARMONY The English reformer Robert Owen came to America in the 1820s to create an experimental community in which to test his own theories of cooperative living. This architect's drawing reveals the grandiose plans Owen and his followers had for the colony, which was in Indiana on the banks of the Wabash River on the site of an earlier social experiment by German idealists. In this plan, which was never constructed, the architecture reflects the sense of order and rationality Owen hoped to bring to the community. The plan was designed "to form a new combination of circumstances, capable of producing permanently greater physical, moral, and intellectual advantages . . . than have ever yet been realized in any age or country." *(The Library of Congress)*

the labor of the community so that all could share as well in the leisure, which was essential for cultivation of the self. The tension between the ideal of individual freedom and the demands of a communal society took their toll on Brook Farm. Many residents became disenchanted and left. When a fire destroyed the central building of the community in 1847, the experiment dissolved.

Among the original residents of Brook Farm was the writer Nathaniel Hawthorne, who expressed his disillusionment with the experiment and, to some extent, with transcendentalism in a series of novels. In *The Blithedale Romance* (1852), he wrote scathingly of Brook Farm itself. In other novels—most notably *The Scarlet Letter* (1850) and *The House of the Seven Gables* (1851)—he wrote equally passionately about the price individuals pay for cutting themselves off from society. Egotism, he claimed (in an indirect challenge to the transcendentalist faith in the self), was the "serpent" that lay at the heart of human misery.

Brook Farm was one of many experimental communities in the years before the Civil War. The Scottish industrialist and philanthropist Robert Owen founded an experimental community in Indiana in 1825, which he named New Harmony. It was to be a "Village of Cooperation," in which every resident worked and lived in total equality. The community was an economic failure, but the vision that had inspired it continued to enchant some Americans. Dozens of other "Owenite" experiments began in other locations in the ensuing years.

New Harmony

Redefining Gender Roles

Many of the new utopian communities were centrally concerned with the relationship between men and women. Some experimented with a radical redefinition of gender roles.

Redefined Gender Roles

Such a redefinition was central to one of the most enduring of the utopian colonies of the nineteenth century: the Oneida Community, established in 1848 in upstate New York by John Humphrey Noyes. The Oneida "Perfectionists," as residents of the community called themselves, rejected traditional notions of family and marriage. All residents, Noyes declared, were "married" to all other residents; there were to be no permanent conjugal ties. But Oneida was not, as horrified critics often claimed, an experiment in unrestrained "free love." It was a place where the community carefully monitored sexual behavior; where women were protected from unwanted childbearing; and where children were raised communally, often seeing little of their own parents. The Oneidans took pride in what they considered their liberation of women from the demands of male "lust" and from the traditional bonds of family.

The Shakers, too, made a redefinition of traditional gender roles central to their society. Founded by "Mother" Ann Lee in the 1770s, the society of the Shakers survived into the twentieth century. (A tiny remnant is left today.) But the Shakers attracted a particularly large following in the mid-nineteenth century and established more than twenty communities throughout the Northeast and Northwest in the 1840s. They derived their name from a unique religious ritual—in which members of a congregation would "shake" themselves free of sin while performing a loud chant and an ecstatic dance.

The most distinctive feature of Shakerism, however, was its commitment to complete celibacy—which meant, of course, that no one could be born into Shakerism; all Shakers had to choose the faith voluntarily. Shakerism attracted about 6,000 members in the 1840s, more women than men. They lived in communities where contacts between men and women were strictly limited, and they endorsed the idea of sexual equality. Within Shaker society, women exercised the greatest power.

Commitment to Celibacy

The Shakers were not, however, motivated only by a desire to escape the burdens of traditional gender roles. They were trying as well to create a society separated and protected from the chaos and disorder that they believed had come to characterize American life as a whole. In that, they were much like other dissenting religious sects and other utopian communities of their time.

The Mormons

Among the most important efforts to create a new and more ordered society within the old was that of the Church of Jesus Christ of Latter-day Saints—the Mormons. Mormonism began in upstate New York through the efforts of Joseph Smith. While still a teenager, he claimed he was visited by God and in 1830, when he was just twenty-four, he published a remarkable document—the Book of Mormon, named for the ancient prophet who he claimed had written it. It was, he said, a translation of a set of golden tablets he had found in the hills of New York, revealed to him by an angel of God. The Book of Mormon told the story of two successful ancient civilizations in America, whose people had anticipated the coming of Christ and were rewarded when Jesus actually came to America after his resurrection. Ultimately, both civilizations collapsed because of their rejection of Christian principles. But Smith believed their history as righteous societies could serve as a model for a new holy community in the United States.

Joseph Smith

In 1831, gathering a small group of believers around him, Smith began searching for a sanctuary for his new community of "saints," an effort that would continue unhappily for more than fifteen years. Time and again the Latter-day Saints, as they called themselves, attempted to establish peaceful communities. Time and again they met with persecution from their neighbors, who were suspicious of their radical religious doctrines—their claims of new prophets, new scripture, and divine authority. Opponents were also concerned by their rapid growth and their increasing political strength. Near the end of his life, Joseph Smith introduced the practice of polygamy (the right of men to take several wives), which became public knowledge after Smith's death. From then on, polygamy became another target of anti-Mormon opposition.

Driven from their original settlements in Independence, Missouri, and Kirtland, Ohio, the Mormons founded a new town in Illinois that they named Nauvoo. In the early 1840s, it became an imposing and economically successful community. In 1844, however, bitter enemies of Joseph Smith published an inflammatory attack on him. Smith ordered his followers to destroy the offending press, and he was subsequently arrested and imprisoned in Carthage, Illinois. There an angry mob attacked the jail and shot and killed him. The Mormons soon abandoned Nauvoo and, under the leadership of Smith's successor, Brigham Young, traveled across the Great Plains and the Rocky Mountains—a society of 12,000 people, in one of the largest single group migrations in American history. They established several communities in Utah, including the present Salt Lake City. There, at last, the Mormons were able to create a lasting settlement.

Utah Founded

Like other experiments in social organization of the era, Mormonism reflected a belief in human perfectibility. God had once been a man, the church taught, and thus every man or woman could aspire to move continuously closer to God. Within a highly developed and centrally directed ecclesiastical structure, Mormons created a haven for people demoralized by the disorder and uncertainty of the secular world. The original Mormons were, for the most part, men and women who felt displaced in their rapidly changing society—economically marginal people left behind by the material growth and social progress of their era. In the new religion, they found a strong and animating faith. In the society it created, they found security and order.

REMAKING SOCIETY

New Reform Efforts

The reform impulse also helped create new movements to remake mainstream society—movements in which, to a striking degree, women formed both the rank and file and the leadership. By the 1830s, such movements had taken the form of organized reform societies.

Revivalism, Morality, and Order

The philosophy of reform arose in part from the optimistic vision of those such as the transcendentalists who preached the divinity of the individual. Another source was Protestant revivalism—the movement that had begun with the Second Great Awakening early in the century and had, by the 1820s, evolved into a powerful force for social reform.

Religious Basis of Reform

The New Light evangelicals embraced the optimistic belief that every individual was capable of salvation through his or her own efforts. Partly as a result, revivalism soon became not only a means of personal salvation but an effort to reform the larger society. In particular, revivalism produced a crusade against personal immorality. "The church," said Charles Grandison Finney, the leading revivalist of his time, "must take right ground on the subject of Temperance, the Moral Reform, and all the subjects of practical morality which come up for decision from time to time."

Evangelical Protestantism added major strength to the crusade against drunkenness. No social vice, temperance advocates argued, was more responsible for crime, disorder, and poverty than the excessive use of alcohol. Women complained that men spent money their families needed on alcohol and that drunken husbands often beat and abused their wives. Temperance also appealed to those who were alarmed by immigration; drunkenness, many nativists believed, was responsible for violence and disorder in immigrant communities. By 1840, temperance had become a major national movement, with powerful organizations and more than a million followers who had signed a formal pledge to forgo hard liquor.

Health, Science, and Phrenology

For some Americans, the search for individual and social perfection led to an interest in new theories of health and knowledge. Threats to public health were critical to the sense of insecurity that underlay many reform movements, especially after the terrible cholera epidemics of the 1830s

THE DRUNKARD'S PROGRESS This 1846 lithograph by Nathaniel Currier shows what temperance advocates argued was the inevitable consequence of alcohol consumption. Beginning with an apparently innocent "glass with a friend," the young man rises step by step to the summit of drunken revelry, then declines to desperation and suicide while his abandoned wife and child grieve. *(The Library of Congress)*

Cholera Epidemics

and 1840s. Cholera is a severe bacterial infection of the intestines, usually a result of consuming contaminated food or water. In the nineteenth century, fewer than half of those who contracted the disease normally survived. Thousands of people died of cholera during its occasional outbreaks, and in certain cities the effects were truly catastrophic. Nearly a quarter of the population of New Orleans died in an 1833 epidemic. Many municipalities established city health boards to try to find solutions to the problems of epidemics. But the medical profession of the time, unaware of the nature of bacterial infections, had no answers.

Instead, many Americans turned to nonscientific theories for improving health. Affluent men and, especially, women flocked to health spas for the celebrated "water cure" (known to modern scientists as hydrotherapy), which purported to improve health through immersing people in hot or cold baths or wrapping them in wet sheets. Although the water cure in fact delivered few of the benefits its promoters promised, it did have some therapeutic value; some forms of hydrotherapy are still in use today. Other people adopted new dietary theories. Sylvester Graham, a Connecticut-born Presbyterian minister and committed reformer, won many followers with his prescriptions for eating fruits, vegetables, and bread made from coarsely ground flour—a prescription not unlike some dietary theories today—instead of meat. (The "Graham cracker" is made from a kind of flour named for him.)

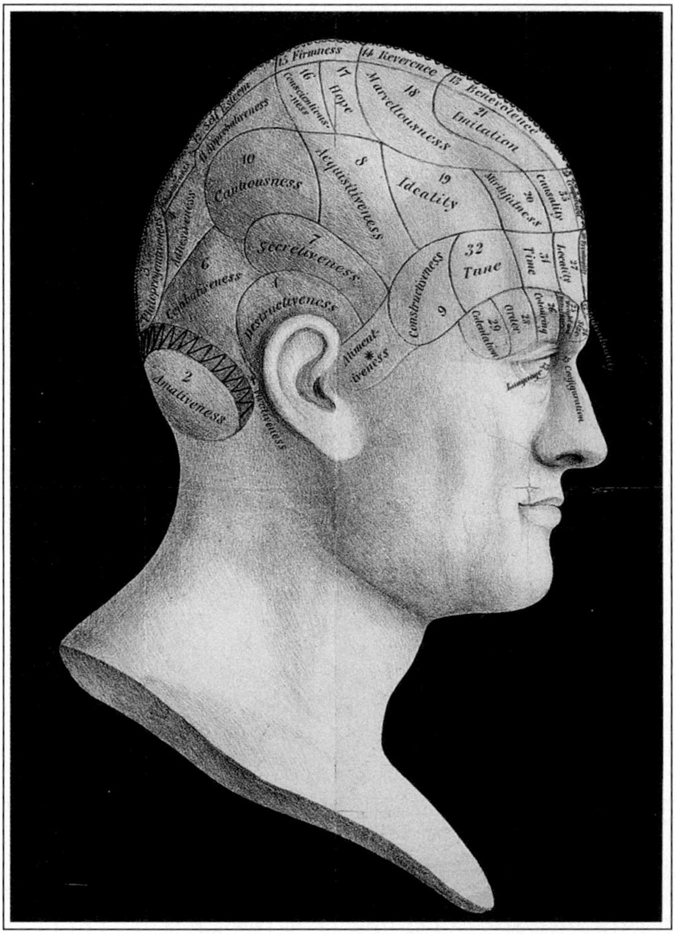

PHRENOLOGY This lithograph illustrates some of the ideas of the popular "science" of phrenology in the 1830s. Drawing from the concepts of the German writer Johann Gaspar Spurzheim, American phrenologists promoted the belief that a person's character and talents could be understood by the formation of his or her skull; that the brain was, in fact, a cluster of autonomous organs, each controlling some aspect of human thought or behavior. In this diagram, the areas of the brain that supposedly control "identity," "acquisitiveness," "secretiveness," "marvelousness," and "hope" are clearly identified. The theory has no scientific basis. *(The Library of Congress)*

Phrenology

Perhaps strangest of all to modern sensibilities was the widespread belief in the new "science" of phrenology, which appeared first in Germany and became popular in the United States beginning in the 1830s through the efforts of Orson and Lorenzo Fowler, publishers of the *Phrenology Almanac.* Phrenologists argued that the shape of an individual's skull was an important indicator of his or her character and intelligence. They made elaborate measurements of bumps and indentations to calculate the size (and, they claimed, the strength) of different areas of the brain. Phrenology seemed to provide a way of measuring an individual's fitness for various positions in life and seemed to promise an end to the arbitrary process by which people matched their talents to occupations and responsibilities. The theory is now universally believed to have no scientific value at all.

Medical Science

In an age of rapid technological and scientific advances, the science of medicine sometimes seemed to lag behind. In part, that was because of the greater difficulty of experimentation in medicine, which required human subjects. In part, it was because of the character of the medical profession, which—in the absence of any significant regulation—attracted many poorly educated people and many quacks. Efforts to regulate the profession were beaten back in the 1830s and 1840s by those who considered the licensing of physicians to be a form of undemocratic monopoly. The prestige of the profession, therefore, remained low.

The biggest problem facing American medicine, however, was the absence of basic knowledge about disease. The great medical achievement of the eighteenth century—the development of a vaccination against smallpox by Edward Jenner—came from no broad theory of infection, but from a brilliant adaptation of folk practices among country people. The development of anesthetics came not from medical doctors at first, but from a New England dentist, William Morton, who was looking for ways to help his patients endure the extraction of teeth. Beginning in 1844, Morton began experimenting with using sulphuric ether. John Warren, a Boston surgeon, soon began using ether to sedate surgical patients. Even these advances met with stiff resistance from some traditional physicians, who mistrusted innovation and experimentation.

Resistance to Scientific Medicine

In the absence of any broad acceptance of scientific methods and experimental practice in medicine, it was very difficult for even the most talented doctors to make progress in treating disease. Even so, halting progress toward the discovery of the germ theory did occur in antebellum America. In 1843, the Boston essayist, poet, and physician Oliver Wendell Holmes published his findings from a study of large numbers of cases of "puerperal fever" (septicemia in children) and concluded that the disease could be transmitted from one person to another. This discovery of contagion met with a storm of criticism, but was later vindicated by the clinical success of the Hungarian physician Ignaz Semmelweis, who noticed that infection seemed to be spread by medical students who had been working with diseased corpses. Once he began requiring students to wash their hands and disinfect their instruments, the infections virtually disappeared.

Education

One of the most important reform movements of the mid-nineteenth century was the effort to produce a system of universal public education. As of 1830, no state had such a system. Soon after that, however, interest in public education began growing rapidly.

Horace Mann's Reforms

The greatest of the educational reformers was Horace Mann, the first secretary of the Massachusetts Board of Education, which was established in 1837. To Mann and his followers, education was the only way to protect democracy, for an educated electorate was essential to the workings of a free political system. Mann reorganized the Massachusetts school system, lengthened the academic year (to six months), doubled teachers' salaries, broadened the curriculum, and introduced new methods of professional training for teachers. Other states followed similar courses: building new schools, creating teachers' colleges, and offering many children access to education for the first time. By the 1850s, the principle (although not yet the reality) of tax-supported elementary schools was established in every state.

Uneven Public Education

Yet the quality of public education continued to vary widely. In some places—Massachusetts, for example—educators were generally capable men and women, often highly trained, who had an emerging sense of themselves as professionals. In other areas, however, teachers were often barely literate, and funding for education was severely limited. In much of the West, where the population was highly dispersed, many children had no access to schools at all. In the South, all African Americans were barred from education, and only about a third of all white children of school age were actually enrolled in schools in 1860. In the North, 72 percent were enrolled, but even there, many students attended classes only briefly and casually.

Among the goals of educational reformers was teaching children a set of social values. These values included thrift, order, discipline, punctuality, and respect for authority. Horace Mann, for example, spoke of the role of public schools in extending democracy and expanding individual opportunity. But he spoke, too, of their role in creating social order: "Train up a child in the way he should go, and when he is old he will not depart from it."

The interest in education also was visible in the growing movement to educate American Indians. Some reformers believed that Indians could be "civilized" if only they could be taught the ways of the white world. Efforts by missionaries and others to educate Indians and encourage them to assimilate were particularly prominent in such areas of the Far West as Oregon, where conflicts with the natives had not yet become acute. Nevertheless, the great majority of Native Americans remained outside the reach of educational reform.

Despite limitations and inequities, the achievements of the school reformers were impressive. By the beginning of the Civil War, the

United States had one of the highest literacy rates of any nation of the world: 94 percent of the population of the North, 83 percent of the white population (and 58 percent of the total population) of the South.

Soaring Literacy Rates

Rehabilitation

The belief in the potential of the individual also sparked the creation of new institutions to help the disabled: institutions that formed part of a great network of charitable activities known as the Benevolent Empire. Among them was the Perkins School for the Blind in Boston. Nothing better exemplified the romantic spirit of the era than the belief of those who founded Perkins that even society's supposedly most disadvantaged members could be helped to discover their own inner strength and wisdom.

Similar impulses produced another powerful movement of reform: the creation of "asylums" for criminals and the mentally ill. In advocating prison and hospital reform, Americans were reacting against one of society's most glaring ills: antiquated jails and mental institutions whose inmates lived in almost inhuman conditions. Beginning in the 1820s, many states built new penitentiaries and mental asylums. New York built the first penitentiary at Auburn in 1821. In Massachusetts, the reformer Dorothea Dix began a national movement for new methods of treating the mentally ill.

Dorothea Dix

The creation of asylums was an attempt to reform and rehabilitate the inmates. New forms of prison discipline were designed to rid criminals of the "laxness" that had presumably led them astray. Solitary confinement and the imposition of silence on work crews (both instituted in Pennsylvania and New York in the 1820s) were meant to give prisoners opportunities to meditate on their wrongdoings and develop "penitence" (hence the name "penitentiary").

Some of the same impulses that produced asylums underlay the emergence of a new "reform" approach to the problems of Native Americans: the idea of the reservation. For several decades, the dominant thrust of the United States' policy toward the Indians had been relocation. The principal motive behind relocation was simple: getting the tribes out of the way of white civilization. But among some whites there had also been another intent: to move the Indians to a place where they would be allowed to develop to a point at which assimilation might be possible.

Reservation Concept Born

It was a small step from the idea of relocation to the idea of the reservation. Just as prisons, asylums, and orphanages would provide society with an opportunity to train and uplift misfits and unfortunates within white society, so the reservations might provide a way to undertake what one official called "the great work of regenerating the Indian race."

The Rise of Feminism

Many of the women who became involved in reform movements in the 1820s and 1830s came to resent the social and legal restrictions that limited their participation. Out of their concerns emerged the first American feminist movement. Sarah and Angelina Grimké, sisters who had become active and outspoken abolitionists, ignored attacks by men who claimed that their activism was inappropriate to their gender. "Men and women were created equal," they argued. "They are both moral and accountable beings, and whatever is right for man to do, is right for women to do." Other reformers—Catharine Beecher, Harriet Beecher Stowe (her sister), Lucretia Mott, Elizabeth Cady Stanton, Susan B. Anthony, and Dorothea Dix—similarly pressed at the boundaries of "acceptable" female behavior.

In 1840, American female delegates arrived at a world antislavery convention in London, only to be turned away by the men who controlled the proceedings. Angered at the rejection, several of the delegates became convinced that their first duty as reformers should now be to elevate the status of women. Over the next several years, Mott, Stanton, and others began drawing pointed parallels between the plight of women and the plight of slaves; and in 1848, in Seneca Falls, New York, they organized a convention to discuss the question of women's rights. Out of the meeting came the "Declaration of Sentiments and Resolutions," which stated that "all men and women are created equal," that women no less than men are endowed with certain inalienable rights. In demanding the right to vote, they launched a movement for woman suffrage that would survive until the battle was finally won in 1920.

"Declaration of Sentiments and Resolutions"

Many of the women involved in these feminist efforts were Quakers. Quakerism had long embraced the ideal of sexual equality and had tolerated, indeed encouraged, the emergence of women as preachers and community leaders. Of the women who drafted the Declaration of Sentiments, all but Elizabeth Cady Stanton were Quakers.

Feminism's Secondary Status

Feminists benefited greatly from their association with other reform movements, most notably abolitionism, but they also suffered as a result. The demands of women were usually assigned a secondary position to what many considered the far greater issue of the rights of slaves.

THE CRUSADE AGAINST SLAVERY

The antislavery movement was not new to the mid-nineteenth century. But only in 1830 did it begin to gather the force that would ultimately enable it to overshadow virtually all other efforts at social reform.

Early Opposition to Slavery

In the early years of the nineteenth century, those who opposed slavery were, for the most part, a calm and genteel lot, expressing moral disapproval but doing little else. To the extent that there was an organized antislavery movement, it centered on the effort to resettle American blacks in Africa or the Caribbean. In 1817, a group of prominent white Virginians organized the American Colonization Society (ACS), which proposed a gradual freeing of slaves, with masters receiving compensation. The liberated blacks would then be transported out of the country and helped to establish a new society of their own. The ACS received some funding from private donors, some from Congress, some from the legislatures of Virginia and Maryland. And it arranged to have several groups of blacks transported out of the United States, some of them to the west coast of Africa, where in 1830 they established the nation of Liberia. (In 1846, Liberia became an independent black republic, with its capital, Monrovia, named for the American president who had presided over the initial settlement.)

American Colonization Society

But the ACS was in the end a negligible force. There were far too many blacks in America in the nineteenth century to be transported to Africa by any conceivable program. And the ACS met resistance, in any case, from blacks themselves, many of whom were now three or more generations removed from Africa and, despite their loathing of slavery, had no wish to emigrate.

Garrison and Abolitionism

In 1830, with slavery spreading rapidly in the South and the antislavery movement seemingly on the verge of collapse, a new figure emerged to transform it: William Lloyd Garrison. Born in Massachusetts in 1805, Garrison was in the 1820s an assistant to the New Jersey Quaker Benjamin Lundy, who published the leading antislavery newspaper of the time. Garrison grew impatient with his employer's moderate tone, so in 1831 he returned to Boston to found his own newspaper, the *Liberator.*

William Lloyd Garrison

Garrison's philosophy was so simple that it was genuinely revolutionary. Opponents of slavery, he said, should not talk about the evil influence of slavery on white society; they should talk about the damage the system did to blacks. And they should, therefore, reject "gradualism" and demand the immediate abolition of slavery and the extension to blacks of all the rights of American citizenship. Garrison wrote in a relentless, uncompromising tone. "I am aware," he wrote in the very first issue of the *Liberator,* "that many object to the severity of my language; but is there not cause for severity? I will be as harsh as truth, and as uncompromising as

Garrison's Revolutionary Philosophy

America in the World

THE ABOLITION OF SLAVERY

The United States abolished slavery through the Thirteenth Amendment to the Constitution in 1865, in the aftermath of a great Civil War. But the effort to abolish slavery did not begin nor end in North America. Emancipation in the United States was part of a worldwide antislavery movement that had begun in the late eighteenth century and continued through the end of the nineteenth.

The end of slavery, like the end of monarchies and aristocracies, was one of the ideals of the Enlightenment, which inspired new concepts of individual freedom and political equality. As Enlightenment ideas spread throughout the western world in the seventeenth and eighteenth centuries, introducing the idea of human rights and individual liberty to the concept of civilization, people on both sides of the Atlantic began to examine slavery anew and to ask whether it was compatible with these new ideas. Some Enlightenment thinkers, including some of the founders of the American Republic, believed that freedom was appropriate for white people, but not for people of color. But others came to believe that all human beings had an equal claim to liberty, and their views became the basis for an escalating series of antislavery movements.

Opponents of slavery first targeted the slave trade—the vast commerce in human beings that had grown up in the seventeenth and eighteenth centuries and had come to involve large parts of Europe, Africa, the Caribbean, and North and South America. In the aftermath of the revolutions in America, France, and Haiti in the late eighteenth and early nineteenth centuries, the attack on the slave trade quickly gained momentum. Its central figure was the English reformer William Wilberforce, who spent years attacking Britain's connection with the slave trade. He argued against it on moral and religious grounds, and eventually, after the Haitian revolution, he argued as well that the continuation of slavery would create more slave revolts. In 1807, he persuaded Parliament to pass a law ending the slave trade within the entire British empire. The British example—when combined with heavy political, economic, and even military pressure from London—persuaded many other nations to make the slave trade illegal as well: the United States in 1808, France in 1814, Holland in 1817, Spain in 1845. Trading in slaves continued within countries and colonies where slavery remained legal (including the United States), and some illegal slave trading continued throughout the Atlantic world. But the sale of slaves steadily declined after 1807. The last known shipment of slaves across the Atlantic—from Africa to Cuba—occurred in 1867.

Ending the slave trade was a great deal easier than ending slavery itself, in which many people had major investments and on which much agriculture, commerce, and industry depended. But pressure to abolish slavery grew steadily throughout the nineteenth century, with Wilberforce once more helping to lead the international outcry against the institution. In Haiti, the slave revolts that began in 1791 eventually abolished not only slavery, but also French rule. In some parts of South America, slavery came to an end with the overthrow of Spanish rule in the 1820s. Simón Bolívar, the great leader of Latin American independence, considered abolishing slavery an important part of his mission, freeing those who joined his armies and insisting on constitutional prohibitions of slavery in several of the Constitutions he helped frame. In 1833, the British parliament passed a law abolishing slavery throughout the British empire and compensated slaveowners for freeing their slaves. France abolished slavery in its empire, after years of agitation from abolitionists within France, in 1848. In the Caribbean, Spain followed Britain in slowly eliminating slavery from its colonies. Puerto Rico abolished slavery in 1873; and Cuba became the last colony in the Caribbean to end slavery, in 1886, in the face of increasing slave resistance and the declining profitability of slave-based plantations. Brazil was the last nation in the Americas, ending the system in 1888. The Brazilian military began to turn against slavery after the valiant participation of slaves in Brazil's war with Paraguay in the late 1860s; eventually educated Brazilians began to oppose the system too, arguing that it obstructed economic and social progress.

In the United States, the power of world opinion—and the example of Wilberforce's movement in England—became an important source of the abolitionist movement as it gained strength in the 1820s and 1830s. American abolitionism, in turn, helped reinforce the movements abroad. Frederick Douglass, the former American slave turned abolitionist, became a major figure in the international antislavery movement and was a much-admired and much-sought-after speaker in England and Europe in the 1840s and 1850s. No other nation paid such a terrible price for abolishing slavery as did the United States during its Civil War, but American emancipation was nevertheless a part of a worldwide movement toward emancipation.

(text continued from page 321)

justice. . . . I am in earnest—I will not equivocate—I will not excuse—I will not retreat a single inch—and I will be heard."

Garrison soon attracted a large group of followers throughout the North, enough to enable him to found the New England Antislavery Society in 1832 and a year later, after a convention in Philadelphia, the American Antislavery Society.

Black Abolitionists

Abolitionism had a particular appeal to the free black population of the North. These free blacks lived in conditions of poverty and oppression at times worse than those of their slave counterparts in the South. For all their problems, however, northern blacks were fiercely proud of their freedom and sensitive to the plight of those members of their race who remained in bondage. Many in the 1830s came to support Garrison. But they also rallied to leaders of their own.

Frederick Douglass

The greatest of the black abolitionists was Frederick Douglass. Born a slave in Maryland, Douglass escaped to Massachusetts in 1838, became an outspoken leader of antislavery sentiment, and spent two years lecturing in England. On his return to the United States in 1847, Douglass purchased his freedom from his Maryland owner and founded an antislavery newspaper, the *North Star*,

FUGITIVE SLAVE LAW CONVENTION Abolitionists gathered in Cazenovia, New York, in August 1850 to consider how to respond to the law recently passed by Congress requiring northern states to return fugitive slaves to their owners. Frederick Douglass is seated just to the left of the table in this photograph of some of the participants. The gathering was unusual among abolitionist gatherings in including substantial numbers of African Americans. *(Madison County Historical Society, Oneida, NY)*

in Rochester, New York. He achieved wide renown as well for his autobiography, *Narrative of the Life of Frederick Douglass* (1845), in which he presented a damning picture of slavery. Douglass demanded not only freedom but full social and economic equality.

Anti-Abolitionism

The rise of abolitionism was a powerful force, but it provoked a powerful opposition as well. Almost all white southerners, of course, were bitterly hostile to the movement. But even in the North, abolitionists were a small, dissenting minority. Some whites feared that abolitionism would produce a destructive war between the sections. Others feared that it would lead to a great influx of free blacks into the North.

Violent Reprisals

The result of such fears was an escalating wave of violence. A mob in Philadelphia attacked the abolitionist headquarters there in 1834, burned it to the ground, and began a bloody race riot. Another mob seized Garrison on the streets of

Boston in 1835 and threatened to hang him. He was saved from death only by being locked in jail. Elijah Lovejoy, the editor of an abolitionist newspaper in Alton, Illinois, was victimized repeatedly and finally killed when he tried to defend his press from attack.

That so many men and women continued to embrace abolitionism in the face of such vicious opposition suggests that abolitionists were not people who made their political commitments lightly or casually. They were strong-willed, passionate crusaders who displayed not only enormous courage and moral strength but at times a fervency that many of their contemporaries found deeply disturbing. The mobs were only the most violent expression of a hostility to abolitionism that many, perhaps most, other white Americans shared.

Abolitionism Divided

By the mid-1830s, the abolitionist crusade had begun to experience serious strains. One reason was the violence of the anti-abolitionists, which persuaded some members of the movement that a more moderate approach was necessary. Another reason was the growing radicalism of William Lloyd Garrison, who shocked even many of his own allies (including Frederick Douglass) by attacking not only slavery but the government itself. The Constitution, he said, was "a covenant with death and an agreement with hell." In 1840, Garrison precipitated a formal division within the American Antislavery Society by insisting that women be permitted to participate in the movement on terms of full equality. He continued after 1840 to arouse controversy with new and even more radical stands: an extreme pacifism that rejected even defensive wars; opposition to all forms of coercion—not just slavery, but prisons and asylums; and finally, in 1843, a call for northern disunion from the South.

Radicals and Moderates

From 1840 on, therefore, abolitionism moved in many channels and spoke with many different voices. The Garrisonians, with their radical and uncompromising moral stance, remained influential. But others operated in more moderate ways, arguing that abolition could be accomplished only as the result of a long, patient, peaceful struggle. They appealed to the conscience of the slaveholders; and when that produced no results, they turned to political action, seeking to induce the northern states and the federal government to aid the cause. They joined the Garrisonians in helping runaway slaves find refuge in the North or in Canada through what became known as the underground railroad. They helped fund the legal battle over the Spanish slave vessel, *Amistad.* Africans destined for slavery in Cuba had seized the ship from its crew in 1839 and tried to return it to Africa. But the U.S. navy had seized the ship and held the Africans as pirates. But with abolitionist support, legal efforts to declare the Africans free (because the slave trade was by then illegal) finally reached the Supreme Court, where the

The Amistad Case

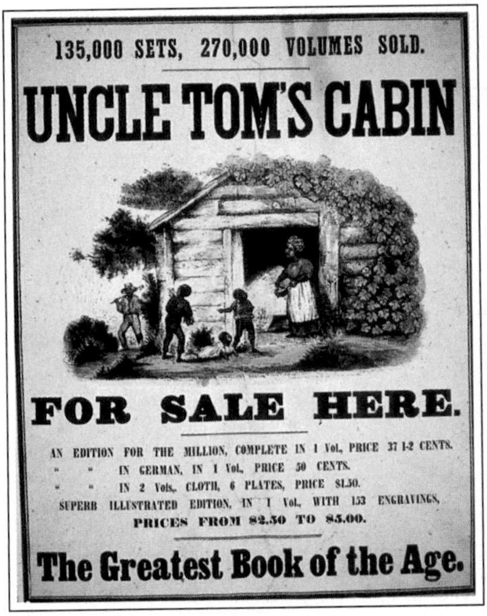

UNCLE TOM'S CABIN *Uncle Tom's Cabin* did much to inflame public opinion in both the North and the South in the last years before the Civil War. When Abraham Lincoln was introduced to Stowe once in the White House, he reportedly said to her: "So you are the little lady that has brought this great war." At the time, however, Stowe was equally well known as one of the most successful American writers of sentimental novels. *(Bettmann/Corbis)*

antislavery position was argued by former president John Quincy Adams. The court declared the Africans free in 1841 and antislavery groups funded their passage back to Africa. After the Supreme Court (in *Prigg* v. *Pennsylvania*, 1842) ruled that states need not aid in enforcing the 1793 law requiring the return of fugitive slaves to their owners, abolitionists won passage in several northern states of "personal liberty laws," which forbade state officials to assist in the capture and return of runaways. The antislavery societies also petitioned Congress to abolish slavery in places where the federal government had jurisdiction—in the territories and in the District of Columbia—and to prohibit the interstate slave trade.

Antislavery sentiment underlay the formation in 1840 of the Liberty Party, which ran Kentucky antislavery leader James G. Birney for president. But this party and its successors never campaigned for outright abolition. They stood instead for "free soil," for keeping slavery out of the territories. Some free-soilers were concerned about the welfare of blacks; others were people who cared nothing about slavery but simply wanted to keep the West a country for whites. But the free-soil position would ultimately do what abolitionism never could: attract the support of large numbers of the white population of the North.

The frustrations of political abolitionism drove some critics of slavery to embrace more drastic measures. A few began to advocate violence; it was a group of prominent abolitionists in New England, for example, who funneled money and arms to John Brown for his bloody uprisings in Kansas and Virginia. (See pp. 350 and 355–356.) Others attempted to arouse public anger through propaganda. The most powerful of all abolitionist propaganda was Harriet Beecher Stowe's novel *Uncle Tom's Cabin*, published as a book in 1852. It sold more than 300,000 copies within a year of publication and was reissued again and again. It succeeded in bringing the message of abolitionism to an enormous new audience—not only those who read the book but those who watched dramatizations of its story by countless theater companies across the nation. Reviled throughout the South, Stowe became a hero to many in the North. And in both regions, her novel helped inflame sectional tensions to a new level of passion.

Uncle Tom's Cabin

Even divided, therefore, abolitionism remained a powerful influence on the life of the nation. Only a relatively small number of people before the Civil War ever accepted the abolitionist position that slavery must be entirely eliminated in a single stroke. But the crusade that Garrison had launched, and that thousands of committed men and women kept alive for three decades, was a constant, visible reminder of how deeply the institution of slavery was dividing America.

CONCLUSION

The rapidly changing society of antebellum America encouraged interest in a wide range of reforms. Writers, artists, intellectuals, and others drew heavily from new European notions of personal liberation and fulfillment—a set of ideas often known as romanticism. But they also strove to create a truly American culture. The literary and artistic life of the nation expressed the rising interest in personal liberation—in giving individuals the freedom to explore their own souls and to find in nature a full expression of their divinity. It also called attention to some of the nation's glaring social problems.

Reformers, too, made use of the romantic belief in the divinity of the individual. They flocked to religious revivals, worked on behalf of such "moral" reforms as temperance, supported education, and articulated some of the first statements of modern feminism. Above all, in the North, they rallied against slavery. Out of this growing antislavery movement emerged a new and powerful phenomenon: abolitionism, which insisted on immediate emancipation of slaves. The abolitionist movement galvanized much of the North. It also contributed greatly to the growing schism between North and South.

FOR FURTHER REFERENCE

Steven Mintz, *Moralists and Moralizers: America's Pre-Civil War Reformers* (1995) and Ronald G. Walters, *American Reformers, 1815–1860* (1978) are good overviews. David Reynolds, *Walt Whitman's America* (1995) is both a cultural biography of Whitman and an evocation of the society Whitman celebrated. Leo Marx, *The Machine in the Garden* (1964) is an influential study of the tension between technological progress and the veneration of nature in the era of early industrialization. Nancy F. Cott, *The Bonds of Womanhood: "Woman's Sphere" in New England, 1780–1835* (1977) argues that nineteenth-century feminism emerged from the separation of home and work in the early nineteenth century. Klaus J. Hansen, *Mormonism and the American Experience* (1981) examines the emergence of the most important new religion in nineteenth-century America. Ellen C. Dubois, *Feminism and Suffrage: The Emergence of an Independent Women's Movement in America, 1848–1869* (1978) examines the origins of the suffrage movement. David Brion Davis, *The Problem of Slavery in the Age of Revolution, 1770–1823* (1975) is an influential study of the rise of antislavery sentiment in the western world. James Brewer Stewart, *Holy Warriors* (1976) is a good summary of the trajectory of abolitionism from the American Revolution through the emancipation. Ronald G. Walters, *The Antislavery Appeal: American Abolitionism After 1830* (1976) emphasizes the religious motivations of antebellum abolitionism. Julie Roy Jeffrey, *The Great Silent Army of Abolitionism: Ordinary Women in the Antislavery Movement* (1988) is a study of the important role women played in fighting slavery.

For quizzes, Internet resources, references to additional books and films, and more, consult this book's Online Learning Center at www.mhhe.com/unfinishednation4.

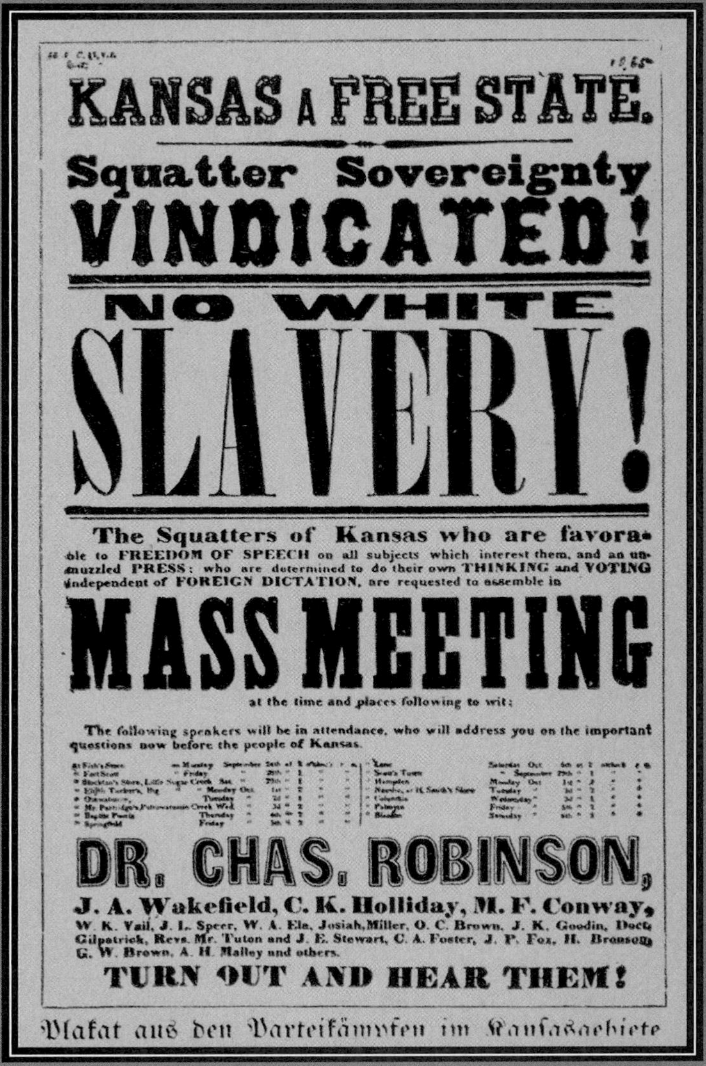

"BLEEDING KANSAS" The battle over the fate of slavery in Kansas was one of the most turbulent events of the 1850s. This 1855 poster invites antislavery forces to a meeting to protest the actions of the "bogus" pro-slavery territorial legislature, which had passed laws that, among other things, made it illegal to speak or write against slavery. "Squatter sovereignty" was another term for "popular sovereignty," the doctrine that gave residents of the prospective state the power to decide the fate of slavery there. *(Bettmann/Corbis)*

TIME LINE

1836	1844	1846	1848	1850	1852	1853
Texas declares independence from Mexico	Polk elected president	Oregon boundary dispute settled U.S. declares war on Mexico Wilmot Proviso	Treaty of Guadalupe Hidalgo Taylor elected president California gold rush begins	Compromise of 1850 Taylor dies; Fillmore becomes president	Pierce elected president	Gadsden Purchase

CHAPTER THIRTEEN

THE IMPENDING CRISIS

Looking Westward
Expansion and War
The Sectional Debate
The Crisis of the 1850s

Until the 1840s, the tensions between North and South remained relatively contained. Had no new sectional issues arisen, it is possible that the two sections might have resolved their differences peaceably over time. But new issues did arise. From the North came the strident and increasingly powerful abolitionist movement. From the South came a newly militant defense of slavery and the way of life it supported. And from the West, more significantly, came a series of controversies that would ultimately tear the fragile Union apart.

LOOKING WESTWARD

More than a million square miles of new territory came under the control of the United States during the 1840s. By the end of the decade, the nation possessed all the territory of the present-day United States except Alaska, Hawaii, and a few relatively small areas acquired later through border adjustments. Many factors accounted for this great new wave of expansion, but one of the most important was an ideology known as "Manifest Destiny."

1854	1855-1856	1856	1857	1858	1859	1860
Kansas-Nebraska Act Republican Party formed	"Bleeding Kansas"	Buchanan elected president	*Dred Scott* decision	Lecompton constitution defeated	John Brown raids Harper's Ferry	Lincoln elected president

Manifest Destiny

Territorial Ambitions

Manifest Destiny reflected both the growing pride that characterized American nationalism in the mid-nineteenth century and the idealistic vision of social perfection that fueled so much of the reform energy of the time. It rested on the idea that America was destined—by God and by history—to expand its boundaries over a vast area.

By the 1840s, the idea of Manifest Destiny had spread throughout the nation, publicized by the new "penny press," which made newspapers available to a far greater proportion of the population than ever before. Some advocates of Manifest Destiny had relatively limited territorial goals; others envisioned a vast new "empire of liberty" that would include Canada, Mexico, Caribbean and Pacific islands, and ultimately, a few dreamed, much of the rest of the world. Henry Clay and others warned that territorial expansion would reopen the painful controversy over slavery. Their voices, however, could not compete with the enthusiasm over expansion in the 1840s, which began with the issues of Texas and Oregon.

Americans in Texas

Twice in the 1820s, the United States had offered to purchase Texas from the Republic of Mexico, only to meet with indignant Mexican refusals. But in 1824, the Mexican government enacted a colonization law offering cheap land and a four-year exemption from taxes to any American willing to move into Texas. Thousands of Americans flocked into the region, the great majority of them white southerners and their slaves, intent on establishing cotton plantations. By 1830, there were about 7,000 Americans living in Texas, more than twice the number of Mexicans there.

American Immigration to Texas

Most of the settlers came to Texas through the efforts of American intermediaries, who received sizable land grants from Mexico in return for promising to bring new residents into the region. The most successful of them was Stephen F. Austin, a young immigrant from Missouri who established the first legal American settlement in Texas in 1822. Austin and others recruited many American immigrants to Texas; in the process, they created centers of power in the region that competed with the Mexican government. In 1830, the Mexican government barred any further American immigration into the region. But Americans kept flowing into Texas anyway.

Friction between the American settlers and the Mexican government was already growing in the mid-1830s when instability in Mexico itself drove General Antonio López de Santa Anna to seize power as a dictator. He increased the powers of the national government at the expense of the state governments, a measure that Texans from the United States assumed Santa Anna was aiming specifically at them. Sporadic fighting between Americans and Mexicans in Texas began in 1835, and in 1836, the American settlers defiantly proclaimed their independence from Mexico.

Independence Declared

Santa Anna led a large army into Texas, where the American settlers were divided into several squabbling factions. Mexican forces annihilated an American garrison at the Alamo mission in San Antonio after a famous, if futile, defense by a group of Texas "patriots" that included, among others, the renowned frontiersman and former Tennessee congressman Davy Crockett. Another garrison at Goliad suffered substantially the same fate. By the end of 1836, the rebellion appeared to have collapsed.

But General Sam Houston managed to keep a small force together. And on April 21, 1836, at the Battle of San Jacinto, he defeated the Mexican army and took Santa Anna prisoner. Santa Anna, under pressure from his captors, signed a treaty giving Texas independence.

Battle of San Jacinto

A number of Mexican residents of Texas *(Tejanos)* had fought with the Americans in the revolution. But soon after Texas won its independence, their positions grew difficult. The Americans did not trust them, feared that they were agents of the Mexican government, and in effect drove many of them out of the new republic. Most of those who stayed had to settle for a politically and economically subordinate status.

One of the first acts of the new president of Texas, Sam Houston, was to send a delegation to Washington with an offer to join the Union. But President Jackson, fearing that adding a large new slave state to the Union would increase sectional tensions, blocked annexation and even delayed recognizing the new republic until 1837.

Annexation Blocked

Spurned by the United States, Texas cast out on its own. England and France, concerned about the growing power of the United States, saw Texas as a possible check on its growth and began forging ties with the new republic. At that point, President Tyler persuaded Texas to apply for statehood again in 1844. But northern senators, fearing the admission of a new slave state, defeated it.

Oregon

Control of what was known as Oregon country, in the Pacific Northwest, was, along with Texas, a major political issue in the 1840s. Both Britain and the United States claimed sovereignty in the region. Unable to resolve their conflicting claims diplomatically, they agreed in an 1818 treaty to allow citizens of each country equal access to the territory. This arrangement, known as "joint occupation," continued for twenty years.

"Joint Occupation"

In fact, at the time of the treaty neither Britain nor the United States had established much of a presence in Oregon country. White settlement in the region consisted largely of American and Canadian fur traders, and the most significant white settlements were scattered fur trading posts. But American interest in Oregon grew substantially in the 1820s and 1830s.

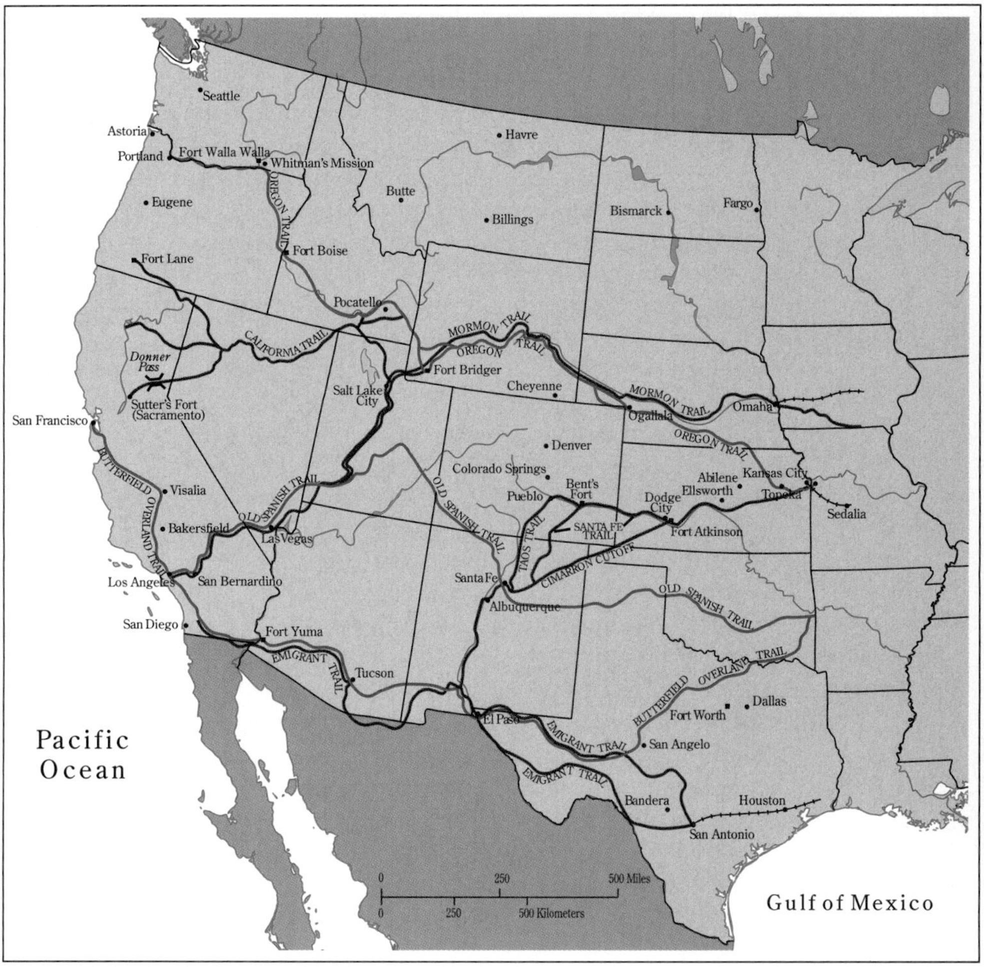

WESTERN TRAILS IN 1860 This map shows how much of western North America had little or no non-Indian population in 1800. As settlers began the long process of exploring and establishing farms and businesses in the West, major trails began to develop to facilitate travel and trade between the region and the more thickly settled areas to the East. Note how many of the trails lead to California and how few of them lead into any of the far northern regions of United States territory. Note too the important towns and cities that grew up along these trails. ◆ *What other, later forms of transportation performed the functions that these trails performed prior to the Civil War?*

Growing American Settlements

By the mid-1840s, white Americans substantially outnumbered the British in Oregon. They had also devastated much of the Indian population, in part through a measles epidemic that spread through the Cayuse. American settlements had spread up and down the Pacific coast, and the new settlers were urging the United States government to take possession of the disputed Oregon Territory.

CROSSING THE PLAINS A long wagon train carries migrants across the Plains toward Montana in 1866. This photograph gives some indication of the rugged condition of even some of the most well-traveled trails. (© *The New-York Historical Society*)

The Westward Migration

The migrations into Texas and Oregon were part of a larger movement that took hundreds of thousands of white and black Americans into the far western regions of the continent between 1840 and 1860. The largest number of migrants were from the Old Northwest (today's Midwest). Most traveled in family groups, until the early 1850s, when the great California gold rush attracted many single men (see pp. 343–344). Most were relatively young people. Few were wealthy, but many were relatively prosperous. Poor people who could not afford the trip on their own usually had to join other families or groups as laborers—men as farm or ranch hands, women as domestic servants, teachers, or, in some cases, prostitutes. Groups heading for areas where mining or lumbering was the principal economic activity consisted mostly of men. Those heading for farming regions traveled mainly as families.

Migrants generally gathered in one of several major depots in Iowa and Missouri (Independence, St. Joseph, or Council Bluffs), joined a wagon train led by hired guides, and set off with their belongings piled in covered wagons, livestock trailing behind. The major route west was the 2,000-mile Oregon Trail, which stretched from Independence across the Great Plains and through the South Pass of the Rocky Mountains. From there, migrants moved north into Oregon or south (along the California trail) to the northern

The Oregon Trail

California coast. Other migrations moved along the Santa Fe Trail, southwest from Independence into New Mexico.

However they traveled, overland migrants faced an arduous journey. Most passages lasted five or six months (from May to November), and there was always pressure to get through the Rockies before the snows began, often not an easy task given the very slow pace of most wagon trains. There was also the danger of disease; many groups were decimated by cholera. Almost everyone walked the great majority of the time, to lighten the load for the horses drawing the wagons. The women, who did the cooking and washing at the end of the day, generally worked harder than the men, who usually rested when the caravan halted.

Only a few expeditions experienced Indian attacks. In the twenty years before the Civil War, fewer than 400 migrants (slightly more than one-tenth of 1 percent) died in conflicts with the tribes. In fact, Indians were usually more helpful than dangerous to the white migrants. They often served as guides, and they traded horses, clothing, and fresh food with the travelers.

Indian Assistance

Despite the traditional image of westward migrants as rugged individualists, most travelers found the journey a very communal experience. That was partly because many expeditions consisted of groups of friends, neighbors, or relatives who had decided to pull up stakes and move west together. And it was partly because of the intensity of the journey. It was a rare expedition in which there were not some internal conflicts before the trip was over; but those who made the journey successfully generally learned the value of cooperation.

EXPANSION AND WAR

The growing number of white Americans in the lands west of the Mississippi put great pressure on the government in Washington to annex Texas, Oregon, and other territory. And in the 1840s, these expansionist pressures helped push the United States into war.

The Democrats and Expansion

In preparing for the election of 1844, the two leading candidates—Henry Clay and Martin Van Buren—both tried to avoid taking a stand on the controversial issue of the annexation of Texas. Sentiment for expansion was mild within the Whig Party, and Clay had no difficulty securing the nomination despite his noncommittal position. But many southern Democrats supported annexation, and the party passed over Van Buren to nominate James K. Polk.

Polk had represented Tennessee in the House of Representatives for fourteen years, four of them as Speaker, and had subsequently served as governor. But by 1844, he had been out of public office for three years.

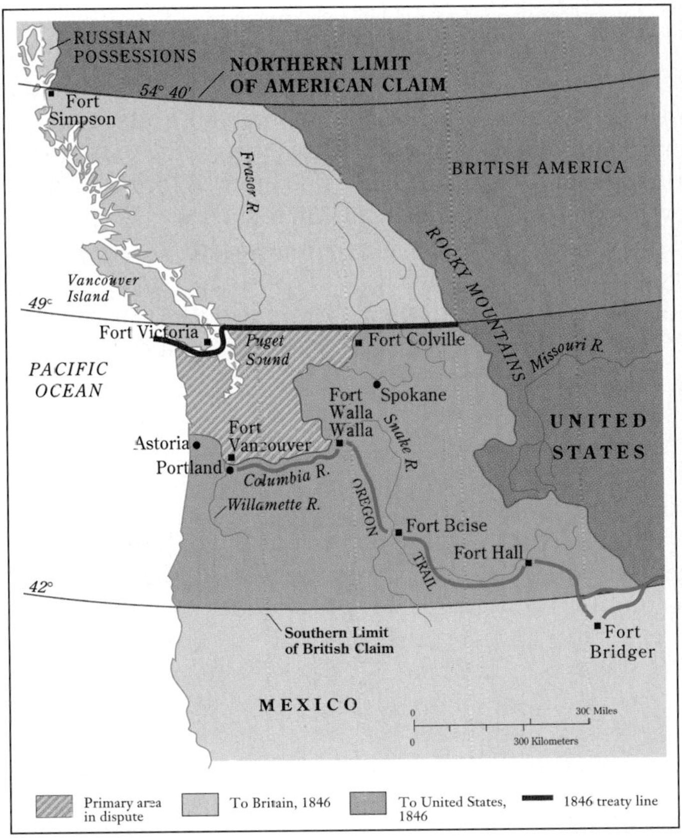

THE OREGON BOUNDARY, 1846 One of the last major boundary disputes between the United States and Great Britain involved the territory known as Oregon—the large region on the Pacific Coast north of California (which in 1846 was still part of Mexico). For years, America and Britain had overlapping claims on the territory. The British claimed land as far south as the present state of Oregon, while the Americans claimed land extending well into what is now Canada. Tensions over the Oregon border at times rose to the point that many Americans were demanding war, some using the slogan "54-40 or fight," referring to the latitude of the northernmost point of the American claim. ◆ *How did President James K. Polk defuse the crisis?*

What made his victory possible was his support for the position, expressed in the Democratic platform, "that the re-occupation of Oregon and the re-annexation of Texas at the earliest practicable period are great American measures." By combining the Oregon and Texas questions, the Democrats hoped to appeal to both northern and southern expansionists. Polk carried the election by 170 electoral votes to 105.

Polk Elected

Polk entered office with a clear set of goals and with plans for attaining them. John Tyler accomplished the first of Polk's goals for him in the last days of his own presidency. Interpreting the election returns as a mandate for the annexation of Texas, the outgoing president won congressional approval for it in February 1845. That December, Texas became a state.

Polk himself resolved the Oregon question. The British minister in Washington brusquely rejected a compromise Polk offered that would establish the United States–Canadian border at the 49th parallel. Incensed, Polk again asserted the American claim to all of Oregon. There was loose talk of war on both sides of the Atlantic—talk that in the United States often took the form of the bellicose slogan "Fifty-four forty or fight!" (a reference to where the Americans hoped to draw the northern boundary of their part of Oregon). But neither country really wanted war. Finally, the British government accepted Polk's original proposal to divide the territory at the 49th parallel. On June 15, 1846, the Senate approved a treaty that fixed the boundary there.

Compromise over Oregon

The Southwest and California

One of the reasons the Senate and the president had agreed so readily to the British offer to settle the Oregon question was that new tensions were emerging in the Southwest. As soon as the United States admitted Texas to statehood in 1845, the Mexican government broke diplomatic relations with Washington. Mexican-American relations grew still worse when a dispute developed over the boundary between Texas and Mexico. Texans claimed the Rio Grande as their western and southern border. Mexico, although still not conceding the loss of Texas, argued nevertheless that the border had always been the Nueces River, to the north of the Rio Grande. Polk accepted the Texas claim, and in the summer of 1845 he sent a small army under General Zachary Taylor to Texas to protect the new state against a possible Mexican invasion.

Texas Boundary Disputed

Part of the area in dispute was New Mexico, whose Spanish and Indian residents lived in a multiracial society that had by the 1840s endured for nearly a century and a half. In the 1820s, the Mexican government had invited American traders into the region, hoping to speed development of the province. And New Mexico, like Texas, soon began to become more American than Mexican. A flourishing commerce soon developed between Santa Fe and Independence, Missouri.

California

Americans were also increasing their interest in California. In this vast region lived members of several western Indian tribes and perhaps 7,000 Mexicans. Gradually, however, white Americans began to arrive: first maritime traders and captains of Pacific whaling ships, who stopped to barter goods or buy supplies; then merchants, who established stores, imported merchandise, and developed a profitable trade with the Mexicans and Indians; and finally pioneering farmers, who entered California from the east, by land, and settled in the Sacramento Valley. Some of these new settlers began to dream of bringing California into the United States.

President Polk soon came to share their dream and committed himself to acquiring both New Mexico and California for the United States. At the same time that he dispatched the troops under Taylor to Texas, he sent secret instructions to the commander of the Pacific naval squadron to seize the California ports if Mexico declared war. Representatives of the president quietly informed Americans in California that the United States would respond sympathetically to a revolt against Mexican authority there.

The Mexican War

Having appeared to prepare for war, Polk turned to diplomacy and dispatched a special minister to try to buy off the Mexicans. But Mexican leaders rejected the American offer to purchase the disputed territories. On January 13, 1846, as soon as he heard the news, Polk ordered Taylor's army in Texas to move across the Nueces River, where it had been stationed, to the Rio Grande. For months, the Mexicans refused to fight. But finally, according to disputed American accounts, some Mexican troops crossed the Rio Grande and attacked a unit of American soldiers. On May 13, 1846, Congress declared war by votes of 40 to 2 in the Senate and 174 to 14 in the House.

War Declared

Whig critics charged that Polk had deliberately maneuvered the country into the conflict and had staged the border incident that had precipitated the declaration. Many argued that the hostilities with Mexico were draining resources and attention away from the more important issue of the Pacific Northwest; and when the United States finally reached its agreement with Britain on the Oregon question, opponents claimed that Polk had settled for less than he should have because he was preoccupied with Mexico. Opposition intensified as the war continued and as the public became aware of the casualties and expense.

Victory did not come as quickly as Polk had hoped. The president ordered Taylor to cross the Rio Grande, seize parts of northeastern Mexico, beginning with the city of Monterrey, and then march on to Mexico City itself. Taylor captured Monterrey in September 1846, but he let the Mexican garrison evacuate without pursuit. Polk now began to fear that Taylor lacked the tactical skill for the planned advance against Mexico City. He also feared that, if successful, Taylor would become a powerful political rival (as, in fact, he did).

In the meantime, Polk ordered other offensives against New Mexico and California. In the summer of 1846, a small army under Colonel Stephen W. Kearny captured Santa Fe with no opposition. Then Kearny proceeded to California, where he joined a conflict already in progress that was being staged jointly by American settlers, a well-armed exploring party led by John C. Frémont, and the American navy: the so-called Bear Flag Revolt. Kearny brought the disparate American forces together under his command, and by the autumn of 1846 he had completed the conquest of California.

Bear Flag Revolt

But Mexico still refused to concede defeat. At this point, Polk and General Winfield Scott, the commanding general of the army and its

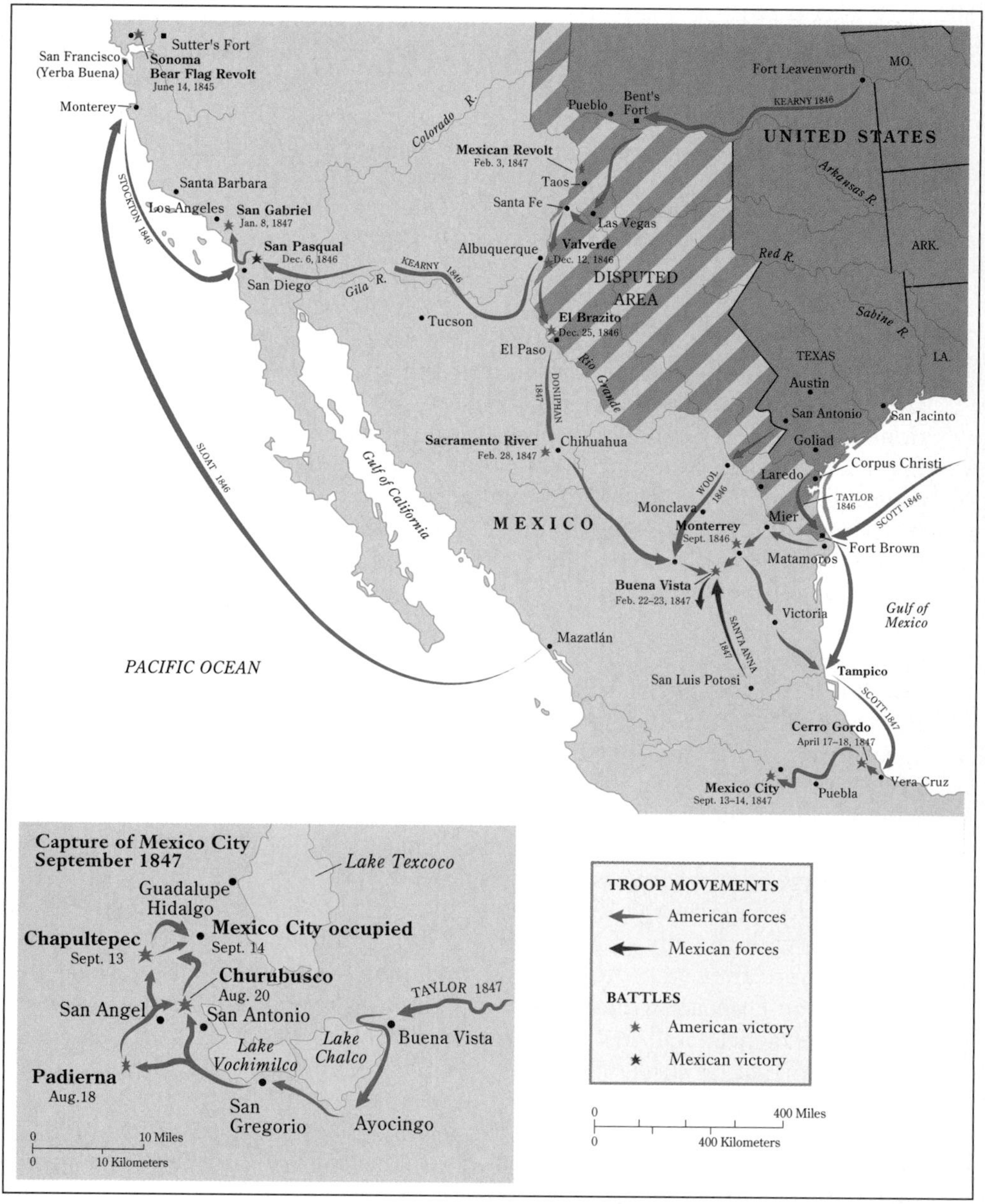

THE MEXICAN WAR, 1846–1848 Shortly after the settlement of the Oregon border dispute with Britain, the United States entered a war with Mexico over another contested border. This map shows the movement of Mexican and American troops during the fighting, which extended from the area around Santa Fe south to Mexico City and west to the coast of California. Note the American use of its naval forces to facilitate a successful assault on Mexico City, and other assaults on the coast of California. Note, too, how unsuccessful the Mexican forces were in their battles with the United States. Mexico won only one battle—a relatively minor one at San Pasqual near San Diego—in the war. ◆ *How did President Polk deal with the popular clamor for the United States to annex much of present-day Mexico?*

For an interactive version of this map go to www.mhhe.com/unfinishednation4ch13maps

STEPHEN KEARNY IN SANTA FE Colonel Stephen Kearny led a small U.S. military party to Santa Fe in 1846 and seized the town without opposition. In this 1909 drawing (which the artist Kenneth Chapman acknowledged was not entirely accurate), Kearny raises the American flag over the "old palace" in Santa Fe. The image appeared on a U.S. postage stamp in 1946. *(Kenneth Chapman,* Drawing of Steven Kearny in Santa Fe, *1909. Courtesy of the Museum of New Mexico)*

finest soldier, launched a bold new campaign. Scott assembled an army at Tampico, which the navy transported down the Mexican coast to Veracruz. With an army that never numbered more than 14,000, Scott advanced 260 miles along the Mexican National Highway toward Mexico City, kept American casualties low, and never lost a battle before finally seizing the Mexican capital. A new Mexican government took power and announced its willingness to negotiate a peace treaty.

President Polk continued to encourage those who demanded that the United States annex much of Mexico itself. At the same time, he was growing anxious to get the war finished quickly. Polk had sent a special presidential envoy, Nicholas Trist, to negotiate a settlement. On February 2, 1848, he reached agreement with the new Mexican government on the Treaty of Guadalupe Hidalgo, by which Mexico agreed to cede California and New Mexico to the United States and acknowledge the Rio Grande as the boundary of Texas. In return, the United States promised to assume any financial claims its new citizens had against Mexico and to pay the Mexicans $15 million. Trist had obtained most of Polk's original demands, but he had not satisfied the new, more expansive dreams of acquiring additional territory in Mexico itself. Polk angrily claimed that Trist had violated his instructions, but he soon realized that he had no choice but to accept the treaty to silence a bitter

Treaty of Guadalupe Hidalgo

battle growing between ardent expansionists demanding the annexation of "All Mexico!" and antislavery leaders charging that the expansionists were conspiring to extend slavery to new realms. The president submitted the Trist treaty to the Senate, which approved it by a vote of 38 to 14.

THE SECTIONAL DEBATE

James Polk tried to be a president whose policies transcended sectional divisions. But conciliating the sections was becoming an ever more difficult task, and Polk gradually earned the enmity of northerners and westerners alike, who believed his policies favored the South at their expense.

Slavery and the Territories

In August 1846, while the Mexican War was still in progress, Polk asked Congress to appropriate $2 million for purchasing peace with Mexico. Representative David Wilmot of Pennsylvania, an antislavery Democrat, introduced an amendment to the appropriation bill prohibiting slavery in any territory acquired from Mexico. The so-called Wilmot Proviso passed the House but failed in the Senate. Southern militants contended that all Americans had equal rights in the new territories, including the right to move their slaves (which they considered property) into them.

Wilmot Proviso

As the sectional debate intensified, President Polk supported a proposal to extend the Missouri Compromise line through the new territories to the Pacific coast, banning slavery north of the line and permitting it south of the line. Others supported a plan, originally known as "squatter sovereignty" and later by the more dignified phrase "popular sovereignty," which would allow the people of each territory to decide the status of slavery there. The debate over these various proposals dragged on for many months.

Growing Sectional Debate

The presidential campaign of 1848 dampened the controversy for a time as both Democrats and Whigs tried to avoid the slavery question. When Polk, in poor health, declined to run again, the Democrats nominated Lewis Cass of Michigan, a dull, aging party regular. The Whigs nominated General Zachary Taylor of Louisiana, hero of the Mexican War but a man with no political experience whatsoever. Opponents of slavery found the choice of candidates unsatisfying, and out of their discontent emerged the new Free-Soil Party, whose candidate was former president Martin Van Buren.

Taylor won a narrow victory. But while Van Buren failed to carry a single state, he polled an impressive 291,000 votes (10 percent of the total), and the Free-Soilers elected ten members to Congress. The emergence of the Free-Soil Party as

Free-Soil Party

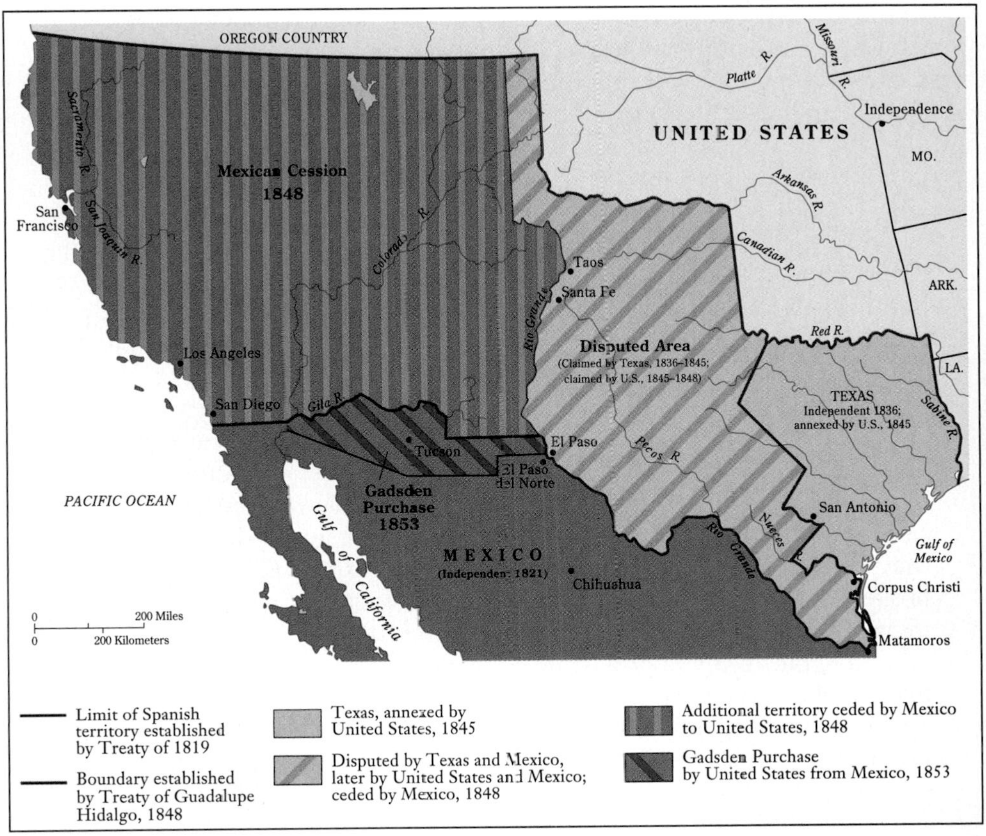

SOUTHWESTERN EXPANSION, 1845–1853 The annexation of much of what is now Texas in 1845, the much larger territorial gains won in the Mexican War in 1848, and the purchase of additional land from Mexico in 1853 completed the present continental border of the United States. ◆ *What great event shortly after the Mexican War contributed to a rapid settlement of California by migrants from the eastern United States?*

For an interactive version of this map go to www.mhhe.com/unfinishednation4ch13maps

an important political force signaled the inability of the existing parties to contain the political passions slavery was creating. It was an important part of a process that would lead to the collapse of the second party system in the 1850s.

The California Gold Rush

By the time Taylor took office, the pressure to resolve the question of slavery in the far western territories had become more urgent as a result of dramatic events in California. In January 1848, a foreman working in a sawmill owned by John Sutter (one of California's leading ranchers) found traces of gold in the foothills of the Sierra Nevada. Within months, news of the discovery had spread throughout the nation and much of the world. Almost immediately, hundreds of thousands of people began flocking to California in a frantic search for gold.

The atmosphere in California at the peak of the gold rush was one of almost crazed excitement and greed. Most migrants to the Far West prepared carefully before making the journey. But the California migrants (known as "Forty-niners") threw caution to the winds. They abandoned farms, jobs, homes, families; they piled onto ships and flooded the overland trails. The overwhelming majority of the Forty-niners (perhaps 95 percent) were men, and the society they created on their arrival in California was unusually fluid and volatile because of the almost total absence of women, children, or families.

"Forty-niners"

The gold rush also attracted some of the first Chinese migrants to the western United States. News of the discoveries created great excitement in China, particularly in impoverished areas. It was, of course, extremely difficult for a poor Chinese peasant to get to America; but many young, adventurous people (mostly men) decided to go anyway—in the belief that they could quickly become rich and then return to China. Emigration brokers loaned many migrants money for passage to California, which the migrants were to pay off out of their earnings there.

The gold rush was producing a serious labor shortage in California, as many male workers left their jobs and flocked to the gold fields. That created opportunities for many people who needed work (including Chinese immigrants). It also led to a frenzied exploitation of Indians that resembled slavery in all but name. A new state law permitted the arrest of "loitering" or orphaned Indians and their assignment to a term of "indentured" labor.

Indians Exploited

The gold rush was of critical importance to the growth of California, but not for the reasons most of the migrants hoped. There was substantial gold in the hills of the Sierra Nevada, and many people got rich from it. But only a tiny fraction of the Forty-niners ever found gold. Some disappointed migrants returned home after a while. But many stayed in California and swelled both the agricultural and urban populations of the territory. By 1856, for example, San Francisco—whose population had been 1,000 before the gold rush—was the home of over 50,000 people. By the early 1850s, California, which had always had a diverse population, had become even more heterogeneous. The gold rush had attracted not just white Americans but Europeans, Chinese, South Americans, Mexicans, free blacks, and slaves who accompanied southern migrants. Conflicts over gold intersected with racial and ethnic tensions to make the territory an unusually turbulent place.

Rising Sectional Tensions

Zachary Taylor believed statehood could become the solution to the issue of slavery in the territories. As long as the new lands remained territories, the federal government was responsible for deciding the fate of slavery within them. But once they became states, he thought, their own governments would be able to settle the slavery question. At Taylor's urging, California quickly adopted a constitution that prohibited slavery, and in December 1849 Taylor asked Congress to admit California as a free state.

Sectional Conflict over Slavery

Congress balked, in part because of several other controversies concerning slavery that were complicating the debate. One was the effort of antislavery forces to abolish slavery in the District of Columbia. Another was the emergence of personal liberty laws in northern states, which barred courts and police officers from helping to return runaway slaves to their owners. But the biggest obstacle to the president's program was the white South's fear that new free states would be added to the northern majority. The number of free and slave states was equal in 1849—fifteen each. But the admission of California would upset the balance; and New Mexico, Oregon, and Utah—all candidates for statehood—might upset it further.

Even many otherwise moderate southern leaders now began to talk about secession from the Union. In the North, every state legislature but one adopted a resolution demanding the prohibition of slavery in the territories.

The Compromise of 1850

Clay's Compromise Debated

Faced with this mounting crisis, moderates and unionists spent the winter of 1849–1850 trying to frame a great compromise. The aging Henry Clay, who was spearheading the effort, believed that no compromise could last unless it settled all the issues in dispute between the sections. As a result, he took several measures that had been proposed separately, combined them into a single piece of legislation, and presented it to the Senate on January 29, 1850. Among the bill's provisions were the admission of California as a free state; the formation of territorial governments in the rest of the lands acquired from Mexico, without restrictions on slavery; the abolition of the slave trade, but not slavery itself, in the District of Columbia; and a new and more effective fugitive slave law. These resolutions launched a debate that raged for seven months.

But in July, after six months of impassioned wrangling, a new, younger group of leaders emerged and took control of the debate from the old "triumvirate" of Webster, Clay, and Calhoun. The new leaders of the Senate were able, as the old leaders had not been, to produce a compromise. One spur to the compromise was the disappearance of the most powerful obstacle to it: the president. On July 9, 1850, Taylor suddenly died—the victim of a violent stomach disorder. He was succeeded by Millard Fillmore of New York—a dull, handsome, dignified man who understood the political importance of flexibility. He supported compromise and used his powers of persuasion to swing northern Whigs into line.

The new leaders also benefited from their own pragmatic tactics. Stephen A. Douglas, a senator from Illinois, proposed breaking up the

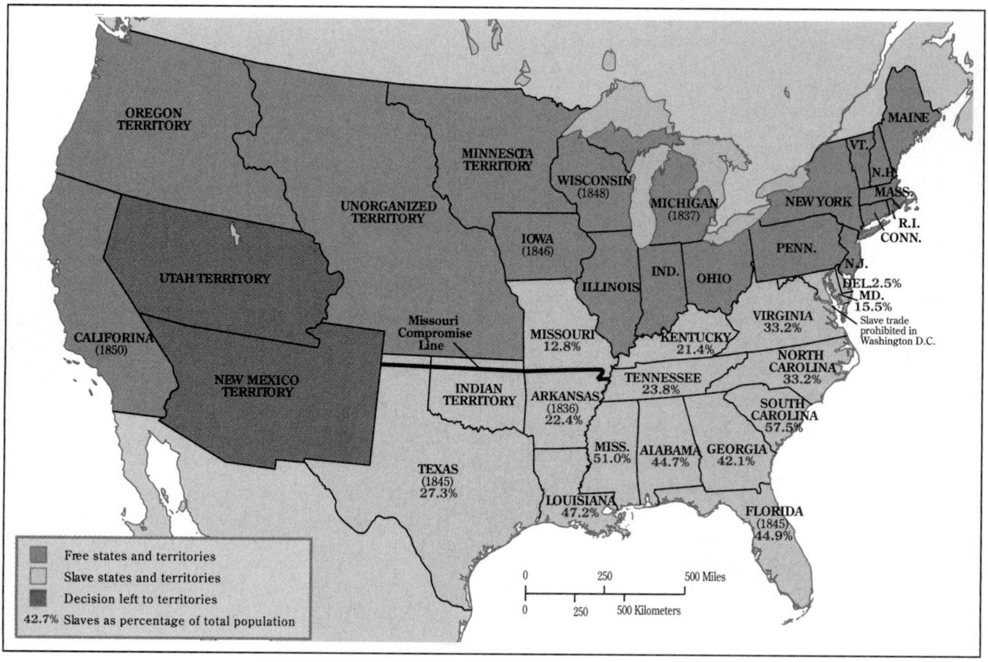

SLAVE AND FREE TERRITORIES UNDER THE COMPROMISE OF 1850 The acquisition of vast new western lands raised the question of the status of slavery in new territories organized for statehood by the United States. Tension between the North and South on this question led in 1850 to a great compromise, forged in Congress, to settle this dispute. The compromise allowed California to join the Union as a free state and introduced the concept of "popular sovereignty" for other new territories.◆ *How well did the compromise of 1850 work?*

For an interactive version of this map go to www.mhhe.com/unfinishednation4ch13maps

"omnibus bill" that Clay had envisioned as a great, comprehensive solution to the sectional crisis and to introduce instead a series of separate measures to be voted on one by one. Thus representatives of different sections could support those elements of the compromise they liked and oppose those they did not. Douglas also gained support with complicated backroom deals linking the compromise to such nonideological matters as the sale of government bonds and the construction of railroads. As a result of his efforts, by mid-September Congress had enacted and the president had signed all the components of the compromise.

Compromise Achieved

The Compromise of 1850 was a victory of self-interest. Still, members of Congress hailed the measure as a triumph of statesmanship; and Millard Fillmore, signing it, called it a just settlement of the sectional problem, "in its character final and irrevocable."

THE CRISES OF THE 1850s

For a few years after the Compromise of 1850, the sectional conflict seemed briefly to be forgotten amid booming prosperity and growth. But the tensions between North and South remained.

The Uneasy Truce

Both major parties endorsed the Compromise of 1850 in 1852, and both nominated presidential candidates unidentified with sectional passions. The Democrats chose the obscure New Hampshire politician Franklin Pierce and the Whigs the military hero General Winfield Scott. But the sectional question was a divisive influence in the election anyway, and the Whigs were the principal victims. They suffered massive defections from antislavery members angered by the party's evasiveness on the issue. Many of them flocked to the Free-Soil Party, whose antislavery presidential candidate, John P. Hale, repudiated the Compromise of 1850. The divisions among the Whigs helped produce a victory for the Democrats in 1852.

Franklin Pierce attempted to maintain harmony by avoiding divisive issues, particularly slavery. But it was an impossible task. Northern opposition to the Fugitive Slave Act intensified quickly after 1850, when southerners began appearing occasionally in northern states to pursue people they claimed were fugitives. Mobs formed in some northern cities to prevent enforcement of the law, and several northern states also passed their own laws barring the deportation of fugitive slaves. White southerners watched with growing anger and alarm as the one element of the Compromise of 1850 that they had considered a victory seemed to become meaningless as a result of northern defiance.

Fugitive Slave Act Opposed

"Young America"

One of the ways Franklin Pierce hoped to dampen sectional controversy was through his support of a movement in the Democratic Party known as "Young America." Its adherents saw the expansion of American democracy throughout the world as a way to divert attention from the controversies over slavery. The great liberal and nationalist revolutions of 1848 in Europe stirred them to dream of a republican Europe with governments based on the model of the United States. They dreamed as well of acquiring new territories in the Western Hemisphere.

But efforts to extend the nation's domain could not avoid becoming entangled with the sectional crisis. Pierce had been pursuing unsuccessful diplomatic attempts to buy Cuba from Spain (efforts begun in 1848 by Polk). In 1854, however, a group of his envoys sent him a private document

Ostend Manifesto

from Ostend, Belgium, making the case for seizing Cuba by force. When the Ostend Manifesto, as it became known, was leaked to the public, antislavery northerners charged the administration with conspiring to bring a new slave state into the Union.

The South, for its part, opposed all efforts to acquire new territory that would not support a slave system. The kingdom of Hawaii agreed to join the United States in 1854, but the treaty died in the Senate because it contained a clause prohibiting slavery in the islands. A powerful movement to annex Canada to the United States similarly foundered, at least in part because of slavery.

Slavery, Railroads, and the West

What fully revived the sectional crisis, however, was the same issue that had produced it in the first place: slavery in the territories. By the 1850s, the line of substantial white settlement had moved beyond the boundaries of Missouri, Iowa, and what is now Minnesota into a great expanse of plains, which many white Americans had once believed was unfit for cultivation. Now it was becoming apparent that large sections of this region were, in fact, suitable for farming. In the states of the Old Northwest, therefore, prospective settlers urged the government to open the area to them, provide territorial governments, and dislodge the Indians located there so as to make room for white settlers. There was relatively little opposition from any segment of white society to this proposed violation of Indian rights. But the interest in further settlement raised two issues that did prove highly divisive and that gradually became entwined with each other: railroads and slavery.

As the nation expanded westward, the problem of communication between the older states and the areas west of the Mississippi River became more and more critical. As a result, broad support began to emerge for building a transcontinental railroad. The problem was where to place it—and in particular, where to locate the railroad's eastern terminus, where the line could connect with the existing rail network east of the Mississippi. Northerners favored Chicago, while southerners supported St. Louis, Memphis, or New Orleans. The transcontinental railroad had become part of the struggle between the North and the South.

Transcontinental Railroad and Slavery

Pierce's secretary of war, Jefferson Davis of Mississippi, removed one obstacle to a southern route. Surveys indicated that a railroad with a southern terminus would have to pass through an area in Mexican territory. But in 1853 Davis sent James Gadsden, a southern railroad builder, to Mexico, where he persuaded the Mexican government to accept $10 million in exchange for a strip of land that today comprises part of Arizona and New Mexico. The so-called Gadsden Purchase only accentuated the sectional rivalry.

Gadsden Purchase

The Kansas-Nebraska Controversy

As a senator from Illinois and the acknowledged leader of northwestern Democrats, Stephen A. Douglas naturally wanted the transcontinental railroad for his own section. He also realized the strength of the principal argument against the northern route: that it would run mostly through country with a substantial Indian population. As a result, he introduced a bill in January 1854 to organize (and thus open to white settlement) a huge new territory, known as Nebraska, west of Iowa and Missouri.

Douglas knew the South would oppose his bill because it would prepare the way for a new free state; the proposed territory was north of the Missouri Compromise line (36°3′) and hence closed to slavery. In an effort to make the measure acceptable to southerners, Douglas inserted a provision that the status of slavery in the territory would be determined by the territorial legislature. In theory, the region could choose to open itself to slavery. When southern Democrats demanded more, Douglas agreed to an additional clause explicitly repealing the Missouri Compromise. He also agreed to divide the area into two territories—Nebraska and Kansas—instead of one. The new, second territory (Kansas) was somewhat more likely to become a slave state. In its final form the measure was known as the Kansas-Nebraska Act. President Pierce supported the bill, and after a strenuous debate, it became law in May 1854 with the unanimous support of the South and the partial support of northern Democrats.

Kansas-Nebraska Act

No piece of legislation in American history produced so many immediate, sweeping, and ominous consequences. It divided and destroyed the Whig Party. It divided the northern Democrats (many of whom were appalled at the repeal of the Missouri Compromise) and drove many of them from the party. Most important of all, it spurred the creation of a new party that was frankly sectional in composition and creed. People in both major parties who opposed Douglas's bill began to call themselves Anti-Nebraska Democrats and Anti-Nebraska Whigs. In 1854, they formed a new organization and named it the Republican Party. It instantly became a major force in American politics. In the elections of that year, the Republicans won enough seats in Congress to permit them, in combination with allies among the Know-Nothings, to organize the House of Representatives.

Republican Party Established

"Bleeding Kansas"

White settlers began moving into Kansas almost immediately after the passage of the Kansas-Nebraska Act. In the spring of 1855, elections were held for a territorial legislature. There were only about 1,500 legal voters in Kansas by then, but thousands of Missourians, some traveling in armed bands into Kansas, swelled the vote to over 6,000. The result was that pro-slavery forces elected a majority to the legislature, which immediately legalized slavery. Outraged free-staters elected their own delegates to a constitutional convention, which met at Topeka and adopted a constitution excluding slavery. They then chose their own governor and legislature and petitioned Congress for statehood. President Pierce denounced them as traitors and threw the full support of the federal government behind the pro-slavery territorial legislature. A few months later a pro-slavery federal marshal assembled a large posse, consisting mostly of Missourians, to arrest the free-state leaders, who had set up their headquarters in Lawrence. The posse sacked the town, burned the "governor's" house, and destroyed several printing presses. Retribution came quickly.

Among the most fervent abolitionists in Kansas was John Brown, a grim, fiercely committed zealot who had moved to Kansas with his sons so that they could fight to make it a free state. After the events in Lawrence, he gathered six followers (including four of his sons) and in one night murdered five pro-slavery settlers. This terrible episode, known as the Pottawatomie Massacre, led to more civil strife in Kansas—irregular, guerrilla warfare conducted by armed bands, some of them more interested in land claims or loot than in ideologies. Northerners and southerners alike came to believe that the events in Kansas illustrated (and were caused by) the aggressive designs of the other section. "Bleeding Kansas" became a symbol of the sectional controversy.

Pottawatomie Massacre

Another symbol soon appeared, in the United States Senate. In May 1856, Charles Sumner of Massachusetts rose to give a speech entitled "The Crime Against Kansas." In it, he gave particular attention to Senator Andrew P. Butler of South Carolina, an outspoken defender of slavery. The South Carolinian was, Sumner claimed, the "Don Quixote" of slavery, having "chosen a mistress . . . who, though ugly to others, is always lovely to him, though polluted in the sight of the world, is chaste in his sight . . . the harlot slavery."

The pointedly sexual references and the general viciousness of the speech enraged Butler's nephew, Preston Brooks, a member of the House of Representatives from South Carolina. Several days after the speech, Brooks approached Sumner at his desk in the Senate chamber during a recess, raised a heavy cane, and began beating him repeatedly on the head and shoulders. Sumner, trapped in his chair, rose in agony with such strength that he tore the desk from the bolts holding it to the floor. Then he collapsed, bleeding and unconscious. So severe were his injuries that he was unable to return to the Senate for four years. Throughout the North, he became a hero—a martyr to the barbarism of the South. In the South, Preston Brooks became a hero, too. Censured by the House, he resigned his seat, returned to South Carolina, and stood successfully for reelection.

Sumner Caned

The Free-Soil Ideology

What had happened to produce such deep hostility between the two sections? In part, the tensions were reflections of the two sections' differing economic and territorial interests. But they were also reflections of a hardening of ideas in both North and South.

In the North, assumptions about the proper structure of society came to center on the belief in "free soil" and "free labor." Most white northerners came to believe that the existence of slavery was dangerous not because of what it did to blacks but because of what it threatened to do to whites. At the heart of American democracy, they argued, was the right of all citizens to own property, to control their own labor, and to have access to opportunities for advancement.

"Free Soil" and "Free Labor"

According to this vision, the South was the antithesis of democracy—a closed, static society, in which slavery preserved an entrenched aristocracy. While the North was growing and prospering, the South was stagnating, rejecting the values of individualism and progress. The South was, northern free-laborites further maintained, engaged in a conspiracy to extend slavery throughout the nation and thus to destroy the openness of northern capitalism and replace it with the closed, aristocratic system of the South. The only solution to this "slave power conspiracy" was to fight the spread of slavery and extend the nation's democratic (i.e., free-labor) ideals to all sections of the country.

"Slave Power Conspiracy"

This ideology, which lay at the heart of the new Republican Party, also strengthened the commitment of Republicans to the Union. Since the idea of continued growth and progress was central to the free-labor vision, the prospect of dismemberment of the nation was unthinkable.

The Pro-Slavery Argument

In the South, in the meantime, a very different ideology was emerging out of a rapid hardening of position among southern whites on the issue of slavery. It was a result of many things: the Nat Turner uprising in 1831, which terrified southern whites; the expansion of the cotton economy into the Deep South, which made slavery unprecedentedly lucrative; and the growth of the Garrisonian abolitionist movement, with its strident attacks on southern society. The popularity of Harriet Beecher Stowe's *Uncle Tom's Cabin* was perhaps the most glaring evidence of the power of those attacks, but other abolitionist writings had been antagonizing white southerners for years.

In response to these pressures, a number of white southerners produced a new intellectual defense of slavery. Professor Thomas R. Dew of the College of William and

Intellectual Defense of Slavery

Mary helped begin that effort in 1832. Twenty years later, apologists for slavery summarized their views in an anthology that gave their ideology its name: *The Pro-Slavery Argument.* John C. Calhoun stated the essence of the case in 1837: Slavery was "a good—a positive good." It was good for the slaves because they enjoyed better conditions than industrial workers in the North. Slavery was good for southern society as a whole because it was the only way the two races could live together in peace. It was good for the entire country because the southern economy, based on slavery, was the key to the prosperity of the nation.

Above all, southern apologists argued, slavery was good because it served as the basis for the southern way of life—a way of life superior to any other in the United States, perhaps in the world. White southerners looking at the North saw a spirit of greed, debauchery, and destructiveness. "The masses of the North are venal, corrupt, covetous, mean and selfish," wrote one southerner. Others wrote with horror of the factory system and the crowded, pestilential cities filled with unruly immigrants. But the South, they believed, was a stable, orderly society, free from the feuds between capital and labor plaguing the North. It protected the welfare of its workers. And it allowed the aristocracy to enjoy a refined and accomplished cultural life. It was, in short, an ideal social order in which all elements of the population were secure and content.

Black Inferiority Assumed

The defense of slavery rested, too, on increasingly elaborate arguments about the biological inferiority of African Americans, who were, white Southerners claimed, inherently unfit to take care of themselves, let alone exercise the rights of citizenship.

Buchanan and Depression

In this unpromising climate, the presidential campaign of 1856 began. Democratic Party leaders wanted a candidate who, unlike President Pierce, was not closely associated with the explosive question of "Bleeding Kansas." They chose James Buchanan of Pennsylvania, who as minister to England had been safely out of the country during the recent controversies. The Republicans, participating in their first presidential contest, endorsed a Whiggish program of internal improvements, thus combining the idealism of antislavery with the economic aspirations of the North. As eager as the Democrats to present a safe candidate, the Republicans nominated John C. Frémont, who had made a national reputation as an explorer of the Far West and who had no political record. The Native American, or Know-Nothing, Party was beginning to break apart, but it nominated former president Millard Fillmore, who also received the endorsement of a sad remnant of the Whig Party.

Election of 1856

After a heated, even frenzied campaign, Buchanan won a narrow victory over Frémont and Fillmore. At the time of his inauguration, Buchanan was, at age sixty-five, the oldest president, except for William Henry Harrison, ever to have taken office. Whether because of age and physical infirmities or because of a more fundamental weakness of character, he became a painfully timid and indecisive president at a critical moment in history.

In the year Buchanan took office, a financial panic struck the country, followed by a depression that lasted several years. In the North, the depression strengthened the Republican Party because distressed manufacturers, workers, and farmers came to believe that the hard times were the result of the unsound policies of southern-controlled Democratic administrations. They expressed their frustrations by moving into an alliance with antislavery elements and thus into the Republican Party.

The Dred Scott *Decision*

On March 6, 1857, the Supreme Court of the United States projected itself into the sectional controversy with one of the most controversial and notorious decisions in its history—its ruling in the case of *Dred Scott* v. *Sandford.* Dred Scott was a Missouri slave, once owned by an army surgeon who had taken Scott with him into Illinois and Wisconsin, where slavery was forbidden. In 1846, after the surgeon died, Scott sued his master's widow for freedom on the grounds that his residence in free territory had liberated him from slavery. The claim was well grounded in Missouri law, and in 1850 the circuit court in which Scott filed the suit declared him free. By now, John Sanford, the brother of the surgeon's widow, was claiming ownership of Scott, and he appealed the circuit court ruling to the state supreme court, which reversed the earlier decision. When Scott appealed to the federal courts, Sanford's attorneys claimed that Scott had no standing to sue because he was not a citizen.

The Supreme Court (which misspelled Sanford's name in its decision) was so divided that it was unable to issue a single ruling on the case. The thrust of the various rulings, however, was a stunning defeat for the antislavery movement. Chief Justice Roger Taney, who wrote one of the majority opinions, declared that Scott could not bring a suit in the federal courts because he was not a citizen. Blacks had no claim to citizenship, Taney argued. Slaves were property, and the Fifth Amendment prohibited Congress from taking property without "due process of law." Consequently, Taney concluded, Congress possessed no authority to pass a law depriving persons of their slave property in the territories. The Missouri Compromise, therefore, had always been unconstitutional.

Taney's Sweeping Decision

The ruling did nothing to challenge the right of an individual state to prohibit slavery within its borders, but the statement that the federal government was powerless to act on the issue was a drastic and startling one. Southern whites were elated: the highest tribunal in the land had sanctioned parts of the most extreme southern argument. In the North, the decision produced widespread dismay. Republicans threatened that when they won control of the national government, they would reverse the decision—by "packing" the Court with new members.

Deadlock over Kansas

President Buchanan timidly endorsed the *Dred Scott* decision. At the same time, he tried to resolve the controversy over Kansas by supporting its admission to the Union as a slave state. In response, the pro-slavery territorial legislature called an election for delegates to a constitutional convention. The free-state residents refused to participate, claiming that the legislature had discriminated against them in drawing district lines. As a result, the pro-slavery forces won control of the convention, which met in 1857 at Lecompton, framed a constitution legalizing slavery, and refused to give voters a chance to reject it. When an election for a new territorial legislature was called, the antislavery groups turned out to vote and won a majority. The new legislature promptly submitted the Lecompton constitution to the voters, who rejected it by more than 10,000 votes.

Both sides had resorted to fraud and violence, but it was clear nevertheless that a majority of the people of Kansas opposed slavery. Buchanan, however, pressured Congress to admit Kansas under the Lecompton constitution. Stephen A. Douglas and other western Democrats refused to support the president's proposal, which died in the House of Representatives. Finally, in April 1858, Congress approved a compromise: The Lecompton constitution would be submitted to the voters of Kansas again. If it was approved, Kansas would be admitted to the Union; if it was rejected, statehood would be postponed. Again, Kansas voters decisively rejected the Lecompton constitution. Not until the closing months of Buchanan's administration in 1861 did Kansas enter the Union—as a free state.

Lecompton Constitution Rejected

The Emergence of Lincoln

Given the gravity of the sectional crisis, the congressional elections of 1858 took on a special importance. Of particular note was the United States Senate contest in Illinois, which pitted Stephen A. Douglas, the most prominent northern Democrat, against Abraham Lincoln, who was largely unknown outside Illinois.

Lincoln was a successful lawyer who had long been involved in state politics. He had served several terms in the Illinois legislature and one undistinguished term in Congress. But he was not a national figure like Douglas, and so he tried to increase his visibility by engaging Douglas in a series of debates. The Lincoln-Douglas debates attracted enormous crowds and received wide attention.

Lincoln-Douglas Debates

At the heart of the debates was a basic difference on the issue of slavery. Douglas appeared to have no moral position on the issue and, Lincoln claimed, did not care whether slavery was "voted up, or voted down." Lincoln's opposition to slavery was more fundamental. If the nation could accept that blacks were not entitled to basic human rights, he argued, then it could accept that other groups—immigrant laborers, for example—could be deprived of rights, too. And if slavery were to extend into the western territories, he argued, opportunities for poor white laborers to better their lots there would be lost.

Lincoln's Argument

Lincoln believed slavery was morally wrong, but he was not an abolitionist. That was in part because he could not envision an easy alternative to slavery in the areas where it already existed. He shared the prevailing view among northern whites that the black race was not prepared to live on equal terms with whites. He and his party would "arrest the further spread" of slavery. They would not directly challenge it where it already existed, but would trust that the institution would gradually die out there of its own accord.

Douglas's position satisfied his followers sufficiently to produce a Democratic majority in the state legislature, which returned him to the Senate, but it aroused little enthusiasm. Lincoln, by contrast, lost the election but emerged with a growing following both in and beyond the state. And outside Illinois, the elections went heavily against the Democrats. The party retained control of the Senate but lost its majority in the House, with the result that the congressional sessions of 1858 and 1859 were bitterly deadlocked.

John Brown's Raid

The battles in Congress, however, were almost entirely overshadowed by an event that enraged and horrified the entire South. In the fall of 1859, John Brown, the antislavery zealot whose bloody actions in Kansas had inflamed the crisis there, staged an even more dramatic episode, this time in the South itself. With private encouragement and financial aid from some prominent eastern abolitionists, he made elaborate plans to seize a mountain fortress in Virginia from which, he believed, he could foment a slave insurrection in the South. On October 16, he and a group of eighteen followers attacked and seized control of a United States arsenal in Harpers Ferry, Virginia. But the slave uprising Brown hoped to inspire did not occur, and he quickly found himself besieged in the arsenal by citizens, local militia companies, and before long United States troops under the command of Robert E. Lee. After ten of his men were killed, Brown surrendered. He was promptly tried in a Virginia court for treason and sentenced to death. He and six of his followers were hanged.

John Brown Hanged

No other single event did more than the Harpers Ferry raid to convince white southerners that they could not live safely in the Union. John Brown's raid, many southerners believed (incorrectly) had the support of the Republican Party, and it suggested to them that the North was now committed to producing a slave insurrection.

JOHN BROWN Even in this formal photographic portrait (taken in 1859, the last year of his life), John Brown conveys the fierce sense of righteousness that fueled his extraordinary activities in the fight against slavery. *(The Library of Congress)*

The Election of Lincoln

As the presidential election of 1860 approached, the Democratic Party was torn apart by a battle between southerners, who demanded a strong endorsement of slavery, and westerners, who supported the idea of popular sovereignty. The party convention met in April in Charleston, South Carolina. When the convention endorsed popular sovereignty, delegates from eight states in the lower South walked out. The remaining delegates could not agree on a presidential candidate and finally adjourned after agreeing to meet again in Baltimore in June. The decimated convention at Baltimore nominated Stephen Douglas for president. In the meantime, disenchanted southern Democrats met in Richmond and nominated John C. Breckinridge of Kentucky.

Democrats Divided

The Republican leaders, in the meantime, were trying to broaden their appeal so as to attract every major interest group in the North that feared the South was blocking its economic aspirations. The platform endorsed such traditional Whig measures as a high tariff, internal improvements, a homestead bill, and a Pacific railroad to be built with federal financial assistance. It supported the right of each state to decide the status of slavery within its borders. But it also insisted that neither Congress nor territorial legislatures could legalize slavery in the territories. The Republican convention chose Abraham Lincoln as the party's presidential nomi-

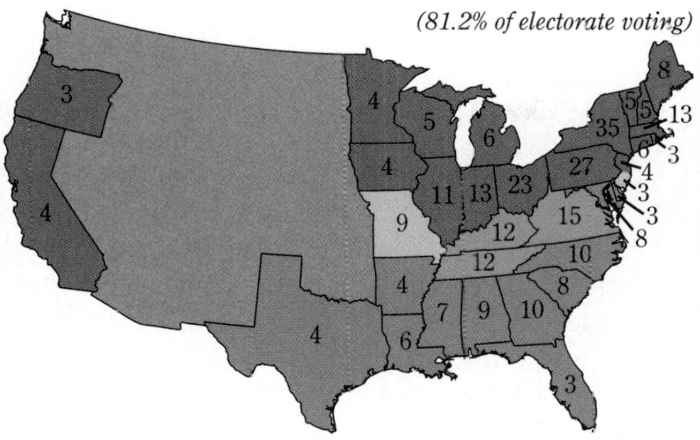

	ELECTORAL VOTE	POPULAR VOTE (%)
Abraham Lincoln *(Republican)*	180	1,865,593 (39.8)
J. C. Breckinridge *(Southern Democratic)*	72	848,356 (18.1)
John Bell *(Constitutional Union)*	39	592,906 (12.6)
Stephen A. Douglas *(Northern Democratic)*	12	1,382,713 (29.5)
Nonvoting territories		

THE ELECTION OF 1860 The stark sectional divisions that helped produce the Civil War were clearly visible in the results of the 1860 presidential election. Abraham Lincoln, the antislavery Republican candidate, won virtually all the free states. John Breckinridge, a strong pro-slavery southern Democrat, carried most of the South. Lincoln won under 40 percent of the popular vote, but because of the four-way division in the race, managed to win a slim majority of the electoral vote. ◆ *What impact did the election of Lincoln have on the sectional crisis?*

For an interactive version of this map go to www.mhhe.com/unfinishednation4ch13maps

nee. Lincoln was appealing because of his growing reputation for eloquence, because of his firm but moderate position on slavery, and because his relative obscurity ensured that he would have none of the drawbacks of other, more prominent (and therefore more controversial) Republicans.

Disunion

In the November election, Lincoln won the presidency with a majority of the electoral votes but only about two-fifths of the fragmented popular vote. The Republicans, moreover, failed to win a majority in Congress. Even so, the election of Lincoln became the final signal to many white southerners that their position in the Union was hopeless. And within a few weeks of Lincoln's victory, the process of disunion began—a process that would quickly lead to a prolonged and bloody war between two groups of Americans, each now convinced that it shared no common ground with the other.

CONCLUSION

In the decades following the War of 1812, a vigorous sense of nationalism pervaded much of American life, helping to smooth over the growing differences among the very different societies emerging in the regions of the United States. During the 1850s, however, the forces that had worked to hold the nation together in the past fell victim to new and much more divisive pressures that were working to split the nation apart.

Driving the sectional tensions of the 1850s was a battle over national policy toward the western territories and over the place of slavery within them. Should slavery be permitted in the new states? And who should decide whether to permit it or not? There were strenuous efforts to craft compromises and solutions to this dilemma: the Compromise of 1850, the Kansas-Nebraska Act of 1854, and others. But despite these efforts, positions on slavery continued to harden in both the North and South. Bitter battles in the territory of Kansas over whether to permit slavery there; growing agitation by abolitionists in the North and pro-slavery advocates in the South; the Supreme Court's controversial *Dred Scott* decision in 1857; the popularity of *Uncle Tom's Cabin* throughout the decade; and the emergence of a new political party—the Republican party—openly and centrally opposed to slavery: all worked to destroy the hopes for compromise and push the South toward secession.

In 1860, all pretense of common sentiment collapsed when no political party presented a presidential candidate capable of attracting national support. The Republicans nominated Abraham Lincoln of Illinois, a little-known politician recognized for his eloquent condemnations of slavery in a Senate race two years earlier. The Democratic party split apart, with its northern and southern wings each nominating different candidates. Lincoln won the election easily, but with less than forty percent of the vote. And almost immediately after his victory, the states of the South began preparing to secede from the Union.

FOR FURTHER REFERENCE

Richard White, *It's Your Misfortune and None of My Own: A History of the American West* (1991) is an excellent presentation of the social and economic history of the region. Anders Stephanson, *Manifest Destiny* (1995) briefly traces the origins of American expansion ideology. Robert M. Johannsen, *To the Halls of Montezuma: The Mexican War in the American Imagination* (1985) examines public attitudes toward the conflict. Paul D. Lack, *The Texas Revolutionary Experience: A Political and Social History, 1835–1836* (1992) chronicles Texas's route to independence from Mexico. Malcolm Rorabaugh, *Days of Gold: The California Gold Rush and the American Nation* (1997) is an account of this seminal event in the history of the West. Susan Lee Johnson, *Roaring Camp: The Social World of the Gold Rush* (2000) examines the experiences of men and women involved in the frenzy. David M. Pletcher, *The Diplomacy of Annexation: Texas, Oregon, and the Mexican War* (1973) is the standard work on war and diplomacy in the 1840s. William W. Freehling, *The Road to Disunion, Vol. 1: Secessionists at Bay, 1776–1854* (1990) explores the successful containment of sectionalism prior to the 1850s. David Potter, *The Impending Crisis, 1848–1861* (1976) is a thorough summary of the decisive decade. Eric Foner, *Free Soil, Free Labor, Free Men* (1970) traces the emergence of the Republican Party. Leonard L. Richards, *The Slave Power: The Free North and Southern Domination, 1780–1860* (2000) examines the long history of sectional tension. Michael Holt, *The Political Crisis of the 1850s* (1978) challenges Foner by emphasizing ethnic and religious alignment in northern politics. Don E. Fehrenbacher, *The Dred Scott Case* (1978) explains the Supreme Court's most infamous decision.

For quizzes, Internet resources, references to additional books and films, and more, consult this book's Online Learning Center site at www.mhhe.com/unfinishednation4.

YOUNG SOLDIER This somber 1864 painting by Winslow Homer portrays a young Union soldier—perhaps a drummer boy. When they were not playing music, drummers and buglers performed other functions in camp, as barbers, valets, and members of burial teams. Boys as young as 12 and 13 sometimes joined the army and grew up quickly in the rough surroundings of the camps. *(*Young Soldier, *by Winslow Homer, 1864. Cooper-Hewitt Museum, Smithsonian Institution. Gift of Charles Savage Homer, 1912-12-110/Art Resource, NY)*

TIME LINE

1861	1862	1863
Confederate States of America formed	Battles of Shiloh, Antietam, Second Bull Run	Emancipation Proclamation
Davis president of Confederacy	Confederacy enacts military draft	Battle of Gettysburg
Conflict at Fort Sumter		Vicksburg surrenders
First Battle of Bull Run		Union enacts military draft
		New York City antidraft riots

CHAPTER FOURTEEN

THE CIVIL WAR

The Secession Crisis
The Mobilization of the North
The Mobilization of the South
Strategy and Diplomacy
Campaigns and Battles

By the end of 1860, the cords that had once bound the Union together had snapped. The relatively stable second party system had collapsed, replaced by a new one that accentuated rather than muted regional controversy. The federal government was no longer the remote, unthreatening presence it once had been; the need to resolve the status of the territories had made it necessary for Washington to deal directly with sectional issues. The election of 1860 brought these tensions to a head and precipitated the most terrible war in the nation's history.

THE SECESSION CRISIS

Almost as soon as the news of Abraham Lincoln's election reached the South, militant leaders began to demand an end to the Union.

The Withdrawal of the South

South Carolina, long the hotbed of southern separatism, seceded first, on December 20, 1860. By the time Lincoln took office, six other southern states—Mississippi (January 9, 1861), Florida (January 10), Alabama

	1864	1865	
	Battle of the Wilderness	Lee surrenders to Grant	
	Sherman's March to the Sea	13th Amendment	
	Lincoln reelected		

(January 11), Georgia (January 19), Louisiana (January 26), and Texas (February 1)—had withdrawn from the Union. In February 1861, representatives of the seven seceded states met at Montgomery, Alabama, and formed a new nation—the Confederate States of America. President James Buchanan told Congress in December 1860 that no state had the right to secede from the Union but that the federal government had no authority to stop a state if it did.

The seceding states immediately seized the federal property within their boundaries. But they did not at first have sufficient military power to seize two fortified offshore military installations: Fort Sumter, on an island in the harbor of Charleston, South Carolina, garrisoned by a small force under Major Robert Anderson; and Fort Pickens, in the harbor of Pensacola, Florida. Buchanan refused to yield Fort Sumter when South Carolina demanded it. Instead, in January 1861, he ordered an unarmed merchant ship to proceed to Fort Sumter with additional troops and supplies. Confederate guns turned it back. Still, neither section was yet ready to concede that war had begun. And in Washington, efforts began once more to forge a compromise.

Confederacy Established

The Failure of Compromise

Crittenden Compromise Rejected

Gradually, the compromise efforts came together around a proposal first submitted by Senator John J. Crittenden of Kentucky and known as the Crittenden Compromise. The heart of the plan was a proposal to reestablish the Missouri Compromise line and extend it westward to the Pacific coast. Slavery would be prohibited north of the line and permitted south of it. Southerners in the Senate seemed willing to accept the plan. But the compromise would have required the Republicans to abandon their most fundamental position—that slavery not be allowed to expand—and they rejected it.

And so nothing had been resolved when Abraham Lincoln arrived in Washington for his inauguration. In his inaugural address, Lincoln insisted that acts of force or violence to support secession were insurrectionary and that the government would "hold, occupy, and possess" federal property in the seceded states—a clear reference to Fort Sumter.

But Union forces at Fort Sumter were running short of supplies. So Lincoln sent a relief expedition to the fort and informed the South Carolina authorities that he would send no troops or munitions unless the supply ships met with resistance. The new Confederate government ordered General P. G. T. Beauregard, commander of Confederate forces at Charleston, to take the fort. When Anderson refused to give up, the Confederates bombarded it for two days, April 12–13, 1861. On April 14, Anderson surrendered. The Civil War had begun.

Fort Sumter Seized

Almost immediately, four more slave states seceded from the Union and joined the Confederacy: Virginia (April 17, 1861), Arkansas (May 6),

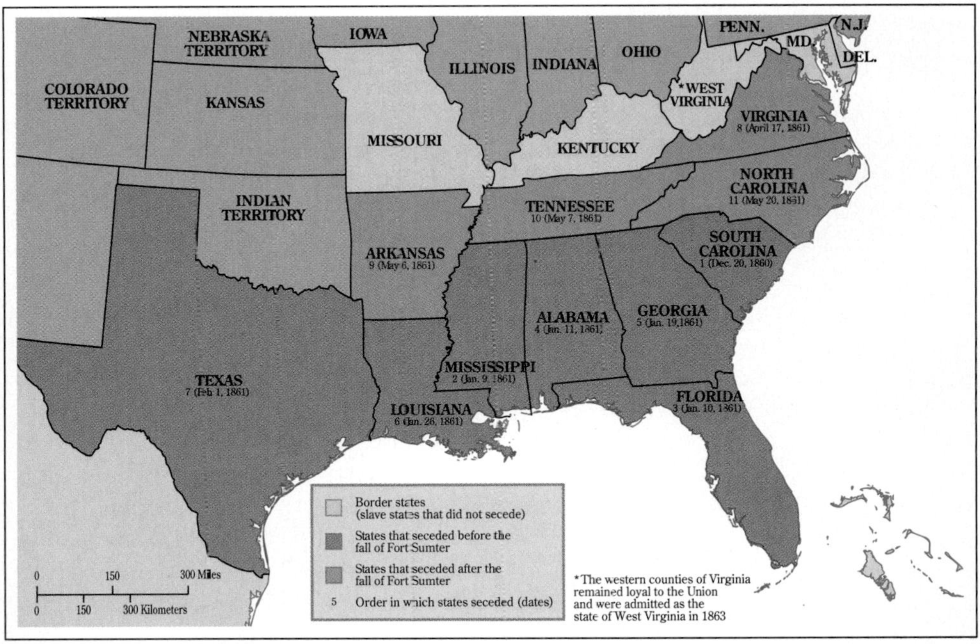

THE PROCESS OF SECESSION The election of Lincoln, the candidate of the antislavery Republican party, to the presidency had the immediate result of inspiring many of the states in the deep South to secede from the Union, beginning with South Carolina only a little more than a month after the November election. Other states nearer the northern border of the slaveholding region remained in the Union for a time, but the U.S. attempt to resupply Fort Sumter (and the bombardment of the fort by the new Confederate army) mobilized the upper South to secede as well. Only enormous pressure from the federal government kept the slaveholding states of Maryland, Kentucky, and Missouri in the Union. ◆ *What accounted for the creation of the state of West Virginia during the Civil War?*

For an interactive version of this map go to www.mhhe.com/unfinishednation4ch14maps

Tennessee (May 7), and North Carolina (May 20). The four remaining slave states, Maryland, Delaware, Kentucky, and Missouri—under heavy political pressure from Washington—remained in the Union.

The Opposing Sides

The North's Material Advantage

All the important material advantages for waging war lay with the North. It had an advanced industrial system and was able by 1862 to manufacture almost all its own war materials. The South had almost no industry at all.

In addition, the North had a much better transportation system than did the South, and in particular more and better railroads. During the war, the already inferior Confederate railroad system steadily deteriorated and by the beginning of 1864 had almost collapsed.

Debating the Past

THE CAUSES OF THE CIVIL WAR

Abraham Lincoln, in his 1865 inaugural address, looked back at the beginning of the terrible war that was now nearing its end and said, "All knew [that slavery] was somehow the cause of the war." Few historians dispute that. But disagreement has been sharp over whether slavery was the only, or even the principal cause of the war.

The debate began even before the war itself. In 1858, Senator William H. Seward of New York took note of the two competing explanations of the sectional tensions that were then inflaming the nation. On one side, he said, stood those who believed the conflicts to be "accidental, unnecessary, the work of interested or fanatical agitators." Opposing them stood those (among them Seward himself) who believed there to be "an irrepressible conflict between opposing and enduring forces."

The "irrepressible-conflict" argument dominated historical discussion of the war from the 1860s to the 1920s. War was inevitable, some historians claimed, because there was no room for compromise on the central issue of slavery. Others de-emphasized slavery and pointed to the economic differences between the agrarian South and the industrializing North. Charles and Mary Beard, for example, wrote in 1927 of the "inherent antagonisms" between the interests of planters and those of industrialists. Still others cited social and cultural differences between the two sections as the source of an irrepressible conflict. Slavery, the historian Allan Nevins argued, was only one factor in the cultural divergence that was making residents of the North and South "separate peoples." There were fundamental differences in "assumptions, tastes, and cultural aim" that made it virtually impossible for the two societies to live together in peace.

More recent proponents of irrepressible-conflict arguments similarly emphasize culture and ideology but define the concerns of the North and the South in different terms. Eric Foner, writing in 1970, argued that the moral concerns of abolitionists and the economic concerns of industrialists were less important in explaining Northern hostility to the South than was the broad-based "free-labor" ideology of the region. Northerners opposed slavery because they feared it might spread into their own region and threaten the position of free white laborers.

Other historians have argued that the war was not inevitable, beginning with a group of scholars in the 1920s known as the revisionists. James G. Randall and Avery Craven were the two leading proponents of the view that the differences between the North and the South were not so great as to require a war, that only a "blundering generation" of leaders caused the conflict. Michael Holt revived the revisionist argument in a 1978 book, in which he too emphasized the partisan ambitions of politicians. But Holt also helped introduce another element to the debate. He was, along with Paul Kleppner, Joel Silbey, and William Gienapp, one of the creators of an "ethnocultural" interpretation of the war, which emphasizes that the collapse of the party system—which was central to the coming of the conflict—was a result less of the debate over slavery than of such ethnocultural issues as temperance and nativism. These scholars challenge the arguments of Eric Foner and others that the "free-labor ideal" of the North—and the challenge slavery and its possible expansion into the territories posed to that ideal—was the principal reason for the conflict.

(text continued from page 363)

Southern Advantages

But the South had advantages as well. The Southern armies were, for the most part, fighting a defensive war on familiar land with local support. The Northern armies, on the other hand, were fighting mostly within the South amid hostile local populations; they had to maintain long lines of communication. The commitment of the white population of the South to the war was, with limited exceptions, clear and firm. In the North, opinion about the war was more divided, and support for it remained shaky until very near the end. A major Southern victory at any one of several crucial moments might have proved decisive by breaking the North's will to continue the struggle. Finally, the dependence of the English and French textile industries on American cotton inclined many leaders in those countries to favor the Confederacy; and Southerners hoped, with some reason, that one or both might intervene on their behalf.

THE MOBILIZATION OF THE NORTH

In the North, the war produced considerable discord, frustration, and suffering. But it also produced prosperity and economic growth. With the South now gone from Congress, the Republican Party had almost unchallenged supremacy. During the war, it enacted an aggressively nationalistic program to promote economic development.

Economic Nationalism

Homestead and Morrill Acts

Two acts of 1862 assisted the rapid development of the West. The Homestead Act permitted any citizen or prospective citizen to purchase 160 acres of public land for a small fee after living on it for five years. The Morrill Act transferred substantial public acreage to the state governments, which could now sell the land and use the proceeds to finance public education. This act led to the creation of many new state colleges and universities, the so-called land-grant institutions. Congress also passed a series of tariff bills that by the end of the war had raised duties to the highest level in the nation's history—a great boon to domestic industries eager for protection from foreign competition, but a hardship for many farmers and other consumers.

Congress also moved to spur completion of a transcontinental railroad. It created two new federally chartered corporations: the Union Pacific Railroad Company, which was to build westward from Omaha, and the Central Pacific, which was to build eastward from California. The two projects were to meet in the middle and complete the link.

National Bank Acts

The National Bank Acts of 1863–1864 created a new national banking system. Existing or newly formed banks could join the system if they had enough capital and were willing to invest one-third of it in government securities. In return, they could issue United States Treasury notes as currency. The new system eliminated much (although not all) of the chaos and uncertainty in the nation's currency.

More difficult than promoting economic growth was financing the war itself. The government tried to do so in three ways: levying taxes, issuing paper currency, and borrowing. Congress levied new taxes on almost all goods and services; and in 1861 the government levied an income tax for the first time. But taxation raised only a small proportion of the funds necessary for financing the war, and strong popular resistance prevented the government from raising the rates.

Financing the War

At least equally controversial was the printing of paper currency, or "greenbacks." The new currency was backed not by gold or silver but simply by the good faith and credit of the government. The value of the greenbacks fluctuated according to the fortunes of the Northern armies. Early in 1864, with the war effort bogged down, a greenback dollar was worth only 39 percent of a gold dollar. Even at the close of the war, with confidence high, it was worth only 67 percent of a gold dollar.

By far the largest source of financing for the war was loans. The Treasury persuaded ordinary citizens to buy over $400 million worth of bonds. But public bond purchases constituted only a small part of the government's borrowing, which in the end totaled $2.6 billion, most of it from banks and large financial interests.

Raising the Union Armies

At the beginning of 1861, the regular army of the United States consisted of only 16,000 troops, many of them stationed in the West to protect white settlers from Indians. So the Union, like the Confederacy, had to raise its army mostly from scratch. Lincoln called for an increase of 23,000 in the regular army, but the bulk of the fighting, he knew, would have to be done by volunteers in state militias. When Congress convened in July 1861, it authorized enlisting 500,000 volunteers for three-year (as opposed to the customary three-month) terms.

This voluntary system of recruitment produced adequate forces only briefly, during the first flush of enthusiasm for the war. By March 1863, Congress was forced to pass a national draft law. Virtually all young adult males were eligible to be drafted, although a man could escape service by hiring someone to go in his place or by paying the government a fee of $300.

To many who were accustomed to a remote and inactive national government, conscription was strange and threatening. Opposition to the law was widespread, particularly among laborers, immigrants, and Democrats opposed to the war. Occasionally it erupted into violence. Demonstrators against the draft rioted in New York City for four days in July 1863. Over 100 people died. The rioters lynched several African Americans and burned down black homes, businesses, and even an orphanage. It was the bloodiest riot in American history. Only the arrival of federal troops halted the violence.

New York City Draft Riots

Wartime Leadership and Politics

When Abraham Lincoln arrived in Washington early in 1861, many Republicans considered him a minor politician from the prairie who would be easily controlled by the real leaders of his party. The new president understood his own (and his party's) weaknesses, and he assembled a cabinet representing every faction of the Republican Party and every segment of Northern opinion. But Lincoln was not cowed by the distinguished figures around him. He moved boldly to use the war powers of the presidency, blithely ignoring inconvenient parts of the Constitution because, he said, it would be foolish to lose the whole by being afraid to disregard a part.

Bold Use of Presidential Powers

He sent troops into battle without asking Congress for a declaration of war, arguing that the conflict was a domestic insurrection. He increased the size of the regular army without receiving legislative authority to do so. He unilaterally proclaimed a naval blockade of the South.

Lincoln's greatest political problem was the widespread popular opposition to the war, mobilized by those in the Democratic Party who were known as Peace Democrats (or, by their enemies, "Copperheads"). Lincoln ordered military arrests of civilian dissenters and suspended the right of habeas corpus (the right of an arrested person to receive a speedy trial). At first, Lincoln used these methods only in sensitive areas such as the border states; but in 1862, he proclaimed that all persons who discouraged enlistments or engaged in disloyal practices were subject to martial law.

"Copperheads"

By the time of the presidential election of 1864, the North was in political turmoil. The Republicans had suffered heavy losses in 1862, and in response leaders of the party tried to create a broad coalition of all the groups that supported the war. They called the new organization the Union Party, but it was, in reality, little more than the Republican Party and a small faction of War Democrats. The Union Party nominated Lincoln for another term as president and Andrew Johnson of Tennessee, a War Democrat who had opposed his state's decision to secede, for the vice presidency.

The Democrats nominated George B. McClellan, a celebrated former Union general, and adopted a platform denouncing the war and calling for a truce. McClellan repudiated that demand, but the Democrats were clearly the peace party in the campaign, trying to profit from growing war weariness. For a time, Lincoln's prospects for reelection seemed doubtful.

George B. McClellan

At this crucial moment, however, several Northern military victories, particularly the capture of Atlanta, Georgia, early in September, rejuvenated Northern morale and boosted Republican prospects. Lincoln won reelection comfortably, with 212 electoral votes to McClellan's 21.

The Politics of Emancipation

Despite their surface unity in supporting the war and their general agreement on most economic matters, the Republicans disagreed sharply with one another on the issue of slavery. Radicals—led in Congress by such men as Representative Thaddeus Stevens of Pennsylvania and Senators Charles Sumner of Massachusetts and Benjamin Wade of Ohio—wanted to use the war to abolish slavery immediately and completely. Conservatives favored a more cautious policy—in part so as to placate the border slave states that remained, precariously, within the Union.

Confiscation Act

Nevertheless, momentum began to gather behind emancipation early in the war. In 1861, Congress passed the Confiscation Act, which declared that all slaves used for "insurrectionary" purposes (that is, in support of the Confederate military effort) would be considered freed. Subsequent laws in the spring of 1862 abolished slavery in the District of Columbia and in the western territories and provided for the compensation of owners. In July 1862, Radicals pushed through Congress the second Confiscation Act, which declared free the slaves of persons supporting the insurrection and authorized the president to employ African Americans as soldiers.

As the war progressed, many in the North seemed slowly to accept emancipation as a central war aim; nothing less, they believed, would justify the enormous sacrifices the struggle had required. As a result, the Radicals gained increasing influence within the Republican Party—a development that did not go unnoticed by the president, who decided to seize the leadership of the rising antislavery sentiment himself.

The Emancipation Proclamation

On September 22, 1862, after the Union victory at the Battle of Antietam, the president announced his intention to use his war powers to issue an executive order freeing all slaves in the Confederacy. And on January 1, 1863, he formally signed the Emancipation Proclamation, which declared forever free the slaves inside the Confederacy. The proclamation did not apply to the border slave states, which had never seceded from the Union; nor did it affect those parts of the Confederacy already under Union control (Tennessee, western Virginia, and southern Louisiana). It applied, in short, only to slaves over which the Union had no control. But the document was of great importance because it clearly and irrevocably established that the war was being fought not only to preserve the Union but also to eliminate slavery. Eventually, as federal armies occupied much of the South, the proclamation became a practical reality and led directly to the freeing of thousands of slaves.

AFRICAN-AMERICAN TROOPS Although most of the black soldiers who enlisted in the Union army during the Civil War performed noncombat jobs behind the lines, there were also black combat regiments—members of one of which are pictured here—that fought with great success and valor in critical battles. *(The Library of Congress)*

The Thirteenth Amendment

Even in areas not directly affected by the proclamation, the antislavery impulse gained strength. By the end of the war, two Union slave states (Maryland and Missouri) and three Confederate states occupied by Union forces (Tennessee, Arkansas, and Louisiana) had abolished slavery. In 1865, finally, Congress approved and the states ratified the Thirteenth Amendment, which abolished slavery as an institution in all parts of the United States. After more than two centuries, legalized slavery finally ceased to exist in the United States.

African Americans and the Union Cause

About 186,000 emancipated blacks served as soldiers, sailors, and laborers for the Union forces. The services of African Americans to the Union military were significant in many ways, not least because of the substantial obstacles many blacks had to surmount in order to enlist.

Growing Black Enlistment

In the first months of the war, blacks were largely excluded from the military. A few black regiments eventually took shape in some of the Union-occupied areas of the Confederacy. But once Lincoln issued the Emancipation Proclamation, black enlistment increased rapidly and the Union military began actively to recruit African-American soldiers and sailors in both the North and, where possible, the South.

Some of these men were organized into fighting units, of which the best known was probably the Fifty-fourth Massachusetts infantry which (like most black regiments) had a white commander: Robert Gould Shaw, a member of an aristocratic Boston family.

Low Status of Black Soldiers

Most black soldiers, however, were assigned menial tasks behind the lines such as digging trenches and transporting water. Even though many fewer blacks than whites died in combat, the African-American mortality rate was actually higher than the rate for white soldiers because so many black soldiers died of disease from working long, arduous hours in unsanitary conditions. Conditions for blacks and whites were unequal in other ways as well. Black soldiers were paid a third less than were white soldiers (until Congress changed the law in mid-1864). Black fighting men captured by the Confederates were sent back to their masters (if they were escaped slaves) or executed. In 1864, Confederate soldiers killed over 260 black Union soldiers after capturing them in Tennessee.

Women, Nursing, and the War

The war thrust women into new and often unfamiliar roles. They took over positions vacated by men as teachers, salesclerks, office workers, and mill and factory hands. Above all, women entered nursing, a field previously dominated by men. The United States Sanitary Commission, an organization of civilian volunteers led by Dorothea Dix, mobilized large numbers of female nurses to serve in field hospitals. By the end of the war, women were the dominant force in nursing.

Traditional Gender Norms Reinforced

Female nurses encountered considerable resistance from male doctors, many of whom thought it inappropriate for women to be taking care of male strangers. The Sanitary Commission countered such arguments by presenting nursing in domestic terms: as a profession that made use of the same maternal, nurturing roles women played as wives and mothers.

Some women came to see the war as an opportunity to win support for their own goals. Elizabeth Cady Stanton and Susan B. Anthony, who together founded the National Woman's Loyal League in 1863, worked simultaneously for the abolition of slavery and the awarding of suffrage to women.

National Woman's Loyal League

THE MOBILIZATION OF THE SOUTH

Early in February 1861, representatives of the seven states that had seceded from the Union met at Montgomery, Alabama, to create a new Southern nation. When Virginia seceded several months later, the leaders of the Confederacy moved to Richmond.

There were, of course, important differences between the new Confederate nation and the nation it had left. But there were also important similarities between the Union and the Confederacy.

Confederate Government

The Confederate constitution was almost identical to the Constitution of the United States, with several significant exceptions. It explicitly acknowledged the sovereignty of the individual states (although not the right of secession). And it specifically sanctioned slavery and made its abolition (even by one of the states) practically impossible.

The constitutional convention at Montgomery named a provisional president and vice president: Jefferson Davis of Mississippi and Alexander H. Stephens of Georgia. They were later elected by the general public, without opposition, for six-year terms. Davis had been a moderate secessionist before the war. Stephens had argued against secession. The Confederate government, like the Union government, was dominated throughout the war by men of the political center.

Jefferson Davis

Davis was a reasonably able administrator, and encountered little interference from the generally tame members of his unstable cabinet. But he rarely provided genuinely national leadership. He spent too much time on routine items, and unlike Lincoln, he displayed a punctiliousness about legal and constitutional requirements inappropriate to the needs of a new nation at war.

There were no formal political parties in the Confederacy, but its congressional and popular politics were badly divided nevertheless. Some white Southerners opposed secession and war altogether. Most white Southerners supported the war, but as in the North many were openly critical of the government and the military, particularly as the tide of battle turned against the South.

States' rights had become such a cult among many white Southerners that they resisted virtually all efforts to exert national authority, even those necessary to win the war. States' rights enthusiasts restricted Davis's ability to impose martial law and suspend habeas corpus. They obstructed conscription. Governors such as Joseph Brown of Georgia and Zebulon M. Vance of North Carolina tried at times to keep their own troops apart from the Confederate forces. But the national government was not impotent. It experimented, successfully for a time, with a "food draft," which permitted soldiers to feed themselves by seizing crops from farms in their path. The government impressed slaves to work as laborers on military projects. The Confederacy seized control of the railroads and shipping; it imposed regulations on industry; it limited corporate profits. States' rights sentiment was a significant handicap, but the South nevertheless took dramatic steps in the direction of centralization.

Damaging Emphasis on States' Rights

Money and Manpower

Financing the Confederate war effort was a monumental task. The Confederate congress tried at first to requisition funds from the individual

CONFEDERATE VOLUNTEERS Smiling and apparently confident, young Southern soldiers pose for a photograph in 1861, shortly before the First Battle of Bull Run. The Civil War was one of the first military conflicts extensively chronicled by photographers. *(Cook Collection, Valentine Museum)*

states; but the states were as reluctant to tax their citizens as the congress was. In 1863, therefore, the congress enacted an income tax. But taxation produced only about 1 percent of the government's total income. Borrowing was not much more successful. The Confederate government issued bonds in such vast amounts that the public lost faith in them, and efforts to borrow money in Europe using cotton as collateral fared no better.

Disastrous Inflation

As a result, the Confederacy had to pay for the war through the least stable, most destructive form of financing: paper currency, which it began issuing in 1861. By 1864, the Confederacy had issued the staggering total of $1.5 billion in paper money. The result was a disastrous inflation—a 9,000 percent increase in prices in the course of the war (in contrast to 80 percent in the North).

Conscription Act

Like the United States, the Confederacy first raised armies by calling for volunteers. And as in the North, by the end of 1861 voluntary enlistments were declining. In April 1862, therefore, the congress enacted the Conscription Act, which subjected all white males between the ages of eighteen and thirty-five to military service for three years. As in the North, a draftee could avoid service if he furnished a substitute. But since the price of substitutes was high, the provision aroused such opposition from poorer whites that it was repealed in 1863.

Even so, conscription worked for a time, in part because enthusiasm for the war was intense and widespread among white men in most of the South. At the end of 1862, about 500,000 soldiers were in the Confederate army. That number did not include the many slave men and women recruited by the military to perform such services as cooking, laundry, and manual labor. Small numbers of slaves and free blacks enlisted in the Confederate army, and a few participated in combat.

After 1862, however, conscription began producing fewer men, and by 1864 the Confederate government faced a critical manpower shortage. The nation was suffering from intense war weariness, and many had concluded that defeat was inevitable. Nothing could attract or retain an adequate army any longer. In a frantic final attempt to raise men, the congress authorized the conscription of 300,000 slaves, but the war ended before the government could attempt this incongruous experiment.

Critical Manpower Shortage

Economic and Social Effects of the War

The war cut off Southern planters and producers from markets in the North, and a Union blockade of Confederate ports made the sale of cotton overseas much more difficult. The war robbed those farms and industries that did not have large slave populations of a male work force. In the North, production of all goods increased during the war; in the South, it declined by more than a third. Above all, the fighting itself wreaked havoc on the Southern landscape, destroying farmland, towns, cities, and railroads. As the war continued, the shortages, the inflation, and the carnage created increasing instability in Southern society. Resistance to conscription, food impressment, and taxation increased throughout the Confederacy, as did hoarding and black-market commerce.

Southern Economic Woes

The war forced many women (and some men) to question the prevailing assumption of their society that females were not suited for the public sphere, since so many women had to perform untraditional, nondomestic tasks during the conflict. The war also decimated the male population. After the war, women outnumbered men in most Southern states by significant margins. The result was a large number of unmarried or widowed women who had no choice but to find employment.

New Roles for Women

Even before emancipation, the war had far-reaching effects on the lives of slaves. Confederate leaders enforced slave codes with particular severity. Even so, many slaves—especially those near the front—escaped their masters and crossed Union lines.

America in the World

THE CONSOLIDATION OF NATIONS

The American Civil War was an event largely rooted in conditions particular to the United States. But it was also a part of a worldwide movement in the nineteenth century to create large, consolidated nations. America's expansion into the western regions of the continent—and its efforts to incorporate those areas into the nation—was one of the principal causes of the controversies over slavery that led to the Civil War. A commitment to preserving the Union—to consolidating, rather than dismantling, the nation—was one of the principal motives for the North's commitment to fighting a war against the seceding states. Similar efforts at expansion, consolidation, and unification were occurring in many other nations at around the same time.

The consolidation of the nation states was, of course, not new to the nineteenth century. Spain, Britain, Russia, and other nations had united disparate states and regions into substantial nations in the fifteenth, sixteenth, and seventeenth centuries. But nationalism took on new force in the nineteenth century. That was partly because of growing sentiment among peoples who shared language, culture, ethnicity, and tradition and who came to believe that a consolidated nation was the best vehicle for strengthening their common bonds. Nationalism was also a product of the centralization of governments in many areas of the world, and the development within them of the ability to administer large territories from above. The revolutions in America and France in the late eighteenth century—and the subsequent strengthening of the French concept of nationhood under Napoleon in the early nineteenth century—inspired new nationalist enthusiasms in other parts of Europe.

In 1848, a wave of nationalist revolutions erupted in Italy, France, and Austria, challenging the imperial powers that many Europeans believed were subjugating national cultures. Those revolutions failed, but they helped lay the groundwork for the two most important national consolidations of nineteenth-century Europe.

One of them occurred in Germany, which was divided into numerous small, independent states in the early nineteenth century but where popular sentiment for German unification had been growing for decades. It was spurred in part by new histories of the German *volk* (people) and by newly constructed images of German traditions, visible in such literature as Grimm's fairy tales—an effort to record and popularize German folk traditions and make them the basis of a shared sense of a common past. In 1862, King Wilhelm I of Prussia—one of the most powerful of the scattered German states—appointed an aristocratic landowner, Otto von Bismarck, as his prime minister. Bismarck harnessed the growing nationalism throughout the various German states and helped develop a strong popular base for unification. He did so in part by launching Prussian wars against Denmark, Austria, and France—wars Prussia easily won, inspiring pride in German power that extended well beyond Prussia itself. The Franco-Prussian War of 1870 was particularly important, because Prussia fought it to take possession of the French provinces of Alsace and Lorraine—provinces the Prussians claimed were part of the German "national community" because its people, although legally French citizens, were ethnically and linguistically German. In 1871, capitalizing on the widespread nationalist sentiment the war had created throughout the German-speaking states, Bismarck persuaded the German king to proclaim himself emperor (or *Kaiser*) of a new empire that united all German peoples except those in Austria and Switzerland.

The second great European movement for national unification occurred in Italy, which had long been divided into regional kingdoms, city-states, and regions controlled by the Vatican. Some areas of Italy were at one time or another dominated by the French, the Spanish, and the Austro-Hungarian empire. Beginning in the early nineteenth century, Italian nationalists formed what became known as the Young Italy movement, under the leadership of Giuseppe Mazzini. The movement demanded an end of foreign control in Italy and the unification of the Italian people into a single nation. It promoted an idea of the nation as a kind of family, and of its territories as a family home. Peoples with common language, culture, and tradition, Mazzini believed, should be free to unite and govern themselves. But even greater than this growing popular nationalism as a cause of Italian unification were the efforts of powerful and ambitious leaders. The most powerful Italian state in the mid-nineteenth century was the kingdom of the Piedmont and Sardinia in the northwestern part of the peninsula. Its king, Victor Emmanuel II, appointed his own version of Bismarck—Camillo di Cavour—as prime minister in 1852. Cavour joined forces with nationalists in other areas of Italy in an effort to drive the Spanish and the Austrians out of Italian territory. Having first won independence for northern Italy, he joined forces with the southern nationalist leader Giuseppe Garibaldi, who helped win independence in the South and then agreed to a unification of the entire Italian nation under Victor Emmanuel in 1860.

Other nations in these years were also trying to create, preserve, and strengthen nation states. Some failed to do so—Russia, which despite the reform efforts of several tsars, never managed to create a stable nation state from among its broad and diverse peoples; Austria, whose empire could never consolidate its claim over a similarly diverse group of national groups; Turkey, whose Ottoman empire (known as "the sick man of Europe") remained frail despite the efforts of leaders to strengthen it; and China, which likewise tried and failed to produce reforms that would consolidate its vast lands effectively. But others succeeded. Meiji Japan, for example, instituted a series of reforms in the 1880s and 1890s that created a powerful new Japanese nation-state.

In fighting and winning the Civil War, the nationalists of the northern parts of the United States not only preserved the unity of their nation. They also became part of a movement toward the consolidation of national cultures and national territories that extended through many areas of the globe.

(text continued from page 373)

STRATEGY AND DIPLOMACY

The social and economic circumstances of the North and the South helped shape the outcome of the war. But much rested on the military and diplomatic strategies that the two sides employed.

The Commanders

The most important Union military commander was Abraham Lincoln, whose previous military experience consisted only of brief service in his state militia. Lincoln made many mistakes, but he was on the whole a successful commander in chief because he knew how to exploit the North's material advantages. He realized, too, that the proper objective of his armies was the destruction of the Confederate armies and not the occupation of Southern territory. It was fortunate for the North that Lincoln had a good grasp of strategy, because many of his generals did not.

From 1861 to 1864, Lincoln tried time and again to find a chief of staff capable of orchestrating the Union war effort. He turned first to General Winfield Scott, the aging hero of the Mexican War. But Scott was unprepared for the magnitude of the new conflict and soon retired. Lincoln then appointed the young George B. McClellan, who was the commander of the Union forces in the East, the Army of the Potomac; but the proud, arrogant McClellan had a wholly inadequate grasp of strategy and in any case returned to the field in March 1862. For most of the rest of the year, Lincoln had no chief of staff at all. And when he eventually appointed General Henry W. Halleck to the post, he found him an ineffectual strategist. Not until March 1864 did Lincoln finally find a general he trusted to command the war effort: Ulysses S. Grant, who shared Lincoln's belief in unremitting combat and in making enemy armies and resources, not enemy territory, the target of military efforts.

U.S. Grant

Lincoln's handling of the war effort faced constant scrutiny from the Committee on the Conduct of the War, a joint investigative committee of the two houses of Congress. Established in December 1861 and chaired by Senator Benjamin E. Wade of Ohio, it complained constantly of the inadequate ruthlessness of Northern generals, which Radicals on the committee attributed (largely inaccurately) to a secret sympathy among the officers for slavery. The committee's efforts often seriously interfered with the conduct of the war.

Davis's Ineffective Command

Southern military leadership centered on President Davis, who was a trained soldier but who failed ever to create an effective central command system. Early in 1862, Davis named General Robert E. Lee as his principal military adviser. But in fact, Davis had no intention of sharing control of strategy with anyone. After a few months, Lee left Richmond to command forces in the field, and for the next two years Davis planned strategy alone. In February 1864, he named General Braxton Bragg as a military adviser, but Bragg never provided much more than technical advice.

At lower levels of command, men of markedly similar backgrounds controlled the war in both the North and the South. Many of the professional officers on both sides were graduates of the United States Military Academy at West Point and the United States Naval Academy at Annapolis. Amateur officers played an important role in both armies as command-

ULYSSES S. GRANT One observer said of Grant (seen here posing for a photograph during the Wilderness campaign of 1864): "He habitually wears an expression as if he had determined to drive his head through a brick wall, and was about to do it." It was an apt metaphor for Grant's military philosophy, which relied on constant, unrelenting assault. One result was that Grant was willing to fight when other Northern generals held back. Another was that Grant presided over some of the worst carnage of the Civil War. *(The Library of Congress)*

ers of volunteer regiments. In both North and South, such men were usually economic or social leaders in their communities who rounded up troops to lead. Sometimes this system produced officers of real ability; more often it did not.

The Role of Sea Power

The Union had an overwhelming advantage in naval power, and it gave its navy two important roles in the war. One was enforcing a blockade of the Southern coast. The other was assisting the Union armies in field operations.

Union Blockade

ROBERT E. LEE Lee was a moderate by the standards of Southern politics in the 1850s. He opposed secession and was ambivalent about slavery. But he could not bring himself to break with his region, and he left the U.S. army to lead Confederate forces beginning in 1861. He was (and remains) the most revered of all the white Southern leaders of the Civil War. For decades after his surrender at Appomattox, he was a symbol to white Southerners of the "Lost Cause." *(Bettmann/Corbis)*

The blockade of the South, which began in the first weeks of the war, kept most oceangoing ships out of Confederate ports, but for a time small blockade runners continued to slip through. Gradually, however, federal forces tightened the blockade by seizing the Confederate ports themselves. The last important port in Confederate hands—Wilmington, North Carolina—fell to the Union early in 1865.

Monitor versus Merrimac

The Confederates made a bold attempt to break the blockade with an ironclad warship, constructed by plating with iron a former United States frigate, the *Merrimac.* On March 8, 1862, the refitted *Merrimac,* renamed the *Virginia,* left Norfolk to attack a blockading squadron of wooden ships at nearby Hampton Roads. It destroyed two of the ships and scattered the rest. But the Union government had already built ironclads of its own. And one of them, the *Monitor*, arrived off the coast of Virginia only a few hours after the *Virginia*'s dramatic foray. The next day, it met the *Virginia* in battle. Neither vessel was able to sink the other, but the *Monitor* put an end to the *Virginia's* raids and preserved the blockade.

The Union navy was particularly important in the western theater of the war, where the major rivers were navigable by large vessels. The navy transported supplies and troops and joined in attacking Confederate strong points. The South had no significant navy of its own and could defend against the Union gunboats only with ineffective fixed land fortifications.

Europe and the Disunited States

Judah P. Benjamin, the Confederate secretary of state for most of the war, was an intelligent but undynamic man who attended mostly to routine administrative tasks. William Seward, his counterpart in Washington, gradually became one of the outstanding American secretaries of state. He had invaluable assistance from Charles Francis Adams, the American minister to London. The gap between the diplomatic skills of the Union and the Confederacy proved to be a decisive factor in the war.

William Seward

At the beginning of the conflict, the sympathies of the ruling classes of England and France lay largely with the Confederacy. That was partly because the two nations imported much Southern cotton; but it was also because they were eager to weaken the United States, an increasingly powerful rival to them in world commerce. But France was unwilling to take sides in the conflict unless England did so first. And in England, the government was reluctant to act because there was powerful popular support for the Union—particularly from the large and influential English antislavery movement. After Lincoln issued the Emancipation Proclamation, antislavery groups worked particularly avidly for the Union. Southern leaders hoped to counter the strength of the British antislavery forces by arguing that access to Southern cotton was vital to the English and French textile industries. But English manufacturers had a surplus of both raw cotton and finished goods on hand in 1861 and could withstand a temporary loss of access to American cotton. Later, as the supply of cotton began to diminish, both England and France managed to keep at least some of their mills open by importing cotton from Egypt, India, and other sources. Equally important, even the 500,000 English textile workers thrown out of jobs as a result of mill closings continued to support the North. In the end, therefore, no European nation offered diplomatic recognition to the Confederacy or intervened in the war. No nation wanted to antagonize the United States unless the Confederacy seemed likely to win, and the South never came close enough to victory to convince its potential allies to support it.

Tension with Britain

Even so, there was considerable tension, and on occasion near hostilities, between the United States and Britain. The Union government was angry when Great Britain, France, and other nations declared themselves neutral early in the war, thus implying that the two sides to the conflict had equal stature. Washington was insisting that the conflict was simply a domestic insurrection, not a war between two legitimate governments.

The Trent Affair

A more serious crisis, the so-called *Trent* affair, began in late 1861. Two Confederate diplomats, James M. Mason and John Slidell, had slipped through the then-ineffective Union blockade to Havana, Cuba, where they boarded an English steamer, the *Trent*, for England. Waiting in Cuban waters was the American frigate *San Jacinto*, commanded by the impetuous Charles Wilkes. Acting without authorization, Wilkes stopped the British vessel, arrested the diplomats, and carried them in triumph to Boston. The British government demanded the release of the prisoners, reparations, and an apology. Lincoln and Seward, aware that Wilkes had violated maritime law and unwilling to risk war with England, eventually released the diplomats with an indirect apology.

A second diplomatic crisis produced problems that lasted for years. Unable to construct large ships itself, the Confederacy bought six ships, known as commerce destroyers, from British shipyards. The United States protested that this sale of military equipment to a belligerent violated the laws of neutrality, and the protests became the basis, after the war, of a prolonged battle over damage claims (known as the *Alabama* claims, a name derived from one of the ships) by the United States against Great Britain.

CAMPAIGNS AND BATTLES

In the absence of direct intervention by the European powers, the two contestants in North America were left to resolve the conflict between themselves. They did so in four long years of bloody combat. More than 618,000 Americans died in the course of the Civil War, far more than the 112,000 who perished in World War I or the 405,000 who died in World War II. There were nearly 2,000 deaths for every 100,000 of population during the Civil War. In World War I, the comparable figure was only 109; in World War II, 241.

Staggering Casualties

The Technology of War

Much of what happened on the battlefield in the Civil War was a result of new technologies that transformed the nature of combat.

The most obvious change in the character of warfare in the 1860s was the nature of the armaments that both sides used in battle. Among the most important was the introduction of repeating weapons. Samuel Colt had patented a repeating pistol (the revolver) in 1835, but more important for military purposes was the repeating rifle, introduced in 1860 by Oliver Winchester. Also significant were greatly improved cannons and artillery, a result of advances in iron and steel technology of the previous decades.

It was now impossibly deadly to fight battles as they had been fought for centuries, with lines of infantry soldiers standing erect in the field firing volleys at their opponents until one side withdrew. Soldiers quickly learned that the proper position for combat was staying low to the ground and behind cover. For the first time in the history of organized warfare, therefore, infantry did not fight in formation, and the battlefield became a more chaotic place. Gradually, the deadliness of the new weapons encouraged armies on both sides to spend a great deal of time building elaborate fortifications and trenches to protect themselves from enemy fire. The sieges of Vicksburg and Petersburg, the defense of Richmond, and many other military events all produced the construction of vast fortifications around the cities and around the attacking armies. (They became the predecessors to the great network of trenches that became so central a part of World War I.)

Deadlier Weaponry

Other weapons technologies were less central to the fighting of the war, but important nevertheless. There was sporadic use of the relatively new technology of hot-air balloons, employed intermittently to provide a view of enemy formations in the field. Ironclad ships such as the *Merrimac* (or *Virginia*) and the *Monitor* suggested the dramatic changes that would soon overtake naval warfare, but did not have a great impact on the fighting of the Civil War. Torpedoes and submarine technology also made a fleeting appearance in the 1860s, showing the way to future innovations in warfare but not playing a major role in the Civil War.

Critical to the conduct of the war, however, were two other relatively new technologies: the railroad and the telegraph. The railroad was particularly important in a war in which millions of soldiers were being mobilized and transferred to the front. Transporting such enormous numbers of soldiers, and the supplies necessary to sustain them, by land or by horse and wagon would have been almost impossible. Railroads made it possible for these large armies to be assembled and moved from place to place. However, they also limited the mobility of the armies. Commanders were forced to organize their campaigns at least in part around the location of the railroads rather than on the basis of the best topography or most direct land route to a destination. The dependence on the rails—and the resulting necessity of concentrating huge numbers of men in a few places—also encouraged commanders to prefer great battles with large armies rather than smaller engagements with fewer troops.

Military Importance of Railroads

The impact of the telegraph on the war was limited both by the scarcity of qualified telegraph operators and by the difficulty of bringing telegraph wires into the fields where battles were being fought. Things improved somewhat after the new U.S. Military Telegraph Corps, headed by Thomas Scott and Andrew Carnegie, trained and employed over 1,200 operators. Gradually, too, both the Union and Confederate armies learned to string telegraph wires along the routes of their troops, so that field commanders were able to stay in close touch with one another during battles.

The Opening Clashes, 1861

The Union and the Confederacy fought their first major battle of the war in northern Virginia. A Union army of over 30,000 men under the command of General Irvin McDowell was stationed just outside Washington. About thirty miles away, at Manassas, was a slightly smaller Confederate army under P. G. T. Beauregard. If the Northern army could destroy the Southern one, Union leaders believed, the war might end at once. In mid-July, McDowell marched his inexperienced troops toward Manassas. Beauregard moved his troops behind Bull Run, a small stream north of Manassas, and called for reinforcements, which reached him the day before the battle.

First Battle of Bull Run

On July 21, in the First Battle of Bull Run, or First Battle of Manassas, McDowell almost succeeded in dispersing the Confederate forces. But the Southerners managed to stop a last strong Union assault and then began a savage counterattack. The Union troops suddenly panicked, broke ranks, and retreated chaotically. McDowell was unable to reorganize them, and he had to order a retreat to Washington—a disorderly withdrawal complicated by the presence along the route of many civilians, who had ridden down from the capital, picnic baskets in hand, to watch the battle from nearby hills. The Confederates, as disorganized by victory as the Union forces were by defeat, did not pursue. The battle was a severe blow to Union morale and to the president's confidence in his officers.

Elsewhere, Union forces achieved some small but significant victories in 1861. Nathaniel Lyon, who commanded a small regular army force in St. Louis, moved his troops into southern Missouri to face secessionists trying to lead the state out of the Union. On August 10, at the Battle of Wilson's Creek, he was defeated and killed—but not before he had seriously weakened the striking power of the Confederates.

West Virginia Established

Meanwhile, a Union force under George B. McClellan moved east from Ohio into western Virginia. By the end of 1861, it had "liberated" the antisecession mountain people of the region, who created their own state government loyal to the Union; the state was admitted to the Union as West Virginia in 1863.

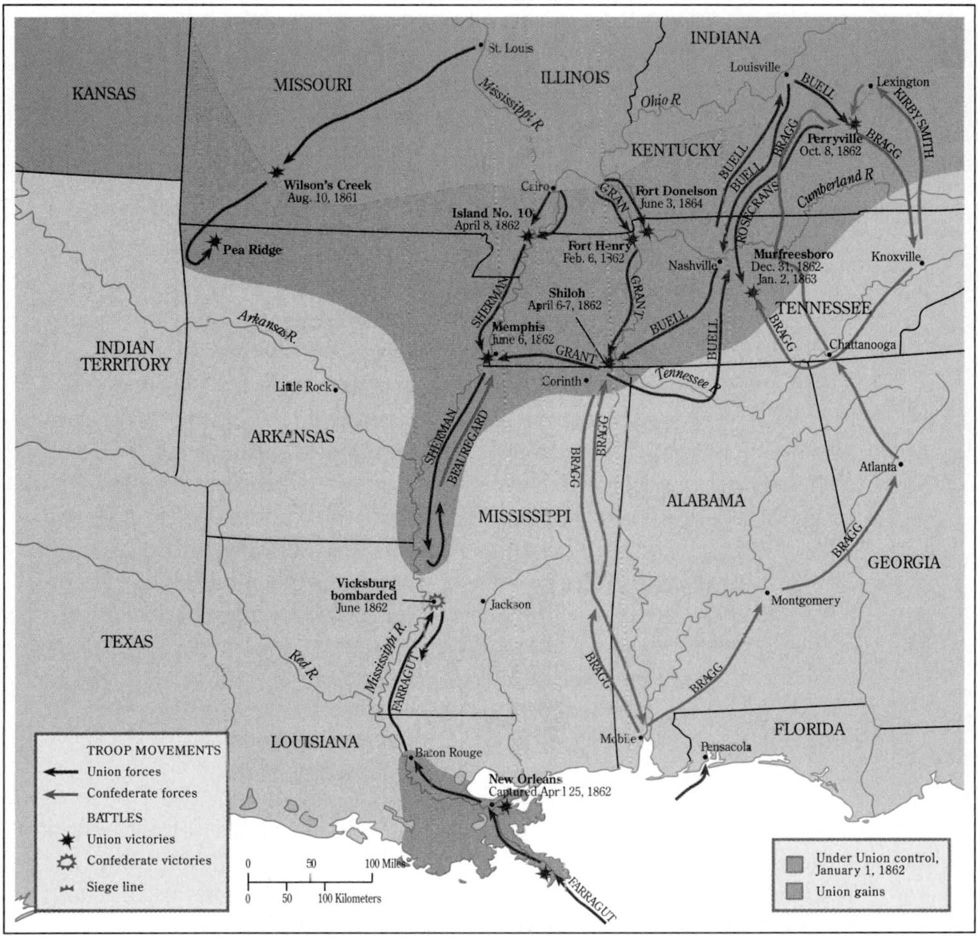

THE WAR IN THE WEST, 1861–1863 While the Union armies in Virginia were meeting with repeated frustrations, the Union armies in the West were scoring notable successes in the first two years of the war. This map shows a series of Union drives in the western Confederacy. Admiral David Farragut's ironclads led to the capture of New Orleans—a critical Confederate port—in April 1862, while forces further north under the command of Ulysses S. Grant drove the Confederate army out of Kentucky and western Tennessee. These battles culminated in the Union victory at Shiloh, which led to Union control of the upper Mississippi River. ◆ *Why was control of the Mississippi so important to both sides?*

For an interactive version of this map go to www.mhhe.com/unfinishednation4ch14maps

The Western Theater, 1862

After the battle at Bull Run, military operations in the East settled into a long and frustrating stalemate. The first decisive operations in 1862 occurred in the western theater. Here Union forces were trying to seize control of the southern part of the Mississippi River. Northern soldiers advanced on the southern Mississippi from both the north and south, moving down the river from Kentucky and up from the Gulf of Mexico toward New Orleans.

In April, a Union squadron of ironclads and wooden vessels commanded by David G. Farragut smashed past weak Confederate forts near the mouth of the Mississippi, and from there sailed up to New Orleans. The city was virtually defenseless because the Confederate high command had expected the attack to come from the north. The surrender of New Orleans on April 25, 1862, was an important turning point in the war. From then on, the mouth of the Mississippi was closed to Confederate trade, and the South's largest city and most important banking center was in Union hands.

New Orleans Seized

Farther north in the western theater, Confederate troops under the command of Albert Sidney Johnston were stretched out in a long defensive line around two forts in Tennessee, Fort Henry and Fort Donelson. Early in 1862, Ulysses S. Grant attacked Fort Henry, whose defenders, awed by the ironclad riverboats accompanying the Union army, surrendered with almost no resistance on February 6. Grant then moved both his naval and ground forces to Fort Donelson, where the Confederates put up a stronger fight but finally, on February 16, had to surrender. Grant thus gained control of river communications and forced Confederate troops out of Kentucky and half of Tennessee.

With about 40,000 men, Grant now advanced south along the Tennessee River. At Shiloh, Tennessee, he met a force almost equal to his own, commanded by Albert Sidney Johnston and P. G. T. Beauregard. The result was the Battle of Shiloh, April 6–7. In the first day's fighting (during which Johnston was killed), the Southerners drove Grant back to the river. But the next day, reinforced by 25,000 fresh troops, Grant recovered the lost ground and forced Beauregard to withdraw. After the narrow Union victory at Shiloh, Northern forces occupied Corinth, Mississippi, and took control of the Mississippi River as far south as Memphis.

Shiloh

Braxton Bragg, now in command of the Confederate army in the West, gathered his forces at Chattanooga, in eastern Tennessee, where he faced a Union army trying to capture Chattanooga. The two armies maneuvered for advantage inconclusively in northern Tennessee and southern Kentucky for several months until they finally met, on December 31–January 2, in the Battle of Murfreesboro, or Stone's River. Bragg was forced to withdraw to the South in defeat.

By the end of 1862, therefore, Union forces had made considerable progress in the West. But the major conflict remained in the East.

The Virginia Front, 1862

McClellan's Peninsular Campaign

During the winter of 1861–1862, George B. McClellan, commander of the Army of the Potomac, concentrated on training his army of 150,000 men

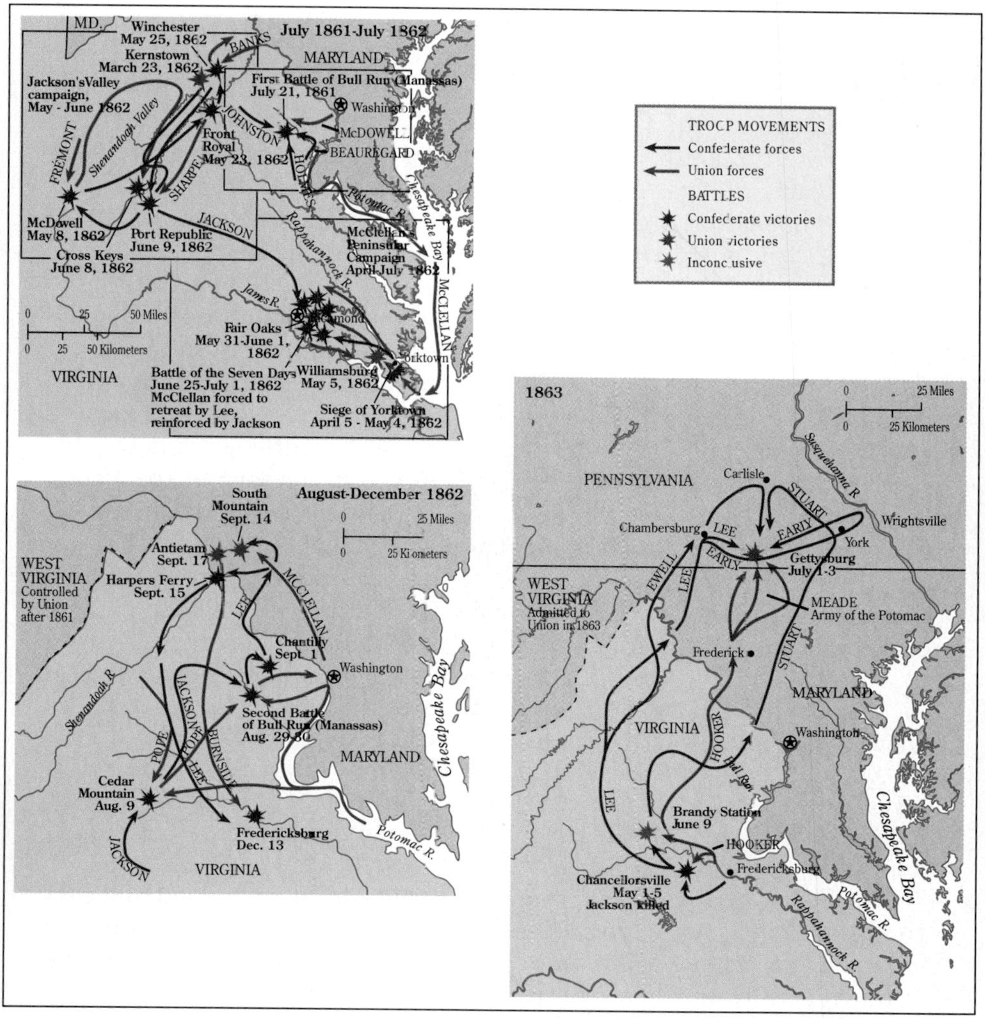

THE VIRGINIA THEATER, 1861–1863 Much of the fighting during the first two years of the Civil War took place in what became known as the Virginia theater—although the campaigns in this region eventually extended north into Maryland and Pennsylvania. The Union hoped for a quick victory over the newly created Confederate army. But as these maps show, the southern forces consistently thwarted those hopes. The map at top left shows the battles of 1861 and the first half of 1862, almost all of them won by the Confederates. The map at lower left shows the last months of 1862, during which the southerners again defeated the Union in most of their engagements—although northern forces drove the Confederates back from Maryland in September. The large map on the right shows the troop movements that led to the climactic battle of Gettysburg in 1863. ◆ *Why were the Union forces unable to profit more from material advantages during these first years of the war?*

For an interactive version of this map go to www.mhhe.com/unfinishednation4ch14maps

near Washington. Finally, he designed a spring campaign to capture the Confederate capital at Richmond. But instead of heading overland directly toward Richmond, McClellan chose a complicated route that he thought would circumvent the Confederate defenses. The navy would carry his troops down the Potomac to a peninsula east of Richmond, between the York and James Rivers; the army would approach the city from there. The combined operations became known as the Peninsular campaign.

McClellan set off with 100,000 men, reluctantly leaving 30,000 members of his army behind, under General Irvin McDowell, to protect Washington. McClellan eventually persuaded Lincoln to send him the additional men. But before the president could do so, a Confederate army under Thomas J. ("Stonewall") Jackson staged a rapid march north through the Shenandoah Valley, as if preparing to cross the Potomac and attack Washington. Lincoln postponed sending reinforcements to McClellan, retaining McDowell's corps to head off Jackson. In the Valley campaign of May 4–June 9, 1862, Jackson defeated two separate Union forces and slipped away before McDowell could catch him.

Meanwhile, McClellan was battling Confederate troops under Joseph E. Johnston outside Richmond in the two-day Battle of Fair Oaks, or Seven Pines (May 31–June 1), and holding his ground. Johnston, badly wounded, was replaced by Robert E. Lee, who then recalled Stonewall Jackson from the Shenandoah Valley. With a combined force of 85,000 to face McClellan's 100,000, Lee launched a new offensive, known as the Battle of the Seven Days (June 25–July 1), in an effort to cut McClellan off from his base on the York River. But McClellan fought his way across the peninsula and set up a new base on the James.

Robert E. Lee

McClellan was now only twenty-five miles from Richmond and in a good position to renew the campaign. But despite continuing pressure from Lincoln, he did not advance. The president finally ordered the army to move back to northern Virginia and join a smaller force under John Pope. The president hoped to begin a new offensive against Richmond on the direct overland route that he himself had always preferred. As the Army of the Potomac left the peninsula by water, Lee moved north with the Army of Northern Virginia to strike Pope before McClellan could join him. Pope was as rash as McClellan was cautious, and he attacked the approaching Confederates without waiting for the arrival of all of McClellan's troops. In the Second Battle of Bull Run, or Manassas (August 29–30), Lee threw back the assault and routed Pope's army, which fled to Washington. With hopes for an overland campaign against Richmond now in disarray, Lincoln removed Pope from command and put McClellan back in charge of all the federal forces in the region.

Lee soon went on the offensive again, heading north through western Maryland, and McClellan moved out to meet him. McClellan had the good luck to get a copy of Lee's orders, which revealed that a part of the Confederate army, under Stonewall Jackson, had separated from the rest to

SKIRMISH AT ANTIETAM The American public followed the course of the Civil War through newspaper reports and, at times, through published drawings of the battlefields by traveling artists who sketched important events for publication. Photographers chronicled the war as well. But cameras in the 1860s could not easily capture action scenes, and very few newspapers or magazines were technologically equipped to publish photographs. So drawings such as this one by A. R. Waud—of a Brooklyn, New York, regiment fighting Southern cavalry at the battle of Antietam—were much in demand. *(Bettmann/Corbis)*

attack Harpers Ferry. But instead of attacking quickly before the Confederates could recombine, McClellan stalled and gave Lee time to pull most of his forces together behind Antietam Creek, near the town of Sharpsburg. There, on September 17, McClellan's 87,000–man army repeatedly attacked Lee's force of 50,000, with staggering casualties on both sides. Late in the day, just as the Confederate line seemed ready to break, the last of Jackson's troops arrived from Harpers Ferry to reinforce it. McClellan might have broken through with one more assault. Instead, he allowed Lee to retreat into Virginia. Technically, Antietam was a Union victory; but in reality, McClellan had squandered an opportunity to destroy much of the Confederate army. In November, Lincoln finally removed McClellan from command for good.

Antietam

McClellan's replacement, Ambrose E. Burnside, was a short-lived mediocrity. He tried to move toward Richmond by crossing the Rappahannock River at Fredericksburg. There, on December 13, he launched a series of attacks against Lee, all of them bloody, all of them hopeless. After losing a large part of his army, he withdrew to the north bank of the Rappahannock. He was relieved at his own request. The year 1862 ended, therefore, with a series of frustrations for the Union.

1863: Year of Decision

At the beginning of 1863, General Joseph Hooker was commanding the still-formidable Army of the Potomac, which remained north of the Rappahannock, opposite Fredericksburg. Taking part of his army, Hooker crossed the river above Fredericksburg and moved toward the town and Lee's army. But at the last minute, he drew back to a defensive position in a desolate area of brush and scrub trees known as the Wilderness. Lee divided his forces for a dual assault on the Union army. In the Battle of Chancellorsville, May 1–5, Stonewall Jackson attacked the Union right and Lee himself charged the front. Hooker barely managed to escape with his army. Lee had frustrated Union objectives, but he had not destroyed the Union army. And his ablest officer, Jackson, was fatally wounded in the course of the battle.

Chancellorsville

While the Union forces were suffering repeated frustrations in the East, they were winning some important victories in the West. In the spring of 1863, Ulysses S. Grant was driving at Vicksburg on the Mississippi River. Vicksburg was well protected on land and had good artillery coverage of the river itself. But in May, Grant boldly moved men and supplies—over land and by water—to an area south of the city, where the terrain was reasonably good. He then attacked Vicksburg from the rear. Six weeks later, on July 4, Vicksburg—whose residents were by then literally starving as a result of the prolonged siege—surrendered. At almost the same time, the other Confederate strong point on the river, Port Hudson, Louisiana, also surrendered to a Union force that had moved north from New Orleans. The Union had achieved one of its basic military aims: control of the whole length of the Mississippi. The Confederacy was split in two, with Louisiana, Arkansas, and Texas cut off from the other seceded states. The victories on the Mississippi were one of the great turning points of the war.

Vicksburg

During an early stage of the siege of Vicksburg, Lee proposed an invasion of Pennsylvania, which would, he argued, divert Union troops north. Further, he argued, if he could win a major victory on Northern soil, England and France might come to the Confederacy's aid. The war-weary North might even quit the war before Vicksburg fell.

In June 1863, Lee moved up the Shenandoah Valley into Maryland and then entered Pennsylvania. The Union Army of the Potomac, commanded first by Hooker and then (after June 28) by George C. Meade, moved north, too. The two armies finally encountered one another at the small town of Gettysburg, Pennsylvania. There, on July 1–3, 1863, they fought the most celebrated battle of the war.

Meade's army established a strong, well-protected position on the hills south of the town. Lee attacked, but his first assault on the Union forces on Cemetery Ridge failed. A day later, he ordered a second, larger effort. In what is remembered as Pickett's Charge, a force of 15,000 Confederate soldiers

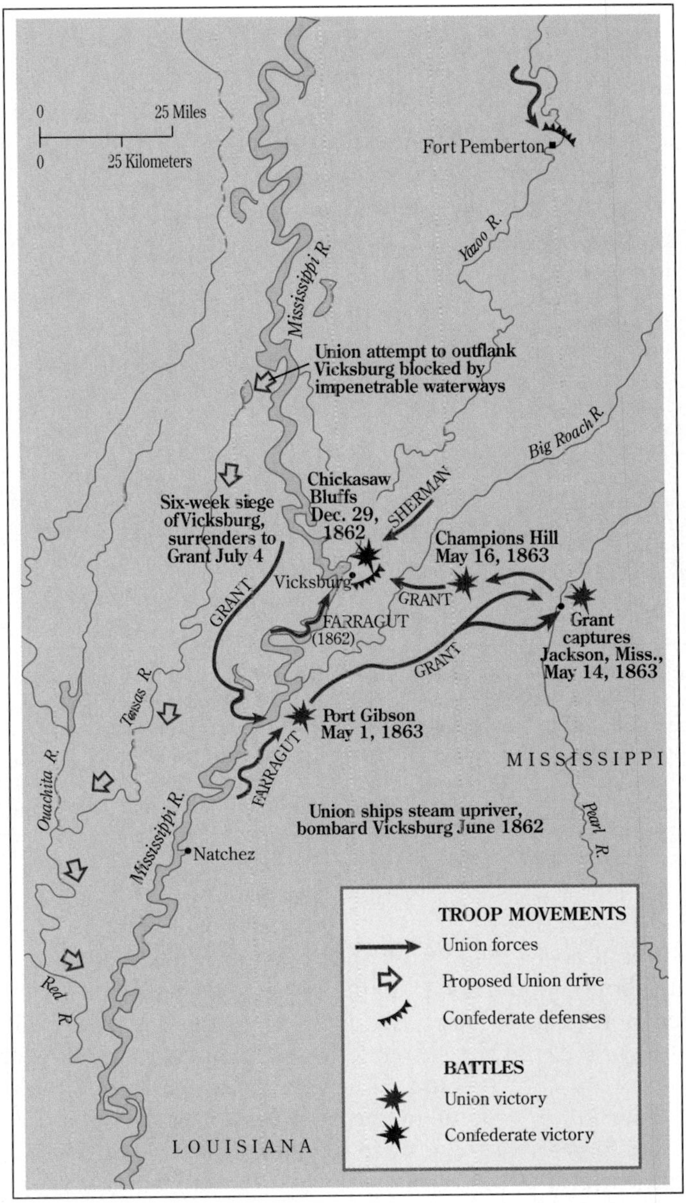

THE SIEGE OF VICKSBURG, MAY–JULY 1863 In the spring of 1863, Grant began a campaign to win control of the final piece of the Mississippi River still controlled by the Confederacy. To do that required capturing the southern stronghold at Vicksburg—a well-defended city sitting above the river. Vicksburg's main defenses were to its north, so Grant boldly moved men and supplies around the city and attacked it from the south. Eventually, he cut off the city's access to the outside world, and after a six-week siege, its residents finally surrendered. ◆ *What impact did the combined victories at Vicksburg and Gettysburg have on northern commitment to the war?*

For an interactive version of this map go to www.mhhe.com/unfinishednation4ch14maps

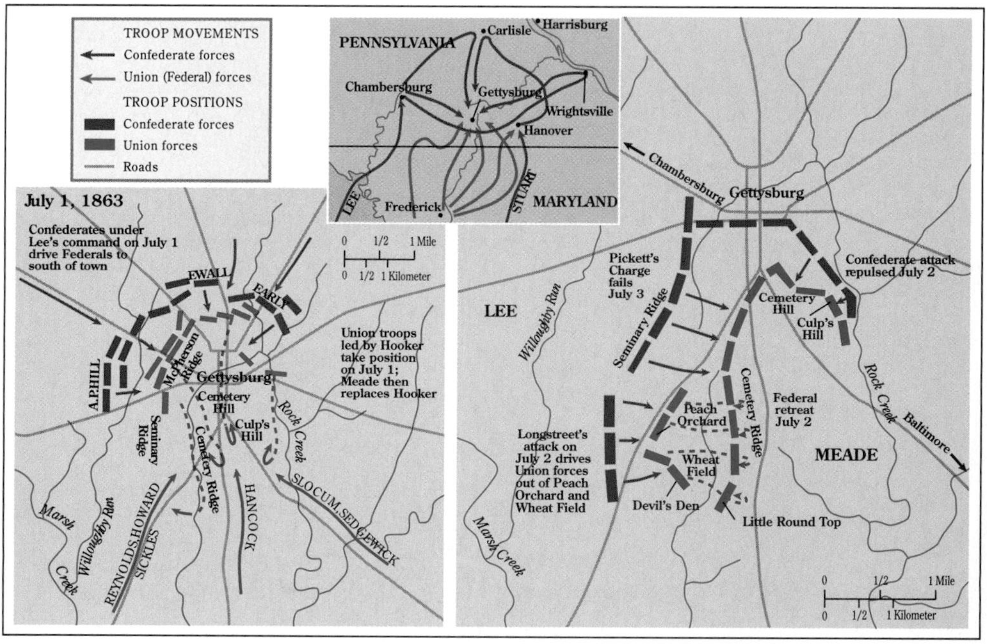

GETTYSBURG, JULY 1–3, 1863 Gettysburg was the most important single battle of the Civil War. Had Confederate forces prevailed at Gettysburg, the future course of the war might well have been very different. The map on the left shows the distribution of Union and Confederate forces at the beginning of the battle, July 1, after Lee had driven the northern forces south of town. The map on the right reveals the pattern of the attacks on July 2 and 3. Note, in particular, Pickett's bold and costly charge, whose failure on July 3 was the turning point in the battle and, some have argued, the war. ◆ *Why did Robert E. Lee believe that an invasion of Pennsylvania would advance the Confederate cause?*

advanced for almost a mile across open country while being swept by Union fire. Only about 5,000 made it up the ridge, and this remnant finally had to surrender or retreat. By now, Lee had lost nearly a third of his army. On July 4, the same day as the surrender of Vicksburg, he withdrew from Gettysburg. The retreat was another major turning point in the war. Never again were the weakened Confederate forces able seriously to threaten Northern territory.

Gettysburg

Before the end of the year, there was another important turning point, this one in Tennessee. After occupying Chattanooga on September 9, Union forces under William Rosecrans began an unwise pursuit of Bragg's retreating Confederate forces. The two armies engaged in western Georgia, in the Battle of Chickamauga (September 19–20). Union forces could not break the Confederate lines and retreated back to Chattanooga.

Bragg now began a siege of Chattanooga itself, seizing the heights nearby and cutting off fresh supplies to the Union forces. Grant came to the rescue. In the Battle of Chattanooga (November 23–25), the reinforced Union army drove the

Battle of Chattanooga

Confederates back into Georgia. Union forces had now achieved a second important objective: control of the Tennessee River.

The Last Stage, 1864–1865

By the beginning of 1864, Ulysses S. Grant had become general in chief of all the Union armies. Grant believed in using the North's great advantage in troops and material resources to overwhelm the South. He planned two great offensives for 1864. In Virginia, the Army of the Potomac would advance toward Richmond and force Lee into a decisive battle. In Georgia, the western army, under William T. Sherman, would advance east toward Atlanta and destroy the remaining Confederate force, now under the command of Joseph E. Johnston.

Grant's Northern Campaign

The northern campaign began when the Army of the Potomac, 115,000 strong, plunged into the rough, wooded Wilderness area of northwestern Virginia in pursuit of Lee's 75,000-man army. After avoiding an engagement for several weeks, Lee turned Grant back in the Battle of the Wilderness (May 5–7). Without stopping to rest or reorganize, Grant resumed his march toward Richmond and met Lee again in the bloody, five-day Battle of Spotsylvania Court House, in which 12,000 Union troops and a large, but unknown, number of Confederates fell. Grant kept moving, but victory continued to elude him. Lee kept his army between Grant and the Confederate capital and on June 1–3 repulsed the Union forces again, just northeast of Richmond, at Cold Harbor.

Grant now moved his army east of Richmond and headed south toward the railroad center at Petersburg. If he could seize Petersburg, he could cut off the capital's communications with the rest of the Confederacy. But Petersburg had strong defenses; and once Lee came to the city's relief, the assault became a prolonged siege.

In Georgia, meanwhile, Sherman was facing less ferocious resistance. With 90,000 men, he confronted Confederate forces of 60,000 under Johnston. As Sherman advanced, Johnston tried to delay him by maneuvering. The two armies fought only one real battle—Kennesaw Mountain, northwest of Atlanta, on June 27—where Johnston scored an impressive victory. Even so, he was unable to stop the Union advance toward Atlanta. Sherman took the city on September 2 and burned it.

Atlanta Taken

Hood now tried unsuccessfully to draw Sherman out of Atlanta by moving back up through Tennessee and threatening an invasion of the North. Sherman sent Union troops to reinforce Nashville. In the Battle of Nashville on December 15–16, 1864, Northern forces practically destroyed what was left of Hood's army.

"March to the Sea"

Meanwhile, Sherman had left Atlanta to begin his soon-to-be-famous "March to the Sea." Living off the land, destroying supplies it could not use, his army cut

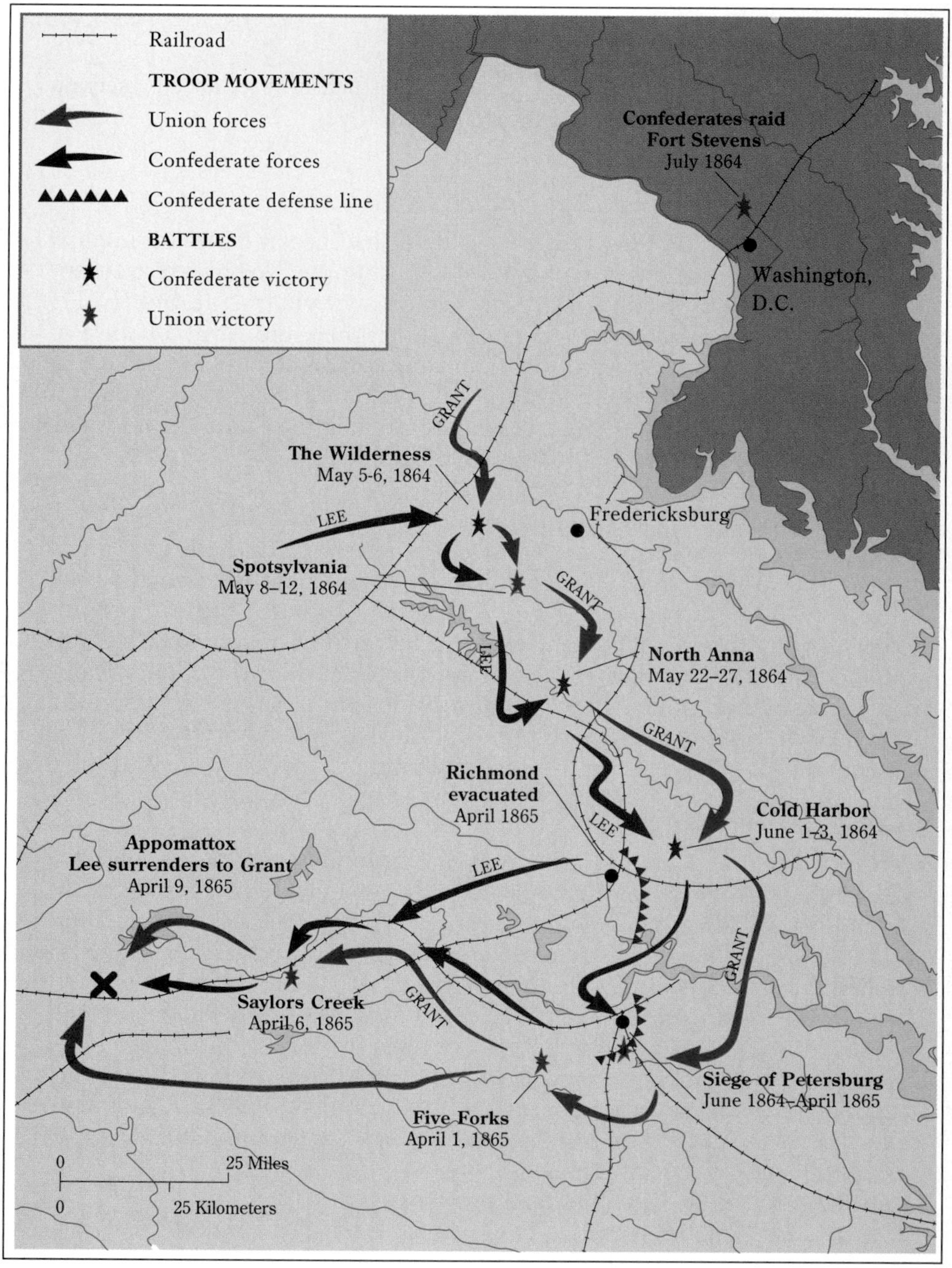

VIRGINIA CAMPAIGNS, 1864–1865 From the Confederate defeat at (and retreat from) Gettysburg until the end of the war, most of the eastern fighting took place in Virginia. By now, Ulysses S. Grant was commander of all Union forces and had taken over the Army of the Potomac. Although Confederate forces won a number of important battles during the Virginia campaign, the Union army grew steadily stronger and the southern forces steadily weaker. Grant believed that the Union strategy should reflect the North's greatest advantage: its superiority in men and equipment. ◆ *What effect did this decision have on the level of casualties?*

For an interactive version of this map go to www.mhhe.com/unfinishednation4ch14maps

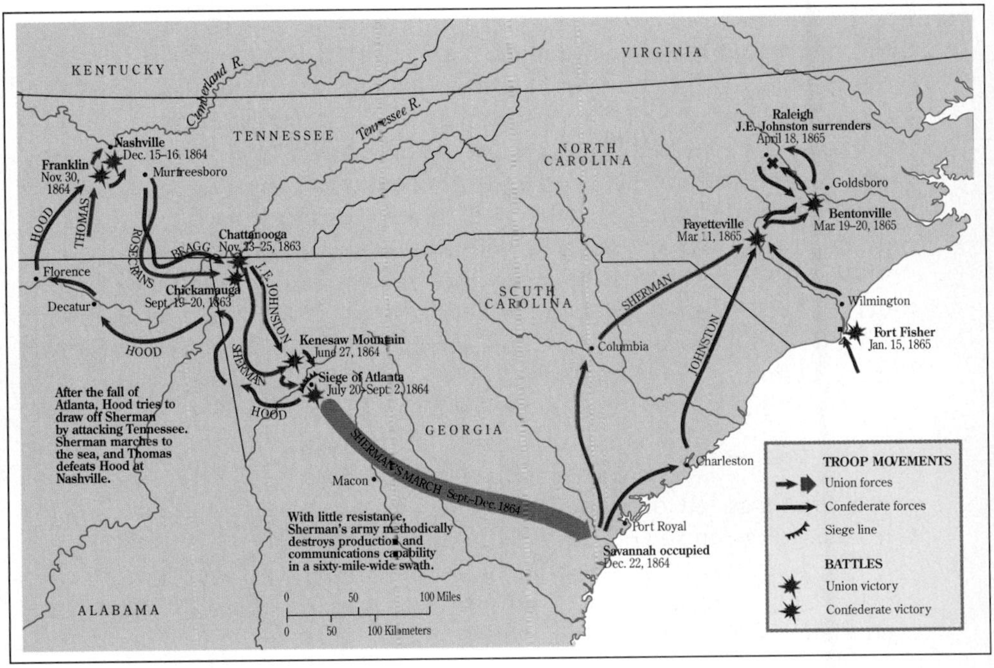

SHERMAN'S MARCH TO THE SEA, 1864–1865 While Grant was wearing Lee down in Virginia, General William Tecumseh Sherman was moving east across Georgia. After a series of battles in Tennessee and northwest Georgia, Sherman captured Atlanta and then marched unimpeded to Savannah, on the Georgia coast—deliberately devastating the towns and plantations through which his troops marched. Note that after capturing Savannah by Christmas 1864, Sherman began moving North through the Carolinas. A few days after Lee surrendered to Grant at Appomattox, Confederate forces further south surrendered to Sherman. ◆ *What did Sherman believe his devastating March to the Sea would accomplish?*

For an interactive version of this map go to www.mhhe.com/unfinishednation4ch14maps

a sixty-mile-wide swath of desolation across Georgia. Sherman sought not only to deprive the Confederate army of war materials and railroad communications but also to break the will of the Southern people by burning towns and plantations along his route. By December 20, he had reached Savannah, which surrendered two days later. Early in 1865, Sherman continued his destructive march, moving northward through South Carolina. He was virtually unopposed until he was well inside North Carolina, where a small force under Johnston could do no more than cause a brief delay.

In April 1865, Grant's Army of the Potomac—still engaged in the prolonged siege at Petersburg—finally captured a vital railroad junction southwest of the town. Without rail access to the South, and plagued by heavy casualties and massive desertions, Lee informed the Confederate government that he could no longer defend Richmond. Within hours, Jefferson Davis, his cabinet, and as much of the white population as could find transportation fled. That night, mobs roamed the city, setting devastating fires. And the next morning, Northern forces entered the Confederate capital. With them was Abraham Lincoln, who walked through the streets of the burned-out city surrounded by black men and women cheering him as the "Messiah" and "Father Abraham." In one particularly stirring moment, the president turned to a former slave kneeling on the street before him and said: "Don't kneel to me. . . . You must kneel to God only, and thank Him for the liberty you will enjoy hereafter."

With the remnant of his army, now about 25,000 men, Lee began moving west in the forlorn hope of finding a way around the Union forces so that he could move south and link up with Johnston in North Carolina. But the Union army pursued him and blocked his escape route. Lee finally recognized that further bloodshed was futile. He arranged to meet Grant at a private home in the small town of Appomattox Courthouse, Virginia, where on April 9 he surrendered what was left of his forces. Nine days later, near Durham, North Carolina, Johnston surrendered to Sherman.

Appomattox Courthouse

The long war was now effectively over. Jefferson Davis was finally captured in Georgia. A few Southern diehards continued to fight, but even their resistance collapsed before long.

CONCLUSION

The American Civil War began with high hopes and high ideals on both sides. In the North and the South alike, thousands of men enthusiastically enlisted in local regiments and went off to war. Four years later, over 600,000 of them were dead and many more maimed and traumatized for life. A fight for "principles" and "ideals"—a fight few people had thought would last more than a few months—had become one of the longest wars, and by far the bloodiest war, in American history, before or since.

During the first two years of fighting, the Confederate forces seemed to have all the advantages. They were fighting on their own soil. Their troops seemed more committed to the cause than those of the North. Their commanders were exceptionally talented, while Union forces were, for a time, erratically led. Gradually, however, the Union's advantages began to assert themselves. The North had a stabler political system led by one of the greatest leaders in the nation's history. It had a much larger population, a far more developed industrial economy, superior financial institutions, and a better railroad system. By the middle of 1863, the tide of the war had shifted; over the next two years, Union forces gradually wore down the Confederate armies before finally triumphing in 1865.

The war strengthened the North's economy, giving a spur to industry and railroad development. It greatly weakened the South's, by destroying millions of dollars of property and depleting the region's young male population. Southerners had gone to war in part because of their fears of growing northern dominance. The war itself, ironically, confirmed and strengthened that dominance.

But most of all, the Civil War was a victory for millions of African-American slaves. The war produced Abraham Lincoln's epochal Emancipation Proclamation and, later, the Thirteenth Amendment to the Constitution, which abolished slavery altogether. It also encouraged hundreds of thousands of slaves literally to free themselves, to desert their masters and seek refuge behind Union lines—at times to fight in the Union armies. The future of the freed slaves was not to be an easy one, but three and a half million people who had once lived in bondage emerged from the war as free men and women.

FOR FURTHER REFERENCE

James McPherson, *Battle Cry of Freedom* (1988) is a fine general history of the Civil War. Shelby Foote, *The Civil War: A Narrative*, 3 vols. (1958–1974) recounts the military history of the war with great literary power. David A. Mindell, *Technology and Experience aboard the USS Monitor* (2000) is an excellent study of the role of technology in major Civil War naval battles. David Herbert Donald, *Lincoln* (1995) is the best modern biography of the sixteenth president. Douglas Southall Freeman, *Robert E. Lee*, 4 vols. (1934–1935), William McFeely, *Grant* (1981), and Brooks D. Simpson, *Ulysses S. Grant: Triumph Over Adversity, 1822–1865* (2000) are significant biographies of the two most important Civil War generals. Philip Shaw Paludan, *"A People's Contest": The Union at War, 1861–1865* (1988) is a good account of the social impact of the war in the North. Iver Bernstein, *The New York City Draft Riots* (1990) examines an important event away from the battlefield. Alvin Josephy, *The Civil War in the West* (1992) remedies a long-neglected aspect of the war. Emory Thomas, *The Confederate Nation* (1979) is a fine one-volume history of the Confederacy. Ira Berlin et al., eds., *Free At Last: A Documentary History of Slavery, Freedom and the Civil War* (1992) is a superb compilation of primary sources from slaves and slaveowners relating to the demise of slavery during the Civil War years. Ira Berlin et al., *Slaves No More: Three Essays on Emancipation and the Civil War* (1992), the companion volume to the documents in *Free At Last*, argues that slaves and freedmen played an active role in destroying slavery and redefining freedom. Jeannie Attie, *Patriotic Toil: Northern Women and the American Civil War* (1998) examines the role of women. Catherine Clinton and Nina Silber, *Divided Houses* (1992) is a collection of essays in the "new social history" from various historians demonstrating the importance of gender to the history of the Civil War. *The Civil War* (1989), Ken Burns's outstanding popular and award-winning, nine-hour epic documentary has shaped the recent popular image of the conflict for many Americans.

For quizzes, Internet resources, references to additional books and films, and more, consult this book's Online Learning Center site at www.mhhe.com/unfinishednation4.

THE GENIUS OF FREEDOM This 1874 lithograph portrays a series of important moments in the history of African Americans in the South during Reconstruction—among them the participation of black soldiers in the Civil War, a speech by a black representative in the South Carolina legislature, and the movement of African-American workers from slavery into a system of free labor. It also portrays some of the white leaders (among them Lincoln and Charles Sumner) who had promoted the cause of the freedman. *(Chicago Historical Society)*

TIME LINE

1863	1864	1865	1866	1867	1868	1869
Lincoln announces Reconstruction plan	Lincoln vetoes Wade-Davis bill	Lincoln assassinated; Johnson is president Freedmen's Bureau Joint Committee on Reconstruction	Republicans gain in congressional elections	Congressional Reconstruction begins	Grant elected president Johnson impeached and acquitted 14th Amendment ratified	Congress passes 15th Amendment

CHAPTER FIFTEEN

RECONSTRUCTION AND THE NEW SOUTH

The Problems of Peacemaking
Radical Reconstruction
The South in Reconstruction
The Grant Administration
The Abandonment of Reconstruction
The New South

Few periods in the history of the United States have produced as much bitterness or created such enduring controversy as the era of Reconstruction—the years following the Civil War during which Americans attempted to reunite their shattered nation. To many white Southerners, Reconstruction was a vicious and destructive experience—a period when vindictive Northerners inflicted humiliation and revenge on the prostrate South. Northern defenders of Reconstruction, in contrast, argued that their policies were the only way to prevent unrepentant Confederates from restoring Southern society to what it had been before the war.

To most African Americans at the time, and to many people of all races since, Reconstruction was notable for other reasons. Neither a vicious tyranny, as white Southerners charged, nor a thoroughgoing reform, as many Northerners hoped, it was, rather, a small but important first step in the effort to secure civil rights and economic power for the former slaves. Reconstruction did not provide African Americans with either the legal protections or the material resources to assure them anything like real equality. Most black men and women who continued to live in what came to be known as the New South had little power to resist their oppression for many decades.

And yet for all its shortcomings, Reconstruction did help African Americans create some new institutions and some important legal precedents that helped them survive and that ultimately, well into the twentieth century, became the basis of later efforts to win freedom and equality.

1872	1873	1875	1877	1883	1890s	1895	1896
Grant reelected	Panic and depression	"Whiskey ring" scandal	Hayes wins disputed election	Supreme Court upholds segregation	Jim Crow laws in South	Atlanta Compromise	*Plessy* v. *Ferguson*
			Compromise of 1877 ends Reconstruction				

THE PROBLEMS OF PEACEMAKING

In 1865, when it became clear that the war was almost over, no one in Washington was certain about what to do. Abraham Lincoln could not negotiate a treaty with the defeated government; he continued to insist that the Confederate government had no legal right to exist. Yet neither could he simply readmit the Southern states into the Union.

The Aftermath of War and Emancipation

The Devastated South

The South after the Civil War was a desolate place. Towns had been gutted, plantations burned, fields neglected, bridges and railroads destroyed. Many white Southerners—stripped of their slaves through emancipation and stripped of the capital they had invested in now worthless Confederate bonds and currency—had almost no personal property. More than 258,000 Confederate soldiers had died in the war, and thousands more returned home wounded or sick. Some white Southerners faced starvation and homelessness.

If conditions were bad for Southern whites, they were far worse for Southern blacks—the three and a half million men and women now emerging from bondage. As soon as the war ended, hundreds of thousands of them left their plantations in search of a new life in freedom. But most had nowhere to go, and few had any possessions except the clothes they wore.

Competing Notions of Freedom

For blacks and whites alike, Reconstruction became a struggle to define the meaning of freedom. But the former slaves and the defeated whites had very different conceptions of what freedom meant.

Some blacks believed the only way to secure freedom was to have the government take land away from white people, who owned virtually all of it, and give it to black people, who owned virtually none. Others asked only for legal equality, confident that they could advance successfully in American society once the formal obstacles to their advancement disappeared. But whatever their particular demands, virtually all former slaves were united in their desire for independence from white control. Throughout the post-Civil War South, African Americans separated themselves from white institutions—pulling out of white-controlled churches and establishing their own, creating clubs and societies for their own people, and in some cases starting their own schools.

Black Desire for Independence

For most white Southerners, freedom meant something very different. It meant the ability to control their own destinies without interference from the North or the federal government. And in the immediate af-

RICHMOND, 1865 By the time Union forces captured Richmond in early 1865, the Confederate capital had been under siege for months and much of the city lay in ruins, as this photograph reveals. On April 4, President Lincoln, accompanied by his son Tad, visited Richmond. As he walked through the streets of the shattered city, hundreds of former slaves emerged from the rubble to watch him pass. "No triumphal march of a conqueror could have equalled in moral sublimity the humble manner in which he entered Richmond," a black soldier serving with the Union army wrote. "It was a great deliverer among the delivered. No wonder tears came to his eyes." *(The Library of Congress)*

termath of the war, they attempted to exercise this version of freedom by trying to restore their society to its antebellum form. When these white Southerners fought for what they considered freedom, they were fighting above all to preserve local and regional autonomy and white supremacy.

In the immediate aftermath of the war, the federal government's contribution to solving the question of the future of the South was modest. Federal troops remained in the South to preserve order and protect the freedmen. And in March 1865, Congress established the Freedmen's Bureau, an agency of the army directed by General Oliver O. Howard. The Freedmen's Bureau distributed food to millions of former slaves. It established schools, staffed by missionaries and teachers who had been sent to the South by Freedmen's Aid Societies and other private and church groups in the North. It made a modest effort to settle blacks on lands of their own. But the Freedmen's Bureau was not a permanent solution. It had authority to operate for only one year, and it was, in any case, far too small to deal effectively with the enormous problems facing Southern society. By the time the war ended, other proposals for reconstructing the defeated South were emerging.

The Freedmen's Bureau

A MONUMENT TO THE CONFEDERATE DEAD This monument in the town square of Greenwood, South Carolina, was typical of many such memorials erected all across the South in the aftermath of the Civil War. They served to commemorate the soldiers who had died in the struggle, but also to remind white Southerners of what was by the 1870s already widely known and romanticized as the "Lost Cause." *(Museum of the Confederacy, Richmond, Virginia)*

Plans for Reconstruction

Control of Reconstruction was in the hands of the Republicans, who were divided in their approach to the issue. Conservatives within the party insisted that the South accept the abolition of slavery, but they proposed few other conditions for the readmission of the seceded states. The Radicals, led by Representative Thaddeus Stevens of Pennsylvania and Senator Charles Sumner of Massachusetts, urged a much harsher course, including dis-

Thaddeus Stevens and Charles Sumner

enfranchising large numbers of Southern whites, protecting black civil rights, and confiscating the property of wealthy white Southerners who had aided the Confederacy and distributing the land among the freedmen. There was also a group of Republican Moderates, who rejected the most stringent demands of the Radicals but supported extracting at least some concessions from the South on black rights.

President Lincoln favored a lenient Reconstruction policy, and he believed that Southern Unionists (mostly former Whigs) could become the nucleus of new, loyal state governments in the South. Lincoln announced his Reconstruction plan in December 1863, more than a year before the war ended. It offered a general amnesty to white Southerners—other than high officials of the Confederacy—who would pledge an oath of loyalty to the government and accept the elimination of slavery. When 10 percent of a state's total number of voters in 1860 took the oath, those loyal voters could set up a state government. Lincoln also proposed extending suffrage to those African Americans who were educated, owned property, and had served in the Union army. Three Southern states—Louisiana, Arkansas, and Tennessee, all under Union occupation—reestablished loyal governments under the Lincoln formula in 1864.

The Radical Republicans were outraged at the mildness of Lincoln's program and refused to admit representatives from the three "reconstructed" states to Congress. In July 1864, they pushed their own plan through Congress in the form of the Wade-Davis Bill. It called for the president to appoint a provisional governor for each conquered state. When a majority of the white males of a state pledged their allegiance to the Union, the governor could summon a state constitutional convention, whose delegates were to be elected by voters who had never borne arms against the United States. The new state constitutions would be required to abolish slavery, disenfranchise Confederate civil and military leaders, and repudiate debts accumulated by the state governments during the war. Only then would Congress readmit the states to the Union. Like the president's proposal, the Wade-Davis Bill left the question of political rights for blacks up to the states.

Wade-Davis Bill

Congress passed the bill a few days before it adjourned in 1864, and Lincoln disposed of it with a pocket veto. His action enraged the Radical leaders, and the pragmatic Lincoln realized he would have to accept at least some of the Radical demands.

The Death of Lincoln

What plan he might have produced no one can say. On the night of April 14, 1865, Lincoln and his wife attended a play at Ford's Theater in Washington. As they sat in the theater, John Wilkes Booth, an actor fervently committed to the Southern cause, entered the presidential box from the rear and shot Lincoln in the head. Early the next morning, the president died.

John Wilkes Booth

ABRAHAM LINCOLN This haunting photograph of Abraham Lincoln, showing clearly the weariness and aging that four years as a war president had created, was taken in Washington only four days before his assassination in 1865. *(The Library of Congress)*

The circumstances of Lincoln's death earned him immediate martyrdom. They also produced something close to hysteria throughout the North, especially because it quickly became clear that Booth had been the leader of a conspiracy. One of his associates shot and wounded Secretary of State William Seward on the night of the assassination, and another abandoned at the last moment a scheme to murder Vice President Andrew Johnson. Booth himself escaped on horseback into the Maryland countryside, where, on April 26, he was cornered by Union troops and shot to death in a blazing barn. Eight other people were convicted by a military tribunal of participating in the conspiracy. Four were hanged.

To many Northerners, however, the murder of the president seemed evidence of an even greater conspiracy—one masterminded and directed by the unrepentant leaders of the defeated South. Militant Republicans exploited such suspicions relentlessly in the ensuing months.

Johnson and "Restoration"

Leadership of the Moderates and Conservatives fell to Lincoln's successor, Andrew Johnson of Tennessee. A Democrat until he had joined the Union ticket with Lincoln in 1864, he became president at a time of growing partisan passions.

Johnson's Reconstruction Plan

Johnson revealed his plan for Reconstruction—or "Restoration," as he preferred to call it—soon after he took office, and he implemented it during the summer of 1865 when Congress was in recess. Like Lincoln, he offered some form of amnesty to Southerners who would take an oath of allegiance. In most other respects, however, his plan resembled the Wade-Davis Bill. The president appointed a provisional governor in each state and charged him with inviting qualified voters to elect delegates to a constitutional convention. In order to win readmission to Congress, a state had to revoke its ordinance of secession, abolish slavery and ratify the Thirteenth Amendment, and repudiate Confederate and state war debts.

Hardening Northern Attitudes

By the end of 1865, all the seceded states had formed new governments—some under Lincoln's plan, some under Johnson's—and awaited congressional approval of them. But Radicals in Congress vowed not to recognize the Johnson governments, for, by now, Northern opinion had become more hostile toward the South than it had been a year earlier when Congress had passed the Wade-Davis Bill. Delegates to the Southern conventions had angered much of the North by their apparent reluctance to abolish slavery and by their refusal to grant suffrage to any blacks. Southern states had also seemed to defy the North by electing prominent Confederate leaders to represent them in Congress.

RADICAL RECONSTRUCTION

Reconstruction under Johnson's plan—often known as "presidential Reconstruction"—continued only until Congress reconvened in December 1865. At that point, Congress refused to seat the representatives of the "restored" states and created a new Joint Committee on Reconstruction to frame a Reconstruction policy of its own. The period of "congressional" or "Radical" Reconstruction had begun.

The Black Codes

Meanwhile, events in the South were driving Northern opinion in even more radical directions. Throughout the South in 1865 and early 1866, state legislatures were enacting sets of laws known as the Black Codes, which authorized local officials to apprehend unemployed blacks, fine

Debating the Past

RECONSTRUCTION

Debate over the nature of Reconstruction has been unusually intense. Indeed, few issues in American history have raised such deep and enduring passions.

Beginning in the late nineteenth century and continuing well into the twentieth, a relatively uniform and highly critical view of Reconstruction prevailed among historians. William A. Dunning's *Reconstruction, Political and Economic* (1907) was the principal scholarly expression of this prevailing view. Dunning portrayed Reconstruction as a corrupt and oppressive outrage imposed on a prostrate South by a vindictive group of Northern Republican Radicals. Unscrupulous carpetbaggers flooded the South and plundered the region. Ignorant African Americans were thrust into political offices for which they were unfit. Reconstruction governments were awash in corruption and compiled enormous levels of debt. The Dunning interpretation dominated several generations of historical scholarship. It also helped shape such popular images of Reconstruction as those in the novel and film *Gone with the Wind.*

W. E. B. Du Bois, the great African-American scholar, offered one of the first alternative views in *Black Reconstruction* (1935). To Du Bois, Reconstruction was an effort by freed blacks (and their white allies) to create a more democratic society in the South, and it was responsible for many valuable social innovations. In the early 1960s, John Hope Franklin and Kenneth Stampp, building on a generation of work by other scholars, published new histories of Reconstruction that also radically revised the Dunning interpretation. Reconstruction, they argued, was a genuine, if flawed, effort to solve the problem of race in the South. Congressional Radicals were not saints, but they were genuinely concerned with protecting the rights of former slaves. Reconstruction had brought important, if temporary, progress to the South and had created no more corruption there than governments were creating in the North at the same time. What was tragic about Reconstruction, the revisionists claimed, was not what it did to Southern whites but what it failed to do for Southern blacks. It was, in the end, too weak and too short-lived to guarantee African Americans genuine equality.

In more recent years, some historians have begun to question the assessment of the first revisionists that, in the end, Reconstruction accomplished relatively little. Leon Litwack argued in *Been in the Storm So Long* (1979) that former slaves used the protections Reconstruction offered them to carve out a certain level of independence for themselves within Southern society: strengthening churches, reuniting families, and resisting the efforts of white planters to revive the gang labor system.

Eric Foner's *Reconstruction: America's Unfinished Revolution* (1988) also emphasized how far African Americans moved toward freedom and independence in a short time and how important they were in shaping the execution of Reconstruction policies. Reconstruction, he argues, "can only be judged a failure" as an effort to secure "blacks' rights as citizens and free laborers." But it "closed off even more oppressive alternatives. . . . The post-Reconstruction labor system embodied neither a return to the closely supervised gang labor of antebellum days, nor the complete dispossession and immobilization of the black labor force and coercive apprenticeship systems envisioned by white Southerners in 1865 and 1866. Nor were blacks, as in twentieth-century South Africa, barred from citizenship, herded into labor reserves, or prohibited by law from moving from one part of the country to another. . . . The doors of economic opportunity that had opened could never be completely closed."

(text continued from page 403)

them for vagrancy, and hire them out to private employers to satisfy the fine. Some of the codes forbade blacks to own or lease farms or to take any jobs other than as plantation workers or domestic servants.

Congress first responded to the Black Codes by passing an act extending the life of the Freedmen's Bureau and widening its powers so that it could nullify work agreements forced on freedmen under the Black Codes. Then, in April 1866, Congress passed the first Civil Rights Act, which declared blacks to be citizens of the United States and gave the federal government power to intervene in state affairs to protect the rights of citizens. Johnson vetoed both bills, but Congress overrode him on each of them.

Johnson's Vetoes

The Fourteenth Amendment

In April 1866, the Joint Committee on Reconstruction proposed a new amendment to the Constitution, which Congress approved in early summer and sent to the states for ratification. The Fourteenth Amendment offered the first constitutional definition of American citizenship. Everyone born in the United States, and everyone naturalized, was automatically a citizen and entitled to all the "privileges and immunities" guaranteed by the Constitution, including equal protection of the laws by both the state and national governments. There could be no other requirements for citizenship. The amendment also imposed penalties on states that denied suffrage to any adult male inhabitants. (The wording reflected the prevailing view in Congress and elsewhere that the franchise was properly restricted to men.) Finally, it prohibited former members of Congress or other former federal officials who had aided the Confederacy from holding any state or federal office unless two-thirds of Congress voted to pardon them.

Citizenship for African Americans

Congressional Radicals offered to readmit to the Union any state whose legislature ratified the Fourteenth Amendment. Only Tennessee did so. All the other former Confederate states, along with Delaware and Kentucky, refused, leaving the amendment temporarily without the necessary approval of three-fourths of the states.

But by now, the Radicals were growing more confident and determined. Bloody race riots in New Orleans and other Southern cities were among the events that strengthened their hand. In the 1866 congressional elections, Johnson actively campaigned for Conservative candidates, but he did his own cause more harm than good with his intemperate speeches. The voters returned an overwhelming majority of Republicans, most of them Radicals, to Congress. In the Senate, there were now 42 Republicans to 11 Democrats; in the House, 143 Republicans to 49 Democrats. Congressional Republicans were now strong enough to enact a plan of their own even over the president's objections.

Radicals Ascendant

The Congressional Plan

The Radicals passed three Reconstruction bills early in 1867 and overrode Johnson's vetoes of all of them. These bills finally established, nearly two years after the end of the war, a coherent plan for Reconstruction.

Under the congressional plan, Tennessee, which had ratified the Fourteenth Amendment, was promptly readmitted. But Congress rejected the Lincoln-Johnson governments of the other ten Confederate states and, instead, combined those states into five military districts. A military commander governed each district and had orders to register qualified voters (defined as all adult black males and those white males who had not participated in the rebellion). Once registered, voters would elect conventions to prepare new state constitutions, which had to include provisions for black suffrage. Once voters ratified the new constitutions, they could elect state governments. Congress had to approve a state's constitution, and the state legislature had to ratify the Fourteenth Amendment. Once that happened, and once enough states ratified the amendment to make it part of the Constitution, then the former Confederate states could be restored to the Union.

By 1868, seven of the ten former Confederate states (Arkansas, North Carolina, South Carolina, Louisiana, Alabama, Georgia, and Florida) had fulfilled these conditions (including ratification of the Fourteenth Amendment, which now became part of the Constitution) and were readmitted to the Union. Conservative whites held up the return of Virginia and Texas until 1869 and Mississippi until 1870. By then, Congress had added an additional requirement for readmission—ratification of another constitutional amendment, the Fifteenth, which forbade the states and the federal government to deny suffrage to any citizen on account of "race, color, or previous condition of servitude." Ratification by the states was completed in 1870.

Fifteenth Amendment

To stop the president from interfering with their plans, the congressional Radicals passed two remarkable laws of dubious constitutionality in 1867. One, the Tenure of Office Act, forbade the president to remove civil officials, including members of his own cabinet, without the consent of the Senate. The principal purpose of the law was to protect the job of Secretary of War Edwin M. Stanton, who was cooperating with the Radicals. The other law, the Command of the Army Act, prohibited the president from issuing military orders except through the commanding general of the army (General Grant), who could not be relieved or assigned elsewhere without the consent of the Senate.

Tenure of Office Act

The congressional Radicals also took action to stop the Supreme Court from interfering with their plans. In 1866, the Court had declared in the case of *Ex parte Milligan* that military tribunals were unconstitutional in places where civil courts were functioning. Radicals in Congress immediately proposed several bills that would require two-thirds of the justices to support any decision overruling a law of Congress, would deny

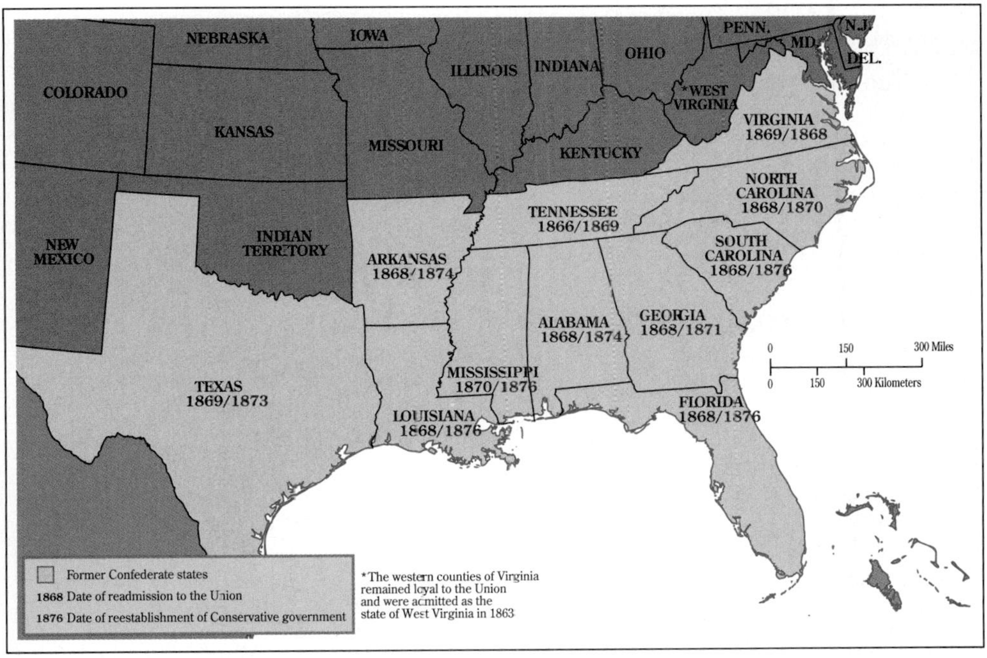

RECONSTRUCTION, 1866–1877 This map shows the former Confederate states and provides the dates when each was readmitted to the Union as well as a subsequent date when each state managed to return political power to traditional white, conservative elites—a process white southerners liked to call "redemption." ◆ *What had to happen for a state to be readmitted to the Union? What had to happen before a state could experience "redemption"?*

the Court jurisdiction in Reconstruction cases, would reduce its membership to three, and would even abolish it. The justices apparently took notice. Over the next two years, the Court refused to accept jurisdiction in any cases involving Reconstruction.

The Impeachment of the President

President Johnson had long since ceased to be a serious obstacle to the passage of Radical legislation, but he was still the official charged with administering the Reconstruction programs. As such, the Radicals believed, he remained a major impediment to their plans. Early in 1867, they began looking for a way to impeach him and remove him from office. A search for grounds for impeachment began. Republicans found them, they believed, when Johnson dismissed Secretary of War Stanton despite Congress's refusal to agree. Elated Radicals in the House quickly impeached the president and sent the case to the Senate for trial.

The trial before the Senate lasted throughout April and May 1868. The Radicals put heavy pressure on all the Republican senators, but the Moderates vacillated. On the first three charges to come to a vote, seven Republi-

The President Acquitted

cans joined the Democrats and independents to support acquittal. The vote was 35 to 19, one short of the constitutionally required two-thirds majority. After that, the Radicals dropped the impeachment effort.

THE SOUTH IN RECONSTRUCTION

Reconstruction may not have accomplished what its framers intended, but it did have profound effects on the South.

The Reconstruction Governments

"Scalawags" and "Carpetbaggers"

Critics labeled Southern white Republicans with the derogatory terms "scalawags" and "carpetbaggers." Many of the "scalawags" were former Whigs who had never felt comfortable in the Democratic Party or farmers who lived in remote areas where there had been little or no slavery. The "carpetbaggers" were white men from the North, most of them veterans of the Union army who looked on the South as a new frontier, more promising than the West. They had settled there at war's end as hopeful planters, businessmen, or professionals.

Freedmen

The most numerous Republicans in the South were the black freedmen, most of whom had no previous experience in politics and tried, therefore, to build institutions through which they could learn to exercise their power. In several states, African-American voters held their own conventions to chart their future course. Freedmen had created their own churches after emancipation, and this religious independence also helped give them unity and self-confidence.

African Americans played a significant role in the politics of the Reconstruction South. They served as delegates to the constitutional conventions. They held public offices of practically every kind. Between 1869 and 1901, twenty blacks served in the United States House of Representatives, two in the Senate. They served, too, in state legislatures and in various other state offices. Southern whites complained loudly about "Negro rule" during Reconstruction, but in the South as a whole, the percentage of black officeholders was always far lower than the percentage of blacks in the population.

The record of the Reconstruction governments is mixed. Critics at the time and later denounced them for corruption and financial extravagance, and there is some truth to both charges. But the corruption in the South, real as it was, was hardly unique to the Reconstruction governments. Corruption had been rife in some antebellum and Confederate governments, and it was at least as rampant in the Northern states. And the large state expenditures of the Reconstruction years were huge only in

A CELEBRATION OF RECONSTRUCTION The celebrated cartoonist Thomas Nast—best known for his savage caricatures of machine politicians in New York's Tammany Hall—drew this celebratory, and optimistic, image of Reconstruction not long after the end of the Civil War: a classical goddess restoring the former Confederate states to their rightful place within a symbolic fasces that represented union. In fact, the Reconstruction process proved much more difficult than this hopeful image suggested. *(North Wind Picture Archives)*

comparison with the meager budgets of the antebellum era. They represented an effort to provide the South with desperately needed services that antebellum governments had never offered.

Education

Perhaps the most important of the accomplishments of the Reconstruction governments was a dramatic improvement in Southern education. In the first years of Reconstruction, much of the impetus for educational reform in the South came from outside groups—from the Freedmen's Bureau, from Northern private philanthropic organizations, from the many Northern white women who traveled to the South to teach in freedmen's schools—and from African Americans themselves. Over the opposition of many Southern whites, who feared that education would give blacks "false notions of equality," these

Establishment of Black Schools

reformers established a large network of schools for former slaves—4,000 schools by 1870, staffed by 9,000 teachers (half of them black), teaching 200,000 students. In the 1870s, Reconstruction governments began to build a comprehensive public school system in the South. By 1876, more than half of all white children and about 40 percent of all black children were attending schools in the South (although almost all such schools were racially segregated). Several black "academies," offering more advanced education, also began operating. Gradually, these academies grew into an important network of black colleges and universities.

Landownership and Tenancy

Land Reform Thwarted

The most ambitious goal of the Freedmen's Bureau, and of some Republican Radicals in Congress, was to reform landownership in the South. The effort failed. By June 1865, the bureau had settled nearly 10,000 black families on their own land—most of it drawn from abandoned plantations in areas occupied by the Union armies. By the end of that year, however, Southern plantation owners were returning and demanding the restoration of their property. President Johnson supported their demands, and the government eventually returned most of the confiscated lands to their original white owners.

Even so, the distribution of landownership in the South changed considerably in the postwar years. Among whites, there was a striking decline in landownership, from 80 percent before the war to 67 percent by the end of Reconstruction. Some whites lost their land because of unpaid debt or increased taxes; some left the marginal lands they had owned to move to more fertile areas, where they rented. Among blacks, during the same period, the proportion who owned land rose from virtually none to more than 20 percent.

Rapid Growth of Sharecropping

Still, most blacks, and a growing minority of whites, did not own their own land during Reconstruction, and some who acquired land in the 1860s had lost it by the 1890s. Instead, they worked for others in one form or another. Many black agricultural laborers—perhaps 25 percent of the total—simply worked for wages. Most, however, became tenants of white landowners—that is, they worked their own plots of land and paid their landlords either a fixed rent or a share of their crop (hence the term "sharecropping"). As tenants and sharecroppers, blacks enjoyed at least a physical independence from their landlords and had the sense of working their own land, even if in most cases they could never hope to buy it. But tenantry also benefited landlords in some ways, relieving them of the cost of purchasing slaves and of responsibility for the physical well-being of their workers.

Incomes and Credit

In some respects, the postwar years were a period of remarkable economic progress for African Americans in the South. The per capita income of blacks (when the material benefits of slavery are counted as income) rose 46 percent between 1857 and 1879, while the per capita income of whites declined 35 percent. African Americans were also able to work less than they had under slavery. Women and children were less likely to labor in the fields, and adult men tended to work shorter days. In all, the black labor force worked about one-third fewer hours during Reconstruction than it had been compelled to work under slavery—a reduction that brought the working schedule of blacks roughly into accord with that of white farm laborers.

But other developments were limiting these gains. While the black share of profits was increasing, the total profits of Southern agriculture were declining. Nor did the income redistribution of the postwar years lift many blacks out of poverty. Black per capita income rose from about one-quarter of white per capita income (which was itself low) to about one-half in the first few years after the war. After this initial increase, however, it rose hardly at all.

Persistent Black Poverty

Blacks and poor whites alike often found themselves virtually imprisoned by the crop-lien system. Few of the traditional institutions of credit in the South—the "factors" and banks—returned after the war. In their stead emerged a new system of credit, centered in large part on local country stores—some of them owned by planters, others owned by independent merchants. Blacks and whites, landowners and tenants—all depended on these stores. And since farmers did not have the same steady cash flow as other workers, customers usually had to rely on credit from these merchants in order to purchase what they needed. Most local stores had no competition. As a result, they were able to set interest rates as high as 50 or 60 percent. Farmers had to give the merchants a lien (or claim) on their crops as collateral for the loans (thus the term "crop-lien system," generally used to describe Southern farming in this period). Farmers who suffered a few bad years in a row, as many did, could become trapped in a cycle of debt from which they could never escape.

The "Crop-lien System"

One effect of this burdensome credit system was that some blacks who had acquired land during the early years of Reconstruction gradually lost it as they fell into debt. Another was that Southern farmers became almost wholly dependent on cash crops—and most of all on cotton—because only such marketable commodities seemed to offer any possibility of escape from debt. The relentless planting of cotton contributed to an exhaustion of the soil. The crop-lien system, in other words, was not only helping to impoverish small farmers; it was also contributing to a general decline in the Southern agricultural economy.

AFTER SLAVERY Although most freed slaves remained agricultural laborers after Emancipation, a considerable number moved off the land in search of new occupations and new homes. For many, that meant living for some time without stable employment or a permanent home. This photograph from the late 1860s shows a group of former slaves at a county almshouse in the South. *(Bettmann/Corbis)*

The African-American Family in Freedom

Families Reunited

A major reason for the rapid departure of so many blacks from plantations was the desire to find lost relatives and reunite families. Thousands of African Americans wandered through the South looking for husbands, wives, children, or other relatives from whom they had been separated. Former slaves rushed to have their marriages, previously without legal standing, sanctified by church and law.

Within the black family, the definition of male and female roles quickly came to resemble that within white families. Many women and children ceased working in the fields. Such work, they believed, was a badge of slavery. Instead, many women restricted themselves largely to domestic tasks. Still, economic necessity often compelled black women to engage in income-producing activities: working as domestic servants, taking in laundry, or helping their husbands in the fields. By the end of Reconstruction, half of all black women over the age of sixteen were working for wages.

THE GRANT ADMINISTRATION

American voters in 1868 yearned for a strong, stable figure to guide them through the troubled years of Reconstruction. They turned trustingly to General Ulysses S. Grant.

The Soldier President

Grant Elected

Grant could have had the nomination of either party in 1868. But believing that Republican Reconstruction policies were more popular in the North, he accepted the Republican nomination. The Democrats nominated former governor Horatio Seymour of New York. The campaign was a bitter one, and Grant's triumph was surprisingly narrow. Without the 500,000 new black Republican voters in the South, he would have had a minority of the popular vote.

Grant entered the White House with no political experience, and his performance was clumsy and ineffectual from the start. Except for Hamilton Fish, whom Grant appointed secretary of state, most members of the cabinet were ill-equipped for their tasks. Grant relied chiefly on established party leaders—the group most ardently devoted to patronage, and his administration used the spoils system even more blatantly than most of its predecessors. Grant also alienated the many Northerners who were growing disillusioned with the Radical Reconstruction policies, which the president continued to support. Some Republicans suspected, correctly, that there was also corruption in the Grant administration itself.

Liberal Republicans

By the end of Grant's first term, therefore, members of a substantial faction of the party—who referred to themselves as Liberal Republicans—had come to oppose what they called "Grantism." In 1872, hoping to prevent Grant's reelection, they bolted the party and nominated their own presidential candidate: Horace Greeley, veteran editor and publisher of the *New York Tribune*. The Democrats, somewhat reluctantly, named Greeley their candidate as well, hoping that the alliance with the Liberals would enable them to defeat Grant. But the effort was in vain. Grant won a substantial victory, polling 286 electoral votes to Greeley's 66.

The Grant Scandals

During the 1872 campaign, the first of a series of political scandals came to light that would plague Grant and the Republicans for the next eight years. It involved the French-owned Crédit Mobilier construction company, which had helped build the Union Pacific Railroad. The heads of Crédit Mobilier had used their positions as Union Pacific stockholders to steer large fraudulent contracts to their construction company, thus bilking the Union Pacific of millions. To prevent investigations, the directors had given Crédit Mobilier stock to key members of Congress. But in 1872, Congress did conduct an investigation, which revealed that some highly placed Republicans—including Schuyler Colfax, now Grant's vice president—had accepted stock.

The "Whiskey Ring"

One dreary episode followed another in Grant's second term. Benjamin H. Bristow, Grant's third Treasury secretary, discovered that some of his officials and a group of distillers operating as a "whiskey ring" were cheating the government out of taxes by filing false reports. Then a House investigation revealed that William W. Belknap, secretary of war, had accepted bribes to retain an Indian-post trader in office (the so-called Indian ring). Other, lesser scandals added to the growing impression that "Grantism" had brought rampant corruption to government.

The Greenback Question

Compounding Grant's, and the nation's, problems was a financial crisis, known as the Panic of 1873. It began with the failure of a leading investment banking firm, Jay Cooke and Company, which had invested too heavily in postwar railroad building. There had been panics before—in 1819, 1837, and 1857—but this was the worst one yet.

Debtors now pressured the government to redeem federal war bonds with greenbacks, which would increase the amount of money in circulation. But Grant and most Republicans wanted a "sound" currency—based solidly on gold reserves—which would favor the interests of banks and other creditors. There was approximately $356 million in paper currency issued during the Civil War that was still in circulation. In 1873, the Treasury issued more in response to the panic. But in 1875, Republican leaders in Congress passed the Specie Resumption Act. It provided that after January 1, 1879, the greenback dollars would be redeemed by the government and replaced with new certificates, firmly pegged to the price of gold. The law satisfied creditors, who had worried that debts would be repaid in paper currency of uncertain value. But "resumption" made things more difficult for debtors, because the gold-based money supply could not easily expand.

Specie Resumption Act

In 1875, the "greenbackers" formed their own political organization: the National Greenback Party. It failed to gain widespread support, but it did keep the money issue alive. The question of the proper composition of the currency was to remain one of the most controversial and enduring issues in late-nineteenth-century American politics.

National Greenback Party

Republican Diplomacy

The Johnson and Grant administrations achieved their greatest successes in foreign affairs. The accomplishments were the work not of the presidents themselves but of two outstanding secretaries of state: William H. Seward and Hamilton Fish.

An ardent expansionist, Seward acted with as much daring as the demands of Reconstruction politics and the Republican hatred of President Johnson would permit. Seward accepted a Russian offer to sell Alaska to the United States for $7.2 million, despite criticism from many who derided the purchase as "Seward's Folly." In 1867, Seward also engineered the American annexation of the tiny Midway Islands, west of Hawaii.

Purchase of Alaska

Hamilton Fish's first major challenge was resolving the longstanding controversy with England over the American claims that it had violated neutrality laws during the Civil War by permitting English shipyards to build ships (among them the *Alabama*) for the Confederacy. American demands that England pay for the damage these vessels had caused became known as the "*Alabama* claims." In 1871, after a number of failed efforts, Fish forged an agreement, the Treaty of Washington, which provided for international arbitration.

"Alabama Claims" Resolved

THE ABANDONMENT OF RECONSTRUCTION

As the North grew increasingly preoccupied with its own political and economic problems, interest in Reconstruction began to wane. By the time Grant left office, Democrats had taken back seven of the governments of the former Confederate states. For three other states—South Carolina, Louisiana, and Florida—the end of Reconstruction had to wait for the withdrawal of the last federal troops in 1877.

The Southern States "Redeemed"

In the states where whites constituted a majority—the states of the upper South—overthrowing Republican control was relatively simple. By 1872, all but a handful of Southern whites had regained suffrage. Now a clear majority, they needed only to organize and elect their candidates.

In other states, where blacks were a majority or where the populations of the two races were almost equal, whites used intimidation and violence to undermine the Reconstruction regimes. Secret societies—the Ku Klux Klan, the Knights of the White Camellia, and others—used terrorism to frighten or physically bar blacks from voting. Paramilitary organizations—the Red Shirts and White Leagues—armed themselves to "police" elections and worked to force all white males to join the Democratic Party. Strongest of all, however, was the simple weapon of economic pressure. Some planters refused to rent land to Republican blacks; storekeepers refused to extend them credit; employers refused to give them work.

Ku Klux Klan

The Republican Congress responded to this wave of repression with the Enforcement Acts of 1870 and 1871 (better known as the Ku Klux Klan Acts), which prohibited states from discriminating against voters on the basis of race and gave the national government the authority to prosecute crimes by individuals under federal law. The laws also authorized the president to use federal troops to protect civil rights—a provision President Grant used in 1871 in nine counties of South Carolina. The Enforcement Acts, although seldom enforced, discouraged Klan violence, which declined by 1872.

Waning Northern Commitment

But this Northern commitment to civil rights in the South did not last very long. After the adoption of the Fifteenth Amendment in 1870, some reformers convinced themselves that their long campaign on behalf of black people was now over, that with the vote blacks ought to be able to take care of themselves. Former Radical leaders such as Charles Sumner and Horace Greeley now began calling themselves Liberals, cooperating with the Democrats, and denouncing what they viewed as black-and-carpetbag misgovernment. Within the South itself, many white Republicans now moved into the Democratic Party.

Flagging Interest in Civil Rights

The Panic of 1873 further undermined support for Reconstruction. In the congressional elections of 1874, the Democrats won control of the House of Representatives for the first time since 1861. Grant reduced the use of military force to prop up the Republican regimes in the South.

By the end of 1876, only three states were left in the hands of the Republicans—South Carolina, Louisiana, and Florida. In the state elections that year, Democrats (after using terrorist tactics) claimed victory in all three. But the Republicans claimed victory as well and were able to remain in office because of the presence of federal troops.

The Compromise of 1877

Grant had hoped to run for another term in 1876, but most Republican leaders—shaken by recent Democratic successes and the scandals with which Grant was associated—resisted. Instead, they settled on Rutherford B. Hayes, three-time governor of Ohio and a champion of civil service reform. The Democrats united behind Samuel J. Tilden, the reform governor of New York, who had been instrumental in overthrowing the corrupt Tweed Ring of New York City's Tammany Hall.

Although the campaign was a bitter one, there were few differences of principle between the candidates. The November election produced an apparent Democratic victory. Tilden carried the South and several large Northern states, and his popular margin over Hayes was nearly 300,000 votes. But disputed returns from Louisiana, South Carolina, Florida, and Oregon, whose electoral votes totaled 20, threw the election in doubt. Hayes could still win if he managed to receive all 20 disputed votes.

Disputed Election

The Constitution had established no method to determine the validity of disputed returns. The decision clearly lay with Congress, but it was not clear with which house or through what method. (The Senate was Republican, and the House was Democratic.) Members of each party naturally supported a solution that would yield them the victory. Finally, late in January 1877, Congress tried to break the deadlock by creating a special electoral commission composed of five senators, five representatives, and five justices of the Supreme

Special Electoral Commission

AFRICAN-AMERICAN WORK AFTER SLAVERY Black men and women engaged in a wide range of economic activities in the aftermath of slavery. But discrimination by white Southerners and the former slaves' own lack of education limited most of them to relatively menial jobs. Many black women (including this former slave) earned money for their families by working as "washer women," doing laundry for white people. *(Historic New Orleans Collection)*

Court. The congressional delegation would consist of five Republicans and five Democrats. The Court delegation would include two Republicans, two Democrats, and the only independent, Justice David Davis. But when the Illinois legislature elected Davis to the United States Senate, the justice resigned from the commission. His seat went instead to a Republican justice. The commission voted along straight party lines, 8 to 7, awarding every disputed vote to Hayes.

Behind the resolution of the deadlock, however, lay a series of elaborate compromises among leaders of both parties. When a Democratic filibuster threatened to derail the commission's report, Republican Senate leaders met secretly with Southern Democratic leaders to work out terms by which the Democrats would support Hayes. As the price of their cooperation, the Southern Democrats exacted several pledges from the Republicans: the appointment of at least one Southerner to the Hayes cabinet, control of federal patronage in their areas, generous internal improvements, federal aid for the Texas and Pacific Railroad, and withdrawal of the troops. Many powerful Southern Democrats believed that Republican programs of federal support for business and industry would help their region develop economically.

Federal Troops Withdrawn

In his inaugural address, Hayes announced that the South's most pressing need was the restoration of "wise, honest, and peaceful local self-government," and he soon withdrew the troops and let white Democrats take over the remaining southern state governments. That produced charges that he was paying off the South for acquiescing in his election. But the election had already created such bitterness that not even Hayes's promise to serve only one term could mollify his critics.

The president and his party hoped to build up a "new Republican" organization in the South committed to modest support for black rights. But although many white Southern leaders sympathized with Republican economic policies, resentment of Reconstruction was so deep that supporting the party was politically impossible. The "solid" Democratic South, which would survive until the mid-twentieth century, was taking shape.

The Legacy of Reconstruction

Lasting Contributions

Reconstruction made important contributions to the efforts of former slaves to achieve dignity and equality in American life. There was a significant redistribution of income. There was a more limited but not unimportant redistribution of landownership. Perhaps most important, there was a large, and largely successful, effort by African Americans themselves to carve out a society and culture of their own and to create or strengthen their own institutions.

Reconstruction was not as disastrous an experience for Southern white elites as most believed at the time. Within little more than a decade after the end of a devastating war, the white South had regained control of its own institutions and, to a great extent, restored its traditional ruling class to power. The federal government imposed no drastic economic reforms on the region, and indeed few lasting political changes of any kind other than the abolition of slavery.

Reconstruction was notable, finally, for its limitations. For in those years the United States failed in its first serious effort to resolve its oldest and deepest social problem—the problem of race. What was more, the experience so disillusioned white Americans that it would be nearly a century before they would try again to combat racial injustice.

Limits of Reconstruction

Given the odds confronting them, however, African Americans had reason for considerable pride in the gains they were able to make during Reconstruction. And future generations could be grateful for two great charters of freedom—the Fourteenth and Fifteenth Amendments to the Constitution—which, although widely ignored at the time, would one day serve as the basis for a "Second Reconstruction" that would renew the drive to bring freedom to all Americans.

THE NEW SOUTH

The agreement between southern Democrats and northern Republicans that helped settle the disputed election of 1876 was supposed to be the first step toward developing a stable, permanent Republican Party in the South. In that respect, at least, it failed. In the years following the end of Reconstruction, white southerners established the Democratic Party as the only viable political organization for the region's whites. Even so, the South did change in some of the ways the framers of the Compromise of 1877 had hoped.

The "Redeemers"

Many white southerners rejoiced at the restoration of what they liked to call "home rule." But in reality, political power in the region was soon more restricted than at any time since the Civil War. Once again, most of the South fell under the control of a powerful, conservative oligarchy, whose members were known variously as the "Redeemers" or the "Bourbons."

"Home Rule"

In some places, this post-Reconstruction ruling class was much the same as the ruling class of the antebellum period. In Alabama, for example, the old planter elite retained much of its former power. In other areas, however, the Redeemers constituted a genuinely new ruling class. They were merchants, industrialists, railroad developers, and financiers. Some of them were former planters, some of them northern immigrants, some of them ambitious, upwardly mobile white southerners from the region's lower social tiers. They combined a commitment to "home rule" and social conservatism with a commitment to economic development.

The various Bourbon governments of the New South behaved in many respects quite similarly. Virtually all the new Democratic regimes lowered taxes, reduced spending, and drastically diminished state services. One state after another eliminated or reduced its support for public school systems.

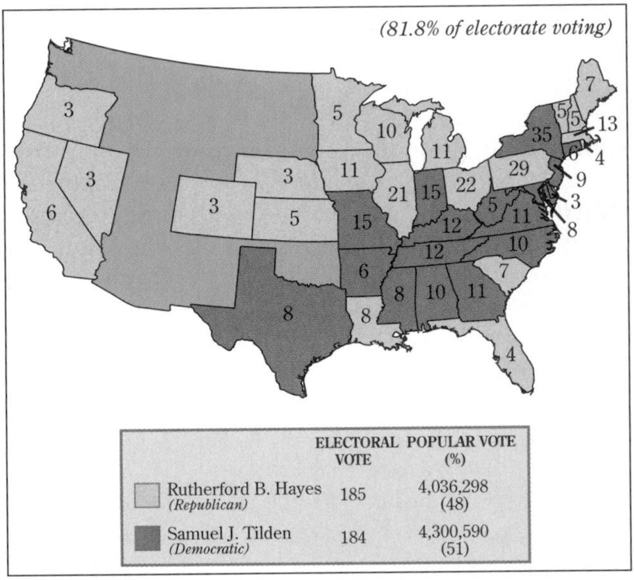

THE ELECTION OF 1876 The election of 1876 was one of the most controversial in American history. As in the elections of 1824, 1888, and 2000, the winner of the popular vote—Samuel J. Tilden—was not the winner of the electoral college, which he lost by one vote. The final decision as to who would be president was not made until the day before the official Inauguration in March. ◆ *How did the Republicans turn this apparent defeat into a victory?*

For an interactive version of this map go to www.mhhe.com/unfinishednation4ch15maps

Industrialization and the "New South"

Many white southern leaders in the post-Reconstruction era hoped to see their region become the home of a vigorous industrial economy, a "New South." Henry Grady, editor of the *Atlanta Constitution*, and other New South advocates seldom challenged white supremacy, but they did promote the virtues of thrift, industry, and progress—qualities that prewar southerners had often denounced in northern society.

Henry Grady

Southern industry did expand dramatically in the years after Reconstruction. Most visible was the growth in textile manufacturing. In the past, southern planters had usually shipped their cotton out of the region to manufacturers in the North or in Europe. Now textile factories appeared in the South itself—many of them drawn to the region from New England by the abundance of water power, the ready supply of cheap labor, the low taxes, and the accommodating conservative governments. The tobacco-processing industry, similarly, established an important foothold in the region. In the lower South, and particularly in Birmingham, Alabama, the iron (and, later, steel) industry grew rapidly.

Substantial Railroad Development

Railroad development also increased substantially in the post-Reconstruction years. Between 1880 and 1890, trackage in the South more than doubled. And in 1886, the South changed the gauge (width) of its trackage to correspond with the standards of the North. No longer would it be necessary for cargoes heading into the South to be transferred from one train to another at the borders of the region.

Yet southern industry developed within strict limits, and its effects on the region were never even remotely comparable to the effects of industrialization on the North. The southern share of national manufacturing doubled in the last twenty years of the century, but it was still only 10 percent of the total. The region's per capita income increased 21 percent in the same period, but average income in the South was still only 40 percent of that in the North; in 1860 it had been more than 60 percent. And even in those industries where development had been most rapid—textiles, iron, railroads—much of the capital had come from, and many of the profits thus flowed to, the North.

The growth of industry in the South required the region to recruit a substantial industrial work force for the first time. From the beginning, a high percentage of the factory workers were women. Heavy male casualties in the Civil War had helped create a large population of unmarried women who desperately needed employment. Hours were long (often as much as twelve hours a day), and wages were far below the northern equivalent; indeed, one of the greatest attractions of the South to industrialists was that employers were able to pay workers there as little as one-half what northern workers received. Life in most mill towns was rigidly controlled by the owners and managers of the factories. They rigorously suppressed attempts at protest or union organization. Company stores sold goods to workers at inflated prices and issued credit at exorbitant rates (much like country stores in agrarian areas), and mill owners ensured that no competing merchants were able to establish themselves in the community.

Worker Exploitation

Some industries, such as textiles, offered virtually no opportunities to African-American workers. Others—tobacco, iron, and lumber, for example—did provide some employment for blacks. Some mill towns, therefore, were places where the black and white cultures came into close contact. This juxtaposition of cultures inhibited the growth of racial harmony and increased the determination of white leaders to take additional measures to protect white supremacy.

Tenants and Sharecroppers

The most important economic reality in the post-Reconstruction South was the impoverished state of agriculture. The 1870s and 1880s saw an acceleration of the process that had begun in the immediate postwar years: the imposition of systems of tenantry and debt peonage on much of the region; the reliance on a few cash crops rather than on a diversified agricultural system; and increasing absentee ownership of valuable farmlands. During Reconstruction, perhaps

Impoverished Agriculture

a third or more of the farmers in the South were tenants; by 1900 the figure had increased to 70 percent.

Tenantry took several forms. Farmers who owned tools, equipment, and farm animals usually paid an annual cash rent for their land. But many farmers (including most black ones) had no money or equipment at all. Landlords would supply them with land, a crude house, a few tools, seed, and sometimes a mule. In return, the farmers would promise the landlord a large share of the annual crop. After paying their landlords and their local furnishing merchants (who were often the same people), these "sharecroppers" seldom had anything left to sell on their own.

African Americans and the New South

The "New South creed" was not the property of whites alone. Many African Americans were attracted to the vision of progress and self-improvement as well. Some blacks succeeded in elevating themselves into a distinct middle class. These were former slaves (and, as the decades passed, their offspring) who managed to acquire property, establish small businesses, or enter professions. This rising group of African Americans believed strongly that education was vital to the future of their people, and they expanded the network of black colleges and institutes that had taken root during Reconstruction into an important educational system.

Booker T. Washington

The chief spokesman for this commitment to education was Booker T. Washington, founder and president of the Tuskegee Institute in Alabama. Born into slavery, Washington had worked his way out of poverty after acquiring an education (at Virginia's Hampton Institute). He urged other blacks to follow the same road to self-improvement.

Washington's message was both cautious and hopeful. African Americans should attend school, learn skills, and establish a solid footing in agriculture and the trades. Industrial, not classical, education should be their goal. Blacks should, moreover, refine their speech, improve their dress, and adopt habits of thrift and personal cleanliness; they should, in short, adopt the standards of the white middle class. Only thus, he claimed, could they win the respect of the white population.

In a famous speech in Georgia in 1895, Washington outlined a controversial philosophy of race relations that became widely known as the Atlanta Compromise. Blacks, he said, should forgo agitating for political rights and concentrate on self-improvement and preparation for equality. Washington offered a powerful challenge to those whites who wanted to discourage African Americans from acquiring an education or winning any economic gains. But his message was also intended to assure whites that blacks would not challenge the system of segregation, which southern governments were in the process of creating.

Atlanta Compromise

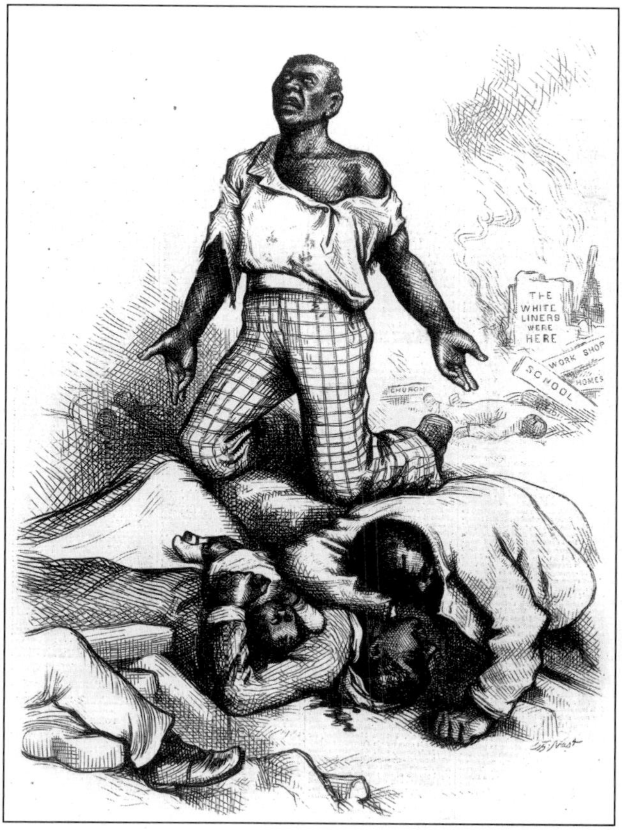

"IS THIS A REPUBLICAN FORM OF GOVERNMENT?" The New York artist and cartoonist Thomas Nast marked the end of Reconstruction in 1876 with this biting cartoon in *Harper's Weekly*, expressing his dismay at what he considered the nation's betrayal of the former slaves, who still had not received adequate guarantees of their rights. The caption of the cartoon continued: "Is *this* protecting life, liberty, or property? Is *this* equal protection of the laws?" *(The Newberry Library, Chicago, Illinois)*

The Birth of Jim Crow

Few white southerners had ever accepted the idea of racial equality. That the former slaves acquired any legal and political rights at all after emancipation was in large part the result of their own efforts and critical federal support. That outside support all but vanished after 1877, when federal troops withdrew and the Supreme Court stripped the Fourteenth and Fifteenth Amendments of much of their significance. In the so-called civil rights cases of 1883, the Court ruled that the Fourteenth Amendment prohibited state governments from discriminating against people because of race but did not restrict private organizations or individuals from doing so.

Eventually, the Court also validated state legislation that institutionalized the separation of the races. In *Plessy* v. *Ferguson* (1896), a case involving a Louisiana law that required

Plessy v. Ferguson

TUSKEGEE INSTITUTE, 1881 From these modest beginnings, Booker T. Washington's Tuskegee Institute in Alabama became the preeminent academy offering technical and industrial training to black men. It deliberately de-emphasized the traditional liberal arts curricula of most colleges. Washington considered such training less important than developing practical skills. *(Bettmann/Corbis)*

separate seating arrangements for the races on railroads, the Court held that separate accommodations did not deprive blacks of equal rights if the accommodations were equal. In *Cumming* v. *County Board of Education* (1899), the Court ruled that communities could establish schools for whites only, even if there were no comparable schools for blacks.

Even before these decisions, white southerners were working to separate the races to the greatest extent possible. They were particularly determined to strip African Americans of the right to vote. In some states, disenfranchisement had begun almost as soon as Reconstruction ended. But in other areas, black voting continued for some time after Reconstruction—largely because conservative whites believed they could control the black electorate and use it to beat back the attempts of poor white farmers to take control of the Democratic Party.

In the 1890s, however, franchise restrictions became much more rigid. During those years, some small white farmers began to demand complete black disenfranchisement—because they objected to the black vote being used against them by the Bourbons. At the same time, many members of the conservative elite began to fear that poor whites might unite politically with poor blacks to challenge them.

Black Disenfranchisement

In devising laws to disenfranchise black males, the southern states had to find ways to evade the Fifteenth Amendment, which prohibited states from denying anyone the right to vote because of race. Two devices emerged before 1900 to accomplish this goal. One was the poll tax or some form of property qualification; few blacks were prosperous enough to meet such requirements. Another was the "literacy" or "understanding" test, which required voters to demonstrate an ability to read and to interpret the Constitution. Even those African Americans who could read had a hard time passing the difficult test white officials gave them. The laws affected poor white voters as well as blacks. By the late 1890s, the black vote had decreased by 62 percent, the white vote by 26 percent.

Jim Crow Laws

Laws restricting the franchise and segregating schools were only part of a network of state and local statutes—known as the Jim Crow laws—that by the first years of the twentieth century had institutionalized an elaborate system of segregation reaching into almost every area of southern life. Blacks and whites could not ride together in the same railroad cars, sit in the same waiting rooms, use the same washrooms, eat in the same restaurants, or sit in the same theaters. Blacks had no access to many public parks, beaches, or picnic areas; they could not be patients in many hospitals. Much of the new legal structure did no more than confirm what had already been widespread social practice in the South. But the Jim Crow laws also stripped blacks of many of the modest social, economic, and political gains they had made in the late nineteenth century.

More than legal efforts were involved in this process. The 1890s witnessed a dramatic increase in white violence against blacks, which, along with the Jim Crow laws, served to inhibit black agitation for equal rights. The worst such violence—lynching of blacks by white mobs—reached appalling levels. In the nation as a whole in the 1890s, there was an average of 187 lynchings each year, more than 80 percent of them in the South. The vast majority of victims were black. Those who participated in lynchings often saw their actions as a legitimate form of law enforcement, and some victims of lynchings had in fact committed crimes. But lynchings were also a means by which whites controlled the black population through terror and intimidation.

Ida B. Wells

The rise of lynchings shocked the conscience of many white Americans in a way that other forms of racial injustice did not. In 1892 Ida B. Wells, a committed black journalist, launched what became an international anti-lynching movement with a series of impassioned articles after the lynching of three of her friends in Memphis, Tennessee, her home. The movement gradually gathered strength in the first years of the twentieth century, attracting substantial support from whites in both the North and South (particularly from white women). Its goal was a federal anti-lynching law, which would allow the national government to do what state and local governments in the South were generally unwilling to do: punish those responsible for lynchings.

But the substantial southern white opposition to lynchings stood as an exception to the general white support for suppression of African Americans. Indeed, just as in the antebellum period, the shared commitment to white supremacy helped dilute class animosities between poorer whites and the Bourbon oligarchies. Economic issues tended to play a secondary role to race in southern politics, distracting people from the glaring social inequalities that afflicted blacks and whites alike.

CONCLUSION

Reconstruction was a profoundly important moment in American history. Despite the bitter political battles in Washington and throughout the South, culminating in the unsuccessful effort to remove President Andrew Johnson from office, the most important result of the effort to reunite the nation after its long and bloody war was a reshaping of the lives of ordinary people in all regions of the nation.

In the North, Reconstruction solidified the power of the Republican Party. The rapid expansion of the northern economy continued and accelerated, drawing more and more of its residents into a burgeoning commercial world.

In the South, Reconstruction fundamentally rearranged the relationship between the region's white and black citizens. Only for a while did Reconstruction permit African Americans to participate actively and effectively in southern politics. After a few years of widespread black voting and significant black officeholding, the forces of white supremacy forced most African Americans to the margins of the southern political world, where they would mostly remain until the 1960s.

In other ways, the lives of southern blacks changed dramatically and permanently. Overwhelmingly, they left the plantations. Some sought work in towns and cities. Some left the region altogether. But the great majority began farming on small farms of their own—not as landowners, except in rare cases, but as tenants and sharecroppers on land owned by whites. The result was a form of economic bondage, driven by debt, only scarcely less oppressive than the legal bondage of slavery. Within this system, however, African Americans managed to carve out a much larger sphere of social and cultural activity than they had ever been able to create under slavery. Black churches proliferated in great numbers. African-American schools emerged in some communities, and black colleges began to operate in the region. Some former slaves owned businesses and flourished.

Strenuous efforts by "New South" advocates to advance industry and commerce in the region produced significant results in a few areas. But the South on the whole remained what it had always been: an overwhelmingly rural society with a sharply defined class structure. It was also a region with a deep commitment among its white citizens to the subordination of African Americans—a commitment solidified in the 1890s and the early twentieth century when white southerners erected an elaborate legal system of segregation (the "Jim Crow" laws). The promise of the great Reconstruction amendments to the Constitution—the Fourteenth and Fifteenth—remained largely unfulfilled in the South as the century drew to its close.

FOR FURTHER REFERENCE

Eric Foner, *Reconstruction: America's Unfinished Revolution, 1863–1877* (1988), the most important modern synthesis of Reconstruction scholarship, emphasizes the radicalism of Reconstruction and the agency of freed people in the process of political and economic renovation. David W. Blight, *Race and Reunion: The Civil War in American Memory* (2001) is an excellent study of the ways in which Americans reinterpreted the Civil War in the late nineteenth century. Amy Dru Stanley, *From Bondage to Contract: Wage Labor, Marriage, and the Market in the Age of Slave Emancipation* (1998) and Jeffrey R. Kerr-Ritchie, *Freedpeople in the Tobacco South: Virginia, 1860–1900* (1999) are important examinations of African-American labor during and after Emancipation. Thomas Holt, *Black over White: Negro Political Leadership in South Carolina During Reconstruction* (1977) examines Reconstruction in the state where black political power reached its apex. C. Vann Woodward, *Origins of the New South* (1951), a classic work on the history of the South after Reconstruction, argues that a rising middle class defined the economic and political transformation of the New South. Edward Ayers, *The Promise of the New South* (1992) offers a rich portrait of social and cultural life in the New South. Jacqueline Jones, *Labor of Love, Labor of Sorrow* (1985) examines the lives of African-American women after Emancipation. Mia Bay, *The White Image in the Black Mind: African-American Ideas about White People, 1830–1925* (2000) is a valuable study of African-American attitudes toward white society. Leon Litwack, *Been in the Storm So Long: The Aftermath of Slavery* (1979) is a major study of the experiences of freed slaves. C. Vann Woodward, *The Strange Career of Jim Crow* (rev. 1974) claims that segregation emerged only gradually across the South after Reconstruction. The "Woodward Thesis" has been challenged by, among others, Joel Williamson, *After Slavery: The Negro in South Carolina During Reconstruction* (1965); John W. Cell, *The Highest Stage of White Supremacy: The Origins of Segregation in South Africa and the American South* (1982); and Howard N. Rabinowitz, *Race Relations in the Urban South, 1865–1890* (1978).

For quizzes, Internet resources, references to additional books and films, and more, consult this book's Online Learning Center site at www.mhhe.com/unfinishednation4.

***AMERICAN PROGRESS*, 1872** John Gast, an artist in Brooklyn, New York, painted this tribute to westward expansion—a picture of hardy pioneers marching toward the frontier, protected by the goddess of progress—at the request of a publisher of travel guides. Engravings adapted from the painting appeared in one guidebook, and color reproductions were offered to customers as a bonus for subscribing to others. It is an example of the wide-ranging promotional effort—by railroads, landowners, farm-equipment manufacturers, even guidebook publishers—designed to persuade Americans to move into the western territories in the late nineteenth century. *(Oil on canvas,* American Progress, *1872, by John Gast; Autry Museum of Western Heritage, Los Angeles)*

TIME LINE

1862	1865-1867	1866	1869	1873	1874	1876
Homestead Act	Sioux Wars	Western cattle bonanza begins	Transcontinental railroad completed	Barbed wire invented	Black Hills gold rush	Battle of Little Bighorn

CHAPTER SIXTEEN

THE CONQUEST OF THE FAR WEST

The Societies of the Far West
The Changing Western Economy
The Romance of the West
The Dispersal of the Tribes
The Rise and Decline of the Western Farmer

By the mid-1840s migrants from the eastern regions of the nation had settled in the West in substantial numbers. Farmers, ranchers, and miners all found opportunity in the western lands. By the end of the Civil War, the West had become legendary in the eastern states. No longer the Great American Desert, it was now the "frontier": an empty land awaiting settlement and civilization; a place of wealth, adventure, opportunity, and untrammeled individualism.

In fact, the real West of the mid-nineteenth century bore little resemblance to its popular image. It was a diverse land, with many different regions, many different climates, many different stores of natural resources. And it was extensively populated. The English-speaking migrants of the late nineteenth century did not find an empty, desolate land. They found Indians, Mexicans, French and British Canadians, Asians, and others, some of whose families had been living in the West for generations.

1877	1882	1885	1887	1889	1890	1893
Desert Land Act	Chinese Exclusion Act	Twain's *Huckleberry Finn*	Dawes Act	Oklahoma opened to white settlement	Battle of Wounded Knee	Turner's "Frontier Thesis"

THE SOCIETIES OF THE FAR WEST

The Far West was in fact many lands. It contained some of the most arid territory in the United States, and some of the wettest and lushest. It contained the flattest plains and the highest mountains. And it contained many peoples.

The Western Tribes

The largest and most important western population group before the great white migration from the East was the Indian tribes. Some were members of eastern tribes who had been forcibly resettled west of the Mississippi. But most were members of tribes indigenous to the West.

The western tribes had developed a number of patterns of civilization. More than 300,000 Indians (among them the Serrano, Chumash, Pomo, Maidu, Yurok, and Chinook) had lived on the Pacific coast before the arrival of Spanish settlers, supporting themselves through a combination of fishing, foraging, and simple agriculture. The Pueblos of the Southwest had long lived largely as farmers and had established permanent settlements there.

Plains Indians

The most widespread Indian groups in the West were the Plains Indians. They were, in fact, made up of many different tribal and language groups. Some lived more or less sedentary lives as farmers. But many of the Plains tribes subsisted largely through hunting buffalo. Riding small but powerful horses, the tribes moved through the grasslands following the herds. When a band halted, it constructed tepees as temporary dwellings. The buffalo, or bison, provided the economic basis for the Plains Indians' way of life. The flesh of the large animal was their principal source of food, and its skin supplied materials for clothing, shoes, tepees, blankets, robes, and utensils. "Buffalo chips"—dried manure—provided fuel; buffalo bones became knives and arrow tips; buffalo tendons formed the strings of bows.

The Plains warriors proved to be the most formidable foes white settlers had encountered. But the various tribes were usually unable to unite against white aggression. At times, tribal warriors faced white forces who were being assisted by guides and even fighters from other, usually rival, tribes. Some tribes, however, were able to overcome their divisions and unite effectively. By the mid-nineteenth century, for example, the Sioux, Arapaho, and Cheyenne had forged a powerful alliance that dominated the northern plains. That proved no protection, however, against the greatest danger to the tribes: ecological and economic decline. Indians were highly vulnerable to eastern infectious diseases. Smallpox epidemics, for example, decimated the Pawnees in Nebraska in the 1840s. And the tribes were, of

Indian Disadvantages

course, at a considerable disadvantage in any long-term battle with an economically and industrially advanced people. They were, in the end, outmanned and outgunned.

Hispanic New Mexico

For centuries, much of the Far West had been part of, first, the Spanish Empire and, later, the Mexican Republic. When the United States acquired its new lands there in the 1840s, it acquired many Mexican residents at the same time.

In New Mexico, the centers of Spanish-speaking society were the farming and trading communities the Spanish had established in the seventeenth century. Descendants of the original Spanish settlers (and more recent migrants from Mexico) engaged primarily in cattle and sheep ranching. When the United States acquired title to New Mexico in the aftermath of the Mexican War, General Stephen Kearny—who had commanded the American troops in the region during the conflict—tried to establish a territorial government out of the approximately 1,000 Anglo-Americans in the region, ignoring the over 50,000 Hispanics. There were widespread fears among the Hispanics and Indians that the new American rulers of the region would confiscate their lands. In 1847, before the new government had established itself, Taos Indians rebelled; they killed the new governor and other Anglo-American officials before being subdued by United States Army forces. New Mexico remained under military rule for three years, until the United States finally organized a territorial government there in 1850. The United States Army finally broke the power of the Navajo, Apache, and other tribes in the region. The defeat of the tribes led to substantial Hispanic migration into other areas of the Southwest and as far north as Colorado.

Taos Indian Rebellion

The Anglo-American presence in the Southwest grew rapidly once the railroads established lines into the region in the 1880s and early 1890s. With the railroads came extensive new ranching, farming, and mining. The expansion of economic activity in the region attracted a new wave of Mexican immigrants, who moved across the border in search of work. The English-speaking proprietors of the new enterprises restricted most Mexicans to the lowest-paying and least stable jobs.

Hispanic California and Texas

In California, Spanish settlement began in the eighteenth century with a string of Christian missions along the Pacific coast. The missionaries and the soldiers who accompanied them gathered most of the coastal Indians into their communities, some forcibly and some by persuasion. In the 1830s, after the new Mexican government began reducing the power of the church, the mission society largely collapsed. In its place emerged a secular Mexican aristocracy, which controlled a chain of large estates in the fertile lands west of the Sierra mountains. For them, the acquisition of California by the United States was disastrous. So vast were the numbers of English-speaking immigrants that the *californios* (as the Hispanic residents of the region were

Anglo-American Onslaught

known) had little power to resist the onslaught. English-speaking prospectors organized to exclude them, sometimes violently, from the mines during the gold rush. Many *californios* also lost their lands—either through corrupt business deals or through outright seizure.

Increasingly, Mexicans and Mexican Americans became part of the lower end of the state's working class, clustered in *barrios* in Los Angeles or elsewhere or laboring as migrant farmworkers. Even small Hispanic landowners who managed to hang on to their farms found themselves unable to raise livestock, as once-communal grazing lands fell under the control of powerful Anglo ranchers.

Hispanics Oppressed

A similar pattern occurred in Texas after it joined the United States. Many Mexican landowners lost their land—some as a result of fraud and coercion, some because even the most substantial Mexican ranchers could not compete with the enormous Anglo-American ranching kingdoms that were emerging. In 1859, angry Mexicans, led by the rancher Juan Cortina, raided the jail in Brownsville and freed all the Mexican prisoners inside. But such resistance had little long-term effect. As in California, Mexicans in southern Texas became an increasingly impoverished working class relegated largely to unskilled farm or industrial labor.

The Chinese Migration

At the same time that ambitious or impoverished Europeans were crossing the Atlantic in search of opportunities in the New World, many Chinese were crossing the Pacific in hopes of better lives. Not all came to the United States. Many Chinese moved to Hawaii, Australia, Latin America, South Africa, and even the Caribbean—some as "coolies" (indentured servants whose condition was close to slavery).

Increasing Chinese Immigration

A few Chinese traveled to the American West even before the gold rush, but after 1848 the flow increased dramatically. By 1880, more than 200,000 Chinese had settled in the United States. Almost all came as free laborers. For a time, white Americans welcomed the Chinese as a conscientious, hardworking people. Very quickly, however, white opinion turned hostile—in part because the Chinese were so industrious and successful that some white Americans began considering them rivals.

In the early 1850s, large numbers of Chinese immigrants joined the hunt for gold. Many of them were well-organized, hardworking prospectors, and for a time some of them enjoyed considerable success. But opportunities for Chinese to prosper in the mines were fleeting. In 1852, the California legislature began trying to exclude the Chinese from gold mining by enacting a "foreign miners" tax. Gradually, the effect of the discriminatory laws, the hostility of white miners, and the declining profitability of the surface mines drove most Chinese out of prospecting.

A CHINESE FAMILY IN SAN FRANCISCO Like many other Americans, Chinese families liked to pose for photographic portraits in the late nineteenth century. And like many other immigrants, they often sent them back to relatives in China. This portrait of Chun Duck Chin and his seven-year-old son Chun Jan Yut was taken in a studio in San Francisco in the 1870s. Both father and son appear to have dressed up for the occasion, in traditional Chinese garb, and the studio—which likely took many such portraits of Chinese families—provided a formal Chinese backdrop. The son is holding what appears to be a chicken, perhaps to impress relatives in China with the family's prosperity. *(The National Archives and Records Administration)*

As mining declined as a source of wealth and jobs for the Chinese, railroad employment grew. Beginning in 1865, over 12,000 Chinese found work building the transcontinental railroad. In fact, Chinese workers formed 90 percent of the labor force of the Central Pacific. The company preferred them to white laborers because they worked hard, made few demands, and accepted relatively low wages.

Transcontinental Railroad

Work on the Central Pacific was arduous and often dangerous. In the winter, many Chinese tunneled into snow banks at night to create warm sleeping areas for themselves, even though such tunnels frequently collapsed, suffocating those inside. In the spring of 1866, 5,000 Chinese railroad workers rebelled against the terrible conditions of their work and went on strike demanding higher wages and a shorter workday. The company isolated them, surrounded them with strikebreakers, and starved them into submission. The strike failed, and most of the workers returned to their jobs.

In 1869 the transcontinental railroad was completed, and thousands of Chinese lost their jobs. Some moved into agricultural work, usually in menial positions. Increasingly, however, the Chinese flocked to cities. By far the largest single Chinese community was in San Francisco. Much of community life there, and in other "Chinatowns" throughout the West, revolved around organizations that functioned as something like benevolent societies and filled many of the roles that political machines often served in immigrant communities in eastern cities. They were often led by prominent merchants. (In San Francisco, the leading merchants—known as the "Six Companies"—often worked together to advance their interests in the larger community of the city and state.) These organizations became, in effect, employment brokers, unions, arbitrators of disputes, defenders of the community against outside persecution, and dispensers of social services. They also organized the elaborate festivals and celebrations that were such a conspicuous and important part of life in Chinatowns.

"Chinatowns"

Other Chinese organizations were secret societies, known as "tongs." And some of the tongs were violent criminal organizations, involved in the opium trade and prostitution. Few people outside the Chinese communities were aware of their existence, except when rival tongs engaged in violent conflict (or "tong wars").

In San Francisco and other western cities, the Chinese usually occupied the lower rungs of the employment ladder. Many worked as common laborers, servants, and unskilled factory hands. Some established their own small businesses, especially laundries. They moved into this business not because of experience—there were few commercial laundries in China—but because laundries could be started with very little capital and required only limited command of English. By the 1890s, Chinese constituted over two-thirds of all the laundry workers in California.

Growing Gender Balance

During the earliest Chinese migrations to California, virtually all the relatively small number of women who made the journey did so because they had been sold into prostitution in China. As late as 1880, nearly half the Chinese women in California were prostitutes. Gradually, however, the number of Chinese women increased, and Chinese men in America became more likely to seek companionship in families.

Anti-Chinese Sentiments

As Chinese communities grew larger and more conspicuous, anti-Chinese sentiment among white residents became increasingly strong. Anti-Chinese activities, some of them violent, reflected the resentment of many white workers toward Chinese laborers for accepting low wages and thus undercutting union members. As the political value of attacking the Chinese grew in California, the Democratic Party took up the call. So did the Workingmen's Party of California—created in 1878 by Denis Kearney, an Irish immigrant—which gained significant political power in the state in large part on the basis of its hostility to the Chinese. By the mid-1880s, anti-Chinese agitation and violence had spread up and down the Pacific coast and into other areas of the West.

In 1882, Congress responded to the political pressure and the growing violence by passing the Chinese Exclusion Act, which banned Chinese immigration into the United States for ten years and barred Chinese already in the country from becoming naturalized citizens. Congress renewed the law for another ten years in 1892 and made it permanent in 1902. It had a dramatic effect on the Chinese population, which declined by more than 40 percent in the forty years after the act's passage.

Chinese Exclusion Act

Migration from the East

The scale of the post–Civil War migration to the American West dwarfed everything that had preceded it. In previous decades, the settlers had come in thousands. Now they came in millions. Most of the new settlers were from the established Anglo-American societies of the eastern United States, but substantial numbers—over 2 million between 1870 and 1900—were foreign-born immigrants from Europe: Scandinavians, Germans, Irish, Russians, Czechs, and others.

They came to the West for many reasons. Settlers were attracted by gold and silver deposits, by the shortgrass pasture for cattle and sheep, and ultimately by the sod of the plains and the meadowlands of the mountains. The completion of the great transcontinental railroad line in 1869, and the construction of the many subsidiary lines that spread out from it, encouraged settlement. So did the land policies of the federal government. The Homestead Act of 1862 permitted settlers to buy plots of 160 acres for a small fee if they occupied the land they purchased for five years and improved it.

Homestead Act of 1862

Supporters of the Homestead Act believed it would create new markets and new outposts of commercial agriculture for the nation's growing economy. But a unit of 160 acres, while ample in much of the East, was too small for the grazing and grain farming of the Great Plains. Eventually, the federal government provided some relief. The Timber Culture Act (1873) permitted homesteaders to receive grants of 160 additional acres if they planted 40 acres of trees on them. The Desert Land Act (1877) provided that claimants could buy 640 acres at $1.25 an acre provided they irrigated part of their holdings within three years. These and other laws ultimately made it possible for individuals to acquire as much as 1,280 acres of land at little cost.

Political organization followed on the heels of settlement. By the mid-1860s, territorial governments were in operation in the new provinces of Nevada, Colorado, Dakota, Arizona, Idaho, Montana, and Wyoming. Statehood rapidly followed. Nevada became a state in 1864, Nebraska in 1867, and Colorado in 1876. In 1889, North and South Dakota, Montana, and Washington won admission; Wyoming and Idaho entered the next year. Congress denied Utah statehood until its Mormon leaders convinced the government in 1896 that polygamy (the practice of men taking several wives) had been abandoned. At the turn of the century, only Arizona, New Mexico, and Oklahoma remained outside the Union.

New Western States

THE CHANGING WESTERN ECONOMY

Among many other things, the great wave of Anglo-American and European settlement transformed the economy of the Far West. The new American settlers tied the West firmly to the growing industrial economy of the East.

Labor in the West

As commercial activity increased, many farmers, ranchers, and miners found it necessary to recruit a paid labor force—not an easy task for people far away from major population centers. The labor shortage of the region led to higher wages for some workers than were typical in most areas of the East. But working conditions were often arduous, and job security was almost nonexistent. Once a railroad was built, a crop harvested, a herd sent to market, a mine played out, hundreds and even thousands of workers could find themselves suddenly unemployed. Competition from Chinese immigrants also forced some Anglo-Americans and Europeans out of work.

Multiracial Working Class

Even more than in many parts of the East, the western working class was highly multiracial. English-speaking whites worked alongside African Americans and immigrants from southern and eastern Europe, as they did in the East. Even more, they worked with Chinese, Filipinos, Mexicans, and Indians. But the work force was highly stratified along racial lines. In almost every area of the western economy, white workers (whatever their ethnicity) occupied the upper tiers of employment: management and skilled labor. The lower tiers—unskilled work in the mines, on the railroads, or in agriculture—consisted overwhelmingly of nonwhites.

COLORADO BOOM TOWN After a prospector discovered silver nearby in 1890, miners flocked to the town of Creede, Colorado. For a time in the early 1890s, 150 to 300 people arrived there daily. Although the town was located in a canyon so narrow that there was room for only one street, buildings sprouted rapidly to serve the growing community. Like other such boom towns, however, Creede's prosperity was short-lived. In 1893 the price of silver collapsed, and by the end of the century, Creede was almost deserted. *(Henry Ford Museum and Greenfield Village)*

The western economy was, however, no more a single entity than the economy of the East. In the late nineteenth century, the region produced three major industries, each with a distinctive history and distinctive characteristics: mining, ranching, and commercial farming.

The Arrival of the Miners

The first economic boom in the Far West came in mining. The mining boom began around 1860 and flourished until the 1890s. Then it abruptly declined.

Mining Booms

News of a gold or silver strike in an area would start a stampede reminiscent of the California gold rush of 1849, followed by several stages of settlement. Individual prospectors would exploit the first shallow deposits of ore largely by hand, with pan and placer mining. After these surface deposits dwindled, corporations moved in to engage in lode or quartz mining, which dug deeper beneath the surface. Then, as those deposits dwindled, commercial mining either disappeared or continued on a restricted basis, and ranchers and farmers moved in and established a more permanent economy.

The first great mineral strikes (other than the California gold rush) occurred just before the Civil War. In 1858, gold was discovered in the Pike's Peak district of what would soon be the territory of Colorado; the following year, 50,000 prospectors stormed in. Denver and other mining camps blossomed into "cities" overnight. Almost as rapidly as it had developed, the boom ended. Later, the discovery of silver near Leadville supplied a new source of mineral wealth.

While the Colorado rush of 1859 was still in progress, news of another strike drew miners to Nevada. Gold had been found in the Washoe district. But even more plentiful and more valuable was the silver found in the great Comstock Lode (first discovered in 1858 by Henry Comstock) and other Washoe veins. The first prospectors to reach the Washoe fields came from California, and from the beginning, Californians dominated the settlement and development of Nevada. In a remote desert without railroad transportation, the territory produced no supplies of its own, and everything had to be shipped from California to Virginia City, Carson City, and other roaring camp towns. When the first placer (or surface) deposits ran out, Californian and eastern capitalists bought the claims of the pioneer prospectors and began to use the more difficult process of quartz mining, which enabled them to retrieve silver from deeper veins. For a few years these outside owners reaped tremendous profits: from 1860 to 1880 the Nevada lodes yielded bullion worth $306 million. After that, the mines quickly played out.

Comstock Lode Discovered

The next important mineral discoveries came in 1874, when gold was found in the Black Hills of southwestern Dakota Territory. Prospectors swarmed into the remote area. Like the others, the boom flared for a time, until surface resources faded and corporations took over from the miners. One enormous company, the Homestake, came to dominate the fields. The Dakotas, like other boom areas of the mineral empire, ultimately developed a largely agricultural economy.

Although the gold and silver discoveries generated the most popular excitement, in the long run other, less glamorous natural resources proved more important to the development of the West. The great Anaconda copper mine launched by William Clark in 1881 marked the beginning of an industry that would remain important to Montana for many decades. In other areas, mining operations had significant success with lead, tin, quartz, and zinc.

Gender Disparity

Men greatly outnumbered women in the mining towns, and younger men in particular had difficulty finding female companions of comparable age. Those women who did gravitate to the new communities often came with their husbands. Single women, or women whose husbands were earning no money, did work for wages at times, as cooks, laundresses, and tavern keepers. And in the sexually imbalanced mining communities, there was always a ready market for prostitutes.

The thousands of people who flocked to the mining towns in search of quick wealth and failed to find it often remained as wage laborers in corporate mines after the boom period, working in almost uniformly terrible conditions. In the 1870s, one worker in every thirty was disabled in the mines, and one in every eighty was killed. That rate fell later in the nineteenth century, but mining remained one of the most dangerous and arduous working environments in the United States.

The Cattle Kingdom

A second important element of the changing economy of the Far West was cattle ranching. The open range—the vast grasslands of the public domain—provided a huge area on the Great Plains where cattle raisers could graze their herds.

Mexican Roots

The western cattle industry was Mexican and Texan by ancestry. Long before citizens of the United States entered the Southwest, Mexican ranchers had developed the techniques and equipment that the cattlemen and cowboys of the Great Plains later employed: branding, roundups, roping, and the gear of the herders—their lariats, saddles, leather chaps, and spurs. Americans in Texas adopted these methods and carried them to the northernmost ranges of the cattle kingdom. Texas also had the largest herds of cattle in the country. From Texas, too, came the small, muscular horses (broncos and mustangs) that enabled cowboys to control the herds.

At the end of the Civil War, an estimated 5 million cattle roamed the Texas ranges. Eastern markets were offering good prices for steers in any condition, and the challenge facing the cattle industry was getting the animals from the range to the railroad centers. Early in 1866, some Texas cattle ranchers began driving their combined herds, some 260,000 head, north to Sedalia, Missouri, on the Missouri Pacific Railroad. The caravan suffered heavy losses. But the drive proved that cattle could be driven to distant markets and pastured along the trail. This earliest of the "long drives," in other words, established the first, tentative link between the isolated cattle breeders of west Texas and the booming urban markets of the East.

With the precedent of the long drive established, the next step was to find an easier route through more accessible country. Market facilities grew up at Abilene, Kansas, on the Kansas Pacific Railroad, and for years the town reigned as the railhead of the cattle kingdom. But by the mid-1870s, agricultural development in western Kansas was eating away at the open-range land. Cattlemen had to develop other trails and other market outlets. As the railroads began to reach farther west, Dodge City and Wichita in Kansas, Ogallala and Sidney in Nebraska, Cheyenne and Laramie in Wyoming, and Miles City and Glendive in Montana all began to rival Abilene as major centers of stock herding.

There had always been an element of risk and speculation in the open-range cattle business. Rustlers and Indians frequently seized large numbers of animals. But as settlement of the plains increased, new forms of competition arose. Sheep breeders from California and Oregon brought their flocks onto the range to compete for grass. Farmers ("nesters") from the

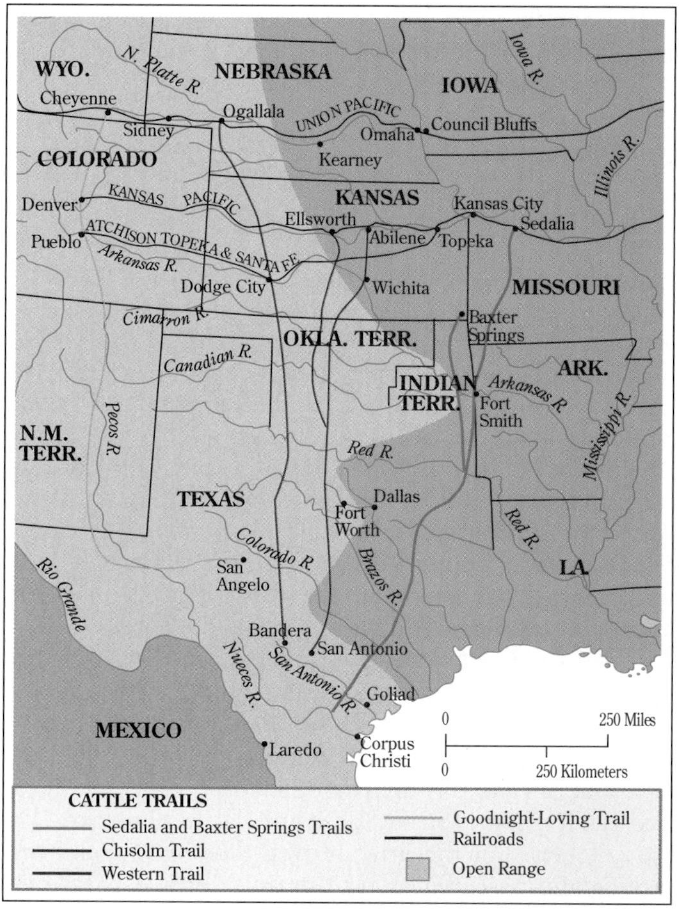

THE CATTLE KINGDOM, c. 1866–1887 Cattle ranching and cattle drives are among the most romanticized features of the nineteenth-century West. But they were also hard-headed business ventures, made possible by the growing eastern market for beef and the availability of reasonably inexpensive transportation to take cattle to urban markets. This map shows two important characteristics of the "cattle kingdom" in the 1860s and 1870s. One is the vast expanse of "open range." ◆ *Why was that necessary for the great cattle drives, and what eventually ended it?* The other is the dense network of trails and railroads that together made possible the commerce in cattle.

For an interactive version of this map go to www.mhhe.com/unfinishednation4ch16maps

East threw fences around their claims, blocking trails and breaking up the open range. A series of "range wars"—between sheepmen and cattlemen, between ranchers and farmers—erupted out of the tensions between these competing groups.

"Range Wars"

Accounts of the lofty profits to be made in the cattle business tempted eastern, English, and Scottish capital to the plains. Increasingly, the structure of the cattle economy became corporate; in one year, twenty corporations with a combined capital of $12 million were chartered in Wyoming.

The result of this frenzied, speculative expansion was that the ranges, already severed and shrunk by the railroads and the farmers, became overstocked. There was not enough grass to support the crowding herds or sustain the long drives. Two severe winters, in 1885–1886 and 1886–1887, with a searing summer between them, stung and scorched the plains. Hundreds of thousands of cattle died; streams and grass dried up; princely ranches and costly investments disappeared in a season.

The open-range industry never recovered; the long drive finally disappeared for good. Railroads displaced the trail as the route to market for livestock. But established cattle ranches survived, grew, and prospered, eventually producing more beef than ever.

Decline of the Open-range Industry

THE ROMANCE OF THE WEST

The West occupied a special place in the Anglo-American imagination in the nineteenth century. Many white Americans continued to consider it a romantic place, a wilderness where individuals could experience true freedom.

The Western Landscape and the Cowboy

"Rocky Mountain School"

Part of the reason was the spectacular natural landscape of the West. Painters of the new "Rocky Mountain School"—of whom the best known were Albert Bierstadt and Thomas Moran—celebrated the new West in grandiose canvases, some of which were taken on tours around the eastern and midwestern states and attracted enormous crowds, eager for a vision of the Great West.

Gradually, the interest in paintings of the West inspired a growing wave of tourism among people eager to see the natural wonders of the region. In the 1880s and 1890s, resort hotels began to spring up near some of the most spectacular landscapes in the region.

Even more appealing than the landscape was the rugged, free-spirited lifestyle that many Americans associated with the West. Many nineteenth-century Americans came to romanticize, especially, the figure of the cowboy. Western novels such as Owen Wister's *The Virginian* (1902) romanticized the cowboy's supposed freedom from traditional social constraints, his affinity with nature, even his supposed propensity for violence. Wister's character—one of the most enduring in popular American literature—was a semi-educated man whose natural decency, courage, and compassion made him a powerful symbol of the supposed virtues of the "frontier." But *The Virginian* was only the most famous example of a type of literature that soon swept throughout the United States: novels and stories about the West, and about the lives of cowboys in particular, that appeared in boys' magazines, pulp novels, theater, and even serious literature.

Cowboys Mythologized

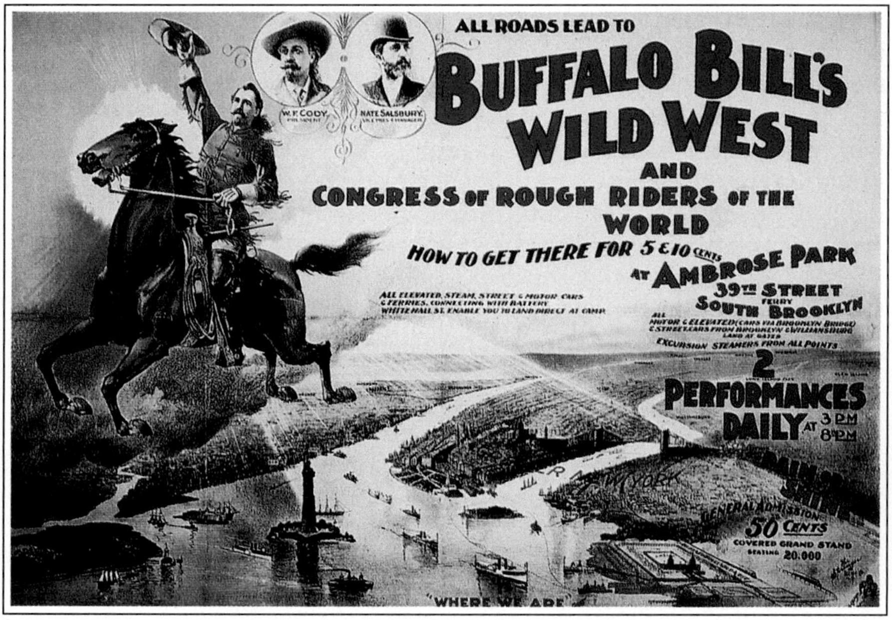

PROMOTING THE WEST Buffalo Bill's Wild West show was popular all over the United States, and indeed through much of the world. He was so familiar a figure that many of his posters contained only his picture with the words "He is Coming." This more conventional poster announces a visit of the show to Brooklyn. *(Culver Pictures, Inc.)*

One reason for the widespread admiration of the cowboy was the remarkable popularity of the Wild West shows that traveled throughout the United States and Europe. The most successful were the shows of Buffalo Bill Cody, a former Pony Express rider and Indian fighter, and the hero of popular dime novels for children. Cody's Wild West show, which had dozens of imitators, exploited his own fame. But it was mainly popular for its romanticization of the West and of the life of the cowboy. It included re-enactments of Indian battles and displays of horsemanship and riflery (many of them by the famous sharpshooter Annie Oakley). Buffalo Bill and his imitators confirmed the popular image of the West as a place of romance and glamour and helped keep that image alive for later generations.

The Idea of the Frontier

Yet it was not simply the particular character of the new West that made it so important to the nation's imagination. It was also that many Americans considered it the last frontier. Since the earliest moments of European settlement in America, the image of uncharted territory to the west had always comforted and inspired those who dreamed of starting life anew.

Mark Twain gave voice to this romantic vision of the frontier in a series of novels and memoirs. In *The Adventures of Tom Sawyer* (1876) and *The Adventures of Huckleberry Finn* (1885), he produced characters who repudiated the constraints of organized society and attempted to escape into a more natural world. For Huck Finn, the vehicle of escape was a small raft on the Mississippi, but the yearning for freedom reflected a larger vision of the West as the last refuge from the constraints of civilization.

Romantic Vision of the Frontier

The painter and sculptor Frederic Remington also captured the romance of the West. His paintings and sculptures portrayed the cowboy as a natural aristocrat, much like Wister's *Virginian*, living in a natural world in which all the normal supporting structures of "civilization" were missing. Remington became one of the most beloved and successful artists of the nineteenth century.

Theodore Roosevelt also contributed to the romanticizing of the West. He traveled to the Dakota badlands in the mid-1880s to help himself recover from the sudden death of his young wife. In the 1890s, he published a four-volume history, *The Winning of the West*, with a heroic account of the spread of white civilization into the frontier.

The clearest and most influential statement of the romantic vision of the frontier came from the historian Frederick Jackson Turner, in a memorable paper he delivered to a meeting of the American Historical Association in Chicago in 1893 entitled "The Significance of the Frontier in American History." In it he boldly claimed that the experience of expansion into the frontier had stimulated individualism, nationalism, and democracy. It had kept opportunities for advancement alive. It had made Americans the distinctive people that they were. "Now," Turner concluded portentously, "the frontier has gone and with its going has closed the first period of American history."

Frederick Jackson Turner

In accepting the idea of the "passing of the frontier," many Americans were acknowledging the end of one of their most cherished myths. As long as it had been possible for them to consider the West an empty, open land, it was possible to believe that there were constantly revitalizing opportunities in American life. Now there was a vague and ominous sense of opportunities foreclosed.

"Passing of the Frontier"

THE DISPERSAL OF THE TRIBES

Having imagined the West as a "virgin land" awaiting civilization by white people, many Americans tried to force the region to match their image of it. That meant, above all, ensuring that the Indian tribes would not remain obstacles to the spread of white society.

White Tribal Policies

The traditional policy of the federal government was to regard the tribes simultaneously as independent nations (with which the United States

Debating the Past

THE FRONTIER AND THE WEST

The emergence of the history of the American West as an important field of scholarship can be traced to the paper Frederick Jackson Turner delivered at a meeting of the American Historical Association in 1893: "The Significance of the Frontier in American History." Turner stated his thesis simply. The settlement of the West by white Americans—"the existence of an area of free land, its continuous recession, and the advance of American settlement westward"—was the central story of the nation's history. The process of westward expansion had transformed a desolate and savage land into modern civilization. It had also continually renewed American ideas of democracy and individualism.

In the first half of the twentieth century, virtually everyone who wrote about the West echoed at least part of Turner's argument. Ray Allen Billington's *Westward Expansion* (1949) was almost wholly consistent with the Turnerian model. In *The Great Plains* (1931) and *The Great Frontier* (1952), Walter Prescott Webb similarly emphasized the bravery and ingenuity of white settlers in the Southwest.

Serious efforts to displace the Turner thesis as the explanation of western American history began after World War II. In *Virgin Land* (1950), Henry Nash Smith examined many of the same heroic images of the West that Turner and his disciples had presented; but he treated those images less as descriptions of reality than as myths. Earl Pomeroy challenged Turner's notion of the West as a place of individualism, innovation, and democratic renewal. "Conservatism, inheritance, and continuity bulked at least as large," he claimed. Howard Lamar, in *Dakota Territory, 1861–1889* (1956) and *The Far Southwest* (1966), emphasized the highly diverse characters of different areas of the West.

The western historians who began to emerge in the late 1970s launched an even more emphatic attack on the Turner thesis and the idea of the "frontier." "New" western historians such as Richard White, Patricia Nelson Limerick, William Cronon, Donald Worster, Peggy Pascoe, and many others challenged the Turnerians on a number of points.

Turner saw the nineteenth-century West as "free land" awaiting the expansion of Anglo-American settlement and American democracy. The "new western historians" have rejected the concept of an empty "frontier," emphasizing instead the elaborate and highly developed civilizations that already existed in the region. White, English-speaking Americans, they have argued, did not so much settle the West as conquer it. And they continue to share the region not only with the Indians and Hispanics who preceded them there, but also with African Americans, Asians, Latin Americans, and others who flowed into the West at the same time they did.

The Turnerian West was a place of heroism, triumph, and above all progress, dominated by the feats of brave white men. The West the new historians describe is a less triumphant (and less masculine) place in which bravery and success coexist with oppression, greed, and failure; in which decaying ghost towns, bleak Indian reservations, impoverished barrios, and ecologically devastated landscapes are as characteristic of western development as great ranches, rich farms, and prosperous cities.

To Turner and his disciples, the nineteenth-century West was a place where rugged individualism flourished and replenished American democracy. The new scholars point out that the region was inextricably tied to a national and international capitalist economy. Westerners depended on government-subsidized railroads for access to markets, federal troops for protection from Indians, and (later) government-funded dams and canals for irrigating their fields and sustaining their towns.

And while Turner defined the West as a process—a process of settlement that came to an end with the "closing of the frontier" in the late nineteenth century—the new historians see the West as a region. Its history does not end in 1890. It continues into our own time.

(text continued from page 443)

could negotiate treaties) and as wards of the president (who would exercise paternalistic authority over the Indians). The concept of Indian sovereignty had supported the government's attempt before 1860 to erect a permanent frontier between whites and Indians. But the belief in tribal sovereignty, and the treaties or agreements with the Indians, were not strong enough to withstand the pressure of white settlers eager for access to Indian lands.

By the early 1850s, the idea of establishing one great enclave in which many tribes could live gave way to a new reservations policy known as "concentration." In 1851, the government assigned all the tribes their own defined reservations, confirmed by individual treaties—treaties often illegitimately negotiated with unauthorized "representatives" chosen by whites, people known sarcastically as "treaty chiefs." The new arrangement had many benefits for whites and few for the Indians. It divided the tribes from one another and made them easier to control. It allowed the government to force tribes into scattered locations and to take over the most desirable lands for white settlement. But it did not survive as the basis of Indian policy for long.

"Concentration" Policy

In 1867, Congress established the Indian Peace Commission, composed of both soldiers and civilians, to recommend a new and presumably permanent Indian policy. The commission recommended that the government move all the Plains tribes into two large reservations—one in Indian Territory (Oklahoma), the other in the Dakotas. At a series of meetings with the tribes, government agents cajoled, bribed, and tricked their representatives into agreeing to treaties establishing the new reservations.

But this "solution" worked little better than previous ones. Part of the problem was the abysmal way in which corrupt or incompetent agents of the Bureau of Indian Affairs administered the reservations. But the problem was also a result of the relentless slaughtering by whites of the buffalo herds that supported the tribes' way of life. After the Civil War, professional and amateur hunters—even casual visitors shooting from passing trains—swarmed over the plains, killing the huge animals. Some Indian tribes (notably the Blackfeet) also began killing large numbers of buffalo to sell in the booming new market. In 1865, there had been at least 15 million buffalo; a decade later,

Buffalo Herds Decimated

HELD UP BY BUFFALO Once among the most numerous creatures in North America, the buffalo became almost extinct as a result of indiscriminate slaughter by white settlers and travelers, who often fired at herds from moving trains simply for the sport of it. This scene was painted around 1880 by N. H. Trotter. *(*Held up by Buffalo, *by N.H. Trotter, c. 1880. Smithsonian Institution)*

fewer than a thousand of the great beasts survived. By destroying the buffalo herds, whites were destroying the Indians' source of food and supplies and their ability to resist white advance.

The Indian Wars

There was almost incessant fighting between whites and Indians from the 1850s to the 1880s, as Indians struggled against the growing threats to their civilizations. Indian warriors attacked wagon trains, stagecoaches, and isolated ranches, often in retaliation for earlier attacks on them by whites. As the United States Army became more deeply involved in the fighting, the tribes began to focus more of their attacks on white soldiers.

Growing Indian Resistance

At times, this small-scale fighting escalated. During the Civil War, the eastern Sioux in Minnesota, cramped on a small reservation and exploited by corrupt white agents, suddenly rebelled. Led by Little Crow, they killed more than 700 whites before being subdued by a force of regulars and militiamen. Thirty-eight of the Indians were hanged, and the tribe was exiled to the Dakotas.

At the same time, fighting flared up in eastern Colorado, where the Arapaho and Cheyenne were coming into conflict with white miners settling in the region. Bands of Indians attacked stagecoach lines and settlements in an effort to regain territory they had lost. In response to these incidents, whites called up a large territorial militia. The governor urged all friendly Indians to congregate at army posts for protection before the army began its campaign. One Arapaho and Cheyenne band under Black Kettle, apparently in response to the invitation, camped near Fort Lyon on Sand Creek in November 1864. Some members of the party were warriors, but Black Kettle believed he was under official protection and exhibited no hostile intention. Nevertheless, Colonel J. M. Chivington led a volunteer militia force—largely consisting of unemployed miners, many of whom were apparently drunk—to the unsuspecting camp and massacred 133 people, 105 of them women and children. Black Kettle himself escaped the Sand Creek massacre. But four years later, in 1868, he and his Cheyennes, some of whom were now at war with the whites, were caught on the Washita River, near the Texas border, by Colonel George A. Custer. White troops killed the chief and his people.

Sand Creek Massacre

At the end of the Civil War, white troops stepped up their wars against the western Indians on several fronts. The most serious and sustained conflict was in Montana, where the army was attempting to build a road, the Bozeman Trail, to connect Fort Laramie, Wyoming, to the new mining centers. The western Sioux resented this intrusion into the heart of their buffalo range. Led by one of their great chiefs, Red Cloud, they so harried the soldiers and the construction party that the road could not be used.

But it was not only the United States military that harassed the tribes. It was also unofficial violence by white vigilantes who engaged in what became known as "Indian hunting." Sometimes the killing was in response to Indian raids on white communities. But considerable numbers of whites were committed to the goal of literal "elimination" of the tribes whatever their behavior, a goal that rested on the belief in the essential inhumanity of Indians and the impossibility of white coexistence with them. In California, civilians killed close to 5,000 Indians between 1850 and 1880—one of many factors (disease and poverty being the more important) that reduced the Indian population of the state from 150,000 before the Civil War to 30,000 in 1870.

"Indian Hunting"

The treaties negotiated in 1867 brought a temporary lull to many of the conflicts. But new forces soon shattered the peace again. In the early 1870s, more waves of white settlers, mostly miners, began to penetrate some of the lands in Dakota Territory supposedly guaranteed to the tribes in 1867. Indian resistance flared anew. In the northern plains, the Sioux rose up in 1875 and left their reservation. When white officials ordered them to return, bands of warriors gathered in Montana and united under two great leaders: Crazy Horse and Sitting Bull. Three army columns set out to round them up and force them back onto the reservation. With the expedition, as colonel of the famous Seventh Cavalry, was the colorful and controversial George A. Custer. At the Battle of the Little Bighorn in southern Montana in 1876, an unprecedentedly large army, perhaps 2,500 tribal warriors, surprised Custer and part of his regiment, surrounded them, and killed every man.

Custer Defeated

But the Indians did not have the political organization or the supplies to keep their troops united. Soon the warriors drifted off in bands to elude pursuit or search for food, and the army ran them down singly and returned them to Dakota. The power of the Sioux quickly collapsed. They accepted defeat and life on reservations.

One of the most dramatic episodes in Indian history occurred in Idaho in 1877. The Nez Percé were a small and relatively peaceful tribe, some of whose members had managed to live unmolested in Oregon into the 1870s without ever signing a treaty with the United States. But under pressure from white settlers, the government forced them to move onto a reservation. With no realistic prospect of resisting, the Indians began the journey to the reservation; but on the way, several younger Indians, drunk and angry, killed four white settlers.

Chief Joseph

The leader of the band, Chief Joseph, persuaded his followers to flee from the expected retribution. American troops pursued and attacked them, only to be driven off in a battle at White Bird Canyon. After that, the Nez Percé scattered in several directions and became part of a remarkable chase. Joseph moved with 200 warriors and 350 women, children, and old people in an effort to reach Canada. Pursued by four columns of American soldiers, the Indians covered 1,321 miles in seventy-five days, repelling or evading the army time and again. They were finally caught just short of the Canadian boundary. Some escaped and slipped across the border; but Joseph and most of his followers, weary and discouraged, finally gave up. "Hear me, my chiefs," Joseph said after meeting with the American general Nelson Miles. "I am tired. My heart is sick and sad. From where the sun now stands, I will fight no more forever."

The last Indians to maintain organized resistance against the whites were the Chiricahua Apaches. The two ablest chiefs of this fierce tribe were Mangas Colorados and Cochise. Mangas was murdered during the Civil War by white soldiers who tricked him into surrendering, and in 1872 Cochise agreed to peace in exchange for a reservation that included some of the tribe's traditional land. But Cochise died in 1874, and his successor, Geronimo, fought on for more than a decade longer, establishing bases in the mountains of Arizona and Mexico and leading warriors in intermittent raids against white outposts. With each raid, however, the number of warring Apaches dwindled, as some warriors died and others drifted away to the reservation. By 1886, Geronimo's band consisted of only about 30 people, including women and children, while his white pursuers numbered perhaps 10,000. Geronimo recognized the odds and surrendered.

The Apache wars were the most violent of all the Indian conflicts, and they produced brutality on both sides. But it was the whites who committed the most flagrant atrocities. That did not end with the conclusion of the Apache wars. Another tragic encounter occurred in 1890 as a result of a religious revival among the Sioux—a revival that itself symbolized the

THE SURRENDER OF GERONIMO The great Apache warrior Geronimo (front row, third from right) sits with members of his diminished band after surrendering to United States troops in 1886. The two men at front row, left, are Geronimo's half brothers. The young boy in the front row, right, is his son. *(Smithsonian Institution, National Anthropological Archives, Bureau of American Ethnology Collection)*

catastrophic effects of the white assaults on Indian civilization. As other tribes had done in trying times in the past, many of these Indians turned to a prophet who led them in a religious revival.

This time the prophet was Wovoka, a Paiute who inspired a fervent spiritual awakening that began in Nevada and spread quickly to the plains. The new revival emphasized the coming of a messiah, but its most conspicuous feature was a mass, emotional "Ghost Dance," which inspired ecstatic, mystical visions among many participants. One of these visions was an image of a retreat of white people from the plains and a restoration of the great buffalo herds. White agents on the Sioux reservation watched the dances in bewilderment and fear; some believed they might be the preliminary to hostilities.

"Ghost Dance"

On December 29, 1890, the Seventh Cavalry tried to round up a group of about 350 cold and starving Sioux at Wounded Knee, South Dakota. Fighting broke out in which about 40 white soldiers and up to 200 of the Indians died. An Indian may have fired the first shot, but the battle soon turned into a one-sided massacre, as the white soldiers turned their new machine guns on the Indians and mowed them down in the snow.

Wounded Knee Massacre

The Dawes Act

Even before the Ghost Dance and the Wounded Knee tragedies, the federal government had moved to destroy forever the tribal structure that had always been the cornerstone of Indian culture. Reversing its policy of nearly fifty years, Congress abolished the practice by which tribes owned reservation lands communally. Some supporters of the new policy believed they were acting for the good of the Indians, whom they considered a "vanishing race" in need of rescue by white society. The action was designed to force Indians to become landowners and farmers, to abandon their collective society and culture and become part of white civilization.

The Dawes Severalty Act of 1887 provided for the gradual elimination of most tribal ownership of land and the allotment of tracts to individual owners: 160 acres to the head of a family, 80 acres to a single adult or orphan, 40 acres to each dependent child. Adult owners were given United States citizenship, but unlike other citizens, they could not gain full title to their property for twenty-five years (supposedly to prevent them from selling the land to speculators).

Assimilation Promoted

In applying the Dawes Act, the Bureau of Indian Affairs relentlessly promoted the idea of assimilation that lay behind it. Not only did agents of the bureau try to move Indian families onto their own plots of land; they also took many Indian children away from their families and sent them to boarding schools run by whites. They moved as well to stop Indian religious rituals and encouraged the spread of Christianity and the creation of Christian churches on the reservations.

Few Indians were prepared for this wrenching change. In any case, white administration of the Dawes Act was so corrupt and inept that ultimately the government simply abandoned most efforts to enforce it. Much of the reservation land, therefore, was never distributed to individual owners.

THE RISE AND DECLINE OF THE WESTERN FARMER

The arrival of the miners, the empire building of the cattle ranchers, the dispersal of the Indian tribes—all served as a prelude to the decisive phase of white settlement of the Far West. Even before the Civil War, farmers had begun moving into the plains region, challenging the dominance of the ranchers and the Indians. By the 1870s, what was once a trickle had become a deluge. Farmers poured into the plains and beyond, enclosed land that had once been hunting territory for Indians and open range for cattle, and established a new agricultural region.

For a time in the late 1870s and early 1880s, the new western farmers flourished, enjoying the fruits of an agricultural economic boom. Beginning in the mid-1880s, however, the boom turned to bust, and the western agricultural economy began a long, steady decline.

From Boom to Bust

Farming on the Plains

Many factors combined to produce the surge of western agricultural settlement, but the most important was the railroads. Before the Civil War, the Great Plains had been accessible only through a difficult journey by wagon. But beginning in the 1860s, a great new network of railroad lines developed. They made huge areas of settlement accessible for the first time.

The building of the transcontinental line—completed in 1869 when the two lines met at Promontory Point, Utah—was a dramatic and monumental achievement. But the construction of subsidiary lines in the following years proved of greater importance to the West. State governments, imitating Washington, subsidized railroad development by offering direct financial aid, favorable loans, and more than 50 million acres of land (on top of the 130 million acres the federal government had already provided). Although built and operated by private corporations, the railroads were in many respects public projects.

The railroads spurred agricultural settlement by making access to the Great Plains easier. But the railroad companies also actively promoted settlement. The companies set rates so low for settlers that almost anyone could afford the trip west. And they sold much of their land at very low prices and with liberal credit to prospective settlers.

Cheap Rail Rates

Contributing further to the great surge of white agricultural expansion was a pronounced but temporary change in the climate of the Great Plains. For several years in succession, beginning in the 1870s, rainfall in the Plains states was well above average. White Americans now rejected the old idea that the region was the Great American Desert.

Even under the most favorable conditions, farming on the plains presented special problems. First was the problem of fencing. Farmers had to enclose their land, but materials for traditional wood or stone fences were unavailable. In the mid-1870s, however, two Illinois farmers, Joseph H. Glidden and I. L. Ellwood, solved this problem by developing and marketing barbed wire, which became standard equipment on the plains and revolutionized fencing practices all over the country and the world.

The second problem was water. Water was scarce even when rainfall was above average. After 1887, a series of dry seasons began, and lands that had been fertile now returned to semidesert. Some farmers dealt with the problem by using deep

Scarce Water

wells pumped by steel windmills, by turning to what was called dryland farming (a system of tillage designed to conserve moisture in the soil by covering it with a dust blanket), or by planting drought-resistant crops. In many areas of the plains, however, only large-scale irrigation could save the endangered farms. But irrigation projects of the necessary magnitude required government assistance, and neither the federal nor the state governments were prepared to fund the projects.

Most of the people who moved into the region had previously been farmers in the Middle West, the East, or Europe. In the booming years of the early 1880s, with land values rising, the new farmers had no problem obtaining extensive and easy credit. But the arid years of the late 1880s—during which crop prices were falling while production was becoming more expensive—changed the farmers' prospects. Tens of thousands of farmers could not pay their debts and were forced to abandon their farms.

Reverse Migration

There was, in effect, a reverse migration: white settlers moving back east, sometimes turning once-flourishing communities into desolate ghost towns. Those who remained continued to suffer from falling prices (for example, wheat, which had sold for $1.60 a bushel at the end of the Civil War, dropped to 49 cents in the 1890s) and persistent indebtedness.

Commercial Agriculture

By the late nineteenth century the sturdy, independent farmer of popular myth was being replaced by the commercial farmer—attempting to do in the agricultural economy what industrialists were doing in the manufacturing economy. Commercial farmers specialized in cash crops that were sold in national or world markets. They did not often make their own household supplies or grow their own food but bought them from merchants. This kind of farming, when it was successful, raised farmers' living standards. But it also made them dependent on bankers and interest rates, railroads and freight rates, national and European markets, world supply and demand. And unlike the capitalists of the industrial order, they could not regulate their production or influence the prices of what they sold.

Between 1865 and 1900, farm output increased dramatically, not only in the United States but in Brazil, Argentina, Canada, Australia, New Zealand, Russia, and elsewhere. At the same time, modern forms of communication and transportation—the telephone, the telegraph, steam navigation, railroads—were creating new markets around the world for agricultural goods. Beginning in the 1880s, worldwide overproduction led to a

Overproduction

drop in prices for most agricultural goods and hence to great economic distress for many of the more than 6 million American farm families. By the 1890s, 27 percent of the farms in the country were mortgaged; by 1910, 33 percent. In 1880, 25 percent of all farms had been operated by tenants; by 1910, the proportion had grown to 37 percent. Commercial farming made some people fabulously wealthy. But the farm economy as a whole was suffering a significant decline relative to the rest of the nation.

The Farmers' Grievances

American farmers were painfully aware that something was wrong. But few yet understood the implications of national and world overproduction. Instead, they concentrated their attention and anger on more immediate, more comprehensible—and no less real—problems: inequitable freight rates, high interest charges, and an inadequate currency.

Grievances against Railroads

The farmers' first and most burning grievance was against the railroads. In many cases, the railroads charged higher rates for farm goods than for other goods, and higher rates in the South and West than in the Northeast. Railroads also controlled elevator and warehouse facilities in buying centers and charged arbitrary storage rates.

Farmers also resented the institutions controlling credit—banks, loan companies, insurance corporations. Since sources of credit in the West and South were few, farmers had to take loans on whatever terms they could get, often at interest rates of from 10 to 25 percent. Many farmers had to pay these loans back in years when prices were dropping and currency was becoming scarce. As a result, expansion of the currency became an increasingly important issue to farmers.

Belief in Conspiracy

A third grievance concerned prices. A farmer could plant a large crop at a moment when its price was high and find that by the time of the harvest the price had declined. Farmers' fortunes rose and fell in response to unpredictable forces. But many farmers became convinced (often with some reason) that "middlemen"—speculators, bankers, regional and local agents—were conspiring with one another to fix prices so as to benefit themselves at the growers' expense. Many farmers also came to believe (again, not entirely without reason) that manufacturers in the East were colluding to keep the prices of farm goods low and the prices of industrial goods high. Although farmers sold their crops in a competitive world market, they bought manufactured goods in a domestic market protected by tariffs and dominated by trusts and corporations.

The Agrarian Malaise

These economic difficulties helped produce a series of social and cultural resentments. In part, this was a result of the isolation of farm life. Farm families in some parts of the country were virtually cut off from the outside world. During the winter months and spells of bad weather, the loneliness and boredom could become nearly unbearable. Many farmers lacked access to adequate education for their children, to proper medical facilities, to recreational or cultural activities, to virtually anything that might give them a sense of being members of a community. Older farmers felt the sting of watching their children leave the farm for the city. They felt the humiliation of being ridiculed as "hayseeds" by the new urban culture that was coming to dominate American life.

Isolation and Obsolescence

The result of this sense of isolation and obsolescence was a growing malaise among many farmers, a discontent that would help create a great national political movement in the 1890s. It found reflection, too, in the literature that emerged from rural America. Writers in the late nineteenth century might romanticize the rugged life of the cowboy and the western miner. For the farmer, however, the image was usually different. Hamlin Garland, for example, reflected the growing disillusionment in a series of novels and short stories. In the past, Garland wrote in the introduction to his novel *Jason Edwards* (1891), the agrarian frontier had seemed to be "the Golden West, the land of wealth and freedom and happiness." Now, however, the bright promise had faded. The trials of rural life were crushing the human spirit. "So this is the reality of the dream!" a character in *Jason Edwards* exclaims. "A shanty on a barren plain, hot and lone as a desert. My God!" Once, sturdy yeoman farmers had viewed themselves as the backbone of American life. Now they were becoming painfully aware that their position was declining in relation to the rising urban-industrial society to the east.

CONCLUSION

To many Americans in the late nineteenth century, the West seemed an untamed "frontier" in which hardy pioneers were creating a new society. The reality of the West in these years, however, was very different from this enduring image. White Americans were moving into the vast regions west of the Mississippi at a remarkable rate in the years after the Civil War, and many of them were indeed settling in lands far from any civilization they had ever known. But the West was not an empty place. It contained a large population of Indians, with whom the white settlers sometimes lived uneasily and sometimes battled, but almost always in the end pushed aside and (with help from the federal government) relocated onto lands whites did not want. There were significant numbers of Mexicans in some areas, small populations of Asians in others, and African Americans moving in from the South in search of land and freedom. The West was not a barren frontier, but a place of many cultures.

The West was also closely and increasingly tied to the emerging capitalist-industrial economy of the East. The miners who flooded into California, Colorado, Nevada, the Dakotas, and elsewhere were responding to the demand in the East for gold and silver, but even more for iron ore, copper, lead, zinc, and quartz. Cattle and sheep ranchers produced meat, wool, and leather for eastern consumers and manufacturers. Farmers grew crops for sale in national and international commodities markets.

The West certainly looked different from the East. But the growth of the West was very much a part of the growth of the rest of the nation. And the culture of the West, despite the romantic images of pioneering individuals embraced by easterners and westerners alike, was at its heart as much a culture of economic growth and capitalist ambition as was the culture of the rest of the nation.

FOR FURTHER REFERENCE

Frederick Jackson Turner's *The Frontier in American History* (1920) is a classic argument on the centrality of the frontier experience to American democracy, an argument that frames much recent history of the West, which reject the Turner thesis. Patricia Nelson Limerick's *The Legacy of Conquest: The Unbroken Past of the American West* (1987) argues that the West was not a frontier but rather an inhabited place conquered by Anglo-Americans. Richard White, *"It's Your Misfortune and None of My Own": A History of the American West* (1991), is an outstanding general history of the region that revises many myths about the West. Ronald Takaki, *Strangers from a Different Shore: A History of Asian Americans* (1989), surveys the Asian-American experience as immigrants to America's western shore. John Mack Faragher, *Women and Men on the Overland Trail* (1979) examines the social experience of westering migrants and Peggy Pascoe, *Relations of Rescue: The Search for Female Authority in the American West, 1874–1939* (1990) describes the female communities of the West. William Cronon, *Nature's Metropolis and the Great West* (1991) describes the relationships among economies and environments in the West. Jon Gjerde, *The Minds of the West: Ethnocultural Evolution in the Rural Middle West, 1830–1914* (1997) examines the impact of the ethnicity on the shaping of the agrarian West. Robert Wooster, *The Military and United States Indian Policy, 1865–1902* (1988) examines the military campaigns against the Indians in the late nineteenth century. Frederick E. Hoxie, *A Final Promise: The Campaign to Assimilate the Indians, 1880–1920* (1984) examines U.S. policies toward Native Americans in the years after the end of the Indian Wars, and Mark David Spence, *Dispossessing the Wilderness: Indian Removal and the Making of the National Parks* (1999) revises a familiar story. John Mack Faragher, *Daniel Boone* (1992) is a study of one of the West's most fabled figures, and Joy S. Kasson, *Buffalo Bill's Wild West: Celebrity, Memory, and Popular History* (2000) describes one of the regon's most accomplished mythmakers. Richard Slotkin, *The Fatal Environment: The Myth of the Frontier in the Age of Industrialization* (1985) and *Gunfighter Nation* (1992) are provocative cultural studies of the idea of the West. Henry Nash Smith, *Virgin Land* (1950) is a classic study of the West in American culture. *The West* (1996), a documentary film by Stephen Ives and Ken Burns, offers a broad history of the region, along with a companion book of the same title by Geoffrey C. Ward.

For quizzes, Internet resources, references to additional books and films, and more, consult this book's Online Learning Center site at www.mhhe.com/unfinishednation4.

SMELTING WORKS AT DENVER The painter Thomas Moran was best known for his enormous canvases depicting the natural landscapes and rugged outdoor societies of the late-nineteenth-century West. In this 1892 watercolor, however, he captures another, less renowned feature of western life: the emergence of industrial manufacturing in the rapidly developing region.
*(*Smelting Works at Denver, *1892, by Thomas Moran. Watercolor and gouache over black chalk, 34.9 x 42.2 cm. © Cleveland Museum of Art, 1998, Bequest of Mrs. Henry A. Everett for the Dorothy Burnham Everett Collection, 1938.56)*

TIME LINE

1859	1866	1870	1873	1876	1877	1879	1881
First oil well drilled	National Labor Union founded	Rockefeller founds Standard Oil	Carnegie Steel founded	Bell invents telephone	Nationwide railroad strike	Edison invents electric light bulb	American Federation of Labor founded
	First transatlantic cable		Economic panic				

CHAPTER SEVENTEEN

INDUSTRIAL SUPREMACY

Sources of Industrial Growth
Capitalism and Its Critics
The Ordeal of the Worker

"Twenty-five years after the death of Lincoln, America had become, in the quantity and value of her products, the first manufacturing nation of the world. What England had accomplished in a hundred years, the United States had achieved in half the time." So wrote the historians Charles and Mary Beard in the 1920s, expressing the amazement many Americans felt when they considered the remarkable expansion of their industrial economy in the late nineteenth century.

In fact, America's rise to industrial supremacy was not as sudden as such observers suggested. The nation had been building a manufacturing economy since early in the nineteenth century. But Americans were clearly correct in observing that the accomplishments of the last three decades of the nineteenth century overshadowed all the earlier progress.

The remarkable growth did much to increase the wealth and improve the lives of many Americans. But such benefits were very unequally shared. While industrial titans and a growing middle class were enjoying a prosperity without precedent in the nation's history, workers, farmers, and others were experiencing an often painful ordeal that slowly edged the United States toward a great economic and political crisis.

1886	1888	1892	1893	1894	1901	1903	1914
Haymarket bombing	Bellamy's *Looking Backward*	Homestead steel strike	Depression begins	Pullman strike	Morgan creates U.S. Steel	Wright brothers' airplane flight	Ford introduces factory assembly lines

SOURCES OF INDUSTRIAL GROWTH

Many factors contributed to the growth of American industry: abundant raw materials; a large and growing labor supply; a surge in technological innovation; the emergence of a talented and often ruthless group of entrepreneurs; a federal government eager to assist the growth of business; and an expanding domestic market for the products of manufacturing.

Industrial Technologies

The rapid emergence of new technologies, together with the discovery of new materials and productive processes, was one of the principal sources of late-nineteenth-century industrial growth. Some of the most important innovations were in communications. In 1866, Cyrus W. Field laid a transatlantic telegraph cable to Europe. During the next decade, Alexander Graham Bell developed the first telephone with commercial capacity. By 1900 there were 1.35 million telephones, and by 1920 13.3 million. And the Italian inventor Guglielmo Marconi was taking the first steps toward the development of radio in the 1890s; the technology he developed quickly found its way to the United States. Other inventions that speeded the pace of business organization were the typewriter (by Christopher L. Sholes in 1868), the cash register (by James Ritty in 1879), and the calculating or adding machine (by William S. Burroughs in 1891).

Alexander Graham Bell

Among the most revolutionary innovations was the introduction in the 1870s of electricity as a source of light and power. Among the pioneers of electric lighting were Charles F. Brush, who devised the arc lamp for street illumination, and Thomas A. Edison, who invented the incandescent lamp (or lightbulb). Edison and others designed improved generators and built large power plants to furnish electricity to whole cities. By the turn of the century, electric power was becoming commonplace in street railway systems, in the elevators of urban skyscrapers, in factories, and increasingly in offices and homes.

Impact of Electric Power

Particularly important to trade and industry was the development of new, high-efficiency steam engines capable of powering larger ships at faster speeds than ever imagined in the past. The new high-speed freighters, for example, made it cheaper for Britain to buy wheat grown in Canada and the United States than to grow it at home. The introduction of refrigerated ships in the 1870s made it possible to transport meat from North America and even Australia and Asia to Europe.

The Technology of Iron and Steel Production

Perhaps the most important technological development in a nation whose economy rested so heavily on railroads and urban construction was the revolutionizing of iron and steel production. Iron production had devel-

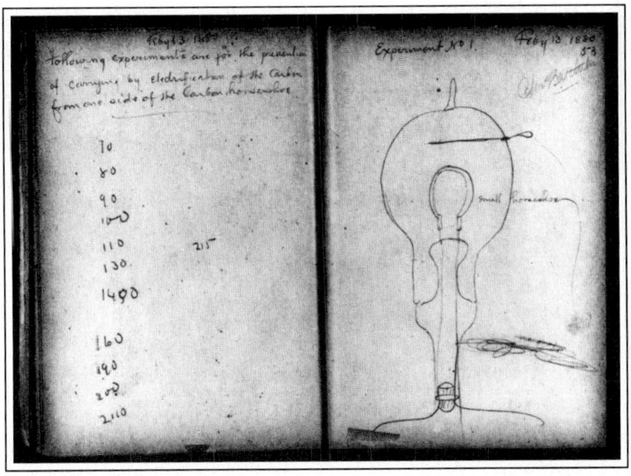

EDISON'S NOTEBOOK This page from one of Thomas Edison's notebooks shows sketches of and notes on some of his early experiments with an incandescent lamp—what we know as an electric lightbulb. Edison was not only the most celebrated inventor of his day, but by the early twentieth century one of the greatest popular heroes in American life in a time when scientific and technological progress was considered the defining feature of the age. *(U.S. Department of the Interior, National Park Service, Edison National Historic Site)*

oped slowly in the United States through most of the nineteenth century, mostly driven by the demand for iron rails for railroads; steel production had developed hardly at all by the end of the Civil War. In the 1870s and 1880s, however, iron production soared as railroads added 40,000 new miles of track, and steel production made great strides toward what would soon be its dominance in the metals industry.

The rise of steel was itself the product of technological discovery. An Englishman, Henry Bessemer, and an American, William Kelly, had developed, almost simultaneously, a process for converting iron into the much more durable and versatile steel. (The process, which took Bessemer's name, consisted of blowing air through molten iron to burn out the impurities and create a much stronger metal.) The Bessemer process also relied on the discovery by the British metallurgist Robert Mushet that ingredients could be added to the iron during conversion to transform it into steel, to give it additional strength. In 1868, the New Jersey ironmaster Abram S. Hewitt introduced from Europe another method of making steel—the open-hearth process. These techniques made possible the production of steel in great quantities and large dimensions, for use in the manufacture of locomotives, steel rails, and girders for the construction of tall buildings.

Bessemer Process

The steel industry emerged first in western Pennsylvania and eastern Ohio. That was partly because iron ore could be found there in abundance. It was also because the new forms of steel production created a demand for new kinds of fuel—and particularly for the anthracite (or hard) coal that was plentiful in Pennsylvania. Later, new techniques made it possible to use soft bituminous coal, also easily mined in western Pennsylvania. As a result, Pittsburgh quickly became the center of the steel world. But the industry was growing so fast that new sources of ore were soon necessary. The upper peninsula of Michigan, the Mesabi Range in Minnesota, and the area around Birmingham, Alabama, became important ore-producing centers, and new centers of steel production grew up near them: Cleveland, Detroit, Chicago, and Birmingham, among others.

New Blast Furnaces

Until the Civil War, iron and steel furnaces were mostly made of stone and usually built against the side of a hill to reduce construction demands. In the 1870s and after, however, furnaces were redesigned as cylindrical iron shells lined with brick. These massive new furnaces were 75 feet tall and higher and could produce over 500 tons a week.

New Transportation Systems

As the steel industry spread, new transportation systems emerged to serve it. The steel production in the Great Lakes region was possible only because of the availability of steam freighters that could carry ore on the lakes. The demand for vessels capable of transporting oil and the development of the new and more powerful steam engine encouraged, in turn, the design of larger and heavier freighters. Shippers used new steam engines to speed the unloading of ore, a task that previously had been performed, slowly and laboriously, by men and horses.

There was even a closer relationship between the emerging steel companies and the railroads. Steel manufacturers provided rails and parts for cars to the railroads; railroads were both markets for and transporters of manufactured steel. But the relationship soon became more intimate than that. The Pennsylvania Railroad, for example, literally created the Pennsylvania Steel Company.

Rise of the Petroleum Industry

The steel industry's need for lubrication for its machines helped create another important new industry in the late nineteenth century—oil. (Not until later did oil become important primarily for its potential as a fuel.) The existence of petroleum reserves in western Pennsylvania had been common knowledge for some time. Not until the 1850s, however, after Pennsylvania businessman George Bissell showed that the substance could be burned in lamps and that it could also yield such products as paraffin, naphtha, and lubricating oil, was there any sense of its commercial value. Bissell raised money to begin drilling; and in 1859, Edwin L. Drake, one of Bissell's employees, established the first oil well near Titusville, Pennsylvania, which was soon producing 500 barrels of oil a month. Demand for petroleum grew quickly, and promoters soon developed other fields in Pennsylvania, Ohio, and West Virginia.

The Airplane and the Automobile

Among the technological innovations that were to have the farthest-reaching impact on the United States was the invention of the automobile. Two technologies were critical to its development. One was the creation of gasoline (or petrol), which was the result of an extraction process developed in the late nineteenth century in the United States by which lubricating oil and fuel oil were removed separately from crude oil. As early as the 1870s, designers in France, Germany, and Austria had begun to develop an "internal combustion engine," which used the expanding power of burning gas to drive pistons. A German, Nicolaus August Otto, created a gas-powered "four-stroke" engine in the mid-1860s, which was a precursor to automobile engines. But he did not develop a way to untether it from gas lines to be used portably in machines. One of Otto's former employees, Gottfried Daimler, later perfected an engine that could be used in automobiles.

The American automobile industry developed rapidly in the aftermath of these breakthroughs. Charles and Frank Duryea built the first gasoline-driven motor vehicle in America in 1903. Three years later, Henry Ford produced the first of the famous cars that would bear his name. In 1895, there were only four automobiles on the American highways. By 1917, there were nearly 5 million.

Henry Ford

The search for a means of human flight was as old as civilization, and had been almost entirely futile until the late nineteenth century when engineers, scientists, and tinkerers in both the United States and Europe began to experiment with a wide range of aeronautic devices. Balloonists began to consider ways to make dirigibles useful vehicles of transportation. Others experimented with kites and gliders.

Two brothers in Ohio, Wilbur and Orville Wright, owned a bicycle shop in which they began to construct a glider that could be propelled through the air by an internal-combustion engine. Four years after they began their experiments, Orville made a celebrated test flight near Kitty Hawk, North Carolina, in which an airplane took off by itself and traveled 120 feet in 12 seconds under its own power before settling back to earth. By the fall of 1904, they had improved the plane to the point where they were able to fly over 23 miles, and in the following year they began to take a few passengers on their flights with them.

The Wright Brothers

Although the first working airplane was built in the United States, aviation technology was slow to gain a foothold in America. Most of the early progress in airplane design occurred in France, where there was substantial government funding for research and development. The U.S. government created the National Advisory Committee on Aeronautics in 1915, twelve years after the Wright brothers' flight, and American airplanes became a significant presence in Europe during World War I. But the prospects for commercial flight seemed dim until the 1920s, when Charles Lindbergh's famous solo flight from New York to Paris electrified the nation and the world.

Research and Development

The rapid development of new industrial technologies persuaded many business leaders to sponsor their own research to keep up with the rapid changes in industry. General Electric, fearful of technological competition, created one of the first corporate laboratories in 1900. The emergence of corporate research and development laboratories coincided with a decline in government support for research. That helped corporations to attract skilled researchers who had found themselves without their traditional forms of support. It also decentralized the sources of research funding and ensured that inquiry would move in many different directions, and not just along paths determined by the government.

Corporate Research and Development

A rift began to emerge between scientists and engineers. Engineers—both inside and out of universities—became increasingly tied up with the research and development agendas of corporations. Many scientists continued to scorn this "commercialization" of knowledge and preferred to stick to basic research that had no immediate practical applications. Even so, American scientists were more closely connected to practical challenges than were their European counterparts, and some joined engineers in corporate research and development laboratories, which over time began to sponsor not just practical but also basic research.

The Science of Production

Central to the growth of the automobile and other industries were changes in the techniques of production. By the turn of the century, many industrialists were embracing the new principles of "scientific management," often known as "Taylorism" after its leading theoretician, Frederick Winslow Taylor. Taylor himself, and his many admirers, argued that scientific management made it possible to manage human labor to make it compatible with the demands of the machine age. But scientific management was also a way to increase the employer's control of the workplace. Taylor urged employers to reorganize the production process by subdividing tasks. This would speed up production; it would also make workers more interchangeable and thus diminish a manager's dependence on any particular employee. If properly managed by trained experts, he claimed, workers using modern machines could perform simple tasks at much greater speed, greatly increasing productive efficiency.

"Taylorism"

The most important change in production technology in the industrial era was the emergence of mass production and, along with it, the moving assembly line, which Henry Ford introduced in his automobile plants in 1914. The assembly line was both a particular place—a factory through which automobiles moved as they were being assembled by workers who specialized on particular tasks—and a concept. The concept stressed the complete interchangeability of parts. General Motors adopted the same philosophy, and even proceeded to demonstrate it at a motor works in England in 1906—when three Cadillacs were dismantled, their engines disassembled, the pieces mixed up with one another, and then completely reassembled by

Assembly Line

THE ASSEMBLY LINE Workers in the Ford Motor Company's plant in Highland Park, Michigan, guide auto bodies down a ramp onto chassis that have moved into position from below. This was the final stage of the assembly line, which Henry Ford pioneered and which by 1914 (when this photograph was taken) had become common in other industries as well. *(Henry Ford Museum and Greenfield Village)*

several mechanics, who then turned on the engines and drove them onto a track. Automobile production relied on other technologies, too, in particular the intensive use of electricity—to drive the assembly line, to light the factories, and to run the critical ventilating systems to keep dust from interfering with the machines. The revolutionary assembly-line technique enabled Ford to raise the wages and reduce the hours of his workers while cutting the base price of his Model T from $950 in 1914 to $290 in 1929. It became a standard for many other industries.

Railroad Expansion and the Corporation

But the principal agent of industrial development in the late nineteenth century was the expansion of the railroads. Railroads gave industrialists access to distant markets and distant sources of raw materials. They were the nation's largest businesses and created new forms of corporate organization. And they were America's biggest investors, stimulating economic growth through their own enormous expenditures on construction and equipment.

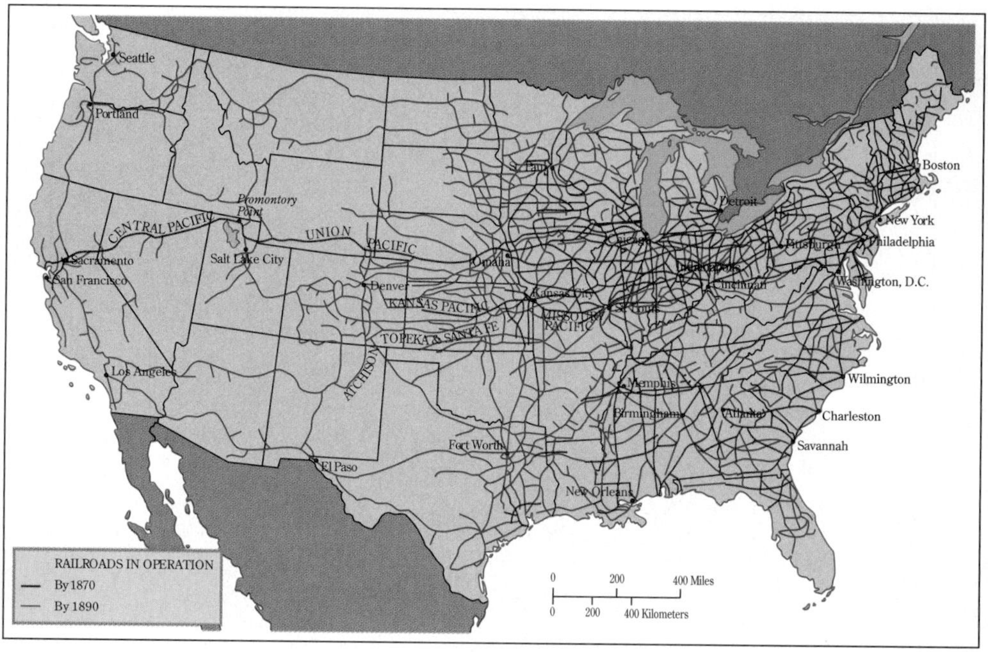

RAILROADS, 1870–1890 This map illustrates the rapid expansion of railroads in the late nineteenth century. In 1870, there was already a dense network of rail lines in the Northeast and Middle West, illustrated here by the red lines. The green lines show the further expansion of rail coverage between 1870 and 1890, much of it in the South and the areas west of the Mississippi River. ◆ *Why were railroads so essential to the nation's economic growth in these years?*

For an interactive version of this map go to www.mhhe.com/unfinishednation4ch17maps

Importance of Government Subsidies

Total railroad trackage increased from 30,000 miles in 1860 to 193,000 in 1900. Subsidies from federal, state, and local governments (along with foreign loans and investments) were vital to this expansion. Equally important was the emergence of great railroad combinations, many of them dominated by one or two individuals. The achievements (and excesses) of these tycoons—Cornelius Vanderbilt, James J. Hill, Collis R. Huntington, and others—became symbols to much of the nation of concentrated economic power. But railroad development was less significant for the individual barons it created than for its contribution to the growth of a new institution: the modern corporation.

There had been various forms of corporations in America since colonial times, but the modern corporation emerged as a major force only after the Civil War. By then, railroad magnates and other industrialists realized that their great ventures could not be financed by any single person.

Under the laws of incorporation passed in many states in the 1830s and 1840s, business organizations could raise money by selling stock to members of the public; after the Civil War, one industry after another began doing so.

What made the stocks more appealing than they had been in the past was that investors now had only "limited liability"—that is, they risked only the amount of their investments; they were not liable for any debts the corporation might accumulate beyond that point. The ability to sell stock to a broad public made it possible for entrepreneurs to gather vast sums of capital and undertake great projects.

"Limited Liability"

The Pennsylvania and other railroads were among the first to adopt the new corporate form of organization. But incorporation quickly spread beyond the railroad industry. In steel, the central figure was Andrew Carnegie, a Scottish immigrant who had worked his way up from modest beginnings and in 1873 opened his own steelworks in Pittsburgh. Soon he dominated the industry. With his associate Henry Clay Frick, he bought up coal mines and leased part of the Mesabi iron range in Minnesota, operated a fleet of ore ships on the Great Lakes, and acquired railroads. He financed his vast undertakings not only out of his own profits but out of the sale of stock. Then, in 1901, he sold out for $450 million to the banker J. Pierpont Morgan, who merged the Carnegie interests with others to create the giant United States Steel Corporation—a $14 billion enterprise that controlled almost two-thirds of the nation's steel production.

U.S. Steel Created

There were similar developments in other industries. Gustavus Swift developed a relatively small meatpacking company into a great national corporation. Isaac Singer patented a sewing machine in 1851 and created I. M. Singer and Company—one of the first modern manufacturing corporations.

Large, national business enterprises needed more systematic administrative structures. As a result, corporate leaders introduced a set of managerial techniques that relied on systematic division of responsibilities, a carefully designed hierarchy of control, careful cost-accounting procedures, and perhaps above all a new breed of business executive: the "middle manager," who formed a layer of command between workers and owners. Efficient administrative capabilities helped make possible another major feature of the modern corporation: consolidation.

Businessmen created large, consolidated organizations primarily through two methods. One was "horizontal integration"—the combining of a number of firms engaged in the same enterprise into a single corporation. The consolidation of many different railroad lines into one company was an example. Another method, which became popular in the 1890s, was "vertical integration"—the taking over of all the different businesses on which a company relied for its primary function. Carnegie Steel, which came to control not only steel mills but mines, railroads, and other enterprises, was an example of vertical integration.

"Horizontal Integration" and "Vertical Integration"

The most celebrated corporate empire of the late nineteenth century was John D. Rockefeller's Standard Oil. Shortly after the Civil War, Rockefeller launched a refining company in Cleveland and immediately began trying to eliminate his competition. Allying himself with other wealthy capitalists, he proceeded methodically to buy out competing refineries. In 1870, he formed the Standard Oil Company of Ohio, which in a few years had acquired twenty of the twenty-five refineries in Cleveland, as well as plants in Pittsburgh, Philadelphia, New York, and Baltimore.

So far, Rockefeller had expanded only horizontally. But soon he began expanding vertically as well. He built his own barrel factories, terminal warehouses, and pipelines. Standard Oil owned its own freight cars and developed its own marketing organization. By the 1880s, Rockefeller had established such dominance within the petroleum industry that to much of the nation he served as a leading symbol of monopoly.

Standard Oil

Rockefeller and other industrialists saw consolidation as a way to cope with what they believed was the greatest curse of the modern economy: "cutthroat competition." Most businessmen claimed to believe in free enterprise and a competitive marketplace, but in fact they feared that substantial competition could spell instability and ruin for all.

As the movement toward combination accelerated, new vehicles emerged to facilitate it. The railroads began with so-called pool arrangements—informal agreements among various companies to stabilize rates and divide markets (arrangements that would, in later years, be known as cartels). But if even a few firms in an industry were unwilling to cooperate (as was almost always the case), the pool arrangements collapsed.

The failure of the pools led to new techniques of consolidation. At first, the most successful such technique was the creation of the "trust"—pioneered by Standard Oil in the early 1880s and perfected by the banker J. P. Morgan. Under a trust agreement, stockholders in individual corporations transferred their stocks to a small group of trustees in exchange for shares in the trust itself. Owners of trust certificates often had no direct control over the decisions of the trustees; they simply received a share of the profits of the combination. The trustees themselves, on the other hand, might literally own only a few companies but could exercise effective control over many.

In 1889, the state of New Jersey helped produce a third form of consolidation by changing its laws of incorporation to permit companies to buy up other companies. Other states soon followed. That made the trust unnecessary and permitted actual corporate mergers. Rockefeller, for example, quickly relocated Standard Oil to New Jersey and created there what became known as a "holding company"—a central corporate body that would buy up the stock of various members of the Standard Oil trust and establish direct, formal ownership of the corporations in the trust.

"Holding Company"

By the end of the nineteenth century, 1 percent of the corporations in America were able to control more than 33 percent of the manufacturing. A system of economic organization was emerging that lodged enormous power in the hands of very few men—the great bankers of New York such as J. P. Morgan, industrial titans such as Rockefeller (who himself gained control of a major bank), and others.

The industrial giants of the era were clearly responsible for substantial economic growth. They were also creating the basis for one of the greatest public controversies of their era: a raging debate over concentrated economic and political power that continued well into the twentieth century.

CAPITALISM AND ITS CRITICS

The rise of big business was not without its critics. Farmers and workers saw in the growth of the new corporate power centers a threat to their ability to control their own destinies. Middle-class critics pointed to the corruption that the new industrial titans seemed to produce. The growing criticisms challenged the captains of industry to create a defense of the new corporate economy.

Survival of the Fittest

The new rationale for capitalism rested squarely on an older ideology of individualism. The new industrial economy, its defenders argued, was not shrinking opportunities for individual advancement. It was providing every individual with a chance to succeed and attain great wealth.

Ideology of Individualism

There was an element of truth in such claims, but only a small element. Before the Civil War there had been few millionaires in America; by 1892 there were more than 4,000. Some of them—Carnegie, Rockefeller, and a few others—were in fact "self-made men." But most of the new business tycoons had begun their careers from positions of privilege and wealth. Nor was their rise to power and prominence always a result simply of hard work and ingenuity, as they liked to claim. It was also a result of ruthlessness and, at times, rampant corruption.

Nevertheless, most tycoons continued to claim that they had attained their wealth and power through hard work, acquisitiveness, and thrift. Those who succeeded, they argued, deserved their success, and those who failed had earned their failure through their own laziness, stupidity, or carelessness. Such assumptions became the basis of a popular social theory of the late nineteenth century: Social Darwinism, the application of Charles Darwin's laws of evolution and natural selection among species to human society. Just as only the fittest survived in the process of evolution, the Social Darwinists argued, so in human society only the fittest individuals survived and flourished in the marketplace.

Social Darwinism

The English philosopher Herbert Spencer was the first and most important proponent of this theory. Society, he argued, benefited from the elimination of the unfit and the survival of the strong and talented. Spencer's teachings found prominent supporters among American intellectuals, most notably William Graham Sumner of Yale, who promoted similar ideas in lectures, articles, and a famous 1906 book, *Folkways.*

Social Darwinism appealed to corporate leaders because it seemed to legitimize their success and confirm their virtues. It was not, however, an

Corporate Wealth Legitimated

ideology that had very much to do with the realities of the corporate economy. At the same time that businessmen were celebrating the virtues of competition and the free market, they were making active efforts to protect themselves from competition and to replace the natural workings of the marketplace with control by great combinations. Vicious competitive battle was in fact the very thing that American businessmen most feared and tried to eliminate.

The Gospel of Wealth

Some businessmen attempted to temper the harsh philosophy of Social Darwinism with a gentler, if in some ways equally self-serving, idea: the "gospel of wealth." People of great wealth, advocates of this idea argued, had not only great power but great responsibilities. It was their duty to use their riches to advance social progress. Andrew Carnegie elaborated on the

Gospel of Wealth

creed in his 1901 book, *The Gospel of Wealth*, in which he wrote that people of wealth should consider all revenues in excess of their own needs "trust funds" to be used for the good of the community. Carnegie was only one of many great industrialists who devoted large parts of their fortunes to philanthropic works.

The notion of private wealth as a public blessing existed alongside another popular concept: the notion of great wealth as something available to all. Russell H. Conwell, a Baptist minister, became the most prominent spokesman for the idea by delivering one lecture, "Acres of Diamonds," more than 6,000 times between 1880 and 1900. Conwell told a series of stories, which he claimed were true, of individuals who had found opportunities for extraordinary wealth in their own backyards. (One such story involved a modest farmer who discovered a vast diamond mine in his own fields in the course of working his land.) Most of the millionaires in the country, Conwell claimed (inaccurately), had begun on the lowest rung of the economic ladder and had worked their way to success.

Horatio Alger

Horatio Alger was the most famous promoter of the success story. Alger was originally a minister in a small town in Massachusetts but was driven from his pulpit as a result of a scandal connected to his active, but usually hidden, homosexuality. He moved to New York, where he wrote his celebrated novels: *Ragged Dick*, *Tom the Bootblack*, *Sink or Swim*, and many others, more than 100 in all. The basic story was almost always the same: A young boy, perhaps an orphan, makes his perilous way through life on the rough streets of the city

A NEWSBOY'S STORY Alger's novels were even more popular after his death in 1899 than they had been in his lifetime. This reprint of one of his many "rags-to-riches" stories—about a New York newsboy's rise to wealth and success—was typical of his work. *(Private Collection)*

by selling newspapers or peddling matches. One day, his energy and determination catches the eye of a wealthy man, who gives him a chance to improve himself. Through honesty, charm, hard work, and aggressiveness, the boy rises in the world to become a successful man.

The purpose of writing, Alger claimed, was twofold. He wanted to "exert a salutary influence upon the class of whom [I] was writing, by setting before them inspiring examples of what energy, ambition, and an honest purpose may achieve." He also wanted to show his largely middle-class readers "the life and experiences of the friendless and vagrant children to be found in all our cities."

But Alger's intentions probably had little to do with the success of his books. Most Americans of the late nineteenth and early twentieth centuries were attracted to Alger because his stories helped them to believe that it is possible for individuals to rise in the world with willpower and hard work, that anyone can become a "self-made man." Alger's admirers came to ignore his own misgivings about industrialism and to portray his books purely as a celebration of (and justification for) laissez-faire capitalism and the accumulation of wealth.

Alternative Visions

Alongside the celebrations of competition and the justifications for great wealth stood a group of alternative philosophies, challenging the corporate ethos and at times capitalism itself.

One such philosophy emerged in the work of the sociologist Lester Frank Ward. In *Dynamic Sociology* (1883) and other books, he argued that civilization was not governed by natural selection but by human intelligence, which was capable of shaping society as it wished. In contrast to Sumner, who believed that state intervention to remodel the environment was futile, Ward thought that an active government engaged in positive planning was society's best hope.

Socialist Labor Party

Other Americans adopted more radical approaches to reform. Some dissenters found a home in the Socialist Labor Party, founded in the 1870s and led for many years by Daniel De Leon, an immigrant from the West Indies. Although De Leon attracted a modest following in the industrial cities, the party never became a major political force and never polled more than 82,000 votes. A dissident faction of De Leon's party, eager to forge stronger ties with organized labor, broke away and in 1901 formed the more enduring American Socialist Party.

Henry George's "Single Tax"

Other radicals gained a wider following. Among them was the California writer and activist Henry George. His angrily eloquent *Progress and Poverty*, published in 1879, became one of the best-selling nonfiction works in American publishing history. George blamed social problems on the ability of a few monopolists to grow wealthy as a result of rising land values. An increase in the value of land, he claimed, was not a result of any effort by the owner. It was an "unearned increment," produced by the growth of society around the land. Such profits were rightfully the property of the community. And so George proposed a "single tax" on land, to replace all other taxes, which would return the increment to the people. The tax, he argued, would destroy monopolies, distribute wealth more equally, and eliminate poverty.

Rivaling George in popularity was Edward Bellamy, whose utopian novel *Looking Backward*, published in 1888, sold more than 1 million copies. It described the experiences of a young Bostonian who went into a hypnotic sleep in 1887 and awoke in the year 2000 to find a new social order in which want, politics, and vice were unknown. The new society had emerged through a peaceful, evolutionary process: the large trusts of the late nineteenth century had continued to grow in size and to combine with one another until ultimately they formed a single, great trust, controlled by the government, which distributed the abundance of the industrial economy equally among all the people. "Fraternal cooperation" had replaced competition. Class divisions had disappeared. Bellamy labeled the philosophy behind this vision "nationalism."

"MODERN COLOSSUS OF (RAIL) ROADS" Cornelius Vanderbilt, known as the "Commodore," accumulated one of America's great fortunes by consolidating several large railroad companies under his control in the 1860s. His name became a synonym not only for enormous wealth, but also (in the eyes of many Americans) for excessive corporate power—as suggested in this cartoon, showing him standing astride his empire and manipulating its parts. *(Culver Pictures, Inc.)*

The Problems of Monopoly

Economic Concentration Challenged

Relatively few Americans shared the views of those who questioned capitalism itself. But as time went on, a growing number of people were becoming deeply concerned about the growth of monopoly.

By the end of the century, a wide range of groups had begun to assail monopoly and economic concentration. They blamed monopoly for creating artificially high prices. In the absence of competition, they argued, monopolistic industries could charge whatever prices they wished; railroads, in particular, charged very high rates along some routes because, in the absence of competition, they knew their customers had no choice but to pay them. Artificially high prices, moreover, contributed to the economy's instability, as production consistently outpaced demand. Beginning in 1873, the economy fluctuated erratically, producing severe recessions every five or six years, each worse than the last.

THE ORDEAL OF THE WORKER

Most workers in the late nineteenth century experienced a real rise in their standard of living. But they did so at the cost of arduous and often dangerous working conditions, diminishing control over their own work, and a growing sense of powerlessness.

The Immigrant Work Force

The industrial work force expanded dramatically in the late nineteenth century. The source of that expansion was a massive migration into industrial cities—immigration of two sorts. The first was the continuing flow of rural Americans into factory towns and cities—people disillusioned with or bankrupted by life on the farm. The second was the great wave of immigration from abroad (primarily from Europe, but also from Asia, Canada, Mexico, and other areas) in the decades following the Civil War—an influx greater than that of any previous era. The 25 million immigrants who arrived in the United States between 1865 and 1915 were more than four times the number who had arrived in the previous fifty years.

Rapidly Expanding Working Class

In the 1870s and 1880s, most of the immigrants came from England, Ireland, and northern Europe. By the end of the century, however, the major sources of immigrants had shifted, with large numbers of southern and eastern Europeans (Italians, Poles, Russians, Greeks, Slavs, and others) moving into the country and into the industrial work force.

The new immigrants were coming to America in part to escape poverty and oppression in their homelands. But they were also lured by expectations of new opportunities. Railroads tried to lure immigrants into their western landholdings by distributing misleading advertisements overseas. Industrial employers actively recruited immigrant workers under the Labor Contract Law, which—until its repeal in 1885—permitted them to pay for the passage of workers in advance and deduct the amount later from their wages. Even after the repeal of the law, employers continued to encourage the immigration of unskilled laborers,

Labor Contract Law

often with the assistance of foreign-born labor brokers, such as the Greek and Italian *padrones*, who recruited work gangs of their fellow nationals.

Growing Ethnic Tensions

The arrival of these new groups introduced heightened ethnic tensions into the dynamics of the working class. Low-paid Poles, Greeks, and French Canadians began to displace higher-paid British and Irish workers in the textile factories of New England. Italians, Slavs, and Poles emerged as a major source of labor for the mining industry. Chinese and Mexicans competed with Anglo-Americans and African Americans in mining, farmwork, and factory labor in California, Colorado, and Texas.

Wages and Working Conditions

At the turn of the century, the average income of the American worker was $400 to $500 a year—below the $600 figure that many believed was the minimum required to maintain a reasonable level of comfort. Nor did workers have much job security. All were vulnerable to the boom-and-bust cycle of the industrial economy, and some lost their jobs because of technological advances. Even those who kept their jobs could find their wages suddenly and substantially cut in hard times. Few workers, in other words, were ever very far from poverty.

Harsh Work Conditions

American laborers faced a wide array of other hardships as well. For first-generation workers accustomed to the patterns of agrarian life, there was a difficult adjustment to the nature of modern industrial labor: the performance of routine, repetitive tasks on a strict and monotonous schedule. To skilled artisans whose once-valued tasks were now performed by machines, the new system was impersonal and demeaning. Most factory laborers worked ten-hour days, six days a week; in the steel industry they worked twelve hours a day. Industrial accidents were frequent.

The decreasing need for skilled work in factories induced many employers to increase the use of women and children, whom they could hire for lower wages than adult males. By 1900, 20 percent of all manufacturing workers were women. Women worked in all areas of industry, even in some of the most arduous jobs. Most women, however, worked in a few industries where unskilled and semiskilled machine labor (as opposed to heavy manual labor) prevailed. The textile industry remained the largest single industrial employer of women. (Domestic service remained the most common female occupation overall.) Women worked for wages well below the minimum necessary for survival (and well below the wages paid to men working the same jobs).

Child Labor

At least 1.7 million children under sixteen years of age were employed in factories and fields; 10 percent of all girls aged ten to fifteen, and 20 percent of all boys, held jobs. Under public pressure, thirty-eight states passed child labor laws in the

SPINDLE BOYS Young boys, some of them barefoot, clamber along the great textile machines in a Georgia cotton mill adjusting spindles. Many of them were the children of women who worked in the plants. The photograph is by Lewis Hine. *(Bettmann/Corbis)*

late nineteenth century. But 60 percent of child workers were employed in agriculture, which was typically exempt from the laws. And even for children employed in factories, the laws merely set a minimum age of twelve years and a maximum workday of ten hours, standards that employers often ignored in any case.

Emerging Unionization

Laborers attempted to fight back against such conditions by creating national unions. By the end of the century, however, their efforts had met with little success.

There had been craft unions in America, representing small groups of skilled workers, since well before the Civil War. Alone, however, individual unions could not hope to exert significant power in the economy. And during the turbulent recession years of the 1870s, unions faced the additional problem of widespread public hostility. When labor disputes with employers turned bitter and violent, as they occasionally did, much of the public instinctively blamed the workers for the trouble, rarely the employers. Particularly alarming to middle-class Americans was the emergence of the "Molly Maguires"

"Molly Maguires"

in the anthracite coal region of western Pennsylvania. This militant labor organization sometimes used violence and even murder in its battle with coal operators. Much of the violence attributed to the Molly Maguires, however, was deliberately instigated by informers and agents employed by the mine owners, who wanted a pretext for ruthless measures to suppress unionization.

Railroad Strike of 1877

Excitement over the Molly Maguires paled beside the near hysteria that gripped the country during the railroad strike of 1877, which began when the eastern railroads announced a 10 percent wage cut. The strike soon expanded into something approaching a class war. Strikers disrupted rail service from Baltimore to St. Louis, destroyed equipment, and rioted in the streets of Pittsburgh and other cities. State militias were called out, and in July President Hayes ordered federal troops to suppress the disorders in West Virginia. In Baltimore, eleven demonstrators died and forty were wounded in a conflict between workers and militiamen. In Philadelphia, the state militia killed twenty people when the troops opened fire on thousands of workers and their families who were attempting to block the railroad crossings. In all, over 100 people died before the strike finally collapsed several weeks after it had begun. The great railroad strike was America's first major, national labor conflict.

The Knights of Labor

The first major effort to create a genuinely national labor organization was the founding in 1869 of the Noble Order of the Knights of Labor, under the leadership of Uriah S. Stephens. Membership was open to all who "toiled," a definition that included all workers, most business and professional people, and virtually all women—whether they worked in factories, as domestic servants, or in their own homes. The only excluded groups were lawyers, bankers, liquor dealers, and professional gamblers. The Knights of Labor championed an eight-hour workday and the abolition of child labor, but they were more interested in long-range reform of the economy. The Knights hoped to replace the "wage system" with a new "cooperative system," in which workers would themselves control a large part of the economy.

Terence V. Powderly

For several years, the Knights remained a secret fraternal organization. But in the late 1870s, under the leadership of Terence V. Powderly, the order moved into the open and entered a period of spectacular expansion. By 1886, it claimed a total membership of over 700,000. Local unions or assemblies associated with the Knights launched a series of railroad and other strikes in the 1880s in defiance of Powderly's wishes. Their failure helped discredit the organization. By 1890, the membership of the Knights had shrunk to 100,000. A few years later, the organization disappeared altogether.

The AFL

Even before the Knights began to decline, a rival association appeared. In 1881, representatives of a number of craft unions formed the Federation of Organized Trade and Labor Unions of the United States and Canada. Five years later, this body took the name it has borne ever since, the American Federation of Labor (AFL).

Rejecting the Knights' idea of one big union for everybody, the Federation was an association of essentially autonomous craft unions that represented mainly skilled workers. Samuel Gompers, the powerful leader of the AFL, concentrated on labor's immediate objectives: wages, hours, and working conditions. As one of its first objectives, the AFL demanded a national eight-hour workday and called for a general strike if the goal was not achieved by May 1, 1886. On that day, strikes and demonstrations for a shorter workday took place all over the country.

Samuel Gompers

In Chicago, a center of labor and radical strength, a strike was already in progress at the McCormick Harvester Company. City police had been harassing the strikers, and labor and radical leaders called a protest meeting at Haymarket Square on May 1. When the police ordered the crowd to disperse, someone threw a bomb that killed seven policemen and injured sixty-seven others. The police, who had killed four strikers the day before, fired into the crowd and killed four more people. Conservative, property-conscious Americans—frightened and outraged—demanded retribution. Chicago officials finally rounded up eight anarchists and charged them with murder, on the grounds that their statements had incited whoever had hurled the bomb. All eight scapegoats were found guilty after a remarkably injudicious trial. Seven were sentenced to death. One of them committed suicide, four were executed, and two had their sentences commuted to life imprisonment.

Haymarket Bombing

To most middle-class Americans, the Haymarket bombing was an alarming symbol of social chaos and radicalism. "Anarchism" now became in the public mind a code word for terrorism and violence, even though most anarchists were relatively peaceful. For the next thirty years, the specter of anarchism remained one of the most frightening concepts in the American imagination. It was a constant obstacle to the goals of the AFL and other labor organizations, and it did particular damage to the Knights of Labor. However much they tried to distance themselves from radicals, labor leaders were always vulnerable to accusations of anarchism, as the violent strikes of the 1890s occasionally illustrated.

Labor Discredited

The Homestead Strike

The Amalgamated Association of Iron and Steel Workers was the most powerful trade union in the country. Its members were skilled workers, in great demand by employers, and thus had long been able to exercise significant power in the workplace. In the mid-1880s, however, demand for skilled workers was in decline as new production methods changed the steelmaking process. In the Carnegie system, which was coming to dominate the steel industry, the union was able to maintain a foothold in only one of the corporation's three major factories—the Homestead plant near Pittsburgh.

Henry Clay Frick

By 1890, Carnegie and his chief lieutenant, Henry Clay Frick, had decided that the Amalgamated "had to go." Over the next two years, they repeatedly cut wages at Homestead. At first, the union acquiesced, aware that it was not strong enough to wage a successful strike. But in 1892, when the company stopped even discussing its decisions with the union and gave it two days to accept another wage cut, the Amalgamated called for a strike.

Frick abruptly shut down the plant and called in 300 guards from the Pinkerton Detective Agency to enable the company to hire nonunion workers. The hated Pinkertons were well-known strikebreakers. They approached the plant by river, on barges, on July 6, 1892. The strikers poured gasoline on the water, set it on fire, and then met the Pinkertons at the docks with guns and dynamite. A pitched battle broke out. After several hours of fighting, which killed three guards and ten strikers and injured many others, the Pinkertons surrendered and were escorted roughly out of town.

Government Intervention

But the workers' victory was temporary. The governor of Pennsylvania, at the company's request, sent the state's entire National Guard contingent, some 8,000 men, to Homestead. Production resumed, with strikebreakers now protected by troops. And public opinion turned against the strikers when a radical made an attempt to assassinate Frick. Slowly, workers drifted back to their jobs, and finally—four months after the strike began—the Amalgamated surrendered. By 1900, every major steel plant in the Northeast had broken with the Amalgamated. Its membership shrank from a high of 24,000 in 1891 (two-thirds of all eligible steelworkers) to fewer than 7,000 a decade later.

The Pullman Strike

A dispute of greater magnitude, if less violence, was the Pullman strike in 1894. The Pullman Palace Car Company manufactured railroad sleeping and parlor cars, which it built and repaired at a plant near Chicago. There the company constructed a 600-acre town, Pullman, and rented its trim, orderly houses to the employees. George M. Pullman, owner of the company, saw the town as a model—a solution to the problems of industrial workers. But many residents chafed at the regimentation (and the high rents). In the winter of 1893–1894, the Pullman Company slashed wages by about 25 percent, citing its own declining revenues in the depression, without reducing the rent it charged its employees. Workers went on

BREAKING THE PULLMAN STRIKE Company C of the 15th United States Infantry, called into service by President Grover Cleveland to break a widespread railroad strike in 1894, poses here before a special patrol train near Rock Island, Illinois. The strike began when workers at the Pullman Palace Car Company outside Chicago walked off the job to protest wage cuts and rent increases. Their walkout generated broad support from other railroad workers and even from the governor of Illinois, John Peter Altgeld, who refused to call out the state militia to keep the trains running. Cleveland, however, had little sympathy for striking workers and he used his authority as president to protect the delivery of the mails to call out federal troops to break the strike. *(Bettmann/Corbis)*

American Railway Union

strike and persuaded the militant American Railway Union, led by Eugene V. Debs, to support them by refusing to handle Pullman cars and equipment. Within a few days thousands of railroad workers in twenty-seven states and territories were on strike, and transportation from Chicago to the Pacific coast was paralyzed.

Unlike most elected politicians, the governor of Illinois, John Peter Altgeld, was a man with demonstrated sympathies for workers and their grievances. He refused to call out the militia to protect employers. Bypassing Altgeld, railroad operators asked the federal government to send regular army troops to Illinois, using the pretext that the strike was preventing the movement of mail on the trains. In July 1894, President Grover Cleveland ordered 2,000 troops to the Chicago area. A federal court issued an injunction forbidding the union to continue the strike. When Debs and his associates defied it, they were arrested and imprisoned. With federal troops protecting the hiring of new workers and with the union leaders in a federal jail, the strike quickly collapsed.

Sources of Labor Weakness

The last decades of the nineteenth century were years in which labor, despite militant organizing efforts, made few real gains. Industrial wages rose hardly at all. Labor leaders won a few legislative victories—the abolition of the Contract Labor Law, the establishment of an eight-hour day for government employees, compensation for some workers injured on the job, and others. But many such laws were not enforced. There were widespread strikes and protests, and many other working-class forms of resistance, large and small, but few real gains. The end of the century found most workers with less political power and less control of the workplace than they had had forty years before.

Few Gains for Labor

Workers failed to make greater gains for many reasons. The principal labor organizations represented only a small percentage of the industrial work force; the AFL, the most important, excluded unskilled workers, and along with them most women, blacks, and recent immigrants. Divisions within the work force contributed further to union weakness. Tensions among different ethnic and racial groups kept laborers divided.

Another source of labor weakness was the shifting nature of the work force. Many immigrant workers came to America intending to earn some money and then return home. The assumption that they had no long-range future in the country eroded their willingness to organize. Other workers were in constant motion, moving from one job to another, one town to another, seldom in a single place long enough to establish any institutional ties or exert any real power.

Sources of Labor Weakness

Above all, perhaps, workers made few gains in the late nineteenth century because they faced corporate organizations of vast wealth and power, which were generally determined to crush any efforts by workers to challenge their prerogatives. And as the Homestead and Pullman strikes suggest, the corporations usually had the support of local, state, and federal authorities, who were willing to send in troops to "preserve order" and crush labor uprisings on demand.

Despite the creation of new labor unions, despite a wave of strikes and protests, workers in the late nineteenth century failed on the whole to create successful organizations or to protect their interests. In the battle for power within the emerging industrial economy, almost all the advantages seemed to lie with capital.

Capital's Strength

CONCLUSION

In the four decades following the end of the Civil War, the United States propelled itself into the forefront of the industrializing nations of the world. Large areas of the nation remained overwhelmingly rural, to be sure. But even so, America's economy, and along with it the nation's society and culture, was being profoundly transformed.

New technologies, new forms of corporate management, and new supplies of labor helped make possible the rapid growth of the nation's industries and the construction of its railroads. The factory system contributed to the growth of the nation's cities. Immigration provided a steady supply of new workers for the growing industrial economy. The result was a steady increase in national wealth, rising living standards for much of the population, and the creation of great new fortunes.

But industrialization did not spread its fruits evenly. Large areas of the country, most notably the South, and large groups in the population, most notably minorities, women, and recent immigrants, profited relatively little from economic growth. Industrial workers experienced arduous conditions of labor. Small merchants and manufacturers found themselves overmatched by great new combinations.

Industrialists strove to create a rationale for their power and to persuade the public that everyone had something to gain from it. But many Americans remained skeptical of modern capitalism, and some—workers struggling to form unions, reformers denouncing trusts, socialists envisioning a new world, and many others—created broad and powerful critiques of the new economic order. Industrialization brought both progress and pain to late-nineteenth-century America. Controversies over its effects defined the era and would continue to define the first decades of the twentieth century.

FOR FURTHER REFERENCE

Robert Wiebe's *The Search for Order, 1877–1920* (1968) is a classic analysis of America's evolution from a society of island communities to a national urban society. Alfred D. Chandler, Jr., describes the new business practices that made industrialization possible in *The Visible Hand: The Managerial Revolution in American Business* (1977) and *Scale and Scope: The Dynamics of Industrial Capitalism* (1990). Olivier Zunz offers a provocative analysis of the social underpinnings of the new corporate order in *Making America Corporate, 1870–1920* (1990) and *Why the American Century?* (1998). David F. Noble, *America by Design: Science, Technology, and the Rise of Corporate Capitalism* (1977) and David Hounshell, *From the American System to Mass Production, 1800–1932* (1984) discuss the explosion of science and technology in the era of rapid industrialization. Daniel Rodgers, *The Work Ethic in Industrial America, 1850–1920* (1978) is an important intellectual history of the way Americans viewed industrial workers. David Montgomery, *The Fall of the House of Labor: The Workplace, the State, and American Labor Activism, 1865–1925* (1987) analyzes the way industrialization shaped (and was shaped by) the workers, their expertise, and the strong cultural traditions of the shop floor. Kevin Kenny, *Making Sense of the Molly Maguires* (1998) examines labor radicalism and Elliott J. Gorn, *Mother Jones: The Most Dangerous Woman in America* (2001) explores the career of a celebrated labor firebrand. Alice Kessler-Harris documents the tremendous movement of women into the work force in this period in *Out to Work: A History of Wage-Earning Women in the United States* (1982). John L. Thomas, *Alternative America: Henry George, Edward Bellamy, Henry Demarest Lloyd, and the Adversary Tradition* (1983) examines some important critics of corporate capitalism.

For quizzes, Internet resources, references to additional books and films, and more, consult this book's Online Learning Center site at www.mhhe.com/unfinishednation4.

MILWAUKEE, 1900 In the middle years of the nineteenth century, Americans were dazzled by large paintings of the dramatic landscape of the Far West. By the beginning of the twentieth century, they were at least as interested in the new landscape of the city—with its tall buildings, its new technologies, and its dramatic design. This painted photograph of downtown Milwaukee is typical of many images of American city centers in this period, with its focus on a particularly dramatic large building and its presentation of such urban wonders as streetcars and electrical wires. Such images were often reproduced on postcards. *(Photo by William Henry Jackson/Detroit Publishing Company. Reproduced by permission of Christopher Cardozo, Inc.)*

TIME LINE

1869	1870	1871	1872	1876	1882	1884	1890
First intercollegiate football game	NYC opens first elevated railroads	Boston and Chicago fires	Boss Tweed convicted	Baseball's National League founded	Congress restricts Chinese immigration	First "skyscraper" in Chicago	Riis's *How the Other Half Lives*

CHAPTER EIGHTEEN

THE AGE OF THE CITY

The New Urban Growth
The Urban Landscape
Strains of Urban Life
The Rise of Mass Consumption
Leisure in the Consumer Society
High Culture in the Urban Age

The face of American society changed in countless ways in response to the growth of industry and commerce. No change was more profound, however, than the growing size and influence of cities. Having begun its life as a primarily agrarian republic, the United States in the late nineteenth century was becoming an urban nation.

THE NEW URBAN GROWTH

The great movement of people from the countryside to the city was not unique to the United States. But Americans found urbanization particularly jarring. The urban population increased sevenfold in the half-century after the Civil War. And in 1920, the census revealed that for the first time, a majority of the American people lived in "urban" areas—defined as communities of 2,500 people or more.

Natural increase accounted for only a small part of the urban growth. Urban families experienced a high rate of infant mortality, a declining fertility rate, and a high death rate from disease. Without immigration, cities would have grown relatively slowly.

1891	1894	1895	1897	1901	1903	1906	1910
Basketball invented	Immigration Restriction League formed	Crane's *The Red Badge of Courage*	Boston opens first subway in America	Baseball's American League founded	First World Series	San Francisco earthquake and fire Sinclair's *The Jungle*	NCAA founded

The Migrations

The late nineteenth century was an age of unprecedented geographical mobility, as Americans left the declining agricultural regions of the East at a dramatic rate. Some of those who left were moving to the newly developing farmlands of the West. But almost as many were moving to the cities of the East and the Midwest.

Unprecedented Geographical Mobility

Among those leaving rural America for industrial cities in the 1880s were southern blacks. They were escaping the poverty, debt, violence, and oppression they faced in the rural South. They were also seeking new opportunities in cities. Factory jobs for blacks were rare and professional opportunities almost nonexistent. Urban blacks tended to work as cooks, janitors, and domestic servants, as well as in other service occupations. Because many such jobs were considered women's work, black women often outnumbered black men in the cities.

The most important source of urban population growth in the late nineteenth century, however, was the arrival of great numbers of new immigrants from abroad. Some came from Canada, Latin America, and—particularly on the West Coast—China and Japan. But the greatest number came from Europe. After 1880, the flow of new arrivals began to include large numbers of people from southern and eastern Europe. By the 1890s, more than half of all immigrants came from these regions.

Southern and Eastern European Immigrants

In earlier years, most new immigrants from Europe (particularly Germans and Scandinavians) had arrived with at least some money and education. Most of them arrived at one of the major port cities on the Atlantic coast (the greatest number in New York, through the famous immigrant depot on Ellis Island) and then headed west. But the new immigrants of the late nineteenth century generally lacked the capital to buy farmland and lacked the education to establish themselves in professions. So, like similarly poor Irish immigrants before the Civil War, they settled overwhelmingly in industrial cities, where they worked largely in unskilled jobs.

The Ethnic City

By 1890, most of the population of the major urban areas consisted of immigrants: 87 percent of the population in Chicago, 80 percent in New York, 84 percent in Milwaukee and Detroit. Equally striking was the diversity of the new immigrant populations. In other countries experiencing heavy immigration in this period, most of the new arrivals were coming from one or two sources. But in the United States, no single national group dominated.

Diverse Immigrant Populations

Most of the new immigrants were rural people, and for many the adjustment to city life was painful. To help ease the transition, some national groups formed close-knit ethnic communities within the cities, neighbor-

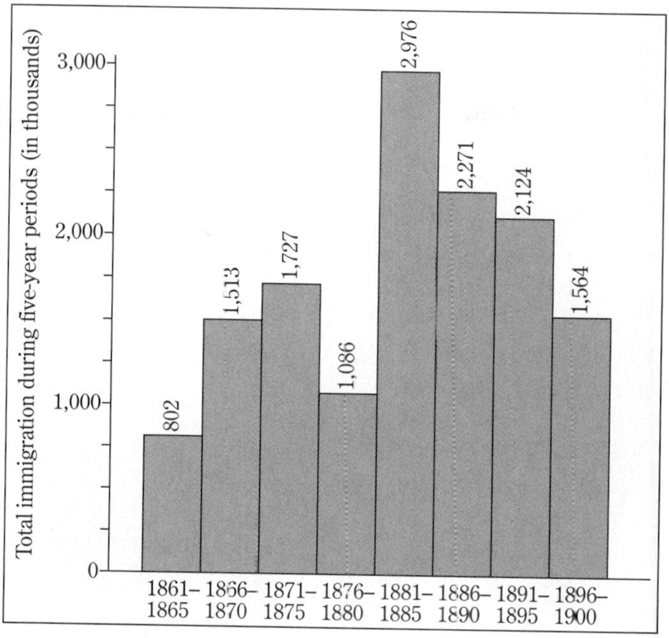

TOTAL IMMIGRATION, 1860–1900 Over 10 million immigrants from abroad entered the United States in the last forty years of the nineteenth century, with particularly high numbers arriving in the 1880s and 1890s. This chart shows the pattern of immigration in five-year intervals. ◆ *What external events might help explain some of the rises and falls in the rates of immigration in these years?*

hoods often called "immigrant ghettoes." Ethnic neighborhoods offered newcomers much that was familiar. They could find newspapers and theaters in their native languages, stores selling their native foods, and church and fraternal organizations that provided links with their national pasts. Many immigrants also maintained close ties with their native countries. They stayed in touch with relatives who had remained behind. Some (perhaps as many as a third in the early years) returned to their homelands after a relatively short time; others helped bring the rest of their families to America.

The cultural cohesiveness of the ethnic communities clearly eased the pain of separation from the immigrants' native lands. What role it played in helping immigrants become absorbed into the economic life of America is a more difficult question to answer. Some ethnic groups (Jews and Germans in particular) advanced economically more rapidly than others (for example, the Irish). One explanation is that, by huddling together in ethnic neighborhoods, immigrant groups tended to reinforce the cultural values of their previous societies. When those values were particularly well suited to economic advancement, as was—for example, the high value Jews placed on education—ethnic identification may have helped members of a group to improve their lots. When other values predominated—maintaining community solidarity, strengthening family ties, preserving order—progress could be less rapid.

Importance of Ethnic Ties

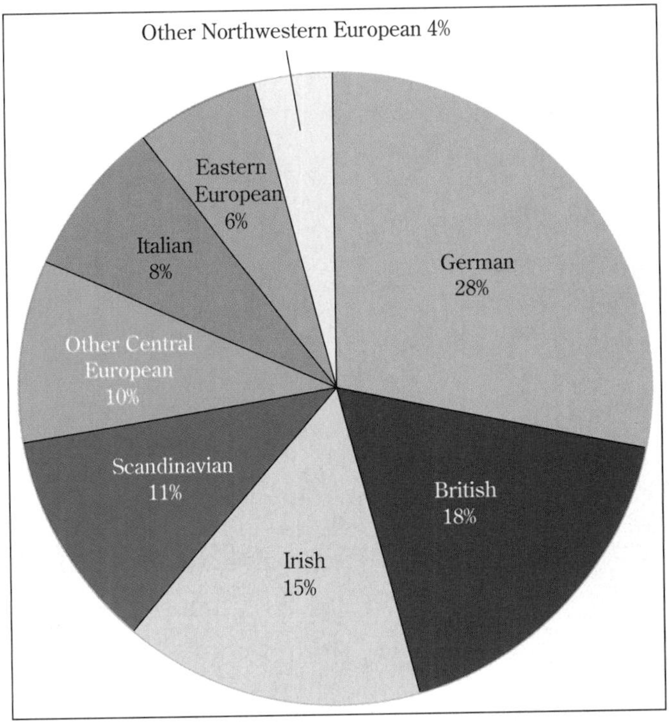

SOURCES OF IMMIGRATION FROM EUROPE, 1860–1900 This pie-chart shows the sources of European immigration in the late nineteenth century. The largest number of immigrants continued to come from traditional sources (Britain, Ireland, Germany, Scandinavia), but the beginnings of what in the early twentieth century would become a major influx of immigrants from new sources—southern and eastern Europe in particular—are already visible here. Immigration from other sources—Mexico, South and Central America, and Asia—was also significant during this period. ◆ *Why would these newer sources of European and other kinds of immigration create controversy among older-stock Americans?*

But other factors were at least as important in determining how well immigrants fared. Immigrants who aroused strong racial prejudice among native-born whites found it very difficult to advance whatever their talents. Those white immigrants who arrived with a valuable skill or with some capital did better than those who did not. And over time, those who lived in cities where people of their own nationality came to predominate—for example, the Irish in New York and Boston, or the Germans in Milwaukee—gained an advantage as they learned to exert their political power.

Assimilation and Exclusion

Despite the many differences among the various immigrant communities, virtually all groups had certain things in common. Most immigrants shared the experience of living in cities. Most were young; the majority of newcomers were between fifteen and forty-five years old. And in most communities of the foreign-born, the strength of ethnic ties had to compete against another powerful force: the desire for assimilation.

Many of the new arrivals had come to America with romantic visions of the New World. And however disillusioning they might find their first contact with the United States, they usually retained the dream of becoming true "Americans." Second-generation immigrants were particularly likely to attempt to break with the old ways. Young women, in particular, sometimes rebelled against parents who tried to arrange (or prevent) marriages or who opposed women entering the workplace.

Assimilation Encouraged

Native-born Americans encouraged immigrants to assimilate in countless ways. Public schools taught children in English, and employers often insisted that workers speak English on the job. Most non-ethnic stores sold mainly American products, forcing immigrants to adapt their diets, clothing, and lifestyles to American norms. Church leaders were often native-born Americans or more assimilated immigrants who encouraged their parishioners to adopt American ways. Some even embraced reforms to make their religion more compatible with the norms of the new country. Reform Judaism, imported from Germany in the late nineteenth century, was an effort by American Jewish leaders (as it had been by German ones) to make their faith less "foreign" to the dominant culture.

The arrival of these vast numbers of new immigrants, and the way many of them clung to old ways and created distinctive communities, provoked fear and resentment among some native-born Americans in much the same way earlier arrivals had done. The rising nativism provoked political responses. In 1887, Henry Bowers, a self-educated lawyer, founded the American Protective Association, a group committed to stopping immigration. By 1894, membership in the organization reportedly reached 500,000, with chapters throughout the Northeast and Midwest. That same year, five Harvard alumni founded a more genteel organization—the Immigration Restriction League—in Boston. They proposed screening immigrants through literacy tests and other standards, to separate the "desirable" from the "undesirable."

Immigration Restriction League

The government responded to popular concern about immigration even earlier. In 1882 Congress excluded the Chinese, denied entry to "undesirables"—convicts, paupers, the mentally incompetent—and placed a tax of 50 cents on each person admitted. Later legislation of the 1890s enlarged the list of those barred from immigrating.

But these laws kept out only a small number of aliens, and more ambitious restriction proposals made little progress in Congress. That was because immigration was providing a cheap and plentiful labor supply to the rapidly growing economy, and many argued that America's industrial (and indeed agricultural) development would be impossible without it.

Cheap Immigrant Labor

America in the World

GLOBAL MIGRATIONS

The great waves of immigration that transformed American society in the nineteenth and early twentieth centuries were not unique to the United States. They were part of a great, global movement of peoples—unprecedented in history—that affected every continent. These great migrations were the product of two related forces: population growth and industrialization.

The population of Europe grew faster in the second half of the nineteenth century than it had ever grown before and than it has ever grown since—almost doubling between 1850 and the beginning of World War I. The population growth was a result of growing economies able to support more people and of more efficient and productive agriculture that helped end debilitating famines. But the rapid growth nevertheless strained the resources of many parts of Europe and affected, in particular, rural people, who were now too numerous to live off the available land. Many decided to move to other parts of the world where land was more plentiful.

At the same time, industrialization drew millions of people out of the countryside and into cities—sometimes into cities in their own countries, but often to industrial cities in other, more economically advanced nations. Historians of migration speak of "push" factors (pressures on people to leave their homes) and "pull" factors (the lure of new lands) in explaining population movements. The "push" for many nineteenth-century migrants was poverty and inadequate land at home; for others it was political and religious oppression. The "pull" was the availability of land or industrial jobs in other regions or lands—and, for some, the prospect of greater freedom abroad. Faster, cheaper, and easier transportation—railroads and steamships, in particular—also aided large-scale immigration.

From 1800 to the start of World War I, fifty million Europeans migrated to new lands overseas—people from almost all areas of Europe, but in the later years of the century (when migration reached its peak) mostly from poor rural areas in southern and eastern Europe. Italy, Russia, and Poland were among the biggest sources of late-nineteenth-century migrants. Almost two thirds of these immigrants came to the United States. But nearly twenty million Europeans migrated to other lands. Migrants from England and Ireland (among others) moved in large numbers to those areas of the British empire with vast, seemingly open lands: Canada, Australia, New Zealand, and South Africa. Large numbers of Italians moved to Argentina and other parts of South America. Many of these migrants moved to open land in these countries; established themselves as farmers, using the new mechanical farming devices made possible by industrialization; and in many places—Australia, New Zealand, Argentina, South Africa, and the United States—evicted the native residents of their territories and created societies of their own. Many others settled in the industrial cities that were growing up in all these regions and formed distinctive ethnic and national communities within them.

But it was not only Europeans who were transplanting themselves in these years. Tremendous numbers of migrants—usually poor, desperate people—left Asia, Africa, and the Pacific Islands in search of better lives. Most of them could not afford the journey abroad on their own. They moved instead as indentured servants (in much the same way many English migrants moved to America in the seventeenth century), agreeing to a term of servitude in their new land in exchange for food, shelter, and transportation. Recruiters of indentured servants fanned out across China, Japan, areas of Africa and the Pacific Islands, and above all, India. French and British recruiters brought hundreds of thousands of Indian migrants to work in plantations in their own Asian and African colonies. Chinese laborers were recruited to work on plantations in Cuba and Hawaii, mines in Malaya, Peru, South Africa, and Australia, and railroad projects in Canada, Peru, and the United States. African indentured servants moved in large numbers to the Caribbean, and Pacific Islanders tended to move to other islands or to Australia.

The immigration of European peoples to new lands was largely voluntary and brought most migrants to the United States, where indentured servitude was illegal. But the migration of non-European peoples often involved an important element of coercion and brought relatively small numbers of people to the United States. This non-European migration was a function of the growth of European empires, and it was made possible by the imperial system—by its labor recruiters, by its naval resources, by its law, and by its economic needs. Together, these various forms of migration produced one of the greatest population movements in the history of the world and transformed not just the United States, but much of the globe.

(text continued from page 487)

THE URBAN LANDSCAPE

The city was a place of remarkable contrasts. It had homes of almost unimaginable size and grandeur and hovels of indescribable squalor. It had conveniences unknown to earlier generations and problems that seemed beyond the capacity of society to solve.

The Creation of Public Space

In the eighteenth and early nineteenth centuries, cities had generally grown up haphazardly. By the mid-nineteenth century, however, reformers, planners, architects, and others began to call for a more ordered vision of the city.

Among the most important innovations of the mid-nineteenth century were great city parks, which reflected the desire of a growing number of urban leaders to provide an antidote to the congestion of the city landscape. Parks, they argued, would allow city residents a healthy, restorative escape from the strains of urban life by reacquainting them with the natural world. The most successful promoters of this notion of the park as refuge were the landscape designers Frederick Law Olmsted and Calvert Vaux, who together in the late 1850s designed New York's Central Park. They deliberately created a public space that would look as little like the city as possible. Instead of the ordered, formal spaces common in some European cities, they created instead a space that seemed to be entirely natural. Central Park was from the start one of the most popular and admired public spaces in the world.

Central Park

At the same time that cities were creating great parks, they were also creating great public buildings: libraries, art galleries, natural history museums, theaters, concert and opera halls. New York's Metropolitan Museum of Art was only the largest and best known of many great museums taking shape in the late nineteenth century. In one city after another, new and lavish public libraries appeared as if to confirm the city's role as a center of learning and knowledge.

Wealthy residents of cities were the principal force behind the creation of the great art museums, concert halls, opera houses, and at times even parks. As their own material and social aspirations grew, they wanted the public life of the city to provide them with amenities to match their expectations. Becoming an important patron of a major cultural institution was an especially effective route to social distinction.

As both the size and the aspirations of the great cities increased, urban leaders launched monumental projects to remake the way their cities looked. Some cities began to clear away older neighborhoods and streets and create grand, monumental avenues lined with new and more impressive buildings. A particularly important event in inspiring this effort to remake the city was the 1893 Columbian Exposition in Chicago, a world's fair constructed to honor the 400th anniversary of Columbus's first voyage to America. At the center of the wildly popular exposition was a cluster of neoclassical buildings—the "Great White City"—arranged symmetrically around a formal lagoon. It became the inspiration for what became known as the "city beautiful" movement, led by the architect of the Great White City, Daniel Burnham. The movement strove to impose a similar order and symmetry on the disordered life of cities around the country. Only rarely, however, were planners able to overcome the obstacles of private landowners and complicated urban politics to realize more than a small portion of their dreams.

Daniel Burnham

The effort to remake the city did not focus only on redesigning the existing landscapes. It occasionally led to the creation of entirely new ones. In Boston in the late 1850s, a large area of marshy tidal land was gradually filled in to create the neighborhood known as "Back Bay." The landfill project was one of the largest public works projects ever undertaken in America to that point. But Boston was not alone. Chicago reclaimed large areas from Lake Michigan as it expanded and at one point raised the street level for the entire city to help avoid the problems the marshy land created. In New York and other cities, the response to limited space was not so much creating new land as annexing adjacent territory. A great wave of annexations expanded the boundaries of many American cities in the 1890s and beyond.

"Back Bay"

The Search for Housing

One of the greatest urban problems was providing housing for the thousands of new residents who were pouring into the cities every day. For the prosperous, housing was seldom a worry. The availability of cheap labor

A TENEMENT LAUNDRY Immigrant families living in tenements, in New York and in many other cities, earned their livelihoods as they could. This woman, shown here with her children, was typical of many working-class mothers who found income-producing activities they could pursue in the home (in this case laundry). The room, dominated by large vats and piles of other people's laundry, is also the family's home, as the crib and religious pictures make clear. *(Bettmann/Corbis)*

reduced the cost of building and permitted anyone with even a moderate income to afford a house. Some of the richest urban residents lived in palatial mansions located in exclusive neighborhoods in the heart of the city—Fifth Avenue in New York, Back Bay and Beacon Hill in Boston, Society Hill in Philadelphia, Lake Shore Drive in Chicago, Nob Hill in San Francisco, and many others.

Many of the moderately well-to-do took advantage of less expensive land on the edges of the city and settled in new suburbs, linked to the downtowns by trains or streetcars. Chicago in the 1870s, for example, connected nearly 100 residential suburbs to the downtown by railroad. Real estate developers worked to create and promote suburban communities that would appeal to the nostalgia for the countryside that many city dwellers felt. Affluent suburbs in particular were notable for lawns, trees, and houses designed to look manorial. Even more modest communities strove to emphasize the opportunities suburbs provided for owning land.

Railroad Suburbs

Most urban residents, however, could not afford either to own a house in the city or to move to the suburbs. Instead, they stayed in the city centers and rented. Landlords tried to squeeze as many rent-paying residents as possible into the smallest available space. In Manhattan, for example, the average population density in 1894 was 143 people per acre—a rate far higher than that of any other American or European city then or since. In the cities of the South—Charleston, New Orleans, Richmond—poor blacks lived in crumbling former slave quarters. In Boston, immigrants moved into cheap three-story wooden houses ("triple deckers"). In Baltimore and Philadelphia, the new arrivals crowded into narrow brick row houses. And in New York and many other cities, they lived in tenements.

Jacob Riis

The word "tenement" had originally referred simply to a multiple-family rental building, but by the late nineteenth century it had become a term for slum dwellings only. The first tenements, built in 1850, had been hailed as a great improvement in housing for the poor. But most were, in fact, miserable places, with many windowless rooms and little or no plumbing or heating. Jacob Riis, a Danish immigrant and New York newspaper reporter and photographer, shocked many middle-class Americans with his sensational (and some claimed sensationalized) descriptions and pictures of tenement life in his 1890 book, *How the Other Half Lives.* But the solution reformers often adopted was simply to raze slum dwellings without building any new housing to replace them.

Urban Technologies: Transportation and Construction

Urban growth posed monumental transportation challenges. The numbers of people who needed to move every day from one part of the city to another mandated the development of mass transportation. Streetcars drawn on tracks by horses had been introduced into some cities even before the Civil War. But the horsecars were not fast enough, so many communities developed new forms of mass transit. In 1870, New York opened its first elevated railway, whose noisy, steam-powered trains moved rapidly above the city streets on massive iron structures. New York, Chicago, San Francisco, and other cities also experimented with cable cars, towed by continuously moving underground cables. Richmond, Virginia, introduced the first electric trolley line in 1888, and in 1897 Boston opened the first American subway. At the same time, cities were developing new techniques of road and bridge building. One of the great technological marvels of the 1880s was the completion of the Brooklyn Bridge in New York—a dramatic steel-cable suspension span designed by John A. Roebling.

Skyscrapers

Cities were growing upward as well as outward. In Chicago, the construction in 1884 of the first modern "skyscraper"—by later standards a relatively modest building, ten stories high—launched a new era in urban architecture. Critical to the creation of the skyscraper was a new technology of construction, which emerged as a result of several related developments. One was the creation of new kinds of steel girders, capable of supporting much greater tension than the metals of the past. Still another was the invention and development of the passenger elevator. And another was the search for ways to protect cities from the ravages of great fires, which caused such terrible destruction in wood-frame cities of the late nineteenth century. Steel-frame construction was, among other things, a way to make cities more fireproof. Once the technology existed to permit the construction of tall buildings, there were few obstacles to building taller and taller structures. The early Chicago skyscrapers paved the way for some of the great construction marvels later in the twentieth century: the Chrysler Building and the Empire State Building in New York, the Lasalle Building in Chicago, and ultimately the vast numbers of steel and glass skyscrapers of the post-1945 cities of America and the world.

STRAINS OF URBAN LIFE

The increasing congestion of the city and the absence of adequate public services produced serious hazards. Crime, fire, disease, and indigence all placed strains on the capacities of metropolitan institutions, and both governments and private agencies were for a time poorly equipped to respond.

Fire and Disease

One serious problem was fire. In one major city after another, fires destroyed large downtown areas. Chicago and Boston suffered "great fires" in 1871. Other cities experienced similar disasters. The great fires were terrible experiences, but they were also important events in the development of the cities involved. They encouraged the construction of fireproof buildings and the development of professional fire departments. They also forced cities to rebuild at a time when new technological and architectural innovations were available. Some of the high-rise downtowns of American cities arose out of the rubble of great fires.

Inadequate Sanitation

An even greater hazard than fire was disease, especially in poor neighborhoods with inadequate sanitation facilities. But an epidemic that began in a poor neighborhood could (and often did) spread easily into other neighborhoods as well. Few municipal officials recognized the relationship of improper sewage disposal and water contamination to such epidemic diseases as typhoid fever and cholera; many cities lacked adequate systems for disposing of human waste until well into the twentieth century. Flush toilets and sewer systems began to appear in the 1870s, but they could not solve the problem as long as sewage continued to flow into open ditches or streams, polluting cities' water supplies.

Environmental Degradation

Modern notions of environmental science were unknown to most Americans in the late nineteenth and early twentieth centuries. But the environmental degradation of many American cities was a visible and disturbing fact of life in those years. The frequency of great fires, the dangers of disease and plague, the extraordinary crowding of working-class neighborhoods were all examples of the environmental costs of industrialization and rapid urbanization.

Improper disposal of human and industrial waste was a common feature of almost all large cities in these years. That contributed to the pollution of rivers and lakes, and also in many cases to the compromising of the city's drinking water. The presence of domestic animals—horses, which were the principal means of transportation until the late nineteenth century, but in poor neighborhoods also cows, pigs, and other animals—contributed as well to the environmental problems.

Air quality in many cities was poor as well. Few Americans had the severe problems that London experienced in these years with its perpetual "fogs" created by the debris from the burning of soft coal. But air pollution from factories and from stoves and furnaces in offices, homes, and other buildings was constant and at times severe. The incidence of respiratory infection and related diseases was much higher in cities than it was in rural areas, and it accelerated rapidly in the late nineteenth century.

Air Pollution

By the early twentieth century, reformers were actively crusading to improve the environmental conditions of cities and were beginning to achieve some notable successes. New sewage and drainage systems were created to protect drinking water from sewage disposal. By 1910, most large American cities had constructed sewage disposal systems, often at great cost, to protect the drinking water of their inhabitants and to prevent the great bacterial plagues that impure water had helped create in the past—such as the yellow fever epidemic in Memphis that killed 5,000 people.

In 1912, the federal government created the Public Health Service, which was charged with preventing such occupational diseases as tuberculosis and anemia and carbon dioxide poisoning, which were common in the garment industry and other trades. It attempted to create common health standards for all factories; but since the agency had few powers of enforcement, it had limited impact. The creation of the Occupational Health and Safety Administration in 1970, which gave government the authority to require employers to create safe and healthy workplaces, was a legacy of the Public Health Service's early work.

Public Health Service

Urban Poverty, Crime, and Violence

Above all, perhaps, the expansion of the city spawned widespread and often desperate poverty. Public agencies and private philanthropic organizations offered some relief. But they were generally poorly funded, and in any case dominated by middle-class people who believed that too much assistance would breed dependency. Most tried to restrict aid to the "deserving poor"—those who truly could not help themselves. Charitable organizations conducted elaborate "investigations" to separate the "deserving" from the "undeserving". Other charitable societies—for example, the Salvation Army, which began operating in America in 1879—concentrated more on religious revivalism than on the relief of the homeless and hungry.

Middle-class people grew particularly alarmed over the rising number of poor children in the cities, some of them orphans or runaways. These "street arabs," as they were often called, attracted more attention from reformers than any other group—although that attention produced no lasting solutions to their problems.

Poverty and crowding bred crime and violence. The American murder rate rose rapidly in the late nineteenth century, from 25 murders for every million people in 1880 to over 100 by the end of the century. That reflected in part a very high level of violence in some nonurban areas: the American South, where lynching and homicide were particularly high; and the West, where the rootlessness and instability of new communities (cow towns, mining camps, and the like) created much violence. But the cities contributed their share to the increase in crime as well. Native-born Americans liked to believe that crime was a result of the violent proclivities of immigrant groups, and they cited the rise of gangs and criminal organizations in various ethnic communities. But native-born Americans in the cities were as likely to commit crimes as immigrants. The rising crime rates encouraged many cities to develop larger and more professional police forces. But police forces themselves could spawn corruption and brutality, particularly since jobs on them were often filled through political patronage.

Growing Crime Rate

Some members of the middle class, fearful of urban insurrections, felt the need for even more substantial forms of protection. Urban national guard groups built imposing armories on the outskirts of affluent neighborhoods and stored large supplies of weapons and ammunition in preparation for uprisings that, in fact, virtually never occurred.

The city was a place of strong allure and great excitement. Yet it was also a place of alienating impersonality and, to some, a place of degradation and exploitation. Theodore Dreiser's novel *Sister Carrie* (1900) exposed one troubling aspect of urban life: the plight of single women (like Dreiser's heroine, Carrie) who moved from the countryside into the city and found themselves without any means of support. Carrie first took an exhausting and ill-paying job in a Chicago shoe factory; then she drifted into a life of "sin," exploited by predatory men.

Sister Carrie

The Machine and the Boss

Newly arrived immigrants were much in need of institutions to help them adjust to American urban life. For many residents of the inner cities, the principal source of assistance was the political "machine."

The urban machine owed its existence to the power vacuum that the chaotic growth of cities had created. It was also a product of the potential voting power of large immigrant communities. Out of that combination emerged the "urban" bosses. The principal function of the political boss was simple: to win votes for his organization. That meant winning the loyalty of his constituents. To do so, a boss might provide them with occasional relief—a basket of groceries or a bag of coal. He might step in to save those arrested for petty crimes from jail. When he could, he found work for the unemployed. Above all, he rewarded many of his followers with patronage: with jobs in city government or in such city agencies as the police (which the machine's elected officials often controlled); with jobs building or operating the new transit systems; and with opportunities to rise in the political organization itself.

Function of the "Urban" Boss

Machines were also vehicles for making money. Politicians enriched themselves and their allies through various forms of graft and corruption. A politician might discover in advance where a new road or streetcar line was to be built, buy land near it, and sell it at a profit when property values rose as a result of the construction. There was also covert graft. Officials received kickbacks from contractors in exchange for contracts to build public projects, and they sold franchises for the operation of public utilities. The most famously corrupt city boss was William M. Tweed, boss of New York City's Tammany Hall in the 1860s and 1870s, whose extravagant use of public funds on projects that paid kickbacks to the organization landed him in jail in 1872.

William M. Tweed

The urban machine was not without competition. Reform groups frequently mobilized public outrage at the corruption of the bosses and often succeeded in driving machine politicians from office. But the reform organizations typically lacked the permanence of the machine.

THE RISE OF MASS CONSUMPTION

In the last decades of the nineteenth century a distinctive middle-class culture began to exert a powerful influence over the whole of American life. Other groups in society advanced less rapidly, or not at all, but almost no one was unaffected by the rise of the new urban, consumer culture.

Patterns of Income and Consumption

Incomes were rising for almost everyone in the industrial era, although at highly uneven rates. The most conspicuous result of the new economy was the creation of vast fortunes, but perhaps the most important result for society as a whole was the growth and increasing prosperity of the middle class. The salaries of clerks, accountants, middle managers, and other "white-collar" workers rose by an average of a third between 1890 and 1910. Doctors, lawyers, and other professionals, for example, experienced a particularly dramatic increase in both the prestige and the profitability of their professions. Working-class incomes rose in those years as well, although from a much lower base and often more slowly. The iron and steel industries saw workers' hourly wages increase by a third between 1890 and 1910; but industries with large female work forces—shoes, textiles, and paper—saw more modest increases, as did almost all industries in the South. Wages for African Americans, Mexicans, and Asians also rose more slowly than those for other workers.

Rising Income

Rising incomes created new markets for consumer goods. Affordable products and new merchandising techniques soon made many consumer goods available to this mass market for the first time. A good example of such changes was the emergence of ready-made clothing. In the early nineteenth century, most Americans had made their own clothing. The invention of the sewing machine and the spur that the Civil War (and its demand for uniforms) gave to the manufacture of clothing helped create an enormous industry devoted to producing ready-made garments. By the end of the century, almost all Americans bought their clothing from stores. Partly as a result, much larger numbers of people became concerned with personal style. Interest in women's fashion, for example, had once been a luxury reserved for the relatively affluent. Now middle-class and even working-class women could strive to develop a distinctive style of dress.

Ready-made Clothing

Buying and preparing food also became a critical part of the new consumerism. The development and mass production of tin cans in the 1880s created a large new industry devoted to packaging and selling canned food and condensed milk. Refrigerated railroad cars made it possible for perishable foods to be transported over long distances without spoiling. Artificially frozen ice enabled many households to afford iceboxes. The changes brought improved diets and better health. Life expectancy rose six years in the first two decades of the twentieth century.

Chain Stores, Mail-Order Houses, and Department Stores

Changes in marketing also altered the way Americans bought goods. New "chain stores" could usually offer a wider array of goods at lower prices than the small local stores with which they competed. The Atlantic and Pacific Tea Company (the A & P) began a national network of grocery stores in the 1870s. F. W. Woolworth built a chain of dry goods stores. Sears and Roebuck established a large market for its mail-order merchandise by distributing an enormous catalog each year.

THE MONTGOMERY WARD DEPARTMENT STORE This advertising poster for the Montgomery Ward department store in downtown Chicago dates from about 1880. The designer has stripped away the outside walls to reveal the vast array of goods inside what the poster calls "the enormous establishment." *(Chicago Historical Society)*

Marshall Field

In larger cities, the emergence of great department stores helped transform buying habits and turn shopping into a more alluring and glamorous activity. Marshall Field in Chicago created one of the first American department stores—a place deliberately designed to produce a sense of wonder and excitement. Similar stores emerged in New York, Brooklyn, Boston, Philadelphia, and other cities.

Women as Consumers

The rise of mass consumption had particularly dramatic effects on American women. Women's clothing styles changed much more rapidly and dramatically than men's, which encouraged more frequent purchases. Women generally bought and prepared food for their families, so the availability of new food products changed not only the way everyone ate, but also the way women shopped and cooked. Canning and refrigeration meant greater variety in the diet. It also meant that food did not always have to be eaten on the day it was purchased.

The consumer economy produced new employment opportunities for women as salesclerks and waitresses. And it spawned the creation of a new movement in which women were to play a vital role: the consumer protection movement. The National Consumers League, formed in the 1890s under the leadership of Florence Kelley, attempted to mobilize the power of women as consumers to force retailers and manufacturers to improve wages and working conditions.

National Consumers League

LEISURE IN THE CONSUMER SOCIETY

Closely related to the growth of consumption was a growing interest in leisure time. Members of the urban middle and professional classes had large blocks of time during which they were not at work—evenings, weekends, even paid vacations. Working hours in many factories declined, from an average of nearly seventy hours a week in 1860 to under sixty in 1900. Even farmers found that the mechanization of agriculture gave them more free time. The lives of many Americans were becoming more compartmentalized, with clear distinctions between work and leisure. The change produced a search for new forms of recreation and entertainment.

Redefining Leisure

It also produced a redefinition of the idea of "leisure." In earlier eras, relatively few Americans had considered leisure a valuable thing. On the contrary, many equated it with laziness or sloth. In the late nineteenth century, however, the beginnings of a redefinition of leisure appeared. The economist Simon Patten was one of the first intellectuals to articulate this new view of leisure. In *The Theory of Prosperity* (1902), *The New Basis of Civilization* (1910), and other works, he challenged the centuries-old assumption that the normal condition of civilization was a scarcity of goods. In earlier times, Patten argued, fear of scarcity had caused people to place a high value on thrift, self-denial, and restraint. But in modern industrial societies, new economies could create enough wealth to satisfy not just the needs, but also the desires, of all.

Simon Patten

As Americans became more accustomed to leisure as a normal part of their lives, they began to look for new experiences with which to entertain themselves. In cities, in particular, the demand for popular entertainment produced a rich mix of spectacles, recreations, and other activities.

Mass entertainment occasionally bridged differences of class, race, or gender. But it could also be sharply divided. Saloons and some sporting events tended to be male preserves. Shopping and going to tea rooms and luncheonettes was more characteristic of female leisure. Theaters, pubs, and clubs were often specific to particular ethnic communities or particular work groups. When the classes did meet in public spaces—as they did, for example, in city parks—there was often considerable conflict over what constituted appropriate public behavior. Elites in New York City, for example, tried to prohibit anything but quiet, "genteel" activities in Central Park, while working-class people wanted to use the public spaces for sports and entertainments.

Spectator Sports

Baseball

Among the most important responses to the search for entertainment was the rise of organized spectator sports, and especially baseball. A game much like baseball—known as "rounders" and derived from cricket—had enjoyed limited popularity in Great Britain in the early nineteenth century. Versions of the game began to appear in America in the early 1830s. By the end of the Civil War, interest in the game had grown rapidly. More than 200 amateur or semiprofessional teams and clubs existed, many of which joined a national association and proclaimed a set of standard rules. As the game grew in popularity, it offered opportunities for profit. The first salaried team, the Cincinnati Red Stockings, was formed in 1869. Other cities fielded professional teams, and in 1876 the teams banded together in the National League. A rival league, the American Association, soon appeared. It eventually collapsed, but in 1901 the American League emerged to replace it. And in 1903, the first modern World Series was played, in which the American League Boston Red Sox beat the National League Pittsburgh Pirates. By then, baseball had become an important business and a great national preoccupation.

Baseball had great appeal to working-class males. The second most popular game, football, appealed at first to a more elite segment of the male population, in part because it originated in colleges and universities. The first intercollegiate football game in America occurred between Princeton and Rutgers in 1869. Early intercollegiate football bore only an indirect relation to the modern game; it was more similar to what is now known as rugby. By the late 1870s, however, the game was becoming standardized and was taking on the outlines of its modern form.

Basketball was invented in 1891 at Springfield, Massachusetts, by Dr. James A. Naismith, a Canadian working as athletic director for a local college. Boxing, which had long been a disreputable activity concentrated primarily among the urban lower classes, became by the 1880s a more popular and, in some places, more reputable sport.

Basketball Invented

Participation in the major sports of the era was almost exclusively the province of men, but several sports emerged in which women became important participants. Golf and tennis both experienced a rapid increase in participation among relatively wealthy men and women. Bicycling and croquet also enjoyed widespread popularity in the 1890s among women as well as men. Women's colleges introduced their students to more strenuous sports as well—track, crew, swimming, and (beginning in the late 1890s) basketball.

Music, Theater, and Movies

Other forms of popular entertainment developed in the cities in response to the large potential markets there. Many ethnic communities maintained their own theaters. Urban theaters also introduced new and distinctively American entertainment forms: the musical comedy, which evolved gradually from the comic operettas of Europe; and vaudeville, a form of theater adapted from French models, which remained the most popular urban entertainment into the first decades of the twentieth century. It consisted of a variety of acts (musicians, comedians, magicians, jugglers, and others) and was, at least in the beginning, inexpensive to produce. As the economic potential of vaudeville grew, some promoters—most prominently Florenz Ziegfeld of New York—staged much more elaborate spectacles.

Vaudeville

Vaudeville was also one of the few entertainment media open to black performers. They brought to it elements of the minstrel shows they had earlier developed for black audiences in the late nineteenth century. Some minstrel singers (including the most famous, Al Jolson) were whites wearing heavy makeup (or "blackface"), but most were black. Entertainers of both races performed music based on the gospel and folk tunes of the plantation and on the jazz and ragtime of black urban communities. Performers of both races also tailored their acts to prevailing white prejudices, ridiculing blacks by acting out demeaning stereotypes.

The most important form of mass entertainment was the movies. Thomas Edison and others had created the technology of the motion picture in the 1880s. Soon after that, short films became available to individual viewers watching peepshows in pool halls, penny arcades, and amusement parks. Soon, larger projectors made it possible to project the images onto big screens, which permitted substantial audiences to see films in

A NICKELODEON, 1905 Before the rise of great movie palaces, urban families flocked to "nickelodeons," smaller theaters that charged five cents for admission and that showed many different films each day, including serials—dramas that drew audiences back into theaters day after day with new episodes of a running story. *(Brown Brothers)*

theaters. By 1900, Americans were becoming attracted in large numbers to these early movies—usually plotless films of trains or waterfalls or other spectacles. The great D. W. Griffith carried the motion picture into a new era with his silent epics—*The Birth of a Nation* (1915), *Intolerance* (1916), and others—which introduced serious (if notoriously racist) plots and elaborate productions to filmmaking. Motion pictures were the first truly mass entertainment medium.

D. W. Griffith

Patterns of Public and Private Leisure

Particularly striking about popular entertainment in the late nineteenth and early twentieth centuries was its public quality. Many Americans spent their leisure time in places where they would find not only entertainment but also other people. Thousands of working-class New Yorkers spent evenings in dance halls, vaudeville houses, and concert halls. More affluent New Yorkers enjoyed afternoons in Central Park, where a principal attraction was seeing other people (and being seen by them). Moviegoers

POSTCARD FROM LUNA PARK Visitors to Coney Island sent postcards to friends and relatives by the millions, and those cards were among the most effective promotional devices for the amusement parks. This one shows the brightly-lit entrance to Luna Park, Coney Island's most popular attraction for many years. *(Bettmann/Corbis)*

were attracted not just by the movies themselves but by the energy of the audiences at lavish new "movie palaces," just as sports fans were drawn by the crowds as well as by the games.

Perhaps the most striking example of popular, public entertainment was Coney Island, the famous and self-consciously fabulous amusement park and resort on a popular beach in Brooklyn. The greatest of the Coney Island attractions, Luna Park, opened in 1903. It provided rides and stunts, and also lavish reproductions of exotic places and spectacular adventures: Japanese gardens, Venetian canals with gondoliers, a Chinese theater, a simulated trip to the moon, and re-enactments of such disasters as burning buildings and earthquakes. A year later, a competing company opened Dreamland, which tried to outdo even Luna Park with a 375-foot tower, a three-ring circus, chariot races, and a Lilliputian village from *Gulliver's Travels.* The popularity of Coney Island in these years was phenomenal. Thousands of people flocked to the large resort hotels that lined the beaches. Many thousands more made day trips out from the city by train and (after 1920) subway. In 1904, the average daily attendance at Luna Park alone was 90,000 people.

Coney Island

Most people who found Coney Island appealing did so in part because it provided them with an escape from the genteel standards of behavior that governed so much of American life at the time. In the amusement parks of Coney Island, decorum was often forgotten, and people delighted in finding themselves in situations that in any other setting would have seemed embarrassing or improper: women's skirts blown above their heads with hot air; people pummeled with water and rubber paddles by clowns; hints of sexual freedom as strangers were forced to come into physical contact with one another on rides and amusements.

Not all popular entertainment, however, involved public events. Many Americans amused themselves privately by reading novels and poetry. The so-called dime novels, cheaply bound and widely circulated, became popular after the Civil War, with detective stories, tales of the "Wild West," sagas of scientific adventure, and novels of "moral uplift." Publishers also distributed sentimental novels of romance, which developed a large audience among women, as did books about animals and about young children growing up. Louisa May Alcott's *Little Women*, most of whose readers were women, sold more than 2 million copies.

Dime Novels

The Technologies of Mass Communication

American publishing and journalism experienced an important change in the decades following the Civil War. Between 1870 and 1910, the circulation of daily newspapers increased nearly ninefold (from under 3 million to more than 24 million), a rate three times as great as the rate of population increase. And while standards varied widely from one paper to another, American journalism was developing the beginnings of a professional identity. Salaries of reporters increased; many newspapers began separating the reporting of news from the expression of opinion; and newspapers themselves became important businesses.

The transformation of publishing and journalism was to a large degree a result of new technologies of communication. The emergence of national press services, for example, was a product of the telegraph, which made it possible to supply papers throughout the country with news and features from around the nation and the world. By the turn of the century important newspaper chains had emerged as well, linked together by their own internal wire services. The most powerful was owned by William Randolph Hearst, who by 1914 controlled nine newspapers and two magazines. New printing technologies were making possible more elaborate layouts, the publication of color pictures, and, by the end of the century, the printing of photographs. These advances not only helped publishers make their own stories more vivid; they also made it possible for them to attract more advertisers.

William Randolph Hearst

The Telephone

The most important new technology of communication was the telephone, which Alexander Graham Bell had first demonstrated in 1876 (see p. 458). In its first years, the telephone was a relatively impractical tool. Those who subscribed to telephone service had to have direct wire links to everyone else they wished to call. In 1878, the first "switchboard" opened in New Haven, Connecticut, opening the way for more practical uses of the telephone. Once there was a switchboard, a telephone subscriber needed only a line to the central telephone office from which connections could be made to any other subscriber. A new occupation—the "telephone operator"—was born. The Bell System, which controlled all American telephone service, hired young white women to work as operators, hoping that a pleasant female voice would make the experience of using the telephone (and the inconvenience of the frequent technological problems that accompanied it) more appealing, or less irritating, to customers. Telephone signals were very weak at first, and callers could seldom reach anyone more than a few miles away. In an effort to increase the range of telephones, engineers created the "repeater," which periodically strengthened the signal as it moved over distances. By 1914, however, the repeaters had improved to the point that it was now practical to envision a transcontinental line.

The Bell System

In its early years, the telephone was an almost entirely commercial instrument. Of the nearly 7,400 telephone customers in the New York-New Jersey area in 1891, 6,000 were businesses and organizations. Even the residential telephones tended to belong to doctors or business managers.

The growing reach of the telephone in the early years of the twentieth century made the Bell System (formally named American Telephone and Telegraph, or AT&T) one of the most powerful corporations in America and a genuine monopoly. Central to its success was an early decision by executives that the company would exclusively build and own all telephone instruments and then lease them to subscribers. That made it possible for AT&T to control both the equipment and the telephone service itself, and to exclude any competitors in either field. It also gave AT&T effective control over the local telephone companies allied with it and made the nation's telephone system into an effective cartel.

HIGH CULTURE IN THE URBAN AGE

In addition to the important changes in popular culture that accompanied the rise of cities and industry, there were profound changes in the realm of "high culture." The distinction between "highbrow" and "lowbrow" culture was largely new to the industrial era. In the early nineteenth century, most cultural activities had targeted people of all classes. By the late nineteenth century, however, elites were developing a cultural and intellectual life quite separate from the popular amusements of the urban masses.

Literature and Art in Urban America

One of the strongest impulses in American literature was the effort to re-create urban social reality. This trend toward realism found an early voice in Stephen Crane, who—although perhaps best known for his novel of the Civil War, *The Red Badge of Courage* (1895)—created a sensation in 1893 when he published *Maggie: A Girl of the Streets*, a grim picture of urban poverty and slum life. Theodore Dreiser, Frank Norris, and Upton Sinclair were similarly drawn to social issues as themes. Kate Chopin, a southern writer who explored the oppressive features of traditional marriage, encountered widespread public abuse after publication of her shocking novel, *The Awakening*, in 1899. It described a young wife and mother who abandoned her family in search of personal fulfillment. William Dean Howells, in *The Rise of Silas Lapham* and other works, described what he considered the shallowness and corruption in ordinary American lifestyles.

Literary Realism

American art through most of the nineteenth century had been overshadowed by the art of Europe. By 1900, however, a number of American artists broke from the Old World traditions and experimented with new styles. Winslow Homer was vigorously American in his paintings of New England maritime life and other native subjects. James McNeil Whistler was one of the first Western artists to introduce Oriental themes into American and European art.

By the first years of the new century, some American artists were turning decisively away from the traditional academic style (a style perhaps most identified in America by the brilliant portraitist John Singer Sargent). Members of the so-called Ashcan School produced work startling in its naturalism and stark in its portrayal of the social realities of the era. John Sloan portrayed the dreariness of American urban slums; George Bellows caught the vigor and violence of his time in paintings and drawings of prizefights; Edward Hopper explored the starkness and loneliness of the modern city. The Ashcan artists were also among the first Americans to appreciate expressionism and abstraction; and they showed their interest in new forms in 1913 when they helped stage the famous "Armory Show" in New York City, which displayed works of the French postimpressionists and of some American moderns.

Ashcan School

The Impact of Darwinism

Perhaps the most profound intellectual development in the late nineteenth century was the widespread acceptance of the theory of evolution, associated most prominently with the English naturalist Charles Darwin. Darwin argued that the human species had evolved from earlier forms of life through a process of "natural selection." History, Darwin suggested, was not the working out of a divine plan. It was a random process dominated by the fiercest or luckiest competitors.

EDWARD HOPPER, *AUTOMAT* Edward Hopper was one of a growing group of American painters in the early twentieth century who chose to chronicle not the world of wealth and power, the characteristic subject of earlier artists, but the harsh, gritty world of the modern city. Hopper's work was distinctive for its evocation of the loneliness of urban life. This 1927 painting of a scene in an "automat" in New York City is characteristic of his work. *(Des Moines Art Center Permanent Collection. Purchased with funds from the Edmundson Art Foundation, Inc., 1958.2. Photo by Michael Tropea, Chicago)*

Resistance to Evolution

The theory of evolution met widespread resistance at first from educators, theologians, and even many scientists. By the end of the century, however, the evolutionists had converted most members of the urban professional and educated classes. Even many middle-class Protestant religious leaders had accepted the doctrine, making significant alterations in theology to accommodate it. Unseen by most urban Americans at the time, however, the rise of Darwinism was contributing to a deep schism between the new, cosmopolitan culture of the city—which was receptive to new ideas such as evolution—and the more traditional, provincial culture of some rural areas—which remained more wedded to fundamentalist religious beliefs and older values. Thus the late nineteenth century saw not only the rise of a liberal Protestantism in tune with new scientific discoveries but also the beginning of an organized Protestant fundamentalism.

Darwinism helped spawn other new intellectual currents. There was the Social Darwinism of William Graham Sumner and others, which industrialists used so enthusiastically to justify their favored position in American life. But there were also more sophisticated philoso-

"Pragmatism"

phies, among them a doctrine that became known as "pragmatism." William James, a Harvard psychologist (and brother of the novelist Henry James), was the most prominent publicist of the new theory, although earlier intellectuals such as Charles S. Peirce and later ones such as John Dewey were also important to its development and dissemination. According to the pragmatists, modern society should rely for guidance not on inherited ideals and moral principles but on the test of scientific inquiry. No idea or institution (not even religious faith) was valid, they claimed, unless it worked, unless it stood the test of experience.

A similar concern for scientific inquiry was influencing the social sciences. Sociologists such as Edward A. Ross and Lester Frank Ward urged applying the scientific method to the solution of social and political problems. Historians such as Frederick Jackson Turner and Charles Beard argued that economic factors more than spiritual ideals had been the governing force in historical development. John Dewey proposed a new approach to education that placed less emphasis on the rote learning of traditional knowledge and more on flexible, democratic schooling.

The implications of Darwinism also promoted the growth of anthropology and encouraged some scholars to begin examining other cultures in new ways. Some white Americans began to look at Indian society, for example, as a coherent culture with its own norms and values that were worthy of respect and preservation, even though they were different from those of white society.

Toward Universal Schooling

The growing demand for specialized skills and scientific knowledge naturally created a growing, and changing, demand for education. The late nineteenth century, therefore, was a time of rapid expansion and reform of American schools and universities.

Spread of Free Public Schooling

One example was the spread of free public primary and secondary education. By 1900, compulsory school attendance laws were in effect in thirty-one states and territories. Education was still far from universal. Rural areas lagged far behind urban-industrial ones in funding public education. In the South, many blacks had access to no schools at all. But for many white men and women, educational opportunities were expanding dramatically.

Educational reformers tried to extend educational opportunities to the Indian tribes as well, in an effort to "civilize" them and help them adapt to white society. In the 1870s, reformers recruited small groups of Indians to attend Hampton Institute (a primarily black college). In 1879 they organized the Carlisle Indian Industrial School in Pennsylvania. Like many black colleges, Carlisle emphasized practical "industrial" education. Ultimately, however, these reform efforts failed, in part because it was unpopular with its intended beneficiaries.

Universities and the Growth of Science and Technology

Colleges and universities were also proliferating rapidly in the late nineteenth century. They benefited particularly from the Morrill Land Grant Act of 1862, by which the federal government had donated public land to states for the establishment of colleges. Sixty-nine "land-grant" institutions were established in the last decades of the century—among them the state university systems of California, Illinois, Minnesota, and Wisconsin. Other universities benefited from millions of dollars contributed by business and financial titans. Rockefeller, Carnegie, and others gave generously to such schools as Columbia, Chicago, Harvard, Northwestern, Princeton, Syracuse, and Yale. Other philanthropists founded new universities or reorganized older ones and perpetuated their family names—Vanderbilt, Johns Hopkins, Cornell, Duke, Tulane, and Stanford.

Economic Impact of Higher Education

These and other universities played a vital role in the economic development of the United States in the late nineteenth century and beyond. The land-grant institutions were specifically mandated to advance knowledge in "agriculture and mechanics." From the beginning, therefore, they were committed not just to abstract knowledge, but to making discoveries that would be of practical use to farmers and manufacturers. As they evolved into great state universities, they retained that tradition and became the source of many of the great technological and scientific discoveries that helped American industry and commerce to advance. Private universities emerged that served many of the same purposes: the Massachusetts Institute of Technology, founded in 1865, which soon became the nation's premier engineering school; Johns Hopkins University in Baltimore, founded in 1876, which did much to advance medical scholarship; the Rockefeller Institute for Medical Research in New York (later Rockefeller University); the Carnegie Institution. By the early twentieth century, even much older and more traditional universities were beginning to form relationships with the private sector and the government, doing research that did not just advance knowledge for its own sake but that was directly applicable to practical problems of the time.

Medical Science

Both the culture of and the scientific basis for medical care was changing rapidly in the early twentieth century. Most doctors were beginning to accept the new medical assumption that there were underlying causes to particular symptoms—that a symptom was not itself a disease. They were also beginning to make use of new or improved technologies—the X-ray, improved microscopes, and other diagnostic devices in laboratories—that made it possible to classify, and distinguish among, different diseases. Laboratory tests could now identify infections such as typhoid and dysentery. That did not in itself help doctors treat diseases, but it was a critical first step toward finding effective treatment. At about the same time, pharmaceutical research was beginning to produce some important new medicines. Aspirin was first synthesized in 1899. Other researchers were beginning to experiment with chemicals that might destroy diseases in the blood, an effort that eventually led to the various forms of chemotherapy that are still widely used in treating cancer. In 1906, an American surgeon, G. W. Crile, became the first physician to use blood transfusion in treatment, which revolutionized surgery. In the past, patients often lost so much blood during operations that extensive surgery could be fatal for that reason alone. With transfusions, it became possible to conduct much longer and more elaborate operations.

Germ Theory Accepted

The widespread acceptance by the end of the nineteenth century of the germ theory of disease had important implications. Physicians quickly discovered that exposure to germs did not by itself necessarily cause disease, and they began looking for the other factors that determined who got sick and who did not. Among the factors they eventually discovered were general health, previous medical history, diet and nutrition, and eventually genetic predisposition. The awareness of the importance of infection in spreading disease also encouraged doctors to sterilize their instruments, use surgical gloves, and otherwise purify the medical environment of patients.

Declining Mortality

By the early twentieth century, American physicians and surgeons were generally recognized as among the best in the world, and American medical education was beginning to attract students from many other countries. These improvements in medical knowledge and training, along with improvements in sanitation and public health, did much to reduce infection and mortality in most American communities.

Education for Women

The post–Civil War era saw an important expansion of educational opportunities for women, although such opportunities continued to lag far behind those available to men and were denied to black women.

Women's Colleges

Most public high schools accepted women readily, but opportunities for higher education were fewer. At the end of the Civil War, only three American colleges were coeducational. In the years after the war, many of the land-grant colleges and universities in the Midwest and such private universities as Cornell and Wesleyan began to admit women along with men. But coeducation was less crucial to women's education in this period than was the creation of a network of women's colleges. Mount Holyoke in central Massachusetts had begun its life in 1836 as a "seminary" for women; it became a full-fledged college in the 1880s, at about the same time that entirely new female institutions were emerging: Vassar, Wellesley, Smith, Bryn Mawr, Wells, and Goucher. A few of the larger private universities created separate colleges for women on their campuses (Barnard at Columbia and Radcliffe at Harvard, for example).

The female college was part of an important phenomenon in the history of modern American women: the emergence of distinctive women's communities outside the family. Most faculty members and many administrators were women (usually unmarried). And the life of the college produced a spirit of sorority and commitment among educated women that had important effects in later years. Most female college graduates ultimately married, but they married at a more advanced age than their non-college counterparts. A significant minority, perhaps over 25 percent, did not marry at all, but devoted themselves to careers. The growth of female higher education clearly became for some women a liberating experience, persuading them that they had roles to perform in their rapidly changing urban-industrial society other than those of wives and mothers.

Emergence of Women's Communities

CONCLUSION

The extraordinary growth of American cities in the last decades of the nineteenth century led to both great achievements and enormous problems. Cities became centers of learning, art, and commerce. They produced great advances in technology, transportation, architecture, and communications. They provided their residents—and their many visitors—with varied and dazzling experiences, so much so that people increasingly left the countryside to move to the city.

But cities were also places of congestion, filth, disease, and corruption. With populations expanding too rapidly for services to keep up, most American cities in this era struggled with makeshift techniques to solve the basic problems of providing water, disposing of sewage, building roads, running public transportation, fighting fire, stopping crime, and preventing or curing disease. City governments, many of them dominated by political machines and ruled by party bosses, were often models of inefficiency and corruption—although in their informal way they also provided substantial services to the working-class and immigrant constituencies who needed them most. Yet they also managed to oversee great public projects: the building of parks, museums, opera houses, and theaters, usually in partnership with private developers.

The city brought together races, ethnic groups, and classes of extraordinary variety—from the families of great wealth that the new industrial age was creating to the vast working class, much of it consisting of immigrants, that crowded into densely packed neighborhoods sharply divided by nationality. The city also spawned new forms of popular culture. It created temples of consumerism: shops, boutiques, and above all the great department stores. And it created forums for public recreation and entertainment: parks, theaters, athletic fields, amusement parks, and later movie palaces.

Urban life created anxiety among those who lived within the cities and among those who observed them from afar. But in fact, American cities adapted reasonably successfully over time to the great demands their growth made of them and learned to govern themselves if not entirely honestly and efficiently, at least adequately to allow them to survive and grow.

FOR FURTHER REFERENCE

Lewis Mumford, author of *The City in History* (1961), was America's foremost critic and chronicler of urbanization through the mid-twentieth century. John Bodnar provides a synthetic history of immigration in *The Transplanted: A History of Immigrants in America* (1985), which challenges an earlier classic study by Oscar Handlin, *The Uprooted: The Epic Story of the Great Migrations that Made the American People*, 2nd ed. (1973). Henry Yu, *Thinking Orientals: Migration, Contact, and Exoticism in Modern America* (2001) is a provocative examination of aspects of Asian immigration. Desmond King, *Making Americans: Immigration, Race, and the Origins of Diverse Democracy* (2000) examines responses to immigration. The new urban mass culture of America's cities is the subject of William Leach, *Land of Desire: Merchants, Power, and the Rise of a New American Culture* (1993) and Kathy Peiss, *Cheap Amusements: Working Women and Leisure in Turn-of-the-Century New York* (1986). Sven Beckert, *The Moneyed Metropolis: New York City and the Consolidation of the American Bourgeoisie, 1850–1896* (2001) and Stuart Blumin, *The Emergence of the Middle Class: Social Experience in the American City, 1760–1900* (1989) examine the rise of the urban middle class. Sarah Deutsch, *Women and the City: Gender, Space, and Power in Boston, 1870–1940* (2000), reveals the world of women in the emergence of the modern city. T. J. Jackson Lears, *No Place of Grace: Antimodernism and the Transformation of American Culture, 1880–1920* (1981) chronicles patterns of resistance to the new culture. Roy Rosenzweig and Elizabeth Blackmar, *The Park and the People: A History of Central Park* (1992) studies the creation of America's most famous public park. Edwin G. Burroughs and Mike Wallace, *Gotham: A History of New York City to 1898* (1998) is a thorough history of New York's remarkable growth. Christine Stansell, *American Moderns: Bohemian New York and the Creation of a New Century* (2001) examines the rise of a modern urban sensibility. John F. Kasson, *Amusing the Million: Coney Island at the Turn of the Century* (1978) is an illustrated history and interpretation of the amusement park's place in American culture. *Coney Island* (1991), a film by Ric Burns, presents a colorful history of America's favorite seaside resort. The documentary film *Baseball* (1994) by Ken Burns—and the companion book by the same name, by Geoffrey C. Ward—provide sweeping narratives of the national pastime, its origins in the age of the city, and its wider social context of race relations, immigration, and popular culture. *New York* (1999–2001), a film by Ric Burns, is a sweeping documentary history of the city, accompanied by a companion book, Ric Burns et al., *New York: An Illustrated History* (1999).

For quizzes, Internet resources, references to additional books and films, and more, consult this book's Online Learning Center site at www.mhhe.com/unfinishednation4.

A PARTY OF PATCHES, *JUDGE* MAGAZINE, JUNE 6, 1891 This political cartoon suggests the contempt and fear with which many easterners, in particular, viewed the emergence of the People's Party in 1891. *(Kansas State Historical Society)*

TIME LINE

1867	1880	1881	1883	1884	1887	1888
National Grange founded	Garfield elected president	Garfield assassinated Arthur becomes president	Pendleton Act	Cleveland elected president	Interstate Commerce Act	Benjamin Harrison elected president

CHAPTER NINETEEN

FROM STALEMATE TO CRISIS

The Politics of Equilibrium
The Agrarian Revolt
The Crisis of the 1890s

The enormous changes America was experiencing in the late nineteenth century strained not only the nation's traditional social arrangements but its political institutions as well. Industrialization and urbanization had produced considerable progress, but they had also created disorder and despair. Gradually, Americans began to look to government for leadership in their search for stability and social justice. Yet American government during much of this period was ill equipped to deal with the new challenges confronting it. In the face of unprecedented dilemmas, it responded with apparent passivity and confusion. Its leaders, for the most part, seemed political mediocrities. The issue with which it was concerned were often irrelevant to the nation's most serious problems. Rather than taking active leadership of the nation's dramatic transformation, the American political system for nearly two decades after the end of Reconstruction was locked in a rigid stalemate—watching the remarkable changes that were occurring in the nation and doing little to affect them. The result was a set of problems and grievances that festered and grew without any natural outlet. And it was not surprising, under the circumstances, that in the 1890s the United States entered a period of national crisis.

1890	1892	1893	1894	1896	1900
Sherman Antitrust Act	Cleveland elected president	Economic depression begins	Coxey's Army	McKinley elected president	Gold Standard Act
Sherman Silver Purchase Act	People's Party formed	Sherman Silver Purchase Act repealed			
McKinley Tariff					

THE POLITICS OF EQUILIBRIUM

To modern eyes, the nature of the American political system in the late nineteenth century appears in many ways paradoxical. The two political parties enjoyed a strength and stability that neither was ever to know again. And yet the federal government was doing relatively little of importance. In fact, most Americans in those years engaged in political activity not because of an interest in particular issues but because of broad regional, ethnic, or religious sentiments.

The Party System

The most striking feature of the late-nineteenth-century party system was its remarkable stability. From the end of Reconstruction until the late 1890s, the electorate was divided almost precisely evenly between the Republicans and the Democrats. Sixteen states were solidly and consistently Republican, and fourteen states (most of them in the South) were solidly and consistently Democratic. Only five states were usually in doubt, and their voters generally decided the results of national elections, often on the basis of voter turnout. The Republican Party captured the presidency in all but two of the elections of the era, but the party was not really as dominant as those victories suggest. In the five presidential elections beginning in 1876, the average popular-vote margin separating the Democratic and Republican candidates was 1.5 percent. The congressional balance was similarly stable, with the Republicans generally controlling the Senate and the Democrats generally controlling the House.

Stability and Stalemate

As striking as the balance between the parties was the intensity of public loyalty to them. Voter turnout in presidential elections between 1860 and 1900 averaged over 78 percent of all eligible voters (as compared with only about 50 percent in recent decades). Even in nonpresidential years, from 60 to 80 percent of the voters turned out to cast ballots for congressional and local candidates. Large groups of potential voters were disfranchised in these years: women in most states; almost all blacks and many poor whites in the South. But for adult white males outside the South, there were few franchise restrictions. The remarkable turnout represented a genuinely mass-based politics.

High Turnout

What explains this extraordinary loyalty to the two political parties? It was not, certainly, that the parties took distinct positions on important public issues. They did so rarely. Party loyalties reflected other factors. Region was perhaps the most important. To white southerners, loyalty to the Democratic Party was a matter of unquestioned faith. It was the vehicle by which they had triumphed over Reconstruction, the vehicle by which they preserved white supremacy. To many northerners, Republican loyalties were equally intense. To them, the party of Lincoln remained a bulwark against slavery and treason.

Cultural Basis of Party Loyalty

Religious and ethnic differences also shaped party loyalties. The Democratic Party attracted most of the Catholic voters, most of the recent immigrants, and most of the poorer workers. The Republican Party appealed to northern Protestants, citizens of old stock, and much of the middle class. Among the few substantive issues on which the parties took clearly different stands were matters connected with immigrants. Republicans tended to support measures restricting immigration and to favor temperance legislation, which many believed would help discipline immigrant communities. Catholics and immigrants viewed such proposals as assaults on them and their cultures; the Democratic Party followed their lead.

Party identification, then, was usually more a reflection of cultural inclinations than a calculation of economic interest. Individuals might affiliate with a party because their parents had done so, or because it was the party of their region, their church, or their ethnic group. Most clung to their party loyalties with great persistence and passion.

The National Government

Weak Federal Government

One reason the two parties managed to avoid substantive issues was that the federal government did relatively little. The government in Washington was responsible for delivering the mails, for maintaining a national military, for conducting foreign policy, and for collecting tariffs and taxes. It had few other responsibilities and few institutions with which it could have undertaken additional responsibilities even if it had chosen to do so.

There was one significant exception. From the end of the Civil War to the early twentieth century, the federal government administered a system of annual pensions for Union Civil War veterans who had retired from work and for their widows. At its peak, this pension system was making payments to a majority of the male citizens (black and white) of the North and to many women as well. Some reformers hoped to make the system permanent and universal, but their efforts failed, in part because the Civil War pension system was awash in party patronage and corruption. Other reformers—believers in "good government"—saw elimination of the pension system as a way to fight graft, corruption, and party rule. When the Civil War generation died out, the pension system died with it.

In most other respects, the United States in the late nineteenth century was a society without a modern, national government. The most powerful national political institutions were the two political parties. The national leaders of both parties were primarily concerned not with policy but with office—with winning elections and controlling patronage.

Presidents and Patronage

The power of party bosses had an important effect on the power of the presidency. The office had great symbolic importance, but its occupants were unable to do very much except distribute government appointments. A new president and his tiny staff had to make almost 100,000 appointments; and even in that function, presidents had limited latitude, since they had to avoid offending the various factions within their own parties.

Sometimes that proved impossible, as the presidency of Rutherford B. Hayes (1877–1881) demonstrated. By the end of his term, two groups—the Stalwarts, led by Roscoe Conkling of New York, and the Half-Breeds, captained by James G. Blaine of Maine—were competing for control of the Republican Party. The dispute between the Stalwarts and the Half-Breeds had little basis in substance. Rhetorically, the Stalwarts favored traditional, professional machine politics, while the Half-Breeds favored reform. In fact, both groups were mainly interested in a larger share of the patronage pie. Hayes tried to satisfy both and ended up satisfying neither.

Stalwarts and Half-Breeds

The battle over patronage overshadowed all else during Hayes's unhappy presidency. His one important substantive initiative—an effort to create a civil service system—attracted no support from either party. And his early announcement that he would not seek reelection only weakened him further.

The Republicans managed to retain the presidency in 1880 in part because they agreed on a ticket that included a Stalwart and a Half-Breed. After a long convention deadlock, they nominated James A. Garfield, a veteran congressman from Ohio and a Half-Breed, for president and Chester A. Arthur of New York, a Stalwart and Conkling henchman, for vice president. The Democrats nominated General Winfield Scott Hancock, a minor Civil War commander with no national following. Benefiting from the end of the recession of 1879, Garfield won a decisive electoral victory, although his popular-vote margin was very thin.

Garfield began his presidency by trying to defy the Stalwarts in his appointments and by showing support for civil service reform. He soon found himself embroiled in an ugly public quarrel with both Conkling and other Stalwarts. It was never resolved. On July 2, 1881, only four months after his inauguration, Garfield was shot twice while standing in the Washington railroad station by an apparently deranged gunman (and unsuccessful office seeker) who shouted, "I am a Stalwart and Arthur is president now!" Garfield lingered for nearly three months but finally died.

Garfield Assassinated

Chester A. Arthur, who succeeded Garfield, had spent a political lifetime as a devoted, skilled, and open spoilsman and a close ally of Roscoe Conkling. But on becoming president, he tried—like Hayes and Garfield before him—to follow an independent course and even to promote reform. To the dismay of the Stalwarts, Arthur kept most of Garfield's appointees in office and supported civil service reform. In 1883, Congress

REVOLT AMONG REPUBLICANS Many Republican reformers, believers in "good government," were aghast when their party nominated James G. Blaine for president in 1884. Blaine, a former Speaker of the House, U.S. senator, and secretary of state, was the leader of the "Half-Breed" faction of the party, the faction that claimed to support cautious reform. But he was controversial even among reformers after a long career of wily political maneuvering and because of the scandals that continually attached themselves to his name. This cartoon by Joseph Keppler in the political magazine *Puck* shows Republican leaders responding with horror to "the writing on the wall," and to the dire consequences they believed would follow the nomination of Blaine. Blaine himself, at left, hides behind the *New York Herald-Tribune*, the principal organ of the reformers and a critic of Blaine. *(New York Public Library)*

Pendleton Act

passed the first national civil service measure, the Pendleton Act, which required that some federal jobs be filled by competitive written examinations rather than by patronage. Relatively few offices fell under civil service at first, but its reach extended steadily so that by the mid-twentieth century most federal employees were civil servants.

Cleveland, Harrison, and the Tariff

In the unsavory election of 1884, the Republican candidate for president was Senator James G. Blaine of Maine—known to his adoring admirers as "the Plumed Knight" but to thousands of other Americans as a symbol of seamy party politics. A group of disgruntled "liberal Republicans," known derisively by their critics as the "mugwumps," announced they would bolt the party and support an honest Democrat. Rising to the bait, the Democrats nominated Grover Cleveland, the "reform" governor of New York.

In a campaign filled with personal invective, what may have decided the election was the last-minute introduction of a religious controversy. Shortly before the election, a delegation of Protestant ministers called on

Blaine in New York City; their spokesman, Dr. Samuel Burchard, referred to the Democrats as the party of "rum, Romanism, and rebellion." Blaine was slow to repudiate Burchard's indiscretion, and Democrats quickly spread the news that Blaine had tolerated a slander on the Catholic Church. Cleveland's narrow victory was probably a result of an unusually heavy Catholic vote for the Democrats in New York.

Cleveland Elected

Grover Cleveland was respected, if not often liked, for his stern and righteous opposition to politicians, grafters, pressure groups, and Tammany Hall. He was the embodiment of an era in which few Americans believed the federal government could, or should, do very much. Cleveland had always doubted the wisdom of protective tariffs (taxes on imported goods designed to protect domestic producers). The existing high rates, he believed, were responsible for the annual surplus in federal revenues, which was tempting Congress to pass "reckless" and "extravagant" legislation, which he frequently vetoed. In December 1887, therefore, he asked Congress to reduce the tariff rates. Democrats in the House approved a tariff reduction, but Senate Republicans defiantly passed a bill of their own actually raising the rates. The resulting deadlock made the tariff an issue in the election of 1888.

The Democrats renominated Cleveland and supported tariff reductions. The Republicans settled on former senator Benjamin Harrison of Indiana, who was obscure but respectable; and they endorsed protection. The campaign was the first since the Civil War to involve a clear question of economic difference between the parties. It was also one of the most corrupt elections in American history. Harrison won an electoral majority of 233 to 168, but Cleveland's popular vote exceeded Harrison's by 100,000.

Election of 1888

New Public Issues

Benjamin Harrison's record as president was little more substantial than that of his grandfather, who had died a month after taking office. Harrison had few visible convictions, and he made no effort to influence Congress. And yet during Harrison's passive administration, public opinion was beginning to force the government to confront some of the pressing social and economic issues of the day. Most notably, perhaps, sentiment was rising in favor of legislation to curb the power of trusts.

By the mid-1880s, fifteen western and southern states had adopted laws prohibiting combinations that restrained competition. But corporations found it easy to escape limitations by incorporating in states such as New Jersey and Delaware that offered them special privileges. If antitrust legislation was to be effective, its supporters believed, it would have to come from the national government. Responding to growing popular demands, both houses of Congress passed the Sherman Antitrust Act in July 1890, almost without dissent. Most

Sherman Antitrust Act

members of Congress saw the act as a largely symbolic measure. For over a decade after its passage, the Sherman Act—indifferently enforced and steadily weakened by the courts—had virtually no impact. As of 1901, the Justice Department had instituted many antitrust suits against unions, but only fourteen against business combinations; there had been few convictions.

Tariff Rates Raised

The Republicans were more interested, however, in the issue they believed had won them the 1888 election: the tariff. Representative William McKinley of Ohio and Senator Nelson W. Aldrich of Rhode Island drafted the highest protective measure ever proposed to Congress. Known as the McKinley Tariff, it became law in October 1890. But Republican leaders apparently misinterpreted public sentiment, for the party suffered a stunning reversal in the 1890 congressional election. The Republicans' substantial Senate majority was slashed to 8; in the House, the party retained only 88 of the 323 seats. Nor were the Republicans able to recover in the course of the next two years. In the presidential election of 1892, Benjamin Harrison once again supported protection; Grover Cleveland, renominated by the Democrats, once again opposed it. A new third party, the People's Party, with James B. Weaver as its candidate, advocated more substantial economic reform. Cleveland won 277 electoral votes to Harrison's 145 and had a popular margin of 380,000. Weaver showed some significant strength, but still ran far behind. For the first time since 1878, the Democrats won a majority of both houses of Congress.

The policies of Cleveland's second term were much like those of his first—hostile to active efforts to deal with social or economic problems. Again, he supported a tariff reduction, which the House approved but the Senate weakened. Cleveland denounced the result but allowed it to become law as the Wilson-Gorman Tariff.

But public pressure was growing in the 1880s for other reforms, among them regulation of the railroads. Farm organizations in the Midwest (most notably the Grangers) had persuaded several state legislatures to pass regulatory legislation in the early 1870s. But in 1886, the Supreme Court—in *Wabash, St. Louis, and Pacific Railway Co.* v. *Illinois*, known as the *Wabash* case—ruled one of the Granger Laws in Illinois unconstitutional. According to the Court, the law was an attempt to control interstate commerce and thus infringed on the exclusive power of Congress. Later, the courts limited the powers of the states to regulate commerce even within their own boundaries.

Interstate Commerce Act

Effective railroad regulation, it was now clear, could come only from the federal government. Congress grudgingly responded to public pressure in 1887 with the Interstate Commerce Act, which banned discrimination in rates between long and short hauls, required that railroads publish their rate schedules and file them with the government, and declared that all interstate rail rates must be "reasonable and just." A five-person agency, the Interstate Commerce Commission (ICC), was to administer the act. But it had to rely on the courts to enforce its rulings. For almost twenty years after its passage, the Interstate Commerce Act—which was, like the Sherman Act, haphazardly enforced and narrowly interpreted by the courts—was without much practical effect.

THE AGRARIAN REVOLT

No group watched the performance of the federal government in the 1880s with more dismay than American farmers. The serious problems that afflicted them helped produce one of the most powerful movements of political protest in American history: what became known as Populism.

The Grangers

National Grange of the Patrons of Husbandry

Farmers had been making efforts to organize politically for several decades before the 1880s. The first major farm organization was the National Grange of the Patrons of Husbandry, founded in 1867. From it emerged a network of local organizations that tried to teach new scientific agricultural techniques to members. But when the depression of 1873 caused a sharp decline in farm prices, membership rapidly increased and the direction of the organization changed. Granges in the Midwest began to organize marketing cooperatives, and they promoted political action to curb the monopolistic practices of the railroads and warehouses. At their peak, Grange supporters controlled the legislatures in most of the midwestern states. The result was the Granger Laws of the early 1870s, by which many states imposed strict regulations on railroad rates and practices. But the destruction of the new regulations by the courts, combined with the political inexperience of many Grange leaders and the return of prosperity in the late 1870s, produced a dramatic decline in the power of the association by the end of the decade.

The Alliances

The successor to the Granges began to emerge even before the Granger movement had faded. As early as 1875, farmers in parts of the South were banding together in so-called Farmers' Alliances. By 1880, the Southern Alliance had more than 4 million members; and a comparable Northwestern Alliance was taking root in the plains states and the Midwest.

Like the Granges, the Alliances formed cooperatives and other marketing mechanisms. They established stores, banks, processing plants, and other facilities for their members—to free them from dependence on the hated "furnishing merchants" who kept so many farmers in debt. Some Alliance leaders, however, saw the movement in larger terms: as an effort to

Social Goals of the Farmers' Alliances

build a new kind of society in which economic competition might give way to cooperation. Alliance lecturers traveled throughout rural areas lambasting the concentrated power of the great corporations and financial institutions.

Although the Alliances quickly became far more widespread than the Granges had ever been, they suffered from similar problems. Their cooperatives did not always work well, partly because the market forces operating against them were sometimes too strong to be overcome and partly because the cooperatives themselves were often mismanaged. These economic frustrations helped push the movement into a new phase at the end of the 1880s: the creation of a national political organization.

In 1889, the Southern and Northwestern Alliances agreed to a loose merger. The next year the Alliances held a national convention at Ocala, Florida, and produced a statement of their goals known as the Ocala Demands. In the 1890 off-year elections, candidates supported by the Alliances won partial or complete control of the legislatures in twelve states. They also won six governorships, three seats in the Senate, and approximately fifty in the House of Representatives. Many of the successful Alliance candidates were simply Democrats who had benefited—often passively—from Alliance endorsements. But dissident farmers drew enough encouragement from the results to contemplate further political action.

Alliance leaders discussed plans for a third party at meetings in Cincinnati in May 1891 and St. Louis in February 1892. Then, in July 1892, 1,300 exultant delegates poured into Omaha, Nebraska, to proclaim the creation of the new party, approve an official set of principles, and nominate candidates for the presidency and vice presidency. The new organization's official name was the People's Party, but the movement was more commonly referred to as Populism.

People's Party Established

The election of 1892 demonstrated the potential power of the new movement. The Populist presidential candidate—James B. Weaver of Iowa, a former Greenbacker—polled more than 1 million votes. Nearly 1,500 Populist candidates won election to state legislatures and local offices. The party elected three governors, five senators, and ten congressmen. It could also claim the support of many Republicans and Democrats in Congress who had been elected by appealing to Populist sentiment.

The Populist Constituency

Already, however, there were signs of the limits of Populist strength. Populism had great appeal to farmers, and particularly to small farmers with little long-range economic security. But Populism failed to move much beyond that group. Its leaders made energetic efforts to include labor within the coalition. In addition to courting the Knights of Labor, the new party added a labor plank to its platform—calling for shorter hours for workers and restrictions on immigration, and

Populism's Limited Appeal

Debating the Past

POPULISM

The scholarly debates over the nature of Populism have tended to reflect a larger debate over the nature of popular mass movements. To some historians, mass uprisings seem dangerous and potentially antidemocratic; and to them, the Populist movement has usually appeared ominous. To others, such insurgency is evidence of a healthy democratic resistance to oppression; and to them, Populism has generally seemed more appealing.

The latter view shaped the first, and for many years the only, general history of Populism: John D. Hicks's *The Populist Revolt* (1931). Hicks portrayed Populism as an expression of the healthy, democratic sentiments of the West. Populists were reacting rationally and constructively to the harsh impact of eastern industrial growth on agrarian society, and they were proposing potentially valuable reforms to restrict the power of the new financial titans. Populism was, he wrote, "the last phase of a long and perhaps a losing struggle—the struggle to save agricultural America from the devouring jaws of industrial America."

In the early 1950s, scholars sensitive to the nature of European fascism and contemporary communism took a more suspicious view of mass popular politics and a more hostile view of Populism. The leading figure in this reinterpretation was Richard Hofstadter. In *The Age of Reform* (1955), he conceded that the Populists had genuine grievances and advanced some sensible reforms. But he concentrated on revealing what he called the "soft" and "dark" sides of the movement. Populism, Hofstadter claimed, rested on a romanticized and obsolete vision of the role of farmers in American society. And it was permeated with bigotry and ignorance.

Hofstadter's harsh portrait inspired a series of spirited challenges. Norman Pollack, beginning in 1962, argued that the agrarian revolt rested not on nostalgic and romantic concepts but on a sophisticated and even radical vision of reform. A year later, Walter T. K. Nugent attempted to show that Populists were not bigoted, that they not only tolerated but welcomed Jews and other minorities into their party. And in 1976, Lawrence Goodwyn published *Democratic Promise,* which described Populism as a "cooperative crusade" battling against the "coercive potential of the emerging corporate state."

At the same time that historians were debating the meaning of Populism, they were also arguing over who the Populists were. Hicks, Hofstadter, and Goodwyn, for all their many disagreements, shared a belief that Populists were victims of economic distress—usually one-crop farmers in economically marginal regions victimized by drought and debt. Others, however, have suggested that this description is, if not wrong, at least inadequate. Sheldon Hackney maintained in 1969 that Populists in Alabama were not only economically troubled but socially rootless, "only tenuously connected to society by economic function, by personal relationships, by stable community membership, by political participation, or by psychological identification with the South's distinctive myths." Peter Argersinger, Stanley Parsons, James Turner, and others have similarly suggested that Populists tended to be people who were socially and even geographically isolated. Steven Hahn's 1983 study *The Roots of Southern Populism* described the poor farmers of "upcountry" Georgia who became Populists as people almost entirely unconnected to the modern capitalist economy. They were reacting to a real economic threat to their way of life: the intrusion into their world of a new commercial order of which they were not a part and from which they were unlikely to benefit.

There has, finally, been continuing debate over the legacy of Populism. Michael Kazin, in *The Populist Persuasion* (1994), is one of a number of scholars who have argued that a Populist tradition has survived throughout much of the twentieth century, influencing movements as different as those led by Huey Long in the 1930s, George Wallace in the 1960s, and Ross Perot in the 1990s.

(text continued from page 523)

denouncing the use of private detective agencies as strikebreakers in labor disputes. But Populism never attracted any substantial labor support, in part because the economic interests of labor and the interests of farmers were often at odds.

In the South in particular, white Populists struggled with the question of accepting African Americans in the party. Indeed there was an important black component to the movement—a network of "Colored Alliances" that by 1890 numbered over 1.25 million members. But most white Populists were willing to accept the assistance of blacks only as long as it was clear that whites would remain indisputably in control. When southern conservatives began to attack the Populists for undermining white supremacy, the interracial character of the movement quickly faded.

Populist Ideas

The Populists' Reform Program

The Populists spelled out their program of reform first in the Ocala Demands of 1890 and then, even more clearly, in the Omaha platform of 1892. They proposed a system of "subtreasuries," a network of government-owned warehouses, where farmers could deposit their crops. Using those crops as collateral, growers could then borrow money from the government at low rates of interest and wait for the price of their goods to go up before selling them. In addition, the Populists called for the abolition of national banks, which they believed were dangerous institutions of concentrated power; the end of absentee ownership of land; the direct election of United States senators (which would weaken the power of conservative state legislatures); and other devices to improve the ability of the people to influence the political process. They called as well for regulation and (after 1892) government ownership of railroads, telephones, and telegraphs. And they demanded a system of government-operated postal savings banks, a graduated income tax, the inflation of the currency, and, later, the remonetization of silver.

A POPULIST GATHERING Populism was a response to real economic and political grievances. But like most political movements of its time, it was also important as a cultural experience. For farmers in sparsely settled regions in particular, it provided an antidote to isolation and loneliness. This gathering of Populist farmers in Dickinson County, Kansas, shows how the political purposes of the movement were tightly bound up with its social purposes. *(Kansas State Historical Society)*

Some Populists were openly anti-Semitic. Others were anti-intellectual, antieastern, and antiurban. But bigotry was not the dominant force behind Populism. The movement was a serious and at times highly intelligent effort to find solutions to real problems. Populism was less a critique of industrialization or capitalism than a challenge to what the Populists considered the brutal and chaotic way in which the economy was developing. Progress and growth should continue, they urged, but should be strictly defined by the needs of individuals and communities.

THE CRISIS OF THE 1890S

The rising agrarian protest was only one of many indications of the national political crisis emerging in the 1890s. There was a severe depression, which began in 1893. There was widespread labor unrest and violence. There was the failure of either major party to respond to the growing distress. And there was the rigid conservatism of Grover Cleveland, who took office for the second time just at the moment that the economy collapsed.

The Panic of 1893

The Panic of 1893 precipitated the most severe depression the nation had ever experienced. It began in March 1893, when the Philadelphia and Reading Railroads declared bankruptcy, unable to meet demands for payment by British banks from which they had borrowed large sums. Two months later, the National Cordage Company failed as well. Together, the two corporate failures triggered a collapse of the stock market. And since many of the major New York banks were heavy investors in the market, a wave of bank failures soon began. That caused a contraction of credit, which meant that many of the new, aggressive businesses that had recently begun operations soon went bankrupt.

America's Interconnected Economy

The depression reflected, among other things, the degree to which all parts of the American economy were now interconnected. And the depression showed how dependent the economy was on the health of the railroads, which remained the nation's most powerful corporate and financial institutions. When the railroads suffered, as they did beginning in 1893, everything suffered.

Once the panic began, its effects spread with startling speed. Within six months, more than 8,000 businesses, 156 railroads, and 400 banks failed. Already low agricultural prices tumbled further. Up to 1 million workers, 20 percent of the labor force, lost their jobs. The depression was unprecedented not only in its severity but also in its persistence. Although there was slight improvement beginning in 1895, prosperity did not fully return until after 1898.

The depression produced widespread social unrest, not least among the enormous numbers of unemployed workers. In 1894, Jacob S. Coxey, an Ohio businessman and Populist, began advocating an inflation of the currency and a massive public works program to create jobs for the unemployed. When it became clear that his proposals were making no progress in Congress, Coxey organized a march of the unemployed (known as "Coxey's Army") to Washington to present his demands to the government. Congress took no action on the demands.

Homestead and Pullman Strikes

There were major labor upheavals as well during the decade—of which the Homestead and Pullman strikes were only the most prominent examples (see pp. 476–479). To many middle-class Americans, the worker unrest was a sign of dangerous social instability, even perhaps a revolution. Labor radicalism—some of it real, much of it imagined—was seldom far from the public mind, heightening the general sense of crisis.

The Silver Question

Populists, and many others, blamed the depression on an inadequate supply of money. Conservatives blamed it on a lack of commitment to a "sound currency." The "money question," therefore, became one of the burning issues of the era.

COXEY'S ARMY Jacob S. Coxey's "army" of the unemployed marches toward Washington in 1894 to demand relief from the federal government. Although several thousand people started out from various parts of the country to join the army, only about 400 actually reached the Capital. The protest disbanded after Coxey and several others were arrested for "trespassing" on the grounds of the United States Capitol. *(Culver Pictures, Inc.)*

The heart of the debate was over what would form the basis of the dollar, what would lie behind it and give it value. Today, the value of the dollar rests on little more than public confidence in the government. But in the nineteenth century, most people assumed that currency was worthless if there was not something concrete behind it—precious metal (specie), which holders of paper money could collect if they presented their currency to a bank or to the Treasury.

During most of its existence as a nation, the United States had recognized two metals—gold and silver—as a basis for the dollar, a formula known as "bimetallism." In the 1870s, however, that had changed. The official ratio of the value of silver to the value of gold for purposes of creating currency (the "mint ratio") was 16 to 1: sixteen ounces of silver equaled one ounce of gold. But the actual commercial value of silver was much higher than that. Owners of silver could get more by selling it for manufacture into jewelry and other objects than they could by taking it to the mint for conversion to coins. So they stopped taking it to the mint, and the mint stopped coining silver.

"Bimetallism"

In 1873, Congress passed a law that seemed simply to recognize the existing situation by officially discontinuing silver coinage. Few objected at the time. But later in the 1870s, the market value of silver fell well below the official mint ratio of 16 to 1. Silver was suddenly available for coinage again, and it soon became clear that Congress had foreclosed a potential method of expanding the currency. Before long, many Americans concluded that a conspiracy of big bankers had been responsible for the "demonetization" of silver, and they referred to the law as the "Crime of '73."

Two groups of Americans were especially determined to undo the "Crime of '73." One consisted of silver-mine owners and their allies, now understandably eager to have the government take their surplus silver and pay them much more than the market price. The other group consisted of discontented farmers, who wanted an increase in the quantity of money—an inflation of the currency—as a means of raising the prices of farm products and easing payment of the farmers' debts. The inflationists demanded that the government return at once to "free silver"—that is, to the "free and unlimited coinage of silver" at the old ratio of 16 to 1. Congress responded weakly to these demands with the Sherman Silver Purchase Act of 1890, which required the government to purchase (but not coin) silver and pay for it in gold.

"Free Silver"

At the same time, the nation's gold reserves were steadily dropping. And the Panic of 1893 intensified the demands on those reserves. President Cleveland believed that the chief cause of the weakening gold reserves was the Sherman Silver Purchase Act. Early in his second administration, therefore, Congress responded to his request and repealed the act—although only after a bitter and divisive battle that helped create a permanent split in the Democratic Party.

Sherman Silver Purchase Act Repealed

"A Cross of Gold"

Republicans, watching the failure of Cleveland and the Democrats to deal effectively with the depression, were confident of success in 1896. Party leaders, led by the Ohio boss Marcus A. Hanna, settled on former congressman William McKinley, author of the 1890 tariff act and now governor of Ohio, as the party's presidential candidate. The tariff, they believed, should be the principal issue in the campaign. But their platform also opposed the free coinage of silver except by agreement with the leading commercial nations (which everyone realized was unlikely). Thirty-four delegates from the mountain and plains states walked out in protest and joined the Democratic Party.

McKinley Nominated

The Democratic convention of 1896 was unusually tumultuous. Southern and western delegates, eager for a way to compete with the Populists, were determined to seize control of the party from conservative easterners and incorporate some Populist demands—among them free silver—into the Democratic platform. They wanted as well to nominate a pro-silver candidate. The divided platform committee presented two reports to the convention. The majority report, the work of westerners and southerners, called for tariff reduction, an income tax, "stricter control" of trusts and railroads, and—most prominently—free silver. The minority report, the product of the party's eastern wing, echoed the Republican platform by opposing the free coinage of silver except by international agreement.

Defenders of the gold standard seemed to prevail in the debate, until the final speech. Then William Jennings Bryan, a handsome, thirty-six-year-old congressman from Nebraska, mounted the podium to address the convention. He delivered a defense of free silver that became one of the most famous political speeches in American history. The closing passage sent his audience into something close to a frenzy: "If they dare to come out in the open and defend the gold standard as a good thing, we will fight them to the uttermost. Having behind us the producing masses of this nation and the world, supported by the commercial interests, the laboring interests and the toilers everywhere, we will answer their demand for a gold standard by saying to them: 'You shall not press down upon the brow of labor this crown of thorns; you shall not crucify mankind upon a cross of gold.' " It became known as the "Cross of Gold" speech.

"Cross of Gold" Speech

In the glow of Bryan's speech, the convention voted to adopt the pro-silver platform. Perhaps more important, the agrarians embraced Bryan as their leader. The following day, Bryan was nominated for president on the fifth ballot.

The Populists had expected both major parties to adopt conservative programs and nominate conservative candidates, leaving the Populists to represent the growing forces of protest. But now the Democrats had stolen much of their thunder. The Populists faced the choice of naming their own candidate and splitting the protest vote or endorsing Bryan and losing their identity as a party. Many Populists argued that "fusion" with the Democrats would destroy their party. But the majority concluded that there was no viable alternative. Amid considerable acrimony, the convention voted to support Bryan. In a feeble effort to maintain their independence, the Populists repudiated the Democratic nominee for vice president and chose their own, Tom Watson of Georgia.

"Fusion"

The Conservative Victory

The campaign of 1896 produced desperation among conservatives. The business and financial community contributed lavishly to the Republican campaign. From his home at Canton, Ohio, McKinley conducted a dignified "front-porch" campaign before pilgrimages of the Republican faithful, customary behavior in an age when many Americans considered it undignified for anyone to campaign too openly for the presidency.

Emergence of Modern Campaigning

Bryan showed no such restraint. He became the first presidential candidate in American history to stump the country systematically. He traveled 18,000 miles (mostly in the West and South) and addressed an estimated 5 million people. His revivalistic, camp-meeting style pleased old-stock Protestants, but it alienated many of the immigrant Catholics and other ethnics who normally voted Democratic. Employers, meanwhile, warned workers that a Bryan victory would cost them their jobs.

On election day, McKinley polled 271 electoral votes to Bryan's 176 and received 51.1 percent of the popular vote to Bryan's 47.7. Bryan car-

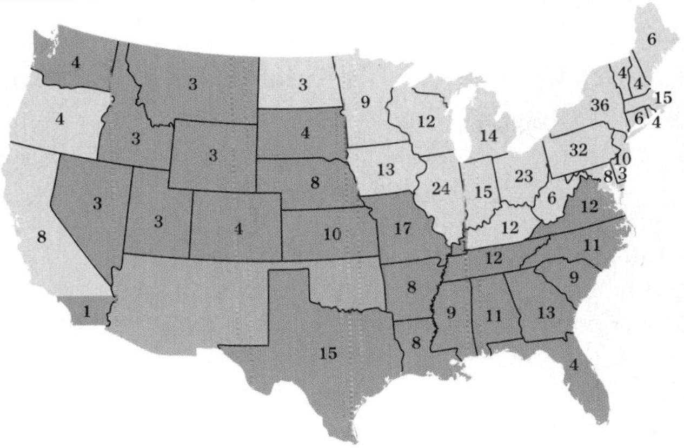

	ELECTORAL VOTE	POPULAR VOTE (%)
William McKinley *(Republican)*	271	7,104,779 (51.1)
William Jennings Bryan *(Democratic)*	176	6,502,925 (47.7)

ELECTION OF 1896 The results of the presidential election of 1896 are, as this map shows, striking for the regional differentiation they reveal. William McKinley won the election by a comfortable but not enormous margin, but his victory was not broad-based. He carried all the states of the Northeast and the industrial Midwest, along with California and Oregon, but virtually nothing else. Bryan carried the entire South and almost all of the agrarian West.
◆ *What campaign issues in 1896 help account for the regional character of the results?*

For an interactive version of this map go to www.mhhe.com/unfinishednation4ch19maps

ried only those areas of the South and West where miners or struggling staple farmers predominated. The Democratic program, like that of the Populists, had been too narrow to win a national election.

Demise of the Populist Party

For the Populists and their allies, the election results were a disaster. They had gambled everything on their "fusion" with the Democratic Party and lost. Within months of the election, the People's Party began to dissolve.

McKinley and Prosperity

The administration of William McKinley saw a return to relative calm. McKinley and his allies worked actively and energetically on only one issue: the need for higher tariff rates. Within weeks of McKinley's inauguration, the administration won approval of the Dingley Tariff, raising duties to the highest point in American history. The administration dealt more gingerly with the explosive silver question (an issue McKinley himself had never considered very important in any case). McKinley sent a commission to Europe to explore the possibility of a silver agreement with Great Britain and France. As he and everyone else anticipated, the effort produced no agreement. The Republicans then enacted the Currency, or Gold Standard, Act of 1900, which confirmed the nation's commitment to the gold standard.

Gold Standard Act

And so the "battle of the standards" ended in victory for the forces of conservatism. Economic developments at the time seemed to vindicate them. Prosperity returned beginning in 1898. Foreign crop failures sent United States farm prices surging upward, and American business entered another cycle of booming expansion. Prosperity and the gold standard, it seemed, were closely allied.

But while the free-silver movement had failed, it had raised an important question for the American economy. In the quarter-century before 1900, the nations of the Western world had experienced a spectacular growth in productive facilities and population. Yet the supply of money had not kept pace with economic progress. Had it not been for a dramatic increase in the gold supply in the late 1890s (a result of new techniques for extracting gold from low-content ores and the discovery of huge new gold deposits in Alaska, South Africa, and Australia), Populist predictions of financial disaster might in fact have proved correct. In 1898, two and a half times as much gold was produced as in 1890, and the currency supply was soon inflated far beyond anything Bryan and the free-silver forces had proposed.

By then, however, Bryan—like many other Americans—was becoming engaged with another major issue: the nation's growing involvement in world affairs and its increasing flirtation with imperialism.

CONCLUSION

For nearly three decades after the battles over Reconstruction, the electorate was relatively evenly divided between the two major parties, which differed with one another on only a few issues. The national government, never fully dominated by either party, remained small and inconsequential. Except for Indian tribes, people engaged in international trade (who were thus subject to tariffs), and the many northern Civil War veterans who received federal pensions, few Americans had any direct contact with the government in Washington except to receive mail from the federal post office. A series of worthy and generally dull presidents presided over this political system as unwitting symbols of its stability and passivity.

Beneath the placid surface of national politics, however, great social issues were creating deep divisions in American life. Battles between employers and workers intensified. American farmers became increasingly resentful of their declining fortunes. Men and women throughout the country grew angry about corruption in government and excessive power in the hands of a few corporate leaders. When a great depression began in 1893, these social tensions exploded to the surface.

The most visible sign of the challenge to politics was the Populist movement. The Populists created their own political party, showed impressive strength in several elections, and then—in 1896—joined with the Democrats to nominate the great Nebraska orator William Jennings Bryan for president. But the forces for insurgency were, in the end, no match for the forces of established institutions. After a campaign notable for its hysterical attacks on Bryan and on the issue with which he was identified ("free silver," making silver a basis for issuing currency in addition to gold), Bryan lost the election to William McKinley. Perhaps more important, the election became the occasion for a great electoral realignment that left the Republicans the clear majority party for the next three decades.

The Republican victory did not, however, end the battle over power and corruption in American life. It simply redirected it into other channels. The challenges to the old politics soon made themselves felt as more conventional reform movements that became known, collectively, as progressivism.

FOR FURTHER REFERENCE

Morton Keller, *Affairs of State: Public Life in Late Nineteenth-Century America* (1977) is an important study of politics and government after Reconstruction. Nell Irvin Painter, *Standing at Armageddon: The United States, 1877–1919* (1987) explores the multicultural dimensions of industrialization, emphasizing the particularly cataclysmic effect of industrialization on minority populations and on race relations. Martin J. Sklar, *The Corporate Reconstruction of American Capitalism, 1890–1916* (1988), offers an interpretation of the evolution of American business practice and, by extension, American politics and society. Two significant books charting the growing capacities of the American state during this period are Theda Skocpol, *Protecting Soldiers and Mothers: The Political Origins of Social Policy in the United States* (1992) and Stephen Skowronek, *Building a New American State: The Expansion of National Administrative Capacities, 1877–1920* (1982). Richard Hofstadter's *The Age of Reform: From Bryan to FDR* (1955) and Lawrence Goodwyn's *The Populist Moment* (1978) offer sharply contrasting characterizations of the Populist and progressive reform movements of this time. Other important studies of Populism include John D. Hicks, *The Populist Revolt* (1931), a classic account, and Steven Hahn, *The Roots of Southern Populism: Yeoman Farmers and the Transformation of the Georgia Upcountry* (1983). Michael Kazin, *The Populist Persuasion: An American History* (1995) places Populist ideas in a broad historical context.

For quizzes, Internet resources, references to additional books and films, and more, consult this book's Online Learning Center site at www.mhhe.com/unfinishednation4.

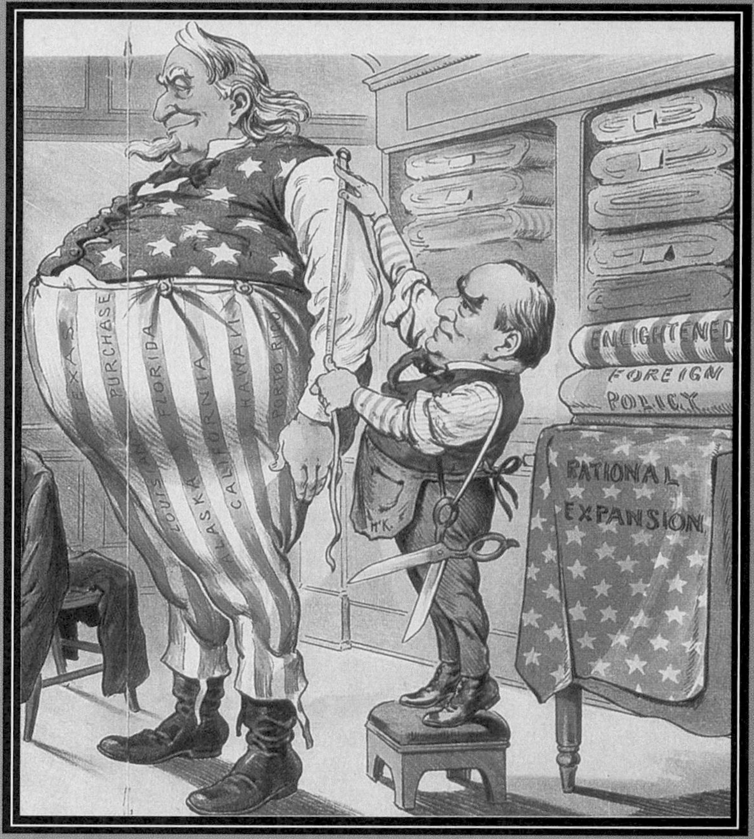

"MEASURING UNCLE SAM FOR A NEW SUIT," BY J. S. PUGHE, IN *PUCK* MAGAZINE, 1900 President William McKinley is favorably depicted here as a tailor, measuring his client for a suit large enough to accommodate the new possessions the United States obtained in the aftermath of the Spanish-American War. The cartoon tries to link this expansion with earlier, less controversial ones such as the Louisiana Purchase. *(Culver Pictures, Inc)*

TIME LINE

1875	1878	1887	1889	1890	1893	1895
Reciprocity treaty with Hawaii	U.S. gains base at Pago Pago	U.S. gains base at Pearl Harbor	First Pan-American Congress	Mahan's *The Influence of Sea Power upon History*	Revolution in Hawaii	Venezuelan boundary dispute

CHAPTER TWENTY

THE IMPERIAL REPUBLIC

Stirrings of Imperialism
War with Spain
The Republic as Empire

Throughout the first half of the nineteenth century, as the population of the United States grew and pressed westward, the government, through purchase or conquest, had continually acquired new lands: the trans-Appalachian West, the Louisiana Territory, Florida, Texas, Oregon, California, New Mexico, Alaska. It was the nation's "Manifest Destiny," many Americans believed, to expand into new realms.

In the last years of the nineteenth century, with little room left for territorial growth on the North American continent, those who favored expansion set their eyes beyond the nation's shore. The United States began to consider joining England, France, Germany, and others in the great imperial drive that was bringing much of the nonindustrial world under the control of the industrial powers of the West.

STIRRINGS OF IMPERIALISM

For over two decades after the Civil War, the United States expanded geographically hardly at all. By the 1890s, however, some Americans were ready—indeed, eager—to resume the course of Manifest Destiny that had inspired their ancestors to wrest an empire from Mexico.

1898	1898–1902	1899	1900	1901	1946
Battleship *Maine* sunk	Philippines revolt	Open Door notes	Boxer Rebellion	Platt Amendment	U.S. grants Philippines independence
War with Spain			McKinley reelected		
Treaty of Paris					
U.S. annexes Hawaii, Philippines, Puerto Rico					

The New Manifest Destiny

Several developments helped shift American attention to lands across the seas. The experience of subjugating the Indian tribes had established a precedent for exerting colonial control over dependent peoples. The supposed "closing of the frontier" produced fears that natural resources would soon dwindle. The depression that began in 1893 encouraged some businessmen to look for new markets abroad. Americans were, moreover, well aware of the imperialist fever that was raging through Europe. It was leading the major powers to partition most of Africa among themselves and to turn covetous eyes on the Far East and the feeble Chinese Empire. Some Americans feared that their nation would soon be left out, that the Europeans would seize all these potential markets for themselves.

Sources of Imperialism

Scholars and others found a philosophic justification for expansionism in Charles Darwin's theories. They contended that nations or "races," like biological species, struggled constantly for existence and that only the fittest could survive. For strong nations to dominate weak ones was, therefore, in accordance with the laws of nature.

Alfred Thayer Mahan

The ablest and most effective advocate of imperialism was Alfred Thayer Mahan, a captain and later admiral in the navy. Mahan's thesis—presented in *The Influence of Sea Power upon History* (1890) and other works—was simple: Countries with sea power were the great nations of history. Effective sea power required, among other things, colonies. Mahan believed America should, at the least, acquire defensive bases in the Caribbean and the Pacific and take possession of Hawaii and other Pacific islands. Mahan feared that the United States did not have a large enough navy to play the great role he envisioned. But during the 1870s and 1880s, the government launched a shipbuilding program that by 1898 had moved the United States to fifth place among the world's naval powers, and by 1900 to third.

Hemispheric Hegemony

James G. Blaine, who served as secretary of state in the Republican administrations of the 1880s, led the early efforts to expand American influence into Latin America. In October 1889, he helped organize the first Pan-American Congress, which attracted delegates from nineteen nations. The delegates agreed to create the Pan-American Union, a weak international organization located in Washington that served as a clearinghouse for distributing information to the member nations. But they rejected Blaine's more substantive proposals: an inter-American customs union and arbitration procedures for hemispheric disputes.

Venezuelan Dispute

The second Cleveland administration also took a lively interest in Latin America. In 1895, it supported Venezuela in a dispute with Great Britain over the boundary between

LAUNCHING THE *MAINE*, 1889 The battleship *Maine* played a major role in American military history when it blew up in the harbor of Havana, Cuba, in 1898, and help precipitate the Spanish-American War. But it was also significant as part of the growing naval strength the United States was developing in the late nineteenth century. This engraving from *Harper's Weekly* portrays the launching of the *Maine* from the New York Navy Yard in November 1889. *(Naval Historical Center)*

Venezuela and British Guiana. When the British ignored American demands that the matter be submitted to arbitration, the Cleveland administration began threatening England with war. The British government finally realized that it had stumbled into a genuine diplomatic crisis and agreed to arbitration.

Hawaii and Samoa

Hawaii Coveted

The islands of Hawaii in the mid-Pacific had been an important way station for American ships in the China trade since the early nineteenth century. By the 1880s, officers of the expanding United States Navy were looking covetously at Pearl Harbor on the island of Oahu as a possible permanent base for American ships. Pressure for an increased American presence in Hawaii was emerging from another source as well: the growing number of Americans who had taken up residence on the islands.

Settled by Polynesian people beginning in about 1500 B.C., Hawaii had developed an agricultural and fishing society in which different islands (and different communities on the same islands), each with its own chieftain, lived more or less self-sufficiently. When the first Americans arrived in Hawaii in the 1790s on merchant ships from New England, there were perhaps a half-million people living there.

IMPERIALISM

Empires were not, of course, new to the nineteenth century, when the United States acquired its first overseas colonies. They have existed since the early moments of recorded history—in Greece, Rome, China, and many other parts of the world; and they continued into the sixteenth and seventeenth centuries with vast imperial projects undertaken by Spain, Portugal, France, the Netherlands, and Great Britain in the Americas.

But in the mid- and late-nineteenth century, the construction of empires took on a different form from those of earlier eras, and the word "imperialism" emerged for the first time to describe it. In many places, European powers now created colonies not by sending large numbers of migrants to settle and populate new lands, but instead by creating military, political, and business structures that allowed them to dominate and profit from the existing populations. This new imperialism changed the character of the colonizing nations themselves, enriching them greatly and producing new classes of people whose lives were shaped by the demands of imperial business and administration. It changed the character of colonized societies even more, by drawing them into the vast nexus of global industrial capitalism and by introducing European customs, institutions, and technologies to the subject peoples.

As the popularity of empire grew in the West in the late nineteenth century, efforts to justify it grew as well. Champions of imperialism argued that the acquisition of colonies was essential for the health, even the survival, of their own industrializing nations. Colonies were sources of raw materials vital to industrial production; they were markets for manufactured goods; and they could be suppliers of cheap labor. But defenders of empire also argued that imperialism was good for the colonized people. Many saw colonization as an opportunity to export Christianity to "heathen" lands, and great new missionary movements emerged in Europe and America in response. More secular apologists argued that imperialism helped bring colonized people into the modern world. The British poet Rudyard Kipling was perhaps the most famous spokesman for empire. In his celebrated poem "The White Man's Burden," he spoke of the duty of the colonizers to lift up primitive peoples: to "fill full the mouth of famine and bid the sickness cease."

The growth of empire was not simply a result of need and desire. It was also a result of the new capacities of the imperial powers. The invention of steamships, railroads, telegraphs, and other modern vehicles of transportation and communication; the construction of canals (particular the Suez Canal, completed in 1869, and the Panama Canal, completed in 1914); the birth of new military technologies (repeating rifles, machine guns, and modern artillery): all contributed to the ability of western nations to reach, conquer, and control distant lands.

The greatest imperial power of the nineteenth century, indeed one of the greatest imperial powers in all of human history, was Great Britain. By 1800, despite its recent loss of the colonies that became the United States, it already possessed vast territory in North America, the Caribbean, and the Pacific—most notably Canada and Australia. But in the second half of the nineteenth century, Britain greatly expanded its empire. Its most important acquisition was India, one of the largest and most populous countries in the world. Britain had carried on a substantial trade with India for many years and had gradually increased its economic and military power there. In 1857, when native Indians revolted against British authority, British forces brutally crushed the rebellion and established formal colonial control over India. British officials, backed by substantial military power, now governed India through a large civil service staffed mostly by people from England and Scotland, but with some Indians serving in minor positions. The British invested heavily in railroads, telegraphs, canals, harbors, and agricultural improvements, to enhance the economic opportunities available to them. They created schools for Indian children, in an effort to draw them into British culture and make them supporters of the imperial system.

In those same years, the British extended their empire into Africa and other parts of Asia. The great imperial champion Cecil Rhodes expanded a small existing British colony at Capetown into a substantial colony that included much of what is now South Africa. In 1895, he added new territories to the north, which he named Rhodesia (and which today are Zimbabwe and Zambia). Others spread British authority into Kenya, Uganda, Nigeria, and much of Egypt. British imperialists simultaneously extended the empire into east Asia, with the acquisition of Singapore, Hong Kong, Burma, and Malaya; and they built a substantial presence—although not formal colonial rule—in China.

Other European states, watching the vast expansion of the British empire, quickly jumped into the race for colonies. France created colonies in Indochina (Vietnam and Laos), Algeria, west Africa, and Madagascar. Belgium moved into the Congo in west Africa. Germany established colonies in the Cameroons, Tanganyika, and other parts of Africa, and in the Pacific islands north of Australia. Dutch, Italian, Portuguese, Spanish, Russian, and Japanese imperialists created colonies as well in Africa, Asia, and the Pacific—driven both by a calculation of their own commercial interests and by the frenzied competition that had developed among rival imperial powers. And in 1898, the United States was drawn into the imperial race. Americans entered it in part inadvertently, as an unanticipated result of the Spanish-American War. But they also sought colonies as a result of the deliberate efforts of homegrown proponents of empire (among them Theodore Roosevelt), many of them heavily influenced by British friends and colleagues, who believed that in the modern industrial-imperial world a nation without colonies would have difficulty remaining, or becoming, a true great power.

(text continued from page 537)

Battles among rival communities were frequent, as ambitious chieftains tried to consolidate power over their neighbors. In 1810, after a series of such battles, King Kamehameha I established his dominance over the other chieftains on Hawaii. He welcomed American traders and helped them develop a thriving trade between Hawaii and China. But Americans soon wanted more than trade. Missionaries began settling there in the early nineteenth century, and in the 1830s, William Hooper, a Boston trader, became the first of many Americans to buy land and establish a sugar plantation on the islands.

Growing American Dominance

The arrival of these merchants, missionaries, and planters was devastating to native Hawaiian society. The newcomers inadvertently brought infectious diseases to which the Hawaiians, like the American Indians before them, were tragically vulnerable. By the mid-nineteenth century, more than half the native population had died. But the Americans brought other incursions as well. Missionaries worked to replace native religion with Christianity. Other white settlers introduced liquor, firearms, and a commercial economy, all of which eroded the traditional character of Hawaiian society. By the 1840s, American planters had spread throughout the islands; and an American settler, G. P. Judd, had become prime minister of Hawaii under King Kamehameha III, who had agreed to establish a constitutional monarchy. Judd governed Hawaii for over a decade.

In 1887, the United States negotiated a treaty with Hawaii that permitted it to open a naval base at Pearl Harbor. By then, growing sugar for export to America had become the basis of the Hawaiian economy—as a result of an 1875 agreement allowing Hawaiian sugar to enter the United States duty-free. The American-dominated sugar plantation system displaced native Hawaiians from their lands and relied heavily for workers on Asian immigrants, whom the Americans considered more reliable and more docile than the natives.

Queen Lilinokalani

Native Hawaiians did not accept these changes without protest. In 1891, they elevated a powerful nationalist to the throne: Queen Liliuokalani. But her brief reign coincided with newly militant efforts by the Americans to seize power, efforts that came as a result of an act of Congress. In 1890, Congress had eliminated the 1875 exemption from tariffs for Hawaiian sugar planters. The result was devastating to the economy of the islands, and American planters concluded that the only way for them to recover was to become part of the United States (and hence exempt from its tariffs). In 1893 they staged a revolution and called on the United States for protection. After the American minister ordered marines from a warship in Honolulu harbor to go ashore to aid the rebels, the queen yielded her authority.

Hawaii Annexed

A provisional government, dominated by Americans, immediately sent a delegation to Washington to negotiate a treaty of annexation. Debate over the treaty continued until 1898, when Congress finally approved the agreement.

Three thousand miles south of Hawaii, the Samoan islands had also long served as a port for American ships in the Pacific trade. As American commerce with Asia increased, business groups in the United States regarded Samoa with new interest, and the American navy began eyeing the Samoan harbor at Pago Pago. In 1878, the Hayes administration extracted a treaty from Samoan leaders for an American naval station there. It bound the United States to arbitrate any differences between Samoa and other nations.

But Great Britain and Germany were also interested in the islands, and they too secured treaty rights from the native princes. For the next ten years the three powers jockeyed for dominance in Samoa. Finally, the three powers agreed to create a tripartite protectorate over Samoa, with the native chiefs exercising only nominal authority. The three-way arrangement failed to halt the intrigues and rivalries of its members, and in 1899, the United States and Germany divided the islands between them, compensating Britain with territories elsewhere in the Pacific. The United States retained the harbor at Pago Pago.

Pago Pago Taken

WAR WITH SPAIN

Imperial ambitions had thus begun to stir within the United States well before the late 1890s. But a war with Spain in 1898 turned those stirrings into overt expansionism.

Controversy over Cuba

The Spanish-American War emerged out of events in Cuba. Cubans had been resisting Spanish rule intermittently since at least 1868, when they began a long but ultimately unsuccessful fight for independence. Many Americans had sympathized with the Cubans during that first ten-year struggle, but the United States did not intervene.

Cuban Revolt

In 1895, the Cubans rose up again. This rebellion produced a ferocity on both sides that horrified Americans. The Cubans deliberately devastated the island to force the Spaniards to leave. The Spanish, commanded by General Valeriano Weyler (known in the American press as "Butcher" Weyler), confined civilians in certain areas to hastily prepared concentration camps, where they died by the thousands, victims of disease and malnutrition. The Spanish had used equally savage methods during the earlier struggle in Cuba without shocking American sensibilities. But the revolt of 1895 attracted unprecedented attention in the United States. That was partly because a growing population of Cuban émigrés in the United States—centered in Florida, New York, Philadelphia, and Trenton, New Jersey—gave extensive support to the Cuban Revolutionary Party (whose headquarters was in New York). They helped publicize its leader, José Martí, who was killed in Cuba in 1895. Later, Cuban Americans formed other clubs and associations to support the cause of *Cuba Libre* (Free Cuba).

"Yellow Press"

But it was also because the events in Cuba were reported more fully and flamboyantly by American newspapers, and particularly by the new "yellow press" of William Randolph Hearst and Joseph Pulitzer. Pulitzer's *World*, which began publishing in New York in 1883, launched the age of yellow journalism—a

863,956 WORLDS CIRCULATED YESTERDAY

"Circulation Books Open to All."

The World.

863,956 WORLDS CIRCULATED YESTERD

"Circulation Books Open to All."

VOL. XXXVIII. NO. 13,3

NEW YORK, THURSDAY, FEBRUARY 17, 189

PRICE

MAINE EXPLOSION CAUSED BY BOMB OR TORPEDO

Capt. Sigsbee and Consul-General Lee Are in Doubt---The World Has Sent Special Tug, With Submarine Divers, to Havana to Find Out---Lee Asks for an Immediate Court of Inquiry---Capt. Sigsbee's Suspicions.

CAPT. SIGSBEE, IN A SUPPRESSED DESPATCH TO THE STATE DEPARTMENT, SAYS THE ACCIDENT WAS MADE POSSIBLE BY AN ENE

Dr. E. C. Pendleton, Just Arrived from Havana, Says He Overheard Talk There of a Plot to Blow Up the Ship---C Zalinski, the Dynamite Expert, and Other Experts Report to The World that the Wreck Was Not Accidental---Washington Officials Ready for Vigorous Action if Spanish Responsibility Can Be Shown---Divers to Be Sent Down to Make Careful Examinations.

THE YELLOW PRESS AND THE WRECK OF THE *MAINE* No evidence was ever found tying the Spanish to the explosion in Havana harbor that destroyed the American battleship *Maine* in February 1898. Indeed, most evidence indicated that the blast came from inside the ship, a fact that suggests an accident rather than sabotage. Nevertheless, the newspapers of Joseph Pulitzer and William Randolph Hearst ran sensational stories about the incident that were designed to arouse public sentiment in support of a war against the Spanish. This front-page from Pulitzer's *New York World* is an example of the lurid coverage the event received. Circulation figures at the top of the page indicate, too, how successful the coverage was in selling newspapers. *(The Granger Collection, New York)*

term probably derived originally from the lavish use of color in the *World*, and the color yellow (an especially difficult one to print) in particular. But before long, the term came to be used to describe a sensationalist style of reporting and writing, and a self-conscious effort to reach a mass market. The success of the *World*, whose circulation reached 250,000 by 1886, spawned imitators in New York and elsewhere. Most prominent among them was Hearst's *New York Journal*, which cut its price to one cent after Hearst bought it in 1895 (Pulitzer quickly followed suit), copied many of the *World*'s techniques, and within a year raised its circulation to 400,000. The competition between these two great "yellow" journals soon drove both to new levels of sensationalism. Their success inspired newspapers in other cities around the nation to copy their techniques.

The civil war in Cuba gave both papers their best opportunities yet for combining sensational reporting with shameless appeals to patriotism and moral outrage. They avidly published exaggerated reports of Spanish atrocities against the Cuban rebels, fanning popular anger toward Spain. When the American battleship *Maine* mysteriously exploded in Havana harbor in 1898, both papers immediately blamed Spanish authorities (without any evidence). The *Journal* offered a $50,000 reward for information leading to the conviction of those responsible for the explosion, and it crowded all other stories off its front page. In the three days following the *Maine* explosion, the *Journal* sold over 3 million copies, a new world's record for newspaper circulation. The *World* exploited the destruction of the *Maine* less successfully (although not for lack of trying), but it soon made up for it in its highly sensationalized coverage of the war itself. Hearst boasted at times that the conflict in Cuba was "the *Journal*'s war" and even sent a cable to one of his reporters in Cuba saying: "You furnish the pictures, and I'll furnish the war."

Despite the mounting storm of indignation against Spain, President Cleveland refused to intervene in the conflict. But when McKinley became president in 1897, he formally protested Spain's "uncivilized and inhuman" conduct, causing the Spanish government (fearful of American intervention) to recall Weyler, modify the concentration policy, and grant the island a qualified autonomy.

But whatever chances there were for a peaceful settlement vanished as a result of two dramatic incidents in February 1898. The first occurred when a Cuban agent stole a private letter written by Dupuy de Lôme, the Spanish minister in Washington, and turned it over to the American press. It described McKinley as a weak man and "a bidder for the admiration of the crowd." This was no more than what many Americans, including some Republicans, were saying about their president. But coming from a foreigner, it created intense popular anger. Dupuy de Lôme promptly resigned.

de Lôme Letter

While excitement over the de Lôme letter was still high, the American battleship *Maine* blew up in Havana harbor with a loss of more than 260 people. Many Americans assumed that the Spanish had sunk the ship, particularly when a naval court of inquiry reported that an external explosion by a submarine mine had caused the disaster. (Later evidence suggested that the disaster was actually the result of an accidental explosion inside one of the engine rooms.) War hysteria swept the country, and Congress unanimously appropriated $50 million for military preparations.

The Maine

McKinley still hoped to avoid a conflict. But others in his administration (including Theodore Roosevelt) were clamoring for war. In March 1898, at McKinley's request, Spain agreed to stop the fighting and eliminate its concentration camps; but it refused to negotiate with the rebels and reserved the right to resume hostilities at its discretion. That satisfied neither public opinion nor Congress. A few days later, McKinley asked for and, on April 25, received a congressional declaration of war.

"A Splendid Little War"

Secretary of State John Hay called the Spanish-American conflict "a splendid little war," an opinion that most Americans seemed to share. Declared in April, it was over in August. That was in part because Cuban rebels had already greatly weakened the Spanish resistance, which made the American intervention in many respects little more than a "mopping up" exercise. Only 460 Americans were killed in battle or died of wounds, although some 5,200 perished of disease: malaria, dysentery, and typhoid, among others. Casualties among Cuban insurgents, who continued to bear the brunt of the struggle, were much higher.

Logistical Difficulties

Yet the American war effort was not without difficulties. United States soldiers faced serious supply problems: a shortage of modern rifles and ammunition, uniforms too heavy for the warm Caribbean weather, inadequate medical services, and skimpy, almost indigestible food. The regular army numbered only 28,000 troops and officers, most of whom had experience in quelling Indian outbreaks but none in larger-scale warfare. That meant that, as in the Civil War, the United States had to rely heavily on National Guard units, organized by local communities and commanded for the most part by local leaders without military experience.

A significant proportion of the American invasion force consisted of black soldiers. Some were volunteer troops put together by black communities. Others were members of the four black regiments in the regular army, who had been stationed on the frontier to defend white settlements against Indians and were now transferred east to fight in Cuba. As the black soldiers traveled through the South toward the training camps, some resisted the rigid segregation to which they were subjected. Black soldiers in Georgia deliberately made use of a "whites only" park; in Florida, they beat a soda-fountain operator for refusing to serve them; in Tampa, white provocations and black retaliation led to a night-long riot that left thirty wounded.

Racial Tensions in the Military

Racial tensions continued in Cuba itself, where African Americans played crucial roles in some of the important battles of the war (including the famous charge at San Juan Hill) and won many medals. Nearly half the Cuban insurgents fighting with the Americans were black, but unlike their American counterparts they were fully integrated into the rebel army. The sight of black Cuban soldiers fighting alongside whites as equals gave African Americans a stronger sense of the injustice of their own position.

Seizing the Philippines

Assistant Secretary of the Navy Theodore Roosevelt was an ardent imperialist and an active proponent of war. As the tension with Spain rose, Roosevelt unilaterally strengthened the navy's Pacific squadron and instructed its commander, Commodore George Dewey, to attack Spanish naval forces in the Philippines, a colony of Spain, in the event of war.

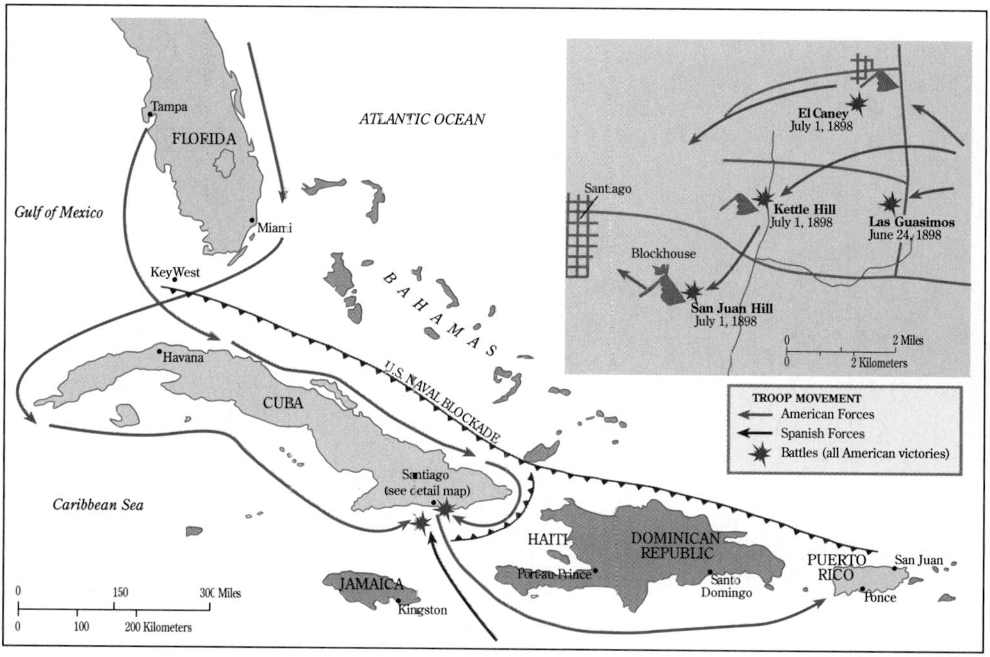

THE SPANISH-AMERICAN WAR IN CUBA, 1898 The military conflict between the United States and Spain in Cuba was a brief affair. The Cuban rebels and an American naval blockade had already brought the Spanish to the brink of defeat. The arrival of American troops was simply the final blow. In the space of about a week, U.S. troops won four decisive battles in the area around Santiago in southeast Cuba—one of them (the Battle of Kettle Hill) the scene of Theodore Roosevelt's famous charge up the adjacent San Juan Hill. This map shows the extent of the American naval blockade, the path of American troops from Florida to Cuba, and the location of the actual fighting. ◆ *What were the implications of the war in Cuba for Puerto Rico?*

For an interactive version of this map go to www.mhhe.com/unfinishednation4ch20maps

Immediately after war was declared, Dewey sailed for the Philippines. On May 1, 1898, he steamed into Manila Bay and completely destroyed the aging Spanish fleet there. Dewey, immediately promoted to admiral, became the first hero of the war. Several months later, after the arrival of an American expeditionary force, the Spanish surrendered the city of Manila itself.

Dewey Victorious

The Battle for Cuba

Cuba, however, remained the principal focus of American military efforts. At first, the American commanders planned a long period of training before actually sending troops into combat. But when a Spanish fleet under Admiral Pascual Cervera slipped past the American navy into Santiago harbor, on the southern coast of Cuba, plans changed quickly. The American Atlantic fleet quickly bottled Cervera up in the harbor. And the army's

THE ROUGH RIDERS Theodore Roosevelt, center, poses with some of the Rough Riders after their famous charge in the Battle of San Juan Hill. The brigade had an unofficial anthem: "Rough, rough, we're the stuff. We want to fight, and we can't get enough." *(Theodore Roosevelt Association)*

commanding general, Nelson A. Miles, hastily altered his strategy and ordered a force of 17,000 to leave Tampa in June to attack Santiago.

General William R. Shafter, the American commander in Cuba, moved toward Santiago, which he planned to surround and capture. On the way he met and defeated Spanish forces at Las Guasimos and, a week later, in two simultaneous battles, El Caney and San Juan Hill. At the center of the fighting (and on the front pages of the newspapers) during all these engagements was a cavalry unit known as the Rough Riders. Nominally commanded by General Leonard Wood, its real leader was Colonel Theodore Roosevelt, who had resigned from the Navy Department to get into the war. Roosevelt rapidly emerged as a hero of the conflict. His fame rested in large part on his role in leading a bold, if perhaps reckless, charge up Kettle Hill (a charge that was a minor part of the larger battle for the adjacent San Juan Hill) directly into the face of Spanish guns. Roosevelt himself emerged unscathed, but nearly a hundred of his soldiers were killed or wounded. He remembered the battle as "the great day of my life."

Theodore Roosevelt's Rough Riders

Although Shafter was now in position to assault Santiago, his army was so weakened by sickness that he feared he could not go on. Disaster seemed imminent. But unknown to the Americans, the Spanish government had by now decided that Santiago was lost and had ordered Cervera to evacuate. On July 3, Cervera tried to escape the harbor. The waiting American squadron destroyed his entire fleet. On July 16, the commander of the Spanish ground forces in Santiago surrendered. At about the same time, an American army landed in Puerto Rico and occupied it against virtually no opposition. On August 12, the United States accepted an end to the war when Spain signed an armistice recognizing Cuban independence, ceding Puerto Rico to the United States, and accepting American occupation of Manila until the two nations reached a final agreement on the Philippines.

Puerto Rico Occupied

Puerto Rico and the United States

The island of Puerto Rico had been a part of the Spanish Empire since Ponce de León arrived there in 1508. The native people of the island, the Arawaks, disappeared almost entirely as a result of infectious diseases, Spanish brutality, and poverty. Puerto Rican society developed, therefore, with a Spanish ruling class and a large African work force for the coffee and sugar plantations that came to dominate its economy.

Puerto Rican resistance to Spanish rule began to emerge in the nineteenth century. Uprisings occurred intermittently beginning in the 1820s; the most important of them—the so-called Lares Rebellion—was, like the others, effectively crushed by the Spanish in 1868. But the growing resistance did prompt some reforms: the abolition of slavery in 1873, representation in the Spanish parliament, and other changes. Demands for independence continued to grow, and in 1898 Spain granted the island a degree of independence. But before the changes had any chance to take effect, control of Puerto Rico shifted to the United States.

American military forces occupied the island during the war. They remained in control until 1900, when the Foraker Act ended military rule and established a formal colonial government. In 1917, Congress passed the Jones Act, which declared Puerto Rico to be United States territory and made all Puerto Ricans American citizens.

Foraker Act

The Puerto Rican sugar industry flourished as it took advantage of the American market that was now open to it without tariffs. As in Hawaii, Americans from the mainland soon established large sugar plantations on the island and hired natives to work them. The growing emphasis on sugar as a cash crop and the transformation of many Puerto Rican farmers into paid laborers led to a reduction in the growing of food for the island and a higher reliance on imported goods. When international sugar prices were high, Puerto Rico did well. When they dropped, the island's economy sagged, pushing the many plantation workers—already desperately poor—into destitution.

The Debate over the Philippines

If the annexation of Puerto Rico produced relatively little controversy, the annexation of the Philippines occasioned a long and impassioned debate. Controlling a nearby

Annexation Debated

Caribbean island fit reasonably comfortably into America's sense of itself as the dominant power in the Western Hemisphere. Controlling a large and densely populated territory thousands of miles away seemed different and, to many Americans, more ominous.

McKinley claimed to be reluctant to support annexation. But, according to his own accounts, he emerged from an "agonizing night of prayer" convinced that there were no acceptable alternatives. Returning the Philippines to Spain would be "cowardly and dishonorable," he claimed. Turning the islands over to another imperialist power (France, Germany, or Britain) would be "bad business and discreditable." Granting them independence would be irresponsible; the Filipinos were "unfit for self government." The only solution was "to take them all and to educate the Filipinos, and uplift and Christianize them." Growing popular support for annexation and the pressure of the imperialist leaders of his party undoubtedly helped him reach this decision of conscience.

The Treaty of Paris, signed in December 1898, brought a formal end to the Spanish-American War. It confirmed the terms of the armistice concerning Cuba, Puerto Rico, and Guam. American negotiators had startled the Spanish by demanding that they also cede the Philippines to the United States, but an offer of $20 million for the islands softened Spain's resistance. The Spanish negotiators accepted all the American terms.

In the United States Senate, however, resistance was fierce. During debate over ratification of the treaty, a powerful anti-imperialist movement arose throughout the country to oppose acquisition of the Philippines. Among the anti-imperialists were some of the nation's wealthiest and most influential figures. Some believed simply that imperialism was immoral, a repudiation of America's commitment to human freedom. Some feared "polluting" the American population by introducing "inferior" Asian races into it. Industrial workers feared being undercut by a flood of cheap laborers from the new colonies. Conservatives feared that the large standing army and entangling foreign alliances they thought imperialism would require would threaten American liberties. Sugar growers and others feared unwelcome competition from the new territories. The Anti-Imperialist League, established by upper-class Bostonians, New Yorkers, and others late in 1898 to fight against annexation, attracted a widespread following in the Northeast and waged a vigorous campaign against ratification of the Paris treaty.

Anti-Imperialist League

Supporters of Annexation

Favoring ratification was an equally varied group. There were the exuberant imperialists such as Theodore Roosevelt. Some businessmen believed annexation would position the United States to dominate the Asian trade. And most Republicans saw partisan advantages in acquiring valuable new territories through a war fought and won by a Republican administration. Perhaps the strongest argument in favor of annexation, however, was the apparent ease with which it could be accomplished. The United States, after all, already possessed the islands.

When anti-imperialists warned of the danger of acquiring heavily populated territories whose people might have to become citizens, the imperialists had a ready answer: The nation's longstanding policies toward Indians—treating them as dependents rather than as citizens—had created a precedent for annexing land without absorbing people.

The fate of the treaty remained in doubt for weeks, until it received the unexpected support of William Jennings Bryan. Bryan was a fervent anti-imperialist who hoped to move the issue out of the Senate and make annexation the subject of a national referendum in 1900, when he expected to be the Democratic presidential candidate again. Bryan persuaded a number of anti-imperialist Democrats to support the treaty so as to set up the 1900 debate. The Senate ratified it finally on February 6, 1899.

Election of 1900

But Bryan miscalculated. If the campaign of 1900 was in fact a debate on the Philippines, as Bryan tried to make it, the election proved beyond doubt that the nation had decided in favor of imperialism. Once again, Bryan ran against McKinley, and once again, McKinley won—even more decisively than in 1896. It was not only the issue of the colonies, however, that ensured McKinley's victory. The Republicans were the beneficiaries of growing national prosperity—and also of the colorful personality of their vice presidential candidate, Theodore Roosevelt.

THE REPUBLIC AS EMPIRE

The new American empire was a small one by the standards of the great imperial powers of Europe. But it created large problems. It embroiled the United States in the politics of both Europe and the Far East in ways the nation had always tried to avoid in the past. It also drew Americans into a brutal war in the Philippines.

Governing the Colonies

Three of the new American dependencies—Hawaii, Alaska, and Puerto Rico—presented relatively few problems. They received territorial status (and their residents American citizenship) relatively quickly: Hawaii in 1900, Alaska in 1912, and Puerto Rico (in stages) by 1917. The navy took control of Guam and Tutuila. The United States had also acquired some of the smallest, least populated Pacific islands; it simply left them alone.

Cuba was a thornier problem. American military forces, commanded by General Leonard Wood, remained there until 1902 to prepare the island for independence. They built roads, schools, and hospitals; reorganized the legal, financial, and administrative systems; and introduced medical and sanitation reforms. But when Cuba drew up a constitution that made no reference to the United States, Congress responded by passing

Platt Amendment

the Platt Amendment in 1901 and pressuring Cuba into incorporating the amendment's terms into its constitution. The Platt Amendment barred Cuba from making treaties with other nations; it gave the United States the right to intervene in Cuba to preserve independence, life, and property; and it required Cuba to permit American naval stations on its territory. The amendment left Cuba with only nominal political independence. And American capital made the new nation an American economic appendage as well. American investors poured into Cuba, buying up plantations, factories, railroads, and refineries. Resistance to "Yankee imperialism" produced intermittent revolts against the Cuban government—revolts that at times prompted United States military intervention. American troops occupied the island from 1906 to 1909 after one such rebellion; they returned again in 1912, to suppress a revolt by black plantation workers. As in Puerto Rico and Hawaii, sugar production—spurred by access to the American market—increasingly dominated the island's economic life and subjected it to the same cycle of booms and busts that so plagued other sugar-producing appendages of the United States economy.

The Philippine War

Americans did not like to think of themselves as imperial rulers in the European mold. Yet like other imperial powers, the United States soon discovered that subjugating another people required strength and at times brutality. That, at least, was the lesson of the American experience in the Philippines, where American forces soon became engaged in a long and bloody war.

The conflict in the Philippines is the least remembered of all American wars. It was also one of the longest (it lasted from 1898 to 1902) and one of the most vicious. It involved 200,000 American troops and resulted in 4,300 American deaths. The number of Filipinos killed in the conflict is still in dispute, but it seems likely that at least 50,000 natives (and perhaps many more) died. The American occupiers faced guerrilla tactics in the Philippines very similar to those the Spanish occupiers had faced prior to 1898 in Cuba. And they soon found themselves drawn into the same pattern of brutality that had outraged so many Americans when Weyler had used them in the Caribbean.

The Filipinos had been rebelling against Spanish rule even before 1898. And as soon as they realized the Americans had come to stay, they rebelled against them as well. Ably led by Emilio Aguinaldo, Filipinos harried the American army of occupation from island to island for more than three years. At first, American commanders believed the rebels had only a small popular following. But by early 1900, General Arthur MacArthur, an American commander in the islands, was writing: "I have been reluctantly compelled to believe that the Filipino masses are loyal to Aguinaldo and the government which he heads."

Emilio Aguinaldo

FILIPINO PRISONERS American troops guard captured Filipino guerrillas in Manila. The suppression of the Filipino insurrection was a much longer and costlier military undertaking than the Spanish-American War, by which the United States first gained possession of the islands. By mid-1900 there were 70,000 American troops in the Philippines, under the command of General Arthur MacArthur (whose son, Douglas, won fame in the Philippines during World War II). *(The Library of Congress)*

To MacArthur and others, that was not a reason to moderate American tactics or conciliate the rebels. It was a reason to adopt more severe measures. Gradually, the American military effort became more systematically vicious and brutal. Captured Filipino guerrillas were summarily executed. On some islands, entire communities were evacuated—the residents forced into concentration camps while American troops destroyed their villages. A spirit of savagery grew among American soldiers, who came to view the Filipinos as almost subhuman and at times seemed to take pleasure in killing almost arbitrarily.

The Philippines Brutally Subjugated

By 1902, reports of the brutality and of the American casualties had soured the American public on the war. But by then, the occupiers had established control over most of the islands. The key to their victory was the March 1901 capture of Aguinaldo, who later signed a document in which he urged his followers to stop fighting and declared his own allegiance to the United States. Fighting continued intermittently until as late as 1906; but American possession of the Philippines was now secure.

In the summer of 1901, the military transferred authority over the islands to William Howard Taft, who became the first civilian governor. Taft gave the Filipinos broad local autonomy. The Americans also built roads, schools, bridges, and sewers; instituted major administrative and financial reforms; and established a public health system. Filipino self-rule slowly increased. But not until July 4, 1946, did the islands finally gain their independence.

Gradual Shift to Self-rule

The Open Door

The acquisition of the Philippines greatly increased the already strong American interest in Asia. Americans were particularly concerned about the future of China, which was now so enfeebled that it provided a tempting target for exploitation by stronger countries. By 1900, England, France, Germany, Russia, and Japan were beginning to carve up China among themselves, pressuring the Chinese government for "concessions" that gave them effective economic control over various regions. In some cases, they simply seized Chinese territories and claimed them as their own "spheres of influence." Many Americans feared the process would soon cut them out of the China trade altogether.

Eager for a way to protect American interests in China without risking war, McKinley issued a statement in September 1898 saying the United States wanted access to China but no special advantages there: "Asking only the open door for ourselves, we are ready to accord the open door to others." Later, Secretary of State John Hay translated the president's words into policy when he addressed identical messages—which became known as the "Open Door notes"—to England, Germany, Russia, France, Japan, and Italy. He asked them to approve three principles: Each nation with a "sphere of influence" in China was to allow other nations to trade freely and equally in its sphere. The principles he outlined would allow the United States to trade with the Chinese without fear of interference.

Hay's "Open Door Notes"

But the Open Door proposals were coolly received in Europe and Japan. Russia openly rejected them; the other powers claimed to accept them in principle but to be unable to act unless all the powers agreed. Hay, unperturbed, simply announced that all the powers had accepted the principles of the Open Door and that the United States expected them to observe those principles. But unless the United States was willing to resort to war, it could not prevent any nation that wanted to violate the Open Door from doing so.

No sooner had the diplomatic maneuvering over the Open Door ended than the Boxers, a secret Chinese martial-arts society, launched a revolt against foreigners in China. The climax of the Boxer Rebellion was a siege of the entire foreign diplomatic corps in the British embassy in Beijing (Peking). The imperial powers (including the United States) sent an international expedi-

The Boxer Rebellion

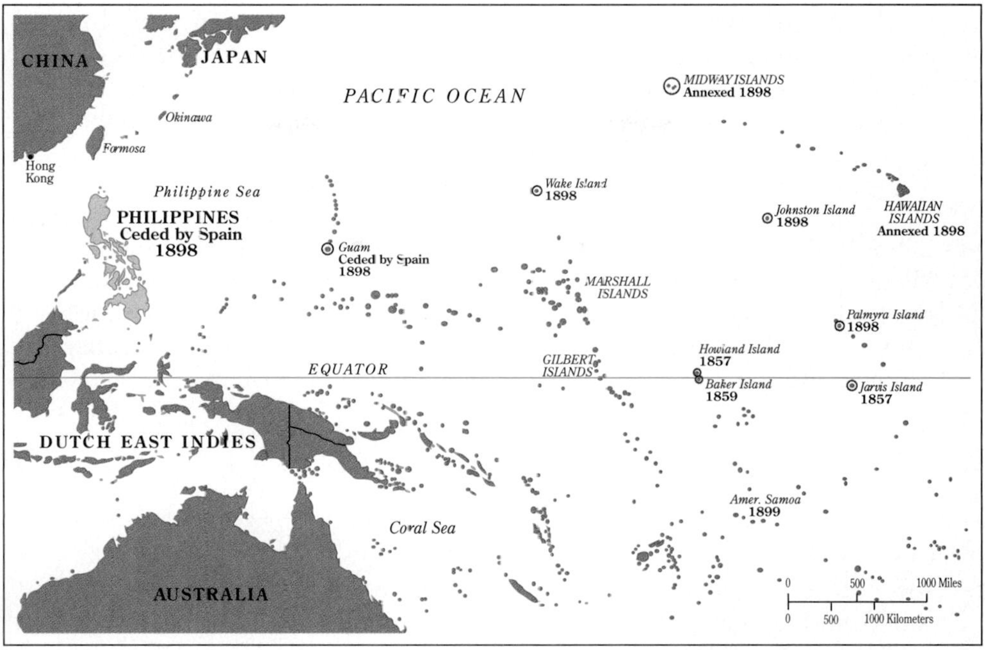

THE AMERICAN SOUTH PACIFIC EMPIRE, 1900 Except for Puerto Rico, all of the colonial acquisitions of the United States in the wake of the Spanish-American War occurred in the Pacific. The new attraction of imperialism persuaded the United States to annex Hawaii in 1898. The war itself gave America control of the Philippines, Guam, and other, smaller Spanish possessions in the Pacific. When added to the small, scattered islands that the United States had acquired as naval bases earlier in the nineteenth century, these new possessions gave the nation a highly far-flung Pacific empire, even if one whose total territory and population remained small by the standards of the other great empires of the age. ◆ *What was the reaction in the United States to the acquisition of this new empire?*

tionary force into China to rescue the diplomats. In August 1900, it fought its way into Beijing and broke the siege.

McKinley and Hay had agreed to American participation so as to secure a voice in the settlement of the uprising and to prevent the partition of China. Hay now won support for his Open Door approach from England and Germany and then induced the other participating powers to accept compensation from the Chinese for the damages the Boxer Rebellion had caused. Chinese territorial integrity survived at least in name, and the United States retained access to its lucrative trade.

A Modern Military System

The war with Spain had revealed glaring deficiencies in the American military system. Had the United States been fighting a more powerful nation, disaster might have resulted. After the war, McKinley appointed Elihu Root, an able New York corporate lawyer, as secretary of war to supervise a major overhaul of the armed forces.

Root's reforms enlarged the maximum size of the regular army from 25,000 to 100,000. They established federal army standards for the National Guard, ensuring that never again would the nation fight a war with volunteer regiments trained and equipped differently from the regular army. They sparked the creation of a system of officer training schools, including the Army Staff College (later the Command and General Staff School) at Fort Leavenworth, Kansas, and the Army War College in Washington, D.C. And in 1903, they established a general staff (named the Joint Chiefs of Staff) to act as military advisers to the secretary of war. As a result of the new reforms, the United States entered the twentieth century with something resembling a modern military system.

Creation of the Modern Military

CONCLUSION

After more than a century of continual national expansion on the North American continent, the United States joined the community of colonial nations in the 1890s and acquired a substantial empire far from its own shores. But the rise of American imperialism was a halting and contested process, whose purposes were never wholly clear.

In the beginning, America's new internationalism took the form of a supposedly humanitarian intervention in a civil war in Spanish Cuba. The American public, inflamed by lurid journalistic accounts of Spanish atrocities inflicted on innocent Cubans, helped push the United States into a short, victorious war with Spain, fought in theory to secure Cuban independence. But through the efforts of some committed internationalists in the McKinley administration, among them Theodore Roosevelt, the Spanish-American War was soon transformed from a fight to free Cuba into a fight to wrest important colonies from Spain. At its end, the United States found itself in possession of substantial new territories in the Caribbean (including Puerto Rico) and an important territory in the Pacific—the Philippines. A vigorous domestic anti-imperialist movement failed to stop the annexationist drive, and by 1899 the United States found itself in possession of colonies.

Taking the colonies proved easier than holding them. In the Philippines, American forces became bogged down in a four-year war with Filipino rebels. The new colonial rulers soon pacified the Philippines, but not before souring much of the American public on the effort. In part as a result, the territories the United States acquired in the aftermath of the Spanish-American War marked not only the beginning but the end of American territorial imperialism.

FOR FURTHER REFERENCE

Walter LaFeber, *The New Empire: An Interpretation of American Expansion, 1860–1898* (1963) and Ernest May, *Imperial Democracy* (1961) are important introductions to the subject. David F. Healy, *U.S. Expansionism: Imperialist Urge in the 1890s* (1970) is a contrasting view. Walter LaFeber, *The Cambridge History of American Foreign Policy, Vol. 2: The Search for Opportunity, 1865–1913* (1993) is an important overview. William Appleman Williams, *The Tragedy of American Diplomacy*, rev. ed. (1972) is a classic revisionist work on the origins and tragic consequences of American imperialism, supplemented by his *Empire as a Way of Life: An Essay on the Causes and Character of America's Present Predicament* (1982). David M. Pletcher, *The Diplomacy of Trade and Investment: American Economic Expansion in the Hemisphere, 1865–1900* (1998) examines the economic roots of American intervention in Latin America. Anders Stephanson, *Manifest Destiny: American Expansionism and the Empire of Right* (1995) is a short and provocative history of Americans' ideology of expansionism. Robert L. Beisner's *Twelve Against Empire* (1968) chronicles the careers of the leading opponents of imperial expansion. Emily S. Rosenberg, *Spreading the American Dream: American Economic and Cultural Expansion, 1890–1945* (1982) is a provocative cultural interpretation. Gerald F. Linderman, *The Mirror of War: American Society and the Spanish-American War* (1974) examines the social meaning of the war within the United States. Stuart Creighton Miller, *"Benevolent Assimilation": The American Conquest of the Philippines, 1899–1903* (1982) describes the American war in the Philippines. Michael Hunt, *The Making of a Special Relationship: The United States and China to 1914* (1983) is a good introduction to the subject. Matthew Frye Jacobson, *Barbarian Virtues: The United States Encounters Foreign Peoples at Home and Abroad, 1876–1917* (2000) is a broad overview of the interplay between imperialism and immigration.

For quizzes, Internet resources, references to additional books and films, and more, consult this book's Online Learning Center site at www.mhhe.com/unfinishednation4.

"VOTES FOR WOMEN," BY B. M. BOYE This striking poster was the prize-winning entry in a 1911 contest sponsored by the College Equal Suffrage League of Northern California. *(Schlesinger Library, Radcliffe Institute, Harvard University)*

TIME LINE

1873	1889	1893	1895	1899	1900
Women's Christian Temperance Union founded	Jane Addams opens Hull House	Anti-Saloon League founded	National Association of Manufacturers founded	Veblen's *A Theory of the Leisure Class*	Galveston, Texas, creates commission government
					Robert La Follette elected Wisconsin governor

CHAPTER TWENTY-ONE

THE RISE OF PROGRESSIVISM

The Progressive Impulse
Women and Reform
The Assault on the Parties
Sources of Progressive Reform
Crusades for Order and Reform

Well before the turn of the century, many Americans had become convinced that the rapid industrialization and urbanization of their society had created intolerable problems—that the nation's most pressing need was to impose order on the growing chaos and to curb industrial society's most glaring injustices. In the early years of the new century, that outlook acquired a name: progressivism.

Not even those who called themselves progressives could always agree on what the word "progressive" really meant, for it was a phenomenon of great scope and diversity. But it was also one that rested on an identifiable set of central assumptions. It was, first, an optimistic vision. Progressives believed, as their name implies, in the idea of progress. They believed that society was capable of improvement and that continued growth and advancement were the nation's destiny. But progressives believed, too, that growth and progress could not continue to occur recklessly, as they had in the late nineteenth century. The "natural laws" of the marketplace, and the doctrines of laissez-faire and Social Darwinism that celebrated those laws, were not sufficient to create the order and stability that the growing society required. Purposeful human intervention was necessary to solve the nation's problems. Progressives did not always agree on the form that intervention should take, but most believed that government should play an important role in the process.

1902	1909	1911	1912	1919	1920
Ida Tarbell's exposé of Standard Oil	Croly's *The Promise of American Life* NAACP formed	Triangle Shirtwaist fire	U.S. Chamber of Commerce founded	18th Amendment (prohibition)	19th Amendment (women suffrage)

Beyond these central premises, progressivism flowed outward in a number of different directions. One powerful impulse was the spirit of "antimonopoly," the fear of concentrated power and the urge to limit and disperse authority and wealth. A second progressive impulse was a belief in the importance of social cohesion: the belief that the welfare of any single person is dependent on the welfare of society as a whole. And a third progressive impulse was a belief in organization and efficiency: the belief that social order was a result of intelligent social organization and rational procedures for guiding social and economic life. These varied reform impulses were not entirely incompatible with one another. Many progressives made use of all these ideas at times, and others as well, as they tried to restore order and stability to their turbulent society.

The Muckrakers and the Social Gospel

Among the first to articulate the new spirit of reform was a group of crusading journalists who began to direct public attention toward social, economic, and political injustices. They became known as the "muckrakers" after Theodore Roosevelt accused one of them of raking up muck through his writings. They were committed to exposing scandal, corruption, and injustice.

At first, their major targets were the trusts and particularly the railroads, which the muckrakers considered dangerously powerful and deeply corrupt. Exposés of the great corporate organizations began to appear as early as the 1860s, when Charles Francis Adams, Jr., and others uncovered corruption among the railroad barons. Decades later, Ida Tarbell produced a scorching study of the Standard Oil trust. By the turn of the century, however, many muckrakers were turning their attention to government and particularly to the urban political machines. Among the most influential was Lincoln Steffens, a reporter for *McClure's Magazine*. His portraits of "machine government" and "boss rule" in cities had a tone of studied moral outrage that was reflected in the title of his series and of the book that emerged from it, *The Shame of the Cities*. The muckrakers reached the peak of their influence in the first decade of the twentieth century. They investigated governments, labor unions, and corporations. They explored the problems of child labor, immigrant ghettoes, prostitution, and family disorganization. They denounced the waste and destruction of natural resources, the subjugation of women, even occasionally the oppression of blacks.

Lincoln Steffens

Many reformers became committed to the idea of what was known as "social justice." A clear expression of that concern was the rise within American Protestantism of the "Social Gospel," the effort to make faith into a tool of social reform. The Salvation Army, which began in England

McCLURE'S MAGAZINE

MAY

LINCOLN STEFFENS'S exposure of another type of municipal grafting; how Pittsburg differs from St. Louis and Minneapolis.

THE END OF THE WORLD, by Professor Newcomb. A powerful story, yet a scientific prediction; pictures by the famous French artist, Henri Lanos.

IDA M. TARBELL on the Standard tactics which brought on the famous oil crisis of 1878.

SIX SHORT STORIES

***MCCLURE'S MAGAZINE*, MAY 1903** *McClure's* was the leading outlet for a form of journalism known as "muckraking," which exposed social and economic scandals in the hope of promoting reform. This issue contains articles by two of the leading muckrakers, Lincoln Steffens and Ida Tarbell. *(Culver Pictures, Inc)*

but soon spread to the United States, was a Christian social welfare organization with a vaguely military structure. By 1900, it had recruited 3,000 "officers" and 20,000 "privates" and was offering both material aid and spiritual service to the urban poor. In addition, many ministers, priests, and rabbis left traditional parish work to serve in the troubled cities. Charles Sheldon's *In His Steps* (1898), the story of a young minister who abandoned a comfortable post to work among the needy, sold more than 15 million copies. The engagement of religion with reform helped bring to progressivism a powerful moral impulse and a concern for the plight of some of society's most impoverished and degraded people.

The Settlement House Movement

One of the strongest elements of progressive thought was the belief that the environment shaped individual development. Ignorance, poverty, even criminality, progressives argued, were not the result of inherent moral or genetic failings or of the workings of providence. They were, rather, the effects of an unhealthy environment. To elevate the distressed, therefore, required an improvement of the conditions in which the distressed lived.

Nothing produced more distress, many reformers believed, than the crowded immigrant neighborhoods of American cities. One response to the problems of such communities, borrowed from England, was the settlement house. The most famous was Hull House, which opened in 1889 in Chicago as a result of the efforts of Jane Addams. It became a model for more than 400 similar institutions throughout the nation. Staffed by members of the educated middle class, settlement houses sought to help immigrant families adapt to the language and customs of their new country.

Hull House

Central to the settlement houses were the efforts of educated women. Indeed, the movement became a training ground for many important female leaders of the twentieth century, among them Eleanor Roosevelt. The settlement houses also helped spawn another important institution of reform: the profession of social work—a profession in which women were to play an important role. The professional social worker combined a compassion for the poor with a commitment to the values of bureaucratic progressivism: scientific study, efficient organization, reliance on experts.

The Allure of Expertise

As the emergence of the social work profession suggests, progressives involved in humanitarian efforts often placed high value on knowledge and expertise. That belief found expression in many ways, among them through the writings of a new group of scholars and intellectuals who envisioned a new civilization in which the expertise of scientists and engineers would be put into the service of the economy and society. Among the most influential of these theorists was the social scientist Thorstein Veblen. Harshly critical of the industrial tycoons of the late nineteenth century—the "leisure class," as he satirically described them in his first major work, *A Theory of the Leisure Class* (1899)—Veblen proposed instead a new economic system in which power would reside in the hands of highly trained engineers. Only they, he argued, could fully understand the "machine process" by which modern society must be governed.

Knowledge and Expertise Valued

In practical terms, the impulse toward expertise and organization helped produce the idea of scientific management, or "Taylorism" (see p. 462). It encouraged the development of modern mass-production techniques and, above all, the assembly line. It inspired a revolution in American education and the creation of a new area of inquiry—social science, the use of scientific techniques in the study of society and its institutions. It also helped create a movement toward organization among the expanding new group of middle-class professionals.

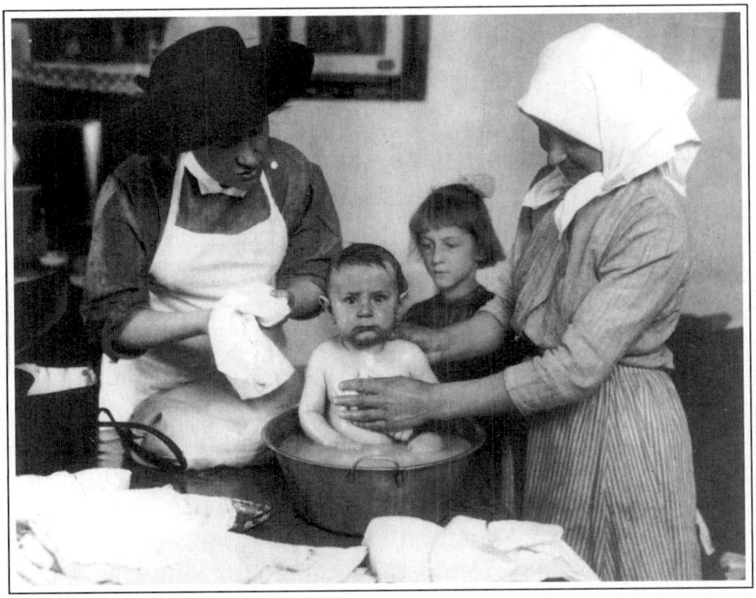

THE INFANT WELFARE SOCIETY, CHICAGO The Infant Welfare Society was one of many "helping" organizations in Chicago and other large cities—many of them closely tied to the settlement houses—that strove to help immigrants adapt to American life and create safe and healthy living conditions. Here, a volunteer helps an immigrant mother learn to bathe her baby sometime around 1910. *(Chicago Historical Society, ICHi–20216)*

The Professions

The late nineteenth century saw a dramatic expansion in the number of Americans engaged in administrative and professional tasks. Industries needed managers, technicians, and accountants as well as workers. Cities required commercial, medical, legal, and educational services. New technologies required scientists and engineers. By the turn of the century, the people performing these services had come to constitute a distinct social group—what some have called a new middle class.

The New Middle Class

By the early twentieth century, the millions of members of this new middle class were building organizations and establishing standards to secure their position in society. As one of their principal vehicles, they created the modern, organized professions. The idea of professionalism had been a frail one in America even as late as 1880. But as the demand for professional services increased, so did the pressures for reform.

Among the first to respond was the medical profession. Throughout the 1890s, doctors who considered themselves trained professionals began forming local associations and societies. In 1901, they reorganized the American Medical Association (AMA) into a national professional society. By 1920, nearly two-thirds of all

American Medical Association

American doctors were members. The AMA quickly called for strict, scientific standards for admission to the practice of medicine. State and local governments responded by creating medical schools in their universities and by passing new laws that required the licensing of all physicians and that restricted licenses to those practitioners approved by the profession.

There was similar movement in other professions. By 1916, lawyers in all forty-eight states had established professional bar associations. Increasingly, aspiring lawyers found it necessary to enroll in graduate programs, and the nation's law schools accordingly expanded greatly. Businessmen supported the creation of schools of business administration and established their own national organizations: the National Association of Manufacturers in 1895 and the United States Chamber of Commerce in 1912. Farmers responded to the new order by forming, through the National Farm Bureau Federation, a network of agricultural organizations designed to spread scientific farming methods, teach sound marketing techniques, and lobby for the interests of their members.

Limiting Entry into the Professions

Among the chief purposes of the new professionalism was guarding entry into the professions. This was only partly an effort to defend the professions from the untrained and incompetent. The admission requirements also protected those already in the professions from excessive competition and lent prestige and status to the professional label. Some professions used their entrance requirements to exclude blacks, women, immigrants, and other "undesirables" from their ranks. Others used them simply to keep the numbers down, to ensure that demand for the services of existing members would remain high.

Women and the Professions

American women found themselves excluded from most of the emerging professions. But a substantial number of middle-class women—particularly those emerging from the new women's colleges and from the coeducational state universities—nevertheless entered professional careers.

A few women managed to establish themselves as physicians, lawyers, engineers, scientists, and corporate managers. Most, however, turned by necessity to those professions that society considered suitable for women.

Teaching and Social Work

Settlement houses and social work provided two professional outlets that were widely considered appropriate for women. The most important, however, was teaching. Indeed, in the late nineteenth century, more than two-thirds of all grammar-school teachers were women, and perhaps 90 percent of all professional women were teachers. For educated black women, in particular, teaching was often the only professional opportunity they could hope to find.

Women also dominated other professional activities. Nursing had become primarily a women's field around the time of the Civil War, when it was still considered a menial occupation, akin to domestic service. But by the early twentieth century, it too was adopting professional standards. Women also found opportunities as librarians. And many women entered academia—often studying at predominantly male institutions that permitted women to earn advanced degrees, among them the University of Chicago, MIT, and Columbia, and then finding professional opportunities in the new and expanding women's colleges.

"Helping" Professions

The "women's professions" had much in common with other professions. But they also had distinctive qualities. Careers such as teaching, nursing, and library work were "helping" professions. Women's workplaces—schools, hospitals, and libraries—had a vaguely "domestic" or "feminine" image, which enabled men (and, indeed, most women) to reconcile the idea of female professional work with prevailing ideas about the proper role of women in society.

WOMEN AND REFORM

The prominent role of women in reform movements is one of the most striking features of progressivism. Women became important reformers even though they could not vote in most states, seldom held office, and had footholds in only a few professions. But their relative insulation from political and professional life in some ways enhanced their ability to wield influence, for it enabled them to tie their causes to the idea of a nonpartisan, nurturing culture uncontaminated by economic or political interests.

The "New Woman"

The phenomenon of the "new woman" was a product of the social and economic changes of the era. By the end of the nineteenth century, almost all income-producing activity had moved out of the home and into the factory or the office. At the same time, many women were having fewer children, and their children were beginning school at earlier ages and spending more time there. For wives and mothers who did not work for wages, home and family were less all-consuming. Hence more and more women began looking for activities outside the home.

There were also more women who lived outside traditional families altogether. Approximately 10 percent of all American women in the last decades of the nineteenth century never married, and single women were among the most prominent female reformers of the time. Some of these women lived alone. Others lived with other women, often in long-term relationships known as "Boston marriages." The divorce rate also rose rapidly, from one divorce for every twenty-one marriages in 1880 to one in nine by 1916; women initiated the great majority of them.

"Boston Marriages"

Higher levels of education also contributed to the prominence of women in reform activities. The proliferation of women's colleges and of coeducational public universities in the late nineteenth century produced the first generation of women in which significant numbers had educations above the high-school level (see pp. 510–511). The new colleges also helped create female communities, within which women could find support for their ambitions and companionship for their activities.

The Clubwomen

In the vanguard of many progressive social reforms was a large network of women's clubs. The clubs began largely as cultural organizations to provide middle- and upper-class women with an outlet for their intellectual energies. In 1892, when women formed the General Federation of Women's Clubs to coordinate the activities of local organizations, there were more than 100,000 members in nearly 500 clubs. By 1917, there were over 1 million members.

Importance of Women's Club

By the early twentieth century, the clubs were becoming less concerned with cultural activities and more concerned with making a contribution to social reform. Much of what they did was uncontroversial: planting trees; supporting schools, libraries, and settlement houses; building hospitals and parks. But many women's clubs also supported such controversial measures as child labor laws, worker compensation, pure food and drug legislation, occupational safety, reforms in Indian policy, and—beginning in 1914—woman suffrage.

Black women occasionally joined clubs dominated by whites. But African Americans also formed clubs of their own, some of which affiliated with the General Federation, but more of which became part of the independent National Association of Colored Women. They modeled themselves on their white counterparts, but some black clubs took positions on issues of particular concern to blacks. Some crusaded against lynching and called for congressional legislation to make lynching a federal crime. Others protested aspects of segregation.

National Association of Colored Women

The women's club movement raised few overt challenges to prevailing assumptions about the proper role of women in society. But it did represent an important effort by women to extend their influence beyond the home and the family. The club movement allowed women to define a space for themselves in the public world without openly challenging the existing, male-dominated order.

Importance of the Club Movement

The importance of the club movement did not, however, lie simply in what it did for middle-class women. It lay also in what those women did for the working-class people they attempted to help. The women's club movement was an important force in winning passage of state (and ultimately federal) laws that regulated the conditions of woman and child labor, that established government inspection of workplaces, that regulated the food and drug industries, and that applied new standards to urban housing. In many of these efforts, the clubwomen formed alliances with other women's groups such as the Women's Trade Union League, founded in 1903 by female union members and upper-class reformers and committed to persuading women to join unions.

Woman Suffrage

The largest single reform movement of the progressive era, indeed one of the largest in American history, was the fight for woman suffrage. It was the culmination of many decades of struggle by women to obtain basic political rights. But it was also the product of forces peculiar to the early twentieth century.

It is sometimes difficult for today's Americans to understand why the suffrage (or right-to-vote) issue could have become the source of such enormous controversy in the early twentieth century. But at the time, suffrage seemed to many of its critics a very radical demand—in part because of the way some of its supporters promoted it. Throughout the late nineteenth century, many suffrage advocates presented their views in terms of "natural rights," arguing that women deserved the same rights as men—including, first and foremost, the right to vote. Elizabeth Cady Stanton, for example, wrote in 1892 of woman as "the arbiter of her own destiny . . . if we are to consider her as a citizen, as a member of a great nation, she must have the same rights as all other members." A woman's role as "mother, wife, sister, daughter" was "incidental" to her larger role as a part of society.

Radical Implications of Suffrage

This was an argument that boldly challenged the views of many men (and even many women) who believed that society required a distinctive female "sphere" in which women would serve first and foremost as wives and mothers. And so a powerful antisuffrage movement emerged. There were antisuffrage organizations, newspapers, and political crusades. Antisuffragists associated suffrage with divorce, promiscuity, and neglect of children. Throughout much of the late nineteenth century, they effectively blocked most efforts by women to gain the vote.

The suffrage movement began to overcome this opposition in the first years of the twentieth century. That was in part because suffragists were becoming better organized and more politically sophisticated than their opponents. Under the leadership of Anna Howard Shaw, a Boston social worker, and Carrie Chapman Catt, a journalist from Iowa, the National American Woman Suffrage Association grew from a membership of about 13,000 in 1893 to over 2 million in 1917.

NAWSA

But the movement also gained strength because many of its leaders began to justify suffrage in less threatening ways. Suffrage, some supporters began to argue, would allow women to bring their special and distinct virtues more widely to bear on society's problems. It was, they claimed, precisely because women occupied a distinct sphere—because as mothers and wives and homemakers they had special experiences and special sensitivities to bring to public life—that woman suffrage could make such an important contribution to politics. In particular, many suffragists argued that enfranchising women would help the temperance movement by giving its largest group of supporters a political voice. Some suffrage advocates claimed that once women had the vote, war would become a thing of the past, since women would—through their maternal instincts and their calming, peaceful influence—help curb the natural belligerence of men.

The principal triumphs of the suffrage movement began in 1910. That year, Washington became the first state in fourteen years to extend suffrage to women. California joined it a year later, and in 1912 four other western states did the same. In 1913, Illinois became the first state east of the Mississippi to embrace woman suffrage. And in 1917 and 1918, New York and Michigan—two of the biggest states in the Union—gave women the vote. By 1919, thirty-nine states had granted women the right to vote in at least some elections; fifteen had allowed them full participation. In 1920, finally, suffragists won ratification of the Nineteenth Amendment, which guaranteed political rights to women throughout the nation.

Nineteenth Amendment Ratified

To some feminists, however, the victory seemed incomplete. Alice Paul, the head of the militant National Woman's Party (founded in 1916), argued that the Nineteenth Amendment alone would not be sufficient to protect women's rights. Women needed more: a constitutional amendment that would provide clear, legal protection for their rights and would prohibit all discrimination on the basis of sex. But for many years Alice Paul's argument found limited favor even among many of the most important leaders of the recently triumphant suffrage crusade.

Alice Paul

THE ASSAULT ON THE PARTIES

Sooner or later, most progressive goals required the involvement of government. Only government, reformers agreed, could effectively counter the powerful private interests that threatened the nation. But American government at the dawn of the new century was, progressives believed, poorly adapted to meet their demands. Before progressives could reform society effectively, they would first have to reform government itself. In the beginning, at least, many progressives believed that such reform should start with an assault on the domination of government and politics by the political parties.

Early Attacks

Attacks on party dominance had been frequent in the late nineteenth century. Greenbackism and Populism, for example, had been efforts to break the hammerlock with which the Republicans and Democrats controlled public life. The Independent Republicans (or mugwumps) had attempted to challenge the grip of partisanship, and former mugwumps became important supporters of progressive political reform activity in the 1890s and later.

The early assaults enjoyed some success. In the 1880s and 1890s, for example, most states adopted the secret ballot. Prior to that, the political parties themselves had printed ballots (or "tickets") with only the party's candidates listed, which they distributed to their supporters, who then simply went to the polls to deposit the tickets in the ballot box. The old system had made it possible for bosses to monitor the voting behavior of their constituents. The new ballot—printed by the government and distributed at the polls, where it was filled out and deposited in secret—helped chip away at the power of the parties over the voters.

Secret Ballot

By the late 1890s, critics of the parties were expanding their goals. Party rule could be broken, they believed, in one of two ways. It could be broken by increasing the power of the people, by permitting them to express their will directly at the polls. Or it could be broken by placing more power in the hands of nonpartisan, nonelective officials. Reformers promoted measures that moved along both those paths.

Municipal Reform

Many progressives believed the impact of party rule was most damaging in the cities. Municipal government, therefore, became the first target of those working for political reform. Muckraking journalists such as Lincoln Steffens were especially successful in arousing public outrage at corruption and incompetence in city politics.

The muckrakers struck a responsive chord among a powerful group of urban middle-class progressives, who set out to destroy the power of machines. They faced formidable opposition. In addition to challenging the powerful city bosses and their entrenched political organizations, they attacked a large group of special interests: saloon owners, brothel keepers, businessmen who had established lucrative relationships with the urban machines and viewed reform as a threat to their profits. Finally, there was the great constituency of urban working people, many of them recent immigrants, for whom the machines were a source of needed jobs and services. Gradually, however, the reformers gained in political strength, and in the first years of the twentieth century, they began to score some important victories.

Urban Machines Challenged

An early and influential success came in Galveston, Texas, where the old city government proved completely unable to deal with the effects of a destructive tidal wave in 1900. Capitalizing on public dismay, reformers won approval of a new city charter that replaced the mayor and council with an elected, nonpartisan commission. In 1907, Des Moines, Iowa, adopted its own version of the commission plan, and other cities followed.

City-Manager Plan

Another approach to reform was the city-manager plan (first adopted in Staunton, Virginia, in 1908), by which elected officials hired an outside expert—often a professionally trained business manager or engineer—to take charge of the government. The city manager would presumably remain untainted by the corrupting influence of politics. By the end of the progressive era, almost 400, mostly smaller cities were operating under commissions, and another 45 employed city managers.

In other cities, reformers organized to challenge the municipal electoral process or to change the distribution of powers within the government. Some cities made the election of mayors nonpartisan or moved them to years when no presidential or congressional races were in progress (to reduce the influence of the large turnouts that party organizations produced on such occasions). Reformers tried to make city-council members run at large so as to limit the influence of ward leaders and district bosses. They tried to strengthen the power of the mayor at the expense of the city council, on the assumption that reformers were more likely to get a sympathetic mayor elected than to win control of the entire council.

Statehouse Progressivism

Other progressives turned to state government as an agent for reform. They looked with particular scorn on state legislatures, whose ill-paid, relatively undistinguished members were, they believed, generally incompetent, often corrupt, and almost always controlled by party bosses. Many reformers began looking for ways to circumvent the legislatures (and the party bosses who controlled them) by increasing the power of the electorate.

Initiative and Referendum

Two of the most important changes were innovations first proposed by Populists in the 1890s: the initiative and the referendum. The initiative allowed reformers to circumvent state legislatures altogether by submitting new legislation directly to the voters in general elections. The referendum provided a method by which actions of the legislature could be returned to the electorate for approval. By 1918, more than twenty states had enacted one or both of these reforms.

The direct primary and the recall were, similarly, efforts to limit the power of parties and improve the quality of elected officials. The primary election was an attempt to take the selection of candidates away from the

ROBERT LA FOLLETTE CAMPAIGNING IN WISCONSIN After three terms as governor of Wisconsin, La Follette began a long career in the United States Senate in 1906, during which he worked uncompromisingly for advanced progressive reforms—so uncompromisingly, in fact, that he was often almost completely isolated. He entitled a chapter of his autobiography "Alone in the Senate." La Follette had a greater impact on his own state, whose politics he and his sons dominated for nearly forty years and where he was able to win passage of many reforms that the federal government resisted. *(State Historical Society of Wisconsin)*

bosses and give it to the people. (In the South, it was also a device for excluding African Americans from voting.) The recall gave voters the right to remove a public official from office through a special election, which could be called after a sufficient number of citizens had signed a petition. By 1915 every state in the nation had instituted primary elections for at least some offices. The recall encountered more strenuous opposition, but some states adopted it as well.

Robet M. La Follette

The most celebrated state-level reformer was Robert M. La Follette of Wisconsin. Elected governor in 1900, he helped turn his state into what reformers across the nation described as a "laboratory of progressivism." The Wisconsin progressives won approval of direct primaries, initiatives, and referendums. They regulated railroads and utilities. They passed laws to regulate the workplace and provide compensation for laborers injured on the job. They taxed inherited fortunes and nearly doubled state levies on railroads and other corporate interests.

Parties and Interest Groups

The reformers did not, of course, eliminate parties from American political life. But they did diminish the parties' centrality. Evidence of that came from, among other things, the decline in voter turnout. In the late nineteenth century, up to 81 percent of eligible voters routinely turned out for national elections. In the early twentieth century, the figure declined markedly. In the presidential election of 1900, 73 percent of the electorate voted. By 1912, the figure had dropped to about 59 percent. Never again did voter turnout reach as high as 70 percent.

Emergence of "Interest Groups"

At the same time that parties were declining, other power centers were emerging to compete with them: what have become known as "interest groups": professional organizations, trade associations representing particular businesses and industries, labor organizations, farm lobbies, and many others. Social workers, the settlement house movement, women's clubs, and others learned to operate as interest groups to advance their demands. A new pattern of politics, in which many individual interests organized to influence government directly rather than operating through party structures, was taking shape.

SOURCES OF PROGRESSIVE REFORM

Middle-class reformers, most of them from the East, dominated the public image and much of the substance of progressivism. But they were not alone in seeking to improve social conditions. Working-class Americans, African Americans, westerners, even party bosses also played crucial roles in advancing some of the important reforms of the era.

Labor, the Machine, and Reform

Although the American Federation of Labor, and its leader Samuel Gompers, remained largely aloof from many of the reform efforts of the time, some unions nevertheless played important roles in reform battles. In San Francisco, for example, workers in the Building Trades Council spearheaded the formation of the new Union Labor Party, committed to a program of reform almost indistinguishable from that of middle-class and elite progressives in the city. Between 1911 and 1913, in significant part because of the new party's efforts, California passed a child labor law, a workmen's compensation law, and a limitation on working hours for women. Union pressures contributed to the passage of similar laws in many other states as well.

One result of the assault on the parties was a change in the party organizations themselves. Party bosses sometimes turned their machines into vehicles of social reform. One example was New York's Tammany

Hall, the nation's oldest and most notorious city machine. Its astute leader, Charles Francis Murphy, began in the early years of the century to fuse the techniques of boss rule with some of the concerns of social reformers. Tammany used its political power on behalf of legislation to improve working conditions and eliminate the worst abuses of the industrial economy.

Triangle Shirtwaist Fire

In 1911, a terrible fire swept through the factory of the Triangle Shirtwaist Company in New York's Washington Square; 146 workers, most of them women, died. Many of them had been trapped inside the burning building because management had locked the emergency exits to prevent unauthorized absences. For the next three years, a state commission studied not only the background of the fire but the general condition of the industrial workplace. By 1914, the commission had issued a series of reports calling for major reforms in the conditions of modern labor. When its recommendations reached the New York legislature, its most effective supporters were not middle-class progressives but two Tammany Democrats from working-class backgrounds: Senator Robert F. Wagner and Assemblyman Alfred E. Smith. With the support of Murphy and the backing of other Tammany legislators, they steered through a series of pioneering labor laws that imposed strict regulations on factory owners and established effective mechanisms for enforcement.

Western Progressives

Reforming the Federal Government

The American West produced some of the most notable progressive leaders of the time: Hiram Johnson of California, George Norris of Nebraska, William Borah of Idaho, and others—almost all of whom spent at least some of their political careers in the United States Senate. That was because for western states, the most important target of reform energies was the federal government, which exercised a kind of authority in the West that it had never possessed in the East.

Many of the most important issues to the future of the West required action above the state level. Disputes over water, for example, almost always involved rivers and streams that crossed state lines. More significant, perhaps, the federal government exercised enormous power over the lands and resources of the western states and provided substantial subsidies to the region in the form of land grants and support for railroad and water projects. Huge areas of the West remained (and still remain) public lands, controlled by Washington; and much of the growth of the West was (and continues to be) a result of federally funded dams and water projects.

Because so much authority in the region rested in federal bureaucracies that state and local governments could not control, political parties in most of the West were relatively weak. That was one reason why western states could move so quickly and decisively to embrace reforms that parties did

W. E. B. DU BOIS AT HIS DESK Although W. E. B. Du Bois, unlike Booker T. Washington, never developed a large popular following, he was the acknowledged leader of the black elite in the late nineteenth and early twentieth centuries. He was the first African American to earn a doctorate at Harvard University, and he published a number of distinguished works of history and sociology during his long career. He also served as editor of *The Crisis*, the newspaper of the NAACP (which he had helped to found). He died in 1963, at the age of ninety-five. *(Photographs and Prints Division, Schomburg Center for Research in Black Culture, The New York Public Library, Astor, Lenox, and Tilden Foundations)*

not like: the initiative, the referendum, the recall, direct primaries. It is also why aspiring politicians were much quicker to look to Washington as a place from which they could influence the future of their region.

African Americans and Reform

The question of race received serious attention from relatively few white progressives, except among those white southerners who believed that the construction of legalized segregation was a progressive reform. But among African Americans themselves, the progressive era produced some significant challenges to existing racial norms.

African Americans faced greater obstacles than any other group in challenging their own oppressed status and seeking reform. That was one reason why so many had embraced the message of Booker T. Washington in the late nineteenth century, to work for immediate self-improvement rather than long-range social change. By the turn of the century, however, a powerful challenge was emerging—to the philosophy of Washington and, more important, to the entire structure of race relations. The chief spokesman for this new approach was W. E. B. Du Bois, a Harvard-trained sociologist and historian.

W. E. B. Du Bois

In *The Souls of Black Folk* (1903), Du Bois launched an open attack on Washington's "Atlanta Compromise," first presented in a speech in Atlanta, which had urged blacks to postpone efforts to achieve political equality and concentrate on self-improvement. Du Bois accused Washington of unnecessarily limiting the aspirations of his race. Rather than content themselves with education at the trade and agricultural schools, Du Bois advocated, talented blacks should accept nothing less than a full university education. They should aspire to the professions. They should, above all, fight for immediate progress on civil rights. In 1905, Du Bois and a group of his supporters met at Niagara Falls—on the Canadian side of the border because no hotel on the American side of the Falls would have them—and launched what became known as the Niagara Movement. Four years later, they joined with white progressives sympathetic to their cause to form the National Association for the Advancement of Colored People (NAACP). In the years that followed, the new organization led the drive for equal rights, using as one of its principal weapons lawsuits in the federal courts.

NAACP Founded

CRUSADES FOR ORDER AND REFORM

Reformers directed many of their energies at the political process. But they also crusaded on behalf of what they considered moral issues. There were campaigns to eliminate alcohol from national life, to curb prostitution, to regulate divorce. There were efforts to restrict immigration and to curb the power of monopoly. There were crusades to resolve what many considered longstanding injustices, of which the most prominent was the campaign for woman suffrage. Proponents of each of those reforms believed that success would help regenerate society as a whole.

The Temperance Crusade

Many progressives considered the elimination of alcohol from American life a necessary step in restoring order to society. Workers in settlement houses and social agencies abhorred the effects of drinking on working-class families: scarce wages vanished as workers spent hours in saloons; drunkenness spawned violence, and occasionally murder. Women, in particular, saw alcohol as a source of some of the greatest problems of working-class wives and mothers, and hoped through temperance to reform abusive or irresponsible male behavior and thus improve women's lives. Employers complained that workers often missed time on the job because of drunkenness or, worse, came to the factory intoxicated and performed their tasks sloppily and dangerously. And political reformers, who looked on the saloon (correctly) as one of the central institutions of the machine,

Debating the Past

PROGRESSIVISM

Until the early 1950s, most historians seemed to agree on the central characteristics of early-twentieth-century progressivism. It was just what many progressives themselves had said it was: a movement by the "people" to curb the power of "special interests." More specifically, it was a protest by an aroused citizenry against the excessive power of urban bosses, corporate moguls, and corrupt elected officials.

In 1951, George Mowry began the process of challenging these assumptions by examining progressives in California and describing them as a small, privileged elite of business and professional figures: people who considered themselves the natural leaders of society and who were trying to recover their fading influence from the new capitalist institutions that had displaced them. Progressivism was not, in other words, a popular, democratic movement; it was the effort of a displaced elite to restore its authority. Richard Hofstadter expanded on this idea in *The Age of Reform* (1955) by describing reformers as people afflicted by "status anxiety," fading elites suffering not from economic but from psychological discontent.

The Mowry-Hofstadter argument soon encountered a range of challenges. In 1963, Gabriel Kolko published his influential study *The Triumph of Conservatism*, in which he rejected both the older "democratic" view of progressivism and the newer "status-anxiety" view. Progressive reform, he argued, was not an effort to protect the people from the corporations; it was, rather, a vehicle through which corporate leaders used the government to protect themselves from competition.

A more moderate reinterpretation came from historians embracing what would later be called the "organizational" approach to twentieth-century American history. First Samuel Hays, in *The Response to Industrialism* (1957), and then Robert Wiebe, in *The Search for Order* (1967), portrayed progressivism as a broad effort by businessmen, professionals, and other middle-class people to bring order and efficiency to political and economic life. In the new industrial society, economic power was increasingly concentrated in large, national organizations, while social and political life remained centered primarily in local communities. Progressivism, Wiebe argued, was the effort of a "new middle class"—a class tied to the emerging national economy—to stabilize and enhance its position in society by bringing those two worlds together.

In the 1970s and 1980s, scholarship on progressivism moved in so many different directions that some historians came to despair of finding any consistent meaning in the term. Much of the new scholarship focused on discovering new groups among whom "progressive" ideas and efforts flourished. Historians found evidence of progressivism in the rising movement by consumers to define their interests; in the growth of reform movements among African Americans; in the changing nature of urban political machines; and in the political activism of working people and labor organizations.

Other scholars attempted to identify progressivism with broad changes in the structure and culture of politics. Richard McCormick, writing in 1981, argued that the crucial change in the "progressive era" was the decline of political parties and the corresponding rise of interest groups working for particular social and economic goals.

At the same time, many historians have focused on the role of women (and the vast network of voluntary associations they created in shaping and promoting progressive reform). Some progressive battles, such historians as Kathryn Sklar, Ruth Rosen, Elaine Tyler May, and Linda Gordon have argued, were part of an effort by women to protect their interests within the domestic sphere in the face of jarring challenges from the new industrial world. This protective urge drew women reformers to such issues as temperance, divorce, prostitution, and the regulation of female and child labor. Other women worked to expand their own roles in the public world, particularly through their support of suffrage. The gendered interests of women reformers are, many historians insist, critical to an understanding of progressivism.

The search for the "essence" of progressivism will undoubtedly continue. But the scholarship of recent decades suggests that the real answer to the nature of progressive reform may be a recognition of its enormous diversity.

(text continued from page 573)

saw an attack on drinking as part of an attack on the bosses. Out of such varied sentiments emerged the temperance movement.

Temperance had been a major reform movement before the Civil War, mobilizing large numbers of people in a crusade with strong religious overtones. Beginning in the 1870s, it experienced a major resurgence. As in the antebellum years, it was a movement led and supported primarily by women. In 1873, temperance advocates formed the Women's Christian Temperance Union (WCTU), led after 1879 by Frances Willard. By 1911, it had 245,000 members and had become the largest single women's organization in American history to that point. In 1893, the Anti-Saloon League joined the temperance movement and, along with the WCTU, began to press for the legal abolition of saloons. Gradually, that demand grew to include the complete prohibition of the sale and manufacture of alcoholic beverages.

WCTU

Pressure for prohibition grew steadily through the first decades of the new century. By 1916, nineteen states had passed prohibition laws. American entry into World War I, and the moral fervor it unleashed, provided the last push to the advocates of prohibition. In 1917, with the support of rural fundamentalists who opposed alcohol on moral and religious grounds, progressive advocates of prohibition steered through Congress a constitutional amendment embodying their demands. Two years later, after ratification by every state in the nation except Connecticut and Rhode Island (with large populations of Catholic immigrants opposed to prohibition), the Eighteenth Amendment became law.

Eighteenth Amendment Ratified

Immigration Restriction

Virtually all reformers agreed that the growing immigrant population had created social problems, but there was wide disagreement on how best to respond. Some progressives believed that helping the new residents adapt to American society was the proper approach. Others argued that the only solution was to limit the flow of new arrivals.

Growing Nativism

In the first decades of the century, the arguments of this second, more pessimistic, group gradually gained strength. New scholarly theories argued that the introduction of immigrants into American society was diluting the purity of the nation's racial stock. The spurious "science" of eugenics spread the belief that human inequalities were hereditary and that immigration was contributing to the multiplication of the unfit. A special federal commission of supposed experts, chaired by Senator William P. Dillingham of Vermont, issued an elaborate report filled with statistics and scholarly testimony. It argued that the newer immigrant groups—largely southern and eastern Europeans—had proved themselves less assimilable than earlier immigrants. Immigration, the report implied, should be restricted by nationality. Even many people who rejected racial arguments supported limiting immigration as a way to solve such urban problems as overcrowding, unemployment, strained social services, and social unrest.

The combination of these concerns gradually won for the nativists the support of some of the nation's leading public figures. Powerful opponents—employers who saw immigration as a source of cheap labor, immigrants themselves, and the immigrants' political representatives—managed to block the restriction movement for a time. But by the beginning of World War I the nativist tide was clearly rising.

The Dream of Socialism

At no time in the history of the United States to that point, and in few times after it, did radical critiques of the capitalist system attract more support than in the period between 1900 and 1914.

Socialist Party of America

The Socialist Party of America grew during the progressive era into a force of considerable strength. In the election of 1900, it had attracted the support of fewer than 100,000 voters; in 1912, its durable leader and perennial presidential candidate, Eugene V. Debs, received nearly 1 million ballots. Strongest in urban immigrant communities (particularly among Germans and Jews), it attracted the loyalties, too, of a substantial number of Protestant farmers in the South and Midwest.

Virtually all socialists agreed on the need for basic structural changes in the economy, but they differed on the extent of those changes and the tactics necessary to achieve them. Some endorsed the radical goals of European Marxists (a complete end to capitalism and private property); others envisioned a more moderate reform that would allow small-scale private enterprise to survive. Militant groups within the party favored direct action. Most conspicuous was the radical labor union the Industrial Workers of the World (IWW), whose members were known to their opponents as "Wobblies." Under the leadership of William ("Big Bill") Haywood, the IWW advocated a single union for all workers. The Wobblies were widely believed to have been responsible for the dynamiting of railroad lines and power stations and other acts of terror, although their use of violence was greatly exaggerated by their opponents.

IWW

More moderate socialists, who advocated peaceful change through political struggle, dominated the party. They emphasized a gradual education of the public to the need for change and patient efforts within the system to achieve it. But by the end of World War I, because the party had refused to support the war effort and because of a growing wave of antiradicalism, socialism was in decline as a significant political force.

Decentralization and Regulation

Many reformers agreed with the socialists that the greatest threat to the nation's economy was excessive centralization of power and concentration of wealth, but they retained a faith in the possibilities of reform within a capitalist system. They argued that the federal government should ensure the survival of genuine economic competition. This viewpoint came to be identified particularly closely with Louis D. Brandeis, a brilliant lawyer and later a justice of the Supreme Court, who spoke and wrote widely (most notably in his 1913 book, *Other People's Money*) about the "curse of bigness."

Challenging Centralized Power

Other progressives were less enthusiastic about the virtues of competition. More important to them was efficiency, which they believed economic concentration encouraged. Government, they argued, should not fight "bigness," but should guard against abuses of power by large institutions. It should distinguish between "good trusts" and "bad trusts." Since economic consolidation was destined to remain a permanent feature of American society, continuing oversight by a strong, modernized government, led by a strong president, was essential. One of the most important spokesmen for this emerging "nationalist" position was Herbert Croly, whose 1909 book, *The Promise of American Life*, became an influential progressive document. One of those who came to endorse that position (although not fully until after 1910) was Theodore Roosevelt, who became for a time the most powerful symbol of the reform impulse at the national level.

Herbert Croly

CONCLUSION

A powerful surge of reform efforts emerged in the last years of the nineteenth century and the first years of the twentieth—reforms intended to deal with the vexing problems that the rise of the modern industrial economy had caused. American reformers at the time thought of themselves as "progressives." But neither then nor since has there ever been wide agreement on what the term "progressive" meant.

The reforms themselves were of a bewildering variety—efforts to improve the moral fabric of families and communities; efforts to make politics more efficient and less corrupt; efforts to tame or discipline the great industrial combinations of the time; efforts to empower some groups and restrict or control others. The ideas that lay behind these reforms were similarly various. "Progressivism" was a remarkably heterogeneous movement, united—if it was united at all—by the common belief among reformers that progress was indeed possible and that purposeful human intervention in the life of society and its economy was necessary. The reform crusades gained strength steadily from the 1880s onward, driven in large part by the energy and commitment of millions of women organized in clubs and other organizations. By the early years of the twentieth century, reform was beginning to transform the character of society and the nature of American politics.

FOR FURTHER REFERENCE

Richard Hofstadter, *The Age of Reform: From Bryan to FDR* (1955) is a classic, and now controversial, analysis of the partly psychological origins of the Populist and progressive movements. Robert Wiebe, *The Search for Order, 1877–1920* (1967) is an important organizational interpretation of the era. Gabriel Kolko makes a distinctly revisionist argument that business conservatism was at the heart of the progressive movement in *The Triumph of Conservatism* (1963). Alan Dawley, *Struggles for Justice: Social Responsibility and the Liberal State* (1991) is a sophisticated synthetic account of progressive movements and their ideas. John Milton Cooper, *The Pivotal Decades: The United States, 1900–1920* (1990) is a good narrative history of the period. Arthur S. Link and Richard L. McCormick, *Progressivism* (1983) is a brief interpretation. Daniel T. Rodgers, *Atlantic Crossings: Social Politics in a Progressive Age* (1998) is an important study of the passage of progressive ideas back and forth across the Atlantic. For powerful insights into pragmatism, an important philosophical underpinning to much reform, see Robert Westbrook, *John Dewey and American Democracy* (1991) and Louis Menand, *The Metaphysical Club: A Story of Ideas* (2001). Thomas L. Haskell, *The Emergence of Professional Social Science* (1977) is an important study of the social sciences and professionalism. Paul Starr, *The Social Transformation of American Medicine* (1982) is a pathbreaking study of the emergence of modern systems of health care. Morton J. Horwirtz, *The Transformation of American Law, 1870–1960: The Challenge to Legal Orthodoxy* (1992) is an important, controversial study of the way the legal world responded to economic and social change. Nancy Cott, *The Grounding of American Feminism* (1987) studies the shifting roles and beliefs of women. Kathryn Kish Sklar, *Florence Kelley and the Nation's Work: The Rise of Women's Political Culture, 1830–1900* (1995) examines the impact of female reformers on the progressive movement and the nation's political culture as a whole. Linda Gordon, *The Great Arizona Orphan Abduction* (1999) is the story of an early twentieth-century event that reveals the power of race, religion, and gender in dealing with immigrants. Paula Giddings, *When and Where I Enter: The Impact of Black Women on Race and Sex in America* (1984) is a good introduction to the intersection of gender and race. Glenda Gilmore, *Gender and Jim Crow: Women and the Politics of White Supremacy in North Carolina, 1896–1920* (1996) examines the role of gender in the construction of segregation. Louis Harlan, *Booker T. Washington: The Making of a Black Leader* (1956) and *Booker T. Washington: The Wizard of Tuskegee* (1983) are parts of an outstanding multivolume biography, as are David Levering Lewis, *W. E. B. Du Bois: Biography of a Race* (1993) and *W. E. B. Du Bois: The Fight for Equality and the American Century* (2000).

For quizzes, Internet resources, references to additional books and films, and more, consult this book's Online Learning Center site at www.mhhe.com/unfinishednation4.

THEODORE ROOSEVELT This heroic portrait of Theodore Roosevelt is by the great American portraitist John Singer Sargent. It hangs today in the White House *(John Singer Sargent/White House Historical Association)*

TIME LINE

1901	1902	1903	1904	1906	1908
McKinley assassinated	Northern Securities antitrust case	Panamanian independence	Roosevelt Corollary	Hepburn Railroad Regulation Act	Taft elected president
Theodore Roosevelt becomes president			Roosevelt elected president	Meat Inspection Act	

CHAPTER TWENTY-TWO

THE BATTLE FOR NATIONAL REFORM

Theodore Roosevelt and the Progressive Presidency
The Troubled Succession
Woodrow Wilson and the New Freedom
The "Big Stick": America and the World, 1901–1917

Efforts to reform the industrial economy encountered repeated frustrations at the state and local levels, so beginning early in the twentieth century, reformers began to look to the federal government. As at the state and local levels, however, the national government—mired in partisan politics—seemed poorly suited to serve as an agent of reform. Progressives attempted to make it more responsive to their demands. Some reformers, for example, urged an end to the system by which state legislatures elected the members of the United States Senate; they proposed instead a direct popular election, which they believed would force the Senate to react more directly to public demands. The Seventeenth Amendment, passed by Congress in 1912 and ratified by the states in 1913, provided for that change.

But even a reformed Congress, progressives believed, could not be expected to provide the kind of coherent leadership their agenda required. Congress was too clumsy, too divided, too tied to local, parochial interests. If the federal government was truly to fulfill its mission, most reformers agreed, it would require leadership from the presidency.

1909	1912	1913	1914	1915	1916
Payne-Aldrich Tariff	Wilson elected president	16th Amendment (income tax)	Federal Trade Commission Act	U.S. troops in Haiti	U.S. troops in Mexico
U.S. troops in Nicaragua		17th Amendment (direct election of U.S. senators)	Panama Canal opened		
		Federal Reserve Act			

THEODORE ROOSEVELT AND THE PROGRESSIVE PRESIDENCY

Roosevelt's Popularity

To a generation of progressive reformers, Theodore Roosevelt was an idol. No president before and few after attracted such attention and devotion. Yet Roosevelt was also in many respects decidedly conservative. He earned his extraordinary popularity less because of the extent of his reforms than because of his ebullient public personality and because he invested the presidency with something of its modern status as the center of national political life.

The Accidental President

When President William McKinley suddenly died in September 1901, the victim of an assassination, Roosevelt (who had been elected vice president less than a year before) was only forty-two years old, the youngest man ever to assume the presidency. Already, however, he had achieved a reputation as something of a wild man. Mark Hanna, who had warned McKinley against selecting Roosevelt as his running mate, exclaimed, "Now look, that damned cowboy is president of the United States!" But Roosevelt as president never openly rebelled against the leaders of his party. He became, rather, a champion of cautious, moderate change.

Roosevelt's Vision of Federal Power

Roosevelt envisioned the federal government not as the agent of any particular interest but as a mediator of the public good, with the president at its center. This attitude found expression in Roosevelt's policies toward the great industrial combinations. At the heart of Roosevelt's policy was his desire to win for government the power to investigate the activities of corporations and publicize the results. The pressure of educated public opinion, he believed, would alone eliminate most corporate abuses.

Roosevelt engaged in a few highly publicized efforts to break up combinations, among them a 1902 suit against a great new railroad combination in the Northwest, the Northern Securities Company. But he was not a trustbuster at heart, and his occasional use of antitrust law did not mark any serious effort to reverse the prevailing trend toward economic concentration.

A similar commitment to establishing the government as an impartial regulatory mechanism shaped Roosevelt's policy toward labor. In the past, federal intervention in industrial disputes had almost always meant action on behalf of employers. Roosevelt was no champion of unions, but he was willing to consider labor's position as well. When a bitter 1902 strike by the United Mine Workers against the anthracite coal industry dragged on long enough to endanger coal supplies for the coming winter, Roosevelt asked both the operators and the miners to accept impartial federal arbitration; and he threatened to dispatch federal troops to seize the mines when the owners refused. They soon relented. Arbitrators awarded the strikers a 10 percent wage increase and a nine-hour day.

Reform was not Roosevelt's main priority during his first years as president. He was too concerned with winning an election in his own right, which meant not antagonizing the conservative Republican Old Guard. By early 1904, Roosevelt had all but neutralized his opposition within the party. He won its presidential nomination with ease. And in the general election, where he faced a pallid conservative Democrat, Alton B. Parker, he captured over 57 percent of the popular vote.

Roosevelt Reelected

The Square Deal

During the 1904 campaign, Roosevelt boasted that he had worked in the anthracite coal strike to provide everyone with a "square deal." In his second term, he set out to extend this square deal further. One of his first targets was the powerful railroad industry. The Interstate Commerce Act of 1887, establishing the Interstate Commerce Commission (ICC), had been an early effort to regulate the industry, but over the years the courts had sharply limited its influence. The Hepburn Railroad Regulation Act of 1906 sought to restore some regulatory authority to the government by giving the ICC authority to inspect the books of railroad companies.

Hepburn Railroad Regulation Act

Roosevelt also pressured Congress to enact the Pure Food and Drug Act, which restricted the sale of dangerous or ineffective medicines. When Upton Sinclair's powerful novel *The Jungle* appeared in 1906, featuring appalling descriptions of conditions in the meatpacking industry, Roosevelt insisted on passage of the Meat Inspection Act, which ultimately helped eliminate many diseases once transmitted in impure meat. Starting in 1907, he proposed even more stringent measures: an eight-hour day for workers, broader compensation for victims of industrial accidents, inheritance and income taxes, regulation of the stock market, and others. But conservative opposition blocked much of this agenda and was responsible for a widening gulf between the president and the conservative wing of his party.

Roosevelt and the Environment

Roosevelt's aggressive policies on behalf of conservation contributed to that gulf. Using executive powers, he restricted private development on millions of acres of undeveloped government land—most of it in the West—by adding them to the previously modest national forest system. When conservatives in Congress restricted his authority over public lands in 1907, Roosevelt and his chief forester, Gifford Pinchot, worked furiously to seize all the forests and many of the water power sites still in the public domain before the bill became law.

Conservation in the West

Roosevelt was the first president to take an active interest in the new and struggling American conservation movement, and his policies had a lasting effect on national environmental policies. Many people who considered themselves "conservationists" in his time promoted policies to protect land for carefully managed development. That was in part a result of the influence of Pinchot, the first director of the National Forest Service (which he had helped create), who supported rational and efficient human use of the wilderness. As a result, the most important legacy of Roosevelt's conservation policy was to establish the government's role as manager of the continuing development of the wilderness.

The Old Guard may have opposed Roosevelt's efforts to extend government control over vast new lands. But they eagerly supported another important aspect of Roosevelt's natural resource policy: public reclamation and irrigation projects. In 1902, the president backed the National Reclamation Act, which provided federal funds for the construction of dams, reservoirs, and canals in the West—projects that would open new lands for cultivation and, years later, provide cheap electric power.

Despite his sympathy with Pinchot's vision of conservation, Roosevelt also shared some of the concerns of the naturalists—those within the conservation movement committed to protecting the natural beauty of the land and the health of its wildlife from human intrusion. Early in his presidency, Roosevelt even spent four days camping in the Sierras with John Muir, the nation's leading preservationist and the founder of the Sierra Club. And he added significantly to the still-young National Park System, whose purpose was to protect public land from any exploitation or development at all.

John Muir

The contending views of the early conservation movement came to a head beginning in 1906 in a sensational controversy over the Hetch Hetchy Valley in Yosemite National Park—a spectacular, high-walled valley highly popular with naturalists such as Muir and his fellow Sierra Club members. But many residents of San Francisco, worried about finding enough water to serve their growing population, saw Hetch Hetchy as an ideal place for a reservoir.

Preservation versus "Rational Use"

For over a decade, a battle raged between naturalists and the advocates of the dam, a battle that consumed the energies of John Muir for the rest of his life. To Pinchot, the issue was the practical one of whether "leaving this valley in a state of nature is greater than using it for the benefit of the city of San Francisco." Muir helped place a referendum question on the ballot in 1908, certain that the residents of the city would oppose the project "as soon as light is cast upon it." Instead, San Franciscans approved the dam by a huge margin. Construction of the dam finally began after World War I.

This setback for the naturalists was not, however, a total defeat. The fight against Hetch Hetchy helped mobilize a new coalition of people committed to preservation, not "rational use," of wilderness and made clear that the casual exploitation of natural wonders would no longer be unopposed.

BOYS IN THE MINES These young boys, covered in grime and no more than twelve years old, pose for the noted photographer Lewis Hine at the entrance to the coal mine in Pennsylvania where they worked—most likely as "breaker boys," crawling into newly blasted areas and breaking up the loose coal. The rugged conditions in the mines were one cause of the great strike of 1902, in which Theodore Roosevelt intervened. *(Lewis Hine/Corbis)*

Panic and Retirement

Despite the flurry of reforms Roosevelt was able to enact, the government still had relatively little control over the industrial economy. That became clear in 1907, when a serious recession began. Conservatives blamed Roosevelt's "mad" economic policies for the disaster. And while the president naturally (and correctly) disagreed, he nevertheless acted quickly to reassure business leaders that he would not interfere with their private recovery efforts.

J. P. Morgan

The great financier J. P. Morgan helped construct a pool of the assets of several important New York banks to prop up shaky financial institutions. The key to the arrangement, Morgan told the president, was the purchase by U.S. Steel of the shares of the Tennessee Coal and Iron Company, currently held by a threatened New York bank. He would, he insisted, need assurances that the purchase would not prompt antitrust action. Roosevelt informally agreed, and the Morgan plan proceeded.

Roosevelt loved being president, and many people assumed he would run for the office again in 1908 despite the longstanding tradition of presidents serving no more than two terms. But the Panic of 1907 and Roosevelt's reform efforts had so alienated conservatives in his own party that he

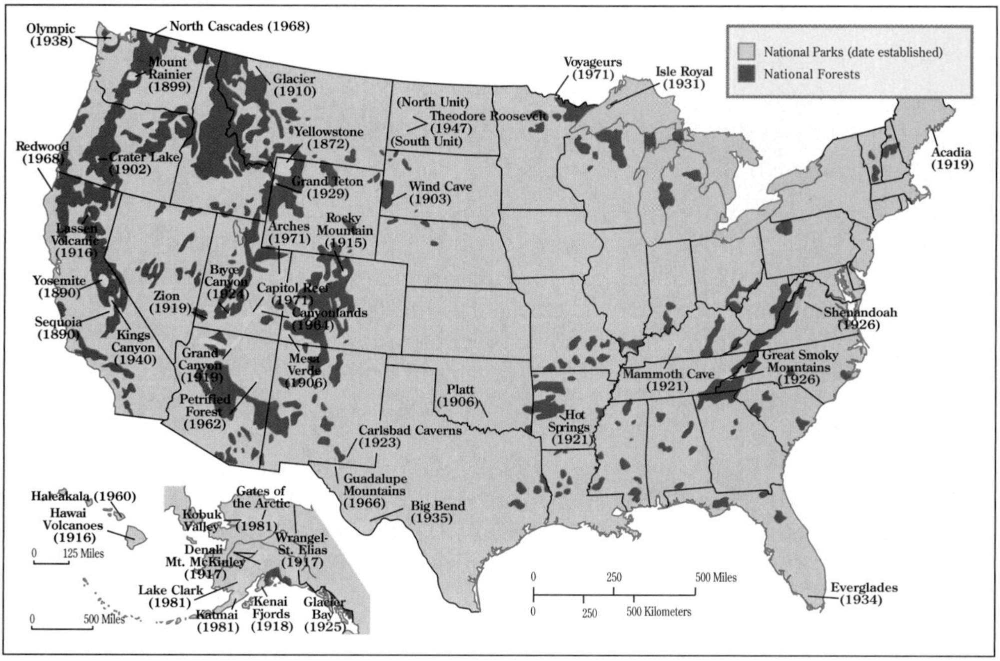

ESTABLISHMENT OF NATIONAL PARKS AND FORESTS This map illustrates the steady growth throughout the late nineteenth and twentieth centuries of the systems of national parks and national forests in the United States. Although Theodore Roosevelt is widely and correctly remembered as a great champion of national parks and forests, the greatest expansions of these systems occurred after his presidency. Note, for example, how many new areas were added in the 1920s. ◆ *What is the difference between national parks and national forests?*

might have had difficulty winning the Republican nomination for another term. In 1904, moreover, he had made a public promise to step down four years later. And so, after nearly eight energetic years in the White House, Theodore Roosevelt, fifty years old, retired from public life—briefly.

THE TROUBLED SUCCESSION

William Howard Taft

William Howard Taft, who assumed the presidency in 1909, had been Theodore Roosevelt's most trusted lieutenant and his hand-picked successor; progressive reformers believed him to be one of their own. But Taft had also been a restrained and moderate jurist, a man with a punctilious regard for legal process; conservatives expected him to abandon Roosevelt's aggressive use of presidential powers. By seeming acceptable to almost everyone, Taft easily won election to the White House in 1908. He received his party's nomination virtually uncontested. His victory in the general election in November—over William Jennings Bryan, running for the Democrats for the third time—was a foregone conclusion.

Four years later, however, Taft would leave office the most decisively defeated president of the twentieth century. Taft's failure was a result in part of his failure to match Roosevelt's personal dynamism. (Contributing to Taft's image as a less than vigorous man was his enormous weight, which at times rose to 350 pounds.) More significant, however, was that having come into office as the darling of progressives and conservatives alike, he soon found that he could not please both groups. Gradually he found himself pleasing the conservatives and alienating the progressives.

Taft and the Progressives

Taft's first problem arose in the opening months of the new administration, when he called Congress into special session to lower protective tariff rates, an old progressive demand. But the president made no effort to overcome the opposition of the congressional Old Guard, arguing that it would violate the constitutional doctrine of separation of powers if he were to intervene in legislative matters. The result was the feeble Payne-Aldrich Tariff, which reduced tariff rates scarcely at all.

Payne-Aldrich Tariff

A sensational controversy broke out late in 1909 that helped destroy Taft's popularity with reformers for good. Many progressives had been unhappy when Taft replaced Roosevelt's secretary of the interior, James R. Garfield, an aggressive conservationist, with Richard A. Ballinger, a more conservative corporate lawyer. Suspicion of Ballinger grew when he attempted to invalidate Roosevelt's removal of nearly 1 million acres of forests and mineral reserves from the public lands available for private development.

In the midst of this mounting concern, Louis Glavis, an Interior Department investigator, charged the new secretary with having once connived to turn over valuable public coal lands in Alaska to a private syndicate for personal profit. Glavis took the evidence to Gifford Pinchot, still head of the Forest Service and a critic of Ballinger's policies. Pinchot took the charges to the president. Taft investigated them and decided they were groundless. But Pinchot was not satisfied. He leaked the story to the press and asked Congress to investigate the scandal. The president discharged him for insubordination, and the congressional committee appointed to study the controversy, dominated by Old Guard Republicans, exonerated Ballinger. But progressives throughout the country supported Pinchot. The controversy aroused as much public passion as any dispute of its time; and when it was over, Taft had alienated the supporters of Roosevelt completely and, it seemed, irrevocably.

Pinchot-Ballinger Controversy

The Return of Roosevelt

During most of these controversies, Theodore Roosevelt was far away: on a long hunting safari in Africa and an extended tour of Europe. To the American public, however, Roosevelt remained a formidable presence. His return to New York in the spring of 1910 was a major public event. Roosevelt insisted that he had no plans to reenter politics, but within a month he announced that he would embark on a national speaking tour before the end of the summer. Furious with Taft, he was becoming convinced that he alone was capable of reuniting the Republican Party.

The real signal of Roosevelt's decision to assume leadership of Republican reformers came in a speech he gave on September 1, 1910, in Osawatomie, Kansas. In it he outlined a set of principles, which he labeled the "New Nationalism," that made clear he had moved a considerable way from the cautious reform conservatism of the first years of his presidency. He argued that social justice was possible only through the efforts of a strong federal government whose executive acted as the "steward of the public welfare." He supported graduated income and inheritance taxes, workers' compensation for industrial accidents, regulation of the labor of women and children, tariff revision, and firmer regulation of corporations.

Roosevelt's "New Nationalism"

Spreading Insurgency

The congressional elections of 1910 provided further evidence of how far the progressive revolt had spread. In primary elections, conservative Republicans suffered defeat after defeat. In the general election, the Democrats won control of the House of Representatives for the first time in sixteen years and gained strength in the Senate. But Roosevelt still denied any presidential ambitions and claimed that his real purpose was to pressure Taft to return to progressive policies. Two events, however, changed his mind. The first, on October 27, 1911, was the announcement by the administration of a suit against U.S. Steel, which charged, among other things, that the 1907 acquisition of the Tennessee Coal and Iron Company had been illegal. Roosevelt had approved that acquisition in the midst of the 1907 panic, and he was enraged by the implication that he had acted improperly.

Roosevelt was still reluctant to become a candidate for president, because Senator Robert La Follette, the great Wisconsin progressive, had been working since 1911 to secure the presidential nomination for himself. But La Follette's candidacy stumbled in February 1912 when, exhausted, and distraught over the illness of a daughter, he appeared to suffer a nervous breakdown during a speech in Philadelphia. Roosevelt announced his candidacy on February 22.

ROOSEVELT AT OSAWATOMIE Roosevelt's famous speech at Osawatomie, Kansas, in 1910 was the most radical of his career and openly marked his break with the Taft administration and the Republican leadership. *(Brown Brothers)*

T. R. versus Taft

For all practical purposes, the campaign for the Republican nomination had now become a battle between Roosevelt, the champion of the progressives, and Taft, the candidate of the conservatives. Roosevelt scored overwhelming victories in all thirteen presidential primaries. Taft, however, remained the choice of most party leaders.

The battle for the nomination at the Chicago convention revolved around an unusually large number of contested delegates: 254 in all. Roosevelt needed fewer than half the disputed seats to clinch the nomination. But the Republican National Committee, controlled by the Old Guard, awarded all but 19 of them to Taft. At a rally the night before the convention opened, Roosevelt addressed 5,000 cheering supporters and announced that if the party refused to seat his delegates, he would continue his own candidacy outside the party. "We stand at Armageddon," he told the roaring crowd, "and we battle for the Lord." The next day, he led his supporters out of the convention, and out of the party. The convention then nominated Taft on the first ballot.

Roosevelt summoned his supporters back to Chicago in August for another convention, this one to launch the new Progressive Party and nominate himself as its presidential candidate. Roosevelt approached the battle feeling, as he put it, "fit as a bull moose" (thus giving his new party an enduring nickname). But by

The "Bull Moose" Party

then, he was aware that his cause was virtually hopeless. That was partly because many of the insurgents who had supported him during the primaries refused to follow him out of the Republican Party. It was also because of the man the Democrats had nominated for president.

WOODROW WILSON AND THE NEW FREEDOM

The 1912 presidential contest was not simply one between conservatives and reformers. It was also one between two brands of progressivism that reflected two different views of America's future. And it was one that matched the two most important national leaders of the early twentieth century in unequal contest.

Woodrow Wilson

Reform sentiment had been gaining strength within the Democratic as well as the Republican Party in the first years of the century. At the 1912 Democratic Convention in Baltimore in June, Champ Clark, the conservative Speaker of the House, was unable to assemble the two-thirds majority necessary for nomination because of progressive opposition. Finally, on the forty-sixth ballot, Woodrow Wilson, the governor of New Jersey and the only genuinely progressive candidate in the race, emerged as the party's nominee.

Wilson had been a professor of political science at Princeton until 1902, when he was named president of the university. Elected governor of New Jersey in 1910, he demonstrated a commitment to reform. During his two years in the statehouse, he earned a national reputation for winning passage of progressive legislation. As a presidential candidate in 1912, Wilson presented a progressive program that came to be called the "New Freedom." Wilson's New Freedom differed from Roosevelt's New Nationalism most clearly in its approach to economic policy and the trusts. Roosevelt believed in accepting economic concentration and using government to regulate and control it. Wilson seemed to side with those who (like Brandeis) believed that the proper response to monopoly was not to regulate it but to destroy it.

"New Freedom"

The 1912 presidential campaign was something of an anticlimax. William Howard Taft, resigned to defeat, barely campaigned at all. Roosevelt campaigned energetically (until a gunshot wound from a would-be assassin forced him to the sidelines during the last weeks before the election), but he failed to draw any significant numbers of Democratic progressives away from Wilson. In November, Roosevelt and Taft split the Republican vote; Wilson held onto most Democrats and won. He polled only a plurality of the popular vote: 42 percent, compared with 27 percent for Roosevelt, 23 percent for Taft, and 6 percent for the socialist Eugene Debs. But in the electoral college, Wilson won 435 of the 531 votes.

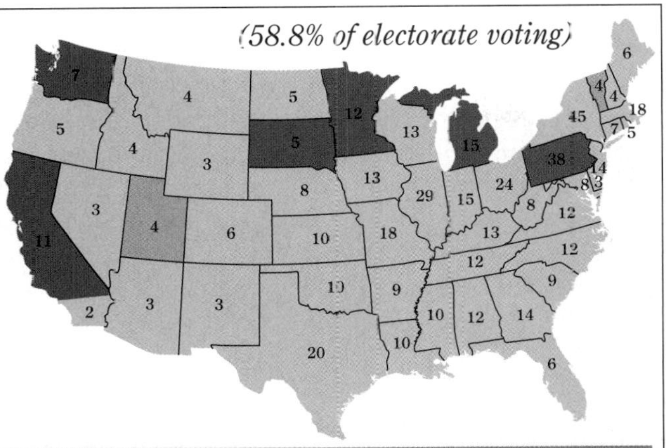

	ELECTORAL VOTE	POPULAR VOTE (%)
Woodrow Wilson *(Democratic)*	435	6,293,454 (41.9)
Theodore Roosevelt *(Progressive/Bull Moose)*	88	4,119,538 (27.4)
William H. Taft *(Republican)*	8	3,484,980 (23.2)
Eugene V. Debs *(Socialist)*	—	900,672 (6.0)
Other parties *(Prohibition; Socialist Labor)*	—	235,025

ELECTION OF 1912 The election of 1912 was one of the most unusual in American history because of the dramatic schism within the Republican party. Two Republican presidents—William Howard Taft, the incumbent, and Theodore Roosevelt, his predecessor—ran against each other in 1912, opening the way for a victory by the Democratic candidate Woodrow Wilson, who won with only about 42 percent of the popular vote. A fourth candidate, the socialist Eugene V. Debs, received a significant 6 percent of the vote. ◆ *What events caused the schism between Taft and Roosevelt?*

For an interactive version of this map go to www.mhhe.com/unfinishednation4ch22maps

The Scholar as President

More than William Howard Taft, more even than Theodore Roosevelt, Wilson concentrated the powers of the executive branch in his own hands. He exerted firm control over his cabinet, and he delegated real authority only to those whose loyalty to him was beyond question. Perhaps the clearest indication of his style of leadership was the identity of his most powerful adviser: Colonel Edward M. House, an intelligent and ambitious Texan whose only claim to authority was his personal intimacy with the president.

In legislative matters, Wilson skillfully used his position as party leader to weld together a coalition that would support his program. Democratic majorities in both houses of Congress made his task easier. Wilson's first triumph as president was the fulfillment of an old Democratic (and progressive) goal: a substantial lowering of the protective tariff. The Underwood-Simmons Tariff, passed in a special session of Congress that Wilson summoned shortly after his inauguration, provided cuts substantial enough, progressives believed, to introduce real competition into American markets and thus to help break the power of trusts. To make up for the loss of revenue under the new tariff, Congress approved a graduated income tax. This first modern income tax imposed a 1 percent tax on individuals and corporations earning over $4,000, with rates ranging up to 6 percent on incomes over $500,000.

Income Tax Adopted

Wilson held Congress in session through the summer to work on a major reform of the American banking system: the Federal Reserve Act, which Congress passed and which the president signed on December 23, 1913. It created twelve regional banks, each to be owned and controlled by the individual banks of its district. The regional Federal Reserve banks would hold a certain percentage of the assets of their member banks in reserve; they would use those reserves to support loans to private banks at an interest (or "discount") rate that the Federal Reserve system would set; they would issue a new type of paper currency—Federal Reserve notes—that would become the nation's basic medium of trade and would be backed by the government. Most important, perhaps, they would be able to shift funds quickly to troubled areas—to meet increased demands for credit or to protect imperiled banks. Supervising and regulating the entire system was a national Federal Reserve Board, whose members were appointed by the president.

In 1914, turning to the central issue of his 1912 campaign, Wilson proposed two measures to deal with the problem of monopoly. There was a proposal to create a federal agency through which the government would help business police itself—a regulatory commission of the type Roosevelt had advocated in 1912. There were also proposals to strengthen the government's ability actually to break up trusts—a decentralizing approach more characteristic of Wilson's 1912 campaign. The two measures took shape as the Federal Trade Commission Act and the Clayton Antitrust Act. The Federal Trade Commission Act created a regulatory agency that would help businesses determine in advance whether their actions would be acceptable to the government. The agency would also have authority to launch prosecutions against "unfair trade practices," which the law did not define, and it would have wide power to investigate corporate behavior. The act, in short, increased the government's regulatory authority significantly. Wilson signed it happily. But he seemed to lose interest in the Clayton Antitrust Bill and did little to protect it from conservative assaults, which

Federal Trade Commission Act

greatly weakened it. The vigorous legal pursuit of monopoly that Wilson had promised in 1912 never materialized.

Retreat and Advance

By the fall of 1914, Wilson believed that the program of the New Freedom was essentially complete. He refused to support the movement for national woman suffrage. Deferring to southern Democrats, he condoned the reimposition of segregation in the agencies of the federal government. When congressional progressives attempted to enlist his support for new reform legislation, he dismissed their proposals as unconstitutional or unnecessary.

The congressional elections of 1914, however, shattered the president's complacency. Democrats suffered major losses in the House of Representatives, and voters who in 1912 had supported the Progressive Party began returning to the Republicans. Wilson would not be able to rely on a divided opposition when he ran for reelection in 1916. By the end of 1915, therefore, Wilson had begun to support a second flurry of reforms. In January 1916, he appointed Louis Brandeis to the Supreme Court, making him not only the first Jew but the most advanced progressive to serve there. Later, he supported a measure to make it easier for farmers to receive credit and one creating a system of workers' compensation for federal employees.

In 1916, Wilson supported the Keating-Owen Act. The measure prohibited the shipment across state lines of goods produced by underage children, thus giving an expanded importance to the constitutional clause assigning Congress the task of regulating interstate commerce. (It would be some years before the Supreme Court would uphold this interpretation of the clause; the Court invalidated the Keating-Owen Act in 1918.) The president similarly supported measures that used federal taxing authority as a vehicle for legislating social change. After the Court struck down Keating-Owen, a new law attempted to achieve the same goal by imposing a heavy tax on the products of child labor. (The Court later struck it down, too.) And the Smith-Lever Act of 1914 demonstrated another way in which the federal government could influence local behavior; it offered matching federal grants to states that agreed to support agricultural extension education.

Limiting Child Labor

THE "BIG STICK": AMERICA AND THE WORLD, 1901–1917

American foreign policy during the progressive years reflected many of the same impulses that were motivating domestic reform. But more than that, it reflected the nation's new sense of itself as a world power.

Roosevelt and "Civilization"

Theodore Roosevelt believed in the value and importance of using American power in the world (a conviction he once described by citing the proverb, "Speak softly, but carry a big stick"). But he had two different standards for using that power.

Roosevelt believed that an important distinction existed between the "civilized" and "uncivilized" nations of the world. "Civilized" nations, as he defined them, were predominantly white and Anglo-Saxon or Teutonic; "uncivilized" nations were generally nonwhite, Latin, or Slavic. But racism was only partly the basis of the distinction. Equally important was economic development. Civilized nations were, by Roosevelt's definition, producers of industrial goods; uncivilized nations were suppliers of raw materials and markets. There was, he believed, an economic relationship between the two parts that was vital to both of them. A civilized society, therefore, had the right and duty to intervene in the affairs of a "backward" nation to preserve order and stability—for the sake of both nations. That belief was one important reason for Roosevelt's early support of the development of American sea power. By 1906, the American navy had attained a size and strength surpassed only by that of Great Britain.

Justifying Intervention

Protecting the "Open Door" in Asia

In 1904 the Japanese staged a surprise attack on the Russian fleet at Port Arthur in southern Manchuria, a province of China that both Russia and Japan hoped to control. Roosevelt, hoping to prevent either nation from becoming dominant there, agreed to a Japanese request to mediate an end to the conflict. Russia, faring badly in the war, had no choice but to agree. At a peace conference in Portsmouth, New Hampshire, in 1905, Roosevelt extracted from the embattled Russians a recognition of Japan's territorial gains and from the Japanese an agreement to cease the fighting and expand no further. At the same time, he negotiated a secret agreement with the Japanese to ensure that the United States could continue to trade freely in the region. But in the years that followed, relations between the United States and Japan steadily deteriorated. Having destroyed the Russian fleet at Port Arthur, Japan now emerged as the preeminent naval power in the Pacific and soon began to exclude American trade from many of the territories it controlled. Roosevelt took no direct action against Japan, but to be sure the Japanese government recognized the power of the United States, he sent sixteen battleships of the new American navy (known as the "Great White Fleet" because the ships were temporarily painted white for the voyage) on an unprecedented journey around the world that included a call on Japan.

"Great White Fleet"

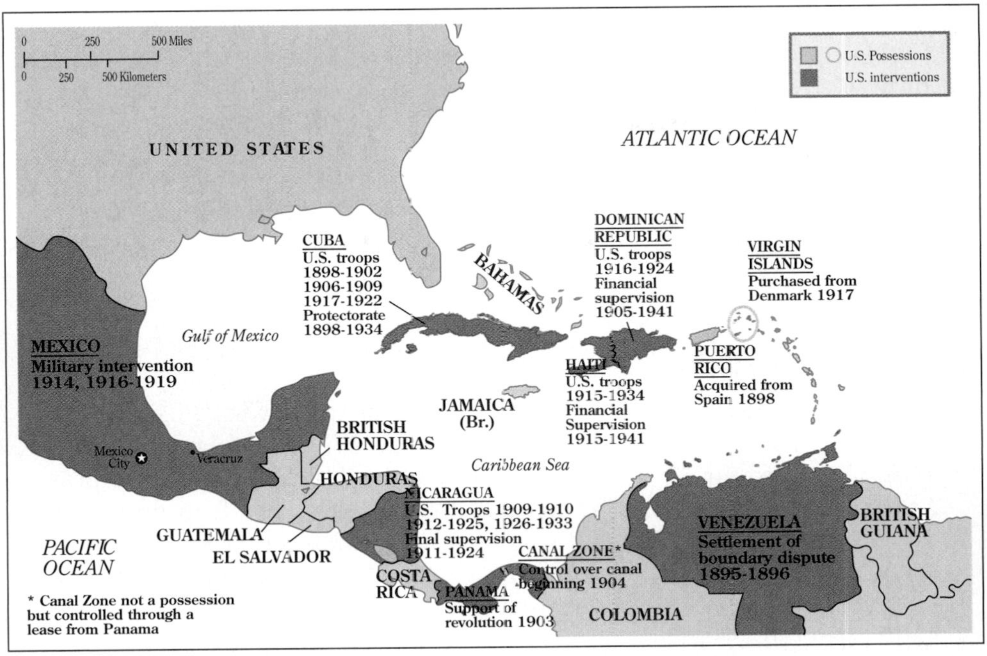

THE UNITED STATES AND LATIN AMERICA, 1895–1941 Except for Puerto Rico, the Virgin Islands, and the Canal Zone, the United States had no formal possessions in Latin America and the Caribbean in the late nineteenth century and the first half of the twentieth. But as this map reveals, the U.S. exercised considerable influence in these regions throughout this period—political and economic influence, augmented at times by military intervention. Note the particularly intrusive presence of the United States in the affairs of Cuba, Haiti, and the Dominican Republic—as well as the canal-related interventions in Colombia and Panama.
◆ *What were some of the most frequent reasons for American intervention in Latin America?*

For an interactive version of this map go to www.mhhe.com/unfinishednation4ch22maps

The Iron-Fisted Neighbor

Roosevelt took a particular interest in events in Latin America. Unwilling to share trading rights, let alone military control, with any other nation, Roosevelt embarked on a series of ventures in the Caribbean and South America. He established a pattern of American intervention in the region that would long survive his presidency.

Crucial to Roosevelt's thinking was an incident early in his administration. In 1902, the government of Venezuela began to renege on debts to European bankers. Naval forces of Britain, Italy, and Germany blockaded the Venezuelan coast in response. Then German ships began to bombard a Venezuelan port amid rumors that Germany planned to establish a permanent base in the region. Roosevelt used the threat of American naval power to pressure the German navy to withdraw.

The incident helped persuade Roosevelt that European intrusions into Latin America could result not only from aggression but from instability or irresponsibility (such as defaulting on debts) within the Latin American nations themselves. As a result, in 1904 he announced what came to be known as the "Roosevelt Corollary" to the Monroe Doctrine. The United States, he claimed, had the right not only to oppose European intervention in the Western Hemisphere but also to intervene itself in the domestic affairs of its neighbors if those neighbors proved unable to maintain order and national sovereignty on their own.

"Roosevelt Corollary" Announced

The immediate motivation for the Roosevelt Corollary, and the first opportunity for using it, was a crisis in the Dominican Republic. A revolution had toppled its corrupt and bankrupt government in 1903, but the new regime proved no better able than the old to make good on the country's $22 million in debts to European nations. Using the rationale provided by the Roosevelt Corollary, Roosevelt established, in effect, an American receivership, assuming control of Dominican customs and distributing 45 percent of the revenues to the Dominicans and the rest to foreign creditors. This arrangement lasted, in one form or another, for more than three decades.

In 1902, the United States granted political independence to Cuba, but only after the new government had agreed to the so-called Platt Amendment (named after Senator Thomas Platt of Pennsylvania) to its constitution. The amendment gave the United States the right to prevent any foreign power from intruding into the new nation. In 1906, when domestic uprisings threatened the island's stability, American troops landed in Cuba, quelled the fighting, and remained there for three years.

Intervention in Cuba

The Panama Canal

The most celebrated accomplishment of Roosevelt's presidency was the construction of the Panama Canal, which linked the Atlantic and the Pacific by creating a channel through Central America. At first, Roosevelt and many others favored a route across Nicaragua, which would permit a sea-level canal requiring no locks. But they soon turned instead to the narrow Isthmus of Panama in Colombia, the site of an earlier, failed effort by a French company to construct a channel. Although the Panama route was not at sea level, it was shorter than the one in Nicaragua, and construction was already about 40 percent complete.

Roosevelt dispatched John Hay, his secretary of state, to negotiate an agreement with Colombian diplomats in Washington that would allow construction to begin without delay. Under heavy American pressure, the Colombian chargé d'affaires, Tomas Herrán, unwisely signed an agree-

OPENING THE PANAMA CANAL The great Miraflores locks of the Panama Canal open in October 1914 to admit the first ship to pass through the channel. The construction of the canal was one of the great engineering feats of the early twentieth century. But the heavy-handed political efforts of Theodore Roosevelt were at least equally important to its completion. *(Bettmann/Corbis)*

ment giving the United States perpetual rights to a six-mile-wide "canal zone" across Colombia; in return, the United States would pay Colombia $10 million and an annual rental of $250,000. The treaty produced outrage in the Colombian senate, which refused to ratify it. Colombia then sent a new representative to Washington with instructions to demand at least $20 million from the Americans plus a share of the payment to the French.

Panamanian Revolt

Roosevelt was furious and began to look for ways to circumvent the Colombian government. Philippe Bunau-Varilla, chief engineer of the French canal project, was a ready ally. In November 1903, he helped organize and finance a revolution in Panama with the support of the United States. Roosevelt landed troops from the USS *Nashville* in Panama to "maintain order." Their presence prevented Colombian forces from suppressing the rebellion, and three days later Roosevelt recognized Panama as an independent nation. The new Panamanian government quickly agreed to the terms the Colombian senate had rejected. Work on the canal proceeded rapidly, and it opened in 1914.

Taft and "Dollar Diplomacy"

Like his predecessor, William Howard Taft worked to advance the nation's economic interests overseas. But he showed little interest in Roosevelt's larger vision of world stability. Taft's secretary of state, Philander C. Knox, worked aggressively to extend American investments into less-developed regions. Critics called his policies "Dollar Diplomacy."

Nicaragua Occupied

It was particularly visible in American policy in the Caribbean. When a revolution broke out in Nicaragua in 1909, the administration quickly sided with the insurgents and sent American troops into the country to seize the customs houses. As soon as peace was restored, Knox encouraged American bankers to offer substantial loans to the new government, thus increasing Washington's financial leverage over the country. When the new pro-American government faced an insurrection less than two years later, Taft again landed American troops in Nicaragua, this time to protect the existing regime. The troops remained there for more than a decade.

Diplomacy and Morality

Woodrow Wilson entered the presidency with relatively little interest or experience in international affairs. Yet he faced international challenges of a scope and gravity unmatched by those of any president before him. Although the greatest test of Wilsonian diplomacy did not occur until World War I, many of the qualities that he would bring to that ordeal were evident in his foreign policy from his first moments in office.

Having already seized control of the finances of the Dominican Republic in 1905, the United States established a military government there in 1916 when the Dominicans refused to accept a treaty that would have made the country a virtual American protectorate. The military occupation lasted eight years. In Haiti, Wilson landed the marines in 1915 to quell a revolution in the course of which a mob had murdered an unpopular president. American military forces remained in the country until 1934, and American officers drafted the new Haitian constitution adopted in 1918. When Wilson began to fear that the Danish West Indies might be about to fall into the hands of Germany, he bought the colony from Denmark and renamed it the Virgin Islands. Concerned about the possibility of European influence in Nicaragua, he signed a treaty with that country's government ensuring that no other nation would build a canal there and winning for the United States the right to intervene in Nicaragua's internal affairs to protect American interests. In all of these actions, Wilson was displaying an approach to Latin America very similar to the approaches of Roosevelt and Taft.

Intervention in Haiti and the Dominican Republic

But Wilson's view of America's role in the Western Hemisphere (and the world) was not entirely similar to the views of his predecessors. That became clear in his dealings with Mexico. For many years, under the friendly auspices of the corrupt dictator Porfirio Díaz, American businessmen had been establishing an enormous economic presence in Mexico. In 1910, however, Díaz had been overthrown by the popular leader Francisco Madero, who promised democratic reform but who also seemed hostile to American businesses in Mexico. The United States quietly encouraged a reactionary general, Victoriano Huerta, to depose Madero early in 1913, and the Taft administration, in its last weeks in office, prepared to recognize the new Huerta regime. Before it could do so, however, the new government murdered Madero, and Woodrow Wilson took office in Washington. The new president instantly announced that he would never recognize Huerta's "government of butchers."

Recognition Withheld

The conflict dragged on for years. At first, Wilson hoped that simply by refusing to recognize Huerta he could help topple the regime and bring to power the opposing Constitutionalists, led by Venustiano Carranza. But when Huerta, with the support of American business interests, established a full military dictatorship in October 1913, the president became more assertive. In April 1914, a minor naval incident provided an excuse for open intervention. An officer in Huerta's army briefly arrested several American sailors from the U.S.S. *Dolphin* who had gone ashore in Tampico. The men were immediately released, but the American admiral demanded that the Huerta forces fire a twenty-one-gun salute to the American flag as a public display of penance. The Mexicans refused. Wilson used the trivial incident as a pretext for seizing the Mexican port of Veracruz.

Wilson had envisioned a bloodless action, but in a clash with Mexican troops in Veracruz, the Americans killed 126 of the defenders and suffered 19 casualties of their own. Now at the brink of war, Wilson began to look for a way out. His show of force, however, had helped strengthen the position of the Carranza faction, which captured Mexico City in August and forced Huerta to flee the country. At last, it seemed, the crisis might be over.

Veracruz Incident

But Wilson was not yet satisfied. He reacted angrily when Carranza refused to accept American guidelines for the creation of a new government, and he briefly considered throwing his support to still another aspirant to leadership: Carranza's erstwhile lieutenant Pancho Villa. When Villa's military position deteriorated, however, Wilson abandoned him and finally, in October 1915, granted preliminary recognition to the Carranza government. By now, however, he had created yet another crisis. Villa, angry at what he considered an American betrayal, retaliated in January 1916 by taking sixteen American mining engineers from a train in northern Mexico and shooting them. Two months later, he led his soldiers across the border into Columbus, New Mexico, where they killed seventeen more Americans.

With the permission of the Carranza government, Wilson ordered General John J. Pershing to

Pershing Expedition

PANCHO VILLA AND HIS TROOPS Pancho Villa (fourth from left) poses with some of the leaders of his army, whose members Americans came to consider bandits once they began staging raids across the U.S. border. He was a national hero in Mexico. *(Brown Brothers)*

lead an American expeditionary force across the Mexican border in pursuit of Villa. The American troops never found Villa, but they did engage in two ugly skirmishes with Carranza's army, in which forty Mexicans and twelve Americans died. Again, the United States and Mexico stood at the brink of war. But at the last minute, Wilson drew back. He quietly withdrew American troops from Mexico, and in March 1917, he at last granted formal recognition to the Carranza regime. By now, however, Wilson's attention was turning elsewhere—to the far greater international crisis engulfing the European continent and ultimately the United States as well.

CONCLUSION

Driven by the great surge of reform energies emerging throughout the United States, American national politics in the early twentieth century itself became an important battleground for progressives. The rise of national reform was a result of many things, but two in particular.

First, many reformers discovered that success required the engagement of the federal government in their efforts. Progressives themselves increasingly turned to Washington as a potential ally in their efforts. Second, two national leaders helped transform the federal government into a visible and muscular vehicle of reform. Theodore Roosevelt's eight years as president changed popular expectations of the office and launched a significant reform agenda. Woodrow Wilson, who defeated not only Roosevelt's ill-fated successor William Howard Taft in 1912, but also Roosevelt himself, running as a third-party challenger, became the most successful legislative president of the early twentieth century by winning passage of a broad and ambitious reform agenda of his own.

Roosevelt, Taft, and Wilson also contributed to a continuation, and indeed an expansion, of America's active role in international affairs, in part as an effort to abet the growth of American capitalism and in part as an attempt to impose American standards of morality and democracy on other parts of the world. Similar mixtures of ideals and self-interest would soon guide the United States into a great world war.

FOR FURTHER REFERENCE

John Milton Cooper, Jr., compares the lives and ideas of the progressive movement's leading national politicians in *The Warrior and the Priest: Woodrow Wilson and Theodore Roosevelt* (1983). John Morton Blum, *The Republican Roosevelt* (1954) is a long-popular brief study. Edmund Morris, *Theodore Rex* (2002) is a popular history of Roosevelt's presidency, and H. W. Brands, *TR* (1997) is a large biography. Donald E. Anderson, *William Howard Taft* (1973) is a useful account of this unhappy presidency. Arthur S. Link is Wilson's most important biographer and the author of *Woodrow Wilson*, 5 vols., (1947–1965). Kendrick A. Clements, *The Presidency of Woodrow Wilson* (1992) is a more recent study. Thomas K. McCraw, *Prophets of Regulation* (1984) is an excellent examination of important figures in the making of modern state capacity. Michael McGerr, *The Decline of Popular Politics* (1986) is a perceptive examination of the decline of public enthusiasm for parties in the North in the late nineteenth and early twentieth centuries. Samuel P. Hays, *The Gospel of Efficiency: The Progressive Conservation Movement, 1890–1920* (1962) makes a pioneering argument about the organizational imperatives behind the conservation movement and Stephen R. Fox, *The American Conservation Movement: John Muir and His Legacy* (1981) is another valuable study. John Opie, *Nature's Nation: An Environmental History of the United States* (1998) is an ambitious synthesis of environmental history. The effects of America's interventionist policies in Latin America are described in John Womack's arresting account of the revolution in Mexico, *Zapata and the Mexican Revolution* (1968). *Theodore Roosevelt*, by David Grubin (1997) is a fine biographical film. *The "Battle for Wilderness"* (1990) is a documentary film about the conservation movement and two of its rival leaders, Gifford Pinchot and John Muir.

For quizzes, Internet resources, references to additional books and films, and more, consult this book's Online Learning Center site at www.mhhe.com/unfinishednation4.

AN APPEAL TO DUTY This most famous of all American war posters, by the artist James Montgomery Flagg, shows a fierce-looking Uncle Sam requesting, almost demanding, Americans to join the army to fight in World War I. With the nation very divided over the wisdom of entering the war, the Wilson administration believed it needed to persuade Americans not only to support the struggle but also—something unusual for Americans—to feel a sense of obligation to the government and its overseas commitments. *(The National Archives and Records Administration)*

TIME LINE

1914	1915	1916	1917
World War I begins	*Lusitania* torpedoed	Wilson reelected	German unrestricted submarine warfare
	Wilson supports preparedness		U.S. enters World War I
			Selective Service Act
			War Industries Board created

CHAPTER TWENTY-THREE

AMERICA AND THE GREAT WAR

The Road to War
"War Without Stint"
The Search for a New World Order
A Society in Turmoil

The Great War, as it was known to a generation unaware that another, greater war would soon follow, began quietly in August 1914 when Austria-Hungary invaded the tiny Balkan nation of Serbia. Within weeks, however, it had grown into a conflagration engaging the armies of most of the major nations of Europe. Americans looked on with horror as the war became the most savage in history and as it dragged on, murderously and inconclusively, for two and a half years. But Americans also believed at first that the conflict had little to do with them. They were wrong. After nearly three years of attempting to affect the outcome of the conflict without becoming embroiled in it, the United States formally entered the war in April 1917.

THE ROAD TO WAR

By 1914, the European nations had created an unusually precarious international system. It careened into war very quickly on the basis of what most historians agree was a minor series of provocations.

1918	1919	1920	1927
Sedition Act	Senate rejects Treaty of Versailles	19th Amendment ratified	Sacco and Vanzetti executed
Wilson's Fourteen Points	Race riots in Chicago and other cities	Palmer Raids and Red Scare	
Armistice ends war	Steel strike and other labor actions	Harding elected president	
Paris Peace Conference			

The Collapse of the European Peace

The major powers of Europe were organized by 1914 in two great, competing alliances. The "Triple Entente," which during the war became known as the "Allies," linked Britain, France, and Russia. The "Triple Alliance," later called the "Central Powers," united Germany, the Austro-Hungarian Empire, and Italy, although Italy withdrew when war began and joined the Allies. The chief rivalry, however, was not between the two alliances but between the great powers that dominated them: Great Britain and Germany.

The Anglo-German rivalry was not the immediate cause of the war. The conflict emerged most directly out of a controversy involving nationalist movements within the Austro-Hungarian Empire. On June 28, 1914, the Archduke Franz Ferdinand, heir to the throne of the tottering empire, was assassinated while paying a state visit to Sarajevo. Sarajevo is the capital of Bosnia, then a province of Austria-Hungary, which Slavic nationalists wished to annex to neighboring Serbia; the archduke's assassin was a Serbian nationalist.

This local controversy quickly escalated through the workings of the system of alliances that the great powers had constructed. Germany supported Austria-Hungary's decision to launch a punitive assault on Serbia. The Serbians called on Russia to help with their defense. The Russians began mobilizing their army on July 30. By August 3, Germany had declared war on both Russia and France and had invaded Belgium. On August 4, Great Britain—ostensibly to honor its alliance with France—declared war on Germany. Russia and the Austro-Hungarian Empire formally began hostilities on August 6. Within months, other smaller nations joined the fighting. By early 1915, virtually the entire European continent (and part of Asia) was embroiled in a major war.

Mobilization for War

Wilson's Neutrality

Wilson called on his fellow citizens in 1914 to remain "impartial in thought as well as deed." But that was impossible, for several reasons. For one thing, many Americans were not, in fact, genuinely impartial. Some sympathized with the German cause; many more sympathized with Britain. Lurid reports of German atrocities in Belgium and France, skillfully exaggerated by British propagandists, strengthened the hostility of many Americans toward Germany.

Sympathy with Britain

Economic realities also made it impossible for the United States to deal with the belligerents on equal terms. The British had imposed a naval blockade on Germany to prevent munitions and supplies from reaching the enemy. As a neutral, the United States had the right, in theory, to trade with whomever it wished. A truly neutral response to the blockade would be either to defy it or to stop trading with Britain as well. But while the United States could survive an interruption of its relatively modest trade with Germany and its allies, it could not easily weather an embargo on its much more extensive trade with Britain and France. So America tacitly accepted the blockade of Germany and continued trading with Britain. By 1915, the United States had gradually transformed itself from a neutral power into the arsenal of the Allies.

The Germans, in the meantime, were resorting to a new and, in American eyes, barbaric tactic: submarine warfare. Unable to challenge British domination on the ocean's surface, the Germans announced early in 1915, enemy vessels would be sunk on sight. Months later, on May 7, 1915, a German submarine sank the British passenger liner *Lusitania* without warning, causing the deaths of 1,198 people, 128 of them Americans. The ship was carrying not only passengers but munitions; but most Americans considered the attack an unprovoked act on civilians.

Submarine Warfare

Wilson angrily demanded that Germany promise not to repeat such outrages, and the Germans finally agreed to his demands. But early in 1916, in response to an announcement that the Allies were now arming merchant ships to sink submarines, Germany proclaimed that it would fire on such vessels without warning. A few weeks later, it attacked the unarmed French steamer *Sussex*, injuring several American passengers. Again, Wilson demanded that Germany abandon its "unlawful" tactics; again, the German government relented.

Preparedness versus Pacifism

Despite the president's increasing bellicosity in 1916, he was still far from ready to commit the United States to war. One obstacle was American domestic politics.

The question of whether America should make military and economic preparations for war provided a preliminary issue over which pacifists and interventionists could debate. Wilson at first denounced the idea of an American military buildup as needless and provocative. In the fall of 1915, however, he endorsed an ambitious proposal by American military leaders for a large and rapid increase in the nation's armed forces.

Pacifists and Interventionists

Still, the peace faction wielded considerable political strength, as became clear at the Democratic Convention in the summer of 1916. The convention became almost hysterically enthusiastic when the keynote speaker punctuated his list of the president's diplomatic achievements with the chant, "What did we do? What did we do? . . . We didn't go to war! We didn't go to war!" That speech helped produce one of the most prominent slogans of Wilson's reelection campaign: "He kept us out of war." During the campaign, Wilson did nothing to discourage those who argued that the Republican candidate, the progressive New York governor

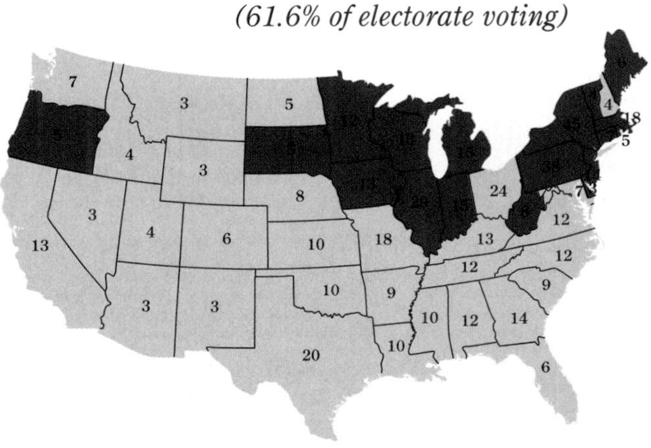

	ELECTORAL VOTE	POPULAR VOTE (%)
Woodrow Wilson *(Democratic)*	277	9,129,606 (49.4)
Charles E. Hughes *(Republican)*	254	8,538,221 (46.1)
A. L. Benson *(Socialist)*	—	585,113 (3.2)
Other parties *(Prohibition; Socialist Labor)*	—	233,909

ELECTION OF 1916 Woodrow Wilson had good reason to be concerned about his re-election prospects in 1916. He had won only about 42 percent of the vote in 1912, and the Republican party—which had been divided four years earlier—was now reunited around the popular Charles Evans Hughes. In the end, Wilson won a narrow victory over Hughes with just under 50 percent of the vote and an even narrower margin in the electoral college. Note the striking regional character of his victory. ◆ *How did Wilson use the war in Europe to bolster his election prospects?*

Charles Evans Hughes, was more likely than he to lead the nation into war. Wilson ultimately won reelection by fewer than 600,000 popular votes and only 23 electoral votes.

A War for Democracy

Tensions between the United States and Germany remained high. But Wilson still required a justification for American intervention that would unite public opinion. In the end, he created that rationale himself. The United States, Wilson insisted, was committed to using the war as a vehicle for constructing a new world order, one based on the same progressive ideals that had motivated a generation of reform efforts in America. In a

MARCHING FOR VICTORY One of the great tasks facing the United States government as it entered World War I in 1917 was to generate popular support for a war that most Americans had been reluctant to enter. The effort to do so produced some alarming violations of civil liberties. It also encouraged an enormous number of parades, rallies, and other popular demonstrations of support for the war. Here, President Wilson marches in a Red Cross parade in Washington shortly after the declaration of war. *(Bettmann/Corbis)*

speech before a joint session of Congress in January 1917, he presented a plan for a postwar order in which the United States would help maintain peace through a permanent league of nations—a "peace without victory." These were, Wilson believed, goals worth fighting for if there was sufficient provocation.

"Peace without Victory"

In January, the military leaders of Germany decided on a dramatic gamble to achieve victory: a series of major assaults on the enemy's lines in France. At the same time, they would begin unrestricted submarine warfare (against American as well as Allied ships) to cut Britain off from vital supplies. Then, on February 25, the British gave Wilson an intercepted telegram sent by the German foreign minister, Arthur Zimmermann, to the government of Mexico. It proposed that in the event of war between Germany and the United States, the Mexicans should join with Germany against the Americans. In return, they would regain their "lost provinces" in the north when the war was over. Widely publicized by British propagandists and in the American press, the Zimmermann telegram inflamed public opinion. Wilson drew additional comfort from another event, in March 1917. A revolution in

Zimmermann Telegram

Russia toppled the reactionary czarist regime and replaced it with a new, republican government. The United States would now be spared the embarrassment of allying itself with a despotic monarchy.

On the rainy evening of April 2, two weeks after German submarines had torpedoed three American ships, Wilson appeared before a joint session of Congress and asked for a declaration of war. Even then, opposition remained. For four days, pacifists in Congress carried on their futile struggle. When the declaration of war finally passed on April 6, fifty representatives and six senators had voted against it.

"WAR WITHOUT STINT"

Armies on both sides in Europe were decimated and exhausted by the time of Woodrow Wilson's declaration of war. The Allies looked desperately to the United States for help in breaking the stalemate.

The Military Struggle

American intervention had its most immediate effect on the conflict at sea. By the spring of 1917, Great Britain was suffering such vast losses from attacks by German submarines that its ability to continue receiving vital supplies from across the Atlantic was in jeopardy. Within weeks of joining the war the United States had begun to alter the balance. A fleet of American destroyers aided the British navy in its assault on the U-boats. Other American warships escorted merchant vessels across the Atlantic. Americans also helped plant antisubmarine mines in the North Sea. The results were dramatic. Sinkings of Allied ships had totaled nearly 900,000 tons in the month of April 1917; by December, the figure had dropped to 350,000; by October 1918, it had declined to 112,000.

Bolshevik Revolution

Many Americans had hoped that providing naval assistance alone would be enough to turn the tide in the war, but it quickly became clear that a major commitment of American ground forces would be necessary as well. Britain and France had few remaining reserves; and after the Bolshevik Revolution in November 1917, a new communist government, led by V. I. Lenin, negotiated a hasty and costly peace between Russia and the Central Powers, thus freeing German troops to fight on the western front.

But the United States did not have a large enough standing army to provide the necessary ground forces in 1917. Only a national draft could provide the needed men. Despite protests, Wilson won passage of the Selective Service Act in mid-May. The draft brought nearly 3 million men into the army.

The engagement of these forces in combat was brief but intense. Not until the spring of 1918 were significant numbers of American troops avail-

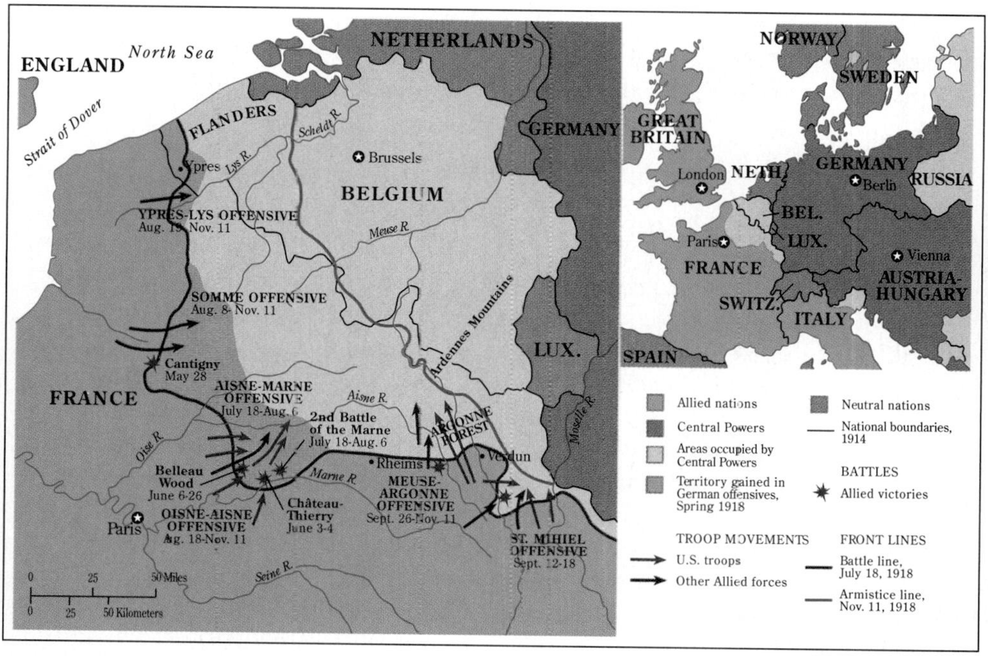

AMERICA IN WORLD WAR I: THE WESTERN FRONT, 1918 These maps show the principal battles in which the United States participated in the last year of World War I. The small map on the upper right helps locate the area of conflict within the larger European landscape. The larger map at left shows the long, snaking red line of the western front in France—stretching from the border between France and southwest Germany all the way to the northeast border between Belgium and France. Along that vast line, the two sides had been engaged in murderous, inconclusive warfare for over three years by the time the Americans arrived. Beginning in the spring and summer of 1918, bolstered by reinforcements from the United States, the Allies began to win a series of important victories that finally enabled them to begin pushing the Germans back. American troops, as this map makes clear, were decisive along the southern part of the front. ◆ *At what point did the Germans begin to consider putting an end to the war?*

For an interactive version of this map go to www.mhhe.com/unfinishednation4ch23maps

able for battle. Eight months later, the war was over. Under the command of General John J. Pershing, the American troops joined the existing Allied forces in turning back a series of new German assaults. In early June, they assisted the French in repelling a bitter German offensive at Château-Thierry, near Paris. Six weeks later, the American Expeditionary Force (AEF) helped turn away another assault, at Rheims, farther south. By July 18, the German advance had been halted. On September 26, an American fighting force of over 1 million soldiers advanced against the Germans in the Argonne Forest. By the end of October, the force had helped push the Germans back toward their own border and had cut the enemy's major supply lines to the front.

Argonne Forest

Faced with an invasion of their own country, German military leaders now began to seek an armistice. Pershing wanted to drive on into Germany itself; but other Allied leaders, after first insisting on terms that made the agreement (in their eyes at least) little different from a surrender, accepted the German proposal. On November 11, 1918, more than four years after it began, the Great War shuddered to a close.

The New Technology of Warfare

World War I was a proving ground for a range of military and other technologies. The trench warfare that characterized the conflict was necessary because of the enormous destructive power of newly improved machine guns and higher-powered artillery. It was no longer feasible to send troops out into an open field. The new weaponry would slaughter them in an instant. Trenches sheltered troops while allowing limited, and usually inconclusive, fighting. But technology overtook the trenches, too, as mobile weapons—tanks and flamethrowers—proved capable of piercing entrenched positions. Most terrible of all, perhaps, new chemical weapons—poisonous mustard gas, which required troops to carry gas masks at all times—made it possible to attack entrenched soldiers without direct combat.

Trench Warfare

The new forms of technological warfare required elaborate maintenance. Faster machine guns required more ammunition. Motorized vehicles required fuel and spare parts and mechanics capable of servicing them. The logistical difficulties of providing so many supplies became a major factor in planning tactics and strategy. Once supplies were unloaded and stored, the process of repacking and moving them forward when troops broke through lines and advanced forward, was hopelessly time-consuming. Late in the war, when Allied armies were advancing toward Germany, they frequently had to stop for days at a time to wait for their equipment.

World War I was the first conflict in which airplanes played a significant role. The planes themselves were relatively simple and not very maneuverable; but anti-aircraft technology was not yet highly developed either, so their effectiveness was still considerable. Planes began to be constructed to serve various functions: bombers, fighters (planes that would engage in "dogfights" with other planes), and reconaissance aircraft.

The most "modern" part of the military during World War I was the navy. New battleships emerged that made use of new technologies such as turbine propulsion, hydraulic gun controls, electric light and power, wireless telegraphy, and advanced navigational aids. Submarines, which had made a brief appearance in the American Civil War, now became significant weapons (as the German U-boat campaign in 1915 and 1916 made clear). The new submarines were driven by diesel engines, which had the advantage of being more compact than steam engines and whose fuel was less explosive than that of gasoline engines.

The new technologies were to a large degree responsible for the most stunning and horrible characteristic of World War I—its appalling level of casualties. A

Appalling Casualties

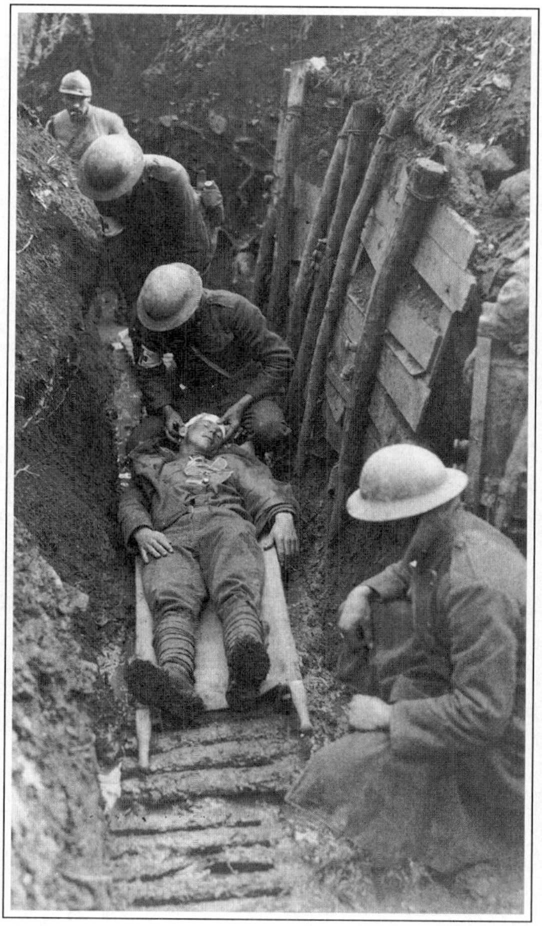

LIFE IN THE TRENCHES For most British, French, German, and ultimately American troops in France, the most debilitating part of World War I was the seeming endlessness of life in the trenches. Some young men lived in these cold, wet, muddy dugouts for months, even years, surrounded by filth, sharing their space with vermin, eating mostly rotten food. Occasional attacks to try to dislodge the enemy from its trenches usually ended in failure and became scenes of terrible slaughter. *(The National Archives and Records Administration)*

million men representing the British Empire (Britain, Canada, Australia, India, and others) died. France lost 1.7 million men; Germany 2 million; the former Austro-Hungarian Empire 1.5 million; Italy 460,000; and Russia 1.7 million. In Britain, one third of the men born between 1892 and 1895 died in the war. Similarly terrible percentages could be calculated for other warring nations. The United States, which entered the war near its end and became engaged only in the last successful offensives, suffered very light casualties in contrast—112,000 dead, half of them victims of influenza, not battle. But the American casualties were very high in the battles in which U.S. troops were centrally involved.

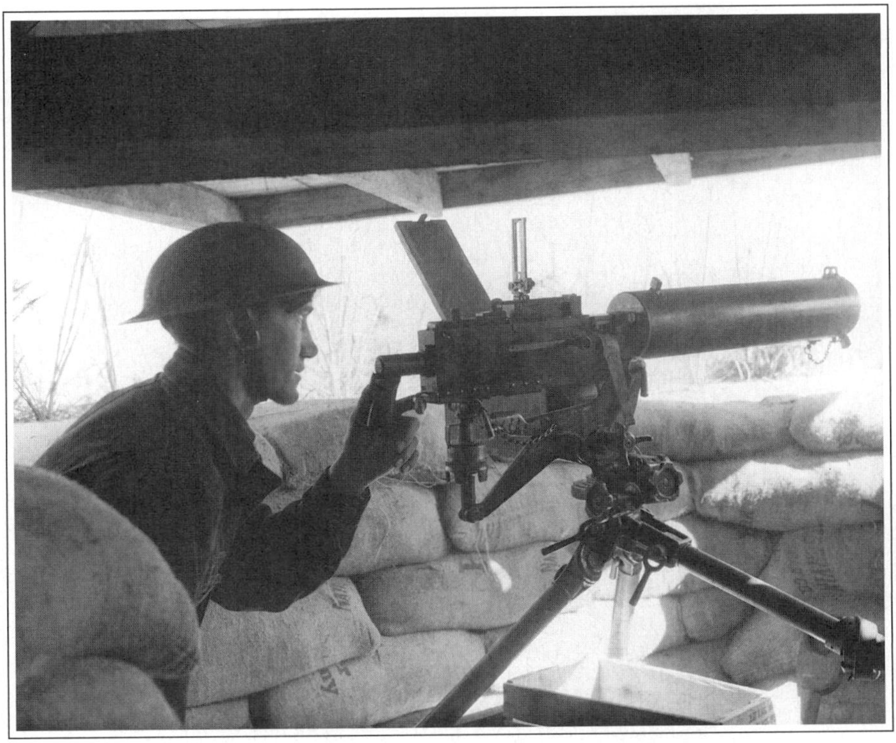

WARTIME TECHNOLOGY An American soldier mans one of the newly improved machine guns that became a staple of World War I combat, in a sandbagged bunker near the front in France. *(Bettmann/Corbis/Hutton-Deutsch Collection)*

Organizing the Economy for War

By the time the war ended, the federal government had appropriated $32 billion for expenses directly related to the conflict—a staggering sum at the time. The entire federal budget had seldom exceeded $1 billion before 1915, and the nation's entire gross national product had been only $35 billion as recently as 1910. To raise the money, the government relied on two devices. First, it launched a major drive to solicit loans from the American people by selling "Liberty Bonds" to the public. By 1920, the sale of bonds, accompanied by elaborate patriotic appeals, had produced $23 billion. At the same time, new taxes were bringing in an additional sum of nearly $10 billion—some from levies on the "excess profits" of corporations, much from new, steeply graduated income and inheritance taxes that ultimately rose as high as 70 percent in some brackets.

"Liberty Bonds"

An even greater challenge was organizing the economy to meet war needs. In 1916, Wilson established the Council of National Defense, composed of members of his cabinet, and the Civilian Advisory Commission, which set up local defense councils in every state and locality. But this early

WOMEN INDUSTRIAL WORKERS In World War II, such women were often called "Rosie the Riveter." Their presence in these previously all-male work environments was no less startling to Americans during World War I. These women are shown working with pneumatic hammers in the Midvale Steel and Ordnance factory in Philadelphia in 1918. *(The National Archives and Records Administration)*

administrative structure soon proved completely unworkable, and members of the Council of National Defense urged a more centralized approach. Instead of dividing the economy geographically, they proposed dividing it functionally by organizing a series of planning bodies, each to supervise a specific sector of the economy. Thus one agency would control transportation, another agriculture, another manufacturing. The administrative structure that slowly emerged from such proposals was dominated by a series of "war boards," one to oversee the railroads (led by Secretary of the Treasury William McAdoo), one to supervise fuel supplies (largely coal), another to handle food (a board that helped elevate to prominence the brilliant young engineer and business executive Herbert Hoover). The boards were not without weaknesses, but they generally succeeded in meeting essential war needs without paralyzing the domestic economy.

War Industries Board

At the center of the effort to rationalize the economy was the War Industries Board (WIB), an agency created in July 1917 to coordinate government purchases of military supplies. Casually organized at first, it stumbled badly until March 1918, when Wilson restructured it and placed it under the control of the Wall Street financier Bernard Baruch. Baruch decided which factories would convert to the production of which war materials, and he set prices for the goods they produced. When materials were scarce, Baruch decided to whom they should go. When corporations were competing for government contracts, he chose among them.

Baruch viewed himself, openly and explicitly, as a partner of business; and within the WIB, businessmen themselves—the so-called dollar-a-year men, who took paid leave from their corporate jobs and worked for the government for a token salary—supervised the affairs of the private economy.

The National War Labor Board, established in April 1918, served as the final mediator of labor disputes. It pressured industry to grant important concessions to workers: an eight-hour day, the maintenance of minimal living standards, equal pay for women doing equal work, recognition of the right of unions to organize and bargain collectively. In return, it insisted that workers forgo strikes and that employers not engage in lockouts.

The Search for Social Unity

Government leaders were painfully aware that public sentiment about American involvement in the war was divided. Many believed that a crucial prerequisite for victory was uniting public opinion behind the war effort. The government approached that task in several ways.

Committee on Public Information

The most conspicuous of its efforts was a vast propaganda campaign orchestrated by the Committee on Public Information (CPI), under the direction of the Denver journalist George Creel. The CPI supervised the distribution of over 75 million pieces of printed material and controlled much of the information available for newspapers and magazines. Creel encouraged journalists to exercise "self-censorship" when reporting war news, and most journalists complied by covering the war largely as the government wished. By 1918, however, government-distributed posters and films were offering lurid (and exaggerated) portrayals of the savagery of the Germans.

Espionage and Sedition Acts

The government also soon began efforts to suppress dissent. CPI-financed advertisements in magazines implored citizens to report to the authorities any evidence among their neighbors of disloyalty, pessimism, or yearning for peace. The Espionage Act of 1917 gave the government new tools with which to combat spying, sabotage, or obstruction of the war effort (crimes that were often broadly defined). More repressive were two measures of 1918: the Sabotage Act of April 20 and the Sedition Act of May 16. These bills expanded the meaning of the Espionage Act to make illegal any public expression of opposition to the war; in practice, they allowed officials to prosecute anyone who criticized the president or the government.

The most frequent targets of the new legislation were anticapitalist groups such as the Socialist Party and the Industrial Workers of the World (IWW). Unlike their counterparts in Europe, American socialists had not dropped their opposition to the war after their country had decided to join it. Many Americans had favored the repression of socialists and radicals even before the war; the wartime policies now made it possible to move against them with full legal sanction. Eugene V. Debs, the humane leader of the Socialist Party and an opponent of the war, was sentenced to ten years in prison in 1918. (A pardon by President Warren G. Harding ultimately won his release in 1921.) Big Bill Haywood and members of the IWW were especially energetically prosecuted. Only by fleeing to the Soviet Union did Haywood avoid imprisonment. In all, more than 11,500 people were arrested in 1918 for the crime of criticizing the government or the war.

Suppressing Dissent

State and local governments, corporations, universities, and private citizens contributed as well to the climate of repression. A cluster of citizens' groups emerged to mobilize "respectable" members of their communities to root out disloyalty. The greatest target of abuse was the German-American community. In the first years of the war in Europe, some had openly advocated American assistance to the Central Powers, and many had opposed United States intervention on behalf of the Allies. But while most German Americans supported the American war effort once it began, public opinion turned bitterly hostile. A campaign to purge society of all things German quickly gathered speed, at times assuming ludicrous forms. Performances of German music were frequently banned. German books were removed from the shelves of libraries. Courses in the German language were dropped from school curricula. Germans were routinely fired from jobs in war industries, lest they "sabotage" important tasks.

THE SEARCH FOR A NEW WORLD ORDER

Woodrow Wilson had led the nation into war promising a just and stable peace at its conclusion. Even before the armistice, he was preparing to lead the fight for what he considered a democratic postwar settlement—for a set of war aims resting on a vision of a new world order.

The Fourteen Points

Wilson's International Vision

On January 8, 1918, Wilson appeared before Congress to present the principles for which he claimed the nation was fighting. He grouped the war aims under fourteen headings, widely known as the Fourteen Points. They fell into three broad categories. First, Wilson's proposals contained a series of eight specific recommendations for adjusting postwar boundaries and for establishing new nations to replace the defunct Austro-Hungarian and Ottoman Empires. Second, there was a set of five general principles to govern international conduct in the future: freedom of the seas, open covenants instead of secret treaties, reductions in armaments, free trade, and impartial mediation of colonial claims. Finally, there was a proposal for a "League of Nations" that would help implement these new principles and territorial adjustments and resolve future controversies.

Wilson's international vision ultimately came to enchant not only much of his own generation (in both America and Europe) but members of generations to come. It reflected his belief that the world was as capable of just and efficient government as were individual nations—that once the international community accepted certain basic principles of conduct, and once it constructed modern institutions to implement them, the human race could live in peace.

Allied Resistance

Despite Wilson's confidence, the leaders of the Allied powers were preparing to resist him even before the armistice was signed. Britain and France in particular were in no mood for a benign and generous peace. At the same time, Wilson was encountering problems at home. In 1918, with the war almost over, Wilson unwisely appealed to the American voters to support his peace plans by electing Democrats to Congress in the November elections. Days later, the Republicans captured majorities in both houses. Domestic economic troubles, more than international issues, had been the most important factor in the voting; but the results damaged his ability to claim broad popular support for his peace plans.

Wilson further antagonized the Republicans when he refused to appoint any important member of their party to the negotiating team that would represent the United States at the peace conference in Paris.

The Paris Peace Conference

Wilson arrived in Europe to a welcome such as few men in history have experienced. When he entered Paris on December 13, 1918, he was greeted, some claimed, by the largest crowd in the history of France. The peace conference itself, however, proved less satisfying.

Negotiating the Peace

The principal figures in the negotiations were the leaders of the victorious Allied nations: David Lloyd George, the prime minister of Great Britain; Georges Clemenceau, the president of France; Vittorio Orlando, the prime minister of Italy; and Wilson, who hoped to dominate them all.

From the beginning, the atmosphere of idealism Wilson had sought to create competed with a spirit of national self-interest. There was also a pervasive sense of unease about the unstable situation in eastern Europe and the threat of communism. Russia, whose new Bolshevik government was still fighting "White" counterrevolutionaries, was unrepresented in Paris; but the radical threat it seemed to pose to Western governments was never far from the minds of the delegates.

In this tense and often vindictive atmosphere, Wilson was unable to win approval of many of the broad principles he had espoused. He was also unable to prevent the other allies from imposing high reparations on the defeated Central Powers. Wilson did manage to win some important victories in Paris in setting boundaries and dealing with former colonies. But his most visible triumph, and the one of most importance to him, was the creation of a permanent international organization to oversee world affairs and prevent future wars. On January 25, 1919, the Allies voted to accept the "covenant" of the League of Nations.

The League of Nations

The Ratification Battle

Wilson presented the Treaty of Versailles (which took its name from the former royal palace outside Paris where the final negotiating sessions had taken place) to the Senate on July 10, 1919. But members of the Senate had many objections to the treaty. Some—the so-called irreconcilables—opposed the agreement in principle. But many other opponents were principally concerned with constructing a winning issue for the Republicans in 1920. Most notable of these was Senator Henry Cabot Lodge of Massachusetts, the powerful chairman of the Foreign Relations Committee, who loathed the president. He used every possible tactic to obstruct the treaty.

Henry Cabot Lodge

Public sentiment clearly favored ratification, so at first Lodge could do little more than play for time. Gradually, however, Lodge's general opposition to the treaty crystallized into a series of "reservations"—amendments to the League covenant further limiting American obligations to the organization. Wilson might still have won approval at this point if he had agreed to some relatively minor changes in the language of the treaty. But the president refused to yield. When he realized the Senate would not budge, he decided to appeal to the public.

He embarked on a grueling, cross-country speaking tour to arouse public support for the treaty. For more than three weeks, he traveled over 8,000 miles by train, speaking as often as four times a day, resting hardly at all. Finally, he reached the end of his strength. After speaking at Pueblo, Colorado, on September 25, 1919, he collapsed with severe headaches.

Canceling the rest of his itinerary, he rushed back to Washington, where, a few days later, he suffered a major stroke. For two weeks, he was close to death; for six weeks more, he was so seriously ill that he could conduct virtually no public business. His wife and his doctor formed an almost impenetrable barrier around him, shielding the president from any official pressures that might impede his recovery.

Wilson ultimately recovered enough to resume a limited official schedule, but he was essentially an invalid for the remaining eighteen months of his presidency. His condition only intensified what had already been his strong tendency to view public issues in moral terms and to resist any attempts at compromise. When the Foreign Relations Committee finally sent the treaty to the

League Membership Rejected

Senate, recommending nearly fifty amendments and reservations, Wilson refused to consider any of them. The effort to win ratification failed.

In the aftermath of this defeat, Wilson became convinced that the 1920 national election would serve as a "solemn referendum" on the League. By now, however, public interest in the peace process had begun to fade.

A SOCIETY IN TURMOIL

Even during the Paris Peace Conference, many Americans were concerned less about international matters than about turbulent events at home. Some of this unease was a legacy of the almost hysterical social atmosphere of the war years; some of it was a response to issues that surfaced after the armistice.

The Unstable Economy

The war ended sooner than almost anyone had anticipated. Without warning, without planning, the nation lurched into the difficult task of economic reconversion. At first, the boom continued, but accompanied by raging inflation. Through most of 1919 and 1920, prices rose at an average of more than 15 percent a year. Finally, late in 1920, the economic bubble burst as inflation began killing the market for consumer goods. Between 1920 and 1921, the gross national product declined nearly 10 percent; 100,000 businesses went bankrupt; and nearly 5 million Americans lost their jobs.

Postwar Recession

Well before this severe recession began, there was a dramatic increase in labor unrest. The raging inflation of 1919 wiped out the modest wage gains workers had achieved during the war; many laborers were worried about job security as hundreds of thousands of veterans returned to the work force; arduous working conditions continued to be a source of discontent. Employers aggravated the resentment by using the end of the war to rescind benefits they had been forced to concede to workers in 1917 and 1918—most notably recognition of unions. The year 1919, therefore, saw an unprecedented wave of strikes. In January, a walkout by shipyard workers in Seattle, Washington, evolved into a general strike that brought the entire city to a virtual standstill. In September, there was a strike by the Boston police force, which was demanding recognition of its union. Seattle had remained generally calm; but with its police off the job, Boston erupted in violence and looting.

Labor Unrest

These and other strikes aroused widespread middle-class hostility to the unions, a hostility that played a part in defeating the greatest strike of 1919: a steel strike that began in September, when 350,000 steelworkers in several midwestern cities demanded an eight-hour day and recognition of their union. The steel strike was long and bitter and climaxed in a riot in Gary, Indiana, in which eighteen strikers were killed. Steel executives managed to keep most plants running with nonunion labor, and public opinion was so hostile to the strikers that the AFL timidly repudiated them. By January, the strike—like most of the others in 1919—had collapsed.

The Demands of African Americans

The black men who had served in the armed forces during the war (367,000 of them) came home in 1919 and marched down the main streets of the industrial cities with other returning troops. And then (in New York and other cities) they marched again through the streets of black neighborhoods such as Harlem, led by jazz bands, cheered by thousands of African Americans, who believed that the glory of black heroism in the war would make it impossible for white society ever again to treat African Americans as less than equal citizens.

In truth, the fact that black soldiers had fought in the war had almost no impact at all on white attitudes. But it did have a profound effect on black attitudes: it accentuated African-American bitterness—and increased determination of blacks to fight for their rights. Nearly half a million migrated from the rural South to industrial cities (often enticed by northern "labor agents," who offered them free transportation) in search of the factory jobs the war was rapidly generating. This was the beginning of what became known as the "Great Migration." Within a few years, the nation's racial demographics were transformed; suddenly there were large black communities crowding into northern cities, in some of which very few African Americans had lived in the past.

"Great Migration"

By 1919, however, the racial climate had become savage and murderous. In the South, there was a sudden increase in lynchings: more than seventy blacks, some of them war veterans, died at the hands of white mobs in 1919 alone. In the North, black factory workers faced widespread layoffs as returning white veterans displaced them from their jobs. And as whites became convinced that black workers with lower wage demands were hurting them economically, animosity grew rapidly.

Wartime riots in East St. Louis and elsewhere were a prelude to a summer of much worse racial violence in 1919. In Chicago, a black teenager swimming in Lake Michigan on a hot July day happened to drift toward a white beach. Whites on shore allegedly stoned him unconscious; he sank and drowned. Angry blacks gathered in crowds and marched into white neighborhoods to retaliate; whites formed even larger crowds and roamed into black neighborhoods. For more than a week, Chicago was virtually at war. In the end, 38 people died—15 whites and 23 blacks—and 537 were injured; over 1,000 people were left homeless. The Chicago riot was the worst but not the only racial violence

Chicago Race Riot

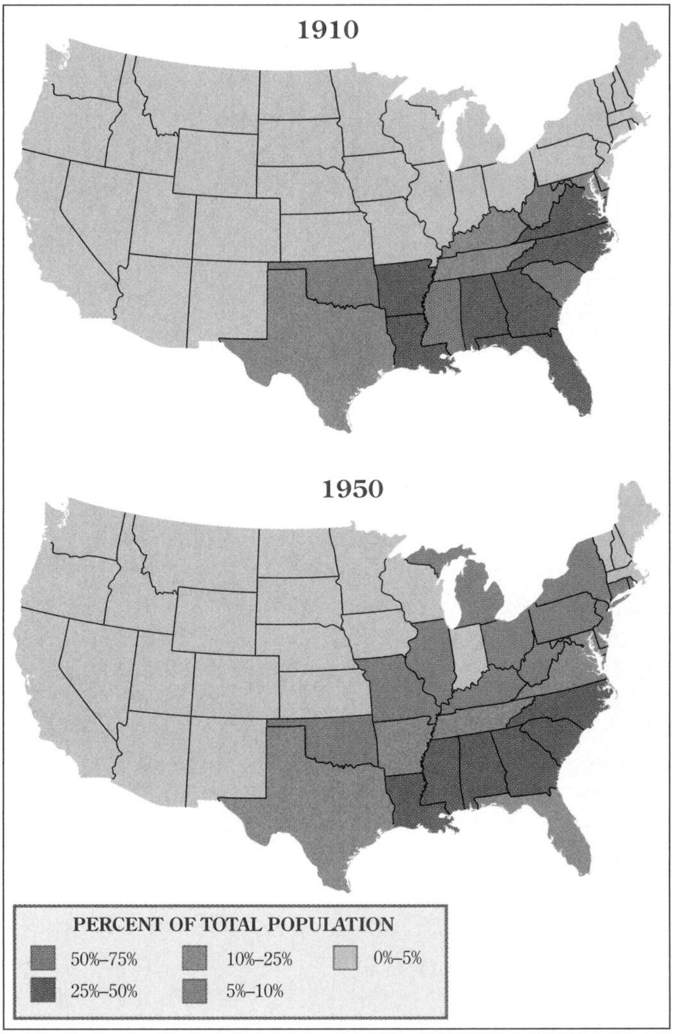

AFRICAN-AMERICAN MIGRATION, 1910–1950 Two great waves of migration produced a dramatic redistribution of the African-American population in the first half of the twentieth century—one around the time of World War I, the other during and after World War II. The map on the top shows the very heavy concentration of African Americans in the South as late as 1910. The map on the bottom shows both the tremendous increase of black populations in northern states by 1950, and the relative decline of black populations in parts of the South. Note in particular the changes in Mississippi and South Carolina. ◆ *Why did the wars produce such significant migration out of the South?*

during the so-called red summer of 1919; in all, 120 people died in such racial outbreaks in the space of little more than three months.

Racially motivated urban riots were not new. But the 1919 riots were different in one respect: they did not just involve white people attacking blacks; they also involved blacks fighting back. The NAACP signaled this change by urging blacks not just to demand government protection but also to defend themselves. The poet Claude McKay, one of the major figures of what would shortly be known as the Harlem Renaissance, wrote a poem after the Chicago riot called "If We Must Die":

> Like men we'll face the murderous cowardly pack.
> Pressed to the wall, dying, but fighting back.

At the same time, a black Jamaican, Marcus Garvey, began to attract a wide following in the United States with his ideology of black nationalism. Garvey encouraged African Americans to reject assimilation into white society and develop pride in their own race and culture. His Universal Negro Improvement Association (UNIA) launched a chain of black-owned grocery stores and pressed for the creation of other black businesses. Eventually, Garvey began urging his supporters to leave America and return to Africa, where they could create a new society of their own. In the 1920s, the Garvey movement experienced explosive growth for a time. It began to decline, however, after Garvey was indicted in 1923 on charges of business fraud. He was deported to Jamaica two years later. But the allure of black nationalism survived in black culture long after Garvey himself was gone.

Universal Negro Improvement Association

The Red Scare

Much of the public considered the industrial warfare and the racial violence in 1919 a frightening omen of instability and radicalism. This was in part because other evidence emerging at the same time also seemed to suggest the existence of a radical menace. After the Russian Revolution of November 1917, communism was no longer simply a theory; it was now the basis of an important regime. Concerns about the communist threat grew in 1919 when the Soviet government announced the formation of the Communist International (or Comintern), whose purpose was to export revolution around the world.

Popular Fears of Radicalism

In America, meanwhile, there was, in addition to the great number of imagined radicals, a modest number of real ones. These small groups of radicals were presumably responsible for a series of bombings in the spring of 1919 that produced great national alarm. In April, the post office intercepted several dozen parcels addressed to leading businessmen and politicians that were triggered to explode when opened. Two months later, eight bombs exploded in eight cities within minutes of one another, suggesting a nationwide conspiracy.

In response to these and other provocations, what became known as the Red Scare began. Nearly thirty states enacted new peacetime sedition laws imposing harsh penalties on those who promoted revolution. There were spontaneous acts of violence against supposed radicals in some communities, and more calculated efforts by universities and other institutions

SACCO AND VANZETTI The artist Ben Shahn painted this view of the anarchists Nicola Sacco and Bartolomeo Vanzetti, handcuffed together in a courtroom in 1927 waiting to hear if the appeal of their 1921 verdicts for murdering a Boston paymaster would succeed. It did not, and the two men were executed later that year. Just before his execution, Vanzetti said: "Never in our full life can we hope to do such work for tolerance, for man's understanding of man, as now we do by an accident. Our words—our lives—our pains—nothing! The taking of our lives—lives of a good shoemaker and a poor fish-peddler—all! That last moment belongs to us—that agony is our triumph." *(© Estate of Ben Shahn/Licensed by VAGA, New York, NY. Digital Image © The Museum of Modern Art/Licensed by SCALA/Art Resource, NY)*

to expel radicals from their midst. But the greatest contribution to the Red Scare came from the federal government. On New Year's Day, 1920, Attorney General A. Mitchell Palmer and his ambitious young assistant, J. Edgar Hoover, orchestrated a series of raids on alleged radical centers throughout the country and arrested more than 6,000 people. Most of those arrested were ultimately released, but about 500 who were not American citizens were summarily deported.

A. Mitchell Palmer

The ferocity of the Red Scare soon abated, but its effects lingered well into the 1920s. In May of 1920, two Italian immigrants, Nicola Sacco and Bartolomeo Vanzetti, were charged with the murder of a paymaster in Braintree, Massachusetts. The case against them was weak and suffused with nativist prejudices and fears; but because both men were confessed anarchists, they faced a widespread public presumption of guilt. They were convicted and sentenced to death. Over the next several years, public support for Sacco and Vanzetti

Sacco and Vanzetti

grew to formidable proportions. But on August 23, 1927, amid widespread protests around the world, Sacco and Vanzetti, still proclaiming their innocence, died in the electric chair.

The Retreat from Idealism

On August 26, 1920, the Nineteenth Amendment, guaranteeing women the right to vote, became part of the Constitution. To the woman suffrage movement, this was the culmination of nearly a century of struggle. To many progressives it seemed to promise new support for reform. Yet the passage of the Nineteenth Amendment marked not the beginning of an era of progressive reform but the end of one.

Disillusionment and Reaction

Economic problems, labor unrest, racial tensions, and the intensity of the antiradicalism they helped create—all combined in the years immediately following the war to produce a general sense of disillusionment. That became particularly apparent in the election of 1920. Woodrow Wilson wanted the campaign to be a referendum on the League of Nations, and the Democratic candidates, Governor James M. Cox of Ohio and Assistant Secretary of the Navy Franklin D. Roosevelt, dutifully tried to keep Wilson's ideals alive. The Republican presidential nominee, however, offered a different vision. He was Warren Gamaliel Harding, an obscure Ohio senator. Harding offered no ideals, only a vague promise of a return, as he later phrased it, to "normalcy." He won in a landslide. The Republican ticket received 61 percent of the popular vote and carried every state outside the South. The party made major gains in Congress as well. To many Americans it seemed that, for better or worse, a new era had begun.

CONCLUSION

For a time after the outbreak of war in Europe in 1914, most Americans—President Wilson among them—wanted nothing so much as to stay out of the conflict. Gradually, however, as the war dragged on and on and the tactics of Britain and Germany began to impinge on American trade and on freedom of the seas, the United States found itself drawn slowly into the conflict. In April 1917, finally, Congress agreed to the president's request that the United States enter the war as an ally of Britain.

American forces quickly broke the stalemate that had bogged the European forces down in years of inconclusive trench warfare. Within a few months of the arrival of substantial numbers of American troops in Europe, Germany agreed to an armistice and the war shuddered to a close. American casualties, although not inconsiderable, were negligible compared to the millions suffered by the European combatants.

The social experience of the war in the United States was, on the whole, dismaying to reformers. Although the war enhanced some reform efforts—most notably prohibition and woman suffrage—it also introduced an atmosphere of intolerance and repression into American life. The aftermath of the war was even more disheartening to progressives, both because of a brief but highly destabilizing recession and because of a wave of repression directed against labor, radicals, African Americans, and immigrants in 1919 and 1920.

At the same time, Woodrow Wilson's bold and idealistic dream of a peace based on the principles of democracy and justice suffered a painful death. The Treaty of Versailles, which he helped to draft, was itself far from what Wilson had hoped. It did, however, contain a provision for a League of Nations, which Wilson believed could transform the international order. But the League quickly became controversial in the United States; and despite strenuous efforts by the president—efforts that hastened his own physical collapse—the treaty was defeated in the Senate. In the aftermath of that traumatic battle, the American people turned away from Wilson and his ideals and prepared for a very different era.

FOR FURTHER REFERENCE

Ernest R. May, *The World War and American Isolation* (1959), is an authoritative account of America's slow and controversial entry into the Great War. Frank Freidel provides a sweeping account of the American soldier's battlefield experience during World War I in *Over There: The Story of America's First Great Overseas Crusade* (1964). David Kennedy, *Over Here: The First World War and American Society* (1980) is an important study of the domestic impact of the war. Robert D. Cuff, *The War Industries Board: Business-Government Relations During World War I* (1973) is a good account of mobilization for war in the United States. Ronald Schaffer, *America in the Great War: The Rise of the War Welfare State* (1991) examines the ways in which mobilization for war created new public benefits for various groups, including labor. Maureen Greenwald, *Women, War, and Work* (1980) describes the impact of World War I on women workers. John Keegan, *The First World War* (1998) is a superb military history. Thomas Knock, *To End All Wars: Woodrow Wilson and the Quest for a New World Order* (1992) is a valuable recent study of the battle for peace. Arno Mayer, *Wilson vs. Lenin* (1959) and *Politics and Diplomacy of Peacemaking: Containment and Counterrevolution* (1965) are important revisionist accounts of the peacemaking process. America's stormy debate over immigration and national identity before, during, and after World War I is best captured by John Higham, *Strangers in the Land: Patterns of American Nativism* (1955). William M. Tuttle, Jr., in *Race Riot: Chicago in the Red Summer of 1919* (1970) recounts the terrible riots of 1919 that showed America violently divided along racial and ideological lines. Paul L. Murphy, *World War I and the*

Origins of Civil Liberties (1979) shows how wartime efforts to quell dissent created new support for civil liberties. *The Great War—1918* (1997) is a documentary film chronicling the experiences of American soldiers in the closing battles of World War I through their letters and diaries.

For quizzes, Internet resources, references to additional books and films, and more, consult this book's Online Learning Center site at www.mhhe.com/unfinishednation4.

THE FLAPPER, 1927 The popular Condé Nast fashion magazine, *Vogue*, portrayed a fashionably dressed "flapper" on its cover in 1927. The short hair and the cap pulled down low over the forehead were both part of the flapper style. What had begin as a fashion among working-class women had by 1927 moved into stylish high society. *(Georges Lepape/©Vogue, The Condé Nast Publications, Inc.)*

TIME LINE

1914–1920	1920	1922	1923	
Great Migration of blacks to the North	Prohibition begins Harding elected president	Lewis's *Babbitt*	Harding dies; Coolidge becomes president Harding administration scandals revealed	

CHAPTER TWENTY-FOUR

THE NEW ERA

The New Economy
The New Culture
A Conflict of Cultures
Republican Government

The 1920s are often remembered as an era of affluence, conservatism, and cultural frivolity. In reality, however, the decade was a time of significant, even dramatic social, economic, and political change. It was an era in which the American economy not only enjoyed spectacular growth but developed new forms of organization. It was a time in which American popular culture reshaped itself to reflect the increasingly urban, industrial, consumer-oriented society of the United States. And it was a decade in which American government experimented with new approaches to public policy. That was why contemporaries liked to refer to the 1920s as the "New Era"—an age in which America was becoming a modern nation.

At the same time, however, the decade saw the rise of a series of spirited and at times effective rebellions against the modern developments that were transforming American life. The intense cultural conflicts that characterized the 1920s were evidence of how much of American society remained unreconciled to the modernizing currents of the New Era.

1924	1925	1927	1928
National Origins Act passed	Fitzgerald's *The Great Gatsby*	Lindbergh's solo transatlantic flight	Hoover elected president
Coolidge elected president	Scopes trial	First sound motion picture, *The Jazz Singer*	
Ku Klux Klan membership peaks			

THE NEW ECONOMY

After the recession of 1921–1922, the United States began a long period of almost uninterrupted prosperity and economic expansion. Less visible at the time, but equally significant, was the survival (and even the growth) of inequalities and imbalances.

Technology, Organization, and Economic Growth

No one could deny the remarkable feats of the American economy in the 1920s. The nation's manufacturing output rose by more than 60 percent. Per capita income grew by a third. Inflation was negligible. A mild recession in 1923 interrupted the pattern of growth; but when it subsided early in 1924, the economy expanded with even greater vigor.

Rise of the Automobile Industry

The economic boom was a result of many things, but one of the most important causes was technology. The automobile industry, as a result of the development of the assembly line and other innovations, now became one of the most important industries in the nation. It stimulated growth in other, related industries as well. Auto manufacturers purchased the products of steel, rubber, glass, and tool companies. Auto owners bought gasoline from the oil corporations. Road construction became an important industry. The increased mobility that the automobile made possible increased the demand for suburban housing, fueling a boom in the construction industry.

Other new industries benefiting from technological innovations contributed as well to the economic growth. Radio began to become a popular technology. Early radio had been able to broadcast little beside pulses, which meant that radio communication could occur only through the Morse Code. But with the discovery of the theory of modulation, pioneered by the Canadian scientist Reginal Fessenden, it became possible to transmit speech and music. Many people built their own radio sets at home for very little money, benefiting from the discovery that inexpensive crystals could receive signals over long distances (but not very well over short ones). These "short wave" radios, which allowed individual owners to establish contact with each other, marked the beginning of what later became known as "ham radio." Once commercial broadcasting began, families flocked to buy more conventional radio sets, which could receive high-quality signals over short and medium distances. They were powered by vacuum tubes that were much more reliable than earlier models. By 1925, there were two million sets in American homes, and by the end of the 1920s almost every family had one.

Commercial Aviation

Commercial aviation developed slowly in the 1920s, beginning with the use of planes to deliver mail. On the whole, airplanes remained curiosities and sources of entertainment. But technological advances—the development of the radial engine and the creation of pressurized cabins—were laying the groundwork for the great increase in commercial travel in the 1930s and beyond. Trains became faster and more efficient as well with the development of the diesel-electric engine. Electronics, home appliances, plastics and synthetic fibers such as nylon, aluminum, magnesium, oil, electric power, and other industries fueled by technological advances—all grew dramatically. Telephones continued to proliferate. By the late 1930s, there were approximately 25 million telephones in the United States, approximately one for every six people.

The seeds of future technological breakthroughs were also visible in the 1920s and 1930s. In both England and America, scientists and engineers were working to transform primitive calculating machines into devices capable of performing more complicated tasks. By the early 1930s, researchers at MIT, led by Vannevar Bush, had created an instrument capable of performing a variety of complicated tasks—the first analog computer. A few years later, Howard Aiken, with financial assistance from Harvard and MIT, built a much more complex computer with memory, capable of multiplying eleven-digit numbers in three seconds.

Genetic Research

Genetic research had begun in Austria in the mid-nineteenth century through the work of Gregor Mendel, a Catholic monk who performed experiments on the hybridization of vegetables in the garden of his monastery. His findings attracted little attention during his lifetime, but in the early twentieth century they were discovered by several investigators and helped shape modern genetic research. Among the American pioneers was Thomas Hunt Morgan of Columbia University and later Cal Tech, whose experiments with fruit flies revealed how several genes could be transmitted together. He also revealed the way in which genes were arranged along the chromosome. His work helped open the path to understanding how genes could recombine—a critical discovery that led to more advanced experiments in hybridization and genetics.

Growing Industrial Consolidation

Large sectors of American business were accelerating their drive toward national organization and consolidation. Certain industries—notably those dependent on large-scale mass production, such as steel and automobiles—seemed naturally to move toward concentrating production in a few large firms. Others—industries less dependent on technology and less susceptible to great economies of scale—proved more resistant to consolidation.

The strenuous efforts by industrialists throughout the economy to find ways to curb competition reflected a strong fear of overcapacity. Even in the booming 1920s, industrialists remembered how too-rapid expansion and overproduction had helped produce recessions in 1893, 1907, and 1920. The great, unrealized dream of the New Era was to find a way to stabilize the economy so that such collapses would never occur again.

THE STEAMFITTER Lewis Hine was among the first American photographers to recognize his craft as an art. In this carefully posed photograph from the mid-1920s, Hine made a point that many other artists were making in other media: The rise of the machine could serve human beings, but might also bend them to its own needs. *(Courtesy George Eastman House)*

Workers in an Age of Capital

Despite the remarkable economic growth, more than two-thirds of the American people in 1929 lived at no better than what one major study described as the "minimum comfort level." Half of those were at or below the level of "subsistence and poverty."

American labor experienced both the successes and the failures of the 1920s as much as any other group. On the one hand, most workers saw their standard of living rise during the decade. Some employers adopted paternalistic techniques that came to be known as "welfare capitalism." Henry Ford, for example, shortened the workweek, raised wages, and instituted paid vacations. By 1926, nearly 3 million industrial workers were eligible for at least modest pensions on retirement. When labor grievances surfaced despite these efforts, workers could voice them through the so-called company unions that were emerging in many industries—workers' councils and shop committees, organized by the corporations themselves. But welfare capitalism, in the end, gave workers no real control over their own fates. Company unions were feeble vehicles. And welfare capitalism survived only as long as industry prospered. After 1929, with the economy in crisis, the entire system collapsed.

Welfare Capitalism

Welfare capitalism affected only a relatively small number of workers in any case. Most laborers worked for employers interested primarily in keeping their labor costs low. Workers as a whole, therefore, received wage increases that were proportionately far below the growth of the economy as a whole. At the end of the decade, the average annual income of a worker remained below $1,500 a year, when $1,800 was considered necessary to maintain a minimally decent standard of living. Only by relying on the earnings of several family members at once could many working-class families make ends meet.

The New Era was a bleak time for labor organization, in part because many unions themselves were relatively conservative and failed to adapt to the realities of the modern economy. The American Federation of Labor (led by the cautious William Green) remained wedded to the concept of the craft union, in which workers were organized on the basis of particular skills. The AFL sought peaceful cooperation with employers. In the meantime, the number of unskilled industrial workers was rising rapidly. They received little attention from the craft unions.

Bleak Time for Labor

But whatever the weaknesses of the unions, the strength of the corporations was the principal reason for the absence of effective labor organization in the 1920s. After the turmoil of 1919, corporate leaders worked hard to spread the doctrine that a crucial element of democratic capitalism was the protection of the "open shop" (a shop in which no worker could be required to join a union). The crusade for the open shop, euphemistically titled the "American Plan," became a pretext for a harsh campaign of union-busting. As a result, union membership fell from more than 5 million in 1920 to under 3 million in 1929.

"American Plan"

Women and Minorities in the Work Force

A growing proportion of the work force consisted of women, who were concentrated in what have since become known as "pink-collar" jobs—low-paying service occupations. Large numbers of women worked as secretaries, salesclerks, and telephone operators and in other nonmanual service capacities. Because technically such positions were not industrial jobs, the AFL and other labor organizations were uninterested in organizing these workers. Similarly, the half-million African Americans who had migrated from the rural South into the cities during the Great Migration after 1914 had few opportunities for union representation. The skilled crafts represented in the AFL usually excluded blacks. Most blacks, however, worked in jobs in which the AFL took no interest at all—as janitors, dishwashers, garbage collectors, domestics, and other service capacities. A. Philip Randolph's Brotherhood of Sleeping Car Porters was one of the few important unions dominated and led by African Americans.

Brotherhood of Sleeping Car Porters

In the West and the Southwest, the ranks of the unskilled included considerable numbers of Asians and Hispanics. In the wake of the Chinese

Exclusion Acts, Japanese immigrants increasingly took the place of the Chinese in menial jobs in California. They worked on railroads, construction sites, and farms and in many other low-paying workplaces. Some Japanese managed to escape the ranks of the unskilled by forming their own small businesses or setting themselves up as truck farmers; and many of the Issei (Japanese immigrants) and Nisei (their American-born children) enjoyed significant economic success—so much so that California passed laws in 1913 and 1920 to make it more difficult for them to buy land. Other Asians—most notably Filipinos—also swelled the unskilled work force and generated considerable hostility. Anti-Filipino riots in California beginning in 1929 helped produce legislation in 1934 virtually eliminating immigration from the Philippines.

Rising Mexican Immigration

Mexican immigrants formed a major part of the unskilled work force throughout the Southwest and California. Nearly half a million Mexicans entered the United States in the 1920s. Most lived in California, Texas, Arizona, and New Mexico; and by 1930, most lived in cities. Large Mexican barrios grew up in Los Angeles, El Paso, San Antonio, Denver, and many other cities and towns. Some of the residents found work locally in factories and shops; others traveled to mines or did migratory labor on farms but returned to the cities between jobs. Mexican workers, too, faced hostility and discrimination from the Anglo population of the region, but there were few efforts actually to exclude them. Employers in the relatively underpopulated West needed this ready pool of low-paid, unskilled, and unorganized workers.

Agricultural Technology and the Plight of the Farmer

Like industry, American agriculture in the 1920s was embracing new technologies. The number of tractors on American farms quadrupled during the 1920s, especially after they began to be powered by internal combustion engines (like automobiles) rather than by the cumbersome steam engines of the past. They helped to open 35 million new acres to cultivation. Increasingly sophisticated combines and harvesters were proliferating, helping to make it possible to produce more crops with fewer workers.

Agricultural researchers were already at work on other advances: the invention of hybrid corn (made possible by advances in genetic research), which became available to farmers in 1921 but was not grown in great quantities for a decade or more; and the creation of chemical fertilizers and pesticides, which also began to have limited use in the 1920s but which proliferated quickly in the 1930s and 1940s.

The new technologies greatly increased agricultural productivity, but the demand for agricultural goods was not rising as fast as production.

Declining Food Prices

The results were substantial surpluses, a disastrous decline in food prices, and a severe drop in farmers' income beginning early in the 1920s. More than 3 million people left

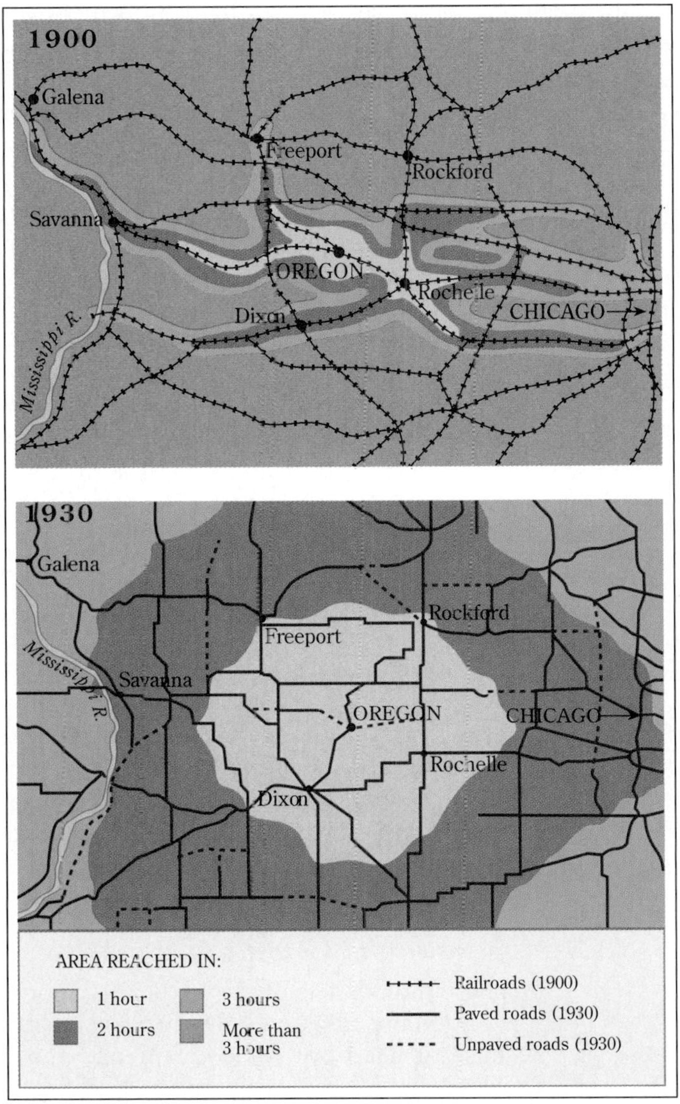

BREAKING DOWN RURAL ISOLATION: THE EXPANSION OF TRAVEL HORIZONS IN OREGON, ILLINOIS This map uses the small town of Oregon, Illinois—west of Chicago—to illustrate the way in which first railroads and then automobiles reduced the isolation of rural areas in the first decades of the twentieth century. The gold and purple areas of the two maps show the territory that residents of Oregon could reach within two hours. Note how small that area was in 1900 and how much larger it was in 1930, by which time an area of over a hundred square miles had become easily accessible to the town. Note, too, the significant network of paved roads in the region by 1930, few of which had existed in 1900. ◆ *Why did automobile travel do so much more than railroads to expand the travel horizons of small towns?*

For an interactive version of this map go to www.mhhe.com/unfinishednation4ch24maps

agriculture altogether in the course of the decade. Of those who remained, many lost ownership of their lands and had to rent instead from banks or other landlords.

In response, some farmers began to demand relief in the form of government price supports. One price-raising scheme in particular came to dominate agrarian demands: the idea of "parity." Parity was a complicated formula for setting an adequate price for farm goods and ensuring that farmers would earn back at least their production costs no matter how the national or world agricultural market might fluctuate. Champions of parity urged high tariffs against foreign agricultural goods and a government commitment to buy surplus domestic crops at parity and sell them abroad.

McNary-Haugen Bill

The legislative expression of the demand for parity was the McNary-Haugen Bill, named after its two principal sponsors in Congress and introduced repeatedly between 1924 and 1928. In 1926 and again in 1928, Congress approved a bill requiring parity for grain, cotton, tobacco, and rice, but President Coolidge vetoed it both times.

THE NEW CULTURE

The urban and consumer-oriented culture of the 1920s helped Americans in all regions to live their lives and perceive their world in increasingly similar ways. That same culture exposed them to a new set of values. But different parts of American society experienced the new culture in very different ways.

Consumerism and Communications

Growing Consumer Culture

The United States of the 1920s was a consumer society. Many more people than ever before could buy items not just because of need but for convenience and pleasure. Middle-class families purchased electric refrigerators, washing machines, and vacuum cleaners. People wore wristwatches and smoked cigarettes. Women purchased cosmetics and mass-produced fashions. Above all, Americans bought automobiles. By the end of the decade, there were more than 30 million cars on American roads.

No group was more aware of the emergence of consumerism (or more responsible for creating it) than the advertising industry. In the 1920s, partly as a result of techniques pioneered by wartime propaganda, advertising came of age. Publicists no longer simply conveyed information; they sought to identify products with a particular lifestyle. They also encouraged the public to absorb the values of promotion and salesmanship and to admire those who were effective "boosters" and publicists. One of the most successful books of the 1920s was *The Man Nobody Knows*, by adver-

THE ELECTRIC REFRIGERATOR The development of new appliances for the home was an important part of the boom in the production and sale of consumer goods in the 1920s. Executives of the Delcom Light Company, a subsidiary of General Motors, pose here in front of the first Frigidaire electric refrigerator as it is readied for shipping from Dayton, Ohio, in 1921. *(Bettmann/Corbis)*

tising executive Bruce Barton. It portrayed Jesus Christ as not only a religious prophet but also a "super salesman." Barton's message, a message in tune with the new spirit of the consumer culture, was that Jesus had been a man concerned with living a full and rewarding life in this world and that twentieth-century men and women should be concerned with doing the same.

Bruce Barton

The advertising industry could never have had the impact it did without the emergence of new vehicles of communication that made it possible to reach large audiences quickly and easily. Newspapers were being absorbed into national chains. Mass-circulation magazines attracted broad, national audiences. The movies were becoming an ever more popular and powerful form of mass communication; over 100 million people saw films in 1930, as compared with 40 million in 1922.

The most important communications vehicle, however, was radio. The first commercial radio station in America, KDKA in Pittsburgh, began broadcasting in 1920, and the first national radio network, the National Broadcasting Company, was formed in 1927.

Birth of Commercial Radio

Psychology and Psychiatry

The increasing affluence and the growing consumerism of the 1920s produced new psychological challenges. The rise of anxiety and alienation as characteristic ailments of the consumer age coincided with the rise of new theories of psychology and psychiatry. Together these two phenomena helped entrench and expand important emerging fields in medicine and science.

Psychiatry had been spreading in the United States since the early twentieth century, driven in part by the growing awareness of the theories of Sigmund Freud and Carl Jung. Although Freud and Jung differed sharply on many points, they both helped legitimize the idea of exploring the unconscious as a way of discovering the roots of mental problems. Psychoanalysis, which Freud pioneered and Jung also advanced, began to attract American adherents as early as 1912 and spread significantly in the 1920s.

John B. Watson of Johns Hopkins University challenged the Freudian belief in introspection and the exploration of the unconscious. Instead, he argued that mental ailments, like physical ones, should be treated by observation and treatment of symptoms—of behavior. The point of therapy was to modify behavior—to discourage undesirable behavior and reinforce "acceptable" actions. Although many psychiatrists dismissed behavioralism and its associated therapies as treating symptoms rather than causes, it demonstrated significant success in treating such disorders as alcoholism, drug addiction, and phobias.

Behavioralism

Although psychoanalysis and other forms of therapy could be performed by psychologists without medical training, the biggest growth in psychiatry was as a field of medicine. At first, medical psychiatrists worked mostly in mental institutions. But as mental hospitals evolved from places where patients came for treatment and then were discharged to places where chronically ill people (many of them aged) resided indefinitely, psychiatrists began to move into other venues—into conventional hospitals and most notably into private practice. Psychiatry began to expand its claims and to offer services not just to the mentally ill, but to otherwise stable individuals experiencing difficulties with everyday life. A new theory of "dynamic" psychiatry emerged early in the twentieth century; and by the 1920s, it had helped psychiatrists to offer therapy for ordinary anxieties, not just severe mental disturbance.

Psychology and psychiatry were, from the beginning, fields in which women played a much larger role than in most areas of medicine. That was in part because training in psychology was considered valuable for occupations in which women had been traditionally dominant—teaching, social work, nursing. Women who had medical training often found it easier to establish themselves in psychiatry than in other, more traditionally male-dominated areas of medicine.

Opportunities for Women

Women in the New Era

College-educated women were no longer pioneers in the 1920s. There were now two and even three generations of graduates of women's or coeducational colleges and universities, and some were making their presence felt in professional areas that in the past women had rarely penetrated. The "new professional woman" was a vivid and widely publicized image in the 1920s. In reality, however, most employed women were nonprofessional, lower-class workers. Middle-class women, in the meantime, remained largely in the home.

Motherhood Redefined

Yet the 1920s constituted a new era for middle-class women nonetheless. In particular, the decade saw a redefinition of motherhood. Shortly after World War I, John B. Watson and other behavioralist began to challenge the long-held assumption that women had an instinctive capacity for motherhood. Maternal affection was not, they claimed, sufficient preparation for child rearing. Instead, mothers should rely on the advice and assistance of experts and professionals: doctors, nurses, and trained educators.

For many middle-class women, these changes devalued what had been an important and consuming activity. Many attempted to compensate by devoting new attention to their roles as wives and companions. And many women now openly considered their sexual relationships with their husbands not simply as a means of procreation, as earlier generations had been taught to do, but as an important and pleasurable experience in its own right, as the culmination of romantic love.

Margaret Sanger

One result was growing interest in birth control. The pioneer of the American birth-control movement, Margaret Sanger, began her career as a promoter of the diaphragm and other birth-control devices out of a concern for working-class women; she believed that large families were among the major causes of poverty and distress in poor communities. By the 1920s, she was becoming more effective in persuading middle-class women to see the benefits of birth control. Nevertheless, some birth-control devices remained illegal in many states (and abortion remained illegal nearly everywhere).

"Flappers"

Some women concluded that in the New Era it was no longer necessary to maintain a rigid, Victorian female "respectability." They could smoke, drink, dance, wear seductive clothes and makeup, and attend lively parties. Those assumptions became the basis of the "flapper"—the modern woman whose liberated lifestyle found expression in dress, hairstyle, speech, and behavior. The flapper lifestyle had a particular impact on lower-middle-class and working-class single women, who were flocking to new jobs in industry and the service sector. At night, such women flocked to clubs and dance halls in search of excitement and companionship.

Despite all the changes, most women remained highly dependent on men and relatively powerless when men exploited that dependence. The

National Woman's Party, under the leadership of Alice Paul, attempted to fight that powerlessness through its campaign for the Equal Rights Amendment, although it found little support in Congress. Responding to the suffrage victory, women organized the League of Women Voters and the women's auxiliaries of both the Democratic and Republican Parties. Female-dominated consumer groups grew rapidly and increased the range and energy of their efforts.

Women activists won a brief triumph in 1921 when they helped secure passage of the Sheppard-Towner Act, which provided federal funds to states to establish prenatal and child health-care programs. From the start, however, the Act produced controversy. Alice Paul and her supporters opposed the measure, complaining that it classified all women as mothers. More important, the American Medical Association fought Sheppard-Towner, warning that it would introduce untrained outsiders into the health-care field. In 1929, Congress terminated the program.

The Disenchanted

Modern Society Critiqued

Many artists and intellectuals coming of age in the 1920s were experiencing a fundamental disenchantment with modern America. One result of this alienation was a series of savage critiques of modern society by a wide range of writers, some of whom were known as the "debunkers." Among them was the Baltimore journalist H. L. Mencken, who delighted in ridiculing religion, politics, the arts, even democracy itself. Sinclair Lewis published a series of savage novels—*Main Street* (1920), *Babbitt* (1922), *Arrowsmith* (1925), and others—in which he lashed out at one aspect of modern bourgeois society after another. Intellectuals of the 1920s claimed to reject the "success ethic" that they believed dominated American life. The novelist F. Scott Fitzgerald, for example, attacked the American obsession with material success in *The Great Gatsby* (1925). The roster of important American writers active in the 1920s may have no equal in any other period. It included Fitzgerald, Lewis, Ernest Hemingway, Thomas Wolfe, John Dos Passos, Ezra Pound, T. S. Eliot, Gertrude Stein, Edna Ferber, William Faulkner, and Eugene O'Neill.

"Harlem Renaissance"

It also included a remarkable group of black artists. In New York City, a new generation of African-American intellectuals created a flourishing artistic life widely described as the "Harlem Renaissance." The Harlem poets, novelists, and artists drew heavily from their African roots in an effort to prove the richness of their own racial heritage. The poet Langston Hughes captured much of the spirit of the movement in a single sentence: "I am a Negro—and beautiful." Other black writers in Harlem and elsewhere—James Weldon Johnson, Countee Cullen, Zora Neale Hurston, Claude McKay, Alain Locke—as well as black artists and musicians helped to establish a thriving, and at times highly politicized, culture rooted in the historical legacy of their race.

A CONFLICT OF CULTURES

The modern, secular culture of the 1920s did not go unchallenged. It grew up alongside an older, more traditional culture, with which it continually and often bitterly competed.

Prohibition

When the prohibition of the sale and manufacture of alcohol went into effect in January 1920, it had the support of most members of the middle class and most of those who considered themselves progressives. Within a year, however, it had become clear that the "noble experiment," as its defenders called it, was not working well. Prohibition did substantially reduce drinking in most parts of the country. But it also produced conspicuous and growing violations. Before long, it was almost as easy to acquire illegal alcohol in many parts of the country as it had once been to acquire legal alcohol. And since an enormous, lucrative industry was now barred to legitimate businessmen, organized-crime figures took it over.

Failure of Prohibition

Many middle-class progressives who had originally supported prohibition soon soured on the experiment. But an enormous constituency of provincial, largely rural, Protestant Americans continued vehemently to defend it. To them, prohibition represented the effort of an older America to defend traditional notions of morality. Drinking, which they associated with the modern city and with Catholic immigrants, became a symbol of the new culture they believed was displacing them.

As the decade proceeded, opponents of prohibition (or "wets," as they came to be known) gained steadily in influence. Not until 1933, however, when the Great Depression added weight to their appeals, were they finally able to effectively challenge the "drys" and win repeal of the Eighteenth Amendment.

"Wets" versus "Drys"

Nativism and the Klan

The fear of immigrants that many prohibitionists expressed found other expressions as well. Agitation for a curb on foreign immigration to the United States had begun in the nineteenth century, and as with prohibition, it had gathered strength in the years before the war largely because of the support of middle-class progressives. In the years immediately following the war, when immigration began to be associated with radicalism, popular sentiment on behalf of restriction grew rapidly.

In 1921, Congress passed an emergency immigration act, establishing a quota system by which annual immigration from any country could not exceed 3 percent of the number of persons of that nationality who had been in the United States in 1910. The new law cut immigration from

800,000 to 300,000 in any single year, but the nativists remained unsatisfied. The National Origins Act of 1924 banned immigration from east Asia entirely. It also reduced the quota for Europeans from 3 to 2 percent. The quota would be based, moreover, not on the 1910 census, but on the census of 1890, a year in which there had been far fewer southern and eastern Europeans in the country. What immigration there was, in other words, would heavily favor northwestern Europeans. Five years later, a further restriction set a rigid limit of 150,000 immigrants a year. In the years that followed, immigration officials seldom permitted even half that number actually to enter the country.

National Origins Act of 1924

To defenders of an older, more provincial America, the growth of large communities of foreign peoples, alien in their speech, their habits, and their values, came to seem a direct threat to their own embattled way of life. Among other things, this provincial nativism helped instigate the rebirth of the Ku Klux Klan as a major force in American society. The first Klan, founded during Reconstruction, had died in the 1870s. But in 1915, a new group of white southerners met on Stone Mountain near Atlanta and established a modern version of the society. Nativist passions had swelled in Georgia and elsewhere in response to the case of Leo Frank, a Jewish factory manager in Atlanta convicted in 1914 (on very flimsy evidence) of murdering a female employee; a mob stormed Frank's jail and lynched him. The premiere (also in Atlanta) of D. W. Griffith's film *The Birth of a Nation*, which glorified the early Klan, also helped inspire white southerners to join a new one.

Rise of the New Klan

At first the new Klan, like the old, was largely concerned with intimidating blacks. After World War I, however, concern about blacks gradually became secondary to concern about Catholics, Jews, and foreigners. At that point, membership in the Klan expanded rapidly and dramatically, not just in the small towns and rural areas of the South but in industrial cities in the North and Midwest. By 1924, there were reportedly 4 million members, including many women, organized in separate, parallel units, and the largest state Klan was not in the South but in Indiana. Beginning in 1925, a series of scandals involving the organization's leaders precipitated a slow but steady decline in the Klan's influence.

Most Klan units (or "klaverns") tried to present their members as patriots and defenders of morality, and some did nothing more menacing than stage occasional parades and rallies. Often, however, the Klan also operated as a brutal, even violent, opponent of "alien" groups. Klansmen systematically terrorized blacks, Jews, Catholics, and foreigners. At times, they did so violently, through public whipping, tarring and feathering, arson, and lynching. What the Klan feared, however, was not simply "foreign" or "racially impure" groups; it feared anyone who posed a challenge to traditional values.

DARROW AND BRYAN IN DAYTON Although the Scopes trial was chiefly significant for the issues it raised, it attracted national attention in 1925 at least as much because of its two celebrated attorneys: Clarence Darrow, the best-known defense attorney in America and a personification of the modern, skeptical, secular intellect; and William Jennings Bryan, the great political leader who had become, in the last years of his life, an ardent defender of Christian fundamentalism. *(UPI/Corbis-Bettmann)*

Religious Fundamentalism

Fundamentalists and Modernists

Another cultural controversy of the 1920s was the result of a bitter conflict over the place of religion in contemporary society. By 1921, American Protestantism was already divided into two warring camps. On one side stood the modernists: mostly urban, middle-class people who were attempting to adapt religion to the teachings of modern science and to the realities of their modern, secular society. On the other side stood the fundamentalists: provincial, largely (although far from exclusively) rural men and women fighting to preserve traditional faith and to maintain the centrality of religion in American life. The fundamentalists insisted the Bible was to be interpreted literally. Above all, they opposed the teachings of Charles Darwin, whose theory of evolution had openly challenged the biblical story of the Creation.

By the mid-1920s, to the great alarm of modernists, fundamentalism was gaining political strength in some states with its demands for legislation to forbid the teaching of evolution in public schools. In Tennessee in March 1925, the legislature actually adopted a measure making it illegal for any public school teacher "to teach any theory that denies the story of the divine creation of man as taught in the Bible."

When the fledgling American Civil Liberties Union (ACLU) offered free counsel to any Tennessee educator willing to defy the law and become the defendant in a test case, a twenty-four-year-old biology teacher in the town of Dayton, John T. Scopes, agreed to have himself arrested. And when the ACLU decided to send the famous attorney Clarence Darrow to defend Scopes, the aging William Jennings Bryan (now an important fundamentalist spokesman) announced that he would travel to Dayton to assist the prosecution. Journalists from across the country flocked to Tennessee to cover the trial. Scopes had, of course, clearly violated the law; and a verdict of guilty was a foregone conclusion, especially when the judge refused to permit "expert" testimony by evolution scholars. Scopes was fined $100, and the case was ultimately dismissed in a higher court because of a technicality. Nevertheless, Darrow scored an important victory for the modernists by calling Bryan himself to the stand to testify as an "expert on the Bible." In the course of the cross-examination, which was broadcast by radio to much of the nation, Darrow made Bryan's stubborn defense of biblical truths appear foolish and finally tricked Bryan into admitting the possibility that not all religious dogma was subject to only one interpretation.

Scopes Trial

The Scopes trial put fundamentalists on the defensive and discouraged many of them from participating openly in politics. But it did not resolve the conflict between fundamentalists and modernists. The issue continued to smolder for decades.

The Democrats' Ordeal

The anguish of provincial Americans attempting to defend an embattled way of life proved particularly troubling to the Democratic Party during the 1920s. More than the Republicans, the Democrats consisted of a diverse coalition of interest groups, including prohibitionists, Klansmen, and fundamentalists on one side and Catholics, urban workers, and immigrants on the other.

Divided Democrats

At the 1924 Democratic National Convention in New York, a bitter conflict broke out over the platform when the party's urban wing attempted to win approval of planks calling for the repeal of prohibition and a denunciation of the Klan. Both planks narrowly failed. More serious was a deadlock in the balloting for a presidential candidate. Urban Democrats supported Alfred E. Smith, the Irish Catholic governor of New York; rural Democrats backed William McAdoo, Woodrow Wilson's Treasury secretary, who had skillfully positioned himself to win the support of southern and western delegates suspicious of modern urban life. For 103 ballots, the convention dragged on, until finally both Smith and McAdoo withdrew and the party settled on a compromise: the corporate lawyer John W. Davis.

Al Smith

A similar schism plagued the Democrats again in 1928, when Al Smith finally secured his party's nomination for president. He was not, however, able to unite his divided party—in part because of widespread anti-Catholic sentiment, especially in the South. He was the first Democrat since the Civil War not to carry the entire South. Outside the South, he carried no states at all except Massachusetts and Rhode Island. Smith's opponent, and the victor in the presidential election, was a man who perhaps more than any other personified the modern, prosperous, middle-class society of the New Era: Herbert Hoover.

REPUBLICAN GOVERNMENT

For twelve years, beginning in 1921, both the presidency and the Congress rested in the hands of the Republican Party. For most of those years, the federal government enjoyed a warm and supportive relationship with the American business community. Yet the government of the New Era was more than the passive, pliant instrument that critics often described. It attempted to serve in many respects as an agent of economic change.

Harding and Coolidge

Nothing seemed more clearly to illustrate the unadventurous character of 1920s politics than the characters of the two men who served as president during most of the decade: Warren G. Harding and Calvin Coolidge.

Harding, who was elected to the presidency in 1920, was an undistinguished senator from Ohio. He had received the Republican presidential nomination as a result of an agreement among leaders of his party, who considered him, as one noted, a "good second-rater." Harding appointed capable men to the most important cabinet offices, and he attempted to stabilize the nation's troubled foreign policy. But he seemed baffled by his responsibilities, as if he recognized his own unfitness. "I am a man of limited talents from a small town," he reportedly told friends on one occasion. "I don't seem to grasp that I am President." Harding's intellectual limits were compounded by personal weaknesses: his penchant for gambling, illegal alcohol, and attractive women.

Warren Harding

Harding lacked the strength to abandon the party hacks who had helped create his political success. One of them, Ohio party boss Harry Daugherty, he appointed attorney general. Another, New Mexico Senator Albert B. Fall, he made secretary of the interior. Members of the so-called Ohio Gang filled important offices throughout the administration. Unknown to the public, Daugherty, Fall, and others were engaged in fraud and corruption. The most spectacular scandal involved the rich naval oil reserves at Teapot Dome, Wyoming, and Elk Hills, California. At the urging of Fall, Harding transferred control of those reserves from the Navy Department to the Interior Department. Fall then secretly leased them to two wealthy businessmen and received in return nearly half a million dollars in "loans" to ease his

Teapot Dome Scandal

(56.9% of electorate voting)

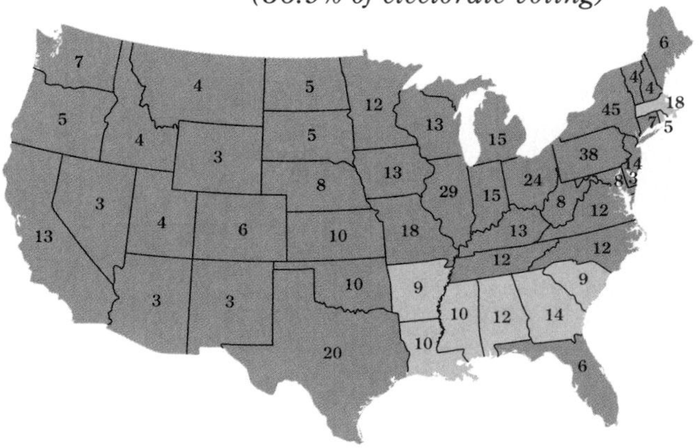

	ELECTORAL VOTE	POPULAR VOTE (%)
Herbert Hoover *(Republican)*	444	21,391,381 (58.2)
Alfred E. Smith *(Democratic)*	87	15,016,443 (40.9)
Norman Thomas *(Socialist)*	—	267,835 (0.7)
Other parties *(Socialist Workers, Prohibition)*	—	62,890

ELECTION OF 1928 The election of 1928 was, by almost any measure, highly one-sided. Herbert Hoover won over 58 percent of the vote to Alfred Smith's 41. Smith carried only Massachusetts, Rhode Island, and some traditionally Democratic states in the South.
◆ *Why did Smith do so poorly even in traditionally Democratic areas of the country in 1928?*

For an interactive version of this map go to www.mhhe.com/unfinishednation4ch24maps

private financial troubles. Fall was ultimately convicted of bribery and sentenced to a year in prison; Harry Daugherty barely avoided a similar fate for his part in another scandal.

In the summer of 1923, only months before Senate investigations and press revelations brought the scandals to light, a tired and depressed Harding left Washington for a speaking tour in the West. In Seattle late in July, he suffered severe pain, which his doctors wrongly diagnosed as food poisoning. A few days later, in San Francisco, he died. He had suffered two major heart attacks.

In many ways, Calvin Coolidge, who succeeded Harding in the presidency, was utterly different from his predecessor. Where Harding was genial, garrulous, and debauched, Coolidge was dour, silent, even puritanical. In other ways, however, Harding and Coolidge were similar figures. Both took essentially passive approaches to their office.

Elected governor of Massachusetts in 1919, Coolidge had won national attention with his laconic response to the Boston police strike that year: "There is no right to strike against the public safety." That was enough to make him his party's vice presidential nominee in 1920. Three years later, after Harding's death, he took the oath of office from his father, a justice of the peace, by the light of a kerosene lamp.

Calvin Coolidge

If anything, Coolidge was even less active as president than Harding, partly as a result of his conviction that government should interfere as little as possible in the life of the nation. In 1924, he received his party's presidential nomination virtually unopposed. Running against John W. Davis, he won a comfortable victory: 54 percent of the popular vote and 382 of the 531 electoral votes. Coolidge probably could have won renomination and reelection in 1928. Instead, in characteristically laconic fashion, he walked into a press room one day and handed each reporter a slip of paper containing a single sentence: "I do not choose to run for president in 1928."

Government and Business

However passive the New Era presidents may have been, much of the federal government was working effectively and efficiently during the 1920s to adapt public policy to the widely accepted goal of the time: helping business and industry operate with maximum efficiency and productivity. The close relationship between the private sector and the federal government that had been forged during World War I continued. Secretary of the Treasury Andrew Mellon, a wealthy steel and aluminum tycoon, devoted himself to working for substantial reductions in taxes on corporate profits and personal incomes and inheritances. Largely because of his efforts, Congress cut them all by more than half. Mellon also worked closely with President Coolidge after 1924 on a series of measures to trim dramatically the already modest federal budget. The administration even managed to retire half the nation's World War I debt.

Sharp Tax Reductions

The most prominent member of the cabinet was Commerce Secretary Herbert Hoover. During his eight years in the Commerce Department, Hoover constantly encouraged voluntary cooperation in the private sector as the best avenue to stability. But the idea of voluntarism did not require that the government remain passive; on the contrary, public institutions, Hoover believed, had a duty to play an active role in creating the new, cooperative order. Above all, Hoover became the champion of the concept of business "associationalism"—a concept that envisioned the creation of national organizations of businessmen in particular industries. Through these trade associations, private entrepreneurs

"Associationalism"

could, Hoover believed, stabilize their industries and promote efficiency in production and marketing.

Some progressives derived encouragement from the election of Herbert Hoover to the presidency in 1928. Hoover easily defeated Al Smith, the Democratic candidate. And he entered office promising bold new efforts to solve the nation's remaining economic problems. But Hoover had few opportunities to prove himself. Less than a year after his inauguration, the nation plunged into the severest and most prolonged economic crisis in its history—a crisis that brought many of the optimistic assumptions of the New Era crashing down and launched the nation into a period of unprecedented social innovation and reform.

CONCLUSION

The remarkable prosperity of the 1920s shaped much of what exuberant contemporaries liked to call the "New Era." In the years after World War I, America built a vibrant and extensive national culture. Its middle class moved increasingly into the embrace of the growing consumer culture. Its politics reorganized itself around the needs of a booming, interdependent industrial economy—rejecting many of the reform crusades of the previous generation, but also creating new institutions to help promote economic growth and stability.

Beneath the glittering surface of the New Era, however, were great controversies and injustices. Although the prosperity of the 1920s was more widely spread than at any time in the nation's industrial history, more than half the population failed to achieve any real benefits from the growth. A new, optimistic, secular culture was attracting millions of urban, middle-class people. But many other Americans looked at it with alarm and fought against it with great fervor. The unprepossessing conservative presidents of the era suggested a time of stability, but in fact few eras in modern American history have seen so much political and cultural conflict.

The 1920s ended in a catastrophic economic crash that has colored the image of those years ever since. The crises of the 1930s should not obscure the real achievements of the New Era economy. Neither, however, should the prosperity of the 1920s obscure the inequity and instability in those years that helped produce the difficult years to come.

FOR FURTHER REFERENCE

Frederick Lewis Allen, *Only Yesterday* (1931) is a classic popular history of the 1920s. Michael Parrish, *Anxious Decades: America in Prosperity and Depression, 1920–1941* (1992) is a good recent survey. Ellis Hawley, *The Great War and the Search for a Mod-*

ern Order (1979) describes the effect of World War I on American ideas, culture, and society. William E. Leuchtenburg, *The Perils of Prosperity* (rev. ed. 1994) reveals the class divisions and culture dislocation that accompanied economic prosperity in the 1920s. David Brody, *Workers in Industrial America* (1980) includes important essays on welfare capitalism and other labor systems of the 1920s. T. J. Jackson Lears, *Fables of Abundance: A Cultural History of Advertising in America* (1994) and Roland Marchand, *Advertising the American Dream* (1985) are valuable inquiries into the role of advertising in the new consumer culture. James J. Flink, *The Car Culture* (1975) examines ways in which the automobile transformed American life. Susan Smulyan, *Selling Radio: The Commercialization of American Broadcasting, 1920–1934* (1994) chronicles the emergence of commercial radio. Robert Lynd and Helen Merrell Lynd, *Middletown* (1929) is a classic sociological study of how an American city encountered the consumer culture and economy of the 1920s. Ann Douglas, *Terrible Honesty: Mongrel Manhattan in the 1920s* (1995) examines the cultural and political history of the New Era in New York City. Lynn Dumenil, *The Modern Temper: America in the 1920s* (1995) examines the reactions of Americans to modern culture. George Chauncey, *Gay New York: Gender, Urban Culture, and the Making of the Gay Male World, 1890–1940* (1994) is an excellent work in a relatively new field of history. The decline of the feminist movement in the 1920s is explored in Nancy Cott, *The Grounding of American Feminism* (1987). Gary Gerstle, *American Crucible* (2000) is an important study of the changing role of race and ethnicity in defining American nationhood in the twentieth century. Andrew Gyory, *Closing the Gate: Race, Politics, and the Chinese Exclusion Act* (1998) examines an early chapter in immigration restriction. Nathan I. Huggins chronicles the cultural and political efflorescence of black Harlem during these years in *Harlem Renaissance* (1971), as does David Levering Lewis in *When Harlem Was in Vogue* (1981). George Marsden, *Fundamentalism and American Culture* (1980) is a good study of some of the religious battles that came to a head in the 1920s. Grant Wacker, *Heaven Below: Early Pentecostals and American Culture* (2001) examines the emergence of modern pentecostalism. Edward J. Larson, *Summer for the Gods: The Scopes Trial and America's Continuing Debate Over Science and Religion* (1997) is a valuable analysis of the Scopes Trial. Leonard Moore, *Citizen Klansmen: The Ku Klux Klan in Indiana, 1921–1928* (1991) is a challenging view of the Klan. Kathleen M. Blee, *Women and the Klan: Racism and Gender in the 1920s* (1991) recreates the female world of the Klan. David Burner, *The Politics of Provincialism* (1967) is a good study of the ordeal of the Democratic Party in the 1920s. Morton Keller, *Regulating a New Economy: Public Policy and Economic Change in America, 1900–1933* (1990) and *Regulating a New Society: Public Policy and Social Change in America, 1900–1933* (1994) are important studies of New Era public policy. *Coney Island* (1990) is a documentary film recreating the drama and fantasy of Coney Island. *That Rhythm, Those Blues* (1997) is a film documenting the one-night stands, makeshift housing, and poor transportation that were all a step toward the big time at the famed Apollo Theatre on Harlem's 125th Street. *Mr. Sears' Catalogue* (1997) is a film exploring how the Sears catalog became a symbol for the ambitions and dreams of a sprawling, fast developing America.

For quizzes, Internet resources, references to additional books and films, and more, consult this book's Online Learning Center site at www.mhhe.com/unfinishednation4.

DETAIL FROM *PRIVATE CAR* (1932), BY LECONTE STEWART
Thousands of men (and some women) left their homes during the Great Depression and traveled from city to city looking for work, often hopping freight trains for a free, if illegal, ride. *(Museum of Church History & Art, Salt Lake City, Utah)*

TIME LINE

1929	1930	1931	1932
Stock market crash; Great Depression begins	Hawley-Smoot Tariff	Scottsboro defendants arrested	Reconstruction Finance Corporation established
Agricultural Marketing Act	Drought begins in Dust Bowl		Bonus Army in Washington
			Franklin D. Roosevelt elected president

CHAPTER TWENTY-FIVE

THE GREAT DEPRESSION

The Coming of the Depression
The American People in Hard Times
The Depression and American Culture
The Ordeal of Herbert Hoover

"We in America today," Herbert Hoover proclaimed in August 1928, "are nearer to the final triumph over poverty than ever before in the history of any land." Only fifteen months later, those words would return to haunt him, as the nation plunged into the severest and most prolonged economic depression in its history—a depression that continued in one form or another for a full decade, not only in the United States but throughout much of the world.

THE COMING OF THE DEPRESSION

The sudden financial collapse in 1929 came as an especially severe shock because it followed so closely a period in which the New Era seemed to be performing another series of economic miracles—miracles that seemed especially evident in the remarkable performance of the stock market.

1934	1935	1936	1939	1940
Southern Tenant Farmers Union organized	American Communist Party proclaims Popular Front	Mitchell's *Gone with the Wind*	Steinbeck's *The Grapes of Wrath*	Wright's *Native Son*

Soaring Stock Market

In February 1928, stock prices began a steady ascent that continued, with only a few temporary lapses, for a year and a half. Between May 1928 and September 1929, the average price of stocks rose over 40 percent. Trading mushroomed from 2 or 3 million shares a day to over 5 million, and at times to as many as 10 or 12 million. There was, in short, a widespread speculative fever that grew steadily more intense, particularly once brokerage firms began encouraging the mania by offering absurdly easy credit to those buying stocks.

The Great Crash

"Black Tuesday"

In the autumn of 1929, the market began to fall apart. On October 29, "Black Tuesday," after a week of steadily rising instability, all efforts to save the market failed. Sixteen million shares of stock were traded; the industrial index dropped 43 points (or nearly 10 percent), wiping out all the gains of the previous year; stocks in many companies became virtually worthless. Within a month stocks had lost half their September value, and despite occasional, short-lived rallies, they continued to decline for several years after that.

Popular folklore has established the stock market crash as the beginning, and even the cause, of the Great Depression. But although October 1929 might have been the most visible early sign of the crisis, the Depression had earlier beginnings and more important causes.

Causes of the Depression

Economists, historians, and others have argued for decades about the causes of the Great Depression. But most agree on several things. They agree, first, that what is remarkable about the crisis is not that it occurred, but that it was so severe and that it lasted so long. Most observers agree, too, that a number of different factors account for the severity of the crisis.

Poor Economic Diversification

One of those factors was a lack of diversification in the American economy in the 1920s. Prosperity had depended excessively on a few basic industries, notably construction and automobiles. In the late 1920s, those industries began to decline. Expenditures on construction fell from $11 billion to under $9 billion between 1926 and 1929. Automobile sales fell by more than a third in the first nine months of 1929. Newer industries were emerging to take up the slack—among them petroleum, chemicals, electronics, and plastics—but had not yet developed enough strength to compensate for the decline in other sectors.

Uneven Distribution of Wealth

A second important factor was the maldistribution of purchasing power and, as a result, a weakness in consumer demand. As industrial and agricultural production increased, the proportion of the profits going to potential consumers was too small to create an adequate market for the goods the economy was producing. Even in 1929, after nearly a decade of economic growth, more than half the families in America lived on the edge of or below the minimum subsistence level.

A third major problem was the credit structure of the economy. Farmers were deeply in debt, and crop prices were too low to allow them to pay off what they owed. Small banks were in constant trouble as their customers defaulted on loans; large banks were in trouble, too. Although most American bankers were very conservative, some of the nation's biggest banks were investing recklessly in the stock market or making unwise loans. When the market crashed and the loans went bad, some banks failed and others made the crisis worse by contracting the already scarce credit and calling in loans that borrowers could not pay.

A fourth factor contributing to the Depression was America's position in international trade. Late in the 1920s, European demand for American goods began to decline. That was partly because European industry and agriculture were becoming more productive and partly because some European nations were having financial difficulties of their own. But it was also because the European economy was being destabilized by the international debt structure that had emerged in the aftermath of World War I.

International Debt Structure

The international debt structure, therefore, was a fifth factor contributing to the Depression. When the war came to an end in 1918, all the European nations that had been allied with the United States owed large sums of money to American banks, sums much too large to be repaid out of their shattered economies. That was one reason why the Allies had insisted on reparation payments from Germany and Austria. Reparations, they believed, would provide them with a way to pay off their own debts. But Germany and Austria were no more able to pay the reparations than the Allies were able to pay their debts.

The American government refused to forgive or reduce the debts. Instead, American banks began making large loans to European governments, which used them to pay off their earlier loans. Thus debts (and reparations) were being paid only by piling up new and greater debts. At the same time, American protective tariffs were making it difficult for Europeans to sell their goods in American markets. Without any source of foreign exchange with which to repay their loans, they began to default. The collapse of the international credit structure was one of the reasons the Depression spread to Europe after 1931.

Progress of the Depression

The stock market crash of 1929 did not so much cause the Depression, then, as help trigger a chain of events that exposed larger weaknesses in the American economy. During the next three years, the crisis grew steadily worse.

Debating the Past

CAUSES OF THE GREAT DEPRESSION

What were the causes of the Great Depression? Economists and historians have debated this question since the economic collapse began and still have not reached anything close to agreement on it. In the process, however, they have illustrated several very different theories about how a modern economy works.

During the Depression itself, different groups offered interpretations of the crisis that fit comfortably with their own self-interests. Some corporate leaders claimed that the Depression was the result of a lack of "business confidence," that businessmen were reluctant to invest because they feared government regulation and high taxes. The Hoover administration blamed international economic forces and sought, therefore, to stabilize world currencies and debt structures. New Dealers, determined to find a domestic solution to the crisis, argued that the Depression was a crisis of "underconsumption," that low wages and high prices had made it too difficult to buy the products of the industrial economy; and that a lack of demand had led to the economic collapse. Other groups offered equally self-serving explanations.

Scholars in the years since the Great Depression have also created interpretations that fit their view of how the economy works. One of the first important postwar interpretations came from the economists Milton Friedman and Anna Schwartz, in their *Monetary History of the United States* (1963). In a chapter entitled "The Great Contraction," they argued for what has become known as the "monetary" interpretation. The Depression, they claimed, was a result of a drastic contraction of the currency (a result of mistaken decisions by the Federal Reserve Board, which raised interest rates when it should have lowered them). These deflationary measures turned an ordinary recession into the Great Depression. The monetary argument fits comfortably with the ideas that Milton Friedman, in particular, has advocated for many years: that sound monetary policy is the best way to solve economic problems—as opposed to fiscal policies, such as taxation and spending.

A second, very different argument is known as the "spending" interpretation, an interpretation supported by many liberal, Keynesian economists. It is identified with, among others, the economist Peter Temin, and his book *Did Monetary Forces Cause the Great Depression?* (1976). Temin's answer to his own question is "no." The cause of the crisis was not monetary contraction (although the contraction made it worse), but a drop in investment and consumer spending, which preceded the decline in the money supply and helped to cause it. Here again, there are obvious political implications. If a decline in spending was the cause of the Depression, then the proper response was an effort to stimulate demand—raising government spending, increasing purchasing power, redistributing wealth. The New Deal never ended the Depression because it did not spend enough. World War II did end it because it pumped so much public money into the economy.

Another important explanation comes from the historian Michael Bernstein. In *The Great Depression* (1987) he avoids trying to explain why the economic downturn occurred and asks, instead, why it lasted so long. The reason the recession of 1929 became the Depression of the 1930s, he argues, was the timing of the collapse. The recession began as an ordinary cyclical downturn. Had it begun a few years earlier, the basic strength of the automobile and construction industries in the 1920s would have led to a reasonably speedy recovery. Had it begun a few years later, a group of newer, emerging industries would have helped produce a recovery in a reasonably short time. But the recession began in 1929, too late for the automobile and construction industries to help and too soon for emerging new industries—aviation, petrochemicals and plastics, aluminum, and others—to help, since they were still in their infancies.

The political implications of this argument are less obvious than those of some other interpretations. But one possible conclusion is that if economic growth depends on the successful development of new industries to replace declining ones, then the most sensible economic policy for government is to target investment and other policies toward the growth of new economic sectors. One of the reasons World War II was so important to the long-term recovery of the U.S. economy, Bernstein's argument suggests, was not just that it pumped money into the economy, but that much of that money contributed to developing new industries. This is, in other words, an explanation of the Depression that seems to support some of the economic ideas that became popular in the 1980s and 1990s calling for a more direct government role in stimulating the growth of new industries.

In the end, however, no single explanation of the Great Depression has ever seemed adequate to most scholars. The event, the economist Robert Lucas once argued, is simply "inexplicable" by any rational calculation. There is no one, wholly persuasive answer to the question of what caused it.

(text continued from page 651)

Banking Crisis

The most serious problem at first was the collapse of much of the banking system. Over 9,000 American banks either went bankrupt or closed their doors to avoid bankruptcy between 1930 and 1933. Partly as a result of these banking closures, the nation's money supply shrank by perhaps a third or more between 1930 and 1933. The declining money supply meant a decline in purchasing power, and thus deflation. Manufacturers and merchants began reducing prices, cutting back on production, and laying off workers. Some economists argue that a severe depression could have been avoided if the Federal Reserve system had acted responsibly. But late in 1931, in a misguided effort to build international confidence in the dollar, it raised interest rates, which contracted the money supply even further.

Plunging GNP

The American gross national product plummeted from over $104 billion in 1929 to $76.4 billion in 1932—a 25 percent decline in three years. By 1932, according to the relatively crude estimates of the time, 25 percent of the American work force was unemployed. (Some argue that the figure was even higher.) For the rest of the decade, unemployment averaged nearly 20 percent, never dropping below 15 percent. Up to another one-third of the work force was "underemployed"—experiencing major reductions in wages, hours, or both.

THE UNEMPLOYED, 1930 Thousands of unemployed men wait to be fed outside the Municipal Lodgers House in New York City. *(The Library of Congress)*

THE AMERICAN PEOPLE IN HARD TIMES

Someone asked the British economist John Maynard Keynes in the 1930s whether he was aware of any historical era comparable to the Great Depression. "Yes," Keynes replied. "It was called the Dark Ages, and it lasted 400 years." The Depression did not last 400 years. It did, however, bring unprecedented despair to the economies of the United States and much of the Western world.

Unemployment and Relief

In the industrial Northeast and Midwest, cities were becoming virtually paralyzed by unemployment. Cleveland, Ohio, for example, had an unemployment rate of 50 percent in 1932; Akron, 60 percent; Toledo, 80 percent. Unemployed workers walked through the streets day after day looking for jobs that did not exist. An increasing number of families were turning to state and local public relief systems, just to be able to eat. But those systems, which in the 1920s had served only a small number of indigents, were totally unequipped to handle the new demands being placed on them. In many cities, therefore, relief simply collapsed. Private charities attempted to supplement the public relief efforts, but the problem was far beyond their capabilities as well.

In rural areas conditions were in many ways worse. Farm income declined by 60 percent between 1929 and 1932. A third of all American farmers lost their land. In addition, a large area of agricultural settlement in the Great Plains was suffering from a catastrophic natural disaster: one of the worst droughts in the history of the nation. Beginning in 1930, the region, which came to be known as the "Dust Bowl" and which stretched north from Texas into the Dakotas, experienced a steady decline in rainfall and an accompanying increase in heat. The drought continued for a decade, turning what had once been fertile farm regions into virtual deserts.

"Dust Bowl"

Many farmers, like many urban unemployed, left their homes in search of work. In the South, in particular, many dispossessed farmers—black and white—simply wandered from town to town, hoping to find jobs or handouts. Hundreds of thousands of families from the Dust Bowl (often known as "Okies," since many came from Oklahoma) traveled to California and other states, where they found conditions little better than those they had left. Many worked as agricultural migrants, traveling from farm to farm picking fruit and other crops at starvation wages.

African Americans and the Depression

Most African Americans had not shared very much in the prosperity of the previous decade. But they did share the hardships of the Great Depression.

As the Depression began, over half of all black Americans still lived in the South. Most were farmers. The collapse of prices for cotton and other staple crops left some with no income at all. Many left the land altogether—either by choice or because they had been evicted by landlords who no longer found the sharecropping system profitable. Some migrated to southern cities. But there, unemployed whites believed they had first claim to what work there was, and some now began to take positions as janitors, street cleaners, and domestic servants, displacing the blacks who formerly occupied those jobs. By 1932, over half the blacks in the South were without employment.

Soaring Black Unemployment

Unsurprisingly, therefore, many black southerners—perhaps 400,000 in all—left the South in the 1930s and journeyed to the cities of the North. But conditions there were little better than those in the South. In New York, black unemployment was nearly 50 percent. In other cities, it was higher. Two million African Americans—half the total black population of the country—were on some form of relief by 1932.

Traditional patterns of segregation and disenfranchisement in the South survived the Depression largely unchallenged. But a few particularly notorious examples of racism did attract the attention of the nation.

America in the World

THE GLOBAL DEPRESSION

The Great Depression began in the United States. But it did not end there. The American economy was the largest in the world, and its collapse sent shock waves across the globe. By 1931, the American depression had become a world depression, with important implications for the course of global history.

The origins of the worldwide depression lay in the pattern of debts that had emerged during and after World War I, when the United States loaned billions of dollars to European nations. In 1931, with American banks staggering and in many cases collapsing, large banks in New York began desperately calling in their loans from Germany and Austria. That precipitated the collapse of one of Austria's largest banks, which in turn created panic through much of central Europe. The economic collapse in Germany and Austria meant that those nations could not continue paying reparations to Britain and France (required by the Treaty of Versailles of 1919), which meant in turn that Britain and France could not continue paying off their loans to the United States. This spreading financial crisis was accompanied by a dramatic contraction of international trade, precipitated in part by the Hawley-Smoot Tariff in the United States, which established the highest import duties in history and stifled much global commerce. Depressed agricultural prices—a result of worldwide overproduction—also contributed to the downturn. By 1932, worldwide industrial production had declined by more than a third, and world trade had plummeted by nearly two thirds. By 1933, thirty million people in industrial nations were unemployed, five times the number of four years before.

But the Depression was not confined to industrial nations. Imperialism and industrialization had drawn almost all regions of the world into the international industrial economy. Colonies and nations in Africa, Asia, and South America—critically dependent on exporting raw materials and agricultural goods to industrial countries—experienced a collapse in demand for their products and thus rising levels of poverty and unemployment. Some nations—among them the Soviet Union and China—remained relatively unconnected to the global economy and suffered relatively little from the Great Depression. But in most parts of the world, the Depression caused tremendous social and economic hardship.

It also created political turmoil. Among the countries hardest hit by the Depression was Germany, where industrial production declined by 50 percent and unemployment reached 35 percent in the early 1930s. The desperate economic conditions there contributed greatly to the rise of the Nazi party and its leader Adolf Hitler, who became chancellor in 1933. Japan suffered greatly as well, dependent as it was on world trade to sustain its growing industrial economy and purchase essential commodities for its needs at home. And in Japan, as in Germany, economic troubles produced political turmoil and aided the rise of a new militaristic regime. In Italy, the fascist government of Benito Mussolini, which had first taken power in the 1920s, also saw militarization and territorial expansion as a way out of economic difficulties.

In other nations, governments sought solutions to the Depression through reform of their domestic economies. The most prominent example of that was the New Deal in the United States. But there were important experiments in other nations as well. Among the most common responses to the Depression around the world was substantial government investment in public works. In the United States, Britain, France, Germany, Italy, the Soviet Union, and other countries, there was substantial investment in roads, bridges, dams, public buildings, and other large projects. Another response was the expansion of government-funded relief for the unemployed. All the industrial countries of the world experimented with one or another form of relief, often borrowing ideas from one another in the process. And the Depression helped create new approaches to economics, in the face of the apparent failure of classical models of economic behavior to explain, or provide solutions to, the crisis. The great British economist John Maynard Keynes revolutionized economic thought in much of the world. His 1936 book *The General Theory of Employment, Interest, and Money*, despite its bland title, created a sensation by arguing that the Depression was a result not of declining production, but of inadequate consumer demand. Governments, he said, could stimulate their economies by increasing the money supply and creating investment—through a combination of lowering interest rates and public spending. Keynesianism, as Keynes's theories became known, began to have an impact in the United States in 1938, and in much of the rest of the world in subsequent years.

The Great Depression was an important turning point not only in American history, but in the history of the twentieth-century world. It transformed ideas of public policy and economics in many nations. It toppled old regimes and created new ones. And perhaps above all, it was a major factor—maybe the single most important factor—in the coming of World War II.

(text continued from page 655)

The most celebrated was the Scottsboro case. In March 1931, nine black teenagers were taken off a freight train in northern Alabama (in a small town near Scottsboro) and arrested for vagrancy and disorder. Later, two white women who had also been riding the train accused them of rape. In fact, there was overwhelming evidence, medical and otherwise, that the women had not been raped at all; they may have made their accusations out of fear of being arrested themselves. Nevertheless, an all-white jury in Alabama quickly convicted all nine of the "Scottsboro boys" (as they were known to both friends and foes) and sentenced eight of them to death.

"Scottsboro Boys"

The Supreme Court overturned the convictions in 1932, and a series of new trials began. The International Labor Defense, an organization associated with the Communist Party, came to the aid of the accused youths and began to publicize the case. Although the white southern juries who sat on the case never acquitted any of the defendants, all of the accused eventually gained their freedom—although the last of the Scottsboro defendants did not leave prison until 1950.

BLACK MIGRANTS The Great Migration of blacks from the rural South into the cities had begun before World War I. But in the 1930s and 1940s the movement accelerated. Jacob Lawrence, an eminent African-American artist, created a series of paintings entitled, collectively, *The Migration of the Negro*, to illustrate this major event in the history of African Americans. *(Jacob Lawrence,* The Migration of the Negro Panel no. 57, *1940–41. Acquired 1942, The Phillips Collection, Washington, DC. Artwork Copyright 2002 Gwendolyn Knight Lawrence, courtesy of the Jacob and Gwendolyn Lawrence Foundation)*

Hispanics and Asians in Depression America

Similar patterns of discrimination confronted many Mexicans and Mexican Americans. The Hispanic population of the United States had been growing steadily since early in the century, largely in California and other areas of the Southwest through massive immigration from Mexico. Chicanos (as Mexican Americans are sometimes known) filled many of the same menial jobs there that blacks had traditionally filled in other regions. Some farmed small, marginal tracts; some became agricultural migrants. It had always been a precarious existence, and the Depression made things significantly worse. Unemployed whites in the Southwest demanded jobs held by Hispanics, jobs that whites had previously considered beneath them. Thus Mexican unemployment rose quickly to levels far higher than those for whites. Some officials arbitrarily removed Mexicans from relief rolls or simply rounded them up and transported them across the border. Perhaps half a million Chicanos left the United States for Mexico in the first years of the Depression.

Hispanic Resistance

There were, occasionally, signs of organized resistance by Mexican Americans themselves, most notably in California, where some formed a union of migrant farmworkers. But harsh repression by local growers and the public authorities allied with them prevented such organizations from having much impact. As a result, many Hispanics began to migrate to cities such as Los Angeles, where they lived in a poverty comparable to that of urban blacks in the South and Northeast.

Asians Marginalized

For Asian Americans, too, the Depression reinforced longstanding patterns of discrimination and economic marginalization. In California, where the largest Japanese-American and Chinese-American populations were, even educated Asians had always found it difficult, if not impossible, to move into mainstream professions. Japanese-American college graduates often found themselves working in family fruit stands. For those who found jobs in the industrial or service economy, employment was precarious; like blacks and Hispanics, Asians often lost jobs to white Americans desperate for work. Japanese farmworkers, like Chicano farmworkers, suffered from the increasing competition for even these low-paying jobs from white migrants from the Great Plains.

Chinese Americans fared no better. The overwhelming majority worked, as they had for many years, in Chinese-owned laundries and restaurants. Those who moved outside the Asian community could rarely find jobs above the entry level. Chinese women, for example, might find work as stock girls in department stores but almost never as salesclerks. Educated Chinese men and women could hope for virtually no professional opportunities outside the world of the Chinatowns.

Women and Families in the Great Depression

The economic crisis served in many ways to strengthen the widespread belief that a woman's proper place was in the home. Most men and many women believed that with employment so scarce, what work there was should go to men. There was a particularly strong belief that no woman whose husband was employed should accept a job. Indeed, from 1932 until 1937, it was illegal for more than one member of a family to hold a federal civil service job.

Growing Female Employment

But the widespread assumption that married women, at least, should not work outside the home did not stop them from doing so. Both single and married women worked in the 1930s because they or their families needed the money. By the end of the Depression, 25 percent more women were working than had been doing so at the beginning. This occurred despite considerable obstacles. Professional opportunities for women declined because unemployed men began moving into professions that had previously been considered women's fields. Female industrial workers were more likely to be laid off or to experience wage reductions than their male counterparts. But white women also had certain advantages in the workplace. The nonprofessional jobs that women traditionally held—salesclerks, stenographers, and other service positions—were less likely to disappear than the predominantly male jobs in heavy industry.

Black women suffered massive unemployment, particularly in the South, because of a great reduction of domestic service jobs. As many as half of all black working women lost their jobs in the 1930s. Even so, at the end of the 1930s, 38 percent of black women were employed, as compared with 24 percent of white women. That was because black women—both married and unmarried—had always been more likely to work than white women, less out of preference than out of economic necessity.

The economic hardships of the Depression years placed great strains on American families. Middle-class families found themselves plunged suddenly into uncertainty, because of unemployment or the reduction of incomes among those who remained employed. Some working-class families had achieved a precarious prosperity in the 1920s but saw their gains disappear in the 1930s. Such circumstances caused many families to change the way they lived. Some women returned to sewing clothes for themselves and their families and to preserving their own food. Others engaged in home businesses such as taking in laundry or boarders. Many households expanded to take in relatives.

Declining Marriage and Birth Rates

But the Depression also worked to erode the strength of many family units. There was a decline in the divorce rate, but largely because divorce was now too expensive for some. More common was the informal breakup of families, particularly the desertion of families by unemployed men trying to escape the humiliation of being unable to earn a living. The marriage rate and the birth rate both declined for the first time since the early nineteenth century.

THE DEPRESSION AND AMERICAN CULTURE

The Great Depression was a traumatic experience for millions of Americans. Out of the crisis emerged probing criticisms of American life. But the Depression also produced powerful confirmations of more traditional values and reinforced many traditional goals. There was not one Depression culture, but many.

Depression Values

Prevailing Values Reinforced

Prosperity and industrial growth had done much to shape American values in the 1920s. Mainstream culture, at least, had celebrated affluence and consumerism. Many Americans assumed, therefore, that the experience of hard times would have profound effects on the nation's social values. In general, however, American social values seemed to change relatively little in response to the Depression. Instead, many people responded to hard times by redoubling their commitment to familiar ideas and goals.

No assumption would seem to have been more vulnerable to erosion during the Depression than the belief that anyone displaying sufficient talent and industry could become a success. And in some respects, the economic crisis did work to undermine the traditional "success ethic" in America. Many people began to look to government for assistance; many learned to blame corporate moguls and others for their distress. Yet the Depression did not destroy the success ethic.

The survival of the ideals of work and individual responsibility was evident in many ways, not least in the reactions of those most traumatized by the Depression: people who suddenly found themselves without employment. Some expressed anger and struck out at the economic system. Many, however, seemed to blame themselves. At the same time, millions responded eagerly to reassurances that they could, through their own efforts, restore themselves to prosperity and success. Dale Carnegie's *How to Win Friends and Influence People* (1936), a self-help manual preaching individual initiative, was one of the best-selling books of the decade.

Dale Carnegie

Artists and Intellectuals in the Great Depression

Not all Americans, of course, responded to the crisis of the Depression so passively. Artists and intellectuals engaged in a broad effort to dramatize the problem of rural poverty. Among those involved in this venture was a group of documentary photographers, many of them employed by the federal Farm Security Administration in the late 1930s, who traveled through the South recording the nature of agricultural life. Men such as Walker Evans, Arthur Rothstein, Russell Lee, and Ben Shahn and women such as Margaret Bourke-White and Dorothea Lange produced memorable studies of farm families and their surroundings, studies designed to show the savage impact of a hostile environment on its victims. Many writers, similarly, devoted themselves to exposés of social injustice. Erskine Caldwell's *Tobacco Road* (1932), which later became a long-running play, was an exposé of poverty in the rural South. Richard Wright, a major African-American writer, exposed the plight of residents of the urban ghetto in novels such as *Native Son* (1940).

But the cultural products of the 1930s that attracted the widest popular audiences were those that diverted attention away from the Depression. And they came to Americans primarily through the two most powerful instruments of popular culture in the 1930s—radio and the movies.

Radio

Almost every American family had a radio in the 1930s. In cities and towns, radio consoles were as familiar a part of the furnishing of parlors and kitchens as tables and chairs. Even in remote rural areas without access to electricity, many families purchased radios and hooked them up to car batteries when they wished to listen.

Radio's Mass Popularity

Listening to radio is generally considered a private experience—something people do alone, or with their families, in their homes. But in some communities, radio was often a community experience. Young people would place radios on their front porches and invite friends by to sit, talk, or dance. In poor urban neighborhoods, people would gather on a street or in a backyard to listen to sporting events or concerts. Within families, the radio often drew parents and children together to listen to favorite programs.

What did Americans hear on the radio? Although radio stations occasionally carried socially and politically provocative programs, the staple of broadcasting was escapism: comedies such as *Amos n' Andy* (with its humorous if demeaning picture of urban blacks); adventures such as *Superman*, *Dick Tracy*, and *The Lone Ranger;* and other entertainment programs.

Escapist Programming

Radio brought a new kind of comedy to a wide audience. Jack Benny, George Burns and Gracie Allen, and other masters of elaborately timed jokes and repartee began to develop broad followings. Soap operas were enormously popular as well, especially with women who were alone in the house during the day. (That was why they became known as soap operas; soap companies—whose advertising was targeted at women—generally sponsored them.)

Radio provided Americans with their first direct access to important public events, and radio news and sports divisions grew rapidly to meet the demand. Some of the most dramatic moments of the 1930s were a result of radio coverage of celebrated events: the World Series, the Academy Awards, political conventions. When the German dirigible the *Hindenburg* crashed in flames in Lakehurst, New Jersey, in 1937, it produced an enormous national reaction largely because of the live radio account by a broadcaster overcome with emotion who cried out, as he watched the terrible crash, "Oh the humanity! Oh the humanity!" The actor/director Orson Welles created another memorable event on Halloween night, 1938, when he broadcast a radio play about aliens whose spaceship landed in central New Jersey and who had set off toward New York armed with terrible weapons. The play took the form of a news broadcast, and it created panic among millions of people who believed for a while that the events it described were real.

The Movies

In the first years of the Depression, movie attendance dropped significantly. By the mid-1930s, however, most Americans had resumed their moviegoing habits to at least some extent in part because the movies (all of them now with sound, and by the end of the decade many of them in color) were becoming more appealing.

Hollywood's Self-Censorship

Hollywood continued to exercise tight control over its products in the 1930s through its resilient censor Will Hays, who ensured that most movies carried no sensational or controversial messages. The studio system—through which a few large movie companies exercised iron control over actors, writers, and directors—also worked to ensure that Hollywood films avoided controversy.

Neither the censor nor the studio system, however, could (or wished to) prevent films from exploring social questions altogether. A few films, such as King Vidor's *Our Daily Bread* (1932) and John Ford's adaptation of *The Grapes of Wrath* (1940), did explore political themes. Gangster movies such as *Little Caesar* (1930) and *The Public Enemy* (1931) portrayed a dark, gritty, violent world with which few Americans were familiar, but their desperate stories were popular nevertheless with those engaged in their own difficult struggles.

But the most effective presentation of a social message, even if a muted one, came from the brilliant Italian-born director Frank Capra. Capra had a deep and somewhat romanticized love for his adopted country, and he translated that love into a vaguely populistic admiration for ordinary people. He contrasted the decency of small-town America and the common man with what he considered the grasping opportunism of the city and the greedy capitalist marketplace. In *Mr. Deeds Goes to Town* (1936), a simple man from a small town inherits a large fortune, moves to the city, and—not liking the greed and dishonesty he finds there—gives the money away and moves back home. In *Mr. Smith Goes to Washington* (1939), a decent man from a western state is elected to the United States Senate, refuses to join in the self-interested politics of Washington, and dramatically exposes the corruption and selfishness of his colleagues. Capra's films, outstandingly popular in the 1930s, helped audiences find solace in a vision of an imagined American past—in the warmth and goodness of idealized small towns and the decency of ordinary people.

Frank Capra

More often, however, the commercial films of the 1930s, like most radio programs, were deliberately and explicitly escapist: lavish musicals such as *Gold Diggers of 1933*, "screwball" comedies (such as Capra's *It Happened One Night*), or the many films of the Marx Brothers—films designed to divert audiences from their troubles and, often, indulge their fantasies about quick and easy wealth.

The 1930s saw the beginning of Walt Disney's long reign as the champion of animation and children's entertainment. After producing cartoon shorts for theaters in the late 1920s, many of them starring the newly created character of Mickey Mouse, Disney began to produce feature-length animated films, starting in 1937 with *Snow White.* Other enormously popular films of the 1930s were adaptations of popular novels: *The Wizard of Oz* and *Gone with the Wind*, both released in 1939.

Walt Disney

Hollywood did little to challenge the conventions of popular culture on issues of gender and race. Women in movies were portrayed overwhelmingly as wives and mothers, or if not, as sexually attractive people engaged in elaborate flirtations with men. Mae West portrayed herself in a

A NIGHT AT THE OPERA The antic comedy of the Marx Brothers provided a popular and welcome escape from the rigors of the Great Depression. The Marx Brothers, shown here in a poster for one of their most famous films, effectively lampooned dilemmas that many Americans faced in their ceaseless, and usually unsuccessful, efforts to find an easy route to wealth and comfort. *(Everett Collection)*

series of successful films as an overtly sexual woman manipulating men through her attractiveness. Few films included important African-American characters. Most of the black men and women who did appear in movies were portrayed as servants or farmhands or entertainers.

Popular Literature and Journalism

The social and political strains of the Great Depression found voice much more successfully in print than they did on the airwaves or the screen. Much literature and journalism in the 1930s dealt directly or indirectly with the tremendous disillusionment, and the increasing radicalism, of the time.

Not all literature, of course, was challenging or controversial. The most popular books and magazines of the 1930s, in fact, were as escapist and romantic as the most popular radio shows and movies. Two of the best-selling novels of the decade were romantic sagas set in earlier eras: Margaret Mitchell's *Gone with the Wind* (1936) and Hervey Allen's *Anthony Adverse* (1933). Leading magazines focused more on fashions, stunts, scenery, and the arts than on the social conditions of the nation. The enormously popular new photographic journal *Life*, which began publication in 1936, had the largest readership of any publication in the United States (with the exception of the *Reader's Digest*). It devoted some attention to politics and to the economic conditions of the Depression, but it was best known for stunning photographs of sporting and theater events, natural landscapes, and impressive public projects. One of its most popular features was "*Life* Goes to a Party," which took the chatty social columns of daily newspapers and turned them into glossy photographic glimpses of the rich and famous.

Other Depression writing, however, was frankly and openly challenging to the dominant values of American popular culture. Some of the most significant literature offered corrosive portraits of the harshness and emptiness of American life: John Dos Passos's *U.S.A.* trilogy (1930–1936), which attacked what he considered the materialistic madness of American culture; Nathanael West's *Miss Lonelyhearts* (1933), the story of an advice columnist overwhelmed by the sadness he encounters in the lives of those who consult him; Jack Conroy's *The Disinherited* (1933), a harsh portrait of the lives of coalminers; and James T. Farrell's *Studs Lonigan* (1932), a portrait of a lost, hardened working-class youth.

John Dos Passos

The Popular Front and the Left

In the later 1930s, much of the political literature adopted a more optimistic, although often no less radical, approach to society. This was in part a result of the rise of the Popular Front, a broad coalition of "antifascist" groups on the left, of which the most important was the American Communist Party. The party had long been a harsh and unrelenting critic of American capitalism and the government it claimed was controlled by it. But in 1935, under instructions from the Soviet Union, the party softened its attitude toward Franklin Roosevelt (whom Stalin now saw as a potential ally in the coming battle against Hitler) and formed loose alliances with many other "progressive" groups. The party began to praise the New Deal and John L. Lewis, a powerful (and strongly anticommunist) labor leader, and it adopted the slogan "Communism is twentieth-century Americanism." In its heyday, the Popular Front did much to enhance the reputation and influence of the Communist Party. It also helped mobilize writers, artists, and intellectuals behind a critical, democratic sensibility.

The importance to many American intellectuals of the Spanish Civil War of the mid-1930s was a good example of how the left helped give meaning and purpose to individual lives. The war in Spain pitted the fascists of Francisco Franco (who was receiving support from Hitler and Mussolini) against the existing republican government. It attracted a substantial group of young Americans—more than 3,000 in all—who formed the Abraham Lincoln Brigade and traveled to Spain to join in the fight against the fascists. The

Abraham Lincoln Brigade

American Communist Party was instrumental in creating the Lincoln Brigade, and directed many of its activities.

The party was active as well in organizing the unemployed in the early 1930s and staged a hunger march in Washington, D.C., in 1931. Party members were among the most effective union organizers in some industries. And the party was virtually alone among political organizations in taking a firm stand in favor of racial justice; its active defense of the Scottsboro defendants was but one example of its efforts to ally itself with the aspirations of African Americans.

The American Communist Party was not, however, the open, patriotic organization it tried to appear. It was always under the close and rigid supervision of the Soviet Union. Most members obediently followed the "party line" (although there were many areas in which Communists were active for which there was no party line, areas in which members acted independently). The subordination of the party leadership to the Soviet Union was most clearly demonstrated in 1939, when Stalin signed a nonaggression pact with Nazi Germany. Moscow then sent orders to the American Communist Party to abandon the Popular Front and return to its old stance of harsh criticism of American liberals; and Communist Party leaders in the United States immediately obeyed—although thousands of disillusioned members left the party as a result.

The Socialist Party of America, under the leadership of Norman Thomas, also cited the economic crisis as evidence of the failure of capitalism and sought vigorously to win public support for its own political program. Among other things, it attempted to mobilize support among the rural poor. The Southern Tenant Farmers Union, supported by the party and organized by a young socialist, H. L. Mitchell, attempted to create a biracial coalition of sharecroppers, tenant farmers, and others to demand economic reform. Neither the STFU nor the party itself, however, made any real progress toward establishing socialism as a major force in American politics.

Southern Tenant Farmers Union

Antiradicalism was a powerful force in the 1930s. Hostility toward the Communist Party, in particular, was intense at many levels of government. Congressional committees chaired by Hamilton Fish of New York and Martin Dies of Texas investigated communist influence wherever they could find (or imagine) it. White southerners tried to drive communist organizers out of the countryside, just as growers in California and elsewhere tried (unsuccessfully) to keep communists from organizing Mexican-American and other workers.

Even so, at few times before (and few since) in American history did being part of the left seem so respectable and even conventional among workers, intellectuals, and others. Thus the 1930s witnessed an impressive, if temporary, widening of the ideological range of mainstream art and politics. The New Deal, for example, sponsored artistic work through the Works Projects Administration that was frankly challenging to the capitalist norms of the 1920s. The filmmaker Pare Lorentz, with funding from New Deal agencies, made a series of powerful documentaries—*The Plow that Broke the Plains* (1936), *The River* (1937)—that combined a celebration of New Deal programs with a harsh critique of the exploitation of people and the environment that industrial capitalism had produced.

A less confrontational grappling with the social misery of the 1930s was a remarkable book by the novelist James Agee and the photographer Walker Evans, *Let Us Now Praise Famous Men* (1941). Agee and Walker had traveled to rural Alabama in the mid-1930s on an assignment from *Fortune* magazine to produce an article about sharecropping and rural poverty. The long, rambling, highly emotional text that Agee produced, accompanied by extraordinary photographs of three families of white southern sharecroppers, was too long and too unconventional for *Fortune*. But the book that eventually appeared is an enduring portrait of a distressed area of what Agee called "human existence," but also a passionate tribute to the strength and even nobility of the struggling people he had come to know.

Let Us Now Praise Famous Men

Perhaps the most successful chronicler of social conditions in the 1930s was the novelist John Steinbeck, particularly in his celebrated novel *The Grapes of Wrath*, published in 1939. In telling the story of the Joad family, migrants from the Dust Bowl to California who encounter an unending string of calamities and failures, he offered a harsh portrait of the exploitive features of agrarian life in the West, but also a tribute to the endurance of his main characters—and to the spirit of community they represent.

The Grapes of Wrath

THE ORDEAL OF HERBERT HOOVER

Herbert Hoover began his presidency in March 1929 believing, like most Americans, that the nation faced a bright and prosperous future. For the first six months of his administration, he attempted to expand the policies he had advocated during his eight years as secretary of commerce. The economic crisis that began before the year was out forced the president to deal with a new set of problems, but for most of the rest of his term, he continued to rely on the principles that had always governed his public life.

The Hoover Program

Hoover's first response to the Depression was to attempt to restore public confidence in the economy. "The fundamental business of this country, that is, production and distribution of commodities," he said in 1930, "is on a sound and prosperous basis." He then summoned leaders of business, labor, and agriculture to the White House and urged them to adopt a program of

Failure of Voluntary Cooperation

voluntary cooperation for recovery. He implored businessmen not to cut production or lay off workers; he talked labor leaders into forgoing demands for higher wages or better hours. But by mid-1931, economic conditions had deteriorated so much that the structure of voluntary cooperation he had erected collapsed.

Hoover also attempted to use government spending as a tool for fighting the Depression. The president proposed to Congress an increase of $423 million—a significant sum by the standards of the time—in federal public works programs, and he exhorted state and local governments to fund public construction. But the spending was not nearly enough in the face of such devastating problems. And when economic conditions worsened, he became less willing to increase spending, worrying instead about keeping the budget balanced.

Even before the stock market crash, Hoover had begun to construct a program to assist the already troubled agricultural economy. In April

Agricultural Marketing Act

1929, he proposed the Agricultural Marketing Act, which established the first major government program to help farmers maintain prices. A federally sponsored Farm Board would make loans to national marketing cooperatives or establish corporations to buy surpluses and thus raise prices. At the same time, Hoover attempted to protect American farmers from international competition by raising agricultural tariffs. The Hawley-Smoot Tariff of 1930 contained increased protection on seventy-five farm products. But neither the Agricultural Marketing Act nor the Hawley-Smoot Tariff ultimately helped American farmers significantly.

By the spring of 1931, Herbert Hoover's political position had deteriorated considerably. In the 1930 congressional elections, Democrats won control of the House and made substantial inroads in the Senate. Many Americans held the president personally to blame for the crisis and began calling the shantytowns that unemployed people established on the outskirts of cities "Hoovervilles." Democrats urged the president to support more vigorous programs of relief and public spending. Hoover, instead, seized on a slight improvement in economic conditions early in 1931 as proof that his policies were working.

International Economic Collapse

The international financial panic of the spring of 1931 destroyed the illusion that the economic crisis was coming to an end. Throughout the 1920s, European nations had depended on loans from American banks to allow them to make payments on their debts. After 1929, when they could no longer get such loans, the financial fabric of several European nations began to unravel. In May 1931, the largest bank in Austria collapsed. Over the next several months, panic gripped the financial institutions of neighboring countries. The American economy rapidly declined to new lows.

By the time Congress convened in December 1931, conditions had grown so desperate that Hoover supported a series of measures designed to keep endangered banks afloat and protect homeowners from foreclosure on their mortgages. Most important was a bill passed in January 1932 establishing the Reconstruction Finance Corporation (RFC), a government agency whose purpose was to provide federal loans to troubled banks, railroads, and other businesses. Unlike some earlier Hoover programs, the RFC operated on a large scale. In 1932, it had a budget of $1.5 billion for public works alone.

Failure of the RFC

Nevertheless, the new agency failed to deal directly or forcefully enough with the real problems of the economy to produce any significant recovery. The RFC lent funds only to financial institutions with sufficient collateral; much of its money went to large banks and corporations. At Hoover's insistence, it helped finance only those public works projects that promised ultimately to pay for themselves (toll bridges, public housing, and others). Above all, the RFC did not have enough money to make any real impact on the Depression, and it did not even spend all the money it had.

Popular Protest

For the first several years of the Depression, most Americans were either too stunned or too confused to raise any effective protest. By the middle of 1932, however, dissident voices began to be heard.

Farmers' Holiday Association

In the summer of 1932, a group of unhappy farm owners gathered in Des Moines, Iowa, to establish a new organization: the Farmers' Holiday Association, which endorsed the withholding of farm products from the market—in effect a farmers' strike. The strike began in August in western Iowa, spread briefly to a few neighboring areas, and succeeded in blockading several markets, but in the end it dissolved in failure.

A more celebrated protest movement emerged from American veterans. In 1924, Congress had approved the payment of a $1,000 bonus to all those who had served in World War I, the money to be paid beginning in 1945. By 1932, however, many veterans were demanding that the bonus be paid immediately. Hoover, concerned about balancing the budget, rejected their appeal. In June, more than 20,000 veterans, members of the self-proclaimed Bonus Expeditionary Force, or "Bonus Army," marched into Washington, built crude camps around the city, and promised to stay until Congress approved legislation to pay the bonus. Some of the veterans departed in July, after Congress had voted down their proposal. Many, however, remained where they were.

Their continued presence in Washington embarrassed President Hoover. Finally, in mid-July, he ordered police to clear the marchers out of several abandoned federal buildings in which they had been staying. A few marchers threw rocks at the police, and someone opened fire; two veterans fell dead. Hoover called the incident evidence of uncontrolled violence and radicalism, and he ordered the United States Army to assist the police in clearing out the buildings.

CLEARING OUT THE BONUS MARCHERS In July 1932, President Hoover ordered the Washington, D.C. police to evict the Bonus Marchers from some of the public buildings and land they had been occupying. The result was a series of pitched battles (one of them visible here), in which both veterans and police sustained injuries. Such skirmishes persuaded Hoover to call out the army to finish the job. *(Bettmann/Corbis)*

Demise of the "Bonus Army"

General Douglas MacArthur, the army chief of staff, carried out the mission himself and greatly exceeded the president's orders. He led the Third Cavalry, two infantry regiments, a machine-gun detachment, and six tanks down Pennsylvania Avenue in pursuit of the Bonus Army. The veterans fled in terror. MacArthur followed them across the Anacostia River, where he ordered the soldiers to burn their tent city to the ground. More than 100 marchers were injured.

The incident served as perhaps the final blow to Hoover's already battered political standing. The Great Engineer, the personification of the optimistic days of the 1920s, had become a symbol of the nation's failure to deal effectively with its startling reversal of fortune.

The Election of 1932

As the 1932 presidential election approached, few people doubted the outcome. The Republican Party dutifully renominated Herbert Hoover for a second term of office, but few delegates believed he could win. The Democrats, in the meantime, gathered jubilantly in Chicago to nominate the governor of New York, Franklin Delano Roosevelt.

(56.9% of electorate voting)

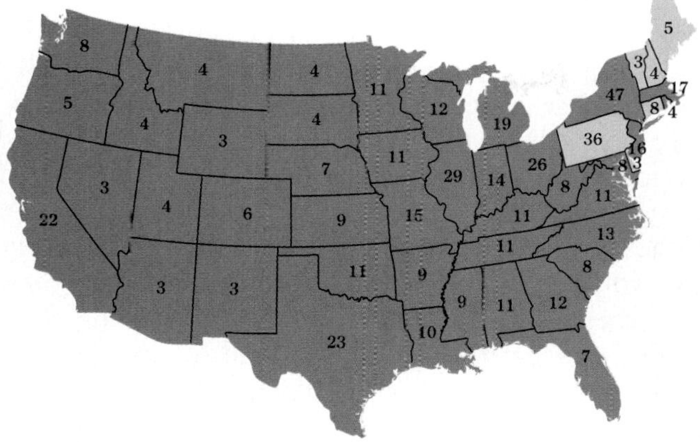

	ELECTORAL VOTE	POPULAR VOTE (%)
Franklin D. Roosevelt *(Democratic)*	472	22,821,857 (57.4)
Herbert Hoover *(Republican)*	59	15,761,841 (39.7)
Norman Thomas *(Socialist)*	—	881,951 (1.2)
Other candidates *(Communist, Prohibition, Socialist Labor, Liberty)*	—	271,355

ELECTION OF 1932 Like the election of 1928, the election of 1932 was exceptionally one-sided. But this time, the landslide favored the Democratic candidate, Franklin Roosevelt, who overwhelmed Herbert Hoover in all regions of the country except New England. Roosevelt obviously benefited primarily from popular disillusionment with Hoover's response to the Great Depression. ◆ *But what characteristics of Roosevelt himself contributed to his victory?*

For an interactive version of this map go to www.mhhe.com/unfinishednation4ch25maps

Franklin Delano Roosevelt

Roosevelt had been a well-known figure in the party for many years already. A Hudson Valley aristocrat, a distant cousin of Theodore Roosevelt, and a handsome, charming young man, he progressed rapidly: from a seat in the New York State legislature to a position as assistant secretary of the navy under Woodrow Wilson during World War I to his party's vice presidential nomination in 1920 on the ill-fated ticket with James M. Cox. Less than a year later, he was stricken with polio. Although he never regained use of his legs (and could walk only by using crutches and braces), he built up sufficient physical strength to return to politics in 1928. When Al Smith received the Democratic nomination for president that year, Roosevelt was elected to succeed him as governor. In 1930, he easily won reelection.

Roosevelt worked no miracles in New York, but he did initiate enough positive programs of government assistance to be able to present himself as a more energetic and imaginative leader than Hoover. In national politics, he avoided divisive cultural issues and emphasized the economic grievances that most Democrats shared. He was able as a result to assemble a broad coalition within the party and win his party's nomination. In a dramatic break with tradition, he flew to Chicago to address the convention in person and accept the nomination. In the course of his acceptance speech, Roosevelt aroused the delegates with his ringing promise: "I pledge you, I pledge myself, to a new deal for the American people." Neither then nor in the subsequent campaign did Roosevelt give much indication of what that program would be. But Herbert Hoover's unpopularity virtually ensured Roosevelt's election.

FDR Elected

Roosevelt won by a landslide. He received 57.4 percent of the popular vote to Hoover's 39.7. In the electoral college, the result was even more overwhelming. Hoover carried Delaware, Pennsylvania, Connecticut, Vermont, New Hampshire, and Maine. Roosevelt won everything else. Democrats won majorities in both houses of Congress. It was a convincing mandate, but it was not yet clear what Roosevelt intended to do with it.

The "Interregnum"

The period between the election and the inauguration (which in the early 1930s lasted more than four months) was a season of growing economic crisis. Presidents-elect traditionally do not involve themselves directly in government. But in a series of brittle exchanges with Roosevelt, Hoover tried to exact from the president-elect a pledge to maintain policies of economic orthodoxy. Roosevelt genially refused.

Banking Collapse

In February, only a month before the inauguration, a new crisis developed when the collapse of the American banking system suddenly and rapidly accelerated. Depositors were withdrawing their money in panic; and one bank after another was closing its doors and declaring bankruptcy. Hoover again asked Roosevelt to give prompt public assurances that there would be no tinkering with the currency, no heavy borrowing, no unbalancing of the budget. Roosevelt again refused.

March 4, 1933, was, therefore, a day of both economic crisis and considerable personal bitterness. On that morning, Herbert Hoover rode glumly down Pennsylvania Avenue with a beaming, buoyant Franklin Roosevelt, who would shortly be sworn in as the thirty-second president of the United States.

THE CHANGING OF THE GUARD Long before the event actually occurred, Peter Arno of the *New Yorker* magazine drew this image of Franklin D. Roosevelt and Herbert Hoover traveling together to the Capitol for Roosevelt's inauguration. It predicted with remarkable accuracy the mood of the uncomfortable ride—Hoover glum and uncommunicative, Roosevelt buoyant and smiling. This was to have been the magazine's cover for the week of the inauguration, but after an attempted assassination of the president-elect several weeks earlier in Florida (in which the mayor of Chicago was killed), the editors decided to substitute a more subdued drawing. *(FDR & Hoover by Peter Arno,* New Yorker, *1933. Franklin Delano Roosevelt Library)*

CONCLUSION

The Great Depression changed many things in American life. It created unemployment on a scale never before experienced in the nation's history. It put enormous pressures on families, on communities, on state and local governments, and ultimately on Washington—which during the innovative but ultimately failed presidency of Herbert Hoover was unable to produce policies capable of dealing effectively with the crisis. In the nation's politics and culture, there were strong currents of radicalism and protest; and many middle-class Americans came to fear that a revolution might be approaching.

In reality, while the Great Depression shook much of American society and culture, it actually toppled very little. The capitalist system survived, damaged for a time but never truly threatened. The values of materialism and personal responsibility were shaken, but never overturned. The American people in the 1930s were more receptive than they had been in the 1920s to evocations of community, generosity, and the dignity of common people. They were more open to experiments in government and business and even private lives than they had been in earlier years. But for most Americans, belief in the "American way of life" remained strong throughout the long years of economic despair.

FOR FURTHER REFERENCE

Donald Worster scathingly indicts agricultural capitalism for its destruction of the plains environment in *Dust Bowl: The Southern Plains in the 1930s* (1979). In *The Great Depression: Delayed Recovery and Economic Change in America, 1929–1939* (1987), Michael Bernstein argues that we should ask not so much why the economy crashed in 1929 but rather why the expected recovery from the crash was so slow. Richard Pells, *Radical Visions and American Dreams: Culture and Social Thought in the Depression Years* (1973) is an important survey of the cultural and intellectual history of the 1930s. Studs Terkel, *Hard Times* (1970) is an excellent oral history of the Depression. Susan Ware analyzes the effect of the Great Depression on women in *Holding Their Own: American Women in the 1930s* (1982). The Communist Party's most popular period in the United States is the subject of Harvey Klehr's *The Heyday of American Communism: The Depression Decade* (1984) and, from quite different viewpoints, Robin D. G. Kelley, *Hammer and Hoe: Alabama Communists During the Great Depression* (1990) and Michael Denning, *The Cultural Front: The Laboring of American Culture in the Twentieth Century* (1997). Joan Hoff Wilson, *Herbert Hoover: Forgotten Progressive* (1975) argues that

President Hoover was in many ways a surprisingly progressive thinker about the American social order.

The Great Depression (1993), a multipart film by Blackside Productions, is an eloquent picture of many aspects of the depression decade. *Union Maids* (1997) is a vivid film history of women organizing in the 1930s. *The Lemon Grove Incident* (1985) is a film providing a rare glimpse of Mexican-American civil rights activism over school integration in the early 1930s.

For quizzes, Internet resources, references to additional books and films, and more, consult this book's Online Learning Center site at www.mhhe.com/unfinishednation4.

WPA POSTER, 1930S The Works Progress Administration, which this striking poster celebrates, was the New Deal's most prominent experiment in work relief. In addition to providing jobs for unemployed farmers and industrial workers (as depicted here), it created programs to assist writers, artists, actors, and others. *(The Library of Congress)*

TIME LINE

1933	1934	1935
"First New Deal" legislation	American Liberty League founded	Supreme Court invalidates NRA
Prohibition ends	Long's Share-Our-Wealth Society established	"Second New Deal" legislation, including Social Security and Wagner Acts
		Lewis breaks with AFL

CHAPTER TWENTY-SIX

THE NEW DEAL

Launching the New Deal
The New Deal in Transition
The New Deal in Disarray
Limits and Legacies of the New Deal

During his twelve years in office Franklin Roosevelt became more central to the life of the nation than any president had ever been. Most important, his administration constructed a series of programs that permanently altered the federal government and its relationship to society. By the end of the 1930s, the New Deal (as the Roosevelt administration was called) had not ended the Great Depression; only World War II did that. But it had created many of the broad outlines of the political world we know today.

LAUNCHING THE NEW DEAL

Roosevelt's first task upon taking office was to alleviate the panic that was creating chaos in the financial system. He did so in part by force of personality and in part by very rapidly constructing an ambitious and diverse program of legislation.

1936	1937	1938	1939
Supreme Court invalidates Agricultural Adjustment Act	Roosevelt's "Court-packing" plan	Fair Labor Standards Act	Marian Anderson sings at Lincoln Memorial
CIO established	Supreme Court upholds Wagner Act		
Roosevelt reelected	Severe recession		
Sit-down strikes			

Restoring Confidence

Much of Roosevelt's early success was a result of his ebullient personality. He was the first president to make regular use of the radio; and his friendly "fireside chats," during which he explained in simple terms his programs and plans to the people, helped build public confidence in the administration. But Roosevelt could not rely on image alone. On March 6, two days after taking office, he issued a proclamation closing all American banks for four days until Congress could meet in special session to consider banking reform legislation. So great was the panic about bank failures that the "bank holiday," as the president euphemistically described it, created a general sense of relief and hope.

"Bank Holiday" Declared

Three days later, Roosevelt sent to Congress the Emergency Banking Act, a generally conservative bill designed primarily to protect the larger banks from being dragged down by the weakness of smaller ones. The bill provided for Treasury Department inspection of all banks before they would be allowed to reopen, for federal assistance to some troubled institutions, and for a thorough reorganization of those banks in the greatest difficulty. Congress passed the bill within a few hours of its introduction. Whatever else the new law accomplished, it helped dispel the panic. Three-quarters of the banks in the Federal Reserve system reopened within the next three days, and $1 billion in hoarded currency and gold flowed back into them within a month. The immediate banking crisis was over.

Emergency Banking Act

On the morning after passage of the Emergency Banking Act, Roosevelt sent to Congress another measure—the Economy Act—designed to convince the public (and especially the business community) that the federal government was in safe, responsible hands. The act proposed to balance the federal budget by cutting the salaries of government employees and reducing pensions to veterans by as much as 15 percent. Like the banking bill, this one passed through Congress almost instantly. Later that spring, Roosevelt signed the Glass-Steagall Act of June 1933, which gave the government authority to curb irresponsible speculation by banks. More important, perhaps, it established the Federal Deposit Insurance Corporation, which guaranteed all bank deposits up to $2,500. In other words, even if a bank should fail, small depositors would be able to recover their money. (Later, in 1935, Congress passed another major banking act that transferred much of the authority once wielded by the regional Federal Reserve banks to the Federal Reserve Board in Washington.)

To restore confidence in the stock market, Congress passed the so-called Truth in Securities Act of 1933, requiring corporations issuing new securities to provide full and accurate information about them to the public. Another act, of June 1934, established the Securities and Exchange Commission (SEC) to police the stock market. Roosevelt also signed a bill to legalize

Securities and Exchange Commission

THE RADIO PRESIDENT Franklin D. Roosevelt was the first American president to master the use of radio. Beginning in his first days in office, he regularly bypassed the newspapers (many of which were hostile to him) and communicated directly with the people through his famous "fireside chats." He is shown here speaking in 1938, urging communities to continue to provide work relief for the unemployed. *(Franklin Delano Roosevelt Library)*

the manufacture and sale of beer with a 3.2 percent alcohol content—an interim measure pending the repeal of prohibition, for which a constitutional amendment (the Twenty-first) was already in process. The amendment was ratified later in 1933.

Agricultural Adjustment

These initial actions were largely stopgaps, to buy time for more comprehensive programs. The first was the Agricultural Adjustment Act, which Congress passed in May 1933. Under the provisions of the act, producers of seven basic commodities (wheat, cotton, corn, hogs, rice, tobacco, and dairy products) would decide on production limits for their crops. The government, through the Agricultural Adjustment Administration (AAA), would then tell individual farmers how much they should produce and would pay them subsidies for leaving some of their land idle. A tax on food processing (for example, the milling of wheat) would provide the funds for the new payments. Farm prices were to be subsidized up to the point of parity.

The AAA helped bring about a rise in prices for farm commodities in the years after 1933. Gross farm income increased by half in the first three years of the New Deal, and the agricultural economy as a whole emerged from the 1930s much more stable and prosperous than it had been in many years. The AAA did, however, favor larger farmers over smaller ones. By distributing payments to landowners, not those who worked the land, the government did little to discourage planters who were reducing their acreage from evicting tenants and sharecroppers and firing field hands.

Large Farmers Favored

In January 1936, the Supreme Court struck down the crucial provisions of the Agricultural Adjustment Act, arguing that the government had no constitutional authority to require farmers to limit production. But within a few weeks the administration had secured passage of new legislation (the Soil Conservation and Domestic Allotment Act), which permitted the government to pay farmers to reduce production so as to "conserve soil," prevent erosion, and accomplish other secondary goals.

Farm Security Administration

The administration launched several efforts to assist poor farmers as well. The Resettlement Administration, established in 1935, and its successor, the Farm Security Administration, created in 1937, provided loans to help farmers cultivating submarginal soil to relocate to better lands. But the programs moved no more than a few thousand farmers. More effective was the Rural Electrification Administration, created in 1935, which worked to make electric power available for the first time to thousands of farmers through utility cooperatives.

Industrial Recovery

Ever since 1931, leaders of the United States Chamber of Commerce and many others had been urging the government to adopt an antideflation scheme that would permit trade associations to cooperate in stabilizing prices within their industries. Existing antitrust laws clearly forbade such practices, and Herbert Hoover had refused to endorse suspension of the laws. The Roosevelt administration was more receptive. In exchange for relaxing antitrust provisions, however, New Dealers insisted on other provisions. Business leaders would have to make important concessions to labor—recognize the workers' right to bargain collectively through unions—to ensure that the incomes of workers would rise along with prices. And to help create jobs and increase consumer buying power, the administration added a major program of public works spending. The result of these and many other impulses was the National Industrial Recovery Act, which Congress passed in June 1933.

National Recovery Administration Established

At its center was a new federal agency, the National Recovery Administration (NRA), under the direction of the flamboyant and energetic Hugh S. Johnson. Johnson called on every business establishment in the nation to accept a temporary "blanket code": a minimum wage of between 30 and 40 cents an hour, a maximum workweek of thirty-five to forty hours, and the abolition of child labor. At the same time, Johnson negotiated another, more specific set of codes with leaders of the nation's major industries. These industrial codes set floors below which no company would lower prices or wages in its search for a competitive advantage, and they included provisions for maintaining employment and production. He quickly won agreements from almost every major industry in the country.

SALUTING THE BLUE EAGLE Several thousand San Francisco schoolchildren assembled on a baseball field in 1933 to form the symbol of the National Recovery Administration: an eagle clutching a cogwheel (to symbolize industry) and a thunderbolt (to symbolize energy). This display is evidence of the widespread (if brief) popular enthusiasm the NRA produced. NRA administrators drew from their memories of World War I Liberty Loan drives and tried to establish the Blue Eagle as a symbol of patriotic commitment to recovery. *(Bettmann/Corbis)*

From the beginning, however, the NRA encountered serious difficulties. The codes themselves were hastily and often poorly written. Large producers consistently dominated the code-writing process and ensured that the new regulations would work to their advantage and to the disadvantage of smaller firms. And the codes at times did more than simply set floors under prices; they actively and artificially raised them—sometimes to levels higher than the market could sustain.

Section 7(a)

Other NRA goals did not progress as quickly as the efforts to raise prices. Section 7(a) of the National Industrial Recovery Act promised workers the right to form unions and engage in collective bargaining and encouraged many workers to join unions for the first time. But Section 7(a) contained no enforcement mechanisms. The Public Works Administration (PWA), established to administer the National Industrial Recovery Act's spending programs, only gradually allowed the $3.3 billion in public works funds to trickle out.

Failure of the NRA

Perhaps the clearest evidence of the NRA's failure was that industrial production actually declined in the months after the agency's establishment despite the rise in prices that the codes had helped to create. By the spring of 1934, the NRA was besieged by criticism. That fall, Roosevelt pressured Johnson to resign and established a new board of directors to oversee the NRA. Then in 1935, the Supreme Court intervened.

In 1935, a case came before the Court involving alleged NRA code violations by the Schechter brothers, who operated a wholesale poultry business confined to Brooklyn, New York. The Court ruled unanimously that the Schechters were not engaged in interstate commerce (and thus not subject to federal regulation) and, further, that Congress had unconstitutionally delegated legislative power to the president to draft the NRA codes. The justices struck down the legislation establishing the agency. Roosevelt denounced the justices for their "horse-and-buggy" interpretation of the interstate commerce clause. He was rightly concerned, for the reasoning in the Schechter case threatened many other New Deal programs as well.

Regional Planning

The AAA and the NRA largely reflected the beliefs of New Dealers who favored economic planning but wanted private interests (farmers or business leaders) to dominate the planning process. Other reformers believed that the government itself should be the chief planning agent in the economy. Their most conspicuous success was an unprecedented experiment in regional planning: the Tennessee Valley Authority (TVA).

Tennessee Valley Authority

Progressive reformers had agitated for years for public development of the nation's water resources as a source of cheap electric power. In particular, they had urged completion of a great dam at Muscle Shoals on the Tennessee River in Alabama—a dam begun during World War I but left unfinished when the war ended. But opposition from the utilities companies had been too powerful to overcome.

In 1932, however, one of the great utility empires—that of the electricity magnate Samuel Insull—collapsed spectacularly, amid widely publicized exposés of corruption. Hostility to the utilities soon grew so intense that the companies were no longer able to block the public power movement. The result was legislation supported by the president and enacted by Congress in May 1933 creating the Tennessee Valley Authority. The TVA was authorized to complete the dam at Muscle Shoals and build others in the region, and to generate and sell electricity from them to the public at reasonable rates. It was also intended to be an agent for a comprehensive redevelopment of the entire region: for encouraging the growth of local industries, for supervising a substantial program of reforestation, and for helping farmers improve productivity.

Opposition by conservatives ultimately blocked many of the ambitious social planning projects proposed by the more visionary TVA administrators, but the Authority revitalized the region in numerous ways. It improved water transportation. It virtually eliminated flooding in the region. It provided electricity to thou-

Benefits of the TVA

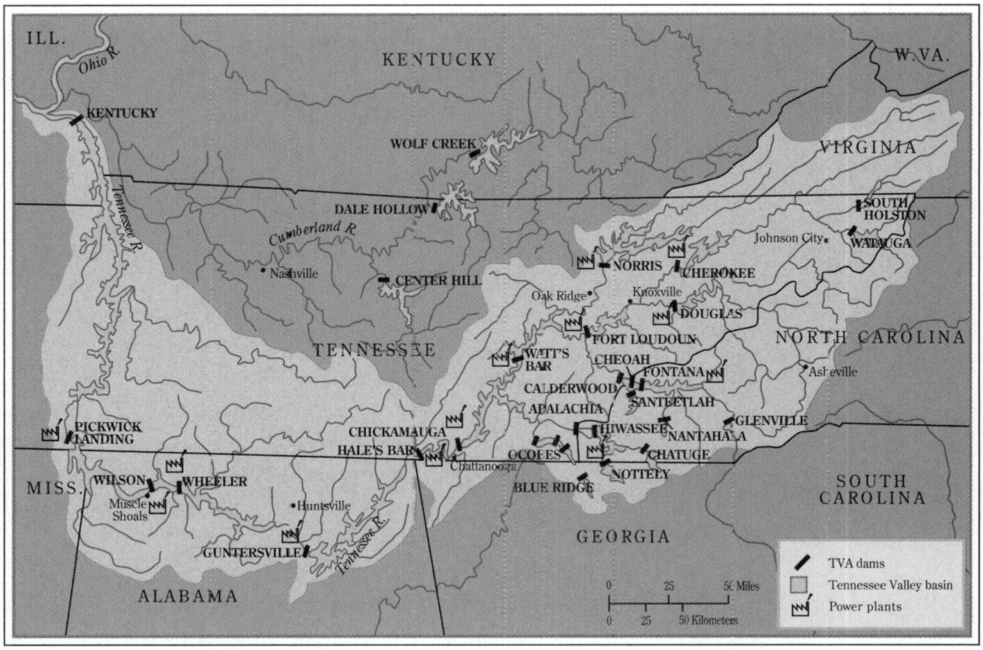

THE TENNESSEE VALLEY AUTHORITY The Tennessee Valley Authority was one of the largest experiments in government-funded public works and regional planning in American history to that point. The federal government had helped fund many projects in its history—canals, turnpikes, railroads, bridges, dams, and others. But never before had it undertaken a project of such great scope, and never before had it maintained such close control and ownership over the public works it helped create. This map illustrates the broad reach of the TVA within the Tennessee Valley region, which spanned seven states. TVA dams throughout the region helped control floods and also provided a source for hydroelectric power, which the government sold to consumers. Note the dam near Muscle Shoals, Alabama, in the bottom left of the map. It was begun during World War I, and efforts to revive it in the 1920s helped create the momentum that produced the TVA. ◆ *Why were progressives so eager to see the government enter the business of hydroelectric power in the 1920s?*

sands who had never before had it. Throughout the country, largely because of the "yardstick" provided by the TVA's cheap production of electricity, private power rates declined. Even so, the Tennessee Valley remained a generally impoverished region despite the TVA's efforts.

The Growth of Federal Relief

The Roosevelt administration did not consider relief to the unemployed its most important task, but it recognized the necessity of doing something to help impoverished Americans survive until the government could revive the economy to the point where relief might not be necessary. Among Roosevelt's first acts as president was the establishment of the Federal Emergency Relief Administration (FERA), which provided cash grants to states to prop up *FERA* bankrupt relief agencies. To administer the program, he chose the director of the New York State relief agency, Harry Hopkins. Both Hopkins and Roosevelt had misgivings about establishing a government "dole." They felt somewhat more comfortable with another form of government assistance: work relief. Thus when it became clear that the FERA grants were not enough, the administration established a second program: the Civil Works Administration (CWA). Between November 1933 and April 1934, it put more than 4 million people to work on temporary projects. Some of the projects were of lasting value, such as the construction of roads, schools, and parks; others were little more than make-work. To Hopkins, however, the important thing was pumping money into an economy badly in need of it and providing assistance to people with nowhere else to turn.

Civilian Conservation Corps

Roosevelt's favorite relief project was the Civilian Conservation Corps (CCC). The CCC created camps in national parks and forests and in other rural and wilderness settings. There young unemployed men from the cities worked in a semimilitary environment on such projects as planting trees, building reservoirs, developing parks, and improving agricultural irrigation.

Mortgage relief was a pressing need for millions of farm owners and homeowners. The Farm Credit Administration, which within two years refinanced one-fifth of all farm mortgages in the United States, was one response to that problem. The Frazier-Lemke Farm Bankruptcy Act of 1933 was another. It enabled some farmers to regain their land even after the foreclosure of their mortgages. Despite such efforts, however, 25 percent of all American farm owners had lost their land by 1934. Homeowners were similarly troubled, and in June 1933 the administration established the Home Owners' Loan Corporation, which by 1936 had refinanced the mortgages of more than 1 million householders. A year later, Congress established the Federal Housing Administration to insure mortgages for new construction and home repairs.

THE NEW DEAL IN TRANSITION

Seldom has an American president enjoyed such remarkable popularity as Franklin Roosevelt did during his first two years in office. But by early 1935, the New Deal found itself the target of fierce public criticism. In the spring of 1935, partly in response to these growing attacks, Roosevelt launched an ambitious new program of legislation that has often been called the "Second New Deal."

Critics of the New Deal

Some of the most strident attacks on the New Deal came from critics on the right. In August 1934, a group of the most fervent (and wealthiest) Roosevelt opponents, led by members of the Du Pont family, formed the

"AN ATTACK ON THE NEW DEAL" This cartoon by William Gropper appeared in *Vanity Fair* in 1935 to illustrate a long excerpt from an anti-New Deal editorial that had appeared a few weeks before in the Republican newspaper, the New York *Herald Tribune.* The cartoon echoes the newspaper's references to Jonathan Swift's famous satire, *Gulliver's Travels.* In this case, Gulliver is Uncle Sam, and the Lilliputians who tie him down with a thousand tiny cords are New Deal agencies and laws. "Here is a giant if there ever was one," the *Herald Tribune* wrote, "the most powerful nation the world has ever seen. It has the makings of good times, [but] it does not make them. Why? Because the Lilliputians of the New Deal will not let it. These busy little folk cannot bear the thought of letting the great giant, America, escape." *(Courtesy Vanity Fair © 1935 (renewed 1963, 1991) by The Condé Nast Publications, Inc.)*

American Liberty League Established

American Liberty League, designed specifically to arouse public opposition to the New Deal's "dictatorial" policies and its supposed attacks on free enterprise. But the new organization was never able to expand its constituency much beyond the northern industrialists who had founded it.

Roosevelt's critics on the far left also managed to produce alarm among some supporters of the administration, but like the conservatives, they proved to have only limited strength. The Communist Party, the Socialist Party, and other radical and semiradical organizations were at times harshly critical of the New Deal. But they too failed ever to attract genuine mass support.

More menacing to the New Deal than either the far right or the far left was a group of dissident political movements that defied easy ideological classification. Some gained substantial public support within particular states and regions. And three men succeeded in mobilizing genuinely national followings. Dr. Francis E. Townsend, an elderly California physician, rose from obscurity to lead a movement of more than 5 million members with his plan for federal pensions for the elderly. According to the Townsend Plan, all Americans over the age of sixty would receive monthly government pensions of $200, provided they retired (thus freeing jobs for younger, unemployed Americans) and spent the money in full each month (which would pump needed funds into the economy). By 1935, the Townsend Plan had attracted the support of many older men and women.

Dr. Francis Townsend

Father Charles E. Coughlin, a Catholic priest in the Detroit suburb of Royal Oak, Michigan, achieved even greater renown through his weekly sermons broadcast nationally over the radio. He proposed a series of monetary reforms—remonetization of silver, issuing of greenbacks, and nationalization of the banking system—that he insisted would restore prosperity and ensure economic justice. At first a warm supporter of Franklin Roosevelt, by late 1934 Coughlin had become disheartened by what he claimed was the president's failure to deal harshly enough with the "money powers." In the spring of 1935, he established his own political organization, the National Union for Social Justice.

Father Charles Coughlin

Most alarming of all to the administration was the growing national popularity of Senator Huey P. Long of Louisiana. Long had risen to power in his home state through his strident attacks on the banks, oil companies, and utilities and on the conservative political oligarchy allied with them. Elected governor in 1928, he launched an assault on his opponents so thorough and forceful that they were soon left with virtually no political power whatsoever. But he also maintained the overwhelming support of the Louisiana electorate, in part because of his flamboyant personality and in part because of his solid record of conventional progressive accomplishments: building roads, schools, and hospitals; revising the tax codes; distributing free textbooks; lowering utility rates. Barred by law from succeeding himself as governor, he ran in 1930 for a seat in the United States Senate and won easily.

Long, like Coughlin, supported Franklin Roosevelt for president in 1932. But within six months of Roosevelt's inauguration he had broken with the president. As an alternative to the New Deal, he advocated a drastic program of wealth redistribution, a program he ultimately named the Share-Our-Wealth Plan. The government, he claimed, could end the Depression easily by using the tax system to confiscate the surplus riches of the wealthiest men and women in America and distribute these surpluses to the rest of the population. That would, he claimed, allow the govern-

Long's Share-Our-Wealth Plan

ment to guarantee every family a minimum "homestead" of $5,000 and an annual wage of $2,500. In 1934, Long established his own national organization: the Share-Our-Wealth Society, which soon attracted a large following through much of the nation. A poll by the Democratic National Committee in the spring of 1935 disclosed that Long might attract more than 10 percent of the vote if he ran as a third-party candidate, possibly enough to tip a close election to the Republicans.

Members of the Roosevelt administration considered dissident movements—and the broad popular discontent they represented—a genuine threat to the president. An increasing number of advisers were warning Roosevelt that he would have to do something dramatic to counter their strength.

The "Second New Deal"

Roosevelt launched the so-called Second New Deal in the spring of 1935 in response both to the growing political pressures and to the continuing economic crisis. The new proposals represented, if not a new direction, at least a shift in the emphasis of New Deal policy. Perhaps the most conspicuous change was in the administration's attitude toward big business. Symbolically at least, the president was now willing to attack corporate interests openly. In March, for example, he proposed to Congress an act designed to break up the great utility holding companies. The Holding Company Act of 1935 was the result, although furious lobbying by the utilities led to amendments that sharply limited its effects.

Holding Company Act

Equally alarming to affluent Americans was a series of tax reforms proposed by the president in 1935. Apparently designed to undercut the appeal of Huey Long's Share-Our-Wealth Plan, the Roosevelt proposals called for establishing the highest and most progressive peacetime tax rates in history—although the actual impact of these rates was limited.

The Supreme Court decision in 1935 to strike down the National Industrial Recovery Act also invalidated Section 7(a) of the act, which had guaranteed workers the right to organize and bargain collectively. A group of progressives in Congress led by Senator Robert E. Wagner of New York introduced what became the National Labor Relations Act of 1935. The new law, popularly known as the Wagner Act, provided workers with a crucial enforcement mechanism missing from the 1933 law: the National Labor Relations Board (NLRB), which would have power to compel employers to recognize and bargain with legitimate unions. The president was not entirely happy with the bill, but he signed it anyway. That was in large part because American workers themselves had by 1935 become so important and vigorous a force that Roosevelt realized his own political future would depend in part on responding to their demands.

National Labor Relations Board

Labor Militancy

The emergence of a powerful trade union movement in the 1930s occurred partly in response to government efforts to enhance the power of unions, but it was also a result of the increased militancy of American workers and their leaders. During the 1920s, most workers had displayed relatively little militancy. In the 1930s, however, many of the factors that had impeded militancy vanished or grew weaker. Business leaders and industrialists lost (at least temporarily) the ability to control government policies. Equally important, new and more militant labor organizations emerged.

The American Federation of Labor remained committed to the idea of the craft union: organizing workers on the basis of their skills. But that concept had little to offer unskilled laborers, who now constituted the bulk of the industrial work force. During the 1930s, therefore, a newer concept of labor organization challenged the craft union ideal: industrial unionism. Advocates of this approach argued that all workers in a particular industry should be organized in a single union, regardless of what functions the workers performed. All autoworkers should be in a single automobile union; all steelworkers should be in a single steel union. United in this way, workers would greatly increase their power.

Leaders of the AFL craft unions for the most part opposed the new concept. But industrial unionism found a number of important advocates, most prominent among them John L. Lewis, the leader of the United Mine Workers. At first, Lewis and his allies attempted to work within the AFL, but friction between the new industrial organizations Lewis was promoting and the older craft unions grew rapidly. At the 1935 AFL convention, Lewis became embroiled in a series of angry confrontations with craft union leaders before finally walking out. A few weeks later, he created the Committee on Industrial Organization. When the AFL expelled the new committee and all the industrial unions it represented, Lewis renamed the committee the Congress of Industrial Organizations (CIO) and became its first president.

CIO Founded

The CIO expanded the constituency of the labor movement. It was more receptive to women and to blacks than the AFL had been, in part because CIO organizing drives targeted previously unorganized industries (textiles, laundries, tobacco factories, and others) where women and minorities constituted much of the work force. The CIO was also more militant than the AFL. By the time of the 1936 schism, it was already engaged in major organizing battles in the automobile and steel industries.

Organizing Battles

Out of several competing auto unions, the United Auto Workers (UAW) was gradually emerging preeminent in the early and mid-1930s. But although it was gaining recruits, it was making little progress in winning recognition from the corporations. In December 1936, however, autoworkers employed a controversial and effective new technique for challenging corporate opposition: the sit-down strike. Employees in several General Motors plants in Detroit simply sat down inside the plants, refusing either to work or to leave, thus preventing the company from using strikebreakers. The tactic spread to other locations, and by February 1937 strikers had occupied seventeen GM plants. The strikers ignored court orders and local police efforts to force them to vacate the buildings. When Michigan's governor refused to call up the National Guard to clear out the strikers, and when the federal government also refused to intervene on behalf of employers, General Motors relented. In February 1937 it became the first major manufacturer to recognize the UAW; other automobile companies soon did the same.

Sit-down Strike

In the steel industry, the battle for unionization was less easily won. In 1936, the Steel Workers' Organizing Committee (SWOC; later the United Steelworkers of America) began a major organizing drive involving thousands of workers and frequent, at times bitter, strikes. In March 1937, to the surprise of almost everyone, United States Steel, the giant of the industry, recognized the union rather than risk a costly strike. But the smaller companies (known collectively as "Little Steel") were less accommodating. On Memorial Day 1937, a group of striking workers from Republic Steel gathered with their families for a picnic and demonstration in South Chicago. When they attempted to march peacefully (and legally) toward the steel plant, police opened fire on them. Ten demonstrators were killed; another ninety were wounded. Despite a public outcry against the "Memorial Day Massacre," the harsh tactics of Little Steel companies succeeded. The 1937 strike failed.

"Memorial Day Massacre"

But the victory of Little Steel was one of the last gasps of the kind of brutal strikebreaking that had proved so effective in the past. In 1937 alone, there were 4,720 strikes—over 80 percent of them settled in favor of the unions. By the end of the year, more than 8 million workers were members of unions recognized as official bargaining units by employers (as compared with 3 million in 1932). By 1941, that number had expanded to 10 million and included the workers of Little Steel, whose employers had finally recognized the SWOC.

Rapid Union Growth

Social Security

From the first moments of the New Deal, important members of the administration had been lobbying for a system of federally sponsored social insurance for the elderly and the unemployed. In 1935, Roosevelt gave public support to what became the Social Security Act, which Congress passed the same year. It established several distinct programs. For the elderly, there were two types of assistance. Those who were presently destitute could receive up to $15 a month in federal assistance. More important for the future, many Americans presently working were incorporated into a pension system, to which they and their employers would contribute through a payroll tax; it would provide them with an income on retirement. Pension payments would not begin until 1942 and even then would provide only $10 to $85 a month to recipients. And broad categories of workers (including domestic servants and agricultural laborers) were excluded from the program. But the act was a crucial first step in building the nation's most important social program for the elderly.

In addition, the Social Security Act created a system of unemployment insurance, which employers alone would finance. It also established a system of federal aid to people with disabilities and a program of aid to dependent children.

The framers of the Social Security Act wanted to create a system of "insurance," not "welfare." And the largest programs (old-age pensions and unemployment insurance) were in many ways similar to private insurance programs. But the act also provided considerable direct assistance based on need—to the elderly poor, to those with disabilities, to dependent children and their mothers. These groups were widely perceived to be small and genuinely unable to support themselves. But in later generations the programs for these groups would expand until they assumed dimensions that the planners of Social Security had not foreseen.

Need-based Direct Assistance

New Directions in Relief

Social Security was designed primarily to fulfill long-range goals. But millions of unemployed Americans had immediate needs. To help them, the Roosevelt administration established in 1935 the Works Progress Administration (WPA). Like the Civil Works Administration and other earlier efforts, the WPA established a system of work relief for the unemployed. But it was much bigger than the earlier agencies.

Harry Hopkins

Under the direction of Harry Hopkins, the WPA was responsible for building or renovating 110,000 public buildings and for constructing almost 600 airports, more than 500,000 miles of roads, and over 100,000 bridges. In the process, the WPA kept an average of 2.1 million workers employed and pumped needed money into the economy.

The WPA also displayed remarkable flexibility and imagination. The Federal Writers Project of the WPA, for example, gave unemployed writers a chance to do their work and receive a government salary. The Federal Arts Project, similarly, helped painters, sculptors, and others to continue their careers. The Federal Music Project and the Federal Theater Project oversaw the production of concerts and plays, creating work for unemployed musicians, actors, and directors. Other relief agencies emerged alongside the WPA. The National Youth Administration (NYA) provided work and scholarship assistance to high-school and college-age men and women. The Emergency Housing Division of the Public Works Administration began federal sponsorship of public housing.

WPA MURAL ART The Federal Arts Project of the Works Progress Administration commissioned an impressive series of public murals from the artists it employed. Many of these murals adorned post offices, libraries, and other public buildings constructed by the WPA. William Gropper, the same artist who drew the cartoon on p. 685, painted *Construction of the Dam*, a detail of which is seen here, is typical of much of the mural art of the 1930s in its celebration of the workingman. Workers are depicted in heroic poses, laboring in unison to complete a great public project. *(Detail,* Construction of the Dam *by William Gropper (Mural Study, Department of the Interior), c. 1937. Oil on canvas, overall: 27¼ × 87¼ inches. Smithsonian American Art Museum, Washington, DC/Art Resource, NY)*

The new welfare system dealt with men and women in very different ways. For men, the government concentrated mainly on work relief—on such programs as the CCC, the CWA, and the WPA. The principal government aid to women was not work relief but cash assistance—most notably through the Aid to Dependent Children program of Social Security, which was designed largely to assist single mothers. This disparity in treatment reflected a widespread assumption that men should constitute the bulk of the paid work force. In fact, millions of women were already employed by the 1930s.

The 1936 "Referendum"

By the middle of 1936—with the economy visibly reviving—there could be little doubt that Roosevelt would win a second term. The Republican Party nominated the moderate governor of Kansas, Alf M. Landon, who waged a generally pallid cam-

paign. Roosevelt's dissident challengers now appeared powerless. One reason was the violent death of their most effective leader, Huey Long, who was assassinated in Louisiana in September 1935. Another reason was the ill-fated alliance among Father Coughlin, Dr. Townsend, and Gerald L. K. Smith (an intemperate henchman of Huey Long), who joined forces that summer to establish a new political movement—the Union Party, which nominated an undistinguished North Dakota congressman, William Lemke.

The result was the greatest landslide in American history to that point. Roosevelt polled just under 61 percent of the vote to Landon's 36 percent and carried every state except Maine and Vermont. The Democrats increased their already large majorities in both houses of Congress.

Electoral Realignment

The election results demonstrated the party realignment that the New Deal had produced. The Democrats now controlled a broad coalition of western and southern farmers, the urban working classes, the poor and unemployed, and the black communities of northern cities, as well as traditional progressives and committed new liberals—a coalition that constituted a substantial majority of the electorate. It would be decades before the Republican Party could again create a lasting majority coalition of its own.

THE NEW DEAL IN DISARRAY

Roosevelt emerged from the 1936 election at the zenith of his popularity. Within months, however, the New Deal was mired in serious new difficulties.

The Court Fight

The 1936 mandate, Franklin Roosevelt believed, made it possible for him to do something about the Supreme Court. No program of reform, he had become convinced, could long survive the conservative justices, who had already struck down the NRA and the AAA.

In February 1937, Roosevelt sent a surprise message to Capitol Hill proposing a general overhaul of the federal court system; included among the many provisions was one to add up to six new justices to the Supreme Court. The courts were "overworked," he claimed, and needed additional manpower and younger blood to enable them to cope with their increasing burdens. But Roosevelt's real purpose was to give himself the opportunity to appoint new, liberal justices and change the ideological balance of the Court.

Conservatives were outraged at the "Court-packing plan," and even

"Court-Packing Plan" Defeated

many Roosevelt supporters were disturbed by what they considered evidence of the president's hunger for power. Still, Roosevelt might well have persuaded Congress to approve at least a compromise measure had not the Supreme Court itself intervened. Of the nine justices, three reliably supported the New Deal, and four reliably opposed it. Of the remaining two, Chief Justice Charles Evans Hughes often sided with the progressives and Associate Justice Owen J. Roberts usually voted with the conservatives. On March 29, 1937, Roberts, Hughes, and the three progressive justices voted together to uphold a state minimum-wage law—in the case of *West Coast Hotel* v. *Parrish*—thus reversing a 5-to-4 decision of the previous year invalidating a similar law. Two weeks later, again by a 5-to-4 margin, the Court upheld the Wagner Act, and in May it validated the Social Security Act. Whatever the reasons for the decisions, the Court's newly moderate position made the Court-packing bill seem unnecessary. Congress ultimately defeated it.

On one level, Franklin Roosevelt had achieved a victory. The Court was no longer an obstacle to New Deal reforms. But the Court-packing episode did lasting political damage to the administration. From 1937 on, southern Democrats and other conservatives voted against Roosevelt's measures much more often than they had in the past.

Retrenchment and Recession

By the summer of 1937, the national income, which had dropped from $82 billion in 1929 to $40 billion in 1932, had risen to nearly $72 billion. Other economic indices showed similar advances. Roosevelt seized on these improvements as a justification for trying to balance the federal budget. Between January and August 1937, for example, he cut the WPA in half, laying off 1.5 million relief workers. A few weeks later, the fragile boom collapsed. The index of industrial production dropped from 117 in August 1937 to 76 in May 1938. Four million additional workers lost their jobs. Economic conditions were soon almost as bad as they had been in the bleak days of 1932–1933.

Sources of "Roosevelt Recession"

The recession of 1937, known to the president's critics as the "Roosevelt recession," was a result of many factors. But to many observers at the time (including, apparently, the president himself), it seemed to be a direct result of the administration's unwise decision to reduce spending. And so in April 1938, the president asked Congress for an emergency appropriation of $5 billion for public works and relief programs, and government funds soon began pouring into the economy once again. Within a few months, another tentative recovery seemed to be under way.

At about the same time, Roosevelt sent a stinging message to Congress, vehemently denouncing what he called an "unjustifiable concentration of economic power" and asking for the creation of a commission to examine that concentration with an eye to major reforms in the antitrust laws. In response, Congress established the Temporary National Economic Committee (TNEC), whose members included representatives of both houses of Congress and officials from several executive agencies. Later in 1938, the administration successfully supported one of its most ambitious pieces of labor legislation, the Fair Labor Standards Act, which for the first time established a national minimum wage and a forty-hour work week, and which also placed strict limits on child labor.

End of the New Deal

Despite these achievements, however, by the end of 1938 the New Deal had essentially come to an end. Congressional opposition now made it difficult for the president to enact any major new programs. But more important, perhaps, the threat of world crisis hung heavy in the political atmosphere, and Roosevelt was gradually growing more concerned with persuading a reluctant nation to prepare for war than with pursuing new avenues of reform.

LIMITS AND LEGACIES OF THE NEW DEAL

The New Deal made major changes in American government, some of them still controversial today. It also left important problems unaddressed.

African Americans and the New Deal

One group the New Deal did relatively little to assist was African Americans. The administration was not hostile to black aspirations. Eleanor Roosevelt spoke throughout the 1930s on behalf of racial justice and put continuing pressure on her husband and others in the federal government to ease discrimination against blacks. The president himself appointed a number of blacks to significant second-level positions in his administration, creating an informal network of officeholders that became known as

The "Black Cabinet"

the "Black Cabinet." Eleanor Roosevelt, Interior secretary Harold Ickes, and WPA director Harry Hopkins all made efforts to ensure that New Deal relief programs did not exclude blacks, and by 1935 an estimated 30 percent of all African Americans were receiving some form of government assistance. One result was a historic change in black electoral behavior. As late as 1932, most American blacks were voting Republican, as they had been doing since the Civil War. By 1936, more than 90 percent of them were voting Democratic.

Blacks supported Franklin Roosevelt, but they had few illusions that the New Deal represented a major turning point in American race relations. The president was, for example, never willing to risk losing the support of southern Democrats by supporting legislation to make lynching a federal crime or to ban the poll tax, one of the most potent tools by which white southerners kept blacks from voting.

Discrimination Reinforced

New Deal relief agencies did not challenge, and indeed reinforced, existing patterns of discrimination. The Civilian Conservation Corps established separate black

ELEANOR ROOSEVELT AND MARY MCLEOD BETHUNE Mrs. Roosevelt was a leading champion of racial equality within her husband's administration, and her commitment had an important impact on the behavior of the government even though she held no official post. She is seen here meeting in 1937 with Aubrey Williams, executive director of the National Youth Administration, and Mary McLeod Bethune, the agency's Director of Negro Affairs. *(UPI/Corbis-Bettmann)*

camps. The NRA codes tolerated paying blacks less than whites doing the same jobs. The WPA routinely relegated black and Hispanic workers to the least-skilled and lowest-paying jobs; when funding ebbed, African Americans, like women, were among the first to be dismissed.

The New Deal was not hostile to black Americans, and it made some contributions to their progress. But it refused to make the issue of race a significant part of its agenda.

The New Deal and the "Indian Problem"

New Deal policy toward the Indian tribes marked a significant break from the approach in the years before Roosevelt, largely because of the efforts of the extraordinary commissioner of Indian affairs in the 1930s, John Collier. Collier was greatly influenced by the work of twentieth-century anthropologists who advanced the idea of cultural relativism—the theory that every culture should be accepted and respected on its own terms.

Collier favored legislation that would, he hoped, reverse the pressures on Native Americans to assimilate and allow them to remain Indians. He effectively promoted legislation—which became the Indian Reorganization Act of 1934—to advance his goals. Among other things, it restored to the tribes the right to own land collectively and to elect tribal governments. In the thirteen years after passage of the 1934 bill, tribal land increased by nearly 4 million acres, and

Indian Reorganization Act

Debating the Past

THE NEW DEAL

Contemporaries of Franklin Roosevelt debated the impact of the New Deal with ferocious intensity: conservatives complaining of a menacing tyranny of the state, liberals celebrating the New Deal's progressive achievements, people on the left charging that the reforms of the 1930s were largely cosmetic and ignored the nation's fundamental problems. Although the conservative critique has found relatively little scholarly expression since Roosevelt's death, the liberal and left positions continued for many years to shape the way historians described the Roosevelt administration.

The dominant view from the beginning was an approving liberal interpretation, and its most important early voice was that of Arthur M. Schlesinger, Jr. He argued in the three volumes of *The Age of Roosevelt* (1957–1960) that the New Deal marked a continuation of the long struggle between public power and private interests, a struggle Roosevelt had moved to a new level. Workers, farmers, consumers and others now had much more protection than they had enjoyed in the past.

At almost the same time, however, other historians were offering more qualified assessments of the New Deal, although they remained securely within the liberal framework. Richard Hofstadter argued in 1955 that the New Deal gave American liberalism a "social-democratic tinge that had never before been present in American reform movements"; but that its highly pragmatic approach lacked a central, guiding philosophy. James MacGregor Burns argued in 1956 that Roosevelt failed to make full use of his potential as a leader and had accommodated himself unnecessarily to existing patterns of power.

William Leuchtenburg's *Franklin D. Roosevelt and the New Deal* (1963) was the first systematic "revisionist" interpretation. Leuchtenburg challenged the views of earlier scholars who had proclaimed the New Deal a "revolution" in social policy. Leuchtenburg could muster only enough enthusiasm to call it a "halfway revolution," one that helped some previously disadvantaged groups (most notably farmers and workers) but that did little or nothing for many others (blacks, sharecroppers, the urban poor).

Harsher criticisms soon emerged. Barton Bernstein in a 1968 essay concluded that the New Deal had saved capitalism, but at the expense of the least powerful. Ronald Radosh, Paul Conkin, and, more recently, Thomas Ferguson and Colin Gordon expanded on these criticisms; the New Deal, they contended, was part of the twentieth-century tradition of "corporate liberalism"—a tradition in which reform is closely wedded to the needs and interests of capitalism.

Most scholars in the 1980s and 1990s, however, seemed largely to have accepted the revised liberal view: that the New Deal was a significant (and most agree valuable) chapter in the history of reform, but one that worked within rigid, occasionally crippling limits. Much of the recent work on the New Deal, therefore, has focused on the constraints it faced. Some scholars (notably the sociologist Theda Skocpol) have emphasized the issue of "state capacity"—the absence of a government bureaucracy with sufficient strength and expertise to shape or administer many programs. James T. Patterson, Barry Karl, Mark Leff, and others have emphasized the political constraints the New Deal encountered—the conservative inhibitions about government that remained strong in Congress and among the public. Frank Freidel, Ellis Hawley, Herbert Stein, and many others point as well to the ideological constraints affecting Franklin Roosevelt and his supporters, the limits of their own understanding of their time. Alan Brinkley, in *The End of Reform* (1995), described an ideological shift within New Deal liberalism that marginalized older concerns about wealth and monopoly power.

The phrase "New Deal liberalism" has come in the postwar era to seem synonymous with modern ideas of aggressive federal management of the economy, elaborate welfare systems, a powerful bureaucracy, and large-scale government spending. But many historians of the New Deal would argue that the modern idea of New Deal liberalism bears only a limited relationship to the ideas that New Dealers themselves embraced.

(text continued from page 695)

Indian agricultural income increased dramatically (from under $2 million in 1934 to over $49 million in 1947). Even with the redistribution of lands under the 1934 act, however, Indians continued to possess, for the most part, only territory whites did not want—much of it arid, some of it desert. And as a group, they continued to constitute the poorest segment of the population.

Women and the New Deal

Symbolically, at least, the New Deal marked a breakthrough in the role of women in public life. Roosevelt appointed the first female member of the cabinet in the nation's history, Secretary of Labor Frances Perkins. He also named more than 100 other women to positions at lower levels of the federal bureaucracy. But the administration was concerned not so much about achieving gender equality as about obtaining special protections for women.

Frances Perkins

The New Deal generally supported the widespread belief that in hard times women should withdraw from the workplace to open up more jobs for men. Frances Perkins, for example, spoke out against what she called the "pin-money worker"—the married woman working to earn extra money for the household. New Deal relief agencies offered relatively little employment for women. The Social Security program excluded domestic servants, waitresses, and other predominantly female occupations.

As with African Americans, so also with women: The New Deal was not actively hostile to feminist aspirations, but it accepted prevailing cultural norms. There was not yet sufficient political pressure from women themselves to persuade the administration to do otherwise. Indeed, some of the most important supporters of policies that reinforced traditional gender roles (such as Social Security) were themselves women.

Prevailing Gender Norms Accepted

The New Deal and the West

One part of American society that did receive special attention from the New Deal was the American West. The West received more government funds per capita through relief programs than any other region.

The largest New Deal public works programs—the great dams and power stations—were mainly in the West, both because the best locations for such facilities were there and because the West had the most need for new sources of water and power. The Grand Coulee Dam on the Columbia River was the largest public works project in American history to that point, and it provided cheap electric power for much of the Northwest. Its construction, and the construction of other, smaller dams and water projects, created a basis for economic development in the region. Without this enormous public investment by the federal government, much of the economic growth that transformed the West after World War II would have been much more difficult, if not impossible, to achieve.

The New Deal, the Economy, and Politics

The most frequent criticisms of the New Deal involve its failure genuinely to revive or reform the American economy. New Dealers never fully recognized the value of government spending as a vehicle for recovery. The economic boom sparked by World War II, not the New Deal, finally ended the crisis. Nor did the New Deal substantially alter the distribution of power within American capitalism, and it had only a small impact on the distribution of wealth among the American people.

The New Deal's Economic Legacy

Nevertheless, the New Deal did have a number of important and lasting effects on both the behavior and the structure of the American economy. It helped elevate new groups—workers, farmers, and others—to positions from which they could at times effectively challenge the power of the corporations. It increased the regulatory functions of the federal government in ways that helped stabilize previously troubled areas of the economy: the stock market, the banking system, and others. And the administration helped establish the basis for new forms of federal fiscal policy, which in the postwar years would give the government tools for promoting and regulating economic growth.

American Welfare State Established

The New Deal also created the rudiments of the American welfare state, through its many relief programs and above all through the Social Security system. The conservative inhibitions New Dealers brought to this task ensured that the welfare system that ultimately emerged would be limited in its impact, would reinforce some traditional patterns of gender and racial discrimination, and would be expensive and cumbersome to administer. But for all its limits, the new system marked a historic break with the nation's traditional reluctance to offer any public assistance whatsoever to its neediest citizens.

Finally, the New Deal had a dramatic effect on the character of American politics. It took a weak and divided Democratic Party, which had been a minority force in American politics for many decades, and turned it into a mighty coalition that would dominate national party competition for more than thirty years. It turned the attention of many voters away from some of the cultural issues that had preoccupied them in the 1920s and awakened in them an interest in economic matters of direct importance to their lives.

CONCLUSION

From the time of Franklin Roosevelt's inauguration in 1933 to the beginning of World War II eight years later, the federal government engaged in a broad and diverse series of experiments designed to relieve the distress of unemployment and poverty; to reform the economy to prevent future crises; and to bring the Great Depression itself to an end. It had only partial success in all those efforts.

Unemployment and poverty remained high throughout the New Deal, although many federal programs provided assistance to millions of people who would otherwise have had none. The structure of the American economy remained essentially the same as it had been in earlier years, although there were by the end of the New Deal some important new regulatory agencies in Washington—and an important new role for organized labor. Nothing the New Deal did ended the Great Depression, but some of its policies kept it from getting worse—and some of them pointed the way toward more effective economic policies in the future.

Perhaps the most important legacy of the New Deal was to create a sense of possibilities among many Americans, to persuade them that the fortunes of individuals need not be left entirely to chance or to the workings of an unregulated market. Many Americans emerged from the 1930s convinced that individuals deserved some protections from the unpredictability and instability of the modern economy, and that the New Deal—for all its limitations—had demonstrated the value of enlisting government in the effort to provide those protections.

FOR FURTHER REFERENCE

William E. Leuchtenburg, *Franklin D. Roosevelt and the New Deal* (1963) is a classic short history of the New Deal. Anthony Badger, *The New Deal: The Depression Years* (1989) is another fine overview. David Kennedy, *Freedom from Fear: The American People in Depression and War, 1929–1945* (1999) is an important narrative history, a volume in the Oxford History of the United States. Geoffrey Ward, *Before the Trumpet: Young Franklin Roosevelt, 1882–1905* (1985) and *A First-Class Temperament: The Emergence of Franklin Roosevelt* (1989) are superb biographical accounts of the pre-presidential FDR. Frank Freidel, *Franklin D. Roosevelt: A Rendezvous with Destiny* (1990) is a one-volume biography by one of FDR's most important biographers. Blanche Wiesen Cook, *Eleanor Roosevelt 1884–1933* (1992) and *Eleanor Roosevelt, vol. 2, The Defining Years, 1933–1938* (1999) are the first two volumes of an important biography. Ellis Hawley, *The New Deal and the Problem of Monopoly* (1967) is a classic examination of the economic policies of the Roosevelt administration in its first five years. Colin Gordon, *New Deals: Business, Labor, and Politics in America, 1920–1935* (1994) is a challenging reinterpretation of the early New Deal years. The transformation of liberalism after 1937 is the subject of Alan Brinkley, *The End of Reform: New Deal Liberalism in Recession and War* (1995). G. Edward White, *The Constitution and the New Deal* (2000) examines the Roosevelt Administration's relationship with the judiciary. Linda Gordon, *Pitied but Not Entitled: Single Mothers and the History of Welfare* (1994) is a pioneering work on women as the recipients and also the authors of government welfare policies. The efforts of Chicago workers to protest and organize is the subject of Lizabeth Cohen, *Making a New Deal: Industrial Workers in Chicago, 1919–1939* (1990). Nelson Lichtenstein, *The Most Dangerous Man in Detroit: Walter Reuther and the Fate of American Labor* (1995) is a valuable study of one of the early leaders of the CIO. Richard Lowitt, *The New Deal and the West* (1984) pays particular attention to water policy and agriculture in the New Deal years. Jordan Schwarz, *The New Dealers: Power Politics in the Age of Roosevelt* (1993) examines the proponents of state-funded economic development of the South and West. Alan Brinkley, *Voices of Protest: Huey Long, Father Coughlin, and the Great Depression* (1982) examines some of the most powerful challenges to the New Deal. Bruce Shulman, *From Cotton Belt to Sunbelt* (1991) explores the New Deal's effort to transform the region Roosevelt and others considered the "nation's number one economic problem," the American South. Harvard Sitkoff, *A New Deal for Blacks* (1978) and Nancy J. Weiss, *Farewell to the Party of Lincoln: Black Politics in the Age of FDR* (1983) take contrasting positions on what the New Deal did for African Americans.

FDR (1994), a documentary by David Grubin, gives viewers a fine view of the private and public life of Franklin D. Roosevelt. One of the president's most vocal and powerful dissidents is featured in another film, by Ken Burns, *Huey Long* (1986). *The World of Tomorrow* (1984) is a provocative documentary on the 1939 World's Fair.

For quizzes, Internet resources, references to additional books and films, and more, consult this book's Online Learning Center site at www.mhhe.com/unfinishednation4.

"DEFENDING MADRID" The Spanish Civil War, in which fascist forces led by Francisco Franco overturned the existing republican government, was an early signal to many Americans of the dangers of fascism and the threat to democracy. This 1938 Spanish war poster contains the words "Defending Madrid is Defending Catalonia," an effort by the government in Madrid to enlist the support of the surrounding regions in the defense of the capital against the fascists. *(Hulton/Archives/Getty Images)*

TIME LINE

	1924	1928	1931	1933	1937	
	Dawes Plan	Kellogg-Briand Pact	Japan invades Manchuria	U.S. recognizes Soviet Union	Roosevelt's "quarantine" speech	
				Good Neighbor Policy		

CHAPTER TWENTY-SEVEN

THE GLOBAL CRISIS, 1921–1941

The Diplomacy of the New Era
Isolationism and Internationalism
From Neutrality to Intervention

Henry Cabot Lodge of Massachusetts, Republican chairman of the Senate Foreign Relations Committee, led the fight that defeated ratification of the Treaty of Versailles in 1919 and 1920. As a result, the United States declined to join the League of Nations; and American foreign policy embarked on an independent course that for the next two decades would attempt, but ultimately fail, to expand American influence and maintain international stability without committing the United States to any lasting relationships with other nations.

Lodge was not an isolationist. He believed the United States should exert its influence internationally. But he believed, too, that the United States should remain unfettered with obligations to anyone else. He said in 1919:

> **We are a great moral asset of Christian civilization. . . . How did we get there? By our own efforts. Nobody led us, nobody guided us, nobody controlled us. . . . I would keep America as she has been—not isolated, not prevent her from joining other nations for . . . great purposes—but I wish her to be master of her own fate.**

In the end, the limited American internationalism of the interwar years proved insufficient to protect the interests of the United States, to create global stability, or to keep the nation from becoming involved in the most catastrophic war in human history.

1938	1939	1940	1941
Munich Conference	Nazi-Soviet nonaggression pact	Tripartite Pact	Lend-lease plan
	World War II begins	America First Committee founded	Atlantic Charter
		Roosevelt reelected	Japan attacks Pearl Harbor
		Destroyers-for-bases deal	U.S. enters World War II

THE DIPLOMACY OF THE NEW ERA

Critics of American foreign policy in the 1920s often described it with a single word: isolationism. But in reality, the United States played a more active role in world affairs in the 1920s than it had at almost any previous time in its history.

Replacing the League

By the time the Harding administration took office in 1921, American membership in the League of Nations was no longer a realistic possibility. But Secretary of State Charles Evans Hughes wanted to find something with which to replace the League as a guarantor of world peace and stability.

Charles Evans Hughes

The most important of such efforts was the Washington Conference of 1921—an attempt to prevent a destabilizing naval armaments race among the United States, Britain, and Japan. Hughes proposed a plan for dramatic reductions in the fleets of all three nations and a ten-year moratorium on the construction of large warships. To the surprise of almost everyone, the conference ultimately agreed to accept most of Hughes's terms. The Five-Power Pact of February 1922 established limits for total naval tonnage and a ratio of armaments among the signatories. For every 5 tons of American and British warships, Japan would maintain 3 and France and Italy 1.75 each.

When the French foreign minister, Aristide Briand, asked the United States in 1927 to join an alliance against Germany, Secretary of State Frank Kellogg (who had replaced Hughes in 1925) proposed instead a multilateral treaty outlawing war as an instrument of national policy. Fourteen nations signed the agreement in Paris on August 27, 1928, amid wide international acclaim. Forty-eight other nations later joined the Kellogg-Briand Pact. It contained no instruments of enforcement.

Kellogg-Briand Pact

Debts and Diplomacy

The first responsibility of diplomacy, Hughes, Kellogg, and others agreed, was to ensure that American overseas trade faced no obstacles. New financial arrangements to deal with international debts were central to that goal. The Allied powers of Europe were struggling to repay $11 billion in loans they had contracted with the United States during and shortly after the war. At the same time, Germany was attempting to pay the reparations levied by the Allies. The United States stepped in with a solution.

The Dawes Plan

Charles G. Dawes, an American banker, negotiated an agreement in 1924 among France, Britain, Germany, and the United States under which American banks would provide enormous loans to the Germans, enabling them to meet

A FORD PLANT IN RUSSIA The success of Henry Ford in creating affordable, mass-produced automobiles made him famous around the world, and particularly popular in the Soviet Union in the 1920s and early 1930s, as the communist regime strove to push the nation into the industrial future. Russians called the system of large-scale factory production "Fordism," and they welcomed assistance from the Ford Motor Company itself, which sent engineers and workers over to Russia to help build large automobile plants such as this one. *(UPI/Corbis-Bettmann)*

their reparations payments; in return, Britain and France would agree to reduce the amount of those payments. Under the Dawes Plan, the United States would lend money to Germany, which would use that money to pay reparations to France and England, which would in turn use those funds (as well as large loans they themselves were receiving from American banks) to repay war debts to the United States. The flow was able to continue only by virtue of the enormous debts Germany and the other European nations were acquiring to American banks and corporations. The American economic involvement in Europe continued to expand until the worldwide depression shattered the system in 1931.

Economic Expansion in Latin America

The government assisted American economic expansion in Latin America even more aggressively. During the 1920s, American military forces maintained a presence in Nicaragua, Panama, and several other countries in the region, while United States investments in Latin America more than doubled. American banks were offering large loans to Latin American governments, just as they were in Europe; and just as in Europe, the Latin Americans were having difficulty earning the money to repay them in the face of the formidable United States tariff barrier.

Hoover and the World Crisis

By 1931, the world financial crisis that had begun in 1929 had produced a rising nationalism in Europe. It soon toppled some existing political leaders and replaced them with powerful, belligerent governments committed to expansion. An expansionist government in Japan created similar problems in Asia. Herbert Hoover confronted the beginning of a process that would ultimately lead to war.

In Latin America, Hoover tried to repair some of the damage earlier American policies had created. He made a ten-week good-will tour through the region before his inauguration. Once in office, he generally abstained from intervening in the internal affairs of neighboring nations and moved to withdraw American troops from Nicaragua and Haiti. He also announced a new policy: America would grant diplomatic recognition to any sitting government in the region without questioning the means it had used to obtain power. He even repudiated the Roosevelt Corollary to the Monroe Doctrine by refusing to permit American intervention when several Latin American countries defaulted on debt obligations to the United States in October 1931.

Roosevelt Corollary Repudiated

In Europe, the administration enjoyed few successes. When Hoover's proposed moratorium on debts failed to attract broad support or produce financial stability, he refused to cancel all war debts to the United States as many economists advised him to do. Several European nations promptly went into default. Efforts to extend the 1921 limits on naval construction fell victim to French and British fears of German and Japanese militarism.

The ineffectiveness of American diplomacy in Europe was particularly troubling in light of the new governments on the Continent. Benito Mussolini's Fascist Party had been in control of Italy since the early 1920s and had become increasingly nationalistic and militaristic. Still more ominous was the growing power of the National Socialist (or Nazi) Party in Germany. By the late 1920s, the Weimar Republic, the nation's government since the end of World War I, had been largely discredited by, among other things, a ruinous inflation. Adolf Hitler, the leader of the Nazis, was growing rapidly in popular favor and would take power in 1933. Hitler believed in the genetic superiority of the Aryan (German) people and in extending German territory to provide *Lebensraum* (living space) for the German "master race." He also displayed a pathological anti-Semitism and a passionate militarism.

More immediately alarming to the Hoover administration was a major crisis in Asia—another early step toward World War II. The Japanese, suffering from an economic depression of their own, were concerned about the increasing power of the Soviet Union and about the insistence of the Chinese leader Chiang Kai-Shek on expanding his government's power in Manchuria, officially a part of China but over which the Japanese had maintained informal economic control since 1905. In 1931, Japan's military leaders staged what was, in effect, a coup in Tokyo. Weeks later, they launched an invasion of northern Manchuria. They had conquered the region by the end of the year. Hoover permitted Secretary of State Henry Stimson to issue stern warnings to the Japanese but barred him from cooperating

Manchuria Invaded

HITLER AND MUSSOLINI The German and Italian dictators, shown here reviewing troops together in Berlin in the mid-1930s, acted publicly as if they were equals. Privately, however, Hitler viewed Mussolini with contempt, and the Italian dictator complained frequently of being treated as a junior partner by his ally. *(Culver Pictures, Inc.)*

with the League of Nations to impose economic sanctions against them. Early in 1932, Japan moved further into China, attacking the city of Shanghai and killing thousands of civilians.

ISOLATIONISM AND INTERNATIONALISM

The administration of Franklin Roosevelt faced a dual challenge as it entered office in 1933. It had to deal with the worst economic crisis in the nation's history, and it had to deal as well with the effects of a decaying international structure.

Depression Diplomacy

Perhaps Roosevelt's sharpest break with the policies of his predecessor was on the question of American economic relations with Europe. Hoover had argued that only by resolving the question of war debts and reinforcing the gold standard could the American economy hope to recover. He had, therefore, agreed to participate in the World Economic Conference, to be held in London in June 1933, to attempt to resolve these issues. By the time the conference assembled, however, Roosevelt had already become convinced that the gold value of the dollar had to be allowed to fall in order for American goods to be able to compete in world markets. Shortly after the conference convened, he released what became known as the "bombshell message," repudiating the orthodox views of most of the delegates and rejecting any agreement on currency stabilization. The conference quickly dissolved.

FDR's "Bombshell Message"

At the same time, Roosevelt abandoned the commitments of the Hoover administration to settle the issue of war debts through international agreement. In April 1934 he signed a bill that prohibited American banks from making loans to any nation in default on its debts. The legislation ended the old, circular system by which debt payments continued only by virtue of increasing American loans; within months, war-debt payments from every nation except Finland stopped for good.

Sixteen years after the Bolshevik Revolution of 1917, the American government still had not officially recognized the government of the Soviet Union. But a growing number of influential Americans were urging a change in policy—largely because the Soviet Union appeared to be a possible source of trade. The Russians, for their part, were hoping for American cooperation in containing Japan. In November 1933, the United States and the Soviet Union agreed to open formal diplomatic relations. Relations with the Soviet Union, however, soon soured once again. American trade failed to establish a foothold in Russia, disappointing hopes in the United States; and the American government did little to reassure the Soviets that it was interested in stopping Japanese expansion in Asia, dousing expectations in Russia. By the end of 1934, the Soviet Union and the United States were once again viewing each other with considerable mistrust.

Soviet Union Recognized

The Roosevelt administration was also taking a new approach toward Latin America, an approach which became known as the "Good Neighbor Policy" and which expanded on the changes the Hoover administration had made. At an Inter-American Conference in Montevideo, Uruguay, in December 1933, Secretary of State Cordell Hull signed a formal convention declaring: "No state has the right to intervene in the internal or external affairs of another."

"Good Neighbor Policy"

The Rise of Isolationism

With the international system of the 1920s now beyond repair, the United States faced a choice between more active efforts to stabilize the world and more energetic attempts to isolate itself from it. Most Americans unhesitatingly chose the latter. Support for isolationism emerged from many quarters. Some Wilsonian

Sources of Isolationism

internationalists had grown disillusioned with the League of Nations and its inability to stop Japanese aggression in Asia. Other Americans were listening to the argument that powerful business interests—Wall Street, munitions makers, and others—had tricked the United States into participating in World War I. An investigation by a Senate committee chaired by Senator Gerald Nye of North Dakota claimed to have produced evidence of exorbitant profiteering and tax evasion by many corporations during the war, and it suggested that bankers had pressured Wilson to intervene in the war so as to protect their loans abroad. (Few historians now lend much credence to these charges.)

Roosevelt continued to hope for at least a modest American role in maintaining world peace. In 1935, he proposed to the Senate a treaty to make the United States a member of the World Court—a largely symbolic gesture. Isolationists such as Father Coughlin and William Randolph Hearst aroused popular opposition to the agreement, and the Senate voted it down.

In the summer of 1935, Mussolini's Italy was preparing to invade Ethiopia. Fearing the invasion would provoke a new European war, American legislators began to design legal safeguards to prevent the United States from being dragged into the conflict. The result was the Neutrality Act of 1935. It established a mandatory arms embargo against both sides in any military conflict and directed the president to warn American citizens against traveling on the ships of warring nations. Thus, isolationists believed, the "protection of neutral rights" could not again become an excuse for American intervention in war. A 1937 law established the so-called cash-and-carry policy, by which warring nations could purchase only nonmilitary goods from the United States and could do so only by paying cash and shipping their purchases themselves.

Neutrality Acts

Isolationist sentiment showed its strength again in 1936–1937 in response to the civil war in Spain. The Falangists of General Francisco Franco, a group much like the Italian fascists, revolted in July 1936 against the existing republican government. Hitler and Mussolini supported Franco, both vocally and with weapons and supplies. Some individual Americans traveled to Spain to assist the republican cause, but the United States government joined with Britain and France in an agreement to offer no assistance to either side.

In the summer of 1937, Japan intensified its six-year-old assault on Manchuria and attacked China's five northern provinces. Roosevelt responded in a speech in Chicago in October 1937. He warned of the dangers of the Japanese actions and argued that aggressors should be "quarantined" by the international community to prevent the contagion of war from spreading. He was deliberately vague about what such a "quarantine" would mean. Even so, public response to the speech was hostile, and Roosevelt drew back. On December 12, 1937, Japanese aviators bombed and sank the United States

"Quarantine" Speech

THE SINO-JAPANESE WAR, 1931–1941

Long before Pearl Harbor, well before war broke out in Europe in 1939, the first shots of what would become World War II had been fired in the Pacific in a conflict between Japan and China.

Having lived in almost complete isolation from the world until the nineteenth century, Japan had emerged from World War I as one of the world's great powers, with a proud and powerful military and growing global trade. But the Great Depression created severe economic problems for the Japanese; and as in other parts of the world, the crisis strengthened the political influence of highly nationalistic armed forces. Out of the military emerged dreams of a new Japanese empire in the Pacific. Such an empire would, its proponents believed, give the nation access to fuel, raw material, and markets for its industries, and land for its agricultural needs and its rapidly increasing population. Such an empire, they also argued, would free Asia from its exploitation by Europe and America and would create a "new world order based on moral principles."

During World War I, Japan had taken territory and economic concessions in China, and had created a particularly strong presence in the northern Chinese region of Manchuria. There, in September 1931, a group of militant young army officers seized on a railway explosion to justify a military campaign through which they conquered the entire province. Both the United States government and the League of Nations demanded that Japan evacuate Manchuria. The Japanese ignored them, and for the next six years consolidated their control over their new territory.

On July 7, 1937, Japan began a wider war when it attacked Chinese troops at the Marco Polo Bridge outside Beijing. Over the next few weeks, Japanese forces overran a large part of southern China, including most of the port cities, killing many Chinese solders and civilians in the process. Particularly notorious was the Japanese annihilation of many thousands of civilians in the city of Nanjing (the number has long been in dispute, but estimates range from 80,000 to over 300,000) in an event that became known in China and the West as the Nanjing Massacre. The Chinese government fled to the mountains. As in 1931, the United States and the League of Nations protested in vain.

The China that the Japanese had invaded was a nation in turmoil. It was engaged in a civil war of its own—between the so-called Kuomintang, a Nationalist party led by Chiang Kai-Shek, and the Chinese Communist Party, led by Mao Zedong; and this internal struggle weakened China's capacity to resist. But beginning in 1937, the two rivals agreed to an uneasy truce and began fighting the Japanese together, with some success—bogging the Japanese military down in a seemingly endless war and imposing great hardships on the Japanese people at home. The Japanese government and military, however, remained determined to continue the war against China, whatever the sacrifices.

One result of the costs of the war in China was a growing Japanese dependence on the United States for steel and oil to meet civilian and military needs. In July 1941, in an effort to pressure the Japanese to stop their expansion, the Roosevelt administration made it impossible for the Japanese to continue buying American oil. Japan now faced a choice between ending its war in China or finding other sources of fuel to keep its war effort (and its civilian economy) going.

They chose to extend the war beyond China in a search for oil. The best available sources were in the Dutch East Indies; but the only way to secure that European colony, they believed, would be to neutralize the increasingly hostile United States in Asia. Visionary military planners in Japan began advocating a daring move to immobilize the Americans in the Pacific before expanding the war elsewhere—with an attack on the American naval base at Pearl Harbor. The first blow of World War II in America, therefore, was the culmination of more than a decade of Japanese efforts to conquer China.

(text continued from page 709)

gunboat *Panay*, almost certainly deliberately, as it sailed the Yangtze River in China. But so reluctant was the Roosevelt administration to antagonize the isolationists that the United States eagerly seized on Japanese claims that the bombing had been an accident, accepted Japan's apologies, and overlooked the attack.

The Failure of Munich

In 1936, Hitler had moved the revived German army into the Rhineland, rearming an area that had been off-limits to German troops since World War I. In March 1938, German forces marched without opposition into Austria, and Hitler proclaimed a union (or *Anschluss*) between Austria, his native land, and Germany, his adopted one. Neither in America nor in most of Europe was there much more than a murmur of opposition.

The Austrian invasion, however, soon created another crisis. Germany had by now occupied territory surrounding three sides of western Czechoslovakia, a region Hitler dreamed of annexing. In September 1938, he demanded that Czechoslovakia cede him the Sudetenland, an area in which many ethnic Germans lived. Although Czechoslovakia was prepared to fight to stop Hitler, it needed assistance from other nations. But most Western governments, including the United States, were willing to pay almost any price to settle the crisis peacefully. On September 29, Hitler met with the leaders of France and Great Britain at Munich in an effort to resolve the crisis. The French and British agreed to accept the German demands in Czechoslovakia in return for Hitler's promise to expand no farther.

"Appeasement"

The Munich agreement, which Roosevelt applauded at the time, was the most prominent element of a policy that came to be known as "appeasement" and that came to be identified (not altogether fairly) largely with British Prime Minister Neville Chamberlain. Whoever was to blame, the policy was a failure. In March 1939, Hitler occupied the remaining areas of Czechoslovakia, violating the Munich agreement unashamedly. And in April, he began issuing threats against Poland.

THE BLITZ, LONDON The German Luftwaffe terrorized London and other British cities in 1940–1941 and again late in the war by bombing civilian areas indiscriminately in an effort to break the spirit of the English people. The effort failed, and the fortitude of the British did much to arouse support for their cause in the United States. *(Brown Brothers)*

At that point, both Britain and France assured the Polish government that they would come to its assistance in case of an invasion; they even tried, too late, to draw the Soviet Union into a mutual defense agreement. But Stalin, who had not even been invited to the Munich Conference, had decided he could expect no protection from the West. He signed a nonaggression pact with Hitler in August 1939, freeing the Germans for the moment from the danger of a two-front war. Shortly after that, Hitler staged an incident on the Polish border to allow him to claim that Germany had been attacked, and on September 1, 1939, he launched a full-scale invasion of Poland. Britain and France, true to their pledges, declared war on Germany two days later. World War II had begun.

FROM NEUTRALITY TO INTERVENTION

"This nation will remain a neutral nation," the president declared shortly after the hostilities began in Europe, "but I cannot ask that every American remain neutral in thought as well." There was never any question that both he and the majority of the American people favored Britain, France, and the other Allied nations in the contest. The question was how much the United States was prepared to do to assist them.

Neutrality Tested

At the very least, Roosevelt believed, the United States should make armaments available to the Allied armies to help them counter the military advantage the large German munitions industry gave Hitler. In September 1939, he asked Congress to revise the Neutrality Acts and lift the arms embargo against any nation engaged in war. Congress maintained the prohibition on American ships entering war zones. But the 1939 law did permit belligerents to purchase arms on the same cash-and-carry basis that the earlier Neutrality Acts had established for the sale of nonmilitary materials.

Cash-and-Carry

After the German armies quickly subdued Poland, the war in Europe settled into a long, quiet lull that lasted through the winter and spring—a "phony war," some called it. But in the spring of 1940, Germany launched a massive invasion known as the "blitzkrieg," to the west—first attacking Denmark and Norway, sweeping next across the Netherlands and Belgium, and driving finally deep into the heart of France. On June 10, Mussolini invaded France from the south as Hitler was attacking from the north. On June 22, finally, France fell, and Nazi troops marched into Paris. A new French regime assembled in Vichy, largely controlled by the German occupiers; and in all Europe, only the shattered remnants of the British and French armies, rescued from the beaches of Dunkirk, remained to oppose the Axis forces.

Fall of France

On May 16, in the midst of the offensive, Roosevelt asked Congress for an additional $1 billion for defense and received it quickly. That was one day after Winston Churchill, the new British prime minister, had sent Roosevelt the first of many long lists of requests for armaments, without which, he insisted, England could not long survive. Some Americans (including the United States ambassador to London, Joseph P. Kennedy) argued that the British plight was already hopeless, that any aid to the English was a wasted effort. But the president was determined to make war materials available to Britain. He even circumvented the cash-and-carry provisions of the Neutrality Acts by giving England fifty American destroyers (most of them left over from World War I) in return for the right to build American bases on British territory in the Caribbean and he returned to the factories a number of new airplanes purchased by the American military so that the British could buy them instead.

Roosevelt was able to take such steps in part because of a major shift in American public opinion. By July 1940, more than 66 percent of the public (according to opinion polls) believed that Germany posed a direct threat to the United States. Congress was, therefore, more willing to permit expanded American assistance to the Allies. Congress was also becoming more concerned about the need for internal preparations for war, and in September it

Burke-Wadsworth Act

approved the Burke-Wadsworth Act, inaugurating the first peacetime military draft in American history.

But a powerful new isolationist lobby—the America First Committee, whose members included such prominent Americans as Charles Lindbergh and Senators Gerald Nye and Burton Wheeler—joined the debate over American policy toward the war. The lobby had at least the indirect support of a large proportion of the Republican Party. Through the summer and fall of 1940, the debate was complicated by a presidential campaign.

The Campaign of 1940

The biggest political question of 1940 was whether Franklin Roosevelt would break with tradition and run for an unprecedented third term. The president himself did not reveal his own wishes. But by refusing to withdraw from the contest, he made it impossible for any rival Democrat to establish a claim to the nomination. And when, just before the Democratic Convention in July, he let it be known that he would accept a "draft" from his party, the issue was virtually settled. The Democrats quickly renominated him and even reluctantly swallowed his choice for vice president: Agriculture secretary Henry A. Wallace, a man too liberal and too controversial for the taste of many party leaders.

The Republicans nominated for president a politically inexperienced Indiana businessman, Wendell Willkie, who benefited from a powerful grassroots movement. Both the candidate and the party platform took positions little different from Roosevelt's: they would keep the country out of war but would extend generous assistance to the Allies. But Willkie was an appealing figure and a vigorous campaigner, and he managed to evoke more public enthusiasm than any Republican candidate in decades. But Roosevelt still won decisively. He received 55 percent of the popular vote to Willkie's 45 percent, and he won 449 electoral votes to Willkie's 82.

FDR Reelected

Neutrality Abandoned

In the last months of 1940, Roosevelt began to make subtle but profound changes in the American role in the war. Great Britain was virtually bankrupt and could no longer meet the cash-and-carry requirements imposed by the Neutrality Acts. The president, therefore, proposed a new system for supplying Britain: "lend-lease." It would allow the government not only to sell but also to lend or lease armaments to any nation deemed "pivotal to the defense of the United States." In other words, America could funnel weapons to England on the basis of no more than Britain's promise to return them when the war was over. Congress enacted the bill by wide margins.

"Lend-lease"

Attacks by German submarines had made shipping lanes in the Atlantic extremely dangerous. The British navy was losing ships more rapidly than it could replace them and was finding it difficult to transport materials across the Atlantic from America. Roosevelt argued that the western Atlantic was a neutral zone and the responsibility of the American nations. By July 1941, therefore, American ships were patrolling the ocean as far east as Iceland.

At first Germany did little to challenge these obviously hostile American actions. By September 1941, however, the situation had changed. Nazi forces had invaded the Soviet Union in June of that year. When the Soviets did not surrender, as many had predicted they would, Roosevelt persuaded Congress to extend lend-lease privileges to them. Now American industry was providing vital assistance to Hitler's foes on two fronts, and the American navy was protecting the flow of those goods to Europe. In September, Nazi submarines began a concerted campaign against American vessels. Roosevelt ordered American ships to fire on German submarines "on sight." In October, Nazi submarines hit two American destroyers and sank one of them, the *Reuben James*, killing many American sailors. Congress now voted to allow the United States to arm its merchant vessels and to sail all the way into belligerent ports. The United States had, in effect, launched a naval war against Germany.

In August 1941, Roosevelt met with Churchill aboard a British vessel off the coast of Newfoundland. The president made no military commitments, but he did join with the prime minister in releasing a document that became known as the Atlantic Charter, in which the two nations set out "certain common principles" on which to base "a better future for the world." It called openly for "the final destruction of the Nazi tyranny" and for a new world order in which every nation controlled its own destiny. It was, in effect, a statement of war aims.

The Atlantic Charter

The Road to Pearl Harbor

Japan, in the meantime, extended its empire in the Pacific. In September 1940, the Japanese signed the Tripartite Pact, a loose defensive alliance with Germany and Italy (although in reality, the European Axis powers never developed a very strong relationship with Japan). In July 1941, Japanese troops moved into Indochina and seized the capital of Vietnam, a colony of France. The United States, having broken Japanese codes, knew Japan's next target was to be the oil-rich Dutch East Indies; and when Tokyo failed to respond to Roosevelt's stern warnings, the president froze all Japanese assets in the United States, severely limiting Japan's ability to purchase needed American supplies.

Japanese Assets Frozen

Tokyo now faced a choice. Either it would have to repair relations with the United States to restore the flow of supplies or it would have to find those supplies elsewhere, most notably by seizing British and Dutch possessions in the Pacific. In October, militants in Tokyo forced the moderate

PEARL HARBOR, DECEMBER 7, 1941 The destroyer U.S.S. *Shaw*, immobilized in a floating drydock in Pearl Harbor in December 1941, survived the first wave of Japanese bombers unscathed. But in the second attack, the Japanese scored a direct hit and produced this spectacular explosion, which blew off the ship's bow. Damage to the rest of the ship, however, was slight. Just a few months later the *Shaw* was fitted with a new bow and rejoined the fleet. *(U.S. Navy Photo)*

prime minister out of office and replaced him with the leader of the war party, General Hideki Tojo.

By late November, the State Department had given up on the possibility of a peaceful settlement. American intelligence, meanwhile, had decoded Japanese messages that made clear a Japanese attack was imminent. But Washington did not know where the attack would take place. Most officials continued to believe that the Japanese would move first not against American territory but against British or Dutch possessions to their south. A combination of confusion and miscalculation caused the government to overlook indications that Japan intended a direct attack on American forces.

Pearl Harbor Attacked

At 7:55 A.M. on Sunday, December 7, 1941, a wave of Japanese bombers attacked the United States naval base at Pearl Harbor in Hawaii. A second wave came an hour later. Within two hours, the United States lost 8 battleships, 3 cruisers, 4 other vessels, 188 airplanes, and several vital shore installations. More than 2,400 soldiers and sailors died, and another 1,000 were injured. The Japanese suffered only light losses.

American forces were now greatly diminished in the Pacific (although by a fortunate accident, no American aircraft carriers—the heart of the

Pacific fleet—had been at Pearl Harbor on December 7). Nevertheless, the raid on Hawaii unified the American people behind war. On December 8, after a stirring speech by the president, the Senate voted unanimously and the House voted 388 to 1 to approve a declaration of war against Japan. Three days later, Germany and Italy, Japan's European allies, declared war on the United States; on the same day, December 11, Congress reciprocated without a dissenting vote.

CONCLUSION

American foreign policy in the years after World War I attempted something that ultimately proved impossible. The United States was determined to be a major power in the world, to extend its trade broadly around the globe, and to influence other nations in ways Americans believed would be beneficial to their own, and the world's, interests. But the United States was also determined to do nothing that would limit its own freedom of action. It would not join the League of Nations. It would not join the World Court. It would not form alliances with other nations. It would operate powerfully—and alone.

But ominous forces were at work in the world that would gradually push the United States into greater engagement with other nations. The economic disarray that the Great Depression created all around the globe, the rise of totalitarian regimes, the expansionist ambitions of powerful new leaders: all worked to destroy the uneasy stability of the post–World War I international system. America's own interests, economic and otherwise, were now imperiled. And America's go-it-alone foreign policy seemed powerless to change the course of events.

Franklin Roosevelt tried throughout the later years of the 1930s to push the American people slowly into a greater involvement in international affairs. In particular, he tried to nudge the United States toward taking a more forceful stand against dictatorship and aggression. A powerful isolationist movement helped stymie him for a time, even after war broke out in Europe. Gradually, however, public opinion shifted toward support of the Allies (Britain, France, and the Soviet Union) and against the Axis (Germany, Italy, and Japan). The nation began to mobilize for war, to supply ships and munitions to Britain, even to engage in naval combat with German forces in the Atlantic. Finally, on December 7, 1941, the surprise Japanese attack on the American base at Pearl Harbor in Hawaii eliminated the last elements of uncertainty and drove the United States—now united behind the war effort—into the greatest and most terrible conflict in human history.

FOR FURTHER REFERENCE

Robert Dallek, *Franklin D. Roosevelt and American Foreign Policy, 1932–1945* (1979) is a comprehensive study of Roosevelt's foreign policy. Akira Iriye, *The Cambridge History of American Foreign Relations, vol. 3: The Globalizing of America, 1913–1945* (1993) is another important study. In *Inevitable Revolutions* (1983), Walter LaFeber recounts America's attempts to halt revolutionary movements throughout the world. James MacGregor Burns, *Roosevelt: the Soldier of Freedom* (1970) and Warren F. Kimball, *The Juggler: Franklin Roosevelt as Wartime Statesman* (1991) are two important studies of the president. Wayne S. Cole, *Charles A. Lindbergh and the Battle Against American Intervention in World War II* (1974) and *Roosevelt and the Isolationists, 1932–1945* (1983) examine prewar isolationism. A. Scott Berg, *Lindbergh* (1998) is an excellent biography of the aviation hero who became such a controversial figure in the 1930s. Charles DeBenedetti, *Origins of the Modern American Peace Movement, 1915–1929* (1978) and *The Peace Reform in American History* (1980) examine antiwar movements in American history, including prior to World War II. Joseph Lash's *Roosevelt and Churchill* (1976) explores the dynamic relationship between the two leaders of the United States and England. Akira Iriye, *The Origins of the Second World War in Asia and the Pacific* (1988) examines the conflict between China and Japan that preceded American intervention in the Pacific War. Gordon Prange, *At Dawn We Slept* (1981) examines the controversial attack on Pearl Harbor from both the Japanese and American sides.

For quizzes, Internet resources, references to additional books and films, and more, consult this book's Online Learning Center site at www.mhhe.com/unfinishednation4.

"STEP ON 'EM" This government poster distributed during World War II suggests the dual character of the American war effort: on the one hand, a military assault on the Axis powers; on the other, the effort at home to expand the nation's industrial capacity and supply the war effort. American production was at least as important to the Allied victory in the war as the successes of American troops in the field. *(The National Archives and Records Administration)*

TIME LINE

1942	1943
Battle of Midway	Americans capture Guadalcanal
Campaign in Northern Africa	Allied invasion of Italy
Japanese Americans interned	Soviet victory at Stalingrad
Manhattan Project begins	
CORE founded	

CHAPTER TWENTY-EIGHT

AMERICA IN A WORLD AT WAR

War on Two Fronts
The American Economy in Wartime
Race and Gender in Wartime America
Anxiety and Affluence in Wartime Culture
The Defeat of the Axis

The attack on Pearl Harbor had thrust the United States into the greatest and most terrible war in the history of humanity, a war that changed the world as profoundly as any event of the twentieth century, perhaps of any century. World War II also transformed the United States in profound, if not always readily visible, ways.

WAR ON TWO FRONTS

Whatever political disagreements and social tensions there may have been among the American people during World War II, there was striking unity of opinion about the conflict itself. But both unity and confidence faced severe tests in the first, troubled months of 1942.

1944	1945
Allies invade Normandy	Roosevelt dies; Truman becomes president
Roosevelt reelected	Germany surrenders
Americans capture Philippines	U.S. drops atomic bombs on Hiroshima, Nagasaki
	Japan surrenders

Containing the Japanese

Ten hours after the strike at Pearl Harbor, Japanese airplanes attacked the American airfields at Manila in the Philippines, destroying much of America's remaining air power in the Pacific. Three days later Guam, an American possession, fell to Japan; Wake Island and Hong Kong followed. The great British fortress of Singapore in Malaya surrendered in February 1942, the Dutch East Indies in March, Burma in April. In the Philippines, exhausted Filipino and American troops gave up their defense of the islands on May 6.

Japanese Victories

American strategists planned two broad offensives to turn the tide against the Japanese. One, under the command of General Douglas MacArthur, would move north from Australia, through New Guinea, and eventually to the Philippines. The other, under Admiral Chester Nimitz, would move west from Hawaii toward major Japanese island outposts in the central Pacific. Ultimately, strategists predicted, the two offensives would come together to invade Japan itself.

Battle of Midway

The Allies achieved their first important victory in the Battle of the Coral Sea, just northwest of Australia, on May 7–8, 1942, when American forces turned back the previously unstoppable Japanese navy. A month later, there was an even more important turning point northwest of Hawaii. An enormous battle raged for four days, June 3–6, 1942, near the small American outpost at Midway Island, at the end of which the United States, despite great losses, was clearly victorious. The American navy destroyed four Japanese aircraft carriers and lost only one of its own; the action regained control of the central Pacific for the United States.

The Americans took the offensive for the first time several months later in the southern Solomon Islands, to the east of New Guinea. In August 1942, American forces assaulted three of the islands: Gavutu, Tulagi, and Guadalcanal. A struggle of terrible ferocity developed at Guadalcanal and continued for six months, inflicting heavy losses on both sides. In the end, however, the Japanese were forced to abandon the island—and with it their last chance of launching an effective offensive to the south. The Americans, with aid from the Australians and the New Zealanders, now began the slow, arduous process of moving toward the Philippines and Japan itself.

Holding Off the Germans

In the European war, the United States was fighting in cooperation with, among others, Britain and the exiled "Free French" forces in the west; and it was trying also to conciliate its new ally, the Soviet Union, which was now fighting Hitler in the east. The army chief of staff, General George C. Marshall, supported a plan for a major Allied invasion of France across the English Channel in the spring of 1943, and he placed a previously little-known general, Dwight D. Eisenhower, in charge of planning the operation. But the Soviet Union,

Dwight Eisenhower

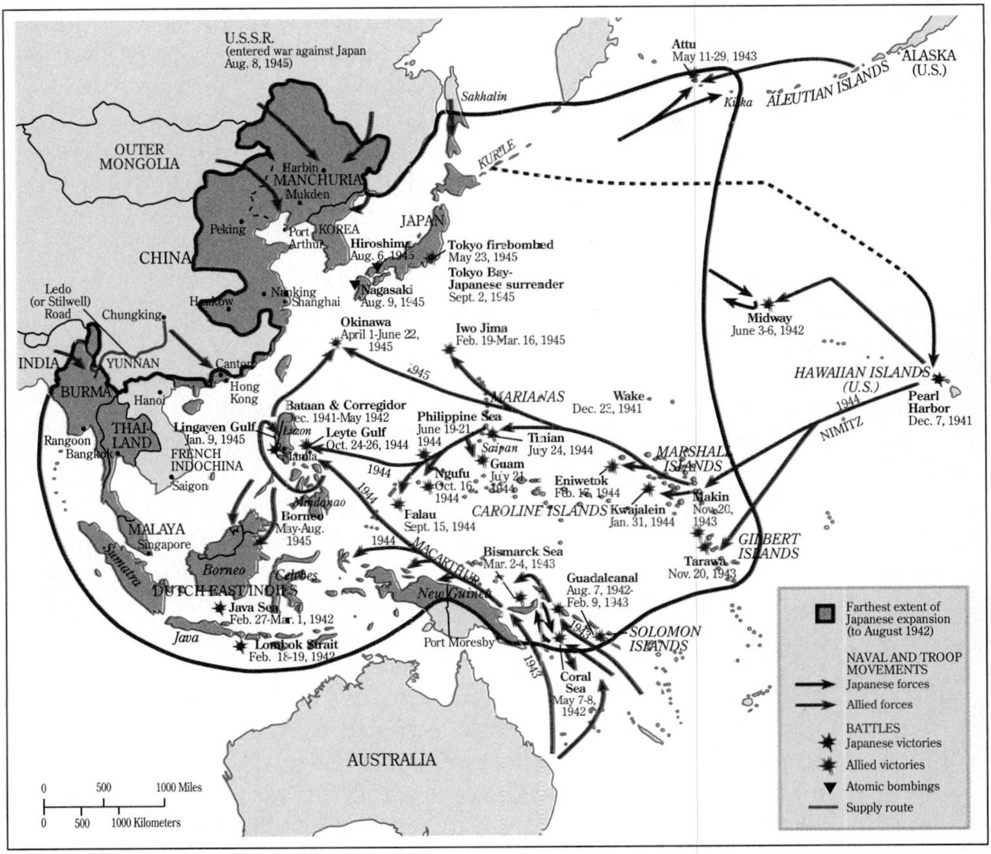

WORLD WAR II IN THE PACIFIC This map illustrates the changing fortunes of the two combatants in the Pacific phase of World War II. The long red line stretching from Burma around to Manchuria represents the eastern boundary of the vast areas of the Pacific that had fallen under Japanese control by the summer of 1942. The blue lines illustrate the advance of American forces back into the Pacific beginning in May 1942 and accelerating in 1943 and after, which drove the Japanese forces back. The American advance was a result of two separate offensives—one in the central Pacific, under the command of Chester Nimitz, which moved west from Hawaii; the other, under the command of Douglas MacArthur, which moved north from Australia. By the summer of 1945, American forces were approaching the Japanese mainland and were bombing Tokyo itself. The dropping of two American atomic bombs, on Hiroshima and Nagasaki, finally brought the war to an end. ◆ *Why did the Soviet Union enter the Pacific War in August 1945, as shown in the upper left corner of the map?*

which was absorbing the brunt of the German war effort, wanted the Allied invasion to begin at the earliest possible moment. The British, on the other hand, wanted first to launch a series of Allied offensives around the edges of the Nazi empire—in northern Africa and southern Europe—before undertaking the invasion of France.

Roosevelt ultimately decided to support the British plan—in part because he was eager to get American forces into combat quickly and knew that a cross-Channel invasion would take a long time to prepare. At the end of October 1942, the British opened a counteroffensive against General Erwin Rommel and the Nazi forces in North Africa that were threatening the Suez Canal. In a major battle at El Alamein, they forced the Germans to retreat from Egypt. On November 8, Anglo-American forces landed at Oran and Algiers in Algeria and at Casablanca in Morocco—areas under the Nazi-controlled French government at Vichy—and began moving east toward Rommel. The Germans threw the full weight of their forces in Africa against the inexperienced Americans and inflicted a serious defeat on them at the Kasserine Pass in Tunisia. General George S. Patton, however, regrouped the American troops and began an effective counteroffensive. With the help of Allied air and naval power and of British forces attacking from the east under Field Marshall Bernard Montgomery (the hero of El Alamein), the American offensive finally drove the last Germans from Africa in May 1943.

The North African campaign had tied up a large proportion of Allied resources. That was one reason why the planned May 1943 cross-Channel invasion of France had to be postponed, despite angry complaints from the Soviet Union. By now, however, the threat of a Soviet collapse seemed much diminished, for during the winter of 1942–1943, the Red Army had successfully held off a major German assault at Stalingrad in southern Russia. Hitler had committed such enormous forces to the battle, and had suffered such appalling losses, that he could not continue his eastern offensive.

Battle of Stalingrad

The Soviet successes persuaded Roosevelt to agree, in a January 1943 meeting with Churchill in Casablanca, to a British plan for an Allied invasion of Sicily. Churchill argued that the operation in Sicily might knock Italy out of the war and tie up German divisions that would otherwise be stationed in France. On the night of July 9, 1943, American and British armies landed in southeast Sicily; thirty-eight days later, they had conquered the island and were moving onto the Italian mainland. In the face of these setbacks, Mussolini's government collapsed and the dictator himself fled north toward Germany. (He was later captured by Italian insurgents and hanged.) Although Mussolini's successor, Pietro Badoglio, quickly committed Italy to the Allies, Germany moved eight divisions into the country and established a powerful defensive line south of Rome. The Allied offensive on the Italian peninsula, which began on September 3, 1943, soon bogged down. Not until May 1944 did the Allies break through the German defenses to resume their northward advance. On June 4, 1944, they captured Rome.

Italy Invaded

The invasion of Italy contributed to postponing the invasion of France by as much as a year, deeply embittering Stalin and giving the Soviets time to begin moving toward the countries of eastern Europe.

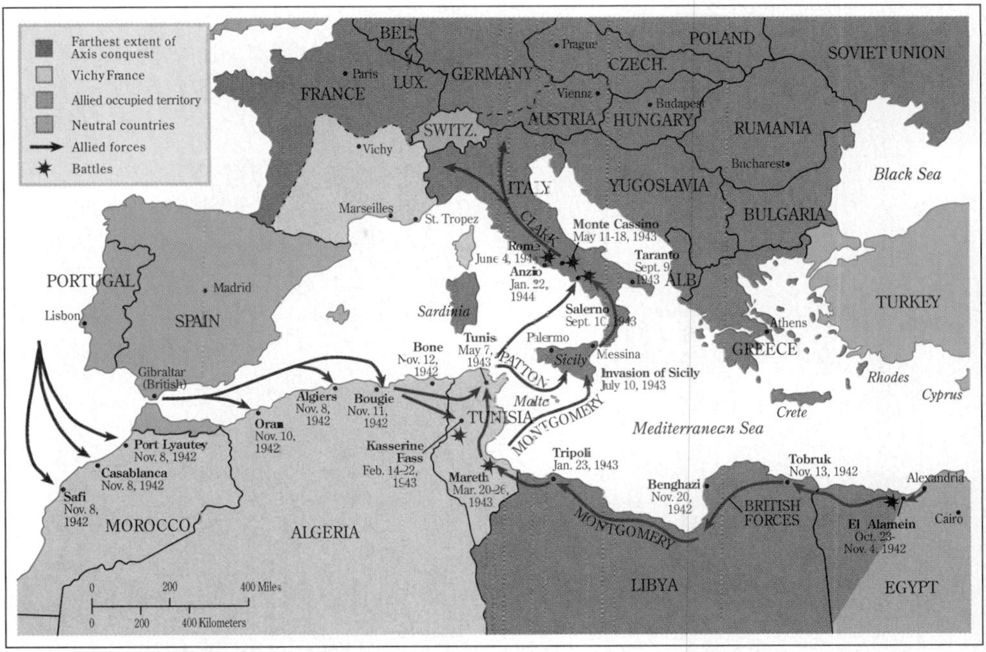

WORLD WAR II IN NORTH AFRICA AND ITALY: THE ALLIED COUNTEROFFENSIVE, 1942–1943 This map shows the Anglo-American offensive in Europe that preceded the great Normandy Invasion of 1944. Eight months after landing in North Africa, U.S. and British forces established their first foothold in Europe when they landed in Sicily in July 1943. ◆ *Why did Stalin have so little enthusiasm for the North African invasion?*

America and the Holocaust

In the midst of this intensive fighting, the leaders of the American government found themselves confronted with one of history's great tragedies: the Nazi campaign to exterminate the Jews of Europe—the Holocaust. As early as 1942, high officials in Washington had incontrovertible evidence that Hitler's forces were rounding up Jews and others (including Poles, homosexuals, and communists) from all over Europe, transporting them to concentration camps in eastern Germany and Poland, and systematically murdering them. (The death toll would ultimately reach 6 million Jews and at least 4 million others.) News of the atrocities was reaching the public as well, and pressure began to build for an Allied effort to end the killing or at least to rescue some of the surviving Jews.

The American government consistently resisted almost all such entreaties. Although by mid-1944 Allied bombers were flying missions within a few miles of the most notorious death camp, at Auschwitz in Poland, the War Department rejected as militarily unfeasible pleas that the planes try to destroy the crematoria at the camp. American officials also refused requests that the Allies try to destroy railroad lines leading to

THE *ST. LOUIS* Many people consider the fate of the German liner *St. Louis* to be a powerful symbol of the indifference of the United States and other nations to the fate of European Jews during the Holocaust, even though its forlorn journey preceded both the beginning of World War II and the beginning of systematic extermination of Jews by the Nazi regime. The *St. Louis* carried a group of over 900 Jews fleeing from Germany in 1939, carrying exit visas of dubious legality cynically sold to them by members of Hitler's Gestapo. It became a ship without a port as it sailed from country to country—Mexico, Paraguay, Argentina, Costa Rica, and Cuba—where its passengers were refused entry time and again. Most of the passengers were hoping for a haven in the United States, but the American State Department refused to allow the ship even to dock as it sailed up the American eastern seaboard. Eventually, the *St. Louis* returned to Europe and distributed its passengers among Britain, France, Holland, and Belgium (where this photograph was taken showing refugees smiling and waving as they prepared to disembark in Antwerp in June 1939). Less than a year later, all those nations except Britain fell under Nazi control. *(Bettmann/Corbis)*

the camp. And the United States resisted pleas that it admit large numbers of Jewish refugees attempting to escape Europe.

Moral Failure

After 1941, there was probably little American leaders could have done, other than defeat Germany in the war, to save most of Hitler's victims. But more forceful action by the United States (and Britain, which was even less amenable to Jewish requests for assistance) might well have saved at least some lives. That they did not take such action, it seems clear in retrospect, constituted a considerable moral failure. But policymakers justified their inaction by insisting that they needed to focus exclusively on the larger goal of winning the war. Any diversion of energy and attention to other purposes, they believed, would distract them from the overriding goal of victory.

THE AMERICAN ECONOMY IN WARTIME

Not since the Civil War had the United States been involved in so prolonged and consuming a military experience as World War II. American armed forces engaged in combat around the globe for nearly four years. American society, in the meantime, experienced changes that reached into virtually every corner of the nation.

Prosperity and the Rights of Labor

World War II had its most profound impact on American domestic life by ending the Great Depression. By the middle of 1941, the economic problems of the 1930s—unemployment, deflation, industrial sluggishness—had virtually vanished before the great wave of wartime industrial expansion.

Massive Government Spending

The most important agent of the new prosperity was government spending, which after 1939 was pumping more money into the economy each year than all the New Deal relief agencies combined had done. In 1939, the federal budget had been $9 billion; by 1945, it had risen to $100 billion. Largely as a result, the gross national product soared: from $91 billion in 1939 to $166 billion in 1945. Personal incomes in some regions grew by as much as 100 percent or more.

The impact of government spending was perhaps most dramatic in the West. The West Coast, naturally, became the launching point for most of the naval war against Japan, and the government created large manufacturing facilities in California and elsewhere to serve the needs of its military. Altogether, the government made almost $40 billion worth of capital investments (factories, military and transportation facilities, highways, power plants) in the West during the war, more than in any other region. By the end of the war, the Pacific Coast had become the center of the growing American aircraft industry and an important center of the shipbuilding industry. Los Angeles, formerly a medium-sized city notable chiefly for its film industry, now became a major industrial center as well.

The war created a serious labor shortage. The armed forces took over 15 million men and women out of the civilian work force at the same time that the demand for labor was rising rapidly. Nevertheless, the supply of workers increased by almost 20 percent during the war—largely through the employment of many people previously considered inappropriate for the work force: the very young, the elderly, minorities, and, most important, several million women.

Union Membership Boosted

The war gave a substantial boost to union membership, which rose from about 10.5 million in 1941 to over 13 million in 1945. That was in part a result of a "maintenance-of-membership" agreement with the government, which ensured that the thousands of new workers pouring into unionized defense plants would be automatically enrolled in the unions. But the government also managed to win two important concessions from union leaders. One was the "no-strike" pledge, by which unions agreed not to stop production in wartime. Another was the so-called Little Steel formula, which set a 15 percent limit on wage increases.

Despite the no-strike pledge, there were nearly 15,000 work stoppages during the war, mostly wildcat strikes (strikes unauthorized by the union leadership). When the United Mine Workers defied the government by striking in May 1943, Congress reacted by passing, over Roosevelt's veto, the Smith-Connally Act (the War Labor Disputes Act), which required that unions wait thirty days before striking and which empowered the president to seize a struck war plant. In the meantime, public animosity toward labor rose rapidly, and many states passed laws to limit union power.

Stabilizing the Boom and Mobilizing Production

The fear of deflation, the central concern of the 1930s, gave way during the war to a fear of inflation, particularly after prices rose 25 percent in the two years before Pearl Harbor. Holding the line against inflation was the task of the Office of Price Administration (OPA), led first by Leon Henderson and then by Chester Bowles. The OPA was successful enough that inflation was a much less serious problem during World War II than it had been during World War I. Even so, the agency was never popular. Black-marketing and overcharging grew in proportions far beyond OPA policing capacity.

Office of Price Administration

From 1941 to 1945, the federal government spent a total of $321 billion—twice as much as it had spent in the entire 150 years of its existence to that point, and ten times as much as the cost of World War I. The national debt rose from $49 billion in 1941 to $259 billion in 1945. The government borrowed about half the revenues it needed by selling $100 billion worth of bonds. Much of the rest it raised by radically increasing income-tax rates, through the Revenue Act of 1942. To simplify collection, Congress enacted a withholding system of payroll deductions in 1943.

In January 1942, the president responded to widespread criticism of earlier efforts to mobilize the economy for war by creating the War Production Board (WPB), under the direction of former Sears Roebuck executive Donald Nelson. Throughout its troubled history, the WPB was never able to win complete control over military purchases; the army and navy often circumvented the board. It was never able to satisfy the complaints of small business, which charged (correctly) that most contracts were going to large corporations. Gradually, the president transferred much of the WPB's authority to a new office located within the White House: the Office of War Mobilization (OWM). But the OWM was only slightly more successful than the WPB.

War Production Board

Despite the administrative problems, however, the war economy managed to meet almost all of the nation's critical war needs. By the beginning of 1944, American factories were, in fact, producing more than the government needed. Their output was twice that of all the Axis countries combined.

Wartime Science and Technology

More than any previous American war, World War II was a watershed for technological and scientific innovation. That was partly because the American government poured substantial funds into research and development beginning in 1940. In that year the government created the National Defense Research Committee, headed by the MIT scientist Vannevar Bush, who had been a pioneer in the early development of the computer. (It later became the Office of Scientific Research and Development.) By the end of the war, the new agency had spent more that $100 million on research, more than four times the amount spent by the government on military research and development in the previous forty years.

National Defense Research Committee

In the first years of the war, all the technological advantages seemed to lie with the Germans and Japanese. Germany had made great advances in tanks and other mechanized armor in the 1930s, particularly during the Spanish Civil War, when it had helped arm Franco's fascist forces. It used its armor effectively during its blitzkrieg in Europe in 1940 and again in North Africa in 1942. German submarine technology was significantly advanced compared to British and American capabilities in 1940. Japan had developed extraordinary capacity in its naval-air technology. Its highly sophisticated fighter planes, launched from distant aircraft carriers, conducted the successful raid on Pearl Harbor in December 1941.

But Britain and America had advantages of their own. American techniques of mass production—the great automotive assembly lines in particular—were converted efficiently to military production in 1941 and 1942 and soon began producing airplanes, ships, tanks, and other armaments in much greater numbers than the Germans and Japanese could produce. Allied scientists and engineers moved quickly as well to improve Anglo-American aviation and naval technology, and particularly to improve the performance of submarines and tanks. By late 1942, Allied weaponry was at least as advanced, and coming to be more plentiful, than that of the enemy.

In addition, each technological innovation by the enemy produced a corresponding innovation to limit the damage of the new techniques. American and British physicists made rapid advances in improving radar and sonar—taking advantage of advances in radio technology in the 1920s and beyond—which helped Allied naval forces decimate German U-boats in 1943 and effectively end their effectiveness in the naval war. Particularly important was

Sonar

BOMBING AXIS FACTORIES The Boeing B-17 bomber was one of the great technological innovations of wartime aviation. It allowed Allied pilots to fly much further into enemy territory on bombing missions. Here, B-17s bomb factories in Austria in 1944. *(Archive Photos/American Stock/Getty Images)*

the creation in 1940 of "centimetric radar," whose narrow beams of short wavelength made radar more efficient and effective than ever before—as the British navy discovered in April 1941 when the instruments on one of its ships detected a surfaced submarine 10 miles away at night and, on another occasion, spotted a periscope at three-quarters of a mile range. With earlier technologies, both things would have been undetectable. This new radar could also be effectively miniaturized, which was critical to its use on airplanes and submarines in particular. These innovations put the Allies far in advance of Germany and Japan in radar technology. The Allies also learned early how to detect and disable German naval mines; and when the Germans tried to counter this progress by introducing an "acoustic" mine, which detonated when a ship came near it, not necessarily just on contact, the Allies developed acoustical countermeasures of their own, which transmitted sounds through the water to detonate mines before ships came near them.

Anglo-American antiaircraft technology—both on land and on sea—also improved, although never to the point where it could stop bombing raids altogether. Germany made substantial advances in the development of rocket technology in the early years of the war, and it managed to launch some rocket-propelled bombs (the V1s and V2s) across the English

Channel, aimed at London. The psychological effects of the rockets on the British people were considerable. But the Germans were never able to create a production technology capable of building enough such rockets to make a real difference in the balance of military power.

Beginning in 1942, British and American forces seized the advantage in the air war by producing new and powerful four-engine bombers in great numbers—among them the British Lancaster B1 and the American Boeing B17F, capable of flying a bomb load of 6,000 pounds for 1,300 miles, and capable of reaching 37,500 feet. Because they were able to fly higher and longer than the German equivalents, they were able to conduct extensive bombing missions over Germany (and later Japan) with much less danger of being shot down. But the success of the bombers rested heavily as well on new electronic devices capable of guiding their bombs to their targets. The Gee navigation system, which was also valuable to the navy, used electronic pulses to help pilots plot their exact location, something that in the past only a highly skilled navigator could do, and then only in good weather. In March 1942, eighty Allied bombers fitted with Gee systems staged a devastatingly effective bombing raid on German industrial and military installations in the Ruhr Valley. In the past, studies had shown that night-bombing raids were at best 30 percent accurate. The Gee system doubled the accuracy rate. Also effective was the Oboe system, a radio device that sent a sonic message to airplanes to tell them when they were within 20 yards of their targets, first introduced in December 1942.

Long-range Bombing

The area in which the Allies had perhaps the greatest advantage was the gathering of intelligence, much of it through Britain's top-secret Ultra project. Some of the advantages the Allies enjoyed came from successful efforts to capture or steal German and Japanese intelligence devices. More important, however, were the efforts of cryptologists to puzzle out the enemy's systems, and advances in computer technology that helped the Allies decipher coded messages sent by the Japanese and the Germans. Much of Germany's coded communication made use of the so-called Enigma machine, which was effective because it constantly changed the coding systems it used. In the first months of the war, Polish intelligence had developed an electro-mechanical computer, which it called the "Bombe," which could decipher some Enigma messages. After the fall of Poland, British scientists, led by the brilliant computer pioneer Alan Turing, took the Bombe, which was too slow to keep up with the increasingly frequent changes of coding the Germans were using, and greatly improved it. On April 15, 1940, the new, improved, high-speed Bombe broke the coding of a series of German messages within hours (not days, as had previously been the case). A few weeks later, it began decrypting German messages at the rate of 1,000 a day, providing the British (and later the Americans) with a constant flow of information about enemy operations that continued—completely unknown to the Germans—until the end of the war. Later in the war, British scientists working for the intelligence

Importance of Code Breaking

services built the first real programmable, digital computer—the Colossus II, which became operational less than a week before the beginning of the Normandy invasion and which was able to decipher an enormous number of intercepted German messages almost instantly.

The United States also had some important intelligence breakthroughs, including, in 1941, a dramatic success by the American Magic operation (the counterpart to the British Ultra) in breaking a Japanese coding system not unlike the German Enigma. The result was that Americans had access to intercepted information that, if properly interpreted, could have alerted them to the Japanese raid on Pearl Harbor in December 1941. But because such a raid had seemed entirely inconceivable to most American officials prior to its occurrence, those who received the information failed to understand or disseminate it in time.

RACE AND GENDER IN WARTIME AMERICA

In most ways, the war loosened traditional barriers that had restricted the lives of minorities and women. There was too much demand for fighting men, too much demand for labor, and too much fluidity and mobility in society for rigid, traditional barriers to survive intact.

African Americans and the War

A. Philip Randolph

In the summer of 1941, A. Philip Randolph, president of the Brotherhood of Sleeping Car Porters, an important union with a primarily black membership, began to insist that the government require companies receiving defense contracts to integrate their work forces. To mobilize support for the demand, Randolph planned a massive march on Washington. Roosevelt finally persuaded Randolph to cancel the march in return for a promise to establish what became the Fair Employment Practices Commission (FEPC) to investigate discrimination against African Americans in war industries.

Wartime Race Riots

The need for labor in war plants greatly increased the migration of African Americans from the rural areas of the South into industrial cities. The migration bettered the economic condition of many African Americans, but it also created urban tensions and occasionally violence. The most serious conflict occurred in Detroit in 1943, when racial friction in the city produced a major riot in which thirty-four people died, twenty-five of them black.

Despite such tensions, the leading black organizations redoubled their efforts during the war to challenge the system of segregation. The Congress of Racial Equality (CORE), organized in 1942, mobilized mass popular resistance to discrimination in a way that the older, more conservative organizations had never done. Randolph, Bayard Rustin, James Farmer, and other, younger African-American leaders helped organize sit-ins and demonstrations in segregated theaters and restaurants.

Pressure for change was also growing within the military. The armed forces maintained their traditional practice of limiting blacks to the most menial assignments, keeping them in segregated training camps and units, and barring them entirely from the Marine Corps and the Army Air Force. But there were signs of change. By the end of the war, the number of black servicemen had increased sevenfold, to 700,000; some training camps were being at least partially integrated; African Americans were being allowed to serve on ships with white sailors; and more black units were being sent into combat. The changes did not come easily. In some of the partially integrated army bases—Fort Dix, New Jersey, for example—riots occasionally broke out when black soldiers protested having to serve in segregated divisions.

Native Americans and the War

Approximately 25,000 Indians performed military service during World War II. Many Native Americans served in combat. Others (mostly Navajos) became "code-talkers," working in military communications and speaking their own language (which enemy forces would be unlikely to understand) over the radio and the telephones. The war had important effects on the Indians who served in the military. It brought them into intimate contact (often for the first time) with white society, and it awakened among some of them a taste for the material benefits of life in capitalist America that they would retain after the war. Some never returned to the reservations, but chose to remain in the non-Indian world and assimilate to its ways.

Navajo "Code-Talkers"

The war had important effects, too, on those Native Americans who stayed on the reservations. Little war work reached the tribes. Government subsidies dwindled. Talented young people left the reservations to serve in the military or work in war production, creating manpower shortages in some tribes. The wartime emphasis on national unity undermined support for the revitalization of tribal autonomy that the Indian Reorganization Act of 1934 had launched. New pressures emerged to eliminate the reservation system and require the tribes to assimilate into white society—pressures so severe that John Collier, the energetic director of the Bureau of Indian Affairs who had done so much to promote the reinvigoration of the reservations, resigned in 1945.

Mexican-American War Workers

Large numbers of Mexican workers entered the United States during the war in response to labor shortages on the Pacific coast and in the Southwest. The American and Mexican governments agreed in 1942 to a program by which *braceros*

Braceros Program

ZOOT-SUITER The baggy pants, the long, loose jacket, the big collar, the exaggerated watch chain, the slicked-back hair—all were features of the outfit known as the zoot suit, which was popular among young Mexican Americans in Los Angeles and elsewhere. The "zoot-suit riots" in Los Angeles in June 1943 were a product of the suspicion with which Anglos (in this case servicemen stationed nearby) looked at the culture of the Chicano communities that were growing rapidly throughout the Southwest. *(UPI/Corbis-Bettmann)*

(contract laborers) would be admitted to the United States for a limited time. Some worked as migrant farm laborers, but many Mexicans were able for the first time to find factory jobs. They formed the second-largest group of migrants (after African Americans) to U.S. cities in the 1940s. They were concentrated mainly in the West, but there were significant Mexican communities in Chicago, Detroit, and other industrial cities.

The sudden expansion of Mexican-American neighborhoods created tensions and occasionally conflict in some American cities. White residents of Los Angeles became alarmed at the activities of Mexican-American teenagers, many of whom were joining street gangs *(pachucos)*. The youths were particularly distinctive because of their style of dress. They wore long, loose jackets with padded shoulders, baggy pants tied at the ankles, long watch chains, broad-brimmed hats, and greased, ducktail hairstyles. The outfit was known as a "zoot suit." In June 1943, animosity toward the "zoot-suiters" produced a four-day riot in Los Angeles, during which white sailors stationed at a base in Long Beach invaded Mexican-American communities and attacked zoot-suiters (in response to alleged zoot-suiter attacks on servicemen). The police did little to restrain the sailors, who grabbed Hispanic teenagers, tore off and burned their clothes, cut off their ducktails, and beat them. When Mexicans tried to fight back, the police moved in and arrested them. In the aftermath of the "zoot-suit riots," Los Angeles passed a law prohibiting the wearing of zoot suits.

"Zoot-Suit Riots"

The Internment of Japanese Americans

Although World War II, unlike World War I, produced little popular animosity toward Germans, it created considerable animosity toward the Japanese. After the attack on Pearl Harbor, government propaganda and popular culture combined to create an image of the Japanese as a devious, malign, and savage people.

Predictably, this racial animosity soon extended to Americans of Japanese descent. There were not many Japanese Americans in the United States—about 127,000, most of them concentrated in a few areas in California. About a third of them were unnaturalized, first-generation immigrants (Issei); two-thirds were naturalized or native-born citizens of the United States (Nisei). Because they generally kept to themselves and preserved traditional Japanese cultural patterns, it was easy for some to imagine that the Japanese Americans were engaged in conspiracies on behalf of their ancestral homeland. (There is no evidence that they actually were.)

In February 1942, in response to pressure from military officials and political leaders on the West Coast and recommendations from the War Department, the president authorized the army to "intern" the Japanese Americans. More than 100,000 people (Issei and Nisei alike) were rounded up, told to dispose of their property however they could (which often meant simply abandoning it), and taken to what the government euphemistically called "relocation centers." In fact, they were facilities little different from prisons, many of them located in the western mountains and desert. Thus a group of innocent, hardworking people (many of them citizens of the United States) were forced to spend up to three years in grim, debilitating isolation, barred from lucrative employment, provided with only minimal medical care, and deprived of decent schools for their children. The Supreme Court upheld the evacuation in a 1944 decision; and although most of the Japanese Americans were released later that year, they were unable to win any significant compensation for their losses until Congress finally acted to redress the wrongs in the late 1980s.

"Relocation Centers"

Chinese Americans and the War

At the same time that the conflict with Japan undermined the position of Japanese Americans, the American alliance with China during World War II significantly enhanced both the legal and social status of Chinese Americans. In 1943, partly to improve relations with the government of China, Congress finally repealed the Chinese Exclusion Acts, which had barred almost all Chinese immigration since 1892. The new quota for Chinese immigrants was minuscule (105 a year), but a substantial number of Chinese women managed to gain entry into the country through other provisions covering war brides and fiancées. Over 4,000 Chinese women entered the United States in the first three years after the war. Permanent residents of the United States of Chinese descent were finally permitted to become citizens.

Declining Prejudice toward Chinese Americans

Racial animosity toward the Chinese did not disappear, but it did decline—in part because government propaganda and popular culture both began presenting positive images of the Chinese (partly to contrast them with the Japanese); in part because Chinese Americans (like African Americans and other previously marginal groups) began taking jobs in war plants and other booming areas suffering from labor shortages and hence moving out of the relatively isolated world of the Chinatowns. A higher proportion of Chinese Americans (22 percent of all adult males) were drafted than of any other national group, and the entire Chinese community in most cities worked hard and conspicuously for the war effort.

Women and Children in Wartime

The number of women in the work force increased by nearly 60 percent during the war, as many women took industrial jobs to replace male workers serving in the military. These wage-earning women were more likely to be married and were, on the whole, older than most of those who had entered the work force in the past.

Many factory owners continued to categorize jobs by gender, reserving the most lucrative positions for men. (Female work, like male work, was also categorized by race: black women were usually assigned more menial tasks, and paid at a lower rate, than their white counterparts.) But some women began now to take on heavy industrial jobs that had long

"Rosie the Riveter"

been considered "men's work." The famous wartime image of "Rosie the Riveter" symbolized the new importance of the female industrial worker. Women joined unions in substantial numbers, and they helped erode at least some of the prejudice, including the prejudice against mothers working, that had previously kept many of them from paid employment.

Most women workers during the war, however, were employed not in factories but in service-sector jobs. Above all, they worked for the government, whose bureaucratic needs expanded dramatically alongside its mili-

WOMEN AT WAR Many American women enlisted in the army and navy women's corps during World War II, but an equally important contribution of women to the war effort was their work in factories and offices—often in jobs that would have been considered inappropriate for them in peacetime but that they were now encouraged to assume because of the absence of so many men. *(The Library of Congress)*

tary and industrial needs. Even within the military, which enlisted substantial numbers of women as WAACs (army) and WAVEs (navy), most female work was clerical.

WAACs and WAVEs

Many mothers whose husbands were in the military had to combine working with caring for their children. The scarcity of child-care facilities or other community services meant that some women had no choice but to leave young children—often known as "latchkey children" or "eight-hour orphans"—at home alone (or sometimes locked in cars in factory parking lots) while they worked.

Perhaps in part because of the family dislocations the war produced, juvenile crime rose markedly in the war years. Young boys were arrested at rapidly increasing rates for car theft and other burglary, vandalism, and vagrancy. The arrest rate for prostitutes, many of whom were teenage girls, rose too, as did the incidence of venereal disease. For many children, however, the distinctive experience of the war years was not crime but work. More than a third of all teenagers between the ages of fourteen and eighteen were employed in the last years of the war, causing some reduction in high-school enrollments.

The return of prosperity helped increase the marriage rate and lower the age at which people married, but many marriages were unable to survive the pressures of wartime separation. The divorce rate rose rapidly. The rise in the birth rate that accompanied the increase in marriages was the first sign of what would become the great postwar "baby boom."

Start of the "Baby Boom"

ANXIETY AND AFFLUENCE IN WARTIME CULTURE

The war created considerable anxiety in American lives. Families worried about loved ones at the front and, as the war continued, many mourned relatives who had died in combat. Women struggled to support families in the absence of husbands and fathers, who had been the principal breadwinners in peacetime. Businesses and communities struggled with shortages of goods and shortages of labor. People living on the two coasts, in particular, worried about enemy invasions and sabotage.

Consumerism Reborn

But the abundance of the war years also created a striking buoyancy in American life. Suddenly people had money to spend again and—despite the many shortages—at least some things to spend it on. In fact, consumerism became, as it had in the 1920s, one of the most powerful forces in American culture and, for many, one of the features of American life that the war was being fought to defend.

Wartime Entertainment and Leisure

The book, theater, and movie industries did record business during the war. Audiences equal to about half the nation's population attended movies each week. Magazines, particularly pictorial ones such as *Life*, reached the peak of their popularity by providing pictures of and stories about the war. Radio ownership and listenership also increased, for the same reason.

Fuel rationing and rubber shortages limited travel by car, but many people traveled nevertheless—by train or bus, or to places relatively close to their homes. Resort hotels, casinos, and racetracks were jammed with customers. More often, however, people sought entertainment in their own communities. Dance halls were packed with young people drawn to the seductive music of bands; soldiers and sailors home on leave, or awaiting shipment abroad, were especially attracted to the dances and the big bands, which became to many of them a symbol of the life they were leaving and that they believed they were fighting to defend.

By far the most popular music in dance halls, and on radio, was the relatively new jazz form known as swing, which, like many other forms of popular music, had emerged from the African-American musical world.

Popularity of Swing

During the heyday of swing, band leaders such as Benny Goodman, Duke Ellington, Tommy Dorsey, and Glenn Miller, were among the most recognized and popular figures in American popular culture, rivaling movie stars in their celebrity. Swing sold more records than any other kind of music. And it became one of the first forms of popular music to challenge racial taboos. Benny Goodman hired the black pianist Teddy Wilson to play with his band in 1935; other white bandleaders followed.

Women and Men in the Armed Services

For men at the front, the image of home was a powerful antidote to the rigors of wartime. They dreamed of music, food, movies, and other material comforts. Many also dreamed of women—wives and girlfriends, but also movie stars and others, who became the source of one of the most popular icons of the front: the pinup. Sailors pasted pinups inside their lockers. Infantrymen carried them (along with pictures of wives, mothers, and girlfriends) in their knapsacks. Fighter pilots gave their planes female names and painted bathing beauties on their nosecones.

For the servicemen who remained in America during the war, and for soldiers and sailors in cities far from home in particular, the company of friendly, "wholesome" women was, the military believed, critical to sustaining morale. The branches of the United Servicemen's Organization (known as USOs) recruited thousands of young women to serve as hostesses in their clubs. They were expected to dress nicely, dance well, and chat happily with lonely men. Other women joined "dance brigades" and traveled by bus to military bases for social evenings with servicemen. They too were expected to be pretty, to dress attractively, and to interact comfortably with men they had never met before and would likely never see again. The "USO girls" and the members of the dance brigades were forbidden to have any contact with men except at parties at the clubs or during dances. Clearly such regulations were often violated. But while the military took elaborate measures to root out gay men and lesbians from their ranks—vigilantly searching for evidence of homosexuality and unceremoniously dismissing gay people with undesirable discharges—the services quietly tolerated illicit heterosexual relationships, which they believed were both natural and, for many men, necessary.

Importance of USOs

As during World War I, the armed services virtually took over many American colleges and universities. Emptied of male students and professors (and many females as well), who left to join the war effort, they turned themselves into training camps for military officers—helped by substantial funding from the federal government.

Retreat from Reform

Late in 1943, Franklin Roosevelt publicly suggested that "Dr. New Deal," as he called it, had served its purpose and should now give way to "Dr. Win-the-War." The statement reflected the president's own genuine shift in concern: victory was now more important than reform. But it reflected, too, the political reality that had emerged during the first two years of war.

Conservative Assault on the New Deal

The greatest assault on New Deal reforms came from conservatives in Congress, who seized on the war as an excuse to do what many had wanted to do in peacetime: dismantle many of the achievements of the New Deal. They were assisted by the end of mass unemployment, which decreased the need for such relief programs as the Civilian Conservation Corps and the Works Progress Administration (both of which Congress abolished). They were assisted, too, by their own increasing numbers. In the congressional elections of 1942, Republicans gained 47 seats in the House and 10 in the Senate.

Republicans approached the 1944 election determined to exploit what they believed was resentment of wartime regimentation and unhappiness with Democratic reform. They nominated as their candidate the young and vigorous governor of New York, Thomas E. Dewey. Roosevelt was unopposed within his party, but Democratic leaders pressured him to abandon Vice President Henry Wallace, an advanced New Dealer and hero of the CIO, and replace him with a more moderate figure. Roosevelt acquiesced in the selection of Senator Harry S. Truman of Missouri. He had won acclaim as chairman of the Senate War Investigating Committee (known as the Truman Committee), which compiled an impressive record uncovering waste and corruption in wartime production.

Roosevelt Reelected

The election revolved around domestic economic issues and, indirectly, the president's health. The president was, in fact, gravely ill, suffering from, among other things, advanced arteriosclerosis. But the campaign seemed momentarily to revive him. He made several strenuous public appearances late in October, which dispelled popular doubts about his health and ensured his reelection. He captured 53.5 percent of the popular vote to Dewey's 46 percent. He won 432 electoral votes to Dewey's 99. Democrats lost 1 seat in the Senate, gained 20 in the House, and maintained control of both.

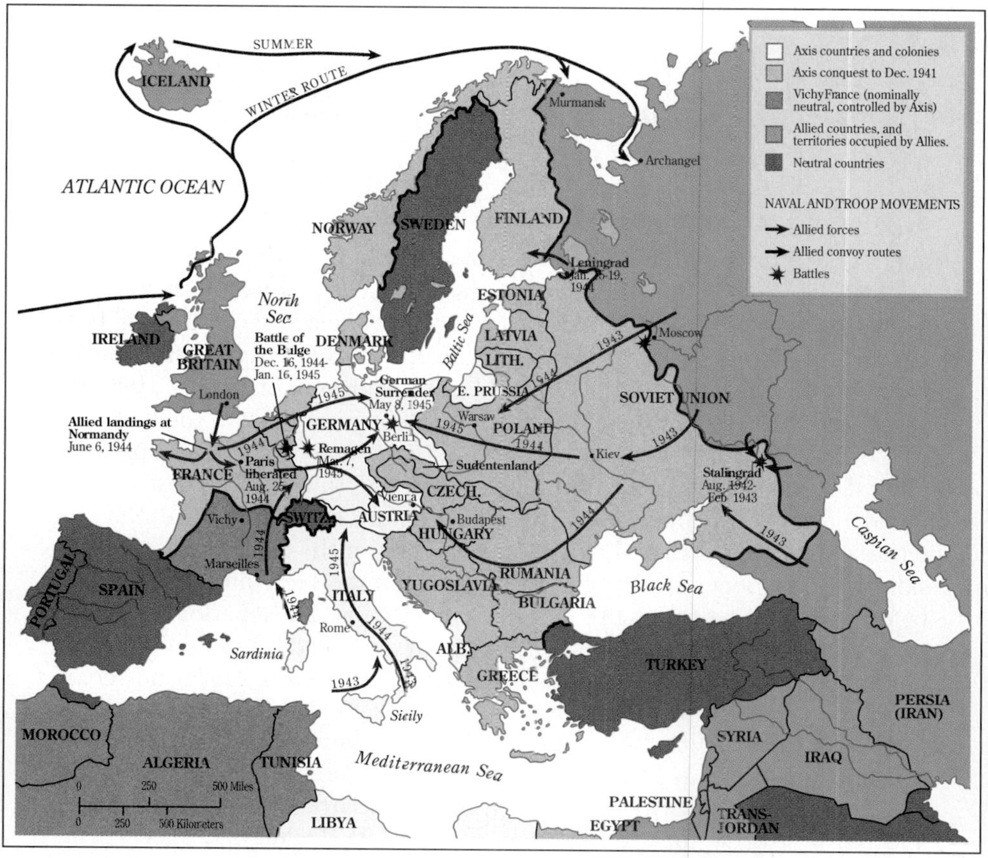

WORLD WAR II IN EUROPE: THE ALLIED COUNTEROFFENSIVE, 1943–1945 This map illustrates the final, climatic movements in the war in Europe—the two great offensives against Germany that began in 1943 and culminated in 1945. From the east, the armies of the Soviet Union, having halted the Germans at Stalingrad and Moscow, swept across eastern Europe toward Germany. From the west and the south, American, British, and other Allied forces moved toward Germany through Italy and—after the Normandy invasion in June 1944—through France. The two offensives met in Berlin in May 1945. Note, too, the northern routes that America and Britain used to supply the Soviet Union during the war. ◆ *What problems did the position of the Allied forces at the end of the war help to produce?*

For an interactive version of this map go to www.mhhe.com/unfinishednation4ch28maps

THE DEFEAT OF THE AXIS

By the middle of 1943, America and its allies had succeeded in stopping the Axis advance both in Europe and in the Pacific. In the next two years, the Allies themselves seized the offensive and launched a series of powerful drives that rapidly led the way to victory.

The Liberation of France

By early 1944, American and British bombers were attacking German industrial installations and other targets almost around the clock, drastically cutting production and impeding transportation. Especially devastating was the massive bombing of such German cities as Leipzig, Dresden, and Berlin. A February 1945 incendiary raid on Dresden created a great firestorm that destroyed three-fourths of the previously undamaged city and killed approximately 135,000 people, almost all civilians.

Invasion of France

An enormous offensive force had been gathering in England for two years before the spring of 1944: almost 3 million troops, and perhaps the greatest array of naval vessels and armaments ever assembled in one place. On the morning of June 6, 1944, this vast invasion force moved into action. The landing came not at the narrowest part of the English Channel, where the Germans had expected and prepared for it, but along sixty miles of the Cotentin Peninsula on the coast of Normandy. While airplanes and battleships offshore bombarded the Nazi defenses, 4,000 vessels landed troops and supplies on the beaches. (Three divisions of paratroopers had been dropped behind the German lines the night before.) Fighting was intense along the beach, but the superior manpower and equipment of the Allied forces gradually prevailed. Within a week, the German forces had been dislodged from virtually the entire Normandy coast.

For the next month, further progress remained slow. But in late July in the Battle of Saint-Lô, General Omar Bradley's First Army smashed through the German lines. George S. Patton's Third Army, spearheaded by heavy tank attacks, then moved through the hole Bradley had created and began a drive into the heart of France. On August 25, Free French forces arrived in Paris and liberated the city from four years of German occupation. By mid-September the Allied armies had driven the Germans almost entirely out of France and Belgium.

The great Allied drive came to a halt, however, at the Rhine River against a firm line of Nazi defenses. In mid-December, German forces struck in desperation along fifty miles of front in the Ardennes Forest. In

Battle of the Bulge

the Battle of the Bulge (named for a large bulge that appeared in the American lines as the Germans pressed forward), they drove fifty-five miles toward Antwerp before they were finally stopped at Bastogne. It was the last major battle on the western front.

While the western Allies were fighting their way through France, Soviet forces were sweeping westward into central Europe and the Balkans.

Germany Invaded

In late January 1945, the Russians launched a great offensive toward the Oder River, inside Germany. By early spring, they were ready to launch a final assault against Berlin. General Omar Bradley, in the meantime, was pushing toward the Rhine from the west. Early in March, his forces captured the city of Cologne, on the river's west bank. The next day, he discovered and seized an undamaged bridge over the river at Remagen; Allied troops were soon pouring

A VICTORY CELEBRATION IN SAN FRANCISCO Soldiers and sailors in San Francisco react jubilantly to the news that the war in Europe has ended. But the news they were celebrating was, in fact, one of the many false rumors of surrender circulating in the spring of 1945. The actual V-E Day occurred several weeks later. *(UPI/Corbis-Bettmann)*

across the Rhine. In the following weeks the British commander, Montgomery, with a million troops, pushed into Germany in the north while Bradley's army, sweeping through central Germany, completed the encirclement of 300,000 German soldiers in the Ruhr.

The German resistance was now broken on both fronts. American forces were moving eastward faster than they had anticipated and could have beaten the Russians to Berlin and Prague. The American and British high commands decided, instead, to halt the advance along the Elbe River in central Germany to await the Russians. That decision enabled the Soviets to occupy eastern Germany and Czechoslovakia.

On April 30, with Soviet forces on the outskirts of Berlin, Adolf Hitler killed himself in his bunker in the capital. And on May 8, 1945, the remaining German forces surrendered unconditionally.

The Pacific Offensive

In February 1944, American naval forces under Admiral Chester Nimitz won a series of victories in the Marshall Islands and cracked the outer perimeter of the Japanese Empire. Within a month, the navy had destroyed other vital Japanese bastions. American submarines, in the meantime, were decimating Japanese shipping and crippling Japan's domestic economy.

In mid-June 1944, an enormous American armada struck the heavily fortified Mariana Islands and, after some of the bloodiest operations of the war, captured Tinian, Guam, and Saipan, 1,350 miles from Tokyo. In September, American forces landed on the western Carolines. And on October 20, General MacArthur's troops landed on Leyte Island in the Philippines. The Japanese now employed virtually their entire fleet against the Allied invaders in three major encounters—which together constituted the decisive Battle of Leyte Gulf, the largest naval engagement in history. American forces held off the Japanese onslaught and sank four Japanese carriers, all but destroying Japan's capacity to continue a serious naval war. In February 1945, American marines seized the tiny volcanic island of Iwo Jima, only 750 miles from Tokyo, but only after the costliest battle in the history of the Marine Corps.

Battle of Leyte Gulf

The battle for Okinawa, an island only 370 miles south of Japan, gave evidence of the strength of the Japanese resistance in these last desperate days. Week after week, the Japanese sent kamikaze (suicide) planes against American and British ships, sacrificing 3,500 of them while inflicting great damage. Japanese troops on shore launched desperate nighttime attacks on the American lines. The United States and its allies suffered nearly 50,000 casualties before finally capturing Okinawa in late June 1945. Over 100,000 Japanese died in the siege.

It seemed likely that the same kind of bitter fighting would await the Americans when they invaded Japan. But there were also some signs early in 1945 that such an invasion might not be necessary. The Japanese had almost no ships or planes left with which to fight. The firebombing of Tokyo in March, in which American bombers dropped napalm on the city and created a firestorm in which over 80,000 people died, further weakened the Japanese will to resist. Moderate Japanese leaders, who had long since concluded the war was lost, were looking for ways to bring the fighting to an end, although they continued to face powerful opposition from military leaders. Whether the moderates could ultimately have prevailed is a question about which historians and others continue to disagree. In any case, their efforts became superfluous in August 1945, when the United States made use of a terrible new weapon it had been developing throughout the war.

Tokyo Firebombed

The Manhattan Project and Atomic Warfare

Reports had reached the United States in 1939 that Nazi scientists had taken the first step toward the creation of an atomic bomb, a weapon more powerful than any ever previously devised. The United States and Britain immediately began a race to develop the weapon before the Germans did.

The search for the new weapon emerged from theories developed by atomic physicists, beginning early in the century, and particularly from

Debating the Past

THE DECISION TO DROP THE ATOMIC BOMB

There has been continuing disagreement since 1945 among historians—and among many others—about how to explain and evaluate President Truman's decision to use the atomic bomb in the war against Japan.

Truman himself, both at the time and in his 1955 memoirs, and many of his contemporaries insisted that the decision was a simple and straightforward one. The alternative to using atomic weapons, he claimed, was an American invasion of mainland Japan that might have cost as many as a million lives. That view has received considerable support from historians. Herbert Feis argued in *The Atomic Bomb and the End of World War II* (1966) that Truman made his decision on purely military grounds—to ensure a speedy American victory. David McCullough, the author of an enormously popular biography of Truman published in 1992, also accepted Truman's own account of his actions largely uncritically, as did Alonzo L. Hamby in *Man of the People* (1995), an important scholarly study of Truman. "One consideration weighed most heavily on Truman," Hamby concluded. "The longer the war lasted, the more Americans killed."

Others have strongly disagreed. As early as 1948, a British physicist, P. M. S. Blackett, wrote in *Fear, War, and the Bomb* that the destruction of Hiroshima and Nagasaki was "not so much the last military act of the second World War as the first major operation of the cold diplomatic war with Russia." The most important critic of Truman's decision is the historian Gar Alperovitz, the author of two influential books on the subject: *Atomic Diplomacy: Hiroshima and Potsdam* (1965) and *The Decision to Use the Atomic Bomb* (1995). Alperovitz dismissed the argument that the bomb was used to shorten the war and save lives. Japan was likely to have surrendered soon even if the bomb had not been used, he claimed. Instead, he argued, the United States used the bomb less to influence Japan than to intimidate the Soviet Union, "to make Russia more manageable in Europe."

John W. Dower's *War Without Mercy* (1986) contributed, by implication at least, to another controversial explanation of the American decision: racism. The Japanese, many Americans came to believe during the war, were almost a subhuman species. Even many of Truman's harshest critics, however, note that it is, as Alperovitz has written, "all but impossible to find specific evidence that racism was an important factor in the decision to attack Hiroshima and Nagasaki."

The debate over the decision to drop the atomic bomb is an unusually emotional one, and it has inspired bitter professional and personal attacks on advocates of almost every position. It illustrates clearly how history has often been, and remains, a powerful force in the way societies define themselves.

some of the founding ideas of modern science developed by Albert Einstein. Einstein's famous theory of relativity had revealed the relationships between mass and energy. More precisely, he had argued that, in theory at least, matter could be converted into a tremendous force of energy. Einstein himself, who was by then living in the United States, warned Franklin Roosevelt that the Germans were developing atomic weapons and that the United States must begin trying to do the same. The effort to build atomic weapons centered on the use of uranium, whose atomic structure made possible the creation of a nuclear chain reaction. A nuclear chain reaction occurs when the atomic nuclei in radioactive matter are split (a process known as nuclear fission) by neutrons. Each fission creates new neutrons that produce fissions in additional atoms at an ever increasing and self-sustaining pace.

Atomic Fission

The construction of atomic weapons had become feasible by the 1940s because of the discovery of the radioactivity of uranium in the 1930s by Enrico Fermi in Italy. In 1939, the great Danish physicist Niels Bohr, sent news of German experiments in radioactivity to the United States, where experiments began in many places. In 1940, scientists at Columbia University began chain-reaction experiments with uranium and produced persuasive evidence of the feasibility of using uranium as fuel for a weapon. The Columbia experiments stalled in 1941, and the work moved to Berkeley and the University of Chicago, where Enrico Fermi (who had emigrated to the United States in 1938) achieved the first controlled fission chain reaction in December 1942.

By then, the army had taken control of the research and appointed General Leslie Groves to reorganize the project—which soon became known as the Manhattan Project, because it was devised in the Manhattan Engineer District Office of the Army Corps of Engineers. Over the next three years, the government secretly poured nearly $2 billion into the Manhattan Project—a massive scientific and technological effort conducted at hidden laboratories in Oak Ridge, Tennessee; Los Alamos, New Mexico; Hanford, Washington; and other sites. Scientists in Oak Ridge, who were charged with finding a way to create a nuclear chain reaction that could be feasibly replicated within the confined space of a bomb, began experimenting with plutonium—a derivative of uranium first discovered by scientists at Berkeley. Plutonium proved capable of providing a practical fuel for the weapon. Scientists in Los Alamos, under the direction of J. Robert Oppenheimer, were charged with the construction of the actual atomic bomb.

J. Robert Oppenheimer

By 1944, the government was secretly funneling over $1 billion a year to the Manhattan Project, and despite many unforeseen problems, the scientists pushed ahead much faster than anyone had predicted. Even so, the war in Europe ended before they were ready to test the first weapon. Just before dawn on July 16, 1945, in the desert near Alamogordo, New Mexico, the scientists gathered to witness the first atomic explosion in history: the detonation of a plutonium-fueled bomb that scientists had named Trinity. The explosion—a blinding flash of light, probably brighter than any ever seen on earth, followed by a huge, billowing mushroom cloud—created a vast crater in the barren desert.

News of the explosion reached President Harry S. Truman (who had taken office in April on the death of Roosevelt) in Potsdam, Germany, where he was attending a conference of Allied leaders. He issued an ultimatum to the Japanese (signed jointly by the British) demanding that they

HIROSHIMA Long after the city was destroyed by the first atomic bomb ever used in warfare, Hiroshima remained a ghostly landscape—an incongruous backdrop for a Japanese couple strolling along the street. *(UPI/Corbis-Bettmann)*

surrender by August 3 or face utter devastation. When the Japanese failed to meet the deadline, Truman ordered the air force to use the new atomic weapons against Japan.

Persistent Controversy

Controversy has continued for decades over whether Truman's decision to use the bomb was justified and what his motives were. Some have argued that the atomic attack was unnecessary—that had the United States agreed to the survival of the emperor (which it ultimately did agree to in any case), or had it waited only a few more weeks, the Japanese would have surrendered. Others argue that nothing less than the atomic bombs could have persuaded the Japanese to surrender without a costly American invasion.

The nation's military and political leaders, however, seemed little concerned about such matters. Truman, who had not even known of the existence of the Manhattan Project until he became president, was, apparently, making what he believed to be a simple military decision. A weapon was available that would end the war quickly; he could see no reason not to use it.

Hiroshima Destroyed

On August 6, 1945, an American B-29, the *Enola Gay*, dropped an atomic weapon on the Japanese industrial center at Hiroshima. With a single bomb, the United States completely incinerated a four-square-mile area at the center of the previously undamaged city. More than 80,000 civilians died, according to later American estimates. Many more suffered the crippling effects of radioactive fallout or passed those effects on to their children in the form of birth defects.

The Japanese government, stunned by the attack, was at first unable to agree on a response. Two days later, on August 8, the Soviet Union declared war on Japan. And the following day, another American plane dropped another atomic weapon—this time on the city of Nagasaki—inflicting 100,000 deaths and horrible damage on yet another unfortunate community. Finally, the emperor intervened to break the stalemate in the cabinet, and on August 14 the government announced that it was ready to give up. On September 2, 1945, on board the American battleship *Missouri*, anchored in Tokyo Bay, Japanese officials signed the articles of surrender.

Surrender of Japan

The greatest war in the history of mankind had come to an end, and the United States had emerged from it not only victorious but in a position of unprecedented power, influence, and prestige. It was a victory, however, that few could greet with unambiguous joy. Fourteen million combatants had died in the struggle. Many more civilians had perished. The United States had suffered only light casualties in comparison with some other nations (and particularly in comparison with Russia and Germany), but the cost had still been high: 322,000 dead, another 800,000 injured. And the world continued to face an uncertain future, menaced by the threat of nuclear warfare and by an emerging antagonism between the world's two strongest nations—the United States and the Soviet Union—that would darken the peace for many decades to come.

CONCLUSION

The United States played a critical, indeed decisive, role in the war against Germany and Italy; and it defeated Imperial Japan in the Pacific largely alone. But America's contributions to and sacrifices in the war paled next to those of its most important allies. Britain, France, and above all the Soviet Union paid a staggering price—in lives, treasure, and social unity—that had no counterpart in the United States. Most American citizens experienced a booming prosperity and only modest privations during the four years of American involvement in the conflict. There were, of course, jarring social changes during the war that even prosperity could not entirely offset: shortages, restrictions, regulations, family dislocations, and perhaps most of all the absence of millions of men, and considerable numbers of women, who went overseas to fight.

American fighting men and women, of course, had very different experiences from those of the people who remained at home. They endured tremendous hardships, substantial casualties, and great loneliness. They fought effectively and bravely. They helped liberate North Africa and Italy from German occupation. And in June 1944, finally, they joined British, French, and other forces in a great and successful invasion of France, which led less than a year later to the destruction of the Nazi regime and the end of the European war. In the Pacific, they turned back the Japanese offensive through a series of difficult naval and land battles. Ultimately, however, it was not the American army and navy that brought the war against Japan to a close. It was the unleashing of the most destructive weapon mankind had ever created—the atomic bomb—on the people of Japan that finally persuaded the leaders of that nation to surrender.

FOR FURTHER REFERENCE

John Morton Blum, *V Was for Victory: Politics and American Culture During World War II* (1976) and Richard Polenberg, *War and Society* (1972) are important studies of the home front during World War II. David Kennedy, *Freedom from Fear: The American People in Depression and War, 1929–1945* (1999) is an important narrative of both the American military experience in the war and the war's impact on American politics and society. Alan Brinkley, *The End of Reform: New Deal Liberalism in Recession and War* (1995) examines the impact of the war on liberal ideology and political economy. Doris Kearns Goodwin, *No Ordinary Time: Franklin and Eleanor Roosevelt: The Home Front in World War II* (1994) is an engaging portrait of the Roosevelts during the war. Susan Hartmann examines the transformation in women's work and family roles during and after the war in *The Homefront and Beyond: American Women in the 1940s* (1982). Richard M. Dalfiume, *Desegregation of the U.S. Armed Forces: Fighting on Two Fronts, 1939–1953* (1969) discusses race relations in the military during World War II and beyond. Barbara Dianne Savage, *Broadcasting Freedom: Radio, War, and the Politics of Race, 1938–1948* (1999) reveals the role of African-American radio in tying the war to the struggle for black freedom. Maurice Isserman, *Which Side Were You On? The American Communist Party During World War II* (1982) portrays the dramatic shifts in Communist Party strategy and status during the war. John W. Dower, *War Without Mercy: Race and Power in the Pacific War* (1986) examines the intense racism that shaped both sides of the war between the United States and Japan. Peter Irons, *Justice at War* (1983) and Roger Daniels, *Concentration Camps USA: Japanese-Americans and World War II* (1981) examine the internment of Japanese Americans. John Keegan, *Six Armies in Normandy: From D-Day to the Liberation of Paris, June 6–August 25, 1944* (1982) is a superb account of the Normandy Invasion. David S. Wyman, *The Abandonment of the Jews: America and the Holocaust, 1941–1945* (1984) is sharply critical of American policy toward the victims of the Holocaust. Richard Rhodes, *The Making of the Atomic Bomb* (1987) is an excellent account of one of the great scientific projects of the twentieth century. Gar Alperovitz, *The Decision to Use the Atomic Bomb and the Architecture of an American Myth* (1995) is an exhaustive and highly critical study of why the United States used atomic weapons in 1945. A sharply different view is visible in Herbert Feis, *The Atomic Bomb and the End of World War II* (1966). John Hersey's *Hiroshima* (1946) reconstructs in minute detail the terrifying experience of the American atomic bomb attack on that Japanese city.

For quizzes, Internet resources, references to additional books and films, and more, consult this book's Online Learning Center site at www.mhhe.com/unfinishednation4.

THE AMERICAN NIGHTMARE Nightmarish visions of what life would be like under communism were staples of American anticommunist propaganda in the early years of the Cold War. This is the cover of a comic book widely distributed beginning in 1947 by Christian groups concerned about inadequate popular awareness of the threat. *(Michael Barson Collection)*

TIME LINE

1945	1946	1947	1948
Yalta and Potsdam Conferences	Atomic Energy Commission established	Truman Doctrine	Berlin blockade
United Nations founded	Iran crisis	Marshall Plan proposed	Truman elected president
		National Security Act	Hiss case begins
		Taft-Hartley Act	

FOR FURTHER REFERENCE

Bruce J. Schulman, *The Seventies: The Great Shift in American Culture, Society, and Politics* (2001) is a good general history of the period. James M. Cannon, *Time and Chance: Gerald Ford's Appointment with History* (1994) is a journalist's account of the Ford presidency. Charles O. Jones, *The Trusteeship Presidency: Jimmy Carter and the United States Congress* (1988) looks at Carter's frustrations in domestic policy, and Gaddis Smith, *Morality, Reason, and Power* (1986) examines his foreign policy. Steven Gillon, *The Democrats' Dilemma: Walter Mondale and the Liberal Legacy* (1992) is a good discussion of the travails of the Democrats in the 1970s. Jerome L. Himmelstein, *To the Right: The Transformation of American Conservatism* (1990) and Godfrey Hodgson, *The World Turned Upside Down: A History of the Conservative Ascendancy in America* (1996) are good introductions to the subject. Lisa McGirr, *Suburban Warriors: The Origins of the New American Right* (2001) is an excellent grass-roots study. E. J. Dionne, *Why Americans Hate Politics* (1991) is a perceptive discussion of the political discontents of the 1980s and early 1990s. Garry Wills, *Reagan's America* (1987) is an interesting, critical interpretation. Lou Cannon, *President Reagan: The Role of a Lifetime* (1990) and Haynes Johnson, *Sleepwalking Through History* (1991) are accounts by journalists who covered the Reagan White House. Frances Fitzgerald, *Way Out There in the Blue: Reagan, Star Wars, and the End of the Cold War* (2000) is a fine history of the Reagan presidency, and its foreign policy in particular. Hedrick Smith, *The Power Game* (1988) is a sweeping portrait of the culture of political Washington during the Reagan years. John Lewis Gaddis, *The United States and the End of the Cold War* (1992) and *We Now Know: Rethinking Cold War History* (1997) examine the transformation of the world order after 1989. Thomas Crothers, *In the Name of Democracy: U.S. Foreign Policy toward Latin America in the Reagan Years* (1991) examines a controversial area of Reagan's international record, including aspects of the Iran-Contra scandal. Herbert Parmet, *George Bush: The Life of a Lone Star Yankee* (1997) is the first major scholarly study of the 41st president.

The Conservative Resurgence (1991) is a documentary film examining the growing conservative trend in American politics during the late 1970s and the 1980s.

For quizzes, Internet resources, references to additional books and films, and more, consult this book's Online Learning Center site at www.mhhe.com/unfinishednation4.

SEPTEMBER 11, 2001 One great American symbol, the Statue of Liberty, stands against a sky filled with the thick smoke from the destruction of another American symbol, New York City's World Trade Center towers, a few hours after terrorists crashed two planes into them. *(Daniel Hatshizer/AP/Wide World Photos)*

TIME LINE

1993	1994	1995	1996	1997
North American Free Trade Agreement ratified	Health care reform fails	Government shutdown	Welfare reform passed	Microsoft antitrust suit begins
	Republicans capture Congress	Crime rates decline	Clinton reelected	Balanced budget agreement
		O. J. Simpson trial		

CHAPTER THIRTY

THE AFFLUENT SOCIETY

The Economic "Miracle"
The Explosion of Science and Technology
People of Plenty
The Other America
The Rise of the Civil Rights Movement
Eisenhower Republicanism
Eisenhower, Dulles, and the Cold War

If America experienced a golden age in the 1950s and early 1960s, as many Americans believed at the time and many continue to believe today, it was largely a result of two developments. One was a booming national prosperity, which profoundly altered the social, economic, and even physical landscape of the United States. The other was the continuing struggle against communism, a struggle that created considerable anxiety but that also encouraged Americans to look even more approvingly at their own society. But if these powerful forces created a widespread sense of national purpose and self-satisfaction, they also helped blind many Americans to serious problems plaguing large groups of the population.

THE ECONOMIC "MIRACLE"

Booming Economic Growth

Perhaps the most striking feature of American society in the 1950s and early 1960s was the booming economic growth that made even the heady 1920s seem pale by comparison. It was a better-balanced and more widely distributed prosperity than that of thirty years earlier. It was not, however, as universal as some Americans liked to believe.

1957	1959	1960	1961	1969
Sputnik launched	Castro seizes power in Cuba	U-2 incident	First American in space	Americans land on moon
Kerouac's *On the Road*				
Little Rock desegregation crisis				

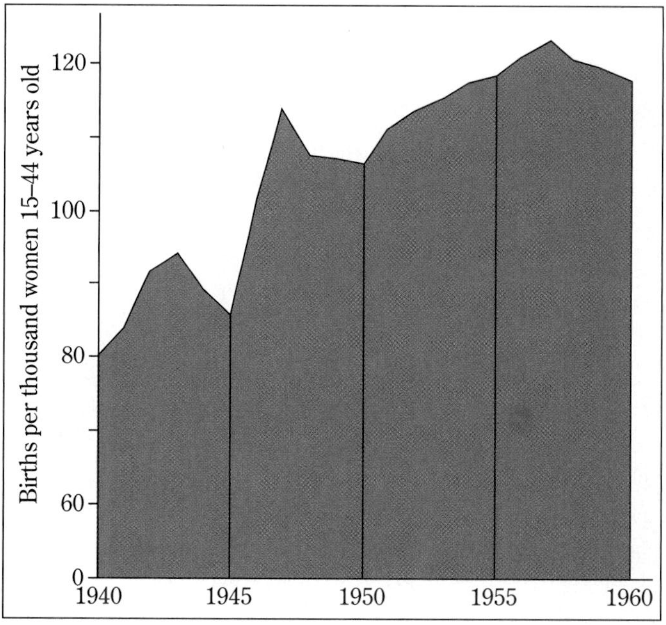

THE AMERICAN BIRTH RATE, 1940–1960 This chart shows how the American birth rate grew rapidly during and after World War II (after a long period of decline in the 1930s) to produce what became known as the "baby boom." At the peak of the baby boom, during the 1950s, the nation's population grew by 20 percent. ◆ *What impact did the baby boom have on the nation's economy?*

Economic Growth

By 1949, despite the continuing problems of postwar reconversion, an economic expansion had begun that would continue with only brief interruptions for almost twenty years. Between 1945 and 1960, the gross national product grew by 250 percent, from $200 billion to over $500 billion. Unemployment remained at about 5 percent or lower throughout the 1950s and early 1960s. Inflation, in the meantime, hovered around 3 percent a year or less.

Government Spending

The causes of this growth were varied. Government spending, which had ended the Depression in the 1940s, continued to stimulate growth through public funding of schools, housing, veterans' benefits, welfare, interstate highways, and above all military spending. Economic growth was at its peak during the first half of the 1950s, when military spending was highest because of the Korean War.

The national birth rate reversed a long pattern of decline with the so-called baby boom, which had begun during the war and peaked in 1957. The nation's population rose almost 20 percent in the decade, from 150 million in 1950 to 179 million in 1960. The baby boom meant increased consumer demand and expanding economic growth.

Suburban Expansion

The rapid expansion of suburbs—whose population grew 47 percent in the 1950s—helped stimulate growth in several important sectors of the economy. The number of privately owned cars more than doubled in a decade. Demand for new homes helped sustain a vigorous housing industry. The construction of roads stimulated the economy as well.

These and other forces helped the American economy to grow nearly ten times as fast as the population in the thirty years after the war. And while that growth was far from equally distributed, it affected most of society. The average American in 1960 had over 20 percent more purchasing power than in 1945, and more than twice as much as during the prosperous 1920s. The American people had achieved the highest standard of living of any society in the history of the world.

The Rise of the Modern West

No region of the country experienced more dramatic changes as a result of the new economic growth than the American West. Its population expanded dramatically; its cities boomed; its industrial economy flourished. By the 1960s, some parts of the West were among the most important (and populous) industrial and cultural centers of the nation in their own right.

Government-Induced Growth

As during World War II, much of the growth of the West was a result of federal spending and investment—on the dams, power stations, highways, and other infrastructure projects that made economic development possible; and on the military contracts that continued to flow disproportionately to factories in California and Texas, many of them built with government funds during the war. But other factors played a role as well. The growing number of automobiles created new demands for petroleum and contributed to the rapid growth of oil fields in Texas and Colorado and of the metropolitan centers serving them: Houston, Dallas, and Denver. State governments in the West invested heavily in their universities. The University of Texas and University of California systems, in particular, became among the nation's largest and best; as centers of research, they helped attract technology-intensive industries to the region. Climate also contributed. Southern California, Nevada, and Arizona, in particular, attracted many migrants from the East because of their warm, dry climates. The growth of Los Angeles after World War II was a remarkable phenomenon: more than 10 percent of all new businesses in the United States between 1945 and 1950 began in Los Angeles. Its population rose by over 50 percent between 1940 and 1960.

Capital and Labor

Corporations enjoying booming growth were reluctant to allow strikes to interfere with their operations; and since the most important labor unions were now so large and entrenched that they could not easily be suppressed

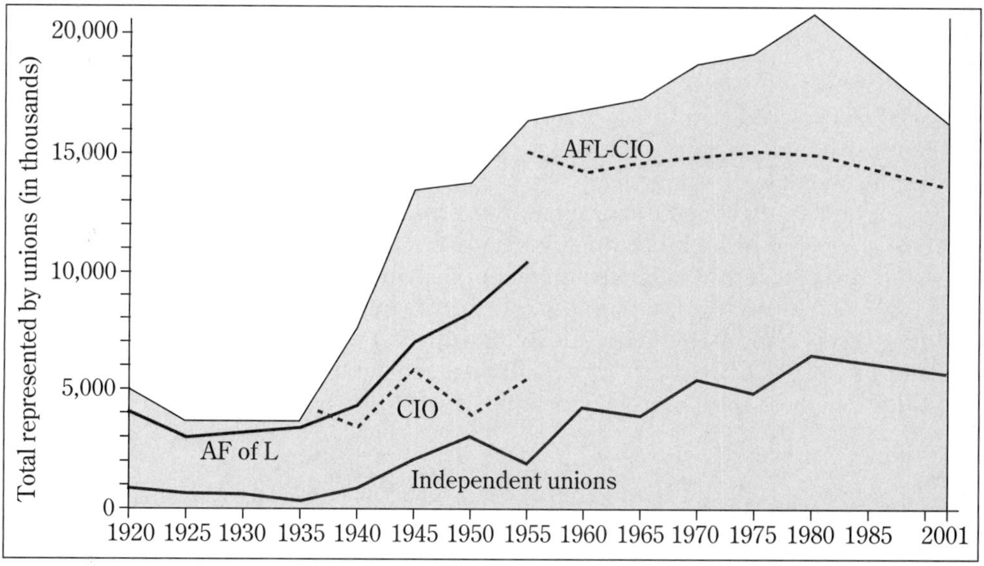

WORKERS REPRESENTED BY UNIONS, 1920–2001 This chart shows the number of workers represented by unions over an eighty-year period. Note the dramatic rise in the unionized work force during the 1930s and 1940s, the slower but still significant rise in the 1960s and 1970s, and the steady decline that began in the 1980s. The chart, in fact, understates the decline of unionized labor in the postwar era, since it shows union membership in absolute numbers and not as a percentage of the rapidly growing work force. Measured in that way, even a consistent number of union members would represent a relative decline for unions.
◆ *Why did unions cease recruiting new members successfully in the 1970s, and why did they begin actually losing members in the 1980s?*

or intimidated, leaders of large businesses made important concessions to them. By the mid-1950s, factory wages in all industries had risen substantially, to an average of $80 per week. In December 1955, the American Federation of Labor and the Congress of Industrial Organizations ended their twenty-year rivalry and merged to create the AFL-CIO, under the leadership of George Meany.

But success also bred stagnation and corruption in some union bureaucracies. In 1957, the powerful Teamsters Union became the subject of a congressional investigation, and its president, David Beck, was charged with the misappropriation of union funds. Beck ultimately stepped down to be replaced by Jimmy Hoffa, whom government investigators pursued for nearly a decade before finally winning a conviction against him in 1967. The United Mine Workers, similarly, became tainted by violence and charges of corruption.

Jimmy Hoffa

THE EXPLOSION OF SCIENCE AND TECHNOLOGY

In 1961, *Time* magazine selected as its "man of the year" not a specific person but "the American Scientist." The choice was an indication of the widespread fascination with which Americans in the age of atomic weapons viewed science and technology.

Medical Breakthroughs

The twentieth century saw more progress in the development of medical science than had occurred in all the centuries before it. A very large proportion of that progress occurred during and after World War II. Particularly important was the development of new antibacterial drugs capable of fighting infections that in the past had been all but untreatable.

Development of Antibacterial Drugs

The development of antibiotics had its origins in the discoveries of Louis Pasteur and Jules-Francois Joubert. Working in France in the 1870s, they produced the first conclusive evidence that virulent bacterial infections could be defeated by other, more ordinary bacteria. Using their discoveries, the English physician Joseph Lister revealed the value of antiseptic solutions to prevent infection during surgery.

But the practical use of antibacterial agents to combat disease did not begin until many decades later. In the 1930s, scientists in Germany, France, and England demonstrated the power of so-called sulfa drugs—drugs derived from an antibacterial agent known as sulfanilamide—which could be used effectively to treat streptococcal blood infections. New sulfa drugs were soon being developed at an astonishing rate, and were frequently improved, with dramatic results in treating what had once been a major cause of death.

Penicillin

In 1928, in the meantime, Alexander Fleming, an English medical researcher, accidentally discovered the antibacterial properties of an organism that he named penicillin. There was little progress in using penicillin to treat human illness, however, until a group of researchers at Oxford University, directed by Howard Florey and Ernest Chain, learned how to produce stable, potent penicillin in sizable enough quantities to make it a practical weapon against bacterial disease. The first human trials of the new drug, in 1941, were dramatically successful, but progress toward the mass availability of penicillin was stalled in England because of World War II. American laboratories took the next crucial steps in developing methods for the mass production and commercial distribution of penicillin, which became widely available to doctors and hospitals around the world by

1948. Since then, a wide range of new antibiotics of highly specific character have been developed so that bacterial infections are now among the most successfully treated of all human illnesses.

There was also dramatic progress in immunization—the development of vaccines that can protect humans from contracting both bacterial and viral diseases. The first great triumph was the development of the smallpox vaccine by the English researcher Edward Jenner in the late eighteenth century. A vaccine effective against typhoid was developed by an English bacteriologist, Almorth Wright, in 1897, and was in wide use by World War I. Vaccination against tetanus became widespread just before and during World War II. Medical scientists also developed a vaccine, BCG, against another major killer, tuberculosis, in the 1920s; but controversy over its safety stalled its adoption, especially in the United States, for many years. It was not widely used in the United States until after World War II, when it largely eliminated tuberculosis until a limited recurrence began in the 1990s.

Viruses are much more difficult to prevent and treat than bacterial infections, and progress toward vaccines against viral infections—except for smallpox—was relatively slow. Not until the 1930s, when scientists discovered how to grow viruses in laboratories in tissue cultures, could researchers study them with any real effectiveness. Gradually, they discovered how to produce forms of a virus capable of triggering antibodies in vaccinated people that would protect them from contracting disease. An effective vaccine against yellow fever was developed in the late 1930s, and one against influenza—one of the great killers of the first half of the twentieth century—appeared in 1945.

A particularly dramatic postwar triumph was the development of a vaccine against polio. In 1954, the American scientist Jonas Salk introduced an effective vaccine against the disease that had killed and crippled thousands of children and adults (among them Franklin Roosevelt). It was provided free to the public by the federal government beginning in 1955. After 1960, an oral vaccine developed by Albert Sabin—usually administered in a sugar cube—made widespread vaccination even easier. By the early 1960s, these vaccines had virtually eliminated polio from American life and from much of the rest of the world.

Salk Vaccine

As a result of these and many other medical advances, both infant mortality and the death rate among young children declined significantly in the first twenty-five years after the war (although not by as much as in Western Europe). Average life expectancy in that same period rose by five years, to seventy-one.

Pesticides

Scientists were also developing new kinds of chemical pesticides, which they hoped would protect crops from destruction by insects and protect humans from such insect-carried diseases as typhus and malaria. Perhaps

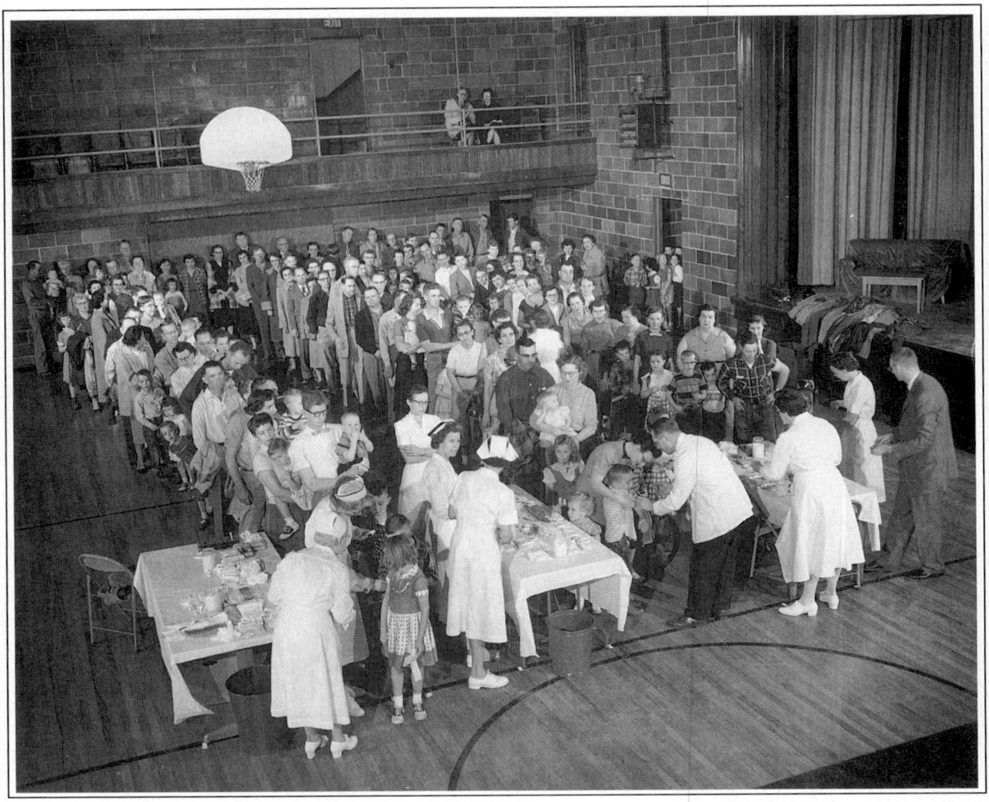

THE SALK VACCINE Dr. Jonas Salk, a medical researcher at the University of Pittsburgh, developed in the mid-1950s the first vaccine that proved effective in preventing polio. In its aftermath, scenes similar to this one—a mass inoculation of families in a school gymnasium in Kansas—repeated themselves all over the country. A few years later, Dr. Albert Sabin of the University of Cincinnati created a vaccine that could be administered more easily, through sugar cubes. *(March of Dimes Birth Defects Foundation)*

the most famous of the new pesticides was dichlorodiphenyltrichloroethane, generally known as DDT, a compound discovered in 1939 by a Swiss chemist named Paul Muller. He had discovered that although DDT seemed harmless to human beings and other mammals, it was extremely toxic to insects. American scientists learned of Muller's discovery in 1942, just as the army was grappling with the insect-borne tropical diseases—especially malaria and typhus—that threatened American soldiers.

DDT

DDT was first used on a large scale in Italy in 1943–1944 during a typhus outbreak, which it quickly helped end. Soon it was being sprayed in mosquito-infested areas of Pacific islands where American troops were fighting the Japanese. The incidence of malaria dropped precipitously. DDT quickly gained a reputation as a miraculous tool for controlling insects, and it undoubtedly saved thousands of lives. Only later did it become evident that DDT had long-term toxic effects on animals and humans.

Postwar Electronic Research

The 1940s and 1950s saw dramatic new developments in electronic technology. Researchers in the 1940s produced the first commercially viable televisions and created a technology that made it possible to broadcast programming over large areas. In the late 1950s, scientists at RCA's David Sarnoff Laboratories in New Jersey developed the technology for color television, which first became widely available in the early 1960s.

Television

In 1948 Bell Labs, the research arm of AT&T, produced the first transistor, a solid-state device capable of amplifying electrical signals, which was much smaller and more efficient than the cumbersome vacuum tubes that had powered most electronic equipment in the past. Transistors made possible the miniaturization of many devices (radios, televisions, audio equipment, hearing aids) and were also important in aviation, weaponry, and satellites. They contributed as well to another major breakthrough in electronics: the development of integrated circuitry in the late 1950s.

Integrated Circuits Invented

Integrated circuits combined a number of once-separate electronic elements (transistors, resistors, diodes, and others) and embedded them into a single, microscopically small device. They made it possible to create increasingly complex electronic devices requiring complicated circuitry that would have been impractical to produce through other means. Most of all, integrated circuits helped advance the development of the computer.

Postwar Computer Technology

Prior to the 1950s, computers had been constructed mainly to perform complicated mathematical tasks, such as those required to break military codes. In the 1950s, they began to perform commercial functions for the first time.

The first significant computer of the 1950s was the Universal Automatic Computer (or UNIVAC), which was developed initially for the U.S. Bureau of the Census by the Remington Rand Company. It was the first computer able to handle both alphabetical and numerical information easily. It used tape storage and could perform calculations and other functions much faster than its predecessor, the ENIAC. Searching for a larger market than the census for their very expensive new device, Remington Rand arranged to use a UNIVAC to predict the results of the 1952 election for CBS television news. It would, they believed, produce valuable publicity for the machine. Analyzing early voting results, the UNIVAC accurately predicted an enormous landslide victory for Eisenhower over Stevenson. Few Americans had ever heard of a computer before that night, and the UNIVAC's television debut became, therefore, a critical breakthrough in public awareness of computer technology.

Remington Rand had limited success in marketing the UNIVAC, but in the mid-1950s the International Business Machines Company (IBM) introduced its first major data-processing computers and began to find a wide market for them among businesses in the United States and abroad. These early successes, combined with the enormous amount of money IBM invested in research and development, made the company the worldwide leader in computers for many years.

IBM

Bombs, Rockets, and Missiles

In 1952, the United States successfully detonated the first hydrogen bomb. (The Soviet Union tested its first H-bomb a year later.) Unlike the plutonium and uranium bombs developed during World War II, the hydrogen bomb derives its power not from fission (the splitting of atoms) but fusion (the joining together of lighter atomic elements with heavier ones). It is capable of producing explosions of vastly greater power than the earlier fission bombs.

Nuclear Fusion

The development of the hydrogen bomb gave considerable impetus to a stalled scientific project in both the United States and the Soviet Union: the effort to develop unmanned rockets and missiles capable of traveling the new weapons—not suitable for delivery by airplanes—to their targets. Both nations began to put tremendous resources into their development. The United States benefited from the emigration to America of some of the German scientists who had helped develop rocketry for Germany during World War II.

In the United States, early missile research was conducted almost entirely by the Air Force, and there were significant early successes in developing rockets capable of traveling several hundred miles. But American and Soviet leaders were both struggling to build longer-range missiles that could cross oceans and continents—intercontinental ballistic missiles, or ICBMs, capable of traveling through space to distant targets. American scientists experimented in the 1950s first with the Atlas and then the Titan ICBM. There were some early successes, but there were also many setbacks, particularly because of the difficulty of massing sufficient, stable fuel to provide the tremendous power needed to launch missiles beyond the atmosphere. By 1958, scientists had created a solid fuel to replace the volatile liquid fuels of the early missiles; and they had also produced miniaturized guidance systems capable of ensuring that missiles could travel to reasonably precise destinations. Within a few years, a new generation of missile, known as the Minuteman, became the basis of the American atomic weapons arsenal. It was capable of traveling several thousand miles. American scientists also developed a nuclear missile capable of being carried and fired by submarines—the Polaris, which is launched from below the surface of the ocean by

ICBMs

compressed air and fires its engines only once it is above the surface. A Polaris was first successfully fired from underwater in 1960.

The Space Program

Sputnik

The American space program eventually developed a rationale of its own. In the beginning, however, it was a byproduct of the rivalry with the Soviet Union. Its origins can perhaps be traced most directly to a dramatic event in 1957, when the Soviet Union announced that it had launched an earth-orbiting satellite—*Sputnik*—into outer space. The United States had yet to perform any similar feats, and the American government (and much of American society) reacted to the announcement with alarm. Federal policy began encouraging (and funding) strenuous efforts to improve scientific education in the schools, to create more research laboratories, and, above all, to speed the development of America's own exploration of outer space. The United States launched its own first satellite, *Explorer I*, in January 1958.

The centerpiece of space exploration, however, soon became the manned space program, established in 1958 along with a new agency, the National Aeronautics and Space Administration (NASA). The first American space pilots, or "astronauts," quickly became the nation's most revered heroes. On May 5, 1961, Alan Shepard became the first American launched into space. But his short, suborbital flight came several months after a Soviet "cosmonaut," Yuri Gagarin, had made a flight in which he had actually orbited the earth. On February 2, 1962, John Glenn (later a United States senator) became the first American to orbit the globe. NASA later introduced the Gemini program, whose spacecraft could carry two astronauts at once.

Apollo

Mercury and Gemini were followed by the Apollo program, whose purpose was to land men on the moon. It had some catastrophic setbacks, most notably a fire in January 1967 that killed three astronauts during a training session. But on July 20, 1969, Neil Armstrong, Edwin Aldrin, and Michael Collins successfully traveled in a space capsule into orbit around the moon. Armstrong and Aldrin then detached a smaller craft from the capsule, landed on the surface of the moon, and became the first men to walk on a body other than earth. Six more lunar missions followed, the last in 1972.

Eventually, the space program became a relatively modest effort to make travel in near-space easier and more practical through the development of the "space shuttle," an airplane-like device launched by a missile but capable both of navigating in space and landing on earth much like a conventional aircraft. The first space shuttle was successfully launched in 1982. The explosion of one shuttle, *Challenger*, in January 1986 shortly after takeoff, killing all seven astronauts, stalled the program for two years. But missions resumed in the late 1980s. The space shuttle has been used to launch and repair communications satellites, to insert the Hubble

Space Telescope into orbit in 1990 (and later to repair its flawed lens), and to service the orbiting Spacelab.

PEOPLE OF PLENTY

Among the most striking social developments of the immediate postwar era was the rapid extension of a middle-class lifestyle and outlook to an expanding portion of the population. The historian David Potter published an influential examination of "economic abundance and American character" in 1954. He called it *People of Plenty.* For the American middle class in the 1950s, at least, it seemed an appropriate label.

The Consumer Culture

Growing Focus on Consumer Goods

At the center of middle-class culture in the 1950s was a growing absorption with consumer goods. That was a result of increased prosperity, of the increasing variety and availability of products, and of the adeptness of advertisers in creating a demand for those products. It was also a result of the growth of consumer credit, which increased by 800 percent between 1945 and 1957 through the development of credit cards, revolving charge accounts, and easy-payment plans. Prosperity fueled such longtime consumer crazes as the automobile, and Detroit responded to the boom with ever-flashier styling and accessories. Consumers also responded eagerly to the development of such new products as dishwashers, garbage disposals, television, hi-fis, and stereos.

Because consumer goods were so often marketed (and advertised) nationally, the 1950s were notable for the rapid spread of great national consumer crazes. For example, children, adolescents, and even some adults became entranced in the late 1950s with the hula hoop—a large plastic ring kept spinning around the waist. The popularity of the Walt Disney-produced children's television show *The Mickey Mouse Club* created a national demand for related products such as Mickey Mouse watches and hats. It also helped produce the stunning success of Disneyland, an amusement park near Los Angeles that re-created many of the characters and events of Disney entertainment programs.

The Suburban Nation

A third of the nation's population lived in suburbs by 1960. The growth of suburbs was a result not only of increased affluence but of important innovations in home building, which made single-family houses affordable to millions of new people. The most famous of the suburban developers, William Levitt, came to symbolize

William Levitt

LEVITTOWN BEFORE THE TREES A section of the Levittown on Long Island in New York, photographed in July 1948, a few months after the first families moved in. The Levitt family pioneered techniques in constructing mass-produced housing that made possible the proliferation of similar inexpensive suburbs in many areas of the country. *(Culver Pictures, Inc.)*

the new suburban growth with his use of mass-production techniques to construct large housing developments, the first of which was on Long Island, near New York City. The houses sold for under $10,000. Many other relatively inexpensive suburban developments soon began appearing throughout the country.

Why did so many Americans want to move to the suburbs? One reason was the enormous importance postwar Americans placed on family life after five years of war. Suburbs provided families with larger homes than they could find (or afford) in the cities, and thus made it easier to raise larger numbers of children. They provided privacy. They also provided a sense of security from the noise and dangers of urban living. They offered space for the new consumer goods—the appliances, cars, boats, outdoor furniture, and other products that many middle-class Americans craved.

Segregated Suburbs

Another factor motivating white Americans to move to the suburbs was race. Most suburbs were restricted to white inhabitants—both because relatively few African Americans could afford to live in them and because formal and informal barriers kept even prosperous blacks out of all but a few. In an era when the black population of most cities was rapidly growing, many white families fled to the suburbs to escape the integration of urban neighborhoods and schools.

The Suburban Family

Traditional Gender Norms Reinforced

For professional men (who tended to work in the city, at some distance from their homes), suburban life generally meant a rigid division between their working and personal worlds. For many middle-class women, it meant an increased isolation from the workplace. Many middle-class husbands considered it demeaning for their wives to be employed. And many women themselves shied away from the workplace when they could afford to, in part because of prevailing ideas about motherhood (popularized by such widely consulted books as Dr. Benjamin Spock's *Baby and Child Care*, first published in 1946) that advised women to stay at home with their children.

Some women, however, had to balance these pressures against other, contradictory ones. As expectations of material comfort rose, many middle-class families needed a second income to maintain the standard of living they desired. As a result, the number of married women working outside the home actually increased in the postwar years. By 1960, nearly a third of all married women were part of the paid work force.

The Birth of Television

Growing Popularity of Television

Television was the result of a series of scientific and technological discoveries, but its impact was largely social and cultural. It quickly became perhaps the most powerful medium of mass communication in history. Experiments in broadcasting pictures (along with sound) had begun as early as the 1920s, but commercial television began only shortly after World War II. Its growth was phenomenally rapid. In 1946, there were only 17,000 sets in the country; by 1957, there were 40 million television sets in use—almost as many sets as there were families. More people had television sets, according to one report, than had refrigerators.

The television industry emerged directly out of the radio industry, and all three of the major networks—the National Broadcasting Company, the Columbia Broadcasting System, and the American Broadcasting Company—had started as radio companies. Like radio, the television business was driven by advertising. The need to attract advertisers determined most programming decisions; and in the early days of television, sponsors often played a direct role in determining the content of the programs they chose to sponsor. Many early television shows bore the names of the corporations that were paying for them: the GE Television Theater, the Chrysler Playhouse, the Camel News Caravan, and others. Some daytime serials (known as "soap operas," because their sponsors were almost always companies making household goods targeted at women) were actually written and produced by Procter & Gamble and other companies.

By the late 1950s, television news had replaced newspapers, magazines, and radios as the nation's most important vehicle of information.

Television advertising helped create a vast market for new fashions and products. Televised athletic events gradually made college and professional sports one of the most important sources of entertainment (and one of the biggest businesses) in America. Television entertainment programming—almost all of it controlled by the three national networks and their corporate sponsors—replaced movies and radio as the principal source of diversion for American families.

Much of the programming of the 1950s and early 1960s created a common image of American life—an image that was predominantly white, middle class, and suburban, and that was epitomized by the popular situation comedies, which showed families in which, as the title of one of the most popular put it, *Father Knows Best*, and in which most women were mothers and housewives striving to serve their children and please their husbands.

Social Conflict Accentuated

Yet television also, inadvertently, created conditions that could accentuate social conflict. Even those unable to share in the affluence of the era could, through television, acquire a vivid picture of how the rest of their society lived. Thus at the same time that television was celebrating the white middle class, it was also contributing to the sense of alienation and powerlessness among groups excluded from the world it portrayed. And television news conveyed with unprecedented power the social upheavals that gradually spread beginning in the late 1950s.

Travel, Outdoor Recreation, and Environmentalism

Although the idea of a paid vacation for American workers, and the connection of that idea with travel, had entered American culture beginning in the 1920s, it was not until the postwar years that vacation travel became truly widespread among middle-income Americans. The construction of the interstate highway system contributed dramatically to the growth of travel. So did the increasing affluence of workers. Even in the 1950s, there was a healthy market for vacation vehicles—trailers and small vans—that some families used while traveling, and that market grew steadily larger in subsequent decades. But the urge to travel was also an expression of some of the same impulses that produced the move to suburbs: a desire to escape the crowding and stress of densely populated areas and find a place where it was possible to experience the natural world.

Nowhere was this surge in travel and recreation more visible than in the nation's national parks, which experienced the beginnings of what became a long-term surge in attendance in the 1950s. People who traveled to national parks did so for many reasons—some to hike and camp; some to fish and hunt (activities that themselves grew dramatically in the 1950s and spawned a large number of clubs), some simply to look in awe at the landscape. But whatever their motives, most visitors came in search of an experience in the wilderness. The importance of that search became clear in the early 1950s in the first of many battles over development of wilderness areas: the fight to preserve Echo Park.

Echo Park is a spectacular valley in the Dinosaur National Monument, on the border between Utah and Colorado, near the southern border of Wyoming. In the early 1950s, the federal government's Bureau of Reclamation—which had been created early in the century to encourage irrigation, develop electric power, and increase water supplies—proposed building a dam across the Green River, which runs through Echo Valley, so as to create a lake for recreation and a source of hydroelectric power. The American environmental movement had been relatively quiet since its searing defeat early in the century in its effort to stop a similar dam in the Hetch Hetchy valley at Yosemite National Park. (See p. 584.) But the Echo Park proposal helped rouse it from its slumber.

In 1950, Bernard DeVoto—a well-known writer and a great champion of the American West—published an essay in *The Saturday Evening Post* entitled "Shall We Let Them Ruin Our National Parks?" It had a sensational impact, arousing opposition to the Echo Valley dam from many areas of the country. The Sierra Club, relatively obscure in previous decades, now sprang into action; the controversy helped elevate a new and aggressive leader, David Brower, who eventually transformed the Club into the nation's leading environmental organization. By the mid-1950s, a large coalition of environmentalists, naturalists, and wilderness vacationers had mobilized in opposition to the dam, and in 1956 Congress—bowing to public pressure—blocked the project and preserved Echo Park in its natural state. The controversy was a major victory for those who wished to preserve the sanctity of the national parks, and it was an important spur to the dawning environmental consciousness that would become so important a decade and more later.

Sierra Club Reborn

Organized Society and Its Detractors

Large-scale organizations and bureaucracies increased their influence over American life in the postwar era, as they had been doing for many decades before. White-collar workers came to outnumber blue-collar laborers for the first time, and an increasing proportion of them worked in corporate settings with rigid hierarchical structures. Industrial workers also confronted large bureaucracies both in the workplace and in their own unions.

The debilitating impact of bureaucratic life on the individual became one of the central themes of popular and scholarly debate. William H. Whyte, Jr., produced one of the most widely discussed books of the decade: *The Organization Man* (1956), which attempted to describe the special mentality of the worker in a large, bureaucratic setting. Self-reliance, Whyte claimed, was losing place to the ability to "get along" and "work as a team" as the most

The Organization Man

valuable trait in the modern character. The sociologist David Riesman made similar observations in *The Lonely Crowd* (1950), in which he argued that the traditional "inner-directed man," who judged himself on the basis of his own values and the esteem of his family, was giving way to a new "other-directed man," more concerned with winning the approval of the larger organization or community.

Novelists, too, expressed misgivings in their work about the impersonality of modern society. Saul Bellow produced a series of novels—*The Adventures of Augie March* (1953), *Seize the Day* (1956), *Herzog* (1964), and many others—that chronicled the difficulties American Jewish men had in finding fulfillment in modern urban America. J. D. Salinger wrote in *The Catcher in the Rye* (1951) of a prep-school student, Holden Caulfield, who was unable to find any area of society—school, family, friends, city—in which he could feel secure or committed.

The Beats and the Restless Culture of Youth

The most derisive critics of bureaucracy, and of middle-class society generally, were a group of young poets, writers, and artists known as the "beats" (or, by disapproving critics, as "beatniks"). They wrote harsh critiques of what they considered the sterility and conformity of American life, the meaninglessness of American politics, and the banality of popular culture. Allen Ginsberg's dark, bitter poem *Howl* (1955) decried the "Robot apartments! invincible suburbs! skeleton treasuries! blind capitals! demonic industries!" of modern life. Jack Kerouac produced the most popular document of the Beat Generation in his novel *On the Road* (1957), an account of a cross-country automobile trip that depicted the rootless, iconoclastic lifestyle of Kerouac and his friends.

Howl

The beats were the most visible evidence of a widespread restiveness among young Americans in the 1950s. Youths in the 1950s never staged rebellions as widespread or as bitter as those of the 1960s, but their restlessness was visible nevertheless. The phenomenon of "juvenile delinquency" attracted tremendous public attention, and in both politics and popular culture there were dire warnings about the growing criminality of American youth. The 1955 film *Blackboard Jungle*, for example, was a frightening depiction of crime and violence in city schools. Scholarly studies, presidential commissions, and journalistic exposés all contributed to the sense of alarm about the spread of delinquency—although in fact youth crime did not dramatically increase in the 1950s.

"Juvenile Delinquency"

Many young people began to wear clothes and adopt hairstyles that mimicked popular images of juvenile criminal gangs. The culture of alienation that the beats so vividly represented had counterparts even in ordinary middle-class behavior: teenage rebelliousness toward parents, youthful fascination with fast cars and motorcycles, increasing sexual activity, assisted by the greater availability of birth-control devices. The popularity of James Dean, in such movies as *Rebel Without a Cause* (1955), *East of Eden* (1955), and *Giant* (1956), was a particularly vivid sign of youth culture in the 1950s. Both in the roles he played (moody, alienated teenagers and young men with a streak of self-destructive violence) and in the way he lived his own life (he died in 1955, at the age of 24, in an automobile accident), Dean became an icon of the unfocused rebelliousness of American youth in his time.

Rock 'n' Roll

One of the most important cultural developments for American youth in the 1950s was the enormous popularity of rock 'n' roll—and of the greatest early rock star, Elvis Presley. Presley became a symbol of a youthful determination to push at the borders of the conventional and acceptable. Presley's sultry good looks, his self-conscious effort to dress in the vaguely rebellious style of urban gangs (motorcycle jackets and slicked-back hair, even though Presley himself was a product of the rural South), and, most of all, the open sexuality of his music and his public performances—all made him wildly popular among young Americans in the 1950s. His first great hit, "Heartbreak Hotel," established him as a national phenomenon in 1956, and he remained a powerful figure in American popular culture until—and indeed beyond—his death in 1977.

Elvis Presley

Presley's music, like that of many early white rock musicians, drew heavily from black rhythm and blues traditions. Sam Phillips, a record promoter who had recorded some of the important black rhythm and blues musicians of his time (among them B. B. King), reportedly said in the early 1950s: "If I could find a white man with a Negro sound, I could make a billion dollars." Soon after that, he found Presley. But there were others as well—among them Buddy Holly and Bill Haley (whose 1955 song "Rock Around the Clock"—used in the film *Blackboard Jungle*—served to announce the arrival of rock 'n' roll to millions of young people)—who were closely connected to African-American musical traditions. Rock drew from other sources too: from country western music (another strong influence on Presley), from gospel music, even from jazz.

Rock 'n' Roll's Black Origins

The 1950s also produced growth in the popularity of African-American bands and singers among both black and white audiences. Chuck Berry, Little Richard, B. B. King, Chubby Checker, the Temptations, and others—many of them recorded by the black producer Berry Gordy, the founder and president of Motown Records in Detroit—never rivaled Presley in their popularity among white youths but did develop significant multiracial audiences of their own.

The rapid rise of rock owed a great deal to innovations in radio and television programming. By the 1950s, radio stations no longer felt obliged to

ELVIS IN CONCERT Elvis Presley ended his career performing before wealthy audiences in Las Vegas, wearing garish sequined suits. But in the early years of his career, as this concert in the late 1950s suggests, both he and his fans were younger—and the connection between them was immediate and intense. *(Bettmann/Corbis)*

present mostly live programming—especially once television took over many of the entertainment functions radio had once performed. Instead, many radio stations devoted themselves almost entirely to playing recorded music. Early in the 1950s, a new breed of radio announcers, known as "disk jockeys," began to create programming aimed specifically at young fans of rock music; and when those programs became wildly successful, other stations followed suit. *American Bandstand*, which began airing in 1957, was a televised showcase for rock 'n' roll hits in which a live audience danced to recorded music. The program helped spread the popularity of rock—and made its host, Dick Clark, one of the best-known figures among young Americans.

Rapidly Growing Record Sales

Radio and television were important to the recording industry, of course, because they encouraged the sale of records, which was increasing rapidly in the mid- and late 1950s, especially in the inexpensive and popular 45 rpm format—small disks that contained one song on each side. Also important were juke boxes, which played individual songs on 45s and which proliferated in soda fountains, diners, bars, and almost every other place where young people were likely to congregate. Sales of records increased from $182 million to $521 million between 1954 and 1960. So eager were record promoters to get their songs on the air that they routinely made secret payments to station owners and disk jockeys to encourage them to showcase their artists. These payments, which became known as "payola," produced a briefly sensational series of scandals when they were exposed in the late 1950s and early 1960s.

THE OTHER AMERICA

It was relatively easy for white, middle-class Americans in the 1950s to believe that the world they knew—a world of economic growth, personal affluence, and cultural homogeneity—was the world virtually all Americans knew, that the values and assumptions they shared were ones that most other Americans shared, too. But such beliefs were false. Large groups of Americans remained outside the circle of abundance and shared neither in the affluence of the middle class nor in many of its values.

On the Margins of the Affluent Society

Michael Harrington

In 1962, the socialist writer Michael Harrington published a celebrated book called *The Other America.* In it, he chronicled the continuing existence of poverty in the United States.

The great economic expansion of the postwar years reduced poverty dramatically but did not eliminate it. In 1960, at any given moment, more than a fifth of all American families (over 30 million people) continued to live below what the government defined as the poverty line (down from a third of all families fifteen years before). Many millions more lived just above the official poverty line, but with incomes that gave them little comfort and no security.

Most of the poor—up to 80 percent—experienced poverty intermittently and temporarily. But approximately 20 percent of the poor were people for whom poverty was a continuous reality from which there was no easy escape. That included approximately half the nation's elderly and a significant proportion of African Americans and Hispanics. Native Americans constituted the single poorest group in the country.

Persistent Poverty

This "hard-core" poverty rebuked the assumptions of those who argued that economic growth would eventually lead everyone into prosperity—that, as many claimed, "a rising tide lifts all boats." It was a poverty that the growing prosperity of the postwar era seemed to affect hardly at all, a poverty, as Harrington observed, that appeared "impervious to hope."

Rural Poverty

Among those on the margins of the affluent society were many rural Americans. In 1948, farmers had received 8.9 percent of the national income; in 1956, they received only 4.1 percent. In part, this decline reflected the steadily shrinking farm population; in 1956 alone, nearly 10 percent of the rural population moved into or was absorbed by cities. But it also reflected declining farm prices. Because of enormous surpluses in basic staples, prices fell 33 percent in those years, even though national income as a whole rose 50 percent at the same time.

Sharecroppers and tenant farmers (most of them African American) continued to live at or below subsistence levels throughout the rural South—in part because of the mechanization of cotton picking beginning in 1944, in part because of the development of synthetic fibers that reduced demand for cotton generally. (Two-thirds of the cotton acreage of the South went out of production between 1930 and 1960.) Migrant farmworkers, a group concentrated especially in the West and Southwest and containing many Mexican-American and Asian-American workers, lived in similarly dire circumstances. In rural areas without much commercial agriculture—such as the Appalachian region in the East, where the decline of the coal economy reduced the one significant source of support for the region—whole communities lived in desperate poverty, increasingly cut off from the market economy. All these groups were vulnerable to malnutrition and even starvation.

The Inner Cities

As prospering white families moved from cities to suburbs in vast numbers, more and more inner-city neighborhoods became repositories for the poor, "ghettoes" from which there was no easy escape. The growth of these neighborhoods owed much to a vast migration of African Americans out of the countryside and into industrial cities. Not all these black migrants were poor, and many found in the city some of the same routes to economic progress that many whites were finding. But African Americans were substantially more likely to live in poverty than most other groups, in part because of the persistence of patterns of discrimination that denied them any real opportunities.

"Ghettoes"

More than 3 million black men and women moved from the South to northern cities between 1940 and 1960. Chicago, Detroit, Cleveland, New York, and other eastern and midwestern industrial cities experienced a major expansion of their black populations—both in absolute numbers and, even more, as a percentage of the whole, since so many whites were leaving at the same time.

Similar migrations from Mexico and Puerto Rico expanded poor Hispanic neighborhoods in many American cities at the same time. Between 1940 and 1960, nearly a million Puerto Ricans moved into American cities (the largest group to New York). Mexican workers crossed the border into Texas and California and swelled the already substantial Latino communities of such cities as San Antonio, Houston, San Diego, and Los Angeles (which by 1960 had the largest Mexican-American population of any city, approximately 500,000 people).

Declining Opportunities for Unskilled Workers

Inner cities were filling up with poor minority residents at the same time that the unskilled industrial jobs they were seeking were diminishing. Employers were moving factories and mills from old industrial cities to new locations in rural areas, smaller cities, and even abroad—places where the cost of labor or of other things were lower. Even in the factories that remained, automation was reducing the number of unskilled jobs. The economic opportunities that had helped earlier immigrant groups to rise up from poverty were unavailable to many of the postwar migrants. Racial discrimination in hiring, education, and housing doomed many members of these communities to continuing, and in some cases increasing, poverty.

THE RISE OF THE CIVIL RIGHTS MOVEMENT

After decades of skirmishes, an open battle began in the 1950s against racial segregation and discrimination, a battle that would prove to be one of the longest and most difficult social struggles of the century. White Americans played an important role in the civil rights movement. But pressure from African Americans themselves was the crucial element in raising the issue of race to prominence.

The Brown Decision and "Massive Resistance"

Plessy v. Ferguson Overturned

On May 17, 1954, the Supreme Court announced its decision in the case of *Brown* v. *Board of Education of Topeka.* In considering the legal segregation of a Kansas public school system, the Court rejected its own 1896 *Plessy* v. *Ferguson* decision, which had ruled that communities could provide African Americans with separate facilities as long as the facilities were equal to those of whites.

LITTLE ROCK An African-American student passes by jeering whites in Arkansas on her way to Central High School in Little Rock, newly integrated by federal court order. The black students later admitted that they had been terrified during the first difficult weeks of integration. But in public, most of them acted with remarkable calm and dignity. *(UPI/Corbis-Bettman)*

The *Brown* decision unequivocally declared the segregation of public schools on the basis of race to be unconstitutional. The justices argued that school segregation inflicted unacceptable damage on those it affected, regardless of the relative quality of the separate schools. Chief Justice Earl Warren explained the unanimous opinion of his colleagues: "We conclude that in the field of public education the doctrine of 'separate but equal' has no place. Separate educational facilities are inherently unequal." The following year, the Court issued another decision (known as *Brown II*) to provide rules for implementing the 1954 order. It ruled that communities must work to desegregate their schools "with all deliberate speed," but it set no timetable and left specific decisions up to lower courts.

In some communities, for example, Washington, D.C., compliance came relatively quickly and quietly. More often, however, strong local opposition (what came to be known in the South as "massive resistance") produced long delays and bitter conflicts. More than 100 southern members of Congress signed a "manifesto" in 1956 denouncing the *Brown* decision and urging their constituents to defy it. Southern governors, mayors, local school boards, and nongovernmental pressure groups (including hundreds of White Citizens' Councils) all worked to obstruct desegregation. By the fall of 1957, only 684 of 3,000 affected school districts in the South had even begun to desegregate their schools.

The Eisenhower administration was not eager to join the battle over desegregation. But in September 1957, it faced a case of direct state defiance of federal authority and felt compelled to act. Federal courts had ordered the desegregation of Central High School in Little Rock, Arkansas. An angry white mob tried to block implementation of the order by blockading the entrances to the school, and Governor Orval Faubus refused to do anything to stop the obstruction. President Eisenhower finally responded by sending federal troops to Little Rock to keep the peace and ensure that the court orders would be obeyed. Only then did Central High School admit its first black students.

Little Rock's Central High School

The Expanding Movement

The *Brown* decision helped spark a growing number of popular challenges to other forms of segregation in the South. On December 1, 1955, Rosa Parks, an African-American woman, was arrested in Montgomery, Alabama, when she refused to give up her seat on a Montgomery bus to a white passenger (as required by the Jim Crow laws that regulated race relations in the city and throughout most of the South). The arrest of this admired woman and local civil-rights leader produced outrage in the city's African-American community, which organized a boycott of the bus system to demand an end to segregated seating.

Rosa Parks

The boycott was almost completely effective. It put economic pressure not only on the bus company but on many Montgomery merchants, because the bus boycotters found it difficult to get to downtown stores and shopped instead in their own neighborhoods. Even so, the boycott might well have failed had it not been for a Supreme Court decision late in 1956, inspired in part by the protest, that declared segregation in public transportation to be illegal. The buses in Montgomery abandoned their discriminatory seating policies, and the boycott came to a close.

Among the most important accomplishments of the Montgomery boycott were the legitimization of a new form of racial protest and the elevation to prominence of a new figure in the movement for civil rights. The man chosen to lead the boycott movement once it was launched was a local Baptist pastor, Martin Luther King, Jr., the son of a prominent Atlanta minister, a powerful orator, and

Martin Luther King, Jr.

a gifted leader. King's approach to black protest was based on the doctrine of nonviolence—that is, of nonviolent resistance to injustice even in the face of direct attack. And he produced an approach to racial struggle that captured the moral high ground for his supporters. For the next thirteen years—as leader of the Southern Christian Leadership Conference (SCLC), an interracial group he founded shortly after the bus boycott—he was the most influential and most widely admired black leader in the country. The popular movement he came to represent soon spread throughout the South and throughout the country.

Causes of the Civil Rights Movement

Several factors contributed to the rise of African-American protest in these years. The legacy of World War II was one of the most important. Millions of black men and women had served in the military or worked in war plants during the war and had derived from the experience a broader view of the world, and of their place in it, than they had been able to develop in their relatively isolated lives prior to the 1940s.

Another factor was the growth of an urban black middle class, which had been developing for decades but which began to flourish after the war. Much of the impetus for the civil rights movement came from the leaders of urban black communities—ministers, educators, professionals—and much of it came as well from students at black colleges and universities, which had expanded significantly in the previous decades. Men and women with education and a stake in society were often more aware of the obstacles to their advancement than poorer and more oppressed people. And urban African Americans had considerably more freedom to associate with one another and to develop independent institutions than did rural blacks, who were often under the very direct supervision of white landowners.

Growing Urban Black Middle Class

Television and other forms of popular culture were another factor in the rising consciousness of racism among African Americans. More than any previous generation, postwar blacks had constant, vivid reminders of how the white majority lived—of the world from which they were effectively excluded. Television also conveyed the activities of demonstrators to a national audience, ensuring that activism in one community would inspire similar protests in others.

Other forces were mobilizing many white Americans to support the movement once it began. One was the Cold War, which made racial injustice an embarrassment to Americans trying to present their nation as a model to the world. Another was the political mobilization of northern blacks, who were now a substantial voting bloc within the Democratic Party; politicians from northern industrial states could not ignore their views. Labor unions with substantial black memberships also played an important part in supporting (and funding) the civil rights movement.

Political Mobilization of Northern Blacks

This great and largely spontaneous social movement emerged, in short, out of an unpredictable combination of broad social changes and specific local grievances. Whatever its causes, it quickly took on a momentum that, by the early 1960s, had made it one of the most powerful forces in America.

EISENHOWER REPUBLICANISM

Dwight D. Eisenhower was the least experienced politician to serve in the White House in the twentieth century. He was also among the most popular and politically successful presidents of the postwar era. At home, he pursued essentially moderate policies, avoiding most new initiatives but accepting the work of earlier reformers. Abroad, he continued and even intensified American commitments to oppose communism but brought to some of those commitments a measure of restraint that his successors did not always match.

"What Was Good for . . . General Motors"

Keynesian Welfare State Accepted

The first Republican administration in twenty years staffed itself with men drawn from the same quarter as those who had staffed Republican administrations in the 1920s: the business community. But by the 1950s, many business leaders had acquired a social and political outlook very different from that of their predecessors of earlier decades. Above all, many of the nation's leading business executives and financiers had reconciled themselves to at least the broad outlines of the Keynesian welfare state the New Deal had launched. Indeed, some corporate leaders had come to see it as something that actually benefited them—by helping maintain social order, by increasing mass purchasing power, and by stabilizing labor relations.

To his cabinet, Eisenhower appointed wealthy corporate lawyers and business executives who were not apologetic about their backgrounds. Charles Wilson, president of General Motors, assured senators considering his nomination for secretary of defense that he foresaw no conflict of interest because he was certain that "what was good for our country was good for General Motors, and vice versa."

Eisenhower's Fiscal Conservatism

Eisenhower's consistent inclination was to limit federal activities and encourage private enterprise. He supported the private rather than public development of natural resources. To the chagrin of farmers, he lowered federal support for farm prices. He also removed the last limited wage and price controls maintained by the Truman administration. He opposed the creation of new social service programs such as national health insurance. He strove constantly to reduce federal expenditures (even during the recession of 1958) and balance the budget. He ended 1960, his last full year in office, with a $1 billion budget surplus.

The Survival of the Welfare State

The president took few new initiatives in domestic policy, but he resisted pressure from the right wing of his party to dismantle those welfare policies of the New Deal that had survived the conservative assaults of the war years and after. Indeed, during his term, he agreed to extend the Social Security system to an additional 10 million people and unemployment compensation to an additional 4 million, and he agreed to increase the minimum hourly wage from 75 cents to $1. One of the most significant legislative accomplishments of the Eisenhower administration was the Federal Highway Act of 1956, which authorized $25 billion for a ten-year project that built over 40,000 miles of interstate highways—the largest public works project in American history. The program was to be funded through a highway "trust fund," whose revenues would come from new taxes on the purchase of fuel, automobiles, trucks, and tires.

Federal Highway Act of 1956

In 1956, Eisenhower ran for a second term, even though he had suffered a serious heart attack the previous year. With Adlai Stevenson opposing him once again, he won by another, even greater landslide, receiving nearly 57 percent of the popular vote and 457 electoral votes to Stevenson's 73. Democrats retained the control of both houses of Congress they had won back in 1954. In 1958—during a serious recession—they increased that control by substantial margins.

The Decline of McCarthyism

The Eisenhower administration did little in its first years in office to discourage the anticommunist furor that had gripped the nation. By 1954, however, the crusade against subversion was beginning to produce significant popular opposition. The clearest signal of that change was the political demise of Senator Joseph McCarthy.

During the first year of the Eisenhower administration, McCarthy continued to operate with impunity. But in January 1954 he attacked Secretary of the Army Robert Stevens and the armed services in general. At that point, the administration and influential members of Congress organized a special investigation of the charges, which became known as the Army-McCarthy hearings. They were among the first congressional hearings to be nationally televised. Watching McCarthy in action—bullying witnesses, hurling groundless (and often cruel) accusations, evading issues—much of the public began to see him as a villain, and even a buffoon. In December 1954, the Senate voted 67 to 22 to condemn him for "conduct unbecoming a senator." Three years later, he died—a victim, apparently, of complications arising from alcoholism.

Army-McCarthy Hearings

THE ARMY-MCCARTHY HEARINGS Senator Joseph McCarthy uses a map to show the supposed distribution of communists throughout the United States during the televised 1954 Senate hearings to mediate the dispute between McCarthy and the U.S. Army. Joseph Welch, chief counsel for the army, remains conspicuously unimpressed. *(UPI/Corbis-Bettmann)*

EISENHOWER, DULLES, AND THE COLD WAR

The threat of nuclear war with the Soviet Union created a sense of high anxiety in international relations in the 1950s. But the nuclear threat also encouraged both superpowers to edge away from direct confrontations. The attention of both the United States and the Soviet Union began to turn instead to the rapidly escalating instability in the nations of the Third World.

Dulles and "Massive Retaliation"

Eisenhower's secretary of state, and (except for the president himself) the dominant figure in the nation's foreign policy in the 1950s, was John Foster Dulles, an aristocratic corporate lawyer with a stern moral revulsion to communism. He entered office denouncing the containment policies of the Truman years as excessively passive, arguing that the United States should pursue an active program of "liberation," which would lead to a "rollback" of communist expansion. Once in power, however, he had to defer to the more moderate views of the president himself.

The most prominent of Dulles's innovations was the policy of "massive retaliation," which he announced early in 1954. The United States would, he explained, respond to communist threats to its allies not by using conventional forces in local conflicts (a policy that had led to so much frustration in Korea) but by relying on "the deterrent of massive retaliatory power" (by which he clearly meant nuclear weapons). In part, the new doctrines reflected Dulles's inclination for tense confrontations, an

"Brinksmanship"

approach he once defined as "brinksmanship"—pushing the Soviet Union to the brink of war in order to exact concessions. But the real force behind the massive-retaliation policy was economics. With pressure growing both in and out of government for a reduction in American military expenditures, an increasing reliance on atomic weapons seemed to promise, as some advocates put it, "more bang for the buck."

France, America, and Vietnam

On July 27, 1953, negotiators at Panmunjom finally signed an agreement ending the hostilities in Korea. Each antagonist was to withdraw its troops a mile and a half from the existing battle line, which ran roughly along the 38th parallel, the prewar border between North and South Korea. A conference in Geneva was to consider means by which to reunite the nation peacefully—although in fact that 1954 meeting produced no agreement and left the cease-fire line as the apparently permanent border between the two countries.

Almost simultaneously, however, the United States was being drawn into a long, bitter struggle in Southeast Asia. Ever since 1945, France had been attempting to restore its authority over Vietnam, its one-time colony, which it had been forced to abandon to the Japanese toward the end of World War II. Opposing the French, however, were the powerful nationalist forces of Ho Chi Minh, determined to win independence for their nation. Ho had hoped for American support in 1945, on the basis of the anticolonial rhetoric of the Atlantic Charter and Franklin Roosevelt's speeches, and also because he had received support from American intelligence forces during World War II while he was fighting the Japanese. He was, however, not only a committed nationalist but a committed communist. The Truman administration ignored him and supported the French, one of America's most important Cold War allies.

Ho Chi Minh

By 1954, Ho was receiving aid from communist China and the Soviet Union. America, in the meantime, had been paying most of the costs of France's ineffective military campaign in Vietnam since 1950. Early in 1954, 12,000 French troops became surrounded in a disastrous siege at the village of Dien Bien Phu. Only American intervention, it was clear, could prevent the total collapse of the French military effort. Yet despite the urgings of Secretary of State Dulles, Vice President Nixon, and others, Eisenhower refused to permit direct American military intervention in Vietnam, claiming that neither Congress nor America's other allies would support such action.

Dien Bien Phu

Without American aid, the French defense of Dien Bien Phu finally collapsed on May 7, 1954, and France quickly agreed to a settlement of the conflict at the same international conference in Geneva that summer that was considering the Korean settlement. The Geneva accords on Vietnam of July 1954, to which the United States was not a direct party, established a supposedly temporary division of Vietnam along the 17TH parallel. The north would be governed by Ho Chi Minh, the south by a pro-Western regime. Democratic elections would be the basis for uniting the nation in 1956. The agreement marked the end of the French commitment to Vietnam and the beginning of an expanded American presence there. The United States helped establish a pro-American government in the south, headed by Ngo Dinh Diem, a member of his country's Roman Catholic minority. Diem refused to permit the 1956 elections, which he knew he would lose. He felt secure in his refusal because the United States had promised to provide him with ample military assistance against any attack from the north.

Cold War Crises

American foreign policy in the 1950s was challenged by both real and imagined crises in far-flung areas of the world. Among them were a series of crises in the Middle East, a region in which the United States had been little involved until after World War II.

Israel Recognized

On May 14, 1948, after years of Zionist efforts and a decision by the new United Nations, the nation of Israel proclaimed its independence. President Truman recognized the new Jewish homeland the next day. But the creation of Israel, while it resolved some conflicts, created others. Palestinian Arabs, unwilling to accept being displaced from what they considered their own country, joined with Israel's Arab neighbors and fought determinedly against the new state in 1948—the first of several Arab-Israeli wars.

Committed as the American government was to Israel, it was also concerned about the stability and friendliness of the Arab regimes in the oil-rich Middle East, in which American petroleum companies had major investments. Thus the United States reacted with alarm as it watched Mohammed Mossadegh, the nationalist prime minister of Iran, begin to resist the presence of western corporations in his nation in the early 1950s. In 1953, the American CIA joined forces with conservative Iranian military leaders to engineer a coup that drove Mossadegh from office. To replace him, the CIA helped elevate the young Shah of Iran, Mohammed Reza Pahlevi, from his position as token constitutional monarch to that of virtually absolute ruler. The Shah remained closely tied to the United States for the next twenty-five years.

Gamal Abdel Nasser

American policy was less effective in dealing with the nationalist government of Egypt, under the leadership of General Gamal Abdel Nasser, which began to develop a trade relationship with the Soviet Union in the early 1950s. In 1956, to punish Nasser for his friendliness toward the communists, Dulles withdrew American offers to assist in building the great Aswan Dam across the Nile. A week later, Nasser retaliated by seizing control of the Suez Canal from the British, saying that he would use the income from it to build the dam himself.

On October 29, 1956, Israeli forces attacked Egypt. The next day the British and French landed troops in the Suez to drive the Egyptians from the canal. Dulles and Eisenhower feared that the Suez crisis would drive the Arab states toward the Soviet Union and precipitate a new world war. By refusing to support the invasion, and by joining in a United Nations denunciation of it, the United States helped pressure the French and British to withdraw and helped persuade Israel to agree to a truce with Egypt.

Cold War concerns affected American relations in Latin America as well. In 1954, the Eisenhower administration ordered the CIA to help topple the new, leftist government of Jacobo Arbenz Guzmán in Guatemala, a regime that Dulles (responding to the entreaties of the United Fruit Company, a major investor in Guatemala fearful of Arbenz) argued was potentially communist.

Jacobo Arbenz Guzmán Overthrown

No nation in the region had been more closely tied to America than Cuba. Its leader, Fulgencio Batista, had ruled as a military dictator since 1952, when with American assistance he had toppled a more moderate government. Cuba's relatively prosperous economy had become a virtual fiefdom of American corporations, which controlled almost all the island's natural resources and had cornered over half the vital sugar crop. American organized-crime syndicates controlled much of Havana's lucrative hotel and nightlife business. In 1957, a popular movement of resistance to the Batista regime began to gather strength under the leadership of Fidel Castro. On January 1, 1959, with Batista having fled to exile in Spain, Castro marched into Havana and established a new government.

Castro soon began implementing drastic policies of land reform and expropriating foreign-owned businesses and resources. When Castro began accepting assistance from the Soviet Union in 1960, the United States cut back the "quota" by which Cuba could export sugar to America at a favored price. Early in 1961, as one of its last acts, the Eisenhower administration severed diplomatic relations with Castro. Isolated by the United States, Castro soon cemented an alliance with the Soviet Union.

Growing Conflict with Cuba

Europe and the Soviet Union

Although the problems of the Third World were moving slowly toward the center of American foreign policy, the direct relationship with the Soviet Union and the effort to resist communist expansion in Europe remained the principal concerns of the Eisenhower administration. Relations between the Soviet Union and the West soured further in 1956 in response to the Hungarian Revolution. Hungarian dissidents had launched a popular uprising in November to demand democratic reforms.

Before the month was out, Soviet tanks and troops entered Budapest to crush the uprising and restore an orthodox, pro-Soviet regime.

The U-2 Crisis

In November 1958, Nikita Khrushchev, who had become Soviet premier and Communist Party chief earlier that year, renewed the demands of his predecessors that the NATO powers abandon West Berlin. When the United States and its allies predictably refused, Khrushchev suggested that he and Eisenhower discuss the issue personally, both in visits to each other's countries and at a summit meeting in Paris in 1960. The United States agreed. Khrushchev's 1959 visit to America produced a cool but polite public response. Plans proceeded for the summit conference and for Eisenhower's visit to Moscow shortly thereafter. Only days before the scheduled beginning of the Paris meeting, however, the Soviet Union announced that it had shot down an American U-2, a high-altitude spy plane, over Russian territory. Its pilot, Francis Gary Powers, was in captivity. Khrushchev lashed out angrily at the American incursion into Soviet air space, breaking up the Paris summit almost before it could begin and withdrawing his invitation to Eisenhower to visit the Soviet Union.

After eight years in office, Eisenhower had failed to eliminate, and in some respects had actually increased, the tensions between the United States and the Soviet Union. Yet Eisenhower had brought to the Cold War his own sense of the limits of American power. He had resisted military intervention in Vietnam. And he had placed a measure of restraint on those who urged the creation of an enormous American military establishment. In his farewell address in January 1961, he warned of the "unwarranted influence" of a vast "military-industrial complex." His caution, in both domestic and international affairs, stood in marked contrast to the attitudes of his successors, who argued that the United States must act more boldly and aggressively on behalf of its goals at home and abroad.

"Military-Industrial Complex"

CONCLUSION

The booming economic growth of the 1950s—and the anxiety over the Cold War that formed a backdrop to it—shaped the politics and the culture of the decade. For most Americans, the 1950s were years of increasing personal prosperity. Sales of private homes increased dramatically; suburbs grew precipitously; young families had children at an astounding rate—creating what came to be known as the postwar "baby boom." After the end of the divisive Korean War, the nation's politics entered a period of relative calm, symbolized by the genial presence in the White House of

Dwight D. Eisenhower, who provided moderate and undemanding leadership through most of the decade.

The nation's culture, too, helped create a broad sense of stability and calm. Television, which emerged in the 1950s as the most powerful medium of mass culture, presented largely uncontroversial programming dominated by middle-class images and traditional values. Movies, theater, popular magazines, and newspapers all contributed to a broad sense of well-being.

But the 1950s were not, in the end, as calm and contented as the politics and popular culture of the time suggested. A powerful youth culture emerged in these years that displayed a considerable level of restiveness and even disillusionment. African Americans began to escalate their protests against segregation and inequality. The continuing existence of widespread poverty among large groups of Americans attracted increasing attention as the decade progressed. These pulsing anxieties, combined with frustration over the continuing tensions of the Cold War, produced by the late 1950s a growing sense of impatience with the calm, placid public culture of the time. That was one reason for the growing desire for action and innovation as the 1960s began.

FOR FURTHER REFERENCE

James T. Patterson, *Grand Expectations: Postwar America, 1945–1974* (1996), a volume in the Oxford History of the United States, is an important general history of the postwar era. John P. Diggins, *The Proud Decades: America in War and Peace, 1941–1960* (1989) and Godfrey Hodgson, *America in Our Time* (1976) are other important surveys. Kenneth T. Jackson, *The Crabgrass Frontier: The Suburbanization of the United States* (1985) is a classic history of a major social movement. Joshua B. Freeman, *Working-Class New York: Life and Labor Since World War II* (2000) is an important study of postwar labor. Eric Barnouw, *Tube of Plenty* (1982) and Karal Ann Marling, *As Seen on TV: The Visual Culture of Everyday Life in the 1950s* (1995) are good studies of the new medium. Elaine Tyler May, *Homeward Bound: American Families in the Cold War* (1988) is a challenging cultural history. Paul Boyer, *By the Bomb's Early Light: American Thought and Culture at the Dawn of the Atomic Age* (1985) examines the impact of the atomic bomb on American social thought. Stephen Ambrose, *Eisenhower the President* (1984) is a good biography and Fred Greenstein, *The Hidden-Hand Presidency* (1982) is a challenge to earlier, dismissive views of Eisenhower's leadership style. Taylor Branch, *Parting the Waters: America in the King Years, 1954–1963* (1988) and *Pillar of Fire: America in the King Years, 1963–1965* (1998) are superb narratives of the early years of the civil rights movement. Richard Kluger, *Simple Justice* (1975) is a classic narrative history of the *Brown* decision and James T. Patterson, *Brown v. Board of Edu-*

cation: A Civil Rights Milestone and Its Troubled Legacy (2001) is an important recent examination. John Egerton, *Speak Now Against the Day: The Generation Before the Civil Rights Movement in the South* (1994) is a history of struggles over white supremacy in the first years after World War II.

The stunning effect of the first Soviet satellite launch in 1957 is vividly portrayed in the documentary film *The Satellite Sky* (1990). *Eisenhower* (1993) is an extensive film portrait, offering a fresh reassessment of his legacy. *An Age of Conformity* (1991) is a film portraying domestic life in the 1940s and 1950s.

For quizzes, Internet resources, references to additional books and films, and more, consult this book's Online Learning Center site at www.mhhe.com/unfinishednation4.

KHE SANH, VIETNAM, 1968 A beleaguered American soldier shows his exhaustion during the 76-day siege of the American marine base at Khe Sanh, which began shortly before the 1968 Tet offensive in Vietnam. American forces sustained record casualties in the fierce fighting at Khe Sanh; the Vietnamese communist forces suffered far more. *(Robert Ellison/Black Star)*

TIME LINE

1960	1961	1962	1963
Kennedy elected president	Freedom rides	Cuban missile crisis	March on Washington
	Bay of Pigs		Kennedy assassinated; Johnson becomes president
	Berlin Wall erected		Civil rights demonstrations in Birmingham

CHAPTER THIRTY-ONE

THE ORDEAL OF LIBERALISM

Expanding the Liberal State
The Battle for Racial Equality
"Flexible Response" and the Cold War
The Agony of Vietnam
The Traumas of 1968

By the late 1950s, a growing restlessness was becoming visible beneath the apparently placid surface of American society. Ultimately, that restlessness would make the 1960s one of the most turbulent and divisive eras of the twentieth century. But at first, it contributed to a bold and confident effort by political leaders to attack social and international problems within the framework of conventional liberal politics.

EXPANDING THE LIBERAL STATE

Those who yearned for a more active government in the late 1950s and who accused the Eisenhower administration of allowing the nation to "drift" hoped for vigorous new leadership. The two men who served in the White House through most of the 1960s—John Kennedy and Lyndon Johnson—seemed for a time to be the embodiment of these liberal hopes.

1964	1965	1967	1968
Johnson launches war on poverty	Malcolm X assassinated	Antiwar movement grows	Tet offensive
Civil Rights Act	Voting Rights Act	Racial violence in Detroit	Martin Luther King, Jr. assassinated
Gulf of Tonkin Resolution	U.S. troops in Vietnam		Robert Kennedy assassinated
Johnson elected president	Racial violence in Watts		Nixon elected president

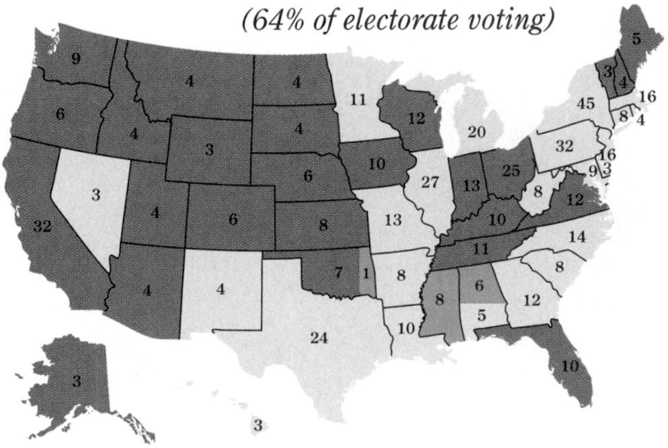

	ELECTORAL VOTE	POPULAR VOTE (%)
John F. Kennedy *(Democratic)*	303	34,227,096 (49.9)
Richard M. Nixon *(Republican)*	219	34,108,546 (49.6)
Harry F. Byrd *(Dixiecrat)*	15	501,643 (0.7)
Other candidates *(Prohibition; Socialist Labor; Constitution; Socialist Workers; National States Rights)*	—	197,029

THE ELECTION OF 1960 The election of 1960 was, in the popular vote at least, one of the closest in American history. John Kennedy's margin over Richard Nixon was less than one-third of one percent of the total national vote, but greater in the electoral college. Note the distribution of electoral strength of the two candidates. Kennedy was strong in the industrial northeast and the largest industrial states of the Midwest, and he retained at least a portion of his party's traditional strength in the South and Southwest. But Nixon made significant inroads into the upper South, carried Florida, and swept most of the Plains and Mountain states. ◆ *What was the significance of this distribution of strength to the future of the two parties?*

For an interactive version of this map go to www.mhhe.com/unfinishednation4ch31maps

John Kennedy

The campaign of 1960 produced two young candidates who claimed to offer the nation active leadership. The Republican nomination went almost uncontested to Vice President Richard Nixon, who promised moderate reform. The Democrats, in the meantime, emerged from a spirited primary campaign united, somewhat uneasily, behind John Fitzgerald Kennedy, an attractive and articulate senator from Massachusetts who had narrowly missed being the party's vice presidential candidate in 1956.

JOHN KENNEDY The new president and his wife, Jacqueline, attend one of the five balls in Washington marking Kennedy's inauguration in 1961. *(Paul Schutzer, Life Magazine, © 1961 Time Warner, Inc./Getty Images)*

John Kennedy was the son of the wealthy, powerful, and highly controversial Joseph P. Kennedy, former American ambassador to Britain. He premised his campaign, he said, "on the single assumption that the American people are uneasy at the present drift in our national course." But his appealing public image was at least as important as his political positions in attracting popular support. He overcame doubts about his youth (he turned forty-three in 1960) and religion (he was Catholic) to win with a tiny plurality of the popular vote (49.9 percent to Nixon's 49.6 percent) and only a slightly more comfortable electoral majority (303 to 219).

Kennedy Elected

The "New Frontier"

Kennedy had campaigned promising a set of domestic reforms he described as the "New Frontier." But his thin popular mandate and a Congress dominated by a coalition of Republicans and conservative Democrats frustrated many of his hopes. Kennedy did manage to win approval of tariff reductions his administration had negotiated, and he began to build a legislative agenda that he hoped he might eventually see enacted—including a call for a significant tax cut to promote economic growth.

More than any other president of the century (except perhaps the two Roosevelts and, later, Ronald Reagan), Kennedy made his own personality an integral part of his presidency and a central focus of national attention. Nothing illustrated that more clearly than the popular reaction to the tragedy of November 22, 1963. Kennedy had traveled to Texas with his wife and Vice President Lyndon Johnson for a series of political appearances. While the presidential motorcade rode slowly through the streets of Dallas, shots rang out. Two bullets struck the president—one in the throat, the other in the head. He was sped to a nearby hospital, where minutes later he was pronounced dead. Lee Harvey Oswald, a confused and embittered Marxist, was arrested for the crime later that day, and then mysteriously murdered by a Dallas nightclub owner, Jack Ruby, two days later as he was being moved from one jail to another. Most Americans at the time accepted the conclusions of a federal commission, chaired by Chief Justice Earl Warren, appointed by President Johnson to investigate the assassination. The commission found that both Oswald and Ruby had acted alone, that there was no larger conspiracy. In later years, however, many Americans came to believe that the Warren Commission report had ignored evidence of a wider conspiracy behind the murders. Controversy over the truth about the assassination continues today.

Lyndon Johnson

The Kennedy assassination was a national trauma—a defining event for almost everyone old enough to be aware of it. At the time, however, much of the nation took comfort in the personality and performance of Kennedy's successor in the White House, Lyndon Baines Johnson. Johnson was a native of the poor "hill country" of west Texas and had risen to become majority leader of the U.S. Senate by dint of extraordinary, even obsessive effort and ambition. Having failed to win the Democratic nomination for president in 1960, he surprised many who knew him by agreeing to accept the second position on the ticket with Kennedy. The events in Dallas thrust him into the White House.

Johnson's rough-edged, even crude personality could hardly have been more different from Kennedy's. But like Kennedy, Johnson was a man who believed in the active use of power. Between 1963 and 1966, he compiled the most impressive legislative record of any president since Franklin Roosevelt. He was aided by the tidal wave of emotion that followed the death of President Kennedy, which helped win support for many New Frontier proposals. But Johnson also constructed a remarkable reform program of his own, one that he ultimately labeled the "Great Society." And he won approval of much of it through the same sort of skillful lobbying in Congress that had made him an effective majority leader.

"Great Society"

Johnson's first year in office was, by necessity, dominated by the campaign for reelection. There was little doubt that he would win—particularly after the Republican Party nominated the very conservative Senator Barry Goldwater of Arizona. In the November 1964 election, the president received a larger plurality, over 61 percent, than any candidate before or since. Goldwater managed to carry only his home state of Arizona and five states in the Deep South. Record Democratic majorities in both houses of Congress, many of whose members had been swept into office only because of the margin of Johnson's victory, ensured that the president would be able to fulfill many of his goals.

The Assault on Poverty

For the first time since the 1930s, the federal government took steps in the 1960s to create important new social welfare programs. The most important of these, perhaps, was Medicare: a program to provide federal aid to the elderly for medical expenses. Its enactment in 1965 came at the end of a bitter, twenty-year debate between those who believed in the concept of national health assistance and those who denounced it as "socialized medicine." But Medicare pacified many critics. For one thing, it avoided the stigma of "welfare" by making Medicare benefits available to all elderly Americans, regardless of need (just as Social Security had done with pensions). That created a large middle-class constituency for the program. The program also defused the opposition of the medical community by allowing doctors serving Medicare patients to practice privately and (at first) to charge their normal fees; Medicare simply shifted responsibility for paying those fees from the patient to the government. In 1966, Johnson steered to passage the Medicaid program, which extended federal medical assistance to welfare recipients and other indigent people of all ages.

Medicare and Medicaid

Medicare and Medicaid were early steps in a much larger assault on poverty—one that Kennedy had been planning in the last months of his life and that Johnson launched only weeks after taking office. The centerpiece of this "war on poverty," as Johnson called it, was the Office of Economic Opportunity (OEO), which created an array of new educational, employment, housing, and health-care programs. But the OEO was controversial from the start, in part because of its commitment to the idea of "Community Action."

Community Action was an effort to involve members of poor communities themselves in the planning and administration of the programs designed to help them. The Community Action programs provided jobs for many poor people and gave them valuable experience in administrative and political work. But despite its achievements, the Community Action approach proved impossible to sustain, both because of administrative failures and because the apparent excesses of a few agencies damaged the popular image of the Community Action programs, and indeed the war on poverty, as a whole.

Failure of the OEO

The OEO spent nearly $3 billion during its first two years of existence, and it helped reduce poverty in some areas. But it fell far short of eliminating poverty altogether. That was in part because of the weaknesses of the programs themselves and in part because funding for them, inadequate from the beginning, dwindled as the years passed and a costly war in Southeast Asia became the nation's first priority.

Cities, Schools, and Immigration

Closely tied to the antipoverty program were federal efforts to promote the revitalization of decaying cities and to strengthen the nation's schools. The Housing Act of 1961 offered $4.9 billion in federal grants to cities for the preservation of open spaces, the development of mass-transit systems, and the subsidization of middle-income housing. In 1966, Johnson established a new cabinet agency, the Department of Housing and Urban Development (whose first secretary, Robert Weaver, was the first African American ever to serve in the cabinet). Johnson also inaugurated the Model Cities program, which offered federal subsidies for urban redevelopment pilot programs.

Federal Aid to Education

Kennedy had fought for federal aid to public education, but he had failed to overcome two important obstacles: Many Americans feared that aid to education was the first step toward federal control of the schools, and Catholics insisted that federal assistance must extend to parochial as well as public schools. Johnson managed to circumvent both objections with the Elementary and Secondary Education Act of 1965 and a series of subsequent measures. The bills extended aid to both private and parochial schools and based the aid on the economic conditions of the students, not on the needs of the schools themselves.

Immigration Act of 1965

The Johnson administration also supported the Immigration Act of 1965, one of the most important pieces of legislation of the 1960s. The law maintained a strict limit on the number of newcomers admitted to the country each year (170,000), but it eliminated the "national origins" system established in the 1920s, which gave preference to immigrants from northern Europe over those from other parts of the world. It continued to restrict immigration from some parts of Latin America, but it allowed people from all parts of Europe, Asia, and Africa to enter the United States on an equal basis. By the early 1970s, the character of American immigration had changed dramatically, with members of new national groups—and particularly large groups of Asians—entering the United States and changing the character of the American population.

Legacies of the Great Society

Taken together, the Great Society reforms meant a significant increase in federal spending. For a time, rising tax revenues from the growing economy nearly compensated for the new expenditures. In 1964, Johnson managed to win passage of the $11.5 billion tax cut that Kennedy had first proposed in 1962 to promote economic growth. The cut increased the federal deficit, but substantial economic growth over the next several years made up for much of the revenue initially lost. As Great Society programs began to multiply, however, and particularly as they began to compete with the escalating costs of America's military ventures, the federal budget rapidly outpaced increases in revenues. In 1961, the federal government had spent $94.4 billion. By 1970, that sum had risen to $196.6 billion.

The high costs of the Great Society programs, the failures of many of them, and the inability of the government to find the revenues to pay for them contributed to a growing disillusionment in later years with the idea of federal efforts to solve social problems. But the Great Society, despite many failures, was also responsible for some significant achievements. It significantly reduced hunger in America. It made medical care available to millions of elderly and poor people who would otherwise have had great difficulty affording it. It contributed to the greatest reduction in poverty in American history. In 1959, according to the most widely accepted estimates, 21 percent of the American people lived below the officially established poverty line. By 1969, only 12 percent remained below that line. Much of that progress was a result of economic growth, but some of it was a result of Great Society programs.

Achievements of the Great Society

THE BATTLE FOR RACIAL EQUALITY

The nation's most important domestic initiative in the 1960s was the effort to provide justice and equality to African Americans. It was the most difficult commitment, the one that produced the severest strains on American society. But it was one that could not be avoided. African Americans were themselves ensuring that the nation would have to deal with the problem of race.

Expanding Protests

John Kennedy was sympathetic to the cause of racial justice, but he was hardly a committed crusader. Like presidents before him, he feared alienating southern Democratic voters and powerful southern Democrats in Congress. His administration hoped to contain the racial problem by expanding enforcement of existing laws and supporting litigation to overturn existing segregation statutes.

But the pressure for change was growing uncontainable even before Kennedy took office. In February 1960, black college students in Greensboro, North Carolina, staged a sit-in at a segregated Woolworth's lunch counter; and in the following months, such demonstrations spread throughout the South, forcing many merchants to integrate their facilities. In the fall of 1960, some of those who had participated in the sit-ins formed the Student Nonviolent Coordinating Committee (SNCC)—a student branch of Martin Luther King, Jr.'s Southern Christian Leadership Council; SNCC worked to keep the spirit of resistance alive.

SNCC

In 1961, an interracial group of students, working with the Congress of Racial Equality (CORE), began what they called "freedom rides." Traveling by bus throughout the South, they tried to force the desegregation of bus stations. They were met in some places with such savage violence on the part of whites that the president finally dispatched federal marshals to help keep the peace and ordered the integration of all bus and train stations.

"Freedom Rides"

Events in the Deep South in 1963 helped bring the growing movement to something of a climax. In April, Martin Luther King, Jr., helped launch a series of nonviolent demonstrations in Birmingham, Alabama. Police Commissioner Eugene "Bull" Connor personally supervised a brutal effort to break up the peaceful marches, arresting hundreds of demonstrators and using attack dogs, tear gas, electric cattle prods, and fire hoses—at times even against small children—in full view of television cameras. Two months later, Governor George Wallace stood in the doorway of a building at the University of Alabama to prevent the court-ordered enrollment of several black students. Only after the arrival of federal marshals did he give way. The same night, NAACP official Medgar Evers was murdered in Mississippi. And in September, a bombing of a black church in Birmingham killed four African-American children.

A National Commitment

The events in Alabama and Mississippi were a warning to the president that he could no longer avoid the issue of race. In an important television address the night of the University of Alabama confrontation, Kennedy spoke eloquently of the "moral issue" facing the nation. Days later, he introduced new legislative proposals prohibiting segregation in "public ac-

THE MARCH ON WASHINGTON, 1963 Martin Luther King, Jr., waves to the vast crowd spreading out from the Lincoln Memorial shortly after delivering his famous "I Have a Dream" speech—the centerpiece of the March on Washington. Initially envisioned as a broad and militant protest against discrimination, it became in the end a moderate, interracial demonstration of support for the civil rights bill President Kennedy had recently proposed to Congress, which passed in 1964. *(UPI/Corbis-Bettmann)*

commodations" (stores, restaurants, theaters, hotels), barring discrimination in employment, and increasing the power of the government to file suits on behalf of school integration.

To generate support for the legislation, and to dramatize the power of the growing movement, more than 200,000 demonstrators marched down the Mall in Washington, D.C., in August 1963 and gathered before the Lincoln Memorial for the largest civil rights demonstration in the nation's history. Martin Luther King, Jr., in one of the greatest speeches of his distinguished oratorical career, aroused the crowd with a litany of images prefaced again and again by the phrase "I have a dream."

March on Washington

The assassination of President Kennedy three months later gave new impetus to the battle for civil rights legislation. The ambitious measure that Kennedy had proposed in June 1963 was stalled in the Senate after having passed through the House of Representatives with relative ease. Early in 1964, after Johnson had applied both public and private pressure, supporters of the measure finally mustered the two-thirds majority necessary to end a filibuster by southern senators; and the Senate passed the most important civil rights bill of the twentieth century.

The Battle for Voting Rights

Having won a significant victory in one area, the civil rights movement shifted its focus to another: voting rights. During the summer of 1964, thousands of civil rights workers, black and white, northern and southern, spread out through the South, but primarily into Mississippi, to work on behalf of black voter registration and participation. The campaign was known as "Freedom Summer," and it produced a violent response from some southern whites. Three of the first freedom workers to arrive in the South—two whites, Andrew Goodman and Michael Schwerner, and one black, James Chaney—were murdered. Local law enforcement officials were involved in the crime.

"Freedom Summer"

The "Freedom Summer" also produced the Mississippi Freedom Democratic Party (MFDP), an integrated alternative to the regular state party organization. Under the leadership of Fannie Lou Hamer and others, the MFDP challenged the regular party's right to its seats at the Democratic National Convention that summer. President Johnson, with King's help, managed to broker a compromise by which members of the MFDP could be seated as observers, with promises of party reforms later on, while the regular party retained its official standing. Many MFDP members rejected the agreement and left the convention embittered.

A year later, in March 1965, King helped organize a major demonstration in Selma, Alabama, to press for the right of blacks to register to vote. Selma sheriff Jim Clark led local police in a brutal attack on the demonstrators, which was televised nationally. Two northern whites participating in the Selma march were murdered in the course of the effort there. The widespread national outrage that followed the events in Alabama helped push Lyndon Johnson to propose and win passage of the Civil Rights Act of 1965, better known as the Voting Rights Act, which provided federal protection to African Americans attempting to exercise their right to vote. But important as such gains were, they failed to satisfy the rapidly rising expectations of American blacks as the focus of the movement began to move from political to economic issues.

Voting Rights Act Approved

The Changing Movement

By 1966, 69 percent of American blacks were living in metropolitan areas and 45 percent were living outside the South. Although the economic condition of most Americans was improving, in many poor urban black communities things were getting significantly worse. More than half of all nonwhite Americans lived in poverty at the beginning of the 1960s.

By the mid-1960s, therefore, the issue of race was moving out of the South and into the rest of the nation and beyond the issue of formal, legal segregation to an attack on the informal practices that often sustained discrimination. That carried the fight into northern cities, which had no Jim Crow laws but much segregation. Many African-American leaders (and their white supporters) soon began demanding that the battle against job discrimination move to a new level. They argued that the only way for employers to prove that they were not discriminating against African Americans was for them to demonstrate that they were hiring minorities. If necessary, they should adopt positive measures to recruit minorities. Lyndon Johnson gave his support to the concept of "affirmative action" in 1965. Over the next decade, affirmative action guidelines gradually extended to virtually all institutions doing business with or receiving funds from the federal government (including schools and universities)—and to many others as well.

"Affirmative Action"

A symbol of the movement's new direction, and of the problems it would cause, was a major campaign in the summer of 1966 in Chicago, in which King played a prominent role. Organizers of the Chicago campaign hoped to direct national attention to housing and employment discrimination in northern industrial cities. But the Chicago campaign evoked vicious and at times violent opposition from white residents of that city and failed to attract wide attention or support in the way events in the South had done.

Urban Violence

Well before the Chicago campaign, the problem of urban poverty had thrust itself into national prominence when riots broke out in black neighborhoods in major cities. There were a few scattered disturbances in the summer of 1964, most notably in New York City's Harlem. The most serious race riot since the end of World War II occurred the following summer in the Watts section of Los Angeles. In the midst of a traffic arrest, a white police officer struck a protesting black bystander with his club. The incident triggered a storm of anger and a week of violence. Thirty-four people died during the uprising, which was eventually quelled by the National Guard. In the summer of 1966, there were forty-three additional outbreaks, the most serious of them in Chicago and Cleveland. And in the summer of 1967, there were eight major disorders, including the largest of them all—a racial clash in Detroit in which forty-three people died.

Riots

Televised reports of the violence alarmed millions of Americans and created both a new sense of urgency and a growing sense of doubt among some whites who had embraced the cause of racial justice only a few years before. A special Commission on Civil Disorders, created by the president in response to the riots, issued a celebrated report in the spring of 1968 recommending massive spending to eliminate the abysmal conditions of the ghettoes. To many white Americans, however, the lesson of the riots was the need for stern measures to stop violence and lawlessness.

Black Power

Disillusioned with the ideal of peaceful change through cooperation with whites, an increasing number of African Americans were turning to a new approach to the racial issue: the philosophy of "black power." Black power meant many different things. But in all its forms, it suggested a shift away from the goal of assimilation and toward increased awareness of racial distinctiveness.

Racial Distinctiveness Emphasized

Perhaps the most enduring impact of the black-power ideology was a social and psychological one: instilling racial pride in African Americans. But black power took political forms as well, and it created a deep schism within the civil rights movement. Traditional black organizations that emphasized cooperation with sympathetic whites—groups such as the NAACP, the Urban League, and King's Southern Christian Leadership Conference—now faced competition from more radical groups. The Student Nonviolent Coordinating Committee and the Congress of Racial Equality had both begun as relatively moderate, interracial organizations. By the mid-1960s, however, these and other groups were calling for more radical and occasionally even violent action against the racism of white society and were openly rejecting the approaches of older, more established black leaders.

Black Panthers

The most radical expressions of the black-power idea came from such revolutionary organizations as the Black Panthers, based in Oakland, California, and the separatist group, the Nation of Islam, which denounced whites as "devils" and appealed to blacks to embrace the Islamic faith and work for complete racial separation. The most celebrated of the Black Muslims, as whites often termed them, was Malcolm Little, who had adopted the name Malcolm X ("X" to denote his lost African surname). He died in 1965 when black gunmen, presumably under orders from rivals within the Nation of Islam, assassinated him. But he remained a major figure in many black communities long after his death—as important to and revered by as many African Americans as Martin Luther King, Jr.

"FLEXIBLE RESPONSE" AND THE COLD WAR

In international affairs as much as in domestic reform, the optimistic liberalism of the Kennedy and Johnson administrations dictated a more active and aggressive approach to dealing with the nation's problems than that of the 1950s.

Diversifying Foreign Policy

The Kennedy administration entered office convinced that the United States needed to be able to counter communist aggression in more flexible ways than the atomic-weapons-oriented defense strategy of the Eisenhower years permitted. In particular, Kennedy was unsatisfied with the nation's ability to meet communist threats in "emerging areas" of the Third World—the areas in which, Kennedy believed, the real struggle against communism would be waged in the future. He gave enthusiastic support to the expansion of the Special Forces (or "Green Berets," as they were soon known)—soldiers trained specifically to fight guerrilla conflicts and other limited wars.

Kennedy also favored expanding American influence through peaceful means. To repair the badly deteriorating relationship with Latin America, he proposed an "Alliance for Progress": a series of projects for peaceful development and stabilization of the nations of that region. Kennedy also inaugurated the Agency for International Development (AID) to coordinate foreign aid. And he established what became one of his most popular innovations: the Peace Corps, which sent young American volunteers abroad to work in developing areas.

"Alliance for Progress"

Among the first foreign policy ventures of the Kennedy administration was a disastrous assault on the Castro government in Cuba. The Eisenhower administration had started the project; and by the time Kennedy took office, the CIA had been working for months to train a small army of anti-Castro Cuban exiles in Central America. On April 17, 1961, with the approval of the new president, 2,000 of the armed exiles landed at the Bay of Pigs in Cuba, expecting first American air support and then a spontaneous uprising by the Cuban people on their behalf. They received neither. At the last minute, as it became clear that things were going badly, Kennedy withdrew the air support, fearful of involving the United States too directly in the invasion. The expected uprising did not occur. Instead, well-armed Castro forces easily crushed the invaders, and within two days the entire mission had collapsed.

Bay of Pigs

Confrontations with the Soviet Union

In the grim aftermath of the Bay of Pigs, Kennedy traveled to Vienna in June 1961 for his first meeting with Soviet Premier Nikita Khrushchev. Their frosty exchange of views did little to reduce tensions between the two nations—nor did Khrushchev's veiled threat of war unless the United States ceased to support a noncommunist West Berlin in the heart of East Germany.

Khrushchev was particularly unhappy about the mass exodus of residents of East Germany to the West through the easily traversed border in the center of Berlin. But he ultimately found a method short of war to stop it. Before dawn on August 13, 1961, the East German government, complying with directives from Moscow, constructed a wall between East and West Berlin. Guards fired on those who continued to try to escape. For nearly thirty years, the Berlin Wall served as the most potent physical symbol of the conflict between the communist and noncommunist worlds.

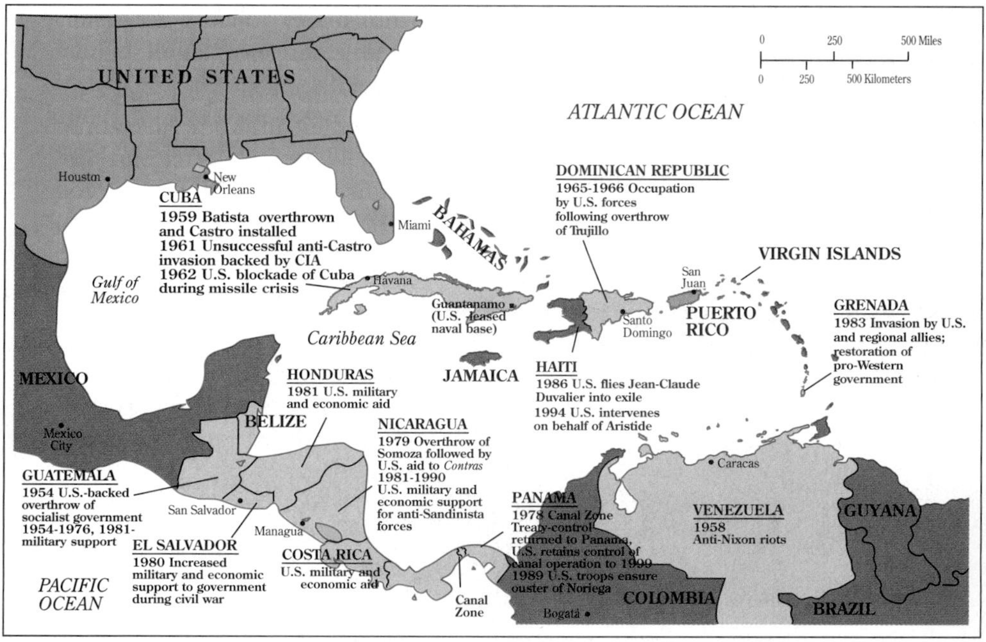

THE UNITED STATES IN LATIN AMERICA, 1954–2001 The Cold War greatly increased the readiness of the United States to intervene in the affairs of its Latin American neighbors. This map presents the many times and ways in which Washington ordered interventions in Central America, the Caribbean, and the northern nations of South America. During much of this period, the interventions were driven by Cold War concerns—by fears that communists might take over nations near the United States as they had taken over Cuba in the early 1960s. ◆ *What other interests motivated the U.S. to exert influence in Latin America, even after the end of the Cold War?*

Cuban Missile Crisis

The rising tensions culminated the following October in the most dangerous and dramatic crisis of the Cold War. During the summer of 1962, American intelligence agencies had become aware of the arrival of a new wave of Soviet technicians and equipment in Cuba and of military construction in progress. On October 14, aerial reconnaissance photos produced clear evidence that the Soviets were constructing sites on the island for offensive nuclear weapons. To the Soviets, placing missiles in Cuba probably seemed a reasonable—and relatively inexpensive—way to counter the presence of American missiles in Turkey (and a way to deter any future American invasion of Cuba). But to Kennedy and most other Americans, the missile sites represented an act of aggression by the Soviets toward the United States. Almost immediately, the president decided that the weapons could not be allowed to remain. On October 22, he ordered a naval and air blockade around Cuba, a "quarantine" against all offensive weapons. Preparations were under way for an American air attack on the missile sites when, late in the evening of October 26, Kennedy received a message from Khrushchev implying that the Soviet Union would remove the missile bases in exchange for an American pledge not to invade Cuba. Ignoring other, tougher Soviet messages, the president agreed. The crisis soon ended.

Johnson and the World

Lyndon Johnson entered the presidency with little prior experience in international affairs. He was eager, therefore, not only to continue the policies of his predecessor but to prove quickly that he too was a strong and forceful leader.

Intervention in the Dominican Republic

An internal rebellion in the Dominican Republic gave him an early opportunity to do so. A 1961 assassination had toppled the repressive dictatorship of General Rafael Trujillo, and for the next four years various factions in the country had struggled for dominance. In the spring of 1965, a conservative regime began to collapse in the face of a revolt by a broad range of groups on behalf of the left-wing nationalist Juan Bosch. Arguing (without any evidence) that Bosch planned to establish a pro-Castro, communist regime, Johnson dispatched 30,000 American troops to quell the disorder. Only after a conservative candidate defeated Bosch in a 1966 election were the forces withdrawn.

From Johnson's first moments in office, however, his foreign policy was almost totally dominated by the bitter civil war in Vietnam and by the expanding involvement of the United States there.

THE AGONY OF VIETNAM

George Kennan, who helped devise the containment doctrine in the name of which America went to war in Vietnam, once called the conflict "the most disastrous of all America's undertakings over the whole 200 years of its history." In retrospect, few would now wholly disagree. Yet at first, the conflict in Vietnam seemed simply one more Third World struggle on the periphery of the Cold War.

America and Diem

Having thrown its support to the new leader of South Vietnam, Ngo Dinh Diem, in the aftermath of the 1954 Geneva accords, and having supported Diem in his refusal to hold the elections in 1956 that the accords had required, the United States found itself drawn steadily deeper into the unstable politics of this fractious new nation.

Growing Support for Diem

Although Diem was an aristocratic Catholic from central Vietnam, an outsider in the south, he was also a nationalist, uncontaminated by collaboration with the French. And he was, for a time, apparently successful. With the help of the American

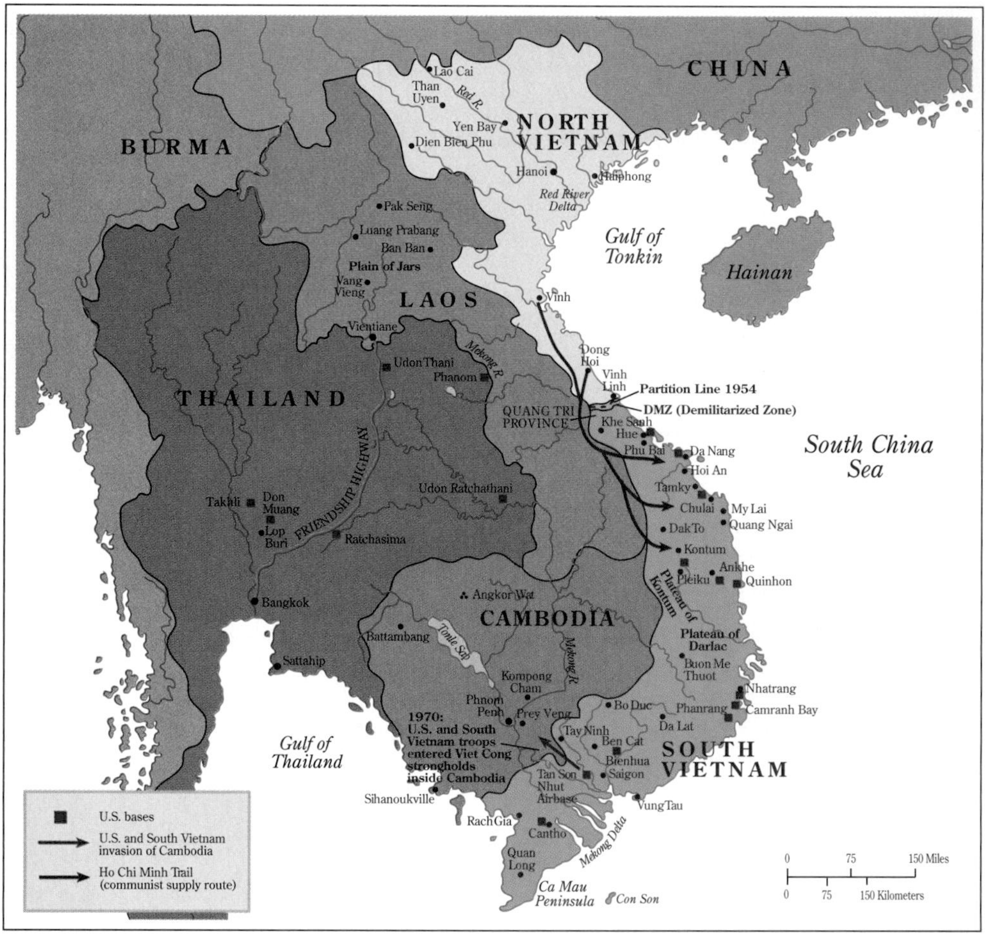

THE WAR IN VIETNAM AND INDOCHINA, 1964–1975 Much of the Vietnam War was fought in small engagements in widely scattered areas and did not conform to traditional notions of combat. But as this map shows, there were traditional battles and invasions and supply routes as well. The red arrows in the middle of the map show the general path of the Ho Chi Minh Trail, the main supply route by which North Vietnam supplied its troops and allies in the South. The blue arrow in southern South Vietnam indicates the point at which American troops invaded Cambodia in 1970. ◆ *What is there in the geography of Indochina, as presented on this map, that helps to explain the great difficulty the American military had in securing South Vietnam against communist attacks?*

CIA, Diem waged an effective campaign against some of the powerful religious sects and the South Vietnamese mafia, which had challenged the authority of the central government. As a result, the United States came to regard Diem as a powerful and impressive alternative to Ho Chi Minh. America poured military and economic aid into South Vietnam.

Diem's early successes in suppressing the sects in Vietnam led him in 1959 to begin a similar campaign to eliminate the supporters of Ho Chi Minh, the Vietminh, who had stayed behind in the south after the partition. That campaign persuaded Ho to resume the armed struggle for national unification. In 1959, the Vietminh cadres in the south created the National Liberation Front (NLF), known to many Americans as the Viet Cong—an organization closely allied with the North Vietnamese government. In 1960, under orders from Hanoi, and with both material and manpower support from North Vietnam, the NLF began military operations in the south. This marked the beginning of what Americans know as the Vietnam War.

By 1961, NLF forces had established effective control over many areas of the countryside. Diem was also by now losing the support of many other groups in South Vietnam, including his own military. In 1963, the Diem regime precipitated a major crisis by trying to discipline and repress the South Vietnamese Buddhists in an effort to make Catholicism the dominant religion of the country. The Buddhists staged enormous antigovernment demonstrations, during which several monks doused themselves with gasoline, sat cross-legged in the streets of downtown Saigon, and set themselves on fire—in view of photographers and television cameras.

American officials pressured Diem to reform his now tottering government, but the president made no significant concessions. As a result, in the fall of 1963, Kennedy gave his approval to a plot by a group of South Vietnamese generals to topple Diem. In early November 1963, the generals staged the coup, assassinated Diem along with his brother and principal adviser, Ngo Dinh Nhu (killings the United States had not wanted or expected), and established the first of a series of new governments, which were, for over three years, even less stable than the one they had overthrown. A few weeks after the coup, John Kennedy too was dead.

Diem Assassinated

From Aid to Intervention

Lyndon Johnson, therefore, inherited what was already a substantial American commitment to the survival of an anticommunist South Vietnam. During his first months in office, he expanded the American involvement in Vietnam only slightly, sending an additional 5,000 military advisers there and preparing to send 5,000 more. Then, early in August 1964, the president announced that American destroyers on patrol in international waters in the Gulf of Tonkin had been attacked by North Vietnamese torpedo boats. Later information raised serious doubts as to whether the administration reported the attacks accurately. At the time, however, virtually no one questioned Johnson's portrayal of the incident as a serious act of aggression. By a vote of 416 to 0 in the House and 88 to 2 in the Senate, Congress hurriedly passed the Gulf of Tonkin Resolution, which authorized the president to "take all necessary measures" to protect American forces and "prevent further aggression" in Southeast Asia. The resolution became, in Johnson's view at least, an open-ended legal authorization for escalation of the conflict.

Gulf of Tonkin Resolution

With the South Vietnamese leadership still in disarray and the communist military pressure on the south growing stronger, more and more of the burden of opposition to the Viet Cong fell on the United States. In February 1965, after communist forces attacked an American military base at Pleiku, Johnson ordered American bombings of the north, in an attempt to destroy the depots and transportation lines responsible for the flow of North Vietnamese soldiers and supplies into South Vietnam. The bombing continued intermittently until 1972. A month later, in March 1965, two battalions of American marines landed at Da Nang in South Vietnam. There were now more than 100,000 American troops in Vietnam.

Four months later, the president announced that American soldiers would now begin playing an active role in the conflict. By the end of the year, there were more than 180,000 American combat troops in Vietnam; in 1966, that number doubled; and by the end of 1967, there were over 500,000 American soldiers there. In the meantime, the air war intensified. By the spring of 1966, more than 4,000 Americans had been killed.

The Quagmire

"Attrition" Strategy

Central to the American war effort in Vietnam was the strategy known to the military as "attrition," one premised on the belief that the United States could inflict more damage on the enemy than the enemy could absorb. But the attrition strategy failed because the North Vietnamese were willing to commit many more soldiers and resources to the conflict than the United States had predicted.

It failed, too, because the United States was wrong in expecting its bombing of the north to eliminate the communists' war-making capacity. North Vietnam was not a modern industrial society, and it had relatively few of the sort of targets against which bombing is effective. The North Vietnamese also responded to the bombing with great ingenuity: creating a network of underground tunnels, shops, and factories; securing substantial aid from the Soviet Union and China; and continually moving the Ho Chi Minh Trail to make it elusive to American bombers. Far from breaking the north's resolve, the bombing seemed actually to strengthen popular commitment to the war.

"Pacification"

Another important part of the American strategy was the "pacification" program, whose purpose was to push the Viet Cong from particular regions and then "pacify" those regions by winning the "hearts and minds" of the people. Routing the Viet Cong was often possible, but the subsequent pacification was more difficult. Gradually, the pacification program gave way to a more heavy-handed relocation strategy, through which American troops uprooted villagers from their homes, sent them fleeing to refugee camps or into the cities (producing by 1967 more than 3 million refugees), and then destroyed the vacated villages and surrounding countryside.

As the war dragged on and victory remained elusive, some American officers and officials began to urge the president to expand the military efforts. But the Johnson administration resisted—in part because it was beginning to encounter obstacles and frustrations at home.

The War at Home

Few Americans, and even fewer influential ones, had protested the American involvement in Vietnam as late as the end of 1965. But as the war dragged on inconclusively, political support for it began to erode.

Growing Antiwar Movement

By the end of 1967, American students opposed to the war had become a significant political force. Enormous peace marches in New York, Washington, D.C., and other cities drew broad public attention to the antiwar movement. In the meantime, a growing number of journalists, particularly reporters who had spent time in Vietnam, helped sustain the movement with their frank revelations about the brutality and apparent futility of the war.

Senator J. William Fulbright of Arkansas, chairman of the Senate Foreign Relations Committee, also turned against the war and in January 1966 began to stage highly publicized and occasionally televised congressional hearings to air criticisms of it. Other members of Congress joined Fulbright in opposing Johnson's policies—including, in 1967, Robert F. Kennedy, brother of the slain president, now a senator from New York. Even within the administration, the consensus seemed to be crumbling. Robert McNamara, who had done much to help extend the American involvement in Vietnam, quietly left the government, disillusioned, in 1968. His successor as secretary of defense, Clark Clifford, became a quiet but powerful voice within the administration on behalf of a cautious scaling down of the commitment.

War-induced Inflation

In the meantime, Johnson's commitment to fighting the war while continuing his Great Society reforms helped cause a rise in inflation, from the 2 percent level it had occupied through most of the early 1960s to 3 percent in 1967, 4 percent in 1968, and 6 percent in 1969. In August 1967, Johnson asked Congress for a tax increase to avoid even more ruinous inflation. In return, congressional conservatives demanded and received a $6 billion reduction in the funding for Great Society programs.

THE TRAUMAS OF 1968

By the end of 1967, the twin crises of the war in Vietnam and the deteriorating racial situation at home had produced great social and political tensions. In the course of 1968, those tensions burst to the surface and seemed to threaten national chaos.

Debating the Past

THE VIETNAM COMMITMENT

The debate over why the United States became involved in the conflict in Vietnam (which is only one of many debates about the meaning of the war) has centered on two different, if related, questions. One is an effort to assess the broad objectives Americans believed they were pursuing in Vietnam. The other is an effort to explain how and why policymakers made the specific decisions that led the United States to a military commitment in Indochina.

Scholars and writers such as Norman Podhoretz, Guenter Lewy, and R. B. Smith, echoing elements of the official government explanation of American intervention in the war in the 1960s, have argued that the communist aggression in Vietnam was part of a Chinese and Soviet design to spread revolution throughout Asia. America, therefore, was not only protecting Vietnam, although that was an important part of its mission; it was also defending the rest of Asia, which would soon be threatened by communism if Vietnam fell. The intervention in Vietnam was a rational and even necessary expression of America's legitimate security interests and its belief in democracy.

Most scholars, however, have been more skeptical. Historians on the left argue that America's intervention in Vietnam was a form of imperialism—part of a larger effort by the United States after World War II to impose a particular political and economic order on the world. "The Vietnam War," Gabriel Kolko wrote in 1985, "was for the United States the culmination of its frustrating postwar effort to merge its arms and politics to halt and reverse the emergence of states and social systems opposed to the international order Washington sought to establish." Others argued that the United States fought in Vietnam to serve the American economic interests that had a stake in the region or in the arms production the war stimulated. More moderate critics blame the Vietnam intervention on the myopia of a foreign policy elite unwilling to question its own unreflective commitment to containing communism everywhere and unable to distinguish between international aggression and domestic insurgency.

Those who have looked less at the nation's broad objectives than at the workings of the policymaking process have also produced competing explanations. David Halberstam's *The Best and the Brightest* (1972) argued that

> policymakers deluded themselves into thinking they could achieve their goals in Vietnam by ignoring, suppressing, or dismissing information that should have suggested that they were wrong; because of arrogance or ideological rigidity, they simply refused to consider that victory was beyond their grasp.

Larry Berman, writing in 1982, offered a somewhat different view. Neither Johnson nor his advisers were unaware of the obstacles to success in Vietnam. Almost everyone suspected that victory would be difficult, even impossible, to attain. The president was not misled or misinformed. But Johnson committed troops to the war anyway, because he feared that allowing Vietnam to fall would ruin him politically and destroy his hopes for building his "Great Society" at home. Leslie Gelb and Richard Betts made a related argument in 1979. Vietnam, they claimed, was the logical, perhaps inevitable result of a political and bureaucratic order shaped by the ideology of the Cold War. However costly the intervention in Vietnam, policymakers concluded, the costs of not intervening and allowing South Vietnam to fall always seemed higher. The war escalated in the 1960s not because American aims changed but because the situation in Vietnam deteriorated to the point where nothing short of intervention would prevent defeat. Only when the national and international political situation itself shifted in the late 1960s and early 1970s—only when it became clear that the political costs of staying in Vietnam were higher than the political costs of getting out—was it possible for the United States to begin disengaging.

(text continued from page 831)

The Tet Offensive

On January 31, 1968, the first day of the Vietnamese New Year (Tet), communist forces launched an enormous, concerted attack on American strongholds throughout South Vietnam. A few cities, most notably Hue, fell temporarily to the communists. But what made the Tet offensive so shocking to the American people, who saw vivid reports of it on television, was the sight of communist forces in the heart of Saigon, setting off bombs, shooting down South Vietnamese officials and troops, and holding down fortified areas (including, briefly, the grounds of the American embassy). The Tet offensive also suggested to the American public something of the brutality of the fighting in Vietnam. In the midst of the fighting, television cameras recorded the sight of a South Vietnamese officer shooting a captured and defenseless young Viet Cong soldier in the head in the streets of Saigon.

Political Defeat

American forces soon dislodged the Viet Cong from most of the positions they had seized. The Tet offensive inflicted enormous casualties on the communists and permanently depleted the ranks of the NLF, forcing North Vietnamese troops to take on a much larger share of the subsequent fighting. But all that had little impact on American opinion. Tet may have been a military victory for the United States, but it was a political defeat for the administration.

In the following weeks, opposition to the war grew substantially. Leading newspapers and magazines, television commentators, and mainstream politicians began taking public stands against the conflict. Public opposition to the war almost doubled. And Johnson's personal popularity rating had slid to 35 percent, the lowest of any president since Harry Truman.

The Political Challenge

Eugene McCarthy

Beginning in the summer of 1967, dissident Democrats tried to mobilize support behind an antiwar candidate who would challenge Lyndon Johnson in the 1968 primaries. When Robert Kennedy turned them down, they recruited Senator Eugene McCarthy of Minnesota. A brilliantly orchestrated campaign

JOHNSON AND HUMPHREY, MARCH 27, 1968 Four days before announcing he would not run for reelection, a grim and tired Lyndon Johnson, accompanied by Vice President Hubert Humphrey, receives a briefing on the military situation in Vietnam. *(Bettmann/Corbis)*

by young volunteers in the New Hampshire primary produced a startling showing by McCarthy in March; he nearly defeated the president.

A few days later, Robert Kennedy entered the campaign, embittering many McCarthy supporters but bringing his own substantial strength among minorities, poor people, and workers to the antiwar cause. Polls showed the president trailing badly in the next scheduled primary, in Wisconsin. On March 31, 1968, Johnson went on television to announce a limited halt in the bombing of North Vietnam—his first major concession to the antiwar forces—and, much more surprising, his withdrawal from the presidential contest.

Robert Kennedy quickly established himself as the champion of the Democratic primaries, winning one election after another. In the meantime, however, Vice President Hubert Humphrey, with the support of President Johnson, entered the contest and began to attract the support of party leaders and of the many delegations that were selected not by popular primaries but by state party organizations. He soon appeared to be the front-runner in the race.

The King Assassination

On April 4, Martin Luther King, Jr., who had traveled to Memphis, Tennessee, to lend his support to striking black sanitation workers in the city, was shot and killed while standing on the balcony of his motel. The assassin, James Earl Ray, who

James Earl Ray

was captured two months later in London, had no apparent motive. Subsequent evidence suggested that he had been hired by others to do the killing, but he himself never revealed the identity of his employers.

King's tragic death produced a great outpouring of grief. Among African Americans, it also produced anger. In the days after the assassination, major riots broke out in more than sixty American cities. Forty-three people died.

The Kennedy Assassination and Chicago

Late in the night of June 6, Robert Kennedy appeared in the ballroom of a Los Angeles hotel to acknowledge his victory in that day's California primary. As he left the ballroom after his victory statement, Sirhan Sirhan, a young Palestinian apparently enraged by pro-Israeli remarks Kennedy had recently made, emerged from a crowd and shot him in the head. Early the next morning, Kennedy died. The shock of this second tragedy in two months cast a pall over the remainder of the presidential campaign.

Democratic National Convention

When the Democrats finally gathered in Chicago in August, for a convention in which Hubert Humphrey was now the only real contender, even the most optimistic observers were predicting turbulence. Inside the hall, delegates bitterly debated an antiwar plank in the party platform that both Kennedy and McCarthy supporters favored. Miles away, in a downtown park, thousands of antiwar protesters were staging demonstrations. On the third night of the convention, as the delegates were beginning their balloting on the now virtually inevitable nomination of Hubert Humphrey, demonstrators and police clashed in a bloody riot in the streets of Chicago. Hundreds of protesters were injured as police attempted to disperse them with tear gas and billy clubs. Aware that the violence was being televised to the nation, the demonstrators taunted the authorities with the chant, "The whole world is watching!" And Hubert Humphrey, who had spent years dreaming of becoming his party's candidate for president, received a nomination that night which appeared at the time to be almost worthless.

The Conservative Response

The turbulent events of 1968 persuaded some observers that American society was in the throes of revolutionary change. In fact, however, the response of most Americans to the turmoil was a conservative one.

George Wallace

The most visible sign of the conservative backlash was the surprising success of the campaign of George Wallace for the presidency. Wallace had established himself in 1963 as one of the leading spokesmen for the defense of segregation when, as governor of Alabama, he had attempted to block the admission of black students to the University of Alabama. In 1968, he became a

1968

The year 1968 was one of the most turbulent in the postwar history of the United States. Much of what made it so traumatic were specifically American events—the growing controversy over the war in Vietnam, the assassinations of Martin Luther King, Jr. and Robert Kennedy, racial unrest across the nation's cities, student protests on campuses throughout America. But the turmoil of 1968 was not confined to the United States. There were tremendous upheavals in many parts of the globe that year.

The most common form of turbulence around the world in 1968 was student unrest. In France, in May 1968, there was a student uprising that far exceeded in size and ferocity anything that occurred in the United States. It attracted the support of French workers and briefly paralyzed Paris and other cities. It contributed to the downfall of the government of Charles de Gaulle a year later. In England, Ireland, Germany, Italy, the Netherlands, Mexico, Canada, Japan, and South Korea, students and other young people demonstrated in great numbers, and at times with some violence, against governments and universities and other structures of authority. Elsewhere, 1968 created more widespread protest, as in Czechoslovakia, where hundreds of thousands of citizens took to the streets in support of what became known as "Prague spring"—a demand for greater democracy and a repudiation of many of the oppressive rules and structures imposed on the nation by its Soviet-dominated communist regimes—until Russian tanks rolled into the city to crush the uprising.

Both at the time and since, many people have tried to explain why so much instability emerged in so many nations at the same time. One factor that contributed to the worldwide turbulence of 1968 was simple numbers. The postwar baby boom had created a very large age cohort in many nations, and by the late 1960s it was coming of age. In the industrial west, the sheer size of the new generation produced a tripling of the number of people attending colleges and universities in fewer than twenty years, and a heightened sense of the power of youth. The long period of postwar prosperity and relative peace in which this generation had grown up contributed to heightened expectations of what the world should offer them—and a greater level of impatience than previous generations had demonstrated with the obstacles that stood in the way of their hopes. A new global youth culture emerged that was in many ways at odds with the dominant culture of older generations. It valued nonconformity, personal freedom, and even rebellion.

A second force contributing to the widespread turbulence of 1968 was the power of global media. Satellite communication introduced in the early 1960s made it possible to transmit live news instantly across the world. Videotape technology and the creation of lightweight portable television cameras enabled media organizations to respond to events much more quickly and flexibly than in the past. The audience for these televised images was by now global and enormous, particularly in industrial nations but even in the poorest areas of the world. Protests in one country were suddenly capable of inspiring protests in others. Demonstrators in Paris, for example, spoke openly of how campus protests in the United States in 1968—for example, the student uprising at Columbia University in New York the previous month—had helped motivate French students to rise up as well. Just as American students were protesting against what they considered the antiquated, paternalistic features of their universities, French students demanded an end to the rigid, autocratic character of their own academic world.

In most parts of the world, the 1968 uprisings came and went without fundamentally altering the institutions and systems they were attacking. But many changes came in the wake of these protests. Universities around the globe undertook significant reforms. Religious observance in mainstream churches and synagogues in the West declined dramatically after 1968. New concepts of personal freedom gained legitimacy, helping to inspire new social movements in the years that followed—among them the dramatic growth of feminism in many parts of the world. The events of 1968 did not produce a revolution, in the United States or in most of the rest of the world, but it did help launch a period of dramatic social, cultural, and political change that affected the peoples of many nations.

(text continued from page 835)

third-party candidate for president, basing his campaign on a host of conservative grievances. He denounced the forced busing of students, the proliferation of government regulations and social programs, and the permissiveness of authorities toward crime, race riots, and antiwar demonstrations. There was never any serious chance that Wallace would win the election, but his standing in the polls rose at times to over 20 percent.

Nixon Elected

A more effective effort to mobilize the conservative middle in favor of order and stability was under way within the Republican Party. Richard Nixon, whose political career had seemed at an end after his losses in the presidential race of 1960 and a California gubernatorial campaign two years later, reemerged as the spokesman for what he sometimes called the "silent majority." By offering a vision of stability, law and order, government retrenchment, and "peace with honor" in Vietnam, he easily captured the nomination of his party for the presidency. And despite a last-minute surge by Humphrey, he hung on to eke out a victory almost as narrow as his defeat in 1960. He received 43.4 percent of the popular vote to Humphrey's 42.7 percent (a margin of only about 500,000 votes), and 301 electoral votes to Humphrey's 191. George Wallace, who like most third-party candidates faded in the last weeks of the campaign, still managed to poll 13.5 percent of the popular vote and to carry five southern states with a total of 46 electoral ballots. Nixon had hardly won a decisive personal mandate. But the election made clear that a majority of the American electorate was more interested in restoring stability than in promoting social change.

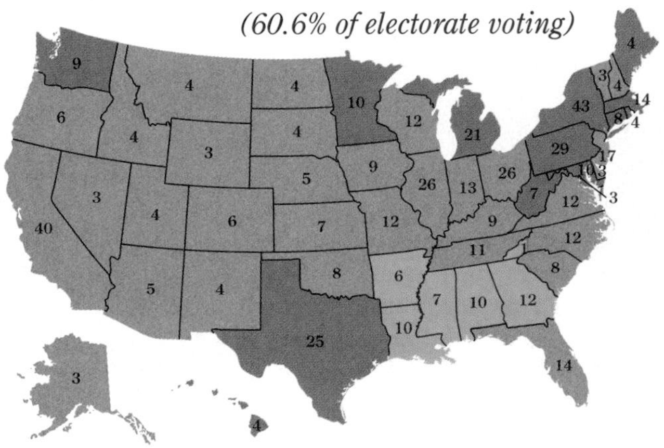

	ELECTORAL VOTE	POPULAR VOTE (%)
Richard M. Nixon *(Republican)*	301	31,770,237 (43.4)
Hubert H. Humphrey *(Democratic)*	191	31,270,533 (42.7)
George C. Wallace *(American Independence)*	46	9,906,141 (13.5)
Other candidates *(Prohibition; Socialist Labor; D. Gregory; Socialist Workers; Peace and Freedom; McCarthy)*	—	218,347

THE ELECTION OF 1968 The 1968 presidential election, which Richard Nixon won, was almost as close as the election of 1960, which he lost. Nixon might have won a more substantial victory had it not been for the independent candidacy of Governor George C. Wallace, who attracted many of the same conservative voters to whom Nixon appealed. ◆ *How does the distribution of Democratic and Republican strength in this election compare to that in 1960?*

For an interactive version of this map go to www.mhhe.com/unfinishednation4ch31maps

CONCLUSION

Perhaps no decade of the twentieth century created more powerful and enduring images in America than the 1960s. It began with the election—and then the traumatic assassination—of an attractive and energetic young president, John Kennedy, who captured the imagination of millions and seemed to symbolize the rising idealism of the time. It produced a dramatic period of political innovation, christened the Great Society by President Lyndon Johnson, which greatly expanded the size and functions of the federal government and its responsibility for the welfare of the nation's citizens. It saw the emergence of a sustained and enormously powerful civil rights movement that won a series of important legal victories, including two civil rights acts that dismantled the Jim Crow system constructed in the late nineteenth and early twentieth centuries.

The very spirit of dynamism and optimism that made the early 1960s so productive also helped bring to the surface problems and grievances that had no easy solutions. The civil rights movement awakened expectations of social and economic equality that laws alone could not provide and that remained in many respects unfulfilled. The peaceful, interracial crusade of the early 1960s gradually turned into a much more militant, confrontational, and increasingly separatist movement toward the decade's end. The idealism among white youths that began the 1960s, and played an important role in the political success of John Kennedy, evolved into an angry rebellion against many aspects of American culture and politics and produced a large upsurge of student protest that rocked the nation at the decade's end. Perhaps most of all, a small and largely unnoticed Cold War commitment to defend South Vietnam against communist aggression from the north led to a large and disastrous American military commitment that destroyed the presidency of Lyndon Johnson, shook the faith of millions in their leaders and their political system, sent thousands of young men to their deaths, and showed no signs of producing a victory. A decade that began with high hopes and soaring ideals ended with ugly and at times violent division, and deep disillusionment.

FOR FURTHER REFERENCE

Allen J. Matusow, *The Unraveling of America: A History of Liberalism in the 1960s* (1984) is a provocative history of this turbulent decade. David Farber, *The Age of Great Dreams: America in the 1960s* (1994) is an intelligent and lively general history. Arthur M. Schlesinger, Jr., *A Thousand Days* (1965) is a celebrated and celebratory memoir of the Kennedy years. Garry Wills, *The Kennedy Imprisonment* (1982) is an important demystification. Robert Dallek, *Lone Star Rising: Lyndon Johnson and His Times, 1908–1960* (1991) and *Flawed Giant: Lyndon B. Johnson, 1960–1973* (1998) are an important biography. Rick Perlstein, *Before the Storm: Barry Goldwater and the Unmaking of the American Consensus* (2001) is an excellent biography of the first postwar hero of the right, and Matthew Dallek, *The Right Moment: Ronald Reagan's First Victory and the Decisive Turning Point in American Politics* (2000) is a good study of the rise of Reagan in the 1960s. Robert Weisbrot, *Freedom Bound: A History of America's Civil Rights Movement* (1990) is a good synthetic history of the movement. John Dittmer, *Local People: The Struggle for Civil Rights in Mississippi* (1994) is an important study of the grass-roots origins of the movement. William Chafe, *Civilities and Civil Rights: Greensboro, North Carolina, and the Black Struggle for Freedom* (1980) is an excellent study of the southern civil rights movement and the white reaction to it. Taylor Branch,

Parting the Waters: America in the King Years, 1959–1963 (1988) and *Pillar of Fire: America in the King Years, 1963–1965* (1998) are good narrative histories of the movement. Nicholas Lemann, *The Promised Land: The Great Black Migration and How it Changed America* (1991) is a challenging study of the postwar African-American migration to northern cities and of the Great Society's response to it. Graham T. Allison, *The Essence of Decision: Explaining the Cuban Missile Crisis* (1971) is an important interpretation of the greatest crisis of the Cold War. Ernest R. May and Philip D. Zelikow, *The Kennedy Tapes: Inside the White House during the Cuban Missile Crisis* (1997) provides the annotated transcripts of the taped meetings of Kennedy's inner circle during the crisis. Robert D. Schulzinger, *A Time for War: The United States and Vietnam, 1945–1975* (1997) is a good general history of the war. Neil Sheehan, *A Bright Shining Lie: John Paul Vann and America in Vietnam* (1988) is a compelling picture of the war as experienced by a significant military figure of the 1960s. Frederik Logevall, *Choosing War: The Lost Chance for Peace and the Escalation of War in Vietnam* (1999); David Kaiser, *American Tragedy: Kennedy, Johnson, and the Origins of Vietnam* (2000); A. J. Langguth, *Our Vietnam/Nuoc Viet Ta: A History of the War, 1954–1975* (2000); and James Mann, *A Grand Delusion: America's Descent into Vietnam* (2001) are important recent studies. Christian J. Appy, *Working-Class War: American Combat Soldiers and Vietnam* (1993) examines the class basis of the army that fought in Vietnam. Larry Berman, *Planning a Tragedy* (1982) and *Lyndon Johnson's War* (1989); Leslie Gelb and Richard Betts, *The Irony of Vietnam: The System Worked* (1979); and David Halberstam, *The Best and the Brightest* (1972) are important interpretations of the American decision to intervene and stay in Vietnam, Dan T. Carter, *The Politics of Rage: George Wallace, The Origins of the New Conservatism, and the Transformation of American Politics* (1995) is a good study of the career of George Wallace. David Farber, *Chicago '68* (1988) examines the turbulent Democratic Convention and, through it, the passions that shaped a traumatic year in recent American history.

Berkeley in the Sixties (1990) is a documentary film portraying the tumultuous student politics at the University of California, Berkeley, and through them larger themes of the decade. *Eyes on the Prize: The American Civil Rights Struggle, 1954–1965* (1986–1987) is a six-part film series by Blackside Productions on the history of the civil rights movement. *Malcolm X: Make it Plain* (1994) is the definitive film biography of Malcolm X. *The Kennedys* (1992) is a film presentation on the lives of President John F. Kennedy and various members of his powerful family. *LBJ* (1991), a film by David Grubin, is a biographical treatment of President Lyndon Johnson. *America's War on Poverty* (1995) is a five-part series on the Kennedy and Johnson administrations' most dramatic welfare initiative.

For quizzes, Internet resources, references to additional books and films, and more, consult this book's Online Learning Center site at www.mhhe.com/unfinishednation4.

"TODAY'S TEENAGERS" The coming of age of the "baby-boom" generation, and the rise of youthful activism, led *Time* magazine to devote a 1965 cover story to "Today's Teen-Agers." As notable as the choice of subject was the choice of artist for the cover image: Andy Warhol, the great pop artist whose serial portraits of both famous and unknown people helped define his era. Warhol's work was instrumental in breaking down barriers between serious art and popular culture, both in its subject matter (celebrities, commercial products) and in its techniques, which drew heavily from commercial art. This series of silk-screened photographs made use of one of his trademark media. *(TIME Magazine, copyright TIME, Inc./Getty Images)*

TIME LINE

1963	1964	1966	1968	1969	1970
Friedan's *The Feminine Mystique*	Free Speech Movement begins	National Organization for Women formed	Turmoil in universities	Antiwar movement's Vietnam "moratoriums"	Cambodian incursion
				Rock concert in Woodstock, NY	

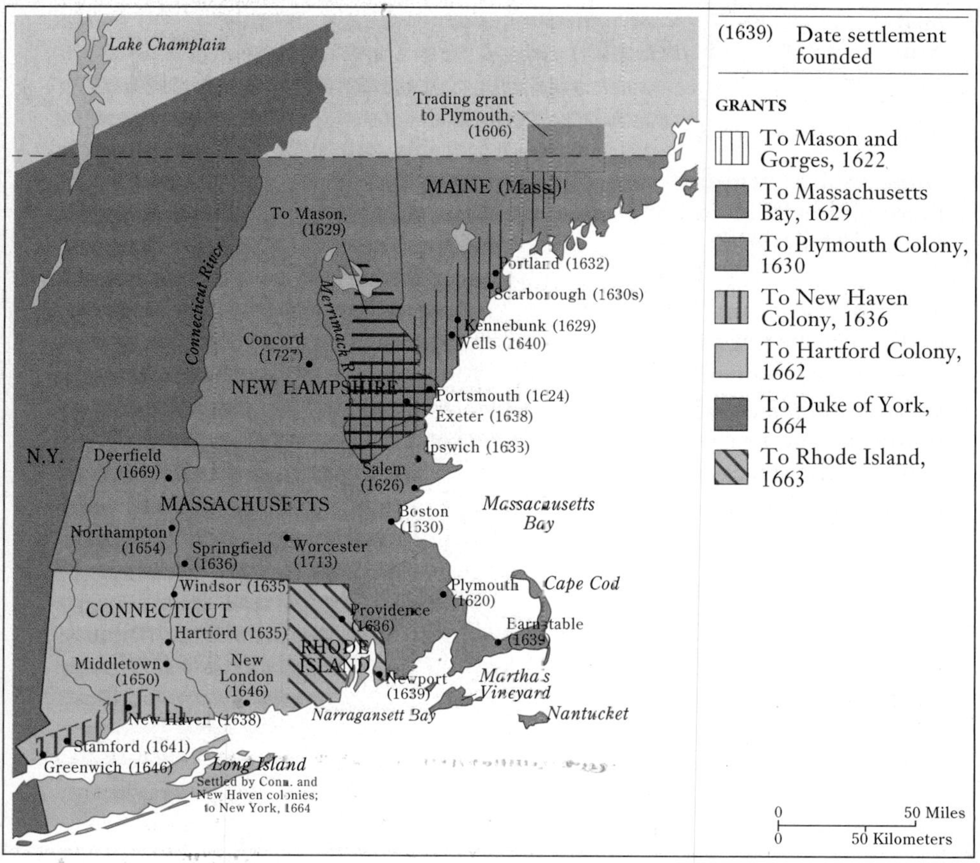

THE GROWTH OF NEW ENGLAND, 1620–1750 The European settlement of New England, as this map reveals, traces its origins primarily to two small settlements on the Atlantic coast. The first was the Pilgrim settlement at Plymouth, which began in 1620 and spread out through Cape Cod, southern Massachusetts, and the islands of Martha's Vineyard and Nantucket. The second, much larger settlement began in Boston in 1630 and spread rapidly through western Massachusetts, north into New Hampshire and Maine, and south into Connecticut. ◆ *Why would the settlers of Massachusetts Bay have expanded so much more rapidly and expansively than those of Plymouth?*

For an interactive version of this map go to www.mhhe.com/unfinishednation4ch2maps

argued that the Massachusetts church should abandon all allegiance to the Church of England. He also proclaimed that the land the colonists were occupying belonged to the natives. The colonial government voted to deport him, but he escaped before they could do so. During the winter of 1635–1636, he took refuge with Narragansett tribesmen; the following spring he bought a tract of land from them, and with a few followers, created the town of Providence. In 1644, after obtaining a charter from Parliament, he established a government similar to that of Massachusetts but without any ties to the church. For a time, Rhode

Island was the only colony in which all faiths (including Judaism) could worship without interference.

Anne Hutchinson

Another challenge to the established religious order in Massachusetts Bay came from Anne Hutchinson, an intelligent and charismatic woman from a substantial Boston family. She argued that many clergy were not among the "elect" and were, therefore, entitled to no spiritual authority. Such teachings (known as the Antinomian heresy) were a serious threat to the spiritual authority of the established clergy. Hutchinson also challenged prevailing assumptions about the proper role of women in Puritan society. As her influence grew, and as she began to deliver open attacks on members of the clergy, the Massachusetts hierarchy mobilized to stop her. In 1638, she was convicted of heresy and sedition and was banished. With her family and some of her followers, she moved to a point on Narragansett Bay not far from Providence. Later she moved south into New York, where in 1643 she and her family died during an Indian uprising.

Maine and New Hampshire

The Hutchinson affair had an important impact on the settlement of the areas north of Massachusetts Bay. New Hampshire and Maine were established in 1629 by two English proprietors. But few settlers moved into these northern regions until the religious disruptions in Massachusetts Bay. In 1639, John Wheelwright, a disciple of Anne Hutchinson, led some of his fellow dissenters to Exeter, New Hampshire. Others soon followed. New Hampshire became a separate colony in 1679. Maine remained a part of Massachusetts until 1820.

Settlers and Natives

The first white settlers in New England had generally friendly relations with the natives. Indians taught whites how to grow vital food crops such as corn, beans, pumpkins, and potatoes; they also taught them new agricultural techniques. European farmers also benefited from the extensive lands Indians had already cleared (and either abandoned or sold). White traders used Indians as partners in some of their most important trading activities. Indeed, commerce with the Indians was responsible for the creation of some of the first great fortunes in British North America. Other white settlers attempted to educate the Indians in European religion and culture. Protestant missionaries converted some natives to Christianity, and a few Indians became at least partially assimilated into white society.

But as in other areas of white settlement, tensions soon developed—primarily as a result of the white colonists' insatiable appetite for land. The particular character of those conflicts emerged as well out of Puritan attitudes toward the natives. The religious leaders of New England came to consider the tribes a threat to their hopes of creating a godly community in the New World. Gradually, the image of Indians as helpful neighbors came to be replaced by the image of Indians as "heathens" and barbarians.

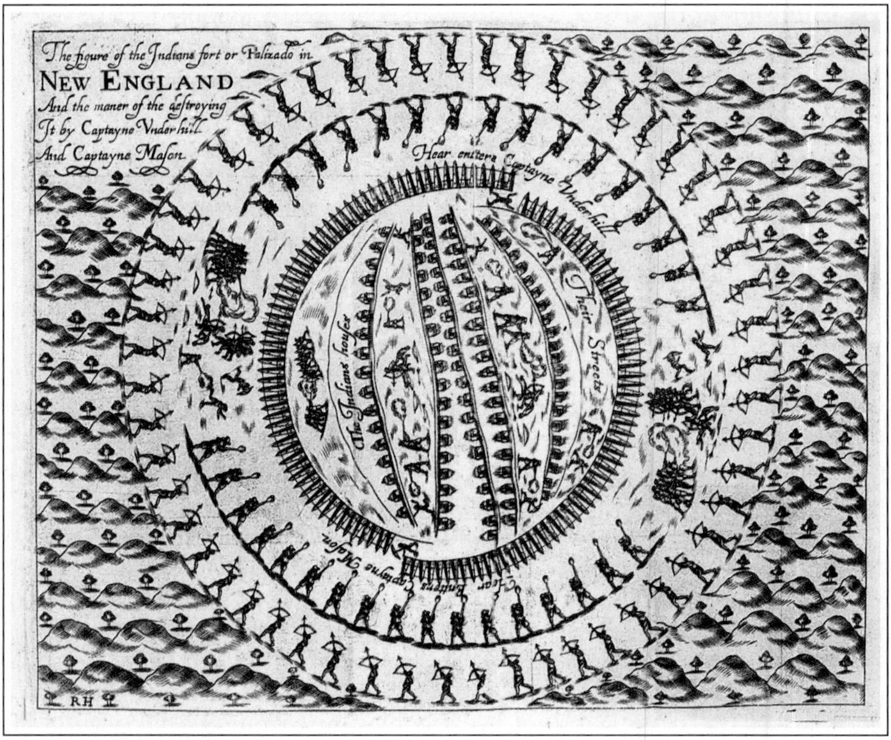

A PEQUOT VILLAGE DESTROYED An English artist drew this view of a fortified Pequot village in Connecticut surrounded by English soldiers and their allies from other tribes during the Pequot War in 1637. The invaders massacred more than 600 residents of the settlement. *(Rare Books Division, New York Public Library, Astor, Lenox and Tilden Foundations)*

King Philip's War and the Technology of Battle

In 1637, hostilities broke out between English settlers in the Connecticut Valley and the Pequot Indians of the region, a conflict (known as the Pequot War) in which the natives were almost wiped out. But the bloodiest and most prolonged encounter between whites and Indians in the seventeenth century began in 1675, a conflict that whites called King Philip's War. The Wampanoags, under the leadership of a chieftain known to the white settlers as King Philip and among his own people as Metacomet, rose up to resist the English. For three years, the natives inflicted terror on a string of Massachusetts towns, killing over a thousand people. But beginning in 1676, the white settlers gradually prevailed, with the help of a group of Mohawk allies who ambushed Metacomet and killed him. Without Metacomet, the fragile alliance among the tribes collapsed, and the white settlers were soon able to crush the uprising.

Metacomet

The character of these and subsequent conflicts between natives and settlers was crucially affected by earlier exchanges of technology between the English and the tribes. In particular, the Indians made effective use of a relatively new weapon introduced to New England by Myles Standish and others: the flintlock rifle. It replaced the earlier staple of colonial musketry, the matchlock rifle, which proved too heavy, cumbersome, and inaccurate to be effective. The matchlock had to be steadied on a fixed object and ignited with a match before firing. The flintlock could be held up without support and fired without a match. Indians using bows and arrows often outmatched settlers using the clumsy matchlocks.

Flintlock Muskets

Many English settlers were slow to give up their matchlocks, but the Indians recognized the advantages of the newer rifles right away and began purchasing them in large quantities. Despite rules forbidding colonists to instruct natives on how to use and repair the weapons, the natives learned to handle the rifles, and even to repair them, very effectively on their own. In King Philip's War, the very high casualties on both sides were a result of the use of these more advanced rifles.

Indians also used more traditional military technologies—especially the construction of forts. The Narragansetts, allies of the Wampanoags in King Philip's War, built an enormous fort in the Great Swamp of Rhode Island in 1675, which became the site of one of the bloodiest battles of the war before English attackers burned it down. After that, a band of Narragansetts set out to build a large stone fort, with the help of a member of the tribe who had learned masonry while working with the English. When English soldiers discovered the stone fort in 1676, after the end of King Philip's War, they killed most of its occupants and destroyed it. In the end, the technological skills of the Indians were no match for the overwhelming advantages of the English settlers in both numbers and firepower.

THE RESTORATION COLONIES

For nearly thirty years after Lord Baltimore received the charter for Maryland in 1632, no new English colonies were established in America. England had to deal with troubles of its own at home.

The English Civil War

After Charles I dissolved Parliament in 1629 and began ruling as an absolute monarch, he steadily alienated a growing number of his subjects. Finally, desperately in need of money, Charles called Parliament back into session in 1640 and asked it to levy new taxes. But he antagonized the members by dismissing them twice in two years; and in 1642, they organized a military force, thus beginning the English Civil War.

The conflict between the Cavaliers (the supporters of the king) and the Roundheads (the forces of Parliament, who were largely Puritans) lasted seven years. In 1649, the Roundheads defeated the king's forces and shocked all of Europe by beheading the monarch. The stern Roundhead leader Oliver Cromwell replaced the king and assumed the position of "protector." But when Cromwell died in 1658, his son and heir proved unable to maintain his authority. Two years later, Charles II, son of the executed king, returned from exile and seized the throne, in what became known as the Restoration.

Oliver Cromwell

Among the results of the Restoration was the resumption of colonization in America. Charles II rewarded faithful courtiers with grants of land in the New World, and in the twenty-five years of his reign he issued charters for four additional colonies: Carolina, New York, New Jersey, and Pennsylvania.

The Carolinas

In successive charters issued in 1663 and 1665, Charles II awarded eight proprietors joint title to a vast territory stretching south from Virginia to the Florida peninsula and west to the Pacific Ocean. Like Lord Baltimore, they received almost kingly powers over their grant, which they prudently called Carolina (a name derived from the Latin word for "Charles"). They reserved tremendous estates for themselves and distributed the rest through a headright system similar to those in Virginia and Maryland. Although committed Anglicans themselves, the proprietors guaranteed religious freedom to all Christian faiths. They also created a representative assembly. They hoped to attract settlers from the existing American colonies and to avoid the expense of financing expeditions from England.

But their initial efforts to profit from settlement in Carolina failed dismally. A few early attempts at colonization were quickly abandoned, and most of the original proprietors soon gave up the project. Anthony Ashley Cooper, however, persisted. He convinced the other proprietors to finance expeditions to Carolina from England, the first of which set sail with 300 people in the spring of 1670. Only 100 people survived the difficult voyage; those who did established a settlement at Port Royal on the Carolina coast. Ten years later they founded a city at the junction of the Ashley and Cooper Rivers, which in 1690 became the colonial capital. They called it Charles Town (it was later renamed Charleston).

Anthony Ashley Cooper

With the aid of the English philosopher John Locke, Cooper (now the earl of Shaftesbury) drew up the Fundamental Constitution for Carolina in 1669. It divided the colony into counties of equal size and divided each county into equal parcels. It also envisioned a social hierarchy with the proprietors themselves (who were to be known as "seigneurs") at the top,

Fundamental Constitution for Carolina

a local aristocracy (consisting of lesser nobles known as "landgraves" or "caciques") below them, and then ordinary settlers ("leet-men"). At the bottom of this stratified society would be poor whites, who would have few political rights, and African slaves. Proprietors, nobles, and other landholders would have a voice in the colonial parliament in proportion to the size of their landholdings.

In reality, Carolina developed along lines quite different from the carefully ordered vision of Shaftesbury and Locke. For one thing, the northern and southern regions of settlement were widely separated and socially and economically distinct from one another. The northern settlers were mainly backwoods farmers. In the south, fertile lands and the good harbor at Charles Town promoted a more prosperous economy and a more stratified, aristocratic society. Settlements grew up rapidly along the Ashley and Cooper Rivers, and colonists established a flourishing trade, particularly (beginning in the 1660s) in rice.

Close ties with the Caribbean

Southern Carolina very early developed close commercial ties to the large (and overpopulated) European colony on the Caribbean island of Barbados. During the first ten years of settlement, in fact, most of the new residents in Carolina were Barbadians, some of whom established themselves as substantial landlords. African slavery had taken root on Barbados earlier than in any of the mainland colonies, and the white Caribbean migrants—tough, uncompromising profit seekers—established a similar slave-based plantation society in Carolina.

Carolina Divided

Carolina was one of the most divided English colonies in America. There were tensions between the small farmers of the Albemarle region in the north and the wealthy planters in the south. And there were conflicts between the rich Barbadians in southern Carolina and the smaller landowners around them. After Lord Shaftesbury's death, the proprietors proved unable to establish order. In 1719, the colonists seized control of the colony from them. Ten years later, the king divided the region into two royal colonies, North Carolina and South Carolina.

New Netherland, New York, and New Jersey

In 1664, Charles II granted his brother James, the duke of York, all the territory lying between the Connecticut and Delaware Rivers. But the grant faced a major challenge from the Dutch, who claimed the entire area.

New Amsterdam Seized

England and the Netherlands were already commercial rivals in Europe, and that rivalry now extended to America. In 1664, vessels of the English navy, under the command of Richard Nicolls, put in at New Amsterdam, the capital of the Dutch colony of New Netherland, and extracted a surrender from the governor, Peter Stuyvesant. Several years later, in 1673, the Dutch reconquered and briefly held their old provincial capital. But they lost it again, this time for good, in 1674.

The duke of York renamed his territory New York. It contained not only Dutch and English but Scandinavians, Germans, French, and a large number of Africans (imported as slaves by the Dutch West India Company), as well as members of several different Indian tribes. James wisely made no effort to impose his own Roman Catholicism on the colony. He delegated powers to a governor and a council but made no provision for representative assemblies.

Unequal Wealth and Power

Property holding and political power remained highly divided and highly unequal in New York. In addition to confirming the great Dutch "patroonships" already in existence, James granted large estates to some of his own political supporters. Power in the colony thus remained widely dispersed among wealthy English landlords, Dutch patroons, fur traders, and the duke's political appointees. By 1685, when the duke of York ascended the English throne as James II, New York contained about four times as many people (around 30,000) as it had twenty years before.

New Jersey Founded

Shortly after James received his charter, he gave a large part of the land south of New York to a pair of political allies, both Carolina proprietors, Sir John Berkeley and Sir George Carteret. Carteret named the territory New Jersey. But the venture in New Jersey generated few profits, and in 1674, Berkeley sold his half interest. The colony was divided into two jurisdictions, East Jersey and West Jersey, which squabbled with one another until 1702, when the two halves of the colony were again joined. New Jersey, like New York, was a colony of enormous ethnic and religious diversity, and the weak colonial government made few efforts to impose strict control over the fragmented society. But unlike New York, New Jersey developed no important class of large landowners.

The Quaker Colonies

Pennsylvania was born out of the efforts of a dissenting English Protestant sect, the Society of Friends, to find a home for their own distinctive social order. The society began in the mid-seventeenth century under the leadership of George Fox, a Nottingham shoemaker, and Margaret Fell. Their followers came to be known as Quakers (from Fox's instruction to them to "tremble at the name of the Lord"). Unlike the Puritans, Quakers rejected the concept of predestination and original sin. All people, they believed, had divinity within themselves and need only learn to cultivate it; all could attain salvation.

The Quakers

The Quakers had no formal church government and no paid clergy; in their worship they spoke up one by one as the spirit moved them. Disregarding distinctions of gender and class, they addressed one another with the terms "thee" and "thou," words commonly used in other parts of English society only in speaking to servants and social inferiors. As confirmed pacifists, they would not take part in wars. Unpopular in England, the Quakers began looking to America for asylum. A few migrated to New England or Carolina, but most Quakers wanted a colony of their own. As members of a despised sect, however, they could not get the necessary royal grant without the aid of someone influential at the court.

Fortunately for the Quaker cause, a number of wealthy and prominent men had converted to the faith. One of them was William Penn, who, over his aristocratic father's objections, converted to Quakerism, took up evangelism, and was sent repeatedly to prison. He soon began working with George Fox to create a Quaker colony in America. When his father died in 1681, Charles II paid a large debt he had owed to the older Penn with an enormous grant to the son of territory between New York and Maryland. At the king's insistence, the territory was to be named Pennsylvania, after Penn's late father.

Pennsylvania Established

Through his informative and honest advertising, Penn soon made Pennsylvania the best-known and most cosmopolitan of all the English colonies in America. More than any other English colony, Pennsylvania prospered from the outset, because of Penn's successful recruiting, his careful planning, and the region's mild climate and fertile soil. Penn sailed to Pennsylvania in 1682 to oversee the laying out, between the Delaware and Schuylkill Rivers, of the city he named Philadelphia ("Brotherly Love"). Penn recognized Indians' claims to the land in the province, and he was scrupulous about reimbursing them for it. The Indians generally respected Penn, and during his lifetime the colony had no major battles with the natives.

But the colony was not without conflict. By the late 1690s, some residents of Pennsylvania were beginning to resist the nearly absolute power of the proprietor. Pressure from these groups grew to the point that in 1701, shortly before he departed for England for the last time, Penn agreed to a Charter of Liberties for the colony. The charter established a representative assembly (consisting, alone among the English colonies, of only one house) that greatly limited the authority of the proprietor. The charter also permitted "the lower counties" of the colony to establish their own representative assembly. The three counties did so in 1703 and as a result became, in effect, a separate colony—Delaware—although until the American Revolution it continued to have the same governor as Pennsylvania.

Charter of Liberties

BORDERLANDS AND MIDDLE GROUNDS

The English colonies clustered along the Atlantic seaboard of North America eventually united, expanded, and became the beginnings of a great nation. But in the seventeenth and early eighteenth centuries, their future was not all clear. In those years, they were small, frail settlements surrounded by other, competing societies and settlements. The British Empire in North America was, in fact, a much smaller and weaker one than the great Spanish Empire to the South, and not, on the surface at least, clearly stronger than the enormous French Empire to the North.

The continuing contest for control of North America, and the complex interactions among the diverse peoples populating the continent, were most clearly visible in areas around the borders of English settlement—the Caribbean and along the northern, southern, and western borders of the coastal colonies. In the regions of the borderlands emerged societies very different from those in the heart of the English seaboard colonies—areas that have been described by recent scholars as "middle grounds," in which diverse civilizations encountered one another and, for a time at least, shaped one another.

Complex Cultural Interactions

The Caribbean Islands

The Chesapeake was the site of the first permanent English settlements in the New World. Throughout the first half of the seventeenth century, however, the most important destinations for English immigrants were the islands of the Caribbean and the northern way station of Bermuda. More than half the English migrants to the New World in the early seventeenth century settled on these islands. The island societies had close ties to English North America.

Before the arrival of Europeans, most of the Caribbean islands had substantial native populations. But beginning with Christopher Columbus's first visit in 1492, and accelerating after 1496, the native population was all but wiped out by European epidemics.

The Spanish Empire claimed title to all the islands in the Caribbean, but created substantial settlement only on the largest of them: Cuba, Hispaniola, and Puerto Rico. English, French, and Dutch traders began settling on some of the smaller islands early in the sixteenth century, despite the Spanish claim to them. After Spain and the Netherlands went to war in 1621 (distracting the Spanish navy and leaving the English in the Caribbean relatively unmolested), the pace of English colonization increased. By mid-century, there were several substantial English settlements on the islands, the most important of them on Antigua, St. Kitts, Jamaica, and Barbados.

The English Caribbean

In their first years in the Caribbean, English settlers experimented unsuccessfully with tobacco and cotton. But they soon discovered that the most lucrative crop was sugar, for which there was a substantial and growing market in Europe. Sugar cane could also be distilled into rum, for which there was also a booming market abroad. Planters were devoting almost all of their land to sugar cane.

Sugar and Slavery

Because sugar was a labor-intensive crop, English planters quickly found it necessary to import laborers. As in the Chesapeake, they began by bringing indentured servants from England. But the arduous work discouraged white laborers. By mid-century, therefore, the English planters in the Caribbean (like the Spanish colonists) were relying more and more heavily on an enslaved African work force, which soon substantially outnumbered them.

On Barbados and other islands where a flourishing sugar economy developed, the English planters were a tough, aggressive, and ambitious breed. Since their livelihoods depended on their work forces, they expanded and solidified the system of African slavery there remarkably quickly. By the late seventeenth century, there were four times as many African slaves as there were white settlers.

Masters and Slaves in the Caribbean

Harsh Conditions for Slaves

Fearful of slave revolts, whites in the Caribbean monitored their labor forces closely and often harshly. Planters paid little attention to the welfare of their workers. Many concluded that it was cheaper to buy new slaves periodically than to protect the well-being of those they already owned, and it was not uncommon for masters literally to work their slaves to death. Few African workers survived more than a decade in the brutal Caribbean working environment—they were either sold to planters in North America or died. Even whites, who worked far less hard than did the slaves, often succumbed to the harsh climate; most died before the age of forty.

Establishing a stable society and culture was extremely difficult for people living in such harsh and even deadly conditions. Those whites who could returned to England with their fortunes and left their estates in the hands of overseers. Europeans in the Caribbean lacked many of the institutions that gave stability to the North American settlements: church, family, community.

Slave Culture and Resistance

Africans in the Caribbean faced much greater difficulties, but because they had no chance of leaving, they created what was in many ways a more elaborate culture than did the white settlers. They started families (although many of them were broken up by death or the slave trade); they sustained African religious and social traditions (and resisted Christianity); and within the rigidly controlled world of the sugar plantations, they established patterns of resistance.

The Caribbean settlements were an important part of the Atlantic trading world in which many Americans became involved—a source of sugar and rum and a market for goods made in the mainland colonies and in England. They were the principal source of African slaves for the mainland colonies. And because Caribbean planters established an elaborate plantation system earlier than planters in North America, they provided models that many mainland people copied.

SUGAR PLANTATION IN THE ANTILLES This nineteenth-century engraving shows a sugar plantation in one of the Caribbean islands of the Antilles. Although the picture gives the sense of an idyllic landscape, sugar plantations were notoriously rugged places for the African slaves who worked there (and whose quarters can be seen on the left). *(Explorer/Mary Evans Picture Library)*

The Southwestern Borderlands

Spain's New World Empire

By the end of the seventeenth century, the Spanish had established a sophisticated and impressive empire. Their capital, Mexico City, was the most dazzling metropolis in the Americas. The Spanish residents, well over a million of them, enjoyed much greater prosperity than all but a few English settlers in North America.

But the principal Spanish colonies north of Mexico—Florida, Texas, New Mexico, Arizona, and California—were relatively unimportant economically to the empire. They attracted religious minorities, Catholic missionaries, independent ranchers fleeing the heavy hand of imperial authority, and Spanish troops defending the northern flank of the empire. But they remained weak and peripheral parts of the great empire to their south.

Spanish New Mexico

New Mexico was the most prosperous and populous of these Spanish outposts—even if far less successful than Spanish settlements in Mexico and South America. By the end of the eighteenth century, New Mexico had a non-Indian population of over 10,000—the largest European settlement west of the Mississippi and north of Mexico—and it was steadily expanding through the region.

California

The Spanish began to colonize California once they realized that other Europeans—among them English merchants and French and Russian trappers—were beginning to establish a presence in the region. Formal Spanish settlement of California began in the 1760s, when the governor of Baja California was ordered to create outposts of the empire further north. Soon a string of missions, forts (or *presidios*), and trading communities were springing up along the Pacific coast: beginning with San Diego and Monterey in 1769 and eventually San Francisco (1776), Los Angeles (1781), and Santa Barbara (1786). The arrival of the Spanish in California had a devastating effect on the native population, which died in great numbers from the diseases the colonists imported. As the new settlements spread, however, the Spanish insisted that the remaining natives convert to Catholicism. That explains the centrality of missions in almost all the major Spanish outposts in California. But the Spanish colonists were also intent on creating a prosperous agricultural economy, and they enlisted Indian laborers to help them do so. California's Indians had no choice but to accede to the demands of the Spanish, although there were frequent revolts by natives against the harsh conditions imposed upon them.

The Spanish considered the greatest threat to the northern borders of their empire to be the growing ambitions of the French. In the 1680s French explorers traveled down the Mississippi Valley to the mouth of the river and claimed the lands for France in 1682. They called the territory Louisiana. Fearful of French incursions further west, the Spanish began to fortify their claim to Texas by establishing new forts, missions, and settlements there, including San Fernando (later San Antonio) in 1731. Much of the region that is now Arizona was also becoming increasingly tied to the Spanish empire and was governed from Santa Fe.

Spanish "Middle Grounds"

The Spanish colonies in the Southwest were the sparsely populated edges of the great Spanish empire to the South—created less to increase the wealth of the empire than to defend it from threats by other European powers in the North. Nevertheless, these Spanish outposts helped create enduring societies that were very unlike those being established by the English along the Atlantic seaboard. The Spanish colonies were not committed to displacing the native populations, but rather to enlisting them. They sought to convert them to Catholicism, to recruit them (sometimes forcibly) as agricultural workers, and to cultivate them as trading partners.

The Southeast Borderlands

A more direct challenge to English ambitions in North America was the Spanish presence in the southeastern areas of what is now the United States. After the establishment of the Spanish claim to Florida in the 1560s, missionaries and traders began moving northward into Georgia and westward into what is now known as the Florida panhandle, and some

The Spanish Threat

ambitious Spaniards began to dream of expanding their empire still further north, into what became the Carolinas, and perhaps beyond. The founding of Jamestown in 1607 dampened those hopes and replaced them with fears. The English colonies, they believed, could threaten their existing settlements in Florida and Georgia. As a result, the Spanish built forts in both regions to defend themselves against the slowly increasing English presence there. Throughout the eighteenth century, the area between the Carolinas and Florida was the site of continuing tension, and frequent conflict, between the Spanish and the English—and, to a lesser degree, between the Spanish and the French, who were threatening their northwestern borders with settlements in Louisiana and in what is now Alabama.

There was no formal war between England and Spain in these years, but that did not dampen the hostilities in the Southeast. English pirates continually harassed the Spanish settlements and, in 1668, actually sacked St. Augustine. The English encouraged Indians in Florida to rise up against the Spanish missions. The Spanish, for their part, offered freedom to African slaves owned by English settlers in the Carolinas if they agreed to convert to Catholicism. About 100 Africans accepted the offer, and the Spanish later organized some to them into a military regiment to defend the northern border of New Spain. By the early eighteenth century, the constant fighting in the region had driven almost all the Spanish out of Florida except for settlers in St. Augustine on the Atlantic coast and Pensacola on the Gulf Coast.

Eventually, after more than a century of conflict in the southeastern borderlands, the English prevailed—acquiring Florida in the aftermath of the Seven Years' War (known in America as the French and Indian War) and rapidly populating it with settlers from their colonies to the North. Before that point, however, protecting the southern boundary of the British empire in North America was a continual concern to the English and contributed in crucial ways to the founding of the colony of Georgia.

The Founding of Georgia

Georgia—the last English colony to be established in what would become the United States—was founded to create a military barrier between the Spanish lands on the southern border of English America, and also to provide a refuge for the impoverished, a place where English men and women without prospects at home could begin anew. Its founders, led by General James Oglethorpe, served as unpaid trustees of a society created to serve the needs of the British Empire.

The need for a military buffer between South Carolina and the Spanish settlements in Florida was particularly urgent in the colony's first years. Oglethorpe, himself a veteran of the most recent Spanish wars with England, was keenly aware of the military advantages of an English

Oglethorpe's Philanthropic Mission

colony south of the Carolinas. Yet his interest in settlement rested even more on his philanthropic commitments. As head of a parliamentary committee investigating English prisons, he had grown appalled by the plight of honest debtors rotting in confinement. Such prisoners, and other poor people in danger of succumbing to a similar fate, could, he believed, become the farmer-soldiers of the new colony in America.

In 1732, King George II granted Oglethorpe and his fellow trustees control of the land between the Savannah and Altamaha Rivers. Their colonization policies reflected the vital military purposes of the colony. They limited the size of landholdings to make the settlement compact and easier to defend against Spanish and Indian attacks. They excluded Africans, free or slave; Oglethorpe feared slave labor would produce internal revolts, and that disaffected slaves might turn to the Spanish as allies. The trustees strictly regulated trade with the Indians, again to limit the possibility of wartime insurrection. They also excluded Catholics for fear they might collude with their coreligionists in the Spanish colonies to the south.

Georgia Founded

Oglethorpe himself led the first colonial expedition to Georgia, which built a fortified town at the mouth of the Savannah River in 1733 and later constructed additional forts south of the Altamaha. In the end, only a few debtors were released from jail and sent to Georgia. Instead, the trustees brought hundreds of impoverished tradesmen and artisans from England and Scotland and many religious refugees from Switzerland and Germany. Among the immigrants was a small group of Jews. English settlers made up a lower proportion of the European population of Georgia than of any other English colony.

Georgia's Political Evolution

Oglethorpe (whom some residents of Georgia began calling "our perpetual dictator") created almost constant dissensions and conflict through his heavyhanded regulation of the colony. He also suffered military disappointments, such as a 1740 assault on the Spanish outpost as St. Augustine, Florida, which ended in failure. Gradually, as the threats from Spain receded, he lost his grip on the colony, which over time became more like the rest of British North America, with an elected legislature that loosened the restrictions on settlers. Georgia continued to grow more slowly than the other southern colonies, but in other ways it now developed along lines roughly similar to those of South Carolina.

Middle Grounds

The struggle for the North American continent was not just one among competing European empires. It was also a series of contests among the many different peoples who shared the continent—the Spanish, English, French, Dutch, and other colonists, on the one hand, and the many Indian tribes with whom they shared the continent, on the other.

In some parts of the British empire—Virginia and New England, for example—English settlers fairly quickly established their dominance, subjugating and displacing most natives until they had established societies that were dominated almost entirely by Europeans. But in other regions, the balance of power was for many years far more precarious. Along the western borders of English settlement, in particular, Europeans and Indians lived together in regions in which neither side was able to establish clear dominance. In these "middle grounds," as they have been called, the two populations—despite frequent conflicts—carved out ways of living together, with each side making concessions to the other.

These were the peripheries of empires, in which the influence of formal colonial government was virtually invisible. European settlers, and the soldiers scattered in forts throughout these regions to protect them, were unable to displace the Indians. So they had to carve out on their own a relationship with the tribes. In that relationship, the Europeans found themselves obligated to adapt to tribal expectations at least as much as the Indian had to adapt to European ones.

To the Indians, the European migrants were both menacing and appealing. They feared the power of these strange people: their guns, their rifles, their forts. But they also wanted the French and British settlers to behave like "fathers"—to help them mediate their own internal disputes, to offer them gifts, to help them moderate their conflicts. Europeans came from a world in which the formal institutional and military power of a nation or empire governed relationships between societies. But the natives had no understanding of the modern notion of a "nation" and thought much more in terms of ceremony and kinship. Gradually, Europeans learned to fulfill at least some of their expectations—to settle disputes among tribes, to moderate conflicts within tribes, to participate solemnly in Indian ceremonies, and to offer gifts as signs of respect.

Paternal Expectations

In the seventeenth century, before many English settlers had entered the interior, the French were particularly adept at creating successful relationships with the tribes. French migrants in the interior regions of the continent were often solitary fur traders, and some of them welcomed the chance to attach themselves to—even to marry within—tribes. They also recognized the importance of treating tribal chiefs with respect and channeling gifts and tributes through them. By the mid-eighteenth century, French influence in the interior was in decline, and British settlers gradually became the dominant European group in the "middle grounds." Eventually, the British learned the lessons that the French had long ago absorbed—that simple commands and raw force were ineffective in creating a workable relationship with the tribes; that they too had to learn to deal with Indian leaders through gifts and ceremonies and mediation. In large western regions—especially those around the Great Lakes—they established a precarious peace with the tribes that lasted for several decades.

"Middle Ground" Accommodation and Adaptation

The Shifting Balance

But as the British (and after 1776) American presence in the region grew, the balance of power between Europeans and natives shifted. Newer settlers had difficulty adapting to the complex rituals that the earlier migrants had developed. The stability of the relationship between the Indians and whites deteriorated. By the early nineteenth century, the "middle ground" had collapsed, replaced by a European world in which Indians were ruthlessly subjugated and eventually removed. Nevertheless, for a considerable period of early American history, the story of the relationship between whites and Indians was not simply a story of conquest and subjugation, but also—in some regions—a story of a difficult but stable accommodation and tolerance.

THE DEVELOPMENT OF EMPIRE

The English colonies in America had begun as separate projects, and for the most part they grew up independent of one another and subject to nominal control from London. Yet by the mid-seventeenth century, the growing commercial success of the colonial ventures was producing pressure in England for a more uniform structure to the empire.

The Navigation Acts

The English government began trying to regulate colonial trade in the 1650s, when Parliament passed laws to keep Dutch ships out of the English colonies. Later, Parliament passed three important Navigation Acts. The first of them, in 1660, closed the colonies to all trade except that carried by English ships, and it required that tobacco and other items be exported from the colonies only to England or to English possessions. The second act, in 1663, required that all goods sent from Europe to the colonies pass through England on the way, where they would be subject to English taxation. The third act, in 1673, imposed duties on the coastal trade among the English colonies, and it provided for the appointment of customs officials to enforce the Navigation Acts. These acts formed the legal basis of England's regulation of the colonies for a century.

The Dominion of New England

Before the Navigation Acts, all the colonial governments except that of Virginia had operated largely independently of the crown, with governors chosen by the proprietors or by the colonists themselves and with powerful representative assemblies. Officials in London recognized that to increase their control over their colonies they would have to create a center of authority less tied to the independent-minded colonial governments, which were unlikely to enforce the new laws.

Lords of Trade

In 1675, the king created a new body, the Lords of Trade, to make recommendations for imperial reform. In 1679, following their advice, he moved to increase his control over Massachusetts. He stripped it of its authority over New Hampshire and chartered a separate, royal colony there whose governor he would himself appoint. And in 1684, citing the colonial assembly's defiance of the Navigation Acts, he revoked the Massachusetts charter.

Charles II's brother James II, who succeeded him to the throne in 1685, went further. He created a single Dominion of New England, which combined the government of Massachusetts with the governments of the rest of the New England colonies and later with those of New York and New Jersey as well. He appointed a single governor, Sir Edmund Andros, to supervise the entire region from Boston. Andros's rigid enforcement of the Navigation Acts and his brusque dismissal of the colonists' claims to the "rights of Englishmen" made him thoroughly unpopular.

Sir Edmund Andros

The "Glorious Revolution"

James II was not only losing friends in America; he was making powerful enemies in England by attempting to control Parliament and the courts and by appointing his fellow Catholics to high office. By 1688, his popular support had all but vanished, and Parliament invited his Protestant daughter Mary and her husband, William of Orange, ruler of the Netherlands, to assume the throne. James II offered no resistance and fled to France. As a result of this bloodless coup, which the English called the "Glorious Revolution," William and Mary became joint sovereigns.

When Bostonians heard of the overthrow of James II, they arrested and imprisoned the unpopular Andros. The new sovereigns in England abolished the Dominion of New England, and restored separate colonial governments. In 1691, however, they combined Massachusetts with Plymouth and made it a single, royal colony. The new charter restored the General Court, but it gave the crown the right to appoint the governor. It also replaced church membership with property ownership as the basis for voting and officeholding.

Dominion of New England Abolished

Andros had been governing New York through a lieutenant governor, Captain Francis Nicholson, who enjoyed the support of the wealthy merchants and fur traders of the province. Other, less favored colonists had a long accumulation of grievances against Nicholson and his allies. The leader of the New York dissidents was Jacob Leisler, a German merchant who had never won acceptance as one of the colony's ruling class. In May 1689, when news of the Glorious Revolution and the fall of Andros reached New York, Leisler raised a militia, captured the city fort, drove Nicholson into exile, and proclaimed himself the new head of government in New York. For two years, he tried in vain to stabilize his power in the colony amid fierce factional rivalry. In 1691, when William and Mary appointed a new governor, Leisler briefly resisted. He was convicted of treason and executed. Fierce rivalry between what became known as the

"Leislerians" and "Anti-Leislerians"

"Leislerians" and the "anti-Leislerians" dominated the politics of the colony for many years thereafter.

In Maryland, many people erroneously assumed that their proprietor, the Catholic Lord Baltimore, who was living in England, had sided with the Catholic James II and opposed William and Mary. So in 1689, an old opponent of the proprietor's government, the Protestant John Coode, led a revolt that drove out Lord Baltimore's officials and led to Maryland's establishment as a royal colony in 1691. The colonial assembly then established the Church of England as the colony's official religion and excluded Catholics from public office. Maryland became a proprietary colony again in 1715, after the fifth Lord Baltimore joined the Anglican Church.

The Glorious Revolution of 1688 in England touched off revolutions, mostly bloodless ones, in several colonies. Under the new king and queen, the representative assemblies that had been abolished were revived, and the scheme for colonial unification from above was abandoned. But the Glorious Revolution in America did not stop the reorganization of the empire. The new governments that emerged in America actually increased the crown's potential authority. As the first century of English settlement in America came to its end, the colonists were becoming more a part of the imperial system than ever before.

Growing Participation in the Imperial System

CONCLUSION

The English colonization of North America was part of a larger effort by several European nations to expand the reach of their increasingly commercial societies. Indeed, for many years, the British empire in America was among the smallest and weakest of the imperial ventures there, overshadowed by the French to the North and the Spanish to the South.

In the British colonies along the Atlantic seaboard, new agricultural and commercial societies gradually emerged—in the South centered on the cultivation of tobacco and cotton, and reliant on slave labor; and in the northern colonies centered on more traditional food crops and based mostly on free labor. Substantial trading centers emerged in such cities as Boston, New York, Philadelphia, and Charleston, and a growing proportion of the population became prosperous and settled in these increasingly complex communities. By the early eighteenth century, English settlement had spread from northern New England (in what is now Maine) south into Georgia.

But this growing British empire coexisted with, and often found itself in conflict with, the presence of other Europeans—most notably the Spanish and the French—in other areas of North America. In these borderlands, societies did not assume the settled, prosperous form they were taking in the Tidewater and New England. They were raw, sparsely populated settlements in which Europeans, including over time increasing numbers of English, had to learn to accommodate not only one another but also the still-substantial Indian tribes with whom they shared these interior lands. By the middle of the eighteenth century, there was a significant European presence across a broad swath of North America—from Florida to Maine, and from Texas to Mexico to California—only a relatively small part of it controlled by the British. But changes were underway within the British empire that would soon lead to its dominance through a much larger area of North America.

FOR FURTHER REFERENCE

Alan Taylor, *American Colonies* (2001) is an excellent general history of the colonial era of American history. William Cronon, *Changes in the Land: Indians, Colonists, and the Ecology of New England* (1983) examines the social and environmental effects of English settlement in colonial America. Richard White, *The Middle Ground: Indians, Empires, and Republics in the Great Lakes Region, 1650–1815* (1991) is an important study of the accommodations that Indians and early European settlers made in the continental interior. David Hackett Fischer and James C. Kelly, *Bound Away: Virginia and the Westward Movement* (2000) examines early western migrations from the Chesapeake. James H. Merrell, *The Indians' New World* (1991) and *Into the American Woods: Negotiators on the Pennsylvaina Frontier* (1999) are among the best examinations of the impact of European settlement on eastern tribes. Joyce E. Chaplin, *Subject Matter: Technology, the Body, and Science on the Anglo-American Frontier, 1500–1676* (2001) is an innovative exploration of the way British settlers viewed Native Americans. Daniel K. Richeter, *Facing East from Indian Country: A Native History of Early America* (2001) is an important study of how European settlement appeared to Indians. Allan Kullikoff, *From British Peasants to Colonial American Farmers* (2000) is an account of early American agriculture. Perry Miller, *The New England Mind: From Colony to Province* (1953) is a classic exposition of the Puritan intellectual milieu. Michael Kammen, *Colonial New York* (1975) illuminates the diversity and pluralism of New York under the Dutch and the English. Edmund Morgan, *American Slavery, American Freedom* (1975) is an excellent narrative of political and social development in early Virginia. Peter Wood, *Black Majority* (1974) describes the early importance of slavery in the founding of South Carolina. Richard S. Dunn, *Sugar and Slaves: The Rise of the Planter Class in the English West Indies, 1624–1713* (1972) is important for understanding the origins of British colonial slavery. David J. Weber, *The Spanish Frontier in North America* (1992) examines the northern peripheries of the Spanish empire.

For quizzes, Internet resources, references to additional books and films, and more, consult this book's Online Learning Center at www.mhhe.com/unfinishednation4.

DR. WILLIAM GLEASON The American artist Winthrop Chandler painted this image of a doctor examining a female patient in 1780. The doctor obviously considers it inappropriate to view a woman lying in bed, so he takes her pulse as she slips her hand through the curtain obscuring her. *(Ohio State Historical Society)*

TIME LINE

1636	1662	1685	1692	1697
Harvard founded	Halfway Covenant	Huguenots migrate to America	Salem witchcraft trials	Slave importations increase

CHAPTER TWENTY-NINE

THE COLD WAR

Even before World War II ended, there were signs of tension between the United States and the Soviet Union. Once the hostilities were over, those tensions quickly grew to create what became known as the "Cold War"—a tense and dangerous rivalry between the two former allies that would cast its shadow over international affairs and American domestic life for decades.

ORIGINS OF THE COLD WAR

No issue in twentieth-century American history has aroused more debate than the question of the origins of the Cold War. Some have claimed that Soviet duplicity and expansionism created the international tensions, others that American provocations and global ambitions were at least equally to blame.

1949	1950	1951	1952
NATO established	NSC-68	Truman fires MacArthur	American occupation of Japan ends
Soviet Union explodes A-bomb	Korean War begins		Eisenhower elected president
Mao victorious in China	McCarthy's anticommunism campaign begins		

Sources of Soviet-American Tension

At the heart of the rivalry between the United States and the Soviet Union in the 1940s was a fundamental difference in the ways the great powers envisioned the postwar world. One vision, first openly outlined in the Atlantic Charter in 1941, was of a world in which nations abandoned their traditional beliefs in military alliances and spheres of influence and governed their relations with one another through democratic processes, with an international organization serving as the arbiter of disputes and the protector of every nation's right of self-determination. That vision appealed to many Americans, including Franklin Roosevelt.

America's Postwar Vision

The other vision was that of the Soviet Union and to some extent of Great Britain. Both Stalin and Churchill had signed the Atlantic Charter. But Britain had always been uneasy about the implications of the self-determination ideal for its own enormous empire. And the Soviet Union was determined to create a secure sphere for itself in Central and Eastern Europe as protection against possible future aggression from the West. Both Churchill and Stalin, therefore, tended to envision a postwar structure in which the great powers would control areas of strategic interest to them, in which something vaguely similar to the traditional European balance of power would reemerge. Gradually, the differences between these two positions would turn the peacemaking process into a form of warfare.

Wartime Diplomacy

Serious strains had already begun to develop in the alliance with the Soviet Union in January 1943, when Roosevelt and Churchill met in Casablanca, Morocco, to discuss Allied strategy. The two leaders could not accept Stalin's most important demand—the immediate opening of a second front in western Europe. But they tried to reassure Stalin by announcing that they would accept nothing less than the unconditional surrender of the Axis powers, thus indicating that they would not negotiate a separate peace with Hitler and leave the Soviets to fight on alone.

In November 1943, Roosevelt and Churchill traveled to Teheran, Iran, for their first meeting with Stalin. By now, however, Roosevelt's most effective bargaining tool—Stalin's need for American assistance in his struggle against Germany—had been largely removed. The German advance against Russia had been halted; Soviet forces were now launching their own westward offensive. Nevertheless, the Teheran Conference seemed in most respects a success. Roosevelt and Stalin established a cordial personal relationship. Stalin agreed to an American request that the Soviet Union enter the war in the Pacific soon after the end of hostilities in Europe. Roosevelt, in turn, promised that an Anglo-American second front would be established within six months.

Teheran Conference

YALTA, 1945 Churchill *(left)* and Stalin *(right)* were shocked at the physical appearance of Franklin Roosevelt *(center)* when he arrived for their critical meeting at Yalta. Roosevelt had enough energy to perform capably at the conference, but he was in fact gravely ill. Two months later, not long after he gave Congress what turned out to be an unrealistically optimistic report of the prospects for postwar peace, he died. *(Bettmann/Corbis)*

On other matters, however, the origins of future disagreements were already visible. Most important was the question of the future of Poland. Roosevelt and Churchill were willing to agree to a movement of the Soviet border westward, allowing Stalin to annex some historically Polish territory. But on the nature of the postwar government in the portion of Poland that would remain independent, there were sharp differences. Roosevelt and Churchill supported the claims of the Polish government-in-exile that had been functioning in London since 1940; Stalin wished to install another, pro-communist exiled government that had spent the war in Lublin, in the Soviet Union. The three leaders left the Teheran Conference with the issue unresolved.

Yalta

More than a year later, in February 1945, Roosevelt joined Churchill and Stalin for a great peace conference in the Soviet city of Yalta. In return for Stalin's renewed promise to enter the Pacific war, Roosevelt agreed that the Soviet Union should receive some of the territory in the Pacific that Russia had lost in the 1904 Russo-Japanese War.

United Nations Established

The negotiators also agreed to a plan for a new international organization, a plan that had been hammered out the previous summer at a conference in Washington, D.C. The new United Nations would contain a General Assembly, in which every member would be represented, and a Security Council, with permanent representatives of the five major powers (the United States, Britain,

France, the Soviet Union, and China), each of which would have veto power. The Security Council would also have temporary delegates from several other nations. These agreements became the basis of the United Nations charter, drafted at a conference of fifty nations beginning April 25, 1945, in San Francisco. The United States Senate ratified the charter in July by a vote of 80 to 2.

On other issues, however, the Yalta Conference produced no real accord. Basic disagreement remained about the postwar Polish government. Stalin, whose armies now occupied Poland, had already installed a government composed of the pro-communist "Lublin" Poles. Roosevelt and Churchill insisted that the pro-Western "London" Poles must be allowed a place in the Warsaw regime. Roosevelt envisioned a government based on free, democratic elections—which both he and Stalin recognized the pro-Western forces would win. Stalin agreed only to a vague compromise by which an unspecified number of pro-Western Poles would be granted a place in the government. He reluctantly consented to hold "free and unfettered elections" in Poland on an unspecified future date. They did not take place for more than forty years.

Disagreements over Poland

Nor was there agreement about the future of Germany. Roosevelt seemed to want a reconstructed and reunited Germany. Stalin wanted to impose heavy reparations on Germany and to ensure a permanent dismemberment of the nation. The final agreement was, like the Polish accord, vague and unstable. The decision on reparations would be referred to a future commission. The United States, Great Britain, France, and the Soviet Union would each control its own "zone of occupation" in Germany—the zones to be determined by the position of troops at the end of the war. Berlin, the German capital, was already well inside the Soviet zone, but because of its symbolic importance it would itself be divided into four sectors, one for each nation to occupy. At an unspecified date, Germany would be reunited. As for the rest of Europe, the conference produced a murky accord on the establishment of governments "broadly representative of all democratic elements" and "responsible to the will of the people."

Problems of the Yalta Accords

The Yalta accords, in other words, were less a settlement of postwar issues than a set of loose principles that sidestepped the most difficult questions. Roosevelt, Churchill, and Stalin returned home from the conference each apparently convinced that he had signed an important agreement. But the Soviet interpretation of the accords differed so sharply from the Anglo-American interpretation that the illusion endured only briefly. In the weeks following the Yalta Conference, Roosevelt watched with growing alarm as the Soviet Union moved systematically to establish pro-communist governments in one Central or Eastern European nation after another and as Stalin refused to make the changes in Poland that the president believed he had promised. Still believing the differences could be settled, Roosevelt

left Washington early in the spring for a vacation at his retreat in Warm Springs, Georgia. There, on April 12, 1945, he suffered a sudden, massive stroke and died.

THE COLLAPSE OF THE PEACE

Harry S. Truman, who succeeded Roosevelt in the presidency, had almost no familiarity with international issues. Nor did he share Roosevelt's apparent faith in the flexibility of the Soviet Union. Truman sided instead with those in the government (and there were many) who considered the Soviet Union fundamentally untrustworthy and viewed Stalin himself with suspicion and even loathing.

The Failure of Potsdam

Truman had been in office only a few days before he decided to "get tough" with the Soviet Union. Stalin had made what the new president considered solemn agreements with the United States at Yalta. The United States should insist that the Soviets honor them. Truman met on April 23 with Soviet Foreign Minister Molotov and sharply chastised him for violations of the Yalta accords.

In fact, Truman had little leverage with which to compel the Soviet Union to carry out its agreements. Russian forces already occupied Poland and much of the rest of Central and Eastern Europe. Germany was already divided among the conquering nations. The United States was still engaged in a war in the Pacific and was neither able nor willing to enter into a second conflict in Europe. Truman insisted that the United States should be able to get "85 percent" of what it wanted, but he was ultimately forced to settle for much less.

Limited American Leverage

He conceded first on Poland. When Stalin made a few minor concessions to the pro-Western exiles, Truman recognized the Warsaw government, hoping that noncommunist forces might gradually expand their influence there. Until the 1980s, they did not. To settle other questions, Truman met in July at Potsdam, in Russian-occupied Germany, with Churchill (who, after elections in Britain in the midst of the talks, was replaced as prime minister by Clement Attlee) and Stalin. Truman reluctantly accepted the adjustments of the Polish-German border that Stalin had long demanded; he refused, however, to permit the Russians to claim any reparations from the American, French, and British zones of Germany. This stance effectively confirmed that Germany would remain divided. The western zones ultimately united into one nation, friendly to the United States, and the Russian zone survived as another nation, with a pro-Soviet, communist government.

The China Problem

American hopes for an open, peaceful world "policed" by the great powers required a strong, independent China. But those hopes faced a major, perhaps insurmountable obstacle: the Chinese government of Chiang Kai-shek. Chiang was generally friendly to the United States, but his government was corrupt and incompetent with feeble popular support. Ever since 1927, the nationalist government he headed had been engaged in a bitter rivalry with the communist armies of Mao Zedong. By 1945, Mao was in control of one-fourth of the population.

Chiang Kai-shek

Some Americans urged the government to try to find a "third force" to support as an alternative to either Chiang or Mao. Truman, however, decided reluctantly that he had no choice but to continue supporting Chiang. For the next several years the United States continued to pump money and weapons to Chiang, even as it was becoming clear that the cause was lost. But Truman was not prepared to intervene militarily to save the nationalist regime.

Instead, the American government was beginning to consider an alternative to China as the strong, pro-Western force in Asia: a revived Japan. Abandoning the strict occupation policies of the first years after the war (when General Douglas MacArthur had governed the nation), the United States lifted all restrictions on industrial development and encouraged rapid economic growth in Japan. The vision of an open, united world was giving way in Asia, as it was in Europe, to an acceptance of a divided world with a strong, pro-American sphere of influence.

Japan Restored

The Containment Doctrine

By the end of 1945, a new American foreign policy was slowly emerging. It became known as containment. Rather than attempting to create a unified, "open" world, the United States and its allies would work to "contain" the threat of further Soviet expansion.

The new doctrine emerged in part as a response to events in Europe in 1946. In Turkey, Stalin was trying to win control over the vital sea lanes to the Mediterranean. In Greece, communist forces were threatening the pro-Western government; the British had announced they could no longer provide assistance. Faced with these challenges, Truman decided to enunciate a firm new policy. In doing so, he drew from the ideas of the influential American diplomat George F. Kennan, who had warned not long after the war that in the Soviet Union the United States faced "a political force committed fanatically to the belief that with the U.S. there can be no permanent modus vivendi," and that the only answer was "a long-term, patient but firm and vigilant containment of Russian expansive tendencies." On March 12, 1947, Truman appeared before Congress and used

Kennan's warnings as the basis of what became known as the Truman Doctrine. "I believe," he argued, "that it must be the policy of the United States to support free peoples who are resisting attempted subjugation by armed minorities or by outside pressures." In the same speech he requested $400 million—for aid to Greece and Turkey. Congress quickly approved the measure.

Truman Doctrine

The American commitment ultimately helped ease Soviet pressure on Turkey and helped the Greek government defeat the communist insurgents. More important, it established a basis for American foreign policy that would survive for more than thirty years.

The Marshall Plan

An integral part of the containment policy was a proposal to aid in the economic reconstruction of Western Europe. There were many motives: humanitarian concern for the European people; a fear that Europe would remain an economic drain on the United States if it could not quickly rebuild and begin to feed itself; a desire for a strong European market for American goods. But above all, American policymakers believed that unless something could be done to strengthen the shaky pro-American governments in Western Europe, those governments might fall under the control of rapidly growing domestic communist parties.

In June 1947, Secretary of State George C. Marshall announced a plan to provide economic assistance to all European nations (including the Soviet Union) that would join in drafting a program for recovery. Although Russia and its Eastern satellites quickly and predictably rejected the plan, sixteen Western European nations eagerly participated. Whatever domestic opposition there was in the United States largely vanished after a sudden coup in Czechoslovakia in February 1948 that established a Soviet-dominated communist government there. In April, Congress approved the creation of the Economic Cooperation Administration, the agency that would administer the Marshall Plan, as it became known. Over the next three years, the Marshall Plan channeled over $12 billion of American aid into Europe, helping to spark a substantial economic revival. By the end of 1950, European industrial production had risen 64 percent, communist strength in the member nations had declined, and opportunities for American trade had revived.

Rebuilding Europe

Mobilization at Home

In 1948, at the president's request, Congress approved a new military draft and revived the Selective Service System. In the meantime, the United States, having failed to reach agreement with the Soviet Union on international control of nuclear weapons, redoubled its own efforts in atomic

research, elevating nuclear weaponry to a central place in its military arsenal. The Atomic Energy Commission, established in 1946, became the supervisory body charged with overseeing all nuclear research, civilian and military alike. And in 1950, the Truman administration approved the development of the new hydrogen bomb, a nuclear weapon far more powerful than the bombs the United States had used in 1945.

The National Security Act of 1947

The National Security Act of 1947 reshaped the nation's major military and diplomatic institutions. A new Department of Defense would oversee all branches of the armed services, combining functions previously performed separately by the War and Navy departments. A National Security Council (NSC), operating out of the White House, would govern foreign and military policy. A Central Intelligence Agency (CIA) would replace the wartime Office of Strategic Services and would be responsible for collecting information through both open and covert methods; as the Cold War continued, the CIA would also engage secretly in political and military operations on behalf of American goals. The National Security Act, in other words, gave the president expanded powers with which to pursue the nation's international goals.

The Road to NATO

The United States was also moving to strengthen the military capabilities of Western Europe. Convinced that a reconstructed Germany was essential to the hopes of the West, Truman reached an agreement with England and France to merge the three western zones of occupation into a new West German republic (which would include the American, British, and French sectors of Berlin, even though that city lay within the Soviet zone). Stalin responded quickly. On June 24, 1948, he imposed a tight blockade around the western sectors of Berlin. If Germany was to be officially divided, he was implying, then the country's Western government would have to abandon its outpost in the heart of the Soviet-controlled eastern zone. Truman refused to do so. Unwilling to risk war through a military challenge to the blockade, he ordered a massive airlift to supply the city with food, fuel, and other needed goods. The airlift continued for more than ten months, transporting nearly 2.5 million tons of material, keeping a city of 2 million people alive. In the spring of 1949, Stalin lifted the now ineffective blockade. And in October, the division of Germany into two nations—the Federal Republic in the west and the Democratic Republic in the East—became official.

Berlin Airlift

The crisis in Berlin accelerated the consolidation of what was already in effect an alliance among the United States and the countries of Western Europe. On April 4, 1949, twelve nations signed an agreement establishing the North Atlantic Treaty Organization (NATO) and declaring that an armed attack against one member would be considered an attack against all. The NATO countries would, moreover, maintain a standing military force in Europe to defend against what many believed was the threat of a

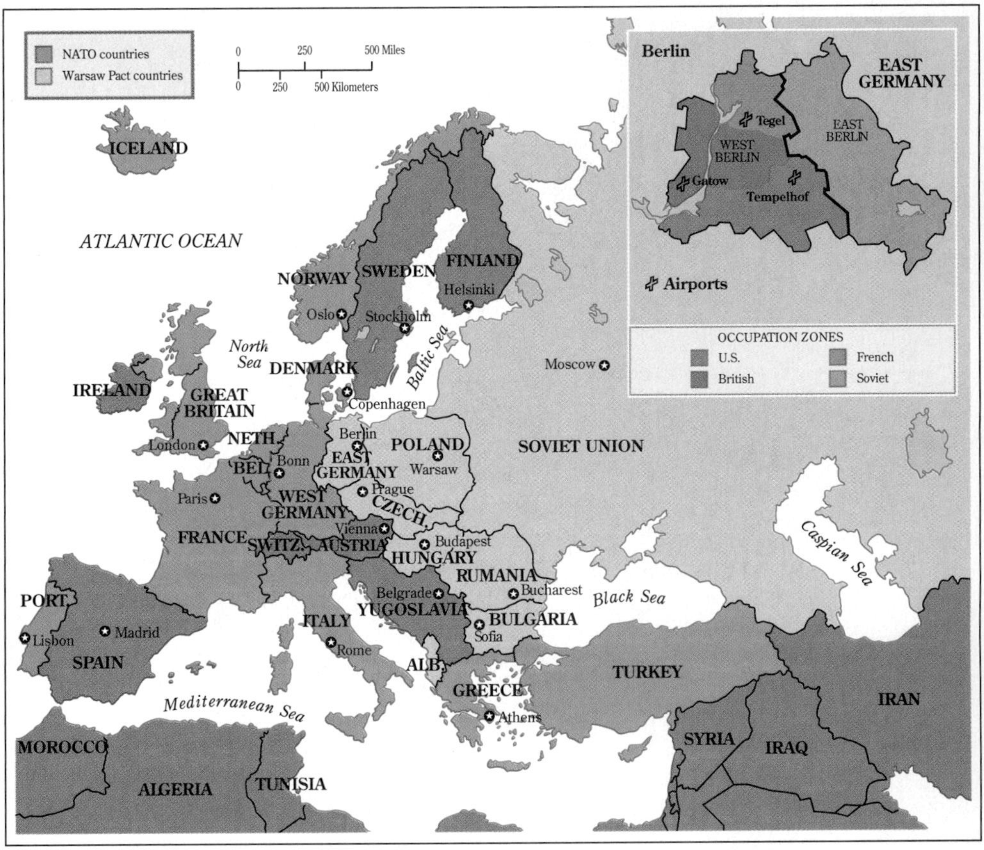

DIVIDED EUROPE AFTER WORLD WAR II This map shows the sharp division that emerged in Europe after World War II between the area under the control of the Soviet Union, and the area allied with the United States. In the east, Soviet control or influence extended into all the nations shaded gold—including the eastern half of Germany. In the west and south, the green-shaded nations were allied with the United States as members of the North Atlantic Treaty Organization (NATO). The countries shaded brown were aligned with neither of the two superpowers. The small map in the upper right shows the division of Berlin among the various occupying powers at the end of the war. Eventually, the American, British, and French sectors were combined to create West Berlin, a city governed by West Germany but entirely surrounded by communist East Germany. ◆ *How did the West prevent East Germany from absorbing West Berlin?*

Soviet invasion. The formation of NATO eventually spurred the Soviet Union to create an alliance of its own with the communist governments in Eastern Europe—an alliance formalized in 1955 by the Warsaw Pact.

Reevaluating Cold War Policy

In September 1949, the Soviet Union successfully exploded its first atomic weapon, years earlier than predicted, an event that shocked and frightened many Americans. So did the collapse of Chiang Kai-shek's nationalist government in China, which occurred with startling speed in the last months

Debating the Past

THE COLD WAR

For more than a decade after the beginning of the Cold War, few historians saw any reason to challenge the official American interpretation of its origins. The breakdown of relations between the United States and the Soviet Union was, most agreed, a direct result of Soviet expansionism and of Stalin's violation of the wartime agreements forged at Yalta and Potsdam. The Soviet imposition of communist regimes in Eastern Europe was part of a larger ideological design to spread communism throughout the world. American policy was the logical and necessary response: a firm commitment to oppose Soviet expansionism and to keep American forces in a continual state of readiness.

Disillusionment with the official justifications for the Cold War began to find expression even in the late 1950s, when anticommunist sentiment in America remained strong and pervasive. William Appleman Williams's *The Tragedy of American Diplomacy* (1959) insisted that the Cold War was simply the most recent version of a consistent American effort in the twentieth century to preserve an "open door" for American trade in world markets. The confrontation with the Soviet Union, he argued, was less a response to Soviet aggressive designs than an expression of the American belief in the necessity of capitalist expansion.

As the Vietnam War grew larger and more unpopular in the 1960s, the scholarly critique of the Cold War quickly gained intensity. Walter LaFeber's *America, Russia, and the Cold War*, first published in 1967, maintained that America's supposedly idealistic internationalism at the close of the war was in reality an effort to ensure a postwar order shaped in the American image—with every nation open to American influence (and to American trade). That was why the United States was so apt to misinterpret Soviet policy, much of which reflected a perfectly reasonable commitment to ensure the security of the Soviet Union itself, as part of a larger aggressive design.

The revisionist interpretations of the Cold War ultimately produced a reaction of their own: what has come to be known as "postrevisionist" scholarship. The most important works in this school have attempted to strike a balance between orthodoxy and revisionism and to identify areas of blame and patterns of misconceptions on both sides of the conflict. An important early statement of this approach was John Lewis Gaddis, *The United States and the Cold War, 1941–1947* (1972), which argued that "neither side can bear sole responsibility for the onset of the Cold War." Both sides had limited options, given their own political constraints and their own preconceptions. Other postrevisionist works—by Thomas G. Paterson, Melvyn Leffler, William Taubman, and others—have elaborated on ways in which the United States and the Soviet Union acted in response to genuine, if not necessarily accurate, beliefs about the intentions of the other. "The United States and the Soviet Union were doomed to be antagonists," Ernest May wrote in 1984. "There probably was never any real possibility that the post-1945 relationship could be anything but hostility verging on conflict."

The collapse of Soviet communism and the dissolution of the Soviet empire has begun to stimulate new interpretations of the Cold War and (by facilitating the opening of Soviet archives) to cast new light on many contested issues. For the moment, however, the dominant scholarly view is one that de-emphasizes the question of who is to blame and emphasizes the ways in which both sides learned to manage a conflict that neither could easily have avoided.

HARRY AND BESS TRUMAN AT HOME Senator Harry Truman and his wife Bess pose for photographers in the kitchen of their Washington apartment, suggesting the "common man" image that Truman retained throughout his public life. The picture was taken shortly before the 1944 Democratic National Convention, which would nominate Truman for vice president. Less than a year later, the Trumans would be living in the White House. *(UPI/Corbis-Bettmann)*

(text continued from page 759)

of 1949. Chiang fled with his political allies and the remnants of his army to the offshore island of Formosa (Taiwan), and the entire Chinese mainland came under the control of a communist government that many Americans believed to be an extension of the Soviet Union. The United States refused to recognize the new communist regime.

Containment Expanded

In this atmosphere of escalating crisis, Truman called for a thorough review of American foreign policy. The result was a National Security Council report, issued in 1950 and commonly known as NSC-68, which outlined a shift in the American position. The first statements of the containment doctrine—the writings of George Kennan, the Truman Doctrine speech—had made at least some distinctions between areas of vital interest to the United States and areas of less importance to the nation's foreign policy and called on America to share the burden of containment with its allies. But the April 1950 document argued that the United States could no longer rely on other nations to take the initiative in resisting communism. It must move on its own to stop communist expansion virtually anywhere it occurred, regardless of the intrinsic strategic or economic value of the lands in question. Among other things, the report

called for a major expansion of American military power, with a defense budget almost four times the previously projected figure.

AMERICA AFTER THE WAR

The crises overseas were not the only frustrations the American people encountered after the war. The nation also faced serious, if short-lived, economic difficulties in adapting to the peace. And it suffered from an exceptionally heated political climate that produced a new wave of insecurity and repression.

The Problems of Reconversion

Despite widespread predictions that the end of the war would return America to depression conditions, economic growth continued after 1945. Pent-up consumer demand from workers who had accumulated substantial savings during the war helped spur the boom. So did a $6 billion tax cut. The Servicemen's Readjustment Act of 1944, better known as the GI Bill of Rights, provided housing, education, and job training subsidies to veterans and increased spending even further.

GI Bill

This flood of consumer demand contributed to more than two years of serious inflation, during which prices rose at rates of 14 to 15 percent annually. Compounding the economic difficulties was a sharp rise in labor unrest. By the end of 1945, there had been major strikes in the automobile, electrical, and steel industries. In April 1946, John L. Lewis led the United Mine Workers out on strike, shutting down the coal fields for forty days. Truman finally forced coal production to resume by ordering government seizure of the mines. But in the process, he pressured mine owners to grant the union most of its demands. Almost simultaneously, the nation's railroads suffered a total shutdown—the first in the nation's history—as two major unions walked out on strike. By threatening to use the army to run the trains, Truman pressured the strikers back to work after only a few days.

Inflation and Labor Unrest

Reconversion was particularly difficult for the millions of women and minorities who had entered the work force during the war. With veterans returning home and looking for jobs in the industrial economy, employers tended to push women, African Americans, Hispanics, and others out of the plants to make room for white males. Some of the war workers, particularly women, left the work force voluntarily, out of a desire to return to their former domestic lives. But as many as 80 percent of women workers, and virtually all black and Hispanic males, wanted to continue working. The postwar inflation, the pressure to meet the growing expectations of a high-consumption society, the rising divorce rate (which left many women responsible for their own economic well-being)—all combined to create a

high demand for paid employment among women. As they found themselves excluded from industrial jobs, therefore, women workers moved increasingly into other areas of the economy (above all, the service sector).

The Fair Deal Rejected

Days after the Japanese surrender, Truman submitted to Congress a twenty-one-point domestic program outlining what he later named the "Fair Deal." It called for expansion of Social Security benefits, the raising of the legal minimum wage from 40 to 65 cents an hour, a program to ensure full employment through aggressive use of federal spending and investment, a permanent Fair Employment Practices Act, public housing and slum clearance, long-range environmental and public works planning, and government promotion of scientific research. Weeks later he added other proposals: federal aid to education, government health insurance and prepaid medical care, funding for the St. Lawrence Seaway, and nationalization of atomic energy.

But most of Truman's programs fell victim to the same public and congressional conservatism that had crippled the last years of the New Deal. Indeed, that conservatism seemed to be intensifying, as the November 1946 congressional elections suggested. Using the simple but devastating slogan "Had Enough?" the Republican Party won control of both houses of Congress. The new Republican Congress quickly moved to reduce government spending and chip away at New Deal reforms. Its most notable action was its assault on the Wagner Act of 1935, in the form of the Labor-Management Relations Act of 1947, better known as the Taft-Hartley Act. It made illegal the closed shop (a workplace in which no one can be hired without first being a member of a union). And although it continued to permit the creation of union shops (in which workers must join a union after being hired), it permitted states to pass "right-to-work" laws prohibiting even that. The Taft-Hartley Act also empowered the president to call for a ten-week "cooling-off" period before a strike by issuing an injunction against any work stoppage that endangered national safety or health. Outraged workers and union leaders denounced the measure as a "slave labor bill." Truman vetoed it. But both houses easily overruled him the same day. The Taft-Hartley Act did not destroy the labor movement. But it did damage weaker unions in relatively lightly organized industries such as chemicals and textiles, and it made much more difficult the organizing of workers who had never been union members at all, especially in the South and the West.

Taft-Hartley Act

The Election of 1948

Truman and his advisers believed that the American public was not ready to abandon the achievements of the New Deal, despite the 1946 election results. As they planned their strategy for the 1948 campaign, therefore, they placed their hopes in an appeal to enduring Democratic loyalties.

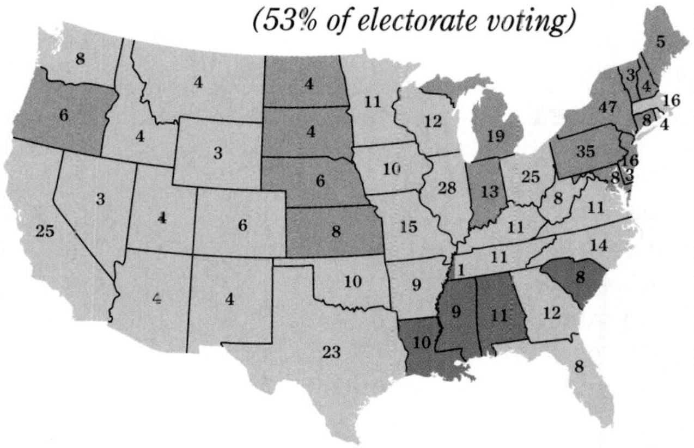

	ELECTORAL VOTE	POPULAR VOTE (%)
Harry S. Truman *(Democratic)*	303	24,105,695 (49.5)
Thomas E. Dewey *(Republican)*	189	21,969,170 (45.1)
Strom Thurmond *(States' Rights)*	39	1,169,021 (2.4)
Henry A. Wallace *(Progressive)*	—	1,156,103 (2.4)
Other Candidates *(Prohibition; Socialist Labor, Socialist, Socialist Workers)*	—	272,713

ELECTION OF 1948 Despite the widespread expectation that the Republican candidate, Thomas Dewey, would easily defeat Truman in 1948, the president in fact won a substantial re-election victory that year. This map shows the broad geographic reach of Truman's victory. Dewey swept most of the Northeast, but Truman dominated almost everywhere else. Strom Thurmond, the States' Rights candidate, carried four states in the South. ◆ *What had prompted Thurmond to desert the Democratic Party and run for president on his own?*

For an interactive version of this map go to www.mhhe.com/unfinishednation4ch29maps

Throughout 1948, Truman proposed one reform measure after another (including, on February 2, the first major civil rights bill of the century). To no one's surprise, Congress ignored or defeated them all, but the president was building campaign issues for the fall.

Divided Democratic Party

There remained, however, the problem of Truman's personal unpopularity—the assumption among much of the electorate that he lacked stature and that his administration was weak and inept—and the deep divisions within the Democratic Party. At the Democratic Convention that summer, two factions abandoned the party altogether. Southern conservatives were

angered by Truman's proposed civil rights bill and by the approval at the convention of a civil rights plank in the platform (engineered by Hubert Humphrey, the reform mayor of Minneapolis). They walked out and formed the States' Rights (or "Dixiecrat") Party, with Governor Strom Thurmond of South Carolina as its nominee. At the same time, some members of the party's left wing joined the new Progressive Party, whose candidate was Henry A. Wallace. Wallace supporters objected to what they considered the slow and ineffective domestic policies of the Truman administration, but they resented even more the president's confrontational stance toward the Soviet Union.

Americans for Democratic Action

Many Democratic liberals who were unhappy with Truman were unwilling to leave the party. The Americans for Democratic Action (ADA), a coalition of anticommunist liberals, tried to entice Dwight D. Eisenhower, the popular war hero, to contest the nomination. Only after Eisenhower had refused did liberals concede the nomination to Truman. The Republicans, in the meantime, once again nominated Governor Thomas E. Dewey of New York. Austere, dignified, and competent, he seemed to offer an unbeatable alternative to the president.

Only Truman, it seemed, believed he could win. As the campaign gathered momentum, he became ever more aggressive, turning the fire away from himself and toward Dewey and the "do-nothing, good-for-nothing" Republican Congress, which was, he told the voters, responsible for fueling inflation and abandoning workers and common people. To dramatize his point, he called Congress into special session in July to give it a chance, he said, to enact the liberal measures the Republicans had recently written into their platform. Congress met for two weeks and, predictably, did almost nothing.

Truman's Stunning Victory

On election night, to the surprise of almost everyone, he won a narrow but decisive and dramatic victory: 49.5 percent of the popular vote to Dewey's 45.1 percent (with the two splinter parties dividing the small remainder evenly between them), and an electoral margin of 303 to 189. Democrats, in the meantime, had regained both houses of Congress by substantial margins.

The Fair Deal Revived

Despite the Democratic victories, the Eighty-first Congress was little more hospitable to Truman's Fair Deal reform than its Republican predecessor had been. Truman did win some important victories, to be sure. Congress raised the legal minimum wage from 40 cents to 75 cents an hour. It approved an important expansion of the Social Security system, increasing benefits by 75 percent and extending them to 10 million additional people. And it passed the National Housing Act of 1949, which provided for the construction of 810,000 units of low-income housing accompanied by long-term rent subsidies.

But on other issues—national health insurance and aid to education among them—Truman made little progress. Nor was he able to persuade Congress to accept the civil rights legislation he proposed in 1949, legislation that would have made lynching a federal crime, provided federal protection of black voting rights, abolished the poll tax, and established a new Fair Employment Practices Commission to curb discrimination in hiring. Southern Democrats filibustered to kill the bill.

Truman did proceed on his own to battle several forms of racial discrimination. He ordered an end to discrimination in the hiring of government employees. He began to dismantle segregation within the armed forces. And he allowed the Justice Department to become actively involved in court battles against discriminatory statutes. The Supreme Court, in the meantime, signaled its own growing awareness of the issue by ruling, in *Shelley* v. *Kraemer* (1948), that the courts could not be used to enforce private "covenants" meant to bar blacks from residential neighborhoods.

Renewed Federal Commitment to Civil Rights

The Nuclear Age

Looming over the political, economic, and diplomatic struggles of the postwar years was the image of the great and terrible mushroom clouds that had risen over Alamogordo in July 1945 and over the ruined Japanese cities of Hiroshima and Nagasaki that atomic weapons had destroyed. Americans greeted the introduction of these terrible new instruments of destruction with fear and awe, but also with expectation. Postwar culture was torn between a dark image of the nuclear war that many Americans feared would be a result of the rivalry with the Soviet Union, and the bright image of a dazzling technological future that atomic power might help to produce.

The fear of nuclear weapons appeared widely in popular culture, but it was often disguised. The late 1940s and early 1950s were the heyday of the *film noir*, a kind of filmmaking that had originated in France and had been named for the dark lighting that was characteristic of the genre. American *film noir* portrayed the loneliness of individuals in an impersonal world—a staple of American culture for many decades—but also suggested the menacing character of the age, the looming possibility of vast destruction. Sometimes, films and television programs addressed nuclear fear explicitly—for example, the celebrated television show of the 1950s and early 1960s, *The Twilight Zone*, which featured dramatic portrayals of the aftermath of nuclear war; or postwar comic books, which depicted powerful superheroes saving the world from destruction.

Film Noir

Such images resonated with the public because awareness of nuclear weapons was increasingly built into their daily lives. Schools and office buildings had regular air raid drills, to prepare people for the possibility of nuclear attack. Radio stations regularly tested the emergency broadcast

systems, which stood in readiness for war. Fallout shelters sprang up in public buildings and private homes, stocked with water and canned goods, to protect citizens in case of war. America was a nation filled with anxiety.

And yet at the same time, the United States was also an exuberant nation, dazzled by its own prosperity and excited by the technological innovations that were transforming the world. Among those innovations was nuclear power. The same scientific knowledge that could destroy the world, many believed, might also lead it into a dazzling future. The *New York Times*, only days after Hiroshima, expressed its own rosy view of the nuclear future:

> The atomic bomb was perfected for war, but the knowledge which made it possible came out of . . . the deathless yearning to know and to use the gifts of nature for the common good. . . . This new knowledge . . . can bring to this earth not death but life, not tyranny and cruelty, but a divine freedom.

That kind of optimism soon became widespread. The "secret of the atom," many Americans soon predicted, would bring "prosperity and a more complete life." A public opinion poll late in 1948 revealed that approximately two-thirds of those who had an opinion on the subject believed that, "in the long run," atomic energy would "do more good than harm." Nuclear power plants began to spring up in many areas of the country, welcomed as the source of cheap and unlimited electricity, their potential dangers scarcely even discussed by those who celebrated their creation.

Atomic Optimism

THE KOREAN WAR

On June 24, 1950, the armies of communist North Korea swept across their southern border and invaded the pro-Western half of the Korean peninsula to the south. Within days, they had occupied much of South Korea, including Seoul, its capital. Almost immediately, the United States committed itself to the conflict.

The Divided Peninsula

When World War II ended, both the United States and the Soviet Union had troops in Korea fighting the Japanese; neither army was willing to leave. Instead, they divided the nation, supposedly temporarily, along the 38TH parallel. The Russians finally departed in 1949, leaving behind a communist government in the north with a strong, Soviet-equipped army. The Americans left a few months later, handing control to the pro-Western government of Syngman Rhee, who was anticommunist but only nominally democratic. He had a relatively small military, which he used primarily to suppress internal opposition.

Syngman Rhee

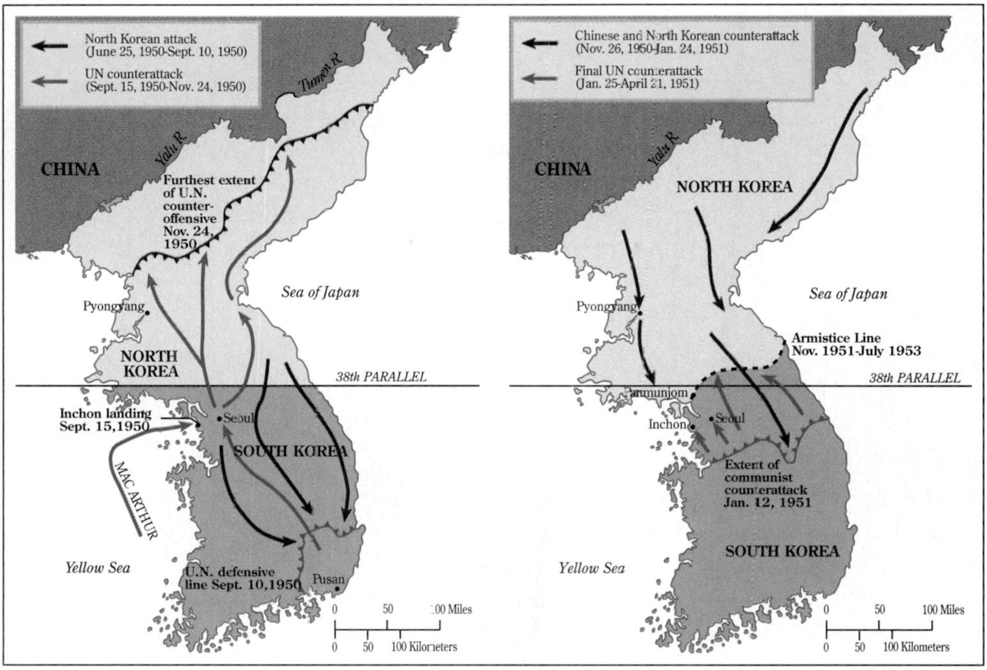

THE KOREAN WAR, 1950–1953 These two maps illustrate the changing fortunes of UN forces (which were mostly American) in Korea during the 1950–1953 war. The map at the left shows the extent of the North Korean invasion of the South in 1950; communist forces for a time controlled all of Korea except a small area around Pusan in the southeast. On September 15, 1950, UN troops under Douglas MacArthur landed in force at Inchon and soon drove the North Koreans back across the border. MacArthur then pursued the North Koreans well into their own territory. The map at right shows the very different circumstances once the Chinese entered the war in November 1950. Chinese forces drove the UN army back below the 38th parallel and, briefly, deep into South Korea, below Seoul. The UN troops fought back to the prewar border between North and South Korea late in 1951, but the war then bogged down into a stalemate that continued for a year and a half. ◆ *What impact did the Korean War have on American politics in the early 1950s?*

The relative weakness of the south offered a strong temptation to nationalists in the North Korean government who wanted to reunite the country. The temptation grew stronger when the American government implied that it did not consider South Korea within its own "defense perimeter." The Soviets may not have approved the invasion in advance, but they supported the offensive once it began.

Almost immediately on June 27, 1950, the president ordered limited American military assistance to South Korea, and on the same day he appealed to the United Nations to intervene. The Soviet Union was boycotting the Security Council at the time (to protest the council's refusal to recognize the new communist government of China) and was thus unable to exercise its veto power. As a result, American delegates were able to win UN agreement to a resolution calling for international assistance to the Rhee government. On June 30, the United States ordered its own ground

WINTER IN KOREA, 1950 An American soldier trudges to the crest of an icy and embattled ridge during the bitter fighting in North Korea between American divisions and Chinese communist forces, who had entered the war as the United Nations forces approached the Korean-Chinese border. *(The National Archives and Records Administration)*

forces into Korea, and Truman appointed General Douglas MacArthur to command the UN operations there. (Several other nations provided assistance and troops, but the "UN" armies were, in fact, overwhelmingly American.)

Inchon

After a surprise American invasion at Inchon in September had routed the North Korean forces from the south and sent them fleeing back across the 38TH parallel, Truman gave MacArthur permission to pursue the communists into their own territory. The president's aim was to create "a unified, independent and democratic Korea." He was moving beyond simple containment and envisioning a rollback of communist power.

From Invasion to Stalemate

For several weeks, MacArthur's invasion of North Korea proceeded smoothly. On October 19, the capital, Pyongyang, fell to the UN forces. Victory seemed near—until the Chinese government, alarmed by the movement of American forces toward its border, intervened. By November 4,

China Intervenes

eight divisions of the Chinese army had entered the war. The UN offensive stalled and then collapsed. Through December 1950, outnumbered American forces fought a bitter, losing battle against the Chinese divisions. Within weeks, communist forces had pushed the Americans back below the 38TH parallel once again and had recaptured the South Korean capital of Seoul. By mid-January 1951 the rout had ceased; and by March the UN armies had managed to regain much of the territory they had recently lost, taking back Seoul and pushing the communists north of the 38TH parallel for the second time. With that, the war degenerated into a protracted stalemate.

From the start, Truman had been determined to avoid a direct conflict with China, which he feared might lead to a new world war. Once China entered the war, he began seeking a negotiated solution to the struggle. But General MacArthur had ideas of his own. The United States was really fighting the Chinese, MacArthur argued. It should, therefore, attack China itself, if not through an actual invasion, then at least by bombing communist forces massing north of the Chinese border. In March 1951, he indicated his unhappiness in a public letter to House Republican leader Joseph W. Martin that concluded: "There is no substitute for victory." His position had wide popular support. The release of the Martin letter struck the president as intolerable insubordination. On April 11, 1951, he relieved MacArthur of his command.

Sixty-nine percent of the American people supported MacArthur, a Gallup poll reported. When the general returned to the United States later in 1951, he was greeted with wild enthusiasm. Public criticism of Truman finally abated somewhat when a number of prominent military figures, including General Omar Bradley, publicly supported the president's decision. But substantial hostility toward Truman remained. In the meantime, the Korean stalemate continued. Negotiations between the opposing forces began at Panmunjom in July 1951, but the talks—and the war—dragged on until 1953.

Truman-MacArthur Controversy

Limited Mobilization

Just as the war in Korea produced only a limited American military commitment abroad, so it created only a limited economic mobilization at home.

Truman set up the Office of Defense Mobilization to fight inflation by holding down prices and discouraging high union wage demands. When these cautious regulatory efforts failed, the president took more drastic action. Railroad workers walked off the job in 1951, and Truman, who considered the workers' demands inflationary, ordered the government to seize control of the railroads. In 1952, during a nationwide steel strike, Truman seized the steel mills, citing his powers as commander in chief. But in a 6-to-3 decision, the Supreme Court ruled that the president had exceeded his authority, and Truman was forced to relent.

The Korean War gave a significant boost to economic growth by pumping new government funds into the economy at a point when many believed it was about to decline. But the war had other, less welcome effects. It came at a time of rising insecurity about America's position in the world and intensified anxiety about communism. As the long stalemate continued, producing 140,000 American dead and wounded, frustration turned to anger. The United States, which had recently won the greatest war in history, seemed unable to conclude what many Americans considered a minor border skirmish in a small country. Many began to believe that something must be deeply wrong—not only in Korea but within the United States as well. Such fears contributed to the rise of the second major campaign of the century against domestic communism.

Rising Insecurity and Frustration

THE CRUSADE AGAINST SUBVERSION

Why did the American people develop a growing fear of internal communist subversion—a fear that by the early 1950s had reached the point of near hysteria? There are many possible answers, but no single definitive explanation.

One factor was obvious. Communism was not an imagined enemy. It had tangible shape, in Josef Stalin and the Soviet Union. Adding to the concern were the Korean stalemate, the "loss" of China, the Soviet development of an atomic bomb. Searching for someone to blame, many were attracted to the idea of a communist conspiracy within American borders. But there were other factors as well, rooted in events in American domestic politics.

HUAC and Alger Hiss

Much of the anticommunist furor emerged out of the search by the Republican Party for an issue with which to attack the Democrats, and out of the efforts of the Democrats to take that issue away from them. Beginning in 1947, the House Un-American Activities Committee (HUAC) held widely publicized investigations to prove that, under Democratic rule, the government had tolerated (if not actually encouraged) communist subversion. The committee turned first to the movie industry, arguing that communists had infiltrated Hollywood and tainted American films with propaganda. Writers and producers, some of them former communists, were called to testify; and when some of them ("the Hollywood Ten") refused to answer questions about their own political beliefs and those of their colleagues, they were sent to jail for contempt. Others were barred from employment in the industry when Hollywood, attempting to protect its public image, adopted a "blacklist" of those of "suspicious loyalty."

The "Hollywood Ten"

ALGER HISS No single figure did more to polarize opinion about the dangers of domestic communism than Alger Hiss, the once-respected diplomat accused in 1948 of having been a spy in the 1930s for the Soviet Union and later convicted of perjury for testifying falsely before a congressional committee. *(UPI/Corbis-Bettmann)*

More alarming to the public was HUAC's investigation into charges of disloyalty leveled against a former high-ranking member of the State Department: Alger Hiss. In 1948, Whittaker Chambers, a former communist agent, now a conservative editor at *Time* magazine, told the committee that Hiss had passed classified State Department documents to him in 1937 and 1938. When Hiss sued him for slander, Chambers produced microfilms of the documents (called the "pumpkin papers," because Chambers had kept them hidden in a pumpkin in his vegetable garden). Hiss could not be tried for espionage because of the statute of limitations (which protects individuals from prosecution for most crimes after seven years have passed). But largely because of the relentless efforts of Richard M. Nixon, a freshman Republican congressman from California and a member of HUAC, Hiss was convicted of perjury and served several years in prison. The Hiss case not only discredited a prominent young diplomat; it cast suspicion on a generation of liberal Democrats. It also transformed Nixon into a national figure and helped him win a seat in the United States Senate in 1950.

The Federal Loyalty Program and the Rosenberg Case

Partly to protect itself against Republican attacks, partly to encourage support for the president's foreign policy initiatives, the Truman administration in 1947 initiated a widely publicized program to review the "loyalty" of federal employees. By 1951, more than 2,000 government employees had resigned under pressure and 212 had been dismissed.

The employee loyalty program became a signal throughout the executive branch to launch a major assault on subversion. The attorney general established a widely cited list of supposedly subversive organizations. The director of the Federal Bureau of Investigation (FBI), J. Edgar Hoover, investigated and harassed alleged radicals. In 1950, Congress passed the McCarran Internal Security Act, which, among other restrictions on "subversive" activity, required that all communist organizations register with the government and publish their records. Truman vetoed the bill. Congress easily overrode his veto.

McCarran Internal Security Act

The successful Soviet detonation of an atomic bomb in 1949, earlier than generally expected, suggested to some people that there had been a conspiracy to pass American atomic secrets to the Russians. In 1950, Klaus Fuchs, a young British scientist, seemed to confirm those fears when he testified that he had delivered to the Russians details of the manufacture of the bomb. The case ultimately moved to an obscure New York couple, Julius and Ethel Rosenberg, members of the Communist Party. The government claimed the Rosenbergs had received secret information from Ethel's brother, a machinist on the Manhattan Project in New Mexico, and had passed it on to the Soviet Union through other agents (including Fuchs). The Rosenbergs were convicted and, on April 5, 1951, sentenced to death. After two years of appeals and public protests, they died in the electric chair on June 19, 1953.

All these factors—the HUAC investigations, the Hiss trial, the loyalty investigations, the McCarran Act, the Rosenberg case—combined with other concerns by the early 1950s to create a fear of communist subversion that seemed to grip the entire country. State and local governments, the judiciary, schools and universities, labor unions—all sought to purge themselves of real or imagined subversives. It was a climate that made possible the rise of an extraordinary public figure.

Growing Fear of Subversion

McCarthyism

Joseph McCarthy was an undistinguished, first-term Republican senator from Wisconsin when, in February 1950, in the midst of a speech in Wheeling, West Virginia, he lifted up a sheet of paper and claimed to "hold in my hand" a list of 205 known communists currently working in the American State Department. No person of comparable stature had

ever made so bold a charge against the federal government; and in the months to come, as McCarthy repeated and expanded on his accusations, he emerged as the nation's most prominent leader of the crusade against domestic subversion.

Within weeks of his charges against the State Department, McCarthy was leveling accusations at other agencies. After 1952, with the Republicans in control of the Senate and McCarthy the chairman of a special subcommittee, he conducted highly publicized investigations of alleged subversion in many areas of the government. McCarthy never produced conclusive evidence that any federal employee was a communist. But a growing constituency adored him nevertheless for his coarse, "fearless" assaults on a government establishment that many considered arrogant, effete, even traitorous. Republicans, in particular, rallied to his claims that the Democrats had been responsible for "twenty years of treason" and that only a change of parties could rid the country of subversion. McCarthy, in short, provided his followers with an issue into which they could channel a wide range of resentments: fear of communism, animosity toward the country's "eastern establishment," and frustrated partisan ambitions. For a time, McCarthy intimidated all but a few people from opposing him. Even the highly popular Dwight D. Eisenhower, running for president in 1952, did not speak out against him, although he disliked McCarthy's tactics and was outraged at, among other things, McCarthy's attacks on General George Marshall.

McCarthy's Soaring Popularity

The Republican Revival

Public frustration over the stalemate in Korea and popular fears of internal subversion combined to make 1952 a bad year for the Democratic Party. Truman, now deeply unpopular, withdrew from the presidential contest. The party united instead behind Governor Adlai E. Stevenson of Illinois. Stevenson's dignity, wit, and eloquence made him a beloved figure to many liberals and intellectuals. But those same qualities seemed only to fuel Republican charges that Stevenson lacked the strength or the will to combat communism sufficiently.

Stevenson's greatest problem, however, was the Republican candidate opposing him. Rejecting the efforts of conservatives to nominate Robert Taft or Douglas MacArthur, the Republicans turned to a man who had no previous identification with the party: General Dwight D. Eisenhower—military hero, commander of NATO, president of Columbia University in New York—who won nomination on the first ballot. He chose as his running mate the young California senator who had gained national prominence through his crusade against Alger Hiss: Richard M. Nixon.

In the fall campaign, Eisenhower attracted support through his geniality and his statesmanlike pledges to settle the Korean conflict. Nixon (after surviving early accusations of financial improprieties, which he effectively

neutralized in a famous television address, the "Checkers speech") exploited the issue of domestic anticommunism by attacking the Democrats for "cowardice" and "appeasement." The response at the polls was overwhelming. Eisenhower won both a popular and an electoral landslide: 55 percent of the popular vote to Stevenson's 44 percent, 442 electoral votes to Stevenson's 89. Republicans gained control of both houses of Congress for the first time since 1946.

Eisenhower Elected

CONCLUSION

Even during World War II itself, when the United States and the Soviet Union were allies, it was evident to leaders in both nations that America and Russia had quite different visions of what the postwar world should look like. Very quickly after the war ended, the once fruitful relationship between the world's two greatest powers quickly soured. Americans came to believe that the Soviet Union was an expansionist tyranny little different from Hitler's Germany. Soviets came to believe that the United States was trying to protect its own dominance in the world by encircling the Soviet Union. The result of these tensions was what became known by the end of the 1940s as the Cold War.

In the early years of the Cold War, the United States constructed a series of policies designed to prevent both war and Soviet aggression. It helped rebuild the shattered nations of Western Europe with substantial economic aid through the Marshall Plan, to stabilize those nations and prevent them from becoming communist. America embraced a new foreign policy—known as containment—that committed it to an effort to keep the Soviet Union from expanding its influence further into the world. The United States and Western Europe formed a strong and enduring alliance, NATO, to defend Europe against possible Soviet advances.

In 1950, however, the armed forces of communist North Korea launched an invasion of the noncommunist South; and to most Americans the conflict quickly came to be seen as a test of American resolve in the Cold War. The Korean War was long, costly, and unpopular, with many military setbacks and frustrations. In the end, however, the United States—working through the United Nations—managed to drive the North Koreans out of the south and stabilize the original division of the peninsula.

The Korean War hardened American foreign policy into a much more rigidly anticommunist form. It undermined the Truman administration, and the Democratic Party, and helped strengthen conservatives and Republicans. It greatly strengthened an already powerful crusade against

communists, and those believed to be communists, within the United States—a crusade often known as McCarthyism, because of the notoriety of Senator Joseph McCarthy of Wisconsin, the most celebrated leader of the effort.

America after World War II was indisputably the wealthiest and most powerful nation in the world. But in the harsh climate of the Cold War, neither wealth nor power could dispel deep anxieties and bitter divisions.

FOR FURTHER REFERENCE

Two books by John Lewis Gaddis, *Strategies of Containment* (1982) and *The United States and the Origins of the Cold War, 1941–1947* (1972) provide a sound introduction to Cold War history. Walter LaFeber, *America, Russia, and the Cold War, 1945–1967* (7th ed. 1993) is a classic survey of American-Soviet relations. Melvyn P. Leffler, *A Preponderance of Power: National Security, the Truman Administration, and the Cold War* (1992) is a superb, densely researched history of the policies of the 1940s. Warren I. Cohen, *The Cambridge History of American Foreign Relations, Vol. 4: America in the Age of Soviet Power, 1945–1991* (1991) is a good general history. Michael Hogan, *The Marshall Plan* (1987) is a provocative interpretation of one of the pillars of the early containment doctrine. David McCullough, *Truman* (1992) is an elegant popular biography, while Alonzo Hamby, *Man of the People: A Life of Harry S. Truman* (1995) is a fine scholarly one. Bruce Cumings, *The Origins of the Korean War* (1980) is an important study of America's first armed conflict of the Cold War. Ellen Schrecker, *Many Are the Crimes: McCarthyism in America* (1998) is an important interpretation of McCarthyism, and David Oshinsky, *A Conspiracy So Immense: The World of Joe McCarthy* (1983) is a fine biography. Richard Fried, *Nightmare in Red* (1990) is a good, short overview of the Red Scare. Frances Stonor Saunders, *The Cultural Cold War* (2000) is a provocative and controversial study. Richard Pells, *The Liberal Mind in a Conservative Age: American Intellectuals in the 1940s and 1950s* (1985) is a valuable overview of postwar intellectual life. Mary L. Dudziak, *Cold War Civil Rights: Race and the Image of American Democracy* (2000) examines the connection between Cold War fervor and civil rights. *The Spy in the Sky* (1996) is a documentary film that tells the story of a team of engineers and pilots racing to design, perfect, and deploy the high-flying U2 spy plane in the 1950s. *Truman* (1997) is an excellent documentary about the 33rd president.

For quizzes, Internet resources, references to additional books and films, and more, consult this book's Online Learning Center site at www.mhhe.com/unfinishednation4.

THE NEW TELEVISION SET Norman Rockwell was one of the best-known American illustrators of the 1930s, 1940s, and 1950s—the creator of countless covers for the popular magazine the *Saturday Evening Post* and of some of the most beloved images of his era. In the 1930s and 1940s, most of his pictures evoked life in small-town America. By the late 1940s, however, he was beginning to portray as well the rise of the new suburban and consumer culture—as this 1949 illustration suggests. The new television antenna rises against the sky almost as if to compete with the older church steeple in the background. *(*The New Television Set *by Norman Rockwell. Los Angeles County Museum of Art. Gift of Mrs. Ned Crowell. Printed by permission of the Norman Rockwell Family Trust. © 1949 The Norman Rockwell Family Trust)*

TIME LINE

1947	1952	1953	1954	1955	1956
Levittown construction begins	Eisenhower elected	Korean War ends	*Brown* v. *Board of Education*	Montgomery bus boycott	Federal Highway Act
			Army-McCarthy hearings		Eisenhower reelected
					Suez crisis

CHAPTER THIRTY-TWO

THE CRISIS OF AUTHORITY

The Youth Culture
The Mobilization of Minorities
The New Feminism
Environmentalism in a Turbulent Society
Nixon, Kissinger, and the War
Nixon, Kissinger, and the World
Politics and Economics in the Nixon Years
The Watergate Crisis

The election of Richard Nixon in 1968 was the result of more than the unpopularity of Lyndon Johnson and the war. It was the result, too, of a broad popular reaction against what many Americans considered a dangerous assault on the foundations of their society and culture. In Richard Nixon such Americans found a man who seemed perfectly to match their mood. Himself a product of a hardworking, middle-class family, he projected an image of stern dedication to traditional values. Yet the presidency of Richard Nixon, far from returning calm and stability to American politics, coincided with, and helped to produce, more years of crisis.

THE YOUTH CULTURE

Perhaps most alarming to many conservatives in the 1960s and 1970s was a pattern of social and cultural protest by younger Americans, who were giving vent to two related impulses. One was the impulse, emerging from the political left, to create a great new community of "the people," which

1971	1972	1973	1974	1975
Nixon imposes wage-price controls	Nixon visits China	U.S. withdraws from Vietnam	Nixon resigns; Ford becomes president	South Vietnam falls
	SALT I	Arab oil embargo		
	"Christmas bombing" of North Vietnam	Agnew resigns		
	Watergate burglary	Supreme Court decides *Roe* v. *Wade*		
	Nixon reelected			

would rise up to break the power of elites and force the nation to end the war, pursue racial and economic justice, and transform its political life.

Personal "Liberation"

The other, at least equally powerful impulse was the vision of personal "liberation." It found expression in part through the efforts of many groups—African Americans, Indians, Hispanics, women, gay people, and others—to define and assert themselves and make demands on the larger society. It also found expression through the efforts of individuals to create a new culture—one that would allow them to escape from what some considered the dehumanizing pressures of the modern "technocracy."

The New Left

Among the products of the racial crisis and the war in Vietnam was a radicalization of many American students, who in the course of the 1960s formed what became known as the New Left. In 1962, a group of students (most of them white) gathered in Michigan to form an organization to give voice to their demands: Students for a Democratic Society (SDS). Their declaration of beliefs, the Port Huron Statement, expressed their disillusionment with the society they had inherited and their determination to build a new politics. In the following years, SDS became the leading organization of student radicalism.

SDS

Campus Unrest

Since most members of the New Left were students, much of their radicalism centered for a time on issues related to the modern university. A 1964 dispute at the University of California at Berkeley over the rights of students to engage in political activities on campus—the Free Speech Movement—was the first outburst of what was to be nearly a decade of campus turmoil. The antiwar movement greatly inflamed and expanded the challenge to the universities; and beginning in 1968, campus demonstrations, riots, and building seizures became almost commonplace. At Columbia University in New York, students seized the offices of the president and others and occupied them for several days until local police forcibly ejected them. Over the next several years, hardly any major university was immune to some level of disruption. Small groups of especially dogmatic radicals—among them the "Weathermen," an offshoot of SDS—were responsible for a few cases of arson and bombing that destroyed campus buildings and claimed several lives.

Not many people ever accepted the radical political philosophy of the New Left. But many supported the position of SDS and other groups on particular issues, and above all on the Vietnam War. Between 1967 and 1969, student activists organized some of the largest political demonstrations in American history to protest the war.

Opposition to the Draft

A related issue that helped fuel the antiwar movement was opposition to the military draft.

THE WAR AT HOME Demonstrators gather on the Mall in Washington in the fall of 1967 for one of the first of the great antiwar demonstrations of the late 1960s. Over time, the antiwar movement helped erode the national consensus on the conflict in Vietnam. But the principal basis for opposing the war was never the moral or economic arguments of the left; it was simply the frustration among many Americans of seeing a war continuing too long and too inconclusively. *(Leif Skoogfors/Woodfin Camp & Associates)*

The gradual abolition of many traditional deferments—for graduate students, teachers, husbands, fathers, and others—swelled the ranks of those faced with conscription (and thus likely to oppose it). Many draft-age Americans simply refused induction, accepting what were occasionally long terms in jail as a result. Thousands of others fled to Canada, Sweden, and elsewhere (where they were joined by deserters from the armed forces) to escape conscription.

The Counterculture

Closely related to the New Left was a new youth culture openly scornful of the values and conventions of middle-class society. The most visible characteristic of the counterculture, as it became known, was a change in personal styles. As if to display their contempt for conventional standards, young Americans flaunted long hair, shabby or flamboyant clothing, and a rebellious disdain for traditional speech and decorum. Also important to the counterculture were drugs: marijuana smoking—which after 1966 became almost as common a youthful diversion as beer drinking had once been—and the use of other, more potent hallucinogens, such as LSD. There was also a new, more permissive view of sex.

Like the New Left, with which it in many ways overlapped, the counterculture challenged the structure of modern American society, attacking what it claimed were its banality, its hollowness, its artificiality, its isolation from nature. The most committed adherents of the counterculture—the hippies, who came to dominate the Haight-Ashbury neighborhood of San Francisco and other places, and the social dropouts, many of whom retreated to rural communes—rejected modern society altogether and attempted to find refuge in a simpler, more "natural" existence. But even those whose commitment to the counterculture was less intense shared a commitment to the idea of personal fulfillment through rejecting the inhibitions and conventions of middle-class culture and giving fuller expression to personal instinct and desire.

Commitment to Personal Fulfillment

The counterculture was only an exaggerated expression of impulses that were coursing through the larger society. Long hair and freakish clothing became the badge not only of hippies and radicals but of an entire generation. The use of marijuana, the freer attitudes toward sex, the iconoclastic (and often obscene) language—all spread far beyond the realm of the true devotees of the counterculture.

One of the most pervasive elements of the new youth society was one that even the least radical members of the generation embraced: rock music. Its growing influence in the 1960s was a result in part of the phenomenal popularity of the Beatles, the English group whose first visit to the United States in 1964 created a remarkable sensation. For a time, most rock musicians—like most popular musicians before them—concentrated largely on uncontroversial romantic themes. By the late 1960s, however, rock had begun to reflect many of the new iconoclastic values of its time. The Beatles, for example, abandoned their once simple and seemingly innocent style for a new, experimental, even mystical approach that reflected the growing popular fascination with drugs and Eastern religions. Other groups, such as the Rolling Stones, turned even more openly to themes of anger, frustration, and rebelliousness. Many popular musicians used their music to express explicit political radicalism as well—especially some of the leading folk singers of the era, such as Bob Dylan and Joan Baez. Rock's driving rhythms, its undisguised sensuality, its often harsh and angry

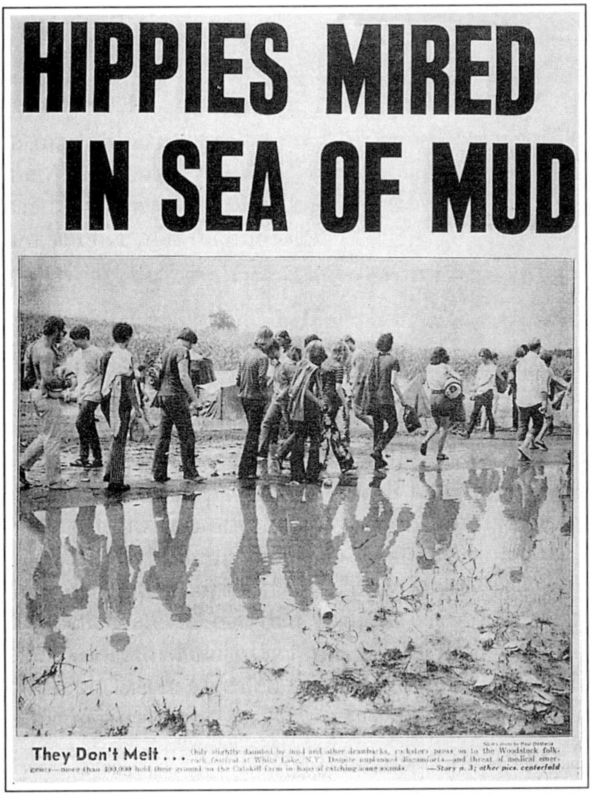
HIPPIES MIRED IN SEA OF MUD

They Don't Melt . . . Only slightly daunted by mud and other drawbacks, rocksters press on to the Woodstock folk-rock festival at White Lake, N.Y. Despite unplanned discomforts—and threat of medical emergency—more than 100,000 held their ground on the Catskill farm in hope of catching some sounds. —Story p. 3; other pics. centerfold

REPORTING WOODSTOCK The *New York Daily News*, whose largely working-class readership was not notably sympathetic toward the young people at Woodstock, ran this slightly derisive front-page story on the concert as heavy rains turned the concert site into a sea of mud. ["They Don't Melt," the caption said.] *(©New York Daily News, L.P. Reprinted with Permission. Archive Photos/Blank Archive/Getty Images)*

tone—all made it an appropriate vehicle for expressing the themes of the social and political unrest of the late 1960s.

Woodstock

A powerful symbol of the fusion of rock music and the counterculture was the great music festival at Woodstock, New York, in the summer of 1969, where 400,000 people gathered on a farm for nearly a week. Despite heavy rain, mud, inadequate facilities, and impossible crowding, the crowd remained peaceful and harmonious. Champions of the counterculture spoke rhapsodically at the time of how Woodstock represented the birth of a new youth culture, the "Woodstock nation." Four months later, however, another great rock concert—at the Altamont racetrack near San Francisco, featuring the Rolling Stones and attended by 300,000 people—exposed a darker side of the youth culture. Altamont became a brutal and violent event at which four people died, several accidentally or from drug overdoses, but one because of injuries received at the hands of members of the Hell's Angels motorcycle gang, who were serving as security guards at the concert and who brutally beat and stabbed a number of people.

THE MOBILIZATION OF MINORITIES

The growth of African-American protest encouraged other minorities to assert themselves and demand redress of their grievances. For Indians, Hispanic Americans, gay men and lesbians, and others, the late 1960s and 1970s were a time of growing self-expression and political activism.

Seeds of Indian Militancy

Few minorities had deeper or more justifiable grievances against the prevailing culture than did American Indians—or Native Americans, as they began defiantly to call themselves in the 1960s. Indians were the least prosperous, least healthy, and least stable group in the nation. And while African Americans attracted the attention (for good or for ill) of many whites, Indians for years had remained largely ignored.

For much of the postwar era, federal policy toward the tribes had been shaped by a determination to incorporate Indians into mainstream American society whether Indians wanted to assimilate or not. Two laws passed in 1953 established the basis of a new policy, which became known as "termination." Through termination, the federal government withdrew all official recognition of the tribes as legal entities, administratively separate from state governments, and made them subject to the same local jurisdictions as white residents. At the same time, the government encouraged Indians to assimilate into the white world and worked to funnel Native Americans into cities, where, presumably, they would adapt themselves to the larger society and lose their cultural distinctiveness.

"Termination"

Despite some individual successes, the new policies were a disastrous failure on the whole. Indians themselves fought so bitterly against them that in 1958 the Eisenhower administration barred further "terminations" without the consent of the affected tribes. In the meantime, the struggle against termination mobilized a new generation of Indian militants and breathed life into the principal Native American organization, the National Congress of American Indians, which had been created in 1944.

The Democratic administrations of the 1960s made no effort to revive termination. Instead, they made modest efforts to restore at least some degree of tribal autonomy. The funneling of OEO money to tribal organizations through the Community Action program was one prominent example. In the meantime, the tribes themselves were beginning to fight for self-determination. The new militancy benefited from the rapid increase in the Indian population, which was growing much faster than that of the rest of the nation (nearly doubling between 1950 and 1970 to a total of about 800,000).

THE OCCUPATION OF ALCATRAZ Alcatraz is an island in San Francisco Bay that once housed a large federal prison that by the late 1960s had been abandoned. In 1969, a group of Indian activists occupied the island and claimed it as Indian land—precipitating a long standoff with authorities. *(AP/Wide World Photos)*

The Indian Civil Rights Movement

In 1961, more than 400 members of 67 tribes gathered in Chicago and issued the Declaration of Indian Purpose, which stressed the "right to choose our own way of life" and the "responsibility of preserving our precious heritage." The meeting was only one example of a growing Indian self-consciousness. The National Indian Youth Council, created in the aftermath of the 1961 Chicago meeting, promoted the idea of Indian nationalism and intertribal unity. In 1968, a group of young, militant Indians established the American Indian Movement (AIM), which drew support from urban areas and reservations alike.

AIM

The new activism produced results. In 1968, Congress passed the Indian Civil Rights Act, which guaranteed reservation Indians many of the protections accorded other citizens by the Bill of Rights, but which also recognized the legitimacy of tribal laws within the reservations. But leaders of AIM and other insurgent groups were not satisfied. In 1968, Indian fishermen, citing old treaty rights, clashed with Washington State officials on the Columbia River and in Puget Sound. The following year, members of several tribes occupied the abandoned federal prison on Alcatraz Island in San Francisco Bay, claiming the site "by right of discovery."

In response to the growing pressure, the Nixon administration appointed Louis Bruce, a Mohawk-Sioux, to the position of commissioner of Indian affairs in 1969; and in 1970 the president promised both increased tribal self-determination and an increase in federal aid. But the protests continued. In November 1972, nearly a thousand demonstrators, most of them Lakota Sioux, forcibly occupied the building of the Bureau of Indian Affairs in Washington for six days. In February 1973, members of AIM seized and occupied the town of Wounded Knee, South Dakota, the site of the 1890 massacre of Sioux by federal troops, for two months, demanding radical changes in the administration of the reservation and insisting that the government honor its long-forgotten treaty obligations.

Wounded Knee Occupied

The Indian civil rights movement, like other civil rights movements of the same time, fell far short of winning full justice and equality for Native Americans. But it helped the tribes win a series of new legal rights and protections that, together, gave them a stronger position than they had enjoyed at any previous time in the twentieth century.

Latino Activism

The fastest-growing minority group in the United States in the 1970s was Latinos, or Hispanic Americans. Large numbers of Mexicans had entered the country during World War II in response to the wartime labor shortage, and many had remained in the cities of the Southwest and the Pacific Coast. By 1960, Los Angeles had a bigger Mexican population than any place except Mexico City.

Growing Latino Population

But the greatest expansion in the Hispanic population of the United States was yet to come. In 1960, the census reported slightly more than 3 million Latinos living in the United States. By 1970, that number had grown to 9 million and by 2000 to 35 million. Hispanics constituted more than a third of all legal immigrants to the United States after 1960. There was also an uncounted but very large number of illegal Latino immigrants in those years (estimates ranged from 7 million to 12 million).

Large numbers of Puerto Ricans (who were entitled to American citizenship by birth) migrated to eastern urban areas, particularly New York, where they formed one of the poorest communities in the city. South Florida's substantial Cuban population began with a wave of middle-class refugees fleeing the Castro regime in the early 1960s. These first Cuban migrants quickly established themselves as a successful and highly assimilated part of Miami's middle class. In 1980, a second, much poorer wave of Cuban immigrants—the so-called Marielietos, named for the port from which they left Cuba—arrived in Florida when Castro temporarily relaxed exit restrictions. Later in the 1980s, large numbers of immigrants (both legal and illegal) began to arrive from Central and South America—from Guatemala, Nicaragua, El Salvador, Peru, and other countries.

Like African Americans and Indians, many Latinos responded to the highly charged climate of the 1960s by strengthening their ethnic identification and by organizing for political and economic power. Affluent Hispanics in Miami filled influential positions in the professions and local government; in the Southwest, Latino voters elected Mexican Americans to seats in Congress and to governorships. A Mexican-American political organization, La Raza Unida, exercised influence in southern California and elsewhere in the Southwest in the 1970s and beyond. One of the most visible efforts to organize Hispanics occurred in California, where an Arizona-born farmworker of Mexican descent, César Chávez, created an effective union of itinerant farmworkers: the United Farm Workers (UFW), a largely Mexican organization.

United Farm Workers

For most Hispanics, however, the path to economic and political power was more difficult. Mexican Americans and others were slow to develop political influence in proportion to their numbers. In the meantime, Hispanics formed one of the poorest segments of the United States population.

Gay Liberation

The last important liberation movement to emerge in the 1960s was the effort by gay men and lesbians to win political and economic rights and social acceptance. Homosexuality has been a generally unacknowledged reality throughout American history. Nonheterosexual men and women were forced for generations either to suppress their sexual preferences, to exercise them surreptitiously, or to live within isolated and often persecuted communities. But by the late 1960s, the liberating impulses that had affected other groups helped mobilize gay men and lesbians to fight for their own rights.

On June 27, 1969, police officers raided the Stonewall Inn, a gay nightclub in New York City's Greenwich Village, and began arresting patrons simply for frequenting the place. The raid was not unusual, but the response was. Gay onlookers taunted the police and then attacked them. Someone started a blaze in the Stonewall Inn itself, almost trapping the policemen inside. Rioting continued throughout Greenwich Village (the center of New York's gay community) through much of the night.

"Stonewall Riot"

The "Stonewall Riot" marked the beginning of the gay liberation movement—one of the most controversial challenges to traditional values and assumptions of its time. New organizations—among them the Gay Liberation Front, founded in New York in 1969—sprang up around the country. Public discussion and media coverage of homosexuality, long subject to an unofficial taboo, quickly and dramatically increased. Gay activists had some success in challenging the longstanding assumption that homosexuality was aberrant behavior; many argued that no sexual preference was any more normal than another.

Most of all, however, the gay liberation movement transformed the outlook of many gay men and lesbians themselves. It helped them to

"come out," to express their preferences openly and unapologetically, and to demand from society a recognition that gay relationships could be as significant and worthy of respect as heterosexual ones. By the early 1980s, the gay liberation movement had made remarkable strides. Even the ravages of the AIDS epidemic, which, in the beginning at least, affected the gay community more disastrously than it affected any other group, failed to halt the growth of gay liberation. In many ways, it strengthened it.

By the early 1990s, gay men and lesbians were achieving many of the same milestones that other oppressed minorities had attained in earlier decades. Openly gay politicians won election to public office. Universities established gay and lesbian studies programs. Laws prohibiting discrimination on the basis of sexual preference made slow, halting progress at the state and local levels. But gay liberation produced a powerful backlash as well, as became evident in 1993 when President Bill Clinton's effort to end the ban on gay men and lesbians serving in the military met a storm of criticism from members of Congress and within the military itself. At the same time, voters in some cities and states were approving referendum questions on their ballots outlawing civil rights protections for gay men and lesbians. And antigay violence continued periodically in communities around the country.

Backlash against Gay Liberation

THE NEW FEMINISM

Women constitute over 50 percent of the United States population. But during the 1960s and 1970s, many women began to identify with minority groups as they renewed demands for a liberation of their own.

The Rebirth

Betty Friedan

The 1963 publication of Betty Friedan's *The Feminine Mystique* is often cited as the first event of contemporary women's liberation. Friedan, who had been a writer for women's magazines in the 1950s, traveled around the country interviewing the women who had graduated with her from Smith College in 1947. Most of these women were living out the dream that postwar American society had created for them: they were affluent wives and mothers living in comfortable suburbs. And yet many of them were deeply frustrated and unhappy, with no outlets for their intelligence, talent, and education. Friedan's book did not so much cause the revival of feminism as help give voice to a movement that was already stirring.

By the time *The Feminine Mystique* appeared, John Kennedy had established the President's Commission on the Status of Women, which

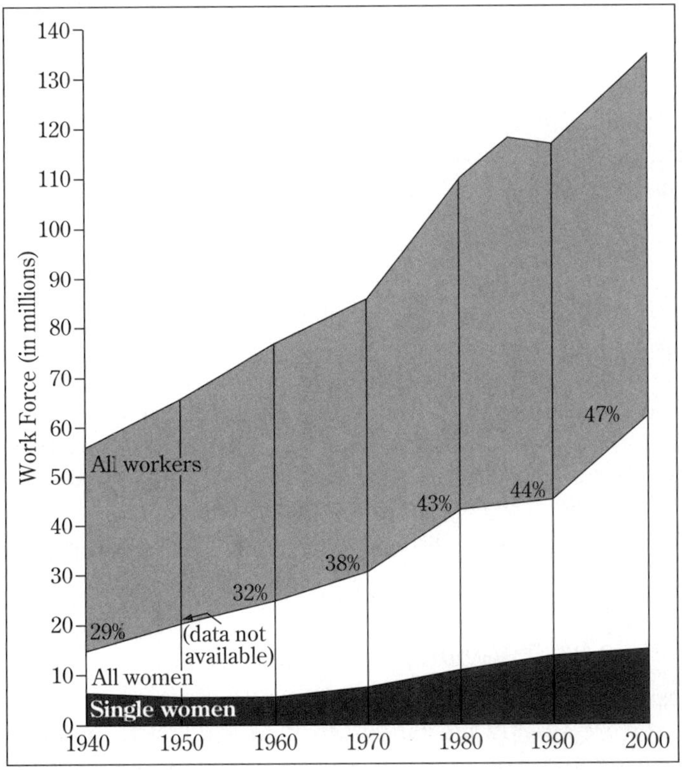

WOMEN IN THE PAID WORK FORCE, 1940–2000 The number of women working for wages steadily expanded from 1940 on, to the point that in 2000, they constituted just under half the total work force. ◆ *What role did this growing participation in the paid work force have on the rise of feminism in the 1960s and beyond?*

brought national attention to sexual discrimination. Also in 1963, the Kennedy administration helped win passage of the Equal Pay Act, which barred the pervasive practice of paying women less than men for the same work. A year later, Congress incorporated into the Civil Rights Act of 1964 an amendment—Title VII—that extended to women many of the same legal protections against discrimination that were being extended to African Americans and other minorities.

NOW

In 1966, Friedan joined with other feminists to create the National Organization for Women (NOW), which was to become the nation's largest and most influential feminist organization. NOW responded to the complaints of the women Friedan's book had examined—affluent suburbanites with no outlet for their interests—by demanding greater educational opportunities for women and denouncing the domestic ideal and the traditional concept of marriage. But the heart of the movement, at least in the beginning, was an effort to address the needs of women in the workplace.

Women's Liberation

By the late 1960s, new and more radical feminist demands were also attracting a large following, especially among younger, white, educated women. Many of them drew inspiration from the New Left and the counterculture. Some were involved in the civil rights movement, others in the antiwar crusade. Many had found that even within those movements, they faced discrimination and exclusion and were subordinated to male leaders.

Increasing Radicalism

In its most radical form, the new feminism rejected the whole notion of marriage, family, and even heterosexual relationships (a vehicle, some women claimed, of male domination). Not many women, not even many feminists, embraced such extremes. But by the early 1970s large numbers of women were coming to see themselves as an exploited group banding together against oppression and developing a culture of their own. In cities and towns across the country, feminists opened women's bookstores, bars, and coffee shops. They founded feminist newspapers and magazines. They created women's health clinics, centers to assist victims of rape and abuse, day-care centers, and, particularly after 1973, abortion clinics.

Expanding Achievements

By the early 1970s, the public and private achievements of the women's movement were already substantial. In 1971, the government extended its affirmative action guidelines to include women—linking sexism with racism as an officially acknowledged social problem. Women made rapid progress, in the meantime, in their efforts to move into the economic and political mainstream. The nation's major all-male educational institutions began to open their doors to women. (Princeton and Yale did so in 1969, and most others soon did the same.)

Women were also becoming an important force in business and the professions. Nearly half of all married women held jobs by the mid-1970s, and almost 90 percent of all women with college degrees worked. The two-career family, in which both the husband and the wife maintained active professional lives, became a widely accepted middle-class norm. (It had been common within the working class for decades.) There were also important symbolic changes, such as the refusal of many women to adopt their husbands' names when they married and the use of the term "Ms." in place of "Mrs." or "Miss" to signal the irrelevance of a woman's marital status in the professional world.

Economic Success

By the mid-1980s, women were serving in both houses of Congress, on the Supreme Court, in numerous federal cabinet positions, as governors of several states, and in many other political positions. In 1981, Ronald Reagan named the first female Supreme Court justice, Sandra Day O'Connor; in 1993, Bill Clinton named the second, Ruth Bader Ginsburg. In 1984, the Democratic Party chose a woman, Representative Geraldine Ferraro of

New York, as its vice presidential candidate. In academia, women were expanding their presence in traditional scholarly fields; they were also creating new fields—women's and gender studies, which in the 1980s and 1990s were among the fastest-growing areas of American scholarship.

Failure of the ERA

In 1972, Congress approved the Equal Rights Amendment (ERA) to the Constitution and sent it to the states. For a while ratification seemed almost certain. By the late 1970s, however, the momentum behind the amendment had died because of a rising chorus of objections to it from people (including many antifeminist women) who feared that it would disrupt traditional social patterns. In 1982, the amendment finally died when the ten years allotted for ratification expired.

The Abortion Issue

A major focus of American feminism since the 1920s has been the effort by women to win greater control of their own sexual and reproductive lives. In its least controversial form, this impulse helped produce an increasing awareness beginning in the 1970s of the problems of rape, sexual abuse, and wife beating. The dissemination of contraceptives and birth-control information became far more widespread and much less controversial than it had been earlier in the century. A related issue, however, stimulated as much popular passion as any question of its time: abortion.

Roe v. Wade

Abortion had once been legal in much of the United States, but by the beginning of the twentieth century it was banned by statute in most of the country and remained so into the 1960s (although many abortions continued to be performed quietly, and often dangerously, out of sight of the law). The women's movement created strong new pressures on behalf of the legalization of abortion. Several states had abandoned restrictions on abortion by the end of the 1960s. And in 1973, the Supreme Court's decision in *Roe* v. *Wade*, based on a new theory of a constitutional "right to privacy" first recognized by the Court only a few years earlier, invalidated all laws prohibiting abortion during the "first trimester"—the first three months of pregnancy. But even then, the issue was far from settled.

ENVIRONMENTALISM IN A TURBULENT SOCIETY

Like feminism, environmentalism entered the 1960s with a long history and relatively little public support. Also like feminism, environmentalism both profited from and transcended the turbulence of the era and emerged by the 1970s as a powerful and enduring force in American life. The rise of this new movement was in part a result of the environmental

degradation in advanced industrial society of the late twentieth century. It was a result, too, of the growth of the science of ecology, which provided environmentalists with new and powerful arguments. And it was a product as well of other social movements that rejected aspects of the modern, industrial, consumer society and called for a return to a more natural existence.

The New Science of Ecology

New Rationale for Environmentalism

Until the mid-twentieth century, most people who considered themselves environmentalists (or, to use the more traditional term, conservationists) based their commitment on aesthetic or moral grounds. They wanted to preserve nature because it was too beautiful to despoil, or because it was a mark of divinity on the world, or because it permitted humans a spiritual experience that would otherwise be unavailable to them. In the course of the twentieth century, however, scientists in the United States and other nations began to create a new rationale for environmentalism. They called it ecology.

Ecology is the science of the inter-relatedness of the natural world. Such problems as air and water pollution, the destruction of forests, the extinction of species, and toxic wastes are not, ecology teaches, separate, isolated problems. All elements of the earth's environment are intimately and delicately linked. Damaging any one of those elements, therefore, risks damaging all the others.

Aldo Leopold

Among the early contributions to popular knowledge of ecology was the work of the writer and naturalist Aldo Leopold. During a career in forest management, Leopold sought to apply the new scientific findings on ecology to his interactions with the natural world. And in 1949, he published a classic of environmental literature, *The Sand County Almanac*, in which he argued that humans had a responsibility to understand and maintain the balance of nature, that they should behave in the natural world according to a code that he called the "land ethic." By then, the science of ecology was spreading widely in the scientific community. Among the findings of ecologists were such now-common ideas as the "food chain," the "ecosystem," "biodiversity," and "endangered species." Rachel Carson's sensational 1962 book, *Silent Spring*, which revealed the dangers of pesticides, was based solidly on the ideas of ecologists and did at least as much as Leopold's work to introduce those ideas to a larger public.

Between 1945 and 1960, the number of professional ecologists in the United States grew threefold, and that number doubled again between 1960 and 1970. Funded by government agencies, by universities, by foundations, and eventually even by some corporations, ecological science gradually established itself as a significant field. By century's end, there were programs in and departments of ecological science in major universities throughout the United States and in many other nations.

Much more than other scientists, however, ecologists tend to fuse their commitment to research and testing with a commitment to publicizing their work and working for responsible public action to deal with environmental crises. Many ecologists argue that environmental problems must be addressed energetically even if firm scientific proof is not yet available to sustain their diagnosis of the problem. To wait for absolute proof, they insist, would be to invite irreversible damage to the environment.

Environmental Advocacy

Re-emergence of Environmental Organizations

The emergence or re-emergence of environmental organizations committed to public action and political lobbying in the 1960s and 1970s was among the most important developments in the growth of an environmental movement. Among the most important environmental organizations were the Wilderness Society, the Sierra Club, the National Audubon Society, the Nature Conservancy, the National Wildlife Federation, and the National Parks and Conservation Association. All of these organizations predated the rise of modern ecological science, but all of them entered the last decades of the twentieth century re-energized and committed to the new concepts of environmentalism. They found allies among other not-for-profit organizations that had no previous experience with environmentalism but now chose to join the battle—among them such groups as the American Civil Liberties Union, the League of Women Voters, the National Council of Churches, and even the AFL-CIO.

Out of these organizations emerged a new generation of professional environmental activists able to contribute to the legal and political battles of the movement. Scientists provided the necessary data. Lawyers fought battles with government agencies and in the courts. Lobbyists used traditional techniques of political persuasion with legislators and other officials—knowing that corporations and other opponents of environmental efforts would be doing the same in opposition to their goals. Perhaps most of all, these organizations learned how to mobilize public opinion on their behalf—an effort much aided by the rise of a popular movement beginning in the early 1970s.

Environmental Degradation

Many other forces contributed as well in the 1960s and 1970s to create what became the environmental movement. Lady Bird Johnson, the wife of the president, helped raise public awareness of the landscape with her energetic "beautification" campaign in the mid-1960s—a campaign unconnected to any ecological concepts, but one that reflected a growing popular dismay at the despoliation of the landscape by rapid economic growth. Members of the counterculture contributed to environmental awareness with their romanticization of the natural world and their repudiation of the "technocracy."

But perhaps the greatest force behind environmentalism was the condition of the environment itself. By the 1960s, the damage to the natural world from the dramatic economic growth of the postwar era was becoming impossible to ignore. Water pollution—which had been a problem in some areas of the country for many decades—was becoming so widespread that almost every major city was dealing with the unpleasant sight and odor, as well as the very real health risks, of polluted rivers and lakes. In Cleveland, Ohio, for example, the Cuyahoga River actually burst into flame from time to time from the petroleum waste being dumped into it; the city declared the river an official fire hazard.

Water Pollution

Perhaps more alarming was the growing awareness that the air itself was becoming unhealthy, that toxic fumes from factories and power plants and, most of all, automobiles were poisoning the atmosphere. Weather forecasts and official atmospheric information began to refer to "smog" levels—using a relatively new word formed from a combination of smoke and fog. In some large cities—Los Angeles and Denver among them—smog became an almost perpetual fact of life, rising steadily through the day, blotting out the sun, and creating respiratory difficulties for many citizens. In 1969, an oil-well platform off Santa Barbara, California had a blowout that spewed hundreds of thousands of gallons of crude oil into the ocean just off the popular beaches of an affluent city. This oil spill had a tremendous impact on the environmental consciousness of millions of Americans. Another, much larger spill—indeed, the largest in American history—occurred off the coast of Alaska in 1989 when the giant tanker *Exxon Valdez* hit a reef in Prince William Sound. The damage it caused to the nearby shoreline, and to the wildlife that inhabited it, also greatly increased environmental consciousness.

Exxon Valdez

Environmentalists brought to public attention some longer-term dangers of unchecked industrial development: the rapid depletion of oil and other irreplaceable fossil fuels; the destruction of lakes and forests as a result of "acid rain" (rainfall polluted by chemical contaminants); the rapid destruction of vast rain forests, in Brazil and elsewhere, which limited the earth's capacity to replenish its oxygen supply; the depletion of the ozone layer as a result of the release of chlorofluorocarbons into the atmosphere, which threatened to limit the earth's protection from dangerous ultraviolet rays from the sun; and global warming, which—if unchecked—would create dramatic changes in the earth's climate and would threaten existing cities and settlements in coastal areas all over the world by causing a rise in ocean levels. Many of these claims became—and remain—controversial. But most environmentalists—and many others—came to believe that while much remained to be learned about all of these developments, the problems were real and deserving of immediate attention.

Earth Day and Beyond

On April 22, 1970, people all over the United States participated in the first "Earth Day." Originally proposed by Wisconsin Senator Gaylord Nelson as a series of teach-ins on college campuses, Earth Day gradually took on a much larger life. Carefully managed by people who wanted to avoid associations with the radical left, it had an unthreatening quality that made it appealing to many people for whom antiwar demonstrations and civil-rights rallies seemed somehow threatening. According to some estimates, over 20 million Americans joined in some part of the Earth Day observances, which may have made it the largest single demonstration in the nation's history.

The cautious, centrist character of Earth Day and related efforts to popularize environmentalism helped create a movement that was less divisive than other, more controversial causes. Gradually, environmentalism became more than simply a series of demonstrations and protests. It became part of the consciousness of the vast majority of Americans—absorbed into popular culture, built into primary and secondary education, endorsed by almost all politicians (even if many of them actually opposed some environmental goals).

EPA Established

It also became part of the fabric of public policy. In 1970, Congress passed and President Nixon signed the National Environmental Protection Act, which created a new agency—the Environmental Protection Agency—to enforce antipollution standards on businesses and consumers. The Clean Air Act, also passed in 1970, and the Clean Water Act, passed in 1972, added additional tools to the government's arsenal of weapons against environmental degradation. The actions of the federal government—and of state and local governments that soon followed its lead—had a measurable, even at times dramatic, impact on many kinds of pollution. Many lakes and rivers that had long been serious environmental hazards became markedly cleaner; restrictions on auto emissions and other air pollutants substantially improved air quality in many cities; industries found it much more difficult to dump toxic wastes in unsafe ways.

But the enlistment of the government behind many of the goals of environmentalists did not put an end to the movement. Different administrations displayed varying levels of support for environmental goals, and advocacy groups remained ready to spring into action to force them to change their positions. And of course new environmental problems continued to emerge even as older ones sometimes found solutions. Environmentalism was simultaneously a movement, a set of public policies, and a broad national ideal—and it was the combination of all those aspects that made it such a continually powerful force in American life.

NIXON, KISSINGER, AND THE WAR

Richard Nixon assumed office in 1969 committed not only to restoring stability at home but to creating a new and more stable order in the world. Central to Nixon's hopes for international stability was a resolution of the stalemate in Vietnam. Yet the new president felt no freer than his predecessor to abandon the American commitment there.

Vietnamization

Henry Kissinger

Despite Nixon's own deep interest in international affairs, he brought with him into government a man who at times seemed to overshadow the president himself in the conduct of diplomacy: Henry Kissinger, a Harvard professor whom Nixon appointed as his special assistant for national security affairs. Kissinger quickly established dominance over Secretary of State William Rogers and Secretary of Defense Melvin Laird, who were both more experienced in public life. Together, Nixon and Kissinger set out to find an acceptable solution to the stalemate in Vietnam.

The new Vietnam policy moved along several fronts. One was the move to "Vietnamize" the conflict—that is, train and equip the South Vietnamese military to assume the burden of combat in place of American forces. In the fall of 1969, Nixon announced the withdrawal of 60,000 American ground troops from Vietnam. By the fall of 1972, relatively few American soldiers remained in Indochina. From a peak of more than 540,000 in 1969, the number had dwindled to about 60,000.

Vietnamization (and the decreased draft calls it produced) did help quiet domestic opposition to the war for a time. It did nothing, however, to break the stalemate in the negotiations with the North Vietnamese in Paris. The new administration decided that new military pressures would be necessary to do that.

Escalation

By the end of 1969, Nixon and Kissinger had decided that the most effective way to tip the military balance in America's favor was to destroy the bases in Cambodia and Laos from which the American military believed the North Vietnamese were launching many of their attacks. Very early in his presidency, Nixon secretly ordered the air force to begin bombing Cambodian and Laotian territory to destroy the enemy sanctuaries. On April 30, Nixon went on television to announce that he was ordering American ground troops across the border into Cambodia to clean out the bases that the enemy had been using for its attacks on South Vietnam.

Literally overnight, the Cambodian invasion restored the dwindling antiwar movement to vigorous life. The first days of May saw the most widespread and vocal antiwar demonstrations ever. A mood of crisis was already mounting when, on May 4, four college students were killed and nine others injured after members of the National Guard opened fire on antiwar demonstrators at Kent State University in Ohio. Ten days later, police killed two African-American students at Jackson State University in Mississippi during a demonstration there.

Kent State

The clamor against the war spread into the government and the press. Congress angrily repealed the Gulf of Tonkin Resolution in December. Then, in June 1971, first the *New York Times* and later other newspapers began publishing excerpts from a secret study of the war prepared by the Defense Department during the Johnson administration. The so-called Pentagon Papers, leaked to the press by former Defense official Daniel Ellsberg, provided evidence the government had been dishonest, both in reporting the military progress of the war and in explaining its own motives for American involvement. The administration went to court to suppress the documents, but the Supreme Court ruled that the press had the right to publish them.

Pentagon Papers

Morale and discipline among American troops in Vietnam were rapidly deteriorating. The 1971 trial and conviction of Lieutenant William Calley, who was charged with overseeing a massacre of more than 100 unarmed South Vietnamese civilians in 1968 near the village of My Lai, attracted wide public attention to the dehumanizing impact of the war on those who fought it—and to the terrible consequences that dehumanization imposed on the Vietnamese people. Less publicized were other, more widespread problems among American troops in Vietnam: desertion, drug addiction, racial bias, refusal to obey orders, even the killing of unpopular officers by enlisted men.

By 1971, nearly two-thirds of those interviewed in public opinion polls were urging American withdrawal from Vietnam. President Nixon, however, believed that a defeat in Vietnam would cause unacceptable damage to the nation's (and his own) credibility. The FBI, the CIA, the White House itself, and other federal agencies increased their efforts to discredit and harass antiwar and radical groups, often through illegal means.

In Indochina, meanwhile, the fighting raged on. American bombing in Vietnam and Cambodia increased. In March 1972, the North Vietnamese mounted their biggest offensive since 1968 (the so-called Easter offensive). American and South Vietnamese forces managed to halt the communist advance, but it was clear that without American support the South Vietnamese would not have succeeded. At the same time, Nixon ordered American planes to bomb targets near Hanoi, the capital of North Vietnam, and Haiphong, its principal port, and called for the mining of seven North Vietnamese harbors.

Easter Offensive

"Peace with Honor"

As the 1972 presidential election approached, the administration stepped up its effort to produce a breakthrough in negotiations with the North Vietnamese. In April 1972, the president dropped his longtime insistence on the removal of North Vietnamese troops from the south before any American withdrawal. Meanwhile, Henry Kissinger met privately in Paris with the North Vietnamese foreign secretary, Le Duc Tho, to work out terms for a cease-fire. On October 26, only days before the presidential election, Kissinger announced that "peace is at hand."

Several weeks later (after the election), negotiations broke down once again. Although both the American and the North Vietnamese governments were ready to accept the Kissinger-Tho plan for a cease-fire, President Nguyen Van Thieu of South Vietnam balked, still insisting on a full withdrawal of North Vietnamese forces from the south. Kissinger tried to win additional concessions from the communists to meet Thieu's objections, but on December 16 talks broke off.

"Christmas Bombing"

The next day, December 17, American B-52s began the heaviest and most destructive air raids of the entire war on Hanoi, Haiphong, and other North Vietnamese targets. Civilian casualties were high, and fifteen American B–52s were shot down by the North Vietnamese; in the entire war to that point, the United States had lost only one of the giant bombers. On December 30, Nixon terminated the "Christmas bombing." The United States and the North Vietnamese returned to the conference table; and on January 27, 1973, they signed an "agreement on ending the war and restoring peace in Vietnam." Nixon claimed that the Christmas bombing had forced the North Vietnamese to relent. At least equally important, however, was the enormous American pressure on Thieu to accept the cease-fire.

The terms of the Paris accords were little different from those Kissinger and Tho had accepted in principle a few months before. There would be an immediate cease-fire. The North Vietnamese would release several hundred American prisoners of war. The Thieu regime would survive for the moment, but North Vietnamese forces already in the south would remain there. An undefined committee would work out a permanent settlement.

Defeat in Indochina

Fall of Saigon

American forces were hardly out of Indochina before the Paris accords began to collapse. In March 1975, finally, the North Vietnamese launched a full-scale offensive against the now greatly weakened forces of the south. Thieu appealed to Washington for assistance. The president (now Gerald Ford) appealed to Congress for additional funding; Congress refused. Late in April 1975, communist forces marched into Saigon, shortly after officials of the Thieu regime and the staff of the American embassy had fled the country in humiliating

THE EVACUATION OF SAIGON A harried U.S. official struggles to keep panicking Vietnamese from boarding an already overburdened helicopter on the roof of the American embassy in Saigon. The hurried evacuation of Americans took place only hours before the arrival of North Vietnamese troops, signaling the final defeat of South Vietnam. *(AP/Wide World Photos)*

disarray. The communist forces quickly occupied the capital, renamed it Ho Chi Minh City, and began the process of reuniting Vietnam under the harsh rule of Hanoi. At about the same time, the Lon Nol regime in Cambodia fell to the murderous forces of the Khmer Rouge—whose brutal policies led to the death of more than a third of the country's people over the next several years.

Such were the dismal results of more than a decade of direct American military involvement in Vietnam. More than 1.2 million Vietnamese soldiers had died in combat, along with countless civilians throughout the region. A beautiful land had been ravaged, its agrarian economy left in

ruins; until an economic revival began in the early 1990s, Vietnam remained one of the poorest and most politically oppressive nations in the world. The United States had paid a heavy price as well. The war had cost the nation almost $150 billion in direct costs and much more indirectly. It had resulted in the deaths of over 57,000 young Americans and the injury of 300,000 more. And the nation had suffered a blow to its confidence and self-esteem from which it would not soon recover.

NIXON, KISSINGER, AND THE WORLD

The continuing war in Vietnam provided an unhappy backdrop to what Nixon considered his larger mission in world affairs: the construction of a new international order. The president had become convinced that the old assumptions of a "bipolar" world—in which the United States and the Soviet Union were the only real great powers—were now obsolete. America must adapt to the new "multipolar" international structure, in which China, Japan, and Western Europe were becoming major, independent forces.

Nixon's Multipolar Vision

The China Initiative and Soviet-American Détente

For more than twenty years, ever since the fall of Chiang Kai-shek in 1949, the United States had treated China, the most populous nation on earth, as if it did not exist. Instead, America recognized the regime-in-exile on the small island of Taiwan as the legitimate government of mainland China. Nixon and Kissinger wanted to forge a new relationship with the Chinese communists—in part to strengthen them as a counterbalance to the Soviet Union. The Chinese, for their part, were eager to end China's own isolation from the international arena.

In July 1971, Nixon sent Henry Kissinger on a secret mission to Beijing. When Kissinger returned, the president made the startling announcement that he would visit China himself within the next few months. That fall, with American approval, the United Nations admitted the communist government of China and expelled the representatives of the Taiwan regime. Finally, in February 1972, Nixon paid a formal visit to China and, in a single stroke, erased much of the deep animosity between the United States and the Chinese communists. Nixon did not yet formally recognize the communist regime, but in 1972 the United States and China began low-level diplomatic relations.

The initiatives in China coincided with an effort by the Nixon administration to improve relations with the Soviet Union, an initiative known by the French word détente. In 1971, American and Soviet diplomats produced the first Strategic Arms Limitation Treaty (SALT I),

DÉTENTE AT HIGH TIDE The visit of Soviet premier Leonid Brezhnev to Washington in 1973 was a high-water mark in the search for détente between the two nations. Here, Brezhnev and Nixon share friendly words on the White House balcony. *(J. P. Laffont/Sygma/Corbis)*

which froze the arsenals of some nuclear missiles (ICBMs) on both sides at present levels. In May of that year, the president traveled to Moscow to sign the agreement. The next year, the Soviet premier, Leonid Brezhnev, visited Washington.

Dealing with the Third World

The policies of rapprochement with communist China and détente with the Soviet Union reflected Nixon's and Kissinger's belief in the importance of stable relationships among the great powers. But the so-called Third World remained the most volatile and dangerous source of international tension.

The Nixon-Kissinger policy toward the Third World was to maintain the status quo without involving the United States too deeply in local disputes. In 1969 and 1970, the president described what became known as the Nixon Doctrine, by which the United States would "participate in the defense and development of allies and friends" but would leave the "basic responsibility" for the future of

Nixon Doctrine

those "friends" to the nations themselves. In practice, the Nixon Doctrine meant a declining American interest in contributing to Third World development; a growing contempt for the United Nations, where underdeveloped nations were gaining influence through their sheer numbers; and increasing support to authoritarian regimes attempting to withstand radical challenges from within.

In 1970, for example, the CIA poured substantial funds into Chile to help support the established government against a communist challenge. When the Marxist candidate for president, Salvador Allende, came to power through an open election despite American efforts, the United States began funneling more money to opposition forces in Chile to help destabilize the new government. In 1973, a military junta seized power from Allende, who was subsequently murdered. The United States developed a friendly relationship with the new, repressive military government of General Augusto Pinochet.

Allende Overthrown

In the Middle East, conditions grew more volatile in the aftermath of the 1967 war, in which Israel had occupied substantial new territories, dislodging many Palestinian Arabs from their homes. The refugees were a source of considerable instability in Jordan, Lebanon, and the other surrounding countries into which they moved. In October 1973, on the Jewish high holy day of Yom Kippur, Egyptian and Syrian forces attacked Israel. For ten days, the Israelis struggled to recover from the surprise attack; finally, they launched an effective counteroffensive against Egyptian forces in the Sinai. At that point, the United States intervened, placing heavy pressure on Israel to accept a cease-fire rather than press its advantage.

The imposed settlement of the Yom Kippur War demonstrated the growing dependence of the United States and its allies on Arab oil. A brief but painful embargo by the Arab governments on the sale of oil to America in 1973 provided an ominous warning of the costs of losing access to the region's resources.

Arab Oil Embargo

A larger lesson of 1973 was that the nations of the Third World could no longer be expected to act as passive, cooperative "client states." And the United States could not depend on cheap, easy access to raw materials as it had in the past.

POLITICS AND ECONOMICS IN THE NIXON YEARS

Nixon ran for president in 1968 promising a return to more conservative social and economic policies and a restoration of law and order. Once in office, however, his domestic policies sometimes continued and even expanded the liberal initiatives of the previous two administrations.

Domestic Initiatives

Many of Nixon's domestic policies were a response to what he believed to be the demands of his constituency—conservative, middle-class people, the "silent majority" who he believed wanted to reduce federal interference in local affairs. He tried, unsuccessfully, to persuade Congress to pass legislation prohibiting school desegregation through the use of forced busing. He forbade the Department of Health, Education, and Welfare to cut off federal funds from school districts that had failed to comply with court orders to integrate. At the same time, he began to reduce or dismantle many of the social programs of the Great Society and the New Frontier. In 1973, he abolished the Office of Economic Opportunity, the centerpiece of the antipoverty program of the Johnson years.

Nixon's "Silent Majority"

Yet Nixon's domestic policies had progressive and creative elements as well. He signed legislation creating the Environmental Protection Agency and establishing the most stringent environmental regulations in the nation's history. He ordered the first affirmative action program for workers on federally funded projects. One of the administration's boldest efforts was an attempt to overhaul the nation's welfare system. Nixon proposed replacing the existing system with what he called the Family Assistance Plan (FAP). It would in effect have created a guaranteed annual income for all Americans: $1,600 in federal grants, which could be supplemented by outside earnings up to $4,000. The FAP won approval in the House in 1970, but the bill failed in the Senate. Nixon also became the first president since Truman to propose a plan for national health insurance, which likewise made no progress in Congress.

From the Warren Court to the Nixon Court

Of all the liberal institutions that aroused the enmity of the conservative "silent majority" in the 1950s and 1960s, none evoked more anger and bitterness than the Supreme Court under Chief Justice Earl Warren. Not only did the Warren Court's rulings on racial matters disrupt traditional social patterns in both the North and the South, but its staunch defense of civil liberties directly contributed, in the eyes of many Americans, to the increase in crime, disorder, and moral decay. In *Engel* v. *Vitale* (1962), the Court ruled that prayers in public schools were unconstitutional, sparking outrage among religious fundamentalists and others. In *Roth* v. *United States* (1957), the Court sharply limited the authority of local governments to curb pornography. In a series of other decisions, the Court greatly strengthened the civil rights of criminal defendants and, many Americans believed, greatly weakened the power of law enforcement officials to do their jobs. For example, in *Gideon* v. *Wainwright* (1963), the Court ruled that every felony defendant was entitled to a lawyer regardless of his or her ability to pay. In *Escobedo* v.

Civil Liberties Expanded

Illinois (1964), it ruled that a defendant must be allowed access to a lawyer before questioning by police. In *Miranda* v. *Arizona* (1966), the Court confirmed the obligation of authorities to inform a criminal suspect of his or her rights. By 1968, the Warren Court had become the target of Americans of all kinds who felt the balance of power in the United States had shifted too far toward the poor, the dispossessed, and the criminal at the expense of the middle class.

Nixon promised to give the Court a more conservative cast. When Chief Justice Earl Warren retired early in 1969, Nixon replaced him with a federal appeals court judge of known conservative leanings, Warren Burger. At about the same time, Associate Justice Abe Fortas resigned his seat after the disclosure of a series of alleged financial improprieties. To replace him, Nixon named Clement F. Haynsworth, a respected federal circuit court judge from South Carolina. But Haynsworth came under fire from Senate liberals, black organizations, and labor unions for his conservative record on civil rights. The Senate rejected him. Nixon's next choice was G. Harrold Carswell, a judge of the Florida federal appeals court of little distinction. The Senate rejected his nomination, too.

Nixon angrily denounced the votes. But he was careful thereafter to choose men of standing within the legal community to fill vacancies on the Supreme Court: Harry Blackmun, a moderate jurist from Minnesota; Lewis F. Powell, Jr., a respected lawyer from Virginia; and William Rehnquist, a member of the Nixon Justice Department.

The new Court, however, fell short of what the president and many conservatives had expected. Rather than retreating from its commitment to social reform, the Court in many areas actually moved further toward it. In *Swann* v. *Charlotte-Mecklenburg Board of Education* (1971), it ruled in favor of the use of forced busing to achieve racial balance in schools. Not even the intense and occasionally violent opposition of local communities as diverse as Boston and Louisville, Kentucky, was able to weaken the judicial commitment to integration. In *Furman* v. *Georgia* (1972), the Court overturned existing capital punishment statutes and established strict new guidelines for such laws in the future. In *Roe* v. *Wade* (1973), one of the most controversial decisions in the Court's modern history, it struck down laws forbidding abortions.

In other decisions, however, the Burger Court did demonstrate a more conservative temperament than the Warren Court had shown. Although the justices approved busing as a tool for achieving integration, they rejected, in *Milliken* v. *Bradley* (1974), a plan to transfer students across municipal lines (in this case, between Detroit and its suburbs) to achieve racial balance. While the Court upheld the principle of affirmative action in its celebrated 1978 decision in *Bakke* v. *Board of Regents of California*, it established restrictive new guidelines for such programs in the future. In *Stone* v. *Powell* (1976), the Court agreed to certain limits on the right of a defendant to appeal a state conviction to the federal judiciary.

Milliken v. Bradley

The Election of 1972

Nixon entered the presidential race in 1972 with a substantial reserve of strength. His energetic reelection committee had collected enormous sums of money to support the campaign. The president himself used the powers of incumbency to strengthen his political standing in strategic areas. And Nixon's foreign policy successes, especially his trip to China, increased his stature in the eyes of the nation.

Nixon was most fortunate in 1972, however, in his opposition. George Wallace, partly at Nixon's urging, entered the Democratic primaries and helped divide the party until a would-be assassin shot the Alabama governor during a rally at a Maryland shopping center in May. Paralyzed from the waist down, Wallace was unable to continue campaigning. In the meantime, the most liberal factions of the party were succeeding in establishing their candidate, Senator George S. McGovern of South Dakota, as the front-runner for the nomination. An outspoken critic of the war and a forceful advocate of advanced liberal positions on many social and economic issues, McGovern profited greatly from party reforms (which he himself had helped to draft) that gave increased influence to women, minorities, and young people in the selection of the Democratic ticket. But in the process, the McGovern campaign came to be associated with aspects of the turbulent 1960s that many middle-class Americans were eager to reject.

George McGovern

On election day, Nixon won reelection by one of the largest margins in history: 60.7 percent of the popular vote compared with 37.5 percent for McGovern, and an electoral margin of 520 to 17. The Democratic candidate had carried only Massachusetts and the District of Columbia. But serious problems, some beyond the president's control and some of his own making, were already lurking in the wings.

The Troubled Economy

Although it was political scandal that would ultimately destroy the Nixon presidency, the most important issue of the early 1970s was the beginning of a long-term transformation of the American economy. For three decades, that economy had been the envy of the world. In fact, however, America's prosperity rested in part on several artificial conditions that were rapidly disappearing by the late 1960s.

The most immediate change was the end of the nation's easy access to cheap raw materials, a change that became a major cause of the serious inflation that plagued the economy through much of the 1970s. For many years, the Organization of Petroleum Exporting Countries (OPEC) had operated as an informal bargaining unit for the sale of oil by Third World nations but had seldom managed to exercise any real strength. But in the early 1970s, OPEC began to assert itself, to use its oil both as an economic tool and as a political weapon. In 1973, in the midst of the Yom Kippur War, Arab members

OPEC

of OPEC announced that they would no longer ship petroleum to nations supporting Israel—that is, to the United States and its allies in Western Europe. At about the same time, the OPEC nations agreed to raise their prices 500 percent (from $3 to $15 a barrel). These twin shocks produced momentary economic chaos in the West. The United States suffered its first fuel shortage since World War II. And although the crisis eased a few months later, the price of energy continued to skyrocket.

The energy crisis eventually subsided, but another, longer-term change in the American economy was the transformation of the nation's manufacturing sector. Ever since World War II, American industry had enjoyed relatively little competition from the rest of the world. By the end of the 1960s, however, both Western Europe and Japan had recovered from the damage their manufacturing sectors had absorbed during World War II; by the early 1970s, they were providing stiff competition to American firms in the sale of automobiles, steel, and many other products both in world markets and within the United States. Some American corporations failed. Others restructured themselves to become more competitive again in world markets. In the process, they closed many older plants and eliminated hundreds of thousands of once-lucrative manufacturing jobs. The high-wage, high-employment industrial economy that had been a central fact of American life since the 1940s was gradually disappearing.

Growing Foreign Competition

The Nixon Response

Nixon's initial answer to these mounting economic problems was a conventional anti-inflationary one. He reduced spending and raised taxes, producing a modest budget surplus in 1969. But when those policies proved difficult to sustain, Nixon turned increasingly to control of the currency. Placing conservative economists at the head of the Federal Reserve Board, he ensured sharply higher interest rates and a contraction of the money supply. Even so, the cost of living rose a cumulative 15 percent during Nixon's first two and a half years in office. Economic growth, in the meantime, declined. The United States was encountering a new dilemma: "stagflation," a combination of rising prices and general economic stagnation.

In the summer of 1971, Nixon imposed a ninety-day freeze on all wages and prices at their existing levels. Then, in November, he launched Phase II of his economic plan: mandatory guidelines for some wage and price increases, to be administered by a federal agency. Inflation subsided temporarily, but the recession continued. Fearful that the recession would be more damaging than inflation in an election year, the administration reversed itself late in 1971: interest rates were allowed to drop sharply, and government spending increased—producing the largest budget deficit since World War II. The

Rising Inflation

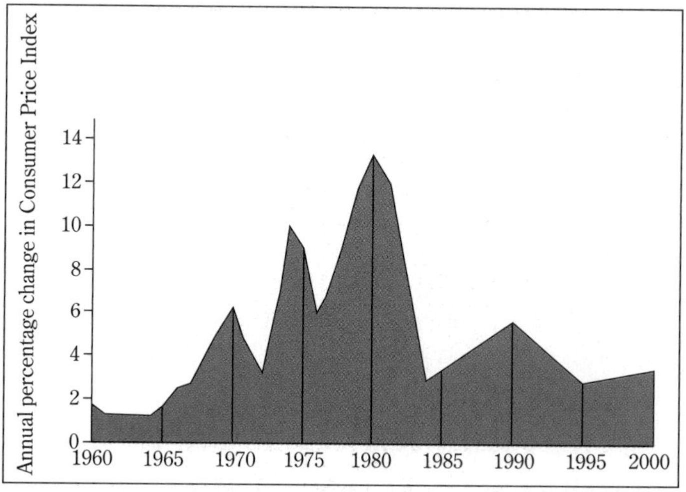

INFLATION, 1960–2000 Inflation was the biggest economic worry of most Americans in the 1970s and early 1980s, and this chart shows why. Having remained very low through the early 1960s, inflation rose slowly in the second half of the decade and then dramatically in the mid- and late 1970s, before beginning a sharp and reasonably steady decline in the early 1980s.
◆ *What caused the great spike in inflation in the 1970s?*

new tactics helped revive the economy in the short term, but inflation rose substantially. In 1973, prices rose 9 percent; in 1974, after the Arab oil embargo and the OPEC price increases, they rose 12 percent—the highest rate since shortly after World War II. The new energy crisis, in the meantime, was quickly becoming a national preoccupation. But while Nixon talked often about the need to achieve "energy independence," he offered few concrete proposals.

THE WATERGATE CRISIS

Although economic problems greatly concerned the American people in the 1970s, another stunning development almost entirely preoccupied the nation beginning early in 1973: the fall of Richard Nixon. The president's demise was a result in part of his own personality. But the larger explanation for the crisis lay in Nixon's view of American society and the world, and of his own role in both. The president believed the United States faced grave dangers from the radicals and dissidents who were challenging his policies. He came increasingly to consider any challenge to his policies a threat to "national security," thus creating a climate in which he and those who served him could justify almost any tactics to stifle dissent and undermine opposition.

The Scandals

Early on the morning of June 17, 1972, police arrested five men who had broken into the offices of the Democratic National Committee in the Watergate office building in Washington, D.C. Two others were seized a short time later and charged with supervising the break-in. When reporters for the *Washington Post* began researching the backgrounds of the culprits, they discovered that among those involved in the burglary were former employees of the Committee for the Re-Election of the President (CRP). One of them had worked in the White House itself. They had, moreover, been paid for the break-in from a secret fund of the reelection committee, a fund controlled by, among others, members of the White House staff.

Public interest in the disclosures grew slowly in the last months of 1972. Early in 1973, however, the Watergate burglars went on trial; and under prodding from federal judge John J. Sirica, one of the defendants, James W. McCord, agreed to cooperate both with the grand jury and with a special Senate investigating committee recently established under Senator Sam J. Ervin of North Carolina. McCord's testimony opened a floodgate of confessions, and for months a parade of White House and campaign officials exposed one illegality after another. Foremost among them was a member of the inner circle of the White House, John Dean, counsel to the president, who leveled allegations against Nixon himself.

Two different sets of scandals emerged from the investigations. One was a general pattern of abuses of power involving both the White House and the Nixon campaign committee, which included, but was not limited to, the Watergate break-in. The other scandal, and the one that became the major focus of public attention for nearly two years, was the way in which the administration tried to manage the investigations of the Watergate break-in and other abuses—a pattern of behavior that became known as the "cover-up." There was never any conclusive evidence that the president had planned or approved the burglary in advance. But there was mounting evidence that he had been involved in illegal efforts to obstruct investigations of the episode.

Watergate "Cover-up"

Nixon accepted the departure of members of his administration implicated in the scandals. But the president continued to insist on his own innocence. There the matter might have rested had it not been for the disclosure during the Senate hearings of a White House taping system that had recorded virtually every conversation in the president's office during the period in question. All those investigating the scandals sought access to the tapes; Nixon, pleading "executive privilege," refused to release them. A special prosecutor appointed by the president to handle the Watergate cases, Harvard law professor Archibald Cox, took Nixon to court in October 1973 in an effort to force him to relinquish the recordings. Nixon, now clearly growing desperate, fired Cox and suffered the humiliation of watching both Attorney General Elliot Richardson and his deputy resign

Watergate Tapes

in protest. This "Saturday night massacre" made the president's predicament much worse. Not only did public pressure force him to appoint a new special prosecutor, Texas attorney Leon Jaworski, who proved just as determined as Cox to subpoena the tapes; but the episode precipitated an investigation by the House of Representatives into the possibility of impeachment.

The Fall of Richard Nixon

Nixon's situation deteriorated further in the following months. Late in 1973, Vice President Spiro Agnew became embroiled in a scandal of his own when evidence surfaced that he had accepted bribes and kickbacks while serving as governor of Maryland and even as vice president. In return for a Justice Department agreement not to press the case, Agnew pleaded no contest to a lesser charge of income-tax evasion and resigned from the government. With the controversial Agnew no longer in line to succeed to the presidency, the prospect of removing Nixon from the White House became less worrisome to his opponents. The new vice president (the first appointed under the terms of the Twenty-fifth Amendment, which had been adopted in 1967) was House Minority Leader Gerald Ford, an amiable and popular Michigan congressman.

The impeachment investigation quickly gathered momentum. In April 1974, in an effort to head off further subpoenas of the tapes, the president released transcripts of a number of relevant conversations, claiming that they proved his innocence. Investigators and much of the public felt otherwise. Even these edited tapes seemed to suggest Nixon's complicity in the cover-up. In July, the crisis reached a climax. First the Supreme Court ruled unanimously, in *United States* v. *Richard M. Nixon*, that the president must relinquish the tapes to Special Prosecutor Jaworski. Days later, the House Judiciary Committee voted to recommend three articles of impeachment.

United States v. Richard Nixon

Even without additional evidence, Nixon might well have been impeached by the full House and convicted by the Senate. Early in August, however, he provided at last the "smoking gun"—the concrete proof of his guilt—that his defenders had long contended was missing from the case against him. Among the tapes that the Supreme Court compelled Nixon to relinquish were several that offered apparently incontrovertible evidence of his involvement in the Watergate cover-up. Only three days after the burglary, the recordings disclosed, the president had ordered the FBI to stop investigating the break-in. Impeachment and conviction now seemed inevitable.

For several days, Nixon brooded in the White House, on the verge, some claimed, of a breakdown. Finally, on August 8, 1974, he announced his resignation—the first president in American history ever to do so. At noon the next day, while Nixon and his family were flying west to their home in California, Gerald Ford took the oath of office as president.

Resignation

Debating the Past

WATERGATE

Thirty years after Watergate—the most famous political scandal in American history—historians and others continue to argue about its causes and significance. Their interpretations tend to fall into several broad categories.

One argument emphasizes the evolution of the institution of the presidency over time and sees Watergate as the result of a much larger pattern of presidential usurpations of power that stretched back at least several decades. Arthur Schlesinger, Jr., helped develop this argument in his 1973 book *The Imperial Presidency*, which argued that the belief of a succession of presidents in the urgency of the Cold War, and in their duty to take whatever measures might be necessary to combat it, led them gradually to usurp more and more power from Congress, from the courts, and from the public. Gradually, presidents began to look for ways to circumvent constraints not just in foreign policy, but in domestic matters as well. Nixon's actions in the Watergate crisis were, in other words, a culmination of this long and steady expansion of covert presidential power. Jonathan Schell, in *The Time of Illusion* (1975), offered a variation of this argument, tying the crisis of the presidency to the pressure that nuclear weapons placed on presidents to protect the nation's—and their own "credibility."

A second explanation of Watergate emphasizes the difficult social and political environment of the late 1960s and early 1970s. Nixon entered office, according to this view, facing an unprecedentedly radical opposition that would stop at nothing to discredit the war and destroy his authority. He found himself, therefore, drawn into taking similarly desperate measures of his own to defend himself from these extraordinary challenges. Nixon made this argument himself in his 1975 memoirs:

> This epidemic of unprecedented domestic terrorism . . . prompted our efforts to discover the best means by which to deal with this new phenomenon of highly organized and highly skilled revolutionaries dedicated to the violent destruction of our democratic system.

The historian Herbert Parmet echoed parts of this argument in *Richard Nixon and His America* (1990). Stephen Ambrose offered a more muted version of the same view in *Richard Nixon* (1989).

Most of those who have written about Watergate, however, search for the explanation not in institutional or social forces, but in the personalities of the people involved, and most notably in the personality of Richard Nixon. Even many of those who have developed structural explanations (Schlesinger, Schell, and Ambrose, for example) return eventually to Nixon himself as the most important explanation for Watergate. Others begin there, perhaps most notably Stanley I. Kutler, in *The Wars of Watergate* (1990) and, more recently, *Abuse of Power* (1997), in which he presents extensive excerpts from conversations about Watergate taped in the Nixon White House. Kutler emphasizes Nixon's lifelong resort to vicious political tactics and his longstanding belief that he was a special target of unscrupulous enemies and had to "get" them before they got him. Watergate was rooted, Kutler argues, "in the personality and history of Nixon himself." A "corrosive hatred," he claims, "decisively shaped Nixon's own behavior, his career, and eventually his historical standing."

Many Americans expressed relief and exhilaration that, as the new president put it, "our long national nightmare is over." But the wave of good feeling could not obscure the deeper and more lasting damage of the Watergate crisis. In a society in which distrust of leaders and institutions of authority was already widespread, the fall of Richard Nixon confirmed for many Americans their most cynical assumptions about the character of American public life.

CONCLUSION

The victory of Richard Nixon in the 1968 presidential election represented a popular repudiation of turbulence and radicalism. It was a call for a restoration of order and stability. But order and stability were not the dominant characteristics of Nixon's troubled years in office. Nixon entered office, rather, when the forces of the left and the counterculture were approaching the peak of their influence. American culture and society in the late 1960s and early 1970s were shaped decisively by, and were deeply divided over, the challenges by young people to the norms by which most Americans had lived. They were also the years in which a host of new liberation movements joined the drive for racial equality, and when, above all, women mobilized effectively and powerfully to demand changes in the way their society treated gender differences.

Nixon had run for office attacking the failure of his predecessor to end the war in Vietnam. But for four years under his presidency, the war—and the protests against it—continued and even in some respects escalated. The division of opinion over the war was as deep as any of the many other divisions in national life. It continued to poison the nation's politics and social fabric until the American role in the conflict finally shuddered to a close in 1973.

But much of the controversy and division in the 1970s was a product of the Nixon presidency itself. Nixon was in many ways a dynamic and even visionary leader, who proposed (but rarely succeeded in enacting) some important domestic reforms and who made important changes in American foreign policy, most notably making overtures to communist China and forging détente with the Soviet Union. He was also, however, a devious, secretive, and embittered man whose White House became engaged in a series of covert activities—many of them connected with the president's reelection campaign in 1972—that produced the most dramatic political scandal in American history. Watergate, as it was called, preoccupied much of the nation for nearly two years beginning in 1972; and ultimately, in the summer of 1974, the scandal forced Richard Nixon—who had been reelected to office only two years before by one of the largest majorities in modern history—to become the first president in American history to resign.

FOR FURTHER REFERENCE

John Morton Blum, *Years of Discord: American Politics and Society, 1961–1974* (1991) is a good overview. James Miller, *"Democracy in the Streets": From Port Huron to the Siege of Chicago* (1987) is a perceptive history of the New Left through its leading organization, SDS. Kristin Luker, *Abortion and the Politics of Motherhood* (1984) is an excellent account of this central battle over the nature of feminism. Daniel Horowitz, *Betty Friedan and the Making of "The Feminine Mystique"* (1998) is a fine study of a major figure in the feminist movement. Margaret Cruikshank, *The Rise of a Gay and Lesbian Liberation Movement* (1992) recounts another important struggle of the 1960s and beyond. David Allyn, *Make Love Not War: The Sexual Revolution: An Unfettered History* (2000) and Beth Bailey, *Sex in the Heartland* (1999) are studies of a major social change. Ronald Takaki, *Strangers from a Distant Shore: A History of Asian Americans* (1989) examines the growing Asian community in postwar America. Stephen Ambrose, *Nixon: The Triumph of a Politician, 1962–1972* (1989), and *Nixon, Ruin and Recovery, 1973–1990* (1992) provide a thorough chronicle of this important presidency. Joan Hoff, *Nixon Reconsidered* (1994) is a more sympathetic account of Nixon's presidency before Watergate. Stanley I. Kutler, *The Wars of Watergate* (1990) is a scholarly study of the great scandal, and Jonathan Schell, *The Time of Illusion* (1975) is a perceptive contemporary account. Marilyn Young, *The Vietnam Wars, 1945–1990* (1991) provides, among other things, a full account of the last years of American involvement in Vietnam and of the conflicts in the region that followed the American withdrawal. Larry Berman, *No Peace, No Honor: Nixon, Kissinger, and Betrayal in Vietnam* (2001) is a study of the end of the war.

Chicago 1968 (1995) is a complex and riveting film portrait of the dramatic events around the Democratic National Convention of 1968. The three-part film series *America in 1968* (1979) examines the political, cultural, and international events of that pivotal year. *Nixon* (1990) is a three-hour film biography of one of the most powerful and controversial figures in modern American history. *Watergate* (1994) is a documentary film on the unmaking of the Nixon presidency, including recent interviews with major participants. *In the Spirit of Crazy Horse* (1990) relates the history of the Lakota Indians on the centennial of the Wounded Knee massacre. *Chicano! History of the Mexican-American Civil Rights Movement* (1996) is a four-part series on the Mexican-American movement from 1967.

For quizzes, Internet resources, references to additional books and films, and more, consult this book's Online Learning Center site at www.mhhe.com/unfinishednation4.

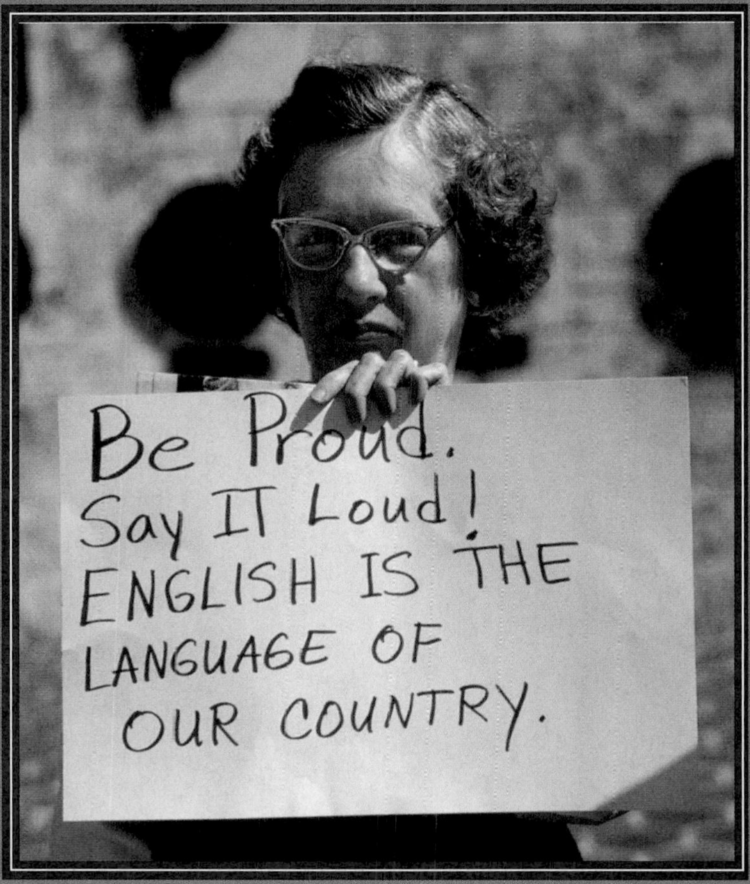

DEMONSTRATING AGAINST BILINGUALISM Among the many divisive issues that sparked controversy in the 1970s and 1980s, and helped fuel the rise of a powerful conservative movement, was the growing number of residents of the United States for whom English was a second language. In California and a few other states educators responded by introducing "bilingualism" into the public school system, to ensure that students whose command of English was poor could receive instruction in their own language—usually Spanish since the largest number of immigrants in the Southwest came from Mexico. Hostility to bilingualism grew rapidly among mostly conservative Americans, who feared that the movement would not stop in the schools. This woman demonstrates in favor of one of the prized causes of the right—the campaign to make English the "official" language of the United States. *(Nathan Benn/Corbis)*

TIME LINE

1974	1976	1977	1978-1979	1980	1981	1982	1983
"Stagflation"	Carter elected president	Panama Canal treaties signed	Camp David accords	U.S. boycotts Moscow Olympics	American hostages in Iran released	Severe recession	U.S. invades Grenada
Ford pardons Nixon		Apple introduces first personal computer	American hostages in Iran	Reagan elected president	Reagan wins tax and budget cuts		
			Soviet Union invades Afghanistan		U.S. military buildup begins		
			U.S. and China restore relations		AIDS first reported in U.S.		
			Three Mile Island nuclear accident				

CHAPTER THIRTY-THREE

FROM "THE AGE OF LIMITS" TO THE AGE OF REAGAN

Politics and Diplomacy after Watergate
The Rise of the New American Right
The "Reagan Revolution"
America and the Waning of the Cold War

The frustrations of the early 1970s—the defeat in Vietnam, the Watergate crisis, the decay of the American economy—inflicted damaging blows to the confident, optimistic nationalism that had characterized so much of the postwar era. Some Americans responded to these problems by announcing the arrival of an "age of limits," in which America would have to learn to live with increasingly constricted expectations. By the end of the decade, however, another response to the challenges was gaining strength—one that combined a conservative retreat from some of the heady visions of the 1960s with a reinforced commitment to the idea of economic growth, international power, and American virtue.

1984	1985	1986	1987	1988	1989	1990	1991	1992
Reagan reelected	Reagan and Gorbachev meet	U.S. bombs Libya	Gorbachev visits U.S.	Bush elected president	Berlin Wall dismantled	Iraq invades Kuwait	Collapse of Soviet regime	Los Angeles race riots
	Crack cocaine appears in U.S. cities	Iran-contra scandal revealed	Stock market falls		Communist regimes collapse		Persian Gulf War	Clinton elected president
					U.S. troops in Panama			
					Human Genome Project launched			

POLITICS AND DIPLOMACY AFTER WATERGATE

In the aftermath of Richard Nixon's ignominious departure from office, many wondered whether faith in the presidency, and in the government as a whole, could easily be restored. The administrations of the two presidents who succeeded Nixon did little to answer those questions.

The Ford Custodianship

Gerald Ford inherited the presidency under unenviable circumstances. He had to try to rebuild confidence in government in the wake of the Watergate scandals. And he had to try to restore prosperity in the face of major economic difficulties.

Nixon Pardoned

The new president's effort to establish himself as a symbol of political integrity suffered a setback only a month after he took office, when he granted Richard Nixon "a full, free, and absolute pardon" for any crimes he may have committed during his presidency. The pardon caused a decline in Ford's popularity from which he never fully recovered. Nevertheless, most Americans considered him a decent man; his honesty and amiability did much to reduce the bitterness and acrimony of the Watergate years.

Economic Problems

The Ford administration enjoyed less success in its effort to solve the problems of the economy. In his efforts to curb inflation, the president called for largely ineffective voluntary efforts. After supporting high interest rates, opposing increased federal spending (through liberal use of his veto power), and resisting pressures for a tax reduction, Ford had to deal with a serious recession in 1974 and 1975. Central to the economic problems was the continuing energy crisis. In the aftermath of the Arab oil embargo of 1973, the OPEC cartel raised the price of oil—by 400 percent in 1974 alone—one of the principal reasons why inflation reached 11 percent in 1976.

Ford retained Henry Kissinger as secretary of state and continued the general policies of the Nixon years. Late in 1974, Ford met with Leonid Brezhnev at Vladivostok in Siberia and signed an arms control accord that was to serve as the basis for SALT II, thus achieving a goal the Nixon administration had long sought. Meanwhile, in the Middle East, Henry Kissinger helped produce a new accord by which Israel agreed to return large portions of the occupied Sinai to Egypt, and the two nations pledged not to resolve future differences by force.

1976 Election

As the 1976 presidential election approached, Ford's policies were coming under attack from both the right and the left. In the Republican primary campaign, Ford faced a powerful challenge from former California governor Ronald Reagan, leader of the party's conservative wing, who spoke for many on the right who opposed any agreements with communists. The president only barely survived the assault to win his party's nomination. The Democrats, in the meantime,

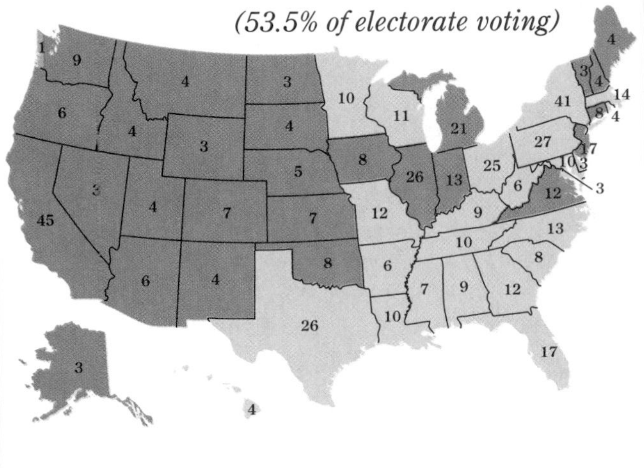

	ELECTORAL VOTE	POPULAR VOTE (%)
Jimmy Carter *(Democratic)*	297	40,828,587 (50.0)
Gerald R. Ford *(Republican)*	240	39,147,613 (47.9)
Ronald Reagan *(Independent Republican)*	1	—
Other candidates *(McCarthy [Ind.], Libertarian)*	—	1,575,459 (2.1)

THE ELECTION OF 1976 Jimmy Carter, a former governor of Georgia, swept the South in the 1976 election and carried enough of the industrial states of the Northeast and Midwest to win a narrow victory over President Gerald R. Ford. His showing indicated the importance to the Democratic Party of having a candidate capable of attracting support in the South, which was becoming increasingly Republican by the 1970s. ◆ *What drove so many southerners into the Republican Party?*

were gradually uniting behind a new and, before 1976, almost entirely unknown candidate: Jimmy Carter, a former governor of Georgia who appealed to the general unhappiness with Washington by offering honesty, piety, and an outsider's skepticism of the federal government. Unhappiness with the economy and a general disenchantment with Ford enabled the Democrat to win a narrow victory. Carter received 50 percent of the popular vote to Ford's 47.9 percent and 297 electoral votes to Ford's 240.

The Trials of Jimmy Carter

Like Ford, Jimmy Carter assumed the presidency at a moment when the nation faced problems of staggering complexity and difficulty. But Carter seemed at times to make his predicament worse by a style of leadership that many considered self-righteous and inflexible.

Carter devoted much of his time to the problems of energy and the economy. Entering office in the midst of a recession, he moved first to reduce unemployment by raising public spending and cutting federal taxes. Unemployment declined, but inflation soared—mostly because of the continuing, sharp increases in energy prices by OPEC. During Carter's last two years in office, retail prices rose at well over a 10 percent annual rate. Like Nixon and Ford before him, Carter responded with a combination of tight money and calls for voluntary restraint. The conservative economists he appointed to head the Federal Reserve Board, determined to stop inflation, helped push interest rates to the highest levels in American history; at times, they exceeded 20 percent.

Soaring Inflation

In the summer of 1979, instability in the Middle East produced a second major fuel shortage in the United States. In the midst of the crisis, OPEC announced another major price increase. Faced with increasing pressure to act, Carter retreated to Camp David, the presidential retreat in the Maryland mountains. Ten days later, he emerged to deliver a remarkable television address. It included a series of proposals for resolving the energy crisis. But it was most notable for Carter's bleak assessment of the national condition and his claim that there was a "crisis of confidence" that had struck "at the very heart and soul of our national will." The address became known as the "malaise" speech (although Carter himself had never used that word), and it helped fuel charges that the president was trying to blame his own problems on the American people. Carter's sudden firing of several members of his cabinet a few days later deepened his political problems.

Human Rights and National Interests

Among Jimmy Carter's most frequent campaign promises was a pledge to build a new basis for American foreign policy, one in which the defense of "human rights" would replace the pursuit of "selfish interests." Carter spoke out sharply and often about violations of human rights in many countries (including, most prominently, the Soviet Union). But the Carter administration also focused on several more traditional concerns. Carter completed negotiations begun several years earlier on a pair of treaties to turn over control of the Panama Canal to the government of Panama. After an acrimonious debate, the Senate ratified the treaties by 68 to 32, only one vote more than the necessary two-thirds majority.

Panama Canal Treaty

Carter's greatest success was in arranging a peace treaty between Egypt and Israel. Middle East negotiations had seemed hopelessly stalled when Egyptian president Anwar Sadat accepted an invitation in November 1977 from Prime Minister Menachem Begin to visit Israel. In Tel Aviv, he announced that Egypt was now willing to accept the state of Israel as a legitimate political entity.

When talks between Israeli and Egyptian negotiators stalled, Carter invited Sadat and Begin to a summit conference at Camp David in September

FORGING THE CAMP DAVID ACCORDS Probably the greatest achievement of Jimmy Carter's generally frustrating presidency was his success in guiding Israel and Egypt toward a peaceful settlement of their longstanding grievances. While hosting Israeli Prime Minister Menachem Begin *(right)* and Egyptian president Anwar Sadat *(left)* at his Camp David retreat in September 1978, he helped the two leaders reach a historic agreement. *(UPI/Corbis-Bettmann)*

1978, and persuaded them to remain there for two weeks while he and others helped mediate the disputes between them. On September 17, Carter escorted the two leaders into the White House to announce agreement on a "framework" for an Egyptian-Israeli peace treaty. On March 26, 1979, Begin and Sadat returned together to the White House to sign a formal peace treaty between their two nations known as the Camp David Accords.

Camp David Accords

In the meantime, Carter continued trying to improve relations with China and the Soviet Union. He responded eagerly to the overtures of Deng Xiaoping, the new Chinese leader who was attempting to open his nation to the outside world. On December 15, 1978, Washington and Beijing announced the resumption of formal diplomatic relations. A few months later, Carter traveled to Vienna to meet with the aging and ailing Brezhnev to finish drafting the new SALT II arms control agreement, which set limits on the number of long-range missiles, bombers, and nuclear warheads on each side. Almost immediately, however, SALT II met with fierce conservative opposition in the United States.

The Year of the Hostages

Ever since the early 1950s, the United States had provided political support and, more recently, massive military assistance to the government of the Shah of Iran, hoping to make his nation a bulwark against Soviet expansion in the Middle East. By 1979, however, the Shah was in deep trouble with his

own people. Many Iranians resented the repressive, authoritarian tactics through which the Shah had maintained his autocratic rule. At the same time, Islamic clergy (and much of the fiercely religious populace) opposed his efforts to modernize and westernize Iranian society. The combination of resentments produced a powerful revolutionary movement. In January 1979, the Shah fled the country.

Ayatollah Ruhollah Khomeini

By late 1979, power in Iran resided with a zealous religious leader, the Ayatollah Ruhollah Khomeini, who was fiercely anti-western and anti-American. In late October 1979, the deposed Shah arrived in New York to be treated for cancer. Days later, on November 4, an armed mob invaded the American embassy in Teheran, seized the diplomats and military personnel inside, and demanded the return of the Shah to Iran in exchange for their freedom. Fifty-three Americans remained hostages in the embassy for over a year.

Afghanistan Invaded

Only weeks after the hostage seizure, on December 27, 1979, Soviet troops invaded Afghanistan, the mountainous Islamic nation lying between the USSR and Iran. The Soviet Union had in fact been a power in Afghanistan for years, and the dominant force since April 1978. But while some observers claimed that the Soviet invasion was a Russian attempt to secure the status quo, Carter claimed it was a Russian "stepping stone to their possible control over much of the world's oil supplies" and the "gravest threat to world peace since World War II." Carter angrily imposed a series of economic sanctions on the Russians, canceled American participation in the 1980 summer Olympic Games in Moscow, and announced the withdrawal of SALT II from Senate consideration.

THE RISE OF THE NEW AMERICAN RIGHT

The jarring social and economic changes in American life in the 1960s and 1970s disillusioned many liberals, perplexed the already weakened left, and provided the right with its most important opportunity in generations to seize a position of authority in American life.

The Sunbelt and Its Politics

The most widely discussed demographic phenomenon of the 1970s was the rise of what became known as the "Sunbelt"—a term created to describe a collection of regions that emerged together in the postwar era to become the most dynamically growing parts of the country. The Sunbelt included the Southeast (particularly Florida), the Southwest (particularly Texas), and above all, California, which became the nation's most populous state in 1964, and continued to grow dramatically in the years that followed. By 1980, the population of the Sunbelt had risen to exceed that of the older industrial regions of the North and the East.

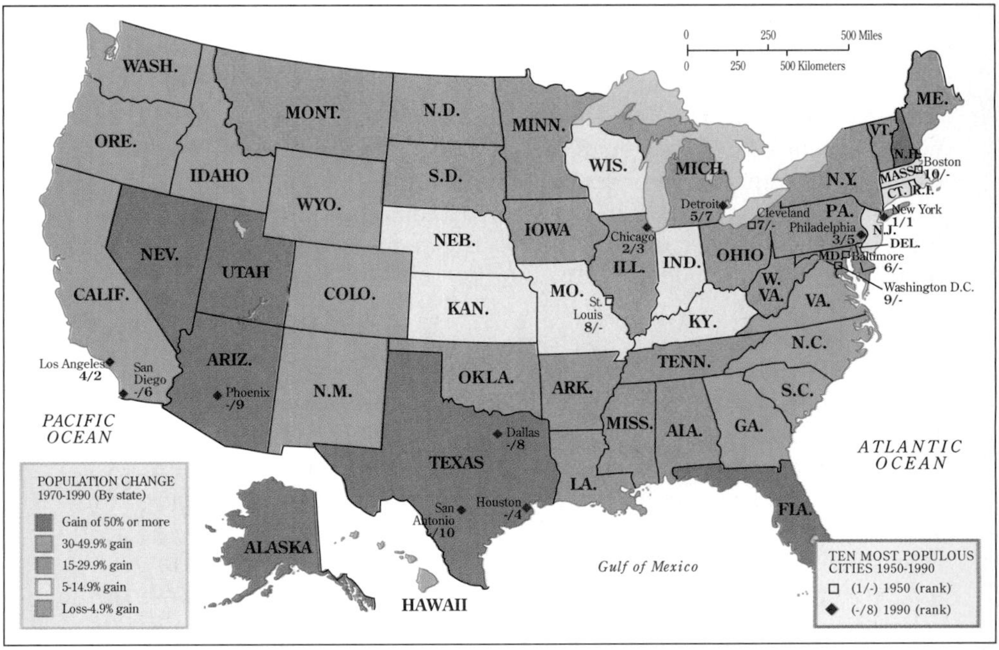

GROWTH OF THE SUNBELT, 1970–1990 One of the most important demographic changes of the last decades of the twentieth century was the shift of population out of traditional population centers in the Northeast and Midwest and toward the states of the so-called "Sunbelt"—most notably the Southwest and the Pacific coast. This map gives a dramatic illustration of the changing concentration of population between 1970 and 1990. The pale green states are those that lost population, while the purple and dark green states are those that made very significant gains (30 percent or more). ◆ *What was the impact of this population shift on the politics of the 1980s?*

The rise of the Sunbelt helped produce a change in the political climate. The strong populist traditions in the South and the West helped produce a strong opposition to the growth of government and a resentment of the proliferating regulations and restrictions that the liberal state was producing. Many of those regulations and restrictions—environmental laws, land-use restrictions, even the fifty-five-mile-per-hour speed limit created during the energy crisis to force motorists to conserve fuel—affected the West more than any other region. White southerners equated the federal government's effort to change racial norms in the region with what they believed was the tyranny of Reconstruction.

Growing Opposition to Government Regulation

The so-called Sagebrush Rebellion, which emerged in parts of the West in the late 1970s, mobilized conservative opposition to environmental laws and restrictions on development. It also sought to portray the West (which had benefited substantially from federal investment) as a victim of government control. Its members complained about the very large amounts of land the federal government owned in many western states and demanded that the land be opened for development.

Sagebrush Rebellion

Suburbanization also fueled the rise of the right. Not all suburbs bred conservative politics, of course; but the most militantly conservative communities in America—among them Orange County in southern California—were mostly suburbs. Many suburbs insulated their residents from contact with different groups—through the relative homogeneity of the population, through the transferring of retail and even work space into suburban office parks and shopping malls. The seemingly tranquil life of the suburb reinforced the conservative view that other parts of the nation—cities in particular—were abandoning the values and norms that society required.

Religious Revivalism

In the 1960s, organized religion had experienced a conspicuous decline. But in the 1970s the United States experienced the beginning of a major religious revival. Some of the new religious enthusiasm found expression in the rise of various cults and pseudo-faiths: the Church of Scientology; the Unification Church of the Reverend Sun Myung Moon; even the tragic People's Temple, whose members committed mass suicide in their jungle retreat in Guyana in 1978. But the most important impulse of the religious revival was the growth of evangelical Christianity.

Surging Evangelicalism

Evangelicals have in common a belief in personal conversion (being "born again") through direct communication with God. Evangelical religion had been the dominant form of Christianity in America through much of its history, and a substantial subculture since the late nineteenth century. In its modern form, it became increasingly visible during the early 1950s, when evangelicals such as Billy Graham and Pentecostals such as Oral Roberts began to attract huge national (and international) followings for their energetic revivalism.

By the late 1970s, evangelical Christians were becoming more visible and more assertive. More than 70 million Americans now described themselves as "born-again" Christians—men and women who had established a "direct personal relationship with Jesus." Christian evangelicals owned their own newspapers, magazines, radio stations, and television networks. They operated their own schools and universities. And one of them ultimately occupied the White House itself—Jimmy Carter, who during the 1976 campaign had talked proudly of his own "conversion experience" and who continued openly to proclaim his "born-again" Christian faith during his years in office.

For Jimmy Carter and for some others, evangelical Christianity had formed the basis for a commitment to racial and economic justice and world peace. For many evangelicals, however, the message of the new religion was very different—but no less political. In the 1970s, some Christian evangelicals became active on the political and cultural right. They were alarmed by what they considered the spread of immorality and disorder in American life; and they were concerned about the way a secular cul-

ture was intruding into their communities and schools and families. Many evangelical men and women feared the growth of feminism and the threat they believed it posed to the traditional family, and they resented the way in which government policies advanced the goals of the women's movement. Particularly alarming to them were Supreme Court decisions eliminating all religious observance from schools and, later, the decision guaranteeing women the right to an abortion.

By the late 1970s, the "Christian right" had become a powerful political force. Jerry Falwell, a fundamentalist minister in Virginia with a substantial television audience, launched a highly visible movement he called the Moral Majority. The Pentecostal minister Pat Robertson began a political movement of his own and, in the 1990s, launched an organization known as the Christian Coalition. These and other organizations of the Christian right opposed federal interference in local affairs; denounced abortion, divorce, feminism, and homosexuality; defended unrestricted free enterprise; and supported a strong American posture in the world. Some denied the scientific doctrine of evolution and instead urged the teaching in schools of the biblical story of the Creation. Their goal was a new era in which Christian values once again dominated American life.

Christian Coalition

The Emergence of the New Right

Evangelical Christians were an important part, but only a part, of what became known as the new right—a diverse but powerful movement that enjoyed rapid growth in the 1970s and early 1980s. It had begun to take shape after the 1964 election, in which Barry Goldwater had suffered his shattering defeat. Energetic organizers responded to that disaster by building a new and powerful set of right-wing institutions to help conservatives campaign more effectively in the future. Beginning in the 1970s, largely because of these organizational advances, conservatives found themselves almost always better funded and organized than their opponents. By the late 1970s, there were right-wing think tanks, consulting firms, lobbyists, foundations, and scholarly centers.

Barry Goldwater

Another factor in the revival of the right was the emergence of a credible right-wing leadership in the late 1960s and early 1970s in the person of Ronald Reagan. Once a moderately successful actor, he had moved into politics in the early 1960s and in 1964 delivered a memorable television speech on behalf of Goldwater. After Goldwater's defeat, he worked quickly to seize the leadership of the conservative wing of the party. In 1966, with the support of a group of wealthy conservatives, he won the first of two terms as governor of California.

The presidency of Gerald Ford also played an important role in the rise of the right. Ford, probably without realizing it, touched on some of the right's rawest nerves. He appointed as vice president Nelson Rockefeller,

the liberal Republican governor of New York and an heir to one of America's great fortunes; many conservatives had been demonizing Rockefeller and his family for more than twenty years. Ford proposed an amnesty program for draft resisters, embraced and even extended the hated Nixon-Kissinger policies of détente, presided over the fall of Vietnam, and agreed to cede the Panama Canal to Panama. When Reagan challenged Ford in the 1976 Republican primaries, the president survived, barely, only by dumping Nelson Rockefeller from the ticket and agreeing to a platform largely written by conservatives.

The Tax Revolt

At least equally important to the success of the new right was a new and potent conservative issue: the tax revolt. It had its public beginnings in 1978, when Howard Jarvis, a conservative activist in California, launched the first successful major citizens' tax revolt in California with Proposition 13, a referendum question on the state ballot rolling back property tax rates. Similar antitax movements soon began in other states and eventually spread to national politics.

Proposition 13

In Proposition 13 and similar initiatives, members of the right succeeded in separating the issue of taxes from the issue of what taxes supported. Instead of attacking popular programs such as Social Security, they attacked taxes themselves and argued that much of the money government raised through taxes was wasted. Virtually no one liked to pay taxes, and as the economy grew weaker and the relative burden of paying taxes grew heavier, that resentment naturally rose.

The Campaign of 1980

By the time of the crises in Iran and Afghanistan, Jimmy Carter was in desperate political trouble—his standing in popularity polls lower than that of any president in history. Senator Edward Kennedy, younger brother of John and Robert Kennedy, challenged him in the primaries. And while Carter managed to withstand the confrontation with Kennedy and win his party's nomination, Carter's campaign aroused little popular enthusiasm as he prepared to face a powerful challenge.

Challenge from Kennedy

The Republican Party, in the meantime, had rallied enthusiastically behind the man who, four years earlier, had nearly stolen the nomination from Gerald Ford. Ronald Reagan was a sharp critic of the excesses of the federal government. He linked his campaign to the spreading tax revolt by promising substantial tax cuts. He also championed a restoration of American "strength" and "pride" in the world.

1980 Election

On election day 1980, the anniversary of the seizure of the hostages in Iran, Reagan swept to victory, winning 51 percent of the vote to 41 percent for Jimmy Carter,

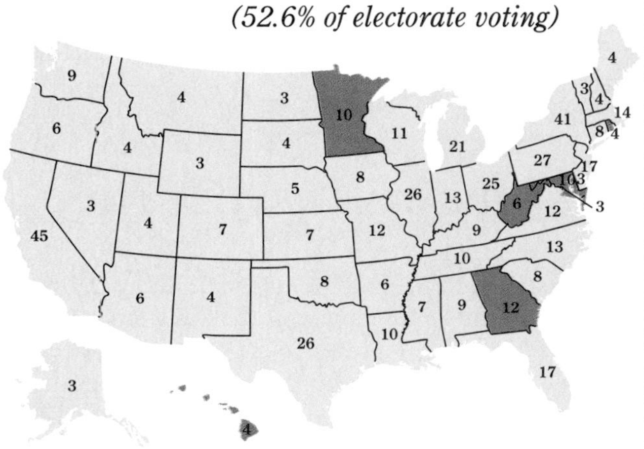

	ELECTORAL VOTE	POPULAR VOTE (%)
Ronald Reagan *(Republican)*	489	43,901,812 (50.7)
Jimmy Carter *(Democratic)*	49	35,483,820 (41.0)
John B. Anderson *(Independent)*	—	5,719,722 (6.6)
Other candidates *(Libertarian)*	—	921,299 (1.1)

THE ELECTION OF 1980 Although Ronald Reagan won only slightly more than half of the popular vote in the 1980 presidential election, his electoral majority was overwhelming—a reflection to a large degree of the deep unpopularity of President Jimmy Carter in 1980. ◆ *What had made Carter so unpopular?*

For an interactive version of this map go to www.mhhe.com/unfinishednation4ch33maps

and 7 percent for John Anderson—a moderate Republican congressman from Illinois who had mounted an independent campaign. The Republican Party won control of the Senate for the first time since 1952; and although the Democrats retained a modest majority in the House, the lower chamber too seemed firmly in the hands of conservatives.

On the day of Reagan's inauguration, the American hostages in Iran were released after their 444-day ordeal. The government of Iran, desperate for funds to support its floundering war against neighboring Iraq, had ordered the hostages freed in return for a release of billions in Iranian assets that the Carter administration had frozen in American banks. Americans welcomed the hostages home with demonstrations of joy and patriotism not seen since the end of World War II. But while the celebration in

1945 had marked a great American triumph, the euphoria in 1981 marked something quite different—a troubled nation grasping for reassurance. Ronald Reagan set out to provide it.

THE "REAGAN REVOLUTION"

Ronald Reagan assumed the presidency in January 1981 promising a change in government more fundamental than any since the New Deal of fifty years before. While his eight years in office produced a significant shift in public policy, they brought nothing so fundamental as many of his supporters had hoped or his opponents had feared. But Reagan succeeded brilliantly in making his own engaging personality the central fact of American politics in the 1980s. He also benefited from the power of the diverse coalition that had united behind him.

The Reagan Coalition

The Reagan coalition included a relatively small but highly influential group of wealthy Americans firmly committed to capitalism and to unfettered economic growth. They believed that the market offers the best solutions to most problems, and they shared a deep hostility to most (although not all) government interference in markets. Central to this group's agenda in the 1980s was opposition to what it considered the "redistributive" politics of the federal government (and especially its highly progressive tax structure) and hostility to the rise of what they believed were "antibusiness" government regulations. Reagan courted these free-market conservatives carefully and effectively, and in the end it was their interests his administration most effectively served.

Free-Market Conservatives

A second element of the Reagan coalition was a small but influential group of intellectuals commonly known as "neo-conservatives," who gave to the right something it had not had in many years—a firm base among "opinion leaders," people with access to the most influential public forums for ideas. Many of these people had once been liberals and, before that, socialists. But during the turmoil of the 1960s, they had become alarmed by what they considered a dangerous and destructive radicalism. Neo-conservatives were sympathetic to the complaints and demands of capitalists, but their principal concern was to reassert legitimate authority and reaffirm Western democratic, anticommunist values and commitments. They considered themselves engaged in a battle to "win back the culture"—from the crass, radical ideas that had polluted it.

"Neo-Conservatives"

RONALD AND NANCY REAGAN The president and the first lady greet guests at a White House social event. Nancy Reagan was most visible in her efforts to make the White House, and her husband's presidency, seem more glamorous than those of most recent administrations. But she also played an important, if quiet, policy role in the administration. *(Dirck Halstead/Getty Images)*

These groups formed an uneasy alliance with what became known as the "new right." The new right shared a fundamental distrust of the "eastern establishment": a suspicion of its motives and goals; a sense that it exercised a dangerous, secret power in American life. These populist conservatives expressed the kinds of concerns that outsiders, non-elites, have traditionally voiced in American society: an opposition to centralized power and influence, a fear of living in a world where distant, hostile forces are controlling society and threatening individual freedom and community autonomy. It was a testament to Ronald Reagan's political skills and personal charm that he was able to generate enthusiastic support from these populist conservatives while at the same time appealing to more elite conservative groups whose concerns were in many ways antithetical to those of the new right.

Reagan in the White House

Reagan's Personal Appeal

Even many people who disagreed with Reagan's policies found themselves drawn to his attractive and carefully honed public image. He turned seventy a few weeks after taking office and was the oldest man ever to serve as president. But through most of his presidency, he appeared to be vigorous, resilient, even youthful. When he was wounded in an assassination attempt in 1981, he joked with doctors on his way into surgery and appeared to bounce back from the ordeal with remarkable speed. Even when things went wrong, as they often did, the blame seldom seemed to attach to Reagan himself (inspiring some Democrats to begin referring to him as the "Teflon president").

Reagan was not much involved in the day-to-day affairs of running the government; he surrounded himself with tough, energetic administrators who insulated him from many of the pressures of the office and who apparently relied on him largely for general guidance, not specific decisions. At times, the president revealed a startling ignorance about the nature of his own policies or the actions of his subordinates. But Reagan did make active use of his office to generate public support for his administration's programs.

"Supply-Side" Economics

Reaganomics

Reagan's 1980 campaign for the presidency had promised to restore the economy to health by a bold experiment that became known as "supply-side" economics or, to some, "Reaganomics." Supply-side economics operated from the assumption that the woes of the American economy were in large part a result of excessive taxation, which left inadequate capital available to investors to stimulate growth. The solution, therefore, was to reduce taxes, with particularly generous benefits to corporations and wealthy individuals, in order to encourage new investments.

Tax Cuts

In its first months in office, the new administration hastily assembled a legislative program based on the supply-side idea. It proposed $40 billion in budget reductions and managed to win congressional approval of almost all of them. In addition, the president proposed a bold three-year, 30 percent reduction on both individual and corporate tax rates. In the summer of 1981, Congress passed it too, after lowering the reductions to 25 percent. Reagan was successful because he had a disciplined Republican majority in the Senate, and because the Democratic majority in the House was weak and riddled with defectors.

Men and women whom Reagan appointed fanned out through the executive branch of government committed to reducing the role of government in American economic life. "Deregulation," an idea many Democrats had begun to embrace in the Carter years, became almost a religion

in the Reagan administration. Secretary of the Interior James Watt had been a major figure in the Sagebrush Rebellion, a movement among western conservatives to fight federal environmental regulations, which they believed had a particularly devastating effect on their region's economy. Watt opened up public lands and water to development. The Environmental Protection Agency (before its directors were indicted for corruption) relaxed or entirely eliminated enforcement of major environmental laws and regulations.

By early 1982, however, the nation had sunk into the most severe recession since the 1930s. The Reagan economic program was not directly to blame for the problems, but neither did it offer a quick solution to them. In 1982 unemployment reached 11 percent, its highest level in over forty years. But before the recession could do great damage to Reagan, the economy recovered more rapidly and impressively than almost anyone had expected. By late 1983, unemployment had fallen to 8.2 percent, and it declined steadily for several years after that. The gross national product had grown 3.6 percent in a year, the largest increase since the mid-1970s. Inflation had fallen below 5 percent. The economy continued to grow, and both inflation and unemployment remained low through most of the decade.

Economic Recovery

The recovery was a result of many things. The years of tight money policies by the Federal Reserve Board had helped lower inflation; perhaps equally important, the Board had lowered interest rates early in 1983 in response to the recession. A worldwide "energy glut" and the virtual collapse of the OPEC cartel had produced at least a temporary end to the inflationary pressures of spiraling fuel costs. And staggering federal budget deficits were pumping billions of dollars into the flagging economy. As a result, consumer spending and business investment both increased. The stock market rose up from its doldrums of the 1970s and began a sustained and historic boom. In August 1982, the Dow Jones Industrial Average stood at 777. Five years later it had passed 2,000. Despite a frightening crash in the fall of 1987, the market continued to grow for more than another decade: in early 2000, the Dow Jones average briefly passed 11,000.

The Fiscal Crisis

The economic revival did little at first to reduce the staggering, and to many Americans alarming, federal budget deficits (the gap between revenue and spending in a single year) or to slow the growth in the national debt (the debt the nation accumulates over time as a result of its annual deficits). By the mid-1980s, this growing fiscal crisis had become one of the central issues in American politics. Having entered office promising a balanced budget within four years, Reagan presided over record budget deficits and accumulated more debt in his eight years in office than the American government had accumulated in

Growing Budget Deficits

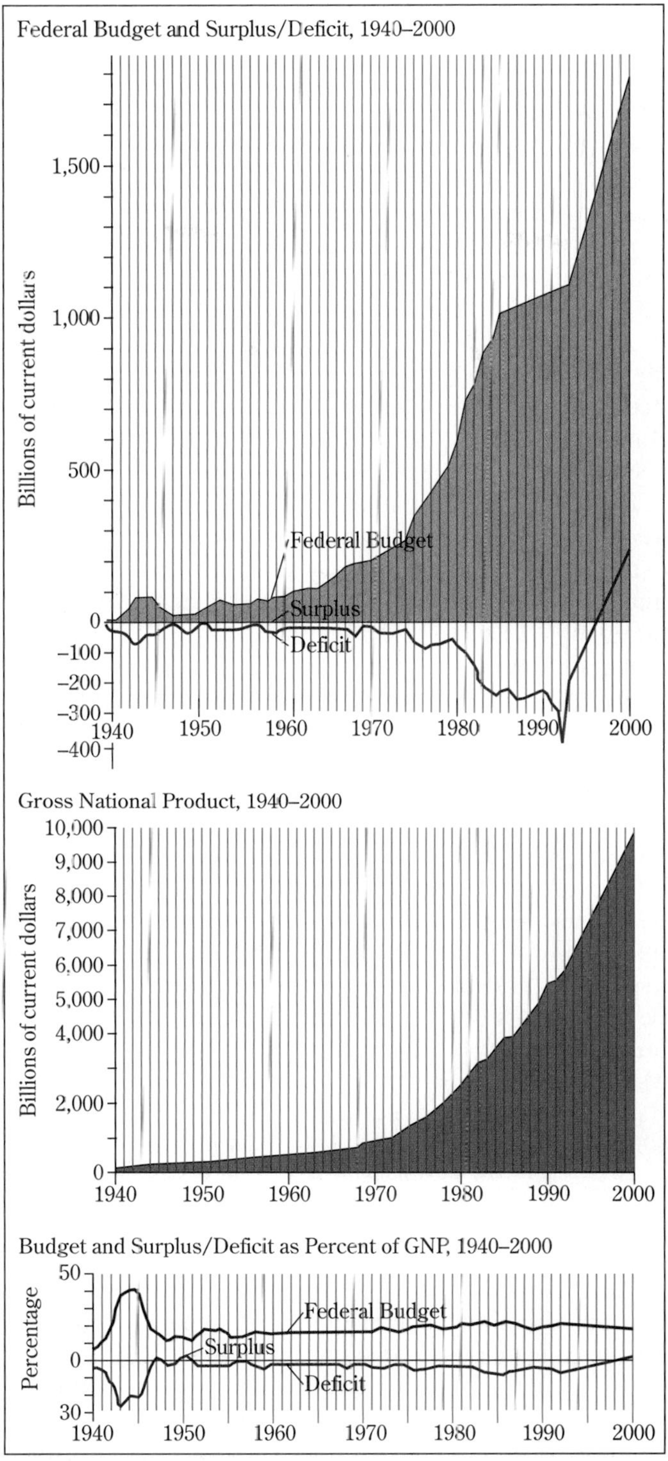

FEDERAL BUDGET SURPLUS/DEFICIT, 1940 TO 2000 These charts help illustrate why the pattern of federal deficits seemed so alarming to Americans in the 1980s, and also why those deficits proved much less damaging to the economy than many predicted. ◆ *What factors contributed to the increasing deficits of the 1980s? How were those deficits eliminated in the 1990s?*

its entire previous history. Before the 1980s, the highest single-year budget deficit in American history had been $66 billion (in 1976). Throughout the 1980s, the annual budget deficit consistently exceeded $100 billion (and in 1991 peaked at $268 billion). The national debt rose from $907 billion in 1980 to nearly $3.5 trillion by 1991.

The enormous deficits had many causes. The budget suffered from enormous increases in the costs of "entitlement" programs (especially Social Security and Medicare), a result of the aging of the population and dramatic increases in the cost of health care. The 1981 tax cuts, the largest in American history, also contributed to the deficit. The massive increase in military spending on which the Reagan administration insisted added much more to the federal budget than its cuts in domestic spending removed.

In the face of these deficits, the administration proposed further cuts in "discretionary" domestic spending, which included many programs aimed at the poorest (and politically weakest) Americans. By the end of Reagan's third year in office, funding for domestic programs had been cut nearly as far as Congress (and, apparently, the public) was willing to tolerate, and still no end to the rising deficit was in sight. By the late 1980s, many fiscal conservatives were calling for a constitutional amendment mandating a balanced budget—a provision the president himself claimed to support. But Congress never approved the amendment.

Reagan and the World

Relations with the Soviet Union, which had been steadily deteriorating in the last years of the Carter administration, grew still chillier in the first years of the Reagan presidency. The president spoke harshly of the Soviet regime (which he once called the "evil empire"), accusing it of sponsoring world terrorism and declaring that any armaments negotiations must be linked to negotiations on Soviet behavior in other areas. Although the president had long denounced the SALT II arms control treaty as unfavorable to the United States, he continued to honor its provisions. But the Reagan administration at first made little progress toward arms control in other areas. In fact, the president proposed the most ambitious (and potentially most expensive) new military program in many years: the Strategic Defense Initiative (SDI), widely known as "Star Wars" (after the popular movie of that name). Reagan claimed that SDI, through the use of lasers and satellites, could provide an effective shield against incoming missiles and thus make nuclear war obsolete. The Soviet Union claimed that the new program would elevate the arms race to new and more dangerous levels (a complaint many domestic critics of SDI shared) and insisted that any arms control agreement begin with an American abandonment of SDI.

"Star Wars"

The escalation of Cold War tensions and the slowing of arms control initiatives helped produce an important popular movement in Europe and

the United States calling for an end to nuclear weapons buildups. In America, the principal goal of the movement was a "nuclear freeze," an agreement between the two superpowers not to expand their atomic arsenals. In what many believed was the largest mass demonstration in American history, nearly a million people rallied in New York City's Central Park in 1982 to support the freeze. Perhaps partly in response to this growing pressure, the administration began tentative efforts to revive arms control negotiations in 1983.

Reagan Doctrine

It also created a new policy, which became known as the Reagan Doctrine, to help groups resisting communism in the Third World. The most conspicuous examples of the new activism came in Latin America. In October 1982, the administration sent American soldiers and marines into the tiny Caribbean island of Grenada to oust an anti-American Marxist regime that showed signs of forging a relationship with Moscow. In El Salvador, whose government was fighting left-wing revolutionaries, the administation provided increased military and economic assistance. In neighboring Nicaragua, a pro-American dictatorship had fallen to the revolutionary "Sandinistas" in 1979; the new government had grown increasingly anti-American (and increasingly Marxist) throughout the early 1980s. The Reagan administration supported the so-called contras, an antigovernment guerrilla movement fighting (without great success) to topple the Sandinista regime.

In other parts of the world, the administration's tough rhetoric seemed to hide an instinctive restraint. In June 1982, the Israeli army launched an invasion of Lebanon in an effort to drive guerrillas of the Palestinian Liberation Organization from the country. An American peacekeeping force entered Beirut to supervise the evacuation of PLO forces from Lebanon. American marines then remained in the city, apparently to protect the fragile Lebanese government. Now identified with one faction in the struggle, Americans became the targets in 1983 of a terrorist bombing of a U.S. military barracks in Beirut that left 241 marines dead. Rather than become more deeply involved in the Lebanese struggle, Reagan withdrew American forces.

The disaster in Lebanon was an example of the changing character of Third World struggles: an increasing reliance on terrorism by otherwise powerless groups to advance their political aims. A series of terrorist acts in the 1980s—attacks on airplanes, cruise ships, commercial and diplomatic posts; the seizing of American and other Western hostages—alarmed and frightened much of the Western world. The Reagan administration spoke bravely about its resolve to punish terrorism; and at one point in 1986, the president ordered American planes to bomb sites in Tripoli, the capital of Libya, whose controversial leader Muammar al-Qaddafi was widely believed to be a leading sponsor of terrorism. In general, however, American leaders had little success in identifying or controlling terrorists.

Terrorism

The Election of 1984

Reagan approached the campaign of 1984 at the head of a united Republican Party firmly committed to his candidacy. The Democrats nominated former vice president Walter Mondale, the early frontrunner, who fought off challenges from Senator Gary Hart of Colorado and the magnetic Jesse Jackson, who had established himself as the nation's most prominent spokesman for minorities and the poor. Mondale brought momentary excitement to the Democratic campaign by selecting a woman, Representative Geraldine Ferraro of New York, to be his running mate and the first female candidate ever to appear on a national ticket.

Reagan Reelected

Reagan's triumphant campaign scarcely took note of his opponents and spoke instead of what he claimed was the remarkable revival of American fortunes and spirits under his leadership. His victory in 1984 was decisive. He won approximately 59 percent of the vote, and carried every state but Mondale's native Minnesota and the District of Columbia. But Reagan was much stronger than his party. Democrats gained a seat in the Senate and maintained only slightly reduced control of the House of Representatives.

To many Reagan supporters, the 1984 election seemed to be the dawn of a new conservative era. But almost no one anticipated the revolutionary changes that would change the world, and America's place in it, within a very few years. The election of 1984, therefore, was not so much the first of a new era as the last of an old one. It was the final campaign of the Cold War.

AMERICA AND THE WANING OF THE COLD WAR

Many factors contributed to the collapse of the Soviet empire. The long, stalemated war in Afghanistan proved at least as disastrous to the Soviet Union as the Vietnam War had been to America. The government in Moscow had failed to address a long-term economic decline in the Soviet republics and the Eastern-bloc nations. Restiveness with the heavy-handed policies of communist police states was growing throughout much of the Soviet empire. But the most visible factor at the time was the emergence of Mikhail Gorbachev, who succeeded to the leadership of the Soviet Union in 1985 and, to the surprise of almost everyone (probably including himself), very quickly became the most revolutionary figure in world politics in at least four decades.

Mikhail Gorbachev

SMASHING THE WALL Once it became clear in November 1989 that the East German government was no longer defending the wall that had divided Berlin for nearly thirty years, Germans on both sides of the divide swarmed over it in celebration. Here, a West German takes a sledgehammer to the already battered wall as East German border guards passively look on. *(Reuters/Corbis-Bettmann)*

The Fall of the Soviet Union

Glasnost and Perestroika

Gorbachev quickly transformed Soviet politics with two dramatic new initiatives. The first he called *glasnost* (openness): the dismantling of many of the repressive mechanisms that had been conspicuous features of Soviet life for over half a century. The other policy Gorbachev called *perestroika* (reform): an effort to restructure the rigid and unproductive Soviet economy by introducing, among other things, such elements of capitalism as private ownership and the profit motive. He also began to transform Soviet foreign policy.

The severe economic problems at home evidently convinced Gorbachev that the Soviet Union could no longer sustain its extended commitments around the world. As early as 1987, he began reducing Soviet influence in Eastern Europe. And in 1989, in the space of a few months, every communist state in Europe—Poland, Hungary, Czechoslovakia, Bulgaria, Romania, East Germany, Yugoslavia, and Albania—either overthrew its government or forced it to transform itself into an essentially noncommunist (and in some cases, actively anticommunist) regime.

In May 1989, students in China launched a mass movement calling for greater democratization. But in June, hard-line leaders seized control of the government and sent military forces to crush the uprising. The result was a bloody massacre on June 3, 1989, in Tiananmen Square in Beijing, in which an unknown number of demonstrators died. The assault crushed the democracy movement and restored hard-liners to power. It did not, however, stop China's efforts to modernize and even westernize its economy.

Tiananmen Square

But China was an exception to a widespread movement toward democratization. Early in 1990, the government of South Africa, long an international pariah for its rigid enforcement of "apartheid" (a system designed to protect white supremacy), began a cautious retreat from its traditional policies. Among other things, it legalized the chief black party in the nation, the African National Congress (ANC), which had been banned for decades, and released from prison the leader of the ANC, Nelson Mandela, who had been in jail for twenty-seven years. Over the next several years, the South African government repealed its apartheid laws. And in 1994, there were national elections in which all South Africans could participate. As a result, Nelson Mandela became the first black president of South Africa.

In 1991, communism began to collapse in the Soviet Union itself. An unsuccessful coup by hard-line Soviet leaders on August 19 precipitated a dramatic unraveling of communist power. Within days, the coup itself collapsed in the face of resistance from the public and crucial elements within the military. Mikhail Gorbachev returned to power, but it soon became evident that the legitimacy of both the Communist Party and the central Soviet government had been fatally injured. By the end of August, many of the republics of the Soviet Union had declared independence; the Soviet government was clearly powerless to stop the fragmentation. Gorbachev himself finally resigned as leader of the now virtually powerless Communist Party and Soviet government, and the Soviet Union ceased to exist.

Collapse of the USSR

The last years of the Reagan administration coincided with the first years of the Gorbachev regime; and while Reagan was skeptical of Gorbachev at first, he gradually became convinced that the Soviet leader was sincere in his desire for reform. At a summit meeting with Reagan in Reykjavik, Iceland, in 1986, Gorbachev proposed reducing the nuclear arsenals of both sides by 50 percent or more, although continuing disputes over Reagan's commitment to the SDI program prevented agreements. But in 1988, the two superpowers signed a treaty eliminating American and Soviet intermediate-range nuclear forces (INF) from Europe—the most significant arms control agreement of the nuclear age. At about the same time, Gorbachev ended the Soviet Union's long and frustrating military involvement in Afghanistan.

The Fading of the Reagan Revolution

For a time, the dramatic changes around the world and Reagan's personal popularity deflected attention from a series of scandals that might well have destroyed another administration. There were revelations of illegality, corruption, and ethical lapses in the Environmental Protection Agency, the CIA, the Department of Defense, the Department of Labor, the Department of Justice, and the Department of Housing and Urban Development. A more serious scandal emerged within the savings and loan industry, which the Reagan administration had helped deregulate in the early 1980s. By the end of the decade the industry was in chaos, and the government was forced to step in to prevent a complete collapse. The cost of the debacle to the public eventually ran to more than half a trillion dollars.

Savings and Loan Crisis

But the most politically damaging scandal of the Reagan years came to light in November 1986, when the White House conceded that it had sold weapons to the revolutionary government of Iran as part of a largely unsuccessful effort to secure the release of several Americans being held hostage by radical Islamic groups in the Middle East. Even more damaging was the revelation that some of the money from the arms deal with Iran had been covertly and illegally funneled into a fund to aid the contras in Nicaragua.

In the months that followed, aggressive reporting and a series of congressional hearings exposed a widespread pattern of covert activities orchestrated by the White House and dedicated to advancing the administration's foreign policy aims through secret and at times illegal means. The principal figure in this covert world appeared at first to be an obscure marine lieutenant colonel assigned to the staff of the National Security Council, Oliver North. But gradually it became clear that North was acting in concert with other, more powerful figures in the administration. The Iran-contra scandal, as it became known, did serious damage to the Reagan presidency—even though the investigations were never able decisively to tie the president himself to the most serious violations of the law.

Oliver North

The Election of 1988

The fraying of the Reagan administration helped the Democrats regain control of the United States Senate in 1986 and fueled hopes in the party for a presidential victory in 1988. Michael Dukakis, a three-term governor of Massachusetts, eventually captured the nomination, even though he was a dry, even dull campaigner. But Vice President George Bush, the largely unopposed Republican candidate, had also failed to spark any real public enthusiasm. He entered the last months of the campaign well behind Dukakis. Beginning at the Republican Convention, however, Bush staged a remarkable turnaround by making his campaign a long, relentless attack on Dukakis, tying him to all

Bush's Negative Campaign

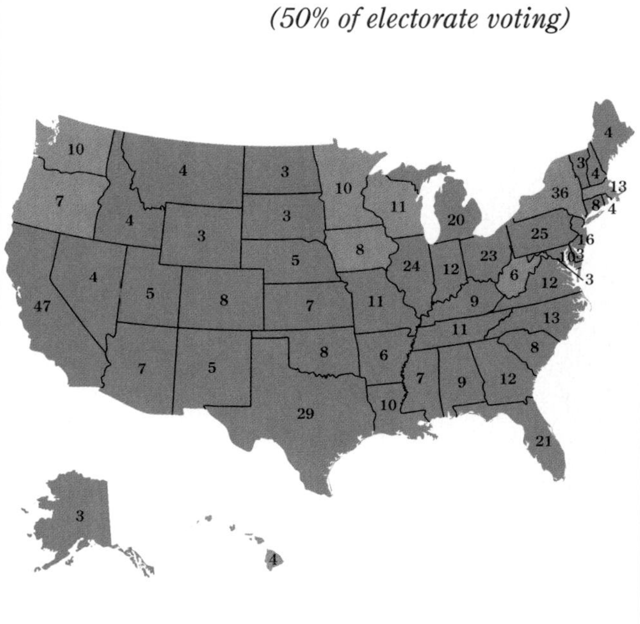

	ELECTORAL VOTE	POPULAR VOTE (%)
George Bush *(Republican)*	426	47, 946, 422 (54.0)
Michael Dukakis *(Democratic)*	112	41, 016, 429 (46.0)

THE ELECTION OF 1988 Democrats had high hopes going into the election of 1988, but Vice President George Bush won a decisive victory over Michael Dukakis, who did only slightly better than Walter Mondale had done four years earlier. ◆ *What made it so difficult for a Democrat to challenge the Republicans in 1988 after eight years of a Republican administration?*

the unpopular social and cultural stances Americans had come to identify with "liberals." Bush won a substantial victory in November: 54 percent of the popular vote to Dukakis's 46 percent, and 426 electoral votes to Dukakis's 112. But Bush carried few Republicans into office with him; the Democrats retained secure majorities in both houses of Congress.

The Bush Presidency

The Bush presidency was notable for the dramatic developments in international affairs with which it coincided and at times helped to advance, and for the absence of important initiatives or ideas on domestic issues.

The broad popularity Bush enjoyed during his first three years in office was partly a result of his subdued, unthreatening public image. But it was primarily because of the wonder and excitement with which Americans

GORBACHEV AND BUSH When Bush became president in 1989, the Cold War with the Soviet Union—although much less intense than it had been several years earlier—was still in progress. By the time he left office in 1993, the Cold War was over; the once "captive nations" of eastern Europe were free of Soviet domination; and the Soviet Union itself had unravelled and dissolved. Much of the impetus for these changes originated with the last Soviet leader, Mikhail Gorbachev, whose efforts at reform unleashed forces he ultimately could not control. But before he lost power, he negotiated a series of historic agreements with the United States—some of them through summit meetings such as this one in Washington in 1990. *(Archive/Ron Sachs/Consolidated News Pictures/Getty Images)*

viewed the dramatic events in the rest of the world. Bush moved cautiously at first in dealing with the changes in the Soviet Union. But like Reagan, he eventually cooperated with Gorbachev and reached a series of significant agreements with the Soviet Union in its waning years. In the three years after the INF agreement in 1988, the United States and the Soviet Union moved rapidly toward even more far-reaching arms reduction agreements.

Arms Reduction

On domestic issues, the Bush administration was less successful—partly because the president himself seemed to have little interest in promoting a domestic agenda and partly because he faced serious obstacles. His administration inherited a staggering burden of debt and a federal deficit that had been out of control for nearly a decade. Any domestic agenda that required significant federal spending was, therefore, incompatible with the president's pledge to reduce the deficit and his 1988 campaign promise of "no new taxes." Bush was constantly concerned about the right wing of his own party and, in his eagerness to ingratiate himself with it, took divisive positions on such cultural issues as abortion and affirmative action that damaged his ability to work with the Democratic Congress.

Despite this political stalemate, Congress and the White House managed on occasion to agree on significant measures. In 1990, the president bowed to congressional pressure and agreed to a significant tax increase as part of a multiyear "budget package" designed to reduce the deficit—thus violating his own 1988 campaign pledge of "no new taxes."

But the most serious domestic problem facing the Bush administration was one for which neither the president nor Congress had any answer: a recession that began late in 1990 and became more serious in 1991 and 1992. Because of the enormous level of debt that corporations (and individuals) had accumulated in the 1980s, the recession caused an unusual number of bankruptcies. It also produced fear and frustration among middle- and working-class Americans.

1990 Recession

The Gulf War

The events of 1989–1991 had left the United States in the unanticipated position of being the only real superpower in the world. The Bush administration, therefore, had to consider what to do with America's formidable political and military power in a world in which the major justification for that power—the Soviet threat—was now gone.

The events of 1989–1991 suggested two possible answers, both of which had some effect on policy. One was that the United States would reduce its military strength dramatically and concentrate its energies and resources on pressing domestic problems. There was, in fact, considerable movement in that direction both in Congress and within the administration. The other was that America would continue to use its power actively, not to fight communism but to defend its regional and economic interests. In 1989, that led the administration to order an invasion of Panama, which overthrew the unpopular military leader Manuel Noriega (under indictment in the United States for drug trafficking) and replaced him with an elected, pro-American regime. And in 1990, that same impulse drew the United States into the turbulent politics of the Middle East.

On August 2, 1990, the armed forces of Iraq invaded and quickly overwhelmed their small, oil-rich neighbor, the emirate of Kuwait. Saddam Hussein, the militaristic leader of Iraq, soon announced that he was annexing Kuwait. After some initial indecision, the Bush administration agreed to lead other nations in a campaign to force Iraq out of Kuwait—through the pressure of economic sanctions if possible, through military force if necessary. Within a few weeks, Bush had persuaded virtually every important government in the world, including the Soviet Union and almost all the Arab and Islamic states, to join in a United Nations–sanctioned trade embargo of Iraq.

Saddam Hussein

At the same time, the United States and its allies (including the British, French, Egyptians, and Saudis) began deploying a massive military force along the border between Kuwait and Saudi Arabia, a force that

ultimately reached 690,000 troops (425,000 of them American). And on January 16, American and allied air forces began a massive bombardment of Iraqi troops in Kuwait and of military and industrial installations in Iraq itself.

The allied bombing continued for six weeks. On February 23, allied (primarily American) forces under the command of General Norman Schwarzkopf began a major ground offensive—not primarily against the heavily entrenched Iraqi forces along the Kuwait border, as expected, but to the north of them into Iraq itself. The allied armies encountered almost no resistance and suffered only light casualties (141 fatalities). Estimates of Iraqi deaths in the war were 100,000 or more. On February 28, Iraq announced its acceptance of allied terms for a cease-fire, and the brief Persian Gulf War came to an end.

General Norman Schwartzkopf

The quick and (for America) relatively painless victory over Iraq was highly popular in the United States. But the tyrannical regime of Saddam Hussein survived, in a weakened form but showing few signs of retreat from its militaristic ambitions.

The Election of 1992

President Bush's popularity reached a record high in the immediate aftermath of the Gulf War. But the glow of that victory faded quickly as the recession worsened in late 1991, and as the administration failed to produce any effective policies for combating it.

Because the early maneuvering for the 1992 presidential election occurred when President Bush's popularity remained high, many leading Democrats declined to run. That gave Bill Clinton, the young five-term governor of Arkansas, an opportunity to emerge early as the front-runner, as a result of a skillful campaign that emphasized broad economic issues instead of the racial and cultural questions that had so divided the Democrats in the past. Clinton survived a bruising primary campaign and a series of damaging personal controversies to win his party's nomination. And George Bush withstood an embarrassing primary challenge from the conservative journalist Pat Buchanan to become the Republican nominee again.

Complicating the campaign was the emergence of Ross Perot, a blunt, forthright Texas billionaire who became an independent candidate by tapping popular resentment of the federal bureaucracy and by promising tough, uncompromising leadership to deal with the fiscal crisis and other problems of government. At several moments in the spring, Perot led both Bush and Clinton in public opinion polls. In July, as he began to face hostile scrutiny from the media, he abruptly withdrew from the race. But early in October, he reentered and soon regained much (although never all) of his early support.

Ross Perot

(55.2% of electorate voting)

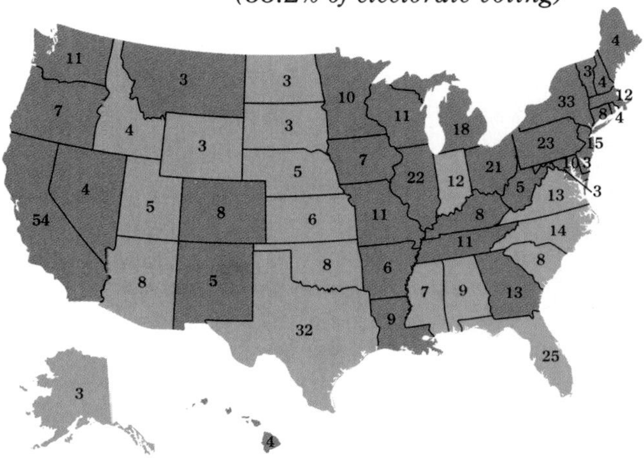

	ELECTORAL VOTE	POPULAR VOTE (%)
Bill Clinton *(Democratic)*	370	44,909,889 (43.01)
George Bush *(Republican)*	168	39,104,545 (37.45)
Ross Perot *(Independent)*	0	19,742,267 (18.91)
Other candidates	—	669,958 (0.63)

THE ELECTION OF 1992 For the first time since 1976, a Democrat captured the White House in the 1992 election. And although the third party candidacy of Ross Perot deprived Bill Clinton of an absolute majority, he nevertheless defeated George Bush by a decisive margin in both the popular and electoral vote. ◆ *What factors had eroded President Bush's once-broad popularity by 1992? What explained the strong showing of Ross Perot?*

For an interactive version of this map go to www.mhhe.com/unfinishednation4ch33maps

Clinton Elected

After a campaign in which the economy and the president's unpopularity were the principal issues, Clinton won a clear, but hardly overwhelming, victory over Bush and Perot. He received 43 percent of the vote in the three-way race, to the president's 38 percent and Perot's 19 percent (the best showing for a third-party or independent candidate since Theodore Roosevelt in 1912). Clinton won 370 electoral votes to Bush's 168; Perot won none. Democrats retained control of both houses of Congress.

CONCLUSION

America in the late 1970s was, by the standards of its own recent history, an unusually troubled nation: numbed by the Watergate scandals, the fall of Vietnam, and perhaps most of all the nation's increasing economic difficulties. The unhappy presidencies of Gerald Ford and Jimmy Carter provided little relief from these accumulating problems and anxieties. Indeed, in the last year of the Carter presidency, the nation's prospects seemed particularly grim in light of severe economic problems, a traumatic seizure of American hostages in Iran, and a Soviet invasion of Afghanistan.

In the midst of these problems, American conservatives were slowly and steadily preparing for an impressive revival. A coalition of disparate but impassioned groups on the right—including a large movement known as the "new right" with vaguely populist impulses—gained strength from the nation's troubles and from their own success in winning support for a broad-ranging revolt against taxes. Their efforts culminated in the election of 1980, when Ronald Reagan became the most conservative man in at least sixty years to be elected president of the United States.

Reagan's first term was a dramatic contrast to the troubled presidencies that had preceded it. He won substantial victories in Congress (cutting taxes, reducing spending on domestic programs, building up the military). Perhaps equally important, he made his own engaging personality one of the central political forces in national life. Easily reelected in 1984, he seemed to have solidified the conservative grip on national political life. In his second term, a series of scandals and misadventures—and the president's own declining energy—limited the administration's effectiveness. Nevertheless, Reagan's personal popularity remained high, and the economy continued to prosper—factors that helped his vice president, George H. W. Bush, to succeed him in 1989.

Bush's presidency was defined not by domestic initiatives, as Reagan's had been—and the perception of its disengagement with the nation's growing economic problems contributed to Bush's defeat in 1992. But a colossal historic event often overshadowed domestic concerns during Bush's term in office: the collapse of the Soviet Union and the fall of communist regimes all over Europe and in other parts of the world. The United States was to some degree a dazzled observer of this process. But the end of the Cold War also propelled the United States into the possession of unchallenged global pre-eminence—and drew it increasingly into the role of international arbiter and peacemaker. The Gulf War of 1991 was only the most dramatic example of the new global role the United States would now increasingly assume.

CHAPTER THIRTY-FOUR

THE AGE OF GLOBALIZATION

A Resurgence of Partisanship
The Economic Boom
Science and Technology in the New Economy
A Changing Society
A Contested Culture
The Perils of Globalization

At 8:45 A.M. on the bright, sunny morning of September 11, 2001, as tens of thousands of workers were beginning a day's work in lower Manhattan, a commercial airliner crashed into the side of one of the two towers of the World Trade Center, the tallest buildings in New York, and exploded in flame. Less than half an hour later, as thousands of workers fled the burning building, another commercial airliner rammed into the companion tower, creating a second fireball. Little more than an hour after that, both towers—their steel girders buckling in response to the tremendous heat—collapsed. One of New York's (and America's) most famous symbols fell to the ground. At about the same time, in Washington, another commercial airliner crashed into a side of the Pentagon—the headquarters of the nation's military—turning part of the building's facade into rubble. And several hundred miles away, still another airplane crashed in a field not far from Pittsburgh, after passengers apparently seized the cockpit and prevented the hijackers from taking the plane to its unknown target.

These four almost simultaneous catastrophes were the result of a single orchestrated plan to bring terrorism—for years the bane of such nations as Israel, Lebanon, Turkey, Italy, Germany, Britain, and Ireland—into the United States, which had previously had relatively little recent experience of it. The people who organized the attack on America were

1998	1999	2000	2001	2002
Lewinsky scandal breaks	Clinton acquitted by Senate	George W. Bush wins contested election	Terrorists destroy World Trade Center and attack Pentagon	Corporate scandals contribute to economic downturn
Democrats gain in congressional elections			U.S. defeats Taliban regime in Afghanistan	
Clinton impeached by House				

Islamic radicals, engaged in what they considered a holy war against "infidels" in the United States. Similarly committed Middle Eastern terrorists had previously attacked American targets overseas—military barracks, a naval vessel, embassies, and consulates—and had tried and failed to organize other episodes of terror within the United States.

The events of September 11 and their aftermath produced significant and perhaps longlasting changes in American life. They also seemed to bring to a close an extraordinary period in modern American history—a time of heady prosperity, bitter partisanship, cultural frivolity and excess, and tremendous social and economic change. And yet there was also at least one great continuity between the world of the 1990s and the world that seemed to begin on September 11, 2001. The United States in the last years of the twentieth century and the first years of the twenty-first, more than at any other time in its history, was becoming more and more deeply entwined in a new age of globalism—an age that combined great promise with great peril.

A RESURGENCE OF PARTISANSHIP

Bill Clinton

Bill Clinton entered office in January 1993 as the first Democratic president since Jimmy Carter, and the first self-proclaimed activist president since Lyndon Johnson. He had a domestic agenda more ambitious than that of any president since the 1960s. But Clinton also had significant political weaknesses. Having won the votes of well under half the electorate, he enjoyed no powerful mandate. Democratic majorities in Congress were frail. The Republican leadership in Congress was highly adversarial and it opposed the president with unusual unanimity on many issues. The president's tendency toward reckless personal behavior gave his many enemies repeated opportunities to discredit him. The Clinton years, therefore, became a time of unusually intense and bitter partisan struggles.

Launching the Clinton Presidency

The new administration compounded its problems with a series of missteps and misfortunes in its first months. The president's effort to end the longtime ban on gay men and women serving in the military met with ferocious resistance, and he was forced to settle for a pallid compromise. Several of his early appointments became so controversial he had to withdraw them. A longtime friend of the president, Vince Foster, serving in the office of the White House counsel, committed suicide in the summer of 1993. His death helped spark an escalating inquiry into some banking and real estate ventures involving the president and his wife in the early 1980s, which became known as the Whitewater affair. An independent counsel began examining these issues in 1993.

Despite its many problems, the Clinton administration could boast of some significant achievements in its first year. The president narrowly won approval of a budget that marked a significant turn away from the policies of the Reagan-Bush years. It included a substantial tax increase on the wealthiest Americans, a significant reduction in many areas of government spending, and a major expansion of tax credits to low-income working people, designed to help lift many struggling families out of poverty.

Clinton was a committed advocate of free trade. After a long and difficult battle against, among others, Ross Perot, the AFL-CIO, and many Democrats in Congress, he won approval of the North American Free Trade Agreement (or NAFTA), which eliminated most trade barriers among the United States, Canada, and Mexico. Later he won approval of other far-reaching trade agreements negotiated in the General Agreement on Trade and Tarriffs (or GATT).

NAFTA

The president's most important and ambitious initiative was a major reform of the nation's health-care system. Early in 1993, he appointed a task force chaired by his wife, Hillary Rodham Clinton, which proposed a sweeping reform designed to guarantee coverage to every American and hold down the costs of medical care. The Clinton plan relied heavily on existing institutions, most notably private insurance companies; and some critics from the left complained that the new system would be too closely tied to an undependable market. But the most substantial opposition came from the right, from those who believed the reform would transfer too much power to the government; and that well-funded opposition doomed the plan. In September 1994, Congress abandoned the health-care reform effort.

The foreign policy of the Clinton administration was at first cautious and even tentative. That was particularly clear in the administration's handling of one of the most troubling international questions of the early 1990s. Yugoslavia, a nation created after World War I out of a group of small Balkan countries, dissolved again into several different nations in the wake of the collapse of its communist government in 1989. Bosnia was among the new nations, and it quickly became embroiled in a bloody civil war between its two major ethnic groups: one Muslim, the other Serbian and Christian backed by the neighboring Serbian republic. All efforts by the other European nations and the United States to negotiate an end to the struggle failed until 1995, when the American negotiator Richard Holbrooke finally brought the warring parties together and crafted an agreement to partition Bosnia.

Bosnia

BREAKING PRECEDENT Bill Clinton broke with precedent in 1993 when he appointed his wife, Hillary Rodham Clinton, to head a task force on health care reform. The prominent role of the first lady in the Clinton administration surprised many Americans, pleasing some and angering others. The Clintons are shown here with Vice President Al Gore, as the first lady talks about health care. Hillary Clinton broke precedent again in 2000 when she was elected to the United States Senate from New York. *(Wally McNamee/Corbis)*

The Republican Resurgence

The trials of the Clinton administration, and the failure of health-care reform in particular, proved enormously damaging to the Democratic Party as it faced the congressional elections of 1994. For the first time in over forty years, Republicans gained control of both houses of Congress.

Throughout 1995, the Republican Congress worked at a sometimes feverish pace to construct one of the most ambitious and even radical legislative programs in modern times. They proposed a series of measures to transfer important powers from the federal government to the states. They proposed dramatic reductions in federal spending, including a major restructuring of the once-sacrosanct Medicare program, to reduce costs. They attempted to scale back a wide range of federal regulatory functions.

President Clinton responded to the 1994 election results by proclaiming that "the era of big government is over" and by shifting his own agenda conspicuously to the center—announcing his own plan to cut taxes and balance the budget. But because the legislative politics of 1995 was becoming part of the presidential politics of 1996, compromise between the president and Congress became very difficult. In November 1995 and again in January

1996, the federal government literally shut down for several days because the president and Congress could not agree on a budget. Republican leaders refused to pass a "continuing resolution" (to allow government operations to continue during negotiations) in hopes of pressuring the president to agree to their terms. That proved to be an epic political blunder. Public opinion turned quickly and powerfully against the Republican leadership, and against much of its agenda. Newt Gingrich, the controversial Republican Speaker of the House, quickly became one of the most unpopular political leaders in the nation, while President Clinton slowly improved his standing in the polls.

The Election of 1996

By the time the 1996 presidential campaign began in earnest, President Clinton—who had seemed so disastrously wounded after the 1994 elections—was in a commanding position to win reelection. Unopposed for the Democratic nomination, he faced a Republican opponent—Senator Robert Dole of Kansas—who inspired little enthusiasm even within his own party. Clinton's revival was in part a result of his adroitness in taking centrist positions that undermined the Republicans on one issue after another, and in championing traditional Democratic issues—such as raising the minimum wage—that were broadly popular. Clinton benefited even more from the disastrous errors by congressional Republicans in 1995 and early 1996. But his greatest strength came from the remarkable success of the American economy and the marked reduction in the federal deficit that had occurred during his presidency. Like Reagan in 1984, he could campaign as the champion of peace, prosperity, and national well-being.

Clinton's Renewed Popularity

As the election approached, both Democrats and Republicans grew uneasy about the failure of the 104th Congress to pass any significant measures. In a flurry of activity in the spring and summer of 1996, the Congress passed several important bills. The most dramatic of them was a welfare reform bill, which President Clinton somewhat uneasily signed, that ended the fifty-year federal guarantee of assistance to families with dependent children and turned most of the responsibility for allocating federal welfare funds (now greatly reduced) to the states. Most of all, it shifted the bulk of welfare benefits away from those without jobs and toward support for low-wage workers. A strong economy in the first few years after the bill passed helped many former welfare recipients move into the paid workforce.

Clinton's buoyant campaign flagged slightly in the last weeks before the election in the face of allegations of improper or illegal fund-raising techniques by the Democrats. But the president nevertheless won a substantial victory. He received just over 49 percent of the popular vote to Dole's 41 percent; Ross Perot, running now as the candidate of what he called the Reform Party, generated much less enthusiasm than he had in 1992 but still received over 8 percent of the vote. Clinton won 379 electoral votes to Dole's 159; Perot

Clinton Reelected

(49% of electorate voting)

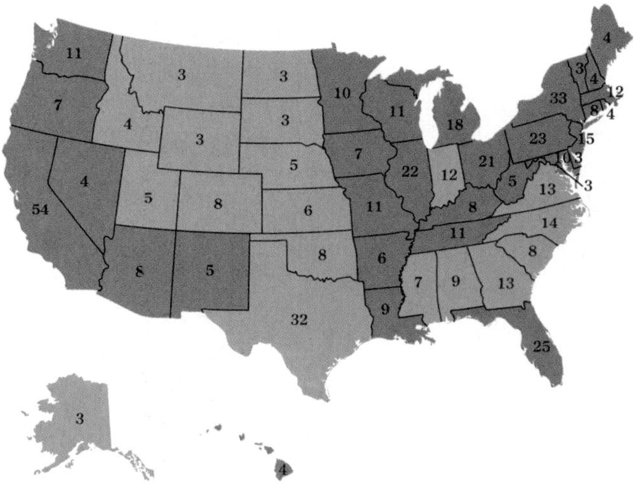

	ELECTORAL VOTE	POPULAR VOTE (%)
Bill Clinton *(Democratic)*	379	47,401,185 (49.3)
Robert Dole *(Republican)*	159	39,197,469 (40.7)
Ross Perot *(Reform)*	0	8,085,294 (8.4)

THE ELECTION OF 1996 Rose Perot did much less well in 1996 than he had in 1992, and President Clinton came much closer than he had four years earlier to winning a majority of the popular vote. Once again, Clinton defeated his Republican opponent, this time Robert Dole, by a decisive margin in both the popular and electoral vote. After the 1994 Republican landslide in the congressional elections, Bill Clinton had seemed permanently weakened. ◆ *What explains his political revival?*

For an interactive version of this map go to www.mhhe.com/unfinishednation4ch34maps

again won none. But the president's victory did not have much effect on other Democrats, who made only modest gains over their disastrous showing in 1994 and failed to regain either house of Congress.

Clinton Triumphant and Embattled

Bill Clinton was the first Democratic president to win two terms as president since Franklin Roosevelt, and he began his second administration with what appeared to be serene confidence. Facing a somewhat chastened but still hostile Republican Congress, he proposed a relatively modest domestic agenda. He also negotiated effectively with the Republican leadership on a plan for a balanced budget, which passed with much fanfare late in 1997. By the end of 1998, the federal budget was generating its first surplus in thirty years. The president finished his fifth year in office more popular than he had ever been before.

That popularity would be important to him in the turbulent year that followed, when the most serious crisis of his presidency suddenly erupted. Clinton had been bedeviled by scandals almost from his first weeks in office. Among his problems was a civil suit for sexual harassment filed against the president by a former state employee in Arkansas, Paula Jones, who charged that Clinton, while governor, had made unwanted sexual advances toward her.

Paula Jones

In early 1998, inquiries associated with the Paula Jones case led to charges that the president had had a sexual relationship with a young White House intern, Monica Lewinsky; that he had lied about it in his deposition before Jones's attorneys; and that he had encouraged Lewinsky to do the same. Those revelations produced a new investigation by the independent counsel in the Whitewater case, Kenneth Starr, a former judge and official in the Reagan Justice Department.

Monica Lewinsky

Starr had been investigating the Whitewater matter for nearly four years without any significant results. But he suddenly resurfaced as a major threat to the president with a vigorous effort to prove that the president had lied under oath and had advised others to lie as well. Clinton forcefully denied the charges, and the public strongly backed him. His popularity soared to record levels—a 79 percent approval rating in one poll, and it remained over sixty percent throughout the year that followed. In the meantime, a federal judge dismissed the Paula Jones case, which had launched the scandal.

But the scandal revived again with great force in August 1998, when Lewinsky struck a deal with the independent counsel and testified about her relationship with Clinton. Starr then subpoenaed Clinton himself, who—faced with the prospect of speaking to a grand jury—finally admitted that he and Lewinsky had had what he called an "improper relationship." A few weeks later, Starr submitted a lengthy and at times salacious report to Congress on the results of his investigation, recommending that Congress impeach the president.

The prospect of impeachment became an issue in the 1998 congressional elections. Democrats believed that the public's strong opposition to impeachment would damage the Republicans, and they turned out to be right. The Republicans lost ten seats in the House, cutting their already thin majority to five, and gained no seats in the Senate.

Impeachment, Acquittal, and Resurgence

Despite the polls and the election results, House leaders resisted all calls for compromise or dismissal of the charges. On December 19, 1998, the House, voting on strictly partisan lines, narrowly approved two counts of impeachment: lying to the grand jury and obstructing justice. The matter then moved to the Senate,

Clinton Acquitted

where a trial of the president—the first since the trial of Andrew Johnson in 1868—began in early January. The Senate trial continued for several weeks without generating any significant public support. It ended with a decisive acquittal of the president. Neither of the charges attracted even a majority of the votes, let alone the two-thirds necessary for conviction.

The investigation into the president's sexual behavior, and the political battle that followed it, illustrated two significant changes in the character of American public life in the 1990s. One was the expanding role of scandal in American politics, driven by an increasingly sensationalist media culture, the legal device of independent counsels, and the intensely adversarial quality of partisan politics. The other was the blurring of the distinction between public and private behavior, which made almost every facet of a politician's life a target of inquiry and exposure.

The last two years of the Clinton presidency were relatively quiet ones domestically. The president had no real hope of major domestic achievements in the face of a hostile Republican Congress. Overseas, however, he was more active than he had ever been before. Beginning in 1998, the United States found itself once again in conflict with Iraqi president Saddam Hussein, who balked at the agreements he had signed at the end of the Gulf War and refused to permit international inspectors to examine military sites in his country. Clinton responded by ordering a series of American bombing strikes at military targets in Iraq.

Serbia Bombed

In 1999, the president faced another crisis in the Balkans. This time, the conflict involved a province of Serbian-dominated Yugoslavia—Kosovo—most of whose residents were Albanian Muslims. A savage civil war erupted there in 1998 between Kosovo nationalists and Serbians. Numerous reports of Serbian atrocities against the Kosovans, and an enormous refugee crisis spurred by Yugoslavian military action in the province, slowly roused world opinion. In May 1999, NATO forces—dominated and led by the United States—began a major bombing campaign against the Serbians, which after little more than a week led the leader of Yugoslavia, Slobodan Milosevic, to agree to a cease-fire. Serbian troops withdrew from Kosovo entirely, replaced by NATO peacekeeping forces. A precarious peace returned to the region.

Clinton finished his eight years in office with his popularity higher than it had been when he had begun. Indeed, public approval of Clinton's presidency—a presidency marked by astonishing prosperity and general world stability as well as persistent scandal—was consistently among the highest of any postwar president.

The Election of 2000

The 2000 presidential election was one of the most extraordinary in American history—not because of the campaign that preceded it, but because of the sensational controversy over its results, which preoccupied the nation for more than five weeks after the actual voting.

ELECTION NIGHT, 2000 The electronic billboard in New York City's Times Square, showing network coverage of the presidential contest, reports George Bush the winner of the 2000 presidential race late on election night. A few hours later, the networks retracted their projections because of continuing uncertainty over the results in Florida. Five weeks later, and then only because of the controversial intervention of the Supreme Court, Bush finally emerged the victor. *(Chris Hondros/Newsmakers)*

George W. Bush—son of the former president and a second-term governor of Texas—rode his famous name and his enormous campaign war chest to overcome a powerful challenge from Senator John McCain of Arizona, a maverick reformer. Vice President Al Gore, an even more prohibitive favorite in the Democratic race, easily beat back a challenge from former Senator Bill Bradley of New Jersey.

Both men ran cautious, centrist campaigns, making much of their relatively modest differences over how to use the large budget surpluses forecast for the years ahead. Although polls showed an exceptionally tight race right up to the end, no one anticipated how close the election would be. In the congressional races, Republicans maintained control of the House of Representatives by a scant five seats, while the Senate split evenly between Democrats and Republicans. (Among the victors in the Senate races was

First Lady Hillary Rodham Clinton, who won a highly publicized race in New York.) In the presidential race, Gore won the national popular vote by the thin margin of about 540,000 votes out of about 100 million cast (or .5%). But on election night, both candidates remained short of the 270 electoral votes needed for victory because no one could determine who had actually won Florida.

Florida Disputed

After a mandatory recount over the next two days, Bush led Gore in the state by fewer than 300 votes. (Ralph Nader, the presidential candidate of the new Green Party, had done poorly nationally but nevertheless drew over 90,000 votes in Florida, which almost certainly denied Gore what would otherwise have been a comfortable victory there.) The technology of voting soon became central to the dispute. In a number of Florida counties, including some of the most heavily Democratic ones, votes were cast by punch-card ballots, which were then counted by machines. But punch cards are notoriously inaccurate, and many voters failed to punch out the appropriate holes adequately, leaving the machines unable to read them. In heavily Democratic Palm Beach County, where the ballot was especially poorly designed, thousands of confused voters punched the wrong hole, or punched two holes when they were supposed to punch one. The Gore campaign asked for hand recounts of punch-card ballots in three critical counties.

Katherine Harris

The Bush campaign immediately struck back in court and through the Republican Secretary of State, Katherine Harris, who had worked actively on the Bush campaign. As the official responsible for certifying elections in the state, she refused to authorize the recounts and declined to extend a deadline for making an official certification. But the Florida Supreme Court voted unanimously to require Harris to permit the hand recounts and to accept the results after the deadline. Such recounts proceeded in two of those counties, but in the third and largest (Dade County, which includes Miami) the local election board—for complicated reasons, which may have included intimidation by Republican demonstrators in the municipal building—abruptly called off the recount, claiming they could not finish in time.

When the new, court-ordered deadline arrived, Harris quickly certified Bush the winner in Florida by a little more than 500 votes. The Gore campaign immediately contested the results in court, asking for the Dade County recount to be reopened. Again they prevailed in the Florida Supreme Court, which ordered hand recounts of all previously uncounted ballots in all Florida counties.

In the meantime, the Bush campaign appealed desperately to the United States Supreme Court to stop the recounts. To the surprise of most observers, the Court issued a stay on Saturday, December 9 (by a vote of 5-4), and late on Tuesday, the Court issued one of the most unusual and controversial decisions in its history. Voting 5-4 again, dividing sharply along party and ideological lines, the conservative majority overruled the Florida Supreme Court's order for a recount, insisted that any

(51% of electorate voting)

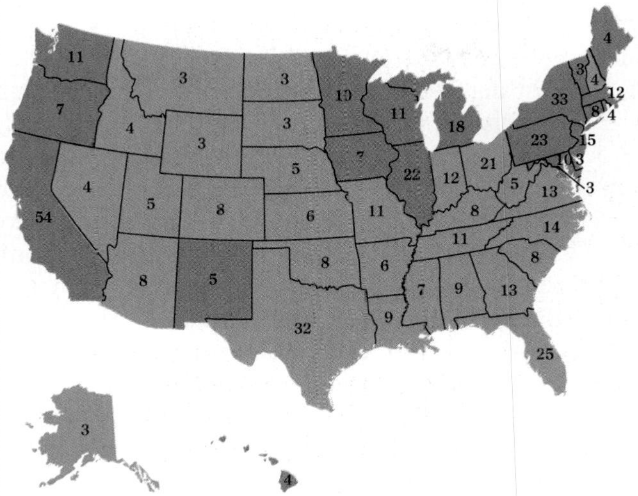

	ELECTORAL VOTE	POPULAR VOTE (%)
Al Gore *(Democratic)*	266	51,003,894 (48)
George W. Bush *(Republican)*	271	50,459,211 (48)

THE ELECTION OF 2000 The 2000 presidential election was one of the closest and most controversial in American history. It also starkly revealed a new pattern of party strength, which had been developing over the previous decade. Democrats swept the Northeast and most of the industrial Midwest and carried all the states of the Pacific Coast. Republicans swept the South, the Plains States, and the Mountain States (with the exception of New Mexico) and held onto a few traditional Republican strongholds in the Midwest. Compare this map to earlier elections, and in particular the election of 1896, and ask how the pattern of party support changed over the course of the twentieth century.

The Supreme Court's Divisive Ruling

revised recount order be completed by December 12 (an obviously impossible demand, since the Court issued its ruling late at night on the 12th), and argued that the standards for evaluating punch-card ballots were too arbitrary and unfair to withstand constitutional scrutiny. The four-member minority bitterly protested the majority's reasoning, and the majority itself appeared deeply divided on some crucial issues. But divided or not, the Court had decided the election. The next day, Gore gave a brief and conciliatory concession speech. Bush then delivered a subdued acknowledgment of one of the most controversial victories in the history of American presidential elections.

The Second Bush Presidency

George W. Bush assumed the presidency in January 2001 burdened both by the controversies surrounding his election and the widespread perception, even among some of his own supporters, that he was ill-prepared for the office. His first eight months in the White House were notable for some important legislative successes but also for little progress in winning over the 52 percent of the electorate that had voted against him.

Bush's Tax Cuts

Bush's principal campaign promise had been that he would use the predicted budget surplus to finance a massive tax reduction. By relying on his own party's control of both houses of Congress (Republicans controlled the 50-50 Senate because the Republican vice president, Richard Cheney, broke all ties), he narrowly won passage of the largest tax cut in American history—$1.35 trillion. But a few weeks later, the administration—and the Republican party—suffered a stunning setback when Senator James Jeffords of Vermont, a moderate Republican unhappy with the conservative policies of both the administration and the Republican leadership in Congress, declared himself an independent and announced he would vote with the Democrats to organize the Senate. Suddenly, Bush's legislative road became much less promising, and over the next several months most of the bills he had proposed made little progress.

In the 2002 midterm elections, however, the Republicans regained control of the Senate (replacing the Democrats' narrow 51–49 margin with a 51–49 division in their favor) and retained a slim majority in the House of Representatives. That enabled the administration and the Republican leadership to move much more aggressively, and with much greater chance of success, to pursue its ambitious agenda.

Having campaigned as a moderate adept at building coalitions across party lines, Bush spent his first two years as president governing as a staunch conservative, allied with the most determinedly right-wing figures in his party. The administration proposed nothing less than a radical shift in both domestic and foreign policy. Domestically, it sought a series of enormous reductions, and even eliminations, of taxes—especially for wealthy Americans, whom conservatives believed were best suited to promote economic growth through investment. It also sought to reduce government regulation of and interference in the market. Internationally, it proposed a dramatically new foreign policy, which asserted the United States to launch "preemptive" wars to eliminate regimes it considered hostile or dangerous and which committed the nation to working toward a world in which all nations embraced America's commitment to free and open markets.

THE ECONOMIC BOOM

The last twenty years of the twentieth century saw remarkable changes in American life—some of them a result of the end of the Cold War, some of them a result of the changing character of the American population and a rapidly evolving culture. But most of these changes were at least in part a product of the dramatic transformation of the American economy.

From "Stagflation" to Growth

The roots of the economic growth of the 1980s and 1990s lay in part in the troubled years of the 1970s. In the face of the sluggish growth and persistent inflation of those years, many American corporations began making important changes in the way they ran their businesses—changes that contributed both to the prosperity of the last decades of the twentieth century, and the growing inequality that accompanied it. Businesses invested heavily in new technology. Corporations began to consider mergers with other companies, to provide a more diversified basis for growth. Many enterprises created more energy-efficient plants and offices. Perhaps most of all, American businesses sought to reduce their labor costs, which were among the highest in the world and which many believed had made the United States uncompetitive against economies that relied on low-wage workers.

Corporate Restructuring

Businesses cut labor costs in many ways. Non-union companies became more successful in staving off unionization drives. Companies already unionized won important concessions from their unions on wages and benefits in exchange for preserving jobs. Some companies moved their operations to areas of the country where unions were weak and wages low. And many companies moved much of their production out of the United States entirely, to such nations as Mexico and China where there were large available labor pools willing to work for much less than American workers earned.

At least as important as the restructuring of existing businesses was the emergence of powerful new sectors of the economy—most notably what became known as the "technology industries." The growth of digital technologies made possible an enormous range of new products and services that quickly became central to American economic life: computers, the Internet, cellular phones, digital music, video cameras, personal digital assistants, and many others. The technology industries employed hundreds of thousands of people, created new consumer needs and appetites, and even spawned their own stock exchange—the NASDAQ—which enjoyed an enormous boom in the late 1990s.

"Technology Industries"

For these and many other reasons, the American economy experienced astonishing growth in the last decades of the twentieth century. The Gross National Product (the total of goods and services produced by the United States) rose from $2.7 trillion in 1980 to over $9.8 trillion in 2000, quadrupling in twenty years. Inflation was low throughout these decades, never rising above 3 percent in any year and for a while in the late 1990s dropping below 2 percent. Stock prices soared to unprecedented levels, and with few interruptions, from the mid-1980s to the end of the century. The Dow Jones Industrial Average, the most common index of stock performance, stood

Surging GNP

at 1,000 in late 1980. Late in 1999, it passed 11,000. Economic growth was particularly dramatic in the last years of the 1990s. In 1997 and 1998, annual growth rates reached five percent for the first time since the 1960s. Most impressive of all was the longevity of the boom. From 1994 to 2000, the economy recorded growth—at times very substantial growth—in every year, indeed in every quarter, something that had never before happened so continuously in peacetime since modern economic measurements began. Except for the relatively brief recession of 1992–1993, the period of dramatic growth actually extended unbroken from late 1983.

Downturn

The most powerful single figure in the American economy—Alan Greenspan, chairman of the Federal Board—warned in 1999 of the "irrational exuberance" with which Americans were pursuing profits in the stock market. The market justified his concern when, in April 2001, there was a sudden and disastrous collapse of the booming technology sector of the economy, which had seen particular growth in the stock values of companies doing business on the Internet. Investors decided that they had greatly overestimated the short-term profitability of Internet-based business. The result was a dramatic sell-off of technology stocks.

The bursting of the "tech bubble" did not have immediate effects on the rest of the market. But in the first months of 2001, the market as a whole began a long slide down from its historic highs of 1999 and 2000. That slide continued for more than a year, so that by the summer of 2002 the Dow Jones Industrial Average—the most commonly cited index of stock values—had lost almost 40 percent of its value. Having once soared above 11,000, it fell for a time in July 2002 below 7,000.

Plummeting Stock Market

In the fall of 2001, the economy as a whole slipped into a recession. And although there was a weak recovery in early 2002, many factors continued to depress growth and to threaten long-term economic sluggishness. Among them was a series of major corporate failures that revealed not just weakness, but corruption and dishonesty, at the heart of the business world. The revelations of corruption began in December 2001 when the Enron Corporation, an energy-trading company based in Houston that had claimed to be the seventh-largest company in America and the world's largest energy merchant, declared bankruptcy. A model to many managers of bold innovation, it conceded that it had vastly inflated its declared earnings through unorthodox and perhaps illegal accounting methods.

Corporate Scandals

The Enron collapse was only the first of a series of corporate scandals that attracted both media and popular attention and did grave damage to public confidence in corporate leadership. One major company after another admitted that their reported earnings greatly exaggerated their real income. Major accounting firms—most notably Arthur Andersen, the Enron accountant—came under intense public and legal scrutiny for failing to give reliable accounts of the corporate finances they were supposed to monitor. And the aggressive innovation that had been so lionized in corporate America in the late nineties suddenly projected a different image—recklessness, occasional lawlessness, and (in the words of Alan Greenspan) "infectious greed."

The Two-Tiered Economy

Although the American economy in the late twentieth century revived triumphantly from the sluggishness of the 1970s and early 1980s, the benefits of the new economy were less widely shared than those of earlier boom times. The increasing abundance created enormous new wealth that enriched those talented, or lucky, enough to profit from the areas of booming growth. The rewards for education increased enormously. In 1995, the average annual income of a person with less than a high-school education was $14,000. A college graduate's average salary was $37,000, and the average salary of someone with an advanced degree was $56,700—four times the level of those who did not graduate from high school. Between 1980 and the mid-1990s, the average family incomes of the wealthiest 20 percent of the population grew by nearly 20 percent (to over $100,000 a year); the average family income of the next 20 percent of the population grew by more than 8 percent. Incomes remained flat for most of the remaining 60 percent of the public, and actually declined for many in the bottom 20 percent.

Poverty in America had declined steadily and at times dramatically in the years after World War II, so that by the end of the 1970s the percentage of people living in poverty had declined to 12 percent (from about 20 percent in preceding decades). But the decline in poverty did not continue. In the 1980s, the poverty rate rose again, at times as high as 18 percent. By the late 1990s, it had dropped to under 13 percent again, but that was about the same as it had been twenty years before.

Rising Poverty Rates

Globalization

The great prosperity of the 1950s and 1960s had rested on, among other things, the relative insulation of the United States from the pressures of international competition. As late as 1970, international trade still played a relatively small role in the American economy as a whole, which thrived on the basis of the huge domestic market in North America.

By the end of the 1970s, however, the world had intruded on the American economy in profound ways. Exports rose from just under $43 billion in 1970 to over $789 billion in 2000. Imports rose even more dramatically: from just over $40 billion in 1970 to over $1.2 trillion in 2000. Most American products, in other words, now faced foreign competition inside the

Mounting Foreign Competition

United States. America had made 76 percent of the world's automobiles in 1950 and 48 percent in 1960. By 2000 the American share was only 21.5 percent. The first American trade imbalance in the postwar era occurred in 1971; only twice since then, in 1973 and 1975, has the balance been favorable.

Costs and Benefits of Globalization

Globalization brought many benefits for the American consumer: new and more varied products, and lower prices for many of them. Most economists, and most national leaders, welcomed the process and worked to encourage it through lowering trade barriers. The North American Free Trade Agreement (NAFTA) and the General Agreement on Trade and Tariffs (GATT) were the boldest of a long series of treaties designed to lower trade barriers stretching back to the 1960s. But globalization had many costs as well. It was particularly hard on industrial workers, who saw industrial jobs disappear as American companies lost market share to foreign competitors and as American companies began exporting work—building plants in Mexico, Asia, and other lower-wage countries to avoid having to pay the high wages workers had won in America.

SCIENCE AND TECHNOLOGY IN THE NEW ECONOMY

The "new economy" that emerged in the last decades of the twentieth century was driven by, and in turn helped to drive, dramatic new scientific and technological discoveries. Much as in the late nineteenth century when technological innovations transformed both society and the economy, so in the late twentieth century, new technologies had profound effects on the way Americans—and peoples throughout the world—lived.

The Personal Computer

The Computer Revolution

The most visible element of the technological revolution to most Americans was the dramatic growth in the use of computers in almost every area of life. By the early 1990s, most Americans were doing their banking by computer. Most retail transactions were conducted by computerized credit mechanisms. Most businesses, schools, and other institutions were using computerized record-keeping. Many areas of manufacturing were revolutionized by computer-driven product design and factory robotics. Scientific and technological research in almost all areas was transformed by computerized methods.

Among the most significant innovations was the development of the microprocessor, first introduced in 1971 by Intel, which represented a notable advance in the technology of integrated circuitry. A microprocessor miniaturized the central processing unit of a computer, making it possible for a small machine to perform calculations that in the past only very large machines could do. Considerable technological innovation was needed before the microprocessor could actually become the basis of what was first known as a "minicomputer" and then a personal computer. But in 1977, Apple launched its Apple II personal computer, the first such machine to be widely available to the public. Several years later, IBM entered the personal computer market with the first "PC." IBM had engaged a small software development company, Microsoft, to design an operating system for their new computer. Microsoft produced a program known as MS-DOS (DOS for "disk operating system"). No PC could operate without it. The PC, and its software, made its debut in August 1981 and immediately became enormously successful. Three years later, Apple introduced its Macintosh computer, which marked another major innovation in computer technology, among other things because its software—very different from DOS—was more graphical and much easier to use than that of the PC. But Apple could not match IBM's marketing power, and by the mid-1980s the PC had clearly established its dominance in the booming personal computer market—a dominance enhanced by the introduction of a new software package to replace DOS in 1985: Windows, also developed by Microsoft, which borrowed many concepts (most notably the Graphical User Interface, or GUI) from the Apple operating system. IBM, however, was not in the end the principal beneficiary of the dominance of its own system, as other companies began marketing their own IBM-compatible personal computers, usually at a lower price than IBMs, and seizing most of the market.

Microsoft

The computer revolution created thousands of new, lucrative businesses: computer manufacturers themselves (IBM, Apple, Compaq, Dell, Gateway, Sun, Digital, and many others); makers of the tiny silicon chips that ran the computers (most notably Intel); and makers of software—chief among them Microsoft, the most powerful new corporation to arise in American life in generations. In the 1990s, Microsoft had a virtual monopoly on the operating systems for most personal computers in the world. It had also moved into new areas: creating other kinds of software (word processing, spreadsheets, databases, communications, personal finance, and many others) and producing software and content for the Internet. In 1997, after many abortive efforts, the Justice Department filed a series of antitrust suits against the giant corporation—a suit that in 2000 produced a strong ruling against the corporation that was later partly overturned by an appeals court.

But if Microsoft was the most conspicuous success story of the computer age, it was only one of many. Whole regions—the so-called Silicon Valley in northern California; areas around Boston, Austin, Texas, and Seattle, Washington; areas in downtown New York City—became centers of booming economic activity servicing the new computer age.

***WIRED* 6.01** The January 1998 issue of *Wired*, a magazine aimed at young, hip, computer-literate readers, expressed the optimistic, even visionary approach to the possibilities of new electronic technologies that was characteristic of many computer and Internet enthusiasts in the 1990s. *Wired*, which began publication in 1992, was careful to differentiate itself from the slick, commercial computer magazines that were principally interested in trumpeting new products. It tried, instead, to capture the simultaneously skeptical and the progressive spirit of a generation to whom technology seemed to define much of the future. *(Designer, John Plunkett; Writer, Louis Rossetto.*

The Internet

Out of the computer revolution emerged another dramatic source of information and communication: the Internet—a vast, geographically far-flung network of computers that allows people connected to the network to communicate with others all over the world. It had its beginning in 1963, in the U.S. government's Advanced Research Projects Agency (ARPA), which funneled federal funds into scientific research projects. In the early 1960s, J. C. R. Licklider, the head of ARPA's Information Processing Technique Office, launched a program to link together computers over large distances. It was known as the Arpanet. For several years, the Arpanet served mainly as a way for people to make use of what were then relatively scarce computer

Arpanet

facilities without having to go to the site of the computer. Gradually, however, both the size and the uses of the network expanded.

This expansion was facilitated in part by two important new technologies. One was a system developed in the early 1960s at the RAND Corporation in the United States and the National Physical Laboratory in England. It was known as "store-and-forward packet switching," and it made possible the transmission of large quantities of data between computers without directly wiring the computers together. There could be a central communications backbone through which messages and information could be routed to individual computers, much as the telegraph and telephone system used centralized carriers that eventually branched off into local connections. The other technological breakthrough was the development of computer software that would allow individual computers to handle the traffic over the network—what became known as the Interface Message Processor.

By 1971, twenty-three computers were linked together in the Arpanet, which served mostly research labs and universities. Gradually, interest in the system began to spread, and with it the number of computers connected to it. By the end of 2001, there were over 650 million computers in use in the world, and over 180 million in the United States, the great majority of them personal computers. The great majority of them had connections to the Internet. In the early 1980s, the Defense Department, an early partner in the development of the Arpanet, withdrew from the project for security reasons. The network, soon renamed the Internet, was then free to develop independently. It did so rapidly, especially after the invention of technologies that made possible electronic mail (or e-mail) and the emergence of the personal computer, which vastly increased the number of potential users of the Internet. In 1984, fewer than a thousand host computers connected to the Internet. A decade later, there were over 6 million. And in 2001, an estimated 400 million people around the world were using the Internet, including 130 million in the United States.

The Internet

As the amount of information on the Internet unexpectedly proliferated, without any central direction, new forms of software emerged to make it possible for individual users to navigate through the vast number of Internet sites. In 1989, a laboratory in Geneva introduced the World Wide Web, which helped establish an orderly system for both the distribution and retrieval of electronic information.

The Internet revolutionized many areas of life. E-mail replaced conventional mail, telephone calls, and even face-to-face conversation for millions of people. Newspapers, magazines, and other publications began to publish on the Internet. It became a powerful marketing tool, through which people can purchase items as small as books and as large as automobiles. It is a site for vast amounts of documentary material for researchers, reporters, students and others. And it is, finally, a highly democratic medium—through which virtually anyone with access to a personal computer can establish a website and present information in a form that is available to virtually anyone in the world who chooses to look at it. New technologies that make it easier to transmit moving images over the Internet—and new forms of "broadband" access that give more users high-speed connections to the Web—promise to expand greatly the functions that the Internet can perform.

Breakthroughs in Genetics

DNA

Aided in part by computer technology, there was explosive growth in the late twentieth century of another area of scientific research: genetics. Early discoveries in genetics by Gregor Mendel, Thomas Hunt Morgan, and others laid the groundwork for more dramatic breakthroughs—the discovery of DNA by the British scientists Oswald Avery, Colin MacLeod, and Maclyn McCarty in 1944; and in 1953, the dramatic discovery by the American biochemist James Watson and the British biophysicist Francis Crick of the double-helix structure of DNA, and thus of the key to identifying genetic codes. From these discoveries emerged the new science—and ultimately the new industry—of genetic engineering, through which new medical treatments and new techniques for hybridization of plants and animals have already become possible.

Human Genome Project

Little by little, scientists began to identify specific genes in humans and other living things that determine particular traits, and to learn how to alter or reproduce them. But the identification of genes was painfully slow; and in 1989, the federal government appropriated $3 billion to fund the National Center for the Human Genome, to accelerate the mapping of human genes. The Human Genome Project set out to identify all of the more than 100,000 genes by 2005. But new technologies for research, and competition from other projects (some of them funded by pharmaceutical companies) drove the project forward faster than expected. In 1998, the genome project announced that it would finish its work in 2003. In the meantime, in 2000, other researchers produced a list of all the genes in the human body, even if their relationship to one another remained unmapped.

In 1997, scientists in Scotland announced that they had cloned a sheep—which they named Dolly—using a cell from an adult ewe; in other words, the genetic structure of the newborn Dolly was identical to that of the sheep from which the cell was taken. The DNA structure of an individual, scientists have discovered, is as unique and as identifiable as a fingerprint. DNA testing, therefore, makes it possible to identify individuals through their blood, semen, skin, or even hair. It played a major role first in the O. J. Simpson trial in 1995 and then in the 1998 investigation into President Clinton's relationship with Monica Lewinsky. Also in 1998, DNA testing appeared to establish with certainty that Thomas Jefferson had fathered a child with his slave Sally Hemings, by finding genetic similarities between descendants of both, thus resolving a political and scholarly dispute stretching back nearly 200 years. Genetic research has already spawned important new areas of medical treatment—and has helped the relatively new biotechnology industry to grow into one of the nation's most important economic sectors.

But genetic research was also the source of great controversy. Some critics feared genetic research on religious grounds, seeing it as an interference with God's plan. Others used moral arguments and expressed fears that it would allow parents, for example, to choose what kinds of children they would have. And a particularly heated controversy emerged over one of the most promising areas of medical research, which involved the use of stem cells, genetic material obtained in large part from undeveloped fetuses—mostly fetuses created by couples attempting in vitro fertilization. (*In vitro fertilization* is the process by which couples unable to conceive a child have a fetus conceived outside the womb using their eggs and sperm and then implanted in the mother.) Anti-abortion advocates denounced the research, claiming that it exploited (and endangered) unborn children. Supporters of stem-cell research—which showed promising signs of offering cures for Parkinson's disease, Alzheimer's disease, ALS, and other previously uncurable illnesses—argued that the stem cells they used came from fetuses that would otherwise be discarded, since in vitro fertilization always produces many more fetuses than can be used. The controversy over stem-cell research became an issue in the 2000 campaign. George W. Bush, once president, kept his promise to anti-abortion advocates and in the summer of 2001 issued a ruling barring the use of federal funds to support research using any stem cells that scientists were not already using at the time of his decision.

Ethical Issues

A CHANGING SOCIETY

The changes in the economy were only one of many factors producing major changes in the character of American society. By the end of the twentieth century, the American population was growing larger, older, and more racially and geographically diverse.

The Graying of America

One of the most important, if often unnoticed, features of American life in the late twentieth century was the aging of the American population. After decades of steady growth, the nation's birth rate began to decline in the 1970s and remained low through the 1980s and 1990s. In 1970, there were 18.4 births for every 1,000 people in the population. By 1996, the rate had dropped to 14.8 births. The declining birth rate and a significant rise in life

Growing Elderly Population

expectancy produced a substantial increase in the proportion of elderly citizens. Almost 13 percent of the population was more than sixty-five years old in 2000, as compared with 8 percent in 1970.

The aging of the population was a cause of the increasing costliness of Social Security pensions. It meant rapidly increasing health costs, both for the federal Medicare system and for private hospitals and insurance companies. It also ensured that the elderly, who already formed one of the most powerful interest groups in America, would remain politically formidable well into the twenty-first century.

It also had important implications for the nature of the work force in the twenty-first century. In the last twenty years of the twentieth century, the number of people aged 25–54 in the native-born work force in the United States grew by over 26 million. In the first ten years of the twenty-first century, the number of workers in that age group will not grow at all. That will put increasing pressure on the economy to employ more older workers. It will also create a greater demand for immigrant workers.

New Patterns of Immigration and Ethnicity

Surging Immigration

The nation's immigration quotas expanded significantly in the last decades of the twentieth century, allowing more newcomers to enter the United States legally than at any point since the beginning of the twentieth century. In 2000, over 28 million Americans—over 10 percent of the total population—consisted of immigrants (people born outside the United States).

The Immigration Reform Act of 1965 (see p. 818–819) had eliminated quotas based on national origin; from then on, newcomers from regions other than Latin America (who were governed by different laws) were generally admitted on a first-come, first-served basis. In 1965, 90 percent of the immigrants to the United States came from Europe. By the mid-1980s, only 10 percent of the new arrivals were Europeans, although that figure rose slightly in the 1990s as emigrants from Russia and eastern Europe—now free to leave their countries—came in increasing numbers. The extent and character of the new immigration was causing a dramatic change in the composition of the American population. By the end of the twentieth century, people of white European background constituted under 80 percent of the population (as opposed to 90 percent a half-century before).

Latino Immigrants

Particularly important to the new immigration were two groups: Latinos (people from Spanish-speaking nations, particularly Mexico) and Asians. Both experienced enormous, indeed unprecedented, growth after 1965. People from Latin America constituted more than a third of the total number of legal immigrants to the United States in every year after 1965—and a much larger proportion of the total number of illegal immigrants. Mexico alone accounted for over one-fourth of all the immigrants living in the United States in 2000.

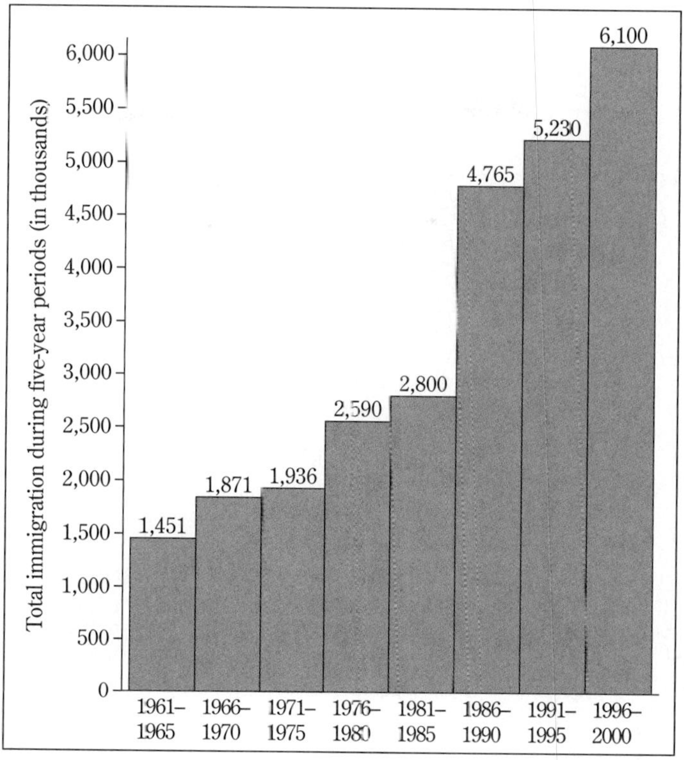

TOTAL IMMIGRATION, 1961–2000 This chart shows the tremendous increase in immigration to the United States in the decades since the Immigration Reform Act of 1965. The immigration of the 1980s and 1990s was the highest since the late nineteenth century.

In the 1980 census, 6 percent of the population (about 14 million) was listed as being of Hispanic origin. By 1997, census figures showed an increase to 11 percent—or 29 million people.

In the 1980s and 1990s, Asian immigrants arrived in even greater numbers than Latinos, constituting more than 40 percent of the total of legal newcomers. They swelled the already substantial Chinese and Japanese communities in California and elsewhere. And they created substantial new communities of immigrants from Vietnam, Thailand, Cambodia, Laos, the Philippines, Korea, and India. By 2000, there were more than 10 million Asian Americans in the United States (4 percent of the population), more than twice the number of fifteen years before.

The Black Middle Class

Remarkable Black Economic Progress

For the black middle class, which by the end of the twentieth century constituted over half of the African-American population of America, progress was remarkable in the more than thirty years after the high point of the

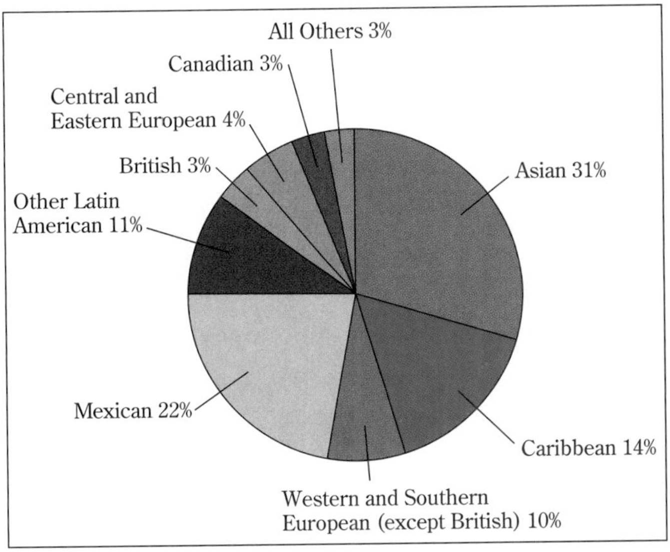

SOURCES OF IMMIGRATION, 1960–1990 The Immigration Reform Act of 1965 lifted the national quotas imposed on immigration policy in 1924 and opened immigration to large areas of the world that had previously been restricted. In 1965, 90 percent of the immigrants to the United States came from Europe. As this chart shows, by 1990 almost the reverse was true. Over 80 percent of all immigrants came from non-European sources. ◆ *What impact did this new immigration have on American politics?*

civil rights movement. Disparities between black and white professionals did not vanish, but they diminished substantially. African-American families moved into more affluent urban and suburban communities. African Americans made up 12 percent of the college population in the 1990s (up from 5 percent twenty-five years earlier). The percentage of black high-school graduates going on to college was virtually the same as that of white high-school graduates by the end of the twentieth century (although a far smaller proportion of blacks than whites managed to complete high school). And African Americans were making rapid strides in many professions from which, a generation earlier, they had been barred or within which they had been segregated. Middle-class blacks, in other words, had realized great gains from the legislation of the 1960s, from the changing national mood on race, from the creation of controversial affirmative action programs, and from their own strenuous efforts.

Poor and Working-Class African Americans

But the rise of the black middle class also accentuated (and perhaps even contributed to) the increasingly desperate plight of other African Americans, whom the economic growth and the liberal programs of the 1960s and beyond had never reached. These impoverished people—sometimes described as the "underclass"—made up as much as a third of the nation's black population. As more successful African Americans moved out of the inner cities, the poor were left virtually alone in their decaying neighborhoods. Fewer than half of young inner-city blacks finished high school; more than 60 percent were unemployed. The black family structure suffered as well from the dislocations of urban poverty. There was a radical increase in the number of single-parent, female-headed black households. In 1970, 59 percent of all black children under 18 lived with both their parents (already down from 70 percent a decade earlier). In 2000, only 38 percent of African-American children lived in such households, while 75 percent of white children did.

Black "Underclass"

Nonwhites were disadvantaged by many factors in the changing social and economic climate of the 1980s and 1990s. Among them was a growing public and political impatience with affirmative action and other programs designed to advance their fortunes. They suffered as well from a steady decline in the number of unskilled jobs in the economy; the departure of businesses from their neighborhoods; the absence of adequate transportation to areas where jobs were more plentiful; and failing schools that did not prepare them adequately for employment. And they suffered, in many cases, from a sense of futility and despair, born of years of entrapment in brutal urban ghettoes.

The anger and despair such conditions were creating among inner-city residents was expressed at times artistically, as in some aspects of the most popular new black musical form of the 1980s and 1990s, rap. The frustration became visible even more graphically in the summer of 1992 in Los Angeles. The previous year, a bystander had videotaped several Los Angeles police officers beating an apparently helpless black man, Rodney King, whom they had captured after an auto chase. Broadcast repeatedly around the country, the tape evoked outrage among whites and blacks alike. But an all-white jury in a suburban community just outside Los Angeles acquitted the officers when they were tried for assault. Black residents of South Central Los Angeles, one of the poorest communities in the city, erupted in anger—precipitating one of the largest racial disturbances of the twentieth century. There was widespread looting and arson. More than fifty people died.

Los Angeles Riots

What Americans had long called "race relations," the way in which white and black Americans viewed each other, grew increasingly sour in these difficult years. Nowhere was this mutual suspicion more evident than in the celebrated trial of the former football star O. J. Simpson, who was accused of murdering his former wife and a young man in Los Angeles in 1994. The long and costly "O. J. trial" was an enormous media sensation for over a year. Throughout the proceedings, opinions about Simpson's guilt broke down strikingly along racial lines. A vast majority of whites believed that he was guilty, and a significant majority of blacks believed he was innocent. Simpson's acquittal in the fall of 1995, after a trial in which the defense tried to

Simpson Trial

"IGNORANCE = FEAR" The artist Keith Haring (whose work was inspired in large part by urban graffiti) created this striking poster in 1989, the year before he himself died of AIDS, to generate support for the battle against the disease. "ACT UP," the organization that distributed it, was among the most militant groups in demanding more rapid efforts to search for a cure. *(Silence = Death, Ignorance = Fear, 1989 © The Estate of Keith Haring)*

portray him as a victim of police racism, caused celebrations in many black communities and a quiet disgust among many whites.

Modern Plagues: Drugs and AIDS

America in the 1980s and 1990s was ravaged by two new and deadly epidemics. One was a dramatic increase in drug use, which penetrated nearly every community in the nation. The enormous demand for illegal drugs, and particularly for "crack" cocaine, spawned what was in effect a multibillion-dollar industry; and those reaping the enormous profits of the trade fought strenuously and often savagely to protect their positions. Political figures of both parties spoke heatedly about the need for a "war on drugs"; but government efforts to stop drug imports and reduce demand had little effect. Drug use declined significantly among middle-class people beginning in the late 1980s, but the epidemic showed no signs of abating in the poor urban neighborhoods where it was doing the most severe damage.

AIDS Epidemic

The drug epidemic was closely related to another scourge of the 1980s and 1990s: the epidemic spread of a new and lethal disease first documented in 1981 and soon named AIDS (acquired immune deficiency syndrome). AIDS is the product of the HIV virus, which is transmitted by the exchange of bodily fluids (blood or semen). The virus gradually destroys the body's immune system and makes its victims highly vulnerable to a number of diseases (particularly to various forms of cancer and pneumonia) to which they would otherwise have a natural resistance. Those infected with the virus (i.e., HIV positive) can live for a long time without developing AIDS, but in the first years of the disease, those who became ill were virtually certain to die. The first American victims of AIDS (and for years the group among whom cases remained the most numerous) were homosexual men. But by the late 1980s, as the gay community began to take preventive measures, the most rapid increase in the spread of the disease occurred among heterosexuals, many of them intravenous drug users, who spread the virus by sharing contaminated hypodermic needles. In 2000, U.S. government agencies estimated that about 780,000 Americans were infected with the HIV virus and that another 427,000 had already died from the disease. But the United States represented only a tiny proportion of the worldwide total of people afflicted with AIDS, an estimated 36.1 million people at the end of 2000. Seventy percent (over 25 million) of those cases were concentrated in Africa. Governments and private groups, in the meantime, began promoting AIDS awareness in increasingly visible and graphic ways—urging young people, in particular, to avoid "unsafe sex" through abstinence or the use of latex condoms. The success of that effort in the United States was suggested by the drop in new cases from 70,000 in 1995 to approximately 40,000 in 2000.

In the mid-1990s, AIDS researchers, after years of frustration, began discovering effective treatments for the disease. By taking a combination of powerful drugs on a rigorous schedule, among them a group known as protease inhibitors, even people with relatively advanced cases of AIDS experienced dramatic improvement. The new drugs gave promise for the first time of dramatically extending the lives of people with AIDS, perhaps to normal life spans. The drugs were not a cure for AIDS; people who stopped taking them experienced a rapid return of the disease. And the effectiveness of the drugs varied from person to person. In addition, the drugs were very expensive and difficult to administer; poorer AIDS patients often could not obtain access to them, and they remained very scarce in Africa and other less affluent parts of the world where the epidemic was rampant. Nevertheless, the new medications restored hundreds of thousands of desperately ill people to health and gave them realistic hopes of long and relatively normal lives.

The Decline in Crime

One of the most striking social developments of the late 1990s was a dramatic reduction in crime rates across most of the United States. The rising incidence of violent crime had been one of the most disturbing facts of American life for two generations—and a central fact of national politics since at least the 1960s. But beginning in the early-1990s, crime began to fall—in many cities, quite dramatically. The government's crime index—which measures the incidence of seven serious crimes—fell by 19.5 percent between 1992 and 2000, with some of the most dramatic reductions occurring in murder and other violent crimes.

Prosperity and declining unemployment were certainly factors. So were new, sophisticated police techniques that helped deter many crimes and that led to the arrest of many criminals who would previously have escaped capture. New incarceration policies—longer, tougher sentences and fewer paroles and early releases for violent criminals—led to a radical increase in the prison population and, consequently, a reduction in the number of criminals at liberty to commit crimes.

New Police Techniques

A CONTESTED CULTURE

Few things created more controversy and anxiety in the 1980s and 1990s than the battles over the character of American culture.

Battles over Feminism and Abortion

Among the principal goals of the New Right as it became more powerful and assertive in the 1980s and 1990s, and as it focused on cultural changes it did not like, was to challenge feminism and its achievements. Leaders of the New Right had campaigned successfully against the proposed Equal Rights Amendment to the Constitution. And they played a central role in the most divisive issue of the late 1980s and 1990s: the controversy over abortion rights.

For those who favored allowing women to choose to terminate unwanted pregnancies, the Supreme Court's decision in *Roe* v. *Wade* (1973) had seemed to settle the question. By the 1980s, abortion was the most commonly performed surgical procedure in the country. But at the same time, opposition to abortion was creating a powerful grassroots movement. The right-to-life movement, as it called itself, found its most fervent supporters among Catholics; and indeed, the Catholic Church itself lent its institutional authority to the battle against legalized abortion. Religious doctrine also motivated the anti-abortion stance of Mormons, fundamentalist Christians, and other groups. The opposition of some other anti-abortion activists had less to do with religion than with their commitment to traditional notions of family and gender relations. To them, abortion was a particularly offensive part of a much larger assault by feminists on the role of women as wives and mothers. It was also, many foes contended, a form of murder. Fetuses, they claimed, were human beings who had a "right to life" from the moment of conception.

Right-to-Life Movement

In the 1970s, Congress and many state legislatures began barring the use of public funds to pay for abortions, thus making them inaccessible for many poor women. The Reagan and both Bush administrations imposed further restrictions on federal funding and even on the right of doctors in federally funded clinics to give patients any information on abortion. Extremists in the right-to-life movement began picketing, occupying, and at times bombing abortion clinics. Several anti-abortion activists murdered doctors who performed abortions.

The changing composition of the Supreme Court in the 1980s and early 1990s (when five new conservative justices were named by Presidents Reagan and Bush) renewed the right-to-life movement's hopes for a reversal of *Roe* v. *Wade*. In *Webster* v. *Reproductive Health Services* (1989), the Court upheld a Missouri law that forbade any institution receiving state funds from performing abortions, whether or not those funds were used to finance the abortions. But the Court stopped short of overturning its 1973 decision.

Through much of the 1970s and 1980s, defenders of abortion had remained confident that *Roe* v. *Wade* protected their right to choose abortion and that the anti-abortion movement was unlikely to prevail. But the changing judicial climate of the late 1980s mobilized defenders of abortion as never before. They called themselves the "pro-choice" movement, because they were defending not so much abortion itself as every woman's right to choose whether and when to bear a child. It quickly became clear that the pro-choice movement was in many parts of the country at least as strong as, and in some areas much stronger than, the right-to-life movement, and it contributed substantially to the election and reelection of Bill Clinton. But abortion rights remained highly vulnerable, given the intensity of feeling among those who opposed them. Clinton's successor, George W. Bush, openly opposed abortion.

Women's Rights Expanded

Other efforts by feminists to protect and expand the rights of women continued. Women's organizations and many individual women worked strenuously in the 1980s and 1990s to improve access to child care for poor women, and to win the right to caregiver leaves for parents, which a law passed by Congress and signed by President Clinton in 1993 helped secure. They also worked to raise awareness of sexual harassment in the workplace, with considerable success. Colleges, universities, the military, government agencies, even many corporations established strict new standards of behavior for their employees in dealing with members of the opposite sex and created grievance procedures for those who believed they had been harassed.

Both the achievements and the limits of their progress on this issue were evident in the sensational controversy in 1991 over Judge Clarence Thomas, President Bush's nominee for a seat on the Supreme Court. Late in the confirmation proceedings, accusations of sexual harassment from Anita Hill, a law professor and former employee of Thomas, became public. Hill's testimony before the Senate Judiciary Committee dramatically polarized both the Senate and the nation. Feminists and others

Anita Hill and Clarence Thomas

tended to believe the accusations and hailed the accuser for drawing national attention to the issue of harassment; but many Americans (and most members of the virtually all-male Senate) apparently did not believe her. Thomas was ultimately confirmed by a narrow margin.

The Changing Left and the Growth of Environmentalism

The New Left of the 1960s and early 1970s did not disappear after the end of the war in Vietnam, but it faded rapidly. Yet a left of sorts did survive, giving evidence in the process of how greatly the nation's political climate had changed. Where 1960s activists had rallied to protest racism, poverty, and war, their counterparts in the 1980s and 1990s more often worked to organize communities to fight for local concerns. A great resurgence of grassroots organizing in many parts of the country was, in part, testament to the legacy of the New Left. Most of all, activists in the 1980s and 1990s organized to stop the proliferation of nuclear weapons and power plants, to save the wilderness, to protect endangered species, to limit reckless economic development, and to otherwise protect the environment.

The environmental movement, which had grown so dramatically in the late 1960s and early 1970s, continued to expand in the last decades of the twentieth century. Several highly visible environmental catastrophes in those years greatly increased their commitment. Among them were a major oil spill off Santa Barbara, California, in 1969; the discovery of large deposits of improperly disposed toxic waste in the residential community of Love Canal in upstate New York in 1978; a frightening accident at the nuclear power plant on Three Mile Island, Pennsylvania in 1979; and the largest oil spill in American history in Alaska in 1989.

Global Warming

In the decades after the first Earth Day, environmental issues gained increasing attention and support. Environmentalists helped block the construction of roads, airports, and other projects (including American development of the supersonic transport airplane, or SST) that they claimed would be ecologically dangerous, taking advantage of new legislation protecting endangered species and environmentally fragile regions. By the end of the 1970s, many scientists were warning that the release of certain industrial pollutants (most notably chlorofluorocarbons) into the atmosphere was depleting the ozone layer of the earth's atmosphere, which protects the globe from the sun's most dangerous rays. They warned, too, of the related danger of global warming, a rise in the earth's temperature as a result of emissions from the burning of fossil fuels (coal and oil). These problems—and such others as the pollution of the oceans and the destruction of rain forests—required international solutions, which were much more difficult to produce. In 1997, representatives of the major industrial nations met in Kyoto, Japan and agreed to a broad treaty banning certain emissions into the atmosphere as a step toward reversing global warming. But in March

2001, under pressure from business leaders, the second Bush administration rejected the treaty.

The concern for the environment, the opposition to nuclear power, the resistance to economic development—all were reflections of a more fundamental characteristic of the post-Vietnam left. In a sharp break from the nation's long commitment to growth and progress, many dissidents argued that only by limiting growth and curbing traditional forms of progress could society hope to survive. Such arguments evoked strong opposition from conservatives and others, who ridiculed the no-growth ideology as an expression of defeatism and despair.

The Fragmentation of Mass Culture

One of the most powerful cultural trends throughout much of the twentieth century was the growing power and the increasing standardization of mass culture. The institutions of the media—news, entertainment, advertising, and others—grew steadily more influential. Almost without exception, they also strove to attract the largest possible audience or market. In doing so, they attempted to standardize their products so that they would be familiar and accessible to everyone. The drive toward standardization was reinforced by the philosophy of the advertising industry to promote most products for the largest possible audience.

Beginning in the 1970s, and accelerating in the 1980s and 1990s, the character of mass culture changed in some important ways. There was, of course, continued standardization in many areas. McDonald's, Burger King, and other fast-food chains became the most widely known restaurants in America (and indeed the world). Huge retail chains—Kmart, Bradlees, Wal-Mart, Barnes & Noble, Blockbuster, the Gap, and others—dominated retail sales in many communities. The most popular Hollywood films attracted larger audiences than ever before; and the most powerful media companies—most notably, Disney—produced merchandise that made their film and television characters familiar to almost everyone in the world. But there was also a very different trend at work at the same time: a tendency in both retailing and entertainment to appeal less to mass markets and more to specific segments of the market.

Growing Cultural Segmentation

This segmentation was first visible in new ideas about advertising that became powerful in the 1970s, ideas known as "targeting." Instead of finding promotional techniques to appeal to everyone, advertisers sought to identify a product with a particular "segment" of the market (men, women, young people, old people, health-conscious people, the rich, people of modest means, children) and create advertisements designed to appeal to it. As if in response, the television networks began to produce programming that focused on particular segments of the audience. Some programs were aimed at women, some at African Americans, some at affluent, urban middle-class viewers, some at more rural and provincial people. Fewer and fewer programs had a truly "mass" audience; more and more aimed at a particular group within that audience.

Even more important was the rapid proliferation of media outlets. As late as the 1970s, American television audiences overwhelmingly watched programs on the three major networks: NBC, CBS, and ABC. In the 1980s, that began to change. One reason was the proliferation of videocassette recorders (VCRs), which were in well over 75 percent of all homes by 2000. Instead of watching network television, viewers could now rent or buy videotapes and watch movies or other programming of their own choosing—available in enormous variety at thousands of video stores all across the country. In the late 1990s, VCRs began to give way to digital video disk players (DVDs), which spread rapidly and seemed likely eventually to displace VCRs altogether. Another reason was the increasing availability of cable and satellite television, which allowed homes to receive many more channels than ever before. The percent of television viewers watching the major networks declined steadily in the 1980s. New networks (among them Fox and Warner Brothers), along with specialized sports, movies, shopping, music, weather, and other channels, began to compete with the traditional leaders, distributing their programming over a combination of broadcast and cable channels. And many people turned away from television altogether and began to explore the powerful new medium of the Internet, with its huge variety of sites tailored to almost every conceivable interest and taste.

New Consumer Technologies

As audiences fragmented among many different stations and media, the phenomenon of the national "shared experience" declined as well. Network news, once the most important source for the vast majority of information, experienced a dramatic decline in viewership. Young people found their own media world in MTV and other cable stations that focused on rock music and other elements of youth culture. Hollywood continued to turn out hugely expensive "blockbusters" in a search for a mass audience. But some filmgoers turned instead to smaller independent films, which targeted particular segments of the population.

The "Culture Wars"

Few issues attracted more attention in the 1990s than the battle over what became known as "multiculturalism." Multiculturalism meant different things to different people, but at its core it was an effort to legitimize the cultural pluralism of the rapidly diversifying American population. That meant acknowledging that "American culture," which had long been defined primarily by white males of European descent, also included other traditions: female, African American, Native American, and increasingly in the late twentieth century, Hispanic, Asian, and Middle Eastern. Particular acri-

"Multiculturalism"

mony emerged out of efforts by some revisionists to portray traditional Western culture as inherently racist and imperialistic. Many critics of multiculturalism complained of a tyranny of "political correctness," by which feminists, cultural radicals, and others introduced a new form of intolerance to public discourse in the name of defending the rights of women and minorities.

The controversies surrounding multiculturalism and "political correctness" were illustrations of a painful change in the character of American society. Traditional patterns of authority faced challenges from women, minorities, and others. The liberal belief in tolerance and assimilation was fraying in the face of the growing cultural separatism of some ethnic and racial groups. But multiculturalism, in many of its forms, was also a way of broadening the definition of American culture to include all the nation's diverse peoples. It was often an expression of confidence in society's ability to tolerate and understand its many differences.

THE PERILS OF GLOBALIZATION

The celebration of the beginning of a new millennium on January 1, 2000 was a notable moment not just because of the dramatic change in the calendar. It was significant above all as a global event—a shared and for the most part joyous experience that united the world in its exuberance. Television viewers around the world followed the dawn of the new century from Australia, through Asia, Africa, and Europe, and on into the Americas. Never had the world seemed more united. But if the millennium celebrations suggested the bright promise of globalization, other events at the dawn of the new century suggested its dark perils.

Opposing the "New World Order"

In the United States and other industrial nations, opposition to globalization—or to what President George H. W. Bush once called "the new world order"—took several forms. To many Americans on both the left and the right, the nation's increasingly interventionist foreign policy was deeply troubling. Critics on the left charged that the United States was using military action to advance its economic interests, most notably in the 1991 Gulf War. Critics on the right claimed that the nation was allowing itself to be swayed by the interests of other nations; they opposed such supposedly humanitarian interventions as the 1993 invasion of Somalia and the American interventions in the Balkans in the late 1990s—both because they insisted no vital American interests were at stake and because they feared that the United States was ceding its sovereignty in these actions to international organizations.

But the most impassioned opposition to globalization in the West came from an array of groups that challenged the claim that the "new world order" was economically beneficial. Labor unions insisted that the rapid expansion of free-trade agreements led to the export of jobs from advanced nations to less developed ones. Other groups attacked working conditions in new manufacturing countries on humanitarian grounds, arguing that the global economy was creating new classes of "slave laborers." Environmentalists argued that globalization, in exporting industry to low-wage countries, also exported industrial pollution and toxic waste into nations that had no effective laws to control them. And still others opposed global economic arrangements on the grounds that they enriched and empowered large multinational corporations and threatened the freedom and autonomy of individuals and communities.

Intervention Criticized

The varied opponents of globalization may have had different reasons for their hostility, but they agreed on the targets of their discontent: not just free-trade agreements, but also the multinational institutions that policed and advanced the global economy. Among them were the World Trade Organization, which monitored the enforcement of the GATT treaties of the 1990s; the International Monetary Fund, which controlled international credit and exchange rates; and the World Bank, which made money available for development projects in many countries. In November 1999, when the leaders of the seven leading industrial nations (as well as the leader of Russia) gathered for their annual meeting in Seattle, Washington, tens of thousands of protestors—most of them peaceful, but some of them violent—clashed with police, smashed store windows, and all but paralyzed the city. A few months later a smaller but still substantial demonstration disrupted meetings of the IMF and the World Bank in Washington. And in July 2001, at a meeting of the same leaders in Genoa, Italy, thousands of demonstrators clashed violently with police in a melee that left one protester dead and several hundred injured. In the days that followed, the number of protesters in Genoa rose to an estimated 50,000. The participants in the meeting responded to the demonstrations by pledging $1.2 billion to fight the AIDS epidemic in developing countries, and also by deciding to hold their next meeting at a remote resort in Canada.

Antiglobalization Protests

Defending Orthodoxy

Outside the industrialized West, many people resented the way the world economy had left them in poverty and had, in their view, exploited and oppressed them. In some parts of the nonindustrialized world—and particularly in some of the Islamic nations of the Middle East—the increasing reach of globalization created additional concerns, less rooted in economics than in religion and culture.

The Iranian Revolution of 1979, in which orthodox Muslims ousted a despotic government whose leaders had embraced many aspects of modern western culture, was one of the first large and visible manifestations of a phenomenon that would eventually reach across the Islamic world and threaten the stability of the globe. In one Islamic nation after another, waves of fundamentalist orthodoxy (known as "Islamism") emerged to defend traditional culture against incursions from the West. The new fundamentalism met considerable resistance within much of Islam—from established governments, from affluent middle classes that had made their peace with the modern industrial world, from women who feared the antifeminist agenda of many of these movements. But it emerged nevertheless as a powerful force—and in a few nations, among them Iran after 1979 and Afghanistan in the late 1990s—the dominant force.

Among some particularly militant fundamentalists, the battle to preserve orthodoxy came to be defined as a battle against the West generally and the United States in particular. Resentment of the West was rooted in the incursion of new and, in their view, threatening cultural norms into traditional societies. It was rooted as well in resentment of the support western nations gave to corrupt and tyrannical regimes in some Islamic countries, and in opposition to western (and particularly American) military incursions into the region. The continuing struggle between Palestinians and Israelis—a struggle defined in the eyes of many Muslims by American support for Israel—added further to their contempt.

Resentment of the West

One product of this combination of resentments was individuals and groups committed to using violence to fight the influence of the West. No fundamentalist movement had any advanced military capabilities. Militants resorted instead to isolated incidents of violence and mayhem, designed to disrupt societies and governments and to create fear among their peoples. Such tactics became known to the world as terrorism.

The Rise of Terrorism

The term "terrorism" was used first during the French Revolution in the 1790s to describe the actions of the radical Jacobins against the French government. The word continued to be used intermittently throughout the nineteenth and early twentieth centuries to describe the use of violence as a form of intimidation against peoples and governments. But the widespread understanding of terrorism as an important fact of modern life is largely a product of the second half of the twentieth century.

Acts of what are now known as terrorism have occurred in many parts of the world. Irish revolutionaries engaged in terrorism regularly against the English through much of the twentieth century. Jews used it in Palestine against the British before the creation of Israel, and Palestinians have used it frequently against Jews in Israel—particularly in the last several decades. Revolutionary groups in Italy, Germany, Japan, and France have engaged in terrorist acts intermittently over the last thirty years.

Origins of Terrorism

The United States, too, has experienced terrorism for many years, much of it against American targets abroad. These included bombing of the Marine barracks in Beirut in 1983, the explosion that brought down an American airliner over Lockerbie, Scotland in 1988, the bombing of American embassies in 1998, the assault on the U.S. naval vessel *Cole* in 2000, and other events around the world. Terrorist incidents were relatively rare, but not unknown, within the United States itself prior to September 11, 2001. Militants on the American left performed various acts of terror in the 1960s and early 1970s. In February, 1993, a bomb exploded in the parking garage of the World Trade Center in New York killing six people and causing serious, but not irreparable, structural damage to the towers. Several men connected with militant Islamic organizations were convicted of the crime. In April 1995, a van containing explosives blew up in front of a federal building in Oklahoma City, killing 168 people. Timothy McVeigh, a former Marine who had become part of a militant anti-government movement on the right, was convicted of the crime and eventually executed in 2001.

Most Americans, however, considered terrorism a problem that mainly plagued other nations. Few thought very much about it as an important concern in their own country. One of the many results of the terrible events of September 11, 2001 was to jolt the American people out of complacency and alert them to the presence of continuing danger. That awareness increased in the weeks after September 11. New security measures began to change the way in which Americans traveled. New government regulations began to alter immigration policies and to affect the character of international banking. Warnings of possible new terrorist attacks created widespread tension and uneasiness. A puzzling and frightening epidemic of anthrax—a potent bacterial agent that can cause illness and death if not properly treated—began in the weeks after September 11 and spread through the mail to media outlets, members of Congress, and random others.

"War against Terrorism"

In the meantime, the United States government launched what President Bush called a "war against terrorism." The attacks on the World Trade Center and the Pentagon, government intelligence indicated, had been planned and orchestrated by Middle Eastern agents of a powerful terrorist network known as Al Qaeda. Its leader, Osama Bin Laden—until 2001 little known outside the Arab world—quickly became one of the best known and most notorious figures in the world. Fighting a shadowy terrorist network spread out among many nations of the world was a very difficult task, and the administration made clear from the beginning that the battle would be waged in many ways, not just militarily. But the first visible act of the war against terrorism was, in fact, a military one. Convinced that the militant "Taliban" government of Afghanistan had sheltered and supported Bin Laden and his organization, the United States began a sustained campaign of bombing against the regime and sent in small numbers of ground troops to help a resistance organization overthrow the Afghan government. The Taliban soon fled in disarray, and with it most of the Al Qaeda forces they had sheltered. How many survived the American onslaught remained unknown for some time, as did the fate of Osama Bin Laden himself.

"Axis of Evil"

In early 2002, President Bush spoke to Congress of an "axis of evil" in the world, which included North Korea, Iran, and Iraq. By the end of 2002, the Bush administration was talking openly of invading Iraq and was amassing troops and weapons in the region, to topple the regime of Saddam Hussein, the enemy of the first Bush administration a decade before. But it was also being drawn, reluctantly, into the turbulent politics of the Middle East, as violence between Israelis and Palestinians escalated. Palestinian "suicide bombers"terrorized the Israeli people. The hard-line Israeli prime minister, Ariel Sharon, sent troops and tanks into Palestinian areas of the West Bank. American leaders seemed torn between their desire to stop the violence and their reluctance to criticize Sharon for combating terrorism.

While the American military built up a presence in the Gulf, the Bush administration made a strenuous but unsuccessful effort to attract broad international support for the proposed war against Hussein and Iraq. The United Nations voted in the fall of 2002 to demand a resumption of inspections of Iraqi weapons—mandated by the settlement of the 1991 Gulf War and ignored by Hussein for the previous several years; and early in 2003, the new inspections began in earnest. Although the Iraqi government disclosed, and even destroyed, some forbidden weapons, the Bush administration insisted that they were not complying adequately with the UN requirements and that only a "regime change" (that is, the ouster of Hussein) would be sufficient evidence of disarmament. One by one, many of America's traditional allies in Europe and the Middle East turned against the American policy, insisting that the United States was moving too rapidly toward war. France, Germany, Russia, and China all opposed a UN Security Council resolution in support of war in Iraq; the Bush administration ultimately abandoned the effort to secure it. Large antiwar demonstrations occurred across much of the world, including within the United States. Anti-American sentiment intensified in Europe, the Middle East, and elsewhere. In the end, only Britain among America's principal allies supported the American effort in Iraq.

War in Iraq

By mid-March 2003, the American military build-up in the Gulf was nearing completion, and President Bush gave Hussein 48 hours to leave the country so as to avert a war. Hussein rejected that demand and on the evening of March 19, American missiles struck Baghdad for the first time since 1991. The next day American and British troops began moving into the Iraqi desert, and the second American war against Iraq in twelve years had begun.

A New Era?

In the immediate aftermath of September 11, 2001, many Americans came to believe that they had entered a new era in their history. The instability that had plagued so much of the rest of the world for years seemed suddenly to have arrived in the United States, shattering long-standing assumptions about safety and security and opening a period of uncertainty and fear. The prospects for the future were clouded further by a significant weakening of the economy that was already well advanced before September 11 and that the events of that day helped to increase.

America United

But fear and uncertainty were not the only results of the September 11 disasters. The reaction to the catastrophe—in New York, in Washington, and in much of the rest of the country—exposed a side of American life and culture that had always existed but that had not always been visible during the booming, self-indulgent years of the 1980s and 1990s. Americans responded to the tragedies with countless acts of courage and generosity, large and small, and with a sense of national unity and commitment that seemed, at least for a time, to resemble the unity and commitment at the beginning of World War II. The displays of courage began with the heroism of firefighters and rescue workers in New York City, who unhesitatingly plunged into the burning towers of the World Trade Center in an effort to save the people inside. Over 300 such workers died when the towers collapsed. In the weeks after the disaster, New York was flooded with volunteers—welders, metal workers, police, firefighters, medical personnel, and many others—who flocked to the city from around the country and the world to assist with rescue and recovery. Charitable donations to help the victims of the disasters exceeded $1 billion, the largest amount ever raised for a single purpose in such a short time in American history. Open and unembarrassed displays of patriotism and national pride—things that many Americans had once scorned—suddenly became fashionable again. Faith in government and its leaders, in decline for decades, suddenly (if not necessarily permanently) surged.

Alongside the many changes that occurred in American life and culture in the months after the attacks, many things remained constant. Most Americans continued to pursue their lives more or less as they always had. Most national institutions continued to function normally. The economy, despite its temporary weakness, remained the strongest, most diverse, and most productive in the world. The nation's traditional strengths—and its traditional problems—remained.

"Nothing has changed. . . . Everything has changed," wrote one prominent journalist in the weeks after September 11. In fact, no one could reliably predict whether the catastrophe would prove to be a fundamental turning point in the course of American and world history, or simply another in the countless changes and adjustments, great and small, that have characterized the nation's experience for centuries.

CONCLUSION

Americans entered the twenty-first century afflicted with many anxieties, doubts, and resentments. Faith in the nation's institutions—most notably, government—was at its lowest point in many decades. Confidence in the nation's leaders had dramatically eroded in the wake of the tawdry scandals and vicious partisanship of the Clinton years and the dispiriting controversy over the results of the 2000 election. Ugly battles over differing standards of morality and different cultural styles disturbed many communities. Vague resentments over the increasingly unequal patterns of income and wealth in the new economy, which few Americans seemed able to translate into a coherent economic agenda, increased the nation's unease.

But the United States at the end of the century was, despite its many problems, a remarkably successful society. It had made dramatic strides in improving the lives of its citizens and in dealing with many of its social problems since the end of World War II. It entered the new century with the strongest economy in the world; with violent crime—one of its most corrosive problems for more than a generation—in a marked decline; and with its power and stature in the world unrivaled.

The traumatic events of September 11, 2001 changed many aspects of American life, not least the nation's sense of its isolation, and insulation, from the problems of the rest of the world. But both the many longstanding problems and the many longstanding strengths of the United States survived the attacks. It seemed safe to predict that the American people would go forward into their suddenly uncertain future not simply burdened by difficult problems, but also armed with great wealth, great power, and perhaps most of all with the extraordinary energy and resilience that has allowed the nation—throughout its long and often turbulent history—to endure, to flourish, and to strive continually for a better future.

FOR FURTHER REFERENCE

John Lewis Gaddis, *The United States and the End of the Cold War* (1992) and *We Now Know: Rethinking Cold War History* (1997) are early examinations of the transformation of the world order. E. J. Dionne, *Why Americans Hate Politics* (1991) is a perceptive discussion of the political discontents of the 1980s and early 1990s. Thomas Byrne Edsall and Mary D. Edsall, *Chain Reaction: The Impact of Race, Rights, and Taxes on American Politics* (1991) is an alternative interpretation of the changes in American politics, focusing primarily on the impact of race. David Marannis, *First in His Class: A Biography of Bill Clinton* (1995) traces Clinton's pre-presidential career. Theda Skocpol,

Boomerang: Clinton's Health Security Effort and the Turn against Government in U.S. Politics (1996) is an account of one of the major setbacks of Clinton's first term. Jeffrey Toobin, *A Vast Conspiracy* (1999) is an account of the scandals that rocked the Clinton presidency. Toobin is also the author of an important account of the disputed 2000 presidential election, *Too Close to Call* (2001). Haynes Johnson, *The Best of Times: America in the Clinton Years* (2001) is an account of the politics and culture of the 1990s. David Halberstam, *War in a Time of Peace: Bush, Clinton, and the Generals* (2001) examines the foreign policy and military ventures of the Bush and Clinton years. Michael A. Bernstein and David E. Adler, *Understanding American Economic Decline* (1994) is an important collection of essays on the changes in the American economy since the 1970s. *Computer: A History of the Information Machine* by Martin Campbell-Kelly and William Aspray (1996) is an introduction to the development of one of the critical technologies of the late twentieth century, and Janet Abbate, *Inventing the Internet* (1999) examines the emergence of the powerful new vehicle of communication. Randy Shilts, *And the Band Played On: Politics, People, and the AIDS Epidemic* (1987) is a provocative discussion of the early years of AIDS in America. Andrew Hacker, *Two Nations: Black and White, Separate, Hostile, Unequal* (1992) and Michael Katz, *The Undeserving Poor: From the War on Poverty to the War on Welfare* (1989) are two contrasting arguments about the nature of African-American life and inner-city poverty. William Julius Wilson, *The Truly Disadvantaged* (1987) and *When Work Disappears* (1996) are important studies of the inner-city poor from one of America's leading sociologists. David A. Hollinger, *Postethnic America: Beyond Multiculturalism* (1995) is an intelligent and spirited comment on the debates over multiculturalism.

For quizzes, Internet resources, references to additional books and films, and more, consult this book's Online Learning Center site at www.mhhe.com/unfinishednation4.

APPENDICES

Documents and Tables

THE UNITED STATES

CANADA
Lake Superior
Lake Michigan
Lake Huron
Lake Ontario
Lake Erie
ATLANTIC OCEAN
Gulf of Mexico
MAINE
VT.
N.H
NEW YORK
MASS.
R.I.
CT.
N.J.
DE.
MD
PENN.
OHIO
MICHIGAN
WISCONSIN
ILLINOIS
INDIANA
W. VA.
VA.
KENTUCKY
TENNESSEE
N.C.
S.C.
GEORGIA
ALABAMA
MISSISSIPPI
LOUISIANA
ARKANSAS
MISSOURI
FLORIDA
WASHINGTON D.C.
Augusta
Portland
Montpelier
Burlington
Concord
Manchester
Boston
Worcester
Providence
Hartford
New Haven
Stamford
Bridgeport
Springfield
Albany
Syracuse
Rochester
Buffalo
Newark
New York
Jersey City
Trenton
Philadelphia
Allentown
Harrisburg
Erie
Pittsburgh
Youngstown
Cleveland
Akron
Toledo
Columbus
Dayton
Cincinnati
Baltimore
Annapolis
Dover
Richmond
Hampton
Norfolk
Newport News
Virginia Beach
Portsmouth
Chesapeake
Roanoke
Charleston
Frankfort
Lexington
Louisville
Evansville
Durham
Raleigh
Greensboro
Winston-Salem
Charlotte
Asheville
Nashville
Knoxville
Chattanooga
Memphis
Greenville
Columbia
Charleston
Atlanta
Augusta
Macon
Savannah
Columbus
Huntsville
Birmingham
Montgomery
Mobile
Pensacola
Tallahassee
Jacksonville
Orlando
Tampa
St. Petersburg
Fort Lauderdale
Hollywood
Hialeah
Miami
Jackson
Biloxi
Shreveport
Baton Rouge
New Orleans
Little Rock
Springfield
Independence
Kansas City
Jefferson City
St. Louis
Springfield
Urbana
Peoria
Chicago
Rockford
Gary
South Bend
Fort Wayne
Indianapolis
Milwaukee
Madison
St. Paul
Cedar Rapids
Davenport
Grand Rapids
Lansing
Flint
Ann Arbor
Detroit
Livonia
Warren
Sterling Heights
0
250
500 Miles
0
250
500 Kilometers
POPULOUS METROPOLITAN AREAS
Cities over 5 million
Cities over 1 million
Cities under 1 million
State Capitals

UNITED STATES TERRITORIAL EXPANSION, 1783–1898

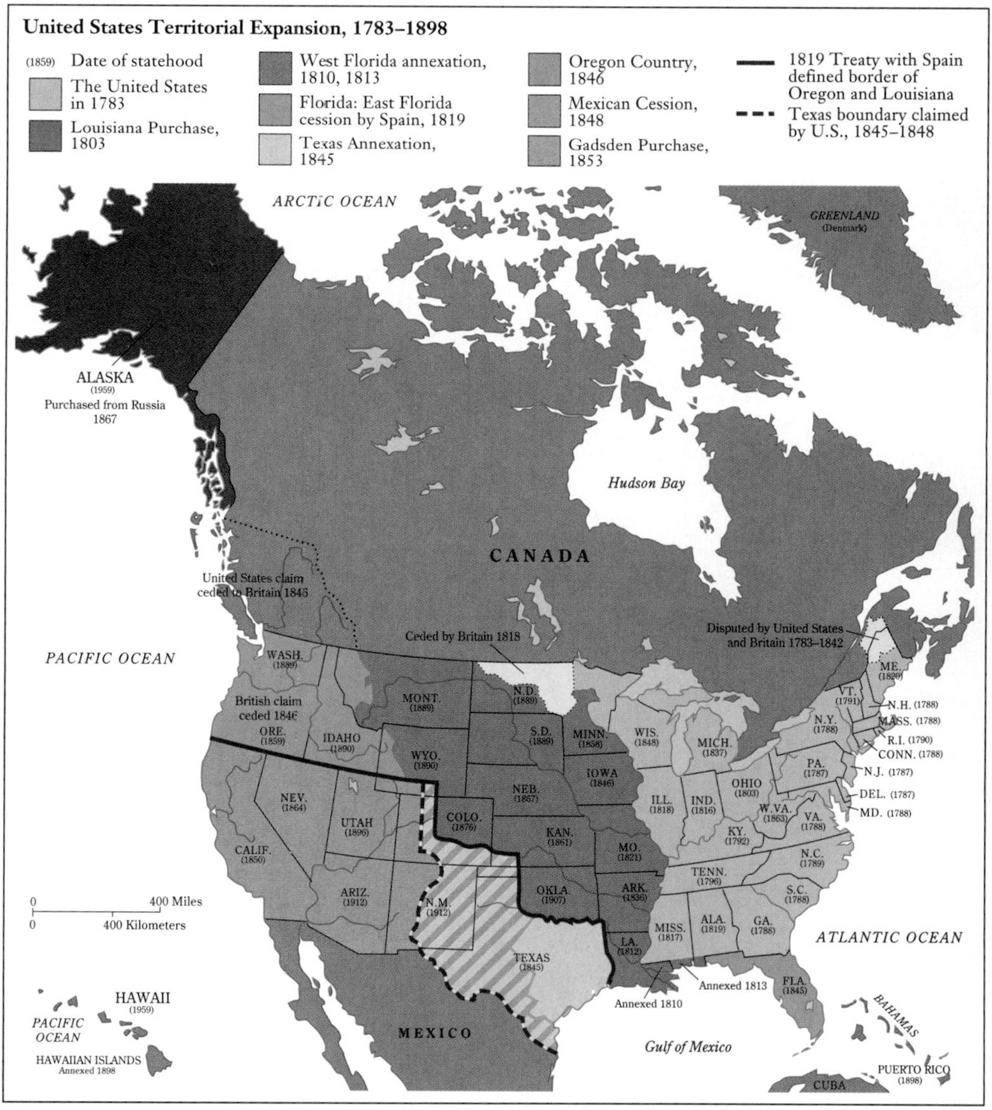

THE DECLARATION OF INDEPENDENCE

In Congress, July 4, 1776,

THE UNANIMOUS DECLARATION OF THE THIRTEEN UNITED STATES OF AMERICA

When, in the course of human events, it becomes necessary for one people to dissolve the political bands which have connected them with another, and to assume, among the powers of the earth, the separate and equal station to which the laws of nature and of nature's God entitle them, a decent respect to the opinions of mankind requires that they should declare the causes which impel them to the separation.

We hold these truths to be self-evident, that all men are created equal; that they are endowed by their Creator with certain unalienable rights; that among these, are life, liberty, and the pursuit of happiness. That, to secure these rights, governments are instituted among men, deriving their just powers from the consent of the governed; that, whenever any form of government becomes destructive of these ends, it is the right of the people to alter or to abolish it, and to institute a new government, laying its foundation on such principles, and organizing its powers in such form, as to them shall seem most likely to effect their safety and happiness. Prudence, indeed, will dictate that governments long established, should not be changed for light and transient causes; and, accordingly, all experience hath shown, that mankind are more disposed to suffer, while evils are sufferable, than to right themselves by abolishing the forms to which they are accustomed. But, when a long train of abuses and usurpations, pursuing invariably the same object, evinces a design to reduce them under absolute despotism, it is their right, it is their duty, to throw off such government and to provide new guards for their future security. Such has been the patient sufferance of these colonies, and such is now the necessity which constrains them to alter their former systems of government. The history of the present King of Great Britain is a history of repeated injuries and usurpations, all having, in direct object, the establishment of an absolute tyranny over these States. To prove this, let facts be submitted to a candid world:

He has refused his assent to laws the most wholesome and necessary for the public good.

He has forbidden his governors to pass laws of immediate and pressing importance, unless suspended in their operation till his assent should be obtained; and, when so suspended, he has utterly neglected to attend to them.

He has refused to pass other laws for the accommodation of large districts of people, unless those people would relinquish the right of representation in the legislature; a right inestimable to them, and formidable to tyrants only.

He has called together legislative bodies at places unusual, uncomfortable, and distant from the depository of their public records, for the sole purpose of fatiguing them into compliance with his measures.

He has dissolved representative houses repeatedly for opposing, with manly firmness, his invasions on the rights of the people.

He has refused, for a long time after such dissolutions, to cause others to be elected; whereby the legislative powers, incapable of annihilation, have returned to the people at large for their exercise; the state remaining, in the meantime, exposed to all the danger of invasion from without, and compulsions within.

He has endeavored to prevent the population of these States; for that purpose, obstructing the laws for naturalization of foreigners, refusing to pass others to encourage their migration hither, and raising the conditions of new appropriations of lands.

He has obstructed the administration of justice, by refusing his assent to laws for establishing judiciary powers.

He has made judges dependent on his will alone, for the tenure of their offices, and the amount and payment of their salaries.

He has erected a multitude of new offices, and sent hither swarms of officers to harass our people, and eat out their substance.

He has kept among us, in time of peace, standing armies, without the consent of our legislatures.

He has affected to render the military independent of, and superior to, the civil power.

He has combined, with others, to subject us to a jurisdiction foreign to our Constitution, and unacknowledged by our laws; giving his assent to their acts of pretended legislation:

For quartering large bodies of armed troops among us:

For protecting them by a mock trial, from punishment, for any murders which they should commit on the inhabitants of these States:

For cutting off our trade with all parts of the world:

For imposing taxes on us without our consent:

For depriving us, in many cases, of the benefit of trial by jury:

For transporting us beyond seas to be tried for pretended offences:

For abolishing the free system of English laws in a neighboring province, establishing therein an arbitrary government, and enlarging its boundaries, so as to render it at once an example and fit instrument for introducing the same absolute rule into these colonies:

For taking away our charters, abolishing our most valuable laws, and altering, fundamentally, the powers of our governments:

For suspending our own legislatures, and declaring themselves invested with power to legislate for us in all cases whatsoever.

He has abdicated government here, by declaring us out of his protection, and waging war against us.

He has plundered our seas, ravaged our coasts, burnt our towns, and destroyed the lives of our people.

He is, at this time, transporting large armies of foreign mercenaries to complete the works of death, desolation, and tyranny, already begun, with circumstances of cruelty and perfidy scarcely paralleled in the most barbarous ages, and totally unworthy the head of a civilized nation.

He has constrained our fellow citizens, taken captive on the high seas, to bear arms against their country, to become the executioners of their friends, and brethren, or to fall themselves by their hands.

He has excited domestic insurrections amongst us, and has endeavored to bring on the inhabitants of our frontiers, the merciless Indian savages, whose known rule of warfare is an undistinguished destruction of all ages, sexes, and conditions.

In every stage of these oppressions, we have petitioned for redress, in the most humble terms; our repeated petitions have been answered only by repeated injury. A prince, whose character is thus marked by every act which may define a tyrant, is unfit to be the ruler of a free people.

Nor have we been wanting in attention to our British brethren. We have warned them, from time to time, of attempts made by their legislature to extend an unwarrantable jurisdiction over us. We have reminded them of the circumstances of our emigration and settlement here. We have appealed to their native justice and magnanimity, and we have conjured them, by the ties of our common kindred, to disavow these usurpations, which would inevitably interrupt our connections and correspondence. They, too, have been deaf to the voice of justice and consanguinity. We must, therefore, acquiesce in the necessity which denounces our separation, and hold them as we hold the rest of mankind, enemies in war, in peace, friends.

We, therefore, the representatives of the United States of America, in general Congress assembled, appealing to the Supreme Judge of the world for the rectitude of our intentions, do, in the name, and by the authority of the good people of these colonies, solemnly publish and declare, that these united colonies are, and of right ought to be, free and independent states: that they are absolved from all allegiance to the British Crown, and that all political connection between them and the state of Great Britain is, and ought to be, totally dissolved; and that, as free and independent states, they have full power to levy war, conclude peace, contract alliances, establish commerce, and to do all other acts and things which independent states may of right do. And, for the support of this declaration, with a firm reliance on the protection of Divine Providence, we mutually pledge to each other our lives, our fortunes, and our sacred honor.

The foregoing Declaration was, by order of Congress, engrossed, and signed by the following members:

John Hancock

New Hampshire
Josiah Bartlett
William Whipple
Matthew Thornton

Connecticut
Roger Sherman
Samuel Huntington
William Williams
Oliver Wolcott

New York
William Floyd
Philip Livingston
Francis Lewis
Lewis Morris

New Jersey
Richard Stockton
John Witherspoon
Francis Hopkinson
John Hart
Abraham Clark

Massachusetts Bay
Samuel Adams
John Adams
Robert Treat Paine
Elbridge Gerry

Pennsylvania
Robert Morris
Benjamin Rush
Benjamin Franklin
John Morton
George Clymer
James Smith
George Taylor
James Wilson
George Ross

Delaware
Caesar Rodney
George Read
Thomas M'Kean

Maryland
Samuel Chase
William Paca
Thomas Stone
Charles Carroll,
of Carrollton

Rhode Island
Stephen Hopkins
William Ellery

Virginia
George Wythe
Richard Henry Lee
Thomas Jefferson
Benjamin Harrison
Thomas Nelson, Jr.
Francis Lightfoot Lee
Carter Braxton

North Carolina
William Hooper
Joseph Hewes
John Penn

South Carolina
Edward Rutledge
Thomas Heyward, Jr.
Thomas Lynch, Jr.
Arthur Middleton

Georgia
Button Gwinnett
Lyman Hall
George Walton

Resolved, That copies of the Declaration be sent to the several assemblies, conventions, and committees, or councils of safety, and to the several commanding officers of the continental troops; that it be proclaimed in each of the United States, at the head of the army.

THE CONSTITUTION OF THE UNITED STATES[1]

We the People of the United States, in Order to form a more perfect Union, establish Justice, insure domestic Tranquility, provide for the common defence, promote the general Welfare, and secure the Blessings of Liberty to ourselves and our Posterity, do ordain and establish this CONSTITUTION for the United States of America.

Article I

Section 1.
All legislative Powers herein granted shall be vested in a Congress of the United States, which shall consist of a Senate and House of Representatives.

Section 2.
The House of Representatives shall be composed of Members chosen every second Year by the People of the several States, and the Electors in each State shall have the Qualifications requisite for Electors of the most numerous Branch of the State Legislature.

No Person shall be a Representative who shall not have attained to the Age of twenty-five Years, and been seven Years a Citizen of the United States, and who shall not, when elected, be an Inhabitant of that State in which he shall be chosen.

[Representatives and direct Taxes[2] shall be apportioned among the several States which may be included within this Union, according to their respective Numbers, which shall be determined by adding to the whole Number of free Persons, including those bound to Service for a Term of Years, and excluding Indians not taxed, three fifths of all other Persons.][3] The actual Enumeration shall be made within three Years after the first Meeting of the Congress of the United States, and within every subsequent Term of ten Years, in such Manner as they shall by Law direct. The Number of Representatives shall not exceed one for every thirty Thousand, but each State shall have at Least one Representative; and until such enumeration shall be made, the State of New Hampshire shall be entitled to chuse three, Massachusetts eight, Rhode-Island and Providence Plantations one, Connecticut five, New York six, New Jersey four, Pennsylvania eight, Delaware one, Maryland six, Virginia ten, North Carolina five, South Carolina five, and Georgia three.

When vacancies happen in the Representation from any State, the Executive Authority thereof shall issue Writs of Election to fill such Vacancies.

The House of Representatives shall chuse their Speaker and other Officers; and shall have the sole Power of Impeachment.

[1]This version, which follows the original Constitution in capitalization and spelling, was published by the United States Department of the Interior, Office of Education, in 1935.
[2]Altered by the Sixteenth Amendment.
[3]Negated by the Fourteenth Amendment.

Section 3.
The Senate of the United States shall be composed of two Senators from each State, chosen by the Legislature thereof, for six Years; and each Senator shall have one Vote.

Immediately after they shall be assembled in Consequence of the first Election, they shall be divided as equally as may be into three Classes. The Seats of the Senators of the first Class shall be vacated at the Expiration of the second Year, of the second Class at the Expiration of the fourth Year, and of the third Class at the Expiration of the sixth Year, so that one-third may be chosen every second Year; and if Vacancies happen by Resignation, or otherwise, during the Recess of the Legislature of any State, the Executive thereof may make temporary Appointments until the next Meeting of the Legislature, which shall then fill such Vacancies.

No Person shall be a Senator who shall not have attained to the Age of thirty Years, and been nine Years a Citizen of the United States, and who shall not, when elected, be an Inhabitant of that State for which he shall be chosen.

The Vice President of the United States shall be President of the Senate, but shall have no vote, unless they be equally divided.

The Senate shall chuse their other Officers, and also a President pro tempore, in the absence of the Vice President, or when he shall exercise the Office of President of the United States.

The Senate shall have the sole Power to try all Impeachments. When sitting for that purpose they shall be on Oath or Affirmation. When the President of the United States is tried, the Chief Justice shall preside: And no person shall be convicted without the Concurrence of two thirds of the Members present.

Judgment in Cases of Impeachment shall not extend further than to removal from Office, and disqualification to hold and enjoy any Office of honor, Trust, or Profit under the United States: but the Party convicted shall nevertheless be liable and subject to Indictment, Trial, Judgment, and Punishment, according to Law.

Section 4.
The Times, Places and Manner of holding Elections for Senators and Representatives, shall be prescribed in each State by the Legislature thereof; but the Congress may at any time by Law make or alter such Regulations, except as to the Places of Chusing Senators.

The Congress shall assemble at least once in every Year, and such Meeting shall be on the first Monday in December, unless they shall by Law appoint a different Day.

Section 5.
Each House shall be the Judge of the Elections, Returns and Qualifications of its own Members, and a Majority of each shall constitute a Quorum to do Business; but a smaller number may adjourn from day to day, and may be authorized to compel the Attendance of absent Members, in such Manner, and under such Penalties, as each House may provide.

Each House may determine the Rules of its Proceedings, punish its Members for disorderly Behaviour, and, with the Concurrence of two thirds, expel a Member.

Each House shall keep a Journal of its Proceedings, and from time to time publish the same, excepting such Parts as may in their Judgment require Secrecy; and the Yeas and Nays of the Members of either House on any question shall, at the Desire of one fifth of those Present, be entered on the Journal.

Neither House, during the Session of Congress, shall, without the Consent of the other, adjourn for more than three days, nor to any other Place than that in which the two Houses shall be sitting.

Section 6.
The Senators and Representatives shall receive a Compensation for their Services, to be ascertained by Law, and paid out of the Treasury of the United States. They shall in all Cases, except Treason, Felony, and Breach of the Peace, be privileged from Arrest during their Attendance at the Session of their respective Houses, and in going to and returning from the same; and for any Speech or Debate in either House, they shall not be questioned in any other Place.

No Senator or Representative shall, during the Time for which he was elected, be appointed to any civil Office under the Authority of the United States, which shall have been created, or the Emoluments whereof shall have been increased, during such time; and no Person holding any Office under the United States shall be a Member of either House during his continuance in Office.

Section 7.
All Bills for raising Revenue shall originate in the House of Representatives; but the Senate may propose or concur with Amendments as on other bills.

Every Bill which shall have passed the House of Representatives and the Senate, shall, before it become a Law, be presented to the President of the United States; If he approve he shall sign it, but if not he shall return it, with his Objections, to that House in which it shall have originated, who shall enter the Objections at large on their Journal, and proceed to reconsider it. If after such Reconsideration two thirds of that House shall agree to pass the bill, it shall be sent, together with the objections, to the other House, by which it shall likewise be reconsidered, and if approved by two thirds of that House, it shall become a Law. But in all such Cases the Votes of both Houses shall be determined by Yeas and Nays, and the Names of the Persons voting for and against the Bill shall be entered on the Journal of each House respectively. If any Bill shall not be returned by the President within ten Days (Sundays excepted) after it shall have been presented to him, the Same shall be a Law, in like Manner as if he had signed it, unless the Congress by their Adjournment prevent its Return, in which Case it shall not be a Law.

Every Order, Resolution, or Vote to which the Concurrence of the Senate and House of Representatives may be necessary (except on a question of Adjournment) shall be presented to the President of the United States; and before the Same shall take Effect, shall be approved by him, or being disapproved by him, shall be repassed by two thirds of the Senate and House of Representatives, according to the Rules and Limitations prescribed in the Case of a Bill.

Section 8.
The Congress shall have Power To lay and collect Taxes, Duties, Imposts and Excises, to pay the Debts and provide for the common Defence and general Welfare of the United States; but all Duties, Imposts and Excises shall be uniform throughout the United States;

To borrow money on the credit of the United States;

To regulate Commerce with foreign Nations, and among the several States, and with the Indian Tribes;

To establish an uniform rule of Naturalization, and uniform Laws on the subject of Bankruptcies throughout the United States;

To coin Money, regulate the Value thereof, and of foreign Coin, and fix the Standard of Weights and Measures;

To provide for the Punishment of counterfeiting the Securities and current Coin of the United States;

To establish Post Offices and post Roads;

To promote the Progress of Science and useful Arts, by securing for limited Times to Authors and Inventors the exclusive Right to their respective Writings and Discoveries;

To constitute Tribunals inferior to the Supreme Court;

To define and punish Piracies and Felonies committed on the high Seas, and Offenses against the Law of Nations;

To declare War, grant Letters of Marque and Reprisal, and make Rules concerning Captures on Land and Water;

To raise and support Armies, but no Appropriation of Money to that Use shall be for a longer Term than two Years;

To provide and maintain a Navy;

To make Rules for the Government and Regulation of the land and naval forces;

To provide for calling forth the Militia to execute the Laws of the Union, suppress Insurrections and repel Invasions;

To provide for organizing, arming, and disciplining the Militia, and for governing such Part of them as may be employed in the Service of the United States, reserving to the States respectively, the Appointment of the Officers, and the Authority of training the Militia according to the discipline prescribed by Congress;

To exercise exclusive Legislation in all Cases whatsoever, over such District (not exceeding ten Miles square) as may, by Cession of particular States, and the acceptance of Congress, become the Seat of the Government of the United States, and to exercise like Authority over all Places purchased by the Consent of the Legislature of the State in which the Same shall be, for the Erection of Forts, Magazines, Arsenals, Dock-yards, and other needful Buildings;—And

To make all Laws which shall be necessary and proper for carrying into Execution the foregoing Powers, and all other Powers vested by this Constitution in the Government of the United States, or in any Department or Officer thereof.

Section 9.

The Migration or Importation of such Persons as any of the States now existing shall think proper to admit, shall not be prohibited by the Congress prior to the Year one thousand eight hundred and eight, but a tax or duty may be imposed on such Importation, not exceeding ten dollars for each Person.

The privilege of the Writ of Habeas Corpus shall not be suspended, unless when in Cases of Rebellion or Invasion the public Safety may require it.

No bill of Attainder or ex post facto Law shall be passed.

No capitation, or other direct, Tax shall be laid unless in Proportion to the Census or Enumeration herein before directed to be taken.

No Tax or Duty shall be laid on Articles exported from any State.

No Preference shall be given by any Regulation of Commerce or Revenue to the Ports of one State over those of another: nor shall Vessels bound to, or from, one State, be obliged to enter, clear, or pay Duties in another.

No Money shall be drawn from the Treasury, but in Consequence of Appropriations made by Law; and a regular Statement and Account of the Receipts and Expenditures of all public Money shall be published from time to time.

No Title of Nobility shall be granted by the United States: And no Person holding any Office of Profit or Trust under them, shall, without the Consent of the Congress, accept of any present, Emolument, Office, or Title, of any kind whatever, from any King, Prince, or foreign State.

Section 10.
No State shall enter into any Treaty, Alliance, or Confederation; grant Letters of Marque and Reprisal; coin Money; emit Bills of Credit; make any Thing but gold and silver Coin a Tender in Payment of Debts; pass any Bill of Attainder, ex post facto Law, or Law impairing the Obligation of Contracts, or grant any Title of Nobility.

No State shall, without the Consent of the Congress, lay any Imposts or Duties on Imports or Exports, except what may be absolutely necessary for executing its inspection Laws; and the net Produce of all Duties and Imposts, laid by any State on Imports or Exports, shall be for the use of the Treasury of the United States; and all such Laws shall be subject to the Revision and Control of the Congress.

No state shall, without the Consent of Congress, lay any duty of Tonnage, keep Troops, or Ships of War in time of Peace, enter into any Agreement or Compact with another State, or with a foreign Power, or engage in War, unless actually invaded, or in such imminent Danger as will not admit of delay.

Article II

Section 1.
The executive Power shall be vested in a President of the United States of America. He shall hold his Office during the Term of four years, and, together with the Vice President, chosen for the same Term, be elected, as follows:

Each State shall appoint, in such Manner as the Legislature thereof may direct, a Number of Electors, equal to the whole Number of Senators and Representatives to which the State may be entitled in the Congress: but no Senator or Representative, or Person holding an Office of Trust or Profit under the United States, shall be appointed an Elector.

[The Electors shall meet in their respective States, and vote by Ballot for two persons, of whom one at least shall not be an Inhabitant of the same State with themselves. And they shall make a List of all the Persons voted for, and of the Number of Votes for each; which List they shall sign and certify, and transmit sealed to the Seat of the Government of the United States, directed to the President of the Senate. The President of the Senate shall, in the Presence of the Senate and House of Representatives, open all the Certificates, and the Votes shall then be counted. The Person having the greatest Number of Votes shall be the President, if such Number be a Majority of the whole Number of Electors appointed; and if there be more than one who have such Majority, and have an equal Number of Votes, then the House of Representatives shall immediately chuse by Ballot one of them for President; and if no Person have a Majority, then from the five highest on the List the said House shall in like Manner chuse the President. But in chusing the President, the Votes shall be taken by States, the Representation from each

State having one Vote; a quorum for this Purpose shall consist of a Member or Members from two-thirds of the States, and a Majority of all the States shall be necessary to a Choice. In every Case, after the Choice of the President, the Person having the greatest Number of Votes of the Electors shall be the Vice President. But if there should remain two or more who have equal votes, the Senate shall chuse from them by Ballot the Vice President.][4]

The Congress may determine the Time of chusing the Electors, and the Day on which they shall give their Votes; which Day shall be the same throughout the United States.

No person except a natural-born Citizen, or a Citizen of the United States, at the time of the Adoption of this Constitution, shall be eligible to the Office of President; neither shall any Person be eligible to that Office who shall not have attained to the Age of thirty-five years, and been fourteen Years a Resident within the United States.

In Case of the Removal of the President from Office, or of his Death, Resignation, or Inability to discharge the Powers and Duties of the said Office, the same shall devolve on the Vice President, and the Congress may by Law provide for the Case of Removal, Death, Resignation, or Inability, both of the President and Vice President, declaring what Officer shall then act as President, and such Officer shall act accordingly, until the disability be removed, or a President shall be elected.

The President shall, at stated Times, receive for his Services a Compensation, which shall neither be increased nor diminished during the Period for which he shall have been elected, and he shall not receive within that Period any other Emolument from the United States, or any of them.

Before he enter on the execution of his Office, he shall take the following Oath or Affirmation:—"I do solemnly swear (or affirm) that I will faithfully execute the Office of President of the United States, and will, to the best of my Ability, preserve, protect, and defend the Constitution of the United States."

Section 2.

The President shall be Commander in Chief of the Army and Navy of the United States, and of the Militia of the several States, when called into the actual Service of the United States; he may require the Opinion, in writing, of the principal Officer in each of the executive Departments, upon any subject relating to the Duties of their respective Offices, and he shall have Power to Grant Reprieves and Pardons for Offenses against the United States, except in Cases of Impeachment.

He shall have Power, by and with the Advice and Consent of the Senate, to make Treaties, provided two-thirds of the Senators present concur; and he shall nominate, and by and with the Advice and Consent of the Senate, shall appoint Ambassadors, other public Ministers and Consuls, Judges of the supreme Court, and all other Officers of the United States, whose Appointments are not herein otherwise provided for, and which shall be established by Law: but the Congress may by Law vest the Appointment of such inferior Officers, as they think proper, in the President alone, in the Courts of Law, or in the Heads of Departments.

The President shall have Power to fill up all Vacancies that may happen during the Recess of the Senate, by granting Commissions which shall expire at the End of their next Session.

[4]Revised by the Twelfth Amendment.

Section 3.
He shall from time to time give to the Congress Information of the State of the Union, and recommend to their Consideration such Measures as he shall judge necessary and expedient; he may, on extraordinary occasions, convene both Houses, or either of them, and in Case of Disagreement between them, with respect to the Time of Adjournment, he may adjourn them to such Time as he shall think proper; he shall receive Ambassadors and other public Ministers; he shall take care that the Laws be faithfully executed, and shall Commission all the Officers of the United States.

Section 4.
The President, Vice President and all civil Officers of the United States, shall be removed from Office on Impeachment for, and Conviction of, Treason, Bribery, or other high Crimes and Misdemeanors.

Article III

Section 1.
The judicial Power of the United States, shall be vested in one supreme Court, and in such inferior Courts as the Congress may from time to time ordain and establish. The Judges, both of the supreme and inferior Courts, shall hold their Offices during good Behaviour, and shall, at stated Times, receive for their Services, a Compensation, which shall not be diminished during their Continuance in Office.

Section 2.
The judicial Power shall extend to all Cases, in Law and Equity, arising under this Constitution, the Laws of the United States, and Treaties made, or which shall be made, under their Authority;—to all Cases affecting ambassadors, other public ministers and consuls;—to all cases of admiralty and maritime Jurisdiction;—to Controversies to which the United States shall be a Party;—to Controversies between two or more States;—between a State and Citizens of another State;[5]—between Citizens of different States—between Citizens of the same State claiming Lands under Grants of different States, and between a State, or the Citizens thereof, and foreign States, Citizens, or Subjects.

In all Cases affecting Ambassadors, other public Ministers and Consuls, and those in which a State shall be Party, the supreme Court shall have original Jurisdiction. In all the other Cases before mentioned, the supreme Court shall have appellate Jurisdiction, both as to Law and Fact, with such Exceptions, and under such Regulations as the Congress shall make.

The trial of all Crimes, except in Cases of Impeachment, shall be by Jury; and such Trial shall be held in the State where the said Crimes shall have been committed; but when not committed within any State, the Trial shall be at such Place or Places as the Congress may by Law have directed.

Section 3.
Treason against the United States, shall consist only in levying War against them, or in adhering to their Enemies, giving them Aid and Comfort. No Person shall be convicted of Treason unless on the Testimony of two Witnesses to the same overt Act, or on Confession in open Court.

[5]Qualified by the Eleventh Amendment.

The Congress shall have power to declare the Punishment of Treason, but no Attainder of Treason shall work Corruption of Blood, or Forfeiture except during the Life of the Person attained.

Article IV

Section 1.
Full Faith and Credit shall be given in each State to the public Acts, Records, and judicial Proceedings of every other State. And the Congress may by general Laws prescribe the Manner in which such Acts, Records and Proceedings shall be proved, and the Effect thereof.

Section 2.
The Citizens of each State shall be entitled to all Privileges and Immunities of Citizens in the several States.

A Person charged in any State with Treason, Felony, or other Crime, who shall flee from Justice, and be found in another State, shall on demand of the executive Authority of the State from which he fled, be delivered up, to be removed to the State having Jurisdiction of the crime.

No Person held to Service or Labour in one State, under the Laws thereof, escaping into another, shall, in Consequence of any Law or Regulation therein, be discharged from such Service or Labour, but shall be delivered up on Claim of the Party to whom such Service or Labour may be due.

Section 3.
New States may be admitted by the Congress into this Union; but no new State shall be formed or erected within the Jurisdiction of any other State; nor any State be formed by the Junction of two or more States, or parts of States, without the Consent of the Legislatures of the States concerned as well as of the Congress.

The Congress shall have Power to dispose of and make all needful Rules and Regulations respecting the Territory or other Property belonging to the United States; and nothing in this Constitution shall be so construed as to Prejudice any Claims of the United States, or of any particular State.

Section 4.
The United States shall guarantee to every State in this Union a Republican Form of Government, and shall protect each of them against Invasion; and on Application of the Legislature, or of the Executive (when the Legislature cannot be convened) against domestic Violence.

Article V

The Congress, whenever two-thirds of both Houses shall deem it necessary, shall propose Amendments to this Constitution, or, on the Application of the Legislatures of two-thirds of the several States, shall call a Convention for proposing Amendments, which, in either Case, shall be valid to all Intents and Purposes, as part of this Constitution, when ratified by the Legislatures of three-fourths of the several States, or by Conventions in three-fourths thereof, as the one or the other Mode of Ratification may be proposed by the Congress; Provided that no Amendment which may be made prior to the Year One thousand eight hundred and eight shall in any Manner affect the first and fourth Clauses in the Ninth Section of the first Article; and that no State, without its Consent, shall be deprived of its equal Suffrage in the Senate.

Article VI

All Debts contracted and Engagements entered into, before the Adoption of this Constitution, shall be as valid against the United States under this Constitution, as under the Confederation.

This Constitution, and the Laws of the United States which shall be made in Pursuance thereof; and all Treaties made, or which shall be made, under the Authority of the United States, shall be the supreme Law of the Land; and the Judges in every State shall be bound thereby, any Thing in the Constitution or Laws of any State to the Contrary notwithstanding.

The Senators and Representatives before mentioned, and the Members of the several State Legislatures, and all executive and judicial Officers, both of the United States and of the several States, shall be bound by Oath or Affirmation to support this Constitution; but no religious Tests shall ever be required as a qualification to any Office or public Trust under the United States.

Article VII

The Ratification of the Conventions of nine States shall be sufficient for the Establishment of this Constitution between the States so ratifying the same.

Done in Convention by the Unanimous Consent of the States present the Seventeenth Day of September in the Year of our Lord one thousand seven hundred and Eighty seven, and of the Independence of the United States of America the Twelfth. In Witness whereof We have hereunto subscribed our Names.[6]

George Washington
President and deputy from Virginia

New Hampshire
John Langdon
Nicholas Gilman

Massachusetts
Nathaniel Gorham
Rufus King

Connecticut
William Samuel Johnson
Roger Sherman

New York
Alexander Hamilton

New Jersey
William Livingston
David Brearley
William Paterson
Jonathan Dayton

Pennsylvania
Benjamin Franklin
Thomas Mifflin
Robert Morris
George Clymer
Thomas FitzSimons
Jared Ingersoll
James Wilson
Gouverneur Morris

Delaware
George Read
Gunning Bedford, Jr.
John Dickinson
Richard Bassett
Jacob Broom

Maryland
James McHenry
Daniel of St. Thomas Jenifer
Daniel Carroll

Virginia
John Blair
James Madison, Jr.

North Carolina
William Blount
Richard Dobbs Spaight
Hugh Williamson

South Carolina
John Rutledge
Charles Cotesworth Pinckney
Charles Pinckney
Pierce Butler

Georgia
William Few
Abraham Baldwin

[6]These are the full names of the signers, which in some cases are not the signatures on the document.

Articles in Addition to, and Amendment of, the Constitution of the United States of America, Proposed by Congress, and Ratified by the Legislatures of the Several States, Pursuant to the Fifth Article of the Original Constitution.[7]

[Article I]

Congress shall make no law respecting an establishment of religion, or prohibiting the free exercise thereof; or abridging the freedom of speech, or of the press; or the right of the people peaceably to assemble, and to petition the Government for a redress of grievances.

[Article II]

A well regulated Militia, being necessary to the security of a free State, the right of the people to keep and bear Arms shall not be infringed.

[Article III]

No Soldier shall, in time of peace, be quartered in any house, without the consent of the Owner, nor in time of war, but in a manner to be prescribed by law.

[Article IV]

The right of the people to be secure in their persons, houses, papers, and effects, against unreasonable searches and seizures, shall not be violated, and no Warrants shall issue, but upon probable cause, supported by Oath or affirmation, and particularly describing the place to be searched, and the persons or things to be seized.

[Article V]

No person shall be held to answer for a capital or otherwise infamous crime, unless on a presentment or indictment of a Grand Jury, except in cases arising in the land or naval forces, or in the Militia, when in actual service in time of War or public danger; nor shall any person be subject for the same offence to be twice put in jeopardy of life or limb; nor shall be compelled in any criminal case to be a witness against himself, nor be deprived of life, liberty, or property, without due process of law; nor shall private property be taken for public use, without just compensation.

[Article VI]

In all criminal prosecutions, the accused shall enjoy the right to a speedy and public trial, by an impartial jury of the State and district wherein the crime shall have been committed, which district shall have been previously ascertained by law, and to be informed of the nature and cause of the accusation; to be confronted with the witnesses against him; to have compulsory process for obtaining witnesses in his favour, and to have the Assistance of Counsel for his defense.

[Article VII]

In suits at common law, where the value in controversy shall exceed twenty dollars, the right of trial by jury shall be preserved, and no fact tried by a jury, shall be otherwise reexamined in any Court of the United States, than according to the rules of the common law.

[7]This heading appears only in the joint resolution submitting the first ten amendments.

[Article VIII]

Excessive bail shall not be required, nor excessive fines imposed, nor cruel and unusual punishments inflicted.

[Article IX]

The enumeration of the Constitution, of certain rights, shall not be construed to deny or disparage others retained by the people.

[Article X]

The powers not delegated to the United States by the Constitution, nor prohibited by it to the States, are reserved to the States respectively, or to the people.

[Amendments I–X, in force 1791.]

[Amendment XI][8]

The Judicial power of the United States shall not be construed to extend to any suit in law or equity, commenced or prosecuted against one of the United States by Citizens of another State, or by Citizens or Subjects of any Foreign State.

[Amendment XII][9]

The Electors shall meet in their respective States and vote by ballot for President and Vice-President, one of whom, at least, shall not be an inhabitant of the same State with themselves; they shall name in their ballots the person voted for as President, and in distinct ballots the person voted for as Vice-President, and they shall make distinct lists of all persons voted for as President, and of all persons voted for as Vice-President, and of the number of votes for each, which lists they shall sign and certify, and transmit sealed to the seat of the government of the United States, directed to the President of the Senate;—The President of the Senate shall, in the presence of the Senate and House of Representatives, open all the certificates and the votes shall then be counted;—The person having the greatest number of votes for President, shall be the President, if such number be a majority of the whole number of Electors appointed; and if no person have such majority, then from the persons having the highest numbers not exceeding three on the list of those voted for as President, the House of Representatives shall choose immediately, by ballot, the President. But in choosing the President, the votes shall be taken by states, the representation from each state having one vote; a quorum for this purpose shall consist of a member or members from two-thirds of the states, and a majority of all the states shall be necessary to a choice. And if the House of Representatives shall not choose a President whenever the right of choice shall devolve upon them, before the fourth day of March next following, then the Vice-President shall act as President, as in the case of the death or other constitutional disability of the President.—The person having the greatest number of votes as Vice-President, shall be the Vice-President, if such number be a majority of the whole number of Electors appointed, and if no person have a majority, then from the two highest numbers on the list, the Senate shall choose the Vice-President; a quorum for the purpose shall consist of two-thirds of the whole number of Senators, and a majority of the whole number shall be necessary to a choice. But no person constitutionally ineligible to the office of President shall be eligible to that of Vice-President of the United States.

[8]Adopted in 1798.
[9]Adopted in 1804.

[Amendment XIII][10]

Section 1.
Neither slavery nor involuntary servitude, except as a punishment for crime whereof the party shall have been duly convicted, shall exist within the United States, or any place subject to their jurisdiction.

Section 2.
Congress shall have power to enforce this article by appropriate legislation.

[Amendment XIV][11]

Section 1.
All persons born or naturalized in the United States, and subject to the jurisdiction thereof, are citizens of the United States and of the State wherein they reside. No State shall make or enforce any law which shall abridge the privileges or immunities of citizens of the United States; nor shall any State deprive any person of life, liberty, or property, without due process of law; nor deny to any person within its jurisdiction the equal protection of the laws.

Section 2.
Representatives shall be apportioned among the several States according to their respective numbers, counting the whole number of persons in each State, excluding Indians not taxed. But when the right to vote at any election for the choice of electors for President and Vice-President of the United States, Representatives in Congress, the Executive and Judicial officers of a State, or the members of the Legislature thereof, is denied to any of the male inhabitants of such State, being twenty-one years of age, and citizens of the United States, or in any way abridged, except for participation in rebellion, or other crime, the basis of representation therein shall be reduced in the proportion which the number of such male citizens shall bear to the whole number of male citizens twenty-one years of age in such State.

Section 3.
No person shall be a Senator or Representative in Congress, or elector of President and Vice-President, or hold any office, civil or military, under the United States, or under any State, who, having previously taken an oath, as a member of Congress, or as an officer of the United States, or as a member of any State legislature, or as an executive or judicial officer of any State, to support the Constitution of the United States, shall have engaged in insurrection or rebellion against the same, or given aid or comfort to the enemies thereof. But Congress may by a vote of two-thirds of each House, remove such disability.

Section 4.
The validity of the public debt of the United States, authorized by law, including debts incurred for payment of pensions and bounties for services in suppressing insurrection or rebellion, shall not be questioned. But neither the United States

[10]Adopted in 1865.
[11]Adopted in 1868.

nor any State shall assume or pay any debts or obligation incurred in aid of insurrection or rebellion against the United States, or any claim for the loss or emancipation of any slave; but all such debts, obligations, and claims shall be held illegal and void.

Section 5.
The Congress shall have the power to enforce, by appropriate legislation, the provisions of this article.

[Amendment XV][12]

Section 1.
The right of citizens of the United States to vote shall not be denied or abridged by the United States or by any State on account of race, color, or previous condition of servitude—

Section 2.
The Congress shall have power to enforce this article by appropriate legislation.

[Amendment XVI][13]

The Congress shall have power to lay and collect taxes on incomes, from whatever source derived, without apportionment among the several States, and without regard to any census or enumeration.

[Amendment XVII][14]

The Senate of the United States shall be composed of two Senators from each State, elected by the people thereof, for six years; and each Senator shall have one vote. The electors in each State shall have the qualifications requisite for electors of the most numerous branch of the State legislatures.

When vacancies happen in the representation of any State in the Senate, the executive authority of such State shall issue writs of election to fill such vacancies: *Provided*, That the legislature of any State may empower the executive thereof to make temporary appointments until the people fill the vacancies by election as the legislature may direct.

This amendment shall not be so construed as to affect the election or term of any Senator chosen before it becomes valid as part of the Constitution.

[Amendment XVIII][15]

Section 1.
After one year from the ratification of this article the manufacture, sale, or transportation of intoxicating liquors within, the importation thereof into, or the exportation thereof from the United States and all territory subject to the jurisdiction thereof for beverage purposes is hereby prohibited.

[12]Adopted in 1870.
[13]Adopted in 1913.
[14]Adopted in 1913.
[15]Adopted in 1918.

Section 2.
The Congress and the several States shall have concurrent power to enforce this article by appropriate legislation.

Section 3.
This article shall be inoperative unless it shall have been ratified as an amendment to the Constitution by the legislatures of the several States, as provided in the Constitution, within seven years from the date of the submission hereof to the States by the Congress.

[Amendment XIX][16]

The right of citizens of the United States to vote shall not be denied or abridged by the United States or by any State on account of sex.

Congress shall have power to enforce this article by appropriate legislation.

[Amendment XX][17]

Section 1.
The terms of the President and Vice-President shall end at noon on the 20th day of January, and the terms of Senators and Representatives at noon on the 3d day of January, of the years in which such terms would have ended if this article had not been ratified; and the terms of their successors shall then begin.

Section 2.
The Congress shall assemble at least once in every year, and such meeting shall begin at noon on the 3d day of January, unless they shall by law appoint a different day.

Section 3.
If, at the time fixed for the beginning of the term of the President, the President elect shall have died, the Vice-President elect shall become President. If a President shall not have been chosen before the time fixed for the beginning of his term or if the President elect shall have failed to qualify, then the Vice-President elect shall act as President until a President shall have qualified; and the Congress may by law provide for the case wherein neither a President elect nor a Vice-President elect shall have qualified, declaring who shall then act as President, or the manner in which one who is to act shall be selected, and such person shall act accordingly until a President or Vice-President shall have qualified.

Section 4.
The Congress may by law provide for the case of the death of any of the persons from whom the House of Representatives may choose a President whenever the right of choice shall have devolved upon them, and for the case of the death of any of the persons from whom the Senate may choose a Vice-President whenever the right of choice shall have devolved upon them.

Section 5.
Sections 1 and 2 shall take effect on the 15th day of October following the ratification of this article.

[16]Adopted in 1920.
[17]Adopted in 1933.

Section 6.
This article shall be inoperative unless it shall have been ratified as an amendment to the Constitution by the legislatures of three-fourths of the several States within seven years from the date of its submission.

[Amendment XXI][18]

Section 1.
The eighteenth article of amendment to the Constitution of the United States is hereby repealed.

Section 2.
The transportation or importation into any State, Territory, or possession of the United States for delivery or use therein of intoxicating liquors, in violation of the laws thereof, is hereby prohibited.

Section 3.
This article shall be inoperative unless it shall have been ratified as an amendment to the Constitution by conventions in the several States, as provided in the Constitution, within seven years from the date of the submission hereof to the States by the Congress.

[Amendment XXII][19]

No person shall be elected to the office of the President more than twice, and no person who has held the office of President, or acted as President, for more than two years of a term to which some other person was elected President shall be elected to the office of the President more than once.

But this Article shall not apply to any person holding the office of President when this Article was proposed by the Congress, and shall not prevent any person who may be holding the office of President, or acting as President, during the term within which this Article becomes operative from holding the office of President or acting as President during the remainder of such term.

This article shall be inoperative unless it shall have been ratified as an amendment to the Constitution by the legislatures of three-fourths of the several states within seven years from the date of its submission to the states by the Congress.

[Amendment XXIII][20]

Section 1.
The District constituting the seat of Government of the United States shall appoint in such manner as the Congress may direct:

A number of electors of President and Vice-President equal to the whole number of Senators and Representatives in Congress to which the District would be entitled if it were a State, but in no event more than the least populous State; they shall be in addition to those appointed by the States, but they shall be considered,

[18]Adopted in 1933.
[19]Adopted in 1961.
[20]Adopted in 1961.

for the purposes of the election of President and Vice-President, to be electors appointed by a State; and they shall meet in the District and perform such duties as provided by the twelfth article of amendment.

Section 2.
The Congress shall have power to enforce this article by appropriate legislation.

[Amendment XXIV][21]

Section 1.
The right of citizens of the United States to vote in any primary or other election for President or Vice President, for electors for President or Vice President, or for Senator or Representative in Congress, shall not be denied or abridged by the United States or any state by reason of failure to pay any poll tax or other tax.

Section 2.
The Congress shall have the power to enforce this article by appropriate legislation.

[Amendment XXV][22]

Section 1.
In case of the removal of the President from office or of his death or resignation, the Vice President shall become President.

Section 2.
Whenever there is a vacancy in the office of the Vice President, the President shall nominate a Vice President who shall take office upon confirmation by a majority vote of both Houses of Congress.

Section 3.
Whenever the President transmits to the President Pro Tempore of the Senate and the Speaker of the House of Representatives his written declaration that he is unable to discharge the powers and duties of his office, and until he transmits to them a written declaration to the contrary, such powers and duties shall be discharged by the Vice President as Acting President.

Section 4.
Whenever the Vice President and a majority of either the principal officers of the executive departments or of such other body as Congress may by law provide, transmit to the President Pro Tempore of the Senate and the Speaker of the House of Representatives their written declaration that the President is unable to discharge the powers and duties of his office, the Vice President shall immediately assume the powers and duties of the office as Acting President.

[21]Adopted in 1964.
[22]Adopted in 1967.

Thereafter, when the President transmits to the President Pro Tempore of the Senate and the Speaker of the House of Representatives his written declaration that no inability exists, he shall resume the powers and duties of his office unless the Vice President and a majority of either the principal officers of the executive departments or of such other body as Congress may by law provide, transmit within four days to the President Pro Tempore of the Senate and the Speaker of the House of Representatives their written declaration that the President is unable to discharge the powers and duties of his office. Thereupon Congress shall decide the issue, assembling within forty-eight hours for that purpose if not in session. If the Congress, within twenty-one days after receipt of the latter written declaration, or, if Congress is not in session, within twenty-one days after Congress is required to assemble, determines by two-thirds vote of both Houses that the President is unable to discharge the powers and duties of his office, the Vice President shall continue to discharge the same as Acting President; otherwise, the President shall resume the powers and duties of his office.

[Amendment XXVI][23]

Section 1.
The right of citizens of the United States, who are eighteen years of age or older, to vote shall not be denied or abridged by the United States or by any State on account of age.

Section 2.
The Congress shall have power to enforce this article by appropriate legislation.

[Amendment XXVII][24]

No law varying the compensation for the services of the Senators and Representatives shall take effect until an election of Representatives shall have intervened.

[23]Adopted in 1971.
[24]Adopted in 1992.

PRESIDENTIAL ELECTIONS

Year	Candidates	Parties	Popular Vote	Percentage of Popular Vote	Electoral Vote	Percentage of Voter Participation
1789	**George Washington (Va.)***				69	
	John Adams				34	
	Others				35	
1792	**George Washington (Va.)**				132	
	John Adams				77	
	George Clinton				50	
	Others				5	
1796	**John Adams (Mass.)**	Federalist			71	
	Thomas Jefferson	Democratic Republican			68	
	Thomas Pinckney	Federalist			59	
	Aaron Burr	Dem.-Rep.			30	
	Others				48	
1800	**Thomas Jefferson (Va.)**	Dem.-Rep.			73	
	Aaron Burr	Dem.-Rep.			73	
	John Adams	Federalist			65	
	C. C. Pinckney	Federalist			64	
	John Jay	Federalist			1	
1804	**Thomas Jefferson (Va.)**	Dem.-Rep.			162	
	C. C. Pinckney	Federalist			14	
1808	**James Madison (Va.)**	Dem.-Rep.			122	
	C. C. Pinckney	Federalist			47	
	George Clinton	Dem.-Rep.			6	

1812	**James Madison (Va.)**	Dem.-Rep.			128	
	De Witt Clinton	Federalist			89	
1816	**James Monroe (Va.)**	Dem.-Rep.			183	
	Rufus King	Federalist			34	
1820	**James Monroe (Va.)**	Dem.-Rep.			231	
	John Quincy Adams	Dem.-Rep.			1	
1824	**John Q. Adams (Mass.)**	Dem.-Rep.	108,740	30.5	84	26.9
	Andrew Jackson	Dem.-Rep.	153,544	43.1	99	
	William H. Crawford	Dem.-Rep.	46,618	13.1	41	
	Henry Clay	Dem.-Rep.	47,136	13.2	37	
1828	**Andrew Jackson (Tenn.)**	Democratic	647,286	56.0	178	57.6
	John Quincy Adams	National Republican	508,064	44.0	83	
1832	**Andrew Jackson (Tenn.)**	Democratic	687,502	55.0	219	55.4
	Henry Clay	National Republican	530,189	42.4	49	
	John Floyd	Independent			11	
	William Wirt	Anti-Mason	33,108	2.6	7	
1836	**Martin Van Buren (N.Y.)**	Democratic	765,483	50.9	170	57.8
	W. H. Harrison	Whig			73	
	Hugh L. White	Whig	739,795	49.1	26	
	Daniel Webster	Whig			14	
	W. P. Magnum	Independent			11	
1840	**William H. Harrison (Ohio)**	Whig	1,274,624	53.1	234	80.2
	Martin Van Buren	Democratic	1,127,781	46.9	60	
	J. G. Birney	Liberty	7,069		—	

*State of residence at time of election.

(continued)

Year	Candidates	Parties	Popular Vote	Percentage of Popular Vote	Electoral Vote	Percentage of Voter Participation
1844	**JAMES K. POLK (TENN.)**	Democratic	1,338,464	49.6	170	78.9
	Henry Clay	Whig	1,300,097	48.1	105	
	J. G. Birney	Liberty	62,300	2.3	—	
1848	**ZACHARY TAYLOR (LA.)**	Whig	1,360,967	47.4	163	72.7
	Lewis Cass	Democratic	1,222,342	42.5	127	
	Martin Van Buren	Free-Soil	291,263	10.1	—	
1852	**FRANKLIN PIERCE (N.H.)**	Democratic	1,601,117	50.9	254	69.6
	Winfield Scott	Whig	1,385,453	44.1	42	
	John P. Hale	Free-Soil	155,825	5.0	—	
1856	**JAMES BUCHANAN (PA.)**	Democratic	1,832,955	45.3	174	78.9
	John C. Frémont	Republican	1,339,932	33.1	114	
	Millard Fillmore	American	871,731	21.6	8	
1860	**ABRAHAM LINCOLN (ILL.)**	Republican	1,865,593	39.8	180	81.2
	Stephen A. Douglas	Democratic	1,382,713	29.5	12	
	John C. Breckinridge	Democratic	848,356	18.1	72	
	John Bell	Union	592,906	12.6	39	
1864	**ABRAHAM LINCOLN (ILL.)**	Republican	2,213,655	55.0	212	73.8
	George B. McClellan	Democratic	1,805,237	45.0	21	
1868	**ULYSSES S. GRANT (ILL.)**	Republican	3,012,833	52.7	214	78.1
	Horatio Seymour	Democratic	2,703,249	47.3	80	
1872	**ULYSSES S. GRANT (ILL.)**	Republican	3,597,132	55.6	286	71.3
	Horace Greeley	Democratic; Liberal Republican	2,834,125	43.9	66	

1876	**RUTHERFORD B. HAYES (OHIO)**	Republican	4,036,298	48.0	185	81.8
	Samuel J. Tilden	Democratic	4,300,590	51.0	184	
1880	**JAMES A. GARFIELD (OHIO)**	Republican	4,454,416	48.5	214	79.4
	Winfield S. Hancock	Democratic	4,444,952	48.1	155	
1884	**GROVER CLEVELAND (N.Y.)**	Democratic	4,874,986	48.5	219	77.5
	James G. Blaine	Republican	4,851,981	48.2	182	
1888	**BENJAMIN HARRISON (IND.)**	Republican	5,439,853	47.9	233	79.3
	Grover Cleveland	Democratic	5,540,309	48.6	168	
1892	**GROVER CLEVELAND (N.Y.)**	Democratic	5,556,918	46.1	277	74.7
	Benjamin Harrison	Republican	5,176,108	43.0	145	
	James B. Weaver	People's	1,041,028	8.5	22	
1896	**WILLIAM MCKINLEY (OHIO)**	Republican	7,104,779	51.1	271	79.3
	William J. Bryan	Democratic People's	6,502,925	47.7	176	
1900	**WILLIAM MCKINLEY (OHIO)**	Republican	7,207,923	51.7	292	73.2
	William J. Bryan	Dem.-Populist	6,358,133	45.5	155	
1904	**THEODORE ROOSEVELT (N.Y.)**	Republican	7,623,486	57.9	336	65.2
	Alton B. Parker	Democratic	5,077,911	37.6	140	
	Eugene V. Debs	Socialist	402,283	3.0	—	
1908	**WILLIAM H. TAFT (OHIO)**	Republican	7,678,908	51.6	321	65.4
	William J. Bryan	Democratic	6,409,104	43.1	162	
	Eugene V. Debs	Socialist	420,793	2.8	—	
1912	**WOODROW WILSON (N.J.)**	Democratic	6,293,454	41.9	435	58.8
	Theodore Roosevelt	Progressive	4,119,538	27.4	88	
	William H. Taft	Republican	3,484,980	23.2	8	
	Eugene V. Debs	Socialist	900,672	6.0	—	

(continued)

Year	Candidates	Parties	Popular Vote	Percentage of Popular Vote	Electoral Vote	Percentage of Voter Participation
1916	**Woodrow Wilson (N.J.)**	Democratic	9,129,606	49.4	277	61.6
	Charles E. Hughes	Republican	8,538,221	46.2	254	
	A. L. Benson	Socialist	585,113	3.2	—	
1920	**Warren G. Harding (Ohio)**	Republican	16,152,200	60.4	404	49.2
	James M. Cox	Democratic	9,147,353	34.2	127	
	Eugene V. Debs	Socialist	919,799	3.4	—	
1924	**Calvin Coolidge (Mass.)**	Republican	15,725,016	54.0	382	48.9
	John W. Davis	Democratic	8,386,503	28.8	136	
	Robert M. LaFollette	Progressive	4,822,856	16.6	13	
1928	**Herbert Hoover (Calif.)**	Republican	21,391,381	58.2	444	56.9
	Alfred E. Smith	Democratic	15,016,443	40.9	87	
	Norman Thomas	Socialist	267,835	0.7	—	
1932	**Franklin D. Roosevelt (N.Y.)**	Democratic	22,821,857	57.4	472	56.9
	Herbert Hoover	Republican	15,761,841	39.7	59	
	Norman Thomas	Socialist	881,951	2.2	—	
1936	**Franklin D. Roosevelt (N.Y.)**	Democratic	27,751,597	60.8	523	61.0
	Alfred M. Landon	Republican	16,679,583	36.5	8	
	William Lemke	Union	882,479	1.9	—	
1940	**Franklin D. Roosevelt (N.Y.)**	Democratic	27,244,160	54.8	449	62.5
	Wendell L. Willkie	Republican	22,305,198	44.8	82	
1944	**Franklin D. Roosevelt (N.Y.)**	Democratic	25,602,504	53.5	432	55.9
	Thomas E. Dewey	Republican	22,006,285	46.0	99	

1948	**HARRY S. TRUMAN (MO.)**	Democratic	24,105,695	49.5	304	53.0
	Thomas E. Dewey	Republican	21,969,170	45.1	189	
	J. Strom Thurmond	State-Rights Democratic	1,169,021	2.4	38	
	Henry A. Wallace	Progressive	1,156,103	2.4	—	
1952	**DWIGHT D. EISENHOWER (N.Y.)**	Republican	33,936,252	55.1	442	63.3
	Adlai E. Stevenson	Democratic	27,314,992	44.4	89	
1956	**DWIGHT D. EISENHOWER (N.Y.)**	Republican	35,575,420	57.6	457	60.6
	Adlai E. Stevenson	Democratic	26,033,066	42.1	73	
	Other	—	—		1	
1960	**JOHN F. KENNEDY (MASS.)**	Democratic	34,227,096	49.9	303	62.8
	Richard M. Nixon	Republican	34,108,546	49.6	219	
	Other	—	—		15	
1964	**LYNDON B. JOHNSON (TEX.)**	Democratic	43,126,506	61.1	486	61.7
	Barry M. Goldwater	Republican	27,176,799	38.5	52	
1968	**RICHARD M. NIXON (N.Y.)**	Republican	31,770,237	43.4	301	60.6
	Hubert H. Humphrey	Democratic	31,270,533	42.7	191	
	George Wallace	American Independent	9,906,141	13.5	46	
1972	**RICHARD M. NIXON (N.Y.)**	Republican	47,169,911	60.7	520	55.2
	George S. McGovern	Democratic	29,170,383	37.5	17	
	Other	—	—		1	
1976	**JIMMY CARTER (GA.)**	Democratic	40,828,587	50.0	297	53.5
	Gerald R. Ford	Republican	39,147,613	47.9	241	
	Other	—	1,575,459	2.1	—	

(continued)

Year	Candidates	Parties	Popular Vote	Percentage of Popular Vote	Electoral Vote	Percentage of Voter Participation
1980	**RONALD REAGAN (CALIF.)**	Republican	43,901,812	50.7	489	52.6
	Jimmy Carter	Democratic	35,483,820	41.0	49	
	John B. Anderson	Independent	5,719,722	6.6	—	
	Ed Clark	Libertarian	921,188	1.1	—	
1984	**RONALD REAGAN (CALIF.)**	Republican	54,455,075	59.0	525	53.3
	Walter Mondale	Democratic	37,577,185	41.0	13	
1988	**GEORGE BUSH (TEX.)**	Republican	47,946,422	54.0	426	50.2
	Michael S. Dukakis	Democratic	41,016,429	46.0	112	
1992	**WILLIAM J. CLINTON (ARK.)**	Democratic	43,728,375	43.0	370	55.0
	George Bush	Republican	38,167,416	38.0	168	
	Ross Perot	Independent	19,237,247	19.0	0	
1996	**WILLIAM J. CLINTON (ARK.)**	Democratic	47,401,185	49.3	379	49.0
	Robert Dole	Republican	39,197,469	40.7	159	
	Ross Perot	Reform	8,085,294	8.4	—	
2000	**GEORGE W. BUSH (TEXAS)**	Republican	50,459,211	47.89	271	51.0
	Albert Gore, Jr.	Democratic	51,003,894	48.41	266	
	Ralph Nader	Green	2,834,410	2.69	—	

POPULATION OF THE UNITED STATES, 1790–2000

Year	Population	Percent Increase	Population per Square Mile	Percent Urban/ Rural	Percent White/ Nonwhite	Median Age
1790	3,929,214		4.5	5.1/94.9	80.7/19.3	NA
1800	5,308,483	35.1	6.1	6.1/93.9	81.1/18.9	NA
1810	7,239,881	36.4	4.3	7.3/92.7	81.0/19.0	NA
1820	9,638,453	33.1	5.5	7.2/92.8	81.6/18.4	16.7
1830	12,866,020	33.5	7.4	8.8/91.2	81.9/18.1	17.2
1840	17,069,453	32.7	9.8	10.8/89.2	83.2/16.8	17.8
1850	23,191,876	35.9	7.9	15.3/84.7	84.3/15.7	18.9
1860	31,443,321	35.6	10.6	19.8/80.2	85.6/14.4	19.4
1870	39,818,449	26.6	13.4	25.7/74.3	86.2/13.8	20.2
1880	50,155,783	26.0	16.9	28.2/71.8	86.5/13.5	20.9
1890	62,947,714	25.5	21.2	35.1/64.9	87.5/12.5	22.0
1900	75,994,575	20.7	25.6	39.6/60.4	87.9/12.1	22.9
1910	91,972,266	21.0	31.0	45.6/54.4	88.9/11.1	24.1
1920	105,710,620	14.9	35.6	51.2/48.8	89.7/10.3	25.3
1930	122,775,046	16.1	41.2	56.1/43.9	89.8/10.2	26.4
1940	131,669,275	7.2	44.2	56.5/43.5	89.8/10.2	29.0
1950	150,697,361	14.5	50.7	64.0/36.0	89.5/10.5	30.2
1960	179,323,175	18.5	50.6	69.9/30.1	88.6/11.4	29.5
1970	203,302,031	13.4	57.4	73.5/26.5	87.6/12.4	28.0
1980	226,545,805	11.4	64.0	73.7/26.3	86.0/14.0	30.0
1990	248,709,873	9.9	70.3	77.5/22.5	80.3/19.7	32.9
2000	281,421,906	13.0	79.6	NA/NA	83.0/17.0	35.3

NA = Not available.

EMPLOYMENT, 1870–2000

Year	Number of Workers (in millions)	Male/Female Employment Ratio	Percentage of Workers in Unions
1870	12.5	85/15	—
1880	17.4	85/15	—
1890	23.3	83/17	—
1900	29.1	82/18	3
1910	38.2	79/21	6
1920	41.6	79/21	12
1930	48.8	78/22	7
1940	53.0	76/24	27
1950	59.6	72/28	25
1960	69.9	68/32	26
1970	82.1	63/37	25
1980	108.5	58/42	23
1985	108.9	57/43	19
1990	118.8	55/45	16
2000	134.3	53/47	13.5

PRODUCTION, TRADE, AND FEDERAL SPENDING/DEBT, 1790–2000

Year	Gross National Product (GNP) (in billions $)	Balance of Trade (in millions $)	Federal Budget (in billions $)	Federal Surplus/ Deficit (in billions $)	Federal Debt (in billions $)
1790	—	–3	.004	+0.00015	.076
1800	—	–20	.011	+0.0006	.083
1810	—	–18	.008	+0.0012	.053
1820	—	–4	.018	–0.0004	.091
1830	—	+3	.015	+0.100	.049
1840	—	+25	.024	–0.005	.004
1850	—	–26	.040	+0.004	.064
1860	—	–38	.063	–0.01	.065
1870	7.4	–11	.310	+0.10	2.4
1880	11.2	+92	.268	+0.07	2.1
1890	13.1	+87	.318	+0.09	1.2
1900	18.7	+569	.521	+0.05	1.2
1910	35.3	+273	.694	–0.02	1.1
1920	91.5	+2,880	6.357	+0.3	24.3
1930	90.7	+513	3.320	+0.7	16.3
1940	100.0	–3,403	9.6	–2.7	43.0
1950	286.5	+1,691	43.1	–2.2	257.4
1960	506.5	+4,556	92.2	+0.3	286.3
1970	992.7	+2,511	196.6	+2.8	371.0
1980	2,631.7	+24,088	579.6	–59.5	914.3
1985	4,087.7	–148,480	946.3	–212.3	1,827.5
1990	5,764.9	–101,012	1,251.8	–220.5	4,064.6
2000	9,860.8	–369.7	1,789.6	+237.0	5,674.2

Index

Note: Page numbers followed by the letter "*i*" refer to illustrations and by the letter "*m*" refer to maps.